W9-DAF-568

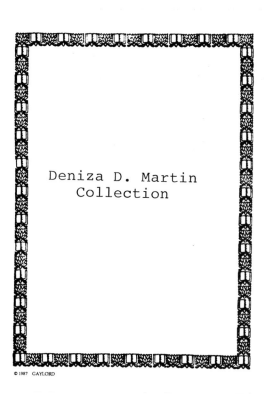

KING ALFRED THE GREAT

KING ALFRED THE GREAT

Alfred P. Smyth

OXFORD UNIVERSITY PRESS · OXFORD

1995

Oxford University Press, Walton Street, Oxford OX2 6DP
Oxford New York
Athens Auckland Bangkok Bombay
Calcutta Cape Town Dar es Salaam Delhi
Florence Hong Kong Istanbul Karachi
Kuala Lumpur Madras Madrid Melbourne
Mexico City Nairobi Paris Singapore
Taipei Tokyo Toronto
and associated companies in
Berlin Ibadan

Oxford is a trade mark of Oxford University Press

Published in the United States
by Oxford University Press Inc., New York

British Library Cataloguing in Publication Data
Data available

Library of Congress Cataloging-in-Publication Data
Smyth, Alfred P.
King Alfred the Great / Alfred P. Smyth.
p.   cm.
Includes bibliographical references (p.   ) and index.
1. Alfred, King of England, 849–899.   2. Great Britain—History—
Alfred, 871–899.   3. Anglo-Saxons—Kings and rulers—Biography.
I. Title.
DA153.S68   1995
942.01′64′092—dc20   95-36713
ISBN 0-19-822989-5

1 3 5 7 9 10 8 6 4 2

Typeset by Graphicraft Typesetters Ltd., Hong Kong
Printed in Great Britain
on acid-free paper by
The Bath Press, Avon

For
Hilary and Edmund

I cannot find anything better in man than that he know,
and nothing worse than that he be ignorant

(King Alfred's version of the *Soliloquies of Augustine*)

ACKNOWLEDGEMENTS

THIS book has been written with the kind help and co-operation of the staff of the Inter-Library Loan Department of the Templeman Library at the University of Kent. Enid Dixon, Olive Lindstrand, Angela Narburgh, and Christine Williams have searched for and located innumerable rare publications through the long arm of their library mail-order service. Their efforts have afforded me access to books from other libraries which I would never otherwise have had the time or resources to visit. Anna Miller has also been tireless in helping me with my bibliographical enquiries. Sally Hewett and Alison Guy in the Master's Office of Keynes College, provided invaluable assistance in the final stages of writing and preparation for the publisher. Without Sally's help and crucial support in lifting so many administrative burdens from my shoulders, I could never have hoped to finish this book as planned. My colleague Richard Gameson has been especially helpful in discussions regarding ninth- and tenth-century book-production and palaeography and in advising on illustrations. Teresa Hankey has helped with textual problems relating to Early Medieval Latin. Graham Anderson, Christopher Chaffin, Arthur Keaveney, and David Nightingale have all generously shared their wisdom with me on matters of Ancient History. My colleagues, Andrew Butcher, Charles Coulson, Richard Eales, and Bruce Webster have generously given of their time in discussing their own areas of specialism. Tony Bex has helped with my understanding of the effects of literacy on oral tradition. Ian Gregor has helped me to understand the special problems involved in writing biography. My students at the University of Kent have been a constant source of inspiration, and on occasion also of excellent ideas. I am indebted to friends and colleagues from other British universities and institutions. Henry Loyn has ever been generous with his ideas and encouragement. Jonathan Shepard has been my guide to the Alfredian countryside of his native Dorset and has shared his knowledge with me of Wimborne, Kingston Lacy, and Badbury Rings. Nigel Ramsey has shared his encyclopædic knowledge of manuscript materials and Patrick Collinson and Kenneth Fincham have helped with discussions on Archbishop Matthew Parker. Marion Archibald kindly supplied me with moulds of specimens of Alfredian coinage and Leslie Webster provided most helpful advice on ninth-century Anglo-Saxon artwork and artefacts. Richard Crampton gave up valuable time on his own scholarly researches on Eastern Europe to explain the mysteries of word-processing to a novice, and Kay Gazzard has kindly helped with compiling the index. Mark Blackburn, James Graham-Campbell, C. Roy Hart, Simon Keynes, Janet Nelson, Ian Stewart, Patrick Wormald, and Barbara Yorke have been especially helpful in supplying me with their own publications and with keeping me up to date on the work of their colleagues. I have chosen not to concentrate at any length on the Alfredian law code in this book, nor have I dealt in detail with economic issues in Alfred's reign. These matters, however urgent, are best deferred until more fundamental problems relating to source materials—which have dogged Alfredian studies for two centuries—have been openly and adequately addressed.

Two deceased friends and scholars have had a major influence on the development of my ideas for this book. Michael Wallace-Hadrill first suggested to me, when I was his student, that I should study the reign of King Alfred and R. H. C. Davis encouraged me by his own scholarly example to review the evidence relating to Alfredian sources with an independent mind. The following scholars and their institutions have afforded me the opportunity of sharing and developing my ideas on King Alfred. They deserve a very special thanks, since it has been peculiarly valuable for me to constructively exchange views on a subject which has become dogmatized to the point of sectarianism: David Bates, Alan Lane, and Peter Edbury at the University of Wales, Cardiff; David Kirby at the University of Wales, Aberystwyth; Christopher Holdsworth, his colleagues and the students of the History Society at the University of Exeter; Jim John, Tom Cross, Bob Farrell, Paul Hyams and John Ruffing, Cornell University; Warren Hollister and his medievalist colleagues at the University of California, Santa Barbara; Joseph Nagy, UCLA, and Daniel Melia at the University of California at Berkeley; Catherine Karkov, Miami University, Ohio; and Amos Booth at the Institut des Universités Americaines, Aix-en-Provence. Amos and his colleagues have followed the progress of this book since its inception. Karl Hammer has always been ready to share his scholarly perspective on the Carolingian world from Pittsburgh. Susan Leigh Fry and her parents provided generous hospitality and friendship during my visit to California. Martin Biddle, David Hinton, Derek Craig, Melissa Dalziel, Charlotte Hodgson, Michael Stansfield, Sheila Hingley, Henrik Jansen, and Mark Redknapp have all been of enormous help in advising on archaeological and archival material. My wife, Margaret, has been especially helpful with her great knowledge of German and with a wide range of bibliographical matters. The typescript has been read by Professor Janet Bately of King's College, University of London, Professor David Kirby, University of Wales at Aberystwyth, and by Professor Michael Herren of the Medieval Institute of Toronto. I owe these scholars an extraordinary debt for bringing their respective scholarly reputations in Old English language, in Early Medieval History, and in Early Medieval Latin to bear on my work. They have saved me from many errors and they have offered me countless helpful suggestions. We have not always found ourselves in agreement on so debatable a subject, but I am grateful for the opportunity for discussion, and for the very positive arguments that have ensued. Ivon Asquith of Oxford University Press was responsible for persuading me to begin work on this book and Tony Morris and Anna Illingworth have shown great patience with an author who had gone long over his allotted time for completion of the work. The staff of the following libraries have shown every kindness during my visits to their manuscript and book collections: The Bodleian Library, Oxford; The British Library; Canterbury Cathedral Archive and Library; Durham Cathedral Archive; Lambeth Palace Library; the Westminster Library; The London Library; the Society of Antiquaries of London; Maynooth College Library; the National Library of Ireland; Bibliothèque

Nationale, Paris; Bibliothèque Municipale, Cambrai; Bibliothèque Municipale, Limoges; and Bibliothèque Méjanes, Aix-en-Provence. The courtesy of the staff of these institutions and their willingness to co-operate in and facilitate the pursuit of historical research is deserving of special recognition. R. I. Page granted permission, on the production of appropriate written evidence for suitability and competence, to consult the Parker manuscript of the Anglo-Saxon Chronicle and Parker's transcript of the Otho manuscript of the *Life* of King Alfred in the library of Corpus Christi College Cambridge. I am grateful to the people of Virolle and Châteauneuf who, for the past twenty years, have provided me and my family with a haven in the French countryside where I have been able, in the midst of friendship and hospitality, to ponder the challenge of writing ninth-century Anglo-Saxon History.

A.P.S.

Châteauneuf-la-Fôret, Limousin
La fête de l'Assomption
15 August 1994

Current address:
Keynes College
The University of Kent
at Canterbury

CONTENTS

LIST OF PLATES

(Between pages 198-199 and pages 422-423)

LIST OF FIGURES

LIST OF MAPS

ABBREVIATIONS

Æthelweard, ed. Campbell	Campbell, A. (ed.), *Chronicon Æthelweardi*
Ann. Bert.	*Annals of St-Bertin (Annales Bertiani)*
Ann. Fuld.	*Annals of Fulda (Annales Fuldenses)*
Ann. Reg. Franc.	*Annales Regni Francorum*
Ann. Ulst.	*Annals of Ulster*
Ann. Ved.	*Annales Vedastini*
ASC	*Anglo-Saxon Chronicle*
ASE	*Anglo-Saxon England*, ed. P. Clemos *et al.* (Cambridge, 1972–)
Birch 313	Charter no. 313 in W. de G. Birch (ed.), *Cartularium Saxonicum*
EHD	*English Historical Documents*
Eng. Hist. Rev.	*English Historical Review*
JEH	*Journal of Ecclesiastical History*
Life of Alfred, ed. Stevenson	Stevenson, W. H. (ed.), *Asser's Life of King Alfred*
Mon. Ger. Hist. SS	*Monumenta Germaniae Historica Scriptores*
Patrologiae	*Patrologiae Cursus Completus*, ed. J.-P. Migne
Proc. Brit. Acad.	*Proceedings of the British Academy*
Quellen z. deut. Gesch. d. Mittelalters	*Ausgewälhte Quellen zur deutschen Geschichte des Mittelalters*
Sawyer 278	Charter no. 278 in P. H. Sawyer, *Anglo-Saxon Charters*
SEHD	*Select English Historical Documents of the Ninth and Tenth Centuries*
Trans. Roy. Hist. Soc.	*Transactions of the Royal Historical Society*

INTRODUCTION

THE life and times of Alfred the Great lie at the heart of Anglo-Saxon studies. The Alfredian era not only occupies a central position, chronologically, in the pre-Conquest history of England, but Alfred's own achievements, the challenges which he faced from the Danish invaders, together with his writings and other writings associated with his reign—all go to make an assessment of this king crucial to our understanding of the development of Anglo-Saxon society as a whole. Alfred's reign marked a turning-point in the Danish wars, and his son and grandsons built on his political and military initiatives eventually to unite England under the rule of one king. That the House of Alfred came to dominate pre-Conquest England owed much to its extraordinarily energetic and fortunate founder in the late ninth century. Alfred's own writings and translations of works of Late Antique authors constitute a unique corpus of material which is vital to our understanding of the development of Old English prose. The Anglo-Saxon Chronicle, which was first compiled during Alfred's reign, sets out the basic framework of Old English history. However much our approach to the study of early English history may change, the Chronicle will forever provide the basic co-ordinates of which all historical narrative and interpretation must take account. Finally, there is the *Life* of King Alfred—the earliest of its kind to survive for an English king—which purports to have been written in AD 893 by the king's tutor and friend, the Welshman, Asser. Asser's *Life* of Alfred has provided generations of students of Old English society not only with information on the life of Alfred the Great, it has also been used as a quarry for the extraction of a multitude of historical vignettes which in turn have been employed by historians and linguists to fill out our understanding of other periods of the Anglo-Saxon past. Any one of Alfred's personal achievements or any one of those sources associated directly or indirectly with him would have made his reign remarkable. The convergence of so much literary and historical material from the reign of this one West Saxon king—set against the dramatic background of the Danish wars—has rendered Alfred's claim to 'greatness' assured and has rendered the study of this remarkable ruler central to our understanding of early English history.

Because of Alfred's self-evident qualities as a ruler and a scholar, as well as claims to greatness made on his behalf by his supposed biographer Asser, this early English king got taken over by nationalist and romantic historians of the nineteenth century. England's Darling was perceived by the Victorians as having saved the nation from the Danish invader, thereby preserving the potential of the country and its people for future greatness in a modern world. Alfred understandably became associated even in the minds of reputable scholars with a sense of pride in being English. In spite of the solid footing on which English historical research had been placed by the middle of the nineteenth century, a core of supposedly irrefutable Alfredian achievements—not all of them securely founded on historical evidence—had already become enshrined in an established canon of Anglo-Saxon historiography. Most damaging of all was the reluctance to face the problems posed by the *Life* of the king which was ascribed to Asser, and the failure to recognize that it was Alfred's own writings, together with the Anglo-Saxon Chronicle, which established the king's reputation on the surest of footings and which ought to take primacy over anything which the so-called Asser might have to say about him. The problems posed by the *Life* of Alfred were peculiarly acute due to the destruction of the only surviving medieval manuscript of the work in the disastrous Cottonian fire of 1731. This fire has left succeeding generations of Alfredian scholars dependent on Archbishop Parker's transcript and a sixteenth-century printed edition of the *Life* as well as on some extracts and summaries of the work as preserved by other later medieval writers. Victorian scholars were presented with the impossible task of trying to reconstruct a text which was for them, incapable of reconstruction. It is not surprising that nineteenth-century scholarly attempts to authenticate the *Life* of Alfred fell prey to subjective and intuitive analysis. It was more unfortunate, still, when the unsatisfactory conclusions reached on this crucial text by the Victorians were given an imprimatur by twentieth-century scholars.

Bishop Stubbs gave a guarded seal of approval to the *Life* of Alfred in his introduction to his edition of William of Malmesbury's *de Gestis regum* for the Rolls Series in 1889. While Stubbs was uneasy about the status of this baffling source his scholarly reservations were soon buried beneath the weight of his ultimate validation of it. His ambivalent and cautious attitude has been repeated throughout the century after he wrote by those scholars who were wise enough to know there was something wrong, but who drew back from the awesome consequences of outright rejection:

In my opinion the present state of the text is such as to inspire some dangerous doubts. I do not wish to be understood as questioning the general truth of the work as history, or as throwing suspicion on its genuineness and authenticity. Of the particular difficulties to which I refer the most important are those which affect Asser himself and his relation to Alfred.

W. H. Stevenson's definitive edition of *Asser's Life of King Alfred*, published in 1904, not only firmed up the argument for the acceptance of that work as an authentic and contemporary biography, it also had the effect of emphasizing the historical value of the *Life* of Alfred at the expense of Alfred's own writings and translations. Because so many of the claims relating to Alfred's personal achievements became inextricably linked with evidence provided by the king's supposed biographer, Asser, and because Stevenson's labyrinthine commentary was essentially a monumental rearguard action in defence of Asser, Alfredian historiography inevitably moved away from a study of Alfred to concentrate instead on a study of Asser. It is not possible, therefore, to write a biography of King Alfred without constant reference to the biography of the king attributed to Asser and without having to deal with the indissolubly related theme of how Alfredian sources have been viewed by historians from the nineteenth century onwards.

All students of King Alfred are indebted to a line of scholars beginning with Stubbs and Stevenson, and descending through Stenton to Whitelock. Dorothy Whitelock was commissioned to write a biography of King Alfred as early as the 1950s and her important published papers on Alfred's writings and charters were intended as a prelude to that biography which was unfortunately not published at the time of her death in August 1982. Although her book on Alfred was declared in her *Times* obituary to have been finished in 1980, and while its publication was declared elsewhere to have been imminent in 1984, it was never seen through the press. While I have not consulted the manuscript of Whitelock's biography of Alfred my debt to her earlier work has been great. More than any other scholar in her field, Whitelock provided a magisterial overview of Anglo-Saxon and Alfredian studies through a lifetime of research from which an entire generation of students have benefited. But Whitelock, however great her learning, inherited a received view of her subject from Stenton—and it was a view which discouraged constructive debate and which allowed for only minor adjustments to be made to what had become a dogmatic approach to Anglo-Saxon history. An evaluation of Asser's *Life* of King Alfred as well as theories relating to the origins and authorship of the Anglo-Saxon Chronicle lay at the heart of Stentonian orthodoxy as propounded by Whitelock—an orthodoxy which was as non-negotiable as it was fundamentally flawed.

Plummer, writing at the end of the nineteenth century, may be said to have represented the last formidable scholar on the historical side of Anglo-Saxon research who worked in an independent ambience which lay outside what was later to become the Stenton–Whitelock axis. Galbraith possessed the courage and reputation to offer an alternative opinion on Alfredian scholarship, but his lack of specialized knowledge within the field inevitably led to the marginalization of his ideas. James Campbell, R. H. C. Davis, E. John, D. P. Kirby, and J. L. Nelson, showed that it was possible to challenge an interpretation of a source such as the Anglo-Saxon Chronicle on a point of detail. Few others dared to offer a reassessment of the evidence and too many contented themselves in the main with rearranging the Stentonian thesis rather than attempting a critical evaluation of it. The inevitable result has been that Alfredian historical research when compared with other areas of Anglo-Saxon scholarship has not moved forward as it ought to have done during the entire half-century since Stenton produced his *Anglo-Saxon England*. When we compare Alfredian historical research with progress made by Janet Bately and others in the study of Old English literature, or with the work of Michael Lapidge and Michael Herren on Early Medieval Anglo-Latin texts, and with the ever-growing volume of numismatic and archaeological research, we are struck by the dead weight of preconceived ideas in Alfredian history which are the hallmark of received tradition in any academic discipline. Significantly, it has been from the contribution by independent scholars that the most lively and thought-provoking historical arguments have emerged. C. R. Hart's prolific series of scholarly and controversial publications on the origins and development of various recensions of the Anglo-Saxon Chronicle have not only moved the debate forward, but have also highlighted what can be achieved by those few able scholars who work outside the networks of patronage which have come to control the subject in England. Real progress has been achieved too, in the area of textual scholarship. Experts in Old English who have wisely shunned the historical impasse have achieved much in establishing which works of translation fall within the Alfredian repertoire and which should be placed outside. The definitive edition of the *Old English Orosius* and of various recensions of the Anglo-Saxon Chronicle point the way to what can yet be achieved. But it is an extraordinary comment on the state of Anglo-Saxon studies to find that for the Old English translation of Gregory's *Dialogues* we must still rely on the 1900 Leipzig edition by Hans Hecht, and that for a comprehensive edition of Alfred's Laws, we are still reliant on the labours of another German scholar, F. Liebermann, who published his work as long ago as 1903. For a complete translation of King Alfred's version of the *Soliloquies* of St Augustine, we must leave England yet again, and seek out Hargrove's dated Yale translation of 1904. Paradoxically, those who worked hardest to prevent a creative discussion on the place of Alfred in early English history did least themselves to make the king's own writings available to us in reliable modern textual editions.

It is not that our debt to scholars such as Stenton and Whitelock is any less because of their extraordinary contribution to many areas of the subject. Our debt to them for their ability to synthesize centuries of historical narrative and to set standards of scholarly exactitude on points of detail remains. What cannot be allowed to stand is the notion that any scholar, however great his or her learning may have been, has had the last word to say on any point of historical interpretation. Nor can any new generation of historians ever hope to successfully interpret a past age in the light of its own unique experience and with the benefits of its own developing methodology, if that generation is committed to keeping faith with the dead.

The study of King Alfred, unlike that of any other Anglo-Saxon ruler—unlike even studies of the Conqueror—has long become enmeshed in polemic and the politics of academe. It has not been possible therefore to construct a historical narrative around the career of this king without first attempting to free the subject from the iron grip of its own historiography. This has resulted in a narrative that inevitably appears more iconoclastic than I would have otherwise wished. Yet Alfred as a historical figure is great enough to survive the criticisms levelled against his detractors and eulogizers—be they the Pseudo-Asser or his modern adherents. I am only too conscious that mine is a narrative, which carries its own weight of polemic. That has been the inevitable consequence of a silence too long held by others. It has never been my intention to provide a definitive narrative of Alfred's life, nor is it my intention to propound an alternative orthodoxy. My purpose is to present one historian's interpretation of the life of Alfred the Great, and in so doing, to refer the debate back into an open forum for all students of history, literature, archaeology, and numismatics to participate in, and to add thereby to our knowledge of this gifted early medieval king.

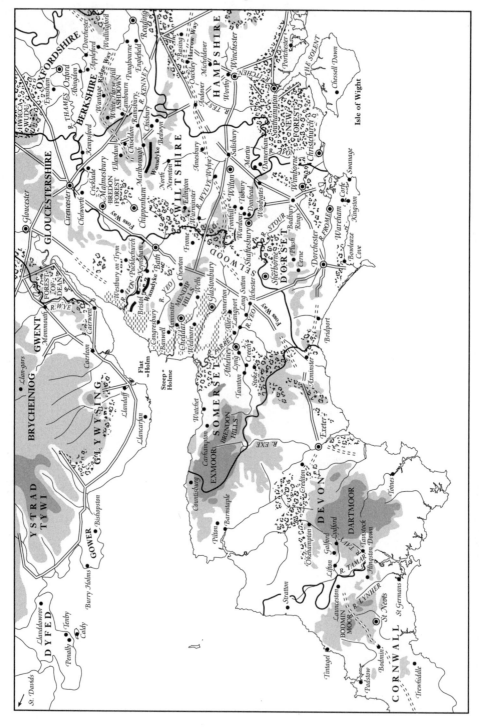

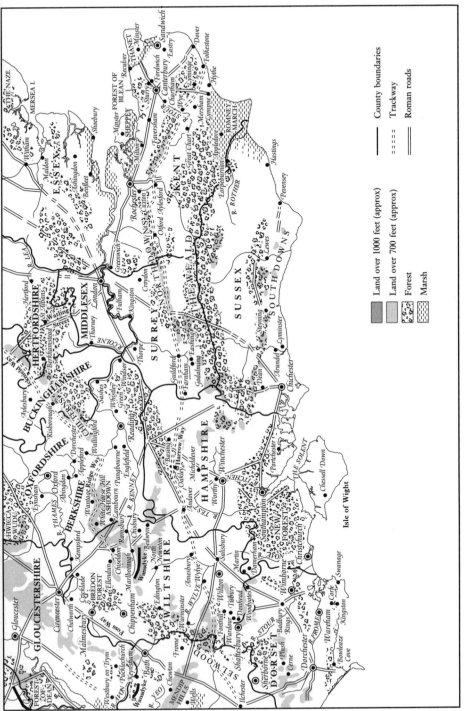

County boundaries
Trackway
Roman roads

Land over 1000 feet (approx)

Land over 700 feet (approx)

Forest

Marsh

Alfred's Kingdom

PART ONE

Narrative of a Reign

I

From Obscurity to Precarious Kingship

MORE DOCUMENTS WRITTEN BY KING ALFRED, OR WRITTEN ABOUT him, have survived from the Middle Ages than for any other Anglo-Saxon king. In spite of this wealth of material, or because of it, few details concerning the king's life have avoided becoming the subject of controversy. The medieval *Life* of King Alfred, attributed to Bishop Asser, is a source whose date and authorship have been furiously contested by Alfredian scholars over two centuries. Information in that *Life* impinges on every aspect of King Alfred's career and a conventional approach to writing the biography of the king would require constant reference to this medieval account of his life and a sustained integration of its material into any narrative of Alfred's reign. Since we shall be engaged in the most radical reappraisal of the value of that work attributed to Asser later on in this study, it is best to attempt a preliminary reconstruction of Alfred's reign independently of whatever information is contained in the controversial *Life* of the king. This does not mean that we prejudge the issue relating to the authenticity of Asser's *Life* of Alfred, or that we dismiss out of hand the material contained there which is unique to that source, but it does allow us to establish a framework for King Alfred's career which is based on a less controversial body of knowledge. The assessment— not to say the deconstruction—of Asser's *Life* of Alfred is best undertaken in isolation from this preliminary survey of Alfred's career, and only when that assessment is undertaken can we finally proceed to an integrated view of the achievements of Alfred the Great.

Even the time and place of Alfred's birth are matters for argument and debate. Alfred was born in 847 or 848. The earliest West Saxon genealogy and regnal list, composed while Alfred was king, states that he was already past 23 years of his life when he succeeded to the throne.[1] His brother, King Æthelred, died after Easter in 871 and Easter in that year fell on 15 April. So, if Alfred were born before mid-April, his year of birth was 848, and if he were born after mid-April, it was 847.[2] The *Life* of King Alfred—a supposedly contemporary biography written by the king's Welsh chaplain, Asser—gives Alfred's year of birth as 849, which is at least one year too late. This *Life* is also alone in claiming that Alfred was born at Wantage in Berkshire,[3] which its author describes as a royal estate (*villa regia*). Wantage presents problems as the place of birth for a West Saxon king's son in the mid-ninth century. Berkshire was a border area between Mercia and Wessex, and Wantage lay well to the north in that area, on the Berkshire Downs. It was on the very periphery of the sphere of West Saxon influence—if indeed it were in Wessex at all at the time of Alfred's birth. Cynewulf, king of Wessex (757–86), once seized territory in Berkshire which included the monastery of Cookham, a few miles north of Maidenhead—a place originally in the possession of King Æthelbald of Mercia (716–57). But Cynewulf of Wessex was later forced to return Cookham to the clergy of the church of Christ Church, Canterbury, who had received it from Æthelbald, and Cynewulf was forced, too, to cede 'many other towns' to Offa, king of the Mercians, who 'brought them under Mercian rule'.[4] The precise time when these disputed lands in the middle Thames valley had reverted to Mercian control was most probably after Offa's victory over Cynewulf at Bensington in Oxford-shire in 779.[5] Wantage was almost certainly still in Mercian hands up to within three or four years of Alfred's birth. A grant by Ceolred, bishop of Leicester, of land at Pangbourne in Berkshire to Brihtwulf, king of Mercia, in 843–4, shows that Pangbourne was then still under Mercian control. In this charter the bishop first granted fourteen hides at Pangbourne to the Mercian king, who then granted the estate to his Mercian ealdorman, Æthelwulf.[6] Pangbourne, on the Thames above Reading, is some sixteen or seventeen miles south-east of Wantage.[7] Stenton who originally dated the annexation of Berkshire by Wessex to 853,[8] later silently retracted in the heat of the Alfredian debate, and suggested that the date of the annexation 'is approximately fixed by the fact that Alfred . . . was born at Wantage in 849'.[9] Keynes and Lapidge followed suit, surmising that Wantage 'presumably fell under West Saxon control in the same decade, if Wantage were a royal estate when Alfred was born'.[10] But we cannot presume anything in relation to Alfredian studies by relying on circular argument, and by relying in particular on a statement which may be at variance with other sounder charter evidence.

What we do know is that southern Berkshire was under the control of the Mercian king in 844, and that its churches were then within the Mercian diocese of Leicester.[11] Berkshire was still under the control of a Mercian, Earldorman Æthelwulf, as late as 871—though whether or not he was the same man as the Mercian ealdorman who received the grant at Pangbourne back in the 840s is impossible to tell. Whitelock[12] and Stenton[13] understood that the Æthelwulf of the Pangbourne charter of 843–4 was the same man who was slain in 871. That is indeed possible, but *Æthelwulf* was an aristocratic name shared by several West Saxon and Mercian magnates in the ninth century. Robertson[14] noted that the thegn (*minister*), Æthelwulf, witnessed charters in AD 862, 863, and 867. Even these three signatories may not refer to the same man. The Æthelwulf who witnessed in the contemporary Kentish charter of AD 863 (Sawyer 332, Birch 507) is not given a title, and he signs at the end of a list of names which follows a long list of Canterbury clergy. The *Edelwulf minister* who witnessed the Canterbury charter of King Æthelred of Wessex in AD 867 (Sawyer 338, Birch 516) is unlikely to have been the ealdorman (*dux*) who was in charge of Berkshire at that time. Robertson makes no allowance for the possibility of different magnates of this name in both Wessex and Mercia. Was the *Ædelwulf dux*, for instance, who witnessed Cialulf's Canterbury grant of AD 888 (*recte* 868) (Sawyer 1204, Birch 519) the same person as the thegn who witnessed Birch 506 and Birch 516 of AD 862 and 867, and what was his relationship to the ealdorman of Berkshire? It seems very likely that the *minister* who witnessed West Saxon charters in the 860s was a different person from the ealdorman of the same name. Other charters supposedly witnessed by *Æthelwulf dux* around this time are all either forgeries or interpolated.[15] A series of five charters issued by Burgred of Mercia, by his queen, or by Mercian bishops do contain the witness of a Mercian Ealdorman (*dux*), Æthelwulf.[16] The *Æthelwulf dux* of these charters was clearly a Mercian. There is furthermore a specific Berkshire connection in the grants relating to Pangbourne (Birch 443) and another (Birch 522) relating to Lockinge at Wantage. This leaves the question of a group of ten West Saxon charters witnessed by an Æthelwulf from as early as 828 in the reign of King Ecgberht, up to 844.[17] Whatever the status of these documents, it is unlikely that the *Æthelwulf dux* who disputed the ownership of property at Dover, Lyminge, and elsewhere in East Kent (Sawyer 1439, Birch 445) was a Mercian ealdorman of Berkshire. On two occasions—in AD 838–9[18] and in AD 841[19]—Æthelwulf signs as *princeps* which might imply that he came of royal West Saxon stock. It is not possible to sort out this tangled record with a high degree of certainty. It is very unlikely that the Æthelwulf who witnessed the grant of King Ecgberht of Wessex in 828 was the same man who was slain by the Danes at Reading in 871. So, too, it is possible but scarcely probable that the Mercian Ealdorman Æthelwulf who witnessed King Wiglaf's grant in favour of Hanbury monastery in Worcestershire in 836[20] was the same Mercian leader who was slain in 871. This earlier Mercian Æthelwulf *dux* of Sawyer 190 is more likely to be the same as the man who witnessed Burgred's grant of AD 855 in favour of Ealhun, bishop of Worcester.[21] That being so, we seem to be dealing with at least five, if not six people of this name:

1. a West Saxon ealdorman (*dux*) who was active from 828–44;
2. a West Saxon thegn (*minister*) active in the period 862–7;
3. a West Saxon ealdorman who witnessed the Canterbury charter (Sawyer 1204) of AD 868;
4. a Mercian ealdorman who was active from 836 to 855;
5. a later Mercian ealdorman active from 860–71;
6. yet another Mercian Ealdorman Æthelwulf, described as *venerabilis dux* who was a party to the settlement of a dispute relating to land at Upton in Blockley, Worcestershire in AD 897 (Sawyer 1442, Birch 575).

When the Great Army of Danes first began to menace Wessex on their seizing Reading in 871, it is significant that the brunt of the early fighting was led by the Mercian, Ealdorman Æthelwulf. It was Æthelwulf who first defeated the invaders at Englefield, west of Reading in Berkshire, only to lose his life four days later in the army of King Æthelred and his brother, Alfred, in an abortive attack on Danish-held Reading. Ealdorman Æthelwulf's Mercian origins are emphasized by the chronicler Æthelweard, who informs us that the body of the slain Berkshire leader was carried secretly away and buried at Derby.[22] There is no conclusive evidence to suggest that Berkshire had become formally part of Wessex even as late as the beginning of Alfred's reign, although it is likely to have been annexed by that time. The Chronicle reports that Ealdorman Æthelwulf brought his Berkshire levy to the aid of the men of Hampshire and successfully defeated 'a great naval force' of vikings which had attacked Winchester in 860. The routing of these invaders who had come from the Somme was of sufficient importance to have found a mention in the *Annals of St. Bertin*.[23] But even if that suggests that Berkshire was by then a tributary of Wessex, it does not necessarily prove that West Saxon's kings had by then also, estates on the Berkshire Downs which they stayed on for any length of time. The complete transfer of a whole shire from the territorial control of one kingdom to another was a major event, and it is difficult to see under what circumstances this disputed borderland reverted to Wessex. It may be that Berkshire was not fully annexed by the West Saxons until after the flight of Burgred, king of the Mercians, to Rome in 874. The Anglo-Saxon Chronicle refers to Wessex as 'the kingdom south of the Thames' (*on þy cynerice be suþan Temese*)[24] in an entry for 871, while Alfred significantly uses that same phrase, *be suðan Temese* in his prose preface to the *Pastoral Care* to describe conditions in Wessex when he became king.[25] But both the Chronicle entry and Alfred's comment were written in the 880s or *c.*890 when the West Saxon territorial position was a lot more secure. If the Thames had marked the frontier in 871, then all of Berkshire had indeed come within the ambit of Wessex by that time, but the precise territorial status of Wantage at the time when Alfred became king does not necessarily have much bearing on its position at the time when he was born. At best, Wantage in 871, lay on the fringes of newly acquired territory and within only eight miles of the Mercian border. Stenton[26] concluded in 1913—long before the status of Asser was to become a major political issue in Anglo-Saxon studies— that Berkshire was not ceded by the Mercians to the West Saxons until 853. That was the year in which Burgred of Mercia had sought Æthelwulf's help in attacking the Welsh, and Stenton surmised that those negotiations involved not only the marriage of Æthelwulf's daughter, Æthelswith, to Burgred, but also the cession of Berkshire to Wessex.[27] It was in that same year, incidentally, that the infant Alfred, was alleged by the Chronicle to have travelled to Rome.[28] Alfred was then 5 or 6 years old, and that being so, it is highly unlikely that he was born in Wantage when that place was in Mercian hands.

The evidence relating to the precise affiliations of Berkshire in the middle of the ninth century is ambiguous and reflects its long-standing disputed border status. This ambiguity was further complicated by forgers of a later age who fabricated grants on the assumption that Berkshire had always been ruled by West Saxon kings. King Ecgberht's grant[29] to Abingdon Abbey of land at Marcham in Berkshire, supposedly made over in AD 835, was recognized by Stenton as a post-Conquest forgery.[30] Fourteenth-century copies of a charter dating to AD 840 record a grant by King Æthelwulf of Wessex to his thegn, Duda, of land at Ashdown, on the Berkshire Downs (Sawyer 288, Birch 431). A twelfth-century copy of a charter (Sawyer 307, Birch 474) regarded by Robertson with suspicion[31] and supposedly issued by King Æthelwulf of Wessex in 854 makes a grant of land at Brightwell in Berkshire to the church of Winchester. This charter belongs to a series supposedly issued at Wilton on 22 April 854 as part of Æthelwulf's tithing, as described in the Chronicle for AD 855–8.[32] Two years later in 856, the same West Saxon king supposedly granted land at Woolstone near Uffington Castle in Berkshire (Sawyer 317, Birch 491). But the witness list is garbled[33] and if this charter were genuine it must have been issued after Æthelwulf's return from Rome, when according to the *Life* of King Alfred,[34] the kingdom was divided between Æthelwulf and his son Æthelbald and the father's power was then confined to 'the eastern districts'—i.e. Kent, Surrey, Sussex, and Essex. No one of these three charters of King Æthelwulf of Wessex include the witness of Ealdorman Æthelwulf, who is otherwise assumed to have been in charge of Berkshire at this time—as the genuine Pangbourne grant to him (Birch 443) implies. The absence of Ealdorman Æthelwulf's name from the witness list to King Æthelwulf's supposed grant of land at Woolstone in 856 is all the more notable, since no less than six ealdormen and six thegns appear there. Yet another charter (Sawyer 335, Birch 504–5) in which King Æthelred of Wessex granted land at Wittenham, Berkshire, to his *princeps* Æthelwulf also presents problems for verification. This charter is dated to 862 and Æthelred had not become king until 866, while one of its witnesses, Bishop Swithun of Winchester, died *c*.862. If this charter could be shown to be substantially genuine, then its *princeps* Æthelwulf would very probably be the same as the man who was slain in King Æthelred's army at Reading in 871. The Æthelwulf described as *dux* and *princeps* who, along with his wife Wulfthryth, received a grant from Bishop Alhwine of Worcester of lands in Worcestershire and elsewhere in Mercia in AD 855 (Sawyer 1273, Birch 490) is probably an earlier Mercian ealdorman of the same name. A grant by Æthelswith, queen of Burgred of Mercia, and dating to 868, does not help to resolve the issue. Æthelswith's grant of land (Sawyer 1201, Birch 522) at Lockinge in Berkshire, to the thegn, Cuthwulf, might seem to confirm Mercian sovereignty in this shire at this time, but the grant is witnessed not only by Æthelswith and Burg[red] of Mercia, but also by Æthelswith's brother, King Æthelred of Wessex, which would suggest there was a joint Mercian–West Saxon interest in the area. The ubiquitous Ealdorman Æthelwulf is also present in the witness list of Æthelswith's grant to Cuthwulf. But the order of names in which King Æthelred of Wessex heads a list of sixteen, with King Burgred's name second last, and Æthelswith's name last of all, is surely suspicious in a grant supposedly issued by a Mercian queen.

Even if Wantage had been part of Wessex as early as the time of Alfred's birth, it would then have provided a most unsafe place for the lying-in of the wife of a West Saxon king. It would have been even more unsafe if we were to entertain Stenton's bizarre idea that at the time of Alfred's birth 'although a Mercian ealdorman [and so, presumably a Mercian king] continued in charge of the shire, the kings of Wessex retained their ancient estates within its borders'.[35] Danish warbands had been probing the defences of the West Saxon kingdom all through the 840s at Southhampton and Portland in Dorset (840); the Romney Marsh in

Kent (841); London and Rochester (842); Carhampton (*c*.843); at the mouth of the Parret in Somerset (*c*.845); and Devon and the Kent coast (851). Wantage, because of its location near the Thames valley, and because of its border position on the Berkshire Downs, was a most unsafe place for a king's wife—given the fondness of viking raiders for holding captives of high social status for ransom. For the vikings were not only notorious slave-traders—their easiest and best spoils were obtained throughout the Christian West through the ransom of high-status captives. The list of magnates and church leaders ransomed from vikings includes victims as far removed in place and time as a northern Irish king taken in 939 and a Christian king of Navarre in 860.[36] The huge sums paid for such victims testify to the profitable nature of the enterprise. Garcia Iniguez of Navarre was ransomed for 90,000 dinars; Charles the Bald of Francia 'drained his church treasuries dry' in order to raise the colossal payment of 686 lbs. of gold and 3,250 lbs. of silver to buy back Louis, abbot of St Denis in 858. The price for Louis may have been extortionate, since he also happened to be a grandson of Charlemagne.[37] In spite of the disarming silence of the Anglo-Saxon Chronicle, England cannot have been any more immune from viking treachery than her neighbours. Occasionally that silence is broken as when we are told that King Alfred's son and successor, Edward the Elder, paid out 40 pounds for the ransom of a bishop of Archenfield in Herefordshire in 914.[38] The going rate on the viking market for the wife of the king of Wessex was no doubt a lot higher than this considerable sum, and Æthelwulf would not have exposed his pregnant queen to await the birth of her son in one of the most insecure border regions of his kingdom.

The Thames and its hinterland had offered a major access route to the first Germanic invaders of Britain back in the fifth and sixth centuries.[39] Even if we accept that Berkshire and the Middle Thames were first settled in the Migration period by Germanic invaders coming down the Icknield Way via rivers flowing into the Wash,[40] Hodgkin's point about the danger posed by the very accessibility of the river Thames to new settlers from later arrivals remains valid.[41] The movements of the Great Army of Danes which attacked Wessex in 871 concentrated its campaign on the lower and middle Thames. Establishing a base at Reading from which they fanned out over the Berkshire Downs, the Danes also, according to the chronicler, Æthelweard, 'laid out a camp near London'.[42] At the time of Alfred's birth, things looked equally bleak for the lower and middle Thames basin. The 'great slaughter' which was recorded in London and Rochester in 842 was followed nine years later by a massive invasion force, put at 350 ships, which stormed London and which was probably launched from a winter base established on Thanet. This attack on the Thames would seem to have been part of a wider movement of Danish marauders who had unleashed themselves against the Frisian and northern Frankish coasts during a time of civil strife within Denmark. Brihtwulf, king of Mercia—in whose territory London (as well as Berkshire) lay—was repulsed with his army, and the victorious Danes pushed 'south across the Thames into Surrey'. Alfred was then an infant of about 3, when his father, Æthelwulf, king of the West Saxons, and his elder brother, Æthelbald, inflicted a crushing defeat on the invaders at *Aclea*, an unidentified battleground in Surrey or Hampshire. The large scale of this viking invasion of the Thames is confirmed by the fact that Æthelwulf's victory drew one of those rare references to English events from a Frankish annalist.[43] The Anglo-Saxon Chronicle does not record every Danish attack during this period of sporadic raiding, for the Chronicle at this point is merely summarizing West Saxon dynastic history, preparing us for the more detailed account of Alfred's reign. A grant by Alfred's future brother-in-law, Burgred king of the Mercians, which was issued in favour of his bishop of Worcester in 855, records that it was drawn up 'when the pagans (*pagani*) were in the province of the Wrekin dwellers'.[44] The presence of these invaders who had penetrated the Severn basin—so incidentally alluded to in this document—went unnoticed by the compiler of the Chronicle. As long as this prolonged emergency lasted, and for as long as viking armies were descending on London, all of the lands in the Thames basin were vulnerable to attack. The most prudent place for Æthelwulf of Wessex to maintain his family and household during those dangerous years prior to his great victory in 851 was at one of the more secure locations in his realm—such as Winchester which was equipped with defences and manpower to withstand sudden assault, and from where his wife and children could be quickly removed to safety into the heart of Wessex. Royal centres such as Wimbourne in Dorset, or Chippenham in Wiltshire, also offered greater safety to a royal wife about to give birth, than the remote and exposed location of Wantage. Even a remote royal centre such as Dorchester,[45] although close to the Channel coast, provided a more secure West Saxon hinterland from would-be raiders than frontier territory along the Berkshire Downs. The fact that Alfred, later in his life, left the estate at Wantage to his own wife Ealhswith, in his *Will*, cannot be used to prove that the place was a royal estate in West Saxon hands in the 840s. On the contrary, Eahlswith was of Mercian origin and Alfred left her only three estates— Edington in Wiltshire, and Lambourn and Wantage in Berkshire.[46] Lambourn is only six miles south of Wantage, and Alfred may have been leaving two adjacent Berkshire estates in former Mercian territory to his Mercian spouse. Lambourn later belonged to Æthelflæd wife of King Edmund[47] and Wantage was left by King Eadred to his mother, Eadgifu,[48] but subsequent West Saxon history of these two estates may have little bearing on the status of Wantage in 847–8. The remarkable expansion of West Saxon power across Mercia in the first half of the tenth century, combined with the upheavels of Danish colonization must have transformed traditional patterns among the Mercian landholding class as well as transforming allegiances in favour of the West Saxon aristocracy especially in border areas such as Berkshire. We cannot be certain where Alfred was born, and on the evidence available, it is unlikely to have been at Wantage.

Alfred was the youngest known surviving son of Æthelwulf, king of the West Saxons. The author of the *Life* of Alfred names his mother as Osburh, supposedly the daughter of Oslac the 'famous' (*famosi*) butler in King Æthelwulf's household.[49] The same author traces the descent of Oslac from Stuf and Wihtgar, two early sixth-century chieftains who ruled in the Isle of Wight. The details of Oslac's

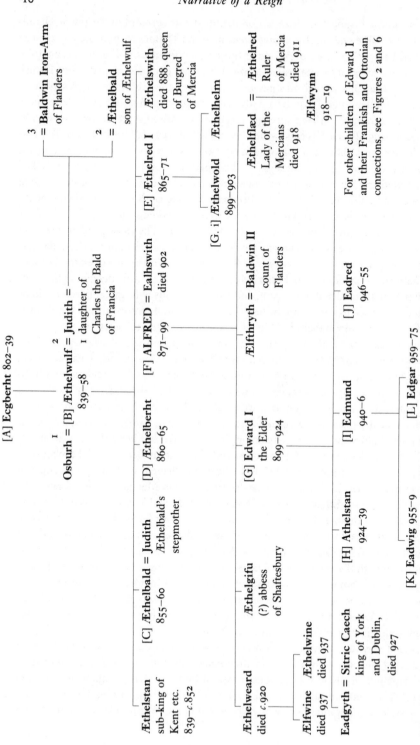

[A] – [L] = order of succession to West Saxon Kingship and (later) to the kingship of England

Fig. 1. The family of King Alfred and his place within the West Saxon dynasty

descent however were based on a garbled version of the Anglo-Saxon Chronicle for the years 530–4.[50] Oslac may or may not be the same as the magnate of that name who witnessed a contemporary charter of Alfred's older brother, King Æthelberht, in 858,[51] but we know nothing about this man or his daughter, Osburh, apart from this passing reference to them in the *Life* of Alfred. Alfred lagged far behind the more senior of his brothers in age. Already some eight or nine years before Alfred's birth, his eldest brother, Æthelstan, ruled as king (under his father, Æthelwulf) over 'the people of Kent, and the kingdom of the East Saxons (Essex) and the people of Surrey and of the South Saxons (Sussex)'.[52] Æthelstan must have been at least twenty-four years older than the infant Alfred. He began his rule over the eastern part of the extended kingdom of Wessex in the same year as his father Æthelwulf succeeded to the whole kingdom in 839 and twelve years later in 851, we find him victorious along with Ealdorman Ealhhere in a naval battle against the vikings off Sandwich in Kent. They captured nine enemy ships and put the rest to flight. This energetic king had probably died by 853. In that year the vikings were back on Thanet and Æthelstan's former ally, Ealhhere 'with the people of Kent', and Huda with the levy from Surrey led a disastrous attack on the viking position in which both ealdormen were slain and many were drowned, presumably in the marshy waters of the Swale. Æthelstan as king of Kent was conspicuously absent from this encounter and we may assume that he had died by 853.

Alfred's sister, Æthelswith, who was married to Burgred king of the Mercians in 853 must have been at least eight or nine years older than Alfred, assuming she was at least 14 at the time of her marriage,[53] which the biographer of King Alfred claims took place at Chippenham.[54] Her husband was eventually driven out of his kingdom after a twenty-two-year reign over Mercia in 874 and died in Rome. His queen, Æthelswith, died in Pavia in 888. Æthelwulf's next oldest son was probably Æthelbald, who took over the kingship during his father's absence on pilgrimage to Rome. Æthelbald's reign began in 855 when his father left for Francia and Italy, and his younger brother Æthelberht then ruled as sub-king of the eastern part of the kingdom.[55] Æthelbald was at least eight years Alfred's senior, given that he was old enough to take charge as king during a time of continuing Danish threat in 855. He may have been considerably older than that, since we find him fighting alongside his father in the West Saxon victory over the vikings at *Aclea* in 851. It is likely that Æthelstan, his brothers Æthelbald and Æthelberht, and perhaps their sister Æthelswith, were the children of a different mother from that of Æthelred and Alfred who came at the end of the family. The mother of Æthelred and Alfred had died by 855, since Æthelwulf acquired yet another wife while visiting the Carolingian court on his way home from Rome in the autumn of 856. This was the 13-year-old Judith, daughter of Charles the Bald, king of the Western Franks, who was married to Æthelwulf at the palace of Verberie on 1 October 856.[56] Judith returned to Wessex with Æthelwulf and on his death in 858, married her stepson, Æthelbald, who had succeeded to the kingship of Wessex. On the death of her second West Saxon husband in 860, Judith 'sold up the possessions which she had acquired in the kingdom of the English' and returned to Senlis in Francia where

she remained under her father's protection and under 'royal and episcopal guardianship' while another suitable husband was being procured for her. But Judith had
acquired a mind of her own by this time in her life, for behind her father's back
'she had changed her widow's clothing and gone off with Count Baldwin [of
Flanders] at his instigation and with the consent of her brother Louis [the Stam-
merer]'.[57] The brief but significant career of this Carolingian princess in the Wessex
of Alfred's childhood was, later on, to be used judiciously by Alfred and his circle,
to point to the prestige of Alfred's father's house. This Carolingian interlude
required careful handling, however, on the part of later Alfredian chroniclers, for
while Judith's marriage lent immense prestige to Æthelwulf's kingship, it also
dignified the kingship of Alfred's older brother, Æthelbald, and it was in Alfred's
interest to emphasize his father's high status and play down that of his brothers.

The Anglo-Saxon Chronicle contains a remarkable entry relating to the infant
Alfred in the year 853: 'And that same year King Æthelwulf sent his son Alfred to
Rome. The Lord Leo was then pope in Rome, and he consecrated him king (*7 he
hine to cyninge gehalgode*) and stood sponsor to him at confirmation.'[58] Apart from
the fact that West Saxon kingship was never in any pope's gift, we need to bear in
mind that Alfred was somewhere between 4 and 6 years old when this royal
consecration was supposed to have taken place. His father, Æthelwulf, was still
very much alive, and as king of Wessex was attacking the Welsh in that very year.
Wessex, under constant threat of viking invasion, had no need for infant kings in
853, and the kingship of Alfred's older brothers—Æthelbald, Æthelberht, and
Æthelred—all still lay in the future. Nor was the sub-kingship of Kent and the
eastern shires of greater Wessex an office to which the sons of a king would
automatically aspire or be given at an age when they could not cope with real
responsibility. We saw how Alfred's eldest brother, Æthelstan, was designated
king in the Chronicle at a time when he was leading Kentish armies in his own
right. His brother, Æthelbald, witnessed charters of AD 854 in his capacity as
ealdorman (*dux*) along with his brother Æthelberht, only one year before he
became king.[59] Earlier, in AD 847, the year perhaps, when Alfred was born, Æthelbald
witnessed a contemporary charter of his father in which he was designated simply
as 'a king's son' (*filius regis*).[60] By AD 850, Æthelbald had graduated to the status
of ealdorman or 'ealdorman and king's son' (*dux filius regis*).[61] So, there was a
natural progression from when a son came to responsible age. He first witnessed
charters as a king's son, and later as a man of office such as ealdorman, and
finally—if the *witan* so decided—as king. There is no question, therefore, that the
record of Alfred's papal consecration as an infant king could ever have been based
on a contemporary or genuine record relating to events of 853—or as some would
have it, of 855. This record was inserted in the Chronicle at the time of its
compilation in Alfred's reign, and it has all the appearance of an insertion designed
to show that even in infancy, Alfred's destiny for the kingship was clearly manifest.
It served a purpose, too, in promoting the standing of Alfred, retrospectively,
above that of his older brothers. Not only is there no comparable record in the
Chronicle relating to the childhood activities of any of Alfred's brothers, but as we

shall see, even records of events during their consecutive reigns as kings of Wessex were drastically summarized or ignored altogether.

Opinions on this record of Alfred's childhood visit to Rome have been bedevilled by doctrinaire views on the origins of the Anglo-Saxon Chronicle and on Alfred's role in that compilation, and they have been complicated , too, by esoteric arguments relating to distinctions between royal anointings, consecrations, and crownings.[62] Leaving aside these issues, for the time being, and concentrating on the Chronicle's bold record that the infant Alfred went through some form of king-making ceremony at the hands of Pope Leo IV, we recognize that a fraudulent claim was being made here, regarding the nature and origins of Alfred's own kingship. That claim could not have been inserted in the Chronicle until after Alfred's succession to the West Saxon kingship in 871, and it had clearly found its way into the record of the Parker Manuscript before the completion of the earliest section of that record or its prototype in the late ninth century. This astonishing and bogus claim, therefore, was presumably inserted in the Chronicle sometime during Alfred's reign and as Nelson pointed out, 'the story of the anointing could not have got into . . . the *Chronicle* . . . without the knowledge and one must assume the approval of Alfred himself'.[63]

Whitelock in her search for evidence to support the Chronicle's assertion that Alfred was party to some kind of papal ceremonial in Rome in 853, pointed to a twelfth-century collection of canonical rulings from the registers of three ninth-century popes. An extract from a letter of Pope Leo IV to Æthelwulf king of Wessex found in that collection would seem to offer us the true explanation of events:

We have now graciously received your son Alfred, whom you were anxious to send at this time to the thresholds of the holy apostles, and we have decorated him, as a spiritual son, with the dignity of the belt and the vestments of the consulate, as is customary with Roman consuls, because he gave himself into our hands.[64]

Here we seem to find support for the notion of Alfred's confirmation as well as for yet another ritual which might have been mistaken for a royal consecration—all at the hands of the pope.[65] This extract—supposedly from the register of Pope Leo IV—only survives in a twelfth-century English compilation,[66] known as the British Collection (*Collectio Britannica*). Ullmann cast grave suspicion over the genuine nature of some of the material relating to letters of Leo IV in this collection[67] and Nelson later offered several cogent reasons for treating Leo's fragmentary letter to King Æthelwulf as an eleventh-century forgery. She argued that there was no ninth-century parallel for a papal conferment of a consulship—an office which lacked all significance at that time; while under eleventh-century reforming popes, such a ceremony would have fitted in well with the claims and ambitions of a papacy seeking after imperial role models. Nelson further pointed out that the claim that Alfred 'gave himself into our hands' was redolent of claims of feudal commendation of the eleventh century.[68] She also compared the account of Alfred's 'consular' ceremony with eleventh-century accounts of papal dealings with

Russian and Spanish rulers and in particular with Gregory VII's letter to Isjaslaw of Russia describing the papal reception of Isjaslaw's son at Rome.[69] She pointed in particular to the phrase relating to Alfred's visit 'to the thresholds of the holy apostles' which also appears in those analogous eleventh-century accounts. This periphrastic reference to Rome, not by name, but as 'the thresholds of the holy apostles' (*ad Sanctorum Apostolorum limina*) was also a hallmark of the writings of Byrhtferth of Ramsey and his circle of Anglo-Latin writers at the turn of the millennium.[70] Numerous instances of the formula *ad limina sanctorum apostolorum* or its variants are found in the *Lives* of St Ecgwine and St Oswald, and the early sections of the *Historia Regum*—all dating to the late tenth or early eleventh century. The phrase was probably promoted by Cluniac writers at Fleury and elsewhere in late-tenth-century Francia and from there it was borrowed into the hermeneutic writings of English monastic reformers *c.*1000 and also taken up independently by Continental writers in circles of the papal reformers.

There is no need here to argue Nelson's case for this record having been compiled as ammunition in the dispute between Gregory VII and William the Conqueror over the issue of fealty to St Peter,[71] nor need we debate precisely how clerks in the papal curia got their hands on a Latin translation of the record of Alfred's supposed visit to Rome in the Anglo-Saxon Chronicle.[72] It will suffice to observe that this record from Leo's letter as preserved in the *British Collection* is too unsafe to provide a basis for any historical argument relating to Alfred's early life and least of all to provide proof of his hallowing or king-making at the hands of a pope. Whitelock's views on this subject depended on her acceptance of the fragmentary letter from Leo IV to King Æthelwulf as genuine, and her conclusions would now be part of the historiographical flotsam of Alfredian studies were it not that they were repeated by scholars who still clung to the notion of Alfred as 'truth-teller' (*veredicus*)[73] and who were reluctant to revise the ideas of a revered master.[74]

Following an idea which is as old as the time of Bishop Stubbs,[75] Whitelock supported Stenton in concluding that the papal ceremony which Alfred attended in Rome 'caused some of Alfred's contemporaries to imagine that the pope had consecrated him king in 853'.[76] Whitelock and Stenton argued separately but in ideological unison[77] that Alfred himself could not possibly have mistaken a ceremony in which he was invested with the insignia of a consul, for one in which he underwent a royal coronation. Indeed no, but they did not allow for the possibility that Alfred later in life may have chosen to mislead readers of the newly compiled Anglo-Saxon Chronicle, or that he may have allowed false information which was flattering to him, to stand unchallenged. There were few or none of Alfred's contemporaries, who were still alive in the 880s and 890s when the Chronicle was compiled, and who had been present at a supposed ceremony in Rome back in 853. Alfred's father and all his brothers were by then long dead—and significantly, none of them were ever supposed to have been present. Alfred's memory of an event such as this, from so far back in his infancy, would have been poor. The account which we have of it, therefore, derives either from the king's own reflections and political assertions later in his life, or from the wishful thinking of his adherents. The question may well be asked as to whether Alfred ever undertook such a journey when he was only an infant. The Rome pilgrimage was a most taxing ordeal—even for an adult—fraught with the danger of fever and other illness as well as the menace posed by vikings in the Channel, robbers on the roads of Francia, and Moslem raiders from the coast of Provence.[78] The Rome journey was fraught with perils even for mature and experienced Frankish travellers of the ninth and tenth centuries who encountered extortionists, assassins, and robbers, as well as risking life and limb in negotiating precipitous Alpine passes.[79]

The author of the *Life* of Alfred rightly imagined that if Alfred had gone to Rome at all, he must have gone in the company of his father, Æthelwulf, who made the pilgrimage two years after the supposed journey of his son in 855. And so, to cover all eventualities, we find in the *Life* of Alfred that the boy Alfred went *twice* to Rome during his childhood—once when he was 'sent' in 853, and again along with his father, when the ageing Æthelwulf set off in 855 and returned in the following year.[80] We may discount the possibility of a West Saxon infant going twice to Rome within two years. Nelson's attempts to reconcile the record of the Chronicle with that of the *Life* of Alfred lack economy and do not match her otherwise sound judgement on this subject. She held that Alfred made only one journey to Rome in the company of his father in 855–6.[81] Alfred in this scenario was later responsible for misinterpreting some kind of ceremony, which took place during his reception by the pope, and he later misreported this as a royal anointing.[82] In order to make this ceremony comparable with the anointing of the sons of Charlemagne by a pope in 781, and with the crowning of Charlemagne by Pope Leo III in 800, Alfred was prompted to portray his own anointing at the hands of yet another Leo—Leo IV (847–55).[83] He, or one of his circle, therefore inserted the record of a separate visit by himself to Rome in 853, when Leo IV was still on the papal throne. Because a double visit to Rome seemed implausible, the 'real' visit of 855 (to Pope Benedict III (855–8)) was subsequently deleted from the records and preserved only in the *Life* of King Alfred ascribed to Asser. There are several objections to this hypothesis. If the Chronicle initially contained the record of only one visit to Rome in 855 by King Æthelwulf and his infant son Alfred, then why should Alfred or anyone else move Alfred's visit back to 853 while leaving the father's journey in its original place at 855? Surely it would have been easier to move the record of the entire Rome journey from 853 to 855 and thereby preserve the supposed truth of the situation—i.e. that Alfred did indeed accompany his father. But this did not happen. There is in fact no evidence from the Chronicle manuscript to suggest that the record of Alfred's journey in 853 was an interpolation. That record appears in the main hand in the body of the text of the earliest Parker Manuscript, and it appears in that manuscript as well as in Manuscript B, along with events of 853—sandwiched between Æthelwulf's Welsh expedition and the account of a battle against vikings on Thanet.[84] The evidence from the Chronicle suggests that the invention of the hallowing of Alfred as king, by Pope Leo, was original to that record. The *Life* of King Alfred supports this view. As we

shall see, that *Life* relies so heavily on the narrative of the Chronicle that for much
of its progress it may be described as a Latin translation of the Chronicle covering
the years of Alfred's life from 851 to 887. The *Life* of Alfred closely follows the
order of events in Manuscripts A and B of the Chronicle in relation to the 'first'
journey to Rome. Alfred's journey is dated to 853 and is recorded, as in the
Chronicle, between Æthelwulf's Welsh expedition and the attack on the vikings in
Thanet. The additional information in the *Life* that Alfred was accompanied by a
great number of nobles, and that Pope Leo 'anointed the child Alfred as king,
ordaining him properly'[85] are embellishments which are characteristic of the style
of that work. The *Life* of Alfred then goes on to follow the Chronicle's record of
Æthelwulf's pilgrimage to Rome in 855, with the added information that King
Æthelwulf took 'his son Alfred with him, for a second time on the same journey,
because he loved him more than his other sons'.[86] We shall return to examine this
passage in the *Life* of King Alfred later on, but two points need stressing at this
stage. First, the evidence of the Chronicle must take priority as a late-ninth
century manuscript source over any argument based on the *Life* of Alfred whose
only surviving manuscript was lost in the eighteenth century. Secondly, the account of Alfred's 853 journey in the *Life* of King Alfred can be shown to be based
on a translation of the Chronicle narrative akin to that preserved in the earliest
Parker Manuscript. The only major variation in the two accounts relates to the
statement in the *Life* of Alfred that King Æthelwulf took his son to Rome for a
second time in 855. That statement must be regarded as an accretion inserted by
the author of the *Life* of Alfred to make a special case for how much Æthelwulf
preferred his son Alfred to his other sons—a dominant theme as we shall see, in
this section of the *Life* of Alfred. This doubling of events by the author of Alfred's
Life is part of the same careless tendency that is evident in his habit of missing out
or confusing entries in the version of the Chronicle which he was translating.[87]
The sequence of events therefore in the Chronicle must be made to stand on its
merits. Of Æthelwulf's journey to Rome in 855 there can be no doubt. It is
supported by the *Life* of Pope Benedict III[88] and by the Frankish *Annals of St.
Bertin*.[89] There is, as we might expect, no mention of an infant Alfred in those
sources. Evidence for Alfred's separate journey in 853 relies entirely on the Chronicle's account, which was fabricated some thirty-five years later to make a special
case for the prestigious nature of Alfred's kingship and to assert the claims of
Alfred and his immediate heirs over those of the other sons of Æthelwulf and their
descendants. In this sense we may indeed argue that Alfred or one of his circle
deliberately ascribed the king-making ceremony to Pope Leo IV in an attempt to
echo the celebrated crowning of Charlemagne by Pope Leo III. The only argument
in favour of the Rome pilgrimage ever having happened at all is Nelson's plea that
'it may be doubted if Alfred could successfully have inserted the story of the papal
anointing into the *Chronicle*, unless it had been widely known that he had indeed
visited Rome in his infancy'.[90] But the historicity of Alfred's journey cannot rest on
his ability to lie successfully about its outcome, some thirty-five years after the
supposed event. Alfred, or one of his supporters, if we are to accept Nelson's

argument, not only fabricated a tale of royal anointing, he also altered the year in which he travelled from AD 855 to AD 853; he claimed he went without his father, and he lied about the pope whom he was supposed to have met—switching Benedict for the seemingly more prestigious Leo. By any standards of scholarly investigation this is a very unsatisfactory case on which to base any historical claim. In the absence of other supporting evidence we can never be sure that Alfred ever went to Rome or met a pope there. The case is worse than unproven, and we have only the meddling of Alfred himself or his supporters, in the historical record, to blame for this impasse.

Alfred was 10 or 11 when his father died in 858. Wessex was then ruled by Alfred's older brother, Æthelbald, whose Carolingian queen was the young Alfred's sister-in-law and erstwhile stepmother. Æthelberht, another of Alfred's older brothers, was ruling as sub-king of Kent, Essex, Surrey, and Sussex. Alfred's brother who was nearest to him in the seniority was Æthelred, who did not become king until 866. Æthelred was at least 16, or thereabouts, in that year, but since he was obviously Alfred's senior, he was more likely to have been 19 or older by then, and he was probably only a few years older than Alfred. When King Æthelwulf died back in 858, few in Wessex could have imagined that either of the young princes, Æthelred or Alfred, would ever come to the kingship. It was not inevitable that the sons of a king should all succeed their father in the kingship, even in the unlikely event that four of those sons should die young. Kings of the West Saxons were chosen from a *stirps regia*, and however narrow the lines of succession in the House of Ecgberht had become, all sons and grandsons of kings must still have been eligible for office. The laconic style of the Anglo-Saxon Chronicle, its economy with the truth, and its overriding desire to promote the image of Alfred as a successful king—all conspire to distract our attention from the fact that it was as late as 868 (the Nottingham expedition) before Alfred began to move close to the kingship. There were almost certainly other contenders in the field—first cousins and nephews and perhaps even other brothers, who are unknown to the record. A certain Oswald, described as a king's son (*filius regis*) witnessed a charter of King Æthelred, along with Alfred in AD 868[91] and we find Oswald's name attached to a charter of Æthelred's sister, Æthelswith, queen of Mercia, in the same year.[92] Although the authenticity of both charters has been questioned, the appearance of this unusual witness is likely to be genuine—perhaps borrowed from an authentic list elsewhere. The same *Oswealdus filius regis* witnessed a charter of AD 875, where his high birth is underlined by the fact that his name appears third after King Alfred and Æthelred, archbishop of Canterbury.[93] Oswald, as a king's son, cannot have been a son of the young Æthelred, but he is likely to have been a son of Æthelstan or less likely of Æthelbald, and as such he could have been as old as his first cousin, Alfred. Alternatively, he might have been yet another son of King Æthelwulf, although his name does not conform to the initial Æ- pattern of Æthelwulf's known sons. Oswald disappears from the record after 875 and the subsequent fate of this atheling is unknown.

Æthelbald only survived his father for two years in the kingship of Wessex. The

Life of King Alfred claims that Æthelbald, with the help of Ealhstan bishop of Sherborne and Eanwulf, ealdorman of Somerset, had raised a rebellion against his father while Æthelwulf was away on pilgrimage in Rome and that on Æthelwulf's return he refused to hand back the kingdom to his father.[94] There is no record of this rebellion elsewhere, and the Chronicle assigns a reign of five years to Æthelbald, implying that he ruled as king of all Wessex from when his father went on pilgrimage in 855. The kingship now passed to Æthelberht in 860. The Danish menace continued to stalk the shires, and Winchester was assailed by a viking army in 860 which was eventually defeated by the levies from Hampshire led by their ealdorman, Osric, assisted by Ealdorman Æthelwulf and his men of Berkshire. In 865 the Kentish peninsula was overrun by a raiding party which had encamped on Thanet and which was large enough to extract a promise of Danegeld from the men of Kent. Æthelberht died after a five-year reign in 865–6 and as in the case of Æthelbald, he was buried in Sherborne. Æthelred became king in 866. The beginning of Æthelred's reign coincided with the arrival of the Great Heathen Army of Danes in England. This was a formidable invading force which was clearly bent on conquest and settlement. For all of Æthelred's reign, events in Wessex can only be observed obliquely and as a sideshow to the momentous happenings in Northumbria and East Anglia which bore the full brunt of the viking onslaught.

The earliest viking activity recorded in the British Isles and Francia consisted of piratical raiding and involved isolated sorties against towns and monasteries in search of loot and quick gains. Targets for these piratical assaults usually lay near coastal waters or along navigable rivers which could be penetrated by viking longships with their shallow draft. This earliest phase lasted from *c*.795 until the middle of the ninth century when more determined efforts at conquest and land-winning (Old Norse *landnám*) began to appear. This transition from raiding to full-scale invasion was heralded by records of viking war-parties wintering in estuaries and offshore islands as at Dublin from 841;[95] on Noirmoutier (at the mouth of the Loire) from 843,[96] Thanet in 851, and Sheppey in 855. It was heralded too, by Norse ability to leave their ships in fortified bases and sweep across large tracts of countryside on foot or on horse. Attempts at settlement in Ireland although confined to coastal strongholds was clearly part of the same movement towards conquest and colonization that we can observe in England. The arrival of the Great Army in England in 865, although some 25 years later than the foundation of Norse Dublin, nevertheless marked a similar turning-point in the viking wars in England, as the establishment of the Dublin base had for Ireland. Furthermore, just as there is clear evidence from contemporary annals to show that viking activity in England was associated with raiding armies in Francia, so too, similar connections are evident between viking campaigns in England and Ireland at this time. The reasons for the Norse drive towards colonization and the conquest of territory in the middle of the ninth century are complex and multi-faceted. Clearly, the phenomenon of larger invading armies bent on conquest was dependent on the availability of young warriors and a concomitant rise in population in the Scandinavian homelands. Circumstance may have varied too, between the more fertile and southerly lands of Denmark which were more immediately influenced by events in the neighbouring Carolingian empire, and those in more distant and less fertile Norway. Those differing circumstances achieve special importance when we realize that Norwegian colonists concentrated their hostile attentions on northern and north-western Scotland and the Irish Sea, while Danish marauders directed their attacks against Saxony, Frisia, Francia, and England. There was, however, one major development in the history of the Christian West which must have had the most profound influence on all Norse activity and that was the visible weakening of the Carolingian empire on the death of the emperor, Louis the Pious, in 840. The division of the empire between the three sons of Louis at the treaty of Verdun in 843; the rivalry and hostility which existed between those brothers and the difficulties which all three of them experienced with their magnates proclaimed the vulnerability of the Christian West throughout every corner of Scandinavia. The invasion of England by the Great Army of Danes in 865 must be seen against the background of Danish attempts to profit from the apparent disintegration of western Francia under the rule of Charles the Bald. From 856 onwards, a series of viking warbands—sometimes acting in unison, but frequently operating on their own account or allying with Charles's enemies—caused havoc on the Seine, the Somme, and the Loire.[97] Charles eventually rid the Seine basin and the heartland of his realm of that particular viking menace, partly through the payment of enormous sums of Danegeld in 865–6 and partly through the judicious defence of the Seine by means of a fortification at Pîtres which prevented the invaders from penetrating further up that river.[98] By July 866 the *Annals of St. Bertin* record the fact that the Seine vikings had withdrawn as far as the sea, and that some of them then headed for the Ijssel district in Frisia.[99] Others undoubtedly headed for eastern England to join a full-scale invading force bent on the conquest of that land. The viking hoard of some 250 coins deposited almost certainly by a member of the Great Army of Danes at Croydon in 871–3[100] contained seven Frankish deniers which had probably been hoarded by their collector since the middle of the 860s. One of the seven coins was a survival piece from the reign of Louis the Pious (814–40), while the remaining six were the *Christiana Religio* types of Charles the Bald, issued between 840 and 864.[101] Such limited numbers of out-of-date Carolingian coins is what we should expect to find in the purse of a viking veteran in England in 872, who had campaigned in Francia in the early 860s.

The immediate target for vikings in England was the conquest of Northumbria—an English kingdom torn apart by rival factions of its aristocracy who had contested its kingship from the beginning of the ninth century. Just as civil strife in Francia had attracted the attention of viking opportunists in the 840s, so now it was to be the turn of Northumbria, and a Danish invading force joined by vikings from northern Francia and Hiberno-Norse Dublin was poised to transform the political map of England. Sawyer believed that the size of viking fleets and armies, and their destructive impact on Western society, was greatly exaggerated by monastic chroniclers in Christendom.[102] More recent economic studies centring on the

logistics of feeding men and horses, while advocating that warbands had to fragment into small raiding parties in order to sustain themselves, support the notion
of large-scale armies transported by hundreds of ships.[103] There is overwhelming
evidence from independent contemporary sources located as far apart as Northumbria and Moslem Spain and from Ireland to Byzantium, to vouch for the size and
destructive power of ninth- and tenth-century Scandinavian warbands. Much of
the controversy and long-running debates on the nature of viking raiding and its
effects on Western civilization have been complicated by a failure on the part of
many scholars to distinguish between different phases in Norse activity. If we
chose to compare data from early piratical raiding with periods of conquest, or
with periods of later settlement and Christianization of Norse settlers, then we can
so confuse the evidence as to allow for the finding of anything we may wish to
discover. Of course Western chroniclers exaggerated the odds that were stacked
against defending native armies, such as the notorious record of 600 Danish ships
on the Elbe in 845[104] or the reported slaying of 9,000 viking horsemen at Saucourt
in northern Francia in 881.[105] But such exaggerations must be set alongside frank
admissions of Norse superiority even when the vikings were outnumbered by
native armies. So, for instance, the *Annals of St. Bertin* record a viking victory at
Melun in 866 in the face of 'what looked like the larger and stronger squadron'
commanded by leading Frankish magnates.[106] Furthermore, the universal reporting of occasional small numbers of viking ships testifies to the ability of annalists
to admit independently to the existence of insignificant raiding parties in England,
Francia, and Ireland. The record of the Anglo-Saxon Chronicle conforms, on the
whole, remarkably well to contemporary evidence from elsewhere in Europe to
show that its assessment of the scale of the Danish threat was accurate and that the
arrival of the Danish invading force in 865 marked a sea change in the struggle for
Anglo-Saxon England. The Danish force was described in the Anglo-Saxon Chronicle as a *micel here* and I make no apologies for so naming it as the *Great Army*, for
to an English chronicler writing in the late 880s, it seemed that this force was
indeed 'great' in relation to anything England had experienced before, and we may
safely accept Stenton's assessment that the size of such an army 'should be reckoned in thousands rather than hundreds'.[107]

   The Danes arrived on the shores of East Anglia, well out of sight of the West
Saxon chronicler who later reported the event and who, not surprisingly, failed to
record the number of invading ships. When at the opening of Alfred's so-called
Last War in 892, yet another 'great Danish army' arrived from Boulogne on the
shores of Kent, the number of ships were then reckoned at 200 or 250. Hæsten
who landed at the same time and settled at Milton Regis in Kent, led an additional
80 ships. These numbers for a large invasion force are in broad agreement with
Frankish records of Weland's command of 200 ships on the Seine in 861 which
were later joined by a further 60 ships.[108] Weland's fleet, incidentally, seems to
have been the same force which attacked Winchester in the previous year.[109] The
viking *Imhar*, who may well have been one of the original leaders of the Great
Army which invaded England in 865–6, is said in the contemporary *Annals of*

Ulster to have led 200 ships back to Dublin in 871 following his campaign in Britain.[110] Guthrum, who may have been a relatively late arrival in Alfred's First War, lost 120 ships in a storm off Swanage in 877, and yet he could still put enough men in the field to capture Exeter and to overrun parts of Western Wessex in 878. For an army to be capable of achieving a victory which had eluded rival English kingdoms for centuries—i.e. the conquest of Northumbria, East Anglia, and Mercia—we may assume that somewhere between 300 and 400 ships landed on the coast of East Anglia in 865, carrying an army of up to 5,000 men. To set the number of ships and men at this high figure is not to give credence to other exaggerated numbers in monastic annals. The Great Army which attacked England was a special invading force in search of territory and farmland. Events of the next twenty years would show how remarkably resilient and successful this force would prove itself to be. Such an army must not be confused with lesser raiding parties such as the handfuls of Danish ships which Alfred is known to have attacked in 882 (4 ships), 885 (16 ships), or 896 (6 ships). Significantly, the Anglo-Saxon chronicler distinguished between the 16 ships which Alfred's fleet encountered at the mouth of the East Anglian Stour and 'a large naval force of vikings (*hie micelne sciphere wicenga*)' which his fleet encountered on their homeward voyage.[111] Frankish and Irish chronicles make similar distinctions between isolated raiding parties and massed fleets. A 'few' ships only (*cum parvis navibus*) are recorded as attacking Meaux in 862.[112] We might compare the account in the *Annals of Ulster* of a Norse fleet of 32 ships on Lough Foyle in 921 when the annalist modestly relates that the Northern Uí Néill king, Fergal son of Domnall, succeeded in slaying the crew of one ship, burning the vessel, and taking its spoil.[113] Medieval annalists may well have rounded up figures for estimating large numbers of enemy ships. But that does not mean that they could not count, or that they exaggerated all estimates. We must at least give them credit for being able to distinguish between large fleets and 'great armies' as opposed to lesser fleets and smaller numbers of fighting men.

The Great Army which probably arrived in the autumn of 865 wintered in East Anglia and entered into a peace with the East Angles who were then ruled by their king, Edmund. Presumably it was under the terms of that peace, that the Danes were equipped with horses and in the following year they rode north, and crossing the Humber seized the city of York on All Saints' Day (1 November) 866. Gillmor has reminded us of the need for such mounted expeditions to include one pack horse to carry supplies for every two to four mounted warriors.[114] But as the Danes rode north in late autumn and early winter, it was possible for such an overwhelming force to seize stored grain stocks *en route*, and it is also very likely that the greater part of this host sailed north to the Humber in the all-important longships. York, the seat of the first Northumbrian Christian king, Edwin, and the city of Alcuin, was now to become a Scandinavian stronghold ruled for the most part by Scandinavian kings who had the closest dynastic ties with Dublin. This new Scandinavian regime was destined to survive north of the Humber until 954 and its influence on northern English society was to endure far beyond that time.

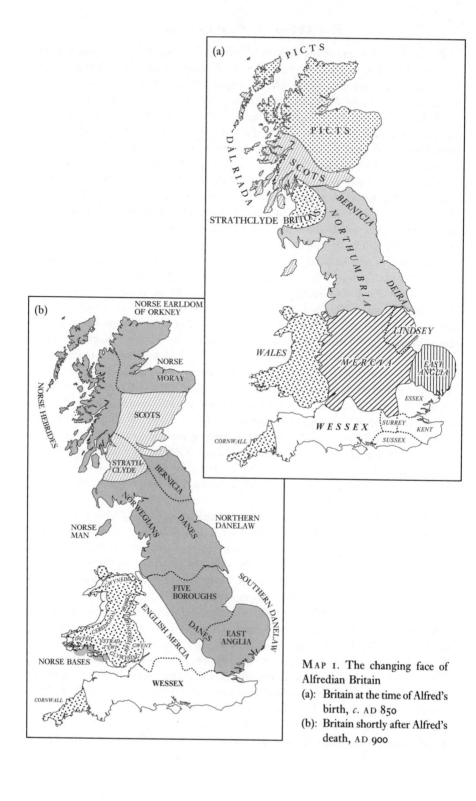

MAP 1. The changing face of Alfredian Britain

(a): Britain at the time of Alfred's birth, *c.* AD 850

(b): Britain shortly after Alfred's death, AD 900

Viking armies were always quick to exploit internecine strife. At the time of the Danish invasion, the Northumbrians had deposed their king, Osberht, and appointed Ælla, 'a king with no hereditary right'.[115] It took the rival Northumbrian factions from early November to the third week in March to patch up their differences and make a combined assault on York. For the Northumbrians to stake all on a pitched battle against a newly arrived enemy who was at full strength was reckless. To try to dislodge that enemy from a defended position was fatal. The vikings, unlike their victims in the British Isles, understood the value of fortifications and the employment of real tactics in warfare. In spite of the heroic rhetoric of Old Norse skaldic poetry, no ruse was too cowardly and no advantage too mean if it achieved the all-important victory and the survival of vulnerable viking warbands.[116] The vikings, time and time again, showed an understandable dislike of risking all on a pitched battle. Fortifications allowed them to dominate a territory while leaving them with the option of refusing a challenge to fight. The force which chose to attack them, on the other hand, experienced all the dangers and disadvantages of exposing themselves while engaged in an assault on a fortified position. The Danes had been allowed almost six months to consolidate their position in York. The Northumbrians launched their counter-attack on 21 or 23 April 867 and the results for them were catastrophic: 'An immense slaughter was made of the Northumbrians, some inside and some outside [the city of York] and both kings were killed and the survivers made peace with the enemy.'[117]

The Danes now consolidated their hold on one of the largest of the Old English kingdoms. One of the terms of the peace imposed on the native survivors was the establishing of a dependent territory in Northumbria beyond the Tyne, which exploited old regional and tribal feelings centred on the territory of the former Anglian kingdom of Bernicia. The Danes based themselves on York and from then on, the Vale of York was under the control—directly or indirectly—of the invaders. In 868 the Danish army was confident enough to move south against Mercia and, following a well-tried tactic, it immediately seized a defensible point—the town of Nottingham—where it spent the winter. The Mercian king, Burgred, and his councillors sent to King Æthelred of Wessex for help. King Æthelred and his brother Alfred—now old enough to take part in a military expedition—led an army into Mercia, joined forces with the Mercians, and laid siege to the vikings in Nottingham. Mercifully, for the English, the Danes declined to be drawn to battle and the result was a stalemate. We are told that the Mercians concluded a peace with the enemy, and a peace made with a viking army, fresh from its triumph in Northumbria, must have entailed the payment of an oppressive tribute—most likely including victuals—so necessary for men and horses in field and garrison conditions—as well as payment in coin and precious metal. This was the young Alfred's first encounter with a viking host, and he was no doubt a witness to the negotiations with those strange warriors who were to prove most powerful and treacherous antagonists. The Anglo-Saxon Chronicle designedly shies away from providing details of any agreement reached with a victorious viking host. But a comparative study of contemporary Frankish sources shows what price had to be paid to buy off a viking warband which was bent on conquest or plunder. We read in Frankish annals of huge sums ranging from 2,412 lbs. of 'purest gold and silver' levied from Charles the Fat at Asselt in 882, to 12,000 lbs. of gold and silver extorted by vikings after the death of Carloman only two years later.[118] We are informed that these immense payments in precious metal, which drained church treasuries of late ninth-century Francia, were 'weighed out under careful inspection'[119] and weighed out, too, 'according to their [viking] scales'.[120] But in addition to a seemingly endless catalogue of Danegeld paid in bullion, we read also of food renders paid to viking warbands in Francia. In 861 Charles the Bald made a large payment to viking allies who were newly returned from their attack on Winchester, and who were besieging the island of Oissel on the Seine. That Carolingian hand-out included not only 5,000 lbs. of silver but also 'a large amount of livestock and corn' and all paid over 'so that the realm should not be looted'.[121] Three years later, the Carolingian, Lothar, paid over to the northman, Rudolf son of Harald, 'a large quantity of flour and livestock and also wine and cider',[122] while in 869, a viking army demanded 'a great sum of silver and quantities of corn, wine and livestock from the local inhabitants' as their price for peace in the Le Mans and Tours regions.[123] The payment of such food renders is what we should expect in the case of large warbands desperately living off the land, and in spite of the Chronicle's silence, we may assume that very similar payments in corn and livestock were made to viking armies in Alfredian England.

It is regularly assumed that it was while on the Nottingham expedition that the young Alfred—he was about 20—was married to Ealhswith, who is said in the *Life* of King Alfred to have been of Mercian origin.[124] But Alfred's wife is nowhere named in the *Life* of the king—so we cannot be even certain that the author is referring to Ealhswith. On the other hand, the names of the parents of Alfred's unnamed wife are given by the author of Alfred's *Life* as Æthelred *alias Mucill*—an ealdorman of the *Gaini* (*Gainorum comitis*)—and Eadburh, a lady supposedly of royal Mercian stock. We know nothing about the *Gaini* or of their whereabouts within Mercia, and the name of this people, as given in the *Life* of King Alfred, does not appear as a proper Old English form.[125] Stenton located the *Gaini* 'in the east of Worcestershire',[126] and his 'strong argument' for so doing was based solely on the supposition that a certain Ealdorman Mucel, 'son of Esne' who was granted an estate at Crowle in Worcestershire from King Wiglaf of Mercia in AD 836[127] was the same person as the grandfather of King Alfred's wife as mentioned in the *Life* of King Alfred. Stenton[128] took Mucel Esne's son to have been the candidate earmarked for being identified with Alfred's father-in-law. If there were to be any substance in this speculation, then Esne's son would have been the father of Alfred's father-in-law. Any connection, however, between the elusive ealdorman of the *Gaini* who is mentioned in the *Life* of Alfred and various ealdormen called Mucel in ninth-century charters is based on an unacceptable chain of supposition. The Mucel who is named in Alfred's biography as an *alias* for Æthelred, ealdorman of the *Gaini*, has been tentatively identified with an Ealdorman Mucel who witnessed two charters in AD 868 along with the two kings' sons, Alfred and Oswald.[129]

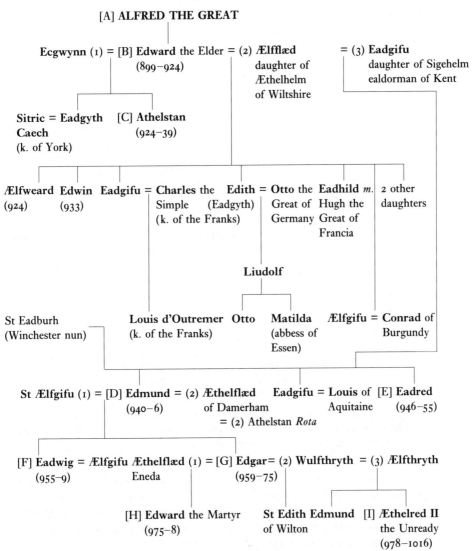

[A] – [I] = order of succession to West Saxon kingship and (later) to the kingship of England. Based on an original genealogy by Anne Williams.

FIG. 2. The descendants of King Alfred the Great

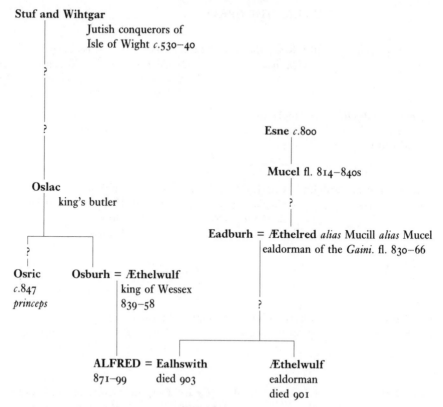

Stuf and Wihtgar
Jutish conquerors of
Isle of Wight *c.*530–40

Esne *c.*800

Mucel fl. 814–840s

Oslac
king's butler

Eadburh = Æthelred *alias* Mucill *alias* Mucel
ealdorman of the *Gaini.* fl. 830–66

Osric   Osburh = Æthelwulf
*c.*847   king of Wessex
princeps   839–58

ALFRED = Ealhswith   Æthelwulf
871–99   died 903   ealdorman
died 901

FIG. 3. The supposed family of King Alfred's mother and of his Queen, Ealhswith. This figure is intended to illustrate speculative theories and few of its details are supported by contemporary or reliable sources

The identification of Alfred's father-in-law with this supposed Mercian Mucel is extremely unsound. The two charters in question have an essentially West Saxon list of witnesses, and the most we can say about the name ascribed to Alfred's father-in-law in the king's biography is that it was current in both Mercian and West Saxon ruling circles in the ninth century.

Mercian magnates with the name *Mucel* (with variants *Mucael/Mucoel* and *(?)Muca*) attested some 32 Mercian charters from 814 to 866.[130] Keynes and Lapidge[131] allocated the period 'from 814 to the 840s' to one Mucel, and identified a second younger man of the same name as attesting 'from the 830s until 866', on the grounds that two men of that name were attesting in the 830s and 840s. In this they were following the notes of the learned A. J. Robertson[132] and of Stevenson.[133] Both Mucels witness for the last time together in the doubtful grant of King Beorhtwulf of Mercia in favour of the monastery of Bredon in Worcestershire,[134] and both men were designated in that document as *princeps*. But the evidence is infinitely more complex than the problem presented by an overlap in time between two Mercian Mucels during the period 836–48. There were also at least two other West Saxon magnates of this name in the middle of the ninth century. King Æthelred's West Saxon charter of AD 868 relating to Worthy in Hampshire[135] was witnessed by a *Mucel dux* and a *Mucel minister*. The latter was almost certainly the same as the thegn (*minister*) called Mucel who witnessed a series of West Saxon charters from AD 850 to AD 867.[136] We seem rather to be dealing with one Mercian Mucel in charters spanning the period from AD 814 to 825, with a further instance at AD 836.[137] A second run of the name occurs in 18 Mercian charters from AD 836 (and more regularly from 840) to 857, followed by further Mercian instances in AD 864[138] and AD 866.[139] Finally, a *Mucel minister* attests in Wessex from AD 850 to AD 868 and a *Mucel dux* also attests West Saxon charters in 868.[140] The West Saxon thegn and ealdorman of that same name attest together in King Æthelred's grant of land at Worthy in Hampshire.[141] The charter of AD 836[142] highlights the complexity of the problem, for it was attested by two Mercian ealdormen of the name Mucel, one of whom was Mucel son of Esne. The Esne may refer to an Ealdorman Esne who attested charters from AD 779 until c.810. Whitelock was, as ever, cautious about connecting Mucel Esne's son with Alfred's supposed father-in-law,[143] but Keynes and Lapidge[144] subsequently constructed a chain of speculation relating to Alfred's supposed Mercian in-laws. So, 'it seems likely' that an earlier Mucel attested from 814 to c.840 and that he 'may be the Mucel son of Esne mentioned in S[awyer] 190' whose father was 'presumably' the Ealdorman Esne of Mercian charters c.800. As for the second Mucel, c.830 to 866, 'it is conceivable' that he was the son of the first Mucel and 'presumably' he was also Alfred's father-in-law. A final link in this preposterous chain of supposition and guesswork—which ultimately derives from Stenton[145]—was the assumption on the part of Keynes and Lapidge that this 'second' Mercian Mucel—Alfred's supposed father-in-law—witnessed a charter[146] of AD 868. That charter, witnessed by the West Saxon king, Æthelred, and dealing with lands in West Saxon Hampshire, includes, not surprisingly, what is essentially a West Saxon witness list. Of those witnesses for instance, Ealdorman Wulfhere was associated with estates in Wiltshire[147] and attested West Saxon charters during the period 854–871/7. Ealdorman Ælfstan attested West Saxon charters from AD 864 down to 875.[148] Ealdorman Wigstan (*alias* Wistan) attested West Saxon charters in AD 863, 864, and 868. The West Saxon thegns, Mannel (*Monnel*) and Beorhtmund both attested King Æthelberht's charter for Sherborne in AD 864,[149] while Mannel also appears in the witness list of King Æthelred's grant relating to St Martin's church in Canterbury in AD 867.[150] Furthermore, no less than eleven of the West Saxon magnates who witnessed King Æthelred's grant of Worthy in Hampshire[151] also witnessed Æthelswith's grant of Lockinge in Berkshire in the same year[152] which may suggest that the *Mucel dux*, who appears in the witness lists of both those charters, was acting in his capacity as a West Saxon rather than a Mercian ealdorman. The entire chain of speculation relating to the identity of Alfred's father-in-law rests on a poorly expressed assumption[153] that the Mucel who witnessed King Æthelred's grant of Worthy in Hampshire in 868 happened to be a Mercian magnate who was visiting Wessex in that year in connection with the marriage of Ealhswith to Alfred. If we are to believe the author of the *Life* of Alfred, however, it was the West Saxon party which travelled to Mercia to attend Alfred's wedding there.[154] The precise dating of Alfred's marriage as well as the notion that the future king was married to a Mercian in 868 is dependent on an uncorroborated statement in the *Life* of Alfred.[155] Even if we were to accept the testimony of the *Life* of Alfred in relation to the information offered there on Alfred's marriage, there is still no conclusive way of identifying his supposed Mercian in-laws.

The only certain point of reference in the subject of Alfred's in-laws is that the Anglo-Saxon Chronicle records the death of 'Ealdorman Æthelwulf (*Aþulf*), the brother of Ealhswith, King Edward's mother' in AD 901.[156] This brother of Ealhswith may or may not be the same as the Mercian Æthelwulf, described as a *venerabilis dux* in the settlement of a dispute over land at Upton in Blockley, Worcestershire,[157] in AD 897, and who is taken on the evidence of this charter to be related to the royal line of Mercia.[158] But given the exclusively West Saxon orientation of the Chronicle at the beginning of the tenth century, and bearing in mind that we have so few reliable charters and witness lists from the beginning of Edward's reign, it is equally, if not more probable, that Ealhswith's brother, Æthelwulf, was a West Saxon magnate. In short, all we may say with certainty of the origins of Alfred's wife is that she was called Ealhswith and that she had a brother, Ealdorman Æthelwulf or Aþulf, who died in 901. If she did come of Mercian royal stock, then she and Alfred may have married in 868 and the marriage may have been arranged to coincide with the expedition of King Æthelred and Alfred to Nottingham in that year. But the supposed Mercian origins of Alfred's wife and the names of her Mercian parents are supplied by the author of the *Life* of Alfred without corroboration from any other source, and the charter evidence, when viewed in isolation of the *Life* of Alfred, may point to a West Saxon origin for Alfred's wife. Ealhswith died three or four years after Alfred in 903.[159]

The Great Army returned to York in 868–9 only to push south again in the following year. The Danes rode across Mercia—under that peace concluded at Nottingham in the year before—and took up winter quarters at Thetford in East Anglia in the autumn or early winter of 869. Thetford was an ideal base for an army intent on further conquest. It was much nearer to the waters of the Wash in the Middle Ages than today[160] and it lay at the centre of a series of roads and trackways which gave swift access to the whole of Norfolk and Suffolk. Edmund as king of the East Angles, must have been party to an earlier peace agreement with the Great Army in 865, but 'that winter [869] King Edmund fought against them, and the Danes had the victory and killed the king and conquered all the land.' Over a century later, Abbo of Fleury, who was then staying at Ramsey Abbey in Huntingdonshire, wrote up the *Life* or *Passion* of King Edmund whom he depicted as a martyr brutally slaughtered in defence of his Christian faith by heathen Danes. Abbo claimed to have got his facts from Archbishop Dunstan of Canterbury, who in turn had heard the story when it was related by a former armour-bearer of Edmund of East Anglia in the presence of King Athelstan (927–39).[161] The account

is highly hagiographical and must be treated with caution, but incidental details in
this *Life* of Edmund may be genuine. Abbo claimed that the Great Army arrived
in part at least by sea, which would make much sense, given that Thetford was so
near to the inner waters of the Wash. Thetford also lay on the Icknield Way which
led from the coast at Holme by the Wash, south through Thetford and on into
south-east Mercia, past Aylesbury and Wallingford, leading on towards Wantage
in Berkshire and the Ridge Way along the Berkshire Downs. Abbo also claimed
that the Danish leader first tried to negotiate tributary status for Edmund and the
East Angles with the stipulation that Edmund share his 'ancient treasures' (the
royal hoard) and his 'hereditary wealth' (royal estates) with the conquerers, and
that Edmund would 'reign in future under him [i.e. Ivar]'.[162] Edmund is said to
have been amenable to these terms only on condition that the Danish leader,
Hinguar (Ivar), become a Christian. Abbo has no mention of Edmund's battle
against the Danes. He relates that the king was taken captive, cruelly tortured in
a way that is suggestive of Norse sacrificial rituals, and that eventually he was
beheaded. Coins struck to commemorate Saint Edmund were circulating in substantial numbers in the Southern Danelaw within twenty or twenty-five years of
Edmund's death which shows that the cult of the East Anglian king was not only
very early but also enjoyed popularity within the territory controlled by his slay-
ers.[163] But the Anglo-Saxon Chronicle is silent on the details of Edmund's end at
the hands of the Danes, leaving us rather, with the impression that Edmund was
slain by them in battle. While it was not in Abbo's interest to detract from
Edmund's status as a martyr by showing his resistence to the Danes in battle,
equally, it was not in the interest of either Alfred or his supporters to celebrate the
martyrdom of a contemporary English king in a West Saxon Chronicle dedicated
to the glorification of the House of Æthelwulf. A chronicle, partly designed as we
shall see, to glorify Alfred's military career was not likely to accommodate accounts
of heroic spiritual behaviour on the part of a neighbouring king which might only
serve to diminish West Saxon achievements. The Chronicle at this point in its
narrative is merely supplying a summary of the campaign of the Great Army of
Danes, and it was not until Wessex became directly involved in the Danish war in
870-1 that the narrative suddenly provides a detailed—almost day by day account—of the action. Its silence therefore, on the events surrounding King
Edmund's death can be put down to a reluctance on the part of the chronicler to
take the spotlight away from Alfred, and partly because of a characteristic lack of
interest in affairs outside of Wessex. There is, however, numismatic evidence to
show that Alfred may have been personally involved in the more commercial
aspect of the promotion of the cult of Edmund. Three St Edmund Memorial coins
found in the Cuerdale hoard (deposited *c*. AD 902) carry a reverse inscription
ALFRED REX DO which have been firmly associated on stylistic, as well as epigraphic
grounds with Alfred's issues from the Canterbury mint (hence *DO* for *Dorovernia*).
These coins, unlike a blundered imitation of the same issue, are of excellent
workmanship and were therefore likely to have been issued from Alfred's Canterbury mint rather than produced in East Anglia as Danish imitations of Alfredian

issues. So, in spite of the silence of the Chronicle on the cult of Edmund and on his heroic stand taken against the Danish invaders, it later suited Alfred's commercial ambitions to promote the cult of his East Anglian neighbour by issuing or adapting a coinage in his memory and on which Alfred's own name appeared.

The Danes, having disposed of Edmund on 20 November 869, next turned their attention to Wessex. Their advance was swift, given that East Anglia, although defeated, had to be secured throughout the winter 869–70. The invaders probably proceeded against Wessex in a pincer movement by land and water, which would explain how their main thrust was focused so far up the Thames basin at Reading. Part of the fleet may have moved south around the coast of Essex and into the Thames, while a land army marched south along the Icknield Way across Ermine Street and Watling Street to reach Reading and the Berkshire Downs. The Danes seized Reading which was ideally placed in a frontier region, giving them access to raiding over Berkshire and northern Hampshire, while at the same time its position on the navigable Thames provided safety and the prospect of a swift withdrawal if circumstances so dictated. Ships were undoubtedly used in this manœuvre, even if they are not mentioned in the Chronicle. Reading's position at the junction of the Thames and the Kennet provided an ideal location for viking longships. According to the author of the *Life* of Alfred, the Danes built a rampart between the two rivers.[164] If we can trust that record, Reading would then have provided the Danes with a location exactly similar to their permanent bases at York and Dublin—between two rivers and with connecting ramparts forming a 'ship-fortress (*longport*)' where warships could be beached in safety.[165] The camp (*castra*) which the chronicler Æthelweard tells us the Danes 'laid out (*metati sunt*)' near London in 872 was also most likely a rampart designed to protect the all-important warships.[166]

King Æthelred of Wessex now faced the gravest crisis, but significantly there is no mention in the Chronicle that he was assisted by his former ally and brother-in-law, Burgred king of the Mercians. When Burgred's kingdom had been invaded three years previously, Æthelred responded to Mercian calls for help and led an expedition to Nottingham which lay some 130 miles north of Winchester. Nottingham lay far beyond West Saxon frontiers, and the supplying of such an expedition must have put a great strain on West Saxon resources. It had been a hazardous military venture, where Æthelred and Alfred had put themselves and their West Saxon war machine at great risk. Earlier, back in 853, Burgred had sought and obtained the presence of King Æthelwulf of Wessex and his army in a campaign against the Welsh. But for the three years from 871 to 874 during which Wessex took the full brunt of viking attack, Burgred held back. It is true that the Mercian ealdorman, Æthelwulf, and his Berkshire yeomen stood yet again in the breach as they had done when Winchester was attacked back in 860, but Burgred was conspicuously absent from the battles with the vikings on the Berkshire Downs. He may have been clinging to the peace which he had negotiated with his enemies at Nottingham in 868, or he may have been hoping that if he kept out of trouble, the danger would go away. If so, he was greatly mistaken. Alternatively, Burgred may have left the defence of Berkshire to his ealdorman, Æthelwulf, if Berkshire had not indeed by now slipped out of Mercian hands and become a part of Wessex. It was certainly Ealdorman Æthelwulf who led the defence. He attacked and defeated a Danish army at Englefield west of Reading, which gave King Æthelred and his brother Alfred four days to get an army together and join the men of Berkshire before Reading. Stenton, who mistakenly concluded that Æthelwulf had been defeated at Englefield,[167] suggested the Mercian ealdorman may have fought with household troops from his own estate at Pangbourne, which lay only three miles from the battlefield at Englefield, along an ancient road leading from Dorchester-on-Thames down to Silchester in northern Hampshire.[168] However that may have been, Reading offered the Danes access to rich pickings from raiding over Berkshire. But an army that had already conquered two kingdoms and attacked a third was not about to risk all it had achieved on isolated raiding forays.

The Great Army had left East Anglia for Reading with one or two major purposes in view—further conquest and or the collection of huge Danegelds in money and in kind to reward and supply an occupying army. The detailed outcome of that conquest may not have been clearly envisaged by the Danish leaders, but a number of options would have been held out to them—control of London and the Thames basin; the establishment of permanent bases on the middle and lower Thames from which Danegeld might be regularly extracted from Wessex; or the eventual conquest of Wessex and eastern and south-eastern Mercia. However great or small their numbers, the Danes could never have hoped to rule all their conquered English territories directly. But it was within their capacity to control and colonize some regions while reducing others to tributary status. This Danish concentration on the Thames during the First War in Wessex reminds us of similar viking concentrations on the Seine and the Loire in the second half of the ninth century, which offered access to large stretches of Frankish territory. It reminds us, too, of viking bases on the middle and upper Shannon, in Lough Ree and elsewhere, in ninth- and tenth-century Ireland.[169] The advantages which these inland river-bases offered to the invaders were twofold. Northmen disliked being separated by long distances or for long periods of time from their ships, while the rivers which gave access to those ships brought the invaders within easy striking distance of targets inland. More crucially, while rivers usually offered English, Irish, and Franks, relatively secure boundaries between one potentially hostile territory and another, the vikings could exploit what were to them, highways between traditional enemies.[170] Nelson described viking involvement in the internal politics and feuding of the late-ninth-century Franks as exploiting 'vertical fault lines' within Carolingian society.[171] It was the rivers of Francia which constituted the reality of those fault lines, which the vikings could exploit by attacking all sides of a river basin at once, or by playing off traditional native enemies against each other. The Thames at Reading also lay on just such a fault line, on a frontier which, as we have seen, had been fought over by Wessex and Mercia from as far back as the middle of the eighth century. A Danish garrison, securely based at

Reading, could strike not only at the heart of Wessex, but could also dominate southern and western Mercia. Besides, the Danes had already concluded a peace with the Mercians in 868 and under cover of that peace, they could now secure their northern flank and concentrate their hostility against Wessex. Burgred had not intervened when the Danes rode across Mercia on their way to annihilate Edmund of East Anglia in October–November 869,[172] nor did he act now when Wessex, ruled by the dynasty of his wife, was attacked by the same seemingly invincible Danish force which had already toppled the Old English kingdoms of Northumbria and East Anglia.

The West Saxons were better placed than other English kingdoms to withstand a Danish assault. Their lands were rich, and the rule of a strong tightly knit dynasty since the accession of Ecgberht back in 802 must have worked for the consolidation of royal patronage throughout the shires. That in turn would have promoted strong local government in the hands of loyal ealdormen whose wealth and authority were secure and who owed their prosperity to the patronage of King Æthelwulf and his succeeding sons. Ninth-century Wessex had escaped the inter-necine strife which had dragged down Northumbria, and it had succeeded, too, in replacing traditional hostility towards the Mercians with friendly ties of marriage and military alliance. Wessex had also escaped the more destructive piratical viking raids of the early ninth century which, because of their intensity and unrelenting nature, had drained other societies in Britain and Ireland of much of their wealth and stamina. Yet Wessex had sufficient experience of sporadic viking warfare to keep its levies on their mettle and to familiarize themselves with viking tactics. Memories of King Æthelwulf's defeat at the hands of thirty-five ships' companies at Carhampton in north-west Somerset in 843, served as a salutary reminder of the consequences of defeat. It was not of course, the function of the Anglo-Saxon Chronicle to dwell on such failures, but Carhampton set off alarm bells even in distant Francia, where the consequences of that viking victory were spelt out: 'the Northmen emerged the winners: plundering, looting, slaughtering everywhere, they wielded power over the land [of the West Saxons] at will.'[173] Fortunately for Wessex, such victorious raiding on the part of the Norsemen was a relatively rare occurrence and this was almost certainly due to the effectiveness of resistance at shire level. Evidence for the capable organization of defence in the West Saxon shires is afforded by several notices in the Chronicle of viking armies being more often engaged by shire levies than by massed armies led by the West Saxon king. So we read of Danes being met in battle by the men of Somerset and Dorset (*c*.845); men of Devon (851); men of Kent (851); men of Kent and Surrey (853); and the men of Hampshire and Berkshire (*c*.860). What is notable about these engagements is the absence of any mention of the West Saxon king, and how often individual ealdormen and their shire levies succeeded on their own initiative in driving off a viking assault. On the other hand, there was cause for real concern at the massed viking army which appeared at Reading in 871. This was not an isolated raiding party which could be beaten off by local yeomen. Ealdorman Æthelwulf of Berkshire clearly appreciated that much, for in spite of his preliminary victory, he waited for the arrival of King Æthelred and his brother, Alfred, before daring to try a direct assault on Reading. And while West Saxon warriors were numerous enough and experienced enough to field a credible deterrent, their leadership may have been comparatively weak. King Æthelred was about 25 when he faced the Great Army at Reading in 871. His brother Alfred was just past 23. Neither men are recorded as having had any previous experience of border warfare or of the ferocity of Norse battles, apart from their abortive trek to Nottingham in 868. They were now about to make their first costly mistake.

Æthelred and Alfred had decided to take Reading by direct assault or at least to draw the Danes into a pitched battle before the town. Either way, the decision was unwise. Attacking forces were always at a disadvantage trying to dislodge vikings from an entrenched position, and we know from contemporary Frankish annalists that the vikings were masters at the use of fortifications in war. The viking position at Jeufosse on the Seine in 856 was described by a contemporary Frankish observer as 'an excellent defensive site for a base camp'.[174] Carloman and his warriors could not attack a viking warband holed-up in Avaux in 882 'without grave danger to themselves' and so wisely, 'as evening drew on they cautiously drew back and took up their posts in nearby *villae*'.[175] Those who did try to take a viking fort by direct assault rarely succeeded. The leaders of a Frankish attack on a viking island-fortress in the Seine were criticized by a commentator on their own side for their 'ill-considered attack' in the very same year, 871, when Æthelred and Alfred led their army against Reading. That Frankish assault on the Seine base in 871 resulted in 'very heavy [Frankish] losses' and from which the leaders themselves 'barely managed to escape, leaving many dead'.[176] Irish kings, too, learnt bitter lessons from their relentless struggle with the Norsemen. The high king, Niall Glundub, ordered his Leinster tributaries to attack a Norse war-camp at Cenn Fuait in 917, when that place was defended by Sitric, grandson of Ivar—that same Ivar who campaigned in Britain in the years prior to 871. The Leinstermen lost their king, together with two tribal kings and their bishop in the assault.[177] Two years later, in 919, Niall Glundub was himself slain in battle while leading his warriors against the vikings at their principal stronghold in Ireland at Dublin.[178] Defending armies in the Christian West found themselves caught between the dilemma of risking their very survival by putting all their men in the field in one battle against a viking host or losing valuable men in a smaller force which could be outnumbered by their enemies. So, while the Northumbrians staked all on one battle and lost at York in 866, Wala, the Carolingian bishop of Metz was reprimanded in the Annals of Fulda because he 'came against them [the Northmen] rashly with a small army and was killed' in 882.[179]

The Norsemen themselves were careful to avoid pitched battles whenever possible,[180] because of the obvious consequences which defeat held for an invading warband which was far from home. Since their first major battle in Wessex was fought at Reading, the Danes had a ready-made line of retreat behind its defences, if things were to go badly wrong for them. Things did go badly wrong—for the West Saxons rather than the Danes. 'A great slaughter was made on both sides' but the Danes had the victory, and the West Saxons left their veteran Mercian ally, Ealdorman Æthelwulf, dead on the field. Here was a leader they could ill afford to have lost—a man who had beaten off the 'great naval force' which attacked Winchester back in 860 and who, only four days before his death at Reading, had struck the first successful blow against the Great Army of Danes since its arrival in England six years before. The twelfth-century Anglo-Norman chronicler Geffrei Gaimar claims that Æthelred and Alfred were driven as far as Whistley Green (*Wiceled*), about six miles east of Reading, and that their army escaped across a ford (on the Loddon) at Twyford ('double ford') which the Danes did not know of.[181] If Gaimer's information is correct, the West Saxon host was being driven north-east, away from home and in danger of being boxed in between the Loddon and the Thames around Wargrave Hill. Yet West Saxon losses cannot have been too heavy, for four days later King Æthelred and Alfred were again in the field, fighting a pitched battle 'against the whole army' at Ashdown—the Old English name for the Berkshire Downs. This engagement gave King Æthelred his first badly needed victory over the invaders. The Chronicle relates that the Danish host was in two divisions—one led by their kings, Bagsecg and Hálfdan, and the other led by the Norse jarls. While King Æthelred fought against the kings' troop, Alfred led a separate assault against the jarls. The Chronicle's account of the arrangement of the Norse army at Ashdown is supported by a contemporary Irish account of a battle fought between Constantine king of Scots and Ragnall, grandson of Ivar, the Danish king of York, at Corbridge on the Tyne, in 918, where the Norse jarls were said to have fought in a separate body from their kings and from the young nobles.[182] This deployment of warriors may have been determined according to the rank or status of Norse leaders or it may reflect the presence of different warbands who preserved their separate identities on the battlefield.[183] The Anglo-Saxon Chronicle lists the enemy dead at Ashdown as the king, Bagsecg, and five jarls—all of which latter we are led to presume were victims of Alfred's victorious contingent. The account is rounded off with the words: 'and both enemy armies were put to flight and many thousands were killed, and they continued fighting until night.' The general siting of this battleground on Ashdown shows that after their successful defence at Reading, the Danes were beginning to move along the Ridge Way leading on into the heart of Wiltshire and towards Salisbury Plain. But no decisive battle had yet been fought, and in spite of the 'many thousands' of Danes reportedly killed, the enemy fell back on Reading and re-emerged to win a victory only a fortnight later. Blocked by the West Saxons at Ashdown, from moving either west along the Mercian–Wessex border or from penetrating Wiltshire, the Danes next pushed south on to the North Downs in Hampshire and defeated King Æthelred and Alfred at Basing, a couple of miles east of Basingstoke. This Danish victory must have put Winchester in some danger, and it was followed two months later by yet another hard-fought Danish victory at *Meretun*, where the Danes fought again in two divisions, and where King Æthelred lost his warrior-bishop, Heahmund of Sherborne 'and many important men'. Heahmund may earlier have served as royal chaplain to King Æthelberht.

The location of the disaster at *Meretun* is unknown. Merton in Oxfordshire was too far north, and being north of the Thames did not fit with the Chronicle's summing up that 'during that year nine general engagements were fought against the Danish army in the kingdom south of the Thames'.[184] Merton in north central Devon is much too far west to suit a location appropriate for a Reading garrison which was acting with caution, while Merton in south London seems too far east for a West Saxon army to risk a pitched battle. Given that all the known recorded battle sites from this campaign of 871–2 were located either at Reading, or on the Berkshire Downs or to the south at Wilton and Basing, we may safely locate *Meretun* in either Berkshire or north Wiltshire or neighbouring Hampshire.[185] This battle of *Meretun* may have been fought at the place of that name where King Cynewulf of Wessex was ambushed and slain by Cyneheard, his enemy and rival in 786.[186] For while the Parker Manuscript of the Chronicle locates the West Saxon defeat of 871 *æt Meretune*,[187] MS B's reading is *æt Merantune*.[188] In the Chronicle's lengthy and heroic account of the slaying of King Cynewulf and of the subsequent slaying of his killer back in 786, we are told in both Manuscripts A and B that the king was visiting a mistress (*on wifcyþþe*) at *Merantune* when he was attacked.[189] There is a possibility—and it is no more than that—that Martin in south-west Hampshire near the Dorset border was the place in question. In 944–6 Alfred's grandson, King Edmund, made a grant to his queen, Æthelflæd, of estates at Pentridge, Damerham, and Martin along the Dorset–Hampshire border.[190] This apparently genuine but fourteenth-century record gives the form of Martin as *cum Mertone*. Martin is only eight miles south of Wilton which was a royal estate in the time of King Æthelwulf, and where Alfred fought his first battle as king in that same eventful year of 871. King Æthelwulf issued two charters from the *villa regali* at Wilton, one contemporary or near-contemporary document confirming an agreement between Archbishop Ceolnoth of Canterbury and King Æthelwulf (along with his father, Ecgberht) in AD 838[191] and another doubtful specimen being a grant by Æthelwulf of lands in Wiltshire issued to his thegn, Wiferd, on Easter Day, 22 April 854.[192] Martin lies between Winchester and Axminster, the burial places of the two major rivals who fell in the bloodbath of 786, but it is some forty miles from Keynsham, the burial place of Bishop Heahmund of Sherborne who was slain by the Danes while fighting for his West Saxon king at *Meretune* in 871. On the other hand, the burial place of high-status magnates who were slain in battle provides little indication of the whereabouts of their place of death. The body of Ealdorman Æthelwulf, for instance, who was slain by the Danes at Reading in 871 was taken to distant Derby for burial.[193] Such magnates were taken for burial to churches which they had endowed during life. It has to be said, however, that we cannot be certain that the events of 786 took place at the same *Merantun* as those of 871, or that any one of those places was definitely at Martin in Hampshire.

The latest enemy victory at *Meretun/Merantune* was followed by two further disastrous events in this dramatic year. A new Danish host—a 'summer army' joined the invaders at Reading—attracted no doubt by rumours of imminent conquest of some of the richest land in Britain. Meanwhile, Æthelred, the West Saxon king, a young man still only in his twenties, died after Easter. The magnates of Wessex buried their lord in Wimborne Minster in Dorset. Wimborne had strong associations with the kings of Wessex. Cuthburh, the sister of King Ine (688–726) had founded a nunnery there. As the Chronicle reminds us: 'Cuthburh . . . had been married to Aldfrith, king of the Northumbrians, and they separated during their lifetime',[194] after which she founded Wimborne. Tetta, yet another of Ine's sisters, had also been an abbess of Wimborne[195] and there is every reason to believe that the house continued as a royal monastery controlled by women of the West Saxon dynasty down to Alfred's time. We know little of the details relating to abbatial succession in Anglo-Saxon monasteries during the ninth century, but given that Anglo-Saxon dynasties had proprietorial interests in their monastic foundations in common with early Irish and Continental Germanic monastic patrons, we may safely assume that West Saxon kings were unlikely to have abandoned their family interest in a community such as Wimborne in Alfred's time. Wimborne was a royal estate in the reign of Edward the Confessor,[196] but the kings of Wessex, having had a family association with a royal monastery founded there in the early eighth century, almost certainly had an estate there at that early time. It was presumably the presence of the estate, which made possible the grant of land for the nunnery in the first instance. The fact that King Æthelred was buried in the minster at Wimborne and that his son, Æthelwold, was later in 900 to choose Wimborne as a base for his rebellion against Edward the son of King Alfred, all suggests that Wimborne was a centre of royal power throughout the ninth century. It was no doubt while they were gathered for Æthelred's funeral in 871, that the West Saxon *witan* or royal councillors elected Alfred to the kingship in his brother's place. The chronicler Æthelweard vouches for Alfred's presence at his brother's funeral at the very time when a new Summer Army arrived to swell the ranks of the invaders in Wessex.[197]

Æthelwulf's youngest son, Alfred, had now come to the kingship of Wessex, against all the odds, when he was still only 23. His grandfather, father, and four of his brothers had all been kings before him, and now as Wessex and Anglo-Saxon society as a whole faced its greatest challenge, it was the turn of this 'last son of King Æthelwulf'[198] to lead the warriors of Wessex against a seemingly numberless, if not invincible foe. Alfred was not untried in battle. The Chronicle trumpets loudly that he accompanied King Æthelred on all that king's recorded campaigns and it claims, too, that Alfred often rode on expeditions or 'raids (*rade*)' in his own right, before he became king in 871, although these are not specified in any detail.[199] The Chronicle at this point in its make-up, focuses exclusively on the progress of the Danish wars and on Alfred's growing military involvement with the Great Army of Danes. No other aspect of the future king's career (with the exception of the Rome pilgrimage) is dealt with in this source apart from his prowess as a military commander and tactician. But if we are to believe Alfred's biographer, we must also accept that he was a pious invalid tormented by an affliction such as piles from his youth[200] and who suffered from yet another mysterious and most painful and debilitating illness from the time of his wedding in 868 up until he was in his forties[201] and presumably until the end of his life.

Alfred's reign opened badly. The men of Wessex had been defeated three times by the Danish garrison at Reading, and now the numbers of that garrison had been replenished by the arrival of a Summer Army. King Æthelred's burial service at Wimborne might seem to have been held well out of reach of the Danes at Reading. But Alfred had his next battle with the invaders one month after becoming king, at Wilton, which lay only twenty miles north of Wimborne and which had easy access to Wimborne along the Roman road to Badbury Rings in Dorset. The Chronicler Æthelweard, who translated a recension of the Anglo-Saxon Chronicle, but whose own Latin rendering of it was so often garbled, does not mention the battle of Wilton by name. He records that while Alfred was attending his brother's funeral, the combined Danish army attacked 'the army of the English [which] was then small, owing to the absence of the king'.[202] The Chronicle proper offers us the earliest and most reliable account that 'Alfred fought with a small force against the whole army at Wilton'[203] and while Æthelweard must also be referring in his garbled way to that same battle at Wilton, we may take it that Alfred was indeed the commander at that English defeat. Alfred may have been staying at Wimborne or at the royal estate at Wilton when the Danes struck. The double monastery for monks and nuns at Wimborne, which was already endowed with 'high and stout walls' prior to 836,[204] would have provided ideal sanctuary for the women and children of the royal kindred of Wessex, as well as a secure place to deposit part at least of the royal hoard of coin and treasure. The proximity of Wilton to Wimborne, and Wilton's status as yet another West Saxon royal centre, may suggest that Alfred was taken by surprise and forced to defend himself at short notice—and hence the smallness of his force. Wilton was the last recorded battle in the first campaign of the Great Army in Wessex, and the compiler of this section of the Chronicle clearly recognized that a watershed had been reached as he attempted to sum up the precarious situation thus far. That summing up, which was attempted more than fifteen years later, seems clearly designed to distract the reader's attention in the 880s and 890s, from the predicament Wessex had found itself in, back in 871:

And during that year nine general engagements were fought against the Danish army in the kingdom south of the Thames, besides the expeditions which the king's brother Alfred and [single] ealdormen and king's thegns often rode on, which were not counted. And that year nine [Danish] earls were killed and one king. And the West Saxons made peace with the enemy that year.[205]

We notice that while nine battles are counted in this summary, only six were described and named, earlier in the Chronicle narrative. Had they or 'the expeditions which the king's brother, Alfred and ealdormen and king's thegns often rode on' been significant West Saxon victories, the compiler of the Chronicle would not have refrained from offering us details. We notice, too, that while a tally of Norse slain is presented, there is no backward glance to Ealdorman Æthelwulf or to

Bishop Heahmund and the 'many important men' of Wessex who had fallen on the West Saxon side. What is crucial to this account is that of six battles recorded, only two were West Saxon victories, and of these only Ashdown was a West Saxon victory involving the leadership of a king (Æthelred). The last three engagements—Basing, *Meretun*, and Wilton—were all West Saxon defeats.

The concentration of battles around West Saxon royal estates may have been due to the fact that such places provided natural centres from where Æthelred and Alfred could rally and organize the support of their thegns. Great estates were also administrative centres where tribute for the invading Danes could be collected in the form of food renders as well as money. It has been suggested with good reason that the presence of the Croydon viking hoard (*c.*871–3) of some 250 coins, as well as ingots and hack-silver, was in some way connected with the great estate there of King Alfred's archbishop of Canterbury.[206] But such explanations do not in themselves explain why battles took place precisely at those places. It looks rather as if the Danes were keeping up pressure on the West Saxon rulers and that they were deliberately intent on driving them off their estates, or on seizing the royal treasure—the source of so much West Saxon wealth and patronage. We are reminded of Ivar's demand to the unfortunate Edmund of East Anglia that he would have him share his 'ancient treasures' and 'hereditary wealth' with his Danish overlords.[207] The association of Danish attacks with royal centres, although conspicuous during Alfred's First War, was not confined to that struggle. King Æthelwulf's defeat at Carhampton back in 843 occurred at a remote place in west Somerset where Alfred later possessed an estate which he left to his son and heir, Edward the Elder.[208] The site of Æthelwulf's great victory over the Danes at *Aclea* (probably in Hampshire or Surrey) in 851 cannot be identified, but it can scarcely be a coincidence that Æthelwulf's father, Ecgberht, issued a charter in favour of his *praefectus*, Wulfheard, at *Acleah* back in 824.[209] Charters were normally issued at royal estates or other centres of royal power, where they could be witnessed by the magnates who made up the *witan* and who were likely to assemble at such places. Although Alfred's Second Danish War clearly saw a radical change of tactics on both sides, we shall see that royal estates continued to loom large in the struggle for the control of Wessex.[210] This, like so much other evidence relating to the viking wars, shows that the Scandinavian invaders of Wessex were well informed on matters of local politics and on economic resources, and that far from their raids being random, they were calculated to maintain constant pressure on the West Saxon king and his household.

Alfred's defeat at Wilton set the seal on a series of Danish victories and hence the notice that 'the West Saxons made peace with the enemy that year'. While Æthelweard claims that the Danes 'took no spoil (*sine spoliis*)' after their victory over Æthelred and Alfred at Basing,[211] he does significantly write of the *dominatione* ('tyrannical rule') of the Great Army in his summing up at the end of the First War in Wessex and adds that 'afterwards they dispersed, carried off plunder and ravaged places'.[212] Because Alfred still had an army in the field, Wessex did not quite lie at the mercy of its invaders. But the West Saxons were now a defeated force and the peace which both the Chronicle and Æthelweard claims they made with the Danes unquestionably involved the payment of geld. The fragmentary record of a coin hoard from Reading containing coins of Burgred of Mercia, Edmund of East Anglia, and of Alfred's brothers—Æthelberht (860–5) and Æthelred I (865–71) most likely dates from this time.[213] But such a modest record of only eleven coins which can now be accounted for in the Reading hoard count as little compared with the thousands of silver pennies that went to make up the huge Danegelds which we know from Frankish sources were levied by the invaders. In 872 the Danes withdrew to London 'and then the Mercians made peace with the army',[214] and Æthelweard adds: 'they fixed cash payments'.[215] Æthelweard informs us, too, that Alfred paid money (*pecuniam*) to the Danes during his Second War at Wareham in 876[216] when he was in less dire straits than after his defeat at Wilton. It is unthinkable that the invaders withdrew to London without taking their share of spoil, and the holy places of Wessex such as Malmesbury, Wimborne, and Glastonbury, together with the bishoprics of Winchester, Sherborne, and Canterbury must all have suffered either in yielding up their treasures for Alfred's tribute as part of the peace (*friþ*), or when, as Æthelweard tells us, places were ravaged by the Great Army in the aftermath of the West Saxon defeat.

Alfred was, after all, in a much more vulnerable position in 872 than Burgred of Mercia. For although Burgred had been forced to pay up, his armies—so far as we know—had not been defeated by the Danes in battle. Nor had Burgred's kingdom, unlike Wessex, been ravaged by a victorious army. When the monks of Abingdon came to write up the history of their house in the twelfth century, they recorded a tradition that the Danes drove out the monks and destroyed the monastery so that only the ruined walls remained.[217] The place was, as Stenton pointed out,[218] 'in the path of one of the raids which compelled the West Saxons to make peace with the invaders at the close of the year [871]'. Abingdon may not have been restored as a monastic church until the time of Abbot Guiatus (Cynath *fl.* AD 930) 'who under Athelstan recovered all things which the Danes, the companions of *Inguar* and *Ubbar* took away'.[219] The silence of the Anglo-Saxon Chronicle on the details of Alfred's plight counts for little, since, as we shall see, this was a carefully edited and monitored source compiled under royal patronage. Alfred, who was a master of playing down the consequences of defeat and bad times, referred only very obliquely in his own writings to those dark days. Nor did he ever attribute them directly to himself or even to the period of his reign. Speaking vaguely of that time 'when I came to the throne (*ða ic to rice feng*)' and when there were supposedly so few scholars south of the Thames, he goes on: 'When I considered all this I remembered also, how I saw before it had been all ravaged and burnt, how the churches throughout the whole of England stood filled with treasures and books.'[220] Whatever the element of exaggeration, Alfred fails to tell us that the period when most destruction of treasures and holy places was accomplished in Wessex can only have been during the first years of his own reign and in the period 876–8. One of the remarkable features which distinguishes the Anglo-Saxon Chronicle from contemporary Frankish and Irish annals is the notable suppression of all mention of viking attacks on West Saxon monasteries. We can be certain that the monasteries of Wessex were targeted by the Danes and that not only Abingdon, but also exposed religious houses such as those in the coastal areas of Kent were destroyed altogether. But the compilers of the Chronicle in Alfred's reign deliberately suppressed what was a major feature of other contemporary annals because records of the destruction of monasteries reflected on Alfred's own ability as a ruler charged with the defence of his Christian people. Alfred chose instead, in his own writings later on in his reign,[221] to distract the reader's attention away from the destruction of West Saxon monasteries, and to concentrate on the decline of learning, which he as a great scholar was going to put right. It was a clever ploy to substitute the idea of cultural decline from within, for the catastrophic events which he had been unable to prevent, and which had assailed his people from without. The Northumbrian, Alcuin, more than half a century before, had chosen to place the blame for the horrors of viking attack on the sins of his people. Alfred's emphasis on internal decline has played into the hands of those modern historians who would have us believe that the viking contribution to the Christian West was all gain in the form of burgeoning trade and the growth of towns, and that any speak of smoke from burning libraries is all down to the bad press of monastic writers. Before Alfred's reign (and the last year of King Æthelred's life), Wessex had known viking raiding—but those early raids had been sporadic and on the whole, as we have seen, they had been successfully repulsed. And a viking raiding party, once it was heavily defeated, would have yielded up not only any loot taken from within the region, but perhaps much else besides. It is even possible that earlier defeats of vikings raiders had enriched the treasury of King Æthelwulf, and it is an indication of West Saxon security that that king could set out for Rome in 855 and return to his kingdom unharmed. But after Alfred's defeat at Wilton in 871, the weakness of his position rendered his reign radically different from that of his grandfather, father, or any of his older brothers.

The situation prevailing in England when the Danes withdrew from Reading to London, probably in the autumn of 871, was very grave indeed. The kingdoms of Northumbria and East Anglia had been conquered and their kings slain. Alfred had been brought to terms after his defeat at Wilton, while his brother-in-law, Burgred, who had done nothing to help him, had renewed his peace with the invaders in 872. The Danes now held Burgred's most important Mercian port of London and dominated the Thames estuary with their fleet. It is true that the Mercian and West Saxon kings with their attendant aristocracies and armies were still to the good. Yet Burgred does not appear to have put up any fight either now or later, and his kingdom was soon to pass without battle into Danish hands. While the West Saxons had mounted crucial and sustained resistance throughout 871, successive military defeats may now have brought them into an even more conspicuously tributary position than that of the Mercians. Although Danish hegemony in Wessex had not yet been tested by a decisive battle, nevertheless Hálfdan and other leaders in his Great Army were now *de facto* overlords of all England. It was little wonder that their remarkable achievement would soon pass into folkore to be celebrated in the English Danelaw and in later Icelandic sagas under the heading of the conquests and exploits of the Sons of Ragnar Lodbrok.[222]

Only the chance survival of a few charters allows us a glimpse of the widespread burden inflicted by the conquerors, of which the Anglo-Saxon Chronicle was otherwise careful to suppress all trace. A grant by Wærferth bishop of Worcester of land at Nuthurst, Warwickshire, to the king's thegn, Eanwulf, shows us how Danish tribute was levied far beyond the Thames basin during their successful campaign from Reading and London in 871–2.[223] Wærferth leased the lands at Nuthurst 'with the unanimous permission of his community in Worcester' to Eanwulf to have for his own life and for that of three of his heirs when the estate would then revert to the monastery at Stratford. In return the bishop received 20 mancuses of tested gold: 'This, however, the above-mentioned bishop agreed to, chiefly because of the very pressing affliction and immense tribute of the barbarians, in that same year [872] when the pagans stayed in London (*pro inmenso tributo barbarorum eodem anno quo pagani sedebant in Lundonia*).'[224] Wærferth had been forced to pawn an ecclesiastical estate in an effort to help his king buy off the Danish warlords. The 20 mancuses which the bishop received amounted to 600 silver pence which had the buying power of about 100 fat oxen. King Alfred left 100 mancuses to each of his ealdormen in his *Will*,[225] but that was a once-off or final bequest to the ten or so leading magnates next to the king, whose loyalty to Alfred's son and successor had to be assured with generous patronage. Bishop Wærferth's transaction shows that Burgred used his bishops to help him levy and collect the Danish tax, and it shows also that the church was a rich and obvious target for the king to fall back on. If Mercia, which so far as we know, never offered major resistance to the Danes, was compelled to provide such an 'immense' tribute to the invaders, then how much greater was the spoil and tribute which the Danes had extracted from the West Saxons who had repeatedly and unsuccessfully opposed the Scandinavians in battle.

Alfred must have found himself under immense pressure from his magnates in the years between 871 and 878 to seek the bulk of his Danegelds from church treasure—treasure that had been accumulated from donations of pious believers over two and a half centuries. We possess a copy of a letter sent from Pope John VIII to Archbishop Æthelred of Canterbury, which was written late in 877 or early 878. This document, originating outside Wessex, and preserved now in a copy made at Monte Casino,[226] provides rare evidence on Alfred's relations with the church of Wessex during the viking wars. It suggests that while Alfred, in his securer later years, may have wished to project himself as a patriotic Christian king, earlier in his reign, he shared in the dilemma confronting all native rulers as to the necessity of buying off Danish invaders either by the appropriation of church land or the sequestration of church treasure. By 877 or early 878, Alfred had still not resolved his struggle with the Great Army, and the pope was clearly replying to earlier allegations made by the Archbishop Æthelred that Alfred had been infringing on the rights of his church. The pontiff acknowledges the hardships which the English metropolitan was enduring—Canterbury exposed to viking attack on the East Kent peninsula was in a most vulnerable position:

And because you, being placed in the life of the present age, which truly is a trial upon earth, daily sustain certain hardships, we not only weep for our own, which we likewise suffer, but we also sorrow with you, suffering alas such things.[227]

But the archbishop's sufferings were only indirectly related to the Danish wars. His immediate problem was with his king, Alfred, who like Burgred, was probably desperate to raise tribute for his Danish masters:

Kindled by zeal for Him [i.e. God] do not cease to resist strenuously not only the king, but all who wish to do any wrong against it [i.e. the Church] . . . for we have been at pains to admonish and exhort your king with a letter from the apostolic see, not to neglect to be obedient to you and a devoted helper for the love of Jesus Christ Our Lord in all things which are beneficial to the holy church committed to you.[228]

Alfred found himself in the same dilemma as his Carolingian contemporary, Charles the Fat, who was castigated by the compiler of the Annals of Fulda for using church treasure to buy peace from the Northmen:

What was still more of a crime, he did not blush to pay tribute to a man [the Danish Godafrid] from whom he ought to have taken hostages and exacted tribute, doing this on the advice of evil men and against the custom of his ancestors the kings of the Franks. He took away the churches treasures, which had been hidden for fear of the enemy, and to his own shame and that of all the army which followed him, gave to those same enemies 2,412 pounds of purest gold and silver.[229]

It would be naïve to imagine that Alfred could have paid the requisite Danish tributes levied in Wessex out of his own royal treasure. That particular Danegeld demanded of Charles the Fat in 882 was relatively small by Frankish standards. Two years later, Frankish vikings were demanding 12,000 pounds of gold and silver,[230] while 5,000–7,000 pounds of silver otherwise seems to have been the Frankish norm for payments of protection money to vikings in the period from 845–85. There is no reason to assume that Alfred was let off any lighter than his Carolingian colleagues. When we bear in mind that Alfred left a total of about 2,000 pounds of silver coin by way of bequests for family and retainers in his *Will*,[231] we realize that to pay a huge Danegeld of say, 5,000 pounds, he would have been compelled to levy a substantial tax on the magnates and leading churchmen throughout his realm. Not surprisingly, we do not have a copy of the letter which Pope John VIII sent to Alfred upbraiding him for infringing on the rights of the English church. Nor do we have any record of Alfred's reply.

Once again, the silence of the historical record from within Alfredian Wessex is offset by the relatively freer reporting of information from the Carolingian empire. The Carolingians, like their Irish contemporaries, had already resorted to raiding church treasuries before viking tribute-gathering had become a problem.[232] The Emperor Lothar while engaged in a struggle with Charles the Bald, looted 'whatever treasure he could find deposited in churches or their strong rooms for safe keeping' in the Le Mans region in 841.[233] It was inevitable that the church would be called upon, later on, by the warrior aristocracy to yield up its treasure to pay off viking warbands. Charles the Fat paid off Sigfrid and Gorm in 882 with 'several thousand pounds of silver and gold which he had seized from the treasury of St Stephen at Metz and from the resting places of other saints'.[234] When the men of Poitiers handed over a tenth of all the booty recovered from a victory over a viking host to the church of St Hilary in 868,[255] they were in effect paying back what had been looted from St Hilary's a few years before. For in 863, when the town was 'ransomed' from the vikings, St Hilary's was burnt,[236] and two years later in 865, Loire vikings sacked Poitiers yet again.[237] And when it came to ransoming or looting, it was primarily church treasure which the vikings were after. Otherwise why should the clergy and nuns of Cologne and Bonn have fled from the Northmen with their treasure to Mainz in 881[238] or the monks of St Martin move their treasure to Orleans in 853, having had advance warning of an impending viking attack on Tours?[239] Archbishop Hincmar had to flee before viking raiders from his cathedral city of Rheims by night, in 882, taking with him the relics of St Remigius and the treasures of his church.[240]

The silence of the Chronicle on the troubles of the West Saxon church may also be due to the fact that Alfred had himself benefited directly from those troubles. The church and especially the monasteries made up the greatest single landholding enclave within Alfred's kingdom, and the exile and annihilation of monastic communities in the face of viking invasion must have presented Alfred with the opportunity of clawing back many monastic estates for the use of the king. The monks of Abingdon remembered Alfred as a mean opportunist who had profited from the Danish onslaught:

After the death of King Æthelred his brother Alfred assumed power. He alienated the vill in which the monastery [of Abingdon] is placed . . . with all its appurtenances from the said monastery, rendering to the victorious Lord an unequal return for the victory with which he was endowed.

A later mid-thirteenth century version of the same Abingdon history refers to Alfred as a Judas who added evil to evil for the Abingdon community.[241] In view of Alfred's towering reputation in the later Middle Ages as the pious law-giver and scholarly king whom forgers might associate with ecclesiastical claims they wished to promote, this deeply negative assessment of Alfred by the Abingdon community may have an authentic ring. It was scarcely in the interests of any monastery to preserve such a negative tradition about a king whose memory was otherwise universally revered, unless that tradition had been as deep-seated historically, as it was bitter.

Ninth-century West Saxon kings were facilitated in profiting from viking destruction of monasteries such as Abingdon and their communities, through an agreement reached between King Ecgberht of Wessex and his son Æthelwulf with monastic houses at the beginning of the viking age. The West Saxon conquest of Kent in the 830s necessitated a settlement between Ceolnoth, archbishop of

Canterbury and Ecgberht of Wessex, at a council held at Kingston in 838.[242] Subsequent confirmations of this settlement made by King Æthelwulf at Wilton in 839 and by all the bishops of the southern province at a synod also held in that year, suggests that the settlement may have applied to all the monastic houses of greater Wessex and not just to Kent alone.[243] Although the precise significance of this accord has been obscured by the inadequate Latin of the scribe who drafted the documents, it appears that King Ecgberht and his son and successor King Æthelwulf, were allowed to exercise 'protection and lordship (*ad protectionem et ad dominium*)'[244] over 'the communities of free monasteries' in their kingdom 'on account of their own [i.e. the monasteries] very great needs'. Ostensibly the king was to act as lay lord and protector in unison with the bishops, who were to act as spiritual lords (*spiritalesque dominos*),[245] and both protecting parties resolved to guarantee the liberty of election, and to ensure the preservation of the regular life. But the agreement also in effect acknowledged the proprietorial rights of royal founders and lay protectors, and opened the door for interference on the part of West Saxon kings. Such an agreement reached in 838–9, ultimately facilitated the rapid appropriation of monastic lands and buildings of religious houses which had been abandoned during viking inroads from *c.*850 onwards.

The exposed coastal monasteries of Kent provide us with a case-study of monastic decline and consequent royal aggrandisement in Alfredian Wessex. As early as 804, Abbess Selethryth of Lyminge had procured a church and property within the walls of Canterbury to provide a refuge for her community on the exposed south coast, and the equally exposed community of St Mildred's at Minster-on-Thanet may have sought the protection of St Mildred's in Canterbury also about this time. While St Mildred's-on-Thanet may have been revived for a short time in the early eleventh century,[246] there is no evidence for the survival of any of the Kentish nunneries after the viking raids of the ninth century. The nuns of Folkestone may have survived up until the time of the synod of Kingston in 838, while monks at Folkestone, Lyminge, and Dover were still to the good in 844.[247] The arrival of the Great Army of Danes in 865 and its series of victories in Wessex in 871 must have spelt the end of the Kentish monasteries outside the walled towns of Canterbury and Rochester. St Augustine's in Canterbury alone of the Kentish houses preserved a continuous existence until its reconstitution in the monastic revival and reform of the late tenth century. By the eleventh century, the churches of Folkestone and Lyminge had no estates of their own in the Domesday survey; Minster-in-Sheppey had declined to the status of a dependent church, while any communities at Hoo, Minster-in-Thanet, and Reculver had by then disappeared.[248] The monastic estates of Reculver had been in the gift of King Eadred by 949 and that of Lyminge in the gift of Edgar by 964.[249] It is likely that these churches together with Minster-in-Thanet, Hoo, Folkestone, and Minster-in-Sheppey all passed by default under direct West Saxon royal control during the reign of Æthelwulf or his sons in the second half of the ninth century. Brooks estimated that monastic estates attached to ninth-century Kentish minsters amounted, at a minimum, to some 300 sulungs of land, or the equivalent of one-quarter of all the landed wealth of Kent.[250] On the other side of the kingdom of greater Wessex there is also evidence for the complete collapse of minsters in places exposed to the viking onslaught. Plymton minster near Plymouth in Devon lay uncomfortably near the Cornish border as well as to the excellent anchorage for viking longships. An admittedly questionable charter from early in the reign of Edward the Elder claims that Bishop Asser of Sherborne handed over Plymton minster and its estates to that king in exchange for lands in Somerset. That same charter—supposedly drawn up *c*.899–909—also alludes to the troubled times which witnessed the burning and plundering of towns and estates.[251] It was these appropriated peripheral estates, and perhaps countless others across the length and breadth of southern England, which Alfred gradually tightened his grip on, in the aftermath of the viking invasions. Faced with the consequences of Danish looting and the repeated payment of Danegelds, it was clearly not in the king's economic interests either to return abandoned monastic lands to scattered communities of dispossessed monks or nuns or to set about refounding such monasteries afresh. The obvious resentment which such a royal policy may have aroused in the archbishop of Canterbury and his episcopal colleagues may well have been the subject of the grievance in the letter of Pope John VIII. Evidence for the appropriation of episcopal and monastic landed wealth by King Alfred and later by his son, Edward, may not be as strong as we would wish it to be. It was in the nature of things to suppress records of unedifying financial transactions which would tell against the reputation of a Christian ruler. Some deserted monastic estates may have reverted to the king by default. Fleming has made a case for more widespread appropriation of monastic lands by King Alfred across Wessex, involving estates of the churches of Winchester, Sherborne, and Malmesbury, for instance. Dumville, who submitted Fleming's findings to an iconoclastic scrutiny, conceded that 'in Greater Wessex, minsters (but not episcopal sees) were put out of action: very likely their lands suffered secularisation . . . both the West Saxon king and his nobles benefited financially from this process'.[252] We might add that the vikings also ultimately stood to gain further tribute from the hard-pressed king and his magnates.

The Great Army pulled back from Reading to London in the autumn or early winter of 871. We are not told whether a Danish garrison was maintained at Reading. The main body of Danes now wintered in London under a second peace concluded with the Mercians. Whatever the exact size of the Danish host—whose ranks had been swelled by the arrival of that Summer Army at Reading sometime before Easter in 871—the invaders would have needed vast supplies of corn, salted meat, or herds of live sheep, cattle, and pigs to sustain them over the winter. There can be little doubt that West Saxon estates across Wiltshire, Hampshire, Berkshire, Surrey, and Kent must have borne the brunt of supplying such provisions. Alfred's bishop, Denewulf of Winchester, complained to King Edward in the years following Alfred's death, that an estate of seventy hides at Beddington in Surrey, belonging to his church at Winchester, had once been 'quite without stock, and stripped bare by heathen men'.[253] Later on, the bishop had succeeded in restocking his farm which then comprised of 9 full-grown oxen, 114 full-grown pigs, 160 varieties of sheep, 7 bondsmen, 20 flitches, and 90 sown acres of corn. Significantly, by *c.*900 the bishop was under pressure from his king to lease this estate against the will of the Winchester community which now 'begged that you desire no more land of that foundation, for it seems to them an unwelcome demand'. Here we have an instance where the West Saxon king is competing with his bishop for the management and profits of an estate which had been reconstituted after viking assaults. Meanwhile over in Kent (*c.*850–60), an estate belonging to a lady, Ealhburg, was considered to be in danger of not being able to pay its annual food-rent to St Augustine's Abbey in Canterbury, because of the ravages of the 'heathen army'.[254] That rent of malt, meat, poultry, bread, lard, cheese, and timber had either been appropriated by a Danish garrison, or equally likely, the workforce of Ealhburg's estate had either been sold into slavery by the vikings or had fled from that fate.

The situation for the native inhabitants of London and in the shires bordering on London, during the time when the Great Army was concentrated in that town, must have been grim. The inhabitants of the London hinterland—in what is now Greater London—must have lived in constant fear of roving viking bands seeking corn and livestock for a huge garrison, as well as slaves for their overseas markets. It is clear from extensive archaeological evidence for the viking occupation of York and Dublin, that the Scandinavian invaders were themselves keen townsmen who packed the crammed areas within those city walls with their own artisans and traders.[255] That being so, native burgers were likely to have been viewed by prospective viking settlers as competitors for space as well as rivals in the market-place. London, unlike York, was not destined to remain for long in Scandinavian hands, but that can have had little bearing on the initial impact which the Great Army had on its first taking London in 871. Nor may we assume, as so many historians tacitly do, that London ceased to experience Danish domination after the withdrawal of the Great Army in 872. That Mercian town was answerable to its Danish masters, until Æthelred of Mercia took control of it with Alfred's agreement in 886. Many London merchants must have fled from the town or hidden their coin and other valuables during the viking occupation. London had been under Burgred's rule and the coin hoard of Burgred's pennies found at Westminster Bridge in *c.*1895 may well have been deposited in 871–2 by a nervous burger who never returned to collect his wealth.[256] A hoard from nearby Waterloo Bridge—containing 96 Burgred pennies, together with one coin of Alfred's predecessor, Æthelred I of Wessex, as well as a possible lunette coin of Alfred himself —bears all the hallmarks of an English owner.[257] The Burgred coins of the Waterloo Bridge hoard are similar to those found at Gravesend, further along the Thames, in Kent. This rich *cache* consisted of over 500 pennies, the great majority of which (427) were coins of Burgred, while 44 coins of Edmund of East Anglia (slain in November 869) and a single Alfredian lunette penny, once again suggests a time of deposition close to the autumn of 871 when the Great Army first descended on London.[258] Some seven miles south of London at Croydon, a hoard of about 250 coins together with ingots and pieces of viking hack-silver was discovered during the building of a railway line from West Croydon Station to Balham.[259] Unlike the Waterloo hoard, the assemblage at Croydon, which was buried in *c*.872, had originally almost certainly belonged to a viking. This is confirmed by the presence of the typical Danish viking hack-silver and the presence of three ingots and a fragment of a fourth, along with 7 Carolingian coins and 3 Kufic Abbasid dirhams. Such an assemblage reflects a collection put together by a viking raider with overseas contacts. The Croydon coin collection was subsequently dispersed, but nearly 150 have since been identified, including those of Burgred of Mercia (94), East Anglia (24 in all—18 of King Edmund), 1 of Ceolnoth, archbishop of Canterbury (833–70), and 56 from Wessex. The West Saxon pennies consisted of 25 of Alfred's brother, Æthelred I, and 31 of Alfred himself.[260] This Croydon hoard can be closely dated to the period 871–3, by the presence of Edmund's East Anglian issues (pre-November 869); Alfred's early lunette-type pennies; by the absence of coins of Ceolwulf II of Mercia who was installed by the Danes in 874; and by the absence of Danish coins from the newly established Danelaw.[261] While it is perilous to speculate on the circumstances of deposition of any hoard, Croydon has interesting late-ninth-century historical associations. It had been a great estate of seventy hides belonging to the archbishops of Canterbury, and it survived as such down to the Reformation. We know it had once belonged to Alfred's archbishop, Æthelred (870–88). Sometime during Æthelred's pontificate—we do not know precisely when—that prelate ceded the Croydon lands to Ealdorman Alfred of Surrey for the lifetime of the latter, in return for Ealdorman Alfred's own estate at Chartham near Canterbury, in Kent.[262] Alfred was one of King Alfred's ealdormen—probably of Surrey—whose will is known to us[263] and who was also remarkable for his record of having ransomed the Golden Gospels 'from the heathen army . . . for pure gold'. He and his wife, Wærburh, presented the rescued gospels to Christ Church Canterbury, probably in the early 870s. The vikings may well have seized the codex originally for the bullion value of its metalwork shrine, and then held the sacred texts for ransom. The safety of those gospels in Canterbury was not assured, for they finally ended up in the Royal Library in Stockholm. Whether Ealdorman Alfred or Archbishop Æthelred was in charge of the Croydon estate when the rich cache of coins was hidden there in 871–3 is impossible to tell. We are equally uncertain of the connection between the owner of the coins, the presence of the Great Army in London, and the possible connection with the Croydon estate. It is true that more coin hoards tend to be discovered in the Greater London region than elsewhere because of intense ground disturbance due to industrial and building activity since the nineteenth century. It is equally true that London was particularly rich in coin throughout the Anglo-Saxon period.[264] Nevertheless coin hoards as a class bespeak unsettled times if not outright panic, and they are also testimony to the burial of what was, on occasion, immense treasure, whose owners were unable ever to recover what they had hidden. The fact that several coin hoards can either firmly or tentatively be associated by numismatists with the movements of the Great Army during its triumphal progress across England in 865–80[265] is in keeping with what contemporary sources tell us of the political crises which this invading force unleashed on the English scene. The preponderance of Burgred's coins in London and the Thames basin in 871 is also a forceful reminder, that while the West Saxon Chronicle portrays this king in a passive light—almost as one doomed to lose his kingdom—in economic terms, he and his Mercian kingdom may have been of greater importance than Alfred and his West Saxon realm.

The constant threat and the stranglehold which a massed viking army posed to the security of the whole of the south-east was unexpectedly removed in 872. The sudden withrawal of the Great Army was not to prove beneficial to Burgred, but for Alfred, it was to afford him the luckiest break of his reign. A revolt against Danish rule in Northumbria summoned the Great Army north from London in the autumn of 872 and the Danes were to be out of Alfred's kingdom for four precious years. The beleaguered king—by no means free of the Danish menace— would now have time and the good sense to review West Saxon mistakes and to build up an effective defence.

The question of Alfred's political relationship with the Danes during the inter-val from his defeat at Wilton in 871 until his victory at Edington in 878 is one that inevitably requires a discussion of Alfred's coinage during this period. It is crucial in all numismatic studies that conclusions reached in relation to coin production, design, and metallic content, be arrived at independently of historical argument, and that only after the numismatist has reached those conclusions which rely on the methodology of his own discipline should he then seek to apply his findings to the historical debate. The serious debasement of Alfred's earliest lunette coinage in relation to the weight of its silver content must surely reflect that king's embattled status, politically and economically, as he struggled to pay off his Danish enemy in the immediate aftermath of defeat in 871–2. The Two Emperor type coinage of Alfred and Ceolwulf of Mercia demands the attention of the historian, since the moneyers who issued those coins also struck coins for Burgred of Mercia. That fact, together with the probable London origin for Alfred's coin and a Mercian (including London) location for Ceolwulf's coinage, underlines the Mercian em-phasis of that entire issue. Alfred's Cross-and-Lozenge coinage from the middle phase of his reign was also issued under Ceolwulf's name—the London mint producing two-thirds for Alfred and one-third for Ceolwulf. Blackburn demon-strated on typological and numismatic grounds that Alfred's Cross-and-Lozenge coinage was on the whole earlier than that of Ceolwulf.[266] Blackburn, in consulta-tion with Keynes, interpreted this evidence to mean that on Burgred's departure from Mercia in 873–4 'Alfred was recognised as the legitimate ruler in London and some other parts of southern Mercia'; that the Two Emperor coin of Alfred was struck in London 'at a time when the people there regarded Alfred as their ruler in preference to Ceolwulf'; and again that 'the people in London, and possibly elsewhere in southern Mercia, would seem to have turned initially to Alfred rather than the Viking or west Mercian nominee Ceolwulf'. In this scenario, Alfred is envisaged as being in control of London until as late as *c.*877, when Ceolwulf is then seen as belatedly taking over a town which the Chronicle would imply had been within his political ambit since 873–4. This is clearly one historical interpretation of the evidence provided by the coinage of Alfred and Ceolwulf, but it can never be admitted as anything more than one of several competing hypotheses. The notion of 'the people in London' taking initiatives in relation to their choice of ruler is surely flawed, as is the idea that because Alfred's name appears on a coin of the 870s it must—because it is Alfred's—reflect greater royal autonomy than an exactly parallel issue of King Ceolwulf. We may only proceed with historical reconstructions on the basis of the evidence provided by the Chronicle. That source tells us that in 871 Alfred was a defeated king; that the Great Army controlled London in 871–2; that on Burgred's flight from his kingdom in 873–4, London as a Mercian town must have remained within the Danish grasp or under their sub-king, Ceolwulf, whom they appointed at that time. Finally in 877, the Danes consolidated their position within Mercia by carving it up between themselves and their tributary Ceolwulf. In the face of this formidable catalogue of evidence—spread across the years 871 to 877—it is not possible to envisage Alfred having any kind of autonomous hold on Mercian London. The counter argument needs to be put, at least, that Alfred as a tributary of the Danes, struck coins during this period which were of precisely the same status as those of Ceolwulf whom the Danes had established as king in Mercia. Rather than viewing every coin with Alfred's name inscribed as evidence for Alfred's 'legitimate authority', it is equally probable that such coins were issued under Danish control and that Alfred's access to the London mint was brought about by his new treaty status vis-à-vis the invaders in the period 871–8. It was the Danes after all, and not the West Saxons, who had so violently redrawn the political map—not just of England but of the whole of Britain. And it was the Danes who had dissolved the frontier between southern Mercia and Wessex and who had ended exclusive Mercian control of London. If this interpretation is correct, then the coin of Hálfdan with the Two Emperors reverse design combined with a monogram reverse of the London Monogram type must surely belong to that leader of the Great Army who controlled London in 871–2 and who settled his men in Northumbria in 875–6. It was this most dangerous of Alfred's enemies who presumably set in place the mechanisms which controlled both Alfred's and Ceolwulf's coin output at this time. For Alfred, such an arrangement may not have been as humiliating or as economically disadvantageous as modern political commentators might imagine. He may have benefited greatly from access to the lucrative London market now under Danish control and he must have availed of Danish supplies of silver to produce this coinage in the first instance. Alfred's restoration of the silver weight of his pennies in the mid-870s and his improvement of the fineness of design are difficult if not impossible to reconcile with his known depressed military situation, unless we accept that he acquired his silver from his Scandinavian overlords who were of course renowned for their access to supplies of silver. As for the Danes, by ruling through their tributary kings they stood to gain tribute and taxation with minimum cost in lives and labour to their own men. This interpretation of Alfred's coinage of the 870s—as essentially the coin of a Danish sub-king—is in keeping with Danish practice throughout the later Danelaw, for the notion of issuing coin through the mints of a tributary king and in his name is not dissimilar to the idea of imitative coinage which was ever a feature of Danelaw issues. The invader was not so concerned with 'status' in the production and distribution of coin: he was more concerned with revenue. Alfred, in spite of his depressed political and economic condition during the precarious interlude between his First and Second War may have had control of the design of his pennies. Alfred may not have been in full control of the production and quantity of his coin in the 870s, but he was most likely free to monitor the activities of his die-cutters and their mints. The invading Danes had little or no experience of coin production, whereas Anglo-Saxon kings had issued coin over centuries. Surely the notion of basing a design on a fourth-century Roman solidus can be attributed to the king, Alfred, whose name it bears, and whom we know from his own writings was obsessed with the heritage of Late Antiquity.

II

The Gathering Storm 872–875

T HE NORTHUMBRIANS HAD EXPELLED THE DANISH UNDER-KING, Ecgberht, and his ally, Archbishop Wulfhere of York in 872.[1] The fact that Burgred had given refuge to Ecgberht and Wulfhere suggests his compliance yet again with the political aims of his Danish overlords. The Danish army wintered at Torksey in Lindsey on its way north in the autumn or early winter of 872 when the Mercians made their third recorded peace with the invaders.[2] The revolt in Northumbria was suppressed: Ecgberht (who had since died) was replaced as Northumbrian under-king, by Ricsige, and Archbishop Wulfhere was reinstated in his see.[3] Burgred's days as king were now numbered. The Danes were complete masters of East Anglia and Northumbria, and although Burgred had made his peace and paid his tribute, he was not a king of Danish choosing. The Danish invaders had good reason to fear a Mercian alliance with Alfred and the West Saxons. It had been that same coalition, after all, which had forced a Danish withdrawal from Nottingham back in 868. It was in the Danish interest to tighten their hold over Mercia and thereby consolidate their territorial gains, which would then stretch from the Firth of Forth to the Thames and London. Late in 873, the Great Army took up winter quarters at Repton 'and drove King Burgred across the sea, after he had held the kingdom 22 years and they conquered all that land'.[4] Burgred was to end his days in Rome and his queen, Æthelswith (sister of King Alfred), clearly followed him either then or later to Italy, where she died in Pavia in 888. Danish arrangements for the government of Mercia were described in the Chronicle some fifteen years or more after they occurred. The view expressed in that record is coloured with the hindsight of Alfred's subsequent victory in 878 and was calculated to denigrate the position of Ceolwulf, the new English under-king appointed by the Danes:

And that same year they gave the kingdom of the Mercians to be held by Ceolwulf, a foolish king's thegn; and he swore oaths to them and gave them hostages, that it should be ready for them on whatever day they wished to have it, and he would be ready, himself and all who would follow him, at the enemies service.[5]

The description of Ceolwulf as an *unwisum cyninges þegne* was devised to emphasize his role as usurper of the kingship once held by Alfred's brother-in-law, Burgred, and suggests too, perhaps his disloyalty to his former king. But in practice little may have changed within Mercia at this time. The Danes had removed one under-king, Burgred, who had been a relative (by marriage) and former ally of King Alfred, and replaced him with a Mercian who was of their own choosing. Nor need we put much store in the Chronicle's carefully chosen title of *þegn* as applied to King Ceolwulf—with its connotations of service to a king. This new ruler was the second of that rather rare Anglo-Saxon name to reign as king of the Mercians. This Ceolwulf II who ruled Mercia as Alfred's contemporary may well have claimed descent from the dynasty of Ceolwulf I—a Mercian king who was deposed in 823—in spite of Stenton's speculation that the first Ceolwulf was the last of his line.[6] Ceolwulf I was a Mercian ruler of the old order, descended from a line of Mercian kings supposedly going back to the kindred of Penda. Ceolwulf I was the last of the truly independent Mercian kings who ruled Mercia before it became tributary for a time, to Alfred's grandfather, Ecgberht of Wessex. It would have made sense for the Danes to promote a representative of an ancient Mercian line which had been independent of Wessex and a man, who presumably as a rival, had not benefited from the patronage of the deposed Burgred. The Danish overthrow of Burgred and the establishment of Ceolwulf II as king of Mercia was seen by the compiler of the Chronicle as somehow connected with the movement of the Danes from Lindsey to Repton: 'In this year [874] the army went from Lindsey to Repton and took up winter quarters there, and drove King Burgred across the sea . . . and the same year they gave the kingdom of the Mercians to be held by Ceolwulf.'

The Danish camp at Torksey in Lindsey was already within Mercian territory, so the move to Repton may well have had special significance for the overthrow of Burgred. Williams[7] pointed out that Repton had been the burial place of King Æthelbald of Mercia (716–57), a ruler who temporarily established Mercian supremacy over the whole of southern England, anticipating the more remarkable achievements of Offa. The church at Repton continued to be closely associated with the Mercian royal house. Ælfflæd, the daughter of Ceolwulf I, may have been the mother of Ceolwulf II[8] and was certainly the mother of Wigstan, who was murdered in 849 by a son of King Beorhtwulf of Mercia. Wigstan was regarded as a saint and his cult centred on his burial place at Repton church, which also housed the remains of his father and grandfather, and had associations with the life of St Guthlac. Repton, then, like Wimborne for the West Saxons, was a holy place with special associations for the old Mercian dynasty descended from Penda. If as Williams argued, the place had special family and cult connections for Ceolwulf II, then the Danish move on Repton can be interpreted as part of a successful coup to replace Burgred not just with any usurper who happened to comply with their wishes, but to replace him with a rival from an ancient and prestigious royal line. If that were so, then the compiler of the Chronicle wilfully misinterpreted those events by a combination of disparagement and silence.

Ceolwulf II had sufficient kingly qualities to win the adherence of his bishops and the Mercian *witan*, ruling 'with the unanimous consent of all my bishops and ealdormen and also of all the chief men of our race'[9] even if Danish backing helped to lend substance to such claims. Viewed from the perspective of his charter evidence, the short reign of Ceolwulf II over the Mercians (874–9) appears

conventional enough. Eleventh-century copies of two of his charters dating from
AD 875 survive—one of which[10] Whitelock deemed to be sufficiently authentic to
merit translation in her *English Historical Documents*. The other,[11] although interpolated and questioned by some scholars, was referred to by Stenton[12] in a context
in which he clearly accepted its overall validity. The beneficiary of the first of these
royal privileges from Ceolwulf II (Sawyer 215) was that same Bishop Wærferth of
Worcester, who only three years earlier had been desperately raising money from
the lease of his estates to pay the Danish tribute. In this charter, on the contrary,
the Danish protégé, Ceolwulf, is seen freeing the diocese of Worcester from the
burden of feeding the king's horses 'and those who lead them'. Ceolwulf also
presented Wærferth with 60 mancuses of gold in return for the lease of six hides
of land at Daylesford, Worcestershire,[13] for the life of Ceolwulf and three of his
successors.[14] Ceolwulf is designated 'by the Grace of God . . . king of the Mercians'
and he appears as a pious ruler wishing to have prayers said for the expiation of his
sins in Mercian monasteries 'for as long as the Christian faith should be observed
in this race'. The witnesses—apart from Ceolwulf and Bishop Wærferth—include
Bishop Deorlaf of Hereford, and Bishop Eadberht probably of Lichfield, as well as
two ealdormen, Beorhtnoð[15] and Æthelhun. The second of the surviving charters
of Ceolwulf (Sawyer 216, Birch 541) is a grant by that king to the monastic
community of St Mary's Minster in Worcester of lands at Overbury, Conderton,
and Pendock in Worcestershire. All of the witnesses of Sawyer 215 reappear in this
charter[16] with the exception of Bishop Deorlaf, but the names of two other ealdormen
(*Atheluuold* and *Alhferht*) together with eight other names of magnates who appear
without title are added. Robinson[17] rejected this Overbury charter as a forgery
because of the repetition of names in the witness list between this document and
Sawyer 215, and because three other names (*Alhferht dux, Kyred* and *Wulfsige*)
were in Robinson's opinion garbled versions of Ealfrith, bishop of Winchester,
Ceolred bishop of Leicester, and of another bishop, Wulfsige. The repetition of
names may have no significance or may even be an argument in favour of the
partial authenticity at least of Sawyer 216. Two charters issued by the same king
in the same year would be expected to have witnesses in common. While lifting
names at random from other charters (genuine or forged) was part of the stock in
trade of the forger's technique, it does not seem plausible that someone forging a
Mercian charter would insert the name of a bishop from such a prominent West
Saxon see as Winchester. The ealdorman, *Alhferht*, listed as a witness in Ceolwulf's
Overbury charter may well be the same as the ealdorman Æthelferth who attended
a witenagemot at Gloucester in AD 896.[18] As for the origins of the names *Kyred* and
Wulfsige, these remain unknown. It is surely unlikely in the extreme that the
church of Worcester would have attributed its forgeries to the short reign of a king
who enjoyed the doubtful distinction in later centuries of having ruled under
Danish overlordship, unless there were some genuine reasons for attributing such
grants to him. The names which we can identify in King Ceolwulf's witness lists
are, as we should expect, names of magnates who had served under his Mercian
predecessors. Deorlaf of Hereford witnessed for Burgred in AD 866[19] and AD 869.[20]

Eadberht of Lichfield and Ealdorman Æthelhun also witnessed this last charter of Burgred in AD 869. Ealdorman Beornoth or Beorhtnoð was probably the same as Beornoð[21] who witnessed the charter of Bishop Ceolred of Leicester which granted the Pangbourne estate, by the river Thames in Berkshire, first to King Brihtwulf of Mercia and then by re-grant from Brihtwulf to Ealdorman Æthelwulf back in AD 843–4.[22] This Ealdorman Beornoth also witnessed charters of Burgred in AD 855,[23] AD 857,[24] AD 862,[25] and AD 866.[26]

Not only did several of the magnates who witnessed Ceolwulf II's charters attest the charters of his predecessors, but several also survived Ceolwulf to serve under Ealdorman Æthelred and his wife Æthelflæd, Lady of the Mercians. Foremost among those magnates was Bishop Wærferth of Worcester who was leasing lands to Æthelred and Æthelflæd as late as AD 904—in the time of Alfred's son, King Edward the Elder.[27] Bishop Wærferth came, as we shall see, to be associated with King Alfred's translation programme and with the translation of the *Dialogues* of Pope Gregory in particular. Bishop Deorlaf of Hereford attested charters of Ealdorman Æthelred of Mercia along with Bishop Wærferth in AD 880,[28] AD 883,[29] and in AD 884.[30] This last charter, issued at a witenagemot held at Prince's Risborough in Buckinghamshire, was also witnessed by two ealdormen, *Beornaþ* and Æthelwald who are most probably the same as Ealdorman Beornoth who witnessed the two charters of Ceolwulf II and Ealdorman *Atheluuold* who witnessed Ceolwulf's Overbury charter (Sawyer 216). The same *Beornoþus* witnessed another charter of Ealdorman Æthelred of Mercia along with Wærferth bishop of Worcester[31] at Droitwich in AD 888. Ealdorman Æthelwold was at the centre of a dispute with Wærferth of Worcester over woodlands at Woodchester in Gloucestershire in AD 896.[32] Æthelwold is not styled ealdorman in the record of this dispute, but he was clearly a man of substance whose *geneat* identified the bounds of the disputed land.[33] It seems very likely that Æthelwold the mass-priest (who was also mentioned as a witness in this dispute) was a different person from the magnate of the same name who was disputing the lands with Bishop Wærferth. Other witnesses to the deliberations at that witenagemot held at Gloucester in 896 were a certain Æthelhun and an ealdorman, Æthelferth. These may well be the same people as *Athelhun dux* and *Alhferth dux* who witnessed Ceolwulf's Overbury charter in AD 875 (Sawyer 216). Ealdorman Æthelferth was also a witness at the witenagemots held at Prince's Risborough in AD 884 (Sawyer 219) and at Droitwich in AD. 888 (Sawyer 220), and given the presence of this magnate in Mercian witness lists, there seems little justification in identifying Ealdorman *Alhferht* of Ceolwulf's Overbury charter with Ealfrith, bishop of Winchester rather than with the Mercian Ealdorman Æthelferth. The charter evidence, therefore, in spite of its limitations, shows that the Mercian *witan* survived the Danish overlordship and remained substantially intact during the reign of the under-king, Ceolwulf II. It seems clear that this king continued to rule through bishops and magnates in southern and western Mercia who were to outlast him and serve under his successors. One of those survivors, Bishop Wærferth of Worcester, was to witness the confirmation of a transaction by King Edward the Elder in AD 904 which made specific reference to earlier dealings of Ceolwulf II.[34] King Edward was confirming a grant of land at Water Eaton in Oxfordshire by a certain Hungið to one Wigfrið. That estate had once belonged to Bishop Wærferth who passed it on to King Ceolwulf, who in turn gave it to Hungið.[35] Far from appearing as a foolish king's thegn, Ceolwulf is seen in these charters as a ruler performing the role expected of him as a great land-owner, and acting as arbiter between other great land-owners in his Mercian realm.

In the early winter of 874 (Anglo-Saxon year 875[36]), the Danish army—having established Ceolwulf II in Mercia—withdrew from Repton. The army then split into two hordes—one going north, back into Northumbria with Hálfdan, and the other moving south and east to Cambridge. The Anglo-Saxon Chronicle, for the first time, is unusually detailed on the identification of the Danish leaders who were involved in this parting of the ways, and since kings from both divisions of this army were active in the field against Alfred, it is appropriate to discuss the Danish leadership at this point. *Healfdene*, whom the Chronicle tells us led his part of the army back to Northumbria from Repton in 874–5, first appears in the Parker Chronicle as a king in the company of *Bagsecg* at the battle of Ashdown in Berkshire, in 871. Hálfdan's appearance at Ashdown—where he fought against King Æthelred, and where his Danish comrade *Bagsecg* was slain—was only eleven days into the First West Saxon War. It is therefore a fair assumption that he had come with the main body of the Great Army from East Anglia, where he had been implicated in the slaying of King Edmund. That deduction is further strengthened by the testimony of the late tenth-century chronicler, Æthelweard, who named the Danish leader of the East Anglian campaign as *Iguuar* or *Iuuar*[37]—a point also supported by Abbo of Fleury, who, writing between 985 and 987, named Edmund's adversary as *Inguar*.[38] A crucial entry in the account of King Alfred's wars in the Anglo-Saxon Chronicle under AD 878 refers to the 'brother of Ivar and Hálfdan (*Inwæres broþur 7 Healfdenes*)'[39] who was slain in Devon in that year. The entry is crucial because it establishes that Ivar (who led the attack on East Anglia) and Hálfdan (who attacked Wessex) were brothers. It also establishes there was a third brother belonging to this dynasty of Danish kings who, like Hálfdan, attacked Wessex and who was clearly yet another leader of the Great Army. Geffrei Gaimar, in the twelfth century, identified this brother of Ivar (*Ywar*) and Hálfdan (*Haldene*) with Ubbe (*Ube*).[40] While the Annals of St Neots do not name the brother who was slain in this incident, directly, they do relate a folk-tale about the Raven banner which, according to the Anglo-Saxon Chronicle, was carried in his army in Devon in 878. The Annals of St Neot's claim this banner had been woven by three sisters of *Hynguar* and *Hubbe*.[41] The twelfth-century Annals of Lindisfarne associate Hálfdan (*Halfdene*), Ubbe (*Ubba*), and Ivar (*Inguar*) as leaders of the heathen army which landed on Sheppey in 855,[42] and later versions of the Anglo-Saxon Chronicle name *Ingware* and *Ubba* as joint leaders of the Great Army in 870.[43] Abbo of Fleury, although not vouching for the brotherly relationship between Ivar and Ubbe, does nevertheless associate both leaders with the conquest of Northumbria in 865–7.[44] Ubbe's (*Huba*) early association with Ivar (*Hinwar*) as two overall

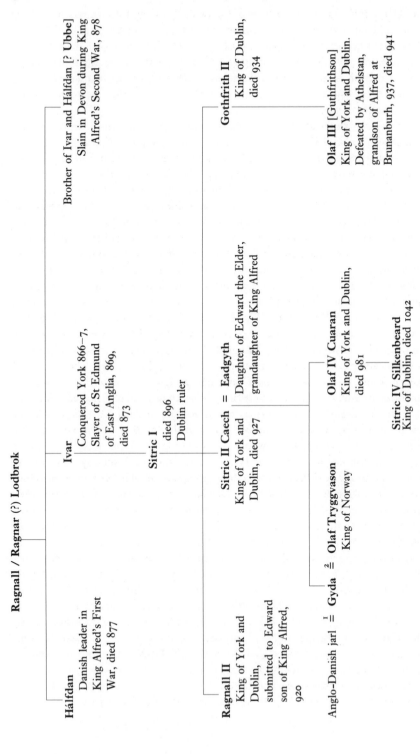

FIG. 4. The dynasty of Ivar: Scandinavian kings of York and Dublin

leaders of the Great Army in the 860s is also vouched for in the *Life* of St Oswald, which was written *c.* AD 1000.[45] It would, indeed, be reasonable to assume that Ubbe was the name of the brother of Ivar and Hálfdan who was slain in Devon in 878. It is also probable, however, that while Ubbe was a genuine leader of the Great Army, he was not related to Ivar and Hálfdan at all, and that the brotherly relationship was suggested in the minds of later chroniclers who were familiar with statements in earlier works such as Abbo's *Life* of St Edmund or the *Life* of St Oswald to the effect that Ubbe was active in the company of Ivar in particular, during the Northumbrian and East Anglian phases of the war. There was an alternative eleventh-century Durham tradition, for instance, which points to Ubbe's possible Frisian connections.[46] But the desire to force connections and to establish precise identifications of viking leaders can raise such an amount of conflicting and inconclusive evidence as to obscure the main narrative of events in ninth-century England. The quest to identify the elusive brother who was slain by the men of Devon in 878 should not be allowed to obscure what we do know from the positive information which the Anglo-Saxon Chronicle provides. That Chronicle gives us the names of several other viking leaders—kings such as Bagsecg, who was slain by the West Saxons in 871, or Oscetel and Anwend who moved south from Repton in 874–5, and who may well have joined Guthrum in the attack on Wessex during Alfred's Second War.

The reference to the brotherly relationship between three viking leaders in the Chronicle at AD 878 has caused unnecessary difficulties for some scholars who have failed to understand its retrospective nature. The Chronicle tells us that in 878, while Alfred had retreated into the woods and marshes (of Somerset) to escape the army of Guthrum, yet another viking army landed further west in Devon. This army, we are told, was led by 'the brother of Ivar and Halfdan'—a reference to two vikings who had been active a few years earlier in the progress of the Great Army, but who by 878 had disappeared from the English scene. Attempts to discredit or devalue this key entry in the Chronicle for AD 878 have been based on a fundamental misunderstanding of historical methodology as well as on a poor understanding of textual evidence. McTurk[47] cast doubt on the Chronicle's statement (under AD 878) that Halfdan and Ivar were brothers, claiming that the Chronicle's 'obscure phrase'[48] relating to 'the brother of Ivar and Hálfdan' was rendered doubtful by Æthelweard's supposed alternative reading of 'Hálfdan, the brother of the tyrant Ivar (*Healfdene, Iguuares tyranni frater*)'.[49] McTurk's interpretation of Æthelweard's text would have us believe that a certain Hálfdan 'the brother of the tyrant Ivar' landed in Devon in 878, where he was slain along with 800 vikings. McTurk misinterpreted the evidence of the Anglo-Saxon Chronicle on several counts. First, he followed de Vries in dismissing the Chronicle's record of the arrival of 'the brother of Ivar and Halfdan' in Devon in the winter of 878 as 'obscure'. On the contrary, the passage is textually straightforward, and contextually it makes excellent sense. Viking leaders such as this unnamed warrior, who descended without warning on Wessex, were easier to identify in terms of Danish leaders who were already known to local inhabitants. By 878, both Ivar and Hálfdan had recently died, but both had been notorious in effecting the conquest of the new Danelaw. Ivar was remembered for the recent slaying of King Edmund of East Anglia and almost certainly for the earlier butchering of Ælla, king of the Northumbrians, in 867. Æthelweard clearly saw 'the tyrant *Iguuar*' as the principal leader of the Great Army which landed in East Anglia in 865–6[50] and therefore by implication that same chronicler must have seen Ivar as the leader of the attack on Northumbria and York in the following year. Later Scandinavian scaldic poetry and Old Icelandic saga-writers would remember Ivar as Ivar the Boneless, who carved a bloody eagle on the mangled body of King Ælle of Northumbria and who offered his royal victim as a sacrifice for Danish victory to the war-god Odin.[51]

Hálfdan had been known personally to the warriors of Wessex as a leader in the First War against Æthelred I and Alfred during 871–2, and his brother Ivar was remembered for having earlier led the attack on Northumbria and East Anglia. When, therefore, a third member of this dynasty descended on Devon in 878—far from being obscure—the chronicler was being very specific in describing this leader as 'the brother of Ivar and Halfdan'. This new, and as yet unknown, invader was identified as a brother of two notorious leaders of the Great Army who were already well known to the West Saxons. McTurk claimed the passage in question was 'relatively unimportant'[52] having less value in relation to the information it gave on Ivar and Hálfdan because it was concerned primarily with their unnamed brother. In this he missed a key point, whereby incidental information in early medieval annals may be all the more reliable because of its peripheral relationship to the prejudices of a compiler. Finally, by preferring the testimony of the late-tenth-century Æthelweard, over that of the near-contemporary Parker Manuscript (version A) of the Chronicle, McTurk was breaking a cardinal rule in the handling of historical textual evidence. Æthelweard's Latin text is garbled at this point, as it so often is elsewhere in his translation. It is by no means certain that Æthelweard meant to convey the notion of 'Halfdan the brother of Ivar' rather than 'the brother of Ivar and of Halfdan' which undoubtedly was the meaning in the earliest version of the Chronicle. Æthelweard's Latin translation is notoriously faulty—his editor noting that 'mistakes and misunderstandings are frequent' and that mistranslations abound in his work.[53] More particularly, Æthelweard's syntax is eccentric and chaotic and he 'very often adopts a peculiar order of words without any rhetorical advantage'.[54] For that reason alone, Æthelweard's *Healfdene, Iguuares tyranni frater*[55] cannot be taken as a superior reading to the Parker Chronicle's *Inwæres broþur 7 Healfdenes*. Besides, Æthelweard was translating the Chronicle—and therefore he provides us with nothing more than a faulty Latin version of a tenth-century exemplar, which we know to have been a revised version of the original text.[56] It is therefore wilful to cast doubt on a passage which appears in Manuscripts A, B (*Ingweres broðor 7 Healfdenes*),[57] and C, D, and E of the original Chronicle, and when we know the equivalent section of the A manuscript (Parker text) is a hundred years older than Æthelweard's time.

De Vries allowed for an interpretation of the Anglo-Saxon Chronicle's reference to the leaders of the Great Army in 878, whereby of the three Danish leaders mentioned (Ivar, Hálfdan, and a third who is not named), only two may have been brothers, and Hálfdan may not have been part of that brotherly relationship at all. de Vries's reasoning was both vague and pedantic. He failed to understand the context of the Anglo-Saxon Chronicle's reporting of events in 878, and so, like McTurk, concluded that the reference to an unnamed 'brother of Ivar and Halfdan' was by nature obscure (*sehr unklar*).[58] He also propounded the dubious and unverifiable platitude that 'leaders, who for a long time were associated, were happily regarded as brothers, or at least as close relatives'.[59] While such an idea may quite legitimately suit the methodology of the folk-tale analyst or the student of saga literature, it is quite inappropriate to a study of a near-contemporary record such as that of the Anglo-Saxon Chronicle.[60] The compiler of the Chronicle was never muddle-headed enough to assume that Alfred of Wessex and Burgred of Mercia were brothers, simply because they had campaigned at Nottingham together in 868. And had he done so, he might have been excused, since Alfred and Burgred were in fact brothers-in-law. Why then should he make such assumptions about their enemies if there not some truth in the notion of their close ties of kinship? de Vries also doubted the reference to Ivar and Hálfdan in 878 as referring to the earlier leaders of the Great Army, because they were not described as kings in the Anglo-Saxon Chronicle's record for 878.[61] This was nothing less than a pedantic quibble. Early Medieval chroniclers could and did achieve accuracy of reporting, while not attaining to a consistency intended to satisfy the 'rigour' of modern scholars. Besides, if de Vries had consulted Æthelweard's text more carefully, he would have noticed that *Healfdene, Iguuares tyranni frater* is alluded to in that very translation of the Chronicle at 878 as 'a king of the barbarians (*barbarum rex*)'.[62]

Our knowledge that Hálfdan, who faced King Æthelred and the ætheling, Alfred, at Ashdown in 871, was the brother of Ivar and of yet another Danish king, who led the Great Army to victory across England in the 860s and 870s, places the invasion of Wessex in its wider and more credible context. The accurate identification of viking leaders—like so much in Early Medieval History—is difficult of absolute proof, and efforts to achieve probable identifications are all too easily vulnerable to iconoclastic critics who find it easier to tell us what we do not know rather than what we may constructively achieve through a careful review of the complex web of available evidence. This complexity of evidence pertains not only to different sources within one society, but to material preserved in different contemporary societies. The cumulative evidence in favour of identifying the Ivar and Hálfdan of Anglo-Saxon records with two vikings of the same names who campaigned in late-ninth-century Ireland is impressive if not, indeed, compelling. The Ivar who slew King Edmund in November 869 died—if we are to accept Æthelweard's account—'shortly afterwards'. Ivar may indeed have died soon after these events, but not immediately. His name does not appear as an active member of the invading force which attacked Wessex from Reading in 871, which was probably the reason why Æthelweard assumed he had died before the Great Army moved on from East Anglia to Reading. But Æthelweard's *Iuuar* was almost

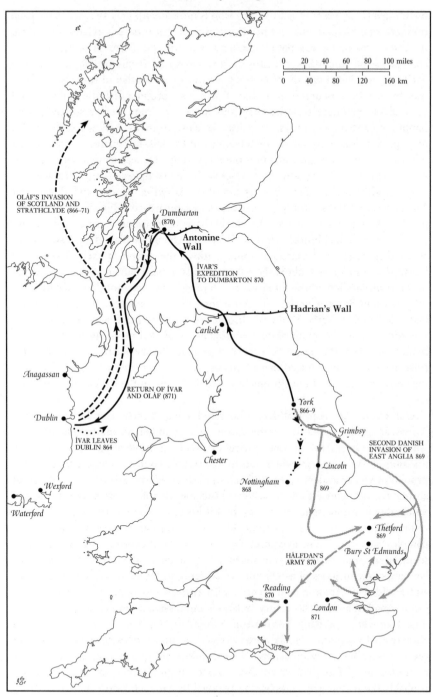

MAP 2. Expeditions of Ivar and Olaf, 864–72

certainly the same as *Imhar* who along with Olaf, a king of Norse Dublin, laid siege to Dumbarton on the Clyde in 870, and who led a great mass of captives back to Dublin in 200 ships in 871. That Imhar of contemporary Irish annals died in 873, and was described at the time of his death as 'king of the Northmen of all Ireland and Britain (*rex Nordmannorum totius Hiberniae et Britanniae*)'[63]—the only viking ever accorded such an all-embracing title in contemporary Irish or Anglo-Saxon records.[64] *Imhar* first appeared in Irish annals in 857 and from then until 863 he is found campaigning in Ireland during five of those seven years.[65] Significantly, he disappears from contemporary Irish records after 863 and he remains out of those records until his reappearance at Dumbarton on the Clyde in 870. That interval, during which Imhar is known (for some of the time at least) to have been in Britain, coincides with the period of activity of *Iuuar/Inguar* in Anglo-Saxon records. The first indication of the arrival of a Danish invading force in England is probably the Anglo-Saxon Chronicle's record of a 'heathen army' which encamped on Thanet in 864–5, followed by the arrival of a 'great heathen army' which wintered in East Anglia in 865–6. Ivar's recorded career with the Great Army stretches from the initial landing in East Anglia in 865–6, through the capture of York in November 866 down to the slaying of Edmund of East Anglia in November 869. *Imhar* was closely and regularly associated while in Ireland with another Norse king, Olaf (*Amhlaimh*), who—*pace* de Vries—was never described in contemporary records as *Imhar*'s brother. *Imhar* and Olaf campaigned together in Ireland during four of the seven years from 857 to 863. They then part company in Irish records until they join forces once more at Dumbarton on the Clyde in 870. During two of four years from 870 to 873 they re-emerge in Irish records as allies who campaigned together once more. *Imhar* was not mentioned by Irish annalists as having joined the army of Olaf which invaded Pictland in 866, which suggests that *Imhar* was not only absent from Ireland during the period 863–71, but that he was not campaigning with Olaf in Scotland either.[66] The crucial element in the record of *Imhar*'s presence at Dumbarton in 870–1 is that it establishes a documentary bridge between the career of the Irish viking who was absent from Ireland between 863 and 871 and the career of *Iuuar/Inguar* who led the Great Army in England from at least 866 until November 869.

We find, furthermore, that Hálfdan, the brother of the Anglo-Danish Ivar who fought against Æthelred and Alfred in Wessex, also had an Irish and Dublin dimension to his career. Hálfdan withdrew with the Great Army from Wessex in 871 and we must presume that he accompanied it northwards to suppress the Northumbrian revolt and to complete the conquest of Mercia at Repton in 874. The Chronicle (under 875) notes Hálfdan's presence at Repton by telling us: 'In this year the army left Repton: Halfdan went with part of the army into Northumbria and took up winter quarters by the River Tyne.' Attempts since the time of de Vries in the early 1920s, to identify this *Healfdene*, the adversary of Alfred in Anglo-Saxon records, with a certain Danish leader Halbden (*Halbdeni*) mentioned in the Annals of Fulda in AD 873[67] have served only to heap confusion on already discredited theories of identifying ninth-century viking leaders. While several

Anglo-Danish vikings such as Hæsten, for instance, did indeed enjoy careers on the Frankish as well as on the English side of the Channel, the Anglo-Danish Hálfdan does not fit into this class. The *Halbden* of Frankish records was the brother of King *Sigifridus*, described as 'king of the Danes',[68] but like his brother, he was clearly a Scandinavian-based ruler negotiating a 'perpetual peace' with the Carolingians which pertained to his Danish territories north of the Eider.[69] Such Danish rulers, based in their home territories can be distinguished in Carolingian sources from their contemporaries, who led destructive forays and colonizing expeditions overseas. The Danish *Healfdene* who campaigned from Reading in 871 and who settled his army in Northumbria in 875–6 is most unlikely ever to have been involved in landlocked territorial dealings along the border between the Continental Danish homeland and Saxony. And although it is not impossible for the English-based *Healfdene* to have been active in Francia in August 873, it is highly improbable. The invader of Wessex almost certainly moved north with his army from Reading in 871. *Healfdene* is associated in the Chronicle with the army at Repton which took up winter quarters there in 874. The real date was probably September–November 873, making it yet more unlikely that the Anglo-Danish *Healfdene* could have been negotiating with the Carolingians in August of that year.

In fact, the Anglo-Danish Hálfdan's career, like that of his brother Ivar, was concerned not only with southern England and Northumbria, but with northern Britain and with the Hiberno-Norsemen of Dublin. *Healfdene*, according to the Anglo-Saxon Chronicle, attacked the Picts and Strathclyde Britons from his Tyne base in 874–5, suggesting he was following an earlier trail which *Imhar* had blazed to Dumbarton in 870.[70] A 'great slaughter' of the Picts is noted in the Annals of Ulster in 875, and although Hálfdan is not mentioned by name in that encounter, his army of *Dubh Gaill* or Danes identifies this expedition with Hálfdan's reported attack in the Anglo-Saxon Chronicle in 874–5.[71] The Irish record's specific mention of Danes stands out in marked contrast to the more familiar Norwegian colonists on the Scottish mainland and in the Scottish Isles.[72] Hálfdan's arm now reached across the Irish Sea where he can be even more firmly identified with the Danish king, *Albann*, in Irish records, than his brother Ivar can with the Irish viking, *Imhar*. Hálfdan slew Eysteinn Óláfsson, the son of Olaf, king of Dublin, in 875. Eysteinn's father, Olaf, had been the erstwhile ally of *Imhar*.[73] The fact that the notice of *Albann*'s slaying of Eysteinn in the Annals of Ulster follows on immediately in that source from the record of the Danish attack on the Picts in 875 may provide a further indication that Hálfdan and his men were involved in both incidents.[74] In the following year, 876, we find Hálfdan back in Northumbria, where according to the Anglo-Saxon Chronicle he 'shared out the land of the Northumbrians, and they proceeded to plough and to support themselves'.[75] This record has rarely been recognized for its very specific reference to the ultimate colonizing goals of the Danish invaders who made up the bulk of the Great Army. We know from place-name and other evidence that Hálfdan's men settled largely in the Vale of York.[76] That ability to colonize the richest parts of Northumbria, in turn presupposes a military superiority on an impressive scale—especially since at least one section of the Danish invading force was still campaigning in the field in Wessex in that same year, 866. Hálfdan had, however, even wider personal ambitions and dynastic obligations than his leadership of the Northumbrian Danes demanded of him. He was slain in a 'small battle' off the Irish coast at Strangford Lough in Co. Down in 877, in what was almost certainly a bid to regain the Dublin kingdom of his brother Ivar.[77] McTurk conceded that there was 'a reasonably strong case' that the *Albann* who was slain according to the Annals of Ulster at Strangford Lough in 877 was the same Danish king as Healfdene who settled his army in Northumbria in 875–6.[78]

Hálfdan/*Albann*'s involvement in events of Scandinavian Dublin, and the Anglo-Saxon Chronicle's statement that Hálfdan/*Healfdene* was the brother of Ivar, is consistent, then, with strong circumstantial evidence that *Iuuar/Inguar* of English records was the same person as the Irish Imhar. This body of evidence which suggests that the Scandinavian kingdom of Dublin owed its origins, in part at least, to the exertions of the same two viking leaders—Ivar and Hálfdan, who were also in the forefront of the conquest of the English Danelaw—makes sense out of the otherwise inexplicable dynastic connection between Scandinavian York and Dublin throughout the first half of the tenth century. That connection between the two towns centred on a single dynasty of Norse kings, and it was consistent as it was sustained.[79] The identification of Ivar and Hálfdan's far-flung contacts and conquests places the leadership of the Great Army of Danes in England in a credible context and helps to illuminate our understanding of the phenomenal success of the invading force which stormed across England in the 860s and 870s, sweeping away forever three kingdoms of the old Heptarchy—Northumbria, East Anglia, and Mercia. The Hiberno-Norse dimension to the activities of the invaders of Alfredian Wessex reveals a co-ordinated attempt by a formidable dynasty of Scandinavian sea-kings to conquer and to colonize a whole series of native kingdoms within the British Isles. It suggests yet again that the Anglo-Saxon Chronicle's repeated reference to a Great Heathen Army ought to be taken seriously. The Hálfdan who confronted King Æthelred and his brother Alfred at Ashdown in 871 was no random or ragged opponent, assumed by Sawyer and by others to have headed a modest collection of ships' companies.[80] He was a most formidable migratory king, who together with his brothers were bent on irrevocably changing the political geography of Britain and Ireland. The Anglo-Saxon Chronicle may not consistently refer to these enemy leaders as kings, but time and time again it does accord the title *cyning* to them and to their associates and successors. Hálfdan is specifically identified in the Chronicle as one of a pair of 'heathen kings (*þa heþnan cyningas*)'.[81] The same is generally true of contemporary Irish and Frankish sources. This, too, is a fact which helps us understand why kings like Alfred and—even more so—rulers like Charles the Simple and Charles the Bald took viking leaders seriously. They entered into repeated negotiations regarding peace treaties, hostages, tribute, trade, and possible baptisms with these men. All this is explicable only if we bear in mind that Carolingian and Anglo-Saxon kings alike recognized

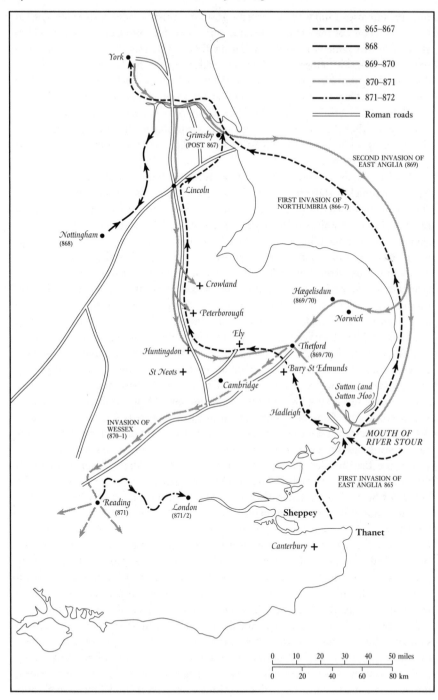

MAP 3. The Danish invasion of England, 865–72

qualities of high status and royal authority in these invading leaders, which answered to qualities which they prized in themselves. The grandsons and great-grandsons of Charlemagne were compelled to do business with Germanic sea-kings on the Seine, Somme, and Loire, in spite of their own pretentions to ruling a Christian *imperium* on the one hand, and in spite of the invaders' observed heathen barbarism on the other. Ivar and Hálfdan—and Guthrum who was soon to follow them—had the military backing of a great warband and the credentials of ancient Germanic kingship, which were calculated to impress the beleaguered kings of the West Saxons. For devout Christian ruler though he was, Alfred belonged to a dynasty which, like the pagan Ynglings in the viking homeland, was proud to trace its descent back to the Germanic war-god, Woden.[82]

By 874 Alfred's respite from attack was coming an end. As his old adversary Hálfdan moved north from Repton, Guthrum and his associates had resolved to return to the south. The unfinished business relating to the future of Wessex, which had been fought over on the Berkshire Downs in 871, was now finally to be resolved.

III

To the Last Ditch at Edington

THE GREAT ARMY WHICH SUPPRESSED THE NORTHUMBRIAN REVOLT IN
872–3 and which established Ceolwulf II in Mercia in the following year,
split into two major divisions after leaving Repton in 874–5. While Hálfdan moved
his men north to the Tyne, Guthrum and his companions moved south again. The
Anglo-Saxon chronicler had good reason to observe the movements of the southern division of this army very closely: 'the three kings, Guthrum, Oscetel and
Anwend, went from Repton to Cambridge with a great force, and stayed there a
year.' But part at least of that same army was soon on the move again, not content
to remain in what was now the Danish-held territory of East Anglia. Those flat
lands, so easily accessible to Denmark, may have been attracting a steady influx of
viking colonists since the conquest that had begun so successfully five years before.
Such a build-up of warriors and settlers could have prompted Guthrum to move
on and make his final move against Wessex. This was now the last remaining
English kingdom, whose king, Alfred, was in a state of uneasy and ambiguous
truce with his Danish overlords. As Guthrum pushed south into Wessex in 875–
6, King Alfred's Second War had begun. The Chronicle records tersely: 'In this
year [876] the enemy army slipped past the army of the West Saxons into Wareham.'
Æthelweard confirms that this was the army 'which was in Cambridge'. The
Chronicle's glib reporting conceals the fact that for Danes to have slipped past the
West Saxon army and to have entrenched themselves in Wareham, this must have
involved a journey of seventy-five or eighty miles across West Saxon territory at
the very least.[1] We hear no more of Oscetel and Anwend—Guthrum being the
leader who focuses the attention of the chronicler from now on—but the names of
the other two leaders were clearly learnt by West Saxon informants after the army
had returned to Wessex in 875–6. The kingly status of all three leaders underlines
yet again the importance of these marauding bands and the serious intent which
underlay their campaign. The chronicler's reference to this 'great force' which
followed those three Danish kings back for a final confrontation with Alfred and
the men of Wessex runs against any notion of these warbands being of little
numerical significance.

It is reasonable to conclude that the bulk of warriors who parted company from
each other at Repton did so along the lines of their allegiances to their war leaders.
While mercenaries were a feature of many viking armies, it was probably more
usual for the composition of warbands to have been rooted in regional and tribal

origins in the Scandinavian homelands. When in 861, a great fleet was prevented from leaving the mouth of the Seine by the onset of winter, the crews 'split up according to their brotherhoods (*sodalitates*) into groups allocated to various ports, from the sea-coast right up to Paris'.[2] The notion that great warbands were composed of groups or *sodalitates* may suggest that men soldiered together who were bound by ties of comradeship going back no doubt in many instances to traditional bonds of kinship and loyalty in the northern homelands.[3] So, Hálfdan would have settled most of those followers in Northumbria whom he had been responsible for, and who had campaigned with him—and earlier with Ivar—from the beginning of the war which had opened with the fall of York back in 866. The army of Guthrum and his followers may have been a more recent arrival in England. We first hear of Guthrum at Repton in 874–5 and it may be that he and his men made up that 'great summer army' which appeared at Reading after the battle of *Meretun* and shortly before the death of King Æthelred in 871.[4] That Summer Army which fought alongside Hálfdan's hordes as 'the whole army' against Alfred at Wilton may nevertheless have retained a separate identity. It is likely that the parting of the ways at Repton in 874–5 was based on a twofold distinction between older campaigners of Ivar's and Hálfdan's day, who were now war-weary and hungry for land, and relative newcomers loyal to Guthrum, who were still hopeful of yet further conquests in the south.

Alfred was faced with a most dangerous enemy in Guthrum in 875–6. Here was a Danish king who was almost certain to have been already familiar with West Saxon terrain and with West Saxon fighting ability. If Guthrum had been present in the battle at Wilton, he would have known how Alfred had been defeated so decisively there, that on the Chronicle's own admission, the West Saxons had been forced to sue for peace. As for Guthrum's intentions towards Wessex, as he invaded that kingdom in 875–6, he must have been resolved on the conquest of at least part of it. Æthelweard, in describing the fragmentation of the Great Army at Repton, relates: 'Then after a year the barbarians divided up the kingdom for themselves into two shares. A leader of the barbarians by name Halfdan took the area of the Northumbrians. . . . Oscytel, Guthrum and Annuth . . . went from Repton to the place called Cambridge.'[5] The kingdom (*regnum*) which the Danish leaders had divided into two shares (*sortes*) would appear to have consisted of the whole of England, and while Hálfdan had seized everything north of the Humber, Guthrum by immediately invading Wessex was laying claim to that territory as part of his southern share. Danish attempts at the conquest of Wessex in this Second War were radically different in some respects from the first Danish campaign which had been based on Reading. The difference relates to both Danish and West Saxon tactics. In the first campaign, the Danish warband under Hálfdan's leadership held tightly together about Reading, cautiously probing West Saxon defences across nearby Berkshire and Hampshire. The West Saxons, on the other hand, embarked on meeting the first Danish threat head-on in a series of pitched battles and perhaps one frontal assault on Reading which for the most part went badly wrong. In the Second War from 875 to 878, we find the Danes constantly on the move, covering huge stretches of countryside, and constantly concluding bogus treaties with Alfred, while constantly giving him and his army the slip. Alfred for his part, now also seemed reluctant to risk a pitched battle, and although the initiative still clearly lay with the Danes, the West Saxon army seems to have adopted the role of trying to contain the activities of the Danish warband by shadowing their progress throughout Wessex. For a large invading force to survive in hostile territory, it had to fragment into small foraging parties to live off the land. By shadowing the main force of invaders with his own large army, Alfred hoped to prevent the Danes from fanning out over the countryside in smaller groups.

It may be that during the years 872–5, Alfred had gained precious time to allow him and his *witan* to think out a strategy and to put Wessex in some state of readiness for the inevitable return of Guthrum and his hordes in 875–6. This is suggested by the first mention of Alfred's warships in 875, which were commanded by the king himself in that year and which captured a Danish ship and put six others to flight.[6] Such an action suggests that Alfred had not been idle since the withdrawal of the Danes from Reading in 872. He may also have been busy fortifying or revamping the fortifications of some key West Saxon centres, although the evidence for Alfredian *burh*-type fortifications at this early stage is ambiguous. We read of the Danes becoming unreachable when they succeeded in getting inside the fortress at Exeter in 877. But whether that fortress (*fæsten*) refers to Alfredian revamped Roman walls of Exeter or to a fort which the Danes constructed for themselves is not clear. Æthelweard does mention that the Danes laid out their own camp (*castra*) within Exeter in the winter of 877–8.[7] Wareham must have had some burghal fortifications by 875–6—not least to protect its nunnery, if by then the community had not fled. It would seem pointless for the Danes to have made a bee-line for the security of that distant place, if it did not provide security for their army as well as a safe anchorage for their ships. We can deduce that the Danish land army was backed up by their fleet along the south coast, for when the army moved off from Wareham to Exeter the fleet (*sciphere*) also sailed west and was shipwrecked off Swanage, which lies just south of the entrace to Poole Harbour, and which in turn gave access from the sea to Wareham.[8] But Æthelweard again casts doubt on the presence of an Alfredian fort at Wareham, for he tells us that the Danes encamped *near* Wareham (*iuxta oppidum quod Vuerham nuncupatur*) rather than actually in that town. Æthelweard's translation of this passage of the Chronicle is corrupt[9] and the original text of the Chronicle which claims the Danes stole past the West Saxons and *into* Wareham must be preferred to Æthelweard's account. Besides, the fact that the Chronicle claims the Danes were in a position to bargain their way out of Wareham—Æthelweard adds that Alfred paid them Danegeld—suggests that they had taken advantage of the defences of that place.

Whatever Alfred's preparations may have been, it was clearly the case that the initiative still lay with the Danish conquerors and this was so, in spite of relentless attempts by the compiler of the Chronicle to erode any impression of Danish

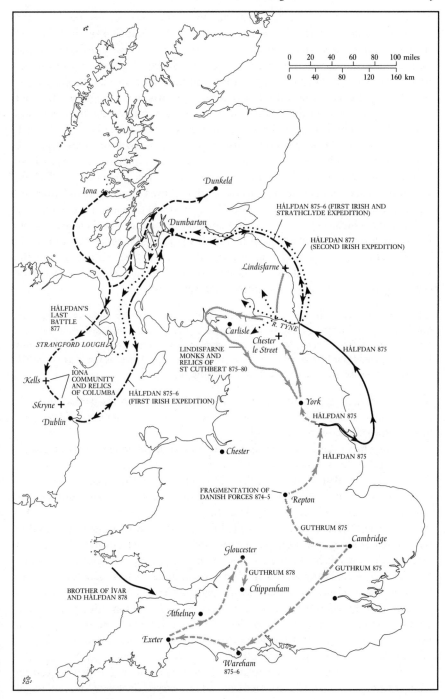

MAP 4. Expeditions of Hálfdan and Guthrum, 875–8

superiority. So, for instance the notion that 'the enemy army slipped past the army of the West Saxons into Wareham' is essentially an admission of the failure of Alfred's men to keep the enemy out of a secure site. Once into Wareham, as formerly at Reading, the invaders, albeit under siege, could dictate terms in an age which was as yet untrained in siege warfare. So the statement that 'the king made peace with the enemy, and they gave him hostages, who were the most important men next to the king in their army and swore oaths to him on the holy ring' was essentially a clumsy attempt by the compiler to cover up either West Saxon incompetence or the inability of native levies to anticipate or control Danish movements. The high status of Danish hostages was a matter which must have been difficult of proof, and in reality an exchange of hostages was more likely to have taken place. Æthelweard reveals the truth of Alfred's predicament by reporting that 'the king . . . gave them money'.[10] The boast that the swearing on the ring 'was a thing which they would not do before for any nation' was equally hollow, for the oath that 'they would speedily leave his [Alfred's] kingdom' was instantly broken. The Anglo-Saxon Chronicle goes on to narrate the sad outcome of the West Saxon decision to allow the Danes out of Wareham which could not be concealed by even the most resourceful of chroniclers:

And then under cover of that, they—the mounted army—stole by night away from the English army to Exeter. . . . And then King Alfred rode after the mounted army with the English army as far as Exeter, but could not overtake them [before they were in the fortress where they could not be reached] and they gave him hostages there, as many as he wished to have, and swore great oaths and then kept a firm peace.[11]

Æthelweard, as ever, provides the more honest comment that 'the barbarians made peace treacherously, being in the same frame of mind as before' providing even more hostages than were asked for![12]

Contemporary Frankish chronicles help us, once again, to understand the logistical and political realities which lie behind the heavily edited and censored account of Alfred's Second War as provided by the Anglo-Saxon Chronicle. The Danish escape by night from Wareham is echoed by the escape of a viking warband by moonlight from Avaux (Ardennes) while they were besieged by Carloman and his troops in 882.[13] That escape was effected because the Carolingians were afraid to remain too close to the besieged Danes within the villa during the hours of darkness. The inability of Alfred and his men to catch up with the enemy before they had entrenched themselves in Exeter reminds us of how Charles the Bald, when he heard of an impending viking attack on Meaux back in 862, 'made all speed in that direction with those men whom he had with him. But he could not catch up with them, because the bridges had been destroyed and the ships taken over by the Northmen.'[14] A few years later Charles sacked several of his magnates because 'these men had achieved nothing of any use at all against the Northmen'.[15] We find the Frankish annalist complaining bitterly yet again in 868 that a squadron led by Carloman, which Charles the Bald had sent across the Seine 'did nothing of any use as far as resisting the Northmen was concerned—and that after all was the purpose for which they had been sent'.[16] The Carolingians were outwitted and outmanœuvred time and time again by the Scandinavian invaders, not only because the vikings moved faster, but because the defenders failed to predict what the vikings' next moves might be, and because the vikings, on their part, were also masters at predicting the tactics of their opponents. So when Charles the Bald had resolved on trying to dislodge a particularly troublesome viking warband from Angers in 873 we are told:

Charles announced that the host would go in the direction of Brittany, so that the Northmen occupying Angers could not surmise that they were going to attack that region, in which case they might have fled away to other places where they could not be so tightly hemmed in.[17]

Had Alfred or his supporters not been so concerned to suppress so much evidence relating to his own discomfort in the Chronicle,[18] we would be in a much better position to assess the odds that had been stacked against him by a highly experienced and resourceful enemy. As things stand, we are left with a bland chronicle which laconically charts the movements of the Danish victors while at the same time disingenuously striving to convey the impression that Alfred was in control. In one important respect, Danish tactics during the Second War had not changed. The Danes consistently sought the safety of a fortified centre and once lodged there, they had to be negotiated out. This was an effective way for the invaders to demand supplies or to plunder at little risk to their own men. But in this Second War, huge distances were being rapidly covered in an attempt to catch the West Saxons off guard and ultimately to seize a portion of the kingdom. It looks very much as though Guthrum's aim was to move his land army and his fleet as rapidly as possible across Wessex to launch his attack proper in the west of the kingdom. The Wareham and Exeter episodes, therefore, may have been no more than a means to an end—i.e. the eventual conquest of north-west Wessex and the annexation of that region to the adjoining parts of Danish-held Mercia. There was clearly a sense of purpose and urgency in Guthrum's rapid drive across Wessex during 875–7, but during this time his army had to be fed and the high morale of his warriors sustained by the acquisition of loot. Viking raiding reached its most destructive levels in Wessex for the second time, and the monasteries of Dorset and Devon—lying in the path of this Danish army—must have borne the brunt of the violence—not to mention the exactions of King Alfred who had been forced to buy off the Danes at Wareham. Æthelweard reveals that while the Danes were at Wareham, 'the greater part of the province was ravaged by them'.[19] Æthelweard's 'province (*prouinciæ*)' refers, almost certainly, to the shire of Dorset rather than to Wessex as a whole, but Devon was soon to provide the next target for viking loot, since Æthelweard goes on to relate how Guthrum's army 'entered the province of Devon (*prouinciam Defenum*) on a wide front'.[20] It was as though the Danes were conscious of having already stripped Berkshire and Hampshire of their food surplus and treasure during the First War, and now it was the turn of Dorset,

Devon—and finally of Wiltshire—to yield up the loot expected of a conquered territory.

The 'firm peace' which the Danes concluded with Alfred at Exeter in 877 was not quite what it seemed. The most important part of the Danish side of the bargain was that they would 'withdraw from the jurisdiction of his boundaries'[21]— leave his kingdom in peace and not return. In August (harvest) 877, Guthrum and his Danes headed north—across Devon, Somerset, and Wiltshire—for Mercia where they 'shared out some of it and gave some to Ceolwulf'. Æthelweard claimed that the Danes drove the native Mercians off the land, ravaged every- where, and built booths in the town of Gloucester.[22] This was no ordinary raiding army: Guthrum and his warriors were clearly bent on territorial conquest and on settlement. It is clear that in the winter of 877–8, Alfred followed Guthrum north and settled down to celebrate Christmas at Chippenham. The place may already have been fortified by Alfred, and if he moved in there with a strong garrison, his action would have made sense. The occupation of Chippenham would, in those circumstances, have been part of Alfred's shadowing tactic to see off Guthrum's army, and to prevent any further looting in north Wiltshire as the invaders departed for Mercia. Alfred's stay at Chippenham could be seen, too, as a move to deter Guthrum's return across the Mercian border from Gloucester into Wessex. But subsequent events were to show that Alfred was in no position to repel an attack from Chippenham when Guthrum did return, and although Guthrum launched a surprise attack in mid-winter, it was none the less unwise of Alfred to have spent Christmas seemingly in a state of unreadiness on what had now become an exposed frontier of his kingdom, in close proximity to such a treacherous foe. It might have seemed to an observer inexperienced in viking treachery that Guthrum's men, like those of Hálfdan had now settled for colonizing parts of Mercia. But Alfred had personal experience of repeated broken viking promises made under 'great oaths' as at Exeter and Wareham, and he must have been aware that Danish leaders would agree to swear to anything provided they were allowed to withdraw unchal- lenged with their booty and captives. Some of Alfred's advisers, who were familiar with Frankish affairs, would have been well aware that treachery and oath-breaking were a hallmark of viking tactics in neighbouring Carolingian lands. One Frankish annalist complained that when Charles the Bald levied a tax to raise 3,000 lbs. of silver to buy off Northmen on the Somme in 860, he was 'deceived by the empty promises of the Danes'.[23] When in 884 the Franks handed over 12,000 lbs. of gold and silver to a viking army, 'even after that [the vikings] did not keep the faith which they had promised, for they killed their hostages and did not cease at all from plundering'.[24] Immediately after the viking leader, Godafrid, had concluded a peace with Charles the Fat in 882, in spite of an exchange of hostages, Frankish warriors who had entered Godafrid's fort in friendship were seized and either slaughtered or held for ransom.[25]

Some of Guthrum's Danes may have intended to settle in parts of Mercia, but Guthrum was intent on one last throw to conquer Wessex. On Twelfth Night (6 January 878) he was back in Alfred's embattled kingdom with a vengeance:

In this year in midwinter after Twelfth Night the enemy army came stealthily to Chippenham, and conquered and occupied the land of the West Saxons and drove a great part of the people across the sea, and conquered and subjected to them most of the others except King Alfred. He journeyed in difficulties with a small force along the woods and in fen fastnesses.[26]

R. H. C. Davis incurred the censure of Whitelock by claiming that the Anglo-Saxon chronicler deliberately exaggerated Alfred's predicament in order to make his victory at Edington later in this year seem all the more impressive.[27] But several features about this 'woods and fen fastnesses' passage proclaim it to be a piece written in favour of Alfred—and although not written perhaps by Alfred himself, then by one of his supporters. The image of Alfred abandoned by 'most' of his people and journeying with 'difficulties' in the wilderness 'with a small force' was calculated to exaggerate the depths to which the fortunes of the king had sunk. We are reminded of the Chronicle's account of Alfred's first battle as king back in 871, when he was said to have fought 'with a small force against the whole army'. The 'woods and fen fastnesses' passage is carefully worded, too, to allow Alfred's victory over Guthrum later in the year, to yield maximum impact. The notion of the abandoned king heroically surviving in the wilderness is close to the image of Alfred in the folk-tale of the Burning Cakes. In that tale,[28] the abandoned and dejected king had sunk to his lowest fortunes. When wandering as a lone fugitive from the Danes, Alfred was supposed to have sought refuge in a herdsman's cabin on Athelney in Somerset. While there, he failed to attend to the cakes which were being cooked by a herdsman's wife. That tale was once dismissed as a twelfth-century invention. It was indeed an invention, but it is found in its earliest form in the late tenth- or early eleventh-century *Life* of St Neot, and the creation of such a story by this relatively early stage was inspired and rendered plausible by the designedly heroic quality of the narrative of Alfred's tribulations at the hands of Guthrum as recorded in the Chronicle. That embroidered passage relating to the 'woods and fen fastnesses' episode was not an absolutely contemporary account. It reflects, rather, how a chronicler, briefed by Alfred or one of his immediate circle, wished to present the trials of an earlier war, viewed from the vantage-point of the winning side some ten years and more, after the event.

The Chronicle's claim that the Danes 'drove a great part of the people across the sea and conquered and subjected to them most of the others except King Alfred' or alternatively that 'the people submitted to the [the Danes] except King Alfred' is flatly contradicted later in the same passage by the account of the victory of the men of Devon over the brother of Ivar and Hálfdan who was slain in Devon along with 840 of his men. Æthelweard tells us that the men of Devon were led by their ealdorman, Odda.[29] So in one shire at least, the local levies, still under their ealdorman, were capable of mounting resistance while their king had gone into hiding elsewhere. There is little reason to doubt that the men of Berkshire, Surrey, Sussex, and Kent were still under the rule of their own ealdormen and diocesan clergy during the weeks and months following Guthrum's invasion of Wessex. As for 'all the people of Somerset and of Wiltshire, and on that part of Hampshire which was on this side of the sea'—they were in a sufficient state of organization—under leaders who clearly had not fled over any seas—to rendezvous with their king at Ecgberht's Stone east of Selwood in the seventh week after Easter.[30] The Chronicle itself states that even while a fugitive on Athelney, Alfred had the support in battle of that 'section of the people of Somerset which was nearest to it', while Æthelweard specifically names Æthelnoth, the ealdorman of Somerset as a leader who helped Alfred construct the fort on Athelney.[31] None of this suggests that the magnates and warriors of Wessex had, as a body, turned their backs either on the peoples of their shires, or on their king. What we do know is that it was Alfred himself who fled before Guthrum's surprise attack on Chippenham, and that he fled to the south and west 'with a small force', joining up with the men of Somerset, when he constructed a fort on Athelney, an island in the Somerset marshes.

Alfred had abandoned Chippenham on 6 January. He built the fort at Athelney at Easter, which in that year fell on 23 March. Since Alfred conducted his campaign against the Danes from Athelney, and since even after his final victory at Edington in north Wiltshire, he withdrew back again to his Somerset base near Aller and Wedmore, it does look as if Guthrum's men had made themselves masters of the open countryside stretching east of Selwood from Chippenham in the north, down to Sherborne and Shaftesbury in the south—if not further south still onto to the Dorset Downs. Guthrum was now in control of the heartland of western Wessex and no doubt he either obtained the submission of Alfred's leading magnates in this fertile region, or he drove them off their lands. Whitelock observed that the men of Devon were absent from the muster which rallied to Alfred at Ecgberht's Stone in the seventh week after Easter (4–7 May).[32] But the Danish warband was highly unlikely to have been in a position to occupy or colonize all of Wessex as an alien power in 878. Guthrum and his associates had earlier parted company with Hálfdan's army at Repton, and it is likely that many of those who had come south and had 'shared out some' of Mercia with Ceolwulf preferred to farm their new estates there than risk another weary war against Wessex. Further losses of men as colonists in East Anglia, together with the loss of 120 ships in a storm off Swanage in 876–7, must have left Guthrum's army severely depleted. Even if Davis underestimated the extent of Guthrum's conquest as being confined to west Wiltshire and north Somerset, Alfred's fight to the finish against Guthrum was indeed localized within north Wiltshire and may not have involved a 'great army (*micel here*)' or 'great force' as on previous campaigns. The levies of Somerset, Wiltshire, and parts of Hampshire who rallied to Alfred's cause at Ecgberht's Stone in those days after Easter in 878 may have been a formidable warband—every bit as great as the armies which rallied behind Æthelred and Alfred during the First War against the Reading garrison in 871–2. The army of even a single shire was clearly not negligible. The men of Devon had, on their own, slain 840 vikings in one battle in that same year as Alfred made his stand at Edington. Even though Guthrum had seized Chippenham in early January, his main strength was still massed about that place in the second week of May. So, in spite of his great and sudden sweep across Wessex in 875–7, once the Dane had achieved his objective, as in the case of the earlier Reading campaign, he now settled down to a cautious waiting game. His initial targeting of Chippenham had clearly been prompted by the prior intelligence of Alfred's presence there, and by his desire to catch the English king off guard. Guthrum's decision to retain Chippenham as his base was determined by its borderland location and its proximity to Danish-held Mercia. The all-important fortress which the Danes occupied at Chippenham may have been built previously by Alfred.

The massed levies of the West Saxons moved north from Ecgberht's Stone to Iley Oak near Eastleigh Wood, two miles south of Warminster. From there they moved to Edington where, sometime between 6 and 12 May, they fought against the 'whole army [of the Danes], put it to flight and pursued it as far as the fortress'. Alfred had at last gained a crucial victory which broke a seemingly endless cycle of defeat followed by oath-swearing and bogus treaties. Edington lies only thirteen miles due south of Chippenham which confirms that Guthrum's men had maintained a defensive stance close to their original base in north Wessex. It is surely more than coincidence that both Edington and Chippenham were royal estates. Alfred left an estate at Edington to his wife Ealhswith in his *Will*,[33] while his great-grandson, King Eadwig, met with his council at Edington in 957.[34] Eadwig's brother, King Edgar, had land to dispose of at Edington in 968.[35] Alfred left an estate at Chippenham in his *Will* to his youngest daughter (Ælfthryth)[36] and Alfred's son and successor, Edward the Elder, is seen from the evidence of a legal dispute, to have been residing at Chippenham at one point in his reign.[37] The invaders—now bent on conquest in Wiltshire—seem, as in the case of the First War, to have been keeping up pressure on centres of West Saxon royal power. Guthrum's surprise attack on Chippenham had almost certainly been directed against Alfred's person. It may be that the Danish attack on Devon, led by the brother of Ivar and Hálfdan, in the same winter of 878, had also been designed to box Alfred in, and ultimately to capture him. The association of Guthrum's army with two royal centres in Wiltshire suggests that the Danish leaders were bent on securing West Saxon royal estates as the first step in their conquest of northern and western Wessex. Guthrum, who was now master of Mercia, may have intended annexing neighbouring portions of Wessex in a *de facto* division of that kingdom with Alfred. Alfred had not previously opposed the Danes in battle since the first month of his kingship back in 871. Like the unlucky Burgred, he had subsequently concluded a peace with his enemies no less than three times—in 871, 876, and 877. We shall never know what terms Alfred had been forced to agree to, and he and his circle, once they had recovered their position in the years after 878, would have been the last to reveal the humiliating reality of that earlier and most difficult time. If Alfred had agreed to hold Wessex for his Danish overlords in the same way as Ceolwulf held Mercia, then Guthrum's seizure of centres such as Chippenham and Edington may be seen in that light. Alfred's brother-in-law, Burgred, king of the Mercians, had also made peace with the Danes in 868, 872, and 873, but when the Danish army descended on Repton in 874, Burgred must

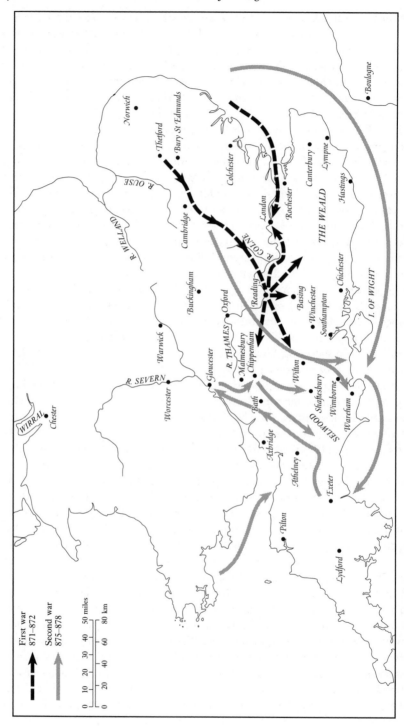

MAP 5. King Alfred's first and second wars

have had compelling reasons for abandoning his kingdom without a battle and heading for Rome.

Burgred would have known of the death of Edmund, king of the East Angles in November 869, and he would have known that Edmund also had concluded an earlier peace with the Danes in 866. Tales circulating within a hundred years of Edmund's death, and written up by Abbo of Fleury, would tell of the horrific tortures which Edmund suffered at the hands of his heathen tormentors, and coins circulating within thirty years of Edmund's death would proclaim him to have died a saint. Later Scandinavian traditions circulating within the English Danelaw would tell of the equally ghoulish fate supposedly meted out to the English king Ælla, of Northumbria, at the hands of Ivar. That leader of the Great Army was supposed to have hacked the body of the English king into the bloody shape of a spread-eagle, as he offered him to Odin as a sacrifice for victory.[38] The skaldic poet, Sigvatr, who composed verses in praise of Cnut the Great *c.*1030 remembered how 'Ivar, who dwelt at York, carved the eagle on Ælla's back'—a reference to the ritual mangling of the body of the captured Northumbrian king. There is no contemporary evidence for such atrocities, although we do have evidence for Raven war-banners and for the Raven coinage issued at York by the great-grandson of Ivar *c.*940. Burgred must have known that an unpleasant end awaited him also, if he disputed the final terms offered Mercia by its new Danish masters. There cannot have been many who witnessed the barbarity of viking war-camps in the wake of victory, and who survived to tell the tale. Victorian naïvety in the portrayal of the 'noble savage', combined with revisionist and post-Christian interpretations of 'heathen integrity' have done much to sanitize our view of pagan barbarism. An eleventh-century Irish account of conditions in a Danish war-camp after a victory over Norwegian rivals suggests a level of barbarism practised by one group of Northmen even against their own Scandinavian enemies, which accounts for the horror which viking marauders instilled into native populations in the Christian West. This account echoes Ibn Fadlan's observations on tenth-century viking behaviour in the East:

Now at this time, Maelsechlainn, king of Tara, sent ambassadors to the Danes. On their arrival, the Danes were cooking, and the supports of their cauldrons were heaps of bodies of the Norwegians, and one end of the spits on which the meat was hung was stuck into the bodies of the Norwegians, and the fire was burning the bodies, so that they belched forth from their stomachs the flesh and fat which they had eaten the night before. The ambassadors reproached the Danes with this [savage conduct]. The Danes replied: 'This is the way they would like to have [had] us'.[39]

Those who rush to the defence of heathen vikings and who see them as 'the long-haired tourists' of the Early Middle Ages, who were given a bad press by narrow-minded monkish chroniclers who enjoyed a monopoly on reporting, do so in face of a formidable body of evidence centring on the ninth and tenth centuries which testifies to a relentless catalogue of treachery and cruelty ranging from Ireland and Spain in the West, to the banks of the Volga in the East. Alfred's retreat westward into Somerset must be seen in the light of the destruction of Ælla and of Edmund, and in the recent flight of his brother-in-law, Burgred, from Mercia.

There is some evidence associating the attack on Wessex in 878 with the cult of the Norse war-god, Odin. One of the contributors to the Anglo-Saxon Chronicle, when reporting the defeat of the army of the brother of Ivar and Hálfdan in Devon, noted that: 'there was captured the banner (*guþfana*) which they called "Raven" (*Hrefn*).'[40] What was so special about this trophy which merited its place in the Anglo-Saxon Chronicle as the only item of booty to have been captured in a land battle by the English in the entire thirteen-year campaign from 865 to 878? The only other captured item mentioned in that time was a single ship which Alfred was said to have seized in 875. What was so special about a Raven banner that earned it a mention in this record, when the chronicler passed over the West Saxon victory at Ashdown in 871, where 'thousands' of Northmen were said to have been slain, and when not one single item of booty was singled out for attention? Æthelweard tells us that when Ealdorman Æthelwulf defeated a party of vikings only three days after their arrival in Reading, in 871, the English 'rejoiced in the spoils of victory', but no particular trophies were singled out for attention.[41] We know that because viking armies were themselves constantly amassing loot, native defenders could be immensely enriched from a victory over a viking host. We read in the Annals of Fulda, how a Frisian army after their victory over a viking fleet 'found such treasure in gold, silver and other kinds of moveable goods that all, from the smallest to the greatest, were made rich'.[42] The banner captured in 878 was clearly in the same category of ritual objects as the Norse 'holy ring (*halgan beage*)' which caught the imagination of the chronicler when describing events of 876.[43] In that year we are told that the Danes concluded a solemn peace with Alfred at Wareham 'and swore oaths to him on the holy ring—a thing they would not do before for any nation'. The authenticity of the record of the Norse oath-ring in 876 is not challenged. The Icelandic *Eyrbyggja saga* describes a sacred ring which was used for oath-swearing in an Icelandic temple, while a Ring of Thor was captured by the Irish high king, Maelsechnaill II, during a raid on Norse Dublin in 994. The eleventh-century *History of the St. Cuthbert* mentions yet another such gold ring 'worn on the right arm' of the Danish king, Guthfrith, during his inauguration in Northumbria in *c.*900.[44] Frankish annalists not only frequently refer to Norse oath-swearing in connection with peace negotiations, but they also suggest that for Norsemen such oaths involved solemn pagan ritual, just as for Christians oaths were sworn on sacred texts or on reliquaries. So in 858, the viking leader, Björn, 'swore fidelity after his own fashion *fidelitatem suatim iurat*' to Charles the Bald,[45] while four years later, Weland and his companions 'swore solemn oaths in their own way *illi se commendavit et sacramenta cum eis quos secum habuit suatim praebuit*'.[46]

The reference in the Chronicle to the Raven banner which was captured by the men of Devon may belong to the original late ninth-century compilation, or it may have been inserted in Manuscript B in the later tenth century. But there is no reason to believe that the Raven banner was any less real than the viking oath-ring, except that while rings might be pressed into ritual service to conclude a peace, Raven banners served a more violent purpose. Norse battle-banners are also among the few captured trophies mentioned in Frankish annals. The West Frankish Robert, Count of Angers, in 865 sent Norse battle-banners (*vexilla Nortmannica*) and weapons (*arma*) which he had captured from the Loire vikings to his master, Charles the Bald.[47] We are told that in the great battle against the vikings on the Dyle in 891, 'terrible battle-banners (*signa horribilia*) moved through the camps' and that 'sixteen [Norse] royal standards (*regia signa*) were carried off [by the Carolingians] and were sent to Bavaria as witness'.[48] The raven was a bird specially associated with war cults in early European societies. It had been so among the pre-Christian Celts and for Germanic warriors it had special associations with battle and with the cult of Odin. Even among the Christian English as late as the reign of Alfred's grandson Athelstan, a gloating reference to the raven feeding on the corpses of slain vikings was deemed in order in a victory poem: 'They [i.e. the Norsemen] left behind them the dusky-coated one, the black raven with its horned beak to share the corpses . . . to enjoy the carrion.'[49] Among the Norsemen, the raven was a symbol of the battle-god's need to be placated with the corpses of the slain.[50] Odin in Norse mythology was credited with having two ravens called *Huginn* ('thought') and *Muninn* ('memory'), and the raven who preyed on the corpses of slain warriors was, by association, seen as a symbol of Odin's acceptance of the sacrifice of the slain. Athelstan's enemy, Olaf Guthfrithsson who was the great-grandson of Alfred's contemporary, Ivar, issued a splendid silver penny from his York mint, displaying the bold image of a raven or spread-eagle, and clearly celebrating the bird of battle.[51]

A passage from *Sverris saga* underlines the role of the Raven banner as an icon capable of procuring victory in battle: 'Let us hoist the standard before the king, and press hard on the Kulflungar. Let the keen blade bite, and let us hew a sacrifice beneath the ravens talons.'[52] Later tradition in the *Annals of St. Neots* held that the banner captured in Devon had been woven by the three daughters of *Lodebroch*, who were the sisters of *Hynguar* and *Hubbe*. The fluttering of that particular raven image forecast victory to the bearers and its drooping forecast defeat.[53] *Orkneyinga saga* describes a similar banner, also supposedly woven by a female relative of a viking warlord—in this case the mother of Earl Sigurd the Stout (*Digri*) of Orkney. That lady had endowed her son's banner with supernatural properties so that: 'they before whom it is borne will be blessed with victory, though it will be the death of him who bears it.'[54] This banner, regarded as a 'fiend (*fjanda*)' by a later saga writer,[55] eventually brought about Earl Sigurd's own death at the battle of Clontarf in 1014. Half a century later, William of Normandy is shown on the Bayeux Tapestry processing before two banners as he rides to battle against Harold at Hastings.[56] The first banner or semicircular pennon in the tapestry has the image of a bird, and the second bears a Christian cross. That cross or more certainly, another shown later on in the tapestry, represents the banner or gonfanon presented by Pope Alexander II in support of William's conquest of

England.[57] The bird on the pennon in the Bayeux Tapestry—significantly carried so close to the person of Duke William—represents the survival of Odin's bird of battle in Norse and later Norman war rituals beyond the middle of the eleventh century. The capture 'of the banner which they called "Raven" ', then, was rightly seen by the West Saxons as symbolic of their triumph as Christian warriors over heathen men relying on the talisman of their pagan war-god, and as such it was singled out for special mention in an otherwise laconic record.

The mention of the Raven battle-banner may suggest that the conflict between Anglo-Saxons and Danish invaders was perceived by contemporaries or by men of the tenth century who were writing on the Christian side, as a struggle between Christians and heathen. That this was so may have been in part due to the propaganda value of Christianity for the English and other beleaguered peoples to use in their war of words against the Danes.[58] But the observed pagan qualities of viking life are not confined to studied pieces of Christian propaganda. The instant comments of contemporary annalists as they recorded the arrival and departure of Scandinavian raiders shows how powerfully the paganism of these enemies impressed itself on native minds. The English evidence for the peculiarly heathen nature of viking culture as it was observed by native commentators is consistent with that from Ireland and Francia at this time. The first viking raid on England— that on Lindisfarne in 793—was ascribed by the compiler of the Anglo-Saxon Chronicle to 'the ravages of heathen men (*heðenra manna*)'. It was a 'heathen army (*hæþene men*)' which had attacked the men of Devon in 851 and 'heathen men (*heþne men*)' who wintered on Thanet in that same year.[59] A 'heathen army (*heþnum herige*)' was back on Thanet in 853 and 'heathen men' were wintering on Sheppey sometime in 855–8.[60] The invaders who confronted Alfred's kingdom of Wessex were first identified as 'a Great Heathen Army (*mycel hæþen here*)' back in 866 and a section of them at least, had probably encamped as a 'heathen army (*heþen here*)' on Thanet in the year before.[61] Bagsecg and Hálfdan who fought against King Æthelred and his brother, Alfred, at Ashdown in 871, were described as 'heathen kings (*þa heþnan cyningas*)'.[62] There was no doubting the heathen nature of King Alfred's enemies in the mind of the Anglo-Saxon Chronicler. Nor can such terminology be easily dismissed as a so-called monkish perception, since the Chronicle—unlike other contemporary productions in Ireland and Francia—was neither ecclesiastically based, nor ecclesiastically orientated in its content.

Irish chroniclers also chose words which emphasized the non-Christian nature of the earliest viking onslaught against monastic houses and territories within Ireland. The word *gentiles* and its Old Irish form *gennti* was consistently applied to viking raiders by the compiler of the Annals of Ulster in the late eighth and early ninth centuries, as *Meic Báis* ('apostates' or 'Sons of Death') was applied to those who joined the Northmens' way of life.[63] In Frankish annals, too, *pagani* is a regular term applied to Northmen, while the native Franks who resisted them or suffered from their depradations, are regularly referred to as 'Christians'. As in Ireland, Norse behaviour in Francia was viewed as something other than that of Christian practice, and we find, for instance, the Frankish magnate, Imino, being castigated by an annalist 'for causing widespread devastation' and for 'behaving the way the Northmen do (*more Nortmannico*)' in the very year in which Alfred made his stand at Edington.[64] Two years previously, a group of newly baptized Northmen who had been received by the emperor, Charles the Bald, had fallen away from the Christian faith and 'like typical Northmen, they lived according to the pagan custom (*moro pagano*) just as before'.[65] The Frankish phrases *more Nortmannico* and *moro pagano* ('according to Norse or pagan custom') echoes the Irish annalist's *more Gentilium* ('according to heathen custom') used of those Irish apostate 'Sons of Death' who had thrown in their lot with viking practice in 847.[66] Those who joined the viking way of life were singled out for special attention in Frankish sources. The Annals of St Bertin tell us of Pippin II of Aquitane who, in 864, abandoned the habit of a monk 'to become a layman and an apostate, [and who] joined company with the Northmen and followed their rites'.[67] It was not Pippin's laicization which had angered the annalist. He recorded the fact that Pippin had been favourably received by Charles the Bald *after* he had abandoned monastic life in 858.[68] Pippin's crime had been his apostacy and his alliance with the viking enemy. When he was eventually indicted at Pîtres in 864, he was accused as 'a traitor to his fatherland and to Christianity (*patriae et christianitatis proditor*)'.[69] Yet another monk who had gone over to Northmen on the Loire and 'had abandoned Christendom' and had been 'extremely dangerous to the Christians', was executed by his Frankish captors in 869.[70]

The ideological polarization between Christian and pagan in the Viking Age is borne out by evidence from several different societies across Latin Christendom, for the participation of leading churchmen in battle against the Northmen. Indeed, it could be argued that it was the threat of viking paganism which accelerated—if it did not in many cases initiate—the personal involvement of Western clergy in medieval warfare. One of the leaders of that Frankish army which attacked the Loire vikings in 869, was Hugh, nephew of the Carolingian, Louis the German, and abbot of St Martin's of Tours.[71] Frankish churchmen were in the forefront of the viking wars, even if Hincmar, archbishop of Rheims, objected to his bishops taking part in viking battles.[72] Just as leading ninth-century Frankish and Irish churchmen and monastic leaders joined in the military defence of their societies, so too, the church in Wessex took an active part in the war against the heathen. We have seen how Bishop Heahmund of Sherborne fell in the army of King Æthelred and his brother Alfred at *Meretun* during the First War in Wessex. There is no reason to assume that this bishop was exceptional. In the civil war between Alfred's son, Edward the Elder, and his first cousin, Æthelwold son of Æthelred, we find that a certain Abbot Cenwulf was slain in Edward's army at the final battle 'between the Dykes and Ouse' in 903.[73] Abbot Cenwulf was fighting on Edward's side and opposing a West Saxon ætheling who, like Pippin II of Aquitane, had defected to the Danes.

The West Saxon chronicler who narrated the progress of the Great Army and the West Saxon opposition to it in the period 866 to 878, settled on the use of the word 'army (*here*)' to indicate the movements of the invaders during that period.

Since the Chronicle narrative is almost exclusively concerned with the progress of the Danish war at this point, and because there was no danger of ambiguity, the term *here* was clearly used for brevity. The change in terminology from 'heathen army' to the simpler 'army' does not mean that the Danes had become any less 'heathen' since their entry into England in 865–71. The emphasis which the chronicler placed on the Danish oath-ring and on their Raven battle-banner, together with the identification of two 'heathen kings' in Wessex in 871, had as we have seen, emphasized the pagan culture of the invaders. It is in the context of this opposition between Christian and pagan opponents that the conversion of Guthrum to Alfred's Christian faith after the Danish defeat at Edington assumes its true importance:

And then the enemy gave him preliminary hostages and great oaths that they would leave his kingdom, and promised also that their king should receive baptism, and they kept their promise. Three weeks later King Guthrum with 30 of the men who were the most import-ant in the army came [to him] at Aller, which is near Athelney, and the king stood sponsor to him at his baptism there; and the unbinding of the chrism took place at Wedmore. And he was twelve days with the king, and he honoured him and his companions greatly with gifts.[74]

The detailed information offered on Guthrum's baptism both in relation to its topographical network and in its precise time sequence, is matched only by that offered for the most important military campaigns in the history of the Danish wars—such as that centred on Reading in 871 or later events of 893. From the chronicler's perspective, therefore, the events at Aller and at Wedmore were of the greatest significance. Alfred at Aller, in June 878, had neutralized the threat to Anglo-Saxon civilization posed by the Danish conquest. For Wessex at least, he had reversed the outcome which the Danish conquest had held for East Anglia, and for those other parts of England where all native resistance had collapsed. Not only had the East Angles lost their Christian king, but they had been conquered by pagan overlords—a point which had not been lost on King Edmund's biographer, Abbo of Fleury. According to Abbo, Edmund had not been averse to submitting to the pagan Ivar, and to sharing his treasures and estates with him, as well as ruling under him, provided only that the conquerer would give up his paganism and embrace Christianity.[75] Abbo's account is not implausible, since the Danish settlement of Northumbria and of Mercia involved the setting up of English subject-kings and the eventual partition of those kingdoms between Danes and English. But Ivar in 869 was in no mood to abandon Odin who, as his *Sigtyr* or 'Victory god', had yielded rich dividends for the Danes. Ivar had been described with some justification even by his Christian enemies as *invictissimus* ('most uncon-querable'),[76] whereas the hapless Edmund, like his royal colleagues, Ælla of North-umbria and Burgred of Mercia, had been in no position to dictate terms. So Edmund, as described by Abbo, suffered the grisly fate of a sacrificial king at the hands of his captors. Alfred, on the other hand, had won his battle at Edington and followed his victory through by besieging his defeated opponents at Chippenham for a fortnight. But a crucial point about Alfred's success—and the one most emphasized in the Chronicle—was the baptism of Guthrum along with thirty of his leading warriors. We know from the Chronicle that the conversion of Guthrum had been made a condition of Alfred's peace in 878, and the Chronicle makes a special point of stating in detail how that condition was met.

It was Alfred's achievement, through the imposition of baptism on Guthrum and his warriors, to have influenced the lives and fortunes not only of the population of Wessex, but of all Guthrum's subjects too—English and Dane alike—from St Albans to the Humber. For even if Alfred had no direct political or military influence over the newly established Danelaw, he was, nevertheless, through the drama surrounding the baptism of Guthrum and his chief men, interfering in the most profound way in the destiny of Guthrum's people. The spiritual parenthood established by Alfred over Guthrum at Aller must inevitably have implied some level of cultural and political superiority, and Guthrum, as the spiritual son of Alfred, was in turn acknowledging the future on-going superiority of a king whose religion he was compelled to adopt. The conversion of this Danish king in the Somerset Levels in the late ninth century was part of a relentless cultural process which can be recognized throughout early medieval Christendom. Guthrum's baptism had, indeed, immediate and long-lasting repercussions on Anglo-Danish society, but in order to understand its full significance, we need to see it in its wider European context, and we need to appreciate, too, that the necessity for Guthrum's baptism was born of an ideological hostility to paganism, not only in England, but on the part of the Christian élite in both Eastern and Western Christendom.

Evidence from ninth- and tenth-century annals in the Christian West show that not only did Christian observers regard Scandinavian invaders as being conspicuously pagan, but that they also treated them with ideological hostility. Historians who deny that the viking wars involved a conflict between Christian and pagan cultures may be correct in assuming that from the viking point of view there was no conscious animosity directed against Christianity as such. But assessments of the Viking Age which fail to take the views of contemporary Christian commentators into account, ignore in effect, what were then the views of an ecclesiastical élite which represented one of the most influential elements within those societies which were under attack. Take, for instance, the vision of some unknown English priest, which had once been narrated to Alfred's father, King Æthelwulf. That vision focused on the future of the 'Christian people (*homines christiani*)' and how they might avert their own destruction:

If Christian people do not quickly do penance for their various vices and crimes and do not observe the Lord's Day in a stricter and worthier way, then a great and crushing disaster will swiftly come upon them . . . and all of a sudden pagan men (*homines pagani*) with an immense multitude of ships will lay waste with fire and sword most of the people and the land of the Christians along with all they possess.[77]

Such passages may easily be dismissed by post-Christian commentators as the rantings of a monk who had an eye to losing his monastic treasure, or who shared in a thought-world formulated earlier by Alcuin, and which tied in the victims of

Scandinavian raiding with well-deserved punishment for sin. What is really significant about this Englishman's vision, however, is that it was thought to have been of such importance that King Æthelwulf of Wessex or his father, King Ecgberht, conveyed its content to the Carolingian emperor, and that it made such an impact on his court it found its way into the Annals of St Bertin. The account of this ninth-century vision shows how the viking menace was perceived as a divinely ordained confrontation between *Christiani homines* and *pagani homines*, and that far from this being restricted to an eccentric monastic preoccupation, on the contrary, it exercised the minds of kings and emperors of the Christian West.

A further insight of a different nature into how the Scandinavian invaders were perceived by native commentators is afforded by the indignation on the part of the compiler of the Annals of St Bertin, in recording Lothar's grant of Walcheren to the pagan Danish king, Harald, in 841. The Frankish chronicler did not, as we might have expected, bemoan the loss of Walcheren as a wealthy island strategically placed near the mouth of the Rhine which dealt with the rich trade of that great river. Instead, he saw the grant as a betrayal of the Christian population there, and his pessimistic attitude, by way of contrast, highlights Alfred's achievement in bringing about the baptism of Guthrum and of the Danish leadership in southern England in 878:

Lothar, to secure the services of Harald . . . now granted him Walcheren and the neighbouring regions as a benefice. This was surely an utterly detestable crime, that those who had brought evil on Christians should be given power over the lands and people of Christians, and over the very churches of Christ; that the persecutors of the Christian faith should be set up as lords over Christians, and Christian folk have to serve men who worshipped demons.[78]

The intermingling of baptismal rituals with political alliances and attempts at subjugation, had been rooted in Byzantium's dealings with the peoples of Eastern Europe since the reign of Justinian in the sixth century.[79] This Byzantine baptismal protocol, although far removed geographically from contemporary events in the Christian West, had nevertheless a direct bearing on Carolingian practice and so, indirectly at least, affected events in Alfredian Wessex. Successive Byzantine emperors of the ninth and tenth centuries exploited baptismal rites in an effort to assert political overlordship, however tenuous, over potentially hostile neighbours who converted to Christianity. Bulgar and Slav converts to Orthodoxy, like the Danish Guthrum, were manipulated in political matters by the imperial government at Constantinople through baptismal rituals and subsequent ecclesiastical contacts. So, the emperor Michael III stood sponsor to the troublesome Khan Boris of the Bulgars at his baptism in 865.[80] Byzantine emperors going back to the days of Heraclius in the early seventh century had wooed Boris's predecessors with the lure of Christian baptism.[81] The emperor Constantine Porphyrogenitus stood as sponsor and godfather to a newly converted Magyar chieftain in 948.[82] The Princess Olga, regent of Russia was baptized by the patriarch of Constantinople in 957, taking Helen as her Christian name to symbolize her new spiritual and political relationship with the Byzantine empire.[83] Vladimir, the first Christian Prince of Kiev took the baptismal name, Basil, in honour of his imperial godfather, Basil II, at his reception into the Christian Church in *c.*988.[84] According to the Anglo-Saxon Chronicle,[85] Guthrum took the West Saxon aristocratic name of Athelstan at his baptism, and the fact that he later issued coins under that name, surely suggests that he took his new-found Christianity seriously—at least from a cultural and economic standpoint.

Nearer home in Francia, politically staged baptisms had an even longer history. Indeed the beginnings of Frankish respectability and the long history of claims by Frankish rulers to the holding of Roman offices may be seen to go back to the baptism of Clovis in 498. Clovis, like Guthrum, found himself in a difficult military and political situation, but according to Gregory of Tours, before Clovis could finally decide in favour of becoming a Christian, he had first to consult his warriors—a reminder of the importance of those '30 of the men who were the most important in the army' who accompanied Guthrum to the font at Aller in 878. No pagan warrior-king could ever abandon Odin in favour of Christ without the backing of his leading men. Those words which Gregory of Tours put into the mouth of Clovis, as that king negotiated with Remigius, bishop of Rheims, might well be applied to Guthrum: 'I myself, most holy father, will gladly hearken to thee; but one thing remaineth. The people that followeth me will not suffer it that I forsake their gods; yet I will go and reason with them according to thy word.'[86] Later Frankish sources highlighted the baptism of prominent Northmen as a special triumph for Carolingian rulers. The emperor Charles the Bald, after the formal closing of the synod of Ponthion in 876, received a delegation of Loire vikings, who were baptized at the hands of Abbot Hugh (son of Conrad).[87] Earlier in 862, the viking leader, Weland 'with his wife and sons' had come to Charles the Bald seeking baptism as a means of cementing an alliance with the Frankish ruler,[88] while in 882, the emperor Charles the Fat personally raised the Norse *dux*, Godafrid, from the font and in the opinion of the cynical annalist made him a co-ruler of his kingdom.[89] The high profile accorded by Frankish annalists to the baptisms of leading Northmen within the Carolingian empire had undoubtedly been influenced by Byzantine diplomacy and by Byzantine court ceremonies. These influences in turn provided Alfred with an understanding of the political importance of baptismal rites held at court and in which the Christian ruler stood as sponsor to newly converted barbarians. We know that Khan Boris of Bulgaria was negotiating the acceptance of Christianity with Louis the German in 864, only months before his baptism at the hands of the Byzantines.[90] The baptism of Danish leaders at the Carolingian court were noted by Frankish annalists from earlier in the reign of Louis the Pious. In 826 the Royal Frankish Annals record the baptism of the Danish king, Harald, together with his wife and a great multitude of Danes at St Albans in Mainz. The emperor Louis the Pious rewarded Harald at his baptism in 826 with many gifts as well as territory at Rüstringen at the mouth of the river Weser.[91] The Anglo-Saxon Chronicle records that Alfred 'honoured him [Guthrum] and his companions with many gifts' at his baptism in Somerset in 878. Alfred by

conferring gifts on Guthrum may have been trying to establish claims of
overlordship, as was certainly implied by Louis's gift-giving to the Dane in 826.
During Alfred's reign in 873, the Carolingian ruler, Charles the Bald, laid siege to
a viking garrison which had entrenched itself in Angers, and having finally forced
their surrender, the terms imposed on the vikings—including the baptism of those
who chose to remain in Francia—compares with the terms which Alfred imposed
on Guthrum:

He [Charles] cowed them so thoroughly that their chiefs came to him and commended
themselves to him, swore exactly the solemn oaths he ordered, and handed over as many,
and as important, hostages as he demanded. The conditions imposed were, that on the day
appointed, they should leave Angers and never again as long as they lived either wreak
devastation in Charles's realm or agree to others' doing so. They requested to be allowed to
stay until February on an island in the Loire, and to hold a market there; and, in February,
they agreed, those of them who had by then been baptised and wished thenceforth to hold
truly to the Christian religion would come and submit to Charles, those still pagan but
willing to become Christian would be baptised under conditions to be arranged by Charles,
but the rest would depart from his realm, never more, as stated above, to return to it with
evil intent.[92]

The circumstances at Edington in 878 and at Angers in 873 may not have been
similar in all respects. Charles the Bald commanded far greater resources than
Alfred, even if in this instance his viking adversaries were as numerous or as strong
as Guthrum and his army clearly remained, after their defeat at Edington. There
are nevertheless striking similarities, not least in the emphasis on enforced baptism
for those vikings wishing to remain within Francia and in the apparently generous
terms offered to a viking enemy, after it had been clearly reduced to near starvation
and encircled by 'a very strong enclosing [Frankish] earthwork'.[93] But for those
Angers vikings who were to remain in Francia, the adoption of Christianity was
obligatory, as it must presumably have been for all of Guthrum's host after he and
his thirty leading warriors provided a lead. Charles like, Alfred, did manage to
throw the invaders out of their entrenched position—in Charles's case at Angers.
Nine years later in 882, Charles the Fat met with less success and a great deal of
criticism from the compiler of the Annals of Fulda, when he attempted to dislodge
a viking warband from a fortress at Asselt on the banks of the Meuse. That
Carolingian emperor led an army 'to be feared by any enemy' against Asselt,
drawing on troops from all over Germany and perhaps also from Lombardy.[94]
Although the Danish fortress was reduced to surrender, Charles, either because of
treachery in his own ranks, or because of disease among both armies[95] finally chose
to negotiate with the Northmen. A central point of those negotiations involved the
baptism of the Danish Godafrid, who was raised from the font by the emperor
himself and granted counties and benefices in the coastal areas of modern Holland.[96] All of those baptisms—like their counterparts in the Byzantine world—
were deliberately staged and invested with political overtones.[97] Viking leaders who
could be inveigled to join the Christian fold were not only expected to observe the
same religion as their Christian neighbours, but they were also expected to enter

into a political relationship with them which, because of their status as godsons to
Christian rulers, would inevitably place them in a relatively inferior political and
cultural position. Not only was Guthrum expected to abandon his Raven banner
and his ring of Thor after Edington and Aller: but he was also clearly expected to
refrain from attacking Christian society and its holy places, and he would have
been expected to confirm his goodwill by swearing, no longer on a pagan ring, but
like Alfred, on Christian Gospels and on Christian reliquaries.

Whitelock rightly pointed to the fragility of the peace concluded in the aftermath of Edington.[98] In addition to promising baptism, Guthrum and his Danes
had also given Alfred 'preliminary hostages and great oaths that they would leave
his kingdom'.[99] That was in late May. They were still hanging about in Wessex in
September, and only sometime later—perhaps in October 878 (Anglo-Saxon year
879)—did they remove themselves to Cirencester. That Mercian town lay ominously close to the West Saxon border and only ten miles north of Malmesbury,
which was one of the holiest places in Wessex. Yet another viking horde arrived in
the Thames and encamped at Fulham, probably in that same autumn of 878. The
stage was set for yet another possible all-out assault on Wessex. But not all viking
warbands acted with common cause. Irish and Frankish annals from the ninth and
tenth centuries are littered with evidence for competition and ferocious hostility
between rivals bands of Northmen. The Anglo-Saxon Chronicle makes a point of
twice distinguishing between the army at Cirencester and 'the army which had
encamped at Fulham' and it records the departure of the Fulham vikings for
Ghent without ever suggesting there had been any contact between the two invading forces. The evidence of the Chronicle is to be preferred here to that of the *Life*
of King Alfred which states that the Fulham vikings joined forces with Guthrum's
Cirencester garrison—a suggestion which may have been inspired by nothing
more than a guess and by a desire on the part of the compiler of the *Life* of Alfred
to lend his work an air of independent authority over the Anglo-Saxon Chronicle
which he had otherwise slavishly translated.[100] It may say something of Alfred's
ability to make the peace with Guthrum stick, that the newcomers at Fulham
decided against staying in England. Or it may reflect on Guthrum's ambition to
monopolize the benefits of his recent peace concluded with Alfred—a peace which
had been remarkably advantageous to Guthrum. So, it may not have been in
Guthrum's interest to invite this new warband at Fulham to share in his English
conquests. In the following year—880 or the autumn of 879—Alfred's victory
could be seen to be secure: 'In this year the army went from Cirencester to East
Anglia, and settled there and shared out the land. And the same year the army
which had encamped at Fulham went overseas into the Frankish empire to Ghent
and stayed there for a year.'[101] Alfred's initial troubles were now at an end, and for
the first time since that day on which he had been elected king, in succession to
Æthelred back in 871, he was now able to devote his mind to other things apart
from the immediate defence of his people.

The account in the Chronicle of the immediate aftermath of Alfred's victory at
Edington reads like an anti-climax. The great build-up which began with Alfred's

riding to meet his shire levies at Ecgberht's Stone, to the battle-rout at Edington
when Guthrum's hordes were pursued all the way back to their fortress, is followed not by the vengeance of the West Saxon victors nor by the immediate
expulsion of the invaders, but by surprisingly long drawn-out negotiations. Instead
of retribution—not to mention execution—we read of Guthrum and his companions
spending twelve days with Alfred and being 'honoured greatly with gifts'—a
strange ending to a war which was presented in the Chronicle as a struggle to the
finish. It is clear that Guthrum still had sufficient men in the field to pose a threat
to Wessex even after his defeat, but Alfred, on the other hand, had turned the
tables by boxing up the defeated Danish warband in their fortress for two weeks.
How can we explain a victor such as Alfred, apparently letting slip such a great
advantage and ultimately negotiating an advantageous deal for his defeated enemies? Because the compiler of the Chronicle exercised such strict control over
what he wanted his readers to know of Alfred's battle at Edington, it is only by
comparing that record yet again with contemporary Frankish experiences, that we
can come to an understanding of Alfred's position in 878. Despite the viking defeat
at Angers in 873 and despite hostage-giving and the swearing of 'great oaths', some
Frankish vikings at Angers were still in a position to negotiate their departure from
the kingdom of Charles the Bald in apparent freedom and without obligation to
become Christian. Those defeated Danes at Angers also negotiated a timetable
which allowed them hold a market on an island in the Loire in the coming February
of 874, although Charles concluded his negotiations with them and had thrown
them out of Angers by October 873.[102] Alfred's enemies also loitered in Wessex for
several months after their defeat at Edington. There were some striking similarities, too, between events at Asselt in 882 and yet again at Edington in 878. The
Carolingian blockade of the Danish fortress at Asselt lasted twelve days—similar
to Alfred's blockade of the Chippenham fortress.[103] The Annals of Fulda afford us
a glimpse of the delicate preliminary moves which allowed negotiations to take
place in what must have been an atmosphere charged with extreme mistrust and
violence. The armies of Charles the Fat had been 'set up in a circle around the city
and so held it besieged for twelve days'.[104] For negotiations to begin, the Franks
although besieging, gave hostages to the Northmen—presumably to guarantee the
safe conduct of the Norse king while he came outside to negotiate with Charles.
Charles and his Danish adversary pulled back to a distance of six miles from the
besieged Danish stronghold to begin their talks. The Danish king then swore an
oath never again to attack Charles's kingdom and he accepted baptism. The Frankish hostages were returned after the peace had been successfully concluded. The
swearing of oaths—not to act in future as an enemy—by viking negotiators was
standard practice in ninth-century Francia. The messengers of the Danish king,
Halbden, swore on their weapons 'according to the custom of that people' in the
presence of Louis the German at Metz in 873, that no one from the Danish
kingdom would harm Louis's realm or his people.[105]

All these negotiations with vikings at Angers in 873, at Edington in 878, and at
Asselt in 882 require an explanation as to why seemingly victorious native rulers

appeared to let the invaders off so lightly. One of the compilers of the Annals of Fulda indignantly castigated Charles the Fat for losing what he saw as a golden opportunity: 'What was still more of a crime, he [Charles the Fat] did not blush to pay tribute to a man from whom he ought to have taken hostages and extracted tribute, doing this on the advice of evil men.'[106] There were, no doubt, many in Wessex in 878, who criticized Alfred for wining and dining with Guthrum, and for showering a Northman with gifts who had already pillaged the holy places of Wessex. The reason for this apparent leniency on the part of native rulers towards vanquished vikings can only have one reasonable explanation—namely that they were confronted with such great numbers of invaders, that even in defeat their armies continued to pose a threat through the sheer difficulty of controlling large numbers of hostile warriors. When a viking force of defeated survivors sought refuge in a fortress and if their numbers were still great, then clearly an important option still remained for the defeated invaders. Rather than surrender unconditionally, they might choose to stake all on a final desperate struggle in which the sheer force of their numbers and the all-important element of desperation would win the day. Such a scenario is depicted in detail in an account in the Annals of Fulda of the fate of a viking army which attacked Frisia in June 873. The native Frisians rose against these invaders and heavily defeated them near Dokkum, in a battle in which the Northmen lost their leader, Rudolf, and in which somewhere between 500 and 800 of their men were slain.[107] The writer in the Annals of Fulda continues:

But the rest, since they could not reach their ships, took refuge in a certain building (*aedificio*). The Frisians laid siege to this and took counsel with each other as to what should be done with them. Different people had said different things, when a Northman who had become a Christian and had long lived among these Frisians and was the leader (*dux*) of their attack, addressed the others as follows: 'O my good fellow-soldiers, it is enough for us to have fought thus far, for it is not due to our strength but to God's that we few have prevailed against so many enemies. You know also that we are absolutely exhausted and many of us are seriously wounded; those who lie here within are in desperation. If we begin to fight against them, we shall not defeat them without bloodshed; if they turn out to be stronger—for the outcome of battle is uncertain—then perhaps they will overcome us and depart in safety, still able to do us harm. It seems more sensible to me therefore, that we should take hostages from them and allow some of them to leave unwounded for the ships. We will meanwhile retain the hostages until they send us all the treasure which they have in the ships, and they will first take an oath that they will never return to King Louis's kingdom'.[108]

Passages such as this show that historians of the Viking Age may have greatly underestimated the size of invading armies in the late ninth century. In this instance, a defending force which had slain several hundred invaders wisely refrained from pressing home a victory against an enemy which remained numerically strong. The Anglo-Saxon Chronicle presents us with additional problems through its sustained economy with truth, and through the device of covering up by silence and resort to cliché. If the Chronicle were correct in telling us that

Alfred 'fought against the whole army and put it to flight' at Edington 'and pursued it as far as the fortress and stayed there a fortnight', then it is unthinkable that after such a battle-rout and—by ninth-century standards—a long siege, Guthrum and his army would be allowed to withdraw and rule independently over the Southern Danelaw. But the phrase 'fought with the whole army (*gefeaht wiþ alne þone here*)' is a cliché used by the chronicler twice in the 871 annal and repeated in the account of Edington in 878.[109] In the account of the battle of Wilton in 871, that phrase was deliberately used in apposition to Alfred's 'small force' in order to excuse his defeat. In 878 it was used by way of climax to the tale of Alfred's return from the 'woods and fen fastnesses' to take on the might of Guthrum and to drive him from his kingdom forever. But the Chronicle's account is the only near-contemporary record we possess, and the reality may have been different. Alfred had indeed been taking the initiative at Edington. His progress from Athelney and his joining forces with the shire levies of Somerset, Wiltshire, and parts of Hampshire shows him on the attack. But it may be that his massed army surprised a Danish foraging party from Chippenham, which may not even have been led by Guthrum or any of his leading men. There is significantly no mention of Guthrum in the account of the actual battle, nor is there any reference to any enemy slain. A Danish force, surprised and outnumbered, would then, predictably, have fallen back on the security of their fortress at Chippenham, where the main strength of Guthrum's garrison may have lain unharmed. In such circumstances, while Alfred had sufficient men to invest the Danish stronghold, there was always that danger, which recurred again and again in Francia, that a desperate viking garrison might stake everything on an attempt to break through the besieging lines. That, and that alone, would account for the necessity to resort to negotiations which proved so favourable to Guthrum and his men.

The problem which confronted Alfred in the aftermath of Edington, like that which brought such criticism on Charles the Fat at Asselt, was clearly much greater than the compiler of the Chronicle was willing to admit. These rulers, unquestionably acting on the advice of their leading men, had decided that negotiation and discretion were the better part of valour—and hence the unexplained volte-face in the Chronicle, where an account of unqualified victory is followed by hard-nosed negotiation and mutual recognition. Just as Alfred had stood godfather to Guthrum, so Charles the Fat stood godfather to Godafrid[110] 'and made the man who before had been the greatest enemy and traitor to his kingdom into a co-ruler over it'.[111] While Guthrum remained twelve days with Alfred, Godafrid 'spent two days there [at Asselt with the emperor Charles] in joy, and then our hostages were sent back from the fortification, and he contrariwise returned home with great gifts'.[112] The Anglo-Saxon Chronicle fails to specify just what gifts Alfred handed over to Guthrum when the two kings made their peace at Wedmore. There may have been an exchange of gifts, as when Horic of Denmark exchanged gifts with the Emperor Louis the Pious in 839[113] for such gift-giving ceremonies between kings were rarely one-sided. The envoys of the Danish Halbden presented Louis the German with a golden hilted sword at Metz in 873[114] and William of Malmesbury tells us King Harold Finehair of Norway presented Athelstan of England with a magnificent viking warship in the tenth century.[115] The Chronicle's reference to the gifts which Alfred gave to Guthrum and his followers may be designed to convey the notion of claims to overlordship on the part of Alfred, but it may also conceal more humiliating realities. All viking leaders had their price for withdrawing from an invaded territory in peace, and Guthrum can have been no exception. Frankish chroniclers specify the gifts which Godafrid and Sigifrid managed to extract from Charles the Fat after their 'peace' and baptism at Asselt in 882. Charles 'to his own shame and that of all the army which followed him, gave those same enemies 2,412 pounds of purest gold and silver'.[116] The Annals of Fulda and the Annals of St Bertin[117] both claim that church treasuries were seized by the emperor to pay off the vikings.[118] Frankish chroniclers were not writing under the watchful eye of their Carolingian rulers, and so could afford to be outspokenly critical of what they saw as Frankish folly in the face of viking brutality and repeated treachery. And churchmen, being the financial losers, objected most strongly to any deals reached with the invaders. If the Anglo-Saxon Chronicle were compiled within King Alfred's own court circle, it would not be surprising to find no criticism of the king's handling of the war with Guthrum or no tantalizing details such as the precise nature of the 'gifts' offered to the departing Danes.[119] If the Frankish experience at Asselt is anything to go by, then the gifts handed over by Alfred at Wedmore amounted to nothing less than a substantial Danegeld. There is no mention in the Anglo-Saxon Chronicle's account of the peace of Wedmore of the enforced Danish return of West Saxon captives or of West Saxon booty. Frankish evidence, once again, warns us against assuming that treaties negotiated with Northmen necessarily meant an attempt to return to the status quo on the part of native rulers who had forced Northmen to the peace-table. So, while Horic was willing to return captives and stolen treasure to Louis the German in 845, such a change of heart would appear to have been made possible only through a pestilence and pressure from the Almighty.[120] Charles the Bald, in one of his stronger moods, was capable of forcing vikings to return all the captives they had seized on the Marne in 862.[121] But Charles was obliged to eat humbler pie four years later when he paid vikings on the Seine 4,000 lbs. of silver 'according to their scales' and agreed to extraordinarily humiliating terms:

Any slaves who had been carried off by the Northmen and escaped from them after the agreement was made were either handed back or ransomed at a price set by the Northmen; and if any one of the Northmen was killed, whatever price the Northmen demanded for him was paid.[122]

After the peace at Asselt, which resulted in the baptism of the Northman, Godafrid, the vikings were clearly allowed to retain their booty and some 200 captives which were shipped back to Scandinavia.[123] We search in vain for such frank reporting in the Anglo-Saxon Chronicle, but the unrelenting silence on all matters which might show Alfred up in an unfavourable light should not blind us to the realities of the hard negotiations which he must have entered into after Edington. Alfred was in a more vulnerable position, *vis-à-vis* the Danes, than his Carolingian neighbours. Not only did the West Saxon king command fewer resources in terms of men, money, and supplies, but Guthrum and his followers had no intention of returning to Scandinavia or departing on a raiding expedition elsewhere. Guthrum was already master of English lands from the Humber to the Thames, and from now on, he and Alfred would have to do business as neighbouring kings.

The text of a treaty drawn up between Alfred and Guthrum shows us in some detail the legal issues which needed to be agreed between the two kings. This document would appear to ascribe London to Alfred's territory—and is therefore dated by historians to after Alfred's occupation of London in 886 and before the death of Guthrum in 890. On the other hand, the Chronicle's account of the immediate aftermath of Edington shows, as we would expect, that Alfred concluded a treaty then, and we find a further reference to a peace (*friþ*) which the East Anglians had violated against King Alfred in 885—one year before Alfred's occupation of London took place. So, whatever its final phase may be dated to, the surviving text of the treaty between Alfred and Guthrum may be reasonably expected to be broadly based on an earlier agreement drawn up at Wedmore or soon after Alfred's victory at Edington in 878:

This is the peace which King Alfred and King Guthrum and the counsellors of all the English race and all the people which is in East Anglia have all agreed on and confirmed with oaths, for themselves and for their subjects, both for the living and those yet unborn, who care to have God's grace or ours.[124]

The Christian tone of the text is noticeable as is the fact that it is a treaty between equals—in no way indicative of a relationship between a conqueror and the vanquished. Nor was the agreement concluded just between Alfred and Guthrum, but between Alfred and the West Saxon and perhaps Mercian *witan*, on the one hand, and Guthrum 'and the people which is in East Anglia'—presumably a reference to the Danish magnates in Guthrum's 'army of the Danes' which is referred to in the last clause of the treaty.[125] The phrase 'all of us estimate Englishman and Dane at the same amount'[126] clearly establishes the principle of equality between the two peoples and the same high levels of wergild set for each side was probably designed as a deterrent against cross-border conflict. It is not at all clear, however, as some scholars have assumed,[127] that 'Englishman' in this text refers to any more than the population directly under Alfred's rule. It would appear that the parties referred to in the text consist of men of high—and certainly of free—status, and we have no idea how native East Anglian magnates fared at this time under Danish overlordship. The English referred to in this treaty would appear to belong geographically and politically to the West Saxon and English Mercian party which is twice referred to in the final provision as 'us'—as opposed to 'them' or the 'army of the Danes'. We know from the Chronicle that in addition to his promising to become a Christian, Guthrum also undertook to withdraw his army from Alfred's kingdom. He would certainly also have taken an oath never to attack Wessex at any time in the future or to assist any other invaders in doing so. Whatever the date of the existing text of the treaty between Alfred and Guthrum, it is curious that this provision is absent, and it may suggest that the short text of this late eleventh or early twelfth-century document is incomplete. A similar treaty drawn up between Æthelred the Unready and a viking army in AD 991[128] asserts that the viking army of Olaf which was under treaty with the English must help them resist any future marauders [I.1], and that any region which gave asylum to other warbands was to be treated as an enemy [I.2]. Such clauses were in line, as we have seen, with Frankish treaties drawn up with viking armies in ninth-century Francia.[129] In 885—while Guthrum was still ruling over the Southern Danelaw, the Anglo-Saxon Chronicle[130] records that 'the Danish army in East Anglia violated their peace with King Alfred' and earlier, in the Chronicle's record for that same year, we are told that Alfred sent a naval force from Kent which attacked viking ships at the mouth of the East Anglian Stour. This clearly shows that Alfred had concluded an earlier treaty with the 'army' of East Anglia, which like that of Æthelred the Unready a century later may have made provision for a pact of non-aggression between English and Danish territories.

Two provisions in the treaty between Alfred and Guthrum refer to the purchase of men, horses, and oxen, and for the provision of hostages as a guarantee of good faith on the part of those on one side who wished to trade with the other. The issues of assessing wergild or compensation for man-slayings, as well as the provision of facilities for mutual trade and the protection of merchants were almost certainly thrashed out between Alfred and Guthrum and their counsellors at Wedmore in 878. Such provisions are also glimpsed at in Frankish accounts of dealings with vikings. We have seen how the Angers vikings negotiated the holding of a market with Charles the Bald, while at Asselt, Godafrid and his warband invited the Frankish warriors into their stronghold to trade with them immediately after the ending of hostilities in 882.[131] In 873 envoys of the Danish king, Sigifrid, appeared before Louis the German near Worms 'seeking to make peace over the border disputes between themselves and the Saxons and so that merchants of each kingdom might come and go in peace to the other, bringing merchandise to buy and sell'.[132] Such contacts inevitably raised issues regarding royal protection and compensation for maiming or man-slayings. When the Danish king, Horic, complained to the emperor Louis the Pious back in 836, that envoys he had sent to the emperor had been slain near Cologne, Louis personally dispatched his *missi* to avenge (*ultus est*) those killings which presumably involved Northmen of the highest social status.[133] Horic was then in a state of peace and friendship with the Carolingian Empire, and it was therefore incumbent on Louis to be seen to be honouring his side of any treaty that may have existed between the two rulers.

It is now time to review the evidence regarding the Chronicle's account of those events in 878 which supposedly transformed Alfred's career from that of an apparently defeated and fugitive king into a successful war-leader who ensured the future independence of his West Saxon realm. Are we to agree with Davis that the Chronicle's version of events is essentially a propaganda exercise in which Alfred's initial difficulties together with the extent of the initial Danish conquest of West

Saxon territory were exaggerated in order to magnify the subsequent achievement of the king? And what if any validity remains in Whitelock's more orthodox assessment of the essential veracity of the Chronicle's account for AD 878 in which Alfred may be assessed as the saviour of his people? Davis was unquestionably correct in seeing the deliberate exaggeration of Alfred's hardships and in seeing that Alfred had, directly or indirectly, influenced the account of this crucial turning-point in his life. But the presence of bias—propaganda may not be the appropriate word—so inevitable in a document of this age, and coming as it may have done from within the royal circle, does not in itself negate or disprove the veracity of the essential sequence of events. In fairness to Whitelock, it has to be said, that had Alfred lost at Edington, then West Saxon and subsequent English history would inevitably have taken a different turn. Leaving aside the inevitability of Alfred's own personal ruin and that of his immediate family, Wessex would either have been colonized by Danish warbands, or more likely partitioned between Danes and a West Saxon enclave ruled by a dynastic group which was pliable to Danish demands. Such a subject-kingdom, diminished and divided within itself, would never have had the resources or determination to win back the Danelaw under English rule. Had Alfred lost at Edington—or had he failed in the subsequent negotiations—then the reign of his son Edward and his grandson Athelstan culminating in the uniting of a single English realm by 927 would never have been.

A study of Carolingian sources shows us how much the compiler of the Anglo-Saxon Chronicle may have deliberately suppressed, but shows us also that what is in the Chronicle is for the most part convincing, even if it is not the whole truth. Alfred was caught off guard while celebrating the end of the Christmas season on an isolated royal estate at Chippenham in January 878. When Guthrum struck, the West Saxon king was highly unlikely to have had an army in the field and may only have been attended by a personal following. Alfred may not have chosen to go west into Somerset—he may have been driven in that direction by an enemy bent on his capture and execution. The arrival of a warband in Devon, consisting of yet another section of the original Great Army, and led by the brother of Ivar and Hálfdan, strongly suggests a concerted action to entrap the last surviving English king. The presence of this warband raises the important question of the whereabouts of Guthrum's own fleet, which he had clearly joined up with, first at Wareham and later at Exeter. In spite of the shipwreck off Swanage, some of Guthrum's ships must have presumably survived. The sea-borne invasion of north Devon in 878, which was led by the brother of Ivar and Hálfdan, may or may not have been part of a pincer movement involving Guthrum's fleet. Happily for Alfred, the threat from the west was removed by Ealdorman Odda and his yeomen of Devon, and whatever the connections of that Devon fleet, its destruction must have weakened Guthrum's position. Guthrum and his army spread out in a north–south direction from Malmesbury to as far south perhaps, as Sherborne, while retaining their main strength about Chippenham in the north. Alfred now fortified his tenuous position at Athelney in the Somerset marshes, with the help of Ealdorman Æthelnoth of Somerset. As a king with any hope of holding on to the loyalty of his magnates, he must have made frantic efforts at this time to maintain contact with his bishops, ealdormen, and thegns, who were scattered from the Cornish border to Kent, to reassure them of his determination to keep up the fight. If that had not been so, his meeting at Ecgberht's Stone 'in the seventh week after Easter' with the men of Somerset, Wiltshire, and Hampshire could never have been organized or made possible. In spite of the Chronicle's silence on this matter, Alfred must have confronted Guthrum with a large army at Edington, and Guthrum's own army may by then have been relatively smaller than hitherto, due to progressive Danish losses as well as attempts at colonization and garrison duties in a hostile land. Alfred's victory at Edington was born of that same determination which the Frankish chronicler ascribed to desperate Northmen fighting in the certain knowledge that defeat can only mean death. Whatever format the fight at Edington took, Alfred and the great men of Wessex, who fought shoulder to shoulder on that day, knew that this was their last-ditch stand. Defeat and capture for West Saxon leaders at Edington, who had defied Guthrum for those seven long years, would have meant certain death for them and the dispossession and enslavement of their kindred. A later poet described the struggle between Alfred's two grandsons— Athelstan and Edmund—on the bloody field at *Brunanburh* in 937, when yet another moment of truth had been reached between the House of Alfred and the viking Olaf Guthfrithsson, great-grandson of Ivar: 'Edward's sons clove the shield wall, hewed the linden-wood shields with hammered swords, for it was natural to men of their lineage to defend their land, their treasure and their homes, in frequent battle against every foe.'[34] But Edington may not have been on the heroic scale of *Brunanburh* and had it been so, it is difficult to envisage that Alfred's publicity machine would have allowed all record of such a titanic struggle to perish. The reality may have been a skirmish between Alfred's massed army and a Danish foraging party from Chippenham. Alternatively, Edington may have involved Alfred in a surprise attack on a substantial Danish warband, garrisoned on a poorly fortified West Saxon royal estate. Edington does not seem to have been a conventional victory won in a pitched battle, in which the winners took all. It was rather an encounter where a surprised or outnumbered Danish enemy took to its heels and fled back to a fortress, where it was coerced into submission. But whatever the scale of the encounter, Edington did yield Alfred that one elusive victory which he had the courage to wait for and to plan. But even with that limited victory in his grasp, huge logistical problems remained. The survivors of Guthrum's horde—which unfortunately for Alfred, included the Danish king himself—were still, in typical viking fashion, trusting to the safety of their fort at Chippenham. As in Francia, the enemy was still probably so numerous that even in defeat it would have to be bought off and negotiated with. It was on recording the details of such negotiations that the Anglo-Saxon chronicler seems to have shied away, for fear of detracting from his account of Alfred's finest hour. Alfred, at last acting from a position of strength, was now able to impose real terms— the acceptance of Christianity and the withdrawal of the Danish army from Wessex. But other issues such as the return of captives and of booty were probably sacrificed in the interests of a permanent Danish withdrawal. Agreements regulating future relations between Wessex and the new neighbouring political order, which in time would come to be known as the Danelaw, also had to be worked out. Guthrum clearly still had sufficient warriors in the field despite shipwreck, colonization, and losses in battle, to withdraw with honour from Wessex and with his vast territorial conquests in Mercia and East Anglia intact. And he may have withdrawn, too, with additional gifts amounting to a huge Danegeld which Alfred and his men would have squeezed from the by now impoverished religious centres of Wessex, such as Glastonbury, Malmesbury, and Sherborne.

However much Alfred himself, or that member of his court circle who compiled the account of events in 878,[135] had endeavoured to dramatize Alfred's victory, there is no denying its lasting consequences. Guthrum's baptism and the wider terms of the peace he concluded with Alfred can best be appreciated in the light of other such treaties between Alfred's immediate descendants and Danish leaders in the next century. Later chroniclers would boast how Alfred's son Edward, and his grandson Athelstan, could bring Danish kings to the peace table. In those rare instances where we can get behind the rhetoric, we find that the results were neither impressive nor enduring. When Athelstan gave his sister Eadgyth, in marriage to Sitric the grandson of Ivar in 925, on condition of Sitric's conversion to Christianity, Roger of Wendover spells out the unhappy outcome: 'But not long afterwards he [Sitric] cast off the blessed maiden and, deserting his Christianity, restored the worship of idols, and after a short while, ended his life miserably as an apostate.'[136] Athelstan travelled to Dacre in the distant Lake District to force Sitric's kinsman, Gothfrith, to terms in 927, only to find that the Northman had made himself scarce before the parley could be convened.[137] Athelstan's brother, Edmund, stood sponsor to Olaf Sitricsson at his baptism and to Ragnald Gothfrithsson at his confirmation in 943, but those two kings of the Northern Danelaw were driven out of Northumbria by that same Edmund in the following year.[138] We can be certain that in both cases the baptism and confirmation which were so quickly rejected by these vikings were but part of a wider political package which they and their magnates, unlike Guthrum, found too burdensome to accept.

The contemporary Frankish experience underlines yet again Alfred's remarkable success in negotiating a lasting working relationship with his Danish adversaries at Edington. We have seen how for the Franks, as well as for the West Saxons, Christian baptism lay at the heart of all major peace treaties concluded with Danish war-leaders. But Frankish evidence shows that viking converts frequently apostatized and apostasy inevitably meant a return to hostile raiding and attacks on monasteries. Charles the Bald appeared to have pulled off a diplomatic coup when Weland, who commanded a fleet of 200 ships on the Seine, presented himself along with his wife and sons for baptism before the Frankish king in 862.[139] But in the following year, Christian vikings from Weland's own fleet were accusing their leader of bad faith and trickery and he lost his life defending his honour, if not his Christianity, in single combat.[140] When Charles the Bald bestowed gifts on newly baptized vikings after the conclusion of the synod at Ponthion in 876, the chronicler complained that 'afterwards, like typical Northmen, they lived according to the pagan custom just as before'.[141] There was clearly a powerful element in Norse paganism, undoubtedly connected with war cults, which Christian rulers were at pains to neutralize through baptism and which Northmen in turn were understandably loath to abandon in favour of untried and novel Christian rituals. Not even Charles the Fat's much publicized conversion of the Danish Godafrid, at Asselt in 882, achieved the desired effect for the beleaguered Franks. Godafrid, having joined the Christian family of dynasts, succeeded in marrying Gisela the sister of Hugh, son of Lothar II, but then 'broke his faith' and launched an attack up the Rhine which ended in his assassination at the hands of the emperor Charles the Fat's men in 885.[142] Norse baptism and subsequent intermarriage with native dynasties proved no more effective in ninth-century Francia than it was to do in tenth-century England. It was Alfred's singular achievement in the case of Guthrum, however, to have tamed an adversary who had been originally bent on his destruction and on the conquest of his kingdom. For Guthrum's baptism and his peace were, as far as we can judge, made to stick. It is true that we read of trouble in the Chronicle between Alfred and Guthrum's East Anglian Danes in 885. It is not clear that Guthrum himself was personally responsible for that breach of the peace, and it would seem that there was no major conflict between Wessex and the Southern Danelaw for the remainder of Guthrum's life. East Anglia was to offer a safe haven and more active resistance to Alfred and his followers during Alfred's Last War in 893–6, but by then Guthrum was in his grave. The Chronicle records Guthrum's death in 890 with a solemnity that reveals nothing but respect for an adversary who had kept his word and his new religious faith: 'And the northern king, Guthrum, whose baptismal name was Athelstan, died. He was King Alfred's godson, and he lived in East Anglia and was the first to settle that land.'[143] We notice how Guthrum's baptism, his aristocratic West Saxon baptismal name, and the fact that he was Alfred's godson, are all placed up front in this record. Few things could afford clearer proof than that in the eyes of the West Saxon court, the baptism of Guthrum had been one of Alfred's finest achievements. And in the eyes of that court, too, Guthrum would remain unique in Anglo-Saxon history as the only viking to achieve respectability and die fully recognized as king in his new English land. And all that was thanks to Alfred's negotiations after Edington in 878 when Guthrum was forced to come to terms not only with Christianity but with all the cultural and political baggage which joining the Anglo-Saxon church entailed. Whether a great battle or just a fortunate skirmish, Edington was indeed Alfred's great victory, when West Saxon and—by extention—Anglo-Saxon society and culture were saved from extinction or premature dilution by overwhelming Scandinavian influence. Alfred's own prose translations, which were to establish early English literature on solid foundations, still lay in the future as did the territorial conquests of his son and grandsons which were eventually to unite England under Alfred's own house. These were achievements which in turn had rendered English life and culture sufficiently resilient as to withstand the later viking onslaughts of the eleventh century. But it was Edington and its aftermath that helped to make all those achievements possible—in late Anglo-Saxon politics, art, literature, and law. Whatever Alfred's shortcomings as a military commander in the future might prove to be, Edington was truly his finest hour. Not even the Anglo-Saxon Chronicle's relentless silence and concealment of truth, which has done so much to obfuscate the record of his reign, can deprive him of the diplomatic achievement of 878 which made Alfred truly a great king.

IV

The Frankish Interlude 880–891

THE BATTLE OF EDINGTON, THE CONVERSION OF GUTHRUM, AND THE Peace of Wedmore constitute a watershed in Alfred's reign. This impression is in part created by, and is certainly reinforced by, the profound change which occurs in the format of the Anglo-Saxon Chronicle after the reporting, in 878–80, of the successful conclusion of the war with Guthrum. The fundamental change in the Chronicle's mode of reporting at this point has had a profound influence on how Alfred's reign has been perceived by historians, and it is a change which has hitherto never been adequately recognized or explained. The controversy surrounding the origins and authorship of the Chronicle will be dealt with elsewhere,[1] but in so far as the Chronicle has had such a formative influence on the narrative of Alfred's reign throughout the decade from 881 to 891, it is necessary to examine the record for those years in some detail. The Anglo-Saxon Chronicle as a continuous narrative can be seen to begin with the account of the arrival of a heathen army on Thanet in 865. Thereafter, we are supplied with a year-by-year record of the progress of the Danish invaders, taking us up to the beginning of Alfred's reign and on to his triumph at Edington in 878 and the departure of his Danish adversaries to East Anglia in 880. This is truly a chronicle in which Alfred and his relationship with the Danish army is at the centre of the narrative. The continuous reporting on the Danish wars is introduced by a summary of earlier major events—most of which deal with viking invaders—from the last years of Ecgberht's reign (c.835) through that of Æthelwulf and of Alfred's older brothers. However summarized this material for 835–64 may be, it nevertheless forms an introduction to the Chronicle proper, preparing us for the reign of Alfred and his struggle with the Danes. In that sense, the brief account of the recent West Saxon past from 835 to 864, on the grounds of its content alone, forms an integral part of the more detailed and continuous narrative from 865 to 878. Prior to c.835, the Anglo-Saxon Chronicle is a pastiche of annals and other historical materials designed to project the narrative backwards and to anchor the story of the West Saxon kingdom in a Late Antique and Early Christian past.[2]

There are some remarkable features in that section where the Chronicle proper begins for the period 865–80. During those fifteen years no foreign news whatever is recorded until we reach the notice of the departure of the Danish warband from Fulham to Ghent in 880. The notice of the burial of King Burgred of Mercia in Rome under 874, looks ahead to some time in the future, and occurs as an integral part of the record of the Danish conquest of Mercia. This section of the Chronicle reveals the essential nature of the compilation and distinguishes it as a record of events from both contemporary Irish annals and from Frankish chronicles. While ninth-century Irish annalists showed a strong interest in the affairs of dominant dynastic groups, they did also concern themselves with rival factions and they provided a random collection of information on ecclesiastical affairs, as well as frequent observations on 'cosmic' marvels. There is no evidence for regular ordering of material or for the sustained development of specific themes. Frankish annalists, on the other hand, do aspire to developing themes—but those themes were diverse and were not solely concerned with the progress of the royal courts or of one particular faction. So the invasions of the Northmen appear in Frankish Chronicles alongside a complex web of information on other external enemies such as Slavs, Magyars, or Saracens, while the papacy and deliberations of church synods may occasionally attract as much of the chronicler's attention as the progress of Carolingian rulers. And, in spite of Frankish chroniclers' overview and thematic approach, earlier annalistic interests of a random sort, including early medieval obsessions with marvels and miracles, continued to be catered for. In the Anglo-Saxon Chronicle from 865 until 880, only one major theme is pursued relentlessly—i.e. the progress of the Danish army across England and Alfred's relationship with that army and his ultimate triumph over it in 878. This theme is pursued even to the exclusion of the regular recording of the deaths of leading churchmen and secular magnates from within Wessex, and it is pursued to the total exclusion of all foreign news. The break after 878–80 could scarcely be more dramatic, therefore, when we observe that for the period 880 to 891, the Anglo-Saxon Chronicle reports more foreign than home news and that during this period there are several years when nothing is reported from within Wessex. The change is twofold. The format of a continuous year-by-year report on Anglo-Saxon affairs which began at 865 is abandoned, and the subject-matter of that report shifts from home to foreign news. It is little wonder that historians have perceived Alfred's reign as being divided into three major sections—the first from 871 to 878 provides the fullest picture of Alfred's life, covering his earliest wars against the Danes; the second from 878 to 891 constitutes his 'rest' period, about which we know little, but when we assume he spent this time in scholarly pursuits, and the third from 891 until his death in 899 constitutes the time of his Last War and his final years. But that structure has been imposed on historians by the nature of the Chronicle narrative—a narrative which historians have only recently and reluctantly come to regard as offering a complex and highly stylized view of events in late ninth-century Wessex. For a Chronicle compiled within Wessex, the remarkable focus on Frankish affairs for the period 880–91—to the exclusion of home news—is surely deserving of more detailed study than it has hitherto received.

The two years after Alfred's victory at Edington are recorded in the Chronicle strictly in terms of a postscript to that victory. In 879 we are informed of the withdrawal of Guthrum's army to Cirencester; of the arrival of a new warband at Fulham, and of a solar eclipse. Eclipses were universally acknowledged in the medieval world as cosmic signs presaging or coinciding with great happenings. Since the Chronicle at this point is retrospective in its reporting, this eclipse was no doubt seen by a later compiler as a cosmic wonder marking the eventful triumph of Alfred over his Danish enemies. The record of the following year (880) is transitional. We are told of the departure of Guthrum's army from Cirencester to East Anglia where it 'settled there and shared out the land'.[3] That record constitutes the final element in a narrative which had been sustained continuously year-by-year from 865. And the seal is set on Alfred's victory by informing us also that the Fulham army departed for Ghent in Francia (*Fronclond*). It is this entry which directs attention away from Wessex and which prepares us for an almost continuous narrative of viking activity within the Frankish empire for the next twelve years. The twelve years from 881 to 892 contain Frankish reporting for all years except 888 and 889. In fact these years are covered by the Anglo-Saxon Chronicle for Frankish events because the death of the emperor Charles the Fat, which took place in January 888, is entered in the Chronicle under 887, while a reference to civil wars in Italy connected with succession struggles within the empire and entered in the Anglo-Saxon Chronicle under 887 refers to the battle of Brescia in the autumn of 888 and the battle of Trebbia which took place in the spring of 889. So, too, the Chronicle's statement under AD 887 that the Danes spent two winters at Chézy on the Marne refers to the winters of January 887 and January 888. For home news, however, the record is almost as sparse as it is full of Frankish information. Alfred's contacts with Pope Marinus in 883, the notice of the death of that pope in 885, the sending of alms or emissaries to Rome in 887, 889, and 890 can all be classified under the heading of foreign contacts rather than home news. It is significant that such exotic contacts are only recorded during this 'foreign' interlude in the Chronicle, and as soon as the narrative returns to deal with its central theme of the Danish wars in Wessex, all references to contacts with the papacy are excluded. If we group the papal entries along with the Frankish, we are left with four years—881, 884, 887, and 889—during which the Chronicle records nothing whatever of West Saxon or even of English internal affairs. On closer scrutiny, the record of home events becomes even sparser still. The notice that 'when the English were encamped against the enemy army at London' in 883 King Alfred sent off his alms to Rome and India was rightly recognized by Whitelock as having 'suspicious features'.[4] Although it occurs in most Chronicle manuscripts and is therefore early, it is absent from the Parker Chronicle and from versions used by Æthelweard and by the compiler of the *Life* of Alfred,[5] and at best the entry may be displaced here in the text. That being so, it is highly likely that the original annual for 883 read, simply: 'In this year the army went up the Scheldt to Condé, and stayed there for a year.'

The record of the death of Guthrum in East Anglia in 890 does not strictly relate to a West Saxon event, which otherwise leaves that year devoid of internal information on Wessex, if we exclude the exotic reference to the taking of alms to Rome. Similarly the 891 record of the arrival of three Irishmen at the court of Alfred, with its emphasis on the construction of their boat, their lack of adequate provisions, their motive for the journey, their exotic names, and the information on the death of the Irish scholar, Swifneh—all constitutes an exotic digression, essentially relating to foreign parts and absolutely atypical of the Chronicle's otherwise dominant military and Danish theme in the Alfredian period. The addition of the years 883, 890, and 891 to the list of years which are devoid of information on the internal affairs of Wessex—not to mention on King Alfred—leaves us with a total of seven such blank years during the twelve-year period from 880 to 891. What survives as English or West Saxon material constitutes a meagre record indeed—Alfred's minor naval battle in 882, a Danish attack on Rochester in 885, and an attack by Alfred on East Anglia in that same year, Alfred's taking of London in 886, and the deaths of Archbishop Æthelred and of Ealdorman Æthelwold in 888. The 885 entry alone contains the kind of detail which we expect from the Chronicle narrative at this point. Significantly, this deals with Alfred's defence against either Danish attack or treachery—providing details of the Danish siege of Rochester and of Alfred's naval expedition against East Anglia. But taken as a whole, this West Saxon record constitutes a rag-bag of disjointed material which was clearly recorded considerably later than the time the events had taken place and when they were only vaguely remembered. Furthermore, this same disjointed record was inserted by a compiler in order to fill in material between the earlier continuous narrative of the doings of the Great Army from 865 to 880 and the subsequent arrival of the Continental viking army in Kent in 891, which heralded the beginnings of Alfred's Last War.

It might be argued that nothing of any note did happen in Wessex between the departure of the Fulham Danes for Francia in 880 and the arrival of a powerful Continental warband in Kent in 891. And the switching of the compiler's attention from Wessex to Francia is easily explained by seeing his central theme as the progress of the Danish armies—one of which had now removed itself to the Frankish side of the Channel. These explanations are at best only partially satisfactory. The notion that nothing of any consequence was going on in Wessex from 881 to 891 is entirely due to the way in which the Chronicle is structured at this point. The Chronicle is our only near-contemporary source of information on Alfred's reign during this decade. The compiler of the *Life* of the king was totally dependent on the Chronicle for basic information on political and military matters during this period of Alfred's life. It is true that much of the Frankish information relates to the progress of the Danes in northern Francia and in that respect the compiler of the Chronicle shows that the progress of the Danish invaders of England was still central to his theme. So when the Continental army sails from Boulogne against East Kent in 891, the Anglo-Saxon chronicler returns to the narrative which he abandoned in 880 and proceeds to tell us once more how King Alfred dealt with this last great challenge of his reign. Once the Danish army has reported back to England in 891, all regular Frankish reporting is abandoned. All of this is indeed true, but it does not explain every aspect of what we may call the Frankish interlude from 881 to 891. First, it was not in the nature of ninth-century annalists and chroniclers to follow the progress of marauding viking armies in any great detail beyond the frontiers of the chroniclers' own kingdoms. It is for this reason that historians find it so difficult to trace the movements of viking armies from Britain across to Ireland or Francia. This section of the Anglo-Saxon Chronicle proves a notable exception to the otherwise essentially tribal horizons of early medieval annalists. So, for instance, when the Anglo-Saxon Chronicle reports the defeat of a great naval force which stormed Winchester in 860, we have to rely on the Annals of St Bertin to identify the attackers as having come from the Somme[6] and we find them back again in Francia in 861 as a fleet of 200 ships under Weland's command on the Seine.[7] All of that Frankish information was either unknown to or of no interest to the Anglo-Saxon chronicler at that point in his narrative.[8] Secondly, the Frankish insertion in the Chronicle is not exclusively concerned with one or more Danish armies in Francia. Danish activity is central to the Frankish insertion, but that also includes sizeable digressions on Frankish dynastic politics. In this, the Frankish insertion differs noticeably from the treatment of West Saxon affairs elsewhere in the Chronicle. Indeed, the Chronicle tells us more about the ramifications of the Carolingian dynasty in the late ninth century than it does about the House of Alfred in Wessex. So, in 885 we are told of the death of Carloman and we are provided with details of his Carolingian pedigree. We are told of the succession of Charles the Fat, given details of the extent of his kingdom, and provided yet again with a pedigree going back to Pippin the father of Charlemagne. In 887, at the notice of the death of Charles the Fat, we are offered a detailed account of the partition of the Frankish empire and the subsequent civil wars. That discussion on Frankish politics contains detail which rivals those accounts of the same events which are preserved in Frankish annals, and for which there is no comparable reporting on West Saxon affairs within the Anglo-Saxon Chronicle. The 887 Frankish narrative is conspicuously alien, then, to the Anglo-Saxon Chronicle in terms of geography and of genre.

We can be certain of one thing about the Frankish insertion in the Anglo-Saxon Chronicle. This is not a cumulative contemporary English record, penned by an Anglo-Saxon observer, who from a vantage-point in Wessex recorded those Frankish events, year by year as news of them reached him across the Channel. If he had done that, we should expect his record of Frankish happenings to differ more substantially in form and content from the basic genre of Frankish chroniclers. Because news from Francia took some time to reach Wessex, we should expect too, to find the Anglo-Saxon chronicler's dating of Frankish events to be on the whole later rather than earlier than the true time of occurrence, whereas in the Anglo-Saxon Chronicle, as we have seen, events of 889 are recorded under 887. That in itself shows us that this material was written up retrospectively, as does the repeated phrase that the Danish army 'stayed there for a year' in 880, 882, 883, and 884. Similar retrospective reporting lies behind the statement that the Danes spent two winters in the Chézy and Yonne areas in 887.[9] Reuter observed that the Chronicle's account of the division of the Carolingian empire in 887 exhibits the hallmarks of a *post ex facto* account which could not have been written up before 889.[10] Since a strictly contemporary West Saxon observer of Frankish events of the

880s could not have known that a Danish army in northern Francia at that time would eventually return to cause havoc in Alfred's kingdom during 891–6, we must assume that the West Saxon chronicler's interest in all this Frankish interlude dates to after the appearance of a viking army from Francia on Kentish soil in 891. That the Old English chronicler obtained his Frankish information from a written source and from a version of Frankish annals in particular is suggested by the nature of the record. The detail in the Anglo-Saxon Chronicle under 885, for instance—that Carloman was killed by a boar—is clearly borrowed from a Frankish annalistic source similar to the record in one version of the Annals of Fulda under 884.[11] So, too, details such as the horsing of the Danish army after a battle in 881; the drowning of viking fugitives after their defeat at the hands of the Bretons in 890, or the notion that the battle of the Dyle was fought against a mounted force of vikings 'before the ships arrived' are all diagnostic of Frankish annalistic detail.[12] The fact that we do not have a Frankish source to hand which tallies in every detail with the Anglo-Saxon account does not negate the argument for textual dependence. When we consider the contradictions and variation in detail between the few Frankish annals which do survive from this period, we realize that the minor divergences from Frankish sources in the Anglo-Saxon Chronicle's Frankish insertion is in keeping rather than at variance with Frankish annalistic tradition. The West Saxon account, for instance, that in 885 'a large naval force assembled among the Old Saxons and twice in the year there occurred a great battle, and the Saxons had the victory and with them there were the Frisians'[13] could refer back to events of 884 or, alternatively, it could be dated to 885. The Annals of Fulda record a viking invasion of Saxony in 884 which was defeated by the East Frankish margrave, Count Henry.[14] The same source adds that 'the Northmen fought not just once or twice with Count Henry, and were defeated'. The similarity between the Anglo-Saxon Chronicle and the Fulda annals in the reporting of this multiple incident is striking. Although the Anglo-Saxon Chronicle reports the invasion of Saxony in similar terms to the Annals of Fulda and in the same year as both sources record the death of Carloman in a boar-hunt in 884, it may also be that the West Saxon account of the viking invasion of Saxony owes something to Continental happenings in 885. The Annals of Fulda record[15] that in 885, the followers of Godafrid, unaware that their leader had been slain, headed off to invade Saxony. The Saxon defenders at first fled, but later regrouped when they were joined by a fleet of Frisian allies—recalling the Anglo-Saxon Chronicle's claim 'and with them were the Frisians'. Whatever the true dates of these incidents and the exact details relating to them may have been, it seems certain that this consecutive thirteen-year section of West Saxon annals on Frankish affairs was copied or summarized from a Frankish text which was taken to England in the 890s.[16]

The remarkably detailed account in the Anglo-Saxon Chronicle on the division of the Carolingian empire into five parts after the death of Charles the Fat also reveals how that record was based on a written Frankish account such as that preserved in the Annals of Fulda.[17] These accounts at first sight appear to be substantially different, but that is not, in fact, the case. The Annals of Fulda go on to

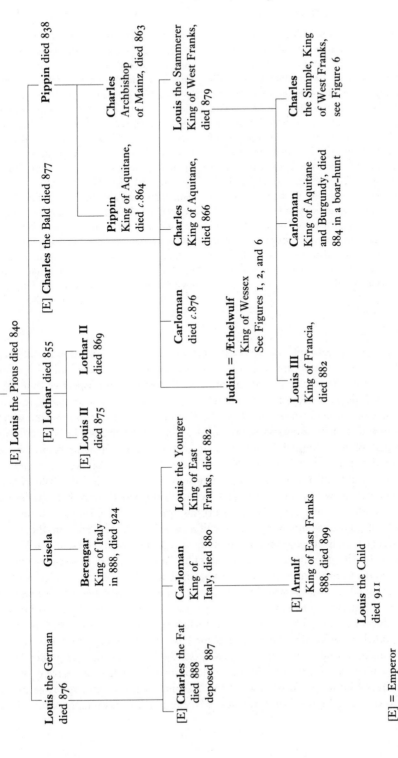

FIG. 5. Carolingian emperors and kings

[E] = Emperor

ANGLO-SAXON CHRONICLE	ANNALS OF FULDA
And that same year Charles, king of the Franks died; and six weeks before he died his brother's son Arnulf had deprived him of the kingdom. The kingdom was then divided into five, and five kings were consecrated to it. It was done however with Arnulf's consent and they said that they would hold it under him, for not one of them was born to it in the male line but him alone. Arnulf then lived in the land east of the Rhine, and Rudolf succeeded to the middle kingdom, and Odo to the western portion; and Berengar and Guido to Lombardy and the lands on that side of the Alps; and they held it with much discord and fought two general engagements, and ravaged the land again and again, and each repeatedly drove out the other.[18]	[887] So, when the emperor Charles came to Frankfurt, these men [from the German duchies] invited Arnulf the son of King Carloman, and chose him for their lord, and without delay decided that he should be made king. . . . And then after Christmas on January 13 [888], [Charles] ended his life happily. [888] . . . While he [Arnulf] delayed there [at Regensburg] many kinglets sprang up in Europe, that is to say the kingdom of his uncle Charles. For Berengar . . . made himself king in Italy; Rudolf . . . decreed that he would hold upper Burgundy in kingly fashion; and then Louis . . . and Wido . . . claimed to hold Belgian Gaul and Provence as kings; Odo . . . usurped the lands as far as the Loire or the province of Aquitane for his own use; and from there Ramnulf decreed that he should be held as king.[19]

report how Odo, Rudolf, and Berengar each in their turn submitted to Arnulf later in 888, while Ramnulf appears to have acknowledged Odo's rule in 889[20]—all of which shows that the Anglo-Saxon annal for 887 with its retrospective statement that the division 'was done with Arnulf's consent'[21] embodies information on a situation which had only materialized by 889. This detailed dynastic information, which was included in the Frankish section of the Chronicle, betrays a keen interest on the part of the compiler in the prestige of the Carolingian empire and in its association with Alfred's father, King Æthelwulf. So, in 885, we are reminded that Carloman and his brother were grandsons 'of that Charles [the Bald] whose daughter Æthelwulf, king of the West Saxons, had married', and that Charles the Fat 'was the son of Louis [the German] the brother of the Charles who was the father of Judith whom King Æthelwulf married'.[22] So the lines in these two separate Carolingian genealogies point to the connection with the House of Wessex and with Alfred's father in particular. The Anglo-Saxon Chronicle pointedly ignored the later marriage of that same Carolingian Judith to Alfred's older brother, King Æthelbald. And it was Æthelbald, and not Alfred, who because of that very marriage attracted the notice of contemporary Frankish chroniclers within the Carolingian empire. The marriage of Æthelbald (*Adalboldus*) to Judith is noted in the Annals of St Bertin under 858 and there is a reference to Judith as 'widow of Æthelbald, a king of the English (*relicta Edelboldi regis Anglorum*)' under 862.[23] Such a mention of Æthelbald in the Anglo-Saxon Chronicle would have detracted from that Chronicle's focusing on Alfred's achievements. The Carolingian marriage involving Alfred's father was not only safe but also advantageous for Alfred and his supporters to emphasize, and like the bogus account of Alfred's childhood hallowing as a king at the hands of the pope back in 853,[24] it served to tie in Alfred's credentials, through his father, with the leading institutions of Western Christendom. And so, just as the ancestry of Charles the Fat on his succession in 885 was tied in with the marriage of Æthelwulf to Judith and traced all the way back to Charlemagne and Pippin, so too, Æthelwulf's own pedigree was traced back through the war-god, Woden, to Adam the first man, in the Chronicle's notice of that king's death in 858.[25]

This Frankish section of the Anglo-Saxon Chronicle, by following the Danish marauders from Wessex to Francia and back to Wessex again, underlined the common menace faced by the Christian Alfred and by contemporary Carolingian rulers who were seen as the guardians of Christendom. And lest the point should be missed, this otherwise laconic West Saxon source—not once, but twice—drew the reader's attention to marriage ties which connected Æthelwulf of Wessex to the kingdom and empire of Alfred's older contemporary, Charles the Bald. Alfred and his scholarly circle would have shared the Frankish annalist's disapproval of the fragmentation of the Empire, and that disapproval comes out in the Chronicle's pronouncement that 'not one of them [the four kings who divided the empire with Arnulf in 887] was born to it in the male line but him [i.e. Arnulf] alone'.[26] We are reminded of how the compiler of the Anglo-Saxon Chronicle dismissed the Northumbrian king, Ælla, who met his death at the hands of the Danes in 867 as 'a king with no hereditary right'.[27] Alfred himself had written of Theodoric in his translation of Boethius's *Consolation of Philosophy* as a tyrannical king who had inherited the empire of Rome from its Gothic conquerors, and who as 'an unrighteous king (*unrihtwisan cyninge*)' might have been quite properly deposed.[28] Alfred or one of his supporters in the 890s may have been using information gleaned from a set of Frankish annals not only to follow the fortunes of a common viking enemy in Francia, but to underline the fact that Alfred's own struggle was showing common cause with his Carolingian betters. The West Saxon compiler of this particular section of the Chronicle could show, too, that through his father, Æthelwulf, Alfred's own kingship was not only legitimate, but by association with his step-mother, Alfred could claim some reflected glory from the Carolingian defenders of Christendom. And the king who allowed a story to circulate which told of his supposed hallowing as a child-king in Rome was also very likely to have been responsible for authorizing insertions within this Frankish interlude in the Chronicle, which told of that same Alfred dispatching alms to Rome and even to distant India no less than five times. And on all occasions the alms or letters were associated personally with King Alfred. These notices, together with the record of the gift of the Holy Cross sent by Pope Marinus to Alfred in 883 and the record of the death of that same 'good pope (*goda papa*)', Marinus, 'who had freed from taxation the English quarter [in Rome] at the request of Alfred, king of the West Saxons' in 885,[29] all form part of the same effort to project an image of Alfred as a king who can be seen on a par with his Carolingian contemporaries—exchanging gifts with a papacy which is seen to value his friendship. This series of Frankish

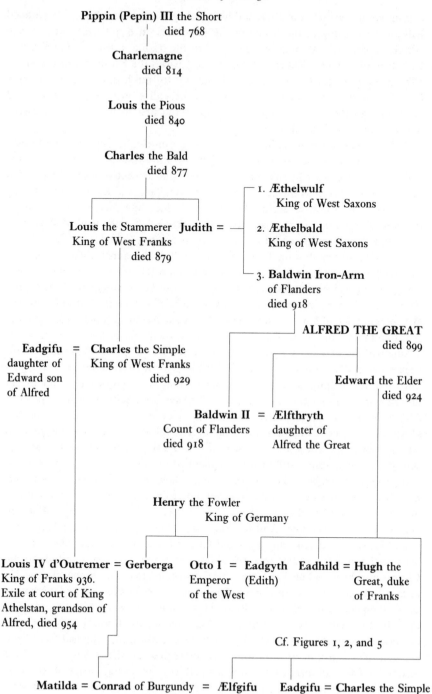

F IG. 6. Carolingian marriage alliances with the house of Alfred and papal entries, although confined to the period 881 to 891, where they act as a fill-in between two separate narratives within the Chronicle, reflect what may be described as Alfred's quasi-imperial ambitions at a time when the Anglo-Saxon Chronicle was being compiled towards the end of the king's life.

When we separate out the Continental reporting in the Chronicle during the interval between Alfred's victory at Edington down to the return of a Danish army to East Kent in 892, we realize that the compiler failed to put a coherent narrative together to cover this part of King Alfred's reign. This was not so much King Alfred's rest period as the time when the Chronicle's record has lapsed. The Chronicle's record for this period resembles the scrappy reporting of the first decade of the reign of Alfred's son, Edward the Elder. We can only approach this material in the knowledge that records do fail us for this time in Alfred's reign, and that the disjointed account which is presented to us constitutes not so many islands of reliable information, as facts pressed into service by a compiler who, on the one hand, wished to fill in glaring gaps in his material and who, on the other hand, wished to show the king in an imperial setting. One feature of the home-based reporting in this period centres on Alfred's efforts to meet the vikings at sea. Alfred was not the first English king to make use of ships in warfare, nor was he the first in his own dynasty to confront the vikings on their own terms at sea. The Northumbrian Ecgfrith launched a naval attack on the coast of eastern Ireland as early as 684,[30] while Alfred's eldest brother, King Æthelstan, 'fought in ships' against viking marauders at Sandwich in Kent in 851 when he and Ealdorman Ealhhere 'slew a great army . . . and captured nine ships and put the others to flight'.[31] The Franks had led the way in confronting the Northmen in their own element. The emperor Charlemagne had taken steps to defend the coasts of northern Francia from viking marauders by the provision of a fleet, as had his son, Louis the Pious.[32] Charlemagne also 'placed strong-points and coastguard stations at all the ports and at the mouths of all rivers considered large enough for the entry of ships, so that the enemy could be bottled up by this military task force.'[33]

It is clear that in the later empire the use of ships to repel viking invaders, while not frequently referred to in Frankish annals, continued to be an option open to the Franks. In 854 the bishops of Orléans and Chartres used their own ships on the Loire to resist viking attempts at sailing up that river from Blois to attack Orléans.[34] In 862 Charles the Bald could not prevent vikings from seizing Frankish ships on the Marne near Meaux.[35] When Charles came to a parley with the viking leaders, Roric and Rodulf, at Maastricht in 872, we learn that the Carolingian arrived by ship down the Meuse.[36] The Frisians, as we saw, deployed their own fleet when helping the Saxons repel a viking attack in 885. Ships of the viking variety had become all-pervasive in the records of mid-ninth-century northern Francia, and those native magnates who did not possess ships of their own could acquire them from the enemy. So, the Breton leader, Salomon, hired twelve Danish ships 'for an agreed fee' in his war against Count Robert of Angers in 862.[37] Alfred's use of ships against his viking enemies, therefore, was neither as novel nor as ambitious as the Chronicle might have us believe. Alfred's first recorded

involvement with ships is found in the Chronicle as early as in 875, when we are
told that the king in that summer 'went out to sea with a naval force (*sciphere*), and
fought against the crews of seven ships, and captured one ship and put the rest to
flight'.[38] During the Frankish interlude in the Anglo-Saxon Chronicle (880–91),
two further reportings of Alfred's naval experiments are recorded. In 882 we are
told:

King Alfred went out with ships to sea and fought against four crews of Danish men, and
captured two of the ships—and the men were killed who were on them—and two crews
surrendered to him. And they had great losses in killed or wounded before they surrendered.[39]

Three years later in 885, the Danish army in East Anglia is reported in the
Chronicle as having broken its peace with King Alfred:[40]

King Alfred sent a naval force from Kent into East Anglia. Immediately they came to the
mouth of the Stour they encountered 16 ships of vikings and fought against them, and
seized all the ships and killed the men. When they turned homeward with the booty, they
met a large naval force of vikings and fought against them on the same day, and the Danes
had the victory.[41]

One notable feature of these incidents is their smallness of scale. In 875, while
the size of Alfred's fleet is not specified, the enemy ships are put at only seven. He
attacked four Danish vessels in 882 and defeated sixteen ships in 885. This suggests that the number of Alfred's own ships was not large—and probably no larger
than the fleet of his brother, Æthelstan—a point supported by the fact that when
the Alfredian fleet dispatched against East Anglia was subsequently attacked by a
'large naval force of vikings (*micelne sciphere wicenga*)' it was defeated. There is no
reason to doubt the number of ships recorded by the Chronicle in these skirmishes.
The record is entirely consistent with similar small-scale viking operations recorded
in contemporary Irish and Frankish annals.[42] On the other hand, it is difficult to
accept that the coast of Wessex was as free from viking raiding—on however small
a scale—during the interval from 880 to 892, as the Chronicle suggests. This
sprawling coastline stretched for 100 miles from Gravesend around the exposed
Kentish peninsula alone, together with another 300 miles from St Margaret's Bay
in Kent to Plymouth. Yet another 100 miles of northern coast stretched from the
Cornish borders to near Bristol, and this remote frontier lay exposed to viking
forays from south-east Ireland and from Norsemen who at this very time infested
the coastal areas of south Wales.[43] The southern coastline along the English Channel was not just exposed to those Danes settled in East Anglia who might be
tempted to break Alfred's and Guthrum's peace. It was much more vulnerable to
roving viking fleets who must have sailed regularly through the Channel at this
time, as well as to those Danish fleets which we know were attacking the Frisian
coast and the Somme and Seine estuaries. The one feature of the Chronicle which
requires us constantly to be on our guard is its silence. A chronicler who suppressed details of Alfred's concessions to Guthrum and of repeated earlier military
mistakes and weakness on the part of the West Saxon king cannot be trusted when
it comes to recording Danish forays along the coast of Wessex. The record as it

stands is designed to show Alfred as a resourceful and energetic king who defeated Guthrum and his hordes in 878 and who then inaugurated an era of peace. It also presents us with the picture of a victorious king who had gone on the offensive against the Danes by organizing his own fleet. There is little doubt that the record is, as ever, broadly correct in its basic reporting, even if there is the characteristic economy with truth. Alfred had fitted out a limited number of warships in readiness against small and sporadic viking raiding parties. That in itself was not a negligible achievement and the chronicler made the most of it. Even small numbers of viking ships' crews, with surprise and ruthless determination on their side, could wreak havoc on larger unsuspecting or unprepared communities. Nor can Alfred be blamed for failing to protect the sprawling coastline of his kingdom with a fleet large enough to secure it from major viking assaults. When a massive fleet of Northmen fell on coastal Frisia in a surprise attack in 837, the emperor Louis the Pious hastened to Nijmegen to review the desperate situation, and the annalist conceded that 'it became clear from the discussion that partly through the sheer impossibility of the task, partly through the disobedience of certain men, it had not been possible for them to offer any resistence to the attackers'.[44] Less than a decade later, Frisia was faring ever worse at the mercy of Norse sea-borne marauders who in 846 had 'gained control of nearly the whole province'.[45] The emperor Lothar, when confronted with 'a vast number of ships (*cum multitudine navium*)' led by the Danish Roric in 850, failed to prevent the devastation of Frisia and was forced to buy the Northman off with a grant of Dorestad and other counties.[46] Alfred, in comparison with this relentless catalogue of Carolingian failure, is seen as indeed an able and perhaps also a fortunate king. But the Chronicle's record of his success against sea-borne viking assault should never be allowed to blind us to the possibility of omissions of records of even major viking successes; to the modesty of Alfred's own naval achievements; and to the inappropriate design of his ships and the incompetence of his crews. The period 893–6 saw intensified coastal raiding around the whole of the West Saxon kingdom, some of which was due to the activities of the army of Hæsten and some of which involved Northumbrian and East Anglian fleets which were taking advantage of the mayhem caused by Hasten's invasion in 892. Such opportunistic raiding, which depended on the fact that Alfred's levies were distracted by a major viking invasion from Francia, may indeed suggest that the period from 880 to 891 was relatively free of sustained and major viking attack in the Wessex region. But since events within Wessex are virtually ignored by the Chronicle for the decade of the 880s, any argument based on silence is weak in the extreme.

The Chronicle informs us that the south coast of Wessex was greatly harassed by Northumbrian and East Anglian marauding bands (*stælhergum*) in 896 who sailed to attack it in their warships (*æscum*) which had been 'built many years before':

Then King Alfred had long-ships (*langscipu*) built to oppose the Danish warships. They were almost twice as long as the others. Some had 60 oars, some more. They were both swifter and steadier and also higher than the others. They were built neither on the Frisian nor the Danish pattern, but as it seemed to him himself that they could be most useful.[47]

This passage was undoubtedly designed to enhance Alfred's image as the scholar king, turning his mind to strategy and boat-building. Closer inspection exposes the enterprise as an impracticable experiment which resulted in disaster. Viking ships were vessels with shallow draught requiring only a few feet of water to float and move in. Alfred's ships—if we can trust the boasting record—were enormous by contemporary standards. The Gokstad ship with its 32 oars may have been one of the largest of its type, although some Norse warships are assumed to have been larger and longer.[48] Yet Alfred's boats were built twice as large as the known example from Gokstad. From the account of their running aground it seems certain that such Alfredian ships would have been difficult to row at sea near the shoreline, or to send up rivers which were choked with weed or silt. They may have been easily capsized and would have been difficult if not impossible to turn in narrow waters. The advantage of their larger crews was outweighed by the possibility of greater losses for every boat which capsized or was sunk. The naïve account in the Chronicle of how these out-sized boats performed when put to the test is remarkable for its uncharacteristic candour. It is as though the strong sense of pride and novelty in the experiment had blinded the chronicler to the failure of the enterprise—yet another of the many indications that the chronicler may have been personally involved in the events which he reported. Alfred dispatched nine of his new ships to take on six viking ships which were causing havoc in the Isle of Wight and along the coast of Devon 'and everywhere along the coast'. Alfred's crews blocked the Danish line of retreat along the seaward end of an estuary. Three Danish ships were beached farther up the estuary, while their crews were raiding inland. The three other Danish ships made an abortive attack on Alfred's fleet—the Danes losing all men on two ships 'at the entrance to the estuary' and with only five escaping on the third. The Chronicle continues:

These got away because the ships of their [West Saxon] opponents ran aground. Moreover, they had run aground very awkwardly: three were aground on that side of the channel on which the Danish ships were aground, and all the others on the other side, so that none of them could get to the others. But when the waters had ebbed many furlongs from the ships, the Danes from the remaining three ships went to the other three which were stranded on their side, and they then fought there. . . . Then however the tide reached the Danish ships before the Christians could launch theirs, and therefore they [i.e. the Danes] rowed away out.[49]

Not only had Alfred's ships all run aground, but his sailors had failed to resist either the current or the vikings from splitting his little fleet into two. And because the novel West Saxon ships were higher than viking longboats, not only did they run aground, but they were even more prone to end up 'stranded (*beebbade*)' in a keeled-over position.[50] Alfred lost 62 of his Frisian and English warrior-sailors in the costly mayhem which ensued about his stranded ships. And even if the Danish losses were indeed higher (120 men), Wessex could ill afford to lose such a select band of sailor-warriors in the company of their skilled Frisian instructors.[51] The Frisians, as we know from Frankish sources, were experienced sailors and had borne the brunt of Danish attacks on the crumbling northern coastal defences of the Carolingian empire. Such men were ideal tutors for the crews of Alfred's modest but cumbersome fleet.[52] The Chronicle's naming of Wulfheard, Æbba, and Æthelhere—all identified as Frisians—as having been slain in this incident is highly unusual, as indeed is the record of the slaying of King Alfred's reeve, Lucuman, and his *geneat*, Æthelfrith. This detailed record of slain foreign allies as well as two royal officials stands out in contrast to the silence of the Chronicle on West Saxon losses sustained in Alfred's earlier battles. As for the ill-fated Alfredian ships which unquestionably were the cause of this West Saxon disaster, not surprisingly we hear no more of them.

The Anglo-Saxon Chronicle's account of the activities of vikings in Francia from 880 down to 892 gives the impression of being a coherent account of the movements of a single warband which had left England in 880. This notion of strict continuity between viking activity in Wessex and later in Francia is created by the compiler's constant reference between 880 and 892 to 'the army (*se here*)'— as if it were that same 'army which had been encamped at Fulham [and which] went overseas into the Frankish empire to Ghent' in 880.[53] So, we are told (881) 'the army went farther inland into the Frankish empire . . .' (882) 'the army went farther into the Frankish empire along the Meuse . . .' (883) 'the army went up the Scheldt to Condé . . .' (884) 'the army went up the Somme to Amiens', while in 885 a portion of that same army came back across the Channel to attack Rochester. In 886 that section of the army which had gone east to Louvain went west again and up the Seine to Paris, and eventually (in 887) up the Marne to Chézy. In 890 'the Danish army' abandoned the Seine for St Lô 'which lies between Brittany and France'. Finally, in 891 we are told 'the Danish army went east' where Arnulf defeated it with a coalition of East Franks, Saxons, and Bavarians—a reference to the victory at the battle of the river Dyle near Louvain.[54] As a result of this crushing defeat, the vikings withdrew from Francia and sailed from Boulogne to attack Wessex by way of East Kent. It is highly plausible that those same vikings who had encamped at Fulham 'by the Thames' back in 879 had maintained their identity as a single warband throughout their subsequent campaign in Francia. It is unlikely, however, that the invaders of East Kent in 892 consisted of precisely the same army which had been at Fulham in 879, tested the defences of Rochester in 885, and had supposedly campaigned up and down the Meuse, Scheldt, Seine, and Marne as one fighting force throughout the 880s. A close inspection of Frankish records for these years suggests that several marauding bands were congregated in the Rhine delta and the rivers flowing into it, and that these armies exploited cross-border tensions along the Scheldt and the Meuse between the magnates of the Middle Kingdom and West Francia. The lower reaches of the Maas up to its junction with the Meuse near Liege had marked a line of partition within the empire in 870, while the Scheldt from its mouth up to and beyond St Quentin marked another line of partition in 843.[55] Such ethnic and political fault lines[56]

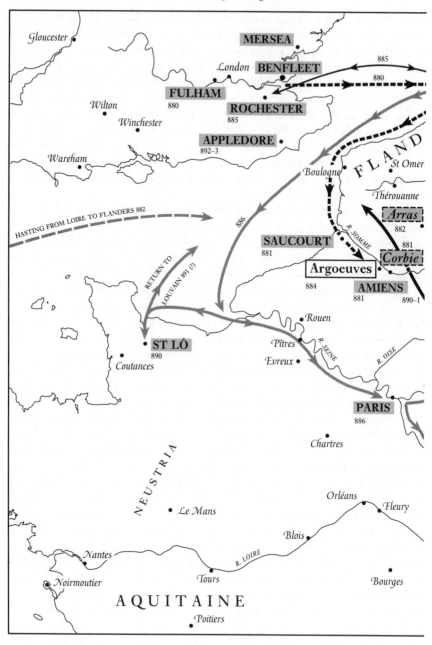

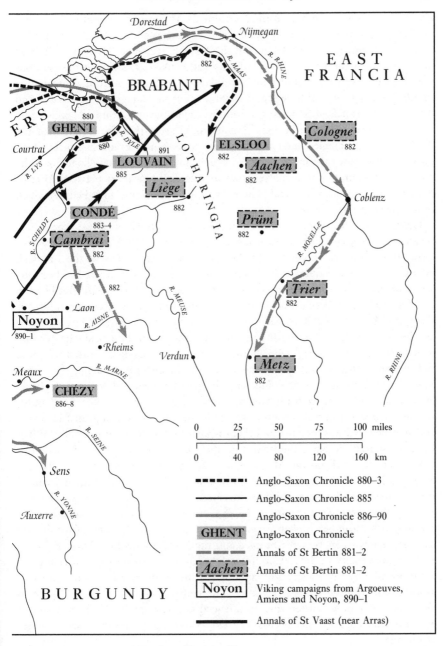

MAP 6. Viking invasion of Northern Francia, 880–92

along navigable rivers provided the Northmen with ideal opportunities for ravaging territory on either side of sensitive frontiers. While Louis the Younger's successful campaign against vikings in the Scheldt region in 881 may have been directed against the Fulham warband who had arrived at Ghent in the previous year, it seems likely that not one, but several disparate groups were all campaigning simultaneously over a wide sweep of countryside from Cologne, Trier, Laon, and Rheims. The Annals of St Vaast confirm the Anglo-Saxon Chronicle's record of a viking presence at Condé in 882,[57] but it would seem that the compiler of the Anglo-Saxon Chronicle edited and simplified a version of Frankish annals which came into his possession in the 890s and which covered the period 880 to 892. The purpose of his simplification of events was to establish continuity between Alfred's war against Guthrum which ended in 878 and the Last War against Hæsten which commenced in 892.

Hæsten is the only named leader on the Danish side in Alfred's Last War, which began with the arrival of two warbands at Appledore and at Milton Regis in East Kent. If we were to accept the Anglo-Saxon Chronicle's view of the Frankish interlude, we would assume that Hæsten who arrived in Kent in 892 had been the leader of that same army which encamped at Fulham back in 878–9. But Hæsten could scarcely have been a leader either at Fulham in 879 or at Ghent in 881, or along the Meuse in 882. The Annals of St Bertin inform us that Hæsten (*Astingus*) had been on the Loire up until 882 and that from there he headed for 'coastal regions (*maritimas partes*)'[58]—no doubt joining in the mayhem caused by those Fulham and other vikings along the Frisian coast and inland along the Maas, Meuse, and Scheldt. But he could scarcely have been part of the same fighting force which had come from Fulham and attacked Ghent in 880. Nor do Frankish annalists name Hæsten as a leading player in an intense campaign in 882 which Hincmar believed was directed to 'bring the kingdom under their control'.[59] When Frankish sources do name the leaders on the viking side who directed operations from a fort at Asselt on the Meuse upstream from Venloo, and who negotiated with Charles the Fat, we read not of Hæsten but of Godafrid, Sigifrid, and Gorm. Hæsten was one of several troublesome migratory Scandinavian kings who was active in the Carolingian empire in the 880s and the fleets which he joined on the invasion of Kent in 892 probably consisted of a number of separate warbands who had been harrying in Western Francia and the Middle Kingdom. Hæsten was to achieve immortality in the folklore of early medieval Normandy as the viking *par excellence* who by his bravery and cunning led his northern warriors to victory in exotic Mediterranean lands (*Suðríki*).[60] The reality may not have been quite so glamorous, but in 892 when this experienced and resourceful Northman landed with a formidable army on the coast of Kent, Alfred was to face the final challenge of his reign.

V

The Last War 892–896

Hæsten, the old english form of the name of the only leader identified with the viking invaders of Kent in the Anglo-Saxon Chronicle in 892, occupies a place in medieval Norman-French folklore on a par with that of Ivar the Boneless and other sons of Ragnar Lodbrok in Anglo-Danish and Icelandic tradition. For just as the sons of Ragnar Lodbrok were remembered as the founders of the Danish colony in England—not least by later generations of Danes within the English Danelaw[1]—so too, Hæsten was remembered within Normandy as a super-hero, whose barbarous exploits contrasted with and prefigured those of Rollo who established the duchy of Normandy in early tenth-century Francia. That later Norman saga tradition ought not be allowed to obscure the essential historicity of Hæsten, whose presence is vouched for in contemporary late ninth-century Frankish annals and in the Anglo-Saxon Chronicle. Those legends relating to Hæsten's supposed adventures, which Dudo of St Quentin recorded in the early eleventh century, are important for what they tell of the impression made by Hæsten on early Norman folk-tradition. Like Harald Finehair of Norway or Knutr the Great of Denmark, or Harald Hardrada, succeeding generations felt impelled to attribute all number of marvels to his name. The Old English form of Hæsten's name is thought to represent an Old Norse form *Haddingr* or less likely *Hásteinn*, with a derivation from *Hallsteinn* now least in favour.[2] Dudo of St Quentin, writing his history of the early dukes of Normandy, c.1020, claimed that *Alstignus/ Hastingus* attacked the church of St Denis, as well as St Medard and St Éloi at Noyon, and Ste Geneviève in Paris.[3] Those raids can probably be dated to 857–9,[4] but are unlikely to have been associated with Hæsten, who may not have begun his Frankish career until 866–9 at the earliest. In the late 860s he was active on the Loire rather than on the Seine. He was very probably involved in a Norse–Breton campaign on the River Sarthe as far as Brissarthe in Anjou[5] in 869, which was reported by Regino of Prüm.[6] Dudo relates that *Alstignus* led an expedition to the Mediterranean where he attacked the city of Luna, mistaking it for Rome.[7] The tale of how *Alstignus*'s men captured Luna by pretending first to seek Christian baptism and then a Christian burial for their supposedly deceased leader is a Norman–Scandinavian folk-motif applied to other legendary and historical leaders from as far apart as Norway, Denmark, and Sicily.[8] William of Jumièges claims that Björn—otherwise Björn járnsíða ('Ironsides'), a supposed son of Ragnar Lodbrok—accompanied Hæsten (*Hastingus*) on the expedition to Luna.[9] This claim is probably based on a confusion, on the part of later Norman writers, of once quite separate Norse traditions relating to earlier viking leaders in Francia. For it is likely that tales which centred on Hæsten were once separate from those which formed about the Sons of Ragnar Lodbrok. According to Dudo, *Alstignus* returned to Francia from his Mediterranean adventures and concluded a peace treaty with a Frankish king, whereby the viking received a substantial Danegeld.[10] William of Jumièges claims, quite implausibly, that *Hastingus* was granted the city of Chartres.[11] The career of the historical *Astingus* of Frankish annals is more mundane and more difficult of recovery. *Astingus* appears on the Loire in the company of Salomen of Brittany in 869–74, where his price for co-operating with the Breton prince was set at 500 cows.[12] In 882 we are informed by the Annals of St Vaast that the Carolingian Louis III did indeed enter into a peace treaty with the historical *Alstingus* on the Loire[13] and the Annals of St Bertin add that *Astingus* left the Loire for 'coastal regions'—presumably of northern Francia and Frisia— also in 882.[14] We next hear of *Alstingus* eight years later in 890 when he entered into negotiations with Rodulf, abbot of St Vaast. There is no means of proving that the *Hastingus/Alstignus* of Dudo of St Quentin ever did lead an expedition to the Mediterranean in which he captured Luna—an expedition which is otherwise dated to 859–61.[15] Nor can we recover the lost years of the career of *Alstingus* between when he campaigned on the Loire in 869 and when he reappeared in Frankish sources in 882. The only solid historical connections between the leader who confronted Alfred in his Last War, with the *Alstingus* of Frankish affairs, is that Alfred's enemy *Hæsten* was almost certainly the same person as the Frankish viking who concluded a peace with Louis III in 882 and was clearly the same person who attacked St Vaast in 890. That Frankish viking, *Alstingus/Alstignus*, had clearly made such a deep impression on his Carolingian victims and on his own Scandinavian following, that his name passed into Norman legend and was immortalized in the Latin History of the early dukes of Normandy by Dudo of St Quentin.

Fortunately for historians who are interested in the career of Hæsten, the monastery of St Vaast, situated near the frontier with Lorraine in the north of Western Francia, was maintaining a set of annals covering this time (873–900), and so Hæsten's presence in the region was noted. The St Vaast annalist tells how, in 889, Odo, king of Western Francia paid off a viking host which was threatening Paris and how that host headed west to attack Coutance and the castle of St Lô (west of Bayeux). In the following year, we learn that in spite of setbacks, the Bretons defended themselves bravely and drove the invaders back to the Seine.[16] The Anglo-Saxon chronicler, following a similar set of Frankish annals included this campaign in his record, adding that the Bretons drove their viking enemies into a river, drowning many of them.[17] The Norse survivors of this expedition, sailed up the Oise from the Seine and set up their winter camp near Noyon, which although on the Oise, also lay near the waters of the Somme to its north (see Map 6). Hæsten (*Alstingus*) now went with his followers to Argoeuves on the Somme just west of Amiens, and Odo took up a monitoring position on the banks of the Oise 'so that the Northmen would not lay waste his kingdom at will'.[18] It was at this time that Hæsten entered into a 'malicious agreement' with Rodulf, abbot of nearby St Vaast, whereby the viking leader 'would be allowed to go unhindered wherever he wanted'. In spite of this accord, Hæsten attacked the monastery and the fortification at St Vaast and in 891 the viking garrison at Noyon devastated the lands between the River Maas and the Scheldt.[19] The Noyon vikings spent the Spring and Summer of 891 in the Channel coastal territories of northern Francia, moving back to the Maas later in that year. King Arnulf of Eastern Francia now drove them back west across the Scheldt as far as Arras, but like so many rulers before and after him, he found viking mobility too much for him, and as 'he could not catch them, he headed back into his kingdom'.[20] The former garrison from Noyon now decided to winter in Louvain, while the vikings from Argoeuves (presumably still under Hæsten's control) settled in Amiens. Arnulf now moved to dislodge the invaders from Louvain and inflicted heavy casualties on them, in a battle on the Dyle recorded also in the Anglo-Saxon Chronicle, the Annals of Fulda, and by Regino of Prüm.[21] It does not seem likely that Hæsten was present at the great viking defeat on the Dyle at Louvain. It is much more probable that he was leading the Amiens garrison, which does not seem to have participated in the Dyle disaster and which was dealt with separately by Odo, king of the Western Franks. Odo moved against Amiens later in 891, but through the negligence of his camp guards he was taken by surprise and his army was forced into flight.[22] After Easter in 892, a great famine and blight drove many of the Frankish inhabitants off the land, and we are told that the Norse survivors of the Louvain disaster 'left Francia and went across the sea' in the autumn of that year.[23]

The Anglo-Saxon Chronicle which had been following the progress of 'the great Danish army' in East Francia 'which we have spoken about before' claims that in 892, that same army withdrew westwards to Boulogne.[24] Its withdrawal had followed a defeat at the hands of King Arnulf in the battle of the River Dyle, near Louvain not long before. So many thousands of Northmen were said to have been slain on the Dyle in 891, that according to the Annals of Fulda, their corpses choked the river-bed and the Dyle appeared to run dry.[25] Whatever the exaggeration, Arnulf had clearly inflicted heavy losses on his viking enemies, which helped to persuade the survivors that it was time to abandon Francia and try their hand in England. They crossed the Channel in 250 ships—sufficient to transport everything in only 'one journey, horses and all', landing four miles up the Lympne estuary, on the southern fringe of the Kentish Weald. There they overpowered 'a few peasants (*cirlisce men*)' who were manning a half-finished fortress in the fen.[26] That fort may have been at Castle Toll, at Newenden in Kent, and a case has been made for identifying it with *Eorpeburnan* listed in the *Burghal Hidage*.[27] Immediately after this landing, Hæsten invaded the Thames estuary with 80 ships and built a fortress at Milton, near Sittingbourne in East Kent. Hæsten, as in the campaign around Amiens and Noyon, appears to have maintained his warband as a separate force in Kent, distinct from the other main band of invaders. The army which had landed on the south coast of Kent encamped at Appledore, is a fortress of the Northmen's

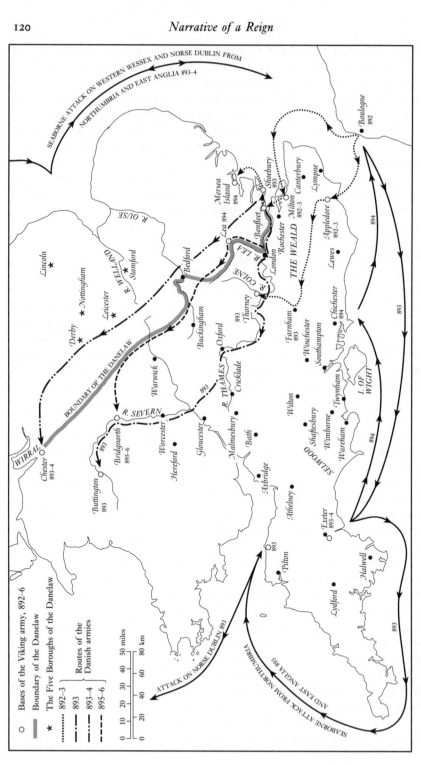

MAP 7. King Alfred's last war, 892–6

own making, and therefore different from the unfinished fort which they had attacked on landing. This combined fleet of 330 ships carried horses and supplies as well as warriors. We also known that women and children accompanied warriors on this expedition. The Chronicle informs us later on, that Hæsten—the only named leader among the Continental invaders in this war—was accompanied at Benfleet by his wife and two sons.[28] Hæsten was clearly not exceptional as a warlord who travelled *en famille*. The Northman Weland, who led a great warband on the Seine, was accompanied by his wife and sons (*cum uxore et filiis*) when introduced to the emperor Charles the Bald in 862.[29] We are told, too, that in 893, before setting out to Chester from Essex, the Danes 'placed their women and ships and property in safety in East Anglia'.[30] Children (*bearnum*) are specifically mentioned as part of the booty captured by the English at Benfleet and taken to London in 893.[31] These brief but crucial references in the Chronicle suggest that this invasion of Kent was a genuine migration of peoples intent on settlement, rather than an isolated raiding party. This in turn is confirmed by the chronicler's statement at the end of the war in 896 that it was 'those that were moneyless (*feohlease*) [who] got themselves ships and went south across the sea to the Seine',[32] while the Danish army proper, divided into two, 'one force going into East Anglia and one into Northumbria'. Those warriors who still lacked coin or booty were not yet in a position to acquire farms, stock them, and raise families, whereas those who had the wherewithal acquired from the Chester raid and elsewhere, now settled down on English soil. So, King Alfred's Last War ended in the consolidation of the Danish colonies in East Anglia and Northumbria. Evidence for the presence of Scandinavian women buried with pagan grave goods in York and Dublin, from the earliest years of those settlements,[33] suggests that large late ninth-century invading armies were bent on colonization from the outset. Scholars who view Scandinavian expansion in the Christian West as a minor irritation on the fringes of Carolingian and other societies have failed to take evidence for the migration of entire families or households into account. That evidence, for the presence of family units, when pieced together from Ireland, England, and Francia, is sufficient to show that viking objectives in relation to colonization were little different from those or the earlier Germanic völkerwanderung of Late Antiquity. Allowing for the presence of women and children, for horses and supplies; and allowing also for different sizes of ships, let us assume that this expedition carried no more than ten warriors to a ship. That estimate is conservative, for whatever the number of non-combatants, a minimum number of warriors was needed to row each vessel and handle its sail on the open sea. Even if that conservative estimate is accepted, we still arrive at a fighting force of 3,300 men landing in East Kent in 892. It is possible that the number of warriors may have been closer to 5,000. It is not safe to assume that this invading army had been so decimated after the defeat on the Dyle, that lack of numbers alone drove the survivors out of Francia. The Norse garrison at Amiens, which earlier had been associated with Hæsten, was still sufficiently strong after the Dyle defeat, so as to successfully resist an attack by Odo, king of the Western Franks. As for the Dyle debacle, while it may have contributed to the viking withdrawal from Francia, it may not have been the major factor in that withdrawal. The Annals of St Vaast make it clear that it was a famine in Francia which drove the Northmen across the Channel—in search no doubt, of their all important provisions.

Alfred met the new challenge which presented itself in East Kent by leading an army 'to take up a position between the two enemy forces' which were encamped at Milton in the north and at Appledore in the south. His objective was to prevent raiding parties from harrying the countryside and moving under cover of the Weald, which the chronicler tells us was then 130 miles long and 30 miles wide. This great expanse of woodland stretched in a north–south direction, isolating the Men of Kent from their neighbours in Sussex and Surrey. The Chronicle's account of King Alfred's Last War is garbled and contrasts sharply with the crisp and laconic reporting of Alfred's earlier campaigns. On the one hand, we are told 'the enemy did not all come out of those encampments [at Appledore and Milton] more than twice: once when they first landed, before the English force was assembled, and once when they wished to leave those encampments'.[34] Yet we are also told that the Weald provided cover for the vikings to set out 'in small bands and mounted companies' wherever it was undefended. And we are told, too, that in spite of Northumbrian oaths and East Anglian hostage-giving, 'yet contrary to those pledges, as often as the other Danish armies went out in full force, they went either with them or on their own behalf'.[35] The invaders of Kent seem to have carried out incessant small-scale raiding to maintain supplies, and the Chronicle suggests that they rarely if ever moved out in full force. Their arrival in southern England had a destabilizing effect on any existing peace between Alfred and the Danelaw. At least one major raiding expedition struck out at Wessex from the safety of the Weald, but the eventual failure of that expedition seems to have resulted in a hasty withdrawal of the entire garrison from Appledore. Æthelweard reports that Hampshire and Berkshire were laid waste by the invaders from the Kentish Weald after Easter in 893.[36] This raiding party was attacked by Alfred's son, Edward, at Farnham in Surrey, and the booty seized by the invaders was recovered.[37] The Danes were defeated and driven across the Thames 'where there was no ford'.[38] They fled up along the Colne, and they were besieged on Thorney island, near Iver in Buckinghamshire.[39] Prince Edward was then joined by Æthelred, ruler of English Mercia.[40] The beleaguered Danes were forced to give hostages and agreed to leave King Alfred's realm. The Appledore fortress was abandoned after the collapse of this expedition. Æthelweard tells us[41] that Danish ships sailed around from 'the harbour of the Lympne' to meet the defeated Danes at Mersea (off the coast of Essex) and took them from there into Danish East Anglia. Meanwhile Alfred was marching from the west to relieve, or come to the assistance of Edward's forces who had been besieging the Danes on Thorney. The Anglo-Saxon Chronicle suggests that Edward's army threw away a crucial opportunity to press home its victory. The supplies of Edward's men were all used up, and they had come to the end of their obligatory period of service in the field. They set off home before Alfred had time to reach them and take over the siege. It would appear that the

Danes remained on Thorney because they could not move their king who had been wounded in the battle at Farnham, but eventually, it would also seem, this warband moved on to meet the ships at Mersea.

The crisis for Alfred now deepened. While he had marched east towards Kent and Essex:

those Danes who lived in Northumbria and East Anglia collected some hundred ships, and went south round the coast and some 40 ships went north around the coast and besieged a fortress on the north coast of Devon, and those who had gone south besieged Exeter.[42]

This was a repetition of the pincer movement executed by Guthrum and by the brother of Ivar and Hálfdan back in 878, only now in 893, it was all on a much greater scale. Hæsten and his associates already had several thousand men poised to cut off the Kentish peninsula, and the choice of position at Appledore and Milton Regis was clearly aimed at overrunning East Kent. In this latest move, 140 warships from the Danelaw, carrying a miniumum of 1,400 warriors—and perhaps many more—were dispatched either to cut off western Wessex or to pin Alfred down while the conquest of Kent and Essex was pursued in the east. The movements of this Danelaw fleet were observed from a strictly West Saxon viewpoint. The 'coast' referred to throughout this annal was the coast of Wessex. So the 40 ships which sailed 'north around the coast', had not sailed on a 1,200-mile voyage around Scotland, but had sailed, rather, down the Channel past Exeter and around the Cornish peninsula to attack north Devon.[43] As soon as Alfred heard of the new threat in the west, he turned back with the greater part of his army and marched to the defence of Exeter. Æthelweard supplies the name of the 'pirate from the land of the Northumbrians' who led the fleet against western Wessex, as *Sigeferð*, whom he tells us 'ravaged twice along the coast on that one expedition'.[44] The 'coast' as ever, for a West Saxon chronicler such as Æthelweard, referred to the coast of Wessex. Stenton, misled by a reference in Æthelweard's Chronicle to events along the Welland and in Kesteven under 894,[45] mistakenly concluded that Sigeferð's expedition was directed up the Welland.[46]

This double pincer executed by the vikings in southern England in 893 gives the lie yet again to any notion that the Northmen were capable of only small-scale random raiding and that well-planned and co-ordinated attacks were beyond their ability. If we accept the Chronicle's reckoning in this report, then a total of 470 ships' crews were deployed around the coast of Wessex in AD 893—330 in the east and 140 in the west. The West Saxon evidence for pincer movements carried out by viking ships reminds us how command of the sea and rivers gave the Northmen flexibility and obvious opportunities for co-ordinated attacks from different directions. Alfred had already had a taste of this tactic when he had been caught as a fugitive between the army of Guthrum and the army of the brother of Ivar and Hálfdan back in 878. Irish annalists too had recognized early on in the ninth century that viking terror could be practised with devastating efficiency by co-ordinating raids on large tracts of territory from two opposing rivers: AD 837: 'A fleet of 60 ships of Northmen on the Boyne. Another fleet of 60 ships on the River

Liffey. These two fleets plundered the Plain of Liffey and the Plain of Brega—
churches, fortifications and homes.'[47] When Weland led his fleet of 200 ships up
the Seine in 861 and laid siege to a camp of rival Northmen on the island of Oissel,
'meanwhile another group of Danes with 60 ships sailed up the Seine and into the
River *Tellas* and from there they reached those who were besieging the fort and
joined up with them.'[48] Two years previously, 'some of the common people living
between the Seine and Loire formed a sworn association among themselves and
fought bravely against the Danes on the Seine.'[49] These unfortunate people, caught
in a vice between viking armies which infested two great rivers of France, were
eventually slain by their own Frankish aristocracy who perceived their action as a
threat to their own position.

Alfred eventually drove the fleet off which was besieging Exeter, but the Chronicle
does not report its final withdrawal until 894 'when they ravaged up in Sussex near
Chichester, and the citizens (*þa burgware*) put them to flight and killed many
hundreds of them, and captured some of their ships'.[50] As for Æthelweard's
Sigeferð, he almost certainly sailed from Devon to attack the son of Ivar (Sigtryggr
Ivarrson) who was then ruling in Dublin, before he returned to his Northumbrian
base.[51] While Alfred 'was occupied in the west in Devon against the naval force',[52]
the remainder of the English and Mercian defence was engaged in a campaign
extending over 'many weeks'[53] and directed against the main body of invaders. The
great army which had come from Boulogne in 892 had by now moved out of Kent
and was directing long-distance raids against north-western Mercia.

One of the reasons why the narrator of the Chronicle presents a confused
account of Alfred's Last War is that he had to cope with describing a struggle
played out simultaneously on two, if not three, separate fronts. When Alfred had
turned back to defend the western side of his kingdom, he sent a small portion of
his forces forward to join up with the citizens (*mid þæm þurgwarum*) of London in
the defence of the east. The Londoners and their meagre reinforcements now
attacked a Danish fort which Hæsten had previously built at Benfleet in Essex.
Hæsten, we are told, was then out on a raid, but the large army 'was at home'.
That 'large army' consisted of the combined armies from Milton and Appledore,
so that by now the invaders had abandoned East Kent for Essex. The English
stormed the Benfleet fortress and in an unusual glimpse of detail relating to the
interior of a Danish war-camp, we learn of captured ships, goods, women and
children, which the English carried off to London or Rochester.[54] But an even
more dramatic revelation follows in the Chronicle:

And Hæsten's wife and two sons were brought to the king; and he gave them back to him,
because one of them was his godson, and the other the godson of Ealdorman Æthelred.
They had stood sponsor to them before Hæsten came to Benfleet, and he had given the king
oaths and hostages, and the king had also made him generous gifts of money, and so he did
also when he gave back the boy and the woman. But as soon as they came to Benfleet and
had made the fortress, Hæsten ravaged his kingdom, that very province which Æthelred,
his son's godfather, was in charge of; and again a second time, he had gone on a raid in that
same kingdom when his fortress was stormed.[55]

The announcement that Alfred had on some previous occasion stood sponsor to Hæsten's son, comes out of the blue, and would never have been reported had it not been for this unexpected English *coup* in capturing the Benfleet fortress. It means that Alfred had at some earlier time, entered into solemn negotiations with Hæsten in the same way as he had with Guthrum back in 878. There was however, this significant difference, that the baptism of Hæsten's household—unlike that of Guthrum—had not worked, and that is the reason why the Anglo-Saxon chronicler failed to report it in the first instance. We note that while Hæsten was said to have originally given Alfred oaths and hostages, Alfred had given Hæsten 'generous gifts of money (*wel feoh*)'.[56] So, Hæsten had been paid a geld as the price for his withdrawal from Kent—a withdrawal that was as sudden as it is otherwise inexplicable. Had the West Saxons or the Men of Kent forced that withdrawal after a battle or successful siege, the chronicler would not have failed to make the most of such a triumph. When Hæsten had built the fortress at Benfleet, he had gone back on an earlier agreement with Alfred and began raiding Mercian territory which was under Æthelred's rule. It is clear from the Chronicle's account, that by the time Hæsten had reached Benfleet, Ealdorman Æthelred was already godfather (*cumpæder*) to Hæsten's son. This implies that Alfred and Hæsten must have initially reached an agreement when Alfred first marched into Kent and encamped between the Appledore and Milton armies in 892. Alfred had probably been forced to come to a settlement with Hæsten when news reached him of the East Anglian and Northumbrian attack on western Wessex. A speedy settlement with Hæsten, at however high a price, would have freed Alfred's army to set off in defence of the West Country. Those negotiations in Kent had been conducted with the help of Alfred's son-in-law, Ealdorman Æthelred of English Mercia. A further Danegeld was paid over when Alfred restored Hæsten's son and wife to the viking leader after they were captured at Benfleet. Those negotiations in Essex amounted to a renewal of the earlier peace, and although Alfred now had high quality captives to bargain with, he may have felt compelled in the face of superior Danish numbers to come to terms yet again.[57] Alfred was also faced with the wellnigh impossible task of defending the exposed Kentish peninsula, with its metropolitan town of Canterbury, from sea-borne attack. This was a region which was not only difficult to defend, but it was also difficult for West Saxon armies to reach—cut off as it was by the barrier of the Weald.

Our meagre knowledge of Hæsten's Frankish career is sufficient to remind us that this viking was an experienced negotiator, well versed in the workings of Christian diplomacy as practised by the Frankish warrior aristocracy. Hæsten was a hardened looter of Frankish churches from Brissarthe in the west to St Vaast in the east—not to speak of epic escapades in Luna—and he would have come to England with an expert knowledge of Frankish military methods, in addition to his own tried tactics in war. Since Hæsten's Frankish career appears to have begun in the late 860s, he was clearly as old if not older than Alfred. If he had been campaigning in his own right as early as 857, then he was considerably older still. But Hæsten, like other Scandinavian leaders in the Christian West, cannot be dismissed as nothing more than a viking marauder. He had negotiated with Breton leaders, with leading Frankish magnates such as Robert of Anjou and Abbot Rodulf of St Vaast, as well as with Odo king of the Western Franks, and with Louis III. Hæsten may well have gone through the motions of receiving Christianity at the hands of one of those Frankish worthies at some stage in his earlier life. Such a previous 'conversion' would explain why the Chronicle reports that Alfred stood godfather to Hæsten's son, rather than to Hæsten himself. We have seen how Hæsten's Norse contemporaries, Weland and Godafrid, had each accepted Christianity under pressure from Charles the Bald and Charles the Fat respectively.[58] Indeed, were Hæsten to go by his knowledge of earlier Frankish experiences, he might have hoped to marry into the House of Alfred—were we not told in the Chronicle that he was already travelling in the company of a wife. His Norse colleague, Godafrid, had been allowed to marry into the Carolingians after his baptism in 882.[59]

The English capture of Benfleet must have dealt a severe blow to the Danes who had now lost ships and supplies, as well as many of their women and children. The two armies which had been based at Benfleet now withdrew further east along the Thames estuary to a new fortress which they erected at Shoebury, where they were joined by a 'great reinforcement (*micel eaca*)' from the East Anglian and Northumbrian Danes. Their tactics continued to replicate those of Guthrum in the Second War—launching expeditions over the next two years against distant and presumably vulnerable targets—all in the same region—in the hope of outmanœuvring the native defence. While Guthrum's target had been north-western Wessex, the latest area singled out for attack was north-west Mercia. The invaders, who according to Æthelweard were led, yet again, by Hæsten,[60] moved up the Thames 'until they reached the Severn, then up along the Severn' to Buttington.[61] Here the Northmen were successfully pinned down in their fortress by a combined army of Mercian and West Saxon defenders. The English side was led by Ealdorman Æthelred of Mercia along with the West Saxon ealdormen, Æthelhelm of Wiltshire and Æthelnoth of Somerset, who led a contingent of thegns and warriors 'from every borough east of the Parret, and both east and west of Selwood'. The Mercians came from 'north of the Thames and west of the Severn' and were joined also by 'some portion of the Welsh people'.[62] The West Saxon leadership at Buttington had been placed in the hands of men who were close to Alfred. Æthelhelm, the ealdorman of Wiltshire, led the embassy which took the alms of 'King Alfred and the West Saxons' to Rome in 887.[63] Ealdorman Æthelnoth was a veteran of the viking wars who, according to the chronicler Æthelweard, had shared Alfred's hardships while 'he lurked in a certain wood with a small force' in Somerset back in 878. That same chronicler also tells us that Ealdorman Æthelnoth led an embassy from King Alfred to the Danes of York in 894. Alfred's objective may have been to establish peace along a border between English Mercia and the Northern Danelaw which at this time stretched south across Lincolnshire as far as the Welland and Kesteven.[64] The English laid siege to Buttington by blockading the Danish fortress on the two sides (*on twa healfe*) of the Severn, which surely implies that the vikings had deployed some ships on this expedition—a conclusion supported by their stated route 'along the Thames . . . and up along the Severn'.[65]

After a siege of 'many weeks' those vikings who had not died of hunger were reduced to eating their horses to avert starvation. A final desperate attempt on the part of the Northmen to break out on the east side of the river ended in their defeat. On the English side 'Ordheah and many other king's thegns' were slain in the desperate struggle at Buttington, and some of the vikings managed to escape by flight back to Essex. But the English carried the day in a most decisive military victory of this war, inflicting 'a very great slaughter' on their enemies. The survivors soon regrouped in Essex, and with the help of further East Anglian and Northumbrian reinforcements, they returned to the attack in the north-west. Moving 'continuously by day and night', before the onset of winter, they occupied Chester 'a deserted city in the Wirral'.[66] As in the case of Alfred's failure to keep the Danes out of Exeter in 877, so now 'the English army could not overtake them [the Danes] before they were inside the fortress'.[67] But the English succeeded in seizing precious stocks of cattle and an abundance of corn outside the fortifications at Chester, and in slaying viking stragglers whom they also found outside. The English siege was apparently abandoned after only two days. In the following spring of 894, the Chester vikings were driven by want of supplies to attack the nearby Welsh and returned with their spoils through Danish held Northumbria and East Anglia where 'the English army could not reach them' until they gained the safety of east Essex and Mersea Island 'which is out in the sea'.[68] The next sortie out of Essex also involved the following of boundaries between English and Danish territory, when in the late autumn or early winter of 894, the vikings 'rowed their ships up the Thames and up the Lea'. As on previous expeditions, they placed their women for safety in East Anglia before they left.[69] Late in 894, they made a fortress by the Lea, 20 miles above London. The object of this exercise seems to have been to procure corn supplies for a great army which had still failed to conquer any territory. In the summer of 895, 'a great part of the citizens (*burgwara*)'—presumably from London—'and also of other people' tried unsuccessfully to dislodge the vikings from the fort on the Lea. The English lost four king's thegns in the struggle. Alfred now arrived with an army in the autumn— probably in early August—so that 'while they [the English] were reaping their corn, the Danes could not deny the people that harvest'.[70] Alfred, on examining the river, began constructing two forts, one on either side of the Lea, with the object of preventing the vikings from taking their ships out along the river with impunity. No sooner had this work begun, than the Danes abandoned their fortress and their ships and struck off for Bridgnorth on the Severn. The Danes, were almost certainly horsed, and we are told that 'the English army rode after the enemy'.

The Danes spent the winter of 895–6 in Bridgnorth, and for a reason which we are not told, they departed thence from English territory in the summer of 896. As ever, they may have been paid off by Alfred and by Æthelred of Mercia. Alfred is likely to have been present at Bridgnorth, before the Danish departure from there, since he had been in command at the Lea and since we know his English army had followed the enemy to the Severn. But the admission that Alfred paid the Danes off yet again to leave his kingdom would have made such an inglorious ending to a campaign, that it could never have been admitted by the compiler of the Anglo-Saxon Chronicle. The reason for the abrupt ending of Alfred's Last War survives as a glaring omission in the Chronicle, and we may even detect an attempt at a cover-up on the part of the compiler, who in spite of his obsession with the detailed recording of Danish movements would have us believe that everything which he had already described was of little consequence:

[896]: Afterwards in the summer of this year the Danish army [at Bridgnorth] divided, one force going into East Anglia and one into Northumbria; and those that were moneyless (*feohlease*) got themselves ships and went south across the sea to the Seine.

By the grace of God the army had not on the whole afflicted the English people very greatly; but they were much more seriously afflicted in those three years by the mortality of cattle and men, and most of all in that many of the best king's thegns who were in the land died in those three years.[71]

Those who accept this record at its face value fall victims to the classic format of the chroniclers' style of reporting. If the deaths of Alfred's thegns from disease, and the scourge of cattle-plague had been the real problem facing the West Saxons, then why the extraordinarily detailed account of a Danish war which threatened not only the survival of Kent, Essex, and English Mercia, but which clearly also destabilized that hard-won settlement which Alfred had achieved with the Danelaw in the years following 878? Besides, not all of Alfred's magnates had died of the pestilence. Ordheah 'and many other king's thegns' fell at Buttington in 893; four more king's thegns were slain on the Lea in 895; and in 896 Alfred lost his reeve Lucuman, his *geneat* or household thegn, Æthelfrith, together with 62 Frisian and English warrior-sailors in a debacle on the coast. The chronicler, who in this record identifies with Alfred's point of view—(in the assessment of the loss of Alfred's thegns)—is consciously trying to minimize the significance of Hæsten's invasion. He may have done so in the knowledge that repeated payments of Danegeld had finally bought that enemy off. A final and substantial settlement in supplies, money, and precious metal is consonant both with the dispersal of the army among the Northumbrian and East Anglian Danish colonists and with the departure of the remainder overseas to Francia. Such a dispersal is consistent with a final settlement at the end of a long campaign which was clearly acceptable to both sides. It virtually replicates the withdrawal and dispersal of Danish armies from Wessex at the end of the Second War in 880. The Last War had not ended indecisively as many historians have assumed. Its ending was little different from that of the struggle with Guthrum. Invaders who had failed to effect a conquest of territory, but who were still a force to be reckoned with, had been bought off, and while most then withdrew from Wessex into the Danelaw, a number of others departed overseas.

The statement that 'the army had not on the whole afflicted the English people very greatly' is part of the special pleading which is a hallmark of the Chronicle's less than honest reporting. Although the defences of Rochester had held firm against the invaders in 885, the East Kent peninsula must have suffered significantly from viking raiding later on in the Last War. The location of Danish bases at Appledore and Milton were suggestive of a deliberate plan to unite Kent to a greater coastal Danelaw stretching from the Straits of Dover through East Anglia to eastern Northumbria.

Æthelweard, whose source at this point was more interested in the fate of Wessex than of Kent, reported that the invaders 'gradually wasted the adjacent provinces of Hampshire and Berkshire'.[72] The Chronicle speaks of raiding parties 'in small bands' and 'in full force'[73] setting out from Kentish bases, and it speaks, too, of Hæsten twice ravaging Ealdorman Æthelred's territory from Benfleet.[74] Most of these raids were probably directed at seizing food supplies, but to appreciate their effect on the local population it is salutary to compare how the annalist at St Vaast viewed the impact of those same followers of Hæsten on the inhabitants of the Somme basin in 884:

The Northmen did not desist from the slaying and taking captive of Christians, tearing down churches, razing fortifications to the ground and burning settlements. On all the streets lay the corpses of clerics, of nobles and of other lay people, of women, young people, and sucklings. There was no street or place where the dead did not lie, and it was for everyone a torment and a pain to see how Christian people had been brought to the point of extermination.[75]

Two years earlier, in 882, Regino described an attack by Northmen on the monastery of Prüm on Twelfth Night. We are told that local peasants were slaughtered by a rampaging enemy who behaved like brute beasts rather than men.[76] Too many modern commentators on viking culture appear to have overlooked the fact that ninth-century Northmen were as yet unaware of the terms of the Geneva Convention. And while the same might be said of the native defending population, they were nevertheless under some social and moral pressure to observe Christian ethics in relation to violence and the inherent dignity of the human person. Ironically, the Anglo-Saxon chronicler's deliberate policy of suppressing details of the devastation and suffering endured at the hands of the Danes in England has helped to promote an unrealistic and distorted image of viking practice in the ninth century, on the part of revisionist historians. We are given no details in the Chronicle of the destruction caused by the Northumbrian and East Anglian Danes when they kept Alfred pinned down in Western Wessex for 'many weeks' in 893. Common sense suggests that such a large force of 140 ships' crews required a constant stream of provisions either by way of tribute, or else from the pillaging of foraging parties. Persistent sorties by the main force of invaders up the Thames and across to the Severn basin meant that ecclesiastical centres in the dioceses of Worcester, Hereford (Archenfield), and the Wrekin, lay at the mercy of raiders who were in search of more substantial loot.

The concentration of Danish attacks on northern and western Mercia during the Last War conforms to an overall pattern of raiding which indicates that the same coherent strategy was pursued by successive bands of invaders in Wessex and Mercia from the first attacks by the Great Army in 871 down to Hæsten's campaigns of 896. In essence an on-going parasitic strategy was pursued, whereby the main targets for attack were isolated for their raiding or settlement potential, and once targeted, such areas were usually avoided by subsequent invaders in favour of more untouched territory, which was capable of yielding more substantial loot. It will be seen from Map 9 how during the period from 871 to 896 successive areas of Wessex and Mercia were milked of loot and tribute, while the same regions were seldom squeezed twice. During the First War, Berkshire, northern Hampshire, and Surrey found themselves in the front line of the Great Army while it was encamped at Reading and London (1A and 1B). During the Second War, the areas targeted were located further to the south and west—south Hampshire and east Dorset lay at the mercy of the Wareham garrison (2A), while western Wessex later yielded up its Danegeld to garrisons at Exeter (2B), north Devon (2C), and Chippenham (2D). The Last War did indeed see a repetition of the earlier western Wessex campaign of 878, but the Chronicle reports that second episode as a diversion to keep Alfred out of the main struggle which concentrated first on Kent and the south-east, and later on the north-west Midlands. The centre of Hæsten's operations carefully avoided territories which had been already squeezed dry by previous invaders. In this final struggle with Alfred, Kent was ravaged from Appledore (3A) and Milton (3B); Essex from Benfleet, Shoebury, and Mersea (3C), and Mercia from Buttington (3D), Chester (3E), and Bridgnorth (3F). Because of its exposed position and the tempting offshore bases on Sheppey and Thanet, Kent may have suffered from more minor raiding in the past than many other regions. Kent had experienced viking raids in 841, 842, 851, 853, 855, and 865. But it was not until 892 that the Chronicle—which had followed the progress of the Great Heathen Army in remarkable detail from its initial landing in East Anglia in 866—reported a major campaign in Kent. Areas singled out for concentrated viking attack were mutually exclusive over the period of the three wars during Alfred's reign. At the very least, we must conclude that successive leaders of invading armies took the record of earlier campaigns into account, and pursued an essentially parasitic strategy of milking regions which, because of their relatively untouched state, were more likely to yield a higher booty in terms of church plate and agricultural supplies. Such evidence which is retrievable from the detailed narrative of the Danish wars in the Anglo-Saxon Chronicle is consistent with information on raiding patterns in contemporary Irish annals. In those sources too, we find evidence for a spread of raiding activity calculated to maximize on the booty to be gained during the ninth century. In the tenth century, on the other hand, when the Northmen settled down to consolidate their hold over Irish coastal towns, we find them working the Christian calendar to their advantage by systematically raiding monastic houses on or around the patron's feastday, while carefully avoiding the outright destruction of the monastic communities which provided them with their source of loot in the first instance.[77] Ninth-century

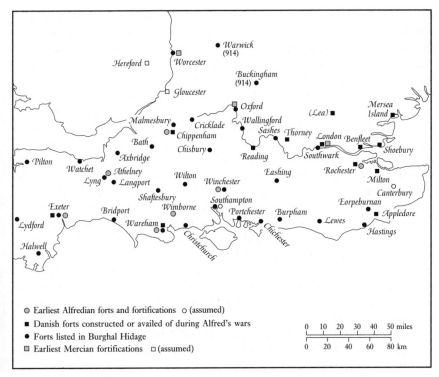

MAP 8. Fortifications from the reign of King Alfred

raiding was much more destructive than in the tenth century for several reasons. The great armies which invaded with the intention of winning territory in the mid-ninth century had to procure supplies urgently or risk rapid starvation. Their descendants who had settled down in the Danelaw and in Dublin during the tenth century were operating from the security of settled bases from which they had developed agricultural and trading links, and other social and religious connections, with neighbouring indigenous societies. Heathen armies of the mid-to late ninth century were not constrained by any such developed relationships with their host communities, and levels of violence and destruction of life and property must have been commensurately higher during that earlier phase of invasion.

Hæsten's ultimate objective was surely colonization. His forts at Benfleet, Shoebury, and Mersea Island were sited progressively closer to the Danish fall-back position in East Anglia, but they were all significantly outside East Anglia proper, and within Essex. Æthelweard specifically states that Benfleet in 885 was 'outside their [the Danes] own boundaries'.[78] But Hæsten's men needed food before they could satisfy their greed for territory, and so the drive for loot and provisions went hand in hand with attempts at conquest. The Chronicle reveals that the stand-off between Alfred's army and the Danes on the Lea in 895 was triggered by a desire on the part of Danes and English alike to seize a crucial corn harvest in that region. So, too, the Danish occupation of Chester in 893 was foiled due to the destruction of their cattle and corn. The far-flung Danish obsession with Buttington, Chester, and Bridgnorth was consistent with a policy aimed at attacking hitherto unexploited territory, and with looting from ecclesiastical centres such as Worcester, Hereford, and Much Wenlock. The distance of these places from the secure Danish bases at Shoebury or on Mersea in coastal Essex obscures the fact that they could be reached in relative safety by way of major rivers which ran along or near to the frontier with the newly established Danelaw. The invaders did succeed in carrying their booty from Wales and elsewhere safely back to Essex by returning through the Northumbrian and East Anglian Danelaw where 'the English army could not reach them'.[79] The only positive piece of information offered on Welsh involvement in this struggle is the Chronicle's statement that 'some portion of the (northern) Welsh people (*sum dæl þæs Norð wealcynnes*)' joined the Mercian and English coalition at Buttington.[80] Hæsten's personal experience of fighting alongside Bretons against a common Frankish enemy in the late 860s must have made him aware of similar ancient ethnic hatreds between Welsh and English that could be exploited in any campaign directed at overrunning north-western Mercia. Had the region from Bridgnorth to Chester been conquered by Hæsten, it would have formed a continuum with the Northumbrian Danelaw on the one hand, and with Danish Mercia as ceded earlier to Guthrum, on the other.

A superficial look at the Chronicle's record of Alfred's Last War presents us with the picture of a great army of Danes engaged in frenetic activity which alternated between the Kentish and Essex sides of the Thames Estuary, on the one hand, and far-off Buttington and Chester, on the other. We are also presented with the fact that Alfred was unable to claim personal credit for a single military victory in this war, unless we include his chasing the Danes away from Exeter in 893, and earlier from Rochester in 885. He was conspicuously absent from the successful English assault on Hæsten's camp at Benfleet, and he played no personal role in the English victory at Buttington—all of which happened in that same year. Buttington was a greater military triumph than Edington, since it entailed not only the siege of a Danish fort, but the routing of the starving survivors who were forced to make a desperate stand there. Æthelweard, in an unusual comment on the Alfredian period, informs us that 'these events, which occurred at Buttington, are vaunted by ancient men'.[81] Buttington was that 'English victory over the Danes in which countless numbers were slain'—a rare contemporary Irish comment on events in late ninth-century England.[82] But Alfred had no part in Buttington—he was then busy pursuing an elusive Northumbrian and East Anglian enemy across western Wessex.

It might be argued that Hæsten's hordes had become a weakened and demoralized force before they arrived in England in 892. Even if the men who made up the army which invaded Kent had not had personal experience of the Frankish victories at Saucourt in 881 and on the Dyle in 891, where the vikings suffered heavy losses, a case might be made for holding that the invaders of Kent had abandoned Francia, ultimately, because of those defeats.[83] But the outcome of Saucourt was ambiguous even in the eyes of contemporary commentators. Hincmar, although he conceded that Louis III, king of the Western Franks, was initially victorious at Saucourt, claims the Frankish army eventually fled from the field,[84] and although the Annals of Fulda record the destruction of 9,000 viking horsemen, that same source reports: 'they renewed their army and increased the number of their horsemen and pillaged many places', including the palace of Aachen where they were said to have stabled their horses in Charlemagne's palace chapel.[85] The battle at Saucourt had been intended by the Franks to put a stop to viking atrocities and raiding on the Somme which had resulted in the capture and occupation by the Northmen of the town of Amiens and the monastery of Corbie. There is no good evidence to show that Saucourt, in spite of being hailed by some as a great Frankish victory,[86] had seriously checked that particular offensive in the longer term. By the end of the next decade, viking activity had intensified between the Somme and the Maas to the extent that outright conquest of some of that region must have seemed within the Northmen's grasp. Their defeat on the Dyle at the hands of Arnulf must have given the invaders a temporary setback, but their immediate reason for abandoning Francia was not military defeat but 'a mighty famine and blight on the earth (*fames valida et sterilitas terrae*)' which drove even the natives off the soil.[87] A famine and crop-failure which drove out the local peasantry would indeed prove disastrous for huge armies on the move and constantly in need of supplies. We are reminded of how Edward the Elder drove out 'a great naval force' which had attacked the Severn Estuary from Brittany in 914. Because the garrisons of Edward's forts from Cornwall to Avonmouth prevented the invaders from foraging on the south side of the Severn Estuary, the invaders 'became very short of food and many men had died of hunger because they could not obtain any food' and so they set off for Dyfed in South Wales and eventually they headed out towards Ireland in that autumn.[88] The large size of many marauding viking armies is confirmed by their crucial need to maintain a food supply. England held out the prospect of loot and provisions in 892, and with much of the land already conquered and settled by Danish warlords, it must have offered even better hopes of land to settle than the crumbling Carolingian empire. But England, as the Alfredian Chronicle reminds us, had its own taste of natural disasters in the form of plagues which attacked humans and cattle. The English epidemic may have been related to a cattle and sheep plague which first struck in Francia during the severe winter of 887,[89] but whose effects were still being felt in Wessex in 896.[90]

Subsequent disasters which befell Hæsten and his fellow vikings in England at Benfleet and Buttington in 893 must have considerably reduced the threat posed by the invaders. It is dangerous, however, to take the Anglo-Saxon chronicler's narrative too much at its face value, or at least to ignore the issues which the chronicler did not wish his readers to take into account. So, if we were to take the record of events at Buttington, as the Anglo-Saxon chronicler wished us to see them, we would assume that the Danes there had been reduced to ruin. We are shown an enemy decimated by hunger and with survivors reduced to eating horses. Yet those same survivors managed to break through Anglo-Saxon lines, slaying many king's thegns in the process, and some subsequently succeeded in returning to their base in Essex. Either the numbers who returned to Essex were very large, or only a small raiding party had set off for Buttington in the first instance. For before the onset of winter in that same year (893) those same Essex Danes were crossing England once more to occupy Chester. None of this suggests that they had received a body blow at Buttington. We are reminded of the Frankish siege of the Danish fort at Asselt when Charles the Fat surrounded that place for twelve days with an immense army.[91] The account of that siege shows that the hardships inflicted on the Northmen within were also endured by the besieging army without 'which began to fall ill and be nauseated by the putrefaction of many corpses'.[92] Besieging armies in the ninth and tenth centuries faced the same problems in relation to disease and in securing a food supply necessary to sustain an army over two weeks or for as long as a siege endured. The English besiegers at Buttington may have only fared marginally better than their victims, and it is significant that the English siege of the vikings in Chester was lifted after only two days. Just as the beleaguered Danes at Buttington appear to have survived in substantial numbers to fight another day, so too, at Asselt in Francia, Godafrid and his Northmen, although apparently reduced to dire straits, were still capable of negotiating highly favourable conditions with Charles the Fat.[93] On balance, when we review the evidence for Alfred's Last War, it is not safe to conclude that the numbers of Danish invaders was low or that they had been decisively weakened either at Benfleet or at Buttington.

One of the more telling indications of the seemingly endless numbers of invaders who descended on Kent and Essex in 892 is the mention in the Anglo-Saxon Chronicle of their ships. Not only does the Chronicle record the largest tally of viking warships during Alfred's Last War—there is nothing comparable for the reign of his son Edward or for that of his grandson Athelstan—but the Chronicle also refers to the breaking up of enemy ships by the English defenders. So, when the English overran the Northmen's fort at Benfleet 'they either broke up or burnt all the ships, or brought them to London or to Rochester'.[94] When the invaders abandoned their ships in their fort on the Lea, two years later in 895, 'the men from London fetched the ships, and broke up all which they could not bring away, and brought to London those which were serviceable.'[95] The impression gained is that the number of ships far exceeded the needs of the native English who wisely resorted to burning and smashing the greatest single asset of their enemies. Irish annals of the early tenth century show that in that country, too, not only native kings, but Norsemen also resorted to breaking up the captured ships of their viking enemies.[96] The proliferation of viking ships in southern England in the period 892–6 is suggestive of very large numbers of invaders, for while those ships were surplus to native English requirements they must have been necessary to invaders who otherwise would not have taken them on hazardous expeditions. The Chronicle's statement that vikings from the Northumbrian and East Anglian Danelaw who harried the south coast of Wessex in 896, sailed 'in warships which they had built many years before' suggests that every available vessel was being pressed into service. In Francia, too, there is every reason to believe that ubiquitous viking long-ships were all in commission and necessary to ferry the large numbers of marauders who were on the move there in the second half of the ninth century. Otherwise there would have been no necessity for invading armies to spend months repairing their warships on the Seine in 862[97] or for repairing old ones and building new ones on that same river in 866.[98] So, while English military successes at Benfleet, Buttington, and on the Lea must have weakened the Danish position, the invaders, as in Francia, were sufficiently numerous and stubborn, to fight back with ever greater determination. And whatever reverses they had suffered, those were not sufficient to deter the invaders from launching their third sortie across England from Essex to Bridgnorth in 895–6. That final expedition and the subsequent threefold dispersion—to East Anglia, Northumbria, and to the Seine—bespeaks the breaking up of a great army which was, up until this time, still largely intact. Attempts to argue away viking numbers, to massage statistics in relation to sizes of fleets and their crews, as well as revisionist attempts to diminish the impact of viking barbarity—none of these approaches offer a convincing explanation for the conclusion of Alfred's Last War. We must seek elsewhere then, for the key to the ultimate West Saxon success in removing Hæsten's threat from Alfred's kingdom.

The key to West Saxon success—and one for which Alfred himself must be given credit—lies in the effectiveness of West Saxon fortifications. The precise contribution of Alfred to the construction of fortifications within Wessex is unnecessarily clouded by the dating of a document known as the *Burghal Hidage* which is quite properly assigned in its present form to the reign of Alfred's son, Edward the Elder. The *Burghal Hidage*, which consists of a list of forts designed to protect Wessex from attack, contains information on the number of hides apportioned for the maintenance of each burh. The hidal allocation was in turn related to the size of the perimeter wall of the burh. The document as it stands can date no earlier than 911, since it contains Oxford in its list—a town annexed by Edward the Elder on the death of Æthelred of Mercia in that year.[99] It may have been completed in its present form before 919 because of the absence of the majority of Mercian burhs from the list. English Mercia did not fall into Edward's hands until after the death of his sister, Æthelflæd, Lady of the Mercians in 918, and after Edward's deposing of her daughter Ælfwynn, in the following year.[100] The inclusion of Buckingham (if it is not an interpolation) suggests the list as it stands must be post-914, the year in which the two Buckingham burhs were built by Edward.[101] Although many historians would accept that the *Burghal Hidage* in its original form must date from Alfred's time—or that the West Saxon burhs which make up the bulk of the document were built in Alfred's reign—nevertheless, the Edwardian date of the document as it stands has served to obscure Alfred's single most important contribution to English military and economic history. The truth is, we are not dependent on the *Burghal Hidage* to show that Alfred initiated fortress building in Wessex. All those writers who are familiar with the Alfredian wars point to the half-finished English fortress near Appledore which the Danes seized in 892. But that is only one example—and a poor example—of Alfredian

fortress building whose origins go back to the war with Guthrum. We have seen
how Wareham and Exeter may well have been given Alfredian defences some time
before 875–6 and how the evidence for an Alfredian fort at Chippenham in 878 is
ambiguous.[102] On the other hand, Alfred's construction of a fort at Athelney after
Easter 878 is beyond question, as was his adoption of a defensive strategy, moving
away from risking his warriors in a pitched battle or from trying to dislodge vikings
from their own defended positions. A viking army which briefly attacked Kent in
885 laid siege to Rochester, whose defences held until Alfred arrived with an army
and drove the invaders back to their ships. Exeter, in 893, also successfully withstood a viking siege, which suggests that the crumbling Roman walls of those
towns had been put in a proper state of defence under Alfred's supervision. The
same must surely have been true of Canterbury, for had the invaders of 885—and
even more so, those of 892–3—been able to storm that town, they would most
certainly have done so, and the Chronicle, in spite of its damning proneness to
silence, could scarcely have ignored such a disaster. Canterbury with the wealth of
its metropolitan church, and caught between two viking armies, would have been
a glittering prize for vikings to seize. We have even more definite evidence not only
for the existence of burhs in Wessex by 893, but also for the organization of their
defence. The Chronicle tells us in the annal for 893 that 'the king had divided his
army into two, so that always half its men were at home, half on service, apart from
the men who guarded the forts (*burga*)'.[103] Whether or not we regard this as a
twofold or threefold division of Alfred's army, we must accept that already the
king had detailed a specific section of his army for the defence of his forts and
fortified towns. In other words, by 893, fortifications were no longer isolated
experiments in Alfredian defence, but had become part of an established system.
Garrisons attached to a *geweorc* or a *burg* need not necessarily have been a static
force anchored in their fortresses. The English army at Buttington drew on 'the
king's thegns who then were at home at the fortresses (*æt þæm geweorcum*) [and
who] assembled from every fort (*burg*) east of the Parret, and both west and east
of Selwood, and also north of the Thames and west of the Severn'.[104]

It is very possible that western forts listed in the *Burghal Hidage* such as
Watchet, Lyng, Langport, Axbridge, Bath, Malmesbury, and Cricklade were already in running order and capable of sending men on a distant expedition as far
as Buttington in 893. When Alfred's nephew Æthelwold was disputing the kingship with Alfred's son, Edward, in 903, he incited the East Anglian Danes to attack
as far as Cricklade.[105] That would have been a pointless exercise, not worthy of
mention in the Chronicle, were it not already a fortified outpost of Wessex in north
Wiltshire and on the Mercian border. Earlier, in late 899 or early 900, Æthelwold
began his challenge to Edward by seizing the residence (*ham*) at *Tweoxneam* or
Christchurch in Hampshire.[106] The place is listed in the *Burghal Hidage* and was
presumably already fortified when Æthelwold chose to make a stand there. So too,
Chichester, which appears in the *Burghal Hidage*, is mentioned in connection with
its 'citizens' or *burgware* who drove off Danish attackers in 894. But *burgware* who
slaughtered Danes and who captured their all-important ships were no ordinary

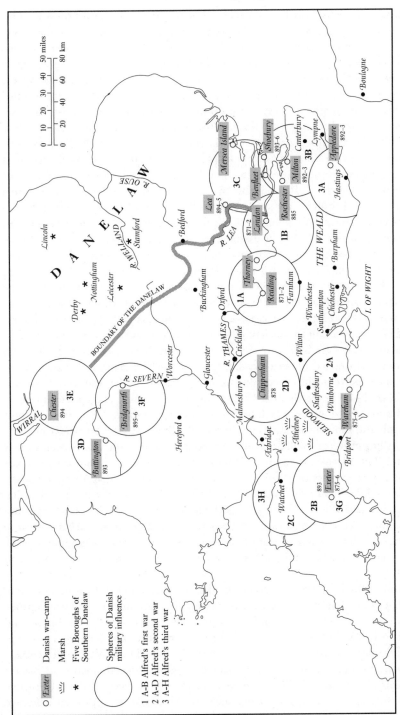

MAP 9. Geographical distribution of Danish wars in the reign of King Alfred

citizens—they must have been the men specifically detailed to guard the *burg*. This term *burgware*—also used of Londoners who attacked a Danish fort on the Lea in 895—is surely further evidence that Alfredian towns had already been provided with their own special defending force by 894–5. While it would be wrong to assume that all *Burghal Hidage* forts were post-Alfredian, it would be equally mistaken to assume that only places listed in the *Burghal Hidage* were fortified centres in late ninth- or early tenth-century Wessex. All the Kentish forts are absent from the list, as are the fortified towns of Canterbury and Rochester. It is difficult to accept that Eashing, which is in the *Burghal Hidage* list, was the only strong point in the whole of Surrey. Its presence in the list was probably due to its status as an estate once owned by King Alfred and which he left in his *Will*, to his nephew, Æthelhelm.[107] It is possible that such forts were only one of several in a neighbourhood, which were singled out in the *Burghal Hidage* for administrative purposes as centres providing garrisons for the defence of an entire locality. So Godalming which lay close to Eashing in Surrey, and where there was also an estate which belonged to Alfred, may have had its own defences. We know that Athelney was fortified, but it is absent from the *Burghal Hidage* and was covered no doubt by the organizational defences of nearby Lyng. We know too, from the Chronicle's account of the succession crisis that followed Alfred's death, that by 899 Wimborne had a fortress capable of withstanding an attack, and that Edward the Elder made use of the ancient defences of nearby Badbury Rings in Dorset.[108] Wimborne may have been a royal residence or *ham*, but it was also provided with gates (*geatu*) which could be defended (*forworht*). Malmesbury and Wareham had their forts, as we might expect, due to their situation on the frontiers of Wessex, which are listed in the *Burghal Hidage*. But other monastic and episcopal centres in addition to Wimborne, which like it are absent from the *Burghal Hidage*, almost certainly had some fortifications by the end of Alfred's reign. Canterbury not only had its line of Roman walls, but its metropolitan cathedral may have been already defended in Alfredian times by an inner fortification which took advantage in part of the city's perimeter wall. Finally, the Chronicle informs us that Alfred personally supervised the building of two forts on the River Lea, 20 miles north of London in 895,[109] and that it was the king himself who studied the layout of the terrain and chose the exact siting for those fortifications. If Alfred paid so much attention to fortress building outside of Wessex proper, it is a reasonable assumption that he had already developed an elaborate network of fortresses throughout Wessex and Kent.

While Alfred deserves full credit for the introduction of fortress building into ninth-century England, the king can scarcely have invented that idea independently of his Danish enemies and of his Frankish neighbours, for the Franks and migratory Danes made greater use of fortifications in warfare than the English of the late ninth century. Early medieval fortress building in the West was essentially Carolingian led, and ultimately Roman in origin. Although there had been a developed tradition of building defensive earthworks in the Celtic and Germanic Iron Age, the notion of integrating such structures into an organized defensive strategy, involving regular manning and provisioning, was alien to barbarian tradition. Alien also to that heroic tradition was the concept of using fortifications as a more effective alternative to deciding military issues than in a pitched battle. So, although the Bernician royal centre at Bamborough was built on a defensive site, the splendid Northumbrian halls at Yeavering were not fortified.[110] King Cynewulf of Wessex was cornered in a *burh* at *Merantune* in 757, which was defended by locked gates (*gatu*). But the place was unlikely to have been a fortress capable of protecting an army or withstanding a siege. It was a secure but modest place, where warriors emerged to confront their attackers and fought to the last man.[111] It cannot be suggested that the Danes had fully absorbed or appreciated the potential for the use of forts in holding down a conquered territory or in the defence of their own. But it is clear from a comparative study of Irish, Anglo-Saxon, and Frankish sources, that by the middle of the ninth century, the vikings had come to appreciate the elementary advantages of fighting in large numbers from defended positions—a military development which was completely at variance with the bravado of pitched battles as purveyed in their own heroic literature. The Danes, who of all the Scandinavians were nearest neighbours to the Carolingians, had adopted the use of fortifications by the early ninth century. The building of the Danevirke—a great earthen barrier, crossing south Slesvig between the Danes and Charlemagne's empire, is graphically described in the Royal Frankish Annals under the year 808.[112] That colossal earthwork—or series of earthworks—which was master-minded by the Danish king, Gothfrith, provides ample testimony to the effective use of fortifications and the necessary organization to build them on such a huge scale by the early ninth century. The initial impetus for the use of forts in ninth-century Scandinavia must have come from the Carolingians, although by the late tenth century, it is very probable that powerful Ottonian and Byzantine influences were also taking hold. For although the forts at Trelleborg, Aggersborg, Fyrkat, and at Nonnebjerg in Odense all appear to date from the late tenth-century onwards,[113]—and may owe much to Byzantium—we do have formidable earlier contemporary evidence for the building of forts and war-camps by ninth-century Scandinavian invaders in the Christian West. In Ireland we have examples of ambitious permanent defences such as the ship-fortress built at Dublin in 841[114] or field forts such as that of Olaf which was sacked at Clondalkin in 867[115] or the fort at Cenn Fuait built by Sitric the grandson of Ivar in 916.[116] Turges, perhaps the most notorious and at one time the most effective of viking leaders who ever attacked Ireland, is reported to have erected a *dún* or fortress on an island in Lough Ree in 845, from which he devastated the monasteries of Connaught and Mide.[117] In Francia we read of the impressive viking fortress at Asselt 'surrounded by a wall'[118] or of a fort built by vikings on the Dyle in 891 where they 'after their fashion, surrounded it by a fortified ditch (*municione septa*)'.[119] The Norse army which descended suddenly on Rochester in 885 laid siege to the town and 'made other fortifications (*fæsten*) round themselves'.[120]—a tactic reminiscent of that employed by perhaps the very same army at Noyon in 890, when they 'set up their camp (*castra*) opposite the town'.[121] Milton, Appledore, Benfleet, Shoebury, and the fort on the Lea were all fortresses of Danish construction during Alfred's Last War. Earlier, as we have seen, they had taken up defensive positions at York, Nottingham, Reading, and London. It was the Danes who first introduced fortress building into England and it was to Alfred's credit that he began aping his enemies in this respect and adopted their type of defensive warfare.

The first real indication that Alfred had moved away from fighting pitched battles and had switched to guerrilla-like warfare, carried on from a defensive position, comes with the record of his building of a fort at Athelney back in 878. While Alfred may have been compelled by circumstances and by successive defeats to rethink West Saxon strategy in his war of survival against the Danes, the idea of fort building came to him simultaneously from two quite different directions. He could unquestionably see that from the very beginning, Danish tactics of occupying York, Nottingham, and Reading had the decided advantage for the invaders of drawing out native defenders and placing defending armies in a most vulnerable position. It was a successful tactic which had led to the collapse of the Northumbrian kingdom in 867. Already at the outset of the Second War, we see Alfred being wary of trying to prise Guthrum and his army from their position in Wareham. But the progression from avoiding direct confrontation with his enemies to building forts for the waging of Alfred's own defensive campaign may have been inspired as much by contemporary Frankish practice, as by Danish example.

Einhard refers to Charlemagne's strong points and coastguard stations (*stationibus et excubiis dispositis*) at those river-mouths which were considered large enough for the entry of Norse longships,[122] and the policy of maintaining coastal defences against Norse attack was maintained by Louis the Pious.[123] Louis maintained a fortress at the imperial centre at Nijmegen which acted as a shield to protect the town of Dorestad from viking attack.[124] The Carolingians employed fortifications in their struggles with each other, as when Louis the German prevented Louis the Pious from crossing the Rhine by occupying forts (*castella*) on the other side of that river.[125] It was Alfred's older contemporary Charles the Bald, who when faced with the infestation of his West Frankish kingdom by competing viking armies, finally met this challenge by the judicious building of bridges and forts at key places along major rivers. In 862 Charles 'followed some indispensable advice' and rebuilt a bridge across the Marne at Trilbardou and stationed troops to guard both banks of the Marne.[126] Three years later in 865, 'on the advice of his faithful men' Charles repaired bridges on the Oise and Marne and set guards on both banks of the Seine.[127] The remarkable emphasis and repeated references accorded by the Annals of St Bertin to a fort built by Charles on the Seine at Pont-de-l'Arche downstream from Pîtres in 862 shows how the construction of that fortress was seen as a turning-point in the viking wars in Francia:

Charles caused all the leading men (*primores*) of his realm to assemble about 1 June, with many workmen and carts, at the place called Pîtres, where the Andelle from one side and the Eure from the other flow into the Seine. By constructing fortifications on the Seine he closed it off to ships sailing up or down the river. This was done because of the Northmen.[128]

Four years later, Charles was relentlessly consolidating his fortifications at Pîtres: 'Charles marched to the place called Pîtres with workmen and carts to complete the fortifications, so that the Northmen might never again be able to get up the Seine beyond that point.'[129] When Charles visited Pîtres two years later, in 868, 'he measured out the fort into sections of a certain number of feet, and assigned responsibility for them to various men of his realm'.[130] In the following year the garrison and maintenance programme had been worked out in more detail:

Charles gave orders that there should be sent to Pîtres one young warrior (*haistaldus*) for every 100 manses, and a cart with two oxen for every 1000 manses . . . These young men were to complete and then guard the fort which the king had ordered to be built at Pîtres out of wood and stone.[131]

A Carolingian capitulary issued from Pîtres in that same year also dealt with the business of fortifications.[132] By 873, when Charles had overcome his remaining viking enemies at Angers, 'the new fort (*castellum novum*) at Pîtres' had by then become a key part of the Frankish military landscape.[133] The construction of this ambitious fortress at a crucial point in the Seine, between 862 and 866, ensured the security of the heartland of Charles's kingdom for the rest of his reign and may well have been instrumental in deflecting viking in-roads away from Western Francia and on to coastal Frisia and to England, which was invaded by the Great Army of Danes in 866.[134]

The steps taken by Charles to block viking access to Frankish rivers were largely replicated by Alfred some twenty-five to thirty years later. Charles's campaign of bridge-building, the guarding of rivers on both banks, and the building of forts on river banks in conjunction with fortified bridges—all reappear in the Anglo-Saxon Chronicle under Alfred's name. We see, too, that the earlier Frankish connection established between the dimensions of a fort and the number of men required for its garrison later reappears in transmuted form in the *Burghal Hidage*. Historians who point out with some plausibility that Henry the Fowler's fortress building in the German Nordmark may have been inspired by Alfred's and by Edward's earlier burghal system in England are more reluctant to recognize or to acknowledge the obvious Carolingian influence on Alfred's defences. The Anglo-Saxon Chronicle would have us believe that Alfred was the sole instigator and developer of a military strategy against the Danes. But Alfred, like Charles, must have had the benefit of the advice 'of his faithful men (*fidelium*)'—in Alfred's case his *witan*, together with the added benefit of Frankish visitors at his West Saxon court, who may even have known Charles the Bald. Alfred's visitors were not only scholars and clerics, but also travellers and traders, such as the Norwegian Ohthere. It is highly probable that from such men the notion of fortifying river banks at key points was first suggested to the West Saxon king. While the idea of revamping older Roman defences around towns such as London, Exeter, Winchester, Canterbury, and Rochester was self-evident, there were none the less Frankish precedents for that policy also. In 869 Charles ordered that the *civitates* of Le Mans and Tours 'should be fortified by their inhabitants, so that they could provide defensive strongholds against the Northmen for the surrounding populations'.[135] Cologne and Bonn had been burnt by the Northmen 'with their churches and buildings' in 881 when the clergy and nuns who survived those attacks fled with their church treasures to the safety of Mainz.[136] This occurred during Alfred's respite from viking attack, and in view of the Anglo-Saxon chronicler's interest in Frankish affairs and access to some Frankish annals, it is possible that Alfred was personally aware of these contemporary events in Francia. If so, he would have known, too, that in 883 'Cologne was rebuilt apart from its churches and monasteries, and its walls were provided with gates, bars, and locks'.[137] Not all Frankish cities had their defences put in order by the 880s: Rheims had no walls capable of withstanding a viking assault in 882.[138] But it cannot be coincidence that Alfred had refortified the principal old Roman towns of his kingdom, and he had adopted a very specific policy of fortifying rivers at points calculated to inhibit viking shipping, when his older contemporary, Charles the Bald, had resorted to precisely those measures a quarter of a century before.

The existence of revamped fortifications around Roman towns in southern England such as Exeter, Winchester, and Canterbury, together with the construction of new forts such as Athelney or Wareham explains the progress of the Last War as reported in the Anglo-Saxon Chronicle and accounts also for Alfred's ultimate triumph. The reasons why the campaigns of his Last War were directed outside Wessex or confined on the periphery of Alfred's kingdom were twofold. First, the heartlands of Wessex had endured earlier intensive raiding at the hands of Hálfdan and of Guthrum, and there were clearly less rich pickings there for Hæsten than if he attacked relatively more untouched territory elsewhere. But an equally pressing reason why Wessex did not have to endure the brunt of Hæsten's armies was surely that it had been heavily fortified by Alfred during the period 878 to 891. It was a combination of these two factors that deflected Danish inroads during the Last War along a south-east to north-west axis across the no man's land between the Danelaw and English Mercia. The lands from Essex to Chester and the Welsh Marches may well have contributed to Danegelds levied by bishops and ealdormen during past campaigns, but they had survived, on the whole, untouched by the destroyer. These lands could not only yield church treasure, but they could also be annexed to the adjacent Danelaw. And so the war was fought essentially outside the frontiers of Wessex proper, and Alfred conducted that war in the same way as he had successfully dealt with Guthrum. He first tried baptism and Christian diplomacy in the hope of neutralizing Hæsten's military and political aggression. When diplomacy collapsed after Hæsten's campaigns from Benfleet, Alfred continued with his well-tried policy of constantly shadowing the main force of the Danish army. However inept that policy may seem, as it is outlined in the Chronicle—with endless chasings of viking armies across the English Midlands— it paid dividends for Alfred in the end. Just as Alfred tracked Guthrum all the way from Wareham to Exeter and from Exeter to Chippenham in 875–8, so in the Last War, the West Saxons and Mercians trekked after Hæsten's army, first to Buttington, and then to Chester and to Bridgnorth, covering huge distances and sometimes with little to show for their efforts. But the policy was calculated to avoid a pitched battle with an enemy which was at some strength, while at the same time keeping that enemy together and preventing small raiding parties from breaking away to gather loot and provisions. Great armies which are unable to find food soon starve, and close examination of the Chronicle's account of the Buttington, Chester, and Lea campaigns shows that lack of provisions was at the heart of the Danish failure to gain the advantage. The Lea episode epitomizes everything on which Alfred based his strategies. He had marched his men to that Danish fort in order to allow the Londoners to reap their harvest and to prevent the Danes from seizing a crucial supply of corn. But having arrived there, Alfred beat the Danes at their own game by building counter-forts along the river which prevented them from moving their all-important ships. The result was that the Danes had to abandon their ships and move on rapidly in the hope of acquiring supplies elsewhere. Alfred predictably sent his men in hot pursuit. And if on such occasions he was— like his Carolingian contemporaries—outrun and outfoxed by the enemy, he did, nevertheless follow on, and by keeping up a relentless pressure, he wore down the invaders by choking off their food supply.

Alfred's war of attrition and his containment strategies, although much more effective, and far less costly than his earlier attempts at fighting an enemy in the open, were not the stuff of which eulogies were made. The entire ethos of early medieval aristocratic culture—reflected in the bravura of heroic poetry and saga— was calculated to view containment and the paying of Danegeld as policies which were as unmanly, as they were unbecoming for a king. The reluctance of the Anglo-Saxon chronicler, and of many modern historians, to explore the possibility of Alfred having paid extensive and repeated Danegelds to his enemies is quite misplaced. If we accept that Alfred's adversaries were indeed so numerous—as others proved also to be in Francia—that they were impossible to expel from a territory after one or even more defeats, then the policy of resorting to payments of protection money makes some sense. The payment of large quantities of geld might seem to have impoverished monastic houses and to have stripped the greater magnates of surplus wealth. But the payment of such tribute was a much more orderly process than the violent seizure of loot by marauding armies, while the burden of such Danegelds could be distributed beyond the immediate region which was at risk from viking marauders. Frankish sources, as ever, afford us better insights into how viking tribute was collected, and suggest, too, that the collection process took a long time. When Sigefrid, a Christian Danish go-between undertook to negotiate between the Franks and Danish warlords (*principes*) who were terrorizing the Somme basin from Amiens in 884, he eventually succeeded in securing a cash settlement 'after long negotiations with coming and going, during which now this and now that [was decided]' and hostages were exchanged.[139] We also learn from Frankish evidence that the burden of payment was passed down the line to the lesser land-owners and servile classes, thereby commuting what initially seemed like a crushing burden to more manageable proportions. When Charles the Bald agreed to pay 3,000 lbs. of silver to Northmen on the Somme in

860, he levied a tax on churches and households and on his greater and lesser traders (*negotiatores*).[140] Six years later Charles raised 4,000 lbs. of silver for Northmen on the Seine by levying a tax on clergy and traders yet again; and by levying 6 denarii on every free household (*mansus*), and from 3 to 1/2 a denarius on lesser servile households.[141] The free peasants, in paying 6 denarii, were handing over the equivalent of about half their usual annual rents due to their lords.[142] It was in striving to raise his share of such a tribute, that Bishop Wærferth of Worcester, as we saw[143] was forced into pawning church estates in Mercia.

Alfred's fort-building programme may have been even more unpopular than his raising of Danegeld. However unpleasant it may have been to hand over one's valuables and surplus wealth, the presence of a marauding army poised to strike must have focused people's minds on the necessity to placate a merciless invader. Fortress building, on the other hand, was a time-consuming and labour-intensive process which was undertaken in the hope that one day it would pay dividends against an invader who might never materialize. It was Alfred's significant achievement not only to have imitated Frankish practice in fortress building, but to have convinced his magnates of the necessity for such long-term investment. Even in modern times, politicians find it difficult to persuade an electorate of the advantages of costly schemes which provide only the mere promise of long-term rewards. Fortress building was just such a programme. It involved persuading West Saxon magnates of the need to provide their slaves and other workmen and craftsmen, and to maintain such a workforce away from home in a costly and lengthy undertaking. When Charles the Bald decided to repair and revamp bridges and fortifications to keep Northmen out of the Seine, Oise, and Marne in 865, this was done 'by men drafted from more distant regions to perform labour services'. But everything in the Middle Ages was controlled by custom, and not even Carolingian rulers—even in times of great crisis—could push their people too far. So this extraordinary workforce was assembled 'on condition that this was treated as a special case of urgent need and that the men who would now repair these bridges should never at any future time suffer any disadvantage through performing labour services on this particular job'.[144] Alfred must have had to plead a myriad of 'special cases of urgent need' when persuading the thegns of Wessex and of Kent to build elaborate fortresses, often in remote frontier areas and which seemed to offer few immediate benefits to them. It may be that the horrors of the First War in Berkshire and Hampshire in 871–2, and of the Second with Guthrum's ravaging of western Wessex in 876–8 were enough to convince the magnates of the need to protect not only their property but also the persons of their families and loved ones from raiders who specialized in looting and slave-trading.

The payment of geld was infinitely preferable to the destructive alternative of Northmen ravaging the land, which meant great loss of life, the destruction of buildings and treasures, the arbitrary driving off of livestock and the rounding up of human captives. Heavy Danegelds may have meant the short-term depression of a local economy. But arbitrary ravaging of territory by a hostile and barbarous army involved the destruction or removal of the native workforce and the destruction of vital structures—markets, buildings, enclosures, water-courses—

so necessary to facilitate recovery after the crisis had past. Alfred walked a tight-rope in his negotiations with such a powerful and treacherous enemy as Hæsten, and—given the extraordinary difficulties which he faced—the West Saxon king succeeded remarkably well. Alfred's problems were legion. If he pressed the confrontation with his enemies too far, he risked being caught off guard or outnumbered in a pitched battle in which everything he had gained for the West Saxons over twenty years would vanish overnight. On the other hand, he had to keep up the pressure on the invaders to make foraging impossible and to prevent indiscriminate raiding. But that in turn risked a major confrontation. And when he chose to settle on cash payments, he had to judge whether the time was right to trust an enemy who had gone back on his word, time and time again. If Alfred were to misjudge his opponents, he risked being rejected by his own people who would see their king as a man who first squeezed them for a viking tax and later proved unable to deliver a peace. We only have to turn to Frankish records to see how an unfortunate population might be raided and butchered by a viking enemy and still have to yield up an additional tribute. The Norse army which had plagued the people of the Somme and the Oise from Amiens in 884, for instance, was still able to extract 12,000 lbs. of silver from the Franks before it agreed to leave the people in peace for a respite lasting no longer than about eight months.[145] The only factor which ensured Northmen would keep their word was when necessity—through hunger or loss of men in battle—dictated it. Alfred had to weigh all those factors, and in the end, his judgement proved correct. The great army which had poured over Kent in 892 had been so wearied of the game of cat-and-mouse, and so worn down by successive losses, that its leaders in 895–6 chose to take a West Saxon and Mercian payment and withdraw.

Alfred's achievement in his Last War had been significant, even if it were lacking in heroics. His foresight in persuading his magnates to build fortifications throughout the kingdom spared Wessex from the worst experience of being at the mercy of an invading army and channelled hostilities further to the north. And by pursuing a policy of relentless monitoring of enemy movements, Alfred prevented the worst excesses from being carried out against his Mercian allies while at the same time he created major supply problems for the invaders. But because of the great strength of his enemies, he was unquestionably forced to come to terms—first with Hæsten in Kent and later at Benfleet, and finally at Bridgnorth. Peace agreements were a two-way process, and for a great Danish host constantly in need of food supplies to stay alive, and constantly in need of loot to bolster the morale of warriors in camp, Danegeld offered the enemy an acceptable way out of their particular dilemma. Excluded from Wessex by a tightly-knit network of fortifications and constantly shadowed throughout Kent, Essex, and the Midlands, a Danish army however large would inevitably be forced to come to terms with a stubborn native defence. The Anglo-Saxon chronicler ought not to have been ashamed of reporting how much Alfred and Æthelred paid their enemies at Bridgnorth. It may have been cheap at the price, to rid the kingdom of this last menace and to allow the native population resume its struggle with the land and its need to trade both internally and with its Danish neighbours. Accounts of Danegeld in Frankish chronicles and from later in the reign of Ethelred the Unready in England have coloured our assessment of this practice. It was understandably detested by monastic chroniclers who, because of the surplus of precious metal in their monasteries, stood to lose most from these payments of protection money. Danegeld has been despised, too, by nationalist writers in Britain and France, who have regarded it as a disgrace on the national escutcheon to have been forced to kowtow to an enemy in however remote a past. For Alfred, it was a prudent policy to rid his kingdom of an enemy which was so evenly matched that it might never otherwise have been overcome. Whatever the immediate loss to Wessex which cash payments may have caused, the infrastructure of its economy remained intact, and its army remained in the field to move forward in the reign of Alfred's son and to go from strength to strength.

The account of Alfred's Last War is rounded off with a self-conscious declaration that 'by the grace of God, the army had not on the whole afflicted the English people very greatly'.[146] An account of Alfred's experiment in designing large warships follows.[147] The Chronicle's last glimpse of Alfred provides, unexpectedly, a draconian image of the king. He is reported to have hung two ships' crews of Northmen in Winchester who had been shipwrecked on the Sussex coast. They were no ordinary castaways, but survivors of a marauding band who had wreaked havoc on Alfred's sailors and on settlements in the Isle of Wight and in coastal Devon.[148] That is the last we hear of the king while he was still alive, in 896. He lived for another three years, but the Chronicle ceases reporting on his reign beyond this point. The only three incidents recorded between the end of the Last War and Alfred's own death are the death of Ealdorman Æthelhelm—a veteran from the victory at Buttington—in 897; the death of Heahstan, bishop of London in the same year, and the death of Æthelred, ealdorman of Devon, four weeks before King Alfred, in 899. Alfred died on 26 October 899, after a twenty-six-and-a-half year reign. Such in detail is the narrative of his military career as we can recover it from the Anglo-Saxon Chronicle and from related sources. We depend so much on the Chronicle for the recovery of that narrative that a comparative approach to any study of Alfred's military career is essential. Not only is the account in the Chronicle unique, as it is also edited and biased, but it reflects, too, an exclusively provincial angle of vision. Even events of major importance within Mercia or East Anglia were of little concern to this West Saxon record. A study of the Chronicle in relation to contemporary Frankish and Irish sources not only raises the relevance of the wars of Alfred's reign onto the higher and wider European stage, but since many of Alfred's enemies also campaigned in Francia and Ireland the comparative approach would seem to be doubly essential. If we wish to gain an understanding of the problems confronting Alfred during his long and eventful struggle with Scandinavian invaders, and if we hope to reach any balanced assessment of his ability to resolve those problems, then we must abandon what are essentially defensive and reverential attitudes to a ninth-century chronicle and examine its record in a critical and comparative light. It is now time to turn to more complex issues relating to Alfred's biography and to the king's own prolific scholarly writings.

PART TWO

A Thousand Years of Deceit

VI

Asser
Battleground of Scholarship
Charnel House of Scholars

A SSER'S *LIFE* OF KING ALFRED OCCUPIES A CENTRAL PLACE IN ENGLISH
historical writing, not only because of its acceptance by scholars as the earliest
extant biography of an English king—and indeed of any English lay person—but
because its subject is Alfred the Great of Wessex whom Asser, the author of the
Life, claims to have known as a tutor and a friend. The immediacy of this extraordinary source is heightened by the author's claim to be writing his biography while
the king was still living—in Alfred's forty-fifth year—in AD 893.[1] Even at this
opening stage in the discussion, we are confronted with problems which have
exercised the minds of scholars for well over a century. Since Asser clearly outlived his royal master by some ten years, dying as bishop of Sherborne in Dorset
in 909,[2] why did he not continue the biography of Alfred up to the latter's death
in 899? By breaking off his account in mid-stream, Asser lost what would have
been for him a golden opportunity to dwell in detail on the king's Last War as a
grand finale to his military career, and he also forfeited the opportunity to discuss
in detail the programme of scholarly writing and translations for which Alfred is
justly famous. And although the author claims to be writing in 893, the biography
follows Alfred's life in strict chronological terms only up to 887.[3] So, questions
immediately present themselves. Did the original *Life*, of which no complete
medieval manuscript survives, follow the career of the king down to the time of his
death, or did Asser break off his narrative at 887 or 893 because he had grown tired
of the project, or because he had no further reason to proceed with it, or because
his sources of information failed him at that point? To these questions we must
return later, but they are by no means the most serious or most urgent in requiring
answers.

This *Life* attributed to Asser presents us with an enduring image of Alfred,
youngest and most favoured son of Æthelwulf of Wessex, destined to outlive and
to succeed all his brothers in the kingship of the West Saxons. It shows us a hero-
king, torn between his duties as leader of the West Saxon warband and the
promptings of his immense piety which drove him to emulate the asceticisms of
the Desert Fathers. All the while as he struggles between the duties imposed by his
public office and the burden of his conscience, he is racked by painful illness which

is endured with saintly fortitude as part of his spiritual struggle against the desires of the flesh. Alfred in this *Life* never achieves the status of an established scholar. He is portrayed rather, as a king obsessed with his own personal need to overcome illiteracy, and he is equally obsessed with the need to enforce literacy on the great men of his realm. He is obsessive, too, in matters of justice, holding post-mortems on 'nearly all the judgements which were passed in his absence anywhere in his realm'. In addition to his extraordinary military, scholarly, and judicial programmes, Alfred we are told offered no less than half of his time, day and night, to the service of God. This work attributed to Asser rounds off its hagiographical portrait of its hero with an overall image of Alfred as a great inventor and a generous patron of the arts. In short, the *Life* shows us Alfred as the idealized Christian king. It is the portrait of Alfred Super-King.

However idealized and sycophantic this *Life* may be, that in itself ought not necessarily to invalidate its claim to have been written during Alfred's lifetime and by a confidant of the king, although it ought to have made supporters for the validity of Asser's authorship more cautious and more critical in their wholesale acceptance of some of the extravagant hagiographical detail offered in this text. As long ago as 1842, Thomas Wright communicated a paper to the Society of Antiquaries in which he cast serious doubts on the authenticity of the *Life* of Alfred as a work composed by Asser, bishop of Sherborne, during the lifetime of the king.[4] Wright was troubled by the unfinished nature of the *Life*, by what he considered to be legendary elements in its make-up—such as Alfred's invention of horn lanterns—and by its heavy reliance on the Anglo-Saxon Chronicle for the providing of detail on Alfred's career. Wright also noted the author's anachronism in referring to the *parochia* or diocese of Exeter which was not formally constituted until AD 1050, and he observed, too, lapses in the author's Latinity from the imperfect into the present tense when speaking of Alfred.[5] This last point cast doubts on whether the subject of the narrative was still alive at the time of writing. Finally, Wright noted the confused and contradictory accounts offered on Alfred's early education and on the mysterious illness which is alleged in the *Life* to have plagued the king's career. Wright's arguments were hampered by his reliance on poor textual editions of the *Life* and by the limitations of textual criticism in his own day. He believed, for instance, the text of the Anglo-Saxon Chronicle (on which the *Life* of Alfred had so heavily relied) to be considerably later than Asser's time, and he was understandably confused by Parker's additions to the original text of the *Life* of Alfred, such as material taken from the Annals of St Neots in the first printed edition of the *Life* in 1574.[6] Wright's study led him to believe that the *Life* of King Alfred was a late tenth- or eleventh-century forgery compiled at St Neots in Huntingdonshire.

W. H. Stevenson brought out his formidable edition of Asser's *Life* in 1904 in which he sought to purify the text of Parker's interpolations and printing errors; and provided scholars with a clear indication of what he considered to belong to the Cottonian manuscript; what parts of the original text had been used by Florence of Worcester; and what were later interpolations.[7] But Stevenson, although he agonized at length over the undoubted problems inherent in the *Life*'s account of Alfred's illnesses and education (to name but two difficulties), was committed to the notion of the authenticity of Asser's authorship.[8] His scholarly commentary has provided the quarry from which all subsequent commentators and translators of the *Life* of Alfred have drawn liberally and not always with due acknowledgement. Stevenson, in his zeal to defend Asser, brushed Wright's arguments aside by the familiar tactic of undermining faith in his opponent's scholarly integrity, through denegrating Wright's strenuous defence of the authenticity of another 'absurd forgery *De situ Britanniae*'.[9] If Wright could be proved wrong in his estimation of one historical text, then who would accept his opinion on another? Considering that Wright's paper appeared more than half a century before Stevenson's edition of the *Life* of Alfred, and bearing in mind that Wright touched on most of the major issues which have caused concern to more recent and able historians, Stevenson's attempts to show up Wright as an unscholarly amateur reaching 'a most lame and impotent conclusion' derived in part 'from later monkish fabrications' was unwarranted and unjust.[10] Wright's concern that this work attributed to Asser was a collection of eulogy and anecdote grafted on to a translation of the Anglo-Saxon Chronicle (and so posing problems regarding its status as a contemporary and independent source on the king) was scorned by Stevenson as 'merely matter of opinion'.[11] The debate over the authenticity or otherwise of Asser's *Life* of King Alfred sadly developed into a battle between linguists constrained, in this particular case, by the limited value of their textual evidence, and historians whose lines of enquiry arose in—Galbraith's words—'from subjective impression' in the first instance.[12] But the dichotomy between a so-called objective linguistic approach, on the one hand, which vaunts the 'archaeology of text' as superior to the more intuitive methods of the historian on the other has been more apparent than real. Stevenson and his textual disciples generated a deluge of annotation and commentary on the *Life* of Alfred which has served to divert attention away from the actual text into a labyrinth of subjective commentary, beset by supposition and circular argument.

If as Maitland observed 'Asser was supremely fortunate in the hands of Mr. Stevenson',[13] he did not fare so happily under the scrutiny of V. H. Galbraith who first expressed his doubts on Asser in his Creighton Lecture at the University of London in 1949 and who later developed his views into open rejection of the source as a contemporary document from Alfred's reign, in a chapter entitled 'Who Wrote Asser's Life of Alfred' in his *Introduction to the Study of History* in 1964. Galbraith, who read Stevenson's 328 pages of Introduction and Notes with great care, concluded of that 1904 edition: 'The whole book is a sustained rearguard action in which every difficulty is looked firmly in the face, and then not so much explained, as explained away.'[14] Galbraith's 'difficulties' and his arguments used to disprove Asser's authorship of the *Life* of Alfred were in many cases similar to those of Wright. He refused to accept Stevenson's explanation for the apparent anachronism in relation to the *parochia* of Exeter; he made much of the contradictions in the account of Alfred's illnesses; of the changes from imperfect to present tense, and of motifs which he viewed as drawn from folklore and legend.[15] Galbraith gave new emphasis to problems presented by other aspects of Asser's text—its debt to Einhard's *Life* of Charlemagne, its dedication to Alfred as 'ruler of all Christians of the island of Britain' (a nonsense in Galbraith's view), and its referring to Alfred as 'king of the Anglo-Saxons', when in his time Alfred ruled only Wessex and parts of Mercia.[16] 'In general', Galbraith concluded, 'it reads like the life of a man no longer alive,' presented in the form of a 'hagiographical picture of Alfred as a neurotic invalid'.[17] He saw the *Life* of Alfred as a forgery which he ascribed to Leofric, bishop of Devon and Cornwall from 1046, and bishop of Exeter from 1050.[18] Galbraith believed the purpose of the forgery was to facilitate or justify the amalgamation of the two bishoprics of Devon and Cornwall, and the moving of Leofric's episcopal seat from Crediton in Cornwall to a safer location in Exeter—hence the prominence given in the *Life* to Alfred's gift of Exeter to Asser.[19] In Galbraith's opinion, Leofric began his work with the notion of writing about a dead king, but stopped at 893 and revised his text by inserting references to Alfred and others in the present tense in order to lend a false aura of contemporaneity to his narrative.[20] This ploy saved Leofric the embarrassment of not knowing much of Alfred's later translations and concealed his ignorance of the precise time when Asser was advanced by King Alfred to the bishopric of Sherborne.

   Galbraith's study, in spite of its dependence on the work of earlier scholars, ranks as one of the most important pieces of historical writing in Great Britain in this century. This is not just because he challenged the authenticity of Asser's authorship of Alfred's *Life* or because he was right or wrong in ascribing that authorship to an eleventh-century bishop of Exeter. Galbraith was essentially asserting the historian's role as presenter of the past—not as individual scholars or as a whole national consciousness might wish to be shown it, but to present it in so far as it can be objectively reconstructed, through the scholarly integrity of one observer's angle of vision. Challenges to the authenticity of the *Life* of Alfred struck deep at the establishment's view of what sort of king Alfred ought to have been. The *Life* of Alfred had served as propaganda not only for medieval English kings and for bishops of the Protestant Reformation: it also had its uses in the romantic and imperial age of nineteenth-century Britain. Those who believed in a divine destiny for the British Empire could conveniently see its origins in Asser's Super-King of Wessex—a man of simple life and virtue, but also a warrior with superhuman resolve and genius. 'The Victorians', Nelson reminded us, 'fashioned Alfred's kingdom in their own image' and that image had a huge bearing on late nineteenth-century scholarship.[21] Wright's voice of dissent in 1841 or that of Howorth in 1876–7[22] failed to win the backing of leading historians such as Edward Freeman (1823–92) or Bishop Stubbs (1825–1901). The ideas of the doubters of Asser were consigned to the wilderness in an imperial Britain that looked upon forgery as a peculiarly villainous craft and which saw any tampering with a major source of English history as tantamount to an unpatriotic act. Queen Victoria and Prince Albert had named their second son after Alfred the Great in 1844, while in death at Frogmore, they themselves were portrayed on monuments with all the trappings of an Alfredian 'Saxon' fantasy. As the nineteenth century neared its end, Britain braced itself to celebrate with millenary fever, the anniversary of her most celebrated and beloved of medieval kings. Winchester acquired its massive statue of Alfred the Great in 1901,[23] and although two major wars with Germany in the early twentieth century killed off the romantic Germanic and Albertian dimension to the Alfred myth in the national consciousness, the West Saxon king-myth survived to present a trimmed-down interpretation of early English greatness. No one can deprive Alfred of the credit for commissioning a modest fleet of longships to withstand Danish sea-borne attacks on his coasts. It was understandable for Lord Rosebery, then former Prime Minister—and carried along by the euphoria of the Alfred mania of 1901—to see 'the British fleet [as] the offspring of his [Alfred's] own poor ships'.[24] It was quite another thing for Stenton to state in his *Anglo-Saxon England* of 1947: 'the recorded beginnings of the English navy lie in the small fleet of large vessels built by Alfred'.[25] The rhetoric generated by Alfredian historiography had, under Stenton, taken on new meaning in a Britain which had endured the menace of invasion in two World Wars. And while the outsized and impracticable longships employed by Alfred in 896 prefigured conquering Dreadnoughts for the late Victorians,[26] for Stenton they had become a symbol of an embattled island's defences against the Reich. Nationalist images and the myths that sustain them die hard, and it took real intellectual courage to go against the tide. Galbraith's papers on Asser in 1949 and 1964 still encountered an academic establishment in hostile mood to any changes in the received teaching on Alfred as enshrined in Stevenson's lengthy commentary on Asser's text. Stenton had already accepted Stevenson as 'the definitive authority' on the *Life* of Alfred[27] prior to Galbraith's bombshell, and he accepted the *Life* attributed to Asser as 'a very naive, but sincerely intimate biography'.[28] Dorothy Whitelock rose to the defence of Asser, Stevenson, and especially of Stenton with *The Genuine Asser*—her riposte to Galbraith, delivered appropriately as *The Stenton Lecture* at the University of Reading in 1967. An additional stated aim of Whitelock was 'to clear Bishop Leofric from the accusation of being a forger'[29] on the assumption that twentieth-century scholars would view the prelate as some latter-day villain. The merits of Whitelock's defence of Asser's authorship have been greatly exaggerated. Many of the points which she raised can still be argued for or against the authenticity of the *Life*, and in her unguarded moments Whitelock indulged in the kind of speculation which she derided in the works of other scholars. Her musings that Asser may have left off from writing the *Life* of Alfred in 893 in order to help the king with the translation of Boethius's *Consolation of Philosophy*[30] shows how she could heap one piece of speculation upon another, for the notion that Asser was connected with the translation of Boethius's *De Consolatione Philosophiae* rests on two unsupported statements of William of Malmesbury.[31] A number of her arguments—such as those regarding Alfred's supposed alliance with Welsh rulers—are inaccurate,[32] while others were patently false. Her idea, for instance, that the author of Alfred's *Life* confined himself 'to datable contemporary records . . . rejecting legendary matter' was a nonsense, as was the notion that a passing reference to St Gueriir was 'the nearest approach to a miraculous element in the *Life*'.[33] Whitelock did succeed in showing that Leofric could not have written the *Life* of Alfred, and her arguments here were based on sound chronological and contextual grounds. She argued that the Cottonian manuscript (Otho A.xii) of the *Life* of Alfred pre-dated Leofric of Exeter by about 50 years,[34] and she rightly pointed out that the Exeter episode in the *Life* constitutes far too minor a feature in that work to justify reasons for constructing an elaborate forgery around an issue which a would-be fabricator allowed to become lost in the body of an otherwise lengthy and irrelevant text.[35] But the effect of her paper on the Asser debate was extraordinary. The contest appeared to have ended in outright victory for the orthodox school, as exemplified by Whitelock and Stenton. In subsequent years a handful of courageous scholars dared to call into question some points of detail in Alfredian sources and to acknowledge the contemporary propaganda value inherent in those sources. Such contributions were sporadic and lacked an overview of the Alfredian debate. They rarely questioned the received dogma on Asser, confining themselves instead to less sensitive Alfredian materials. They were received by the academic establishment as mere fine-tuning—not all of it welcome— to a thesis which was considered unassailable and which remained unchallenged in its essentials. The effect of Whitelock's personal defence of Stenton, and of her *ex cathedra* teaching on Asser's authorship of the *Life* of Alfred, was to elevate all sections of that problematical text to the status of a sacred canon in Anglo-Saxon Studies. For if, as Stevenson once wrote, 'no work of similar extent [as the *Life* of Alfred] has contributed so much to English history',[36] then conversely, no scholar with an eye to reputation or patronage dared—after Whitelock's validation—to deprive English history of such an untouchable source. And so, in 1983, the editors of the Penguin translation of *Asser's Life of King Alfred* felt confident in excluding all reference from their bibliography to either Wright's or Howorth's papers in the nineteenth century, or to Galbraith's Creighton Lecture. They could proclaim that Galbraith's 'case was promptly and comprehensively demolished by Dorothy Whitelock'.[37] They did fear however that Galbraith's 'richly deserved prestige as a medieval historian' was in danger of casting some lingering 'suspicion' upon the subject of Asser's veracity, and so they felt impelled to exorcise the ghost of Galbraith from the subject of Asser's text once and for all by reviewing some 'main points at issue'.[38] In an uncharacteristically brief sortie into the graveyard of Galbraith's arguments, the authors finally liquidated all trace of credibility pertaining to his case and summed up their satisfaction, secure in the knowledge that they held loyally to orthodox tradition: 'In short, the case against the authenticity of Asser's *Life* of King Alfred does not stand up to scrutiny, and any lingering doubts should be laid peacefully to rest.'[39] Few remain who share Galbraith's unease in relation to Asser and his supposed *Life* of the king of Wessex. Yet in spite of the complacent obsequies held for Galbraith's scholarship in 1983, the spirit of historical enquiry in Anglo-Saxon Studies has not been entirely extinguished. It is time to reopen the debate.

Asser's work survived into modern times in one solitary (and by then composite) manuscript (Cotton MS Otho A.xii) as part of the library of Sir Robert Cotton (1571–1631). That unique source was destroyed in the blaze which consumed 114 priceless volumes when Cotton's library was severely damaged in the fire at Ashburnham House in the Little Dean's Yard, Westminster, on 23 October 1731. Cotton had acquired the manuscript of Asser's text by 1621, but one of its previous owners, Matthew Parker (1504–75), archbishop of Canterbury and erstwhile master of Corpus Christi College, Cambridge, published the first printed edition of the text in 1574. Parker had a transcript of the manuscript made for his own use while preparing his edition, which survives as Cambridge Corpus Christi College MS 100.[40] This transcript was assumed by Stevenson[41] to be largely free of annotations and interpolations of Parker and his secretaries, which they are believed to have added to the Cottonian manuscript, and which appear in his printed edition. Similar Parkerian additions and alterations are also present to a lesser extent in yet another and slightly later transcript, BL Cotton Otho A.xii*.[42] Parker's edition was reprinted in Frankfurt in 1602 by Camden who, in addition to reproducing Parker's additions and incorporating his marginal glosses into the original text, also inserted the outrageous anecdote to prove that Oxford already possessed a university in King Alfred's reign.[43] A second new edition of the work was published by Francis Wise at Oxford University Press in 1722.[44] Although this was only nine years before the fire which destroyed the only surviving medieval manuscript, Wise did not personally consult either that manuscript or the Corpus transcript for his edition, and his work incorporated interpolations and errors of Parker and Camden, and of their printers. Wise employed the antiquary, James Hill, who collated the Cotton manuscript with Camden's printed edition, a task which was poorly undertaken, but Hill also supplied a freehand facsimile of the first fourteen lines of the Cotton manuscript of the *Life* for Wise's edition.[45] This precious, though far from satisfactory, piece of evidence relating to the lost manuscript of the *Life* clearly has a bearing on deciding the date of Cotton MS Otho A.xii. It shows us the text of Asser's supposed dedication to his 'esteemed and most holy lord, Alfred' written in rustic capitals followed by the opening lines of the text proper. The text began with a large initial, opening a line of smaller capitals, followed by a second line of rustic capitals, followed in turn by five lines of text in Caroline minuscule. This Caroline script was used for Latin texts in England from *c*.950 onwards.[46] Stevenson dated the script from the drawing supplied by Hill in Wise's edition, to 'the early part of the eleventh century'[47] and the general appearance of the drawing clearly suggests that we are dealing with a pre-Conquest date for the Cotton manuscript text of Asser as a whole. But some words of caution need to be registered at this stage. Parker claimed his manuscript of the *Life* was written in Latin letters—presumably Caroline minuscule as represented in Hill's drawing. But Parker also claimed a resemblance between the script in his Cotton manuscript and that of other manuscripts of King Alfred's translation of the *Pastoral Care*, which were written not in Caroline minuscule, but in Anglo-Saxon characters.[48] Wanley was later (in 1721) to challenge Parker's opinion, by stating that only proper names in the Cotton manuscript of Alfred's *Life* were written in Saxon letters, the main text of the *Life* being in 'the English hand of that time'—i.e. the Caroline minuscule which he dated to *c.*1000.[49] The early eighteenth-century representation of the opening page of the lost Cottonian manuscript *Life* of Alfred does not constitute a proper facsimile. It is a print of an original freehand drawing, admitted by Whitelock to have been 'poorly drawn'.[50] There are several inconsistencies relating to the treatment of certain letters, and there is the overall impression of carelessness evident here as elsewhere in Hill's work. Above all, this visual evidence comes from the early eighteenth century when in this as in other things—compare for instance the picturesque treatment by eighteenth-century artists of antiquarian ruins—draughtsmen did not feel compelled to reproduce what they perceived to be the physical reality of their subject. We would also like to know whether Hill had been in consultation with Humphrey Wanley who also examined the Cotton manuscript for Wise at this time, for if he executed the drawing with Wanley's observations in mind, that clearly would have a bearing on the value of his drawing as independent evidence for the dating of the manuscript. Wanley, who was by the standards of his day, a skilled palaeographer, believed the Cotton manuscript had been written by several hands, and he dated the first and earliest of these to *c.*1000–1 and the remaining hands to much the same time.[51] This precise judgement was based, as Sisam showed, on Wanley's comparison of the manuscript text of Alfred's *Life* with a charter of King Æthelred the Unready (Cotton Augustus ii. 22) dating to 1001.[52] So Hill's facsimile and Wanley's observations both suggest a date of *c.* AD 1000 for the lost Cottonian manuscript of the *Life* of Alfred.

It is scarcely surprising to find that there is frequent disagreement between the accounts of scholars who examined the Cottonian manuscript prior to its destruction. Wanley identified several hands in the manuscript in 1721, but already, back in 1600, Thomas James, the first Bodley's librarian, who saw the work in the library of Lord Lumley, claimed 'it was written by two diverse scribes at the least, whereof the later parte of the book. . . . is by much in my opinion the latest'.[53] Yet even the later hand had some 'Saxon letters', by which James presumably meant that even the later of the two scripts may have been pre-Conquest in date. When James Ussher, archbishop of Armagh,[54] wrote of the Cottonian manuscript sometime before 1639, he dated it to Asser's time (i.e. *c.* AD 900) or shortly afterwards.[55] Ussher's contemporary, Sir John Spelman, returned to the issue of an earlier and later hand in the manuscript, but it is not clear from his report whether what he perceived as the later hand was that of an interpolator or of a main scribe.[56] Spelman did distinguish between this later hand and annotations of Archbishop Parker, written in Parker's characteristically red pen. Wise also discussed an earlier and later hand in the manuscript in 1722 and was informed by those who consulted the manuscript that the later hand was at work from part of chapter 88 to the end of chapter 98.[57] We shall never know whether the script for chapters 99 to 106 at the end of the *Life* reverted to that of the first or earlier hand, or whether it was written by one of those several hands observed by Wanley, who was one of Wise's advisers.[58] The picture is further confused by James's pronouncement[59] that the text in the neighbourhood of chapter 83 was in the later hand—a hand incidentally which he considered to be much later than the first or earlier hand. Several of these commentators, including Wise,[60] show some confusion in distinguishing Archbishop Parker's annotations from other hands in the text. In short, the Cotton manuscript Otho A.xii of the *Life* of Alfred seems to have been written in two main hands, the first of which may have dated to *c.*1000, but we have little indication of the date of the later hand or hands in this manuscript except to say that the manuscript as a whole was considered to be pre-Conquest in date.

Our knowledge of the lost manuscript, then, depends on a surviving freehand drawing of its opening lines; the printed editions of Parker, Camden, and Wise; the transcripts made for Parker's use; and the opinions expressed by a range of scholars and antiquaries who inspected the manuscript prior to its destruction in 1731. We also have access to limited sections of the *Life* as copied by a few later medieval writers. Extracts from the *Life* of Alfred were incorporated into the *Chronicon ex chronicis* attributed to Florence (*alias* John) of Worcester; two sections of the *Historia Regum* attributed to Symeon of Durham; and in the Annals of St Neots. Florence used a manuscript of the *Life* which embodied several of the errors of the lost Cottonian manuscript. Stevenson firmly believed Florence copied from the Cotton manuscript of Alfred's *Life*.[61] Florence may have worked from the actual Cottonian source,[62] correcting and editing as he thought fit, or—less likely— he may have used another recension altogether. Hart and Lapidge convincingly and independently showed that the first five sections of the *Historia Regum* (including abstracts from the *Life* of Alfred) were compiled by Byrhtferth, a monk and teacher at Ramsey Abbey in Huntingdonshire at the turn of the tenth century.[63] Hunter Blair demonstrated that the section in the *Historia Regum* (*HR* 1) dealing with the period 849–87 was based on the series of annalistic entries which formed the framework of the *Life* of Alfred, and he suggested (contradicting Stevenson)[64] that the compiler of that early section the *Historia Regum* (now known to be Byrhtferth) may have worked from a manuscript different from that of Cotton Otho A.xii which was available to Parker and Wise.[65] Whitelock went further and held that the manuscript source behind the extract from the *Life* of Alfred in the first five sections of the *Historia Regum* (*HR* 1) was not only different from Otho A.xii but had a reading that was superior to it. Lapidge was more cautious in his assessment of the textual evidence, suggesting that at least in one case (the designation of place-names with the *æt* formula), Byrhtferth, the compiler of the first five parts of the *Historia* may have altered the original text of the *Life* of Alfred, which could in this one respect at least, have had identical readings with the Cotton manuscript.[66] It is also possible, however, that the *æt* formula for place-names was original to the text of the *Life* of Alfred and that Parker or one of his 'apprentices' expunged it from the Cottonian text in an effort to normalize its Latin. The same might have happened at the hands of an earlier medieval transcriber of Cotton Otho A.xii. In that case the readings preserved in *HR* 1 would represent, as Whitelock suggested, a superior version of the text of Alfred's *Life*.[67] Lapidge was not prepared in his 1982 study to develop his argument further. He contented himself with the guarded suggestion that 'there is some possibility that it was the Cotton manuscript which Byrhtferth used'.[68] Stevenson was of the view that the extracts from Alfred's *Life* in the early section of the *Historia Regum* (*HR* I) followed the Cottonian manuscript.[69] He pointed out, *inter alia*, that *HR* I 'had most of the errors [as shared by the Cotton manuscript] in the reckoning of the king's age'.[70] Lapidge was, presumably, tending towards that view. We must therefore conclude that a manuscript of the *Life* of King Alfred was available for Byrhtferth of Ramsey to include in his historical compilation sometime between 987 and *c.*1015—at about the very time when the Cotton manuscript of the *Life* was written. It is the known existence of the *Life* of Alfred by this early date which invalidates Galbraith's thesis for Leofric's forging of the *Life* in the mid-eleventh century.

Hart[71] showed that the compiler of the first five sections of the *Historia Regum* (*HR* I)—Hart's *Northumbrian Chronicle*—had access to Abbo of Fleury's *Passio* of St Edmund of East Anglia. This, together with an insertion regarding viking attacks on Fleury (under AD 881) suggests he worked after the period 986–8 when Abbo visited and taught at Ramsey Abbey. Hart suggested that *HR* I was completed by Byrhtferth at Ramsey sometime before 1001.[72] Hart also argued for the Cottonian Otho A.xii manuscript of the *Life* of Alfred to have been the source of Byrhtferth's summary from that *Life* which he included in his Northumbrian Chronicle—*HR* I of the *Historia Regum*.[73] Hart went further, making the bold suggestion that since Wanley was able to date the Cotton manuscript of Alfred's *Life* so closely to *c.*1000—because of its remarkable similarity to the charter of Æthelred the Unready from the Worcester scriptorium—then the Cotton *Life* of Alfred also had to have been written by a scribe trained in that same Worcester milieu.[74]

The *Annals of St. Neots* is the name given to a manuscript compilation put together at Bury St Edmunds at some time between *c.*1020 and 1140,[75] and containing annals and extracts from saints' *Lives* which are are mainly concerned with the history of East Anglia. The title *Annals of St. Neots* was given to this collection by the antiquary John Leland who discovered the work when he visited St Neots Priory in Huntingdonshire between 1540 and 1544[76] and who at first may have wrongly ascribed the authorship of the work to Asser.[77] Leland's unique manuscript eventually came into the possession of Parker who collated material from the Annals of St Neots with the Cottonian text of his *Life* of Alfred. This amounted to a double conflation of two medieval texts, because the Annals of St Neots had from their medieval beginnings incorporated large sections of the *Life* of King Alfred. Parker caused immense confusion for all subsequent students of these texts by marrying portions of the Annals of St Neots to the Cottonian manuscript text of the *Life* of Alfred in his 1574 edition. Hart suggested renaming the Annals of St Neots, *The East Anglian Chronicle*, on the grounds that they were largely a chronicle of East Anglian affairs from the time of Julius Caesar's invasion of Britain up to the year 914.[78] The renaming of the source has much to recommend it, but since the older title has become firmly established in the literature, and since the Alfredian debate is already sufficiently complicated, it seems best to retain the title *Annals of St. Neots* however unsatisfactory it may be.[79] Hart tentatively dated the time of actual composition of this work to the late tenth century, ascribing its authorship to a monk of Ramsey Abbey who was a contemporary and perhaps a pupil of Byrhtferth, the author of the first five sections of the *Historia Regum* (*HR* 1)— otherwise known as Hart's *Northumbrian Chronicle*.[80] Hart set the outside limits for the date of authorship as any time from 985 to 1140—the latter date being the time of the latest scribe who worked on the surviving manuscript text.[81]

The Annals of St Neots made extensive use of the *Life* of Alfred, but thirty-two of its chapters were omitted, and some of the remainder were only partially transcribed into the later work.[82] Hart was firmly of the opinion that the compiler of the Annals of St Neots worked from the same Cottonian manuscript of the *Life* of Alfred as that used by Archbishop Parker, and he explained the extensive variant readings of the Annals of St Neots text as due to collations by its compiler with a very early text of the Anglo-Saxon Chronicle (the A text precursor), and by the introduction of explanatory material to elucidate the text of Alfred's *Life*.[83] Whitelock's argument that the Annals of St Neots (in the case of the 885 annal) share with the later part of the *Historia Regum* (*HR* 2) a superior reading of the *Life* of Alfred to that found in Cotton Otho A.xii stands in opposition to Hart's views.[84] Whitelock was essentially agreeing with Stevenson here,[85] for although Stevenson accepted that the manuscript of the *Life* of Alfred which was used in the compilation of the Annals of St Neots agreed very closely with the Cottonian manuscript, he also held that in places, it displayed more correct readings. In the opinion of Stevenson and Whitelock, therefore, the copy of the *Life* of Alfred used by the compiler of the Annals of St Neots was by implication a different manuscript from that of Cotton Otho A.xii. It is not clear what precise relationship was thought by Whitelock to have existed between the manuscript of Alfred's *Life* which lay behind the Annals of St Neots and that consulted by the compilers of the *Historia Regum* (*HR* 1) and—in one instance at least—*HR* 2, save the fact that they all preserved more accurate readings than those in the lost Cotton manuscript which formed the basis of Parker's edition. Whitelock's conclusions on the nature of the manuscript of the *Life* of Alfred, consulted by the compiler of the Annals of St Neots, were based on a much more limited study than that carried out by Hart, but in the case of her evaluation of the 885 annal she seemed to have proved her point that the manuscript of Alfred's *Life* consulted by the compilers of the first part of the *Historia Regum* and of the Annals of St Neots had a better reading than that of the Parker–Cotton text of Alfred's *Life*. Hart's views on the manuscript of Alfred's *Life* which lay behind the Annals of St Neots were summed up as follows:

Such variants as exist [between the text of the Annals of St Neots and the Cottonian manuscript of the *Life* of Alfred] appear to be due entirely to minor errors in transcription, or to the East Anglian chronicler [i.e. compiler of the Annals of St Neots] seeking to elucidate the text of Asser by introducing or substituting words or phrases from other sources, known to be before him as he wrote.[86]

But the readings of the Annals of St Neots and the later part of the *Historia Regum* are so close for that portion of the 885 annal examined by Whitelock, that they must either derive from a common source or else one must depend upon the other. Dumville[87] took an independent stand from his editorial colleague's pronouncements on this problem, declaring that 'at present, it seems impossible to say whether the Compiler of the Annals of St Neots (or, indeed, Byrhtferth of Ramsey or John [i.e. Florence] of Worcester) employed a text of Asser's work superior to that of the Parker–Cotton manuscript'.

The reason for Dumville's agnosticism in 1985 was that he was suspending judgement until the completion of a new edition of the Parker–Cotton text of Alfred's *Life* 'in as accurate a reconstruction as the limits of the surviving evidence will permit'.[88] But the surviving evidence is so limited due to the loss of the Cotton manuscript, and so botched and contaminated by Parker's editorial apprentices, that the reconstruction of the text of Cotton Otho A.xii of the *Life* of King Alfred will forever remain a subjective exercise. To suggest that any future full-scale reconstruction of the Parker–Cotton text could carry the same authority as the lost manuscript of Alfred's *Life* would be to reduce Anglo-Latin textual studies to the level of a pseudo-science. The best we can ever hope to achieve is to tentatively reconstruct those portions of the *Life* which are covered by all the major medieval abstractors—Byrhtferth, Florence of Worcester, and the Compiler of the Annals of St Neots. It is not until these medieval versions of the *Life* of Alfred are accorded parity with, if not primacy over the Parker–Cotton edition, that parts of the text of the *Life* of Alfred can be cited with any degree of certainty.

Because the Annals of St Neots have been associated for so long with the text of the *Life* of King Alfred, an accurate estimation of their date of composition is very important for Alfredian studies. The association between the Annals of St Neots and the *Life* of Alfred goes back much further than the time of Parker, who conflated the two sources in an effort to publish as much material as he could find on the subject of King Alfred. We have seen how from their inception the St Neots annals had themselves incorporated material from the *Life* of Alfred, and it was this which prompted Leland—when he discovered the manuscript in the 1540s to attribute their authorship to Asser.[89] While Hart argued cogently for a late tenth- or early eleventh-century date for the compilation of the Annals of St Neots,[90] Dumville and Lapidge opted for a date of compilation between 1120 and 1140.[91] The fact that Hart's detailed, and on the whole convincing, arguments were dismissed in a two-line footnote,[92] rather than answered point by point, lends little credibility to the pronouncements of his critics. Among Hart's strongest arguments for a date *c.*1000 were his comparisons between the Annals of St Neots and Byrhtferth's *Northumbrian Chronicle*. Both sources, he argued, made use of an early version of the Anglo-Saxon Chronicle, the Royal Frankish Annals, Bede's *Historia Ecclesiastica*, the *Life* of King Alfred, and Abbo's *Passio* of St Edmund. The structural arrangement of this similar material was handled in the same way by the compiler of Byrhtferth's *Northumbrian Chronicle* and by the compiler of the Annals of St Neots, using sets of annals for continuity, and the textual treatment was also very similar in both cases. Dumville and Lapidge failed to provide a convincing explanation as to why a twelfth-century compiler would cut short a historical compilation (beginning at 60 BC) at 914. Their suggestion that by bringing the work to a conclusion in the early tenth century, with the foundation of the Norman duchy, the compilers had fulfilled their remit is not convincing.[93] The editors' notion that the ending of the work in 914 paved the way for a subsequent volume (which no longer exists) was on their own admission—utter speculation.[94] Dumville and Lapidge concluded that the presence of extracts from Norman annals in the Annals of St Neots betrays a post-Conquest date for that compilation.[95] Hart argued for the transmission of this material via pre-Conquest links between Normandy and the English Danelaw.[96] Norman annals—in the usually understood sense of that term—originated in the mid-eleventh century and are considered contemporary from the late eleventh century.[97] It is, of course, possible that a work such as the Annals of St Neots—ending in 914—could have borrowed from a compilation which did not come into existence until *c.*1066, but it is no less probable that the same scattered information which was borrowed by the St Neots compiler was made available from precursor texts of the Norman annals which have since been lost. No surviving set of Norman annals can be shown to be the source of the St Neots entries.[98] Dumville's statement on this extremely complex issue constitutes no more than one writer's unsubstantiated personal opinion and side-steps the glaring lack of detailed study of the Norman texts involved: 'Whatever annalistic or chronicling activity may have occurred in Normandy before this period [*c.*1066], there seems no reason to place the composition of the parent text of these Norman Annals before the second half of the eleventh century.'[99]

Almost all of the so-called Norman material in the Annals of St Neots pre-dates the foundation of the Norman duchy in 911, and belongs, therefore, ultimately to Frankish sources rather than to things Norman. The modern editors of the Annals of St Neots did not provide an adequate explanation for the existence of so many entries from the Norman annals either squeezed in and abbreviated at the ends of lines, or in the margins of the only surviving medieval manuscript of the text.[100] Apart from the 633 entry which is of mixed English and 'Norman' content, all of these marginal or end-of-line annals deal exclusively with 'Norman' annalistic matters and their peripheral position in the manuscript of the Annals of St Neots (although all appear to be written in the main or text hand) could suggest that the twelfth-century scribe of this work was incorporating 'Norman' material into an older compilation. While we may agree with Hart that the surviving text of the Annals of St Neots 'has the appearance of a copy from an exemplar, rather than something being compiled at the time of writing [in the twelfth century] from a variety of sources',[101] it is possible that the two twelfth-century scribes copied an earlier version of the Annals of St Neots dating from *c.*1000 and incorporated into that copy an early series of entries from a later eleventh-century set of Norman annals. The twelfth-century scribes of the surviving manuscript would not, in that case, have been acting as general compilers, but were rather adding in a prepared and coherent set of Norman abstracts into an earlier compilation, of which they were making a new and conflated copy. We must at least acknowledge a quite separate handling of the Norman material by the writers of the twelfth-century manuscript, and when we add to this the cogent reasons offered by Hart for a pre-Conquest date for the core of the annalistic compilation, the possibility of two phases in the development of the Annals of St Neots presents itself.

Alistair Campbell demonstrated that the writer of the *Encomium Emmae Reginae* (a praise poem on Emma, the widowed queen of Cnut who died in 1052) borrowed two glosses from the *Life* of Alfred into his text. The evidence is concise but specific and convincing, and therefore suggests that the author of the *Encomium*, who was connected with either St Omer or St Bertin and who wrote *c.*1041, had consulted a text of Alfred's *Life* or portions of that text, either in Flanders or perhaps in England.[102] The *Encomium* (ii. 8), in relating how Cnut spent a winter in Sheppey (*Sceepei*), glosses that place-name with the phrase: 'that is to say in Latin *insula ovium* ["island of sheep"] (*quod est dictum Latine 'insula ovium'*)'.[103] In chapter 3 of the *Life* of Alfred, Sheppey (*Sceapieg*) is also glossed: *quod interpretatur 'insula ovium'*[104] in a translation of the annal from the Anglo-Saxon Chronicle for 851. Similarly, the *Encomium* (ii. 9) glosses the place-name *Aescenedun* with 'a word which we Latinists can explain as "Hill of Ash Trees" (*quod nos Latini 'montem fraxinorum' possumus interpretari'*,[105] while in chapter 37 of Alfred's *Life*, the place-name *Æscesdun* is glossed (*quod Latine 'mons fraxini' iterpretatur*).[106] The Encomiast's two glosses—which echo the text of the *Life* of Alfred—stand out in contrast to several other place-names in the text of the *Encomium Emmae* which are not so glossed. Campbell also lent all the weight of his great learning and knowledge of medieval Latin texts to claim certainty for his opinion that the author of the *Encomium* (ii. 9) had access to that passage in the Annals of St Neots which describes the Raven banner of the Danish army in Devon in 878.[107] All three passages occur close together in the text of the *Encomium Emmae* and it reasonable to conclude that all three items were borrowed by the author of the *Encomium* from one source. Otherwise we must accept the highly unlikely circumstance whereby this Continental author was sufficiently familiar with both the *Life* of Alfred and the Annals of St Neots as to extract such detailed information from each work. Campbell not unreasonably concluded that the author of the *Encomium* found the St Neots passage on the Raven banner in his copy of the *Life* of Alfred.[108] But although that passage was included in Parker's edition of Alfred's *Life*, Wise later stated that the Raven banner episode was an interpolation from the Annals of St Neots into the Cottonian text.[109] We must, therefore, either go against Wise's judgement and conclude that episodes such as the Raven banner were original to the Cotton manuscript of Alfred's *Life*, or alternatively that the author of the *Encomium* found all three of his borrowed passages in another source. That source can only have been a copy of the Annals of St Neots. The unique twelfth-century Bury St Edmunds manuscript of those annals omits the gloss on Sheppey in its version of the annal for 851.[110] But it does include the gloss on *Aescesdun* under 871[111] and, of course, it provides the source for the Raven banner episode at 878.[112]

Given the medieval association between extracts from the *Life* of Alfred with material such as the Raven banner episode in the Annals of St Neots, the most economical conclusion to be drawn from the evidence of the *Encomium* is to conclude that its author probably consulted a version of the Annals of St Neots which included both the *Aescesdun* and *Sceapeige* glosses, as well as the passage on the Raven banner. If that were so, then the earliest version of the Annals of St Neots must pre-date the composition of the *Encomium* in *c.*1041. Whitelock rightly used the *Encomium Emmae* as proof for the existence of the *Life* of Alfred prior to the time of Bishop Leofric of Exeter.[113] That same *Encomium* also suggests the existence of a version of the Annals of St Neots prior to *c.*1040, and in which case Hart, therefore, may well have been correct, in arguing for a pre-Conquest date for the earliest level of compilation for the Annals of St Neots.

Emma (whose English name was Ælfgifu) was the daughter of Duke Richard I of Normandy (943–96) and sister of Duke Richard II. She was the queen of Æthelred the Unready from 1002 until his death in 1016, and a son of that marriage was the future Edward the Confessor. A year after Æthelred's death, Emma became the queen of Cnut, whom she outlived on his death in 1035, and survived through the reign of her son, Harthacnut, dying as late as 1052. Emma was twice forced into exile during her English career—once when she retreated back to Normandy during a crisis in Æthelred's reign in 1013, and later during the reign of her son, Harthacnut, when she was forced across to Flanders in the period 1037 to 1040. Emma was the Norman influence *par excellence* on early eleventh-century England. She epitomized not only the demographic links which had become firmly established in the early eleventh century between the Danelaw and Normandy, on the one hand, and the Scandinavian homelands, on the other, but in her dynastic and marital relationships she also personally symbolized the broadening of horizons in England's foreign policies. Historians or linguists who view the Norman Conquest of England as the only major cultural watershed in eleventh-century English history fail to appreciate that the careers of magnates such as Emma and her immediate household had paved the way for Norman domination of England half a century before the Conquest. The era of Emma and Cnut the Great suggests itself as an appropriate time for the compilation of the Annals of St Neots on several counts. It was a time when those East Anglian monasteries which had been reconstituted by the reformers at the end of the tenth century were consolidating their position during the relative stability of Cnut's regime. Emma herself was credited in one tradition[114] with having urged Cnut to restore Bury St Edmunds—that place of pilgrimage of the martyred King Edmund, whose *Passio* was freely used by the compiler of the Annals of St Neots. The Annals of St Neots, like all historical compilations of their kind, reflect a self-confidence on the part of their originators, which in the case of this source finds a suitable home in the period *c.*1020–35. That was a time when the great monasteries of East Anglia and their rich lay patrons were most likely to want to indulge their interests in the history of the region. It was also a time when Norman and Anglo-Danish tastes in historical writing had to be catered for. Emma was herself the owner of huge East

Anglian estates in West Suffolk, which were used after her fall from favour in 1043 for the endowment of Bury St Edmunds.[115] Prior to that time, a charter from Cnut in 1021–3[116] confirmed an earlier grant of privileges supposedly conferred on the abbey of Bury St Edmunds by King Edmund (939–46).[117] In addition to Cnut's and Emma's support for Bury St Edmunds,[118] we know that Emma and her son, Harthacnut, also enriched Ramsey Abbey, the one-time home of Byrhtferth and his circle of writers, by granting it an estate at Hemingford in Huntingdonshire in 1040–2.[119] It is entirely in keeping with the evidence to find that a praise-poem on Emma, whose Continental author had associations with St Bertin, should contain echoes of passages from an East Anglian chronicle which was composed shortly before that time in an effort to celebrate the history of the Southern Danelaw under the new-found stability of Cnut. A compilation date of *c.* 1020–35 is somewhat later than that envisaged by Hart, but it is still early enough for the Annals of St Neots to have been compiled under the influence of Byrhtferth's pupils, as Hart maintained.

There were, then, either only one—or less likely as many as two, three, or four—manuscript versions of the *Life* of Alfred extant in the twelfth century. The Cottonian version which was eventually destroyed in 1731 was probably the same manuscript as that used in the Chronicle of Florence of Worcester. Hart, as we have seen, believed that the Cotton manuscript also lay behind the extracts from Alfred's *Life* in the Annals of St Neots, and Lapidge demonstrated that in one instance at least the Cotton manuscript could be shown to have been the exemplar for Byrhtferth's extracts from the *Life* of Alfred in the earlier section of the *Historia Regum* (*HR* 1). There was also part at least, of a text of Alfred's *Life* available in *c.* 1041 to the pro-Danish writer of the *Encomium Emmae* who may have been based in Flanders, and who may have had access to extracts from the *Life* of Alfred in the Annals of St Neots. While we cannot be certain that the Cotton Otho A.xii text lies behind all surviving versions of the *Life* of Alfred, it is equally difficult to show (with the notable exception of the 885 annal in *HR* 2) that any other manuscript version was definitely involved. We can never reach firm conclusions about manuscripts of a text which have all perished except for late copies, and so the precise relationship between the Cotton manuscript and the original text of the *Life* of Alfred will forever elude us. Whitelock argued that since the versions of Asser in the *Historia Regum* and in the Annals of St Neots both share the same errors in a process of miscopying from a common exemplar, and since the Cotton manuscript has a greater number of errors than the other two versions, then the lost Cotton manuscript was at best a copy of a copy of the original text.[120] This does not necessarily have to have been the case, but even if that were true, it does not follow that the original manuscript had to be very much older than its copies.

This discussion on the complicated history of the text sets the background for the debate on the authenticity of Asser's *Life* of Alfred, but it also brings home to us an important point at the outset. It makes us aware of the severe limitations of textual evidence in arguments relating to the date of the work. It cannot be emphasized too often, that all complete medieval manuscripts of the *Life* have perished, and the evidence as it stands cannot prove that there was ever more than one—or at the most two—manuscripts in existence in the eleventh and twelfth centuries. Even Otho A.xii—that sole survivor of the *Life* from the pillaging of monastic libraries in sixteenth-century England[121]—tragically perished in the fire of 1731 before it could be subjected to the scrutiny of modern palaeographers. Reaching textual certainty in regard to this manuscript *Life* of King Alfred is as remote as reaching a final verdict on a report of an early eighteenth-century autopsy. We can never be certain precisely how much Matthew Parker added or deleted from those parts of his manuscript source which are not supported by textual parallels from other medieval writers. And even where alternative medieval textual readings are available, we cannot be certain that Parker's variant forms derive from Cotton Otho A.xii or from Parker's own editorial 'improvements'. That is true of his transcript[122] as well as of his printed text, and Stevenson's optimism regarding the textual purity of that transcript, which was shared by Keynes and Lapidge, can scarcely be justified.[123]

A study of those passages from the *Life* of Alfred in Florence of Worcester, the Annals of St Neots, and the *Historia Regum* (*HR* 1) does allow us to exercise a limited check on Parker's edition. But that check is always only partial, since the last two sources tend to concern themselves with those parts of the *Life* of Alfred which were borrowed from the Anglo-Saxon Chronicle, omitting the more controversial and so-called original biographical aspects of the *Life*. As for Florence, he severely edited out of his Chronicle extensive passages in the *Life* which he either did not find in his manuscript of that work or which he did not believe in, or which he felt were of no interest or help to his own compilation.[124] So, for many crucial passages in the *Life* of Alfred, we have ultimately to rely on Parker's edition, which was, on Stevenson's admission, 'filled with arbitrary alterations and interpolations, which are distinguished in no way from the readings of the original [manuscript]'.[125] Although Stevenson was aware that Parker relied a great deal on his secretaries for help with his scholarly researches,[126] he minimized the complexity of Parker's editorial teamwork and he seemed to have been unaware of the religious and ideological motivation which provided the driving-force for Parker's entire publication programme. Strype described Parker's large and diverse household at Lambeth as 'a kind of flourishing University of learned men: and his domestics, being provoked by the Archbishop's exhortations and precepts, often published to the world the fruits of their studies'.[127] We are told on Parker's authority that 'he had within his house, in wages, drawers [of pictures], and cutters [engravers], painters, limners, writers, and bookbinders'.[128] Strype goes on to inform us that the archbishop

kept such in his family as could imitate any of the old characters admirably well. One of these was Lyly, an excellent writer, and [one] that could counterfeit any antique writing. Him the archbishop customarily used to make old books complete, that wanted some pages; that the character might seem to be the same throughout.[129]

Stevenson[130] conveniently omitted to quote the final sentence from the above passage relating to the 'completion' of old 'books'—which, from the context, must be a reference to manuscripts. Stevenson's argument that interpolations in the Cottonian manuscript (Otho A.xii), in addition to those in Parker's characteristic red ochre pencil, were in the handwriting of Parker's own time must be questioned.[131] Since the manuscript is no longer extant, we have no way of knowing whether a man such as Lyly had tampered with it, however obvious Parker's own interpolations may have been to seventeenth- and eighteenth-century observers. Nor can we be certain as to what later medieval interpolations the Cotton manuscript may have contained. James Hill, who consulted the manuscript in 1722, shortly before its destruction, failed to distinguish between the so-called sixteenth-century Parkerian hands and medieval hands in the Cotton text.[132] Not only did Parker run a household which was a cross between a Tudor university and a medieval monastic scriptorium,[133] but Parker was himself so busy that his role in the production of King Alfred's *Life* may not have been as immediate as is so often supposed. In the years immediately prior to the publication of the *Life*, Parker had lost his wife and was himself in failing health.[134] He was preoccupied with the turmoil of Church and State, coping with a three-cornered struggle between Anglicans, Catholics, and Puritans, and energetically monitoring (in so far as he could) the war of words between all three. Parker died in May 1575, in the year after the publication of the *Life* of Alfred. He had been responsible for ambitious building projects at Lambeth and Cambridge, and engrossed in elaborate preparations for the entertainment of his queen in Canterbury in the autumn of 1573.[135] In spite of his personal devotion to historical scholarship, Parker's role in the publication of the *Life* of Alfred in 1574 may not have been more than that of a general editor. We do know that the *Lives* of the archbishops of Canterbury published under the title of *De Antiquitate Britannicae Ecclesiae* were certainly compiled, if not actually completed, by John Joscelyn, the Essex antiquary, whom we might describe as Parker's chief research assistant in the 1570s.[136] The *De Antiquitate* was published by John Day in 1572—that same publisher who gave Asser to the world only two years later.

As for Parker's own scholarly methods, by the standards of his time they may have been second to none, but it is prudent to bear in mind that this busy sixteenth-century archbishop did not have the benefit of the ubiquitous modern M.Phil seminars in palaeography. And although Joscelyn, Parker's secretary, was a careful scholar and a man of great learning, we need to keep our assessment of that learning within the context of his day. McKisack reminded us that Joscelyn's 'methods of handling his manuscripts were much the same as Parker's. He wrote notes on them for purposes of collation, supplemented and otherwise "improved" the text.'[137] The learned Joscelyn was also capable, like Lyly, of faking an Old English hand.[138] It is true Parker tells us in his preface to the edition of the *Life* of Alfred that it was 'exactly and literally done from the original manuscript' and that the manuscript itself (or perhaps he meant the transcript) could be collated against his printed text by anyone who wished to consult it in Corpus Christi College Cambridge.[139] But Parker did tamper with the text of the Corpus transcript,[140] and with that of the original Cotton manuscript of Alfred's *Life*[141] and according to Stevenson, he had elsewhere indulged in 'wanton falsification' of the Latin text of King Alfred's *Will*.[142] We know, too, that Parker was responsible for an interpolation in the manuscript of the *Textus Roffensis* and for yet another in the *Black Book of the Archdeacon of Canterbury*.[143] In a letter to Cecil in 1565, Parker suggested that he would employ his gifted counterfeiter, Lyly, to add illustrations and missing text to the manuscript of a medieval psalter.[144] Parker's editorial methods were outlined in another letter probably dating to December 1571 and written by him to a peer who is not named. In this letter it is clear that the archbishop had been sent a manuscript which he was then returning to its sender in a printed edition: 'And whereas I have been long in requiting your good will in bestowing this written story upon me, I send the same story to your lordship in print, somewhat more enlarged with such old copies as I had of other of my friends, praying for your lordship to accept it in good part.'[145] So, Parker, at the very time when he must have been planning his edition of King Alfred's *Life*, is here declaring that his editorial approach was to 'enlarge' the text of his exemplar by conflating it with related material from other sources. It was this approach which explains the presence of extensive interpolations from the Annals of St Neots in Parker's 1574 edition of the *Life* of King Alfred. None of this is to suggest that there was necessarily any intention to deceive. The practice of collation and conflation was no doubt viewed as a desirable procedure facilitated by the invention of printing. But since we lack the original manuscript on which Joscelyn or his helpers left their notes, we have little idea of how those editors went about their scissors-and-paste approach. If Parker's 1571 edition of Matthew Paris's *Greater History* is anything to go by, then we must assume that the edition of the *Life* of Alfred also consisted of 'a "mixed" text, made up . . . with unbounded licence and with interpolations which belie the editor's claim [in his preface to Asser] never to have added anything to or subtracted anything from the books he published'.[146] McKisack catalogued a lengthy list of examples of defacing and altering of medieval manuscripts by Parker or his editorial assistants, which affords convincing proof that were the Cottonian *Life* of King Alfred to survive today, we would find erasures and 'corrections' in a counterfeit hand, as well as 'improved' versions of the text pasted over original script, together with a multitude of marginalia.[147]

Parker was, by sixteenth-century standards, an able scholar and a bibliophile to whom we should be grateful for rescuing a vast number of medieval manuscripts from iconoclasm and ruin. To view Parker solely, however, as a renaissance scholar and antiquary would be to misunderstand his publication programme entirely. Parker was a propagandist who employed his scholarly household in a drive to justify the ideological and doctrinal position of the recently established Anglican Church. His agents ransacked the remnants of ruined monastic libraries and private book collections[148] in search of material from an elusive ancient 'British' Church—material which could be used to demonstrate a continuity with the Reformers' otherwise apparently novel doctrinal position.[149] Although Parker was responsible for the collection of huge numbers of medieval books and manuscripts,[150] clearly his decision to proceed with publication was limited to only a special few of these items. That being so, we need to ask the question, as to why the *Life* of Alfred was singled out for a printed edition. In his preface to his edition of Matthew Paris, Parker praised that chronicler for standing out against the usurpations and tyrannies of the papacy.[151] And the thirteenth-century manuscript which Parker used to publish his edition of that work has been drastically 'improved' with eight missing folios added in a counterfeit or 'restoring' hand.[152] In his *Testimony of Antiquity, Showing the Ancient Faith in the Church of England* published in the late 1560s, Parker used Anglo-Saxon sources to attack Catholic doctrine on transubstantiation.[153] The *Life* of King Alfred which Parker, following Leland,[154] firmly attributed to Asser, clearly held a special interest for the archbishop to convince him of its importance for his expensive publication programme. To begin with, Asser was regarded as an ancient 'British'—i.e. Welsh—bishop, and therefore qualified for special attention as a member of an early Church, which was seen by the Reformers as being independent of Rome. Secondly, Alfred was well known to Parker as a translator into Old English of philosophical and religious works. Parker possessed no less than three manuscript copies of King Alfred's translation of the *Pastoral Care*, as well as manuscripts of Gregory's Dialogues and of the Old English Bede.[155] Alfred had therefore vindicated the Reformers' use of the vernacular, some seven centuries before the Reformation began. Finally, one of the more enduring impressions conveyed by the *Life* of Alfred was the account of how the king eagerly learnt to read and translate while discussing passages from Holy Scripture with his chaplain, Asser.[156] Alfred could be presented to the world by Parker as an Anglo-Saxon prototype and as a devout version of a Henrician Protestant king. Here was a figure who might warm the cockles of any Reforming bishop's heart—a lay ruler mulling over the Scriptures, publishing devout texts in the vernacular, and whose biography was written by a cleric from the acceptable ancient British Church. The publication of the *Life* of King Alfred was no mere antiquarian pursuit. It was a typical product of Parker's busy 'shop'—'rough hewn by one of the apprentices' and lacking 'polishing by the foreman' who was otherwise preoccupied with the affairs of his Church and of his queen.[157]

Where does all this information leave Stevenson's lengthy discussion on the various hands of the lost Cottonian manuscript? We know that that manuscript contained glosses in Parker's hand and other glosses from his secretaries. We are also justified in concluding that Parker's editorial household worked in a tradition that was as much late medieval as it was 'modern',[158] and that in spite of his own quite reasonable protestations of editorial integrity, both Parker and his assistant scholars were capable of completing a line or finishing off a sentence without incurring any sense of guilt pertaining to modern invention or forgery.[159] Parker's Cottonian manuscript of the *Life* of Alfred included paper additions interleaved by Parker and his secretaries, which contained extracts from the Annals of St Neots.[160] Other interleaved material may have been inserted in the manuscript as well. The original Cottonian text was either in two or several hands, but that observation is not as relevant as it might seem, since we have no certain way of knowing how close that lost Cotton version was to the original manuscript of King Alfred's *Life*.[161] Faced with this unsatisfactory if not indeed chaotic 'archaeology of text', the historian must turn to his rightful task—a task which would still confront him even if he had the benefit of modern palaeographical and textual criticism advising him on an extant and original manuscript. That task is to study the actual *Life* of King Alfred as it has imperfectly come down to us, and to reach an opinion regarding its consistency and plausibility, in the light of what we know as historians, of England in the ninth and tenth centuries. As we turn now to this task, of analysing the text ascribed to Asser, we are neither unmindful of the textual problems nor overawed by them. If the *Life* of Alfred had dealt with any lesser subject than the darling of early English history, it would long ago have been relegated to its appropriate place among problematical texts of doubtful origin and composition. It only came to be regarded as 'one of the most important . . . of the sources of our early history'[162] because of an understandable—not to say desperate—need, on the part of nineteenth-century writers, to know more about one of England's most important kings. Compared with Bede's *Life* of Cuthbert or Eddius's *Life* of Wilfrid, for instance, we shall see that the biography of Alfred reads as a sad hotch-potch of poorly wrought hagiography and translated annals.

We enter this discussion, equipped with some valuable information and guidelines provided by textual scholars. Clearly, parts at least of the *Life* of Alfred have to be as old as the earliest known medieval writers who made use of them. The earliest known writer who had access to the *Life* of Alfred was Byrhtferth of Ramsey, in or about the year 1000, when Byrhtferth included a summary from Alfred's *Life* in what now survives as the first five sections of the *Historia Regum* (*HR* 1). A faint but clearly recognizable echo of Asser's text appears in the *Encomium Emmae Reginae* c.1041.[163] The presence of lengthy passages borrowed from, or based on the text of the *Life* of Alfred in the Annals of St Neots, and in the twelfth-century works of Florence of Worcester and the later part of the *Historia Regum* (*HR* 2), are valuable in correcting or verifying Parker's edition of the text of the lost Cottonian manuscript. We note too, that however unsatisfactory the freehand facsimile of the opening lines of the Cotton text may be, it has been accepted on palaeographical grounds as roughly dating to the early eleventh century—a date which is in keeping with Wanley's observations on the script of the manuscript in his letter of 1721 and vaguely in line with Ussher's opinions expressed in 1639. This dating of the lost Cottonian manuscript also happens to coincide with the time when Byrhtferth was busy producing his hagiographical, historical, and pseudo-scientific outpourings at Ramsey, and Byrhtferth was the earliest scholar who can be shown to have been familiar with the *Life* of Alfred. It may be that one of Byrhtferth's pupils was the next writer, in the time of Queen Emma (*c.*1020–35), to have made extensive use of the *Life* of Alfred in his compilation of the Annals of St Neots. And it was from this same East Anglian monastic milieu that the author of the *Encomium Emmae* may have been introduced to a version of the Annals of St Neots, which contained, of course, extensive extracts from the *Life* of Alfred.

Thus far, the trail leads back to the turn of the millennium—to the circle of Byrhtferth of Ramsey and perhaps to a single manuscript with palaeographical associations with Worcester—a monastery with close Ramsey connections in the late tenth century. It was at Worcester, too, that Florence *alias* John later incorporated sections of the Cottonian text of the *Life* into his own chronicle. It is now our task to determine if possible, from the text of the *Life* of Alfred that survives to us, whether or not it was written in the lifetime of King Alfred and by a man who claimed to have been on intimate terms with his king.

VII

At His Mother's Knee
Tall Tales of Childhood

IF IT WERE NOT FOR THE *LIFE* OF ALFRED, WE SHOULD KNOW NOTHING of the king's childhood and youth before 868—apart, that is, from the dubious account in the Anglo-Saxon Chronicle of his pilgrimage to Rome as an infant in 853[1] The first historical notice of Alfred in the Chronicle mentions his presence along with King Æthelred I on the West Saxon expedition to Nottingham in 868. By then, Alfred was aged somewhere between 19 and 21, and soon to be king. Alfred's biographer, however, promises his readers to fill the void in the twenty hidden years of Alfred's early life: 'I think that we should return to what specially incited me to this work; that is to say, that I consider that I should insert briefly in this place the little that has come to my knowledge concerning the character of my revered lord, Alfred, king of the Anglo-Saxons, during his childhood and boyhood (*de infantilibus et puerilibus*).'[2]

In this, as in several other instances, the author of the *Life* of Alfred stands in sharp contrast to that of the Frankish Einhard. Indeed, as we shall see, Alfred's biographer may have been deliberately trying to outdo Einhard, whose *Life* of Charlemagne was known and used by him and served as the immediate model for the *Life* of Alfred. Einhard's approach was more cautious than that of the author of Alfred's *Life*: 'I consider that it would be foolish for me to write about Charlemagne's birth and childhood, or even about his boyhood, for nothing is set down in writing about this and nobody can be found still alive who claims to have any personal knowledge of these matters. I have therefore decided to leave out what is not really known.'[3] Alfred's biographer was, we might argue, in a very different position from Einhard. Although Einhard had been a member of Charlemagne's Palace school for twenty-three years, Charlemagne was dead for more than twenty years when Einhard eventually wrote his biography in retirement from the Carolingian court at Seligenstadt. Alfred's biographer, on the other hand, claims that he was writing when Alfred was still at the height of his career and when the author still enjoyed the king's friendship and great generosity at the West Saxon court.[4] If that were true, then Alfred's biographer would indeed have been in a position to question the king and his courtiers about Alfred's childhood, and so the account of that childhood holds one of the keys to the validation or otherwise of the *Life* of King Alfred. This is all the more true because the compiler of the *Life*, unlike Einhard, specifically set himself the task of discussing Alfred's early years.

The literary plan adopted by King Alfred's biographer has been recognized by scholars as far apart in their views as Wright and Stevenson to consist of blocks of biographical prose grafted onto a framework provided by the Anglo-Saxon Chronicle. The *Life* taken as a whole—consisting of a Latin translation of the Alfredian section of the Chronicle; interpolations and glosses added to the Chronicle; and the biographical passages on Alfred—is agreed to have been put together, however crudely, by one compiler.[5] This is also the view accepted in this discussion. Stevenson's edition of 1904 presented the *Life* of Alfred in 106 chapters. The core of the continuous and original biographical narrative of that *Life* (i.e. that part which is independent of the translation of the Anglo-Saxon Chronicle) does not begin until chapter 73 when the author reintroduces the subject of Alfred's marriage.[6] Apart from five chapters which revert to dependence on the Chronicle,[7] this independent narrative is sustained to the end of the work. Significantly, the author of the *Life* had earlier dated Alfred's marriage to 868 in an interpolation to his translation of the Chronicle annal for that year.[8] He informs us under the year 868, that Alfred had taken a Mercian wife—in the same year as Alfred had joined his brother, King Æthelred, on the Nottingham expedition.[9] So, the beginning of the continuous narrative of supposedly original biographical material coincides exactly with that first historical notice of Alfred in the Chronicle. The Chronicle, then, not only provided a basic narrative of non-Alfredian events to cover those years for which Alfred's biographer was devoid of information on the king, but the first genuine reference to Alfred in the Chronicle also triggered a parallel biographical narrative of supposedly supportive and independent information on the part of the king's biographer. If the writer really had personal knowledge of the king, then why did he take the same starting-point—868—as the Anglo-Saxon Chronicle, to begin a narrative on a king who was then already (on the author's reckoning) 20 years old. None of this is suggestive of a writer who was the contemporary of Alfred and who had access to that multiplicity of independent sources of information which we associate with contemporary biography.[10]

Of the first seventy-two chapters in the *Life* of Alfred, which cover the period from Alfred's supposed birth in 849 up to and including 885—or the first 36 years of his life—only twelve[11] contain what we may call biographical narrative of the same genre as those which appear from chapter 73 onwards. Two other chapters[12] contain extensive narrative additions to the account of the Anglo-Saxon Chronicle. And of the twelve anecdotal chapters, only six deal personally with Alfred himself, covering his youth and marriage.[13] The remaining six cover a largely irrelevant discussion on an eighth-century West Saxon queen, Eadburh;[14] on the rebellion of Æthelbald[15] and on Æthelbald's marriage;[16] and on the *Will* of his father, King Æthelwulf.[17] So, before we even begin to analyse the biographer's account of Alfred's early years, we realize that he had severe problems in obtaining information, in spite of frequent protestations throughout the *Life* that the friendly king is alive and to hand, and presumably willing to answer any questions that might be put to him.[18] For instead of consulting his 'revered lord' as the obvious source of information on Alfred's infancy and youth, the king's biographer contented himself with basing no less than sixty of his first seventy-two chapters on the Anglo-Saxon Chronicle—a source which, as we have seen, contained no reliable mention of Alfred prior to 868. The only exception is the translation of the spurious account of Alfred's visit to Rome in 853[19] and in this the author of the *Life* added to the confusion by sending Alfred to Rome for a second time in chapter 11.[20]

The author of the *Life* does offer a little information by way of interpolation and glossing in his translation of the Chronicle narrative, and while some of these insertions may represent a genuine tradition, others clearly do not. We have already seen[21] that the statement that Alfred was born in Wantage in Berkshire[22] is extremely unlikely to have been correct. It flies in the face of common sense, poses real historical problems, and was doubted by Stenton in an earlier and more objective stage of his thinking.[23] The first two chapters of the *Life* present a mere illusion of originality. The genealogy of Alfred offered in chapter 1 is based on a version of the genealogy of Alfred's father, Æthelwulf, which appears in the Chronicle at the notice of Æthelwulf's death, under 855–8.[24] In view of the consistently careless way in which Alfred's biographer handles his other source materials, attempts to show that Asser's source for this genealogy differed in some genuine respects from that of the Chronicle, or that he edited the Chronicle's genealogy of Æthelwulf in the knowledge of other unspecified information[25] amount to frantic attempts to attribute originality to the author of the *Life*. It is not that a genealogy of Alfred is out of place in a *Life* of that king. The main point at issue in relation to chapter 1 is that the author lifted a genealogy otherwise associated with Alfred's father in the Chronicle at 855–8, and transferred it back to 849, supposedly the year of Alfred's birth. Alfred's biographer seems to have fixed the year of Alfred's birth at least one year too late.[26] For Alfred, according to the Genealogical Preface to Manuscript A of the Anglo-Saxon Chronicle, was 23 when he became king in 871, which means that he was born in 847 or 848, and the testimony of that source, dating if not from the later years of Alfred's own life, then certainly to c.900, is to be preferred to anything found in the textual confusion of the *Life* of Alfred.[27] The supposed evidence for Asser's editorial tampering with this genealogy is that the author of the *Life* omitted the name Esla between Elesa and Gewis, and that he omitted three consecutive names (Wig, Freawine, and Freothogar) between Gewis and Brand. We note that the omissions come immediately before and after the name *Gewis*. Since these same names are also lacking in genealogies preserved outside the textual tradition of the Chronicle, the argument goes that the author of the *Life* was drawing on that non-Chronicle genealogical tradition. That may be, but it is equally probable that because the author inserted a gloss on the name of Gewis, he was distracted from his copying and lost out one name before, and three other names after, the subject of his insertion. It is understandable why he left out *Esla*, the name immediately before Gewis. His exemplar—in the Chronicle text—read 'Elesa the son of Esla, the son of Gewis' (*Elesa Esling, Esla Giwising, Gewis Wiging*) and taking the second Esla as a repetition of Elesa, the author of Alfred's *Life* omitted it, as did the compiler of Version D of the Anglo-Saxon Chronicle. The author of the *Life* next inserted one of his characteristic glosses on the name of Gewis—'after whom the Welsh call that whole race [of West Saxons] the Gewisse'. This digression caused the author's eye to skip a whole line of text that followed, and hence the absence of Wig, Freawine, and Freothogar from his genealogy.[28] This derivative material, together with a completely irrelevant and long extract from the *Carmen Paschale* of Sedulius— by way of a gloss on the name of the mythical *Geat* in Alfred's pedigree—form the bulk of the first chapter.

    The rigmarole on Alfred's maternal ancestors which makes up the short chapter 2 is based on a mangled version of two entries in the Chronicle relating to the conquest of the Isle of Wight by the West Saxons, Cerdic and Cynric, under the years 530 and 534.[29] The manipulation of the text of the Chronicle here was intended by the author to demonstrate the nobility of Alfred's maternal kin by inventing the claim that his mother's ancestors included in their number a certain Stuf and Wihtgar, two kinsmen of the founding fathers of the kingdom of Wessex, who are mentioned in the Chronicle under AD 534. There never were any contemporary sources for this early period which might have prompted Asser or anyone else to make such genealogical connections, and there is no evidence to suggest that this tradition is any older than the *Life* of Alfred. Scholars who are tempted to believe that the genealogy of Alfred offered in chapter 1 might contain even a grain of authentic Asserian editorial treatment will be dismayed to find that the author of the *Life* contradicts that genealogy he has just offered, by claiming in chapter 2 that Cynric was the son of Cerdic, in the face of the previous genealogy in which he recorded that Cynric was the son of Creoda and the *grandson* of Cerdic.[30] We are told that Alfred's mother's name was Osburh the daughter of Oslac, a butler (and therefore one of the principal magnates) at the court of Alfred's father, Æthelwulf.[31] This may have been the same Oslac as the magnate of that name who attested a genuine and contemporary charter of King Æthelberht dealing with Kentish estates in 858.[32] Alternatively, this information on Alfred's mother may be just as fictitious as the notion that she was descended from the 'Gothic' (*Gothus*) Stuf and Wihtgar and is certainly as elusive of verification. Had Alfred's mother really claimed such an illustrious decent, we should have expected that exotic tradition in turn to have been prompted by more immediate evidence of royal ancestry. And had Alfred's supposedly famous (*famosi*) grandfather really been active as late as 858, then Alfred's biographer would have met many who had known this man and who could have told of his more immediate distinguished and presumably royal predecessors. This entire claim—because of its remoteness— looks derivative and bookish, and its invention was almost certainly suggested to the author of Alfred's *Life* as he searched through the earliest sections of his copy of the Anglo-Saxon Chronicle—a source which he ransacked in his quest for material for his biography.

    It could be argued that the *Life* of King Alfred contains no more and no less rhetorical invention than that of other ninth-century hagiographical works or of, say, the biographies of Carolingian rulers. It could also be argued that *if* the *Life* of King Alfred does truly represent a contemporary biography of the king, then its version of events carries as much weight as the evidence provided by the Chronicle which was also coming into being towards the close of Alfred's reign. According to that line of reasoning, it would be quite wrong to measure the text of the *Life* of Alfred against the Chronicle because the Chronicle would not then be a demonstrably superior source, and the author of the *Life* of Alfred might be argued to have had access to variant versions of sources which were also consulted by the compilers of the Chronicle. There are however several important issues which cannot be divorced from the information supplied by the author of the *Life* of Alfred on the king's maternal kin and on his Mercian in-laws. First, the information in question, from the *Life* of Alfred, which can be corroborated from elsewhere, can be shown to echo closely material which was available in the Chronicle. That in itself might not be so significant were it not that the reliance by the biographer of King Alfred on the Anglo-Saxon Chronicle is otherwise all-pervasive in his work. His genealogical material and his information on the maternal ancestry of Alfred cannot therefore be studied in isolation from his overall dependence on the Chronicle text. Secondly, the apparently original information supplied on Alfred's Mercian in-laws must be set against the remarkable lack of information supplied by the author on Alfred's own family and associates at the time when the work is supposed to have been written. It is one thing to tell us of Alfred's legendary ancestors on the Isle of Wight. But how does it come about that a writer who tells us of Alfred's Mercian in-laws—distant in place and time—shows no knowledge of Alfred's immediate kinsmen—cousins, sisters, and even brothers—who may well have loomed large in his life but who are not mentioned in other sources? And how does it come about that a writer who claims to have spent long periods in King Alfred's household never once supplies the name of a visiting magnate, clergyman, or scholar—with the exception of the priests, Athelstan and Wærwulf—who is not mentioned in the Chronicle or in the king's own writings? These are related issues that can neither be made to go away nor be argued in isolation.

Having offered us these none-too-promising crumbs of information on Alfred's birth and maternal family origins in the first two chapters, the author of the *Life* of Alfred quickly abandoned any pretensions he may have harboured for a biographical mode. From chapter 3 onwards, he was forced to rely almost verbatim on the Anglo-Saxon Chronicle—a situation which persists until the end of chapter 72, with the exception of the twelve 'anecdotal' chapters referred to above. Indeed, the reliance of the *Life* of Alfred on the Chronicle is so complete, and the two texts are so close, that Alfred's *Life* here, like the Chronicle of Æthelweard, ought to be regarded as yet another recension of a section of the Chronicle, rather than a work in its own right. Turning to those twelve chapters in the earlier part of the *Life* which are not dependent on the Chronicle, we may begin with the tale of Queen Eadburh. Here we have an example of the author's ability to provide a good story—however irrelevant—in lieu of even fictional material relating to King Alfred himself. For Alfred has no part in this tale. After explaining how, when Alfred's father, King Æthelwulf, returned from Rome, he had to remain content with the 'eastern districts' of his kingdom,[33] the author then informs us that Æthelwulf insisted that his new Carolingian bride, Judith, be treated as a queen and that she 'should sit beside him on the royal throne until the end of his life'. The author goes on to explain that ever since the time of a certain 'grasping and wicked queen', the West Saxons had reduced the status of their queens to that of 'king's wife (*regis coniugem*)'.[34] The wicked queen in question[35] was Eadburh the daughter of Offa, king of the Mercians who married Beorhtric, king of the West Saxons. That marriage did indeed take place, according to the Anglo-Saxon Chronicle, in 789.[36] Eadburh—the author tells us—became a tyrant like her father, Offa, eventually poisoning one of Beorhtric's young nobles and accidentally poisoning Beorhtric himself. Her flight from Wessex to Francia followed[37] where she turned up at the court of Charles 'the most famous king of the Franks' who invited her to choose between him and his son. Eadburh foolishly chose the son, inviting the rebuke from Charles: 'Had you chosen me, you would have had my son; but because you have chosen my son, you will have neither him nor me.'[38] Charles then appointed her as abbess of a nunnery, a position which she lost, having been caught in debauchery with a man of her own race. She was eventually reduced to a life of misery dying as a beggar in Pavia.

This in outline is the tale of Eadburh which Alfred's biographer protests he heard 'from my lord the truthful Alfred, king of the Anglo-Saxons, who still often tells me about it, and he likewise had heard it from many reliable sources, indeed to a large extent from men who remembered the event in all its particulars'.[39] The author was himself able to corroborate Alfred's 'truthful' telling of the tale with other versions of it gleaned from 'many who saw' the wretched queen as a beggarwoman in Pavia.[40] There can be few cases where a supposedly ninth-century writer offers more impressive evidence to substantiate the truth of his tale. And yet, the author's protestations of his reliability as a contemporary witness are too many and too loud. We know that Beorhtric died in 802,[41] and since, according to the tale, he died from Eadburh's poison, then Eadburh must have tramped off on her road to ruin, in or around that year. She must also have made her foolish choice of a mate in Francia prior to 814—the year in which Charlemagne died. It is not impossible, but highly improbable that Asser (who supposedly first met King Alfred in *c*.885) ever knew people who had seen Eadburh in Pavia. This was a queen who had fled Wessex 83 years before Asser arrived there. If Asser had met people who had known her in exile, then we must agree with the nervous comment of the Penguin translators that 'she must have lived for a good many years thereafter [i.e. her expulsion from her nunnery]'.[42] Stevenson, straining all the evidence, suggested that if Eadburh had been 15 at her marriage in 789, she would have been eighty in 854 when the infant Alfred was conveniently passing by on his apocryphal way through Pavia from Rome![43]

There is no need to press such meagre and doubtful evidence into such a chronological strait-jacket. The tale of Eadburh as narrated in the *Life* of Alfred is apocryphal and does not lend itself to serious historical analysis. This is the story of a West Saxon queen who ruled in the time of Alfred's grandfather, yet it is told in the form of folk-tale relating to a vaguely remembered and by implication to a more distant past. If Eadburh's misdemeanours really had caused the reduction in status accorded to West Saxon queens, then only two generations in the royal house of Wessex had elapsed since the incident occurred, and the author himself protests that he knew people who had met the lady who caused all the trouble in the first instance. But Alfred's biographer speaks of the matter as if it were a long-established custom whose origins were shrouded in obscurity: 'And because many do not know (I suspect) how this perverse and detestable custom, contrary to the practise of all Germanic peoples, originally arose in the Saxon land, I think I should explain it a little more fully.'[44] The author's real reason for the lengthy and totally irrelevant digression on Eadburh was to fill out his account of Alfred's childhood about which he knew nothing. Even Stevenson was forced to admit that this tale reflects West Saxon bias against the Mercians and that it 'may have been slightly "improved" in transmission'.[45] The confrontation with Charlemagne, involving the outrageous choice offered the exiled queen to choose between Charlemagne and his son, together with the foolish choice of the fallen woman, marks this piece off as a fictional account. Even the notion of Eadburh's reduction to beggary in Pavia has nothing to recommend its historicity. This is essentially a transformation tale,[46] involving the motif of the transformation of a king or queen to menial status. In this case we may describe the tale as the transformation of the *famous queen reduced to penury and deserted by kin*, and the fact that it is here applied to an otherwise historical person does not in any way make the tale itself historical. In essence this is the same general motif as that told of King Alfred and the burning cakes in the late tenth-century *Life* of St Neot.[47] In the latter, it is a king of Wessex who has reversed roles and is reduced to the level of a fugitive, seeking refuge in the swineherd's cottage. The notion of a queen reduced to poverty and ruin is not peculiar to Wessex. Gormlaith, the daughter of the tenth-century Irish high king, Flann Sinna, was herself married to no less than three kings in turn— all of whose careers are well documented in contemporary Irish annals. Unlike Eadburh, we know the eventual fate of Gormlaith. She survived the death of her third and last husband, Niall Glundub, who was slain by the Dublin vikings in 919, and she died 'in penitence' in a nunnery in 948.[48] Yet, if we were to believe the early seventeenth-century translator of the medieval *Annals of Clonmacnoise*, we would have to accept a different and clearly legendary version of events, taking Gormlaith, like Eadburh, out of her retirement in a nunnery: 'after all which royall marriages she begged from doore to doore, forsaken of all her friends and allies, and glad to be relieved by her inferiours'.[49] The parallel with Alfred's biographer's account of Eadburh who 'in the end, accompanied by a single slave boy, and begging every day' ended her life in Pavia[50] is striking and hinges essentially on a reversal of roles motif.

While this tale of Eadburh served to fill out the great blanks in the biographer's knowledge of Alfred's childhood, the immediate cause for its insertion in the text of Alfred's *Life* is not far to seek. After describing Æthelbald's rebellion during his father's absence in Rome and Francia,[51] the author reverts to the text of the Anglo-Saxon Chronicle[52] with the statement: 'When therefore King Æthelwulf returned from Rome, the entire nation was . . . delighted at the arrival of their lord' and he goes on to say that although Æthelwulf was willing to leave his rebellious son, Æthelbald, in charge of Wessex proper, nevertheless the old king insisted that his bride be recognized as a queen who would be allowed 'to sit beside him on the royal throne'. The lengthy tale of the wicked Eadburh is next introduced to explain why her earlier evil conduct in Wessex had led to the demotion of queens in that kingdom. Finally, the author follows on with the account of King Æthelwulf's supposed *Will*, and his death, closing this whole section of King Alfred's *Life* with the notice of Æthelbald's marriage to his father's queen, Judith.[53] There is no mention in the Anglo-Saxon Chronicle of Judith having been given full recognition in Wessex for her queenly status, nor of her marriage to her step-son, Æthelbald, on the death of Æthelwulf in 858. Indeed, Judith is not actually named in the Anglo-Saxon Chronicle in the annal for 855.[54] Yet in other matters of this nature, the compiler of the *Life* of Alfred shows a slavish dependence on the Chronicle. In view of the strong Frankish influence that is apparent throughout the *Life* of Alfred, it seems clear that the author of the *Life* had a copy of Prudentius of Troyes' Annals of St Bertin before him. There he would have seen, not only the notice of Æthelbald's marriage to his Frankish step-mother in 858,[55] but also the detailed account of Æthelwulf's earlier marriage to that same Judith in 856. There, too, he would have read: 'After Hincmar, bishop of Rheims, had consecrated* her and placed a diadem on her head, Æthelwulf formally conferred on her the title of queen, which was something not customary before then to him or to his people.'[56] This was the key passage which triggered off the notion in the *Life* of Alfred of Æthelwulf's insistence that Judith be allowed to 'sit beside him on the royal throne until the end of his life'. The two statements—one in the distant but contemporary Annals of St Bertin, and the other in Alfred's *Life*—both of which focus on the status of queenship traditionally denied the wife of West Saxon kings, and both of which focus on the person of King Æthelwulf, cannot be coincidence. It is also significant that the biographer of Alfred, in taking up this theme of Judith's special regal position on the West Saxon throne, makes something of a nonsense of his subsequent statement that Æthelwulf was forced to accept the reduced status of king of Kent, Surrey, and Sussex, and—we may surmise—ruling there as joint-king alongside his other son, Æthelberht.

Æthelberht would appear to have carried the title of 'king' from as early as 855—before his father headed off for Rome, since he witnessed Æthelwulf's charter concerning lands near Rochester at that time.[57] In that charter, accepted by Whitelock as genuine, Æthelberht witnessed as *Æðberht rex*.[58] Keynes and Lapidge struggled to accommodate the crumbling evidence offered by the *Life* of Alfred by speculating that 'it would appear that on Æthelwulf's return, Æthelberht gave up his kingship and the kingdom was divided between Æthelwulf (assigned Kent,

* (*benedicente*).

Surrey, Sussex, and Essex) . . . and Æthelbald'.[59] By all accounts this would have been a modest and overcrowded throne to offer a Carolingian queen. But the record of Prudentius is ambiguous. It could mean that the West Saxons did not recognize the 'king's wife' as having any special royal status—an unlikely meaning which goes against everything we know of early Germanic and Celtic kingship. The account of Prudentius is more likely to refer to the making of English queens rather than to the inevitable *de facto* importance that accrued to their role as the king's wife, and as the mother of kings. The Carolingian chronicler is telling us that the West Saxons lacked specific coronation rituals to mark the special status of their queens—which was altogether different from saying that English queens lacked status in the first instance. The author of Alfred's *Life* next introduced the folk-tale of Eadburh to explain how Wessex came to despise the role of queens. This was either invented by the author from stock motifs, or it was already to hand as a legend which originally had no bearing on the diminished status of queens either real or imagined. It was essentially a tale prejudicial to women, telling of a wicked queen—a poisoner and enemy of menfolk; and a sexually immoral profligate, who stole the treasure of the West Saxons, and who was eventually reduced to beggary.[60]

The original purpose of the Eadburh tale may have been to denigrate the memory of Offa and his hostile Mercians. The tale, in the precise form in which the author of the *Life* presents it, owed its existence to a marriage between Eadburh and Beorhtric of Wessex which resulted in the exile of Ecgberht, Alfred's grandfather. Just as the author of Alfred's *Life* was prompted to invent a fictional ancestry for Alfred's mother from a perusal of the early section of the Anglo-Saxon Chronicle, so too, the Chronicle may have inspired him to include the tale of Eadburh. Marriages are rarely recorded in the Anglo-Saxon Chronicle, and when they are, it is usually because of their political significance. The marriage of Athelstan's sister to Sitric, the Danish king of Northumbria in 926, or of Emma of Normandy to Æthelred the Unready in 1002 are but two examples of this kind. Even more unusually, for the Chronicle, the marriage of Beorhtric of Wessex to Eadburh of Mercia is referred to twice—once when the event occurred in 789 and again in 839. The 839 mention underlines Eadburh's complicity in the exile of Alfred's grandfather, Ecgberht: 'In this year King Ecgberht died. Earlier before he became king, Offa, king of the Mercians, and Beorhtric, king of the West Saxons, had driven him from England to Francia for three years. Beorhtric had helped Offa because he had married his daughter.'[61]

The prominence accorded this marriage of Beorhtric to Eadburh caught the eye and the imagination of the author of the *Life* of Alfred. Exaggerated tales about the wickedness of a late-eighth and early ninth-century Mercian queen would have gone down well at the court of Alfred or of any of his successors throughout the tenth century and later. The marriage of the historical Eadburh had been designed to deprive the future House of Alfred of all power. The resulting exile of Alfred's grandfather, in Francia, and genuine negotiations and wrangling between Offa and Charlemagne over possible intermarriage between their children, all combined to weave the fictional tale of the hated poisoner, who herself ended her days also as an exile in the Carolingian Empire. It must have taken some time for the historical Eadburh to become transformed into the figure of an impossibly wicked and fallen queen. It is not impossible that such a folk-tale had already come into existence during Alfred's lifetime. But for that to have happened—and taking the text of Alfred's *Life* at its face value—the time-scale was very short. Such developed folk elements had already ousted conventional historical narrative in a tale supposedly written in 893 concerning a woman who lived long enough to have been seen by 'many' men (*a multis videntibus*), who passed their stories on to the author, sometime after 885. And all this concerned a woman who was old enough to have married back in 789.[62] Whether or not we accept the notion that West Saxon queens were not recognized as such in the late ninth century, the insertion of this lengthy episode with its crucial folk-tale elements that have no bearing whatever on Alfred's life—(the author fails even to provide the name of Alfred's own queen!)—only serves to expose that same author's almost complete ignorance of the early years of the king. At the very least, the Eadburh episode reveals a hagiographical and folkloric treatment in common with the other so-called biographical chapters which stand out in isolation in the early section of the *Life* of Alfred in stark contrast to the translation of the Chronicle to which they have been so clumsily grafted.

As we turn to those five chapters which focus directly on Alfred's early life, we need to bear in mind constantly that they allege to have been written when Alfred was still alive. The content of these chapters may be summarized as follows:

Chapter 21. Begins with a careless translation of the entry in the Anglo-Saxon Chronicle for the year 866 in which the East Angles are confused with the East Saxons (of Essex) and in which the Danish homeland is confused with the Danube (*Danubia*)! Asser promises to return to his main theme and furnish some account of Alfred's infancy and childhood.

Chapter 22. Alfred was loved by his parents more than all his brothers. He excelled all his brothers in appearance and manner. He loved learning from the cradle. His education was neglected until his twelfth year or longer. He committed English poems to memory. He excelled as a huntsman and the impression is given that he continues to do so (*laborat non in vanum*) at the time when Asser was supposed to be writing.

Chapter 23. Alfred learnt the contents of a book of Anglo-Saxon poetry in a competition organized by his mother.

Chapter 24. Alfred learnt prayers and offices which he collected in a notebook kept by him in later life which the author claims 'I have seen for myself (*sicut ipsi vidimus*)'. The king's early education was hampered by the absence of good scholars in Wessex.

Chapter 25. Alfred bemoaned the fact that when he once had youth and leisure he had no teachers, and when he was older and preoccupied with 'all kinds of illnesses' and the affairs of kingship, he had no time to study. He longed for learning from infancy up to the present day.

The first thing we can say of these crucial chapters is that they are full of generalities and glaring inconsistencies and that they are really only summaries of similar generalities and contradictions repeated at much greater length later in the *Life*.[63] They have clearly been inspired by that main biographical section of the *Life*, but summarized and inserted back here to supplement the translation of the Chronicle, in order to cover the compiler's nakedness. When we subtract the vague statements about Alfred's love of learning, his scholarly notebook, his lack of teachers, and his mysterious illnesses—all repeated elsewhere in the work—we are left with only one anecdotal and circumstantial piece in this section, namely the story in chapter 23 of how Alfred won a book of poetry from his mother by learning its contents more quickly than any of his brothers. The story runs as follows:

When, therefore, his mother one day was showing him and his brothers a certain book of Saxon poetry which she held in her hand, she said: 'I will give this book to whichever of you can learn it most quickly.' And moved by these words, or rather by Divine inspiration, and attracted by the beauty of the initial letter of the book, Alfred said in reply to his mother, forestalling his brothers, his elders in years though not in grace: 'Will you really give this book to one of us, to the one who can soonest understand and read it aloud to you?' And, smiling and rejoicing, she confirmed it, saying: 'To him will I give it.' Then taking the book from her hand he immediately went to his master, and read it*. And when it was read, he went back to his mother and read it aloud (*recitavit*).[64]

This tale of Alfred attracted by the beauty of the initial letter in the manuscript; of the precocious youngster who beat his older brothers in the competition for the book, and above all the enduring image of the princelings of the House of Wessex all learning together at their mother's knee, has understandably taken its place alongside the story of the Burning Cakes at the very centre of the Alfred myth. It is a story exhibiting all the ingredients which folk-tales are made of, and it shows us the author of Alfred's *Life* at his best, in creating an anecdotal vignette within an otherwise chaotic narrative. Yet the historicity of 'this well-known incident' as Whitelock called it[65] was accepted implicitly by that scholar who quite rightly pointed out that, but for the *Life* of Alfred, it 'would otherwise have been unknown'. For Whitelock, this tale ranked, by implication, among those passages in the *Life* of Alfred which vindicated the reliability of that work because of its unique content and presumably its inherent authenticity. The importance this tale has for our understanding of the *Life* of Alfred is paramount. At first sight it bears a superficial resemblance to a tale told by Notker Balbulus[66] in which boys at the Palace School in Francia were examined personally in prose and poetry by Charlemagne himself and promised rewards or punishments as a result. But however apocryphal Notker's tale may have been, it is infinitely more plausible than this fictitious account of the infant schoolboy Alfred. Charlemagne did no more than to scold the idle sons of his nobles and encouraged the hard work presented by boys of lesser birth. The

---

* Whitelock translates 'he immediately went to his master *who* read it' following Stevenson's suggestion that *et* was an error for *qui* (*EHD*, i. 266 n. 2)—a necessary editorial violation of the original text in order to cover up the shortcomings of a clumsy biographer.

central motif in the Alfred story is essentially that of a quest or competition between a king's sons, in which the youngest shows himself to be better than his brothers, and therefore by implication to be the most suited for kingship—in this case the kingship of Wessex. That point is needlessly and crudely driven home in this anecdote which shows us Alfred 'forestalling his brothers, his elders in years though not in grace'.[67] And these were brothers who all preceded Alfred in the kingship.

The story of Alfred's first book prize is a version of an international folk-tale categorized as *Youngest brother alone succeeds on quest*.[68] The tale is at least as old as the time of Herodotus who tells it in relation to the origin of the kingship of the Scythians.[69] When Heracles fathered three infant boys on a certain viper-woman in Scythia, he instructed her to set the boys a test when they grew up, to establish which one of them was fit to rule Scythia. The successful candidate had to try on a special girdle and to manipulate a bow. Eventually, of the three brothers, Scythes, the youngest, was the only one to pass the test and allowed to remain in Scythia, while his older brothers were banished.[70] The parallels with the Alfred tale are close—in each case the competition, between brothers, was supervised by the mother, and in each case the youngest brother emerged successful over his rivals, although the nature of the tests might naturally favour the older brothers. The motif of the succession of the youngest son to his father's kingship is widespread in medieval and modern folklore, but a particular version of it in the eighth-century Irish *Testament of Cathair Már* has relevance for the Alfred tale if only because of its relatively earlier date. In this tract,[71] Cathair Már, ancestor-god of the Leinstermen, distributes his sovereignty and landed inheritance to his ten sons in turn, but when he comes to his youngest boy, Fiacha, he has nothing left to give him except his blessing. This blessing proves to be a winning card, and the legend was invented after the fact to explain why it was that Fiacha's descendants were the dominant tribe of the Leinstermen who had relatively recently wrested the over-kingship of all Leinster from other tribes claiming a more senior descent from Cathair Már. In this tale the sons play a more passive role than in the Alfredian book contest, but the notion of competition for kingship is no less strong, and it is the youngest son who, like Alfred, eventually triumphs. This Irish tale and the later transmuted version of it applied to Alfred in his *Life* may well owe much to the favoured position accorded younger sons of Old Testament patriarchs—of which the compiler of the *Life* of Alfred must have been well aware. The Testament of Cathair Már is paralleled by Jacob's blessing or testament for his twelve sons in the Book of Genesis,[72] while Alfred's superiority and popularity in contrast to his older brothers, echoes the roles of Jacob, and his sons, Joseph and Benjamin, in Genesis.

In Herodotus's tale the instruments in the test of the brothers consisted of arms (girdle and bow) while in the Alfred story, the mother offered a book to be read. The change in objects merely reflects the shift in atmosphere from the secular warrior society of Herodotus to that of the early medieval monastic scriptorium in which the hagiographical tale of Alfred was invented. And so the competition changes from trying out weapons and armour to a race as to who can read a book fastest. Nor is it surprising that Alfred, the great translator of books, should have been remembered in later folk-tradition for his intellectual precocity. Alfred's fantastic feat in memorizing the book of poetry so quickly reminds us of Adomnan's tale (*c.* AD 695) of how Columba miraculously proof-read a psalter in an instant in the scriptorium on Iona,[73] or of how a pupil of the Irish saint, Óengus the Céli Dé, absorbed more than was necessary of his lesson on the psalms, by sleeping with his head resting on the knee of the saintly Óengus.[74] Such hagiographcial motifs are categorized as *learning or reading in a remarkably short time by magic or miracle.*[75] Yet another parallel to the Alfred tale is the legend of when the infant Patrick was taken for baptism in Britain to the blind priest, Gorianus. The priest's sight was not only restored by miraculous water supplied by the holy infant, but Gorianus was also capable of reading the baptismal rite although hitherto he had never seen a written word.[76] Here we have a motif which uses the miraculous reading formula (albeit here applied to an adult) as a device to forecast the future greatness of an infant saint, just as in Alfred's case the same motif is designed to forecast the future greatness and superiority of a boy-king. Loomis summed up the hagiography of the child-scholar thus: 'The education of the wonder-child is accompanied by miracles which would make any schoolboy envious. Leonorius by divine dispensation was enabled to learn his letters in one day, his conjugations upon a second day, and the art of writing upon a third successive day.'[77] The infant Alfred could hold his own with the greatest of scholar saints, and the remarkable powers attributed to him in his *Life* are essentially miraculous in spite of Whitelock's protestations that his biographer exercised 'restraint . . . in confining himself to datable contemporary records and rejecting legendary matter'.[78] We are specifically told by the author of Alfred's *Life* that Alfred's miraculous powers of reading were accomplished through 'Divine inspiration' (*divina inspiratione*).[79]

Even if we were to overlook the obvious folk-tale element in the story of Alfred and his brothers, learning together at their mother's knee, there are compelling historical arguments for rejecting the tale in its details. Since Æthelwulf married Judith the daughter of the Carolingian king, Charles the Bald, on 1 October 856,[80] then Alfred's mother, Osburh, had already died or had been divorced from Æthelwulf before that date. We can safely assume that Osburh was no longer at the court of Æthelwulf by 855 when the king set off on a pilgrimage to Rome which eventually led to his new marriage on his return through Francia in the following year. So the tale of Alfred learning from his mother relates to the year 855 at the very latest. By the reckoning of the author of Alfred's *Life*, Alfred was only six in 855—scarcely the appropriate age for reading and committing whole books of poetry to memory. If we were to accept the Chronicle's fictionalized account of Alfred's pilgrimage to Rome in 853,[81] then the date of the reading and learning episode may have to be pushed back in time by two or three years. Alfred's journey would have taken up to two years, and on his return to Wessex in 854–5, his father Æthelwulf would by then have been contemplating his own pilgrimage and a search for a new wife. This scenario would put Alfred's age in his mother's schoolroom at somewhere between 4 and 6. But if Alfred were 6 (or at the most 8) in 855, let us investigate the age of his brothers, who made up the competition in this story. His eldest known brother was Æthelstan, who according to the Parker Chronicle, was given the rule of Kent, Essex, Surrey, and Sussex by his father, Æthelwulf, perhaps as early as 839[82]—ten years before Alfred was born. That at least is one possible interpretation of the Chronicle's entry under 839, and even if the entry is retrospective and summational in tone, the last we hear of King Æthelstan concerns his victory over the Danes at Sandwich in 851 (when Alfred was between 2 and or 4). By 855 Athelstan had clearly died, for the two sons who were then prominent in Æthelwulf's kingdom were Æthelbald and Æthelberht. Æthelbald was already old enough in 851 to fight alongside his father in the battle of Aclea,[83] while Æthelberht was witnessing charters and ruling a section of the kingdom for his father from at least as early as 855–6. The author of the *Life* of Alfred himself tells us that when Æthelwulf returned from Rome (*c*.856) he effected a division of the kingdom between his two eldest sons—who were then Æthelbald and Æthelberht.[84] So, at the time when this evocative tale of Alfred's book prize is supposed to have taken place, Alfred's eldest brother was already in his grave, having grown to manhood and ruled a kingdom as his father's sub-king. Two other brothers, Æthelbald and Æthelberht, had clearly outgrown any apocryphal maternal schoolroom. Æthelberht was about to become, or had already become his father's deputy, and the successful warrior, Æthelbald, was waiting in the wings—not to learn at his deceased mother's knee, but to marry his young and prestigious step-mother!

This analysis reduces the number of pupils in Osburh's school significantly. We are left with the infant Alfred, and his brother, Æthelred, who may have been only a few years his senior. There is nothing inherently improbable in the notion that Osburh, while she lived, personally supervised the education of her infant sons. Indeed, if the folk-tale of the book prize in the *Life* of Alfred has anything of value to offer historians, it is surely that it was considered appropriate for an author to portray aristocratic women in pre-Conquest England as being personally involved in the education of their sons. The motif then, tells us more about the educational attainments of Anglo-Saxon women, than anything specific in relation to Alfred or his brothers. When we do apply the tale specifically to Alfred, not only do we find ourselves trying to extract historical detail from a folk-tale, but those details do not, as we have seen, fit the chronological facts. Furthermore, as so often happens when we try to take the text of the *Life* of Alfred too seriously on any issue, we find that the author contradicts his own version of things elsewhere in his narrative. Just as conflicting versions of a genealogy were set out in close proximity in chapters 1 and 2, so here the account of the solicitous mother tutoring her sons and offering prizes in chapter 23 is completely negated by what the author tells us in chapters 22 and 25. For here we are told that when Alfred was young he lacked tutors (*magistros*),[85] and he specifically tells us[86] that due to 'the unworthy negligence of his parents and tutors (*suorum parentum et nutritorum*)' he remained illiterate (*illiteratus*) until the age of 12 or beyond.[87] Yet in the anecdote about his mother's book—in spite of constant and wilful mistranslation by those who cling to the authenticity of Asser—the infant Alfred is shown to be 'reading (*et legit*)' and 'reading aloud (*recitavit*)'.[88] In the folk-tale relating to Osburh, the so-called negligence of the parent is forgotten as is Alfred's supposed illiteracy, and Osburh, instead of tutoring the only two sons who were then available, is made to set up a learning competition among several of her sons who, incidentally, in that same tale, do have the benefit of a tutor (*magister*). In addition to Alfred, the narrative mentions *fratribus suis* and *fratres suos* with the implication that more than two sons were present. It mattered little to the compiler of Alfred's *Life* that some of these men had long since outgrown their schooldays, that Alfred was still too young to compete, or that their mother may well have been dead. The sole point of this apocryphal tale was to glorify Alfred at the expense of his brothers. This anecdote, perhaps more than any other, brings home to us the futility of trying to reconcile the contradictory elements within the text of the *Life* of Alfred, or of trying to explain those contradictions away by claiming the text is a draft or incomplete. This text, for so long attributed to Asser, fails the test of historical analysis because it is essentially hagiographical and didactic, and clearly not a contemporary narrative of events.

Having abandoned a crude literal interpretation of the story of Alfred's first book prize, and recognizing the impossibility of this episode having really happened, it is still useful to explore what purpose the inclusion of this motif served in the *Life* of King Alfred. The immediate purpose of the tale was to underline Alfred's supposed superiority over his brothers, and this superiority is one of the central themes in the *Life* of Alfred as a whole. The theme of Alfred's superiority is a follow-on to the same treatment in the Anglo-Saxon Chronicle, where no doubt the compiler of Alfred's *Life* recognized the high profile accorded Alfred in that source over his brothers.[89] But whereas Alfred's prominence in the Chronicle is handled with some subtlety, its treatment in the *Life* of Alfred is characteristically much cruder, and its lack of historical exactitude betrays a considerable chronological development in the Alfred cult. So in chapter 11 we learn that the reason why Æthelwulf took the infant Alfred to Rome 'in great state' in 855 was 'because he loved him more than his other sons'. In chapter 22 the claims made for Alfred at the expense of his older brothers are more preposterous: 'Now, he was loved by his father and mother, and indeed by everybody, with a united and immense love, more than all his brothers, and was always brought up in the royal court, and as he passed through his childhood and boyhood he appeared fairer in form than all his brothers, and more pleasing in his looks, his words and his ways.'[90]

All of these brothers, we need to remind ourselves, had served as kings of Kent or of all Wessex before Alfred's reign. The exclusive dynastic claims put forward for Alfred here and, by implication for his direct descendants in the tenth century, are obvious. At first sight it is tempting to interpret this treatment of Alfred's predestined superiority as propaganda designed to exclude the heirs of Alfred's brothers from the kingship of Wessex. But as always, it is imprudent to seek for too rational or political a motive behind a text which is riddled with inconsistencies and which was so obviously and so carelessly compiled in haste. We are dealing with a text which is essentially hagiographical in its perceptions of its subject, and the superiority of the infant Alfred over his brothers, together with the superior love which his parents bestowed upon him, is part of that hagiographical dimension. We are reminded of how 'Israel loved Joseph above all his sons'.[91] Precocity in sanctity was not the only quality in infants which litters the pages of medieval saints' *Lives*. The infant Cuthbert—that English holy man *par excellence*—beat boys of his own age and many who were older at 'jumping or running or wrestling or exercising their limbs in any other way',[92] while Alfred's contemporary, the saintly Count Gerald of Aurillac, was also trained in the aristocratic pursuits of the age—hunting, archery, and falconry.[93] Alfred, too, excelled at hunting as a youth,[94] and like Gerald was surrounded by falconers and dog-keepers.[95] But precocity in learning was closely associated with sanctity, and Alfred's feat in reading the contents of his book, was, as we have seen, quintessentially hagiographical in its conception. But the infant Alfred also learnt the 'services of the hours (*celebrationes horarum*)'—clearly part of the Divine Office—and certain Psalms,[96] as did Count Gerald,[97] while Gerald's own biographer, Odo of Cluny, was ridiculed by the canons of Tours for trying to master difficult textual studies when he was a young monk.[98]

This theme of Alfred's superiority is related, as we shall see, to the character assassination of Alfred's older brother, Æthelbald, in the *Life* of Alfred,[99] and emerges yet again in more subtle form in the treatment of Alfred's relationship with his brother, Æthelred. Æthelred's career, as we shall see, was treated with some caution in the Anglo-Saxon Chronicle since that king and his sons (the nephews of King Alfred) still clearly had a following within Wessex at the time when the Chronicle was first compiled. The *Life* of Alfred shows a further development in the handling of that delicate relationship which is seen in the account of the battle of Ashdown fought against the Danes in 871. The *Life*, as in all cases involving Danish battles, follows the Chronicle account implicitly, but the Ashdown episode is one of the rare cases where the *Life* of Alfred incorporates an unusually lengthy interpolation in the Chronicle narrative. The Chronicle tells us that at Ashdown in 871, King Æthelred and his brother Alfred fought against 'the whole army' of Danes which was drawn up in two divisions—one led by Danish kings and the other by Danish earls. Æthelred fought against the kings' division and Alfred against the earls. The outcome was a great English victory—both Danish divisions being put to flight and thousands of the enemy were slain, several of their leaders being named.[100] The *Life* of Alfred follows this basic framework including the list of slain Danish leaders given by the Chronicle. But it adds information which looks disarmingly circumstantial—information which the author protests he 'heard from truthful authorities who saw it',[101] and he adds that more immediate and personal touch by describing 'a rather small and solitary thorn tree (*spinosa arbor*), which I have seen for myself with my own eyes' around which the battle of Ashdown raged.[102] But the main brunt of the author's contribution to a seemingly near-contemporary account of the battle of Ashdown has been largely overlooked by historians:

Alfred and his men reached the battlefield sooner and in better order: for his brother, King Æthelred, was still in his tent at prayer, hearing Mass and declaring firmly that he would not leave that place alive before the priest had finished Mass, and that he would not forsake divine service for that of men; and he did what he said. The faith of the Christian king counted for much with the Lord, as shall be shown more clearly in what follows.[103]

The author of the *Life* now reverts to the Chronicle's account of Æthelred and Alfred's two separate divisions pitted against their Danish opposite numbers and continues:

Since the king was lingering still longer in prayer, and the pagans were ready and had reached the battlefield more quickly, Alfred, then heir apparent, could not oppose the enemy battle lines any longer without either retreating from the battlefield or attacking the enemy forces before his brother's arrival on the scene. He finally deployed the Christian forces against the hostile armies, as he had previously intended even though the king had not yet come, and acting courageously, like a wild boar. . . . he moved his army without delay against the enemy.[104]

The outcome was a resounding West Saxon victory for which King Æthelred was given no further mention much less credit. This tale serves the same purpose as that of Alfred and his brothers competing for their mother's book of poetry, even if the handling is more delicate. Alfred is given all the credit for this victory, fighting against the odds, while his brother, King Æthelred, is excused of cowardice by being cast in the role of a pious king who puts prayer before battle. While this piety is commended, nevertheless, the real point of the tale is to demonstrate how Alfred had to take the field alone without his brother's help and face two Danish divisions unaided. Alfred's practical behaviour in the face of such danger is what counted, and his preparedness to fight, together with his valour, demonstrated to the reader once again that Alfred of all his brothers—including and perhaps especially Æthelred—was destined to be the greatest king of Wessex. When we look again at the Chronicle narrative we realize how this tale from Alfred's *Life* has no basis in fact. In spite of the prominent role which the Chronicle assigned to Alfred during the reign of Æthelred, it does nevertheless show Æthelred as overall leader at Ashdown. It is Æthelred who is mentioned before Alfred in the order of battle, and likewise Æthelred's fallen enemy is mentioned before those of Alfred. This near-contemporary record, compiled after Æthelred I had died and during Alfred's reign, clearly suggests that Æthelred I was in charge of the field at Ashdown. The Chronicle states tersely that: 'the Danes were in two divisions: in the one were the heathen kings Bagsecg and Healfdene, and in the other were the earls. And then King Æthelred fought against the king's troops and King Bagsecg was slain there; and Æthelred's brother Alfred fought against the earls' troop . . . and there were slain Earl Sidroc the Old.'[105] The West Saxons drew up their double battle-line in response to a Danish tactic with which they were confronted, and which presumably required an immediate response. The tactic would seem to have been distinctively Norse, and its very novelty prompted West Saxon as well as Irish chroniclers to record it in the first instance.[106] The author of the *Life* of

Alfred, however, informs us that the order of battle had already been 'arranged on both sides' prior to, or during, King Æthelred's attendance at Mass in his tent.[107] It is not clear whether the two 'sides (*ab utraque parte*)' which arranged the order of battle, referred to two West Saxon divisions or to the West Saxons and vikings.[108] Assuming that it was the West Saxons who decided that Æthelred should fight the Norse kings and that Alfred should oppose the jarls, such a plan would suggest that battle was imminent and unavoidable. The author of King Alfred's *Life*, however, presents us with an unlikely scenario of the battle plan being worked out either before or during King Æthelred's Eucharist, and also before the enemy had even arrived on the battlefield (*locum certaminis*). It is utterly fantastic to assume that even if a plan had been worked out beforehand, King Æthelred would then have refused to leave his tent, vowing to finish his attendance at Mass. But the Mass episode is yet another hagiographical motif, the recognition of which, administers the *coup de grâce* to any remaining credibility in the account of the battle of Ashdown in King Alfred's *Life*. Odo of Cluny tells us that when the saintly Count Gerald was attending Mass with his soldiers in his castle at Aurillac, they were surrounded and attacked by a hostile magnate called Adalelmus. 'A great noise of people shouting arose in the castle and the soldiers who were at Mass with the count wanted to go out, but he stopped them with a word and would not allow them to go until Mass was finished.' Gerald was rewarded by Heaven with the shameful withdrawal of his enemies and with the death of the wicked Adalelmus fourteen days later.[109] The anecdote in Gerald's *Life* may be no more 'real' than that in Alfred's, but in the *Life* of Gerald, the tale is primary in the sense that it focuses on the subject of the *Life* and eminently fulfils its hagiographical function to demonstrate the sanctity of Gerald. In the *Life* of Alfred, on the other hand, the anecdote is transposed and derivative. For by displacing the tale of the *holy man who refuses to leave Mass even while under attack* the author of Alfred's *Life* as ever exposes himself to unresolved contradictions. Had he told the tale of Alfred, it would have fitted in perfectly with his otherwise consistent picture of the West Saxon king as neurotic saint.[110] By applying the story to Æthelred, however, the author achieved his customary short-term gain by showing Alfred as the pragmatist who was best suited to lead his people in war, as opposed to his well-intentioned but over-pious brother. Yet the tale goes against much of what its author tells of Alfred, who is shown elsewhere in his *Life* as a saintly king, prostrating himself in prayer during night vigils, and praying for illness. Not only must the Ashdown episode in the *Life* of Alfred no longer be treated as an historical event, but the motif on which it is based appears in a derivative and later form than that which was written into Gerald's *Life* by Odo of Cluny at about AD 930. That was nearly a quarter of a century after the death of the historical Asser, who by coincidence, died in the same year (909) as Count Gerald of Aurillac.

Æthelred's declaration that he would prefer to be slaughtered at Mass than leave before the end was inserted by the compiler of the *Life* of Alfred as part of the development of his wider theme of the superiority of Alfred over all his brothers. Only Alfred—who took on two divisions of the enemy, single-handed—had what it took to be king. And that is why at this point in the text the outrageous claim is slipped in that Alfred was 'then heir apparent' or *secundarius*.[111] The claim that Alfred was already recognized as 'heir apparent' before he actually assumed the kingship of the West Saxons is made no less than three times in Asser's *Life* and is an extension of the claim for his superiority over his brothers—a claim designed to justify Alfred's eventual succession, and yet another aspect of hagiographical premonition regarding the future greatness of the saint-hero. Earlier in the *Life*[112] we are told that Alfred was already 'accorded the status of "heir apparent"' at the time of his marriage which is dated to Alfred's twentieth year in 868. In chapter 42, which describes the succession of Alfred to the kingship of the West Saxons on the death of his brother Æthelred,[113] we are informed that 'Alfred had been heir apparent while his brothers were alive'. There is no question but that his brothers plural (*viventibus fratribus suis*) are meant, and since the statement is also preserved by the Annals of St Neots,[114] and by Florence of Worcester, then Archbishop Parker and his associates cannot be accused of meddling with this part of Asser's text. The statement that Alfred had been *secundarius* even while his older brothers ruled, is perfectly consistent with the author's other nonsensical statements that Alfred had been singled out for special favour as an infant by his father Æthelwulf— hence Alfred's *second* pilgrimage to Rome.[115] The message is abundantly clear that Alfred alone of all his brothers was worthy of kingship had he been old enough to succeed to it. Indeed the author of Alfred's *Life* goes on to make just that point:

Alfred . . . took over the government of the whole kingdom as soon as his brother had died . . . indeed he could easily have taken it over with the consent of all while his brother Æthelred was alive, had he considered himself worthy to do so, for he surpassed all his brothers both in wisdom and in all good habits; and in particular because he was a great warrior and victorious in virtually all battles.[116]

Leaving aside the claim that he was 'victorious in virtually all battles' which a scrutiny of the Chronicle shows to have been quite false,[117] it seems superfluous to labour the point that the passage just quoted belongs to a world of hagiographical propaganda. Yet since statements such as this are still accepted at their face value by modern commentators on Alfred's *Life*, who, having committed themselves to accepting the *Life* as genuine, are then constrained to accept quite uncritically material which in other contexts would be regarded as nonsense. Stevenson, who gave the lead in this as in most other pronouncements on the *Life* of Alfred, believed that Alfred as *secundarius* was something of 'a viceroy or almost joint-king'—adding 'it agrees with the prominent part that Alfred plays in the Chronicle during his brother's [Æthelred's] reign.'[118] Caught as he was in a circular argument, Stevenson could not have concluded otherwise. A major objective of the Chronicle, as we shall see, was to maximize Alfred's role in the military history of Wessex prior to his accession to kingship.[119] This in turn prompted the author of Alfred's *Life*—who was so dependent on the Chronicle—to develop the notion that Alfred was recognized as being destined for kingship from infancy. There is nothing whatever in the Chronicle to justify the idea of an office of *secundarius* in ninth-century Wessex. Had Alfred ever held such an office, the compiler of the Chronicle would not have been slow to tell us so.[120] So well did the author of the *Life* of Alfred succeed in his task of 'developing' the Chronicle narrative, that serious scholars in the later twentieth century tacitly accepted that the West Saxon *witan* or royal counsellors recognized Alfred as future king while he was still an infant—in his father's lifetime, or on the accession of Æthelbald in 858, of Æthelberht in 860, or of Æthelred in 871.

Apart from the *Life* of Alfred, there is no evidence whatever to suggest that the office of heir apparent had emerged in a recognizable or institutionalized form within the West Saxon dynasty at any time in the pre-Conquest period. The issue of West Saxon succession is needlessly complicated by reference to Binchy's oft-quoted discussion on the office of *tánaise* in Ireland and *gwrthrych* in Wales in the Early Medieval period.[121] These terms were indeed applied in those Celtic societies to the 'expected one' or heir apparent to the kingship. But whether the author of King Alfred's *Life* was or was not a Welshman can have little bearing on the reality of West Saxon—as opposed to Welsh—succession practices. Stevenson was surely nearer to the correct meaning of *secundarius* as 'joint-king' rather than 'heir apparent'. Stevenson was in this supported by Niermeyer and[122] supported also by the context of the *Life* of Alfred whose author has to be forgiven for assuming from his reading of the Anglo-Saxon Chronicle that Alfred did indeed rule jointly with King Æthelred I—that king whose actions are reported there invariably in association with Alfred. Nor can we argue that the Anglo-Saxon term *aetheling* could be construed in any way to mean 'heir apparent' or even *secundarius*—however we define its precise meaning. Dumville in his study of references to the atheling in Anglo-Saxon sources concluded: 'the word aetheling seems therefore to carry no more specific meaning than that of "prince" . . . we may argue that the male descendants of a common grandfather who had been king enjoyed this title.'[123] Dumville pointed to a specific example of several members of the royal house being described as athelings at one particular time, in the case of a genealogical tract dating to *c*.969. In this tract,[124] three sons of King Edgar—Edward, Edmund, and Æthelred—are all described as *æðelingas* or athelings. Dumville's comment is instructive: 'they cannot all have been designated heirs, and Æthelred was at most three years old in 969'.[125] But Alfred was at most 6 when his father is alleged to have sent him to Rome, and he was only 10 or 11 when his father died. Dumville rightly rejected the notion of an 'institutional provision for the succession of a designated heir',[126] but going against his own evidence and judgement, he was willing to make an accommodation for the *Life* of Alfred, conceding that Alfred might have been 'a designated successor' even before Æthelred's reign and (by implication from his argument) from as early as 853 or 855 when Alfred was aged somewhere between 4 and 8.[127] In the face of all the evidence he himself had marshalled to the contrary, Dumville speculated that if a king (such as Æthelwulf) and his chosen successor were strong enough, then he might be able to force an *ad hoc* arrangement on his dynasty and on his magnates, whereby they would accept an heir apparent, or the so-called *secundarius* status which 'Asser' attributed to Alfred.[128] While this allowed

Dumville to accept the veracity of Asser, it compelled him to ignore 'other controversial issues' such as Alfred's 'coronation' by the pope, which he quite wrongly decided were 'not relevant to the problem'.[129] The king who is alleged by modern historians, following a special interpretation of the *Life* of Alfred, to have supposedly left a *Will* which ensured the eventual succession of Alfred, was Æthelwulf of Wessex. But Æthelwulf ended his reign, also on the testimony of that same chaotic *Life* of Alfred, as a failure—one of the few in the history of his dynasty—dispossessed by his son and by a section of his nobles. Such a ruler would have been the last king in Wessex capable of imposing his will on the kingdom and on his successors, regardless of what he might have decided in 855 or in 858. So Dumville followed John's notion—'notwithstanding John's unsatisfactory presentation of his argument'[130]—that King Æthelwulf somehow imposed the infant Alfred's favoured status on the magnates of Wessex, and John developed the special pleading and circular argument further, in that he suggested Æthelwulf purposely sent the infant Alfred to Rome to obtain papal ratification for the special status of a boy within the dynasty.[131] None of these ideas involving King Æthelwulf's supposed 'elaborate plan' for the succession of his infant son[132] stand up to close scrutiny,[133] and all are dependent for their very survival on Whitelock's 'Genuine Asser' thesis.

In his efforts to fill out a narrative on Alfred's childhood and youth, about which he knew nothing, the compiler of Alfred's *Life* inserted six chapters[134] in his work dealing not with Alfred, but with Æthelwulf of Wessex and his son Æthelbald, together with the folk-tale about Eadburh, that earlier wicked Wessex queen. We learn from the Chronicle that sometime between 855 and 858 Æthelwulf of Wessex 'conveyed by charter (*gebocude*) the tenth part of his land throughout all his kingdom to the praise of God and his own eternal salvation'.[135] The implication must be that he gave this land to the church or for benefit of the poor or both. The land in question was more likely to have been part of his own hereditary estates (*propria hereditatas*)—as the text of the *Life* of Alfred suggests[136]—as opposed to lands belonging to the royal demesne. Otherwise it is difficult to envisage how the magnates of Wessex would have been agreeable to such a dramatic diminution of the royal fisc.[137] There is an air of finality about this settlement as if the chronicler were describing the act of an ageing or defeated king who was settling his account with Heaven. The record of Æthelwulf's pilgrimage to Rome which follows immediately on this entry might seem to confirm the impression that Æthelwulf had resigned his kingship to die in Rome as had his predecessors Ceadwalla back in 688 and later Ine, in 726. Like Ine, too, it would seem that Æthelwulf had decided to leave the kingship of Wessex 'to the younger men'—as Bede had so ambiguously put it.[138] We are reminded, too, of Æthelwulf's son-in-law, Burgred of Mercia, who abandoned his Mercian kingship in the face of the viking onslaught in 874 to settle and die an exile in the English quarter in Rome.[139] But Æthelwulf's behaviour towards the end of his reign is more complex, for he not only succeeded in resuming his kingship, but he succeeded also in adding to his own prestige by means of a new marriage with the Carolingian house.[140] It seems highly unlikely that Charles the Bald would have consented to marry off his daughter, Judith, to a retired king or to a returning ruler who was already known to be in serious political trouble in a distant kingdom such as Wessex. Judith was clearly very young at the time, with a profitable and varied married career ahead of her. She later married her English stepson, Æthelbald, in 858, and after his death she eventually eloped with Baldwin, Count of Flanders in 862.[141] The Chronicle, which tells us nothing of any rebellion against Æthelwulf, goes on laconically to record Æthelwulf's death two years after his return.[142] His genealogy, and the succession of his son Æthelbald to Wessex, and of his other son Æthelberht, to Kent, Surrey, Sussex and Essex, are next noted in the Chronicle text. We are told no more of Æthelbald than that he reigned five years and was buried in Sherborne in 860. The Chronicle dates the reign of Æthelbald, therefore, from 855, the time of Æthelwulf's departure for Rome. We have no means of knowing for certain whether Æthelbald was recognized as a *sub regulus* of Wessex during his father's absence or whether he was recognized as a joint-king. The Chronicle deliberately ignored specific events during the period of the rule of Æthelbald and of his brother, Æthelberht, as part of its brief to emphasize the career of Alfred.[143] The Annals of St Neots[144] very reasonably suggest that while Æthelbald reigned for two and a half years after the death of Æthelwulf, he had previously reigned for another two and a half years 'with his father' (*cum patre*). The Annals of St Neots appear to be following an independent tradition here and one which does not survive in MS A of the Chronicle. It is under this same entry that they record the burial of Æthelwulf in Steyning in Sussex—a fact which is also not recorded in the A text. None of the Chronicle texts refer specifically to any difficulties between Æthelwulf and his son Æthelbald in the ruling of Wessex between 855 and 860. The author of the *Life* of Alfred, however,[145] pursued his own special tactic of showing up Alfred in a superior light to his brothers by launching into a character assassination of Æthelbald. He tells us that on Æthelwulf's return, his son Æthelbald tried to expel him from the kingdom and civil war was averted by assigning the less important eastern regions (of Kent, Sussex, and Surrey) to Æthelwulf, while his son retained the kingdom of Wessex proper in the west. It would not have been unusual had such a dynastic squabble actually taken place. The records of the Middle Ages are littered with quarrels between kings and their ambitious and impetuous sons. There are two statements in the Chronicle which might seem to make veiled references to Æthelbald's rebellion. The first is to the effect that when Æthelwulf returned from Rome (in 856–7) 'he came to his people and they were glad of it', and the second is that when Æthelbald (who succeeded his father in 858) died two years later, he was in turn followed by his brother Æthelberht who 'succeeded to the whole kingdom and held it in good harmony and in great peace'.[146] These statements can too easily be invested with a significance which is not warranted by the evidence of the Chronicle text, especially by those trapped in the circular argument which holds that *because* 'Asser' is genuine, then other things must fall into place. The Annals of St Bertin, which are more strictly contemporary than the Anglo-Saxon Chronicle at this time, support the Chronicle's record of the marriage of Æthelwulf to Judith. But these same Frankish annals describe Æthelwulf as 'king of the Western English (*rex occidentalium Anglorum*)' in October 856[147] and show no knowledge of any political storm that may have lain ahead of him on his return to England. The same source confirms that Æthelwulf was still 'king of the Western Saxons (*rex occidentalium Saxonum*)'—and we note the correctness of that title—on his death in 858.[148] The *Life* of Pope Benedict III (855–8), recorded in the *Liber Pontificalis*, confirms that Æthelwulf arrived in Rome during Benedict's pontificate with a great following when he offered splendid gifts to the Holy See.[149] Historians who accept the account of Æthelbald's rebellion in the *Life* of Alfred, assume that the phrase *et regnum proprium suum amisit* as applied to the pilgrim Æthelwulf in Benedict's *Life* confirms that Æthelwulf had 'lost' his kingdom.[150] But the garbled account of Æthelwulf's pilgrimage emphasizes that the West Saxon king came to pray (*causa orationis veniens*) and his prayers concluded, he returned to his own kingdom (*finita causa orationis, reversus est ad proprium regnum suum*)—all of which suggests that he came not as a fugitive but as a pilgrim, and that he still had a kingdom to return to. That being so, we ought to read *amisit* in its primary and rather vague sense of 'to give up' rather than 'to lose', and translate: 'he gave up his own kingdom, coming to Rome . . . for the sake of prayer'. In short, we are entirely dependent on the *Life* of Alfred for any firm evidence whatever to support a case for Æthelbald's rebellion.

The importance of the record of Æthelbald's rebellion in the *Life* of Alfred lies in the way in which the author uses this story firstly to fill out his blank record on Alfred's childhood, and secondly to show Alfred up in the most favourable light by denegrating his older brother. While the charismatic Alfred was loved exceedingly by his parents 'and indeed by everybody', the wicked Æthelbald, on the other hand, was supposed to have raised rebellion against his father and then married his stepmother. Æthelbald in the matter of the rebellion 'was stubborn in this affair and in many other wrong acts'. He was 'an iniquitous and stubborn son (*iniquus et pertinax filius*)', and he was portrayed as a 'conspirator' trying 'to commit a great crime'.[151] As for his marriage to Judith on his father's death in 858, the clerical author of Alfred's *Life* viewed that as 'contrary to God's prohibition and Christian dignity, and also against the usage of all pagans'.[152] The author's expressed horror at the son and successor marrying his stepmother is all part of a design in the *Life* to show Alfred's brothers in an inferior light. King Æthelwulf's Carolingian bride is not actually named in the Chronicle, and her remarriage to Æthelbald is ignored by that source.[153] That in turn suggests yet again that the author of Alfred's *Life* had access to a version of the Annals of St Bertin. It was the entry under 858 in that source which prompted the author of the *Life* to view the remarriage in an incestuous light: 'Æthelwulf, king of the West Saxons, died. His son Æthelbald married his widow (*relictam*), Queen Judith.'[154] It was clearly too prestigious an opportunity to be missed for the young Æthelbald as king of Wessex, not to marry the Carolingian princess, who was in all probability younger than himself. The marriage was not of course contrary to pagan Germanic practice as is shown by the earlier union of King Eadbald of Kent with his Christian stepmother, Bertha—

the widowed queen of his father, Æthelberht.[155] While such 'incestuous' unions were proscribed by the Christian Church, they were none the less condoned across Christendom. The Frankish chronicler recorded Judith's second marriage to her stepson without comment. The purpose of such marriages was primarily political, and not always, as the disapproval of clerics might suggest, inspired by lust. The compiler of the *Life* of Alfred, however, steeped as he was in the biblical lore of his monastic environment, would have been well aware that the contrast he invented between Alfred and Æthelbald, mirrored that between Joseph, whom Israel loved above all his sons,[156] and Joseph's eldest brother, Ruben—Jacob's first-born—who was cursed for defiling his father's bed.[157] We shall see later on,[158] how the author of the *Life* of Alfred invented the supposed wickedness and moral depravity of King Æthelbald of Wessex through a wilful confusion of that king with his namesake, Æthelbald of Mercia (716–57).

The account of Æthelbald's rebellion in the *Life* of Alfred is riddled with inconsistencies and naïvety and lacks that core of circumstantial detail which we should expect from a narrator working in the lifetime of many who would have witnessed the events in question and whom he claims to have consulted (*sicut quorundam hominum relatu audivimus*).[159] He named the leaders of the conspiracy against King Æthelwulf as Ealhstan, bishop of Sherborne, and Eanwulf, ealdorman of Somerset. Alternatively, he cites others as attributing blame either to the bishop and ealdorman alone or to Æthelbald alone. So carelessly did the author of the *Life* assemble his material, and so clumsily did he graft his scant narrative onto that of the Chronicle, that when he came—later on in his narrative—to the entry in the Chronicle under 867 for the death of Ealhstan of Sherborne, he had clearly forgotten about the bishop's earlier support for the supposedly wicked Æthelbald. Otherwise he could not possibly have embellished his translation of the Chronicle's brief notice of Ealhstan's death by adding (italics) that 'he ruled the bishopric *honorably* (*honorabiliter*) for 50 years, went the way of all flesh, and was buried *in peace* (*in pace*) at Sherborne'.[160] The author's careless addition of these three words (*honorabiliter . . . in pace*) may seem slight, but they stand out in glaring contradiction to what he had already written of this apparently conspiratorial and rebellious prelate who was accused of 'great crimes' back in chapter 12. It is highly probable that the author of the *Life* of Alfred invented the conspiracy of Bishop Ealhstan and Ealdorman Eanwulf just as he very probably invented the entire episode regarding Æthelbald's rebellion. At first sight, it might seem that the names of Ealdorman Eanwulf and of Bishop Ealhstan add uncharacteristic circumstantial detail to this episode. Conventional versions of the Anglo-Saxon Chronicle do not record the date of Ealdorman Eanwulf's death. That record may well have been in an earlier version of the Chronicle which was available to the author of Alfred's *Life*. Alternatively, the author may have had access to a copy of Æthelweard's Chronicle which provided a Latin translation of the Chronicle compiled *c*.1000. It cannot be coincidence that Æthelweard not only recorded the death of Ealdorman Eanwulf and of Bishop Ealhstan in the same year (867), but he also linked the record of their two deaths: 'In the same year Eanwulf, ealdorman of Somerset passed away, and also bishop Ealhstan, fifty years after his succession to his see in the bishopric called Sherborne. And there [in Sherborne] his body now rests, and that of the ealdorman just mentioned [lies] in the monastery called Glastonbury.'[161] It was this simple fact alone—that Ealdorman Eanwulf and Bishop Ealhstan had died in the same year—which may have initially prompted the author of Alfred's *Life* to name the same two men as co-conspirators in Æthelbald's rebellion back in 866.

If the author of Alfred's *Life* was inconsistent in his treatment of Bishop Ealhstan, he was uncharacteristically relentless in his hostility towards King Æthelbald. While the Chronicle merely states: 'in this year [860] King Æthelbald died, and his body is buried in Sherborne', the author of the *Life* delivered his final piece of invective against this older brother of Alfred by adding that he 'ruled the government of the kingdom of the West Saxons for two and a half unbridled years (*effrenis annis*) after his father's death'.[162] Asser's treatment of Æthelbald's rebellion embodies the same flawed and extravagant statements as his account of Alfred's eventual succession to the kingship. Just as we are told that Alfred could easily have taken the West Saxon kingship 'with the consent of all' while his brother Æthelred ruled as king, so too, we are asked to believe that 'the nobles of all the Saxon land (*nobiles totius Saxoniae*)' refused to consent to the expulsion of Æthelwulf from his kingdom.[163] This is a nonsense, since we have already been informed that the rebellious Æthelbald 'with all his councillors (*cum omnibus suis consiliariis*)' had the backing of the bishop of Sherborne—one of the most powerful political figures in the realm—together with the ealdorman of Somerset, who must also have commanded a considerable following. Besides, Æthelwulf was eventually supposed to have been forced out of his kingdom and to have accepted 'the eastern regions (*orientales plagae*)' which lay outside of Wessex proper.[164]

The hostility which the author of Alfred's *Life* showed towards Alfred's older brother, Æthelbald, stands out in marked contrast to the more careful handling of the career of Æthelred. This sympathetic treatment of Æthelred's career may have been prompted by nothing more than the very obvious linkage in the Chronicle between 'King Æthelred and his brother Alfred'.[165] Because the two men were reported in the Chronicle as acting so often together, a later reader might assume that they had been constant allies. We shall see that the compiler of the Chronicle was also careful how he approached Æthelred's reign, but for different reasons than the author of Alfred's *Life*. The Anglo-Saxon Chronicle strove to associate Alfred with Æthelred's earlier reign, in order to give Alfred credit for what had been primarily the achievements of his brother. In the *Life* of Alfred, the treatment of King Æthelred has evolved much further. While open hostility is there declared towards Æthelbald, Æthelred continues to be treated with respect. But he is nevertheless shown to have been inferior in childhood as a scholar, and later as a warrior, compared with Alfred. Yet the elaborate point of Alfred's superiority to Æthelred is got across delicately in the account of the battle of Ashdown—albeit as we have seen with inherent contradictions—which contrasts in turn with the crude polemic directed against Æthelbald. The reason for this cautious approach towards Æthelred may have been prompted solely by the Chronicle, or it may relate also to the continued existence of Æthelred's direct descendants as powerful magnates within England at the turn of the tenth century. Although King Æthelred's son, Æthelwold, was slain by Alfred's son and successor, Edward the Elder in 903, it is clear that Æthelwold and his kin had some support from among the Wessex thegns and their fighting men. Æthelred's descendants clearly held on to lands and power. The late tenth-century chronicler, Æthelweard, who was an ealdorman of the western shires of Wessex, claimed, on his own account, to be the great-great-grandson of King Æthelred, and was therefore presumably descended from either Æthelwold or his brother, Æthelhelm.[166] Yet another late tenth-century ealdorman, Ælfhere of Mercia, may also have claimed Æthelred as a royal ancestor,[167] and there may have been others. So it is with this knowledge in mind that we must view the approach shown in the *Life* of Alfred to that king's brothers. While Æthelbald, who seems to have left no descendants, could be safely portrayed as an enemy of his father—a disloyal son, who married his stepmother—it is possible that Æthelred, on the other hand, had to be taken more seriously, both in Alfred's lifetime and throughout the century that followed his death.

It is now time to review the evidence which has emerged from this study of the first seventy-two chapters of the *Life* of King Alfred. Of the twelve of those chapters which are not borrowed from the Anglo-Saxon Chronicle, only six[168] deal with Alfred's life. Chapter 21 contains nothing more on Alfred than a promise to give an account of his childhood. Chapters 22, 24, and 25 contain generalities and glaring contradictions about Alfred's precocity and illiterate childhood which are repeated later on in the work. The folk-tale of the reading competition between Alfred and his brothers,[169] containing impossible and contradictory details, was included as part of a wider scheme designed to glorify Alfred at the expense of all his brothers. Chapter 29 deals with the Mercian origins of Alfred's wife, who is suspiciously unnamed throughout the text, and who was supposed to have been the daughter of the enigmatic Æthelred *alias* Mucel of the equally enigmatic *Gaini*.[170] If the author had been ignorant of the name of Alfred's queen, then he made up for this deficiency by probably inventing the name *Eadburh* for Alfred's mother-in-law. This looks like a crude doubling on the name of the earlier Mercian Eadburh, the wicked queen of Beorhtric of Wessex. The author's protestations that 'I often saw her [Eadburh] myself with my very own eyes for several years before her death' should put us on our guard, just as his claims to have met men who saw the earlier Eadburh in exile, or his supposed sighting of the lone thorn tree on Ashdown, do nothing to erase the essentially fictional nature of those episodes. It is strange that an author who protests about his intimate knowledge of Alfred's deceased mother-in-law cannot supply the name of Alfred's wife, Ealhswith, who outlived Alfred by four years. Chapter 2 deals with the origins of Alfred's mother, Osburh, and was based on a fictional linking with events in the Anglo-Saxon Chronicle relating to the early sixth century. There is no reason, given the author's wilful tendency for invention, to accept anything he says about Alfred's mother's family or about his wife's ancestors, unless those statements can be

clearly supported by evidence from elsewhere.[171] The genealogy offered in chapter
1, like the material relating to Alfred's mother in chapter 2, both derive from the
Chronicle. Part of chapter 37, all of 38, and part of 39 are devoted to the
hagiographical and derivative account of the battle of Ashdown which in turn was
grafted on to the Chronicle's account of that battle.

The remaining six anecdotal chapters, in the first seventy-two chapters of the
Life, all contain information which has nothing to do with Alfred. The folk-tale of
Eadburh, the daughter of King Offa, adds nothing to our knowledge of Alfred and
was inserted to conceal the compiler's ignorance of events in Alfred's own youth,
as was the account of Æthelbald's supposed rebellion, which had the added value
of making Alfred seem superior to an older brother. Chapter 16 deals with King
Æthelwulf's *Will*[172] and the short chapter 17 records the marriage of Æthelbald to
his stepmother. The remaining sixty or so chapters in this first section of the *Life*
of Alfred are all based on a translation of the Anglo-Saxon Chronicle with, here
and there, a number of the author's own very brief interpolations and glosses
added. The *Life* of Alfred was compiled to hagiographical specifications, and that
being so, the scholarly Alfred's precocity for learning as a child had to be
demonstrated, as was his superiority over all his brothers. Alfred's superiority in
looks and in learning all sprang from a higher level of superiority, which the author
of the *Life* construed as being essentially moral. Hence the king, as we shall see,
was portrayed in his later life as a quasi-saint. This explains the hostility shown
towards Æthelbald, who was portrayed by the author as morally flawed, being
effrenus or 'unbridled'. It explains, too, the very special lengths to which the author
went to show that although Æthelred was a worthy man, Alfred was the superior
warrior and more fit to be king. Allied to this theme, is the fictitious notion that
Alfred, although the youngest son, was already a designated 'heir apparent' in the
lifetime of those royal brothers who 'surpassed him in years though not in ability'.
There can be no question of accepting the *Life*'s account of Alfred's childhood,
youth, or indeed of any part of his career before becoming king, as the witness of
a man who knew Alfred in life. This is indeed the tale of a king long dead, about
whom the writer knew nothing and invented much. He did have access to chronicles
(English and Frankish) and other sources which furnished accurate though meagre
information if not on Alfred, then on the background history of his dynasty. The
material used by the author of the *Life* of Alfred would have been available to any
writer with access to a good monastic library at any time in the tenth and first half
of the eleventh centuries. Most of the added plausible detail in this text would
have been common knowledge to any writer who was familiar with England and
with English affairs at that time. This applies to the topographical details relating
to places such as Wareham,[173] or to comments such as that on the crumbling
condition of the walls of York.[174] Other brief insertions in the *Life* may have been
based on no more than reasonable assumptions or plain guesswork, which because
of their nature are difficult of verification. The statement that Burgred of Mercia
married King Æthelwulf's daughter at Chippenham in 853, and that the place was
then a royal estate, comes under this category.[175] The author must have known

from his text of the Anglo-Saxon Chronicle—however much he botched his translation of it[176]—that King Alfred had been celebrating Twelfth Night at Chippenham
in 878, and he also knew[177] that the place was in northern Wessex and therefore
near the border with Mercia. Such a place was likely to have been a royal estate
and would have provided an obvious border location for a West Saxon and Mercian
wedding. For this otherwise careless author, we do not have to invoke the necessity
for his having to undertake, in this instance, any detailed research on documents
whatever. Whitelock believed that if the *Life* of Alfred were a forgery it would have
involved 'a great amount of troublesome research'.[178] It did indeed involve research
but we can see that the author worked in a hurry, constantly cutting corners,
duplicating and omitting material at will, and frequently being found guilty of
gross errors. His famous statement that Alfred was born in Wantage is an example
of where his guesswork may have let him down, while his taking of the Great
Army of Danes into England from the Danube in 866[179] reveals not stupidity, but
rather the blind following as we shall see,[180] of an early Norman bookish tradition.
These are questions to which we must return: but for now the crucial point at issue
is that although we may have textual and (lost) manuscript evidence to date the
Life of Alfred to at least as early as *c*. AD 1000, nevertheless, it is difficult even at
this preliminary stage in this study to accept the work as a contemporary biography written by Asser or by anyone else who had personal knowledge of King
Alfred. Equally important is the recognition of so much rhetorical invention within
the text of the *Life* of this king. Regardless of when the work was written, or by
whom, the presence of so much invention demonstrates that far too much credence
has been given hitherto, to otherwise unsubstantiated statements in this source
regarding the life and times of Alfred the Great.

PLATE 1. King Alfred was remembered four centuries after his death as both a great law-giver and a heroic king who brought the Danish invaders to heel. In this illustration from a Latin translation of the Treaty between Alfred and Guthrum in a *Liber legum antiquorum regum* of *c.*1327, the two kings are shown in the friendly context of a *concilium*—in this case, the concluding of a peace treaty.

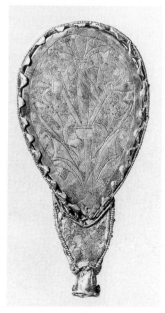

PLATE 2. The Alfred Jewel. An enamel plaque held under a rock crystal and framed in a gold pear-shaped surround. An animal head attachment holds a tube of sheet metal which provides a socket for what may once have been a wooden or ivory stem. The frame carries the remarkable inscription + *AELFRED MEC HEHT GEWYRCAN* ('Alfred had me made'). The jewel was found in 1693, at North Petherton in Somerset and only four miles from Athelney where Alfred built his fortress during the decisive campaign against Guthrum in 878. The figure in the centre of the Jewel may represent Sight as in the Fuller Brooch (Plate 3, below), or it may depict Christ as the incarnate Wisdom of God. Few artifacts may take us closer to the person of an early medieval king, but as ever in Alfredian studies, nothing is quite as simple as it may seem. The crucial matter of function relating to this object still eludes us, and suggestions vary from its possible use as a book-mark to that of a wand of office.

PLATE 3. The Fuller Brooch. Late ninth-century silver Anglo-Saxon disc brooch with niello inlay. Once considered to be a fake, this brooch has been rehabilitated as a genuine late-ninth century piece showing the five senses with Sight in the centre, flanked by Smell (top right), Touch (lower right), Hearing (lower left) and Taste (top left). The brooch had probably found its way into an antiquarian collection by the sixteenth century, though its provenance is unknown. The scheme of ornamental motifs reminds us of Alfred's developed intellectual interests as a philosopher-king.

PLATE 4. Gold finger ring (*left*) with niello inlay, inscribed with the name of King Æthelwulf—the father of Alfred the Great—who ruled as king of Wessex from 839 to 858. The ring was found crushed in a cart rut at Laverstock, Wiltshire, in 1780. The design incorporates two peacocks flanking a tree of life motif. Gold finger ring (*right*) with niello inlay, inscribed with the name of Queen Æthelswith, sister of Alfred the Great, and queen of Burgred, king of the Mercians. Burgred was driven out of Mercia by the Great Army of Danes in 873–4, dying later as an in exile in Rome. Æthelswith followed her husband into exile and died at Pavia in 888. The central motif of the ring shows a haloed *Agnus Dei* (Lamb of God). It was found during ploughing between Aberford and Sherburn in West Yorkshire in 1870.

PLATE 5. Remains of a wall painting on a stone which was re-used in the building of the New Minster at Winchester. Since the New Minster was completed in 903, the painting—from an earlier building—must date from the reign of King Alfred or before. Its art has been compared to the style of Frithestan's vestments (Plate 29).

PLATE 6. The Winchester Reliquary. This gilded copper burse or purse-shaped reliquary is the first complete early medieval portable reliquary to be found in England. Discovered during excavations in Sussex Street, Winchester in 1976 in association with pottery dating *c.* A.D. 900, the reliquary is seen as a possible example of West Saxon craftsmanship from the Alfredian era. The object housed a saint's relic in the cavities of its wooden interior. Its surface has on one side (*left*), [badly damaged], a portrait of Christ seated with a book in his left hand and with the right hand raised in blessing, while on the other side (*right*) is the tree-of-life motif in an acanthus design.

PLATE 7. The Gokstad Ship as it was found in a burial on the western side of Oslofjord in Norway in 1880. This ocean-going viking warship was over 76 feet (23.2 m) long and accommodated 32 oarsmen. Timbers used in the construction of the burial chamber date to *c.* A.D. 900. Not all viking vessels were as splendid as this, but fleets of 200 longships and more, are attested in contemporary chronicles during King Alfred's reign, and so numbers of invading Northmen who overran Alfred's kingdom may be reckoned in thousands rather than hundreds.

PLATE 8. The Trewhiddle Hoard. This assemblage of coins (not shown), a chalice, silver scourge, and other items of jewellery and precious metal was discovered at Trewhiddle near St. Austell in Cornwall in 1774. The material is predominantly Anglo–Saxon and the deposition of this hoard is dated to *c*.868 or to shortly before the reign of King Alfred. The existence of a hoard such as this may be indicative of troubled times in Cornwall, and the cache may represent loot seized by vikings or by Cornishmen on a raid into Wessex.

PLATE 9. (*a*) The Abingdon Sword. This Anglo–Saxon iron pattern-welded sword has its pommel and upper and lower hilt guards mounted with silver and inlaid with niello. Parts of the sword may originally have been adorned with sheet gold and filigree work. The figures on the upper guard may represent the Four Evangelists. Such a splendid weapon would have been appropriate for a Christian warrior such as King Alfred. It dates to probably the end of the king's reign or a little later.

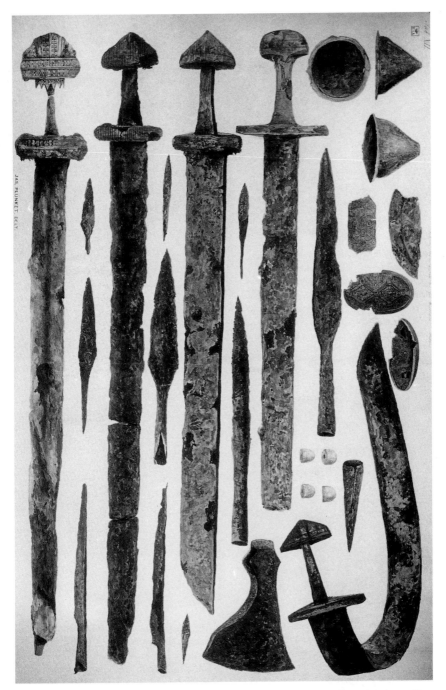

(*b*) Weapons discovered in a viking cemetery during the construction of the Great Southern railway at Kilmainham-Islandbridge west of Dublin in the early nineteenth century. The assemblage contains swords (some with lavishly decorated hilts), shields (only the bosses survive), arrow-heads, spears and a battle-axe. Such weapons were typical of those used by the heathen Northmen who confronted Alfred's warriors in the 870s and 890s. The water-colour drawing from 1847 also shows Scandinavian women's brooches and four gaming pieces.

PLATE 10. (*a*) Late (posthumous) coin of Æthelred I of Wessex (866–71), elder brother of King Alfred, whose reign was designedly over-shadowed by that of Alfred in the account of it preserved in the Anglo-Saxon Chronicle. Closest to Alfred in age, the two brothers reached a settlement over their inheritance at Swinborg in 870–1 which was to split the family and lead to bloody civil war on Alfred's death.

(*b*) Coin of King Burgred of Mercia. Burgred was the brother-in-law and contemporary of King Alfred. He was driven from his kingdom by the Danes in 873–4 and died in exile in Rome.

(*c*) Coin of the Danish king, Guthrum, who led the most serious attack on Alfred's kingdom during the second war and who was eventually brought to terms by Alfred in 878. He then took the baptismal name, Æthelstan, a version of which appears on this coin. Guthrum withdrew to East Anglia where he ruled as king until his death in 890. Guthrum's coinage had close connections with that of King Alfred, in terms of design, inscriptions, moneyers and mints.

(*d*) Unique coin—discovered in 1984 from the Ashdon (Essex) Hoard—of yet another Danish invader who was rehabilitated and ruled as a Christian king of York. Guthfrith (*c*.883–95) established a *rapprochement* with the church of St. Cuthbert and on his death was honoured with a Christian burial within York Minster. King Alfred's ealdorman of Somerset, Æthelnoth, was dispatched to negotiate with Guthfrith's York Danes in 894.

(e) Coin of Archbishop Æthelred of Canterbury 871–88 who ruled over King Alfred's church for the first seven years of that king's reign. He received a letter from Pope John VIII urging him to resist Alfred's encroachments, and Alfred acknowledged him as the premier adviser and witness in the drawing up of the king's will.

(f) Coin of Archbishop Plegmund of Canterbury (890–923). A Mercian scholar, who was acknowledged by King Alfred for his help with the king's translation of Gregory's *Pastoral Care*. Plegmund reorganized the West Saxon diocese and survived to the end of the reign of Alfred's son and successor, Edward the Elder.

(a)

PLATE 11. (a) Coin of King Ceolwulf II of Mercia (873–9). Ceolwulf came to power in Mercia as a Danish tributary king after Burgred's expulsion. His Two-Emperor type coinage establishes an obvious link with the same issue of King Alfred who may also have been regarded by the Danes as their tributary king in the period 871–8. This coinage and Alfred's Two-Emperor type were most likely issued under Danish control.

(b)

(c)

PLATE 11. (*cont.*) Two coins of King Alfred. The example of the Two-Emperor type (*b*) carries the title *REX ANGLO* which does not necessarily mean that Alfred was claiming to be king of more than the people of Wessex. The London Monogram issue (*c*) may or may not date to after Alfred's reported occupation of London in 886. Such a coin could refer to Alfred's new arrangement with the victorious Danish Army which controlled London from 871 onwards. These coins cannot be taken to present realistic portraits of Alfred. The Two-Emperor specimen shows a strong chin and long head, while the London Monogram issue displays an entirely different portrait.

PLATE 12. (*a*) Silver penny of Hálfdan. This coin combines the Two-Emperor design with that of the London Monogram. Two-Emperor type coins were otherwise associated with the kings Alfred and Ceolwulf, and Alfred's issues may date in part at least from the period of Danish supremacy in the years during and following 871–3 when the Danes controlled London and dominated Wessex and Mercia. Since Hálfdan, a leader of the Great Army who defeated Alfred in Wessex in 871–2, also controlled London, it is difficult not to identify this coin with that viking leader. Alternative attributions suggest an association with some unknown Scandinavian leader in the Danelaw.

(*b*) King Alfred's Offering Piece issued late in his reign probably from Winchester and bearing the inscription: *AELFRED REX SAXONUM* ('Alfred, King of the Saxons'). The inscription on the reverse: *ELIMO[OSINA]* meaning 'Alms Money' (*eleemosyna*) reveals the purpose of this ceremonial coinage which weighed as much as seven silver pennies. It was coins such as this which Alfred's ealdormen, may have taken to Rome on behalf of their king and his people throughout the 88os. This remarkable piece was found near Poole in Dorset in 1875

(*c*) Coin of Alfred's son and heir, King Edward the Elder (899–924). The eldest son and second child of Alfred and Ealhswith, this successful and energetic warrior-king built on Alfred's defensive policies and eventually conquered the Southern Danelaw. There is no evidence to suggest that he shared much of his father's great personal love for learning and there is some evidence to show that he regarded his sister, Æthelflæd, and her daughter as rivals on his path to conquest and power. Edward's son, Athelstan, became the first king to rule all England.

PLATE 13. The face of a ninth-century politician and ruthless king, Lothar I (795–855), who quarrelled with his father, the Carolingian emperor Louis the Pious, and with his brothers, Louis, and Charles (Plate 14), over the inheritance of Charlemagne. Such squabbling attracted Scandinavian freebooters to the crumbling Western Empire like moths to a candle and was instrumental, too, in the eventual viking conquest of the greater part of England.

PLATE 14. The Carolingian ruler, Charles the Bald (823–77). Charles was the grandson of the emperor Charlemagne and the father-in-law of Alfred's older brother, King Æthelbald of Wessex. King Alfred may have learnt much from Charles's defensive strategy against viking invaders and imitated his tactic of building forts and fortified bridges at vulnerable points on waterways and rivers. This rakish-looking portrait of Alfred's older and powerful Carolingian contemporary was executed from life sometime between 842 and 869.

PLATE 15. The Isle of Athelney. The place-name *Athelney* may mean 'Island of the princes' and the name may derive from the fact that King Alfred kept his family about him there for safety when he built his fort on that island in the Somerset marshes in 878. The foundation of the monastery on Athelney may date to after Alfred's time. It is not mentioned in the king's *Will*. But the fort at nearby Lyng is listed in the Burghal Hidage and must date, therefore, to at least as early as *c.*914–9.

Plate 16. Burghal Hidage forts. Cricklade (*top*), a fort listed in the Burghal Hidage, was probably already fortified by 903 when the place was mentioned in relation to an attack by a Danish army. Cricklade, on the upper Thames in north Wiltshire, defended the Wessex border from raiders coming out of Mercia. Wareham (*bottom*) retains some of the most dramatic (albeit altered) Alfredian defences of all Burghal Hidage forts. Since the place had a nunnery and lay near the anchorage at Poole Harbour it may well have been fortified by King Alfred before the Danes encamped there in 875–6. Both Cricklade and Wareham have streets laid out on a grid pattern, and the perimeter defences of both towns—originally provided with a bank and wooden revetment—were later reorganized in the reign of Æthelred the Unready.

PLATE 17. A memento of difficult times at Wareham in Dorset. This square silver gilded mount may have been originally designed to adorn a Carolingian horse harness or sword fitting. It may have come to Wareham via Alfredian contacts with his Frankish neighbours, or it may have come there as a piece of viking loot, since many of those Northmen who occupied Wareham in 875–6 may have served on earlier raiding parties in the Carolingian Empire.

PLATE 18. Detail from the Bayeux Tapestry showing a banner with bird image being carried (next but one) behind Duke William of Normandy as he rides out to the battle of Hastings. It was a raven banner such as this—imbued with magical powers of the bird of the Norse war-god, Odin—which the West Saxons captured from their viking enemies in north Devon in 878.

VIII

Neurotic Saint and Invalid King

THE IMAGE OF ALFRED PRESENTED IN THE ANGLO-SAXON CHRONICLE
as a warrior-king fighting off inroads from Danish warbands and otherwise
seeing to the defence of his kingdom is apparent in the *Life* of the the king only in
so far as the compiler relied so heavily on his translation of that same Alfredian
section of the Chronicle. The author of the *Life* of King Alfred made his own
destructive contribution to our understanding of the king's private life and
personality, which is in conflict with much of what we know about Alfred from
contemporary sources. In the words of Galbraith, Asser's king is presented to us
as 'a neurotic invalid' obsessed with his own painful and mysterious medical
condition.[1] The author of Alfred's *Life* first introduces the topic of King Alfred's
poor health in his garbled account of the king's childhood: 'When he [Alfred] was
more advanced in years, he did have teachers and writers to some extent, but he
was not able to study, because he was harassed, nay, rather disturbed, day and
night . . . with illnesses unknown to all the physicians of this island.'[2] This passing
reference to Alfred's illnesses—for there were more than one—sets the tone of his
Life, and the subject of the king's diseases and his sufferings are returned to by the
author, again and again, throughout the work. The first detailed account of one of
the illnesses is introduced into the narrative of the king's wedding in chapter 74.
We are told that after the wedding feast which lasted for a day and a night, Alfred
'was struck without warning in the presence of the entire gathering by a sudden
severe pain that was quite unknown to all physicians'. This illness 'plagued him
remorselessly by day and night from his twentieth year until his forty fifth'—the
year in which the author was claiming to write—or again it continued 'without
remission from his twentieth year up to his fortieth and beyond'.[3] When Alfred
was not suffering from illness, like all neurotics, he was dreading its recurrence: 'If
at any time through God's mercy that illness abated for the space of a day or a
night or even of an hour, his fear and horror of that accursed pain would never
desert him, but rendered him virtually useless—as it seemed to him—for heavenly
and worldly affairs.'[4] Elsewhere the author, when listing Alfred's obligations and
achievements, refers to the king's 'continual bodily infirmities (*cotidianas corporis
infirmitates*)' and to his mysterious 'malady (*dolor*)'.[5] Near the end of the *Life* the
subject is broached once more, but typical of the compiler, he adds nothing to
what he has already told us, apart from highlighting the king's general problem:

The king was pierced by many nails of tribulation, although placed in royal power. For, from his twentieth till his forty-fifth year, in which he now is, he has been constantly afflicted with a most severe attack of an unknown malady (*gravissima incogniti doloris*), so that he has not a single hour's peace, in which he is not either suffering that infirmity (*infirmitatem*) or driven almost to despair by apprehension of it.[6]

According to the author of Alfred's *Life*, the king did not suddenly become an invalid at nineteen. In a confused narrative, the author tells us, that the young and saintly Alfred 'in the first flowering of his youth before he had married his wife' prayed to God for 'some illness which he would be able to tolerate' and thereby, though mortification of the flesh help the prince 'abstain from carnal desire'.[7] Heaven's response was piles (*ficus*)—but of an extraordinarily severe, if not indeed, incapacitating variety:

After some time he contracted the disease of piles through God's gift; struggling with this long and bitterly through many years, he would despair even of life, until that time when, having finished his prayers, God removed it from him completely. But, alas, when it had been removed, another more severe illness seized him at his wedding feast.[8]

Here at least, the compiler's meaning is clear. From early adolescence until his wedding, Alfred, through prayer, had become a martyr to haemorrhoids—suffering 'agonising irritation even from his youth' and despairing 'even of life'. But on his wedding-day (in his twentieth year), he became an even more confirmed invalid. This second illness, which the compiler informs us followed the king throughout his life, was also inflicted by Heaven in answer to Alfred's second prayer that 'Almighty God in his [*sic*] bountiful kindness might substitute for the pangs of the present and agonising infirmity some less severe illness.'[9] It would seem that this second petitioning of Heaven gave Alfred somewhat more than even his supposedly ascetic nature bargained for, and the resulting disease was that which in the words of the compiler 'rendered him virtually useless'.

The notion of Alfred praying for bodily infirmity underlines that much of what the author of his *Life* personally contributes on the *persona* of the king was modelled on a saint's *vita*. Indeed, Alfred emerges as a much more convincing *sanctus* in his *Life* than many other conventional holy men as treated by their biographers. We are told of Alfred that 'even from his childhood he was an enthusiastic visitor of holy shrines, to pray and give alms'.[10] The parallel with Einhard's Life of Charlemagne, here as in several other places in the *Life* of Alfred, is ominously striking. Einhard's account of his hero's spiritual life is credible, even if idealized:

Charlemagne practised the Christian religion with great devotion and piety, for he had been brought up in this faith since earliest childhood. . . . As long as his health lasted he went to church morning and evening with great regularity, and also for early morning Mass, and the late-night hours. . . . He was most active in relieving the poor. . . . He gave alms not only in his own country . . . but also across the sea in Syria, Egypt, Africa, Jerusalem, Alexandria and Carthage.[11]

Alfred, too, according to the compiler of his *Life*

was also in the habit of hearing daily the divine office, the Mass, and certain prayers and psalms, and of observing both the day and the night hours, and of visiting churches at night-time, as we have said, in order to pray without his followers knowing. Moreover, he showed zeal for almsgiving, and generosity both to his countrymen and to strangers from all nations. . . . And many Franks, Frisians, men of Gaul, pagans, Welsh, Scots [*recte* Irishmen] and Bretons willingly submitted to his lordship.[12]

Alfred would listen to lessons from Holy Scripture being read out either 'by his own countrymen, or . . . in the company of foreigners',[13] and we are reminded yet again of Einhard's account of 'stories (*historiae*)' and 'sagas (*res gestae*)' being read aloud to Charlemagne and of how that ruler 'took great pleasure in the books of Saint Augustine and especially in those which are called the *The City of God*'.[14] Charlemagne also, according to Einhard, 'loved foreigners (*peregrinos*) and took great pains to make them welcome', so much so that they were considered to have become a burden on the Frankish realm.[15] Although Charlemagne would only sing his psalms in a discreet voice along with the rest of the choir, and never read a lesson aloud, nevertheless 'he made careful reforms in the way in which the psalms were chanted and the lessons read', and 'he was himself quite an expert at both of these exercises.'[16]

We must allow for the fact that Alfred, like Charlemagne shared the same passion for learning, if not for educational and ecclesiastical and liturgical reform, and Alfred may have consciously sought to emulate some of the cultural achievements of his Frankish predecessor. A number of the parallels between the *Life* of Alfred and the *Life* of Charlemagne, therefore, may well be fortuitous and none of them necessarily invalidate any of Alfred's real achievements. Nor do these parallels show, in themselves, that the *Life* of Alfred was not written by a contemporary of the king. But given that the compiler of Alfred's *Life* is known to have had access to Einhard's work—quoting verbatim from it in parts—we need to be constantly on our guard not to accept everything that is said of Alfred's piety or scholarship, since his biographer had Einhard at hand as a model, offering a mine of plausible information on these very subjects. There is evidence that the author of Alfred's *Life* wished to 'go one better than Einhard' in describing the achievements of his king. If Charlemagne were presented in his biography as pious, then Alfred was presented as a saint. The two men might have attended daily Mass and a punishing round of offices and psalmody, as well as giving alms and putting up with tiresome foreigners, but Alfred the saint, was clearly in a class all on his own:

He very often got up secretly in the early morning at cockcrow and visited churches and relics of the saints in order to pray; he lay there prostrate a long while, turning himself totally to God, praying that Almighty God through his mercy would more staunchly strengthen his resolve in the love of his service by means of some illness which he would be able to tolerate.[17]

Nor was this an aberration contracted in later life. Alfred 'even from his childhood was an enthusiastic visitor of holy shrines, to pray and to give alms',[18] and from his precocious childhood he had kept a book 'by him day and night' in which he had personally collected 'the services of the hours, and then certain psalms and many prayers.' This was a book which the compiler of the *Life* even claimed to have seen himself during Alfred's later years.[19] It was a book which Alfred 'took around with him everywhere for the sake of prayer, and was inseparable from it'. Charlemagne could not compete with the saintly and precocious Alfred here, for Charlemagne's notebook—which, as we shall see, clearly inspired the idea of Alfred's book—was acquired late in life to help an illiterate emperor learn to write, and that was a task which Einhard admitted 'he had begun too late in life'.[20]

This image of the invalid and neurotic Alfred, clutching his childhood book of prayers, keeping secret nightly vigils prostrated in prayer in remote churches, and storming Heaven for diseases to mortify his flesh, must be one of the last medieval fictions still taken seriously by modern scholars. Keynes and Lapidge[21] accepted the chaotic narrative of Alfred's illnesses as 'adequately coherent' but nevertheless conceded that 'Asser's' picture of the king 'as one so obsessed with his poor health', had led those translators of Alfred's *Life* 'to suspect that the illness was in part psychological'. That is, of course, one explanation—that the illnesses were a figment of the king's imagination—Galbraith's *malade imaginaire*.[22] The question must then be posed as to whether such a king—praying for illness and enduring excruciating imagined illnesses—would not have been regarded as mad, by the standards of his age, and by all but the most inobservant and indulgent of his followers? An alternative explanation would be that the illnesses were a figment of the biographer's imagination. The story of King Alfred's illnesses was indeed invented by his biographer, and what may or may not have been genuine tenth-century traditions relating to Alfred's personal piety were distorted out of all recognition into a tale of perpetual 'martyrdom' by his later hagiographer. Can we really accept that a king who was so incapacitated by unremitting illness from early adolescence could possibly have achieved all that we justifiably attribute to Alfred's name? Could such a king, beset by physical illness, ever have summoned the energy to lead relentlessly in war from 871 until 878 and again from 893 until 896? Indeed, 'Asser' claimed to be writing in 893—the very year in which the supposedly stricken king was about to face the last great challenge to his rule. Alternatively, if the illnesses were psychological, and accompanied by the obsessive fears and depressions which the author so vaguely yet so vividly describes, could the sufferer ever have mustered the nervous energy and the impressive powers of long-term concentration and planning necessary to see through his ambitious translation programmes and other intellectual achievements? And would it ever have been possible for the hard-headed and embattled West Saxon *witan* to entrust the kingship to a depressive invalid at the very time, in 871, when they were in need of a dynamic military commander, in full possession of all his physical faculties—not to mention optimism and courage? The answer to these questions must be a resounding 'no'.

Not only is the tale of Alfred's outlandish piety and unremitting sickness at odds with what contemporary sources tell us of the king, but it is also contradicted by what his biographer has to say of Alfred elsewhere in his *Life*. For he writes of this same king that he was such 'a great warrior and victorious in virtually all battles' even as a young man he could, if he had so wished, have taken the kingship from his older brothers.[23] Which of these two fictions are we to believe—that concerning the neurotic saint, or that of Alfred the macho warrior and 'heir apparent'? Could a young man whose piles had reduced him to 'despair even of life'[24] and who spent his nights mortifying the flesh in vigils, be described with any semblance of credibility as 'a keen huntsman, he toiled unceasingly in every branch of hunting, and not in vain; for he was without equal in his skill and good fortune in that art'.[25] And is not the tale of the warrior Alfred cutting short his Mass to fight the Danes, completely at variance with the other elaborate tales of his ascetic exercises? It was Alfred who left his brother King Æthelred to persevere with the Eucharist, while Alfred set off to do the true business of a king, leading his warband to victory against the Danish hordes at Ashdown. In that anecdote, it was Æthelred who emerged as the pious 'wimp' 'declaring firmly that he would not leave that place alive before the priest had finished Mass, and that he would not forsake divine service for that of men'.[26]

The truth is that for the author of the *Life*, any story that served its purpose at a given point in his garbled narrative was pressed into service regardless of how it contradicted what was said of King Alfred elsewhere. This being so, it is impossible to accept anything which is written in the *Life* of King Alfred relating to the alleged illnesses of the king or to his ascetic practices. We know from the contemporary or near-contemporary witness of the Chronicle that Alfred's days were crowded with prolonged military crises which constantly demanded immediate and decisive responses. The very year (868) in which Alfred is alleged to have contracted his most mysterious and crippling illness—at his marriage in Mercia—was a time, when according to the Chronicle he undertook the longest recorded expedition of his life. In that same year he marched with his brother, King Æthelred, at the head of the West Saxon army to Nottingham to confront the Danes who had established their winter quarters there. The year 871 saw Alfred fighting in five recorded pitched battles at Reading, Ashdown, Basing, *Meretun*, and Wilton, 'besides the [lesser] expeditions which . . . Alfred often rode on' in that same hectic year. Alfred's brother, King Æthelred, died sometime after the Danish victory and 'great slaughter' at Meretun. It was at that very moment, during the burial of Æthelred at Wimborne, that we deduce from the chronicler, Æthelweard, news came in of the arrival of a new 'summer army' at Reading which was joined by the Great Heathen Army already in the field.[27] The crisis could not have been greater in that month after Easter in 871. Almost everything depended on the courage and strength of personality of the new king. As leader of the warband, Alfred was ultimately responsible for protecting the lives, property, and lands of every West Saxon warrior and their kith and kin. Those men who stood by their king in the shield-wall admired neither neuroses nor self-inflicted infirmity. Yet the West Saxon *witan*, in their hour of peril, put their trust in Alfred. Were he the sickly ascetic described by his biographer, he could never have stood the pace in the veritable league-table of battles fought that year, nor would he have won the support of his battle-hardened warriors.

It is clear from Alfred's own writings that he was indeed a deeply Christian king, holding deeply Christian views on kingship and on the ordering of Christian society, and the promotion of Christian culture.[28] He had a mind, too, which was reflective and scholarly. But we shall see that Alfred reveals himself in his scholarly writings as a man deeply conscious of his own awesome royal power, and as a ruler who demanded unswerving loyalty from his followers.[29] Alfred also displays in his writings, an ordered mind—and one which his ill-equipped biographer did not share. Indeed, one of the more powerful arguments against contemporary authorship of Alfred's *Life* is that a man of Alfred's power and genius would never have let such an incompetent loose on his own biography. Alfred possessed a bent for organization and direction, and it was this capacity for action more than any other, which enabled the king to push forward his programme of fortress building, on the one hand, and the translation of a whole series of major Latin works into the vernacular, on the other. Everything that contemporary evidence affords us on the personality of Alfred—from the issuing of his law codes to the organization of his army—are all suggestive of a man of high intelligence backed by boundless energy. There is nothing to suggest a morbid interest in asceticism or the endurance of self-inflicted disease, nor is there any evidence for the self-doubt or contradictions such a temperament would reveal under the stresses of public life and the challenge posed by the demands of warrior-kingship. The image of Alfred, the neurotic saintly invalid, as portrayed in the king's *Life*, has endured for only the most unworthy of reasons in twentieth-century English historical scholarship, underpinning as it does the gravest distortion of our assessment of this remarkable medieval king.

We have already seen how the biographer's treatment of Alfred's precocity as a small boy, as well as his superiority over his brothers, conforms to hagiographical models. In the matter of Alfred's illnesses, we can even more clearly identify hagiographical borrowing and invention. True saints were expected either to cure illness in others as wonder workers, or else to endure illness themselves with heroic Christian fortitude. The notion of describing illnesses endured by great men has a pre-Christian pagan and Roman ancestry. Suetonius writes of Julius Caesar's occasional comas and epilepsy, as well as of Augustus' 'several grave and dangerous illnesses'.[30] He describes Gaius (Caligula) as an epileptic from boyhood who also suffered from mental illness, while Claudius was celebrated for his stumbling gait and nervous twitching of the head, together with numerous other disorders which he endured from childhood.[31] For medieval saints, however, illness properly handled, could be a sign of God's special favour—like St Paul's thorn in the flesh—and therefore could be used as evidence to prove the heroic sanctity and wonder-working powers of a holy man. Bede relates how the child, Cuthbert, endured a great tumour on the knee which rendered walking almost impossible, and which was cured by an angel.[32] Later, while still only a young monk, Cuthbert contracted plague, which resulted in a swelling on his thigh and although he recovered from this. 'The swelling which appeared in his thigh gradually left the surface of his body, [and] it sank into the inward parts and, throughout almost the whole of his life, he continued to feel some inward pains, so that, in the words of the apostle, "strength was made perfect in weakness"'.[33] Bede refers to this chronic illness later in the *Life* as Cuthbert's 'old complaint which used to afflict him almost daily',[34] and which was not to be confused with a third and final malady in the form of a long-term suppurating ulcer on one of the saint's swollen feet.[35]

The catalogue of disagreeable illnesses and repulsive symptoms listed in medieval saints' *lives* do indeed reflect the realities of those disease-ridden times. But the reason for exaggerating the infirmities endured by holy men and women was primarily to underline their saintly powers of endurance which was seen as a veritable martyrdom during life. It is in this context that we must interpret the account of Alfred's infirmities. For not only did Alfred, like most saints, endure illness, but he was alleged in his *Life* to have belonged to an exclusive and fanatical class of holy people who wilfully sought to have disease inflicted upon them. This category of ascetic extremists was never numerous, if only because of the dubious theology of suffering which lay behind the idea of self-inflicted disease. The late sixth-century Irish female saint, Ita, was remembered for mortifying her flesh by allowing a hideous beetle to eat into 'the whole of one of her sides' and which she referred to endearingly as her 'fosterling'.[36] There is also the instance of another Irish saint, Molaise of Leighlin, who, like Alfred, prayed to God for the sending of disease. Molaise was said to have had 'thirty diseases in his body for devotion's sake' and when he was once visited by St Magnenn, that saint asked the fanatical Molaise: 'I adjure you by God, to tell me why you ask Him that in your body there must be a score and ten diseases.' Molaise replied that 'sinfulness like a flame pervades my body, therefore I wish to have my purgatory here'.[37]

While the fanatical intensity of Alfred's asceticism is matched only in Irish saints' *lives*, nevertheless the *vita* which provided the model for the *Life* of Alfred and for the specific themes within Alfred's *Life*, was not Irish, but Frankish, and dealt with the same unusual subject of a pious lay ruler. The *Life* of Count Gerald of Aurillac, written by Odo of Cluny *c*.930, portrays that Frankish count as a successful warrior but also as an intensely pious layman who was beset by illness. While the young Alfred had to endure piles, the youthful Gerald 'for a long time was so covered with small boils that it was not thought that he could be cured'.[38] These *pustulae* were clearly more than 'pimples'[39] for because of them Gerald's parents decided that their son would probably 'be unsuited for wordly pursuits' and during his long illness he was 'put more closely to the study of letters'. Later as a young man, Gerald was struck blind from a cataract (*glaucomate caecicatis*) for over a year[40] and he was blind yet again for more than seven years at the end of his life.[41] The key to understanding the treatment of King Alfred's illnesses in his biography lies in a study of the handling of illness in the Cluniac hagiography which, as we shall see, inspired Alfred's *Life*. John of Salerno tells us of Odo (who wrote the *Life* of Gerald), that when Odo was a youth, he too, suffered from illness. In Odo's case he was tormented by a severe headache (*dolor capitis*) from his sixteenth until his nineteenth year—'torn by this pain as the earth by a plough-share'.[42] But Odo's illness was not fortuitous. It was sent by Heaven, because Odo's father had promised his infant son as a monk to the community of St Martin, and it was only when Odo eventually entered the monastery of Tours that the pain receded.[43] Odo's excruciating pain, then, was inflicted by God in order to prompt the sufferer towards the celibate life of a monk. The tale of Gerald's temporary blindness was also narrated by Odo in the context of a heavenly intervention in order to chastise and confirm the Frankish count in his celibate life. Gerald we are told, initially succumbed to the idea of sleeping with the daughter of one of his serfs, but drew back at the eleventh hour, having already enjoyed the preliminary aspects of his temptation: 'The kind and just Lord . . . did not omit to punish his concupiscence by a just punishment. A few days after He struck the offender for a year or more with blindness from cataract.' Gerald, who unlike Alfred had not sought this affliction, nevertheless bore it with Christian fortitude: 'He neither refused bodily medicines, nor eagerly sought them, but waited patiently for the time and manner in which his Lord might see fit to remove the scourge . . . for he knew that every son is chastised.'[44] Gerald, in spite of this sexual misdemeanour, preserved his chastity to the end of his life, and was held up by his Cluniac biographer, as an example of a layman who lived a life of chastity which could be emulated by all monks.[45] It is clear from the *Life* of Alfred that its author also set out to portray Alfred as a saintly lay ruler in the same mould as Gerald. For just as the chaste Gerald was held up as an example to tenth-century reformed Frankish monks, so Alfred was taken up as a model ruler, with deep religious and ascetic tendencies, by English monks of the late tenth-century monastic reform. Alfred prayed for illness in order to control his concupiscence while an adolescent. And Alfred's piety was modelled on that of the saintly Gerald, who like Alfred learnt the psalter as a boy, and recited it almost every day during his later life.[46] Gerald, like Alfred, was devoted to the Night Office[47] and to the Mass[48] and he regularly prayed for long periods alone in church at night.[49] Both rulers excelled at giving alms to the poor and were conscientious judges. The scholarly Gerald always employed a reader at his table, even when guests were present, and reading was suspended only to allow for questions and discussion on the text.[50] Alfred, too, 'by day and night, whenever he had any free time, ordered books to be read before him by such men [as Plegmund or Wærferth], nor indeed did he allow himself to be without one of them'.[51]

Alfred's biographer had taken the idea of his scholar king and transformed him into the mould of a saint modelled on Count Gerald of Aurillac. The choice of Gerald as the lay ruler who lived the life of a quasi-monk and saint, while coping with affairs of the world was an obvious one to provide a model for the kingly Alfred. There was one significant difference, however, between Alfred and Gerald. While Gerald had preserved his chastity, Alfred abandoned his, on his marriage to his Mercian queen. So, while Alfred and Gerald both suffered from irritating skin disorders in adolescence, both, too, were 'punished' by their biographers for later lapses in their sexual morals. Gerald was struck blind for a year for merely toying with the idea of sleeping with his serf's daughter. Alfred was dished out a more punitive sentence for abandoning chastity altogether on his marriage in 868. The author of Alfred's *Life* twice links the king's second and more terrible illness to the day of his wedding. Anglo-Saxon feasting was not unknown for its dramatic happenings. King Harthacnut collapsed and died 'as he stood at his drink' at a wedding bout for his father's retainer on 8 June 1042.[52] Dunstan had to drag away King Eadwig by force after his coronation feast in 955, from a sexual romp with a mother and daughter—with the king's precious crown thrown on the floor and the king 'wallowing [with the women] in evil fashion, as if in a vile sty'.[53] This last anedote from the *Life* of St Dunstan is instructive for our understanding of the handling of the account of Alfred's wedding feast by that king's biographer. The so-called *B* author of the *Life* of St Dunstan was writing *c.* AD 1000 for that same general monastic milieu in which I would claim the *Life* of King Alfred was also produced. The anecdote relating to Eadwig's coronation feast was prejudicial to Eadwig as it was anti-feminist in its tone. For the monastic writer, obsessed with the observation of celibacy on the part of reforming monks in late tenth-century Francia and England, secular feasting was synonymous with sexual licence and debauchery—and all that was inimical to the observation of the all-important monastic *Rule*. The notion of Alfred's wedding feast 'which lasted for a day and a night' also triggered strong anti-secular feelings on the part of the king's monastic biographer, who was writing as we shall see, under marked Cluniac influence. Alfred's second illness is first introduced in chapters 73 and 74 'when he had duly celebrated the wedding', but the author returns to the connection between the king's marriage and his illness later again in chapter 74:

Another more severe illness seized him at his wedding feast (as I have said), which plagued him remorselessly by day and night from his twentieth year until his forty-fifth; and if at any time through God's mercy that illness abated for the space of a day or a night or even of an hour, his fear and horror of that accursed pain would never desert him, but render him virtually useless—as it seemed to him—for heavenly and worldly affairs.[54]

Alfred's biographer makes yet a third connection between the king's marriage and his illness, when he tells us how 'going back to the beginning' he intends to explain how the very first illness was contracted by the king. It is then he tells us how Alfred as a young adolescent—'in the first flowering of youth *before he had married his wife*' first prayed for illness in order to control his lust.[55] So even at the beginning of his account of the king's life, his biographer is fixated on the king's future marriage and has already established a connection in his own mind not only between the king's illnesses and chastity, but between the king's marriage and its concomitant punishment in the form of disease. Saint Alfred, therefore, was punished 'without warning in the presence of the entire gathering' for abandoning chastity on his wedding-day, with a ghastly and incurable illness which haunted him for the rest of his life. A warrior-king, who was never regarded as a *sanctus* by his contemporaries, was conveniently cast in that mould by a later hagiographer who invented an illness for his hero in order to compensate for the otherwise complete lack of evidence for the kind of heroic sanctity expected of a saint. It is incumbent on historians to explain to medical experts researching on the history of medicine, that all studies into the precise nature of King Alfred's diseases, however well intentioned, are doomed to failure. Alfred has been diagnosed as suffering from neuritis, epilepsy, sexually transmitted ano-genital warts, haemorrhoid-like lesions, Crohn's Disease, and it has even been seriously suggested that the king was infected by virtue of his being a passive homosexual.[56] Few monarchs have been credited with such a catalogue of disagreeable disorders. But if the basis for any medical diagnosis is founded on hagiographical motifs, then all attempts to reach firm conclusions on Alfred's imagined illnesses are as futile as trying to test Alfred's infant IQ on the basis of the folk-tale concerning his mother's book-prize. What we can say, is that compared with all four of his older brothers, Alfred lived long and found the stamina to rule for no less than twenty-eight and a half years.

The so-called evidence from the remedies of Elias, the patriarch of Jerusalem, is little more than a red herring in any discussion of Alfred's illnesses. Elias (*c*.879–907) was the author of a 'round robin' sent to Western rulers, of which one was received by Charles the Fat in 881. The purpose of that letter was to raise money for the restoration of churches under the Eastern Patriarch's jurisdiction. The *Leechbook of Bald*, which survives in a mid-tenth century manuscript and which may or may not have been compiled in Alfred's reign, offers further information on Patriarch Elias as a wise medical man. From this work we deduce that Elias sent Alfred a list of remedies for various medical disorders ranging from constipation to 'pain in the spleen'. There is no evidence to prove that Alfred either ever received a copy of Elias's letter seeking funds for his churches, or that Alfred first sought the list of remedies which Elias is supposed to have sent him. The statement in Alfred's *Life* that its author had 'seen and read letters sent to him [Alfred] with gifts from Jerusalem by the patriarch Elias'[57] is not as supportive of 'strong confirmation of the authenticity of the Life' as Stevenson wished to believe.[58] Alfred's biographer only serves to arouse suspicion when he trumpets his role as a contemporary witness, and besides, the precise name *Elias* has only been arrived at through a 'reconstruction' of the supposed original text.[59] Nor can the claim by Alfred's biographer that the king was in contact with the Patriarch of Jerusalem derive much support from the Chronicle's assertion that King Alfred sent alms to distant India in 883. That entry along with other notices of contacts with the papacy was heavily influenced by borrowings from contemporary Frankish annals in what we identified as the Frankish interlude in the Chronicle (880–92), and such records may well have been prompted by Carolingian models. The problem with this type of evidence is that it can never be conclusive, and arguments may go either way. King Alfred's biographer might indeed have seen a written record of Alfredian contact with the Patriarch of Jerusalem. But that record might have been none other than the note in the *Leechbook of Bald* which could have been consulted in the pre-Conquest period, any time from the reign of Alfred onwards.

There is a further crucial element in the Life of King Alfred which suggests the account of the king's illnesses was influenced by the *Life* of Count Gerald. When the young Gerald had already succeeded to his hereditary rule,[60] and when exactly like Alfred 'it was a thing unheard of that he or his soldiers who fought under him were not victorious',[61] he was struck blind for a year because of that unlawful desire to seduce a girl. Odo, the writer of Gerald's *Life*, goes on to say: 'Those about him (*familiares*) knew of the blindness and they concealed it from the peering eyes of strangers (*extraneis*) with the greatest care.'[62] The worry of temporary blindness for the historical Gerald and his *familiares* was that those outside his immediate household (*extranei*) would no longer accept the leadership of a blind lord. The author of Alfred's *Life* relates that when the youthful Alfred prayed for a substitute for his piles he did so 'on the understanding that the new illness would not be outwardly visible on his body, whereby he would be rendered useless and contemptible . . . for he feared leprosy or blindness (*leppram aut caccitatem*) or some such disease, which so quickly render men useless and contemptible.'[63] It had been a similar condition to leprosy which suggested to Gerald's parents that their son might never succeed to the countship, and it was temporary blindness which later had to be concealed from Gerald's followers. Earlier in his life, at the onset of adolescence, the young Alfred first prayed for his earliest disease which was inflicted as piles, but he asked, 'not, however, that God would make him unworthy and useless in worldly affairs'.[64] Alfred's biographer, under the influence of the *Life* of Gerald, showed Alfred laying down these conditions, because writing in the tenth or early eleventh century he well knew his youthful subject had been destined to be king of Wessex—and no one, not even the supposedly saintly Alfred, could have hoped to rule with great physical deformity or disability. Of course, if the historical Alfred had in reality waged fanatical spiritual warfare against concupiscence, and if he really had been the saint which the *Life* pretends him to have been, then clearly he would have gladly accepted all the diseases Heaven might have wished to unleash upon him, because he would neither have expected nor wished for kingship, at that youthful point in his career.

The accounts of Alfred's illnesses in the *Life* of that king, not only show a dependence of the *Life* of Gerald of Aurillac, but they also display an anachronistic approach to the career of Alfred. The many parallels between the lifestyles of Gerald and of Alfred are so close that one *vita* was clearly compiled under the influence of the other. It is impossible to see how the detailed catalogue of Alfred's virtues, as extolled for instance, in chapter 76 of his *Life*, could have been constructed in isolation from the *Life* of Gerald. These and other parallels are collectively and individually so striking that we can be in no doubt as to the connection between the two works. Gerald and Alfred are not only said to have been interested in relics[65]—we are told that both men had quantities of wax made into candles which Gerald 'ordered to be burnt in lights before the altar or the relics of saints, which he had carried about with him'[66] while Alfred's candles also were 'to burn . . . in the presence of the holy relics of a number of God's chosen saints which the king always had with him everywhere'.[67] The parallels in this single point relate to three specific issues all linked within the same concept—the conversion of the wax into candles, the burning of the candles before relics, and the transport of the relics in the company of the ruler. We have already encountered one highly specific motif of *the ruler who refuses to abandon the Mass while under attack* and we have seen while that motif was central to the *Life* of Gerald, it had become transposed in the *Life* of Alfred to illustrate the subsidiary role of Alfred's brother. In the account of Alfred's illnesses, the garbled and convoluted narrative, replete with repetition and exaggerated asceticism, shows this up as derivative material in comparison with the *Life* of Gerald. Gerald's *Life* by contrast, although clearly hagiographical in structure, is well ordered and the detailed description of that ruler's illnesses are plausible, if not indeed believable. Here was a man who suffered from severe skin disease during adolesence, was later troubled by cataracts and ended his life in blindness. There is also the plausible admission of prudence dictating that Gerald's temporary blindness should be concealed from the public domain. Alfred's diseases having been invented, were perforce described in wilfully mysterious terms, and inflicted on their victim with the hindsight that one day, he would succeed to kingship. While the details of precisely how these motifs were borrowed from the *Life* of Gerald into that of Alfred will be examined later on,[68] it is sufficient to show at this stage that in all aspects, the demonstrably near-contemporary *Life* of Gerald provided the source for some key motifs in the more disorganized and highly derivative *Life* of Alfred.

There is one episode in the account of Alfred's illnesses which is suggestive of a post mid-tenth-century date for the composition of the *Life* of that king. We are told that when Alfred was enduring his piles—and sometime before his wedding in 868—he prayed specifically for an alternative illness. This improbable story has an even more improbable location. At that time, Alfred 'had gone to Cornwall to do some hunting and, in order to pray, had made a detour (as is his wont) to a particular church in which St *Gueriir* lies in peace (and now St Neot lies there as well)'.[69] Stevenson[70] was embarrassed by the reference to Saint Neot and arbitrarily ruled this passage to be a later interpolation—in spite of its presence in the version of the text of the *Life* preserved by Florence of Worcester. Keynes and Lapidge allowed the reference to St Neot to take its place in the Alfredian canon.[71] There is no reason on the manuscript evidence, to suppose the passage was not included by the author of Alfred's *Life*, but there is good reason to reject its evidence for the historical Alfred. St Neots, in the depths of Cornwall, was one of the more dangerous, if not one of the most improbable places for a prince of the House of Ecgberht to go hunting in the 860s. The Cornish kings, and therefore also a Cornish aristocracy, had not been displaced by the West Saxons until well into the reign of Alfred's grandson, King Athelstan in the tenth century. William of Malmesbury records how Athelstan, 'attacking' the Cornishmen 'with vigour', drove them out of Exeter 'which they had up to that time inhabited with equal rights with the English; fixing the boundary of their province beyond the river Tamar'.[72] Athelstan pushed the Cornishmen back some thirty-five miles to the west of Exeter, behind what today is the south-eastern boundary of Cornwall. Athelstan's successes against the Cornish have to be seen in a tenth-century context, along with his related successes over the Welsh and the Strathclyde

Britons.[73] But during Alfred's lifetime, all that was still in the distant future. Not only were the Cornishmen still ruled then, however precariously, by their native kings and aristocracy, but those rulers can only have been bitterly hostile to Alfred's dynasty which faced them with nothing less than extinction[74] Alfred's grandfather, Ecgberht, had been the *bête noire* of the Cornishmen. In 815 'King Ecgberht ravaged in Cornwall, from East to West (*from easteweardum oþ westewearde*)'[75] but the Cornishmen were able to mount a counter-attack in 825 when their army fought against the men of Devon at Galford.[76] The location of this battleground, near Lew Trenchard, on the western edge of Dartmoor in Devon, may suggest that the Cornishmen were taking the offensive. We are not told of the outcome, which may have been the chronicler's way of concealing a West Saxon defeat. The absence of any mention of a West Saxon victory at Galford in 825 stands in contrast to the Chronicle's record of Ecgberht's 'victory and great slaughter' of his Mercian enemies in that same year. The Cornishmen were again fielding an army against Ecgberht in 838, this time in alliance with 'a great naval force' of pagan Danes. That coalition was defeated by Ecgberht at Hingston Down to the west of the Tamar.[77] Lack of detailed reporting on Cornish affairs in the Chronicle prior to 871 does not allow us to assume that the Cornishmen were a spent force in Alfred's time. It may well be that serious English colonization of Cornish lands to the west of the Tamar had got under way after Ecgberht's victory in 838, but it must not be forgotten, that even after Alfred had become king, Dumgarth, his British opposite number is recorded in the *Annales Cambriae* as ruling Cornwall until his death in 875.[78] Nor are we justified in assuming that Dumgarth was the last of the Cornish kings.[79] Had Alfred forced Dumgarth or any of his successors into submission, the Anglo-Saxon Chronicle would not have failed to proclaim such an event.[80] And if the biographer of Alfred were truly the king's contemporary and confidant, then why did he trumpet what amounts to the Alfredian conquest of Wales proper (in chapter 80), and yet omit to say anything of supposed West Saxon control of Cornwall? In King Alfred's *Will* the most westerly lands which are itemized by name among his bequests are Stratton in Triggshire in the far north-east of Cornwall, which he left to Edward the Elder, and Lifton in western Devon (near the Cornish border) which he left to Æthelweard.[81] The bequest to Æthelweard of 'all that I have in Cornwall except in Triggshire' specifically referred in the *Will* to the lands which belonged to Lifton. The vagueness of that phrase *all that I have in Cornwall* (*þæt synd ealle þe ic on Wealcynne hæbbe*) may well have been deliberate—meaning 'lands in Cornwall which are capable of being claimed or occupied by the West Saxons'. So, too, although Alfred's father and older brothers had made generous grants of land in the Cornish march, none of these—as Finberg's researches showed—suggest extensive English penetration of Cornish territory in the south and west of the peninsula.[82] Æthelwulf's grant at Monk Okehampton to the north of Dartmoor, in the centre of Devon, was followed by grants of Æthelbald and Æthelberht of estates at Braunton and Tawstock respectively—both near Barnstaple at the mouth of the river Taw in North Devon.[83] The most westerly fortress in the *Burghal Hidage* was at Pilton which was also in the vicinity of Barnstaple. The other westernmost fort in that survey was at Lydford on the eastern side of Dartmoor, eight miles to the east of Alfred's Cornish estates at Lifton. Lydford was but a few miles from Galford, where back in 825 the Cornish army was defeated by Ecgberht. It would seem that the area east of Dartmoor from Launceston to Lydford Gorge was a frontier zone disputed by Cornishmen and Saxons into Alfred's own time. And even if that area had been colonized from the reign of Ecgberht, St Neots, lying twenty miles further west under Bodmin Moor, was still no place for a prince of Ecgberht's line to go hunting in the early 860s. In early medieval Ireland, a day's journey even on a well-travelled route could be less than 25 miles. The chase left its participants at their most vulnerable, as William Rufus was to find to his cost while hunting over home ground in the New Forest, some two centuries later. The youthful Alfred is likely to have hunted near his father's West Saxon estates. He is highly unlikely, as a youth, to have ventured into the untamed forests of Cornwall, just as he was equally unlikely to have been born in Wantage in a Mercian no-man's-land. According to the early eleventh-century *Life* of St Neot, that saint was supposed to have been Alfred's contemporary, and later versions of the cult alleged that Neot was Alfred's brother.[84] At the time when Alfred is supposed to have visited St Neots while still in his youth, the saint was presumably still alive. Can it be a coincidence that the king who, in the early eleventh-century *Life* of St Neot, was credited with a vision of that saint in AD 878, was in his youth alleged to have visited the church where that same St Neot would be buried at some time in the future?[85] The *Life* of Alfred states that St Neots housed, in Alfred's youth, the relics of St Gueriir, implying that Neot settled and was later buried in an earlier foundation, which clearly had associations with an earlier holy man. The *Life* of Neot, on the other hand, describes that saint's Cornish retreat as a hermitage, founded by Neot himself in a wilderness, which only later in the saint's career was elevated to the status of a regular monastery housing a whole community (*fratribus regularibus*).[86] Alfred's hunting activities together with his prostrations and morbid prayers for disease, which he is alleged to have undertaken at St Neots in Cornwall, should be dismissed as a hagiographical fiction.

What prompted the compiler of Alfred's *Life* to turn his hero king into a sickly saint? All biographical writing in early medieval England was rooted in the tradition of saints' *lives*. As such it was obsessed with the dual purpose of the edification of the reader and the demonstration of the heroic sanctity of the subject. Bede's *Ecclesiastical History*, so often praised for the qualities of its historical writing, is steeped in hagiographical tradition. Not only does Bede himself announce that edification is one of his main objectives,[87] but his historical survey contains an endless series of hagiographical motifs, albeit organized and bonded together in a disciplined narrative. In Bede's *Life* of Saint Cuthbert, we have an unashamedly classic hagiographical work, replete with miracle stories to underline the saint's unquestioned sanctity and supernatural powers. The Early English had not participated in the Carolingian revival of royal biography, and although the author of Alfred's *Life* was clearly influenced by Einhard's *Life* of Charlemagne, and perhaps by Thegan's and by the Astronomer's *Life* of Louis the Pious, the ethos of Suetonius' Classical models which lay behind the Carolingian revival, eluded the biographer of Alfred.[88] The author of Alfred's *Life* was writing in a strictly hagiographical and monastic tradition and it was inevitable that in his hands, Alfred super-king, would be transformed into Alfred super-saint. While Einhard's *Life* of the emperor Charlemagne—with its emphasis on learning and the arts— provided an obvious model for Alfred's biographer to emulate, Odo's *Life* of Count Gerald of Aurillac also provided a suitably pious template, appropriate for that reformed monastic readership in late tenth- and early eleventh-century England, for which Alfred's *Life* was composed.[89] The Frankish Gerald was, like Alfred, a lay ruler—but unlike Charlemagne or indeed Alfred, Gerald was genuinely regarded as a saint. Odo's *Life* of Gerald, therefore, provided an especially appropriate model for the needs of an English biographer anxious to present King Alfred to his monastic readers in the guise of a pious and chaste king. Alfred also differed from his contemporary, Edmund, king of the East Angles. Whatever personal qualities of sanctity Edmund did or did not have, no one disputed his death at the hands of the Danes—either in battle or as their prisoner. Alfred, on the other hand, could not be treated as a martyr—in the conventional sense. We shall see that the *Life* of King Alfred was conceived by its author, as part of the same hagiographical programme which produced the *Life* or *Passio* of St Edmund.[90] So, in the absence of clear evidence for Alfred's sanctity, either in the form of a martyr's death, or of extraordinary personal spiritual qualities, that king's biographer made use of Odo's *Life* of Count Gerald. Since Gerald was stricken in childhood and youth with a skin complaint, then Alfred also was burdened with a similar irritation. And while Gerald was temporarily punished for endangering his chastity, Alfred was permanently punished at his wedding, with a gruesomely mysterious and conveniently invisible disease. And neither Gerald nor Alfred could afford, as lay lords, to reveal the outward signs of their maladies. While Gerald patiently endured the afflictions which Heaven had sent him, Alfred was made go one better and pray to the Lord for diseases to be sent his way.

There was good reason why the author of Alfred's *Life* had come to envisage his king in the role of a sickly saintly hero even before he may have encountered the *Life* of Gerald. In Alfred's own writings, we find frequent references to the cares and tribulations of the world as the king protests about the decline and lack of interest in scholarship, the pressures imposed on him by the duties of kingship, and the strong sense that he was a martyr to his royal duties as well as to his more personal commitment to scholarship. It may be that the historical Alfred did have a pessimistic frame of mind. It is more likely that he chose to exaggerate how bad things were, in order to show how he personally had improved them, and to persuade his bishops (in the *Pastoral Care*) of the need for translations. References to the burdensome nature of one's office and to oppressive demands of work were part of the stock-in-trade of rhetorical apparatus employed by early medieval writers.[91] It was incumbent on medieval writers, too, to proclaim their own inadequacies for the task before them. So Einhard speaks for a whole library of authors when he says: 'My own meagre talent, small and insignificant, non-existent almost, is not equal to writing this life and setting it out in full.'[92] Eddius Stephanus beginning his work on his hero Saint Wilfrid bemoaned: 'this task is great and my powers of understanding and eloquence are small.'[93] It is easy to forget that the 'genuine' Alfred wrote, not as a monk, but with all the preoccupations of an early medieval king. A cursory look at that king's prefaces to his own translations, in which his rhetorical laments were taken out of context, could easily have conveyed the erroneous impression of a man who was persecuted either by conventional enemies or by a more mysterious fate. Alfred had good reason to indulge in self-pity, but that is something that must be understood against the background of the Danish menace which was all-pervasive, which had brutally deprived two of his royal contemporaries in Northumbria and East Anglia of life itself, and which had driven his brother-in-law, the king of the Mercians, overseas. Alfred had endured constant attacks against his kingdom and had seen his people slaughtered and carried off into slavery, and we know from the Chronicle he had suffered the personal loss of many of his best thegns. He refers in his own writings to when 'everything was ransacked and burnt' by barbarous enemies, in those 'troubles' when no one knew what would happen, as he tells us in his *Will*,[94] even to his own person. But elsewhere, even when discussing other matters, the Danish menace and the physical and cultural threat it posed was never far from Alfred's mind. References to 'tribulation' endured by rulers in Alfred's translations and in his own prefaces are, of course, rhetorical allusions to the burden of public office and of kingship in particular. Pope Gregory, some of whose works Alfred had studied in great detail, was renowned for enduring the tensions generated between the conflicting obligations imposed by a public career and his personal or spiritual life.[95] Count Gerald of Aurillac, like Alfred, had to rule his people while trying also to pursue the life of the mind:

He was compelled to be occupied in administering and watching over things . . . and to leave that peace of heart . . . to take up the weariness of earthly business. He could scarcely bear to leave the inner solitude of his heart, and he returned to it as soon as he could. . . . Dragged down to earth, he yearned for this spiritual refreshment, but his household and dependants demanded that he should break into his repose and give himself to the service of others.[96]

In the mind of a not very perceptive monastic reader in the late tenth century, Alfred's references to 'tribulation' might very easily have been taken literally. To such an unsophisticated reader, anxious to produce information on the life of Alfred, these ritual complaints could easily have suggested real physical distress endured by the king, and since the precise nature of his 'tribulation' was, understandably, nowhere spelt out in Alfred's writings, his biographer was prompted to envisage it as an illness 'quite unknown to all physicians'. And the *Life* of Gerald, that other conscientious and scholarly ruler, was at hand to provide ideas and details of the the kind of illness Alfred might have endured. In the preface to Gregory's *Dialogues* Alfred speaks of the 'lofty station of worldly office' of his kingship which he holds 'amidst these earthly anxieties', and of the need to 'reflect my mind on heavenly things amidst these earthly tribulations'.[97] Alfred's biographer, approaching the task of compiling a *Life* of the king in the late tenth or early eleventh century—a task which was clearly beyond him—could have misconstrued two basic points. A reader of his blinkered intelligence and lack of sophistication could easily have misinterpreted King Alfred's rhetorical complaints, and the view of the king, meditating in the midst of misfortune, was transposed into two simplistic notions of a saintly king, wrapt up in prayer, and enduring some form of physical disease. In the preface to Gregory's *Pastoral Care*, Alfred states how he began the translation of that work 'among other various and manifold troubles of this kingdom'.[98] The author of the king's *Life* almost certainly had access to both the translation of the *Dialogues* and the *Pastoral Care*. It is only Alfred's biographer who informs us that Wærferth, bishop of Worcester, translated the *Dialogues* of Gregory at King Alfred's command.[99] Alfred's biographer also says of the *Dialogues* that they were translated 'from Latin into English, sometimes rendering sense for sense (*aliquando sensum ex sensu*)'.[100] His knowledge of this phrase must have come from Alfred's own use of it on two occasions—once in that very same passage concerning the 'multifarious afflictions of this kingdom' in the preface to the *Pastoral Care* and yet again at the beginning of Alfred's prose preface to Boethius's *Consolation of Philosophy*.[101] The phrase derives from a Latin tag used by Gregory and Jerome[102] but surely it is more reasonable to argue that the king's biographer, whatever his identity or the time of his writing, would have borrowed a phrase repeatedly used by the king himself from Alfred's own works. Otherwise we must conclude that Alfred's biographer found the phrase in an earlier Latin source, such as Gregory's *Registrum Epistolarum*. It is far-fetched to assume that a careless and unscholarly biographer would have independently discovered a turn of phrase, twice used by Alfred, in a work which for him was inaccessible, both physically and intellectually. The Latin phrase in the *Life* of Alfred is clearly borrowed from the vernacular writings of the king whose *life* his biographer was composing. That being so, we can safely assume that Alfred's biographer was thoroughly familiar with some at least, of the rhetorical lamentations in the king's prefaces to his own translations.

It is from King Alfred's prose preface to Boethius's *Consolation of Philosophy*, that a biographer searching for information on his subject could have developed the more fully blown notion of the invalid king. Here Alfred returns to the theme of 'the various and manifold worldly cares' but now he specifically declares that these cares 'troubled him both in mind and in body'.[103] Furthermore, the king declares these tribulations to have been both unremitting and beyond number: 'These cares are very hard for us to reckon, that in his days came upon the kingdom to which he had succeeded.' Nor was this all. In his concluding prayer at the end of this work, Alfred's biographer could read the king's cry to Heaven: 'Strengthen my mind to your will and to my soul's need, and confirm me against the devil's temptations; and keep far from me foul lust and all iniquity.'[104] Was not here an idea in the making, which later prompted the monastic biographer to describe Alfred as a king 'transfixed by the nails of many tribulations; even though he is invested with royal authority'? And what better way to develop Alfred's undoubted piety than by spinning an elaborate tale of a saintly king praying for illness to curb those very lusts of the flesh which Alfred himself prayed for control over, in the *Consolation of Philosophy*? Not only might the author of Alfred's *Life* have developed the notion of Alfred's struggle with the flesh from the king's translation of this work, but clear echoes of the wording of the concluding prayer in Boethius surface in the *Life* of Alfred. The plea in the concluding prayer to 'strengthen my mind to your will . . . and confirm me against the devil's temptations; and keep far from me foul lust' is taken up by the author of Alfred's *Life* when he turns to describe the king's personal prayer. There he tells us that Alfred:

wished to confirm his own mind in God's commandments, and when he realised that he was unable to abstain from carnal desire, fearing that he would incur God's disfavour if he did anything contrary to His will. . . . he lay there prostrate [praying] a long while, turning himself totally to God, praying that Almighty God through His mercy would more staunchly strengthen his resolve in the love of His service by means of some illness.[105]

Here then, Alfred's biographer took the king's prayer that one step further into hagiographical fiction, by making the king pray for illness to ensure he kept God's commandments. And so the notion of Alfred the neurotic invalid was born in the mind of a late tenth-century writer of limited understanding and ability, and has dogged our understanding of a remarkable king ever since.

IX

Illiterate Scholar, Writer, and Publisher Extraordinary

THE *LIFE* OF ALFRED GIVES AN ACCOUNT OF THE KING'S EDUCATION and scholarly career which is riddled with contradictions even greater than those which beset the report on the king's illnesses. The king who was depicted by his biographer as a brooding invalid was also supposed to have been an illiterate until his thirty-ninth year. And because his biographer miscalculated the year of Alfred's birth, that king was probably past his fortieth birthday when he supposedly read his first Latin sentence. Yet this same king was responsible for one the most significant scholarly achievements in Early Medieval Europe. The garbled and apocryphal tales in the *Life* of Alfred telling of his prolonged state of ignorance have not only distorted our personal understanding of the man, but these tales have been allowed to determine the chronology of the Alfredian renaissance. The entire literary output of King Alfred and his court circle is crammed into the period 890–9 for no better reason than that Alfred is said by the author of his *Life* to have only begun to read in 887.[1] All is thrown into confusion and doubt in relation to Alfred's scholarship when the compiler of his *Life* embarks on describing how Alfred 'first began . . . to read and translate on one and the same day'. These chapters[2] are deservedly notorious, not for the inherent drama in their account of a great king supposedly learning to read, but for the mischief which they have caused for over a thousand years in preventing an accurate historical appreciation of King Alfred's life and work. The compiler, posing as Asser, informs us that it was he who personally taught King Alfred 'to read and to translate' and to begin his study of the Scriptures on the festival of St Martin, 11 November 887.[3] The record of what is supposed to have happened begins with a clear enough statement— the king, in his thirty-ninth year, began to read and to translate (*legere et interpretari*) with Asser's help, on that day when they sat talking together in the royal chamber (*regia cambra*). As the king sat listening to Asser who was reading aloud from a book, Alfred suddenly produced that 'little book' (*libellum*) of his own which he had kept with him from childhood and which was crammed with prayers from the daily Office and the psalms. Alfred wished Asser to copy the passage which he had been reading, into this little book, but since it was found to be full, Asser with Alfred's consent, prepared a new quire (of eight leaves or sixteen pages) to accommodate that passage and others which were pleasing to the king. Eventually this little book in its turn became as large as a psalter and Alfred himself named it his *enchiridion* or 'handbook', 'because he conscientiously kept it to hand by day and by night'.[4]

From the moment the first passage had been entered by Asser into this new booklet, on that day in November, the king 'was eager to read it at once and to translate it into English (*Saxonica lingua*)'. This supposedly instantaneous ability of a middle-aged ruler to read and translate Latin would presuppose that he had earlier mastered reading and writing in the vernacular. That would seem to be supported by an earlier remark in chapter 76 to the effect that Alfred, while already king—and presumably before his miraculous tutorial in 887—was 'reading aloud from books in English (*Saxonicos libros*)'.[5] Alfred's possession of a note-book which was already crammed with his own material, prior to Asser's tutorial, also implies a high degree of literacy. At another time, which was certainly prior to 887, and very probably in 886, we are shown both the king and Asser reading aloud in circumstances where no restrictions on language are specified: 'I read to him whatever books he wished and which we had at hand. For it is his most usual habit either himself to read books aloud or to listen to others who read them, day and night.'[6] These particular reading sessions took place during the eight months after Asser was supposed to have met up with the king at *Leonaford*—a stay which probably would have ended in December 886.[7] This account of a medieval king reading aloud or being read to by his confidants carries in itself no implication of his being a novice at reading. If the passage is to be taken seriously, it implies that the king was already so thoroughly schooled that he could pick up any book in his library and read and discuss it with his scholars. The notion of 'whatever books he wished and which we had at hand' must have applied to works in Latin, since Latin was the language of 'Divine wisdom and the liberal arts (*divinae sapientiae et liberalium artium*)'[8] for which, his biographer assures us, Alfred had developed a great passion. How then, do we interpret the tale of Alfred's miraculous reading and comprehension in 887, when we have already been assured of his competence as a reader and a scholar in 885–6 and indeed, before?

Those scholars who accept the *Life* of King Alfred as genuine, assume that the king first learnt to read in English in his twelfth year or somewhat later,[9] and that he failed to master Latin until his first introduction to that language in November 887, when he was already by medieval standards rapidly approaching old age. But we recall that contradictions relating to Alfred's schooling were already present in the early chapters of the king's *Life*. There we were told that 'by the unworthy carelessness of his parents and tutors, he remained ignorant of letters until his twelfth year, or even longer'.[10] This did not deter the biographer from narrating a miracle story telling how the infant Alfred—who was then no more than 4 or 6— miraculuosly *read* a whole book, learning it faster than any of his older and grown-up brothers. That was a tale which showed that far from his education being neglected, Alfred enjoyed the personal tuition of his mother as well as of a regular tutor. We also recall how the compiler of the *Life* informed us that the precocious Alfred kept a book of his own by him 'day and night' into which he had personally collected 'the daily course, that is the services of the hours, and then certain psalms

and many prayers'.[11] We are specifically told that this was accomplished after his
infant success with the book-reading contest, and the two accounts are consecutive
in the *Life* of the king. Lest there should be any doubt about the childhood origins
of Alfred's literacy, his biographer returns much later in his work to discuss that
'little book' which the infant Alfred 'carried about with him everywhere in his
bosom'. It is unquestionably the same book that is being referred to in chapter 88,
since the author of the *Life* repeats the fact that it contained 'the daily course and
certain psalms and prayers which he had read (*legerat*) in his youth'.[12]

Alfred's personal ability to read from childhood and his continued interest in
learning as an adult, and as king, is put by the author of his *Life* in no doubt. Later
in Alfred's career, we are told there was a school at the king's court 'under the
diligent care of tutors (*magistrorum*)' at which the infant sons of Alfred's nobles
were educated, as well as the king's own children.[13] In his exaggerated way,
Alfred's biographer presents us with a picture of the king personally involving
himself with the instruction of his pupils in the art of writing: 'He himself never
ceased among other occupations, day and night, to train their sons [i.e. of his
magnates] who were being brought up in the royal household, in all good behaviour
and to educate them in letters (*literis*).'[14] This account of the king's school occurs
in his *Life* some twelve chapters ahead of the account of Alfred's learning to master
the rudiments of Latin, and follows immediately on the account of his wedding.
So, in addition to Alfred the warrior, Alfred the saint, Alfred the invalid, and
Alfred the scholar, we are here presented with the picture of Alfred the headmaster.
This narrative relating how Alfred aspired to different degrees of literacy is as
elusive of analysis as other accounts of the king's illnesses or the folk-tale of Queen
Eadburh at the court of Charlemagne. It is quite impossible to reconcile what is
presented as a consistent body of evidence relating to Alfred's lifelong ability to
read, with an equally clear statement by the same author in chapter 77, to the effect
that the king could read nothing whatever. There, the author claims that Alfred
remained completely illiterate even while surrounded by the four scholars, Wærferth
bishop of Worcester, Plegmund archbishop of Canterbury, and the Mercian priests,
Æthelstan and Wærwulf. These men, we are told were ordered to read to the king:
'Therefore he obtained a knowledge of almost all books, although he could not as
yet by himself understand anything from books, for he had not yet begun to read
anything. (*quamvis per se ipsum aliquid adhuc de libris intelligere non posset. Non enim
adhuc aliquid legere inceperat*)'.[15] There could scarcely be a more categorical
pronouncement on Alfred's complete illiteracy than this, and it clearly relates to a
time when he was well established as king. Plegmund and his companions are
alleged to have joined Alfred's court sometime before November 887, and at about
the same time (*his temporibus*) as when Asser himself was said to have been summoned
to the king in 885–6.[16] Since Plegmund lived until as late as 923,[17] he can scarcely
have entered Alfred's service very much before 887. Yet if we are to believe
Alfred's biographer, the king was a complete illiterate up to that time, and he was
a man who had been deprived of tutors by his neglectful parents. But of those
same parents, his mother had presented him with a prize in the form of a book,

which as an infant he had learnt to read, and that same youthful Alfred showed such zeal for reading and writing that he kept his own personal notebook constantly by him which he had filled with devotional prayers. By the time Alfred had succeeded to the kingship and had advanced to his late thirties, he still had to be read to by scholars because of his complete illiteracy, but at the same time it was 'his most usual habit (*usitatissima illius consuetudo*), himself to read books aloud'.[18] To confuse us yet further, we are told Alfred was able to personally supervise the pupils in his 'Royal Household (*regali familia*) School' and 'to instruct them in letters'.[19] Lest there should be any room for special pleading to the effect that this royal academy under Alfred's tutelage was devoted only to the vernacular, his biographer reassures us: 'In that school, books of both languages, Latin, that is, and English (*utriusque linguae libri, Latini scilicet et Saxonicae*), were assiduously read, and they had leisure for writing.'[20] Clearly, as a headmaster who personally coached his pupils through a gruelling curriculum that was pursued 'night and day', Alfred would of necessity have had to have been a master of both languages. And yet on that historic day in November 887, Alfred in the privacy of his study, suddenly and miraculously learnt to read and to translate Latin. The truth is, we cannot believe anything the king's biographer tells us about Alfred's education or personal scholarship, because each anecdote was invented at the whim of the compiler without any thought for consistency to illustrate the marvellous powers— however contradictory—of an otherwise saintly king.

We have seen how the book-reading competition set up by Alfred's mother was firmly rooted in hagiographical motifs designed to show the future greatness of a precocious and saintly infant. So too, Alfred's ability to read and to translate in 887 is narrated as yet another miracle, for it was achieved suddenly (*subito*) and 'by Divine inspiration' (*divino instinctu*)[21]—precisely the same *divina inspiratione* which triggered the folk-tale of how the infant Alfred beat his brothers in the book-reading contest.[22] Even Keynes and Lapidge, who adhered unswervingly to Whitelock's views on the *Life* of Alfred, accepted the account of Alfred's first lesson in reading and translation in 887 as 'a miraculous occasion'[23] but they clearly believed in the miracle.[24] This tale of how a mature and illiterate king came to read Latin, is yet another version of the motif of *the man who reads by magic or miracle*. As a result of Alfred's sudden conversion to understanding Latin, his tutor 'gave great thanks to Almighty God, although silently, with hands outstretched to Heaven, who had planted so great devotion for the study of wisdom (*studium sapientiae devotionem*) in the king's heart.' And again the author repeats the notion of the king's 'devout wish to study Divine wisdom (*studium divinae sapientiae*)'. Those who have studied Latin from infancy appreciate that for an illiterate adult to suddenly graduate to reading and translating the Scriptures in one day is nothing short of a miracle indeed. When we study the detailed explanation which the compiler offers us about Alfred's flash of heavenly inspiration, we find it to have been an even more spectacular achievement than that of a mere beginner mastering the rudiments of a simple Latin sentence. The author's repeated references to Alfred's eager desire to master the meaning of various *testimonia* being read out by

Asser might refer to any 'passages' in a general sense. But the specific references to *divinorum testimoniorum*[25] and to the comparison of Alfred with a busy bee collecting honey from 'the flowers of Holy Scripture (*divinae scripturae flosculos*)'[26] show that these tutorials involved the study of the Scriptures in Latin and that Alfred's miraculous understanding of that language was supposed to have rendered him instantly capable of compiling a thesaurus of passages from Scripture, which the king found personally pleasing and which also spurred him on to exegetical endeavours. In short, Alfred's miraculous entry into Latin studies involved biblical exegesis or what might be described in modern university parlance as post-graduate, if not indeed, post-doctoral research. Ryan pronounced that in spite of the high standard of Classical learning in pre-ninth-century Ireland, 'the palm for the highest form of knowledge was awarded without hesitation' to the study in the monasteries of biblical exegesis.[27] John of Salerno describes how the canons of St Martin's at Tours in the late ninth century ridiculed the studious Odo because he struggled to study those writers 'who expounded the gospels and the prophets'. He tells us that 'croaking like so many crows' the worldly canons advised their eager novice to: 'spare yourself, and leaving these inextricably involved writings, go to the psalms'.[28] That anecdote sheds light on Alfred's supposed scholarly career, for it suggests that in pre-Cluniac Francia the study of biblical exegesis was well-nigh dead, but that the psalter still provided a basic education for most monastic pupils. There is no reason to doubt that the same practice held good for the pre-monastic reform curriculum in ninth-century England. In other words, this hagiographical tale, with its emphasis on Scriptural commentary, reflects a late tenth- or early eleventh-century monastic attitude to advanced biblical learning. None of Alfred's translations that survive, apart from the Psalter, deals specifically with the Scriptures, and none at all concern themselves with biblical exegesis *per se*. Alfred's translations deal with historical, legal, and philosophical matters, which is what we should expect from the hand of a layman. The king's interest in the works of Pope Gregory centred on the wisdom and advice which they contained for lay and secular rulers, and in so far as scriptural material plays a part in Gregory's *Pastoral Care* or the *Dialogues*, it is peripheral to the first of those works and constitutes a popular devotional approach in the second.

The 'illiterate' king was, surprisingly, already in possession of a book which he had had since childhood, and which he himself had filled with personal prayers from the Divine Office and from the Psalms. Such prayers in the ninth century would almost certainly have been written in Latin. We are told on no less than two occasions that the contents of this little book were exclusively devotional, if not indeed liturgical, and if the story were in any way true, it would show that Alfred had been educated in a monastic school.[29] Where else could he have learned the *cursus diurnus* but in one of the monasteries where it constituted the daily prayer rota for the monks? That being so, Alfred would have had a sound knowledge of Latin from childhood, and the Psalms which the compiler insists the boy Alfred had learnt and written into his book, constituted a standard textbook for teaching Latin in that same monastic curriculum where he had learnt the Daily Office.

Indeed, Alfred's biographer himself implies that his own primitive understanding of a training in the liberal arts consisted of nothing more in terms of Latin learning than studying the Psalms. The canons of St Martins at Tours at the end of the ninth century would have agreed.

Of the 'liberal education (*liberali disciplina*)' enjoined on Alfred's two children, Edward and Ælfthryth, Alfred's biographer tells us 'they have learnt carefully psalms and Saxon books, and especially Saxon poems'. Clearly the Psalms were understood here to have made up the necessary Latin component of a bilingual education, for the author, for what he is worth, specifically tells us that Latin as well as English was on the curriculum of Alfred's court school. Alfred tells us in his preface to Gregory's *Pastoral Care* that in his own educational programme as king, Latin was to be taught to those children 'whom one wishes to teach further and to bring to holy orders'. The king also tells us that before his time, people 'derived very little benefit from those books [in monastic libraries], because they could understand nothing of them, since they were not written in their own language'.[30] Are we then to assume that there was an exception in the case of the psalter, and that the younger Alfred had free access to an Old English translation of it from childhood. If that had been so, it is strange that the king himself personally undertook to translate the Psalms into Old English as one of those 'books which are the most necessary for all men to know'. William of Malmesbury may not have been correct in assuming that Alfred died before he had completed that translation, but scholars seem to be agreed that the translation of the first fifty Psalms in the psalter was the last work undertaken personally by the king.[31] So on Alfred's own testimony, and on the evidence of his own translation programme, the Psalms were a closed book to those of his age who knew no Latin. But Alfred is alleged by his biographer to have made his own of the Psalms from childhood, even to the extent of writing them into his own personal prayer book. All this in turn makes complete nonsense of the miraculous tale of Alfred's Latin lesson on Martinmas 887. And yet that apocryphal tale has been taken seriously by linguists and historians and used as a key point in all arguments relating to the dating of the translation programme undertaken by the king.

Just as Alfred's biographer modelled his king's illnesses on the *Life* of Gerald of Aurillac, so, too, he modelled his account of Alfred's education on Einhard's *Life* of Charlemagne. And in both cases Alfred's biographer resorted to gross distortion and exaggeration. While Gerald's plausible and temporary illnesses were transposed in the *Life* of Alfred to show the saintly West Saxon ruler as a life-long martyr to pain and suffering, so Charlemagne's attempts at writing were also borrowed into the *Life* of Alfred. That in turn meant that Alfred, like Charlemagne, could be cast in the role of an illiterate adult, and because Alfred was being portrayed as a saint, this allowed his biographer to produce a miraculous enlightenment which allowed an ignorant king to be turned suddenly into a great scholar. Even Alfred's 'little book', plausible though it may seem, is highly unlikely to have any basis in fact, and was borrowed—together with the notion of Alfred's illiteracy in adulthood— from Einhard's *Life* of Charlemagne. In chapter 25 of Einhard, Alfred's biographer found a portrait of the scholarly life of Charlemagne which profoundly influenced his confused and crude account of King Alfred:

He [Charlemagne] was not content with his own mother tongue, but took trouble to learn foreign languages. He learnt Latin so well that he spoke it as fluently as his own tongue; but he understood Greek better than he could speak it. He paid the greatest attention to the liberal arts; and he had great respect for men who taught them, bestowing high honours upon them. When he was learning the rules of Grammar he received tuition from Peter the Deacon of Pisa, who by then was an old man, but for all other subjects he was taught by Alcuin, surnamed Albinus, another Deacon, a man of the Saxon race who came from Britain and was the most learned man anywhere to be found. Under him the emperor spent much time and effort in studying rhetoric, dialectic and especially astrology. . . . He also tried to learn to write. With this object in view he used to keep writing tablets and notebooks under the pillows on his bed, so that he could try his hand at forming letters during his leisure moments; but although he tried very hard, he had begun too late in life and he made little progress.[32]

Alfred's biographer would not have troubled to recognize the inherent contradictions already present in Einhard's account of an illiterate king who, nevertheless, had mastered arithmetic (*ars computandi*) and who 'had traced the course of the stars', nor could he have been aware of Einhard's indebtedness to Suetonius who describes how Caesar and Augustus both studied under Greek tutors; of how Tiberius wrote in Latin and Greek and preferred the company of Greek professors; of how Claudius published his own literary compositions and began work on his histories while he was still a boy; or of how Nero recited his own poems in the theatre.[33] For Einhard, if the emperors of ancient Rome were capable of such accomplishments, then Charlemagne simply had to be described as speaking Latin 'as fluently as his own tongue'. And for Alfred's biographer, if Charlemagne had a notebook, which he kept under his pillow for practising his pathetic letters, then Alfred would have to be seen to go one better and have a notebook full of prayers which he also kept by him 'day and night' from childhood, and yet another which was crammed full of passages from the Scriptures, and which as a result of his miraculous tutorial with Asser amounted to a notebook of biblical exegesis. And while the great Charlemagne was admitted by his biographer to have remained at best only semi-literate, Alfred, on the other hand, was deliberately portrayed as completely illiterate into his adult life and was then shown to have progressed to miraculous powers of scholarship and learning.

Not only did Alfred's biographer quote or echo several turns of phrase direct from Einhard's *Life* of Charlemagne,[34] but we have already encountered instances where he tried to improve on Einhard to fill out his portrait of King Alfred. So, where Einhard openly confesses his ignorance of the details of Charlemagne's childhood, Alfred's biographer invents feats of extraordinary scholarship for the infant Alfred. Charlemagne and Alfred both shared a natural piety that sent them off to chapel to attend daily Mass and even the Night Office, and both shared a love of foreigners. Both men were specifically stated to have been devoted to the *artes liberales*—Alfred constantly bemoaning the fact that he had neither sufficient respite from troubles of the world nor the proper education to devote the required time to them. Both men also invited in foreign scholars to further their educational programmes. Apart from the supposed long-term public objectives of the educational programmes of both rulers, Charlemagne and Alfred were each believed by their biographers to have personally seen to the education of their children at court. Of Charlemagne, Einhard wrote:

Charlemagne was determined to give his children, his daughters just as much as his sons, a proper training in the liberal arts (*liberalibus studiis*) which had formed the subject of his own studies. . . . He paid such attention to the upbringing (*educando*) of his sons and daughters that he never sat down to table without them when he was at home, and never set out on a journey without taking them with him.[35]

So too, Alfred's biographer tells us that of the king's children, his eldest son, Edward and his sister Ælfthryth 'were always brought up in the royal court (*in curto regio*), with great care from their tutors and nurses. . . . Nor indeed are they allowed to live idly and carelessly without a liberal education (*liberali disciplina*) among the other occupations of this present life which are fitting for nobles.'[36] And of Alfred's youngest boy, Æthelweard, we are told he 'was given over by the divine counsel and the admirable prudence of the king to the pleasures of literary studies, along with almost all the children of noble birth of the whole country, and also many of humble birth under the diligent care of masters'.[37] Charlemagne, too, according to his other biographer, Notker the Stammerer, established a court school under the Irishman, Clement, which was attended not only by the sons of nobles but also by boys of humble birth, and Charlemagne like Alfred later on, was, according to Notker[38] to personally oversee the tuition of those youths. Both Charlemagne and Alfred were said to have become the pupils of their scholarly gurus—Charlemagne studying under the aged Peter of Pisa but more especially under Alcuin, while Alfred according to his biographer employed Wærferth of Worcester and several other scholars, but was personally and especially taught by Asser. It is possible to conclude from Einhard's *Life* of Charlemagne that the emperor had been taught to write by Alcuin—'but for all other subjects he was taught by Alcuin. . . . Under him the emperor spent much time and effort in studying rhetoric. . . . He also tried to learn to write.'[39] The primacy accorded by Einhard to the English scholar, Alcuin, at the court of Charlemagne, and the notion that it was Alcuin who tried to teach Charlemagne to write, may well have prompted Alfred's biographer to ascribe the same role to Asser at the court of King Alfred. A tenth-century writer, striving to model a biography of King Alfred on Einhard's *Life* of Charlemagne, would have read in Alfred's own prose preface to his translation of the *Pastoral Care* how the king had been tutored in that work by Archbishop Plegmund, by 'Asser my bishop', and by the mass-priests, Grimbald and John.[40] All four of these men were acknowledged in the *Life* of Alfred as personally helping King Alfred with his educational programme in a similar way to which Einhard had written of Charlemagne's foreign scholars.[41] The obscure

John was conveniently singled out elsewhere in Alfred's *Life* as the hero of an apocryphal tale.[42] But if the compiler were looking for a figure at King Alfred's court who would fulfil the role he believed Einhard had ascribed to Alcuin *vis-à-vis* Charlemagne, then the superficial resemblance between the names of Alcuin and Asser might have been enough to prompt the compiler of Alfred's *Life* to cast Asser in the mould of Alcuin. He would have read too, in Einhard's preface how that biographer argued for his special qualifications to write the life of his emperor: 'for I am very conscious of the fact that no one can describe these events more accurately than I, for I was present when they took place and, as they say, I saw them with my own eyes (*quibus ipse interfui, quaeque praesens oculata, ut dicunt*).' Alfred's biographer drew, textually, on the opening lines of Einhard's preface to fill out the second part of chapter 73 of the *Life* of Alfred.[43] So we know, therefore, that Alfred's biographer had to have been aware of Einhard's presentation of himself as a contemporary witness—but a few lines further down in that same preface to the *Vita Karoli*. This in turn prompted Alfred's biographer to argue for his own position as a contemporary witness of the events he was narrating, and so he cast himself in the role of Asser—none other than the supposed tutor of King Alfred. And while Einhard properly presented himself, briefly, as a contemporary witness, Alfred's biographer carried his special pleading to extremes—claiming to have personally witnessed Alfred's skill in the hunt (*sicut et nos saepissime vidimus*);[44] to have seen the king's little prayer book from infancy (*sicut ipsi vidimus*);[45] to have seen Alfred's mother-in-law with 'his very own eyes (*quam nos ipsi propriis oculorum nostrorum obtutibus vidimus*)';[46] and to have seen the lone thorn tree on the field at Ashdown also with his 'own eyes (*quam nos ipsi nostris propriis oculis vidimus*)'.[47] And so, the exaggeration was sustained. While not even the great Alcuin could succeed in teaching Charlemagne to write, the compiler of King Alfred's *Life*, posing as Asser and the king's tutor extraordinary, tells how he witnessed the miraculous beginning of Alfred's advanced literacy in Latin.

That there was an association in the mind of Alfred's biographer between Alcuin and Asser is confirmed by the use which he is known to have made of the anonymous *Life* of Alcuin in his *Life* of Alfred. Alfred's biographer echoes the *Life* of Alcuin in showing how King Alfred first persuaded Asser to join his court circle and to show how he later rewarded his tutor for the personal benefits of his scholarship. In the *Life* of Alcuin, the Northumbrian scholar is said to have met Charlemagne at Parma (*c.*780) when he was invited by the Carolingian ruler to join his educational programme. Alcuin begged leave to return to his native land and gain the permission of his king and archbishop before joining Charlemagne's court school. Charlemagne, meanwhile presented Alcuin with two monasteries by way of a 'down payment' for his services—St Peter at Ferrieres and St Lupus at Troyes.[48] On his return to the Carolingian court, Alcuin was rewarded with the glittering prize of the abbacy of the monastery of St Martin at Tours.[49] The account in the *Life* of King Alfred of how Asser was supposed to have entered Alfred's service is modelled closely on this Alcuin–Charlemagne narrative in the *Life* of Alcuin. The first meeting between Asser and Alfred is said to have taken place at Dean in

Sussex.[50] The account of first meeting between Asser and Alfred parallels Alcuin's encounter with Charlemagne at Parma, even down to the plea by Asser to return to seek the permission of his own people. While Alcuin had to consult his king and his archbishop back in Northumbria,[51] Asser supposedly had to seek the advice of his people.[52] And just as Alcuin had a superior in the archbishop of York, so Alfred's biographer, not to be outdone, described one of Asser's kinsmen as 'Archbishop Nobis' of St David's.[53] While it was not unknown for a bishop to be described as an *archiepiscopus* in Celtic monasteries in early medieval Ireland, it was highly unusual. A small number of Irish monasteries such as Armagh, succeeded in developing extensive *parochiae* or monastic confederacies which led to claims of monastic overlordship equivalent to the notion of metropolitan jurisdiction which pertained to the office of archbishop under Graeco-Roman organization. The situation which pertained in Ireland, however, cannot also be assumed—as it was by Whitelock[54]—to have pertained to late ninth-century Wales. Nobis is correctly styled *episcopus* in the *Annales Cambriae*[55] and the application of the title of *archiepiscopus* to that Welshman by the author of the *Life* of Alfred was very probably inspired by the status of Alcuin's superior, Eanbald, archbishop of York. The reference to 'Archbishop Nobis' was also irrelevant if not anachronistic to the account of how and when Asser was supposed to have been summoned by King Alfred. For Alfred's biographer, speaking in the person of Asser, informs us that if he were to join Alfred's household, that might have helped his people who were being attacked by the Welsh king, Hyfaidd. He then adds the circumstantial detail that Hyfaidd's attacks on St David's had led on one occasion to the expulsion of Asser's kinsman, 'Archbishop Nobis'. But Nobis, who was already bishop by 840, had died as early as 873—some twelve years before Asser was supposed to have been summoned by the king. In the turbulent politics of Celtic society, the temporary expulsion of a bishop from his see can scarcely have been a very live issue twelve years after the death of the person involved, and perhaps many more after the incident was supposed to have taken place.[56]

The sequence of monastic rewards given to Alcuin are exactly paralleled by a similar sequence given by Alfred to Asser. For if Charlemagne, according to Einhard 'had great respect for men who taught them [the liberal arts], bestowing high honours upon them', so too, Alfred according to his biographer 'endowed and honoured them [his tutors] with great authority'.[57] While Alcuin first received Ferrières and Troyes and was later given Tours, Asser was said first to have received the modest rewards of Congresbury and Banwell in Somerset, but was later given Exeter 'with all the diocese (*parochia*) belonging to it, in Saxon territory and in Cornwall'.[58] While this notorious passage has inspired heated debate as to whether the *parochia* of Exeter did or did not refer to the 'diocese' centred on that town—which was not created until the mid-eleventh century—its relationship to and dependence on the anonymous *Life* of Alcuin has been virtually ignored.[59] In the account of Asser's bargaining with King Alfred, the king's argument is cast in the form of direct speech—one of the very rare instances in the entire *Life* of Alfred where the king's actual words are ever cited.[60] This, too, is modelled on the dialogue attributed to Charlemagne (*voce blandientis*) and to Alcuin in the *Life* of the Northumbrian saint.[61]

The *Life* of Alcuin, in following the saint's Frankish career, concentrates not on the itinerant Carolingian court, but on the monastery of St Martin at Tours. Was it this strong association with St Martin in the anonymous *Life* of Alcuin that prompted the compiler of the *Life* of Alfred to provide Martinmas as an exact date for the occasion when Alfred miraculously learnt to read and to translate his Scriptures from Latin into English? The festival of St Martin (11 November) was a major landmark in the Old English calendar. The compiler of the Anglo-Saxon Chronicle for the reign of Edward the Elder dated that king's campaigns regularly in relation to Martinmas.[62] It was, of course, an even greater festival in Francia, and one on which special gatherings were held, and on which palace revolutions might be staged. Indeed the very day in the very year on which Alfred is supposed to have begun to read, coincides exactly with the date for the deposition of the Carolingian ruler Charles the Fat (11 November 887)—an episode recorded in the Anglo-Saxon Chronicle. The entry for the year 887 was also the last annal which Alfred's biographer copied and translated from his text of the Anglo-Saxon Chronicle.[63] The dating of Charles's deposition to an assembly connected with Martinmas is recorded by Regino of Prüm and the *Annales Hildesheimenses*.[64] The provision of an exact date for an event is quite out of keeping with other anecdotal and hagiographical vignettes in the *Life* of Alfred, which are conspicuously vague on exact chronology.[65]

The technique of the author of the *Life* of King Alfred was to intersperse tales of hagiographical fiction with ideas of substance and structure which he himself had hastily gleaned from written sources. So, in addition to translating whole sections of the Anglo-Saxon Chronicle into Latin, he also made use of Einhard's *Life* of Charlemagne, the *Life* of Count Gerald, the anonymous *Life* of Alcuin, Alfred's prose preface to the *Pastoral Care*, and perhaps several other works attributable to the king himself. The author may also have had access to genuine traditions of his own day which attested to Alfred's great piety, his lifelong love of church services and prayer, his devotion to scholarship and learning, his possible care for his children's education, and his love of foreigners and foreign scholars. The incalculable damage done by this compiler is that by forcing such traditions into Einhard's mould for Charlemagne, we can never trust the details of any of his claims unless they are supported by other sources. So, for instance, Alfred's personal piety is in evidence throughout the king's own writings, and his collateral descendant Æthelweard wrote of him in the late tenth century that he was a man 'steeped in sacred literature above all things'.[66] We know, too, from the Chronicle that Irish holy men, pilgrims and scholars, sought out Alfred at his court, and we learn from the Old English Orosius that the Norwegian merchant-trader, Ohthere and perhaps also the Baltic traveller, Wulfstan, travelled to the court of this king.[67] It is a fair assumption that these pilgrims and traders were but a few of many travellers who sought out this generous lord, renowned for his enquiring mind, and that Alfred may have personally invited other foreigners to enter his service on a more permanent basis. We must however query whether there is any truth at all behind the account of how the historical Asser entered King Alfred's service, as his late tenth- or early eleventh-century biographer describes. Equally tenuous is the author's account of the 'school' at King Alfred's court and of the king's personal participation in it—if not as an ignorant student then as its patron and head-master.[68] So much of that is based on the notion of Charlemagne's palace school and on Charlemagne's problems with learning to write, that it will never be possible to accept the unsupported testimony of the Pseudo-Asser.

There is little for the historian to salvage, even with caution, from the *Life* of Alfred. We can treat its curiously stilted pronouncements on Alfred's writings and translations as evidence from the late tenth century of the limited impact of Alfred's literary achievements at that point in time. In this the biographer of Alfred may be compared with the writer of the eleventh-century Old English *Life* of St Neot who remembered Alfred in vague terms as having had a successful and peaceful reign,[69] or with Ælfric who refers vaguely and in passing in his *Catholic Homilies* to Alfred's translations of books from Latin into English.[70] By Ælfric's time, the historical Alfred who fought and sometimes lost in his struggle against the Danes had been replaced by a mythologized king 'who often fought against the Danes, until he won the victory and protected his people'.[71] We are reminded of that equally imaginary Alfred who 'was a great warrior and victorious in virtually all battles' as described in the king's own *Life*. Ælfric wrongly attributed the Old English version of what he called the *Historia Anglorum* to King Alfred and claimed that the work was difficult to come by even in translation in his own time (*c.*1000).[72] We may compare, too, the meagre testimony of Alfred's biographer on Alfred's writings with the equally vague Æthelweard, who wrote of King Alfred, that 'he turned unknown numbers of books from the ornate Latin tongue into his own language with such variety and richness, that not only for scholars, but for any who might hear it read, the tearful passion of the book of Boethius would be in a measure brought to life'.[73] Æthelweard rightly identified Boethius's *Consolation of Philosophy* as a translation from Alfred's hand, and just as this scholar and nobleman had access to an early copy of the Chronicle, so too, he may have possessed a copy of Boethius, or he may at least have seen a copy of it in Sherborne or elsewhere. The decision of Alfred's biographer to model his *Life* of Alfred on Einhard's *Life* of Charlemagne was based in part on the obvious similarities between the careers and achievements of the two rulers. Our dilemma is made all the greater by the fact that Alfred's biographer may not have been the first to recognize the genuine similarities between the cultural achievements of Alfred and of Charlemagne. The first person to recognize that may have been King Alfred himself, and it is likely that he was consciously striving to imitate some of the achievements of Charlemagne and his immediate successors. But Alfred's mind and intelligence were far too original, to slavishly ape the Carolingian renaissance, and a closer examination of the Alfredian literary achievement shows it to have been markedly different from that of Charlemagne in several important respects.[74] We know from Alfred's own writings that not only had he personally achieved a far higher level of educational attainment than Charlemagne, but that he possessed a very practical mind, arguing from principles rooted in concrete experience and common sense. Had Alfred's biographer chosen to write down what genuine memories and apocryphal tales that had survived about Alfred in late tenth-century England, he would have left us a biography on the lines of Notker's racy portrait of Charlemagne—and it would have been a work of inestimable worth. Sadly, he chose differently. By forging a contemporary 'life' of King Alfred which drew largely on Einhard, and modelling its supposed author, Asser, on the Carolingian Alcuin, the compiler buried the West Saxon writer-king under a welter of hagiographical legend and wove a Carolingian web about him, from which it is well-nigh impossible for a historian to extricate the real man.

The damage which Alfred's biographer has done in preventing an accurate historical assessment of Alfred's cultural achievement has been immense. The extravagant tales of the king's illnesses and saintly neuroses, while for too long distorting the historian's understanding of the *persona* of Alfred, have not been quite so damaging as the equally fictional and contradictory account of the king's lack of education. For historians and linguists alike have relied on the *Life* of King Alfred to determine the chronology of the king's writings. Since the *Life* of the king asserts that he was unable to read Latin before November 887, then Alfred's literary achievement had to be crammed into the last six or seven years of the king's life. Sisam, who took the account of the king's illiteracy in the *Life* of Alfred to its logical and farcical conclusion, boldly stated that 'nothing in Asser's *Life* suggests that Alfred wrote with his own hand', and went on to claim that on 'Asser's' evidence we must accept that Alfred—even after his miraculous tutorial—dictated his translations to his scholarly amanuenses.[75] Such ideas, however ludicrous, constituted an honest attempt to explore the consequences of the pseudo-biographer's argument. They showed, however, a remarkable lack of understanding of the importance of literacy on the development of individual intellectual thought. Sisam himself clearly believed that it was possible to identify Alfredian vocabulary and phrasing in the writings attributed to the king.[76] That being so, he clearly also accepted that texts attributed to the king reflected—to some extent at least—his own personal style, and were not the product of wholesale reworkings on the part of his helpers.[77] If we assume, along with Sisam, that Alfred remained incapable all his life of writing in the vernacular, then the entire body of textual and literary criticism of specific Alfredian works is instantly devalued if not entirely undermined. For if we accept that what passes as the words and works of Alfred are actually the end-product of a team of glossators and ghost-writers, then it should be well-nigh impossible to attibute any part of these works to any one individual, and least of all, to the king. And even if we were to accept that Alfred was always capable of reading English but remained ignorant of Latin until the last ten years of his life, that would also pose insurmountable problems on the evidence of the works which he himself claimed to have translated.

A noted trait of the works attributable to Alfred, is the high degree of amplification and rearrangement of their original Latin content.[78] Such treatment is not suggestive either of a novice struggling with comprehension problems or of an illiterate working at several removes from a Latin original, and dependent on the help of translators. While Alfred's translations into English are often independent of Latinate forms and reveal their own complex vernacular syntactical structures, nevertheless Latin prose style is agreed to have had a profound influence on the writings of Alfred and his contemporaries.[79] We are assured that 'there is nothing rude or rudimentary' about Alfred's translation of the prose Psalms in the Paris Psalter— a work which stays close to its Latin original.[80] Elsewhere, even in those 'free' passages in his *Soliloquies*, where Alfred departs from his Latin text, it is rightly assumed that the king's knowledge of Latin prose has enabled him to construct complex sentences, employ figures of speech, and above all to think in the abstract while tackling philosophical arguments.[81] Alfred, more than any of his English contemporaries, struggled in his writings to develop Old English prose to a point where it could cope with the abstractions and philosophical vocabulary of Boethius and Augustine. We shall see how Alfred was ultimately defeated by the abstraction of the Aristotelian syllogism when it came to understanding his philosophical Latin texts. But he was inspired to grapple with intellectual problems which were far beyond the reach of his contemporaries—and indeed of his scholarly helpers— for as far as we know, none of those helpers attempted to embark on philosophical commentaries in their own right. The fact that Alfred did not fully succeed in his understanding of either Boethius or Augustine was due not to his illiteracy in Latin, but to the fact that he was a child of the early Middle Ages when knowledge of Antique culture was at its lowest ebb in the Christian West. But could such a man, who was so ambitious to make sense of Boethius and Augustine, really have been ignorant of the original Latin where their concepts, which he sought so hard to possess, were originally enshrined? Alfred, of course, wanted to make the works of Christian philosophers available in English, but he more than anyone else was aware that English had not sufficiently developed as a language to cope with the subtleties of philosophical vocabulary and with the abstract concepts of Plato and Aristotle. It is scarcely credible that a man who was ignorant of the original Latin of Boethius's narrative would, while in middle age, develop either the inclination or the expertise to master such a discourse.[82] We shall see, when we come to look at the content of Alfred's writings that they reveal a scholarly mind of a reflective and philosophical mould, which in turn is suggestive of a man who had loved learning all his life and who was steeped in a lifetime of Latin and Old English scholarship.[83]

It is rare to find those who accept the account of Alfred's deprived education in the *Life* of the king, ever setting out that account alongside the tangible achievement of the king's staggering scholarly output. Because the *Life* of Alfred attributed to Asser remained in a shadowy world of half-truth throughout the twentieth century, a schizophrenic approach to Alfredian studies has been the inevitable outcome. It became too difficult to discuss the career of an illiterate king alongside that of one of the most significant writers in early medieval Europe. For many, the only hope of preserving scholarly integrity was to avoid Asser altogether, or at least to discuss his supposed *Life* in isolation from the historical Alfred of the translations. It is imperative that we confront the evidence of the *Life* with the reality of the king's prolific writings. King Alfred did not furnish a list of his translations which survives, nor is there any contemporary account of the complete literary output of the king. Prefaces to Gregory's *Pastoral Care*, Boethius's *Consolation of Philosophy*, and the *Soliloquies* of Augustine proclaim these translations to be the work of the king himself.[84] A West Saxon translation of the first fifty Psalms of the Psalter preserved in a single manuscript from the mid-eleventh century in the Bibliothèque Nationale in Paris was confidently attributed by Bately to Alfred.[85] It was not until the early twelfth century that William of Malmesbury ventured to supply a list of King Alfred's works,[86] and in addition to the *Pastoral Care*, Boethius's *Consolation*, and part of the Psalter, William added the History of Orosius, Bede's *Gesta Anglorum* (i.e. the *Historia Ecclesiastica* or *Ecclesiastical History*) and 'a book of his own which he called in his native language *Enchiridion*'.[87] William made no mention of the *Soliloqiues* as such, and we now know that the Old English Bede and Orosius were not the works of the king, although they were almost certainly done as part of his translation programme. We must treat what William says of King Alfred and his works with the same caution as we exercise with the author of the *Life* of Alfred. William's information on Alfred was derived from sources as diverse as the *Life* of the king, version E of the Anglo-Saxon Chronicle, and hagiographical works such as the Durham *History* of Saint Cuthbert, as well as manuscripts of Alfred's own translations and folk-tales current in William's own time in the early twelfth century. The Alfred of William of Malmesbury was a king who, like the Danish ruler, Olaf Guthfrithsson half a century later, was reputed to have disguised himself as an entertainer while spying in the camp of his enemies.[88] He had become a king, too, whom West Saxon propaganda from the time of his grandson, Athelstan, liked to show enjoyed the patronage of the Northumbrian saint, Cuthbert—a saint whose cult was far removed from the West Saxons of Alfred's day.[89] Whitelock recognized how dependent William of Malmesbury was on the *Life* of King Alfred. William had borrowed traditions from that source relating to the monasteries of Athelney and Shaftesbury; to Alfred's fighting alone at the beginning of the battle of Ashdown; to the division of his revenues; as well as to material on Alfred's inventions.[90] William's information on the authorship of Gregory's *Dialogues* must have been derived from the compiler of Alfred's *Life*, for William followed that author in attributing the translation of the *Dialogues* to Wærferth, bishop of Worcester. No surviving manuscript of this work acknowledges Wærferth's authorship and we have King Alfred's own first-hand testimony to the effect that the *Dialogues* were produced at his request by more than one scholar—his 'true friends'.[91] In the light of the king's own statement, which clearly takes precedence over the evidence of his confused biographer, it is no longer appropriate for historians to refer to this work as *Werferth's translation of Gregory's 'Dialogues'*.[92]

William of Malmesbury's correct attribution of Boethius's *Consolation of Philosophy* to King Alfred may or may not have been based on the testimony of Æthelweard with which William was familiar. But William went on to state on two

occasions that Asser explained this work to Alfred.[93] Asser's help is acknowledged
by King Alfred only in the preface to the *Pastoral Care*, yet there is no reason why
the historical Asser, as one of the king's editorial team, could not have helped
Alfred with several other works as well. But Alfred's biographer intrudes yet again
to diminish William's testimony here, for William of Malmesbury may have concluded from reading the account of Alfred's miraculous tutorial in the *Life* of the
king (or from an extract from the *Life*), that Asser was indeed the king's tutor *par
excellence*. That being so, it would have been reasonable, as Whitelock suggested,
for William to attribute one of the translations of the king to Asser's helping
hand.[94] We are left to explain the absence of any mention of the *Soliloquies* in
William's list of Alfredian works and the dramatic inclusion in that list of that
'book of his own which in the native language is called *Enchiridion*'. William allows
us to glimpse a few items from the contents of this book—the genealogy of St
Aldhelm (and by implication a West Saxon royal genealogy and regnal list), and an
account of Aldhelm's knowledge of vernacular poetry and how that saint used his
talents as a poet to attract an audience.[95] Material prefixed to one later medieval
Worcester manuscript and marginal notes attached to another refer enigmatically
to a work known as the *Dicta* or 'Sayings' of King Alfred.[96] Some scholars have not
unreasonably assumed that a lost work by King Alfred, containing the very material
of that little handbook described in the *Life* of the king, was preserved at Worcester
into the twelfth century, where it was consulted by William of Malmesbury. If
such a book had indeed existed, then 'it would obviously have transformed our
knowledge of the spiritual and intellectual interests of the king.'[97] It is highly
unlikely, however, that such a book ever existed at Worcester in the later Middle
Ages. We have seen how the motif of the *libellus* or 'little book' which King Alfred
had kept by his side was borrowed from Einhard's *Life* of Charlemagne, and that
Alfred's biographer speaks not of one but of two such books kept by Alfred. One
book, according to the *Life* of Alfred, contained Alfred's own personal prayers,
Psalms and the Daily Office, and had been kept by him from childhood, while a
second book was begun for him supposedly by Bishop Asser to contain random
jottings from Holy Scripture and its commentaries. It is likely that Alfred and his
team of scholars did keep notebooks—but in this as in so much else, Alfred's
biographer has clouded our picture of the king, for the so-called *Enchiridion* of
King Alfred owes much to Einhard.[98] It was Alfred's biographer in turn which
prompted William of Malmesbury to list the *Enchiridion* as a distinct work of King
Alfred rather than the scholarly scrapbook it was alleged in the *Life* of Alfred to
have been. William's gloss on this work—*id est manualem librum* ('that is to say a
hand-book') is copied straight from the text of the *Life* of Alfred, as was the highly
distinctive Greek title of *enchiridion*.[99] Whitelock ingeniously suggested that William
of Malmesbury may have consulted King Alfred's translation of the *Soliloquies* of
St Augustine while visiting Worcester, and that he mistook that work for the
enchiridion or handbook of the king as described in the *Life* of Alfred.[100] Alfred
refers, in his preface to the *Soliloquies*, to constructing an intellectual and spiritual
edifice through the writings of 'St Augustine and St Gregory and St Jerome, and

through many other holy fathers'.[101] Such a reference embedded in a complex metaphor may have suggested to William or to some earlier researcher in Worcester or elsewhere, that what they had found was that very handbook supposedly kept by Alfred himself. The content of the translation of the *Soliloquies* might, on a cursory reading, also have reinforced the notion of an anthology of ideas and writings of Church Fathers, on the subject of immortality and the way in which the human soul comes to know God. For while the work opens with a translation of the first book of Augustine's *Soliloquies*, it moves on to assume a much less specific Augustinian format. King Alfred refers to the work as *þa cwidas* at the beginning and end of the third book of the *Soliloquies*, which Whitelock observed would naturally translate into Latin as *dicta*, and hence, perhaps suggested the title for the *Dicta* or 'Sayings' of King Alfred which are referred to in later medieval Worcester manuscripts.[102] For a work at Worcester, known as the *Dicta* of King Alfred, is referred to in material prefixed to a Worcester manuscript version of the *Chronicon ex Chronicis* attributed to Florence of Worcester and is implied to have contained a list of West Saxon kings.[103] Yet another refence to the *Dicta* occurs in late twelfth-century marginal notes to a Worcester manuscript of the *Liber Pontificalis* and which contains an anecdote on St Jerome.[104] Whitelock's suggestion that the so-called *Dicta* of Alfred and his *Enchiridion* were names given to the same Worcester manuscript of Alfred's translation of the *Soliloquies*—with miscellaneous notes added on later—has much to recommend it. King Alfred's translation of the *Soliloquies* is also called *þa blostman* ('blossoms') at the end of Alfred's Book I and at the beginning and end of Book II. Remarkably, Alfred's biographer also speaks of King Alfred's *enchiridion* as a collection of flowers (*flosculos*) in that very same passage as he describes the development of the handbook:

And he [Alfred] [began] to learn those flowers (*flosculos*), which had been gathered from various masters (*magistris*), and to bring them all into the compass of one book, although in no order as they came to hand, until it grew almost to the size of a psalter. This book he used to call his *Enchiridion*, that is, 'hand-book', because he was most careful to have it at hand by day and night.[105]

It is even possible that Alfred's biographer, having himself seen a manuscript of the Alfredian *Soliloquies* at Worcester, failed to identify it as such and was prompted to invent the notion of a royal scrap-book from his known familiarity with Einhard's account of Charlemagne's education. At any rate, such a false identification is unlikely to have begun with William of Malmesbury. The material on Aldhelm, the West Saxon genealogy, and the note on St Jerome may have consisted of no more than a short collection of notes appended to the end of this manuscript of the *Soliloquies* preserved at Worcester in the twelfth century. There is no evidence whatever, earlier than the time of Alfred's biographer, for the existence of a handbook or notebook belonging to King Alfred. If that book had really been what Alfred's biographer described it to be, we should expect it to have contained not secular and antiquarian learning, such as West Saxon genealogy, but devotional and liturgical prayers, including the Psalms—if it came from Alfred's childhood—

or biblical commentary and passages from Scripture—if it were the mature Alfred's *enchiridion*. Since William of Malmesbury fails to list the *Soliloquies* among Alfred's works, then it is reasonable to assume that he or a predecessor such as Alfred's biographer, confused the so-called 'handbook'—so dramatized in the miracle story in the *Life* of Alfred—with a manuscript of the *Soliloquies* which he consulted at Worcester.

There are two other works which although not acknowledged to be the products of Alfred's own hand (*in toto* at least) are nevertheless either certain or likely to have emanated from the king's court circle, and therefore ultimately must have been produced as a response to his request for translations. The first of these is the *Dialogues* of Pope Gregory, acknowledged by Alfred's own preface to have been written by his 'true friends' at his request. The second work is the Old English translation of Paulus Orosius's *Histories against the Pagans* (*Historiae adversus Paganos*). This great historical enterprise from Late Antiquity was translated into West Saxon by an anonymous writer, but not—as Bately demonstrated—by Alfred himself.[106] The association—however indirectly—of Alfred with the final form of this work at least is confirmed by the inclusion of a lengthy description of the voyages of a Norwegian mariner, Ohthere, followed by an account of Wulfstan, yet another traveller, in Scandinavia. The Ohthere and Wulfstan episodes may have been inserted as an afterthought when the translation of Orosius's *Histories* had been completed[107] and these interpolations may have been compiled by different contributors, who were different in turn from the main translator or translators of Orosius proper.[108] Nevertheless, the interpolation, if such it is, has to be as old as the earliest manuscript which contains it. The account of Ohthere's voyages is as old therefore, as the Lauderdale manuscript[109] of the Old English Orosius, which is written in a hand identical with that of the second scribe of the Parker Manuscript of the Anglo-Saxon Chronicle, and could have been written anytime from Alfred's final years down to *c*.930.[110] The Ohthere episode is inserted abruptly into the geographical introduction to Orosius's *Histories* with the statement: 'Ohthere told his lord King Alfred, that he dwelt northmost of all the northmen.'[111] Alfred's name is introduced in respectful tones—the king was Ohthere's *hlaforde* or 'lord'— and the narrative returns twice to acknowledge King Alfred's association with this unique account. Once we are given the circumstantial detail that Ohthere travelled northwards towards the White Sea with a view to collecting Walrus ivory and that 'some of these teeth they brought to the king'.[112] Later we are told that Ohthere 'had at the time he came to the king, six hundred unsold tame deer'.[113] Ohthere's voyage to the Arctic was clearly based on a first-hand account that was obtained from that traveller for a purpose, and was written down if not in King Alfred's own presence, then certainly in the scholarly circle attached to the king. Two passing and isolated references to Alfred in Ohthere's extensive narrative, which refer to Alfred simply as 'the king (*cyninge*)',[114] suggest this account was compiled when Alfred was alive and when there was no ambiguity as to which king—Alfred, Edward, or even Athelstan—was meant.

The same Alfredian connection can only be assumed for Wulfstan's account of his Baltic voyage. But although the account of this itinerary is not specifically connected with Alfred, it forms a consecutive and coherent narrative with that of Ohthere and is introduced with a similar keynote sentence—'Wulftan said that he went from Hedeby (*Hæðum*) to *Truso* in seven days and nights'.[115] At the very least, Orosius's *Histories* were translated and compiled by a West Saxon who before the final compilation of his work had access to extensive contemporary information originating from Alfred's court. It is also likely that King Alfred had read the translation of Orosius before he had completed his own translation of Boethius's *Consolation of Philosophy*. A direct connection between the Orosius text and that of Alfred's translation of Boethius is established by the presence of a reference to the Gothic kings *Alrica* and *Rædgota* at the end of Orosius's *Histories* and to *Eallerica* and *Rædgota* in the first chapter of the Alfredian Boethius. Bately confirmed, from the textual details and shared errors of this connection, that Alfred's Boethius has borrowed from the Old English Orosius.[116] At a more general level, the style and use of language in Orosius is different from Alfred's own treatment of the *Soliloquies* and the *Consolation of Philosophy*, and no claim for Alfredian authorship of the Orosius can any longer be sustained. Nevertheless, there is a similar treatment on the part of Alfred and the translator of Orosius in their handling of original Latin texts. Both translators were capable of omitting, summarizing, and rearranging material, and generally avoiding a rigid following of the original Latin.[117] That could be suggestive of two scholars working to an agreed format and aiming towards common goals. The content of Orosius's *Histories*, which presented an essentially Christian view of the survey of Antiquity, fitted in admirably, as we shall see, with works such as the Anglo-Saxon Chronicle and the Old English translation of Bede. Finally, we must also take account of the insertion—at however late a stage in the production of the Old English Orosius—of acknowledged Alfredian information on Scandinavian geography supplied by Ohthere. Given what Alfred himself tells us of his ambitious translation programme, it is difficult to exclude the translation of Orosius's *Histories* from that Alfredian scheme.

A third work which has hitherto been excluded from the Alfredian canon on the basis of Stenton's long-standing views on the subject, is the Anglo-Saxon Chronicle.[118] The Chronicle, unlike even those works which were translated by Alfred himself, centres on the king's personal achievement in the war against the Danes. Its preface and pre-ninth-century material were designed to anchor the House of Ecgberht in a Christian and Roman past. In this it conforms to the wider purpose of Orosius's *Histories* and to Bede's *Ecclesiastical History*, and to King Alfred's introduction to his own Law Code.[119] Unlike Gregory's *Dialogues* and the Old English Bede which were written in Mercian dialect,[120] Orosius and the Anglo-Saxon Chronicle were both written in West Saxon. Certain similarities in words and phrases have long been recognized between the texts of the Anglo-Saxon Chronicle and that of Orosius, and this has fuelled a debate between those scholars who allow for an Alfredian dimension in the Chronicle and those who persist in excluding it from the Alfredian canon. Even Whitelock was willing to accept that a compiler of the early section of the Chronicle who wrote of the emperor Titus, under annal 81, 'that he lost the day on which he did no good act (*þæt he þone dæg forlure þe he noht to gode on ne gedyde*)'[121] had borrowed this statement from an almost identical account in the Old English Orosius.[122] Bately later showed, however, that while 'the Chronicle's ultimate source here seems to be Isidore's *Chronicon* . . . Orosius's source owes *something at least* to Jerome'.[123] This may well show that we do not have a case for direct borrowing. But equally, we can not ignore the fact that two writers compiling their work at roughly the same point in time, within the same kingdom, and including subject-matter relating to King Alfred, both picked out the same saying in relation to the same Roman emperor. True, that saying on Titus may have been part of the common currency of medieval apocrypha relating to antiquity (in this case from Suetonius)—and also true, it may have been borrowed from two different sources—but it remains nevertheless common to both texts, and it raises the distinction between common authorship and the common culture which Alfred was personally striving to create at his court. The fact therefore, that modern scholarship may show Plummer was mistaken in seeing a common authorship in the Chronicle and Orosius on the basis of verbal similarities between the two texts,[124] does not prove that there was *no* connection between those two works. It is now thought that several compilers were involved in the earliest sections of the Chronicle prior to its production in the 890s.[125] There is less compelling evidence to suggest that the same may be true for the Old English Orosius.[126] It would seem logical therefore, given that a number of compilers seem to have been working all at the same time on the production of the Chronicle, that evidence for similarity in phrase and lexicography between the Chronicle and Orosius can also be offset by marked differences. But the similarities between the two works remain, and the fact that they persist in the Chronicle throughout Edward the Elder's reign (899–924) does not invalidate an argument either for common authorship in part, or at least for a common scholarly background.[127] Plegmund, archbishop of Canterbury, whose help King Alfred acknowledged with the translation of the *Pastoral Care*, survived through nearly all of Edward's reign, dying as late as 923. The historical Asser survived until 909 and Wærferth of Worcester until 914 or 915. Frithestan who may have had a connection with the compilation or continuation of the Chronicle, for instance, became bishop of Winchester in 909 and ruled that see until 932. We should expect, therefore, that under the influence of such veteran scholars, broad continuity in style and language would have been maintained in their scriptoria from the Alfredian period and hence the continuity of style at certain levels within the Chronicle during most of Edward's reign.[128] Since, as we shall see, the evidence for the time of publication of many Alfredian works suggests they were produced within a few years of each other, that in turn requires an argument for many scholars and scribes copying and compiling, if not translating, contemporaneously. But the common Alfredian purpose and the common Alfredian culture remains, and we have the king's own testimony of purpose, in the prose preface to his *Pastoral Care*, to vouch for it. The onus of proof therefore, is firmly on those scholars who would deny any close connection between Orosius and the Chronicle, on the one hand, and the king's own translations on the other.

Keynes and Lapidge argued for the inclusion of the Old English Bede in the Alfredian canon 'given both its late ninth-century dating as well as the fact that it was apparently distributed to various scriptoria from a central source much in the manner of Alfred's *Pastoral Care*'.[129] Their conclusion therefore, was that 'it is not unreasonable to think of the Old English Bede as the product of one of Alfred's Mercian helpers'.[130] Stenton also viewed the Old English Bede as within the pale of Alfredian scholarship: 'That [it] . . . was produced under Alfred's influence need not be doubted, but its right to a place in the Alfredian canon is by no means secure.'[131] And as the guardian and purifier of that canon, Stenton's views on the subject were taken as final. Sadly for Anglo-Saxon scholarship, it was safer to allow the less controversial Old English Bede into the 'Alfredian canon', than the Anglo-Saxon Chronicle—surrounded as it was by the more highly charged political debate regarding its origins which Stenton had mapped out in letters of granite.[132] Yet the evidence for an Alfredian connection with the Chronicle is infinitely stronger than what in itself is no more than a reasonable assumption regarding the Old English Bede. Keynes and Lapidge conceded that the Chronicle 'fits naturally among the other historical works produced in Alfred's reign (and presumably under his direction)', but they nevertheless felt constrained to declare: 'It should be emphasised, however, that King Alfred need not have been involved personally in the work of compilation, so we cannot assume that the *Chronicle* was in that sense an "official" production.'[133] Whitelock, in a more objective mood, rightly observed that neither the Anglo-Saxon Chronicle, nor the translators of Orosius, Gregory's *Dialogues*, or the *Pastoral Care* had made any use of the Old English Bede. Nor had the translator of Bede in his turn shown any knowledge of those Old English translations.[134] In other studies she questioned the evidence that the Old English Bede was ever copied in a multiplicity of manuscripts in the same way as the *Pastoral Care*.[135] We shall see that evidence for the circulation of multiple copies of the Anglo-Saxon Chronicle in the 890s is not as strong as had hitherto been assumed.[136] Unlike the Anglo-Saxon Chronicle which can be shown to have been constructed as a narrative about King Alfred and his dynasty, and their handling of the Danish wars, the Old English Bede cannot be shown to demonstrate any Alfredian connection.[137] That in itself does not exclude it from the 'canon'. But to include the Old English Bede and to exclude the Anglo-Saxon Chronicle from being an integral part of the king's programme is, as we shall see, to go against sound historical judgement and to deny the integrity of the scholarly foundations of a subject firmly laid down by Plummer a century before.

Stenton and Whitelock accepted the account in the *Life* of Alfred of how that king began to translate Latin at Martinmas 887. Stenton deduced from this that 'it was undoubtedly during the years of peace between 887 and 892 that he acquired the knowledge of Latin which enabled him to produce English translations of five elaborate Latin works between 892 and his death in 899'.[138] But if the king were only acquiring that advanced knowledge of Latin so necessary to cope with the complex philosophical ideas of Boethius and Augustine between 887 and 892, how then could he have actually produced any of his finished works as early as 892? That would be the equivalent of requiring an undergraduate not only to obtain a

First Class result in Final Examinations, but also to produce a complete and publishable edited text during the same years of study. Alfred, of course, was busier than the average undergraduate during his supposed years of adult education. He was engaged in a lengthy and indecisive war against Hæsten and his Danes during the first five years of this supposedly scholarly activity from 892 until 896,[139] and Stenton added the king's Law Code to Alfred's labours at this time, dating it 'towards the end of his reign'.[140] The king's own translations, unlike those of his Mercian helpers who worked on the *Dialogues* and unlike Bede's *Ecclesiastical History*, are full of digressions and personal commentary which presuppose lengthy time for reflection. Even if Alfred were writing during the entire period from 892 until his death, he would still be the envy of a modern British university research selectivity panel.

Whitelock, aware of the corner into which Stenton had painted himself and all his followers, attempted to backtrack on the over-tight writing schedule which Stenton had assigned to the king. But she was careful to hold on to what had become Stentonian dogma regarding the veracity of Asser. So, she argued that because 'Asser' had known of the translation of Gregory's *Dialogues*—a work which she attributed to Wærferth—that work had to pre-date the alleged time of Asser's writing in 893, and for Alfred's Law Code she departed marginally from Stenton's canonical line, by favouring a date in 'the middle of the reign'.[141] But Whitelock failed to perceive the consequences of her own argument. Illiterate medieval kings could and did preside over the promulgation of written laws. But what supposedly illiterate king issued his own written code with a preface written in the first person and in his name in which he provided a Cook's tour of Judaic and ancient legal systems? Alfred's Law Code was no ordinary catalogue of West Saxon customary law. It was a synthesis, carried out under the king's direction, of the legal practice in several Anglo-Saxon kingdoms, introduced by a scholarly preface which already bears all the hallmarks of Alfred's interest in historical issues and in the Christian wisdom of Late Antiquity. As for Gregory's *Dialogues*, would someone who was at best semi-literate, commission an English translation of a Latin text of a work which for all its devotional content was totally alien to the interests of an unlettered barbarian and aristocratic mind?

Whitelock suggested a date 'soon after' 890 for the initial circulation of the Chronicle and she was tacitly moving towards an acceptance of that work as being on the fringes, at least, of the Alfredian canon[142] even though she held out against allowing for any Alfredian involvement in the work. The year 892 coincided with the arrival of the last great Danish invasion of Alfred's reign and the end of what was a period of prolonged and comparative peace for the king, extending for fourteen years from 878. Because the Frankish material for the period 880 to 892 was deliberately copied into the Chronicle in order to establish continuity with the account of Alfred's Last War which ended in 896, it seems clear that the Chronicle can scarcely have been compiled in the form in which we have it, prior to 896.[143] The bunching of texts from the Alfredian era around the year 892 may be more apparent than real. It was dictated by the 'Genuine Asser' thesis which held, among other things, that because Asser translated a text of the Chronicle, therefore that Chronicle text had to pre-date the time in which Asser was allegedly writing in 893. The acknowledgement of Plegmund's help under his title as archbishop in the prose preface or introductory letter to the *Pastoral Care* clearly dates the distribution of that work to after Plegmund's elevation to the see of Canterbury in 890. A manuscript of the *Pastoral Care* (Cotton Tiberius xi) which was probably kept in Alfred's lifetime as a master copy, but which was badly damaged in the Cottonian fire, once contained a note to the effect that 'Archbishop Plegmund has been given his copy, and Bishop Swithulf, and Bishop Wærferth'.[144] Since Swithulf, bishop of Rochester was one of those 'best king's thegns' who died according to the Chronicle 'in those three years' from 894 to 896, we may date the prose preface and distribution of the *Pastoral Care* to the period 890–4/6. In that same prose preface to the *Pastoral Care*, King Alfred expressed the intention of accomplishing the education of free-born English youth 'if we have the peace' to accomplish it.[145] These can scarcely be the concerns of a king embroiled in a life-and-death struggle with invaders who poured over his kingdom and that of the Mercians from 892 until 896. That being so, the distribution of multiple copies of the *Pastoral Care* can be reasonably dated to the interval between 890 and 892.

Both the Chronicle and the *Pastoral Care* may have taken their compilers and researchers several years to prepare. Accepting that Alfred may not have been personally responsible for the production of the Chronicle, its compilers, nevertheless were probably men of substance and responsibility. We know that bishops such as Plegmund and Wærferth who helped Alfred with the *Pastoral Care* were men who had not only great ecclesiastical responsibilities, but as bishops and members of the *witan*, they were held responsible for royal administration such as the provision of burghal defences for Worcester, or the reconstruction of London in 898.[146] That being so, it is reasonable to conclude that the time when Plegmund made his most important contribution to the Alfredian translation programme was before he became archbishop and before he was consigned to the isolated East Kent peninsula. Leaving the melodramatic narrative of the *Life* of Alfred to one side, we have Alfred's own rhetorical complaint on the pressing affairs of kingship—working as he tells us 'among other various and manifold troubles of this kingdom'.[147] So all in all, we might allow for a minimum of five years for the production of a work such as the *Pastoral Care*. This would suggest a date of *c.*885–7 for the commencement of the *Pastoral Care* assuming that it was not issued later than the opening of the prolonged campaigns against the Danes in 892. But the work could have been begun considerably earlier than 885–7—a date which provides no more than a *terminus post quem*.

There has always been a tendency in Alfredian studies—even on the part of those who recognized an Alfredian dimension in the Chronicle, to view that source as being essentially different from the main bulk of the translations proper. But even though the Chronicle was not a translation of a compilation of early annals as such, its production clearly involved the translation of earlier Latin annals and some other Latin sources.[148] Its ninth-century narrative—contributed by several writers—reveals a conscious decision on the part of its editor to write in vernacular West Saxon, and thus abandon the monastic Latin so characteristic of annalistic genre in the Frankish Empire and elsewhere in the Christian West. As for its content and emphasis on the House of Ecgberht and on King Alfred in particular, it was clearly one of those books which in the king's own words 'may be most necessary for all men to know'. Whitelock's belief that the Chronicle had borrowed its entry on the emperor, Titus, from Orosius was successfully challenged as we have seen, by Bately, who dated the final production of the Old English Orosius most likely to between 880 and 892, or again, not before 889 and not after King Alfred's death in 899.[149] If this late dating is correct, we have yet another major work which may also have been completed in or about 890. But the arguments which would date the Old English Orosius to after 889 depend on our very imperfect understanding of when precisely the Magyars or Hungarians first settled permanently in the Danube valley, and on how the reporting of that event reached the translator of Orosius.[150] The absence of any mention of Hungarians in the Danube region, in an earlier discussion in the Orosius, allows for a considerably earlier dating for at least that part of the translation. The presence of the Hungarians in the West became generally known after 899, and their mention later on in the translation, was regarded by Bately as providing a *terminus ante quem* for the Old English Orosius as a whole.[151] Linked to that, was the mention of a wasteland (*westen*) lying between the *Carendran* and the Bulgarians, which she tentatively identified with either Charlemagne's devastations of the mark of Pannonia or with Svatopluk's ravages of 883–4.[152] The Balkans and the Danube Valley were too far removed from Alfred and his world to provide us with an accurate chronology for the dating of an Old English text. It is hazardous to argue from negative evidence or from vague references to a region which was so poorly known in the West, and whose land-route for pilgrims and travellers to Constantinople had been cut for centuries by successive waves of Avars, Bulgars, and migrating Slavs. The Old English Orosius could have been translated any time early in King Alfred's reign, but most likely after the Peace of Wedmore in the period 878–92. Such a date, as Bately acknowledged, is in keeping with an apparent reference to peaceful conditions prevailing in Wessex in *Orosius* [III. xi].[153] That reference to late ninth-century conditions runs as follows: 'We now call it war, when strangers and foreigners (*fremde 7 ellþeodge*) come upon us, and plunder us of some little, and again quickly leave us'. This dismissal on the part of the West Saxon translator, of isolated and short-lived viking raiding parties could relate to any minor raid after the Peace of Wedmore (878) and before the beginning of the Last War (892). We are by no means therefore, constrained by Whitelock's specific identification of this reference with the raid on East Kent in 885,[154] and Bately's more general dating from 878 is to be preferred.

Certainty is not possible to achieve in the matter of dating Alfredian texts but we do have a relative chronology, based on textual relationships to guide us. The Old English Orosius is agreed to pre-date Alfred's Boethius, which in turn is seen to be earlier than the *Soliloquies* with which it shares similarities in diction and phraseology. The *Pastoral Care* can be shown to be earlier than the *Soliloquies* since its Old English translation of Gregory's *Cura Pastoralis* is seen as the source for certain passages in the *Soliloquies* rather than the original Latin text. But if as we shall see, the completion of the *Pastoral Care* was accomplished perhaps several years before its publication or distribution to the bishops in 890–2, then there is no compelling reason to date either the translations of the *Soliloquies* or the *Consolation of Philosophy* by Boethius to the difficult period after 892.

The solution to the problem may lie in the evidence provided by the *Pastoral Care*, which contains King Alfred's prose preface or introductory letter and which survived into the modern era in two manuscripts from the king's own time. In his prose preface, Alfred outlines his plans not only for the translation of the *Pastoral Care* but of those other books in his educational programme 'which are most necessary for all men to know'. He also outlines his plans for the education of all the English freeborn youth in the reading of English, and for the further education of some in Latin also. This preface therefore, as Whitelock correctly observed, is suggestive of a beginning. But its long preamble on the general decline of learning in England and its provision for the translation into English of several books, as well as a schooling programme, shows that it was meant to serve not just as a preface to the *Pastoral Care* but as a blueprint for an entire translation programme of scholarly works. The publication of the *Pastoral Care* was availed of by Alfred to circulate a veritable king's writ, setting out of his cultural programme in general, by way of a letter written expressly to accompany the volume then being copied and distributed among the bishoprics of Wessex and Mercia. The dating of this letter or the so-called prose preface to the *Pastoral Care* need not necessarily provide a date for the earliest Alfredian translation of that entire work. For the *Pastoral Care* had its own preface—the verse preface—which is a true preface, describing Gregory as the original author of the work which 'Augustine brought from the south over the salt sea' to England, and of how 'afterwards King Alfred translated every word of me into English', and had the work copied and distributed to his bishops.'[155] In Sisam's opinion, the prose preface was a later addition to the work, inserted between the original heading of the manuscript and the verse preface. Sisam's explanation for the later insertion of the prose preface was because 'the inclusion in the book itself of Alfred's famous letter to his bishops was an afterthought, made possible by the interval necessary to produce enough copies of the text'.[156]

Sisam suggested[157] that the heading 'This is the preface [telling] how St Gregory composed this book which is called the *Pastoralis*' got separated from the verse preface in the Tiberius and Cambridge University manuscripts by the later insertion of the prose preface. The idea has much to recommend it, and if we accept that, then we can scarcely argue that Alfred was preparing both verse preface and letter 'while copies of the text [of the *Pastoral Care*] were being prepared'.[158] An alternative explanation may be that different prefaces were composed to serve different purposes on different occasions, and the time-lag involved is reflected in the eventual dislocation of the original heading from the earliest verse preface and from the *Pastoral Care* as a whole. Sisam envisaged only a short interval, perhaps, between the writing of the two prefaces, or he did at any rate see the two prefaces as part of the same continuous process, however lengthy. But there is no intrinsic connection between these two prefaces. The prose preface or prefatory letter to the *Pastoral Care* is a general statement of royal policy in regard to the king's translation and cultural programme. The verse preface, on the other hand, was clearly original in the sense that it was composed to introduce Alfred's translation of the *Pastoral Care*. Once we have accepted along with Sisam the secondary nature of the prose preface, there is no compelling reason to view it as an immediate afterthought to the translation of the *Pastoral Care* as a whole. Given the symmetry between the verse preface and verse epilogue, and recognizing that the prose preface serves an altogether different and more general purpose, it may be that the publication of the *Pastoral Care* in *c*.890 involved the copying and wide circulation at that time, of a work which had been completed by the king to satisfy his own personal needs several if not many years before. The fact that Plegmund is referred to by King Alfred as archbishop in the prose preface may merely recognize the status which that prelate enjoyed at the time of the general distribution of the *Pastoral Care* in *c*.890. It is possible that the king's account of how he began his personal involvement in the translation programme might well refer back to a time in the early 88os, and it is equally possible that the helpers whom he names lent their tutorial assistance to the king at different points in time. Certainly the account of how Alfred began his work on the *Pastoral Care* has a retrospective tone particularly in its opening sentence:

When I remembered how the knowledge of Latin had formerly decayed throughout England, and yet many could read English writing, I began among other various and manifold troubles of this kingdom, to translate into English the book which is called in Latin *Pastoralis* and in English 'Shepherd-Book', sometimes word by word and sometimes according to the sense, as I had learnt it from Plegmund my archbishop, and Asser (*Asserie*) my bishop, and Grimbold my mass-priest, and John my mass-priest.[159]

   This does not sound like an author who has just put down his pen from working on the *Pastoral Care*. It reads more like a man looking back over a scholarly career and remembering how it all began. It is more reasonable to assume that the full range of the Alfredian canon was in preparation and production during the fourteen-year interval of peace from 878 until 892 rather than accept a scenario involving a flood of translation in and after 892. Alfred makes it quite clear in his preface to the *Dialogues* that he commissioned his scholarly friends to translate that work for his own personal use.[160] At some later time, a bishop—assumed to be Wulfsige of Sherborne[161] wrote his own preface for a new copy of the *Dialogues* which he had made from King Alfred's exemplar. So in the case of Gregory's *Dialogues*, we can be reasonably certain that this translation was first intended for the king and only afterwards did it achieve a wider circulation. The *Preface* attributed to Wulfsige, and the copying of the accompanying translation of Gregory's *Dialogues* which had been sent to him, represents part of that second stage of wider distribution which

Date	Historical Bench-mark	Traditional Chronology	Revised Chronology
878	End of Alfred's Second War		King Alfred's *Will* (part at least of extant version, 871–888)
882–5		Old English *Bede*	Old English *Bede* (any time in late ninth century)
c.885		Alfred's Law Code [Whitelock]	Alfred's Law code (878–92)
		Wærferth's Translation of *Dialogues* (known to 'Asser')	Translation of *Dialogues* (878–92)
		Histories of Orosius [post 885 Whitelock]	*Histories* of Orosius c.884–889
887		11 November, 887. According to 'Asser', Alfred learnt to read and to translate Latin	*Pastoral Care* (begun c.885) *Boethius Soliloquies* (pre-892)
890	Plegmund became Archbishop of Canterbury (mentioned as archbishop in prefatory letter to *Pastoral Care*)		Distribution of *Pastoral Care* with prefatory letter
892	Beginning of Alfred's Last War	*Pastoral Care* [Whitelock] 'Publication' of Anglo-Saxon Chronicle (later used in *Life* of Alfred)	End of major phase in Alfredian translation programme
893		Supposed time of writing of *Life* of King Alfred attributed to Asser	
894		*Pastoral Care* [Stenton] (*Anglo-Saxon England*, 270)	
894–6	Death of Bishop Swithulf of Rochester (mentioned in connection with distribution of *Pastoral Care*)		
896	End of Alfred's Last War	*Boethius Soliloquies* Alfred's Law Code [Stenton] Psalms of Paris Psalter	Completion of Alfredian section of Anglo-Saxon Chronicle Psalms
899	Death of Alfred		
1000–20			*Life* of King Alfred

FIG. 7. Chronology of Alfredian and related writings

is otherwise apparent in Alfred's letter (or second or prose preface) which accompanied his *Pastoral Care*.[162] It is due to his biographer's clumsy miracle story of Alfred's Latin lesson in 887 that scholars have precluded the possibility of dating any of the Alfredian translations—both by the king himself and by others—to the 880s. It is also thanks to 'Asser' that the production of the Chronicle must be squeezed into the period prior to 893.

King Alfred's *Will* is a document which goes far beyond the simple listing of bequests. Nor was it primarily an oral recitation of those bequests in the presence of witnesses. This *Will* was written down to provide a complex explanation and apology for Alfred's treatment of his nephews and reveals the king's own ideas and complex political manœuvrings.[163] As we should expect—*pace* the author of the *Life* of Alfred—it reflects the mind of an astute and well-educated ruler, who on his own statement claimed to have *written* (*ic ær on oðre wisan awriten*) an earlier *Will*, copies of which he had distributed 'to many men'.[164] We are not entitled to assume that the text of the king's surviving or second *Will* was drawn up by an amanuensis. Alfred himself claims it was drawn up with the 'advice (*mid gepeahtunge*)' of his archbishop, Æthelred, and with the 'witness (*gewitnesse*)' of his West Saxon counsellors. There is no sense in which the king claims the document was drawn up by any of these men on his behalf, and he speaks of himself—yet again in the first person—as the writer of his earlier *Will*. The point is important because Sisam, forgetful of his pronouncements on Alfred's illiteracy which he made elsewhere, used the king's *Will* as evidence for his literary style. Sisam pointed to Alfred's fondness for the use of the insistent *now . . . now* formula in his *Will* as well as in the prose preface to the *Pastoral Care* and the prose preface to Boethius's *Consolation of Philosophy*.[165] King Alfred's surviving or second *Will* was drawn up sometime between 872–3 when Bishop Wærferth (mentioned as such in the *Will*) took charge of Worcester, and the death of Archbishop Æthelred, on whose advice Alfred drew up his *Will*. Archbishop Æthelred died in June 888,[166] and in view of the bequests to all the king's children and to his son-in-law, Æthelred of Mercia, the *Will* was most likely drawn up in the 880s. Alfred's earlier *Will* was written shortly before he became king, for he tells us that he and his brother Æthelred (who was by then king) had made provision for their children—and therefore by implication drew up a formal *Will*—during an assembly at *Swinbeorg* which was probably held in 871.[167] The making of *Wills* and the production of scholarly works were very different activities, but the evidence for King Alfred's two *Wills* in the period 871 to 888 has a bearing on the career of a man who was alleged to have been illiterate and educationally deprived before 887. The lengthy and complicated way in which Alfred argues a case for his privileged place in the succession from his father King Æthelwulf,[168] and his own account of his earlier *Will*, have some light to shed on the career of a king who was otherwise alleged to have been an illiterate:

Now I had previously written differently about my inheritance, when I had more property and more kinsmen, and I had entrusted the documents to many men, and in these same men's witness they were written. Therefore I have now burnt all the old ones which I could discover. If any one of them be shall be found, it has no validity, for it is my will that now it shall be as here stated, with God's help.[169]

Here, already before 888, and very probably also in the 870s, we find Alfred writing in his discursive and dignified way as we should expect from a highly literate king. We find him too, openly striving to suppress earlier written statements of intent, and already displaying that organizational ability which he perfected in his more ambitious translations. The 'many men' to whom he had sent copies of his earlier *Will* were the bishops such as Æthelred and Wærferth, and those other few literate members of his *witan* who could distinguish between a will and any other piece of parchment—that same small group, who were the recipients of his translations. What this *Will* tells us of Alfred is that already in 870 and later in the 880s he appreciated the value of the written word, not just to draw up a primitive list of bequests, but to shore up his position as king, and that he already understood the legal and political advantages of distributing multiple copies to key men in his realm.[170] There is no reason to assume that such a king was incapable of setting up a team of scholars and beginning work both on his Law Code and on his translation programme, as soon as he was safely rid of Guthrum and his hordes back in 878.

Scholarly opinion on the chronology of Alfredian texts is fraught with preconceived notions relating to the time-scale implied for these works in the *Life* of King Alfred as well as contradictory views on the primacy of the *Pastoral Care*. We have already disposed of the necessity to follow the *Life* of Alfred in believing that Alfred did not 'begin his first lessons in holy writings' until 11 November 887. We may ignore too, the argument that because Asser was supposed to have completed his biography of the king in 893 and had failed to mention any of Alfred's own translations, that all of those works were produced between 893 and the death of the king in 899. Because of the intervention of Alfred's Last War, that would effectively confine the entire translation programme into the three-year period 896–9. Whitelock concluded from similarities in phraseology, that the author of the *Life* of Alfred knew of the prose preface to the *Pastoral Care*, but she explained the absence of any reference to that or other works by concluding that the historical Asser left his biography of King Alfred unfinished. Since we are no longer constrained by the spectre of the 'Genuine Asser' and the unedifying process of endless special pleading which has been so necessary to keep that thesis in play, we may look to the fourteen-year period from 878 to 892 as the most obvious time— when Alfred had 'peace' enough—for his literary activities. As for the chronological primacy of the *Pastoral Care*, Alfred's own words on this subject depend on the relative timing of his prose preface to the main text of that work. The king does imply in his prose preface that the *Pastoral Care* was the first work which he translated.[171] But since Alfred's prose preface may have been written a considerable time after the actual translation proper, as well as after its verse preface and epilogue, we are not compelled to date the translation as a whole to 890 or after. The date of writing of the translation of the *Pastoral Care*—as opposed to its copying and distribution—may have been at some time in the late 880s when Alfred had more time to devote to such matters.[172] Whitelock was uneasy about seeing the distribution of the *Pastoral Care* as the time of the first translation of any Alfredian work to be produced, and she very cautiously implied that the *Dialogues* might have been produced earlier for the king's personal use.[173] She did not however distinguish between the time of the translation of the *Pastoral Care* and the possibility of its later circulation.

While the sequence of Alfred's own translations would appear to be *Pastoral Care* followed by *Consolation* and *Soliloquies* in quick succession if not in parallel, we need to be cautious in accepting what are archaeological style typologies in relation to the Alfredian canon. We cannot accept without qualification that a vernacular text which remains most faithful to the original is earlier than one which departs more radically from its Latin exemplar. That notion was encouraged by the idea that as the semi-literate king grew rapidly in precocity, he felt confident enough to depart from his parent text. Such an idea conformed nicely to Alfred's biographer's account of an eager king struggling to translate his Latin with a naïve and pious enthusiasm. To apply this criterion as a general rule for dating Alfred's works would be fallacious. We should not expect, for instance, to find marked deviation from the text of the Latin Psalms at whatever time in his life the king translated them. The Psalms were part of Holy Writ—prayers not only contained within the Scriptures, but part also of the Divine Office and revered for their association with King David. The same is true of Alfred's translation of passages from the Old and New Testaments in the introduction to his Laws. While the Alfredian tendency for expansion and commentary is still present in his treatment of Scripture, that tendency was nevertheless curbed by virtue of the authority of the sacred texts.[174] Those texts which do depart most markedly from their Latin originals are those of a philosophical nature which the king translated himself—most probably for his own speculative enjoyment and for sharing with his inner circle of scholarly friends. The *Pastoral Care*, on the other hand, was intended for Alfred's bishops, and as a practical handbook did not encourage deviation from the original. That is not to say that the *Soliloquies* and *Consolation* may not be later works, but if they are, it may not be because they depart radically from their Latin originals. The Old English translation of the Psalms follows the original text with relative closeness. Keynes and Lapidge believed that this work came last in the entire series and that Alfred 'was possibly prevented by death from completing the task'.[175] That idea was based on William of Malmesbury's statement that Alfred's translation of the Psalms was left unfinished by death. Whitelock rightly believed that Malmesbury was misled by the fact that the Old English translation of the psalms which he consulted—like the surviving manuscript in the Bibliothèque Nationale—only contained the first fifty Psalms and from that he guessed the work was left unfinished. What Malmesbury may not have taken into consideration was that it was normal in the ninth century to divide the Psalter into three groups of fifty Psalms.[176] Taking the closeness of translations to their original as a yardstick for date may be of little help in assessing the relative chronology of works commissioned by the king such as the *Dialogues* of Gregory. Those translations not undertaken personally by the king tend as a group to conform more closely to their Latin originals and there is no way of assessing their relative dating on the grounds of closeness to those originals. The reason why Gregory's *Dialogues* have hitherto been tentatively dated earlier than other Alfredian works was based on the notion that because the author of the *Life* of Alfred knew of this translation, it must have been produced earlier than 893 when the historical Asser was thought to have laid aside his pen. Similarly, the Old English Orosius was once thought to have fitted into the narrow chronological band between 890–3 and 899.[177] Bately, having freed the Orosius from Alfred's direct authorship, and not constrained by the Asser bogey, argued for a date *c.*884–889, or 'not before 889' for that translation.[178] She was rightly sceptical of attempts to date the Ohthere and Wulfstan voyages, since we have no comparable early texts to compare them with,[179] and concluded that we must settle for a date any time in Alfred's reign when these voyages were first reported to the king. It is likely, however, that most, if not all works in the list consisting of Gregory's *Dialogues*, the Old English Bede, and Old English Orosius were begun or completed during the 880s. The fact that Alfred's biographer mentions only the *Dialogues* is meaningless in relation to the dating of other material. His knowledge of the *Dialogues* and their association with Wærferth and King Alfred was very likely dependent on a misreading of a copy of the Old English verse preface to the *Dialogues* of Gregory which Alfred's biographer had consulted.[180]

While we may reject the notion that the entire Alfredian translation programme was compressed into the last decade of Alfred's life, the possibility of the simultaneous production of texts cannot be ruled out altogether. Scholars who speculate on the relative chronology of Alfredian works tend to lose sight of the possibility of a team effort, and focus on the role of Alfred alone. If Alfred were assisted as he himself hints in the *Soliloquies* by 'a few wise and skillful men',[181] then we may envisage a scenario where more than one text was prepared in draft translation at the same time, and where the simultaneous perusal of those drafts led to the mutual influence of one work on another. Alfred, in his overall editorial role would then have had time to consider making his own personal additions to simplify or elucidate a text wherever he thought necessary. It is difficult to envisage a king, even of Alfred's scholarly interests and ability having the time required successfully to complete the translation of any one of these works entirely unaided. It is certainly wrong to consider any of these texts being treated in complete isolation. We shall see[182] that there is evidence for the mutual influence of the translated texts of Boethius's *Consolation* and the *Soliloquies* of Augustine, one upon the other, which in turn is suggestive of simultaneous production. However we interpret the interrelationship between the Old English *Consolation* and the *Soliloquies*, we must assume that the king and his scholars were familiar—either individually or collectively—with a wide range of much of their translated works in the original Latin, for several years before the translation programme was carried through to completion. It is the mischief created by Alfred's biographer which alone was responsible for the bogus notion of an illiterate middle-aged king stumbling across the learning of Late Antiquity which he somehow miraculously managed to present to the world in a very short time largely with the help of Asser. If Alfred did indeed produce or supervise some of his translated works in a relatively short period, that timetable was dictated by the pressing events and crises of his reign. He himself states that the success of his education programme was dependent on whether 'we have peace (*stilnesse*) enough'.[183] It is all the more probable, that such a king, working under great pressure between wars, had long ago in his youth acquired the necessary ambition and intellectual training to enable him to organize such an elaborate and successful series of translations in so difficult a time. Whatever the precise date of those translations, we can safely assume that Alfred and some at least of his helpers were familiar with their Latin originals for many years before turning them into Old English.

This discussion of the list of Alfredian translations and of their relative chronology has led us far from the account in the *Life* of Alfred of a king still struggling with his Latin sentences in middle age, and on the eve of his final and prolonged confrontation with his Danish enemies. It is, however, crucial to attempt an integrated reconstruction of the king's deprived education as described in his *Life*, alongside the reality of his outstanding literary achievement. For when we attempt this, we find that the fictional narrative of the Pseudo-Asser—as we shall now come to call him—inevitably gives way to the substantial discussion of Alfred's historically verifiable major contribution to the development of Old English prose. The *Life* of Alfred cannot hold its own in any discussion involving the reality of Alfred's own writings, where the sheer weight of the king's literary ouput—not to mention his learning—exposes his biographer as a man far removed both in time and in intellectual ability from the king whom he describes. Alfred's writings and the immense breadth of learning and familiarity with Late Antiquity which they contain stand as an indictment of the king's biographer's account of a supposedly illiterate scholar.

X

International Scholars in the Seminar of a King

KING ALFRED'S BIOGRAPHER TELLS US THAT THE KING SUMMONED four scholars from Mercia to help with his personal education—Wærferth, bishop of Worcester, Plegmund, archbishop of Canterbury, and two priests and chaplains, Æthelstan and Wærwulf.[1] And because this is an account of a saintly king, we are told that the initiative to send these men to Alfred began with God (*Deus . . . transmisit*). In a following chapter of King Alfred's *Life*, we learn that Alfred acquired two more scholars—the priest and monk Grimbald from Gaul (*Gallia*), and John, yet another priest and monk, whom we only assume was the same person as John 'the Old Saxon' (i.e. from Continental Saxony), who in another part of the *Life* is said to have been appointed by Alfred as abbot of Athelney.[2] To complete the scholarly team, Alfred's biographer describes how he—'Asser'—was himself 'summoned by the king from the western and farthest parts of Wales'.[3] He makes it clear that Alfred built up this team before he could himself read, and therefore these seven men were supposed to have arrived in Wessex prior to November 887. The reference to Plegmund as archbishop of Canterbury in this context of his first coming to Alfred's court, is anachronistic, and was almost certainly copied from Alfred's reference to 'Plegmund, my archbishop' in the king's prose preface to the *Pastoral Care*, where the Pseudo-Asser also picked up the names of the Mass-priests Grimbald and John—not to speak of Bishop Asser.[4] The names of all of these royal tutors turn up in charters of varying degrees of authenticity relating to King Alfred or to his son, Edward the Elder. Whitelock fully endorsed the notion that the witness of King Alfred's scholarly priests to some charters at least, 'supports what Asser says about the priests invited to Alfred's court'.[5] But charters have to be genuine before they can support anything that anyone says, and it is proof of their authenticity which in this case is singularly lacking. Whitelock was attempting here to authenticate problematic charters with the help of a spurious *Life* of Alfred.

The Pseudo-Asser stresses the constant presence of these supposedly royal tutors in the king's company: 'For by day and night whenever he had any free time, he ordered books to be read before him by such men, nor indeed did he allow himself to be without one of them.'[6] Such scholarly confidants clearly had the ear of their king, and in spite of the non-episcopal rank of many of them, we find their names in the witness lists of royal charters which would seem to confirm their special status—as members of the king's household, if not indeed of his *witan*. There is, however, a serious difficulty in that the names of the great majority of Alfred's supposed tutors turn up in the witness lists, not of Alfred's charters but in those of his son and successor, Edward the Elder. It is difficult to explain how royal chaplains or non-episcopal tutors did not qualify as witnesses to charters in ninth-century Wessex, and then having to account for a drastic change of policy in the opening years of the tenth century under Edward. But no such explanation is required, if it can be shown that the presence of the names of Alfred's non-episcopal tutors in the witness lists of King Edward's charters are not genuine. The Mercian Plegmund, who became archbishop in 890, might (if we could trust the Pseudo-Asser) have been at Alfred's court some years before 887. Plegmund must have been a cleric of the first importance in the years immediately prior to his elevation to Canterbury. Yet there is no evidence for Plegmund witnessing charters of any king prior to his elevation, and even in his role as metropolitan, his presence in Alfredian charters is a rare occurrence. He heads the witness list in what Whitelock, following Stevenson, branded as 'a glaring Rochester forgery'— a grant from King Alfred to Bishop Burhric of Rochester attributed to AD 895[7] and he benefited along with Wærferth, bishop of Worcester, in a grant from Alfred and the rulers of Mercia in *c*.898.[8] As archbishop of Canterbury, Plegmund later confirmed a grant originally issued by a certain Eardwulf to Wighelm back in 875,[9] but his name does not appear in most of the surviving grants involving Mercia in the Alfredian period and it is absent, too, from Alfredian charters dealing with estates nearer to Plegmund's Canterbury base in the 890s. We do not find Plegmund's name, for instance, in the early Canterbury parchment containing a grant by King Alfred to his *dux* Sighelm of land at Fearnleag (Farleigh) on the river Medway in Kent in 898.[10] If we were to abide by the charter evidence alone, Archbishop Plegmund, far from sitting all day in Alfred's schoolroom—as the Pseudo-Asser suggests—seems to have led a more independent life. The same might be said for Wærferth, bishop of Worcester. The charter evidence in relation to Wærferth might seem to bear out the Pseudo-Asser's point that Alfred showered gifts upon his tutors. But Wærferth from the charter evidence appears as a powerful ecclesiastical magnate carefully nursing his Worcester constituency in the days of the Danish sub-king, Ceolwulf, and his career during all of Alfred's reign would also appear to have been firmly Worcester based.

Historians have been too influenced by the Pseudo-Asser's notion of the 'summoning (*a rege advocatus*)',[11] of the historical Asser and his colleagues to reside at the court of the king. The account of Asser's arrival at the court of King Alfred stresses the king's desire that he should reside permanently at his court[12] and has promoted the image of an international scholars' seminar brought together in the royal household where each scholar had—as the Pseudo-Asser implies—become the *familiaris* of the king. Historians who accept the account of Alfred's biographer as genuine, write in vague terms of the king's scholarly 'circle'[13] which is assumed to have moved with Alfred and his court. This image of a Carolingian-type Palace School is further confused with an equally hazy notion of a Household Prep-

School for the sons of the Alfredian aristocracy.[14] Both concepts are derived from the *Life* of Alfred, and neither one has any firm evidence outside of the *Life* to recommend it. The notion of a team of leading household scholars, whose job it was to educate Alfred and then help him achieve his translation programme, is entirely due to the Pseudo-Asser's claim that the historical Asser abandoned his career in Wales to nurture the fragile intellectual life of the king. But that idea may have owed everything to the model presented by the *Life of Alcuin* in relation to that scholar's service at the court of Charlemagne, as well as to the influence of Einhard's description of Charlemagne's Palace School. We have no idea what the personal circumstances of the historical Bishop Asser were, when he assisted King Alfred with the translation of the *Pastoral Care*, and we can never assume on the basis of what the Pseudo-Asser says of those supposed arrangements, that they also applied to Wærferth or to anyone else. It is reasonable to assume that Plegmund and Wærferth ran their dioceses from their episcopal centres and communicated directly with the king on those occasions when they temporarily joined his *witan*. There is no evidence to suggest otherwise.

It is the Pseudo-Asser alone who has left us the image of Alfred as the intellectual invalid, in need of constant tutorial support from his devoted episcopate. The superior evidence of the verse preface to the *Pastoral Care*, on the other hand, shows the opposite to have been the case. That source, which is contemporary with Alfred, claims that it was the king who was striving to educate his bishops 'for some of them needed it [i.e. a copy of the Old English *Pastoral Care*], who knew but little Latin'.[15] That remark must have applied to a number of prelates ruling that short list of bishoprics within Alfred's jurisdiction during the period 880–90—Canterbury, Rochester, Winchester, Sherborne, London, and Worcester. While it is true that Alfred rejoiced at the presence in his realm of 'learned bishops (*gelærede biscopas*)' in his later prose preface to the *Pastoral Care*, clearly that had not been the case when the verse preface had been penned. Apart from Plegmund and Asser, it is not at all clear, as we shall see, which of the others (including even Wærferth) had a firm grasp of Latin.[16] Alfred's translation programme was designed to achieve the dissemination of key texts in English to the bishops within his kingdom. It cannot be assumed that all those bishops were actively involved in the translation programme, although they were expected to facilitate the further copying of the translations in their churches. If we are to seek a Carolingian model for the functioning of the Alfredian renaissance, we ought to look to the near-contemporary scholarly life of Francia under Charles the Bald, rather than back to a Palace School of Charlemagne. It was by modelling Alfred's scholarly career on that of the semi-literate Charlemagne that the Pseudo-Asser drifted into developing his hagiographical tales of Alfred's miraculous mastering of Latin late in life and the consequent formal 'calling' of the seven scholars—which is significantly dealt with by the Pseudo-Asser in three consecutive chapters in his *Life*. There is no compelling evidence to suggest that Alfred summoned these men as a team which was permanently based at his court. The model of a scattered network of scholars— bishops and lesser clerics—working from a distance, but in close association with their scholar-king, is more plausible. It allows for a few key episcopal figures to get on with the running of their dioceses, while helping the king with his scholarly programme, through their patronage and supervision of a few regional scriptoria such as those at Winchester and Worcester. This model still allows Alfred himself a central role in directing the literary output of the movement—through his own written communications—as opposed to the preposterous image of a semi-literate king miraculously nursed through a crash course in advanced Latin. This model does not exclude the possibility of scholars joining the king's household from time to time, either individually or in groups, where they would have combined their scholarly activities with other official duties. But it does reject the notion of a formally constituted school, permanently based in the peripatetic household of a ninth-century West Saxon king.

If Plegmund and Wærferth appear in the charter witness lists strictly in their role as prelates, and so as *ex officio* members of the *witan*, the same is also true of the historical Asser. Indeed the remarkable thing about the 'genuine' Asser is that he never once witnesses a surviving charter of King Alfred—genuine or fake. This is because the historical Asser's career as a diocesan bishop in Wessex was almost certainly confined to the reign of Edward the Elder. Wulfsige, his predecessor in the bishopric of Sherborne, may not have died until 901—two years after Alfred's death—which would date Asser's rule in that diocese to 901–9. The absence of the name of the historical Asser from Alfred's charter witness lists can only be explained by the fact that prior to his becoming bishop of Sherborne in 900–1, either Asser did not attend on the king, or if he were regularly present at Alfred's court, he was not considered an appropriate person to witness the king's charters.[17] Going by the charter evidence alone, there is no record of Asser's presence at King Alfred's court at any time in that king's reign. If we argue that Asser was indeed attending on the king from the 880s onwards but did not enjoy the appropriate status to witness charters, then it would be reasonable to reject as later fabrications, the names of John, Grimbald, and Wærwulf—which do appear on Alfred's witness lists. That is not difficult to do. The names of Grimbald and John appear in Whitelock's 'glaring Rochester forgery' of Alfred's grant to Bishop Burhric[18] which takes account of the only Alfredian charter reference to Grimbald. That 'clumsy twelfth-century forgery' was dismissed by Stevenson, not least because it related to lands in Suffolk which were never at any time under Alfred's jurisdiction.[19] The only other mention of John in an Alfredian charter occurs in Alfred's grant of land at North Newnton, Wiltshire, to Æthelhelm,[20] which Stevenson rejected as spurious, and the only surviving copy of which is found in the fourteenth-century Wilton cartulary. Whitelock, when referring to this charter in 1955 dismissed it as 'spurious'.[21] In later life, she sought to rehabilitate it by demonstrating that the witness list contained many authentic names of Alfredian magnates and that its text contained verbal echoes of other charters, which were however of even more doubtful authenticity.[22] Whitelock may have been correct to point to the authentic nature of many of the names in the witness list of this Alfredian charter in favour of Æthelhelm. But in a charter preserved in so late a manuscript as this, it is impossible to demonstrate that any witness list is authentic in its entirety. Whitelock admitted that in no other Alfredian charter do we find the names of witnesses accompanied by the titles of their offices in the royal household.[23] She then indulged in special pleading to point to 'other periods [when] such titles are occasionally used'. But in no comparable charter which she cited, do we find three consecutive names of magnates accompanied by designations such as *cellerarius*, *thesaurarius*, and *pincerna* respectively. Whitelock also conceded that the nine signatories which are each described as *miles* must, in the original charter—if such there ever were—have been described as *minister*.[24] But as soon as such a concession to later editing is recognized, we can never be certain that the names of *Wærulf* and of John (*Johannes*) were not also added by a later editor or forger who had consulted the text of the Pseudo-Asser. All parties (including Whitelock) are agreed that later forgers made use of references to King Alfred's scholarly team which occur in the *Life* of the king.[25] What makes the appearance of John and Wærwulf's names particularly doubtful in the witness list of the Æthelhelm charter is that they witness consecutively at sixth and seventh place respectively. Later in the reign of Edward the Elder, John and Wærwulf turn up again in two doubtful charters purporting to record grants by King Edward to Bishop Denewulf and the *familia* of Winchester.[26] Not only do the names of these two Alfredian priests appear consecutively yet again in these two Edwardian charters of AD 904, but they appear in precisely the same order:

Johan presbyter
Werulf presbyter

as in Alfred's charter for Æthelhelm back in 892.[27] This repetition in the ordering of names, offsets Whitelock's weak suggestion that the absence of the name of the priest, Athelstan, from the witness list of the Æthelhelm charter argues in favour of the authenticity of that particular list.[28] The reality may be, that the Pseudo-Asser's account of Alfred's calling of his scholarly team, provided forgers with a mine of plausible names which they drew upon and combined at random to fill out the witness lists of spurious charters. If in one instance a forger decided against using all the names which could be culled from the *Life* of Alfred, that can scarcely be argued to lend authenticity to the names which he decided—quite randomly—to include. What we are most certainly not entitled to say on the evidence of the Æthelhelm charter is that 'it supports what Asser says about the priests invited to Alfred's court'.[29]

Wærwulf's name like that of John, appears only twice in the Alfredian lists—once in the doubtful Æthelhelm charter we have discussed, and once in Alfred's lease of land at Chelworth, Wiltshire, to Dudi.[30] This charter for Dudi, also rejected by Stevenson,[31] but reinserted in the canon by Whitelock,[32] is witnessed by one *Verulf*.[33] Whether Alfred's priest Wærwulf, or Ealdorman Werulf (described as *dux*) who witnessed one of Edward's spurious charters of 909 is meant,[34] it is impossible to say. Since the mysterious *Verulf* is sandwiched in the list between Wulfric and Ecgulf who are elsewhere described as *ministri* or thegns, we might expect *Verulf* also to have been one of their class, but since the list has been rearranged,[35] such analysis on such doubtful material seems fruitless. A *Warulf minister* or thegn appears in the witness list of Ealdorman Ordlaf's grant to Malmesbury Abbey[36]—a charter which Whitelock believed to be genuine.[37] A priest Wærwulf, who may or may not, have been one of Alfred's helpers[38] was the recipient of a lease from his bishop, Wærferth of Worcester in 899.[39] The lease was made on account of the long-standing friendship between the two men[40] and since Bishop Wærferth was said by Alfred's biographer to have been involved in the Alfredian translation programme, then his priestly friend mentioned in this grant of land at Ablington in Gloucestershire, is taken to be the Mercian priest of that name also mentioned by Alfred's biographer as one of the king's tutors.[41] Wærferth's lease in favour of Wærwulf was a Mercian transaction, issued in the year of Alfred's death. The king was not involved in the grant, and Wærwulf did not himself witness the grant unless he appears as *Werfrið praesbiter* in the eleventh-century manuscript where this document is preserved.

This leaves only one other person mentioned by the Pseudo-Asser as a member of King Alfred's seminar—the priest and chaplain Æthelstan. There are several people in the Alfredian and Edwardian witness lists with the name of Æthelstan, and not all of them were clerics. The name Æthelstan occurs in three charters of Alfred's reign—two from Winchester[42] and one from Canterbury.[43] The grant from Bishop Ealhferð of Winchester to Earldorman Cuthred[44] includes in its witness list the name of Ealdorman Æthelstan (*Æðelstan dux*), and two thegns of that name appear in the list attached to Alfred's grant to Bishop Denewulf of Winchester in 879–80.[45] None of these men can have been the same person as Alfred's supposed priest (or bishop?) and chaplain (*sacerdos et capellanus*).[46] A priest (*presbiter*) called Athelstan does appear in the witness list of Alfred's grant to Bishop Denewulf[47] who may be the same man as the Athelstan *sacerdos* who witnessed Alfred's grant to Sighelm in 898,[48] although the charters are separated in time by nineteen years. The grant to Sighelm is preserved on an early parchment, which, however early, is later than Alfred's time. Alfred's grant to Denewulf[49] was treated with suspicion by Stevenson and by Whitelock, and is wrongly dated in its extant twelfth-century manuscript version to 979 rather than 879. Even if that charter were to be accepted as genuine, a priest, Athelstan, witnessing a Winchester charter for 879, can scarcely be identified with a Mercian who supposedly did not arrive at Alfred's court until after 885. The proliferation of the name Athelstan both for clerics and laymen in forged charters from this period makes it impossible to be sure of the identity of any particular individual even in those few documents which display any semblance of authenticity. Three thegns called Athelstan turn up in a forged charter of Bishop Denewulf early in the reign of Edward[50] while no less than three priests of the name are found in yet another Denewulf charter[51] in a garbled witness list where there has been clearly reorganization and duplication of names. So, although references to the priest Athelstan in two of Alfred's charters— to Sighelm[52] and to Denewulf[53]—may be genuine, there can be no certainty in an evaluation of documents involving poor manuscript transmission and bedevilled by forgery. For although Bishop Denewulf's grant of land at Ebbesborne, Wilt-shire, to Beornwulf[54] was regarded as authentic by Harmer and Finsberg, never-theless Harmer recognized that a second list of witnesses began with the name of the second *Tata presbyter*, and that *Wigea* who appears in the first list as a deacon, appears in the second as a priest.[55] Charters may in some respects be genuine, therefore, while their witness lists, even if genuine in whole or in part, may have come from elsewhere.

What is clear is that the overall pattern of the occurrence of the name of the priest Athelstan in the charters, conforms to the picture we have already recovered for that of Alfred's other supposed non-episcopal tutors as well as for Bishop Asser—namely that the priestly Athelstan is more securely associated with the reign of Edward the Elder than with King Alfred. While the name of the *sacerdos* or *presbiter*, Athelstan, occurs only twice in Alfredian charters,[56] it is found no less than twenty or twenty-three times (depending on the identity of the three Athelstans without titles in Sawyer 360 and 380) in the charters of Edward the Elder. This does not take account of the Bishop Athelstan who witnessed Edward's grant to Bishop Frithestan of Winchester *c*.909,[57] nor of the various ealdormen or the atheling and future king of that name. In thirteen occurrences, the names of Athelstan and that of the priest Wærwulf are either paired together in the lists or placed in close proximity, which prompted Stevenson rightly to dismiss these examples as drawn from the *Life* of King Alfred. Stevenson had so little faith in any of this material that he was prompted to observe: 'The Winchester chartulary is of such exceedingly bad repute that one cannot feel any confidence in the texts coming from it and bearing the name of Edward the Elder. Æthelstan and Werwulf are mentioned in other charters, but there is not one that is altogether free from doubt.'[58] Even if we were to accept the presence of the priest Athelstan as an authentic record in a few of these Edwardian charters, such as Edward's grant to Ordlaf[59] witnessed by *Aeðelstan mess[epreost]*, or in Edward's grant to Denewulf of land in Tichborne in Hampshire,[60] we are still left to explain the fact that these records relate to the post-Alfredian age. The fourteen occurrences of the name of Asser in Edwardian charters, on the other hand, pose no problem, since by that time the historical Asser would have been witnessing charters in his capacity as bishop of Sherborne. We have to allow for the possibility that the consecration of an Athelstan to the newly created bishopric of Ramsbury in 909 may have prompted the Pseudo-Asser to use this name for one of his Alfredian priest-chaplains, and once inserted in a *Life* of Alfred, the name was proliferated in bogus witness lists attached to forged charters pretending to date from the reign of Edward.

When we come to examine the evidence for the careers of two of the best known of Alfred's helpers—Grimbald and John—we find that Grimbald became the focus of fraudulent tenth- and eleventh-century writers at Winchester, while the tale of 'Abbot John' in the *Life* of Alfred will not stand up to close scrutiny. The sum total of contemporary information we possess on Grimbald is that his help with the translation of the *Pastoral Care* was acknowledged by King Alfred who described him as 'my Mass-priest (*minum mæssepreoste*)'[61] and that he died still enjoying the title of *mæssepreost* in 901—presumably in England, since the notice of his death occurs in the Anglo-Saxon Chronicle.[62] We take a step away from sound historical evidence when we follow the Pseudo-Asser in identifying Grimbald's homeland with 'Gaul'; accepting that he was monk; an expert in [Gregorian] chant; and a scholar of church doctrine and of Holy Scripture.[63] There is no reason why we ought to reject this late tenth-century tradition out of hand, except to observe that the association of Grimbald the *monachus* with an expertise in *ecclesiasticis disciplinis* suspiciously echoes the harping in a suspect letter from Archbishop Fulk of Rheims on this very subject of 'ecclesiastical order' and 'canonical authority', which were supposed to be enforced by Grimbald in Alfred's kingdom. The earliest source of information on Grimbald, outside the mention of him in King Alfred's own writings, the Anglo-Saxon Chronicle and the *Life* of Alfred, occurs in the monastic breviary of Hyde Abbey in the lections for matins on the Feast of St Grimbald on 8 July.[64] The material relating to Grimbald in these lections has been labelled the *Vita Prima* by Grierson and has been dated 'to the second half of the tenth or [less probably] to the eleventh century.'[65] We are dealing here with a hagiographical genre closely related in subject-matter, in its Latin style, and time of composition, to the work of the Pseudo-Asser. It is from the lections in the Hyde breviary that we learn Grimbald's place of birth was Thérouanne and that at the age of 7 he joined the community of the abbey of St Bertin (at St Omer) where he eventually became prior. Grimbald is said to have received the infant Alfred and his companions at St Bertin when Alfred was *en route* to Rome to be crowned king by Pope Leo.[66] It was then that the remarkably precocious Alfred determined to take Grimbald back to Wessex, and when Alfred eventually succeeded to the kingship, he did indeed persuade the abbot and monks of St Bertin to send Grimbald to him.[67] The ridiculous aspects of this tale need not detain us—except to comment on the fact that its author, in writing of the *regni Anglicani* in a mid-ninth century West Saxon context betrays a similar anachronistic approach as the Pseudo-Asser in his opening dedication in the *Life* of Alfred. Indeed, we are dealing here not merely with a parallel genre, but with the intertwining of late tenth-century Winchester elaborations of the Alfred myth.

The so-called twelfth-century *Vita Secunda* of Grimbald, partially preserved by Leland in the sixteenth century,[68] follows the Pseudo-Asser in recording a second visit by Alfred to Rome, and embroiders the tale of Grimbald's summoning to England by naming John the priest and Asser, as members of the English deputation to St Bertin.[69] The *Vita Prima* goes on to relate how on his arrival in England, Grimbald was provided with a 'little monastery (*monasteriolum*)' at Winchester.[70] On the death of Archbishop Æthelred of Canterbury, Grimbald was offered the metropolitan see by Alfred with the approval 'of all the clergy and people',[71] but declined it in favour of Plegmund, whom Grimbald recommended for the job.[72] We are reminded of how the Pseudo-Asser claimed that Alfred could have taken the kingship even while his brother Æthelred was still alive 'with the consent of all'.[73] Yet another bright suggestion of Grimbald's was the building of the New Minster at Winchester under the patronage of Edward the Elder. According to the

Vita Prima, when King Alfred died, the grief-stricken Grimbald was only dissuaded by the new king, Edward, from returning to his Continental monastery, with the promise of a new monastic home in Winchester—the future New Minster. The place was built within two years[74]—dedicated by Archbishop Plegmund to the Virgin and Saints Peter and Paul, and it was at the New Minster that Grimbald died on 8 July 903.[75] The correct date of Grimbald's death was 901, by which time the New Minister at Winchester could scarcely have been completed. But the notion that Grimbald played a leading role in the foundation of the New Minster and that he was offered the archbishopric of Canterbury by King Alfred is clearly a piece of Winchester propaganda dating from the late tenth and early eleventh centuries.

The tradition that Grimbald was offered and refused the archbishopric of Canterbury is echoed in the *Letter* of Fulk, archbishop of Rheims, to King Alfred. Whitelock who regarded this letter as being 'usually accepted as genuine' found it 'difficult to see to whose interest in England it would be to fabricate it'.[76] In this, Whitelock had followed Grierson, who accepted the authenticity of the letter and regarded the surviving manuscript as a tenth-century document originating in the West Country.[77] Keynes and Lapidge, while accepting the letter as genuine, pronounced it to be an eleventh-century copy written 'rather later in the eleventh century' by a scribe from New Minister, Winchester into a Gospel manuscript which had originated at Christ Church Canterbury in the first quarter of the eleventh century.[78] The earliest copy of this supposed letter from Archbishop Fulk therefore, cannot have been entered in the Canterbury Gospel book until that codex had reached Winchester most likely after *c.*1025. This was the time when the Grimbald hagiographical saga—feeding off the related myth of the infant Alfred's pilgrimage to Rome and of Grimbald's supposed refusal of the archbishopric of Canterbury—was at its height. Nelson first expressed scepticism regarding the veracity of Fulk's letter: 'Grimbald was Winchester's man and the letter does much to enhance Grimbald's reputation.'[79] She observed that the letter gives the strong impression that Grimbald, in Archbishop Fulk's mind, was destined for episcopal office in England, rather than for a scholarly role in the king's writing office.[80] Alfred is said to have asked for Grimbald by name 'to be chosen for this office (*officium*) and appointed to the charge of pastoral authority (*curae pastoralis*)'.[81] Grimbald was a candidate proclaimed by the universal church herself 'to be most worthy of pontifical honour (*pontificali honore*) and capable of teaching others'.[82] The future responsibilities ascribed to Grimbald in this letter, purporting to come from Archbishop Fulk, have nothing to do with scholarly help which the historical Grimbald afforded King Alfred, and have everything to do with the teaching and pastoral responsibilities of a future bishop. The thrust of this document is that since the English church had never properly aspired to be observances laid down by canonical decree, it was in need of reform. Indeed, Grimbald is accorded the status approaching that of a papal legate in Fulk's letter. He is to be received with 'due honour (*cum debito honore*)' by the English who 'will observe inviolably all their days the canonical decrees (*decreta canonica*)' and apostolic teaching of the

Church as laid down by Grimbald, their 'pastor and teacher (*pastore et doctore*)'.[83] It is this exaggerated role accorded Grimbald, whereby he is expected to enforce 'canonical authority and the custom of our church' that gives this spurious document away. The Grimbald of this letter was not being sent to Alfred as a scholar who would help with the translation of philosophical and hagiographical Latin texts. The sustained argument beginning with the mission of Augustine from Pope Gregory; the subsequent falling away by the English from moral precepts; the consequent need for reform; the harking back to the apostolic authority of Peter, James, Barnabas, and Paul; the historical appeal to the authority of councils and synods to enforce canonical decrees—all of this argument rooted in the premise of an apostolic tradition, prepares the reader for Grimbald's key role as a reformer, backed by the teaching authority of the church, which can only be interpreted by way of Grimbald's episcopal power. The letter asserts that when the English have received Grimbald with due honour and promised to abide by the apostolic teaching of the church:

When they have done this with divine benediction, receiving him duly consecrated according to the ecclesiastical custom by the authority of the blessed Remigius through our ministry and the laying on of hands, and most fully instructed in all things, they are to escort him with due honour to his own see (*ad propriam sedem*) ... and be constantly instructed by his teaching and example.[84]

This is not Grimbald the mass-priest and scholar chaplain. This is Grimbald, bishop and legate extraordinary. Keynes and Lapidge departed from Whitelock's rendering of this passage and translated Fulk's words to read: 'they shall joyfully take him with the honour due to him to their own home',[85] insisting that Fulk was instructing the West Saxon delegation which had come to collect Grimbald in Francia, to take their newly acquired scholar back to England![86] But England was not Grimbald's home and the phrase *ad propriam sedem* refers to Grimbald and not to his English handlers. The *sedes* in question can only refer to a bishopric if Grimbald's extraordinary teaching authority—not to mention the laying on of hands (*impositionem manuum*)—is to make any sense. Furthermore, the English delegation was supposed to have consisted of not only 'magnates and chief men' of Alfred's kingdom, but it also included a party of *electores*,[87] who as Grierson suggested, were clearly seen to be involved in Grimbald's election to a bishopric. Keynes and Lapidge argued that these *electores* were members of a selection committee 'who had actually chosen Grimbald . . . to assist Alfred in his endeavours'.[88] None of Alfred's scholarly 'endeavours' are even obliquely referred to in this letter, and far from the English 'selectors' choosing Grimbald on their arrival in Francia, Fulk is made to say in his supposed letter that Alfred had already particularly asked for Grimbald by name when he dispatched his delegation to Rheims (*De quorum numero unum a nobis specialiter deposcitis nomine Grimbaldum*).[89] That would seem to make the role of any selection committee in Francia redundant, and we are left with the *electores* whose task it was to present Grimbald as their candidate for the episcopate, and for that solemn and sacramental laying on of hands. Grimbald's authority in this letter was to be transmitted from St Remigius through the agency of Archbishop Fulk, and the *sedes* can only refer to the *cathedra* of a bishop and the consequent apostolic authority that accompanied it. Whatever the date of this letter, Grierson's view still holds good, that Fulk expected Grimbald to be offered a bishopric by King Alfred and that Fulk intended to consecrate Grimbald himself.[90] Nelson viewed the presentation of Remigius as the apostle of the Franks as a product of renewed contacts in the 1040s between Wessex and the see of Rheims, and she suggested that the letter was forged at Winchester during the reign of Edward the Confessor.[91] Even if we were to accept that portions of this document may derive from a genuine source 'improved' in eleventh-century Winchester, we still cannot accept anything said about Grimbald at its face value, since it was the cult of Grimbald that inspired the forgery in the first instance.

Much scholarly effort has been expended on the notion that Grimbald was well placed linguistically to cope with King Alfred's translation of Latin texts into West Saxon dialect. Unfortunately, there is no firm historical basis to sustain any of the speculation regarding Grimbald's mother tongue. We have to rely on the *Vita Prima* for the statement that Grimbald was born at Thérouanne and such a statement may, as Bately wisely warned us, 'be as fabulous as any other of the details given in the *Vita*'[92]—not least of which is the erroneous date of Grimbald's death. The tradition that Grimbald was a monk of St Bertin may or may not preserve a genuine tenth-century Winchester memory of King Alfred's priest. But no one at St Bertin preserved any information on Grimbald until the twelfth century when lections for the observation of his festival were imported from England. Even if Grimbald's association with St Bertin were to be proven at some future time, Bately has shown that there is nothing to suggest that Saxon, or any form of Anglo-Saxon, was spoken in Thérouanne. Although St Bertin was within the German-speaking part of Northern France, Latin and Old French would have been the more usual languages for the inmates of such a prominent Carolingian monastery in the ninth century.[93] In short, we know nothing of Grimbald's Frankish origins, and consequently we do not know whether he spoke French or Flemish or any other Germanic dialect. We can dismiss his teaching authority and other quasi-episcopal functions as set out in Fulk's letter, as attempts in eleventh-century Winchester to glorify their monk with Alfredian connections at the expense of Canterbury. The historical Grimbald, wherever he hailed from, may have played a much more modest role in King Alfred's scholarly programme than historians relying on the *Life* of Alfred, the letter of Archbishop Fulk, and the breviary of Hyde have hitherto supposed. The close connection between this scholar and Archbishop Fulk can only by regarded as dubious. Grimbald was a visiting scholar—probably from Francia—who assisted King Alfred with the translation of the *Pastoral Care* and who died in 901 probably in a monastery in Winchester. More than this we are not entitled to say.

The *Life* of King Alfred informs us[94] that Grimbald was 'summoned' from Gaul. By implication, the priest and monk, John, was summoned from the same place. 'He [Alfred] sent messengers across the sea to Gaul to acquire teachers.

From there he summoned Grimbald. . . . and also John, likewise a priest and monk, a man of very keen intelligence and most learned in all branches of the art of literature, and skilled in many other arts.'[95] It is nowhere actually stated in the *Life* of King Alfred that this priest and monk, John from 'Gaul', was the same person as the priest and monk, John, described in chapter 94 of Alfred's *Life* as 'an Old Saxon by race (*Eald-saxonum genere*)'[96] who was appointed by Alfred as abbot of Athelney.[97] Since contradiction, duplication of records, and inconsistency are the endemic hallmarks of the Pseudo-Asser's work, there is little reason to doubt that the compiler of Alfred's *Life* had only one person called John in mind, a foreign scholar from the Carolingian Empire who helped King Alfred with his scholarly activities and who was also appointed as abbot of Athelney. For earlier in the *Life*, we are told of Grimbald and John, that the king 'endowed and honoured them with great authority (*eos magna potestate ditavit et honoravit*)',[98] so while Winchester tradition developed this concept to mean that Grimbald was offered the metropolitan see of Canterbury, the Pseudo-Asser developed his fictional tale into elevating John to the abbacy of Athelney. Whether John came from Gaul—i.e. Francia proper—or from Saxony, is impossible to decide. W. H. Stevenson was not deterred by the chaotic treatment of John in the *Life* of Alfred, from indulging in a type of speculation which he was quick to ridicule in the writings of his contemporaries: 'The choice of John the Old Saxon and Grimbald as literary assistants by the king was a very wise one, and seems to have been largely dictated by the close relationship of their native tongues with his own.'[99] Mabillon tried to reconcile the conflicting references to John's Gaulish and Saxon origins by speculating that he came from the Westphalian monastery of Corvei via the abbey of Corbie in Picardy.[100] We have even less idea of where John came from than we have of Grimbald's origins, and everything which has been written on this subject is based on the dubious and conflicting traditions preserved in the *Life* of Alfred.

We are told in chapter 92 of the *Life* of Alfred, that the saintly king, 'meditating on the needs of his soul' and being engaged 'day and night' in good works, resolved to found two monasteries—one for men and one for women. We find (in chapter 98) that the monastery for women was built 'near to the east gate of Shaftesbury (*iuxta orientalem portam Sceftesburg*)'.[101] The implication of this statement is that the nunnery was built after the fortifications of the *burh* at Shaftesbury had been constructed. We do not know precisely when that *burh* was first built, but the absence of Shaftesbury from the earliest (eleventh-century) manuscript of the *Burghal Hidage* could suggest that its fortifications were of tenth-century Edwardian date.[102] William of Malmesbury's account of an inscription to the effect that 'In the year of Our Lord's Incarnation 880, King Alfred made this town, in the eighth year of his reign' represents nothing more than later medieval antiquarian wishful thinking of a similar sort to that which prompted other medieval accounts of a supposed funerary inscription for King Arthur and Guinevere in Glastonbury.[103] Not only has William's supposed inscription few parallels in Anglo-Saxon England, but it does not survive, and besides, it contained a chronological error.[104] For AD 880 spanned Alfred's ninth and tenth years in the kingship, rather than his eighth.

Whoever drew up that inscription, assumed the first year of Alfred's reign to have begun in 872, revealing a dependence on a later (eleventh-century) version of the Chronicle such as the C text. Assuming even yet further, that Shaftesbury had indeed been fortified in 880, and assuming that the historical Asser had visited the nunnery some time between then and when he wrote in 892–3, we should not expect the need for a precise topographical location in a town which could not as yet, have had a profusion of prominent landmarks within its newly built walls. But the phrase 'near to the east gate of Shaftesbury' conveys a precise location that is suggestive of a developed urban topography replete with street patterns and a degree of structural congestion. Such a detailed topographical urban location would be more appropriate for a late tenth-century Anglo-Saxon town than for a village protected by a relatively large expanse of fortified wall. Even assuming that Alfred had, quite reasonably, founded a nunnery within the protection of a fortified place, the details of that convent's precise location as supplied by the Pseudo-Asser betray a retrospective tone.

This same retrospective tone is more developed in the Pseudo-Asser's preamble to his account of the founding of Athelney. King Alfred, we are told, could find 'no noble or freeman of his own nation who would of his own accord enter the monastic life—apart from children'.[105] The latter were unsuitable because they could not yet distinguish between good and evil. So, 'for this reason he sought to gather together monks of different race in that monastery [at Athelney]'.[106] The account is as usual flawed with inconsistency and contradiction. It was common practice for monastic houses of all shades of observance to receive oblates into their communities at an early age. The 7-year-old Bede would have been refused entry into Wearmouth had the Pseudo-Asser's rigorous attitude been applied in seventh-century Northumbria,[107] as would the (perhaps imaginary) infant Grimbald at St Bertin.[108] Boys were even a part of the reformed monastic system of the tenth century. Odo was the master of a school of the reformed monastery of Baume in early tenth-century Burgundy, where boys slept in a dormitory within close proximity to the monks.[109] About a century later we read a tale of naughty schoolboys (one of whom later became a bishop) who cracked the monastic bell at Ramsey.[110] The Pseudo-Asser makes a nonsense of his own account when he tells us that King Alfred, 'when he still had not with these [Gauls] the number he wanted, he also procured many of that same Gallic race, some of whom, being children, he ordered to be educated in that same monastery [at Athelney], and to be raised to the monastic order (*ad monachium habitum*) at a later time'.[111] So, it would seem that even if Frankish infants had not yet attained to the age of reason, their presence in Athelney was preferable to that of West Saxon children who were rejected on the grounds that they 'could not yet choose good or refuse evil'. The story is of course a nonsense, and the notion of Alfred as the monastic founder and reformer is a hagiographical accretion of the late tenth century that may bear no relationship to the historical Alfred whatever. The image of a saintly Alfred performing good works ceaselessly by day and night and striving to found monasteries in spite of a scarcity of suitable—i.e. reformed—monks is surely yet another borrowing from

Odo's *Life* of Count Gerald of Aurillac. Count Gerald, like his contemporary King Alfred, is said to have founded his own model monastery beside his castle at Aurillac, and like Alfred he found it almost impossible to recruit true monks or to achieve success with those whom he recruited.

While he went on with building the monastery he was always turning over in his mind where to find monks of good character who would live in the place according to their rule (*sub regulari proposito*). But when the rareness with which they were to be found brought home the difficulty of the task, he became anxious and did not know what to do.[112]

Count Gerald sent noble youths to be trained in the monastery at Vabres near Toulouse, but they on their return to Aurillac became lax and even their superior turned out to be a failure.[113] Gerald was reduced to lamenting the worldliness and quarrelling (*jurgia*) of his monastic recruits at Aurillac, and like Alfred, he planned his benefactions and his prayers 'by day and night':

Consequently his mind was in a turmoil day and night (*diu noctuque*), and he could not forget his wish to gather a community of monks. He often spoke of it with his household and friends (*cum domesticis et familiaribus*). He was so moved by his desire for this that sometimes he exclaimed, 'O, if it might be granted me by some means to obtain religious monks. How I would give them all I possess, and then go through life begging.'[114]

Later, towards the end of his life, Gerald was portrayed weeping in his castle at Aurillac as he looked down on his monastery. When asked why he wept, Gerald replied: 'Because I can by no means bring into effect the desire which I have long had for this place. . . . By the help of God I have easily provided all those things suitable for the use of monks; only the monks are missing; they alone could not be found, and so alone and bereaved I am worn out with sorrow.'[115]

The account of Gerald's interest in monasteries, although hagiographical, was rooted in historical reality. Later, in the middle of the tenth century, Gerbert of Aurillac, the future Silvester II, was to benefit from an education gained in the monastery founded by Count Gerald.[116] Gerald's concern for the preservation of monasticism was understandably stressed by his biographer, Odo, who was the guiding light of early tenth-century Cluniac reform. And that particular episode relating to Gerald's monastic experiment, was recorded in writing by one of the monks of Vabres who witnessed those events.[117] So the parallel sentiments and anecdotes in the *Life* of Gerald are seen to be once again primary in relation to those in the *Life* of Alfred, while the latter, written a century after Gerald's and Alfred's time, are patently derivative, and as we shall see, more developed and fantastic. If Gerald's monastic experiment caused him grief to the end of his life, Alfred's achievement was expected to surpass anything which Gerald had tried to accomplish. But just as Gerald had to cope with the laxity and quarrels of his monks, so, too, Alfred was said to have had initial setbacks. The Pseudo-Asser peopled King Alfred's monastery at Athelney exclusively with 'Gauls' and former pagans, ruled by the Old Saxon abbot, John. It was against this exotic Frankish background that Alfred's biographer regaled his readers with the bizarre tale of the monks' murderous attack upon their abbot at Athelney. And the Pseudo-Asser, as the good hagiographer that he was, introduced this squalid tale with the standard hagiographical preface to the effect that tales of 'good deeds . . . may be praised [and] followed', while tales of 'evil deeds . . . may be cursed and entirely shunned'.[118] It is not that scandalous incidents such as the murder of abbots did not occur. Abbot Athelstan of Ramsey was murdered by an Irish servant in the eleventh century,[119] and yet another foreigner at Ramsey—this time a German abbot, Wythman—was so unpopular that his monks eased him out and on to a pilgrimage to Jerusalem.[120] But the Pseudo-Asser's tale of how two Gallic slaves—servants of a Gallic monk and a deacon in the community at Athelney—waylaid the abbot while he was praying alone in the church has all the outlandish characteristics of folklore and developed hagiography. This motif of the *attack-on-the-holy-man-which-went-wrong* is firmly rooted in the hagiography of tenth-century monastic reformers rather than in a contemporary account of a late ninth-century king. Abbot John, like Columba three centuries before him, was accustomed to rise in the night when his community 'was sleeping soundly in blissful bodily peace', and enter the chapel to pray alone. But whereas Columba was observed by an admiring and aspiring novice,[121] the holy John was waylaid by those who 'were aroused by envy at the devil's prompting against their abbot'.[122] The story of the attempted murder of Abbot John is a cautionary tale directed against those who would impede monastic reform. It reminds us of Abbot Odo of Cluny whose life was threatened by the recalcitrant monks of Fleury, who initially chose to defend themselves to the death against him rather than admit Odo as a reforming abbot.[123] More immediately, it reminds us of Ælfric's tale (*c.*1000) of the abortive attempt by the unreformed clerics at Winchester to poison St Æthelwold, who with the help of King Edgar imposed the strict observance of the Rule in the Old and New Minsters in Winchester.[124] There is a significant difference in the conclusion of these tales by the Pseudo-Asser, on the one hand, and by Ælfric or John of Salerno (the biographer of St Odo) on the other. Ælfric tells us that on recovering from the poison, Bishop Æthelwold 'did not repay his poisoner with any ill'.[125] Odo of Cluny was possessed of even greater powers of forgiveness. He once rewarded a thief with five shillings for his theft of a community horse,[126] and when a felon tried to slay Odo on a Roman street in the 930s, Odo rewarded his assailant with cash and forbade Alberic of Rome from cutting off the culprit's hands.[127] The Pseudo-Asser, on the other hand, records a harsh reprisal against Abbot John's wretched assailants: 'The villains who had committed this deed, *as well as all those who had instigated so great a crime*, were captured and bound and underwent a terrible death through various tortures.'[128] This unedifying tale of gruesome revenge reflects the confusion in the mind of the Pseudo-Asser as to the precise purpose of the anecdotal padding in his *Life* of King Alfred. It is illustrative too, of the undigested mixture of hagiographical and folkloric elements in the *Life*. But the reformist tone of this tale of the attack on Abbot John cannot be doubted, and its clear distinction between English communities which were monastic only in name—and those 'properly observing the rule of this way of life' (*regulam illius* *vitae ordinabiliter tenente*)[129] places the late tenth-century consciousness of the writer in the little doubt. For although, as Wormald observed,[130] such distinctions were formally recognized in Carolingian legislation sponsored by Louis the Pious and his reforming guru, Benedict of Aniane, as early as 816–19, those initiatives had run aground even in Francia by the late ninth century. It was the Pseudo-Asser who, following the *Life* of Gerald, anachronistically ascribed to King Alfred the zeal to return to a Benedictine type *regula* in the monasteries of late ninth-century Wessex.

This is not to deny that Alfred did indeed endow monastic houses enjoying his special patronage. We should expect no less from a king who personally lamented the decline of learning and monastic scholarship. But King Alfred's own *Will* which provides a superior testimony to that of his *Life*, does not suggest that either Athelney or Shaftesbury enjoyed the king's special favour. Indeed the king's *Will* contains no mention of either monastery. The absence of any mention of these two houses, singled out by the Pseudo-Asser as the only two monastic show-pieces in Alfred's so-called reform programme, is all the more remarkable when we discover that several other monasteries do find a mention in Alfred's *Will*. The king left a bequest, as we might expect, to Winchester (i.e. to the Old Minster), involving his personal property at lower Hurstbourne in Hampshire and he confirmed or fulfilled a bequest of his father, King Æthelwulf, in favour of the same community, involving lands at Hurstbourne in Hampshire and at Chiseldon in Wiltshire.[131] Elsewhere in the *Will* he left the considerable sum of 50 pounds to the same community—'to the church in which I shall rest'.[132] He also willed that 'the community at Damerham (*þam hiwum æt Domrahamme*) be given their charters and liberty to choose whatever lord they think best, for my sake and for Ælfflæd and for the friends for whom she interceded and I intercede'.[133] The implication must be that this Damerham community in Hampshire was a nunnery which had enjoyed Alfred's special patronage and whose superior was his friend and perhaps also a kinswoman. King Alfred mentions in his *Will*, yet another community at Cheddar (*þam hiwum æt Ceodre*) with whom he had concluded an earlier agreement and to which he left an estate at Chewton in Somerset.[134]

There is a notable ambiguity in King Alfred's *Will* relating to the precise status of these communities at Cheddar, Damerham, and even at Winchester. Clearly, they must have been monastic at least in name. Their association with royal estates was in keeping with the proprietorial nature of the early English church and explains the king's special interest in these places, which he may have regarded as family monasteries in the same way as his brother Æthelred may have viewed Wimborne, or Æthelbald and Æthelberht viewed the church at Sherborne. Damerham had later associations with Alfred's grandson, King Edmund; with Edmund's queen Æthelflæd; and the place was later associated with Edmund's brother, King Eadred (died 955).[135] Cheddar was a royal estate in the tenth century and Chewton in Somerset, associated in Alfred's *Will* with the Cheddar community, belonged to Queen Edith before 1066.[136] The location of these communities either on royal estates or—as in the case of Winchester—in a town with royal associations, afforded them vital protection during prolonged period of viking attacks. The vague references to 'communities (*þa hiwan*)' in King Alfred's *Will* and their association with centres of royal power is precisely what we should expect in an age described by Eric John as having undifferentiated monastic communities housing aristocratic inmates who held property individually in a prebendary type arrangement.[137] It was a time when the notion of a corporate body of monks holding property in common and living strictly according to the reformed Rule of St Benedict was still a thing of the future. There is no mention in King Alfred's *Will* of Athelney or of Shaftesbury—neither in terms of final bequests nor in terms of confirmation of earlier grants. Nor is there any hint of the notion of reformed monastic communities enjoying the king's special favour anywhere to be found in Alfred's *Will*. If any one monastery could be argued to have enjoyed the king's special patronage, it must surely have been the Old Minster at Winchester, where he planned his burial and which was rewarded with appropriate generosity.[138] In this connection, it is significant that Count Gerald of Aurillac planned the monastery in that Frankish town to be his burial place and rewarded it accordingly in his *Will*.[139]

As for Alfred's daughter, Æthelgifu, while she may be mentioned in her father's *Will* as the middle or second (*þære medemestan*) daughter, there is no confirmation to be found there as to either her religious status or her association with Shaftesbury.[140] It was the Pseudo-Asser[141] who identified Æthelgifu with Alfred's second daughter. According to the Pseudo-Asser, King Alfred established Æthelgifu as abbess in charge of Shaftesbury, where, writing in the present tense, he informs us 'along with her dwell many other noble nuns serving God in the monastic life'.[142] We are not told whether these aristocratic sisters were 'Gauls' or former pagans, or whether (unlike their English brothers) they were daughters of Wessex who had not shied away from the monastic calling. Earlier, the Pseudo-Asser describes Æthelgifu as 'subjected and consecrated to the rules of the monastic life'.[143] The reformist emphasis here on *monasticae vitae regulis* is not only ignored in the contemporary testimony of King Alfred's *Will*, but points yet again to a later tenth-century perspective. Alfred does make a bequest to his middle daughter involving estates at Kingsclere and at Candover in Hampshire.[144] Even allowing for the possibility that it was Æthelgifu who inherited this land as the king's second daughter, there is no reference to her special status as abbess or to her supposed model community at Shaftesbury. It could be that Athelney and Shaftesbury were founded by the king after he drew up his *Will*, i.e. after *c*.888 but before Asser was supposed to have written his *Life* of King Alfred in 892–3. This does not allow much time for that 'particular occasion (*quodam tempore*)' for the community at the new foundation of Athelney—supposedly founded with the highest ideals—to go so badly off the rails.[145] King Alfred's *Will* is a composite document with later additions and revisions to earlier versions. Those earlier versions had, at the king's own command, been destroyed. The surviving document is likely to embody in its final sections what was literally the last will of the king, which could account for the presence there of bequests for his five children and for his son-in-law, Ealdorman

Æthelred of Mercia. If that is so, it is possible that Athelney and Shaftesbury were founded as monasteries after the king's death—most likely in the reign of Edward. In that case, Æthelgifu, in the tradition of many aristocratic English women, may have founded or joined a nunnery towards the end of her life and sometime in the tenth century. The absence of any bequest in Alfred's *Will* to a nunnery at Shaftesbury, stands out in marked contrast to the *Will* of Alfred's grandson, King Eadred, where we do find a bequest of 30 pounds for Shaftesbury.[146] Eadred also made a bequest to the nunnery (Nunnaminster) at Winchester which had been founded by Alfred's queen, Ealhswith, and which, significantly, had been completed, not by Alfred, but by Edward the Elder.[147]

We can never be certain when either Athelney or Shaftesbury were founded and their earliest charters offer us little comfort in this respect. The earliest supposed charter for Athelney[148] in which King Alfred allegedly granted lands at Sutton in Somerset to Athelney Abbey is dated to 852 when Alfred was back in his legendary and precocious infancy. The fourth indiction might indicate that the years 871 or 886 were meant.[149] But Alfred only became king in 871 and his earliest association with the swamps of Athelney was in 878. If we opt for 886 on the other hand, then we have to explain the presence of the name of Bishop Ealhfrith of Winchester (*Elfred* or *Ealferd*) in the witness list, who died in 877—a year before Alfred's earliest association with Athelney.[150] The earliest Alfredian grant to Shaftesbury[151] is equally suspect. Even the trusting Finberg observed that this charter contained interpolations relating to the three fines for obstructing justice, forcible entry, and breach of the king's protection.[152] We might add that the statement in this charter, that Æthelgifu had taken the veil at Shaftesbury because of her poor health, is another indication of the fictional nature of this document.[153] Such references are rare in ninth-century charters, and besides, if Æthelgifu were indeed a weakling, she would have offered poor material for establishing a fervent community about to enforce the rigour of the Benedictine Rule. The reference to Æthelgifu's infirmity in this charter is suggestive of a later tradition. It may be that Æthelgifu's genuine connection with Shaftesbury began after her father's death in the reign of Edward, or that there is no historical basis for her connection with that nunnery at all. It could be that the later association of Queen Ælfgifu, the wife of King Edmund, who was buried at Shaftesbury in 944[154] and who was later venerated there as a saint, prompted speculation of an earlier Alfredian connection through the similarity of the name of Edmund's queen and of the name of his aunt, Æthelgifu, the daughter of King Alfred. The chronicler, Æthelweard, vouches for the fact that miracles were believed to be still taking place at Ælfgifu's tomb at Shaftesbury at the time when he was writing—the same time in fact, when the Pseudo-Asser was compiling his *Life* of Alfred.[155] Such wilful and random confusion of people and places is endemic in the Pseudo-Asser's work, and later genuine tenth-century historical associations were frequently used and distorted by him as part of his capricious and fictional reconstruction of the Alfredian era.[156]

Whatever the precise origins of the monasteries of Athelney and Shaftesbury, we cannot prove a historical Alfredian connection with either house, much less establish that Alfred intended these places to represent the cutting edge of a notional monastic reform in late ninth-century England. We cannot ascribe to Alfred the reforming zeal of a Louis the Pious. Indeed, we have already seen[157] that Alfred may have benefited from the demise of monastic communities under the pressure of the viking wars, by appropriating monastic estates for the royal fisc. The notion of the saintly and reforming Alfred belongs essentially to the writings of the Pseudo-Asser. The 'genuine' Alfred was much more concerned with his own personal pursuit of scholarship and with the dissemination of learning rather than with spiritual development *per se*. The chaos and dislocation suffered by monastic communities in Francia, England, and Ireland, during the height of the viking invasions in the late ninth century, meant that sheer survival rather than reform or a return to the *regula* was the overriding priority. Everything that we know independently of monasticism from all three societies suggests that reform programmes were born during the period of reconstruction from the second quarter of the tenth century onwards. In his very self-conscious analysis of the state of monasticism in Alfredian England, the Pseudo-Asser betrays his distant perspective on the times which he describes. He speculates that the reason for the decline in the observation of the monastic *rule* was due either to 'onslaughts of foreigners, who very often invaded by land or sea, or on account of the nation's too great abundance of riches of every kind'.[158] Significantly, he then opts for the 'abundance of riches' as the main cause of monastic decline which must be a nonsense for a late ninth-century context, when the magnates of Wessex had been enduring a sustained assault from viking armies which had carried off their movable wealth, including their workforce and livestock, and which had milked the church and aristocracy of its coin and precious metal.[159] We recall that Alfred's own episcopal friend, Bishop Wærferth of Worcester, testified to the financial crisis endured by the church in Mercia 'because of the very pressing affliction and immense tribute of the barbarians, in that same year when the pagans stayed in London [872]'.[160] Contemporary Frankish evidence from the early tenth century lays the blame for the disintegration of monastic life and ideals firmly on the viking invaders of the century before. The *Life* of Odo of Cluny, for instance, states that when the community of Fleury reassembled at their monastic home on the Loire after a period of disperal 'far and wide' in the face of viking attack 'it was united in body but with divided minds that they occupied again that holy place'.[161] Such a community, the narrator informs us, was in urgent need of moral regeneration. While it is unquestionably true that monastic fervour and spiritual idealism had already declined in the West before the arrival of viking invaders, it is equally true that the Northmen delivered a mortal blow to monastic organization and to the agrarian infrastructure so vital for sustaining the monastic economy. Monastic treasuries and sometimes whole communities at Tours, Fleury, Noirmoutier, and Limoges— to name but some major centres—were scattered or went into hiding at various times during the viking wars. Such dislocation—however temporary—was detrimental to a way of life which was constructed around the rigid pursuit of a daily timetable involving physical as well as spiritual exercises. It was detrimental, too, for the management of monastic estates, whose leaders had fled and whose servile workforce were preyed upon by viking slave-raiders. The same must certainly have been true of coastal and other isolated monasteries throughout Wessex and Kent, and it was only those centres such as Canterbury, Winchester, or Worcester, which enjoyed royal support and the security of fortifications, which had any real hope of maintaining continuity throughout the latter half of the ninth century.

However complex the evidence may be, it does not point to decadent monastic communities wallowing in the supposed luxury of Alfredian Wessex as the Pseudo-Asser suggests. It may be that Alfred's own reference to 'churches filled with treasures (*maðma*)' in his prefatory letter or prose preface to the *Pastoral Care* prompted the Pseudo-Asser to attribute pre-Alfredian monastic decline to an 'abundance of riches (*divitiarum abundantia*)'.[162] It is conceivable that Alfred may have surrounded himself by a small band of clerics and monks of proven reputation in his retreat at Athelney just as he may have assembled some of his family and many of his most loyal retainers there at that time. The name *Athelney* ('island of the *æthelings* or princes') may derive from Alfred's stay there in 878.[163] But Athelney was very much a passing phase in the military career of the king, and however safe a base it provided for the remnants of a royal army in a desperate situation, it could never have been a secure location for a monastery during the height of the Viking wars—isolated as it was on the very fringes of Wessex. Alfred had sought out the marshes of Athelney in desperation, and such locations—as the ninth-century Fenland monks of Crowland and elsewhere had also learnt—provided no safe haven without constant military protection. As Alfred regained his hold on his kingdom, it is much more likely that the monks who enjoyed his special support would have been located in the towns at the heart of his realm, or near to, or on, his royal estates. It is more likely, that as the cult of Alfred developed in the decades after the king's death, a community was founded in Athelney to commemorate Alfred's association with that place, in a time when under the rule of Edward the Elder or of Athelstan, Athelney had become a safer place for monks to reside in. Alfred's chief preoccupation with monasticism must have been to conserve what little had remained, rather than launch out on the foundation of costly new and risky ventures. It is also highly unlikely that the king would have been imbued with a sense of monastic reform by way of strict observance of the Benedictine Rule, in an age when such programmes had been otherwise lost under the collapse of the Carolingian Empire, and in the face of a permanent emergency created by viking attack. The Pseudo-Asser's suggestion, then, that Alfred was striving to rescue English monasticism from the corrosive effects of luxurious living, reveals an attitude of mind more appropriate to the period of recovery and reconstruction in the later tenth century.

The Pseudo-Asser's wicked society which treated the monastic life with disrepect through 'an abundance of riches' was much more akin to that community of 'evil-living clerics (*malemorigerati clerici*), possessed by pride, insolence and wanton behaviour to such an extent that several of them . . . were continually given over to gluttony and drunkenness' which Bishop Æthelwold encountered in late tenth-century Winchester.[164] Keynes and Lapidge were of the opinion that 'Asser's' comments on the decline of monasticism 'were prompted by Alfred, who seems to have made similar remarks in a letter to Fulco, archbishop of Rheims (as reported in Fulco's reply)'.[165] But Archbishop Fulk's letter can be shown to be no more authentic than the writings of the Pseudo-Asser, and one dubious document cannot be used to shore up the crumbling evidence of another. What can be said however, is that concern for ecclesiastical reform in the letter attributed to Archbishop Fulk shares a similar reformist mentality of the early eleventh century as exhibited in the Pseudo-Asser's *Life* of Alfred. The long digression in the *Life* of Alfred on the monks of Athelney only serves to highlight the biographer's poverty of information relating to Alfred's own all-important association with that place. In contrast to the Pseudo-Asser's derivative account of Alfred's military campaign from Athelney in 878, and the hagiographical tale of Abbot John, the compiler of the Anglo-Saxon Chronicle drew on a circumstantial, if heavily edited account of the Athelney campaign of 878, which was replete with a string of West Country place-names and a detailed timetable of events. The Pseudo-Asser had nothing to add to the Chronicle's account apart from the topographical padding relating to the isolation of the swamp at Athelney itself.[166] The Pseudo-Asser's tale of the goings-on in Athelney among wicked foreign monks who attacked Abbot John, is fundamentally no different from his outlandish folk-tale of the wicked Mercian queen, Eadburh, who poisoned her husband, King Beorhtric, supposedly in the days before Alfred was even born.

The recognition that the tale of Abbot John's adventures at Athelney belong to a fictitious world of hagiography and folklore, and that neither Athelney nor Shaftesbury may have even been founded as monastic communities during Alfred's reign, does not necessarily diminish our estimation of the king. The relegation of Alfred's scholarly helpers—the Mass-priests, Grimbald and John—to their original status as named helpers of unknown origin, who were politely acknowledged, only once, in a preface of the king, cannot effect in any way our assessment of Alfred's own extraordinary scholarly achievements. The realization that the names of these two men, together with the more shadowy figures of the Mercian priest-chaplains, Æthelstan and Wærwulf, mentioned by the Pseudo-Asser, were all wilfully used by the compilers of the witness lists to bogus charters, serves only to clear away the excrescence of half-truth which for too long has choked up Alfredian studies. It is not even necessary to hold that all charters containing the names of Æthelstan and Wærwulf are fraudulent. Because the author of King Alfred's *Life* almost certainly had access to the Worcester archive, he could well have have lifted names of priests from genuine charters which he uncovered there, and his inclusion of the names of those men in the fictional Alfredian seminar would then have ensured the proliferation of their names in later bogus witness lists which clearly did rely on the Pseudo-Asser's *Life* of Alfred. We know from Alfred's *Will* that he was generous to monastic foundations which had a claim on his patronage. We know from the king's scholarly writings that he lamented the decline in English monastic learning and the physical destruction of church treasures.

We know, too, that Alfred stood apart from the great majority of early medieval rulers in that he had a genuine passion for learning and for mastering the book knowledge of Late Antiquity. He himself acknowledges the help of his archbishop, Plegmund; of his bishop, Asser; and of his Mass-priests, Grimbald and John. It is clear that those men helped him with his translation of Gregory's *Pastoral Care*, and no doubt with some other works as well. The mischief accomplished by the author of the *Life* of Alfred and by the forger of the letter from Archbishop Fulk was to draw historians' attention away from the scholarly Alfred to that of an imaginary monastic reformer who employed Grimbald and John not as his scholarly assistants, but as envoys extraordinary from Francia and the archdiocese of Rheims—who had a brief to impose orthodoxy on a supposedly backward Anglo-Saxon Church, and to found monasteries as flagships of what was essentially a late tenth-century ideal of Monastic Reform. To free Alfred from this web of ecclesiastical propaganda and anachronism—not to say hagiographical deformity—is to allow us to see the king in isolation from, and towering above his more modest scholarly helpers, and consequently to view him in a more searching light. Far from diminishing our understanding of Alfred, the rejection of the image of the retarded hagiographical king, surrounded by his improbable reforming minions, liberates us to concentrate on an assessment of the historical Alfred through his own extensive writings which he has left behind.

XI

A Lot of Latin and Less Greek

Pathways to a Thousand-Year-Old Forgery

GALBRAITH'S IDEAS ON THE SPURIOUS NATURE OF ASSER'S *LIFE* OF King Alfred were hunted down and slain by critics who focused on his erroneous notion that the *Life* was forged by Leofric, bishop of Exeter in the middle of the eleventh century. It was a curious judgement on the part of a formidable historian to attribute the *Life* of Alfred to a mid-eleventh-century bishop, particularly since Stevenson had already discounted that possibility on the grounds that the date of the lost manuscript of Asser's *Life* most likely pre-dated the transference of the see of Crediton to Exeter by half a century.[1] Inevitably, once Galbraith's identification of Leofric as the forger had been discredited, his more important ideas on the doubtful status of the *Life* as contemporary biography were quickly swept to one side. It is not of course necessary to identify a forger in order to prove the bogus nature of his fabrication. However, in view of the central position which the *Life* of King Alfred enjoys in Anglo-Saxon scholarship and in Early English historiography generally, it is incumbent on anyone who questions the authenticity of Asser's authorship of the *Life*, to suggest who the forger might have been, or to point at least, to the circle to which he belonged. It is essential, too, to outline, however tentatively, the wider cultural and political background in which the notion of writing such a spurious *Life* was born. Thus far, our examination of Alfred's *Life* has revealed some crucial information, which is of a different nature from the objections which were put forward by Galbraith, but which are essentially supportive of his view of Alfred's *Life* as a forgery. The accounts of the king's childhood, of his education, and of his various illnesses, reveal definite and repeated folklóric and hagiographical elements together with a contradictory narration that are inconsistent with the author's claim to be writing the biography of a friend who was still living. We saw furthermore, that when we remove these clearly identifiable fictional elements from Alfred's *Life*, the account of Alfred's career prior to becoming king is reduced to the bare bones of the Anglo-Saxon Chronicle's narrative. This in turn revealed that the Chronicle had been pressed into service by the author in order to supply a crucial framework to a narrative which was otherwise lacking in historical information. Once we abandon the notion of the *Life* of Alfred as being a contemporary account, we also, in effect, relinquish the idea of Asser's authorship. The account of Alfred's illnesses, his interest in the establishment of a reformed monastic community, and numerous specific motifs in his *Life*, such as the tale of Æthelred's refusal to abandon the Mass in the face of imminent viking attack—are all closely paralleled in the *Life* of Count Gerald of Aurillac, which was written between 936 and 942.[2] The motifs and ideas which are paralleled in both works are, as we have seen, set in a primary context in the *Life* of Gerald, while in Alfred's *Life*, these same motifs are derivative and sometimes— as in the case of the *Æthelred-at-Mass* episode—they are displaced. Other aspects of Alfred's *Life*—especially those passages relating to his interest in monastic foundations—reveal an attitude appropriate to the era of English Monastic Reform in the late tenth and early eleventh centuries.

On entering this most hazardous stage of the study, we are looking for a late tenth-century writer who had an interest in biography and hagiography, and whose Latin prose showed strong Frankish influences in vocabulary and hagiographical motifs, which was suggestive of an education either in Francia or at the hands of a Frankish master. We seek too, a writer whose Anglo-Latin mannerisms owed much to a long-established bombastic and convoluted prose style stretching back to Aldhelm in the seventh century, reinforced by hermeneutic usage imported from Fleury in the tenth.[3] We need also to keep in mind that the Pseudo-Asser's own personal ambition as a writer, far outstretched his ability to organize material or to sustain a coherent narrative free of irritating digressions. We shall also be looking, at the conclusion of this point in our study, for a writer with some know-ledge of Old Welsh or Cornish, and who also had an interest in the etymology of place-names.

We begin with the *Life* of Count Gerald of Aurillac in the French Auvergne. Gerald was almost the exact contemporary of King Alfred. He was born in 855 and died, most probably, on 13 October 909—coincidentally in the same year as the historical Bishop Asser of Sherborne. His *Life*, written by Odo, abbot of Cluny, in *c*.940, is a near-contemporary work compiled by one of the founding fathers of the Cluniac monastic reform movement. Its purpose was to demonstrate not only the sanctity of Gerald but to show to monks and recalcitrant canons in Francia, that even high-born laymen were capable of achieving great sanctity while immersed in worldly preoccupations. Hagiographical this work may be, but its author interviewed several witnesses who had personal knowledge of Count Gerald, some of whom were monks and some of whom were aristocratic laymen. It tells a tale of a saintly magnate of Aquitane who grew up with a sweetness and modesty of mind, but whose parents—like those of Alfred—neglected his education—to the extent that in Gerald's case he was only allowed to study the Psalter.[4] Like Alfred, too, Gerald's adolescence was spent in aristocratic pursuits with his hunting dogs, archery, and falcons. Gerald was plagued by sickness in early youth, and just as Alfred was tormented by piles, so too, Gerald was covered by pustules (*pustulis*) or boils which rendered him unsuited to worldly affairs and enabled him to return to study. He mastered Gregorian chant and grammar, and like Alfred he performed the Divine Office and prayed in chapel alone at night. Gerald recited the Psalms and learnt a whole series of the Scriptures which put his contemporary 'clerical smatterers' to shame.[5] Like Alfred, too, Gerald struggled to preserve his chastity and after a partial succumbing to temptation he was stricken with blindness from a cataract for more than a whole year. Just as Alfred prayed for a disease which 'would not be outwardly visible on his body' so as to render him useless for public office, so too, the long-suffering Count Gerald had his blindness concealed 'with the greatest care' by his followers 'from the peering eyes of strangers'. Gerald succeeded to his father's office but accepted his responsibilities as a reluctant ruler, torn by the tensions between worldly rule and the cultivation of the inner life.[6] So too, the saintly Alfred, although allegedly far better qualified for kingship than his older brothers, did, according to the Pseudo-Asser, come eventually to rule 'almost unwillingly'.[7] Alfred was also, exactly like Gerald, beset by tensions caused by the demands of his worldly office—tensions which were in conflict with the king's natural desire for study and contemplation.[8]

Gerald was a conscientious judge who upheld the cause of the poor and the weak, and who fasted before presiding over his law-court,[9] and although he did not himself write or publish works of learning, he was portrayed none the less as a great scholarly ruler. Like King Alfred, Count Gerald had works read aloud to him, and he divided his time between prayer and contemplation on the one hand, and a busy life of a secular lord and administrator on the other. Gerald's hall was transformed into a seminar where meals were taken listening to readings or to commentaries on readings by those so qualified in learning. Like Alfred, Gerald carefully planned the building of a model monastery which he found difficult to staff with suitably spiritually-minded monks, and like Alfred, he carefully provided for the church and the poor during his life and in his *Will*. Gerald was a lover of pilgrimage journeying to Tours and to Limoges, and like Alfred he visited distant Rome.[10] A detailed study of Odo's *Life* of Gerald shows beyond question that it provided Alfred's biographer with material for the life of that English king. No other account of an early medieval ruler resembles that of the Pseudo-Asser's *Life* of King Alfred more closely than Odo's tenth-century *Life* of Count Gerald. For although Carolingian royal biographies had an obvious influence on Alfred's biographer, nevertheless Alfred's *vita* was essentially hagiographical. As such, the *Life* of Alfred belongs to a genre which is spiritual rather than secular, and it displays few of those pretentions to Roman imperialism which are the hallmark of its Carolingian counterparts. Gerald's *Life* provided an obvious model for a monastic biographer who wished to invest Alfred with saintly qualities—for Gerald, although a saint, was remarkable also for being, like Alfred, a secular lord. Not only did the overall picture of the sickly and saintly scholarly ruler provide what may be described as the major 'original contribution' of the Pseudo-Asser to the *Life* of Alfred, but countless details in the *Life* of Count Gerald have been replicated in Alfred's *Life*. We have already encountered detailed comparisons between the illnesses and education of the two men, and between detailed motifs such as that of the ruler who risked capture or death at the hands of his attacking enemies rather than abandon his presence at Mass during the attack. There are several other detailed comparisons whose significance are best discussed in relation to the identification of the author of the *Life* of Alfred. At this point we need to ask how this *Life* of Count Gerald, if it inspired key elements within the *Life* of Alfred, could ever have reached the hands of Alfred's biographer?

Odo who wrote the *Life* of Gerald had been abbot, first of Baume and later of Cluny in Burgundy. As second abbot of Cluny, he was the successor of Berno (910–26) who, under the auspices of Duke William of Aquitane, began the whole reforming process of Frankish monasteries.[11] Odo was remembered for reforming monasteries in Rome, but he also initiated the reform of monasteries in Aquitane including that at Tulle which lay deep in the Massif Central, half-way between Limoges and Gerald's castle at Aurillac. Odo, like Count Gerald, was deeply immersed in the affairs of Aquitane. Odo's father had been a friend of Duke William of Aquitane, the founder of Cluny, and Odo had as a youth been brought up at Duke William's court.[12] Later in life he had contacts across the Massif with monks at Tulle and Limoges and through discussions with members of those communities who had either known Gerald of Aurillac personally or by repute, he was encouraged to write the *Life* of that count. The most important Frankish monastery which Odo reformed and ruled as abbot—at some personal risk to himself—was Fleury on the Loire. Fleury boasted to be the custodian of the relics of St Benedict of Monte Casino—the father of Western monasticism. Later in the tenth century, Fleury was ruled by Abbo, one of the finest scholars of his day.

With Fleury and its brilliant scholar, Abbo, we arrive at the connection between the *Lives* of Count Gerald of Aurillac and his biographer, Odo of Cluny, on the one hand, and the English environment which produced the *Life* of King Alfred, on the other. England's connection with the house of Fleury went back into the second quarter of the tenth century in the person of Archbishop Oda of Canterbury (941–58). Oda, who became bishop of Ramsbury (in Wiltshire) in *c*.926 was the confidant of Alfred's grandson, King Athelstan. Bishop Oda may even have fought alongside Athelstan at Brunanburh in 937 when the English king overthrew a combined force of Danes and Scots which challenged Athelstan's claim to rule Northumbria, if not indeed all England.[13] In 941 Oda became archbishop of Canterbury and was a leading figure in negotiating a peace between the new and young king, Edmund, and the Danes of York. Oda, perhaps independently of St Dunstan, was one of the first ecclesiastical reformers in tenth-century England who laid the foundations not only of monastic reform but of the rebuilding of an English Church, badly mauled by the viking wars of the previous century. He went to Francia in 936 as one of Athelstan's ambassadors to Hugh, Duke of the Franks, who negotiated the restoration of Athelstan's nephew—the Carolingian Louis d'Outremer—as King of Francia.[14] Duke Hugh was a patron of Fleury which had just been recently reformed by Abbot Odo of Cluny, and it was at Fleury, probably in 936, that Bishop Oda of Ramsbury took his vows of obedience to the Rule of St Benedict. That at any rate would seem to be the reasonable deduction from Byrhtferth of Ramsey's statement in his *Life* of St Oswald that Oda *suscepit monasticae religionis habitum* at Fleury.[15] Later, as Archbishop of Canterbury, Oda was in an even more powerful position to push forward his reforming ideals for English monasticism. In 952 Oda sent his nephew, Oswald, to study at Fleury for six years and that same Oswald was later to become bishop of Worcester (961) and eventually, Archbishop of York (971).[16] Archbishop Oda, before his death in 958, had acquired the site of the ruined monastery of Ely, and he showed a special interest in the restoration of Mercian and East Anglian monasteries of the Danelaw. If Byrhtferth, the biographer of Archbishop Oswald,[17] was correct in believing that Oda was the son of a Danish invader from the notorious Great Army of Ivar and Ubba back in 865,[18] then perhaps Oda saw it as his special mission to rebuild that English monastic church so brutally crushed by his own kinsmen. In August 968, Oda's nephew, Bishop Oswald of Worcester, raised the battle-standard of the *milites Dei* in the Danelaw with his founding or refounding of the monastery of Ramsey in Huntingdonshire with the help of his friend and patron, Ealdorman Æthelwine of East Anglia.[19] The founding of Ramsey was one of the major turning-points in early English religious and cultural history. Neither Canterbury, York, nor Winchester could rival this isolated monastic settlement in the claim that Ramsey, more than any other centre, was responsible for the consolidation and dissemination of a distinctly English scholarly and monastic culture which was to endure the second wave of Danish conquest under Cnut, and whose legacy was to survive the Norman Conquest as well.

The new community at Ramsey had been transferred to there *en masse* from Oswald's reformed monastery at Westbury-on-Trym, near Bristol, where its monks had been trained by Oswald's helper, Germanus. This former Winchester priest had also studied and trained as a monk at Fleury in the period *c*.950–8, before being appointed by Oswald as prior of Westbury.[20] Germanus was moved quickly from Westbury to Ramsey in 968, and after only a year at Ramsey, he was on the move again to become abbot of Winchcombe. Germanus was expelled from Winchcombe in 975 during the upheavals which followed the death of King Edgar, and he retreated back to Fleury. Bishop Oswald soon summoned Germanus back from Francia to help consolidate monastic reform in the English Midlands and East Anglia, and he returned to Ramsey late in 975. Germanus witnesses charters as abbot of Ramsey from 988–9 until 993, but he may have ruled as abbot from much earlier.[21] Not long after the refounding of Ramsey, its role as a leading centre of scholarship and Latin learning in England was assured by the arrival of Abbo of Fleury who spent two years there from *c*.985 until 987.[22] Abbo was already an established scholar by the time he arrived at Ramsey, having studied at Rheims and at Paris and being by now head of the monastic school at Fleury. While at Ramsey, Abbo compiled works on astronomy, a poem on Ramsey, and a treatise on Grammar. More significantly, he composed the *Passio* or *Passion* of the saint and king, Edmund of East Anglia—a contemporary of King Alfred—who had been slain by the Danes in 869. This *Life* of Edmund, the materials of which had been supplied to Abbo by Archbishop Dunstan of Canterbury (yet another champion of monastic reform) served a dual purpose. It obviously served a general spiritual purpose to illustrate the virtues of a heroic Christian king. But personal edification was not the sole function of this production. Abbo's biography of King Edmund—

compiled with only a kernel of historical material—was designed to show would-be English hagiographers how spiritual biography could be used as a tool to further the aims of ecclesiastical reformers. The *Passion* of St Edmund was to provide inspiration for a much more comprehensive biographical collection designed to provide an ideology and a sense of purpose to the entire programme of monastic and spiritual regeneration. As that movement entered on its secondary phase, when the age of its saintly founders—Oda, Dunstan, Æthelwold, and Oswald—was past, Abbo's *Passion* of St Edmund was joined by the *Lives* of St Dunstan, St Æthelwold, and St Oswald, as well as *lives* of earlier figures which were forged at this time, as part of a great literary drive to shore up the spiritual and cultural recovery of the Anglo-Saxon soul in the aftermath of the viking onslaught. One of those inventions was Byrhtferth of Ramsey's *Life* of St Ecgwine, a shadowy early eighth-century bishop of Worcester. Another such bogus production was, as we shall see, the *Life* of King Alfred.

Abbo of Fleury's time at Ramsey constitutes a milestone in the history of Anglo-Latin biography and hagiography. For Abbo's pupil, Byrhtferth of Ramsey, was to follow his Frankish master's lead and make biography the characteristic genre of the second generation of monastic reformers in late tenth- and early eleventh-century England. Byrhtferth of Ramsey is known for his mathematical and astronomical work in his *Manual* or *Enchiridion* which was intended as a handbook to the *Computus*, written partly in Latin and partly in English.[23] He has been identified as the author of the *Life* of St Oswald who founded Byrhtferth's house at Ramsey and of whom Byrhtferth had personal knowledge.[24] Lapidge identified Byrhtferth as the author of the *Life* of St Ecgwine, the third bishop of Worcester, who ruled that diocese in the early eighth century and who was supposed to have founded the monastery of Evesham.[25] Hart and Lapidge independently demonstrated that the *Historical Miscellany* or Northumbrian Chronicle, which makes up the first five sections in the *Historia Regum* attributed to Symeon of Durham (*HR* 1), was also compiled by Byrhtferth of Ramsey.[26] That work contains the earliest surviving version, in summary, from the *Life* of King Alfred. The greatest Frankish influence on Byrhtferth's career must have been that of his teacher, Abbo of Fleury. Byrhtferth inherited from Abbo his obsession with elementary mathematics, astronomy, and natural science generally. But he also absorbed a passion for hagiography and biography which must have been fired by Byrhtferth's own vivid historical imagination. That historical imagination, as we shall see, was to induce Byrhtferth to overstep the bounds of historical writing and take on, in the case of the *Life* of Ecgwine, the role of the forger.

Abbo was not the only Frankish influence from the monastery of Fleury which was at work on Byrhtferth and his scholarly circle. Byrhtferth's master and hero, Bishop Oswald, whose *Life* Byrhtferth was eventually to write, had studied at Fleury for several years, and Byrhtferth's abbot at Ramsey, Germanus, had visited and studied at Fleury on at least two occasions. Bishop Oswald's nephew, another Oswald, who became a monk of Ramsey during Byrhtferth's time there, and who was believed to have been the author of several works (since lost), had also studied at Fleury.[27] Ramsey, at the turn of the millennium, was, in an intellectual and spiritual sense, as closely connected with Fleury, as say, the monastery of Worcester was with Ramsey.[28] So many key people at Ramsey had had personal contacts with Fleury or had been trained there as monks and scholars, that Byrhtferth, his contemporaries, and pupils must have had access not only to Frankish tutors, but also to the many books which those tutors had taken as essential equipment in their baggage. Books and learning were at the heart of Cluniac and related reform movements. John of Salerno informs us that St Odo took a hundred volumes from the library of the monastery of Tours to help equip the monastic school at Baume in Burgundy when he became master there.[29] We learn from the *Life* of Oswald that the founding fathers of Ramsey presented that monastery with gospel books and we can be certain that an excellent library was included among those 'glorious gifts' which it received on its foundation.[30] The wide reading and diffuse scholarly interests of Byrhtferth would alone vouch for the finest library being at Ramsey at the turn of the millenium. In later times, a Ramsey chronicler could inform his readers that in the monastic archives (*in archivis nostris*) the monks preserved a book of verses written by Oswald, a nephew of the saintly founder of Ramsey.[31] That late ninth-century Ramsey writer had been educated at Fleury, and it may well be that his literary output at Ramsey had been greater than has hitherto been recognized. A lavishly endowed foundation such as Ramsey—with its sumptuous altar and expensive organ—was likely to attract more books to its library rather than less, as its reputation became established. We know that Bishop Ælfweard of London presented his books, in a moment of pique in 1044, to Ramsey Abbey rather than to Evesham as might have been expected.[32] That bishop Ælfweard also presented Ramsey with the blood-stained cowl which had covered the head of Archbishop Ælfheah at that moment when, thirty-two years before, he was butchered by a Danish army in 1012.[33] The archbishop's tormentors were successors of those same *pagani* whose menacing deeds appear on almost every page of the Pseudo-Asser's text. Such a gift reminds us how mementos of those holy men who had stood out heroically against Nordic paganism were treasured by reformed monks throughout the eleventh century in England. And gifts such as Bishop Ælfweard's library, which would have benefited the pupils of Byrhtferth and the younger Oswald, had been undoubtedly coming Ramsey's way ever since the piety of St Oswald and the erudition of Abbo of Fleury had established the reputation of Ramsey as a leading centre of learning and scholarly writing in Anglo-Saxon England. Books taken by Fleury monks to Ramsey could have included not only Einhard's *Life* of Charlemagne and the *Life* of Alcuin, which were used by the Pseudo-Asser, but also the writings of St Odo of Cluny, and particularly Odo's biography of the saintly Count Gerald of Aurillac and perhaps John of Salerno's *Life* of Abbot Odo. For Odo of Cluny, even more than the founding abbot, Berno, was viewed by his successors as the instigator and apostle of Monastic Reform, and it was Odo rather than Berno, who had taken Fleury in hand, and given it back its monastic way of life.[34] Odo's literary works must have been dear to Abbo of Fleury's heart, and they provided him with models for the task ahead in England—

namely the writing up of the *Lives* of those English holy men which would provide an inspiration to the disciples of Monastic Reform among the Anglo-Saxons. Odo of Cluny is of interest not only for his sanctity and role as a reformer. He was also the exponent of a newly developing style of Latin writing—a style with roots in the Late Antique and Early Medieval past, but one which developed its own abstruse qualities in early tenth-century Francia. The main features of this hermeneutic style were 'the ostentatious parade of unusual, often very arcane and apparently learned vocabulary'.[35] The characteristic hallmarks of that vocabulary were archaisms—even by the standards of Classical writers, neologisms or made-up words, and loan-words—especially words culled from Greek lexicons or Greek glossaries. Archbishop Oda of Canterbury, who may well have had personal knowledge of Odo of Cluny—and who certainly studied with members of his community—was a leading practitioner of the hermeneutic style of Latin in mid-tenth-century England,[36] while St Oswald who had studied for even longer at Fleury must also have known and practised this style of writing. Ramsey from the time of Abbo of Fleury's teaching there had become the major centre of the hermeneutic school of Latinists in England, as the writings of its star performer, Byrhtferth, amply demonstrate.

If the Pseudo-Asser's *Life* of King Alfred were written in a late tenth- or early eleventh-century Ramsey milieu, we should expect that work to contain Frankish loan-words of that time, and also to exhibit many if not all the characteristics of the hermeneutic style. This can indeed be shown to have been the case. Stevenson itemized some ten or twelve distinctively Frankish words in the *Life* of King Alfred which he considered to have been borrowed by the historical Bishop Asser either through his own personal contact with Francia or through 'foreign clerks in Alfred's service'—no doubt in Stevenson's mind, the elusive Grimbald and John, whose apocryphal careers have caused so much distortion in the historiography of ninth-century England.[37] Remarkably, Stevenson suggested that three of the Frankish borrowings in the *Life* of Alfred—*indiculus* ('letter'), *gronnosa* ('marshy, swampy'), and *famina* ('words, conversation') were tenth-century Frankish borrowings into Anglo-Latin writings—in spite of the fact that such an admission argued against his own sustained thesis for a ninth-century date for the *Life* of Alfred.[38] Furthermore, Stevenson believed that the Frankish-Latin *gronna* and *gronnosa* had been imported from the Fleury school of writers—the same which enjoyed such influence in late tenth-century Ramsey.[39] And in the case of *famina* Stevenson observed that although this word had been used by Aldhelm, its most prevalent English context was the late tenth-century 'when it came into use again . . . with other Frankish-Latin words'.[40] The implication must be that, in Stevenson's view, there was no continuity of use of regard to such a word by English writers of Latin, and therefore if the word were indeed reintroduced in the tenth century, we ought not to expect to find it in genuine ninth-century texts. *Famen* occurs in a charter of King Edgar for AD 964; and in Frithegod's *Life* of St Wilfrid. It also appears in the *B Life* of St Dunstan, in the *Chronicle* of Æthelweard, and in the *B* author's letter to Archbishop Æthelgar of Canterbury.[41] These are mostly the works of late tenth-

or early eleventh-century writers. Frithegod, who was the earliest of this group of authors, was the disciple of Archbishop Oda of Canterbury and was steeped in the hermeneutic style of tenth-century Anglo-Latin.[42] The *B* author of Dunstan's *Life*, who wrote *c*. AD 1000, was also a leading exponent of the hermeneutic style.[43] *Famen*—a word of Late Classical Latin origin—was a Frankish borrowing or reintroduction into English tenth-century Latin.[44] The adverb *oppido* ('very much, exceedingly') on the other hand, was a genuine archaism in the Pseudo-Asser's text. That same archaism, *oppido*, appears also in Byrhtferth's *Life* of St Oswald.[45]

The evidence from English charters is strongly against any argument for continuity between earlier so-called 'hisperic' forms of Anglo-Latin usage and the hermeneutic style proper, of later tenth-century England. Frankish influence on English Latin documents, especially charters, can be seen to develop from modest beginnings in the charters of Alfred's grandson, Athelstan (924–39) leading up to a more fully blown ornate style in those of King Edgar (959–75). The appearance of this hermeneutic element in English Latin charters in the second quarter of the tenth century was a new phenomenon, and Lapidge suggested with good reason, that it may have owed its origin and introduction to the influence of Bishop Oda on Athelstan's writing office.[46] Clearly, Alfred's *Life* belongs to a different genre to that of Anglo-Latin charters, but when viewed against the Latin usage of charters, the *Life* of Alfred would be conspicuously out of place in a ninth-century English context, and entirely at home in a late tenth- or early eleventh-century English environment. To argue otherwise demands an explanation for why a work of such profound significance as the *Life* of Alfred had so little stylistic influence on late ninth- and early tenth-century Anglo-Latin writing—including charters—and why if the *Life* of Alfred were indeed from the late ninth century do scholars then argue that an identical Latin style of writing was reintroduced into England at the end of the tenth century? For were it not for their obsession with linking Alfred's *Life* to the 'genuine Asser', Anglo-Latin scholars from Stevenson onwards, would on their own definition, have instinctively consigned that work, on textual grounds to the turn of the millennium rather than to the later part of the ninth century.

The words *castellum* ('castle or fort'); *satelles* for 'thegn', and the title *senior* (Modern French *seigneur*) for 'lord'—all of which appear in the *Life* of King Alfred—are of Classical Latin origin but appear in Anglo-Latin writings as Frankish borrowings. These words together with the Frankish Latin *fasellus* (or *vassallus*)—which also occurs in the *Life* of Alfred—are all found in St Odo's *Life* of Count Gerald of Aurillac. *Satellites, seniores,* and *castellum* also occur in Byrhtferth of Ramsey's *Life* of St Oswald. Fleury is acknowledged by Stevenson, Crawford, and by subsequent scholars, as having provided a major source of influence for the introduction of the hermeneutic style of Latin writing into late tenth-century England.[47] One of the characteristics of that convoluted style was the inevitable inclusion of tenth-century Frankish vocabulary. The Frankish loan-words in the text of the Pseudo-Asser, therefore, fit perfectly within a late tenth-century Ramsey context and do not of themselves require any special pleading involving premature transmission of such vocabulary by way of Frankish clerks at Alfred's court. Nor need we speculate on the possibility of the historical Asser having studied in Francia in an earlier life—for which there is not a shred of evidence apart from the Frankish literary and linguistic influence within the *Life* of Alfred.[48] It is not impossible that King Alfred's clerks were influenced by contemporary Frankish Latin. But King Alfred and his scholarly circle were committed to translation into the vernacular—the very opposite to the cultivation of arcane Latin so evident both in the *Life* of Alfred and in late tenth-century writers in Anglo-Latin. Indeed, King Alfred was clearly against obscurantism of any kind, and he himself gives as the *raison d'être* for his educational programme 'that we should turn into the language that we can all understand certain books which are the most necessary for all men know'. Is it credible or even possible, that such a king—himself a master of communication in the vernacular—should have allowed his own biography to be written in a disorganized and bombastic style of difficult Latin, exuding what Keynes and Lapidge have admitted to be a 'baroque flavour',[49] and which Stevenson more bluntly described as a 'highly rhetorical' display of 'recondite words' whose author's 'meaning is obscured by a cloud of verbiage'.[50]

Stevenson's great commentary on the *Life* of King Alfred in 1904 has not been superseded, but it was written as a rear-guard action defending the ninth-century status of the text, and it cannot be said to meet the requirements of modern scholarship. The Latinity of other late tenth- and early eleventh-century English writers, both in terms of style, use of language and vocabulary, has since been studied with greater intensity—and it needs to be said with greater objectivity—than that of the biographer of King Alfred. There is conspicuous confusion, however, in the minds of Anglo-Latin scholars, as to their criteria for determining the difference between the hermeneutic texts of the pre-ninth century (going back to the writings of Aldhelm), and tenth- and eleventh-century Latin works in the later hermeneutic style. There is also the erroneous assumption that the identification and exact dating of early medieval Latin styles is a precise science, which allows one to construct a rigorous chronological sequence or typology for a series of texts. Nothing could be further from the truth. Unreal distinctions can be made by linguists between what they see as a definitive hermeneutic Anglo-Latin style of the late tenth century and earlier English Latin works based on a style of Aldhelmian prose. Because the late tenth-century hermeneutic school of English writers included keen students and admirers of Aldhelm, it is often difficult to decide on stylistic evidence alone, whether a work such as the *Life* of Alfred belongs to the ninth century or to the late tenth or early eleventh. Since the later hermeneutic style in England owed so much to Frankish influence, coming by way of monastic reform, then clearly evidence for Frankish borrowings in vocabulary provides one of the major indicators for lateness of date of an Anglo-Latin text. Late tenth-century Anglo-Latin writers cultivated a style involving repetitive, esoteric, if not positively arcane vocabulary, embedded in a convoluted syntax. That style took its inspiration from two distinct sources—the one indigenous, and tracing its origins back ultimately to Aldhelm and his school, the other dependent on powerful and novel Frankish influences, most notably from writers at Fleury as they were known and admired in England and especially at Ramsey in the late tenth century. The indigenous or Aldhelmian strain was not necessarily part of a continuous tradition. Any late tenth-century writer at Winchester, Canterbury, Ramsey, or elsewhere was capable of reading Aldhelm in the original and incorporating his style into his own writings, without being dependent on intermediaries in any way. Indeed we know that Byrhtferth and the late tenth-century Anglo-Latin school were fully conversant with Aldhelm's works.[51] It is rather the case, that the two late tenth-century hermeneutic streams—Frankish and English—were inextricably related, in that Frankish scholarly and literary influences on late tenth-century England, encouraged Anglo-Latin writers to draw on their own earlier arcane Aldhelmian tradition. But the impetus was essentially Frankish, stemming from the movement for monastic reform, and the English scholarly reversion to the convoluted Latin usage of Aldhelm was driven, not so much from a desire to impress stylistically, as to imitate models of Frankish Latin which were associated in the minds of scholarly English monks with the reforming principles and tenets of their Frankish mentors at Fleury and elsewhere. The great majority, if not indeed all the exponents of the Frankish hermeneutic style in England, were themselves steeped in the ideals of monastic reform. Given the indigenous and on-going Aldhelmian element, therefore, which pervades the earlier and later stages of the English hermeneutic tradition, it is the presence of Frankish-Latin borrowings in Anglo-Latin texts such as the *Life* of King Alfred that provides us with crucial evidence to indicate a date of composition later than the middle of the tenth century.

Lapidge's distinction between hisperic—which he confined to Hiberno-Latin texts—and hermeneutic is of no help to this discussion. His definition of hermeneutic applied to all difficult and arcane non-Irish Latin texts going back to Apuleius in the second century.[52] Campbell's usage of the term 'hisperic' may have been imprecise, but his grasp of the history of Anglo-Saxon Latinity is still unrivalled for its clarity and its validity. He pointed to two parallel and contemporaneous strains of Anglo-Saxon Latinity, divided clearly into two chronological phases. The strains were classical and hermeneutic, and they spanned an earlier phase which was pre-viking, or up to *c*. AD 800, and a later which was post-viking from *c*.930 onwards.[53] In the earliest phase, Campbell pointed to Bede as an example of the classical style, and to Aldhelm for the hermeneutic, while for the post-viking period, he rightly saw Ælfric's *Life* of Æthelwold in the classical tradition and the *Life* of Oswald (by Byrhtferth of Ramsey) in the hermeneutic. An essential element in Campbell's view of the history of Anglo-Latin writing was the hiatus caused 'by the barren years of the Danish wars'.[54] It is into this hiatus, that those who hold to the 'genuine Asser' thesis would place the *Life* of King Alfred. But by so doing, they make a work which, as we shall see, exhibits the closest ties to late tenth- and early eleventh-century Anglo-Latin writing stand alone and without context in a period otherwise renowned for its emphasis on the vernacular.[55] The ninth-century hiatus identified by Campbell was real, and it was not confined exclusively to linguistic or literary matters, for it was rather the symptom of a much greater phenomenon. It related to deeply cultural developments connected with English monasticism. The ninth-century viking wars had accelerated the decline of monasticism—not to speak of the annihilation of many great English monasteries, thereby creating a need for reconstruction at the end of the tenth century. That decline and revival of monasticism is reflected in the development of Anglo-Latin literature. The argument relating to the date of Alfred's *Life* is exacerbated by the fact that the ninth century presents us with a hiatus in Latin works in England—the Alfredian renaissance after all, being a vernacular phenomenon.

We begin the analysis of the Latinity of the Pseudo-Asser by turning to the topos of Alfred, who like the busy bee, dutifully crammed his little handbook with an anthology of exegetical class-studies—'those flowers which had been gathered from various masters'. We note the remarkable name which the Pseudo-Asser chose to call the king's notebook: 'This book he used to call his *Enchiridion*, that is "hand book" (*Quem enchiridion suum, id est manualem librum, nominari voluit*).'[56] This exceedingly rare word in Anglo-Latin texts is borrowed from the Greek (τὸ ἐγχειρίδιον) meaning 'handbook', but it is significantly, the very same Greek word used by Byrhtferth of Ramsey to describe his *Manual*:

We have set down in this *Enchiridion*, that is *manualis* in Latin, and *handboc* in English (*enchiridion, þæt ys manualis on Lyden 7 handboc on Englisc*), many things about the computus, because we wished that young men should be able the more easily to understand the Latin and speak with greater freedom to old priests about these things.[57]

The Greek word and its gloss reveals an intimate connection between the text of Byrhtferth's *Manual* and that of the *Life* of Alfred. There is nothing remarkable in this, since we now know that Byrhtferth, as the summarizer of the *Life* of King Alfred in section 5 of the *Historical Miscellany* prefixed to the *Historia Regum*, clearly must have had access to the text of Alfred's *Life*. Lapidge was willing to speculate that Byrhtferth may have borrowed the idea of the *Enchiridion* for his *Manual* from King Alfred's *Life*.[58] But we must now be prepared to see the borrowing in the other direction. The Pseudo-Asser informs us that it was not Bishop Asser, but rather King Alfred himself who wished his class-book to be called *Enchiridion*. There is no evidence whatever to suggest that King Alfred knew any Greek or that he had access to, or an interest in, Greek lexicography. Although his biographer did have access to Einhard, who made extravagant claims for Charlemagne's knowledge of Greek, the Pseudo-Asser was not tempted to transfer those claims to King Alfred. Knowledge of Greek flourished among a select band of Carolingian scholars in the later ninth century led by the Irishman John Scotus Eriugena who died *c.* AD 877. Lecture notes explaining Eriugena's Greek words and phrases subsequently provided pedantic Frankish writers with poorly understood Greek vocabulary, with which they embroidered their ostentatious Latin prose.[59] Those English writers who, in imitation of their Frankish masters, posed as savants of Greek, flourished not in the ninth, but rather—as Lapidge pointed out[60]—in the second half of the tenth century. The use of Greek words, culled from lexicons, accompanied the bombastic Latin hermeneutic style which first made its appearance in the charters of King Athelstan in the 930s and which came to full bloom in the late tenth century, and of which Byrhtferth of Ramsey was the prime exponent. If we concede—as we must—that the naming of King Alfred's handbook and of Byrhtferth's *Manual* are a related phenomena, and bearing in mind that the invention of Alfred's handbook was inspired by Einhard's account of Charlemagne's 'writing-tablets and notebooks (*tabulasque et codicellos*)',[61] it is possible that the title *Enchiridion* was invented not by King Alfred, nor even by the historical Bishop Asser, but by Byrhtferth of Ramsey or one of his circle who were otherwise known as avid collectors of abstruse Greek vocabulary, and who in the case of Byrhtferth, made use of this very Greek term in his own writings.

The significant *enchiridion* does not stand alone as a Greek borrowing in the Pseudo-Asser's text. We also find *graphium* ('charter' or 'document') in chapter 11, and *eulogii* ('text') in chapter 91. These Greek borrowings in the *Life* of Alfred may not compare in their frequency with those in some of Byrhtferth's other works, but there are reasons why this should be so. The great bulk of the text of the *Life* of Alfred—unlike Byrhtferth's *Life* of St Oswald or his *Life* of St Ecgwine—followed a close translation of the Anglo-Saxon Chronicle which left little scope for experimentation with vocabulary. Nor did the *Life* of a king present its author with the same scope for the borrowing of technical terms from the Greek as did Byrhtferth's study of the computus and the natural sciences. It would be unwise to lend too much weight to the actual frequency of Greek borrowings in the works of a late tenth- and early eleventh-century Anglo-Latin writer as a criterion for a test of authorship. What is important, is that Greek borrowings do occur in the Pseudo-Asser's text and that they are otherwise a hallmark of late tenth-century Anglo-Latin writers and—in the case of the very special *enchiridion*—of Byrhtferth of Ramsey in particular. It may well be that the *Life* of Alfred originally contained more Grecisms than it now has, for subsequent normalization and correction on the part of medieval editors or by Archbishop Parker may have erased those obscure forms from the Otho Manuscript of the *Life*. Byrhtferth's summary of the *Life* of Alfred significantly includes at least three more Grecisms—*onoma*,[62] *hypocrissima*,[63] and *pentecontarchus*[64] which are absent from the text as edited by Stevenson. It would have been a simple and natural reaction for a medieval editor or Parker to gloss or to correct *Osbryht vocitatum onomate*[65] for instance, to read *Osbyrht nomine* as it now does in Stevenson's printed edition.[66] Byrhtferth is acknowledged as an accurate transcriber when he is quoting verbatim from Bede or elsewhere,[67] as was the Pseudo-Asser when providing a Latin translation of the Chronicle. We might therefore expect that, as here, when Byrhtferth was following the text of the *Life* of Alfred closely (rather than summarizing whole sections as he does elsewhere), he would have rendered his original accurately. Given that Byrhtferth uses the Grecism *onomate Æthelhelmo*, for instance, in his *Life* of St Oswald,[68] the argument must at least be conceded as possibly going either way. So, Byrhtferth, who used the form *onoma* elsewhere in his works, may have inserted it into his summary of the *Life* of Alfred, where it had not existed in the original. Alternatively, the form *Osbryht . . . onomate* may well have appeared in the original text of the *Life* of Alfred and Byrhtferth so transcribed it in his summary which now survives in the *Historia Regum*. In the absence of the earliest—or indeed of any—complete medieval manuscript of the *Life* we cannot achieve certainty in these discussions. As for the phrase *sub specie hypocrissima* ('under the guise of hypocrisy') found in Byrhtferth's summary of the Pseudo-Asser in connection with the adventure's of the wicked Queen Eadburh, subsequent copiers or editors might well have been prompted to excise this from the text because of the unorthodox and unattested nature of the usage. Stevenson himself observed how Florence of Worcester had carried out editorial 'improvements' on his copy of the *Life* of Alfred[69] and how Florence excised a Frankish Latinism from his exemplar of the *Life* of Alfred on the grounds that it was 'evidently considered as pleonastic'. Such proof of editorial tampering on the part of a later medieval Worcester editor, combined with the evidence from Byrhtferth's early textual version of the Pseudo-Asser—not to speak of the loss of the original Otho manuscript—in no way entitles one to argue from negative evidence in relation to the precise number of Greek borrowings in the surviving text of Alfred's *Life*.

The word *zizania* which occurs in chapter 95 of Stevenson's edition of the *Life* of King Alfred points us to a remarkable conclusion in relation to the authorship of the *Life*. *Zizania* is of Vulgate origin (from the patristic Greek, τὸ ζιζάνιον)— being the diabolically-inspired tare or darnel which was sown among the wheat, as narrated in the Gospel story of Matthew 13: 25.[70] The Pseudo-Asser with his love of arcane vocabulary and of Grecisms could not resist using such a word, and he aptly applied it to tale of the wicked monks who tried to slay Abbot John at Athelney. He excused and explained his lurid tale of monastic violence with the comment: 'throughout Scripture, the foul deeds of the unrighteous are sown among the holy deeds of the righteous, like cockle and tares in the crop of wheat (*sicut zizania et lolium in tritici segetibus, interseminantur*)'.[71] Keynes and Lapidge observed[72] that the author of the *Life* of Alfred was here 'interestingly' conflating two different weeds from two different sources. He was conflating his biblical darnel weeds—*zizania* in the midst of St Matthew's wheat, with Vergil's crops (*Georgics i. 152–4*) which were overcome by the 'wretched tare (*infelix lolium*)'. What is remarkable about all this is that Byrhtferth of Ramsey in his *Life* of St Oswald repeats this very conflation. He tells us that while the saintly Oswald was studying at Fleury, he drove out 'the brambles, thorns, and *zizania* (*vepres et spinas et zizania*)' from his heart, and clothing himself in his baptismal garment (i.e. the monastic habit) he began to tear up by the root the cockle and nettles of sin (*lolium et urticas exstirpare*).[73] So, not only is this exotic word *zizania* found in the text of the Pseudo-Asser and in Byrhtferth's *Life* of Oswald, but it is used in both works in association with *lolium* and in such a specific way to suggest that we might well be dealing with the mind of the same writer—or certainly the same circle of writers—in each case.

In addition to Grecisms, Lapidge itemized the use of Latin diminutives and unusual agentive nouns in *-or* as being a distinct characteristic of Byrhtferth's Latin style. Among the latter he cites *bellator* as turning up in the *Life* of St Oswald and in Byrhtferth's *Historical Miscellany* in the *Historia Regum*.[74] But

Byrhtferth also writes of *bellatores* in his *Life* of St Ecgwine[75] and *bellatores* are mentioned at least twice in the *Life* of King Alfred.[76] As for other examples of this usage in the *Life* of Alfred, we find *operator* ('workman');[77] *administrator* ('administrator'), *coadiutores* ('assistants'), and *inspector*;[78] *rector* ('ruler, regent');[79] *habitator* ('inhabitant');[80] *ductor* ('leader, guide'),[81] and *gubernator* ('ruler').[82] The Pseudo-Asser's fondness for using *gubernator* and its related forms *gubernaculum/gubernacula*, and *guberno*, is found throughout the text of Byrhtferth's *Historical Miscellany* (outside of the summary of the *Life* of Alfred), as well as in his *Manual*, and in the *Life* of St Ecgwine and the *Life* of St Oswald. With the more usual *gubernator*, we may compare Byrhtferth's use of *gubernatrix* in his *Life* of St Oswald,[83] and just as the Pseudo-Asser delighted in what Lapidge described elsewhere as 'verbal playfulness'[84]—playing with word repetition and in varying his word forms as in *semel regni gubernaculum, veluti gubernator praecipuus*, so too, Byrhtferth wrote in his *Manual*: *penetrando circumdat et circumdando adimplet et adimplendo gubernat et gubernando*.[85] As for Byrhtferth's known fondness for diminutives, these turn up also in the text of the Pseudo-Asser as evidenced by *servulus* ('young slave');[86] *campulus* ('piece of ground');[87] *latrunculus* ('bandit, desperado');[88] *foliuncula* ('sheet of parchment')[89] and *opusculum* ('short work').[90]

One of the more definitive hallmarks of Byrhtferth's Latin is his use of uncommon polysyllabic adverbs ending in *-iter*, and it was the identification of those particular adverbs which formed the main plank in Lapidge's argument for attributing authorship of the *Historical Miscellany* in the early sections of the *Historia Regum* as well as the *Life* of St Ecgwine to Byrhtferth of Ramsey.[91] Elsewhere Keynes and Lapidge, although upholding Whitelock's thesis for the 'genuine' ninth-century 'Asser', nevertheless recognized precisely the same tenth-century features in his Latin as those exhibited by Byrhtferth: 'Above all Asser seems to have been obsessed with a love of polysyllabic adverbs, to the point that scarcely a sentence lacks one.'[92] That statement by Lapidge, repeats almost verbatim what he wrote of Byrhtferth of Ramsey:

> Yet another aspect of this same lexical predilection is revealed in the use (it is virtually an abuse) of polysyllabic adverbs terminating in *-iter*. Although adverbs of this sort are used sparingly by most medieval Latin authors, they occur so frequently in the two works [i.e. Byrhtferth's *Life* of Ecgwine and the *Life* of St Oswald] that there is seldom a sentence which does not have one.[93]

Lapidge, like Byrhtferth the subject of his study, revealed here in his own words the 'ingrained mental habits' of a scholar 'where he is too much in a hurry, to pay close attention to the wording of a . . . phrase',[94] but by his own judgement, he inadvertently identified the hand of Byrhtferth of Ramsey or one of his Ramsey circle in the composition of the *Life* of King Alfred. Lapidge never claimed that his word-surveys in Byrhtferth's texts were exhaustive, for indeed the various lists which he offered may be said to represent random samples rather than the result of systematic searches. I make no claim for completeness for the list of polysyllabic adverbs in Appendix A, but I do offer there more than a random sample of those

Latin adverbs occurring in the text of the Pseudo-Asser, set alongside the other
known works of Byrhtferth. My primary concern in this list is with the corpus of
adverbs in the Pseudo-Asser, but it also includes the results of searches throughout
the works of Byrhtferth for other polysyllabic adverbs identified by Lapidge as
being characteristic of Byrhtferth's style. This analysis reveals that of some 47
different polysyllabic adverbs from the *Life* of King Alfred, 28 or 60 per cent occur
elsewhere in the known works of Byrhtferth of Ramsey and some 30 per cent of
those, occur in more than one other of Byrhtferth's works. This analysis excludes
(with one exception) the adverbs in Byrhtferth's summary of the Pseudo-Asser,
since that work must be treated as a variant recension of the original Pseudo-
Asserian text. These statistics present a conservative assessment of the true situation,
for they are unrealistically schematized. For instance, if we take the adverb *affabiliter*
which occurs in Byrhtferth's *Life* of Oswald, we may note that this is absent from
the Pseudo-Asser, but equally we need to register the presence of *affabilitate* in the
Pseudo-Asser's text.[95] We might compare *amabiliter* which appears to be unique to
the Pseudo-Asser[96] with *amicabiliter* in the *Life* of St Oswald. We may compare
immisericorditer common to the *Lives* of Oswald and Ecgwine and to the *Historical
Miscellany* in the *Historia Regum*, with *misericorditer* which occurs in the Pseudo-
Asser, and again in the *Lives* of Oswald and Ecgwine. The instance of the more
unusual *pigriter* ('slothful') in the *Life* of Ecgwine[97] may be set alongside the *pigritia
populi* ('sloth of the people') of the Pseudo-Asser,[98] while *venerabiliter* of the *Historical Miscellany* needs to be compared with the ubiquitous *venerabilis* and
venerabilissimae of the Pseudo-Asser.[99]

Lapidge drew attention to Byrhtferth's fondness for polysyllabic superlatives in
general and for their use in modifying the word *rex* in particular. He noted how the
forms *famosissimus . . . rex* appear no less than twice in the *Life* of St Ecgwine,[100]
but precisely the same phrase is applied to Charlemagne in Stevenson's edition of
the *Life* of Alfred (*Karolum illum famosissimum Francorum regem*), and also in
Byrhtferth's version of that text in his *Historical Miscellany* at that same place in
the Eadburh tale.[101] But it also occurs elsewhere in Byrhtferth's version of the
Pseudo-Asser's text *sub anno* 883 where it is applied to King Alfred,[102] and Byrhtferth
uses it in his *Historical Miscellany* outside his summary of the Pseudo-Asser in
relation to the Frankish king, Carloman *sub anno* 771[103]—all of which suggests that
there is little or no distinction between the style of Byrhtferth's *Historical Miscellany* as a whole, and that of the summary version of the *Life* of Alfred which is
contained within it. Byrhtferth may well have borrowed the usage from the opening lines of Einhard's *Life* of Charlemagne where that writer refers to Charlemagne
as *excellentissimi et . . . famosissimi regis*.[104] The Pseudo-Asser is known to have
borrowed sometimes verbatim from Einhard's work, and it is no coincidence that
both the superlatives *famosissimus* and *excellentissimus* are used by him in his *Life* of
Alfred.[105] Byrhtferth refers, in his *Life* of St Oswald, to King Edgar who was the
patron of the monastic reformers, as *piissimus rex*,[106] and he uses *piissimae* yet again
in his tale of the martyrdom of the Kentish princes, Æthelberht and Æthelred,[107]
which echoes the Pseudo-Asser's dedication of the *Life* of King Alfred to that

Domino meo venerabili piissimoque omnium Britanniae insulae Christianorum rectori, Ælfred, Anglorum Saxonum regi.[108] We shall see how the regnal titles accorded to Alfred in this dedication reflect later tenth-century usage rather than that of the ninth.[109] We note the personal mark of either Byrhtferth or one of his circle in the reference to Alfred as *piissimus rex* in the dedicatory words at the opening of Alfred's *Life*, and we note, too, that Byrhtferth in his version of the *Life* of Alfred in the *Historia Regum*[110] referred to Guthrum's baptism 'at the hand of the most pious king [Alfred] (*sub manu piissimi regis*)'. In the *Life* of St Ecgwine, that saint, supposedly writing in the first person—precisely as the bogus Asser is made to do in the *Life* of King Alfred—refers to his supposed friend Cenred, as *rex famosissimus mihique dilectissimus amicus.*[111] The Pseudo-Asser, as we have seen, uses the superlative *famosissimus*, but he also uses *dilectissimus* in relation to King Alfred's 'thegns [who were] most dear to him' (*dilectissimos suos ministros*).[112] The text of the Pseudo-Asser is indeed littered with polysyllabic superlatives characteristic of Byrhtferth's Latinity, many of which are listed in Appendix A. A systematic study of these words will no doubt show more exact parallels with Byrhtferth's other works, but it may be noted that in addition to *famosissimus* and *dilectissimus*, we also find *munitissima*,[113] *nobilissimos*,[114] *prudentissima*,[115] and *pulcherrima*[116]—all of which appear in Byrhtferth's *Historical Miscellany* in the *Historia Regum*, independently of the summary in that latter work of the Pseudo-Asser. *Pulcherrimus* is also used in the *Life* of St Oswald,[117] while *turpissimus* is common to the Pseudo-Asser[118] and to Byrhtferth's *Life* of St Ecgwine.[119] Two further superlatives from the same phrase in the Pseudo-Asser's text—*opinatissimum atque opulentissimum*[120] also appear in Byrhtferth's short *Epilogue.*[121]

In comparing the Latinity of Pseudo-Asser with that of Byrhtferth and his circle of Ramsey writers, we need to distinguish between particles or other Latin parts of speech which are immutable, and those which turn up in a variety of substantival, adjectival, or adverbial forms. So, the emphatic *immo* which turns up frequently in the *Life* of Alfred also appears (although less often) in both the *Life* of St Oswald and that of St Ecgwine.[122] In cases such as *immo* we can proceed with a mechanical listing of the word. But it is possible to arrive at unreal if not misleading conclusions by analysing various parts of speech found in ninth- and tenth-century texts in a too rigorous Lapidgian grammatical or syntactical isolation from each other. An author's predilection for certain words might well depend on the particular phase in his career in which he was writing or on the nature of the work on which he was engaged, or on the presence or absence of pre-existing texts which he might incorporate into his work. Equally, his choice of words might well relate to a particular root element rather than to an adverbial or adjectival use *per se*. It would be quite wrong in any analysis of Latinity to ignore the obvious relationship which exists in the works of the Pseudo-Asser and of Byrhtferth, between polysyllabic adverbs and superlatives on the one hand, and polysyllabic adjectives with the prefix *in-* and suffix *-bilis* on the other. These polysyllabic adjectives—seen in their separate category—were also identified by Lapidge as characteristic of Byrhtferth's style, and he cited *inedicibilis* from the *Historical Miscellany* as an instance of a rare form in this class.[123] But *inedicibilis* is found in Byrhtferth's version of the *Life* of Alfred in his *Historical Miscellany*[124] and is related to Byrhtferth's use of *inedicibiliter* yet again in the *Historical Miscellany* and in the *Lives* of Oswald and Ecgwine. By the same analogy, we need to connect Byrhtferth's use of *ineffabiliter* in his *Lives* of Oswald and of Ecgwine with his use of *ineffabilis* again in the *Lives* of Oswald and of Ecgwine, and in his *Epilogue*. But *ineffabilis* also appears in the text of the Pseudo-Asser.[125] We note the occurrence of *incomparabiliter*[126] in the *Life* of Alfred, and compare it with *incomparabilis* as found earlier on in that same work.[127] The form *incomparabilis* also occurs in Byrhtferth's *Historical Miscellany* outside of the summary of the *Life* of Alfred,[128] and these forms must be taken together in any analysis, in the same way as we note the alternation between *incessabiliter* and *incessabilius* within the text of the Pseudo-Asser elsewhere.[129] We might cite the Pseudo-Asser's use of *laudabiliter*[130] along with *laudabilis* in the *Lives* of Oswald and of Ecgwine.[131] There are, of course, more direct comparisons between polysyllabic adjectives which we can make, as in the case of *innumerabilis* used by Byrhtferth in his *Life* of St Oswald[132] and which occurs at least six times in the text of the Pseudo-Asser.[133] Byrhtferth was not unique in resorting to polysyllabic adjectives with *in-* and *-bilis*, but that usage which was only one of several distinctive features of the hermeneutic style, was essentially characteristic of the school of writers belonging to the later tenth-century English Monastic Reform. Archbishop Oda of Canterbury, for instance, uses the rare word *intransmeabilis* ('impassable') in his short mid-tenth-century *Preface* to Frithegod's *Life* of St Wilfrid.[134] That same rare word is used by the Pseudo-Asser to describe the topography of Athelney in Somerset.[135] Oda's vocabulary generally, has close similarities with that of the Pseudo-Asser and the works of Byrhtferth of Ramsey which suggests yet again, that the *Life* of King Alfred is textually at home in the later tenth and early eleventh century rather than in the ninth.[136] Clearly, not all the adverbs, adjectives, and superlatives which have been itemized in this discussion are as rare as words such as *intransmeabilis*—some are indeed common. It is surely permissible, however, when this wide range of vocabulary is taken in combination with other factors to use it as a tool to identify if not a particular author, then at least a circle of writers and the general era in which they wrote. This, after all, was the very technique employed by Lapidge and others to identify Byrhtferth of Ramsey specifically as the author of several Anglo-Latin texts.

When recognizing the close similarities between the text of the *Life* of King Alfred and the known works of Byrhtferth of Ramsey, we are not dealing solely with a matter of comparing the same Latin words, or words used as different parts of speech. Both the Pseudo-Asser and Byrhtferth of Ramsey gloried in piling up polysyllabic adverbs, adjectives and superlatives within the same sentence, frequently playing on variations of the same Latin root. When we compare the following passages from the Pseudo-Asser with other known works of Byrhtferth, we are not necessarily looking for word-for-word similarities—though these do occur—or for evidence of direct borrowing. We are looking, primarily for similarities in the use of language and in style, and for the similar manipulation of vocabulary. For random examples of the authors' love of word-play, we have the Pseudo-Asser's: *Sicut enim irrationabiliter in propria vixisse refertur, ita multo irrationabilius in aliena gente vivere deprehenditur,*[137] which we may compare with: *atque lacrymulis lacrymis effusionem* in the *Life* of St Oswald,[138] or with *Eanbaldus . . . in archiepiscopatum genti Northanhymbrorum solempniter confirmatus est . . . qua die celebratur solempnitas* in the *Historical Miscellany.*[139] We may compare here the Pseudo-Asser's *irrationabiliter . . . irrationabilius* with Byrhtferth's *lacrymulis lacrymis* and *solempniter . . . solemptnitas* while bearing in mind that *sollemniter* was also an adverb used by the Pseudo-Asser.[140] We note the succession of polysyllabic adverbs in the following text from the Pseudo-Asser: '*non inaniter incepta, utiliter inventa, utilius servata est. Nam iamdudum in lege scriptum audierat, Dominum decimam sibi multipliciter redditurum promisisse atque fideliter servasse, decimamque sibi multipliciter redditurum fuisse'.*[141]

Here we have *inaniter, utiliter . . . utilius, fideliter,* and the characteristic repetition of *multipliciter,* an adverb also found in Byrhtferth's *Life* of St Oswald.[142] The following passage from the *Life* of St Oswald is part of an account of how Oswald observed a solemn church festival at Ramsey with his monks:

His sollemniter finitis, reversi sunt cuncti ad refectionem quam eis beautus dux praeparaverat dapsiliter ad edendum. Cuncta quae quondam Salomon suis regali potentia fretus dederat, omnia iste non solum carnaliter sed etiam spiritaliter peregerat. Dicatam Christo ecclesiam, quam nobiliter aeditui ornaverunt cortinis et palleis, et mutiphariis accensis luminaribus, quis annuntiet?[143]

Byrhtferth, too, piled up his polysyllabic adverbs within a single sentence—and recalling that 60 per cent of the Pseudo-Asser's repertoire turns up in Byrhtferth's works, we note the presence in this one sentence of *sollemniter, dapsiliter, carnaliter, spiritaliter,* and *nobiliter. Sollemniter/solempniter* occurs in the *Life* of Alfred[144] and in the *Life* of Ecgwine[145] and the *Historical Miscellany.*[146] With *carnaliter* from the *Life* of Oswald, we may compare *corporaliter* in the *Life* of Alfred.[147]

Lapidge drew attention to Byrhtferth's use throughout his writings of the rhetorical question to achieve emphasis, and to Byrhtferth's use of compounds based on *nuntio, expedio, enarro,* or *edico.*[148] In the example quoted above from the *Life* of Oswald, the formula used is that of *quis annuntiet?* The precise formulae used by Byrhtferth when employing this rhetorical device vary considerably, and in addition to his use of those forms cited by Lapidge we may also point to his piling up of rhetorical questions in the sentence *Quid restat? quid superest? quid moramur? cur non dicimus quae restant?* in the *Life* of Ecgwine,[149] or to *Quid dicam? quidve referam?* in the *Life* of St Oswald.[150] The passage beginning *His sollemniter finitis* quoted above from the *Life* of Oswald may also be compared in its rhetorical *quis annuntiet?* in relation to the church of Ramsey, with the Pseudo-Asser's similar rhetorical question in relation to King Alfred's building achievenments:

Quid loquar de . . . civitatibus et urbibus renovandis et aliis, ubi nunquam ante fuerat, construendis? De aedificiis aureis et argenteis incomparabiliter, illo edocente, fabricatis? De aulis et cambris regalibus, lapideis et ligneis suo iussu mirabiliter constructis? ['What of the cities and towns he restored, and the others, which he built where none had been before? Of the buildings made by his instructions with gold and silver, beyond compare? Of royal halls and chambers constructed admirably in stone and timber at his command?']¹⁵¹

The adverb *mirabiliter* from this passage in King Alfred's *Life* occurs in at least three of Byrhtferth's known works, in at least nine instances.¹⁵² The Pseudo-Asser's use of *incomparabiliter* in this same passage may be set against the adjectival form, *incomparabilis*, which appears elsewhere in the *Life* of Alfred,¹⁵³ and which reappears in Byrhtferth's *Historical Miscellany*.¹⁵⁴ That particular passage in chapter 22 of the Pseudo-Asser is resonant with echoes from the writings of Byrhtferth:

> *Sed, proh dolor! indigna suorum parentum et nutritorum incuria usque ad duodecimum aetatis annum, aut eo amplius, illiteratus permansit. Sed Saxonica poemata die noctuque solers auditor, relatu aliorum saepissime audiens, docilibus memoriter retinebat. In omni venatoria arte industrius venator incessabiliter laborat non in vanum; nam incomparabilis omnibus peritia et felicitate in illa arte, sicut in ceteris omnibus Dei donis, fuit sicut et nos saepissime vidimus.* ['But alas, by the unworthy carelessness of his parents and tutors, he [Alfred] remained ignorant of letters until his twelfth year, or even longer. But he listened attentively to Saxon poems by day and night, and hearing them often recited by others committed them to his retentive memory. A keen huntsman he toiled unceasingly in every branch of hunting, and not in vain; for he was without equal in his skill and good fortune in that art, as also in all other gifts of God, as we have ourselves [very] often seen.']¹⁵⁵

This passage—so dependent in its ideas on St Odo's *Life* of Gerald and Einhard's *Life* of Charlemagne—contains the rhetorical lamentation *proh dolor* which recurs several times throughout the *Life* of King Alfred. Crawford identified *heu pro dolor* as a characteristic feature of Byrhtferth's Latin in both his *Manual* and the *Life* of St Oswald.¹⁵⁶ Stevenson, on the other hand, identified *eo amplius* as a characteristic hallmark of the textual style of the *Life* of King Alfred.¹⁵⁷ Remarkably, the combination of *proh dolor . . . eo amplius* occurs in close proximity in the passage quoted above from chapter 22 of Alfred's *Life* and the combination recurs yet again in chapter 74.¹⁵⁸ Precisely the same combination of phrases occur within a single passage in a section of Byrhtferth's *Historical Miscellany* referring to AD 792, and therefore prior to Byrhtferth's summary of the Pseudo-Asser proper:

> *Karolus rex Francorum misit synodalem librum ad Britanniam, sibi a Constantinopoli directum, in quo libro, heu pro dolor! multa inconvenienta et verae fidei contraria reperientes, maxime quod poene omnium orientalium doctorum non minus quam trecentorum vel eo amplius episcoporum unanima assertione confirmatum, imagines adorare debere, quod omnino ecclesia Dei execratur.*¹⁵⁹

Yet another phrase in that passage from chapter 22 of the Pseudo-Asser is *die noctuque* ('by day and by night') which occurs at least eleven times in the text of the Pseudo-Asser.¹⁶⁰ There are in addition related phrases *per diem . . . et noctem*,¹⁶¹ and *unius diei aut noctis*.¹⁶² With these we may compare *diebus ac noctibus* of Byrhtferth's short *Epilogue*,¹⁶³ *non diebus non noctibus*¹⁶⁴ and *diebus et noctibus* in the *Historical Miscellany*.¹⁶⁵ More significant is the occurrence in the Pseudo-Asser's text of *diuturnitas*,¹⁶⁶ a word described by Lapidge as a 'rare abstraction', and therefore for him a diagnostic word in the repertoire of Byrhtferth of Ramsey.¹⁶⁷ *Diuturnitas* occurs in Byrhtferth's *Historical Miscellany* at the end of his account of the Kentish hagiographical legends.[168] The text of the Pseudo-Asser is replete with phrases relating to night and day, which is what we should expect if its author were Byrhtferth or one of Byrhtferth's colleagues or pupils, who was an expert on the measurement of time, and who in the case of Byrhtferth devoted a large part of his *Manual* to discussing the divisions of day and night. We have in the *Life* of Alfred *diuturna et nocturna*,[169] *diuturna*,[170] and *diurno . . . ac nocturno*,[171] and *nocturnarum horarum . . . et diurnarum*.[172] We may compare the phrase *diurnus . . . et nocturnus* in the *Historical Miscellany*,[173] or *peractis nocturnalibus mysteriis* in the *Life* of St Ecgwine.[174] The majority of these phrases relating to time would be commonplace in any medieval Latin narrative, but it is the frequency with which they are repeated, and their variety of form in the *Life* of King Alfred, which links those phrases to the works of Byrhtferth of Ramsey—that master of time studies in his *Manual*.

Lapidge drew attention to Byrhtferth's characteristic continuity phrases which he saw as ultimately deriving from Bede.[175] Such borrowings may not always have involved deliberate cloning of phrases on the part of Byrhtferth, whose intense study of writers such as Bede and Aldhelm must have implanted techniques and turns of phrase in his own subconscious repertoire as a writer. Approaching this subject from an analysis of the Pseudo-Asser's text we find that he, too, made extensive use of continuity passages:

I think I should return to that which particularly inspired me to this work . . . I consider that some small account . . . of Alfred . . . should briefly be inserted at this point (*ad id, quod nos maxime ad hoc opus incitavit, nobis redeundum esse censeo, scilicet aliquantulum . . . de Ælfredi, moribus hoc in loco breviter inserendum esse existimo*).[176]

In order that I may return to that point from which I digressed . . . I shall, as I promised, undertake with God's guidance, to say something albeit succinctly and briefly . . . about the life . . . of Alfred (*ad id, unde digressus sum, redeam . . . aliquantulum quantum notitiae meae innotuerit, de vita . . . Ælfredi . . . Deo annuente, succinctim ac breviter . . . ut promisi, expedire procurabo*).[177]

We may compare the Pseudo-Asser's *digressus sum redeam* with a related passage from Byrhtferth's *Life* of St Oswald: '*Digressi sumus paulisper ab ordine narrationis . . . sed etiam tempus esse dinoscitur ut ad viam nostri sermonis redeamus*',[178] or with '*extra viam paulatim digressimus, sed redeamus ad viam quae nos reducat ad callem justitiae*' from that same saint's *Life*.[179] Returning to the *Life* of King Alfred, the phrase: 'Now that I have related these things, let us return to the proper subject' (*His ita relatis, ad incepta redeamus*)[180] may be compared with Byrhtferth's '*His strictim dictis, ad ordinem revertamur narrationis*' in his *Historical Miscellany*[181] and with the same writer's '*His dictis, redeamus ad nos ipsos*' in his *Manual*[182] or '*His dictis, redeamus uenusto animo unde discesseramus mediocri alloquio*',[183] and '*ad ordinem . . . redeamus propriae relationis*' in the *Life* of St Oswald.[184] Byrhtferth's desire in his known writings to return *ad ordinem* reminds us of the Pseudo-Asser's admission of his inability to handle the chaotic account as he presented it, of King

Alfred's illness: 'For, if I may speak succinctly and briefly although I set things out in the reverse order (*Nam, ut . . . succinctim ac breviter, quamvis praeposterato ordine, loquar*).'[185] The Pseudo-Asser is telling us quite literally that he is presenting his narrative or 'order', back to front!

Several of the continuity phrases in the *Life* of Alfred are couched as announcements for the inclusion of a specific narrative, or apologies for leaving it out: 'At this point I do not think that I can profitably bypass the intention and resolve of his most excellent enterprise . . . (*De voto quoque et proposito excellentissimae meditationis suae . . . praetereundum esse hoc in loco utiliter non existimo*).'[186]

Byrhtferth makes similar statements throughout his works as in this passage from the *Life* of Oswald: '*Rem breviter narrare desidero, quam praeterire non libet ob inertiam desidiae torporis.*'[187]

The Pseudo-Asser may also excuse himself from going into detail:

It is not necessary to mention the other details of his bequests to men in this short work, for fear its readers or those wishing to listen to it should find its verbosity distasteful (*Nam cetera, quae ad humanam dispensationem pertinent, in hoc opusculo inserere necesse non est, ne fastidium prolixitate legentibus vel etiam audire desiderantibus procreaverit*).[188]

Here we have the writer's excuse that he does not wish to bore his readers and indeed his hearers. Significantly, Byrhtferth panders to his hearers (*audientes*) in a similarly apologetic vein in his *Manual*: 'We refrain at this point from discoursing of [the numbers] sixty, eighty and ninety, lest we should disturb our hearers (*De sexagessimo et septuagessimo et octuagesimo, nec non et nonagesimo supsedimus hoc in loco sermocinari, ne forte perturbemus audientes*).'[189] We may compare Byrhtferth's 'we have no desire to treat these subjects further, lest it should prove tedious to educated priests (*nu ne lyst us þas þing leng styrian, þelæspe hyt beo æþryt gelæredum preostum*)',[190] or that same writer's excuse for terminating his long digression in his *Manual* on figures of speech: 'We could say a great deal on these things, but we are afraid that scholars may hate our speaking so fully about their mysteries. . . . But I am eager [to return] to pursue the study of the computus.'[191]

This formula may be compared with the other announcements of Byrhtferth: 'Let these words suffice at this point (*Hoc in loco sufficiant hec dicta*)'[192] or 'Let us pass over these in this place because we wish to come to more important matters (*de his hoc in loco taceamus, quia ad necessiora cupimus peruenire*).'[193] No less than three of these continuity passages of Byrhtferth of Ramsey are linked to the continuity text in chapter 92 of the Pseudo-Asser's *Life* of Alfred (quoted above) by the key formula *hoc in loco* discussed below.

The Pseudo-Asser, like Byrhtferth, also makes announcements for the benefit of ignorant readers: 'And because many do not know, I suspect . . . I think I should explain it a little more fully (*Et quia, ut opinor, multis habetur incognitum . . . paulo latius mihi videtur intimandum*).'[194]

We may compare this with Byrhtferth's plea in his *Manual*: 'Time presses us to speak concisely of the number one thousand—beseeching those who have the knowledge not to be annoyed with what is our pleasure to set forth for those who are ignorant (*Nunc tempus instat ut de millenario strictim loquamar, scientes obsecrans ut oneri non sit quod ignorantibus placet traducere*).'[195] Lapidge cited a closely related passage from the *Life* of St Ecgwine.[196] Similarly, in the *Life* of Alfred, the author protests that he does not itemize the gifts which he received from the king out of vanity: 'I call God to witness that I have not done so [out of vanity], but only to make clear to those who do not know (*nescientibus*) how profuse is his [the king's] generosity.'[197] The Pseudo-Asser's 'those who do not know (*nescientibus*)' may be compared with a similar class of readers who 'do not know (*nescientes*)' and who consequently were in need of Byrhtferth's instruction in the *Historia Regum* and elsewhere in his writings. Continuity phrases and the stated desire on the part of authors that they do not wish to bore their readers are not confined to either Byrhtferth of Ramsey or to the Pseudo-Asser. What is significant, however, is the frequency with which both those writers resort to such signposting. The reason for this frequency in continuity phrasing is also instructive. In the case of both Byrhtferth and the Pseudo-Asser, we are dealing with highly disorganized writers—neither of whom are stupid—but both of whom constantly back-track and display the same extraordinary inability to produce an episodic narrative.

Other closer verbal similarities may be found between the work of the Pseudo-Asser and other known works of Byrhtferth. The Pseudo-Asser in his account of how Alfred first learnt to read and to translate tells us: 'I gave immense thanks, although silently, to Almighty God, with hands outstretched to Heaven (*immensas Omnipotenti Deo grates, qui extensis ad aethera volis, tacitus quamvis, persolvi*).'[198] The passage echoes another in Byrhtferth's *Life* of St Ecgwine: '*Salvatoris gratia concedente propriis arvis redditi sumus, immensas ei grates rependentes, erectis digniter palmis ad aethera*.'[199] It may indeed be argued that both passages are derived ultimately from Aldhelm[200]—and all parties are agreed that the Pseudo-Asser and Byrhtferth had studied Aldhelm—but what is remarkable is that precisely these same phrases should be borrowed by the Pseudo-Asser and by Byrhtferth who have hitherto been regarded as living a whole century apart. Crawford, as long ago as 1929 observed as 'noteworthy . . . the fact that in both the *Manual* and the *Vita Oswaldi* [of Byrhtferth of Ramsey] we never find *in hoc loco*, but always *hoc in loco*.'[201] Indeed Crawford used this 'marked characteristic' to help show that Byrhtferth was none other than the author of the *Life* of St Oswald—a fact now generally accepted. We find this same distinctive Byrhtferthian usage of *hoc in loco* ('in this place') throughout the work of the Pseudo-Asser, two examples of which have been cited in the continuity passages above.[202] Witness the celebrated passage where the biographer informs us that King Alfred rewarded him with Exeter and all its *parochia*:

besides innumerable daily gifts of all kinds of earthly riches, which it would be tedious to enumerate here, lest it should cause weariness to the readers. But do not let anyone think that I have mentioned such gifts in this place out of any vain glory or in flattery, or for the sake of gaining greater honour (*quae hoc in loco percensere longum est, ne fastidium legentibus procreent. Sed nullus existimet, pro vana aliqua gloria aut adulatione aut maioris honoris quaerendi gratia, me talia hoc in loco dona commemorasse*).[203]

The passage may be borrowed in part from Einhard—as are other announcements by the Pseudo-Asser that he does not wish to bore his readers. Nevertheless, the repeated use of *hoc in loco* in this single passage is peculiar to the Pseudo-Asser and to Byrhtferth of Ramsey. And the Pseudo-Asser shows in this very specific usage that he shared the same ingrained mannerisms as Ramsey writers of the early eleventh century.

The Pseudo-Asser and Byrhtferth of Ramsey fell back on the same devices to excuse their scissors-and-paste technique of writing. They each made excessive use of signposting and apologizing to their readers, and both writers too often resorted to 'continuity formulae' which appear in the *Life* of King Alfred and throughout all the major works of Byrhtferth: 'I think I should return to my main subject', 'Having said these things, let us return to the main narrative', 'Having digressed from the main narrative, let us return' or simply 'as I have said'. We also encounter signposting of an apologetic or explanatory variety: 'Because many do not know, I think I should explain this more fully' or alternatively, 'it is not necessary to mention other details for fear of boring readers'. There are, as we might expect, points of difference between the texts of the *Life* of Alfred and those of the other known works of Byrhtferth of Ramsey. We cannot expect such a prolific author, writing, perhaps over half a century in time, to display the exact same characteristics in all his writings. So too, someone in Byrhtferth's circle would not be expected to replicate Byrhtferth's style in every detail. Other scholars have noted variations in Bryhtferth's use of vocabulary and style across the range of his works. The status of the text of the *Life* of King Alfred is also unique in that the original manuscript has not survived, and there is evidence to suggest that even before Archbishop Parker and his team set to work on editing that manuscript, earlier medieval scholars may have sought to 'improve' on its eccentric style. So, for instance, Byrhtferth of Ramsey in his other works frequently refers to Rome as 'the Romulean city' or as 'the threshold of the Apostles'.[204] The Pseudo-Asser (in Stevenson's edition) mentions Rome some eleven times in his *Life* of Alfred, but nowhere in these terms. But all of the references to Rome in King Alfred's *Life* relate directly or indirectly to incidents in the Anglo-Saxon Chronicle which, because the Pseudo-Asser followed his Latin text of the Chronicle so closely, did not allow him scope to embroider his narrative at that point. Both Crawford and Robinson observed that in his other works, Byrhtferth's Latin was at his most 'sober' and lacking in 'efflorescent rhetoric' when he was following an established author such as Bede.[205] Byrhtferth in his summary of the *Life* of Alfred in the *Historical Miscellany* in the *Historia Regum* also writes of Rome simply as *Roma* when he is following passages from the Chronicle. There is however, one notable exception, when Byrhtferth in his *Historical Miscellany* is summarizing the account in the *Life* of Alfred of how King Æthelwulf took his son, Alfred, to Rome and how Æthelwulf arranged in his *Will* for alms to be sent there. In this passage, Byrhtferth does refers to Rome as *Romuleas sedes* and *ad limina principis apostolorum* and *ad limina sancti Petri*.[206] The account of how King Æthelwulf bequeathed 300 mancuses annually to Rome is not found in the Chronicle and is peculiar to the Pseudo-Asser.[207] The schematized division of the bequest into thirds—100 mancuses for oil lamps in St Peter's, 100 for St Paul's, and 100 for the pope's use—looks very Byrhtferthian in its schematization and mathematical symmetry.[208] It may well be therefore, that the Pseudo-Asser, when following the Chronicle closely, referred to Rome simply as *Roma*, but that in the case of the account of Æthelwulf's bequests to Roman churches (which is not in the Chronicle) more 'precocious phrases' for Rome were used by him. Byrhtferth's summary of Alfred's *Life* in his *Historical Miscellany*, after all, has superior medieval manuscript evidence to support it, than that of Parker's printed edition.

A study of the metaphors employed by the biographer of King Alfred shows that they bear a remarkable similarity to those found in the writings of Byrhtferth of Ramsey. On three occasions in the *Life* of Alfred, the biographer uses a nautical image—twice[209] referring to himself as a ship's pilot and to his work as a ship holding its course and seeking a safe harbour—and a third time referring to King Alfred himself as the pilot guiding his treasure-laden ship of state (the kingdom) to that same metaphorical safe harbour. The nautical metaphor was a literary commonplace, and King Alfred in his own writings made frequent use of it. Alfred was probably influenced in this, as in so much else, by his great knowledge of some of the works of Gregory the Great.[210] The nautical metaphors in the *Life* of Alfred are quite different from those used by Alfred in his own writings and bear a close relationship to those of late tenth- and early eleventh-century writers. As early as 1877, Howorth observed that the author of King Alfred's *Life* may have borrowed his nautical metaphors from the late tenth-century Chronicle of Æthelweard.[211] The notion was contemptuously dismissed by Stevenson with the comment: 'This argument would equally prove that Cicero also borrowed from Æthelweard.'[212] But Cicero and Æthelweard were separated by a millennium, whereas Æthelweard and the biographer of Alfred, who both worked on Latin translations of the Anglo-Saxon Chronicle, had more in common than Stevenson was willing to admit. The fact that the nautical metaphor had established itself as a topos in the writings of Jerome, Fortunatus, or Eriugena,—and among earlier English writers such as Aldhelm and Alcuin—cannot *per se* invalidate the possibility that the same metaphor was borrowed by King Alfred's biographer from Æthelweard, or—more probably—that it might date from the same late tenth-century literary milieu as that of Æthelweard and his contemporaries. The Pseudo-Asser tells us he had:

entrusted the ship' to waves and sails, and having sailed quite far away from the land— among such terrible wars, and in year by year reckoning (*inter tantas bellorum clades et annorum enumerationes*), I think I should return to that which particularly inspired me to this work: in other words I consider that some small account (as much as has come to my knowledge) of the infancy and boyhood of my esteemed lord Alfred, king of the Anglo-Saxons, should briefly be inserted at this point.[213]

Later on, in chapter 73, he repeats his hollow pledge:

to return to that point from which I digressed—and so that I shall not be compelled to sail past the haven of my desired rest as a result of my protracted voyage—I shall as I promised, undertake, with God's guidance, to say something . . . about the life, behaviour, equitable character and, without exaggeration, the accomplishments of my lord Alfred, king of the Anglo-Saxons.[214]

For the Pseudo-Asser, his ocean was in part, the relentless following (by way of translation) of the Anglo-Saxon Chronicle, while the safe haven from this boring digression, beckoned in the form of elusive details relating to Alfred's own life—about which the author knew so little. What is remarkable about the parallel use of this same metaphor by the chronicler Æthelweard, is that it is used in precisely the same context by that late tenth-century writer. At a point in the fourth book of his *Chronicle*, Æthelweard brings his narrative down to the death of his own ancestor, King Æthelred I (the older brother of Alfred) in AD 871. At this point in his work, Æthelweard turns aside to address his German cousin (for whom he was compiling his Chronicle in the first instance):

Having just retraced my steps, O revered cousin Matilda, I will begin to give you confirmation with added clarity. Just as a ship which has been carried through the turmoil of the waves for great distances, which she has explored on her careful voyage, comes at last to port, so we enter [port] as if in the manner of sailors. . . . So setting aside my less even style, I will speak of the sons of Æthelwulf. The brothers were five in number. The first was Æthelstan who had taken up government at the same time as his father. The second was Æthelbald, who was also king of the West Saxons. The third was Æthelbyrht, king of the people of Kent. The fourth was Æthelred who succeeded to the kingdom after the death of Æthelbyrht, and who was my great-great-grandfather. The fifth was Alfred successor of all the others to the entire kingdom, who was your great-great-grandfather. Accordingly, sweet cousin Matilda, having gathered these things from remote antiquity, I have made communication to you, and above all I have given attention to the history of our race as far as these two kings, from whom we derive our descent. . . . Therefore let us return to our neglected subject and the death of the above-mentioned King Æthelred. . . . When these things had happened, Alfred got the kingdom after the death of his brothers.[215]

So, for Æthelweard too—like the Pseudo-Asser—the translation of earlier sections of the Anglo-Saxon Chronicle was a preliminary but necessary chore—an ocean leading to a safe harbour—essentially that same harbour which was being sought by the Pseudo-Asser, namely the account of King Alfred's career. It was quite wrong of Stevenson to assess Æthelweard's *Chronicle* as 'merely a brief version of the history of England with no personal details'.[216] On the contrary, it was designed as a work showing King Alfred's central role in the history of the House of Wessex and in demonstrating the connection between Matilda, abbess of Essen (the recipient of the work), with King Alfred and the West Saxon dynasty. The ship's voyage was used by Æthelweard as a central metaphor to make the connection between King Æthelred and his brother Alfred, on the one hand, and the relentless annalistic narrative of English history on the other. Howorth argued that had Æthelweard known of the biography of King Alfred he would most certainly have supplied his cousin with details of that colourful narrative, and concluded therefore, that it was the biographer of King Alfred who had borrowed his nautical metaphors from Æthelweard.[217] That argument, after more than a century, returns to centre stage—not necessarily to demonstrate any direct borrowing of one author from the other, but to show how Æthelweard may indeed have written before the Pseudo-Asser, and how these contemporary writers, inhabiting the same thought-world, shared very similar perceptions of West Saxon history.

As it happens, the nautical metaphor is also used by Byrhtferth of Ramsey in an even more elaborate form near the beginning of his *Manual*:

We have stirred with our oars the waves of the deep pool. We have likewise beheld the mountains around the salt sea stand, and with outstretched sail and prosperous winds, we have succeeded in pitching our camp on the coasts of the fairest of lands. The waves symbolise this profound art [of computation], and the mountains, too, symbolise the magnitude of this art. . . . These things we found at Ramsey, by the merciful grace of God. . . . We have touched the deep sea and the mountains of this work.[218]

Byrhtferth's ocean waves represent the art of computation, while for the Pseudo-Asser the waves were the *annorum enumerationes* and for Æthelweard, 'the turmoil of the waves over the great distances' represented also the history of the English down to the reign of King Alfred. Indeed, for the Pseudo-Asser as for Æthelweard, the ocean represented the translation of the Anglo-Saxon Chronicle into Latin, and the harbour at journey's end represented the central role of King Alfred in English history, as both men perceived that rôle at the end of the millennium. Paradoxically, both Alfred's biographer and Æthelweard, who held King Alfred in such awe, were busy reversing that ruler's cultural achievement. For they both translated the powerfully direct and laconic West Saxon prose of the Anglo-Saxon Chronicle, which had been written in Alfred's reign, into a garbled and pretentious Latin of a sort that Alfred would have most certainly disapproved. And in all this, Byrhtferth's use of the same nautical simile as Æthelweard is important. Of course, Byrhtferth's metaphorical harbour in his *Manual* were those 'distant shores' where he found honey and other delights of scholarship relating to the natural sciences. But such a writer—or one of his circle—seeing himself as a ship's pilot exploring the ocean of knowledge might easily qualify as the man who resorted no less than three times to that same metaphor in the *Life* of King Alfred. It is to Byrhtferth and his circle then—the contemporaries of Æthelweard—that we return, in our efforts to explore the mind of the Pseudo-Asser.

Byrhtferth's metaphor of the pilot on his ocean voyage mixes in other images which that writer developed with regularity in his other known works. In describing the metaphorical journey's end in his pursuit of the art of computation, Byrhtferth not only identified the place with his own monastic home at Ramsey, but he described it as a land of flowers and sweet-tasting honey. It was a place:

Where we perceived the blossom of the lily—that is the beauty of computation—there we scented the perfume of roses—that is we perceived the profundity of reckoning. In that place the noble plain provided us with honey sweet and pleasant to taste. In that place we received myrrh . . . and 'gutta' that is a drop, sweet as honey . . . and *thus*, that is incense. These things we found at Ramsey by the merciful grace of God.[219]

This vision of the land of honey is closely related to yet another of Byrhtferth's metaphors of the honey-bee which he used as a symbol for the scholar toiling with his work or browsing through the 'flowers of Scripture', or for learning in general. Later in his *Manual*, Byrhtferth, in striving to explain the devilishly complicated routine for calculating the correct date of Easter, encourages his pupils to persevere with their calculations in these words:

Behold the chaste bee very often visits far and wide the beautiful flowers for so long that her rough thighs become heavily burdened. And fierce winds meet her and vex the poor thing, so that she can scarcely reach home. When she has ascended her throne in this dazed condition, she is constrained with such gladness in her heart, that she has no hesitation in singing a pleasant song.[220]

Byrhtferth uses the bee metaphor yet again in his *Epilogue*[221] and also in his *Life* of St Oswald, where he compares the studies undertaken at Fleury on the 'flowers of the Scriptures' by the Winchester monk, Germanus, with the work of a honey-bee.[222] The Pseudo-Asser uses the bee metaphor twice in his *Life* of King Alfred. He tells us that Alfred, unable to find scholars within his own kingdom, was inspired by divine promptings to seek them from outside: 'Forthwith, like the prudent bee, which arises in the summer-time at dawn from its beloved cells and, directing its course in swift flight through the unknown ways of the air, alights upon many and various blossoms of herbs, plants and fruits, and finds and carries home what pleases it most.'[223] Later, in his celebrated passage describing how he taught King Alfred to read and to translate, the Pseudo-Asser relates that the eager king began searching daily for interesting passages in the Scriptures which might be transcribed into his notebook: 'like a most productive bee, travelling far and wide wide over the marshes in his quest, he eagerly and unceasingly collected many various flowers of Holy Scripture, with which he densely stored the cells of his mind.'[224]

Stevenson, followed by Keynes and Lapidge, stressed that the bee metaphor in the *Life* of King Alfred was derived from the writings of the late seventh-century Aldhelm.[225] But Aldhelm, as we have seen, had a profound influence on hermeneutic writers of late tenth- and early eleventh-century England. Stevenson recognized that the bee metaphor also enjoyed popularity in the late tenth century (although he did not identify it with Byrhtferth of Ramsey), but his judgement was already constrained by his conviction that the *Life* of Alfred was a ninth-century production. The late tenth-century writer of the *B Life* of St Dunstan likened that saint's studies at Glastonbury to the labours of the honey-bee,[226] and that same author of Dunstan's *Life*, writing *c*.988–90 to Archbishop Æthelgar of Canterbury, informed the prelate in his letter that he was on his way to Winchester to study the works of Aldhelm. Even in that selfsame letter, he employs the metaphor of the 'obedient honey-bee' (*apis obediens*).[227] The question hinges then, not on whether the bee metaphors in the *Life* of Alfred derive from Aldhelm, because ultimately most if not all such English imagery may well derive from that early West Saxon scholar. The question is, rather, do the bee metaphors in King Alfred's *Life* date to the late ninth century, where they would then stand in a conspicuously isolated English context, or do they belong to a significant body of closely related literary *topoi* used by Anglo-Latin writers of the late tenth and early eleventh centuries? To answer this question we must take into the account the fact that Byrhtferth of Ramsey and the Pseudo-Asser have this significant point in common: they both made extensive use of the ship's pilot and the honey-bee metaphors. We note, too, that the biographer of Alfred likened the supposedly saintly king, to a honey-bee searching 'far and wide over the marshes' in his thirst for biblical knowledge. The image of a bee searching for honey in extensive marshland would be more appropriate to a Fenland context in East Anglia than to the prosperous downlands of Alfredian Wessex. The word used by Alfred's biographer for those metaphorical 'marshes' traversed by his scholarly bee was *gronnios*[228] and elsewhere he uses *gronnosa* or 'marshy' to describe the wetlands of Somerset where Alfred retreated during his Athelney campaign.[229] That very rare word *gronna* ('marsh' or 'fen'), was admitted by Stevenson to have been a Frankish import from tenth-century Fleury[230] and its earliest occurrence in England, outside of the *Life* of Alfred, is in King Edgar's foundation charter for Thorney Abbey, dating to 973.[231] That charter, with its 'basically authentic text'[232] was witnessed by St Oswald and by Ealdorman Æthelwine, who were the joint founders of Byrhtferth's monastery at nearby Ramsey. John Leland, the sixteenth-century antiquary, claimed that Byrhtferth had once been a monk at Thorney.[233]

We have already seen how the Pseudo-Asser narrated Alfred's sudden ability in middle age to read and to translate in terms of a conventional miracle story, and we saw too, how Alfred, whose well-documented translation programme centred on historical and largely non-Scriptural themes, was portrayed by the Pseudo-Asser as a saint translating passages from Scripture and indulging in biblical exegesis. The Pseudo-Asser's bee metaphor reinforces the image of Alfred as the saintly monk, collecting 'the various little flowers of Holy Scripture (*multimodos divinae scripturae flosculos*)'.[234] The Pseudo-Asser again refers to these flowers (*flosculos*) 'of the rudiments of Holy Scripture' which King Alfred collected in his *Enchiridion* or handbook.[235] The motif of the 'flowers of the Scriptures' may well also be Aldhelmian in origin, but it was a motif beloved by Byrhtferth who wrote of Germanus at Fleury, for instance, studying the 'flowers of the Scriptures (*flores Scripturarum*)'.[236] The entire context of the Pseudo-Asser's account of King Alfred's learning to read and to pursue a scholarly life, is cast in a late tenth-century monastic mould. And if we need any further confirmation that the imagery of the Pseudo-Asser belongs not to the ninth century, but to the era of the monastic reformers at the end of the tenth, then we need only turn to the text of the *Regularis Concordiae Monachorum* of King Edgar, where we find there in the very charter of the monastic reformers, an instance of the bee metaphor used to describe the *vita regularis* in terms reminiscent both of the letter to Archbishop Æthelgar and of Byrhtferth's *Epilogue*.[237] There we are told that a Winchester synod of reforming clergy, encouraged by King Edgar, 'gathered from their praiseworthy customs [of Fleury and Ghent] much that was good and thus, even as honey is gathered by bees from all manner of wild flowers and collected into one hive, so also the said monastic customs . . . were, by the grace of Christ . . . embodied in this small book'. Byrhtferth of

Ramsey, as a hagiographer, writing in that monastery which was a flagship of Oswald's monastic reform, was steeped in the sentiments of the *Regularis Concordia*. It would have been natural for such a man, or for someone working under his influence, and writing the biography of a supposedly saintly King Alfred, to have transferred the metaphor of the monastic bees and the all-important 'little book' (*codicellus*) of the *Rule*, to the scholarly Alfred collecting 'flowers' or notes on biblical exegesis into his little handbook (*manualem librum*) or *enchiridion*.

Before leaving this study of the Latinity of the *Life* of King Alfred, it is important to remind ourselves of the strengths and limitations of this kind of evidence. The study of early medieval Latin vocabulary and syntax is too blunt an instrument on its own to allow us to point with certainty to either the identity of an individual author or even to the exact place in which he worked. This has not deterred scholars in the past from upholding a ninth-century date for the biography of Alfred on the basis of its Latinity and then by circular argument to proclaim that the *Life* in turn provides us with an example of Latin writing in the Alfredian era. It is important not to fall into the same trap by stretching the evidence too far in the opposite direction. We cannot provide proof on the basis of its Latinity alone that the *Life* of Alfred was produced in a given place at a given time and by a clearly identifiable author. What we can say from this study is that the *Life* exhibits a full-blown hermeneutic style that could date the work from any time in the second half of the tenth century until the end of the first quarter of the eleventh. Such a florid style, replete with arcane vocabulary and syntax could scarcely be placed at the beginning of the development of hermeneutic Latin writing even in the second quarter of the tenth-century. We can also say that the compiler of this work would have been very much at home in the world of scholarly monastic reformers who were based in such centres as Winchester, Canterbury, or Ramsey. Such general conclusions may seem to fall short of expectations raised by individual points of comparison between details in the text of the *Life* of Alfred and those in other works by known authors and by the circle of Byrhtferth of Ramsey in particular. These conclusions do nevertheless assume great importance when set alongside related findings. A comparison of the structure of the *Life* of Alfred will show that it exhibits close similarities to the *Life* of St Ecgwine—a *vita* which together with that of St Oswald and other known works of Byrhtferth of Ramsey can be shown to be otherwise related in their Latinity to the *Life* of Alfred. The *Life* of Alfred—on the basis of its Latinity—would fit quite comfortably within the repertoire of the early eleventh-century Ramsey school. That it does so fit cannot be proved on linguistic grounds alone, but when we add the realization that very specific hagiographical borrowings within the *Life* of Alfred derive from a source—Odo's *Life* of Gerald—which can most easily be accounted for by transmission to Ramsey via Abbo of Fleury and other Frankish and English travellers, then a Ramsey dimension becomes much more compelling. That same Cluniac influence on Ramsey also accounts for other Frankish influences in the *Life* as well as for its clear overtones of the spirit of late tenth-century monastic reform.

XII

A Forger Observed

THE SOURCES FOR AN AUTHOR'S READING AND EARLIER EDUCATION DO not reveal themselves consistently in every work of that writer, nor indeed, does evidence for knowledge of the same works between two writers prove they are identical persons. The works quoted or reflected by the style of an author relate in part to the nature of his particular subject. The *Life* of King Alfred is a text restricted in chronological scope and subject-matter, and it is further severely restricted by being based on a very close Latin translation of the Anglo-Saxon Chronicle. So, although we know that Byrhtferth, and presumably other members of his Ramsey circle, were familiar with Bede's *Historia Abbatum*, that work lay outside the chronological range of Alfred's *Life* and we should not, therefore, expect to find references to it. Similarly, Byrhtferth's knowledge of and interest in Bede's *De Natura Rerum* and *De Temporum Ratione* found scope in his works on the computus and could be accommodated also in a work of wide chronological range such as Byrhtferth's *Historical Miscellany* in the first part of the *Historia Regum*.[1] The author of the *Life* of King Alfred did, on the other hand, almost certainly know Bede's *Ecclesiastical History*, a work in which Byrhtferth was well read.[2] Both Byrhtferth and the Pseudo-Asser were avid students of Aldhelm and their Latin style was heavily indebted to his *De Virginitate*. They were both familiar with the *Carmen Paschale* of Caelius Sedulius, and however well-known that work may have been in the Early Middle Ages, Byrhtferth and the Pseudo-Asser both have the distinction—unusual for medieval writers—of citing Sedulius by name, before they quote him. Byrhtferth cites Sedulius in his *Life* of Oswald and in his *Manual*, while the Pseudo-Asser quotes him in an endeavour to make a false connection between the legendary Geat in the West Saxon royal genealogy and the Roman slave, Geta, a figure in a poem of Sedulius.[3] The learning displayed by the biographer of King Alfred has been underestimated by Stevenson and by later editors because of their prejudicial views on his Latin style. It is also the case, that in order to defend the authenticity of the *Life* of King Alfred, its supporters have tended to argue for its author to have been a poorly read and provincial 'Welsh' writer, thereby excusing the worst excesses in the organization and style of the work. The question has not been asked as to why Alfred would have especially summoned such a poorly educated cleric from furthest Wales, and then have honours heaped upon him as his personal tutor, and agreed to his becoming the king's biographer. Byrhtferth's Latin and his lack of organizational skills, however, can be shown to have been identical in faults and failings with those of the Pseudo-Asser. Lapidge greatly understated Byrhtferth's 'considerable freedom of handling' of his *Life* of St Ecgwine, for instance, which he conceded was 'an eccentric and idiosyncratic document'.[4] This is a *Life* in which its author, as we shall now see, regularly resorted to invention and blatant forgery and in which he indulged in lengthy digressions to conceal his lack of knowledge—all couched in a chaotic and bombastic narrative adorned with archaisms, neologisms, and Grecisms. But Byrhtferth is otherwise accorded the standing of a formidable scholar and as 'one of the most prolific of the authors of the late Anglo-Saxon period'.[5] Lapidge's assessment of Byrhtferth was based on precisely the same observations as he made on the Latin of King Alfred's biographer:

The quality of his Latin prose . . . shows Asser as a man with considerable stylistic pretensions but without any mastery of prose style. His sentences are frequently long and sprawling (in this respect Asser had studied Aldhelm too closely), his syntax unclear and his exposition garbled. As is often the case with authors whose overall command of Latin is insecure, Asser took care to embellish his prose with learned looking words of various sorts: thus grecisms, archaisms, and various other rare words adorn his writing.[6]

But while 'Asser' was judged as a provincial Welshman, Byrhtferth, on the other hand, was acclaimed as a prolific author even if he exemplified all the failings of 'Asser'.

A more dispassionate look at Pseudo-Asser's repertoire, however, reveals a man of much wider learning than has hitherto been supposed. It was surely naïve of Stevenson and his followers first to identify significant Frankish borrowings in the Pseudo-Asser's Latin, and then assume the man was not well read. The evidence must surely suggest the opposite—that a writer who had imbibed Frankish Latin vocabulary and mannerisms must surely either have had an education within the Carolingian Empire or else have been taught by a Carolingian master—a rare quality among Early Medieval English writers. We have recognized the Pseudo-Asser's heavy indebtedness to Odo's *Life* of Count Gerald of Aurillac, and very probably also to John of Salerno's *Life* of St Odo. Earlier Carolingian works consulted by the Pseudo-Asser definitely included Einhard's *Life* of Charlemagne and the anonymous *Life* of Alcuin, with the possible inclusion of the Astronomer's *Life* of the emperor Louis the Pious, the *Life* of Louis by Thegan, and perhaps also the Carolingian *Life* of St Eloi as well as a collection of Frankish annals.[7] He was familiar, too, with Nennius's *Historia Brittonum* and with works of Gregory and Augustine. Much has been made of the Pseudo-Asser's quotation in two instances from the Old Latin translation of the Bible, as opposed to Jerome's Vulgate. This use of a more ancient translation is seen to reflect the genuine Welsh backwardness of King Alfred's biographer and is supposed to reveal that St David's 'was . . . a cultural backwater'[8]—surely a recklessly dismissive comment on a leading Welsh ecclesiastical centre. What is not stressed is that in five other cases, the Pseudo-Asser may well be quoting from the Vulgate[9] and that the two quotations from the Old Latin Bible do not offer firm, much less conclusive, evidence for a Welsh background for the author of King Alfred's *Life*. In one case,[10] the reading is found in the ninth-century St Germain manuscript of the Old Latin Bible and also in the writings of Hilary of Poitiers. The second quotation is adapted from a reading cited by Irenaeus and Jerome.[11] Either of those quotations could have been picked up by the author, through his Frankish contacts, and at second hand from the original Old Latin Bible, which in any case, survived much longer in use in the Gaulish church, than it did in England. A more relevant feature of the Pseudo-Asser's use of the Bible is his frequent resort to biblical quotation in a biography which has much more to do with hagiography than with the life of a secular ruler who was supposed to be still living.

Because of the wall of prejudice which for so long has prevented any possibility of exploring new ways through textual analysis of identifying the background of King Alfred's biographer, students of this subject have been compelled to attribute the grossest errors of that biographer to his supposedly stilted Welsh training rather than to other causes. Let us take for instance, the Pseudo-Asser's account of the arrival of the Great Army of Danes in England in 865–6. He read in his version of the Anglo-Saxon Chronicle, which he usually followed with care, that in 'the same year, a great heathen army came into England and took up winter quarters in East Anglia'.[12] The Pseudo-Asser rendered this passage: 'In the same year , a great pagan fleet arrived in Britain from the Danube, and spent the winter in the kingdom of the East Saxons, which is called "East Anglia" in English.'[13] We note the confusion between the kingdom of the East Saxons (*in regno Orientalium Saxonum*)—i.e. Essex—and East Anglia or *East-Engle*.[14] That confusion might seem out of place in a work which we can now attribute to a Ramsey author, but Byrhtferth of Ramsey showed a similar confusion in his *Life* of St Ecgwine. While inventing that life, he seized on a record which he found in Bede relating to the pilgrimage of King Offa of the *East* Saxons to Rome in AD 709.[15] Bede clearly identified Offa as *regis Orientalium Saxonum* ('of the East Saxons'), but Byrhtferth described Offa in conjunction with Cenred of Mercia with the garbled formula of *rex famossissimus . . . Kænred, et Offa rex Merciorum Orientalium Anglorum* ('the most renowned Cenred and Offa, king[s] of the Mercians [and] of the East Angles [respectively]'.[16] In this case, Byrhtferth had transformed a king of the East Saxons into a king of the East Angles. Byrhtferth was writing in the opening years of the eleventh century when the political status and ethnic make-up of Essex had undergone radical upheaval. Essex had been originally ruled by its own dynasty of East Saxon kings which had been driven off the political map by King Alfred's grandfather, Ecgberht of Wessex in 825.[17] From then until the arrival of the Great Army, Essex had formed part of a West Saxon satellite kingdom along with Kent, Surrey, and Sussex.[18] The political orientation of Essex began to change radically after the establishment of the Danelaw, where some if not most of the Essex hinterland must have fallen under the Danish sphere of influence from 865 until the reoccupation of Colchester by Edward the Elder in 917.[19] Hart has argued that from then until 946, the ealdordom of Essex remained under the jurisdiction of the kings of Wessex,[20] but Hart also conceded that Essex might have formed part of the great East Anglian ealdordom of Athelstan 'Half-King', down to as late as 956.[21] With the death of Ealdorman Byrhtnoth in the Battle of Maldon, which was fought against the Danes in August 991, the fortunes of Essex became more and more integrated with those of East Anglia and east Mercia generally. Ealdorman Leofsige of Essex, who succeeded Byrhtnoth and governed Essex until 1002–3, also ruled all of East Anglia and much of the East Midlands, and with the advent of Cnut, we find that Essex from 1017 was allocated to Thorkell the Tall, Earl of East Anglia.[22] This confusion in the status of Essex—long ago ruled by East Saxons, and later by West Saxons, but now firmly integrated into East Anglia, is perfectly reflected in the writings of Byrhtferth of Ramsey and of the biographer of King Alfred. To Alfred's biographer and to Byrhtferth alike, *East Saxons* had become a term which was interchangeable with *East Angles* and no longer possessed a precise ethnic or political meaning.

The Pseudo-Asser's seemingly most outrageous gloss on the Chronicle's record of the arrival of the Great Army was his statement that the invaders had come from the Danube (*de Danubia*). That was a statement which belonged to 'the transmitted text' of the Pseudo-Asser's work.[23] Keynes and Lapidge attempted to explain what seemed a ludicrous blunder by suggesting that 'Asser' had 'made a mistaken connection between Danes and the Danube'.[24] In this, as in so much else, they followed Stevenson, who was, however, less happy with that explanation.[25] The idea that the Danes hailed from the Danube, was indeed erroneous, but it was derived from early eleventh-century book learning rather than from a lapse of memory or of sanity, on the part of a supposed provincial ninth-century Welsh writer. Dudo of St Quentin, a contemporary of Byrhtferth of Ramsey, who wrote his *History* of the dukes of Normandy between 1015 and 1026, traced the origins of the Northmen, Hæsten (or Hasting) and Rollo, from Dacia, from where they supposedly migrated to attack the Franks.[26] Dudo's reasons for elaborating on this Dacian origin of the founders of the Norman duchy in Francia were inspired by a desire on the part of late tenth- and early eleventh-century Norman writers to provide the recently Christianized and recently settled rulers of Normandy with pseudo-classical credentials. The notion of a Dacian—and consequently Danubian—origin for the Danish invaders of ninth-century Francia was a scholarly conceit prompted by the writings of Jordanes, the sixth-century historian of the Goths. Jordanes described in his *Getica* or *Gothic History* how the Goths and other north Germanic peoples had migrated into Eastern Europe in the second and third centuries, and had settled in Dacia, a region which he defined as being encircled by the Danube and by other rivers.[27] That same Gothic presence in the Danube basin in Late Antiquity was also dimly remembered but vividly celebrated in the heroic literature of Scandinavia—an oral literature, of which Dudo and other Norman writers were aware.[28] Jordanes account of how the defeated Vandals had been settled in Pannonia by Constantine, and were later settled by Stilicho in Gaul, may also have inspired more inventive Norman historians to take in later ninth-century Scandinavian raiders, such as Hæsten, along the same route.[29] Amory suggested that Jordanes' account of the Germanic tribe of *Asdingi* who occupied lands to the north of the Danube[30] may have been the immediate reason for Dudo's invention of a Dacian origin for Hasting/Hæsten. A further fiction on the part of Norman writers was the identification of *Dani* or Danes with the *Danai*, or heroes of the Trojan War, who were supposed to have settled in ancient Illyria.[31] This genealogical fiction secured a bogus place for the *nouveau* society of late tenth-century Normandy in the civilized Classical scheme of things. The *Dani* or 'Danes' were seen to have originated in Dacia—a suitably remote no man's land to the north of the Danube frontier of the Roman Empire—where second-generation Norsemen in Francia could claim a respectable and bogus ancestry, tacked onto a fanciful Greek association. Dudo began the First Book of his *History* by describing how the early north Germanic peoples invaded Dacia—a region which he located with reference to the Danube.[32] There can be little doubt that the statement in the *Life* of Alfred that the Great Army of Danes which attacked England in 865–6 hailed from the Danube betrays a knowledge of the earliest Norman tradition of a Dacian origin for Hæsten.

Although the Old English translation of Orosius deals with the political geography of Danubian lands in eastern Europe, no argument can be made for the historical Asser—or for anyone else—having found a Danubian origin for the Danish invaders of England in that source. Orosius was aware that 'the Dacians (*Datia*), who were formerly Goths (*Gotan*)' once lived in south-east Europe,[33] and that the Goths had occupied lands to the north of the Danube (*Donua*).[34] But there is no suggestion in Orosius—as there is none in Jordanes' *Getica*—of the Danes being located so far to the south and east of their Scandinavian homeland in northern Europe. Indeed the Old English Orosius shows the clearest knowledge of the Danish homeland being located in Scandinavia[35] and contains as we have seen, additional eye-witness accounts of ninth-century travellers to the Baltic region.[36] The idea of a Dacian homeland for ninth-century Danish invaders may not have been invented by Dudo, but it cannot have been much older than his time. It was a product of a recent and growing need in late tenth- and early eleventh-century Normandy to find a respectable origin for Scandinavian barbarians who had established themselves in northern Francia. Byrhtferth and his colleagues and pupils at Ramsey lived and wrote in a part of England which enjoyed a twofold cultural connection with Francia at the beginning of the eleventh century. On the one hand, monks of the reformed foundations of the southern Danelaw had close ties with Fleury and with Flanders. But they were also part of a provincial secular society which had the closest cultural and ethnic links with the Norman duchy. East Anglia and Normandy were two newly Christianized Scandinavian colonies, which from the time of Queen Emma and King Æthelred the Unready (from 1002 onwards), enjoyed the closest ties with each other, and with Denmark. The channels through which Byrhtferth had picked up the literary conceit of a Dacian—and thereby Danubian—origin for his English Northmen was the same channel through which tales of Rollo had found their way into the *Annals of St. Neots*.[37] Of one thing we can be certain. The account of the invasion of England by the Great Army of Danes, as given by King Alfred's biographer, does not contain a series of errors which amount to a nonsense of 'Asser's' own making. The confusion relating to the status of Essex accurately reflects the attitude of an early eleventh-century English writer. The statement that the Danes had come from the Danube, far from revealing the ignorance of a careless and provincial scholar, shows us an author, on the contrary, who maintained the closest contact with current thinking among Norman writers of the late tenth and early eleventh centuries. Such a statement on Danish Danubian origins could not have been made before the last quarter of the tenth century at the earliest.

A study of Byrhtferth of Ramsey's working methods and his handling of historical sources in his other known works sheds a great deal of light on how the *Life* of King Alfred was constructed. The Pseudo-Asser has certain definitive and crucial organizational and stylistic features in common with all the known major works of Byrhtferth. Both writers indulge in lengthy digressions which frequently bear little relationship to the main body of narrative and whose *raison d'être* within the text is to conceal the author's glaring lack of information on his chosen subject. Alternatively, such digressions, although relevant to the work as a whole, have been inserted at the wrong point in the discussion due to the writer's haste or because of his gross lack of organizational ability. The result is that the Pseudo-Asser and Byrhtferth spend a conspicuous amount of their time apologizing to the reader for having gone down green lanes or for having to recapitulate on a subject which has been inadequately dealt with several times earlier on in the narrative. So, the Pseudo-Asser's folk-tale of the wicked Mercian queen, Eadburh, constitutes a similar digression to say, the account of the Mesopotamian city of Nineveh in the *Life* of St Ecgwine, or the discourse on figures of speech in Byrhtferth's *Manual*. The Pseudo-Asser's chaotic handling of his account of King Alfred's many illnesses may be compared stylistically with Byrhtferth's numerous attempts in his *Manual* to explain the mysteries of certain numbers, as for instance, in his endless recapitulation on the significance of the number *four*. The lengthy digression on the life of Archbishop Oda in Byrhtferth's *Life* of St Oswald, however useful to modern historians, constitutes a *life* within a *Life* not unlike the way in which digressions on Æthelwulf and Eadburh constitute a sub-text within the *Life* of Alfred. While the *Life* of Oda constitutes a lengthy introduction to the *Life* of Oswald, the Chronicle provides the Pseudo-Asser with a central narrative and framework for his *Life* of Alfred. And just as Byrhtferth crudely grafted on or forged, irrelevant historical documents in his *Life* of Ecgwine, so, too, the Pseudo-Asser crudely pasted on motifs and inventions from the *Life* of Count Gerald of Aurillac and from Einhard's *Life* of Charlemagne to his biography of Alfred, without any serious attempt at integrating this material into the main narrative.

In his *Life* of St Ecgwine, an early eighth-century bishop of Worcester who founded the monastery of Evesham, Byrhtferth invented an entire biography from hagiographical folk-tales and a combination of forgery and the use of genuine but inappropriate historical material lifted from its proper context elsewhere.[38] Byrhtferth's unscrupulous technique in manufacturing this *life* is best illustrated in his handling of two 'documents'—a forged charter and a garbled version of an eighth-century letter of St Boniface, which had nothing whatever to do with St Ecgwine or his associates. In his zeal to provide Ecgwine with a *Life* which would be seen to compare favourably with biographies of other monastic founders, Byrhtferth showed himself to be an unscrupulous and ruthless forger. He reveals himself as a man with no regard for chronological considerations, who tried to conceal the poverty of his historical narrative by inserting one completely irrelevant historical document and by inventing another. He was a master, too, at fabricating 'historical' statements prompted by vague similarities in names between people who lived in different generations and in different geographical locations. He also invented episodes in the 'life' of his subject by tagging those inventions onto other genuine unrelated incidents, authenticated by Bede and others, thereby enveloping his fabrications in a smoke-screen of respectable historical association. Not only did Byrhtferth invent a charter in which lands were listed which were supposed to have been granted to the monastery at Evesham by various rulers, but as in the case of the Pseudo-Asser, Ecgwine himself was made to write in the first person.[39] More remarkably, the *propria persona* was retained for St Ecgwine through succeeding sections of the *Life* where the saint himself went on to narrate how further land grants were made to his monastery by Æthelwulf son of King Oshere.[40] St Ecgwine continues through a third episode (still writing in the first person) telling how he accompanied King Cenred of Mercia and King Offa of East Anglia (*recte* Essex) on their pilgrimage to Rome where the seal of papal approval was obtained for privileges granted to Evesham.[41] Three further sections follow, describing the proceedings of a bogus synod held *in loco celebri qui vocatur Alnae*, convened by King Cenred and supposedly attended by Archbishop Berhtwald of Canterbury and by St Wilfrid of York.[42] Further privileges were allegedly granted to St Ecgwine's monastery by the luminaries at this synod—men who, like Archbishop Wilfrid or King Cenred, were in fact either dying or already dead[43]—and after the celebration of the Eucharist the proceedings were concluded with the promulgation of the decrees in favour of Evesham and anathemas decreed against those who would infringe upon its rights.[44] This is not conventional hagiography, written simply with a view to edify. This is the work of a forger weaving a web of historical deceit. Nor was the motif solely to promote the claims of Evesham. For Byrhtferth, forgery would seem to have provided an end in itself.

Lapidge was aware that the so-called ancient charter supposedly providing the basis of this narrative in Ecgwine's *Life* was indeed a fabrication[45] but he preferred to view that forgery as earlier than Byrhtferth's time, even though he admitted 'we have no record of it but his [i.e. Byrhtferth's] own'.[46] The evidence would suggest, on the contrary, that all of this supposedly documentary-based material was forged by Byrhtferth himself. The language of these so-called eighth-century sources is that of Byrhtferth of Ramsey throughout, with its plethora of polysyllabic adverbs (including the Pseudo-Asser's *lugubriter* and *unanimiter*),[47] and what Lapidge describes as 'characteristic Byrhtferthian phrases'. Among the latter, we may note Ecgwine's description of Cenred of Mercia as *rex famosissimus* and his use of *rector regni*—both of which reappear in the *Life* of King Alfred.[48] The language of

Byrhtferth might merely suggest that he was, as Lapidge believed, paraphrasing older documents which seemed 'ancient' to him,[49] but this is very unlikely on several counts. First, we are not dealing here with one supposed charter, but with several diverse documents—a charter, an account of a pilgrimage to Rome where papal privileges were procured, and an account of a synod with supposed extracts from its decrees. Not only were all of these spurious consecutive sources alleged to have contained related privileges for the monastery of Evesham, but the assemblage is presented in the *Life* of Ecgwine with connecting narratives and added historical information which reveals the work of a single editor with a powerful historical imagination, even if he was clumsy and showed scant regard for truth or historical accuracy. Finally, all of the material—including most unusually, the spurious charter—is introduced by St Ecgwine himself addressing the reader in the first person—an effective ploy to lend urgency and historical 'weight' to material which can be shown to be otherwise fraudulent. Byrhtferth, or one of his circle, brought this technique to perfection in writing the *Life* of King Alfred in the *propria persona*, posing as Asser, and insisting again and again, how he was a regular witness to various incidents recorded in the life of the king.

A more detailed look at Byrhtferth's handling of his fake documents in the *Life* of Ecgwine convinces us of his personal responsibility for their authorship. The pilgrimage of the kings Cenred and Offa to Rome is dated by Bede to 709 and there is no evidence—apart from that of Byrhtferth—to suggest that St Ecgwine accompanied the kings to Rome.[50] According to the *Liber Pontificalis*, both Cenred and Offa died in Rome on their pilgrimage, and Bede, too, implies that both kings ended their days in monastic retirement there. But it was necessary for Byrhtferth to take Cenred home again to allow him to convene his synod, heaping yet more privileges on Evesham. The notion of the subject of a saint's *Life* being made to undertake a pilgrimage to Rome—fictional or otherwise—was commonplace. But Ecgwine's bogus pilgrimage, undertaken in the company of historically documented pilgrims, reminds us of the Pseudo-Asser's claim that the infant Alfred made not one, but two pilgrimages to that city, and that on the second journey he accompanied King Æthelwulf whose pilgrimage did indeed take place, according to the Anglo-Saxon Chronicle in 856. In the case of Alfred and of Ecgwine, the account of a bogus Rome pilgrimage was fused onto a genuine historical account of a similar pilgrimage, in order to lend a semblance of authenticity to the narrative. Lapidge has observed that it would have been impossible for the terminally ill Wilfrid—who died in April 709—to have attended a synod convened in Mercia by a king who was in Rome in that same year.[51] The supposed presence of St Wilfrid at a synod which decreed certain privileges to Evesham was designed to add further historical and ecclesiastical weight to the series of fabrications presented in the *Life* of Ecgwine. The cult of the Northumbrian Wilfrid had been promoted in England south of the Humber by the removal of that saint's relics to Canterbury by Archbishop Oda in the middle of the tenth century, and by the writing up of a new *Life* for Wilfrid by Frithegod of Canterbury, whose Latin style was shared if not imitated by Byrhtferth of Ramsey.[52] There was a more immediate reason why

Byrhtferth included Wilfrid in the list of dignitaries who attended the synod in 709. Byrhtferth's invention of the Rome pilgrimage of Ecgwine was prompted by his discovery that Bede in his *History* (v. xix) had noted the pilgrimage of Cenred and Offa to Rome. Following immediately on that record, Bede goes on: 'The same year that they [Cenred and Offa] left Britain, the famous bishop Wilfrid ended his days in the district called Oundle.'[53] For Byrhtferth, that tireless inventor of the past—and an inventor who worked in a hurry—this juxtaposition in Bede's narrative of the pilgrimage of Cenred and Offa and the death of Wilfrid was enough to prompt the outrageous idea of sending Ecgwine also on the Rome pilgrimage, and of bringing back all three travellers to join up with the dying Wilfrid at an imaginary synod.

There is no necessity to seek earlier versions behind the bogus documents used by Byrhtferth in his *Life* of St Ecgwine, nor is it necessary or proper for historians to defend Byrhtferth from the charge of forging them. His account of 'another letter' sent by Pope Boniface 'at the same time' as Ecgwine made his pilgrimage to Rome shows just how ruthless Byrhtferth might be in pressing irrelevant documentary material into service when his facts otherwise failed him. According to Byrhtferth, this letter was sent by Pope Boniface—presumably Boniface V (619–25)—to King Eadbald of Kent (616–40) and if so, then such a letter was sent some three generations before 'that time' when St Ecgwine made his imaginary pilgrimage in *c.*709! But none of that deterred Byrhtferth of Ramsey—nor the fact that the opening lines of the letter which he goes on to quote shows it to have been written not by Pope Boniface, but by Boniface the Englishman, and Archbishop of Mainz, to King Æthelbald of Mercia in *c.*747—some 40 years *after* Ecgwine was supposed to have gone on his pilgrimage.[54] Lapidge lamenting that 'we can scarcely surmise what led Byrhtferth to make so egregious an error' suggested that he confused St Boniface's condemnation of Æthelbald's 'incest' with that of Eadbald of Kent as described by Bede.[55] But there was little which those kings had in common to confuse Byrhtferth or any other writer. King Eadbald of Kent bore a different name from Æthelbald of Mercia, and they lived in different centuries and in different kingdoms. Furthermore, their reported vices were also significantly different. Eadbald of Kent had married his stepmother, while Æthelbald of Mercia was not accused of incest, as Lapidge believed. He was accused of sleeping with nuns—a fact luridly highlighted by Boniface at several key points in his letter.[56] Instead of searching for reasons why Byrhtferth had become confused by his sources, it is more reasonable to conclude that he was a careless and ruthless forger who worked in a hurry. The juxtaposition in Bede's *History* yet again, of a reference to a letter from Pope Boniface to King Æthelberht of Kent[57] and the account of Æthelberht's death and the subsequent marriage of his son, Eadbald, to his father's widow[58] undoubtedly prompted this further invention of Byrhtferth's. But the pope who wrote to King Æthelberht of Kent was Boniface IV (608–15), while the author of any supposed letter to Æthelberht's son, King Eadbald, would have been Pope Bonice V (619–25). The truth is that the name of any historical ruler snatched from any century was sufficient to prompt Byrhtferth of Ramsey into making the most preposterous of unhistorical connections. Byrhtferth's treatment of the narrative in the *Life* of St Ecgwine is little different from the Pseudo-Asser who first tells us that King Alfred had his schooling ignored by his parents, then tells us that his mother gave him a prize for his precocious reading as an infant, and concludes by claiming the king was illiterate until his thirty-ninth year. We are reminded, too, of the cavalier confusion of people's names in King Alfred's *Life*, where Alfred is once confused with Charlemagne,[59] where Alfred's son-in-law, Æthelred, is consistently confused with Eadred,[60] and where the Roman slave, Geta, is quite arbitrarily equated with the legendary Saxon, Geat. Byrhtferth quotes only the opening lines of the letter of St Boniface in his *Life* of Ecgwine, and he provides also his version of the closing or valedictory sentence.[61] But those opening lines clearly identify this document not as a letter to King Eadbald of Kent as Byrhtferth claimed it to be, but as the letter from Boniface and seven other German bishops to Æthelbald [of Mercia] 'king of the English'. Byrhtferth tells us that he does not wish to insert all of the letter because of its length[62]—and also, no doubt, because the sermon against fornication had nothing in the world to do with either St Ecgwine or with Ecgwine's pious patron, King Cenred of Mercia! The apology for not including all of the material is in line with the Pseudo-Asser's concern not to bore his readers, and the promise to return to the main theme of his narrative at the end of this outrageous digression, also echoes closely similar continuity phrases inserted in the *Life* of Alfred at the end of equally irrelevant digressions.

There is a much more remarkable point of contact between the passage describing the letter of St Boniface, by Byrhtferth in the *Life* of St Ecgwine, and a related incident in the *Life* of King Alfred. The Pseudo-Asser is our only source for the censuring of King Æthelbald of Wessex, older brother of King Alfred, for having married his stepmother, Judith, daughter of Charles the Bald of Francia. According to the Pseudo-Asser: 'Æthelbald . . . contrary to God's prohibition and Christian dignity, and also against the usage of all pagans, ascending the bed of his father, married Judith.'[63] We note that unlike the confusion in the *Life* of St Ecgwine between the names Eadbald and Æthelbald, here in the *Life* of King Alfred, Æthelbald of Wessex did at least have the same name as Æthelbald of Mercia who received the letter from Boniface protesting against his sexual licence a century before, and it was that correspondence between the names of the two kings which prompted the biographer to censure King Alfred's older brother. As ever, there was neither rhyme nor reason to this fabrication. Byrhtferth, or one of his circle, was familiar with Bede's account of the marriage of Eadbald of Kent with his stepmother, and he transferred Bede's disapproval of that marriage to the much later marriage of King Æthelbald of Wessex. Byrhtferth or one of his associates picked up the notion that the marriage of the West Saxon Æthelbald was contrary to pagan practice both from his knowledge of Bede's account of Eadbald of Kent[64] as well as from his knowledge of the letter from St Boniface the Englishman to King Æthelbald of Mercia—two sources which Byrhtferth had used to fabricate a totally false historical scenario in the *Life* of Ecgwine. As proof of that being so, we need only look at the Pseudo-Asser's comment that the behaviour of the ninth-century Æthelbald of Wessex 'was contrary to the practise of all pagans (*contra omnium paganorum consuetudinem*)'. That in fact, was not the case, but Byrhtferth when he read that letter of St Boniface which he alluded to, so wilfully, in his *Life* of St Ecgwine, had seen there Boniface's claim that fornication 'was held not only by Christians, but even by the pagans as a reproach and a shame (*non solum a Christianis sed etiam ab ipsis paganis in obprobrium et verecundiam deputatur*)'.[65] A copy of the text of that letter of Boniface was presumably available in Ramsey. The censuring of King Æthelbald of Wessex for his marriage to the Carolingian Judith was a late tenth- or early eleventh-century comment on the life of a ninth-century king. It is extremely doubtful, therefore, in the light of the evidence for Alfred's biographer's irresponsible handling of his sources, that the other account in the *Life* of King Alfred, of King Æthelbald's rebellion against his father, King Æthelwulf, has any foundation whatever. This is a conclusion reached in the face of conventional interpretations of a vague statement in the Chronicle that when King Æthelwulf 'came home to his people' in 856, 'they were glad of it.' That comment is assumed to relate—however obliquely—to Æthelbald's rebellion. The account of Æthelbald's supposed rebellion has, as we have seen, its own in-built suspicious elements.[66] It is also closely related to the record of King Æthelbald's 'incestuous' marriage to Judith, and it forms part of an attempt by the biographer of King Alfred to discredit Alfred's older brother.

One of the conspirators who was castigated by the author of King Alfred's *Life* for being involved in Æthelbald's rebellion was, as we saw earlier, Ealhstan, bishop of Sherborne. When Alfred's biographer came to record the death of Bishop Ealhstan under the year 867 in his translation of the Chronicle, he added three words to the Chronicle's record which tells us much about his glossing technique of the Chronicle which is so evident throughout King Alfred's *Life*. The Chronicle relates laconically of Ealhstan: 'he held the bishopric of Sherborne for 50 years, and his body is buried in the cemetery there.'[67] In the translation of the Chronicle in the *Life* of Alfred, the word *honorabiliter* ('honorably') has been added to the statement of Ealhstan's holding of the bishopric, and *in pace* ('in peace') was added as a gloss to the notice of the bishop's burial.[68] The addition makes a nonsense of the earlier allegation that Ealhstan had 'tried to commit so great a crime as to keep the king [Æthelwulf] out of his own kingdom'.[69] But that contradictory word *honorabiliter* inserted as a gloss into the Chronicle's record of Bishop Ealhstan's death is one typical of Byrhtferth of Ramsey. The word *honorabiliter*, used some seven times in the *Life* of King Alfred,[70] is one of those polysyllabic adverbs so popular with Byrhtferth, and that same word turns up in precisely the same context yet again in Byrhtferth's *Life* of St Oswald. In narrating the account of the assassination of King Edward the Martyr in 978, Byrhtferth describes how Ealdorman Ælfhere had the hidden corpse exhumed and prepared for proper burial, whereupon he and his followers 'buried him honorably (*eum honorabiliter sepelierunt*)'.[71] An alternative formula for 'honorable burial' used by the author of the *Life* of King Alfred is *honorifice sepultus [est]* as applied to the record of King

Burgred's burial in the church of St Mary in Rome.[72] Byrhtferth in his _Historical Miscellany_ in the _Historia Regum_ uses precisely the same alternative formula— _sepultum est honorifice_—for the burial of Archbishop Eanbald in York Minster in 796,[73] and for the burial of Abbot Edwin at Gainford in Co. Durham in Northumbria in 801.[74] So we have two variants of the same formula for a burial record used by both Byrhtferth and the Pseudo-Asser. And in the case of Bishop Ealhstan's obituary in the _Life_ of Alfred, the added word _honorabiliter_ may be clearly identified as a gloss from Byrhtferth's school. Its presence in the text of Alfred's biography betrays that inconsistent and careless approach so typical of Byrhtferth towards his historical narrative. Keynes and Lapidge[75] suggested that 'Asser' in his benign gloss-ing of the account of Bishop Ealhstan's death may have been 'defending one of his predecessors from the charges of complicity in the plot against King Æthelwulf'. The idea is a nonsense. If Alfred's biographer had been trying to exonerate Bishop Ealhstan, then why did he _twice_ implicate Ealhstan in a conspiracy for which that same biographer is our sole witness? Furthermore, it is extremely unlikely that the historical Bishop Asser had already become bishop of Sherborne at the time (AD 893) when the biographer of Alfred claims to have been writing, and that same biographer never once claims in his narrative, to be bishop of Sherborne.

Byrhtferth's interest in certain monasteries and in the burial places of certain saints as revealed in his known writings helps us towards a better understanding of the glosses and some of the expanded passages in the _Life_ of King Alfred. For instance, in following a translation of the Chronicle's account that in 876 'the enemy army slipped past the army of the West Saxons into Wareham', the author of the _Life_ of Alfred (chapter 49) adds that Wareham was a 'fortified site' with: 'a convent of nuns situated in the district called _Durngueir_ in Welsh and Dorset in English, between the two rivers _Frauu_ [Frome] and Tarrant, in a very secure position except on the West, where it is joined to the mainland'.[76] Rare additions to the Chronicle's text such as this have been cited by Whitelock as evidence for the fuller treatment of events by King Alfred's biographer, and by implication, for their contemporary and authentic testimony. But it can scarcely be a coincidence that Wareham in Dorset was the very place to which the body of King Edward the Martyr was taken for temporary burial after his murder—a murder so vividly described for us by Byrhtferth in one of his lengthy and irrelevant digressions in his _Life_ of St Oswald.[77] Everything about the martyred King Edward, as the friend of St Dunstan, and of Byrhtferth's hero, Ealdorman Æthelwine of East Anglia (the lay patron and founder of Ramsey), would have been of interest to Byrhtferth. In 980, King Edward's body was reinterred in the nunnery at Shaftesbury,[78] where in 1001 his relics were formally translated in a shrine.[79] That was precisely the time when Byrhtferth of Ramsey was at the height of his powers as a writer and purveyor of saintly biography. The translation of King Edward's relics in 1001 may help to explain not only Byrhtferth's gloss on Wareham in King Alfred's _Life_, but it may also partly help to account for the insertion in that work of the account of King Alfred's supposed founding of Shaftesbury as a model nunnery. Wareham may well have been fortified early in Alfred's reign, in preparation for the Second

War against Guthrum,[80] but the description of Wareham in the *Life* of Alfred as a *castellum* reveals the influence of the author's Frankish training and is otherwise consonant with the late tenth-century tone of the *Life*. Such glosses in the *Life* of Alfred then, far from vouching for a contemporary ninth-century date for the work, may only serve to confirm its later date and its association with Byrhtferth of Ramsey in particular.

The Anglo-Saxon Chronicle tells us that (in southern England) the Vikings wintered for the first time in 851, and MS B (*sub anno* 853) followed by the chronicler Æthelweard, names the place in which they wintered as Thanet.[81] The Parker Manuscript (A) of the Chronicle does not name the location of the winter camp,[82] and perhaps because King Alfred's biographer was following a version of the Chronicle which was close to that of the Parker Manuscript's text down to 893, he may also have found the location missing. The Pseudo-Asser made up the loss by naming the place in which the vikings wintered as Sheppey,[83] which was a blunder, because both Manuscripts A and B of the Chronicle specifically state that Sheppey was wintered on for the first (*ærest*) time, four or five years later, in 855–6.[84] Thanet, then, was clearly the place which the chronicler originally had in mind for the wintering in 851. The Pseudo-Asser went on to insert one of his typical glosses on the word 'Sheppey', of that type which has reassured many scholars as to his authentic ninth-century character. He says of Sheppey that 'an excellent monastery is established on the island' but such a monastery—supposedly flourishing *c*.890—is highly unlikely to have survived an initial viking onslaught in 835,[85] not to mention the enemies' wintering in 855 or the fact that the Danes controlled the Thames estuary from 871 until 878 if not longer. The author of the *Life* of Alfred also added a gloss to the Chronicle's record of a battle fought against vikings on Thanet in 853, supplying its ancient British name.[86] These monasteries, on two of the most isolated and exposed offshore islands in the Thames estuary must have been one of the earliest casualties of the viking age in England. But the Pseudo-Asser's interest in the Kentish islands of Sheppey and Thanet, as in the case of Wareham and Shaftesbury, may not be inconsistent with Byrhtferth's involvement yet again. Byrhtferth, at the beginning of his *Historical Miscellany* in the *Historia Regum* relates the tale of the martyrdom of the royal Kentish saints, Æthelberht and Æthelred.[87] These youths were slain at Eastry in East Kent and were buried in the monastery of Wakering in Essex.[88] Byrhtferth closed his account of the Kentish martyrs by narrating the tale of the foundation of the nunnery of St Mary's on Thanet by the boys' sister, Eormenburga or Domneva (*alias* Eafa, who died in 694), and how she placed her daughter, Mildrith (died 732) in charge of the nunnery there along with seventy nuns. Byrhtferth's interest in Kentish saints and their monasteries must have been encouraged significantly by the translation of the relics of those same martyred Kentish princes, Æthelberht and Æthelred, from Wakering to Ramsey in the reign of Æthelred the Unready (979–1016) at about the time or shortly before Byrhtferth was writing. The translation was accomplished by Ealdorman Æthelwine of East Anglia, the lay founder and patron of Ramsey Abbey.[89] Yet another of the Pseudo-Asser's disarmingly authoritative glosses relates to the condition of the walls of York. Following the Chronicle's account of the viking capture of that city and of the Northumbrian counter-attack in 867, the Pseudo-Asser adds his comment: 'for in those days the city did not yet have firm and secure walls (*Non enim tunc adhuc illa civitas firmos et stabilitos muros illis temporibus habebat*)'.[90] Byrhtferth of Ramsey showed precisely the same antiquarian interest in those once 'firm' walls of York, when he digressed to discuss that topic in his *Life* of St Oswald: '*Est civitas Eboraca metropolis totius gentis Northanimbrorum, quae quondam erat nobiliter aedificata, et firmiter muris constructa; quae nunc est dimissa vetustati.*'[91]

The Anglo-Saxon Chronicle records a solar eclipse 'for one hour of the day' under the year 879—the same year in which it records the withdrawal of Guthrum's army from Chippenham to Cirencester. The recording of eclipses is, as we have seen, a great rarity in this section of the Chronicle and this incident clearly relates to a remarkable total eclipse of the sun on 29 October 878—which by contemporary Anglo-Saxon reckoning fell in the year 879. A penumbral solar eclipse of 26 March 879 would not have been noticed in the southern part of the British Isles.[92] Apparent times for mid-eclipse of the October 878 phenomenon are put by astronomical calculation at about 1 p.m. in eastern Ireland, 1.35–1.42 p.m. at London, and 2.25–2.33 p.m. at Fulda.[93] The Annals of Ulster gives the correct day and month, timing the eclipse to 'about the seventh hour of daylight'.[94] The Annals of Fulda recorded this same eclipse on 29 October, observing that 'the sun was so dimmed for about half an hour after the ninth hour (*post horam nonam*), that stars appeared in the sky and all thought that night was threatening'.[95] None at Fulda was at 2.22 p.m. so the eclipse did indeed occur there just after none. Regino of Prüm timed this same eclipse to *circa horam nonam*.[96] The Anglo-Saxon Chronicle does not provide the exact time of this eclipse, but its compiler timed the duration of the phenomenon to one hour.[97] This was a reasonable approximation for the time of substantial eclipse and stresses the impact which the darkness made on English observers as at Fulda. The Pseudo-Asser added his own gloss to the Chronicle's record. He tells us that the eclipse occurred 'between nones and vespers, but nearer to nones (*inter nonam et vesperam sed propius ad nonam*)'.[98] None at London 'cannot have been before 2.20 p.m. apparent time',[99] and 'Asser' clearly suggests that the eclipse took place some considerable time after that for it to have been timed some way into the bracket 'between nones and vespers'—however much it may have been nearer to nones. In this the Pseudo-Asser was either guessing wildly, or more likely he had a collection of Frankish annals such as those from Fulda to guide him. It seems more than coincidence that his timing of the event is couched in terms which would fit an East Frankish observation but which is more than an hour too late for Wessex. The historical Asser would have observed the eclipse of October 878 some seven years before he arrived at the court of King Alfred from 'the remote westernmost parts of Wales'. If he had observed the eclipse in west Wales, the problem inherent in his observation becomes even greater. The eclipse in western Wales would have been observed shortly after 1 p.m. If the historical Asser had observed it in Wessex it would have been only slightly later. It is little wonder that Stevenson had to send his 'Asser' off as a visitor to the Continent 'at no great distance from Fulda'[100] at the time of this eclipse! D. J. Schove, approaching the records from the perspective of an astronomical historian found that all the contemporary authorities cited above had recorded this eclipse accurately with the significant exception of the author of the *Life* of Alfred. Making due allowance for the precise meaning and calculation of 'nones' and taking other 'strained interpretations' put forward by Stevenson and others into account, 'Asser's' observations still failed to make sense to a scientist. Schove's comment: 'Asser's [timing of the eclipse] is uncomfortably late for England, where mid-eclipse almost certainly occurred before none'[101] calls into serious question the credentials of the author of the *Life* of Alfred as a contemporary witness by a scholar who approached the problem from another discipline and with an independent mind. It was Stevenson, after all, who observed that: 'if it could be proved that the time of day assigned for the eclipse is accurate, it would be a conclusive proof of the authenticity of the *Life*'.[102]

The identification of Byrhtferth or one of his circle as the author of King Alfred's *Life* not only explains the presence there of apparently random comments on the text of the Anglo-Saxon Chronicle, but it also allows us insights into how the Ramsey school of writers worked as compilers of saintly and royal biographies. It has been assumed that while Byrhtferth invented a biography for the shadowy Ecgwine out of legend and thin air, his *Life* of St Oswald, on the other hand, is thought to contain unique and immensely valuable information on his own time. But Byrhtferth's lengthy piece on St Oda of Canterbury—which forms the introduction to Oswald's *Life*—refers to times and places which lay outside the experience and living memory of most men in Byrhtferth's circle, and Byrhtferth could be notoriously unreliable when handling such remote subjects. It is possible, that as Byrhtferth tells us, Oda was the son of a warrior who had invaded England as a member of Ivar's Great Army in 865,[103] and who presumably under the settlement between Alfred and Guthrum in 878, had become a Christian magnate in the southern Danelaw. But when Byrhtferth goes on to relate that the young Oda joined the household of a *miles* or thegn called Æthelhelm, who later (*c*.925) accompanied Oda on pilgrimage to Rome,[104] we need to be on our guard against a writer who, throughout his works, ruthlessly lifted material out of context in order to write a plausible narrative. To begin with, it seems unusual that Oda should have been educated within the household of an aristocratic layman. We should have expected him, as a future cleric and bishop, to have been educated in a monastic setting. There was an Æthelhelm, Ealdorman of Wiltshire, who died in 897[105] whom the Pseudo-Asser learnt from the Anglo-Saxon Chronicle 'took the alms of King Alfred and the West Saxons to Rome' in 887. The Pseudo-Asser noted that fact in chapter 86 of King Alfred's *Life*.[106] Such a man as King Alfred's ealdorman, Æthelhelm of Wiltshire, undertaking such a pilgrimage with such a mission, could well have provided Byrhtferth of Ramsey, writing over a century later, with a ready-made foster-father for the youthful St Oda. And Byrhtferth very conveniently supplied Oda yet again with Æthelhelm as a travelling companion on the pilgrimage to Rome, when Oda is said to have cured him of an illness. It was typical of Byrhtferth's method of writing historical fiction to graft bogus pilgrims onto historically documented journeys to Rome. And while the Pseudo-Asser's ninth-century Æthelhelm took King Alfred's alms (*eleemosynam*) to Rome, so too, St Oda and the tenth-century Æthelhelm made their offerings *tributis piis elemosinis*.[107]

Just as researches in the Anglo-Saxon Chronicle (which were necessary to fill out the narrative for the *Life* of King Alfred) are paralleled by the miniature *Life* of St Oda within the larger *Life* of St Oswald, so too, traditions which Byrhtferth picked up about St Oda may have been pressed into service in the *Life* of King Alfred. The tradition—and Byrhtferth does not put it any stronger than that (*dicunt quidam*)—that Oda's father had come in with the army of Ivar and Ubba,[108] combined with the notion of Oda having been brought up in the Christian faith and educated for ordination, may well have prompted the Pseudo-Asser to suggest in King Alfred's *Life* that even pagan (i.e. Danish) youths might be found studying in the monastery at Athelney: 'In that monastery, I also saw one of pagan race (*paganicae gentis*), brought up there and wearing the monastic habit, quite a young man and not the lowest among them.'[109]

Stevenson suggested that Oda might have been the very boy whom 'Asser' had seen at Athelney some time before 893—an idea which Keynes and Lapidge found 'attractive but unprovable'.[110] Robinson found it chronologically not impossible, but otherwise improbable that Archbishop Oda who died in 958 should have already been a monk at Athelney in or before 893.[111] We are reminded of the straining of chronology and stretching of historical argument which went towards Stevenson's 'proving' that it was possible for the infant Alfred to have glimpsed the fictional Eadburh in her misery, begging on the streets of Pavia![112] Robinson pointed out that in the *Life* of St Oswald, Oda was said to have acquired the monastic habit at Fleury subsequent to an education, not at Athelney, but in the household of the mysterious Ealdorman Æthelhelm.[113] Finally, we should expect to find Oda's earlier days spent outside Wessex if he were indeed a Dane. What is important, however, in this discussion is that several leading commentators on the *Life* of King Alfred have recognized strong links between the account of the Dane at Athelney in Alfred's *Life*, and the notion of Oda being of Danish parentage in the *Life* of St Oswald. There is indeed a strong connection, but it may be in the reverse order to that suggested by Stevenson. It was most likely the Pseudo-Asser writing in Ramsey in the early eleventh century who decided to place a Danish youth in King Alfred's model monastery at Athelney. The Pseudo-Asser's use of *vidimus* ('we saw') in relation to this young man's presence there, is all part of a wider and conspicuous protestation by the author that he was indeed a witness to many of the preposterous things which he describes. The notion that the Danish youth was in a monastic habit (*in monachico habitu*)[114] echoes Byrhtferth's record in the *Life* of Oswald of how Oda received the monastic habit at Fleury (*suscepit monasticae religionis habitum*).[115] For central to both the account of the monastery at Athelney in the *Life* of Alfred, and of Fleury in the *Lives* of Oda and Oswald, is concern for monastic reform and the image of the *habitus* as being a symbol of a life governed by the Benedictine Rule. The *Life* of St Odo of Cluny lays great stress on the importance of wearing the monastic habit, while the *Regularis Concordia* even stipulated that the monk ought to be buried after death, in his monastic garb or *cuculla*.[116]

There are two episodes in the *Life* of King Alfred which betray a Ramsey interest in mathematics and numerology, on the one hand, and in scientific enquiry, on the other, and both of these interests were acquired by Byrhtferth of Ramsey from his Frankish master, Abbo. The saintly Count Gerald of Aurillac was said by his biographer, Odo of Cluny, to have made a *Will* in the presence of his bishop, Gausbert, in which he made over his property to St Peter for the maintenance of his monastery at Aurillac.[117] Gerald was also said to have 'assigned dues to be paid each year to St Peter'. Later on in Gerald's *Life* we read how Gerald left his lands 'to relations and soldiers and even serfs' in some cases with a reversion to the church at Aurillac.[118] Provision was made for the liberation of one hundred of Count Gerald's serfs. Gerald's final or deathbed bequests issued in the presence of another bishop, Amblardus of Clermont, are alluded to yet again in his *Life*, and earlier, 'when all his produce had been rightly tithed, he [Gerald] ordered a ninth part to be set aside so that it might be used to buy various necessaries for the poor'.[119] Much of this is what we should expect from a pious lord anxious to settle his account with God and with his neighbour. In King Alfred's *Will*, the West Saxon king also made provision for the liberation of his serfs—indeed Alfred's provision may have been more generous than Gerald's in this respect.[120] Alfred also made bequests to his bishops and to monasteries such as Winchester and Damerham, but not—as we have noted—to the houses of Athelney and Shaftesbury, which were singled out for special attention by the Pseudo-Asser.[121] Apart from legacies which Alfred left to his family and retainers, there is no evidence in that king's *Will* for precise mathematical ordering in the dividing up of his inheritance. Indeed, as we should expect, the contrary was true, since vagueness was a necessary element in an age when the precise resources of distant estates could never be easily assessed, and when even the king's monetary resources in his royal chest might fluctuate widely in short periods of time. So Alfred ends his *Will* by directing that 'for the good of my soul let such provision be made in livestock, as is feasible, and also becoming, and as ye are willing to grant me.'[122] The number of livestock is not specified and it was left to the discretion of the king's executors to decide what was feasible (*swa hit beon mæge*). Alfred was at his most uncertain in relation to his cash resources: 'I do not know for certain whether there is as much money as this, nor do I know whether there is more, but I think that there is.'[123] And again: 'Now I had made other arrangements in writing concerning my inheritance, when I had more property and more kinsmen.'[124] This authentic muddle-headedness, so apparent in King Alfred's *Will*, has vanished when we turn to the pages of the Pseudo-Asser. Here we are introduced to a different Alfred—a king with an unreal and obsessive interest in mathematical divisions. Alfred, if we are to believe the Pseudo-Asser, commanded his thegns to divide his annual revenues into two equal parts. The first of these halves was reserved for secular use (*secularibus negotiis*) and the second half was reserved for spiritual good works.[125] But whereas the first half was divided into three portions, the second half was divided into quarters. So in the first half, one-third—or one-sixth of the king's total income—was spent on his warriors (*bellatores*) and his household; one-sixth on his craftsmen (*operatores*) 'from many races', and one-sixth on 'foreigners of all races'.[126] Of the second half of Alfred's revenues, a quarter—or one-eighth of his total income—went to 'the poor of every race', one-eighth to the monasteries at Athelney and Shaftesbury, one-eighth to his royal school (*schola*), and one-eighth to other monasteries in Wessex and Mercia, and—resources permitting—to monasteries in Wales, Cornwall, Gaul, Brittany, Northumbria, and sometimes in Ireland.[127] Apart from the unreality of the mathematical divisions, we see that there is no proper distinction between the secular and spiritual provisions, for while needy foreigners are assigned one-sixth of the king's revenues in the first half, the wandering poor 'of every race' receive one-eighth of the total revenues in the second half. We have seen how the dubious accounts of the founding and endowing of Athelney and Shaftesbury find no support in King Alfred's *Will*,[128] and it seems implausible that key churches and monasteries such as those at Winchester, Sherborne, Canterbury, and Worcester would have had to share in a blanket provision along with all other monasteries, at home and abroad, for their allocation of resources. Nor is it credible that the king's *bellatores* and his household thegns—on whom his personal safety and the very survival of his kingdom depended—would only have enjoyed one-sixth of the royal revenues, while five-sixths was spent on charities and luxuries. We have seen how a letter of Pope John VIII to Archbishop Æthelred of Canterbury—that same prelate who witnessed King Alfred's *Will*—suggested on the contrary, that Alfred was a man who had to be 'strenuously resisted' from encroaching on, or usurping the rights of the Church.[129] Most early medieval kings were careful if not resentful about how much land was alienated to the Church. Alfred was no Edgar, either in terms of generosity to churchmen or in the circumstances of his reign. Alfred had a dirty war with heathen vikings on his hands, in which the very survival of the Church was called into question, and he had more need than most kings for financial resources to fight off his enemies. Would such a ruler, pious or not, spend five-sixths of his entire income on the poor and the Church? And even if he were to do so, could he possibly hope to retain the loyalty of the all-important *witan*?

The Pseudo-Asser heaps yet further mathematical improbabilities on his pile of Alfredian statistics, by informing us that while the fighting men and household thegns received one-third of the first half of the kings revenues, service at the king's court was organized on a three-shift rota.[130] More complicated still was the proviso that while each group of one-third of the thegns attended on the king for one month, they were relieved by yet another third which had enjoyed a two-month respite at home.[131] So what is being described, is a rota in three divisions, with each division having its time divided yet further into thirds, spending two-thirds at home and one-third at court. This complex arrangement based on thirds and ninths can in no way be said to be confirmed by the evidence of the Anglo-

Saxon Chronicle under the year 893: 'The king had divided his army into two, so that always half its men were at home, half on service, apart from the men who guarded the burhs.'[132] Although the Chronicle lists three categories of men—those active on military expeditions, those 'at home', and those guarding the burhs—the basic statement here relates to two major categories or 'halves (*healfe*)'—those who were not engaged in warfare and those who were. The garrisons for the burhs presented the Chronicler with something of an anomaly, since fortifications were a new phenomenon, but the entry suggests that garrisons were considered to be a subdivision of those men who were on active service. Too much may have been made of Alfred's so-called military reorganization. It seems to have consisted of nothing more than having half the fighting force in the field and the other half at home in reserve. Such a primitive method of operating was probably as old as warfare itself, and in that very same year of 893, the Chronicle shows that the system, for Alfred, did not function well. English levies who had been investing a Danish force on the island of Thorney in the river Colne raised the siege because 'they had completed their term of service and used up their provisions'.[133] In spite of the fact that 'the king was then on the way there', the besieging English force on the Colne threw away its initiative and set off for home. There is nothing here to substantiate the Pseudo-Asser's elaborate divisions of service into thirds and ninths, nor is there any evidence for a professional fighting force. On the contrary, we are presented with a picture of yeomen, who were entitled by customary law to withdraw from a campaign when their obligatory length of service had been fulfilled and when all their provisions had been consumed.

The essential difference between what the Pseudo-Asser writes about the service provided by Alfred's followers and that described in the Chronicle is that while the Chronicle is speaking of a simple division of fighting men on campaign, the Pseudo-Asser is describing a much more complicated rota of attendance in the king's household. Everything that the Pseudo-Asser tells us of Alfred's allocation of revenues and organization of court service hinges on a stylized mathematical scheme based on thirds, sixths, ninths, and quarters. We are reminded of Byrhtferth of Ramsey's obsession with numerology in his *Manual*. Byrhtferth devotes much time there to explaining repeatedly, the meaning of a quarter and the mystical significance of fours—four seasons, four ages of man, four letters in the name of Adam, four Evangelists, four elements, four virtues, and four winds.[134] Elsewhere in his apocryphal *Life* of St Ecgwine, Byrhtferth promises to divide the work into four parts to cover the four 'ages' of his subject—childhood, adolescence, youth or manhood, and old age.[135] In the *Life* of Ecgwine also, Byrhtferth relates a folk-tale concerning the foundation of the monastery of Evesham, where a grant of forested land acquired from King Æthelred was supposed to have been divided into four sections (like the tetrarchy in biblical Judaea) by St Ecgwine, who placed four swineherds in charge of each section.[136] This tale ought not to be taken seriously, and certainly not literally,[137] and the Pseudo-Asser's division of King Alfred's revenues needs to be approached with similar caution.

Threes, sixes, and nines enjoy an elementary mathematical relationship, and in medieval minds were associated with the mystery of the Holy Trinity. Witness what Byrhtferth has to say of the number six:

The number six, therefore, by its magnitude, its sublimity, and its dignity surpasses the power of expression of our language. Writers on numbers, indeed, are wont to indicate its eminent worth to the children of the church in this way. (diagram). 'For one', he (Augustine) says, 'and two and three make six'. This number as Aurelius Augustine says, is termed a perfect number; because it is made up of its fractions; for it has these three: a sixth, a third, and a half, nor is there any other possible aliquot part to be found in it. The sixth part of it is one; the third is two, and the half three. But one, two and three added together make up this same six. Its perfection is commended to us in Holy Scripture in the words: 'In six days God finished his works.' On the sixth day man was made in the image of God. . . . There were six water pots in Cana of Galilee.[138]

It is a mind such as this, steeped in biblical allegory and obsessed with elementary mathematical relationships, which lies behind the division of Alfred's income into halves, thirds, and sixths; as well as quarters and eighths; and which devised Alfred's supposed rota of military service on the basis of thirds and ninths.

Conspicuously absent from the *Life* of Alfred as it stands in Stevenson's edition is the numerological circumlocution of *bis bina* ('twice two') for *quatuor* or 'four'. *Bis bina* occurs not only throughout the *Enchiridion* or *Manual* of Byrhtferth, but it also occurs in his *Life* of St Ecgwine and in the *Life* of St Oswald.[139] This phrase reflects Byrhtferth's obsession with numerology and in the multiplicative qualities of numbers in particular. We should therefore expect to find this formula in the Pseudo-Asser's *Life* of King Alfred. Byrhtferth promised to divide the *Life* of St Ecgwine into four parts (*in bis binis partibus*),[140] but although the *bis bina* phrase recurs in that *Life*, Byrhtferth also used the conventional *quat(t)uor* when describing the division of the wood at Evesham into four sections.[141] The Pseudo-Asser, in his *Life* of King Alfred, describes how the second half of Alfred's annual income was divided *in quatuor partibus* where we would have expected Byrhtferth to have written *in bis binis partibus*.[142] In this case, Byrhtferth's version of Alfred's *Life* in the *Historia Regum* does not help, since that precise division is not discussed in the concluding summary of the work.[143] The Pseudo-Asser translates the phrase *ymp iiii niht* ('four days later') in the Anglo-Saxon Chronicle's account both of the West Saxon attack on Reading and of the battle of Ashdown in 871, as *post quatuor dies*.[144] But Byrhtferth in his version of that same passage in Alfred's *Life* in the *Historia Regum* renders *post quatuor dies* as *bis binis dierum*[145] which is a remarkable rendering of an inconsequential phrase in the summary of a work done by a careless man who worked in a hurry. It is quite possible that this phrase was already in Byrhtferth's exemplar of the *Life* of Alfred and that the version printed by Archbishop Parker is an edited one. In these discussions, we need to bear in mind constantly that no inherent primacy can be attached to readings in the printed text of Parker, over readings in the shortened version of Alfred's *Life* as supplied in the *Historia Regum*, nor indeed did the lost Otho manuscript necessarily have any claim to a greater antiquity than the earliest version of Byrhtferth's summary in the *Historia Regum*. In other words, the form *quatuor dies* in chapter 36 of Stevenson's edition of Parker's version of the *Life* of Alfred may be a later emendation, and the original reading of Byrhtferth's text may have been the *bis binis dierum* that now survives in Byrhtferth's summary of the Pseudo-Asser's work. Byrhtferth's summary renders the threefold division (*in tribus partibus*) of the first half of King Alfred's revenues as *trifarie*[146]—a phrase that echoes the *bifarie* or 'twofold' division of Alfred's total income as described by the Pseudo-Asser[147] and which reminds us also of Byrhtferth's *quadrifarie* or 'fourfold' explanation of the lunar year in his *Manual*.[148]

If the mathematical mind of Byrhtferth can be discerned in the unreal divisions of Alfred's revenues, it reveals itself much more clearly in the account of King Alfred's celebrated invention of the horn lantern. The Pseudo-Asser's account runs as follows:

He instructed his chaplains to produce an ample quantity of wax, and when they had brought it, he told them to weight it against the weight of pennies on a two-pound balance. When a sufficient amount of wax, equivalent in weight to 72 pennies, had been measured out, he told the chaplains to make six candles out of it, each of equal size, so that each candle would be twelve inches long and would have the inches marked on it. Accordingly once this plan had been devised, the six candles were lit so as to burn without interruption through the twenty-four hours of each day and night.[149]

A lantern, consisting of a wooden frame with translucent windows of shaved horn, was devised to house the candles and protect them from gusts of wind, thereby ensuring a consistent rate of burning and a regular measuring of time. What immediately strikes us about this passage in the Pseudo-Asser is the wealth of technical and statistical detail on offer here. In this it is closely related to the account of Alfred's finances, and the complexity of detail provided in both accounts stands out in stark contrast to the poverty of biographical information on King Alfred himself—in a work which purports to be the life of a king and not a scientific treatise.[150] Much scholarly effort has been expended on the precise nature of this candle clock, with Stevenson calculating that each candle weighed twelve penny-weights or approximately five-eighths of an ounce.[151] It may be irrelevant to ask how long it would have taken such a fragile candle, twelve inches long, to burn itself out, or to ask how such a long and slender candle was fixed in its holder? A more profitable line of enquiry is to ask why it was that King Alfred was supposed to have invented this clock in the first instance? The reason, the Pseudo-Asser offers us was because of Alfred's determination to offer God

one half of his mental and bodily effort both by day and night. But because he could not in any way accurately estimate the duration of the night hours because of darkness, nor of the daytime hours because of the frequent density of the rain and cloud, he began to reflect on how he might be able . . . to preserve the substance of his vow unfailingly until he died, by means of some enduring principle, without any kind of uncertainty.[152]

The notion of Alfred's desire to offer half his life in the service of God, having become so obsessive to the point of wanting to calculate that time with exactitude 'by means of some enduring principle', depends on our acceptance of the hagiographical view of Alfred as a saint. If we accept this story, then we must also view Alfred as a frustrated saintly astronomer-king, who, failing to read the time from the sun and stars, was driven to invent a candle clock to satisfy his obsession with giving half of his life up to prayer and to God. Such a vision does not tally with our understanding either of Alfred from other sources, or of the essentially agrarian life of the warrior aristocracy in the Middle Ages, whose lifestyle was locked into easy and ill-defined rhythms of the seasons. Even if Alfred had adopted a neurotic approach to time-keeping, as he is alleged to have done *vis-à-vis* his illnesses and his spiritual life, the realities of his situation as a warrior-king defending his people and their territory from a Danish enemy constantly on the move would scarcely have allowed or encouraged a time-keeping mentality more appropriate to a twenty-first-century businessman. In fact, this passage reveals more about the biographer's own obsession with precise calculations of time than anything it may tell us of the historical Alfred. We have no evidence outside the account of the Pseudo-Asser to show that Alfred had an interest in astronomy and horology. We have an abundance of evidence to show that Byrhtferth of Ramsey was obsessed by both.

Byrhtferth in his *Manual* discusses tides and phases of the moon. He says that 'the moon rises four points [on the dial] later than it did on the previous day',[153] and he is a mine of miscellaneous information such as that 'the moon shines for twelve hours when it is fifteen days old'.[154] Most of what Byrhtferth writes may be derived from Bede, or from his master Abbo, or elsewhere, but Byrhtferth's all-absorbing interest in the natural sciences is never in doubt. He claims, for instance, that in the year in which he was writing his *Manual* (AD 1011), the moon was twenty-three days old on 1 January.[155] He supplies a chart not only of the phases of the moon, but also of the zodiac, showing the length of time spent by the sun in each constellation.[156] With Byrhtferth's zodiacal chart before us, we note his two references, in his *Life* of St Oswald, to the sun moving through the constellations of Aries, Taurus, and Gemini.[157] Byrhtferth in that same work dated St Oswald's laying of the foundation of the church at Ramsey with reference to the positions of the constellations of Aries and Cygnus.[158] He writes yet again by way of simile in his *Life* of St Oswald of the clouding over of the Pleiades and other stars in the night sky.[159] Byrhtferth, in his *Historical Miscellany* now prefixed to the *Historia Regum*, informs us in his discussion of eclipses that they are not always visible because of cloud-cover.[160] Byrhtferth of Ramsey was clearly a keen observer of the night sky, and it was possibly he, rather than King Alfred, who dreamt up the idea of inventing a candle clock to tell the time on cloudy and rainy nights in Early Medieval England.

Byrhtferth also tells us of the seven divisions of the night—divisions which signposted the monks through their rotas of the Night Office.[161] It was those same 'services of the hours (*celebrationes horarum*)' observed in a 'daily round (*cursum diurnum*)' which the monk-like Alfred was alleged by the Pseudo-Asser to have 'kept by him day and night in a single book' from earliest childhood as he participated in the monastic Day and Night Offices (*horas diurnas et nocturnas*).[162] Byrhtferth discusses minutes, hours, and days and links his discussion with the sun-dial thus:

The word *day* is used in two ways—*naturaliter et vulgariter*, i.e. in a natural and a popular sense. It is the nature of the day to have twenty four hours from the rising of the sun until it shows its light again above. *Vulgaris vel artificialis dies*, that is to say the vulgar or artificial day, is from the beginning of the sun until it sets and returns to the joy of mankind. The day which has twenty four hours has ninety-six points. Four *puncti* that is points, make an hour in the course of the sun, and the 'point' is so called, because the sun ascends point by point on the time piece . . . Observe O Clerk how the sun ascends point by point on the dial of the time-piece.[163]

The man who informs us that each year consists of 35,190 'points' on the sun-dial, or 87,660 minutes, or 1,931,060 'atoms'[164] is just the person to invent the tale of a saintly King Alfred's obsession with time-measuring and time-keeping in order to observe the hours of the Divine Office and to devote half of his life to God. Not only does Byrhtferth speak of sun-dials, sun clocks, and time-measurement, but he of all scholars in ninth- and tenth-century England shows us how to calculate the weight of King Alfred's supposed candles in pennies: 'Priests skilled in the computus say that the day must have 24 hours, and we say that twice six scruples make a *semi-uncia*, that is half an ounce. . . . An ounce consists of 24 pence. There are twelve times twenty pence in a pound.'[165] Even if such information were entirely derivative, it shows at the very least that Byrhtferth was aware of these matters, and that he was intensely interested in them. On Byrhtferth's reckoning, each of King Alfred's candles weighed only half an ounce—even flimsier than those envisaged in Stevenson's calculation. But exact figures are meaningless. What matters is that Byrhtferth combined an interest in weights and coinage; clocks, astronomy, and numerology, and he brought all of these interests to bear in the *Life* of King Alfred.

There are other aspects of this tale of Alfred's candle clock which lead us back once more from Byrhtferth through his master, Abbo of Fleury, to the *Life* of Count Gerald of Aurillac. Alfred, according to his biographer, ordered his chaplains 'to produce an ample quantity of wax' and when they had weighed out seventy-two penny-weights, they made candles for the king which 'were lit so as to burn without interruption through the twenty four hours of each day and night in the presence of the holy relics of a number of God's chosen saints which the king always had with him everywhere'.[166]

It was because the wind gusted through not only doors and buildings where the king lodged, but also 'through the thin material of tents' that Alfred devised the lantern to protect his candles from the gale.[167] Count Gerald of Aurillac also collected wax in large quantities, and like King Alfred, he had it converted into candles to burn not just as a lamp:

His tenants and clerics, who loved him dearly as a father, often brought him bundles of wax, which he with many thanks accepted as great gifts. And he did not allow any of this wax to be burnt for his own use, but he ordered it all to be burnt in lights before the altar or relics of the saints, which he had carried about with him.[168]

So, Gerald, like Alfred, had wax candles burning before those relics which both men were believed to have carried about with them in tents. Gerald was an enthusiastic collector of relics, which he paid for not only with horses and money, but also with tents.[169] The Count had relics of the saints in his tent while he was camped near Sutri on a journey through Italy, and on yet another occasion we read of Gerald sleeping in his tent with 'a candle burning before his bed which was usual'.[170] Byrhtferth,—or one very close to him—who had the *Life* of Count Gerald before him, giving him his model for the saintly and sickly Alfred, seized on the image of the ruler in his tent with wax candles burning in front of his relics, and inspired by his own interest in horology and numerology, fabricated the story of King Alfred's invention of the candle clock. As ever, the passages relating to wax, candles and relics in the *Life* of Gerald, stand in a primary role in relation to those in the later and clearly more derivative *Life* of Alfred. That is not to say that the historical Alfred did not carry relics about with him, or that he lacked an abundance of candles. It is the context in which these matters are narrated in the *Life* of King Alfred that questions whether we are dealing with anything more than mere borrowing of motifs.

XIII

Burning Cakes and a Welsh Dimension

THE TALE OF HOW KING ALFRED BURNED THE CAKES IS TOLD BY THE author of the earliest *Life* of St Neot who wrote very probably in the eleventh century:

There is a place in the remote parts of English Britain far to the west, which in English is called Athelney and which we refer to as 'Athelings' Isle'; it is surrounded on all sides by vast salt marshes and sustained by some level ground in the middle. King Alfred happened unexpectedly to come there as a lone traveller. Noticing the cottage of a certain unknown swineherd (as he later learned), he directed his path towards it and sought there a peaceful retreat; he was given refuge and he stayed there for a number of days, impoverished, subdued and content with the bare necessities. Reflecting patiently that these things had befallen him through God's just judgement, he remained there awaiting God's mercy through the intercession of His servant Neot; for he had conceived from Neot the hope that he nourished in his heart. 'Whom the Lord loves', says the apostle 'He chastises; He scourges every son whom He adopts' [Heb. 12: 6]. In addition to this, Alfred patiently kept the picture of Job's astonishing constancy before his eyes every day. Now it happened by chance one day, when the swineherd was leading his flock to their usual pastures, that the king remained alone at home with the swineherd's wife. The wife concerned for her husband's return, had entrusted some kneaded flour to the husband of sea-borne Venus [Vulcan, the fire god, that is, the oven]. As is the custom among countrywomen, she was intent on other domestic occupations, until, when she sought the bread from Vulcan, she saw it burning from the other side of the room. She immediately grew angry and said to the king (unknown to her as such): 'Look here, man, You hesitate to turn the loaves which you see to be burning, Yet you're quite happy to eat them when they come warm from the oven!'

But the king reproached by these disparaging insults, ascribed them to his divine lot; somewhat shaken, and submitting to the woman's scolding, he not only turned the bread but even attended to it as she brought out the loaves when they were ready.[1]

A major point of this story is that King Alfred was so humbled by the scolding wife that he not only watched the bread and turned it, but he even assisted the crone as she brought out the cooked loaves. In other words, the once all-powerful king was transformed into the most menial of servants in a swineherd's hut. A king, who by definition was the servant of no man, had now become the servant of the lowest of women. We have here an alternative version of the reversal-of-roles motif which was evident in the Pseudo-Asser's tale of the Mercian queen, Eadburh, in the *Life* of King Alfred. Just as Alfred became an outcast at distant Athelney,

Eadburh was also cast out upon the world, friendless and without means, in far-off Pavia; but unlike Alfred, Eadburh was portrayed as a wicked queen who deserved her fate and so she had no St Neot to rescue her. Alfred, as portrayed in the tale of the burning cakes, was not entirely blameless, but unlike Eadburh, he was redeemable. In his efforts to glorify Neot, the author of that saint's *Life* suggested that Alfred was being punished by God for his sins, but because the king had heeded the earlier warnings of Neot, that saint eventually interceded with the Lord to rescue Alfred and restore him to power in Wessex. Ideas and ideals of Anglo-Saxon kingship permeate this folk-tale of King Alfred and the cakes. Alfred is assumed by many modern scholars to have ignored the burning cakes because he was preoccupied with affairs of state. But no such statement is made or implied in this earliest version of the tale. Alfred got himself into trouble with the swineherd's wife, because as a king it was impossible for him to be concerned with menial tasks, and so the cakes burned, not because he was preoccupied or careless, but because he *was* a king. The wife failed to understand, for we are told that Alfred's true identity as king was hidden from her, and the king was forced to suffer her anger and become her servant while retaining his disguise. We are reminded of William of Malmesbury's tale of how the Danish king Olaf Gothfrithsson disguised himself as a harper in order to gain access to King Athelstan's war camp.[2] All went well until Olaf refused to accept a reward for his music-making, thereby revealing his royal identity—for a king might not accept a gift for such a service. Of course, there are points of divergence between the stories. Olaf failed to conceal his royal identity, while Alfred suffered the insult and retained his secret. Nevertheless, both rulers are shown laying aside the trappings of kingship and disguising themselves in menial roles, and both kings inadvertently revealed their true royal status—to their readers at least—Alfred by failing to tend to the cakes, and Olaf by failing to accept a reward. As it happens, William of Malmesbury provides a link between the tale of Alfred hiding *incognito* in the swineherd's cottage as told in St Neot's *Life*, and the folk-tale relating to King Olaf disguised as a harper. For earlier in his *Gesta regum*, William also included a brief notice of Alfred, who while hiding at Athelney, disguised himself as a jester or mimic actor (*mimus*) and 'as a professor of the jocular art (*ut joculatoriae professor artis*)' spied on the Danish war camp of Guthrum.[3]

It was indeed an understatement to claim for this legend of the cakes that 'its authenticity cannot . . . be guaranteed'.[4] Equally, it was a misplaced trust in the value of Alfred's *Life* as a contemporary source which prompted Keynes and Lapidge to question the cakes yarn solely on the grounds that it did not appear among the even more preposterous anecdotes of the Pseudo-Asser. The cakes anecdote is nothing more than a folk-tale invented in the late tenth or early eleventh century, and most probably committed to writing for the first time by the compiler of the earliest *Life* of St Neot. The account of Alfred's reign in the Anglo-Saxon Chronicle was in part responsible for the general development and shaping of such legends for over a century after the king's death. We have seen how the Chronicle fails to tell the full truth in explaining Alfred's victory over

Guthrum in 878, and how that source exaggerated Alfred's predicament before his eventual triumph.[5] The melodramatic tone of the entry for 878 with its exaggerated sense of Alfred's isolation and of desertion by his warriors was bound to fuel the imagination of a later age:

In this year in midwinter after twelfth night the enemy army came stealthily to Chippenham, and occupied the land of the West Saxons and settled there, and drove a great part of the people across the sea, and conquered most of the others; and the people submitted to them, except King Alfred. He journeyed in difficulties through the woods and fen-fastnesses with a small force . . . and afterwards at Easter, King Alfred with a small force made a stronghold at Athelney.[6]

It was Alfred's genuinely beleaguered situation on Athelney in 878 which caught the imagination of a later generation, and someone who read this passage in the Chronicle, developed a marvellous tale of how the king arrived as a lone fugitive at the herdsman's hovel.

An abbreviated version of the tale of Alfred and the cakes appears in an Old English homily on St Neot dating from the early twelfth century. Alfred in this homily is cast in the role of a deserter who in the face of the Danish threat 'abandoned all his soldiers and his chieftains, and all his people, his treasures and treasure chests' and fled to Athelney.[7] There Alfred sought refuge with a swineherd whose spouse, now an 'evil wife' scolded him for warming himself by her fire while neglecting to turn her loaves. Yet another version of the tale appears in the *Annals of St. Neots*, that East Anglian chronicle which was put together in its final form at Bury St Edmunds sometime in the period *c*.1020–35.[8] In this version the swineherd (*subulcus*) has become a cow-herd (*vaccarius*), and although Alfred conceals his identity as king, that point is greatly lost by portraying him 'sitting by the fire . . . busy preparing a bow and arrows and other instruments of war (*bellorum instrumenta*)'.[9] So, although he may not have been recognized as a king, Alfred clearly projected the image of a warrior to his hosts, and therefore demonstrated his social superiority. This version of the tale includes two hexameters enshrining the woman's rebuke to the king, which are borrowed from the tale as told in the *Life* of St Neot. But otherwise the two accounts are not close, except for the important qualification that the tale is introduced in the Annals of St Neots with the statement *ut in uita sancti patris Neoti legitur* ('as is read in the *Life* of the saintly father, Neot').[10]

The story of the burning cakes would take its place beside other later legends of King Alfred and be of no further interest in our quest for the historical king, were it not that the *Life* of St Neot, in which it belongs, holds a key to our understanding of how the image of the legendary Alfred has come to obscure our efforts to reach a realistic assessment of the ninth-century ruler. An investigation into the origin of the St Neot connection with the Alfred legend leads us along a trail outside Alfredian Wessex, both in place and time, and we end up once more in the world of those early eleventh-century monastic reformers in East Anglia—a world dominated by Byrhtferth of Ramsey and his school. The problem is an immensely complicated one, for the texts of the *Life* of King Alfred, the *Life* of St Neot, and the Annals of St Neots have all been transmitted under the mutual influence or borrowing of one from the other. All three texts may, as we shall see, have been compiled within the same Ramsey scriptorium. It is the stubborn insistence—through three generations of modern scholarship—on a ninth-century date for the *Life* of King Alfred which has hitherto prevented a proper understanding of the problem. It is perhaps best to begin with Archbishop Matthew Parker, who included several passages from the Annals of St Neots in his printed edition of *Asser's Life of King Alfred* in 1574. The most celebrated of Parker's interpolations from the Annals of St Neots contained the story of King Alfred and the burning cakes, and undoubtedly served to fix that tale for centuries in the Alfredian canon as well as in the popular imagination.[11] Parker included those interpolations in his edition of the *Life* of King Alfred in the sincere belief that they were also written by Asser, bishop of Sherborne, the contemporary of King Alfred, and for this he has been castigated by a succession of modern editors. Stevenson believed that 'more mischief has been wrought by Parker's interpolation of this long passage [about the burning cakes] than by any of his other falsifications of historic evidence'.[12] Dumville described the outcome of Parker's conflation of several sections of the Annals of St Neots as 'disastrous' and held that it accounts for the subsequent 'disrepute into which Asser's text fell because of Parker's interference'.[13] Parker has been unfairly cast in the role of editorial villain by modern scholars seeking a scapegoat for the confused state of Alfredian textual studies. Parker should be thanked for giving the text of the *Life* of King Alfred to the world as early as he did, particularly in view of the subsequent destruction of the only surviving manuscript of the *Life* in the fire of October 1731. And Parker cannot be blamed or made to take sole responsibility for believing that the Annals of St Neots were also written by Asser. Parker was not the first to have reached that conclusion and it is wrong to hold that he led the field in promoting this error. He was merely following the judgement of the antiquary, John Leland, who discovered the manuscript of the Annals of St Neots in St Neots in Huntingdonshire at the time of the dissolution of the monasteries in 1539. John Bale in 1548 shows that he, too, shared Leland's views on Asser's authorship of the Annals of St Neots,[14] and elsewhere Stevenson observed that John Caius also identified the Annals of St Neots with Asser's authorship in 1568—some six years before Parker's edition of the *Life* of King Alfred was published.[15]

The reason why so many later editors of the *Life* of King Alfred and of the Annals of St Neots have been displeased with Parker's interpolation of the anecdote relating to the burning cakes (and other passages from the Annals of St Neots) into the *Life* of Alfred, is that it complicated their efforts to prove a late ninth-century date for the *Life* of Alfred. The Annals of St Neots and the *Life* of St Neot were compiled more than a century after the time of King Alfred. So, if it could be shown that the interpolations from the Annals of St Neots were original to Parker's manuscript of King Alfred's *Life*, then clearly that could discredit claims for the early eleventh-century date for the manuscript, and it might also discredit claims for a ninth-century date for the *Life* of Alfred itself. It was in the interest of all those who owed allegiance to the 'Genuine Asser' school, to distance the tale of the burning cakes from the text of the *Life* of Alfred. The obvious folkloric elements in the tale of Alfred and the cakes—not to mention its origin in the eleventh-century *Life* of St Neot—did little to bolster credibility in a supposedly contemporary *Life* of a ninth-century king, which had already raised suspicions in the minds of critics for over a century. As it happens, the tale of Alfred and the cakes may indeed be accepted as an interpolation by Parker into the *Life* of King Alfred, but there is no need to treat it as a significantly different tradition in the development of the Alfred myth, from say, the tale of Alfred's winning of the book prize from his mother or the outrageous story of the wicked queen, Eadburh, at the court of Charlemagne. These latter tales do belong to the *Life* of King Alfred, but they may not be any earlier and certainly no more reliable than the tale of the cakes as told in the *Life* of St Neot. Scholarly efforts to purge the Pseudo-Asser's work of impurities introduced into it by Parker and others from sources such as the Annals of St Neots have failed to isolate a demonstrably ninth-century text. Such efforts have been inspired by a desire to prove the 'Genuine Asser' theory and have resulted in a false attribution of contemporaneity to the Pseudo-Asser's biography, and a consequent devaluation of the *Life* of St Neot and the Annals of St Neots in eleventh-century English historiography.

Studies of the Annals of St Neots and of the *Life* of St Neot have been dogged by failing to analyse those works for their own sake, and have been driven by prejudicial views on the relationship between them and the *Life* of King Alfred. A more balanced view of the relationship between these sources may be achieved, if it is assumed that the *Life* of King Alfred was composed not in the late-ninth century, but in the early eleventh, and that consequently it comes closer in time both to the *Life* of St Neot and to some levels at least, within the compilation of the Annals of St Neots. Acceptance that Parker was indeed responsible for adding interpolations in the *Life* of King Alfred from the Annals of St Neots should neither evoke criticism of the sixteenth-century archbishop nor in any sense devalue the standing of the Annals of St Neots as a source in its own right. Parker may be excused his editorial licence, however unfortunate the consequences, since the very nature of the Annals of St Neots inevitably prompted him to conflate them with his edition of the *Life* of King Alfred. The *Annals* are now accepted as a compilation which has drawn heavily from the *Life* of King Alfred (including material from seventy of Stevenson's one hundred and five chapters in his edition of the *Life of King Alfred*) and which has also drawn from a *Life* of St Neot.[16] It was the *Life* of St Neot which ultimately, at least, provided the compiler of the Annals of St Neots with a version of the story of King Alfred and the burning cakes.[17] It is small wonder, then, that Parker and his secretaries, seeing such a huge Alfredian dimension in the Annals of St Neots, and clearly recognizing the overwhelming contribution of the *Life* of King Alfred to the annals for the period 849 to 887, should have decided to draw freely on that source in preparing the first printed edition of the *Life* of King Alfred. The atavistic relationship between

Parker's edition of the *Life* of King Alfred and earlier influences of Alfredian material on the Annals of St Neots are set out diagrammatically in Figure 8.

The source which has the most important bearing on the *Life* of King Alfred is the *Life* of Alfred's supposed relative (*consanguinitate proximum carnis*) and contemporary, St Neot of Cornwall.[18] The twelfth-century British Library manuscript of the earliest *Life* of Neot contains a statement to the effect that King Alfred and St Neot were brothers.[19] Antiquaries of a later age were to latch onto this piece of nonsense and develop an idea that Neot was either a nephew or brother of Alfred. Whitaker concluded that Neot was none other than Alfred's older brother, Æthelstan, who had supposedly resigned from the kingship of Kent, which he had held under his father, Æthelwulf, and retired to Glastonbury under an assumed monastic name of *Neot!*[20] This interpolation—or indeed the notion that Alfred and Neot were in any sense relatives—is not to be taken seriously, but it reflects how closely intertwined the development of the Alfred and Neot myths had become by the early eleventh century at the latest. It shows too, how the Alfred and Neot myths may have been developed within the same literary circle in the same monastic centres, and the identification of that literary circle has a crucial bearing on the background to the authorship of the *Life* of King Alfred in the early eleventh century. Neot, according to his earliest *Life* was born in the territory of the 'eastern Britons (*Orientalium Britonum*)' which might mean in the eastern *parts* of British territory, i.e. eastern Cornwall, or in the confused mind of the writer, it might mean that he was born in the eastern parts of the island of Britain, and hence the phrase that the place is 'now known as England'.[21] He is said to have studied at Glastonbury either under Æthelwold or Ælfheah, later bishops of Winchester. After his ordination to the priesthood, he retreated as an anchorite to Cornwall. The location of his Cornish retreat as *Neotestoce* which was ten milestones from St Petroc's, identifies the place as St Neots, where he spent seven years in solitude before his pilgrimage to Rome.[22] On his return from Rome, he built a monastery at St Neots to house a monastic community and where King Alfred, hearing of his saintly reputation, sought him out. Since Neot was the hero of this particular tradition, the Alfred whom we see in the *Life* of St Neot is seen from a different perspective than that of the Pseudo-Asser's pious king. On the two occasions that Alfred is described as visiting his saintly relative, Neot is shown castigating the king for his wicked deeds (*prauis actionibus*) and later, lecturing him sharply for his evil behaviour that threatened the king with eternal hellfire.[23] Neot advised that gifts be sent to Pope Marinus for the English quarter in Rome. Alfred begged the blessing of St Neot, dispatched the gifts, and received a relic of the true Cross from Pope Marinus in return. Neot died on 31 July and was buried in his own church.[24] His death is supposed to have occurred sometime between Alfred's succession to the kingship of Wessex in 871 and Guthrum's attack on England (*recte* Wessex) at Twelfth Night (6 January) 878. Alfred's retreat in the face of the Danish invasion to Athelney, and his failure to save the cakes of a swineherd's wife from burning, are next described. King Alfred, in his hour of need, had a night vision of St Neot who promised him help on the morrow—help which materialized in the form of warriors rallying to King Alfred's side at Ecgberht's Stone. On the eve of his crucial battle with Guthrum at Edington, Alfred prayed to St Neot who appeared to the king yet again and promised to lead him to victory.[25] Alfred's victory at Edington and the consequent baptism of Guthrum followed. The *vita* proper ends with the notice that Alfred, thanks to the help and correction of Neot, ruled in peace until his death on 25 October 900 and with a reminder that in his time the English quarter in Rome was freed (from taxation).[26]

The account of the translation of the relics of St Neot follows by way of an epilogue to the *Life* of St Neot and was written by the same author as the writer of the *Life* proper. Many years later (after the death of St Neot or of Alfred) Neot appeared in a vision to the sacristan of his shrine instructing him to remove his relics to another location. This man removed the relics of St Neot to the protection of a certain magnate called Æðelricus and his very devout wife, Æðelfled, who lived to the north (*in aquilonarium partium*).[27] The community of St Neots in Cornwall made a vain attempt to recover their relics which miraculously proved to be immovable from their new location and the English king (*Anglorum rex*) who is not named, sanctioned what was in effect the theft of the relics.[28] Cures were wrought at the new location by the saintly remains and the landowner ordered a church to be built on the banks of the Ouse at *Neotesberia* situated between Bedford and Huntingdon. The feast of the translation of the relics from Cornwall to the new St Neots in Huntingdonshire was celebrated on 7 December. The sacristan who stole the relics eventually died and was buried in the new church alongside St Neot.[29]

The purpose of this *Life* is clear. It was written to publicize the fact that relics of a Cornish saint, Neot, had been removed from their Cornish base and rehoused at Eynesbury (henceforth St Neots) in Huntingdonshire. The *Life* reads partly as a proclamation of this event and partly as a naïve explanation, if not cover-up, for what may have been the theft or forcible removal of relics from a church of the Cornish Britons. The Cornishmen had been crushed by Athelstan (924–39) and their church must have suffered materially in consequence. Two related historical analogies present themselves. We have the evidence of Eddius Stephanus from the seventh century for Wilfrid's pillaging of British churches and church lands in the north-west in order to endow his revamped Anglo-Saxon foundation at Ripon.[30] Another analogy which is much nearer in time is provided by Archbishop Oda of Canterbury, who claimed to have taken the relics of that same Wilfrid from Ripon in the 940s because they had suffered neglect there and removed them to Canterbury. Ripon in the 940s was enjoying the protection of the Danes of York, which would explain why the minster at Ripon was looted by King Eadred of Wessex in 948 during that king's harrying in Northumbria. Wilfrid's relics were removed to Canterbury as part of the spoils of war, and as part also of the drive begun by Archbishop Oda to revitalize the Anglo-Saxon Church along his own Wessex-dominated lines.[31] We have seen that the methods used to achieve the reforms set in motion by Oda and later by Dunstan, Æthelwold, and Oswald, were to reform monastic life and disseminate the fruits of that reform through the production of *vitae sanctorum* and the promotion of the cults of monastic reformers and their relics. Archbishop Oda's disciple, Frithegod, was commissioned by him to write a new *Life* of St Wilfrid to mark the translation of that saint's relics to Canterbury. Wilfrid had clearly not been one of the tenth-century reformers, but he had been an early champion of orthodoxy and of monastic reform, in his struggles with a recalcitrant and suspect Celtic Church. Significantly, the Latinity of Frithegod of Canterbury's *Life* of Wilfrid (*Breviloquium Vitae Wilfredi*) bears a close relationship to that of the *Life* of St Neot.[32] While some tenth-century *vitae* such as those of Oswald and of Dunstan publicized the lives of holy men who were instrumental in rebuilding the English monastic church after the viking wars, others were composed or invented around the careers of people who were supposedly responsible for standing out against viking paganism during the dark days of the ninth century. The *Lives* of the kings, Edmund of East Anglia and of Alfred of Wessex, fall into the latter category. The *Life* of Neot, invented for the most part with the help of hagiographical clichés built around key entries in the Anglo-Saxon Chronicle, strove to give that saint credit for Alfred's victory over the pagan Danes by making him responsible for the spiritual reform of the West Saxon king.

An important feature of the programme to revitalize English monasticism was a conscious effort to reconstruct monasticism within those areas of the Danelaw where it had suffered most in the ninth century, and Ramsey, as we have seen, lay at the heart of that Danelaw enterprise. This is the context in which the writing of the *Life* of St Neot must be viewed. The author of the *Life* of King Alfred portrayed that king as a neurotic supplicant struggling to control unchaste desires while visiting a church in distant Cornwall. There he prayed for an illness to replace an existing malady, which would help control his passions. That Cornish church of St Gueriir was connected by the Pseudo-Asser with St Neot. There was clearly a connection between this confused tradition and that in the *Life* of St Neot, which shows Alfred visiting Neot and later entertaining visions of him, as a result of which the king achieved his military success. Alfred's struggles with his evil impulses were developed further in St Neot's *Life* where the king was now shown to have reached a stage of wickedness, such that he needed censuring and direction from the saint. But with Neot's help, Alfred was restored to both spiritual and military greatness, and the prestige of both the House of Wessex and of a Danelaw monastery were seen to benefit thereby. A further point of interest in both the *Lives* of Alfred and of Neot is the notion of monks leading a regular life in the late ninth century. Alfred was portrayed by the Pseudo-Asser as being anxious to reform monasticism in Wessex, and with founding two model communities at Athelney and at Shaftesbury. Neot, too, after his return from his pilgrimage to Rome founded a monastery at St Neots in Cornwall where he assembled a community living according to the rule (*aggregatis fratribus regularibus*).[33] Such notions of a regular life for monks had not become current in England for a century after Alfred's and Neot's time, and reflects, as we have seen, the preoccupations of the later reformers.

The new St Neots was founded *c*.980 beside Eynesbury in Huntingdon—the

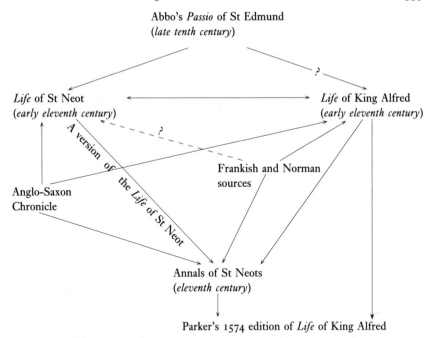

FIG. 8. Atavistic relationship between the *Life* of King Alfred, the Annals of St Neots, and the *Life* of St Neot

place, according to the *Liber Eliensis* having lain desolate after the viking wars. The surrounding countryside had been conquered by King Edward the Elder in a sustained campaign which resulted in the capture of Bedford in 915 and of Huntingdon in 917—two places specifically mentioned in St Neot's *Life*. In 939–41, however, all of this area reverted into the hands of Olaf Gothfrithsson, the pagan Danish king of York, and it was not until the capture of Archbishop Wulfstan of York by King Eadred of Wessex in 952 and the subsequent slaying of Eric Bloodaxe, the last Danish king of York in 954, that even the southern Danelaw can be said to have reverted to secure English rule.[34] We can assume that those members of the half-Christian Danish aristocracy of the Southern Danelaw who submitted willingly to Edward the Elder and his sons, survived into the later tenth century with some of their privileges intact. It was at this very time that Archbishop Oda, drawing on his experience of Fleury's reformed monasticism, set the reform movement in motion—a movement which was brought to completion in East Anglia under Oda's nephew, Bishop Oswald, who founded Ramsey in *c*.968. St Neots, which lay only 16 miles to the south of Ramsey, was founded *c*.980, and sometime between then and 1013 it was endowed with the relics of a Cornish saint, whose *Life* was written up to proclaim that event.

At a broader level, the *Life* of St Neot served as part of a wider programme, spearheaded by Ramsey, to disseminate edifying Christian sentiments throughout the infant Scandinavian church of the Danelaw. But in this *Life*, Neot's supposed association with King Alfred, and Alfred's own spiritual reform and consequent triumph over the pagan Danes, provided potent political propaganda for the West Saxon kings and their Church among the Danish settlers of eastern England. This movement for monastic reform was supported not only by pious lay magnates such as Ealdorman Æthelwine of East Anglia, but also by King Edgar, and this royal backing gave the Cluniac and other Continental elements in English reform a distinctly English flavour. Eadred was clearly responsible, directly or indirectly, for the arrival of Wilfrid's relics in the hostile south in the 950s. The *Life* of St Neot specifically tells us the *Anglorum rex*—who is not named—sanctioned the removal of the relics of St Neot from Cornwall to Huntingdonshire.[35] Further-more, we gather from the *Liber Eliensis* that Ealdorman Æthelwine of East Anglia, the generous lay patron who established Oswald's monks at Ramsey, also had a hand in the founding of St Neots.[36] St Neots in Huntingdonshire, therefore, which began life as a satellite of Ely, had a close association with Ramsey from the outset, and by 991, Ealdorman Æthelwine the co-founder of Ramsey was recognized as the patron also of St Neots.[37]

We know nothing about the historical Neot, except that he was remembered as a holy man whose cult was centred on St Neots in Cornwall. We also deduce that his Cornish community was robbed of his relics with the support of an English king in the late tenth century. The *Life* of St Neot was manufactured to promote the new foundation in Huntingdonshire. Its author knew little or nothing of Neot, and his statements relating to his education at Glastonbury, his relationship with King Alfred and his support for that king may have no factual basis. Indeed, the notion that Neot's primary claim to fame was that he enabled Alfred to defeat the Danes, while serving a useful political purpose, also demonstrates the poverty of information on the Cornish saint which was available to the writer of his *Life*. On the other hand, the fact that the writer of St Neot's life made use of the Alfred myth to promote the cult of the re-established Neot, tells us much about how the literary and political side of the reform movement functioned in the early eleventh century. It tells us of the importance of Alfred's own cult to the West Saxon dynasty and to monastic reformers alike. Although Alfred plays a secondary role to that of Neot in St Neot's *Life*, it is clear that Alfred was viewed from an early eleventh-century perspective in that source, as the saviour of England against the heathen Dane. Alfred is shown journeying to Cornwall to consult Neot as a guru on two occasions, and he was also the subject of two nightly visions of Neot who promised him victory against the Danes. We are reminded of late tenth-century Durham traditions which alleged that King Alfred had been favoured with a vision of St Cuthbert who also promised him victory over the Danish enemy.[38] Signific-antly, Alfred was believed to have had his encouraging vision from St Cuthbert in 878 when he was beleaguered on Athelney—precisely the same time and location attributed to the Neot vision.[39] The St Neot and Cuthbert visions are part of the same general phenomenon relating to that period from the mid-tenth to the early eleventh centuries in England. While it was flattering for monastic communities to associate their patron saints with the great victory of Alfred over the Danes in 878, it was equally beneficial for the West Saxon dynasty to bring the now legendary Alfred into contact with saints and their regional bases which once lay far beyond the reach of Alfredian Wessex, but which by the turn of the millennium had come under West Saxon control. Athelstan was the first English king to exercise lordship over the church of Cuthbert at Chester-le-Street (and Lindisfarne) in 934. Hagiographical tales of Alfred's visions of Cuthbert served the useful purpose of projecting West Saxon influence over Northumbria, back into Alfredian times. Similarly, Alfred's contacts with, and his later visions of Neot, served to emphasize that the West Saxon hold over Cornwall and East Anglia in the late tenth century was much older than in fact it really was.

Neot's supposed pilgrimage to Rome has no more historical evidence to back it than the similar journey which Byrhtferth of Ramsey attributed to St Ecgwine. Neot's Rome pilgrimage was part of the stock in trade of hagiographical narrative, but it may have been immediately prompted by the record of Alfred's problematical pilgrimage as recorded in the Anglo-Saxon Chronicle. The author of Neot's *Life* was so desperate for material that he made Neot advise Alfred to send gifts to Pope Marinus and then recorded the pope's return gift of a relic of the true Cross—all of which papal information was lifted from the Chronicle[40] and then woven into a fictitious narrative. There are surprisingly few miracles attributed to Neot in his *Life*, and those that are recorded there are all part of the stock in trade of hagiographers' motifs. There can be few lives of English saints from the early Middle Ages with such a poor historical content, and were it not for the association with King Alfred, the *Life* of St Neot even at a hagiographical level would have been a poorly constructed work indeed. It is remarkable solely for its legendary content relating to the miraculous assistance which Alfred received from Neot in his struggle with the Danish Guthrum, and, of course, for the legend of King Alfred and the burning cakes. There are a number of serious chronological errors or contradictions in the *Life* of Neot which indicate that its author was both very careless and also far removed from the events he described. Guthrum's invasion of northern Wiltshire in January 878 is recorded as an invasion of England (*Brittannie Anglice insulam*) with the implication that this was Guthrum's first appearance on the scene.[41] The author seems unaware that Guthrum is mentioned in the Anglo-Saxon Chronicle as campaigning in England from 875—an oversight which is all the more remarkable because the writer of the *Life* did consult a version of the Chronicle for the account of Alfred's struggle with Guthrum in 878. More serious is the statement that Neot studied at Glastonbury under the direction of *Apeluuoldus* later bishop of Winchester.[42] Æthelwold, who was bishop of Winchester from 963 until 984, and who had indeed been professed at Glastonbury, lived a century later than the supposed lifetime of Neot. Matters are not helped by the scribe of the mid-twelfth-century MS B of the *Life* of Neot who substituted the name *Helphego* for that of Neot's mentor at Glastonbury.[43] But Alphege, or Ælfheah, was the later contemporary of Æthelwold, whom he succeeded in the bishopric of Winchester in 984, and Alphege was martyred by the Danes as late as 1012. It may be that the author of the *Life* of St Neot had confused a genuine tradition of Bishop Æthelwold's role in the founding of the new St Neots beside Eynesbury in Huntingdonshire, with the notion that Æthelwold had been Neot's monastic mentor. For the *Liber Eliensis* claims that it was Bishop Æthelwold who took the initiative in founding a monastery at Eynesbury-St Neots.[44] This confusion in the *Life* of St Neot regarding his precise association with Bishop Æthelwold could also have arisen if Æthelwold had also been instrumental in acquiring the relics of Neot for the Eynesbury monastery. Whatever the reason for this blunder, it might suggest that the earliest version of the *Life* of Neot cannot have been written too early in the eleventh century. On the other hand, historical accuracy is not a characteristic of the nearby Ramsey school which, as we shall see, produced this *Life*, and a careless approach to historical material does not in itself necessarily prove the author was very far removed from the events he describes. We have seen how Byrhtferth not only invented charters to lend a semblance of authenticity to his *Life* of Ecgwine, but he also knew little about Archbishop Oda who lived in the first half of the tenth century and showed himself capable of invention of material on that prelate when his facts failed him.

The author of the *Life* of St Neot claims that Neot was responsible for advising Alfred to send gifts for the English quarter in Rome, and in return Pope Marinus sent Alfred a relic of the true Cross. He found this information in a version of the Chronicle where he must have seen that it was entered there under 883 and 885. But according to the *Life* of Neot, the saint was already dead by 878 and he appeared to Alfred in a series of visions from beyond the grave in that year. Such a careless writer might well have invented the name of a prominent monastic reformer such as Æthelwold to act as the spiritual director of Neot while he was supposed to have been at Glastonbury, regardless of the violence that such a statement did to the chronology of his work. The author of the *Life* of Alfred, after all, happily confused King Eadred (946–55) with Æthelred, Lord of the Mercians (*c.*883–911).

The date at which the earliest *Life* of St Neot was written is agreed in general terms to have been somewhere in the period 1000–1050. Keynes and Lapidge pronounced the *Life* to have been 'composed not long after the transfer, probably in the late tenth century, of the relics of St Neot from their original location in Cornwall to a priory at Eynesbury (soon renamed St Neots) in Huntingdonshire'.[45] Elsewhere, however, Dumville and Lapidge favoured a time *c.*1050 'after the memory of Æthelwold had receded but before the Norman refoundation'[46] to allow time for the author to take the liberty of placing Neot and Æthelwold in the same generation. The *Vita* only records a single miracle after the church of St Neot had been constructed in Huntingdonshire, which suggests the *Life* cannot have been written too long after *c.*980, while by 1010–14, the relics of Neot had been removed from Eynesbury and eventually located at Crowland to protect them from the renewed viking attacks of that time.[47] So there is a strong case for favouring *c.*980–1014 as the time of writing.[48] The fact that the *Vita* was 'written either at or for St Neots in Huntingdonshire'[49] is proved not only by the emphasis on the translation of the relics to that newly built monastery, but also because knowledge of the date of the festival of the translation (7 December) is unique to the *Life* and to liturgical manuscripts connected with St Neots. This *Life*, therefore, was composed at precisely the time when Byrhtferth of Ramsey, his Ramsey contemporaries, and his pupils in his remarkable school were active in the production of *vitae sanctorum* to help the promotion of monasticism and monastic reform especially in the Midlands and East Anglia. It may be significant that two of the earliest manuscripts of St Neot's *Life*, dating from the twelfth century, contain material with direct Cluniac connections. The British Library MS Add. 38130 contains, in addition to Bede's *Ecclesiastical History*, the earliest *Life* of St Neot (MS A), two Latin homilies on St Neot, and Abbo of Fleury's *Preface* to his *Passio Sancti Eadmundi*.[50] This manuscript has almost certainly an East Anglian provenance. The Corpus Christi College Cambridge MS 161 contains the *Life* of Neot (MS C) in a collection of English saints' *Lives*, but also includes four *Lives* of abbots of Cluny. This Corpus Christi Cambridge manuscript of the *Life* of Neot was written at St Augustine's, Canterbury.[51] Although these manuscripts are probably a century later in time, from when the *Life* of St Neot which they contain was first written, their Cluniac and Fleury associations may well point back to the original East Anglian monastic milieu in which the *Life* was composed. We have seen how Byrhtferth had virtually invented a *Life* for St Ecgwine of Evesham at the invitation of that community. Lapidge surmised that Byrhtferth undertook that particular task at the invitation of Abbot Ælfweard of Evesham, a kinsman of Cnut and former Ramsey monk who in *c.*1014 was busy acquiring the relics of St Wigstan and later those of St Odulf of Brabant for Evesham.[52] Lapidge suggested with equally good reason, that Byrhtferth of Ramsey may also have been invited to celebrate the translation to Ramsey of the relics of the seventh-century Kentish martyrs, Æthelberht and Æthelred. The relics of those saints had been brought to Ramsey through the powerful offices of Ealdorman Æthelwine, the lay patron of Ramsey and of St Neots, *c.*980–90.[53] St Neots lay close to Ramsey and both houses shared a number of the same powerful benefactors. So, the possibility that the earliest *Life* of St Neot was also composed at Ramsey or by a monk with Ramsey connections, to mark the acquiring by the Eynesbury monks of the Cornish relics, is strong.[54] When we turn to examine the Latinity of the *Life* of St Neot, we find that the possibility of a Ramsey connection with the production is confirmed yet further.

A study of the Latinity of the *Life* of St Neot takes us at once into the world of Byrhtferth of Ramsey and his immediate circle. Agentive nouns in *-or* such as *lapidator* or *opitulator*[55] recall the usage in the *Life* of King Alfred and the works of Byrhtferth, as do the occurrence of adverbs in *-im*, such as *diurnatim*[56]—which Keynes and Lapidge identified as a hallmark of the author of the *Life* of Alfred.[57] Among those adverbs in the *Life* of Neot which Lapidge characterized as being 'more unusual still' is *incommutabiliter*.[58] This word is one of those many polysyllabic adverbs in *-iter* of which some fourteen different examples turn up in the short text of the *Life* of St Neot, and of which several are repeated there many times.[59] Lapidge failed to note the presence of these words in the text of the *Life* of Neot or to identify them as a hallmark of Byrhtferth's style, although he did acknowledge the presence of other Byrhtferthian traits in this work.[60] Lapidge also failed to point out that the very rare form *incommutabiliter* is also found in chapter 103 of the *Life* of King Alfred.[61] Other examples of polysyllabic adverbs which are common to the *Life* of St Neot, the *Life* of Alfred, and works attributed to Byrhtferth are *fideliter*, *graviter*, *pariter*, *qualiter*, *viriliter*, and a form in -*e* in *honorifice*.[62] The forms *acriter*, *corporaliter*, *incommutabiliter*, and *specialiter* are also peculiar to the *Life* of King Alfred and the *Life* of St Neot. There is the same interchange between the use of polysyllabic adverbs and that of polysyllabic adjectives in the *Life* of Neot which we have already encountered in the works of Byrhtferth and in the *Life* of King Alfred. We may point to *innumerabilis*[63] and *irrationabilis*,[64] both of which occur in the *Life* of King Alfred, where *irrationabiliter* occurs alongside *irrationabilius*.[65] Other forms which appear in the *Life* of St Neot are *inexcusabilis*,[66] and *inestimabilis*.[67] The adjectival form *inenarrabilis* turns up both in the *Life* of St Neot[68] and in Byrhtferth's *Historical Miscellany* in the *Historia Regum*[69] and may be compared with the apparently unique adverbial form *inenarrabiliter* also found in Byrhtferth's *Historical Miscellany*.[70] Yet another feature of the *Life* of St Neot is the frequent occurrence of polysyllabic superlatives which is also a characteristic of the *Life* of King Alfred and of the works of Byrhtferth generally. In this category, as with the adverbs, some specific words such as *frequentissimus*,[71] *munitissimus*,[72] and *piissimus*[73] occur in both the *Lives* of King Alfred and of St Neot. And just as the Pseudo-Asser frequently used superlatives when describing rulers such as Alfred who was *piissimus*, or Charlemagne who was *famosissimus*, so too, the author of the *Life* of Neot referred to Pope Marinus as *reuerentissimus*[74] and to the wood of the Holy Cross as *preciosissimi ligni*.[75] The Pseudo-Asser referred to that same cross of Christ as *sanctissimae ac venerabilissimae crucis*.[76]

Lapidge pointed to the use of archaisms and Grecisms in the *Life* of St Neot which gives the author's style 'an awkward, archaic flavour'.[77] Both of these characteristics are evident in the *Life* of King Alfred and in Byrhtferth's known works. Lapidge suggested elsewhere, that Byrhtferth's fondness for Greek vocabulary may have been due to the fact that 'he learned some smattering of Greek from Abbo [of Fleury]'.[78] The occurrence of *immo* at least three times in the short *Life* of Neot[79] reminds us of its frequent use in the *Life* of Alfred, and the word *curricula* identified by Stevenson as a favourite word in the Pseudo-Asser's text, is also employed on at least two occasions by the author of St Neot's *Life*.[80] Lapidge's observation[81] that the author of the *Life* of Neot employed eccentric word order— involving the transposition especially of the verb—to achieve syntactical mannerisms reminds us of Byrhtferth's own lengthy digression in his *Manual* to explain figures of speech, beginning with prolepsis which he explains as 'anticipation . . . when the noun which ought to be behind, is in front [and] the same thing applies to the verb'.[82] Other characteristic elements which link the style of the author of the *Life* of St Neot to that of the *Life* of Alfred and the works of

Byrhtferth are the frequent occurrences of diminutives such as *locula, tuguriolum*, and *puellula* in the St Neot text. The observation that the author of the *Life* of St Neot strove to write prose which 'is consciously poetic in effect . . . achieved by the use of tags from Classical poets, hexametrical cadences and rhyming clauses'[83] reminds us that the Pseudo-Asser resorted to the use of alliteration and showed a fondness for what was in effect, poetic prose.[84] We recall, too, that the Pseudo-Asser also embellished his prose with the inclusion of hexameters,[85] as well as a lengthy inclusion from the *Carmen Paschale* of Caelius Sedulius. Byrhtferth of Ramsey also quoted at some length and with acknowledgement, from Sedulius in his *Life* of St Oswald[86] and in his *Manual*.[87] Lapidge elsewhere argued from the fact that another poem—this time Bede's *De Die Iudicii*—was cited extensively by Byrhtferth and by the author of the *Life* of St Ecgwine showed that the two writers were identical.[88] Bede's *De Die Iudicii* was, like Sedulius, 'not unknown in late Anglo-Saxon England',[89] but the 'extensive citation' by apparently different authors was rightly seen by Lapidge as a 'striking coincidence'. Precisely the same argument applies in our efforts to identify the authors of the *Life* of Alfred and of the *Life* of Neot. The detailed chronological terms of reference provided in the *Life* of St Neot are so narrow, even compared with the *Life* of King Alfred, and the text as a whole is so short, that its author did not allow himself much scope to reveal to us his knowledge of Christian and Classical literature. He does also, however, draw on Sedulius's *Carmen Paschale* and his poetic tags drawn from such authors as Ovid, Lucan, and Vergil, together with a metaphor from Persius[90] are not inconsistent with the learning of Byrhtferth of Ramsey and his circle. The distinctive use of rhyming Latin prose interspersed with rhyming verse as found in the *Life* of St Neot is a rare occurrence among Anglo-Latin writers but is found in the *Translation and Miracles of Swithun* (*Translatio et Miracula S. Swithuni*) a Winchester work composed *c*.975.[91] Bishop Æthelwold, who introduced reformed monks to replace the degenerate clerks of Winchester and who had completed his new cathedral church there in 971, almost certainly commissioned the writing of the *Translation and Miracles of St. Swithun*. This piece was written by Lantfred of Winchester to commemorate the translation of Swithun's relics to the new cathedral and to publicize the cult attached to the new shrine.[92] Lantfred was part of a task-force of Continental monks imported by Æthelwold from Fleury and Corbie to help implement his monastic reforms, and the *Translation of St. Swithun* was a propaganda piece designed to further that cause. As such it performed precisely the same function as the *Life and Translation of St. Neot* and because of Bishop Æthelwold's connection with Ramsey and St Neots, there is every reason to believe that Lantfred of Winchester's work was known in those houses in the early eleventh century. The presence of rhyming prose, therefore, in the *Life* of Neot may not be so indicative of an inherent quality in the style of its author so much as evidence that the writer of St Neot's *Life* had access to Lantfred's *Translation of St. Swithun* as a model for his work.

The opinion of Dumville and Lapidge that there are no 'similarities in diction' between the *Life* of Alfred and the earliest *Life* of St Neot[93] does not stand up to scrutiny. We have already encountered a common arcane vocabulary and stylistic traits which the editors of those texts failed to recognize. While it is true that the author of the *Life* of Neot may have independently translated the text of the Chronicle rather than having followed the Pseudo-Asser's translation of it to describe events of 878, there is nevertheless other evidence which points to a close relationship in style between translations of passages from the Chronicle in both the *Lives* of Alfred and of Neot. One passage in question, originated in the Anglo-Saxon Chronicle's account under the year 885, of how Pope Marinus 'had sent him [Alfred] great gifts, including part of the cross on which Christ suffered'.[94] The Pseudo-Asser translated that passage thus:

The pope also sent many gifts to King Alfred, among which he gave not a small piece of that most holy and venerable Cross, on which our Lord Jesus Christ hung for the salvation of all mankind. (*Dedit etiam non parvam illius sanctissimae ac venerabilissimae crucis partem, in qua Dominus noster Iesus Christus pro universali hominum salute pependit*).[95]

The author of the earliest *Life* of St Neot rendered this same passage: '*Ob eterne enim memorie signum preciosissimi ligni salutifere crucis partem - in qua uita salus orbis penali morte pependit.*'[96] The Pseudo-Asser's rendering of this passage and that of the author of the *Life* of Neot have two notable features in common. While the Anglo-Saxon Chronicle refers laconically to 'part of the Cross on which Christ suffered (*þære rode del þe Crist on þrowude*)' the *Life* of St Neot and the *Life* of Alfred both include embellishments using polysyllabic superlatives—*preciosissimi* and *sanctissimae ac venerabilissimae*, respectively. But both the Latin versions re-place the Chronicle's notion of a cross on which Christ *suffered* (*þrowude*) and replace it with the idea of a cross on which Christ *hung* (*in qua . . . pependit*). The rendering of this passage by Alfred's biographer and by the author of the *Life* of Neot are related, and calls into question the statement that there are no 'similar-ities in diction between ["]Asser["] and *Vita I*' of St Neot.[97] While the *Life* of Alfred may not have been the immediate source for the corresponding passage relating to Pope Marinus and the Holy Cross in the *Life* of Neot, or vice versa, it is possible nevertheless, that both passages were written in the same scriptorium by authors who were contemporaneous, or by the same author, who at different times in his career was independently translating the same passage in the Anglo-Saxon Chronicle.[98]

There are several other verbal echoes between the text of the Pseudo-Asser's *Life* of King Alfred and the *Life* of St Neot. We have more general similarities in the relationship, for instance, between *Iam vero florem attingens iuuentutis*[99] and the repeated use of *primaevo iuventutis suae flore* of the *Life* of Alfred. Other phrases, such as the account of St Neot's reputation—*ad eum multitudo utriusque sexus populi conflueret*[100]—closely echo the description of King Alfred's marriage in that King's *Life*, which was *inter innumerabiles utriusque sexus populos, sollemniter celebraret.*[101] So too, the description of Athelney in the *Life* of Neot as 'a place in the remote parts of English Britain far to the west (*locus in ultimis Anglorum Brittannie partibus ad occidentem*)'[102] is paralleled by the Pseudo-Asser's account of himself as coming 'from the remote westernmost part of Wales (*de occiduis et ultimis Britanniae finibus*).'[103] And the explanation of the place-name 'Athelney' in that same passage in the *Life* of Neot is related to similar etymological explanations offered throughout the *Life* of Alfred. In addition to remarkable similarities in vocabulary, and the use of parts of speech and phrases, the *Life* of St Neot shares with the *Life* of King Alfred the use of the bee and honey-making metaphor which, as we saw, was a characteristic device of Byrhtferth of Ramsey and of late tenth- and early eleventh-century Anglo-Latin writers in his circle.[104]

Two features in particular within the text of the *Life* of St Neot suggest that it is the work of either Byrhtferth or of someone in his Ramsey circle. One is the reference to St Neot's resolve to visit Rome which is described as the 'thresholds of the princes of the apostles Peter and Paul (*principum apostolorum Petri et Pauli uisitare proposuit limina*)'.[105] This method of describing Rome is defined elsewhere by Lapidge as a definitive feature in the style of Byrhtferth and is found in his *Life* of Oswald, his *Life* of Ecgwine, and in his section of the *Historia Regum*.[106] Further crucial evidence for the personal influence of Byrhtferth in the text of the *Life* of St Neot is the method employed by that author to describe his numberings of years and distances. He describes six years in terms of 'twice three years (*bis ter annis*)'; seven years in terms of 'a five-year period plus two (*uno integro lustro annisque duobus paucis*)'; and twenty-two years as 'twice ten plus two (*bis deni et duo*)'. When telling us that St Neots in Huntingdonshire was nine miles from Bedford and five from Huntingdon, he uses 'thrice three (*ter tribus*)' for nine and 'twice two plus one (*bis duobus addito uno*)' for five.[107] This multiplicative treatment of numerals in the *Life* of St Neot reflects the influence of Byrhtferth's personal obsession with numerology and with word-play on elementary arithmetic. In his discussion on Byrhtferth's style in relation to the *Historical Miscellany* in the *Historia Regum*, Lapidge concluded:

Concern with the details of computus engendered in Byrhtferth an exceptional interest in numerology, an interest which is evinced on nearly every page of his writings, ranging from his excessive use of distributive numerals in multiplicative combinations (e.g. *bis bina* for *quatuor*) to the extensive discussion of the symbolical significance of the numbers 1 to 1000 that forms part IV of [his] *Enchiridion* [or Handbook].[108]

One historical source which was certainly used by the writer of St Neot's *Life* was the Anglo-Saxon Chronicle. Indeed, it may be said that the entire *Life* hinges on the Chronicle's account of King Alfred's retreat to Athelney in 878. For earlier vague statements in the *Life* about Neot's monastic training, his Rome pilgrimage and reprimanding of King Alfred, all lead up to the climactic, and only 'original' element in the work, where Neot is shown rescuing the seemingly defeated king in the marshes at Athelney. This centre-piece to the *Life* of St Neot was constructed by taking the Anglo-Saxon Chronicle's account of events of 878 as the author's basic framework. This provided information on King Alfred's retreat to Athelney in the face of Guthrum's invasion, and it also provided a stage by stage report on Alfred's military recovery and his ultimate victory at Edington, later in the same year. Onto this historical narrative of the Chronicle, the author grafted the legend of Alfred's visions of St Neot and the account of the crucial supernatural help which Neot was supposed to have given the king to achieve his victory over the Danes. We are reminded of the Pseudo-Asser's approach to his *Life* of Alfred, where the Anglo-Saxon Chronicle was used to provide the entire framework of the *Life*, and onto which were grafted hagiographical and apocryphal tales of illness, illiteracy, and scientific invention. Where, then, did the author of the *Life* of Neot find the idea of using Neot as Alfred's visionary guru? We have seen how there was clearly a connection between the visions which King Alfred supposedly experienced of St Cuthbert in the Durham tradition, and those of Neot which Alfred was also said to have enjoyed in the *Life* of that saint. Not only were the visions of the same basic content—i.e. the promise of victory over the Danes, or at least the promise of Alfred's restoration to this kingdom—but in both cases, Alfred was supposed to have had his visions while beleaguered on Athelney. The tale of Alfred's vision of St Cuthbert is found in the eleventh-century *Historia de Sancto Cuthberto* and is later repeated in a variant form by William of Malmesbury.[109] But the tale of Cuthbert's heavenly visit to King Alfred at Athelney was known to Byrhtferth of Ramsey when he incorporated his summary of the *Life* of King Alfred into that *Historical Miscellany* which is now the First Part of the *Historia Regum* attributed to Symeon of Durham. Before going on to relate the building of the fort at Athelney and Alfred's victory over Guthrum at Edington, Byrhtferth writes:

That infamous army [of Danes] left Exeter and went to the royal estate at Chippenham and spent the winter there. At this time, King Alfred endured great tribulations and led a difficult life. At length, encouraged by St Cuthbert in a fitting vision (*apto oraculo*), he fought against the Danes, and in the very time and place the saint had commanded, he was victorious. And ever afterwards, he was terrible and invincible to his enemies, and he held St Cuthbert in especial honour.[110]

Byrhtferth then backtracks to relate the Danish invasion of Devon from Dyfed in Wales; how Alfred constructed his fort at Athelney and his eventual triumph at Edington—all of which is derived from the Latin translation of the Chronicle as found in chapters 54–6 of the *Life* of Alfred. Clearly, Byrhtferth inserted this notice of Cuthbert's appearance to King Alfred as an addition to his version of the *Life* of Alfred in his Historical Miscellany. But it is also evident from this brief note on Cuthbert's apparition to King Alfred, that it, too, is a summary of a lengthier account, such as that preserved in the *Historia de Sancto Cuthberto*. Byrhtferth had gained access to the Durham hagiographical legend of Alfred's vision of St Cuthbert in the same way as he had acquired the so-called York annals which form yet another section of his *Historical Miscellany* in *Historia Regum*. He most likely acquired this Northumbrian historical lore through contacts established via Oswald, the founder of Ramsey, who ended his life as Archbishop of York in 992.[111] Whatever the precise route by which Byrhtferth acquired the tale of King Alfred's vision of St Cuthbert, there can be no doubt that he did have access to it. That being the case, we may conclude that the earliest textual version of the tale of the Cuthbert apparition was older than the time of composition of the *Life* of St Neot,[112] and that Byrhtferth or someone in his circle, having discovered the Cuthbert legend, reshaped it to form the centre-piece in a *Life* of Neot which he had been commissioned to write, and on which he had little or no genuine information. It was by just such a reusing of older material and by a ruthless distortion of historical matter, that Byrhtferth invented an entire *Life* for St Ecgwine of Evesham.

A remarkable feature of the *Life* of St Neot is the strong impression it conveys of a British—i.e. Welsh or Cornish—association, if not origin, for its author. The writer of this *Life* refers to eastern Cornwall as 'Britain which is now called England (*Britannie, que nunc Anglia dicitur*)',[113] and he refers to England as a whole in terms of 'English Britain' (*Brittannie Anglice*).[114] The author introduces the story of King Alfred and the burning cakes with a description of Athelney. His account of 'a place in the remote parts of English Britain far to the west, which is called Athelney in English, and which we refer to as "Athelings' Isle" (*locus in ultimis Anglorum Brittannie partibus ad occidentem situs cui nomen lingua Saxonum est Ethelingaige—quod apud nos sonat "clitonum insula"*)'[115] is open to conflicting interpretations. It may suggest the author is making a distinction between his élite circle of Latin readers and those who use the vernacular (i.e. Old English), or he may be attempting to distinguish between English and British (i.e. Cornish) speakers. The account of King Alfred's sojourn at Athelney, when he burned the cakes, is retold in the mid-thirteenth century Chronicle of John of Wallingford, and since that account follows closely, in all its essential details, the text of the earliest *Life* of St Neot, it throws an important light on what the author of Neot's *Life* may have meant when he wrote that 'among us [the place] is called island of the princes'. John of Wallingford's version of the description of Athelney refers to it as 'a place in the remote parts of England to the far west, and [which] is called "the land of nobles" by the Britons (*diciturque a Brithonibus clitonum patria*)'.[116] John of Wallingford followed the earliest *Life* of St Neot (*Vita I*) in explaining the etymology of Athelney; in noting Athelney's location among salt marshes and the presence of level ground in its interior. He noted too, the fact that Alfred lodged with a swineherd (and not a cow-herd) and he followed the *Life* of Neot in sending the swineherd off with his flocks to pasture on the day when Alfred sat at home with the herdsman's wife and burnt the cakes. He noted that the king patiently awaited the prophesied help of Neot and that he modelled himself on Job. Finally, to complete the picture of how closely John of Wallingford followed his text of St Neot's *Life*, he also included the quotation in the earliest *Life* of Neot from Heb. 12: 6, in relation to King Alfred's misfortunes: 'He [God] scourges every son whom he adopts.' It is just possible, therefore, that John of Wallingford's remark that Athelney was called '"land of princes" by the Britons' was in the text of the *Life* of St Neot which he was following.

The ambiguity surrounding the ethnic origin of the author of the *Life* of St Neot reveals itself yet again in his reference to a war-camp 'near Selwood as it is called in the language of the English (*iuxta siluam Sæalwudu cognominatam Anglorum lingua*)'.[117] Taken on its own, such a comment might signify nothing more than an English Latin scholar distancing himself from his own vernacular.[118] It was common for Anglo-Latin writers—including Bede—to provide Latin translations of Old English and (occasionally) even of Celtic place-names.[119] But the closest parallel for the gloss on the place-name, *Selwood*, in the *Life* of Neot is found in the *Life* of King Alfred, where the writer refers to 'the eastern part of Selwood Forest, *Silva Magna* in Latin, and *Coit Maur* in Welsh (*in orientali parte saltus, qui dicitur Seluudu, Latine autem "silva magna", Britannice "Coit Maur"*)'.[120] It is interesting to note that the author of the *Life* of St Neot glossed the place-name 'Selwood' with the phrase *cognominatam Anglorum lingua* at that point where he is describing the exact same campaign of 878, which in the *Life* of Alfred caused the place-name 'Selwood' to be glossed with the Latin and Welsh forms of its name. Nor can we argue that in this instance the writer of St Neot's *Life* was following the Anglo-Saxon Chronicle, because the Chronicle's account of events in 878 does not contain any gloss on the name of Selwood. The summary of events presented in the *Life* of Neot at this point shows some awareness of the corresponding passage relating to Selwood in the *Life* of King Alfred, or vice versa.

Dumville and Lapidge were so impressed by the Celtic element in the earliest *Life* of St Neot that they favoured a Cornish British-speaking origin for the author of the *Life*.[121] Those editors believed that while the author's knowledge of Cornish topography was sound, he was ignorant of East Anglian geography 'in important ways'.[122] This is not the case, and indeed the contrary can be shown to be true. It did not take a detailed knowledge of Cornish territory to surmise that in the tenth and eleventh centuries Cornwall contained thick forests and clear rivers and that it was near the sea.[123] A modest command of topographical clichés was all that was required to achieve such an obvious description, which might, indeed, apply to any area throughout the length of the Cornish or indeed of many other peninsulas. The knowledge that St Neot's hermitage lay 'nearly ten milestones from the monastery of St Petroc'[124] is more than offset by another more detailed statement to the effect that St Neots in Huntingdonshire was 'nine milestones from Bedford and five miles from Huntingdon'.[125] Dumville and Lapidge claimed, quite mistakenly, that the author of the *Life* of St Neot believed the river Ouse entered the sea at Wells-next-the-Sea in Norfolk, when in fact it debouches at King's Lynn some 35 miles east and south, around the coast of the Wash.[126] If the author of the *Life* were guilty of such an error, it might indeed suggest that he had little first-hand knowledge of the Huntingdon and Cambridgeshire areas. For although the course of the Ouse and the configuration of the Fens in the Middle Ages were very different from what they are today, nevertheless since St Neots was actually on the Ouse, and Ramsey near the edge of its fens, a writer based at either monastery would be expected to know that the great river did not enter the ocean at Wells-next-the Sea. But the author of the *Life* of St Neot has been falsely accused of this error by his Cambridge editors, who appear to know less about the topography of their region than their medieval subject. The author of the earliest *Life* of Neot

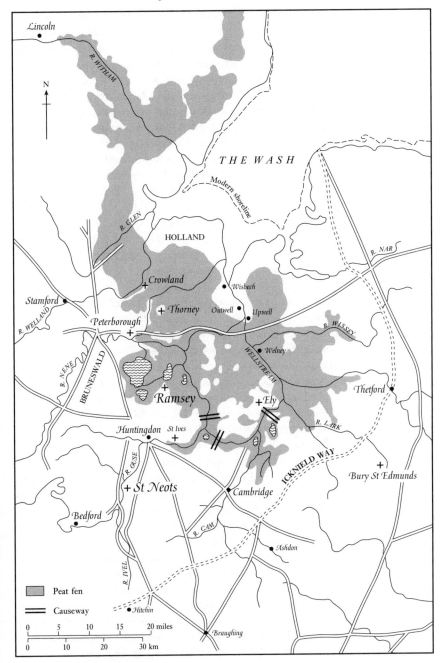

M AP 10. Ramsey and St Neots in the Fenland, *c.* AD 1000 (with acknowledgement to C. R. Hart)

tells us in his hexameters, that after reaching a place called *Guella*, the Ouse entered the sea at a place which was *sub Oylandia*. A glance at Hill's map of the region around the Wash in Anglo-Saxon times[127] reveals that it is an oversimplified if not a false notion to assume the Ouse ever joined the sea at King's Lynn in the eleventh century. King's Lynn was effectively part of a long island strip running east–west along the southern shores of the present Wash, and the Ouse joined the great marshes of the Fens long before it could ever have reached King's Lynn. The river emptied itself into the vast coastal marshland some ten to twelve miles south-east of King's Lynn and just to the north of Upwell Fen. The associated place-names, *Upwell* and *Outwell* 'once' as Ekwall informs us, 'formed a whole, the name being *Wella* "the spring" '[128] and it is this *Wella*—as Hart convincingly suggested[129]—which the author of the *Life* of St Neot singled out as *Guella*, a place 'below Holland (*sub Oylanda*)'. In other words, the Ouse joined the sea somewhere north of Outwell, and east of Wisbech, and below the parts of Holland which lie to the south and west of the Wash.[130] Wells-next-the-Sea, therefore, ought never to have entered into the argument, and the author of the *Life* of St Neot, far from being ignorant of East Anglian geography displays a very detailed knowledge of it, as we might expect from a writer who was based at Ramsey or St Neots. Hart also reminded us that Ealdorman Æthelwine, the lay founder of Ramsey Abbey, bestowed on that community twenty fishermen at this same *Welles* together with their annual catch of 60,000 eels.[131] The monks of Ramsey had every reason to know the whereabouts of their rich fisheries at 'Wells below Holland'.

The editors of the *Life* of St Neot have seen in the author's spelling of three East Anglian place-names, evidence for the fact that he was 'a British-speaking native of Cornwall'.[132] The three place-names in question—Ely, Wells, and the river Ivel, are rendered by the author of the *Life* as *Aileci, Guella*, and *Heblus*, respectively, when we would expect *Elig, Wella/Welles*, and *Gifla* or *Givle* in tenth- and eleventh-century Anglo-Saxon documents. The argument for the presence of Cornishisms in the three place-names cited above, runs thus: the place-name 'Ely' was written *Elig* in Old English but pronounced [Eli]. For the writer of the *Life* of Neot to render the name as *Aileci* he had to consciously convert the written -*g* in *Elig* to -*c*-, under the influence of the Old Cornish spelling system. Similarly, he converted the initial *W* in *Wella* to *Gu*. Such an argument requires our acceptance of the fact that the writer was engaged in a bookish exercise, transposing written forms of those East Anglian place-names into written Old Cornish or Old Welsh, and he was not influenced by the contemporary pronunciation of the names. The author was clearly indulging in conscious antiquarianism, for the place-names in question lay in thoroughly English territory, far removed from any British cultural or linguistic influence. Dumville and Lapidge argued that since the supposed British forms used by the author of the earliest *Life* of Neot were based on a written tradition rather than on any hypothetical Old Cornish pronunciation,[133] this shows the author was a Cornishman 'who had spent long enough in Anglo-Saxon schools to learn to read Old English and to adopt Anglo-Saxon practices of writing Latin ostentatiously'.[134] Precisely the same argument has been advanced by those who hold that the *Life* of King Alfred was indeed written by a Welshman, who supposedly learned to translate the Anglo-Saxon Chronicle into hermeneutic Latin. The pseudo-Asser, we recall, like the author of the *Life* of Neot, also indulged in providing antiquarian British forms of English place-names which were located deep in English territory. This recognition by the editors of Neot's *Life* that its author could well have been a Briton writing within an English monastic milieu in the pre-Conquest period has crucial relevance for the undeniably Welsh dimension within the *Life* of King Alfred. That hitherto supposedly unique Welsh dimension has provided what amounted to unassailable corroboration of the statement by the author of Alfred's *Life* that he was indeed none other than the Welsh bishop, Asser. Not only does a study of the *Life* of Neot show that Welsh linguistic traits within the *Life* of Alfred are no longer unique, but many of those traits are mirrored in detail by the text of the *Life* of Neot. The author of the *Life* of St Neot may indeed have been a Briton. But there remains the possibility that he was an Englishman with an antiquarian interest in things Welsh. His treatment of place-names, after all, could have been based exclusively on book-learning. The hermeneutic style of early eleventh-century Anglo-Latin writers is the all-pervasive characteristic of the author of the *Life* of St Neot. His knowledge of Classical Greek—itself derived from glossaries—is a much more prominent feature of the *Life* of Neot than any knowledge of Cornish. No scholar has as yet suggested that the eight, or so, clear Grecisms in the *Life* of Neot[135] are suggestive of an origin for the author in Constantinople. Since the supposed Cornish forms are based on a manuscript tradition, it may be possible to conclude that the Ramsey writer, obsessed as he was with archaisms and with antiquarian glossating and glossaries, acquired his taste for providing British forms of English place-names from his extensive reading in Ramsey's well-stocked monastic library?[136] Alternatively, we must allow that he may, indeed, have had a Cornish or Welsh origin.

The Brittonic forms applied by the author of the *Life* of St Neot to three Anglo-Saxon place-names, combined with the impression he may have been trying to convey of not being an Englishman, recall the most controversial feature in the *Life* of King Alfred. The Pseudo-Asser also presents us with some ten Welsh or British forms of English place-names, and just as the author of Neot's *Life* renders *Wella* as *Guella*, so too, the author of King Alfred's *Life* calls the river Wylye in Wiltshire, *Guilou*[137] rather than giving its English form of *Wilig* or the like. Similarly, while the author of Neot's *Life* writes of that island 'which in English is called Athelney and which we refer to as "Athelings' Isle"', so, too, the Pseudo-Asser describes a fort at *Cynuit* or Countisbury in Devon fortified by 'ramparts thrown up in our fashion'.[138] The reader is being invited in both the quoted examples to view his author as something other than English. The Welsh element in the *Life* of King Alfred is more prominent than anything we can detect in that of St Neot, if only because the *Life* of Alfred is a much lengthier work and its author proclaims himself to be Asser, a Welsh cleric from St David's. It is the Brittonic elements in the *Life* of King Alfred which form the most controversial part of that text, and it is to these that we must now turn in the knowledge that similar, if less numerous but no less distinctive Brittonic forms, are also present in the *Life* of St Neot.

The most serious objection to accepting Byrhtferth of Ramsey or one of his associates as the author of the *Life* of King Alfred must surely be the entrenched notion that the *Life* was written by a Welshman—Bishop Asser of Sherborne—and that it was written for a Welsh readership. The evidence that the author was Welsh—and indeed, was a Welsh speaker—might seem, on the face of it, to be strong. Welsh etymologies are offered for the English place-names Thanet (*Ruim*), Nottingham (*Tig Guocobauc*), Dorset (*Durngueir*), Exeter (*Cairuuisc*), the Forest of Selwood (*Coit Maur*), and Cirencester (*Cairceri*).[139] Four other Welsh forms of place-names are offered—*Guilou* (River Wylye, near Wilton); *Abon* (River Avon), the fortress of *Cynuit* in Devon, and the church of St *Gueriir* in Cornwall.[140] Directional details are given in three instances in a Latinized version of the Welsh idiom, whereby 'on the right hand (*i parth dehou*)' means 'on the south side' and 'on the left hand (*i parth cled*)' signifies 'on the north side'. So, we are told the Danes at Reading constructed a rampart 'on the right-hand side (*a dextrali parte*) of the royal estate' there;[141] that the royal estate at Chippenham was in the 'left-hand part (*in sinistrali parte*)' of Wiltshire;[142] that Asser first met King Alfred 'in the territory of right-hand Saxons (*Dexteralium Saxonum*) which in English is called Sussex';[143] and during that meeting, Alfred asked Asser to relinquish 'all that I had on the left-hand and western side of the Severn (*in sinistrali et occidentali Sabrinae parte*)'.[144] Finally, Asser informs us that 'all the districts of right-hand Wales (*dexteralis Britanniae partis*) belonged to Alfred'.[145]

Eleven out of fourteen of these Welsh formulae relating both to place-name spelling and directions have one significant thing in common. They are all inserted in the text of the *Life* of Alfred by way of a gloss on the translation of the Anglo-Saxon Chronicle. The three exceptions consist of directional idioms which occur in chapters 79 and 80; one (chapter 79) describing the 'summoning' of Asser from Wales to King Alfred's court, and the other (chapter 80) outlining the politics of Alfredian Wales. A major characteristic of the Welsh material in the Pseudo-Asser is the fact that it either occurs in the form of glosses or it is tightly condensed into those two exclusively 'Welsh' chapters (79 and 80). In other words, the Welsh material in the *Life* of King Alfred is even less well integrated into the text of the *Life* than other ill-conceived insertions in that work, such as tales of the king's childhood or accounts of his illnesses. For the Welsh material to furnish conclusive evidence of Welsh authorship, it would need to be much more convincingly integrated throughout the text of the Pseudo-Asser so as to betray 'the habitual patterns of one mind expressing itself in characteristic ways' through predictable formulaic expressions.[146] But this is not the case with the Pseudo-Asser. His knowledge and interest in the meaning of English place-names shows clearly that he understood Old English. We are reminded of the author of the *Life* of Neot, who in spite of his supposed knowledge of Welsh or Cornish, clearly understood the meaning of the English place-name *Athelney*. It would have been a remarkable feat for a man such as the historical Asser, who had come from 'the remote westernmost part of Wales' in 885, to be expounding the etymologies of Anglo-Saxon place-names when he was supposed to be writing King Alfred's *Life* in Latin in 893. The Welsh learning displayed both by the Pseudo-Asser and by the author of the *Life* of Neot was essentially antiquarian. There is nothing spontaneous about the Welshness in the *Life* of Alfred, and it is important to observe that the Welsh etymologies relate to six English rather than to Welsh place-names.[147] The 'Welshness' of those English place-names was an academic matter relating to the remote past, and in the case of Nottingham and Selwood the supposed Welsh renderings bear no relationship to the later English forms.

The use of Welsh directional idioms in relation to the royal estates at Chippenham and Reading may otherwise betray anachronistic features. Chippenham provided a location for meetings of the *witan* in the tenth century, but that in itself does not prove it was a *villa regis* as early as the reign of Alfred. On the contrary, we have evidence to suggest that up to the end of King Alfred's life, the estate at Chippenham had not yet become part of the royal demesne. It was, of course, in Alfred's possession. He had spent Twelfth Night there in 878, but in his *Will* he left Chippenham to his youngest daughter, which may suggest that his estate there did not pertain to the kingship of Wessex *per se*.[148] The fact that Chippenham had become 'a major royal estate before 1066'[149] tells us little of King Alfred's day, but suggests that Byrhtferth or one of his Ramsey associates, having read in his Latin translation of the Chronicle that Alfred was stationed there in 878, would reasonably assume that it was already a *villa regia* in the ninth century. The same argument applies to Reading. It occupied an important frontier position and it may well have belonged to the royal kindred from before Alfred's time. But it was held by female members of the dynasty as late as the 970s or 980s, when Æthelflæd, second wife of King Edmund bequeathed it to Edward the Martyr or to Æthelred the Unready.[150] We are only certain of Reading's position as a royal estate during the reign of Edward the Confessor. Information on the status of these places as royal estates may be compared with the similar gloss on Chézy in Francia,[151] which was either supplied to the Ramsey biographer by Abbo of Fleury or by one of his Frankish colleagues, or was otherwise inserted into the text as an inspired guess.

The Pseudo-Asser was not consistent in his use of the Welsh directional idiom. Such habits—relating to a turn of phrase so fundamental to his own language ought to have been so ingrained as to preclude any lapses. But when the Pseudo-Asser tells us that Surrey was 'situated on the southern bank of the River Thames' he chooses the conventional *meridianus* for 'southern'.[152] So, too, he tells us Wilton was on the southern bank (*in meridiana ripa*) of the Wylye;[153] Cirencester in the southern part (*in meridiana parte*) of the Hwicce;[154] Reading on the southern bank (*in meridiana ripa*) of the Thames;[155] and York on the northern bank (*in aquilonali ripa*) of the Humber.[156] Nor can we argue that these inconsistencies in the use of directional idioms arose from the corrections of later 'improving' medieval editors, since the conventional Latin forms *aquilonalis* and *meridianus* appear in relation to the siting of York and Reading respectively in the version of Alfred's *Life* preserved in Byrhtferth's *Historical Miscellany*.[157] In other words, the inconsistencies go back to the original text of Alfred's *Life*. Where is the genuine and spontaneous Welshness in this? Is it not rather that the writer has nodded off, and that those Anglo-Latin formulae which came naturally to betray 'the habitual patterns of his mind' have taken over from the author's self-conscious posturing as a Briton?

The Pseudo-Asser's genuinely 'formulaic expressions'[158] are—as we have seen from countless examples—very much in keeping with those of Byrhtferth of Ramsey and his early eleventh-century milieu. The Welsh material in the *Life* of King Alfred is also mirrored by the Ramsey writer's use of Welsh material in the *Life* of Neot. That remains true even if the Welsh insertions in the *Life* of King Alfred look suspiciously foreign to the main text of that work in every sense. The isolated structuring of the Welsh information betrays it as yet another clumsy addition which was probably inserted into the *Life* in one operation. If the author of King Alfred's *Life* were indeed 'a native speaker of Welsh' as Keynes and Lapidge insisted,[159] then we should expect a proportionately high number of Celtic borrowings spread evenly throughout his Latin text. Stevenson could point to only three words of Celtic origin—*graphium*, *gabulum*, and *gronna*[160] in the entire *Life* of Alfred, and all three of these can be shown to have come into the writer's repertoire from sources other than from Wales. *Graphium* ('charter, document') was acknowledged by Lapidge to be a Grecism[161] and it was culled by the Pseudo-Asser from his Greek glossary. *Gabulum* coming originally from Old Irish *gabul* ('a fork'), had already been borrowed into the Latin of Varro and was used by the early eighth-century Aldhelm[162]—a writer who had the greatest influence on the Pseudo-Asser and on Byrhtferth of Ramsey. This Aldhelmian word occurs in the Pseudo-Asser's text[163] close to several other Aldhelmian motifs spread across chapters 88 and 89. Significant, too, for the Byrhtferth dimension is the presence of this 'otherwise very rare [word] in English Latin'[164] in two charters of Cnut in favour of Abingdon, dating to 1032–3.[165] Abingdon, like Ramsey, was a centre for monastic reform, founded by St Æthelwold of Winchester who had also been responsible for the refounding of Ely, Peterborough, and Thorney—all within the Fenland home of Byrhtferth of Ramsey. Finally, on Stevenson's own admission, while *gronna* ('a marsh') may have begun life in Irish Latinity, 'no argument as to the nationality of the writer of the present work can be founded upon it'[166] because 'it was introduced into England, probably from Fleury, with other Franco-Celtic Latin words in the tenth century'.[167] And so the case collapses even for these three words as direct Celtic-Latin borrowings in the Pseudo-Asser's text, and we are left with a work where the only meaningful linguistic and literary influences are either tenth-century Frankish or earlier English Aldhelmian.

While there is no conclusive proof that the writer of King Alfred's *Life* was a Welsh speaker, there is, of course, positive evidence from his treatment of English place-names, to suggest that he could at least read Old English. Those who press their opinions—and they are no more than opinions—on the Welsh origin of the author of the *Life* of Alfred have failed to take into account the remarkable knowledge of Old English possessed by this man who translated the Alfredian section of the Anglo-Saxon Chronicle into Latin. More than that, he translated the Old

English idiom *wælstowe gew(e)ald ahton* ('they held the place of slaughter', i.e. 'they won the battle') with a word-for-word Latin rendering of *loco funeris dominati sunt*. When the Pseudo-Asser used that Latin phrase, describing the English victory over those vikings who had sacked Winchester in 860, he was following his idiomatic text of the Chronicle word for word.[168] Even Stevenson who firmly believed in the Welshness of his Asser, was forced to comment: 'It is surprising that a Welshman should have used this literal translation of an O[ld] E[nglish] phrase, for, as we are informed by Professor Rhys, no such expression is recorded in Welsh.'[169] It was one thing for a Welshman to translate an unfamiliar English idiom, word for word into Latin, when he found that idiom in his West Saxon text. But this supposed Welshman even invented the same English idiom when it was not in his original text. So, while the Chronicle simply says of the English victors at Aclea in 851, that 'they had the victory there' (*þær sige namon*),[170] the Pseudo-Asser, following those 'habitual patterns of one mind expressing itself in characteristic [English] ways' rendered that simple Old English sentence in Latin as *et loco funeris dominati sunt*.[171] Few aspects of the *Life* of Alfred could reveal the English mind of its author more clearly than this.

The fact that the majority of the Welsh material in the *Life* of King Alfred occurs in the form of glosses does not in itself preclude the Welshness of the author. But the Welsh material in the *Life* is invariably used to gloss English place-names and never used to explain place-names in Wales proper, as we might expect if the author had indeed come from Wales, and was truly at home with the Welsh language. Nor can we argue that this was so, because he was writing exclusively for Welshmen who had no need for an explanation of their own place-names. Medieval Welsh and Irish texts abound with etymologies to satisfy the fascination for etymology which Celtic readers held in regard to their own familiar place-names. Nor is the exclusive glossing of place-names within England in the *Life* of Alfred confined to the offering of Welsh forms of names. Etymologies in Latin are also offered on English place-names such as Sheppey, Englefield, Berkshire, Ashdown, and *Aclea*. We are reminded of the comment offered by the author of St Neot's *Life* on the place-name *Selwood* ('as it is called in the language of the English')[172] which, as we have seen, bears a relationship to the text of the *Life* of King Alfred. The Pseudo-Asser's technique throughout the *Life* of Alfred was basically to gloss the Latin translation of the Chronicle thinly, and to add his own material here and there in separate chapters. But the Welsh material is neither integrated enough, nor sufficiently wide-ranging to offer proof of Welsh authorship for the *Life* as a whole. The Welsh forms offered for his place-names in England, are—precisely like those in the *Life* of St Neot—essentially antiquarian and, as we shall see, they are derived from book-learning. This cannot preclude the possibility that the author of the *Life* of King Alfred and of the *Life* of St Neot was Welsh or Cornish, but we must at least allow for the possibility that their knowledge of things Celtic had been acquired.

The archaic or retrospective tone of the Pseudo-Asser's Welsh information is nowhere better illustrated than in his gloss on the place-name *Thanet*. He describes this as 'the island called Thanet (*Tenet*) in English and *Ruim* in Welsh'. But in the early tenth-century, a genuine Welsh bard—the author of *Armes Prydein*—who referred to the English as 'the scavengers of Thanet (*kechmyn Danet*)' twice gave the Kentish island its contemporary English name.[173] That patriotic Welsh poet, who was striving to rouse the Welsh kings to battle against the English and hoping to drive the English off old British lands back into the sea at Sandwich, might well have used a Welsh form for Thanet, had he access to it. The same poet refers to Winchester, for instance, as *Caer Wynt*.[174] But the Pseudo-Asser's knowledge of the obsolete word *Ruim* for Thanet did not necessarily stem from any Welshness on his part. It owed its existence to his knowledge of Nennius's early ninth-century *Historia Brittonum* which source also provided him with information on the worship of the Old English ancestor-god, Geat.[175] This crucial evidence for the Pseudo-Asser's book-learning in relation to Welsh information has implications for all his glosses relating to things Welsh. The notion that Nottingham was called *Tig Guocobauc* in Welsh and *Speculum Domus* ('House of Caves') in Latin—a name that bears no relationship to the English *Snotengaham*—must also have come from a written source.[176] Nottingham, unlike Cirencester (*Cairceri*), Dorset (*Durngueir*), or Exeter (*Cairuuisc*), was far removed from Wales, and far removed in time from when it was under British rule. The Pseudo-Asser's interest in Nottingham as a place-name is exactly paralleled by the author of St Neot's *Life* and his antiquarian treatment of Brittonic forms of East Anglian place-names such as Ely or the river Ivel. At first sight, there seems nothing odd about a supposedly early Medieval Welsh writer of a *Life* of King Alfred referring to the Severn by its Classical name of *Sabrina*.[177] Ninth-century Frankish annalists and biographers regularly referred to the Seine for instance, by its Classical name of *Sequana*. The Welsh historian Nennius used the classical *Sabrina* for the river Severn throughout his work,[178] and the form *Sabrina* was also used by the compiler of the *Annales Cambriae*.[179] But while Nennius used the Classical *Sabrina* throughout his *Historia Brittonum*, he also—by way of contrast to the Pseudo-Asser—sometimes referred to the Severn by way of the vernacular *Habren*.[180] What is remarkable is that while the Pseudo-Asser used the same word for the Severn as Ptolemy, Gildas, and Bede, he came up with a contemporary Frankish word, *Signe*, for the Seine, in preference to the Classical *Sequana* of ninth-century Frankish writers.[181] Few things could more clearly demonstrate where the most powerful contemporary cultural influences on the author of King Alfred's *Life* were coming from, than this. When a tenth- or eleventh-century author writes of the Welsh *Sabrina*, he shows he has been consulting his books. When he writes of the Frankish *Signe*, he shows that he is either a Frank, or else that he is someone writing under the strongest of contemporary Frankish influences. Byrhtferth of Ramsey, the pupil of the learned Abbo of Fleury or any one of Byrhtferth's Ramsey circle who had been trained at Fleury could be expected to write in this way.

Recognizing the book-learning that lies behind so much of the Pseudo-Asser's Welsh information, it is quite feasible that a scholar with an antiquarian outlook such as that certainly possessed by Byrhtferth of Ramsey may have acquired the modest amount of Welsh nomenclature and sporadic use of Welsh directional idioms as displayed in the *Life* of Alfred, from books consulted either at Ramsey or in the library at Worcester, which was also accessible to Byrhtferth. An alternative explanation suggests itself in the form of a Cornish or Welsh monk of the community of St Neots in Huntingdonshire, who provided Byrhtferth or one of his circle with the necessary knowledge of Brittonic which enabled him to experiment with those forms in the *Life* of Neot and eventually to develop the more ambitious idea of presenting the *Life* of Alfred as the work of the Welsh bishop, Asser. It is doubtful if St Neots in East Anglia had preserved any meaningful contacts with the Cornish house from which the relics of the saint had been stolen. Indeed, the evidence would point in the other direction. To deprive a monastic house of the relics of its founding saint in the early Middle Ages was to rob it of its spiritual and economic *raison d'être*, and the only connection between the two St Neot monasteries may have been that a dominant English community had deprived a house in a conquered Cornish territory of the bones of its patron saint. Hart suggested that the author of the earliest *Life* of Neot had been brought as a novice by Ealdorman Æthelwine of East Anglia (the lay founder of Ramsey) from one of that ealdorman's West Country estates.[182] This would explain the author's knowledge of Cornish topography and perhaps also his grasp of Celtic nomenclature. So a third possibility presents itself, whereby the author of the *Lives* of St Neot and of King Alfred was himself a Cornish émigré at Ramsey or St Neots. But the complex interrelationship between the Celtic elements in the *Life* of Neot with those in the *Life* of Alfred, together with the undeniably shared elements in style and vocabulary which those two works have in turn, with the known works of Byrhtferth of Ramsey and his circle, requires that we suspend final judgement on precise authorship until much more work has been done on all the texts under discussion. It may be, for instance, that the hand of the indefatigable Byrhtferth lies behind all of the works which have been attributed to him. On the other hand, Lapidge may have been seeking after too great a precision in attributing the authorship of the *Lives* of Ecgwine and of Oswald, together with the *Historical Miscellany* in the *Historia Regum* to Byrhtferth alone. Armitage Robinson long ago cautioned us against attributing everything to Byrhtferth which carried the hallmarks of his Ramsey school:

> The abundance of coincidences in phrase and material to which he [Crawford] has pointed must not lead us to forget that among the pupils of Abbo at Ramsey there may have been contemporaries of Byrhtferth who had the same training in the older literature as himself, one of whom might have had no less capacity of commemorating the virtues and achievements of the saintly founder.[183]

While bearing that caveat in mind, it is, nevertheless legitimate, in view of all the evidence, to attribute the *lives* of Alfred and of St Neot to the circle of Byrhtferth of Ramsey, if not to Byrhtferth himself. We know that Byrhtferth was personally interested in the etymology of place-names, as witnessed by his lengthy digression on the derivation and meaning of the word 'Ramsey' in his *Life* of St Oswald.[184]

Once he, or an associate had embarked on the experiment of writing King Alfred's *Life* in the person of a Welsh bishop, Asser, he was then committed to injecting some plausibly Welsh-looking material into his work. The material most useful and most accessible to a non-Welsh medieval researcher would have been of an etymological nature, and written in Latin in the format of a glossary. Such a work could have been consulted by Byrhtferth in precisely the same way as he culled pretentious words from his Greek lexicon.

When we look at what the Pseudo-Asser tells us about his first coming to King Alfred from Wales, we find that the same inconsistencies, the similar borrowing of motifs from other sources, and a downright disregard for common sense pervades the narrative as elsewhere throughout the *Life* of Alfred. The writer tells that he was summoned by the king 'from the most westernmost part of Britain'—a phrase recalling the author's location of Athelney in the *Life* of Neot—and that he first met Alfred at the royal estate at Dean.[185] This narrative of the 'summoning' of Asser forms a continuation of the summoning of Grimbald and John in the previous chapter and was, as we have seen, based on an imitation of the notion of Charlemagne's Palace School as described by Einhard and in the *Life* of Alcuin. Indeed the Pseudo-Asser borrowed from Einhard's *Vita Caroli* in this very part of the *Life* of Alfred when telling us of the many gifts which King Alfred gave him.[186] When Alfred's biographer goes on to describe his reluctance to join the king's household without first consulting his *familia* at St David's, and later when he itemizes the gifts of monasteries which he received from the king, we recall that he was drawing from the Frankish *Life* of Alcuin of York.[187] The proposed agreement between Asser and King Alfred, whereby Asser was to spend six months with Alfred and six months back in Wales, or alternatively, three months with Alfred and three months in Wales,[188] smacks of Byrhtferth's love of symmetry and halves and quarters—as in his account of the division of Alfred's revenues. When Asser is supposed to have returned to King Alfred's court for the implementation of his plan, we are told he spent not three or six, but eight months in the king's service.[189] In the interim however, when Asser had intended consulting his people, he was seized by a violent fever and forced to convalesce at Winchester for twelve months and a week 'by day and by night without any remission or hope of recovery'.[190] King Alfred, for his part, wrote to Asser requesting the reason for the delay and urging him to join the king as soon as possible. Stevenson, embarrassed by the nonsense of Asser lying ill in Alfred's chief town for a whole year without the king's knowledge, and finding it difficult to reconcile that Asser lay up in Winchester having already told us he had gone home (*ad patriam remeavimus*), adopted North's suggestion that the author of the *Life* had originally written *Guentonia* for *Wintonia*, and so by a pseudo-linguistic slight of hand, Asser was made to convalesce in Caerwent in Monmouthshire on the road to St David's![191] Indeed, so embedded in the Alfredian canon has this emendation become, that Keynes and Lapidge boldly translated their version of the Pseudo-Asser's text to read: 'I was seized by a violent fever in the monastery of Caerwent.'[192] There was never any justification, for tampering so freely with an early eleventh-century text. *Wintonia*

is what we are left with, and *Wintonia* means Winchester. In another context, free
from the polemic of the Asser debate, Stevenson unhesitatingly identified *Wentonia*
in a mid-ninth century text by Rægenbold as relating to Winchester.[193] *Wintonia* of
chapter 79 in the *Life* of King Alfred is clearly the same *Wintonia* which the
Pseudo-Asser tells us in chapter 18 of the same text was attacked by a great
heathen army arriving by sea in 860.[194] There is no doubt whatever that the
Wintonia mentioned in 860 translates the *Wintanceaster* (Winchester) of the Anglo-
Saxon Chronicle for that year.[195] As for the inconsistency and contradiction, that
is the stuff of which the *Life* of King Alfred is made, and to edit it away is to do
violence to the text and to the truth.

Yet another celebrated ambiguity—if not a glaring anachronism—in the *Life* of
Alfred is the author's claim that the king rewarded his services first with the two
monasteries of Congresbury and Banwell (in Somerset) and later added Exeter
'with all the diocese belonging to it, in Saxon territory and in Cornwall'.[196] Exeter,
as Galbraith explained, was not formally constituted as the seat of a diocese or
parochia until 1050.[197] In King Alfred's reign, the bishop of Sherborne had episcopal charge over the whole of western and south-western Wessex. On the death of
the historical Bishop Asser of Sherborne in 909, his unwieldy diocese was divided
into three, with bishoprics centred on Sherborne as before (for Dorset); and with
two new bishoprics centred on Wells (for Somerset), and Crediton (for the ex-
panding conquered territories in Cornwall).[198] In 1050, Bishop Leofric of Crediton
had his seat moved from Crediton to Exeter, and it was this event which prompted
Galbraith to attribute the forging of King Alfred's *Life* to Leofric. Galbraith
argued that Leofric had a vested interest in promoting earlier claims for Exeter as
a diocesan centre. But there is clearly not sufficient propaganda promoting the
claims of Exeter in the Pseudo-Asser's work to warrant the notion that the entire
Life of King Alfred was written to further Exeter's claim. Besides, the manuscript
of the *Life* which was destroyed in the fire of 1731 would seem to have pre-dated
the establishment of the diocese of Exeter in 1050 by several decades. Numerous
attempts have been made over the past century to explain away the Pseudo-Asser's
narrative here, and more recently by commentators anxious to suppress Galbraith's
thesis and to restore credibility in the contemporary nature of King Alfred's
biography. Their ideas range from the notion that Asser had been made a suffra-
gan bishop of Exeter prior to his known elevation to Sherborne *c.*900, to developed
interpretations of the author's use of the word *parochia*.[199] Since Asser was a
Welshman, the argument goes, then by *parochia* he would not have meant an
episcopal charge over a diocese, but rather the jurisdiction of an abbot over a
monastery at Exeter and over 'its dependent lands with all its rights'.[200] But such
special pleading has its own built-in problems. Celtic abbots ruled their monastic
familiae de facto with the same power as bishops in a Roman ecclesiastical organization. Although a Celtic abbot might not be able to ordain clergy or perform
other sacramental functions of a bishop, the monastic *caput* of a *parochia*—including those for women—were known to have their own resident bishops to perform
these vital functions. Since Celtic churches were organized on a monastic basis,

then monasteries whose abbots ruled as heads of a *familia* ruled the entire network of a monastic confederacy with rights over monks and their clergy, and revenues— including revenues for instance, from burial fees—in the same way as a bishop under the Roman system controlled his parish clergy and their church lands. One major difference may have been that the monastic *familia* was a scattered confederacy whose *parochia* may not often have exhibited the clearly defined and tidy territorial aspect of Roman diocesan organization. If the Welsh Asser, therefore, were to have claimed such jurisdictional powers for a *parochia* based on Exeter, then he would *de facto*, as a bishop who was thoroughly conversant with English ways, be claiming episcopal authority over a diocese based on a town which was not known to have been a bishopric until 1050. In other words, when the Celtic notion of *parochia* is transposed into a West Saxon context—particularly by a writer who was himself a bishop, and who was supposed to have had an intimate knowledge of both societies—then the '*parochia* of Exeter' can only have meant a diocese based on that town.

Byrhtferth of Ramsey was a man who compiled a *Life* of St Ecgwine out of thin air, and who, when it came to writing about his own much-admired contemporary—Byrhtnoth, hero of the Battle of Maldon—even got the date of that heroic struggle badly wrong by stating that Archbishop Dunstan died after, rather than before, Byrhtnoth was slain.[201] That glaring error appears in the *Life* of St Oswald, as does the confusion between Edmund and his half-brother, King Edward the Martyr, and the statement that King Edgar died many years after his consecration.[202] A writer such as the Pseudo-Asser who actually confused the name of his subject, King Alfred, with that of his role model, Charlemagne; who consistently confused King Alfred's son-in-law, Ealdorman Æthelred of Mercia, with Eadred, and who accepted the early eleventh-century Frankish conceit that the Danes had come from the Danube, can be excused for sending the Welshman Asser back home to Winchester to convalesce, or for associating him with an imaginary diocese at Exeter. From an early eleventh-century perspective, a writer such as Byrhtferth or any of his associates located at distant Ramsey might have been dimly aware that the three dioceses of Sherborne, Wells, and Crediton were a post-Alfredian creation, but they would have been vague about what had gone before. They would have known from the Anglo-Saxon Chronicle that Sherborne did possess a bishop in King Alfred's time, but that he was not Asser. They would also have seen from their copy of the Chronicle that Exeter loomed large in the history of the viking wars, and was so important to King Alfred that he abandoned a campaign against vikings in Kent and Essex to return and save his West Saxon town in the far west of his kingdom.[203] That event was recorded in 893 and we have seen how the Pseudo-Asser was prompted to pretend that he was writing in 893 because that was the year in which one particular copy of the Chronicle which he had consulted, ended abruptly, depriving him of further basic information on King Alfred's life. But the very last year in that copy of the Chronicle would have provided him with a record of a major Danish assault from the sea on Exeter which was successfully beaten off by King Alfred. Exeter would have been a fitting place, for a forger based in Ramsey, to invent as King Alfred's gift to his favourite tutor.[204] It has to be said, however, that the mention of the *parochia* of Exeter in a *Life* which was written in the early eleventh century continues to present the same problem of anachronism as it once presented to those who held out for a ninth-century date for the *Life* of Alfred.

The second of the two so-called Welsh chapters—chapter 80 of King Alfred's *Life*—contains a brief discussion, consisting of only 151 words. But it contains a narrative densely packed with political and dynastic information on late-ninth century Wales. The narrative opens with the bold statement that 'at that time and for a considerable time before then, all the districts of southern Wales belonged to King Alfred, and still do'.[205] This statement is patently not true. We note first of all the plea for contemporaneity of writing in the phrase 'and they still do belong to him (*et adhuc pertinent*)'—always a suspicious element in the forger's text, striving to impress on his readership that he is ever, the genuine Asser. Common sense suggests that if the Cornish peninsula survived under the rule of its own kings into the reign of King Alfred's grandson, Athelstan, then South Wales remained free of West Saxon overlordship for at least as long. The southern Welsh rulers of Dyfed, Brycheiniog, and Glywysing were cut off by the great expanse of the Bristol Channel from all contact with Wessex, whose own northern coasts along that Channel (in Devon and Somerset) formed a virtually impassable frontier of forest and marsh. The Pseudo-Asser himself informs us that the army of the brother of Hálfdan and Ivar attacked north Devon from a winter base in Dyfed in south-west Wales in 878,[206] and from then until the reign of Edward the Elder in 914, the Bristol Channel was clearly a major entry point into western Britain for viking marauders. The viking invasion of 914 shows that while Edward successfully defended the coast of Wessex along the Bristol Channel 'from Cornwall east as far as Avonmouth' there were some raiding parties which broke through his coastal defences along the Bristol Channel, and the viking fleet ravaged at will along the southern Welsh coast.[207] Such accounts show that South Wales and the Bristol Channel lay hopelessly exposed to sea-borne raiders—not only from Scandinavia, but also from Brittany and Ireland. We cannot seriously entertain the idea, therefore, that Alfred or his immediate predecessors 'for a considerable time before then' were either in a position physically to subdue the southern Welsh, or indeed to reach them with effective aid in any military crisis. Added to all this was the reality that Alfred and his older brothers and their father, Æthelwulf, had more than enough on their hands to ward off Danish attacks on the West Saxon heartlands. They were clearly not in a position to embark on dangerous adventures in South Wales at a time when Mercia still retained its independence, under King Burgred, up until 874. Indeed the only evidence we have for a West Saxon expedition against the Welsh proper is the record of King Æthelwulf's raid in 853. But the Chronicle makes it clear that the initiative for that raid came from Burgred and his Mercian *witan*, and that Æthelwulf joined in as Burgred's ally in order 'to help him [i.e. Burgred] to bring the Welsh under subjection to him'.[208] So if any portion of Wales had been brought into a tributary position to the English 'for a

considerable time before' Alfred's reign, it was surely subject to Mercia rather than
to Wessex. The earliest evidence we have for West Saxon overlordship in Wales
proper comes from the end of the reign of Edward the Elder and from more
plausible accounts of submissions on the part of Welsh rulers to King Athelstan in
c.927 as recorded in the Anglo-Saxon Chronicle and later by William of
Malmesbury.[209]

The Pseudo-Asser, having told us of the subjection of southern Wales to King
Alfred, proceeds to supply us with a *Who's Who* of rulers in the region. This may
be set out as follows:

Hyfaidd, with all the inhabitants of the kingdom of Dyfed
   [driven by the might of the six sons of Rhodri (Mawr) submitted to King
   Alfred]
Hywell ap Rhys, king of Glywysing and
Brochfael and Ffernfael, sons of Meurig and kings of Gwent
   [driven by the might and tyrannical behaviour of Ealdorman Eadred and the
   Mercians sought King Alfred's protection]
Elise ap Tewdwr king of Brycheiniog
   [driven by the might of the same sons of Rhodri (Mawr) submitted to King
   Alfred]
Anarawd ap Rhodri and his brothers
   [abandoned his alliance with the Northumbrians and submitted to King Alfred
   in person].

Most of the Welsh rulers mentioned in this short and compact chapter can be
shown from Welsh annals and other fragmentary sources to have been active in the
880s and 890s in their respective kingdoms in Wales. As a list of late-ninth century
Welsh rulers, this chapter from the *Life* of Alfred would seem to supply us with
genuine information, and so it may well be the most valuable section in the entire
work. This information stands out among the 106 chapters of Stevenson's edition
of King Alfred's *Life* for its density of information, the consistency of its Welshness
and the consistency of content in regard to dynastic information. All this stands
out in stark contrast to the remainder of this vague and sprawling biography. It
is a remarkable fact that King Alfred's biographer supplies us with the names of
six Welsh rulers—Hyfaidd, Hywell, Brochfael, Ffernfael, Elise, and Anarawd—
together with names of four territories—Dyfed, Glywysing, Gwent, and Brycheiniog
—as well as the names of four kings' fathers—Rhys, Meurig, Tewdwr, and Rhodri
[Mawr]. It could, of course, be argued that this furnishes undoubted proof of the
Welsh origins of the biographer of King Alfred. Yet that same biographer, who
alleged to have been a confidant and tutor of the king, offers us not one single
name of a follower of Alfred or of a member of his household who is not mentioned in the Anglo-Saxon Chronicle. So ignorant was he of Alfredian Wessex and
of the king's household, that he failed even to give the name of King Alfred's wife,
and in this very chapter on Welsh rulers, he confuses the name of King Alfred's
son-in-law, Æthelred of Mercia, with that of Eadred. The explanation for the

relative wealth of information on Wales—as compressed into chapter 80—in contrast to the poverty and glaring ignorance in the rest of the *Life*, is not that the Pseudo-Asser was a Welshman, but that he used a genuine Welsh source on late ninth-century Welsh history, and inserted it *en masse* into this short chapter. What the author of the *Life* may well have used was a historical source equivalent to the Irish synchronisms or a set of king-lists setting out contemporary Welsh rulers from the late ninth century. This he then used for his own purposes, transforming it from a mere list—accurate though it may have been—into a political commentary to suit his own designs. And in claiming that all of these Welsh kings submitted to Alfred, he achieved two goals at once. He glorified the subject of his biography and he also provided his forgery with a powerful semblance of authenticity for its Welsh authorship which has proved impervious to historical criticism.

The Pseudo-Asser claimed that all of the rulers in his list submitted to King Alfred—Hyfaidd of Dyfed and Elise of Brycheiniog driven by the sons of Rhodri Mawr; and Hywell of Glywysing and Brochfael and Ffernfael of Gwent under pressure from Ealdorman Eadred (*recte* Æthelred) of Mercia. Finally, the bullying Anarawd ap Rhodri and his brothers abandoned their alliance with (Danish) Northumbria and came to submit to King Alfred in person. In this optimistic account of things, not only did the southern Welsh princes submit, but their northern Welsh persecutors from Gwynedd—the sons of Rhodri, who were overlords of Powys and Ceredigion, also came into Alfred's camp. In short, the whole of Wales was at King Alfred's feet. Had all that really happened before the Pseudo-Asser was supposed to have written in 893, is it possible that the Anglo-Saxon Chronicle would have ignored the most momentous development in Anglo-Welsh relations since the *adventus Saxonum* back in the fifth century? It is simply not possible that the Chronicle, in which the military and political career of King Alfred was one of prime concern, would have ignored a triumph which anticipated the achievements of Edward I in the thirteenth century. It would have been a triumph too, which had massive repercussions for the progress of the Danish wars which were also at the centre of the Chronicle's theme. The Chronicle does touch briefly on Welsh help given to the English in their victory over the Danes at Buttington 'on the bank of the Severn' in 893. But the Chronicle is significantly vague on what that Welsh help consisted of. It comprised 'some portion of the Welsh people (*sum dæl þæs Norðwealcynnes*)'.[210] We are not told which Welsh, how many, or from where? They might have been levies from within English districts along the Welsh borders, or they might have been Welshmen from a Welsh kingdom. But for the writer of the Chronicle, the Welsh were still a distant people whose affairs scarcely impinged on the concerns of Wessex. It was not until the reign of Alfred's son, Edward, and later in the reign of his grandson Athelstan, that Welsh submission to the House of Alfred began to become an issue of some importance for the West Saxons. To a writer such as Byrhtferth of Ramsey, who was writing several decades after the submission of the Welsh to King Edgar at Chester in 973, it seemed natural to project such events back into Alfred's time. But as Davies reminded us, the nature even of tenth-century Welsh submissions remains obscure, and evidence for the appearance of Welsh kings at the English court belongs to the tenth century rather than to the ninth.[211] From 928 to 956 kings of Dyfed, Gwynedd, Brycheiniog, and Gwent-Glywysing occasionally witnessed English charters. But Welsh submission to the House of Wessex followed on from the West Saxon conquest of the Danelaw and consequent West Saxon unification of England under Alfred's immediate descendants. Welsh submissions followed those momentous Anglo-Danish events of the tenth century, they did not drive them. It is false to use the doubtful testimony of the *Life* of King Alfred as evidence for a Welsh coalition organized by Alfred, which in turn helped him in his struggle with the Danes. The opposite was in fact the case. Welsh independence was more secure while Wessex was kept busy with a dangerous Danish enemy. As the power of Wessex grew *vis-à-vis* the Danes, a Welsh bard in his poem *Armes Prydein* read the signs of the times correctly, and begged his countrymen to join a Norse alliance in order to keep Athelstan or his brother Edmund in their place.[212] That alliance failed, and the submission of Welsh rulers to Wessex was a continuing and inevitable consequence. For as the English—i.e. West Saxon—frontier was pushed relentlessly northwards through the Danelaw, and as Mercia, too, became subsumed into the new English realm, it was inevitable that Mercia's old enemies, the Welsh, should also be forced to respond to West Saxon claims of overlordship. Those were the political realities of the time of Alfred's grandsons and of the later tenth century. All of that was far into the future, when back in the late ninth century, Alfred was fighting for the survival of Wessex. We search in vain to find royal Welsh witnesses to the charters of King Alfred, and not even industrious forgers of a later age unearthed names of Welsh witnesses from now lost genuine documents, to add to their own bogus lists.

One piece of information which the Pseudo-Asser provided in his Welsh chapter has been the subject of close scrutiny. He tells us that Hyfaidd, along with 'all the inhabitants of the kingdom of Dyfed, driven by the might of the six sons of Rhodri, had subjected himself to [Alfred's] royal overlordship'. Stevenson expressed some disquiet in 1904, that the reference by Alfred's biographer to 'the six sons of Rhodri Mawr' did not tally with information available from other sources, which seemed to identify only four sons.[213] Dumville's investigation into the number of Rhodri's sons yielded little comfort to those who had put their faith in the 'genuine' Asser. Stevenson's four sons of Rhodri were those mentioned in the *Annales Cambriae*—one of whom, Gwriad, was slain by the Saxons (*a Saxonibus*) in 877. Yet, the time when these sons were supposed to have submitted to Alfred must, on Dumville's own ruling, have been between 878 after Alfred had overcome Guthrum, and 893 the year in which 'Asser' was supposed to have been writing.[214] With Gwriad already dead, that left only three sons who were politically active in contemporary Welsh records. Matters become yet further complicated when we turn to thirteenth- and fourteenth-century genealogical collections, of which one mentions seven sons of Rhodri and another gives us eight.[215] When all the sons mentioned in these later medieval genealogical tracts are added up, we arrive at a total of ten sons in all. Dumville was compelled in the face of these difficulties to abandon the notion of the Pseudo-Asser's 'Six sons of Rhodri' altogether, on the grounds that his text at this point was corrupt. In spite of his admission that 'here Stevenson's text [of the *Life* of Alfred] depends directly on no witness earlier in date than the second half of the sixteenth century',[216] this did not deter Dumville from inventing 'the best available approximation to Asser's [*sic*] words'.[217] Without any alternative readings to guide him from Byrhtferth's version of Alfred's *Life* in the *Historia regum*, from the Annals of Neots or from Florence (*alias* John) of Worcester, Dumville amended Parker's text of *sex filiorum Rotri vi compulsus* ('driven by [fear of] the might of the six sons of Rhodri') to read: *filiorum Rotri vi compulsus* ('driven by the might of the sons of Rhodri').[218] By this sleight of hand, Dumville could claim that 'Rhodri's six sons may thus be banished by some quick strokes of the editorial pen',[219] and through such an unsatisfactory approach, we arrive at a so-called 'reconstructed text' of the *Life* of King Alfred. Dumville's reconstruction, which is admitted to be founded on supposition[220] and conjecture[221] goes against what little evidence we have of the original manuscript reading. The Early Modern editions of the *Life* of Alfred, together with the surviving sixteenth-century transcripts, all read: *sex filiorum* for the 'six sons' of Rhodri. Wise also reported *sex* to have been the reading of the lost Cotton manuscript.[222] The alteration of Parker's *sex filiorum Rotri vi compulsus* to 'reconstruct' a supposed original *ui filiorum Rotri compulsus* requires that two changes rather than one were made to the original manuscript reading. It requires first that the *sex* of Parker's text previously read *vi* ('by the force') and was later misconstrued as the Roman numeral *vi* ('six'). But it also requires that Parker added yet another *vi* to his transcript between the words *Rotri* and *compulsus*. But why should Parker be blamed for inventing the 'six sons of Rhodri'? It would seem that in the absence of other medieval manuscript textual readings from this section of the *Life* of Alfred, any uncomfortable aspects of this chaotic text can be conveniently blamed on a sixteenth-century archbishop.

Even if we were to accept Dumville's subjective tamperings with the *Life* of Alfred and abandon the notion of the elusive 'six' sons of Rhodri, we are still left with serious historical anomalies in the Pseudo-Asser's account of late ninth-century Welsh politics and political geography. The *Annals Cambriae* record that in 895, 'Anarawd came with the English (*cum Anglis*) to lay waste Ceredigion and Ystrad Tywi'.[223] By this time—supposedly three years after 'Asser' had written— Anarawd ap Rhodri and his brothers had abandoned their hostility against the south Welsh kingdoms and had, supposedly, submitted to King Alfred in person. What was the sense, therefore, in this supposedly Alfredian ally, attacking Alfred's other and older allies in Ceredigion and Ystrad Tywi? Dumville offered the suggestion that Anarawd 'was enjoying a military benefit of the new alliance' with Alfred. But Anarawd and his brothers already controlled all of North Wales from Anglesey to the far south of Ceredigion and Powys. Alfred was a wise enough king to know that if he supported Anarawd in his conquests further south in Wales (even if say, Ceredigion had rebelled against Alfred), it would have been foolish to allow Anarawd to dominate all of Wales from the inaccessible north. By Dumville's own reckoning, Anarawd's attack on Ystrad Twywi in 895 was directed against territory which the author of the *Life* of Alfred had declared had 'belonged to King Alfred for a long time before'.[224] Dumville was, understandably confused by the Pseudo-Asser's account of things in Wales during the period 878 to 893. If, as the Pseudo-Asser claimed, the sons of Rhodri—be they four, six, seven, or ten—had been harrying Dyfed and putting such pressure on its king, Hyfaidd, to rush into an alliance with Alfred, then why as late as 895, were Rhodri's sons still only trying to control Ceredigion—a kingdom which lay between them and Dyfed? Dumville, asked: 'Had the Scandinavians taken control?' Such comments put one in mind of a historical card game, where the joker is a viking who may be played when a player wishes to extricate himself from a desperate situation. The only conclusion we can agree with from Dumville's investigation is that 'our knowledge of the political structure of Wales in the year around 900 is lamentably deficient' and that being so, we must refrain from inventing a history for a country that is based on the evidence of a text which elsewhere can be shown to be riddled with inconsistency, invention, and deceit. Anarawd's English allies in 895 were more likely to have been Mercian rather than West Saxon. We know little or nothing of Scandinavian involvement in local Welsh politics, but we may assume that as in Ireland, the vikings took sides in inter-tribal wars, without ever being able to dominate any one faction or any one territorial kingdom. There is no evidence whatever—apart from the *Life* of Alfred—to suggest that Alfred ever enjoyed an overlordship over the northern Welsh kingdoms of Gwynedd or Powys, and it is highly unlikely that either he or his son, Edward, ever even considered that southern Welsh territories actually 'belonged' to the West Saxon dynasty in any meaningful sense.

Among the many unjustified assumptions found in the contentious literature on King Alfred that have eventually been firmed up into 'facts' is the belief that the *Life* of the king was not only written by a Welshman, but that it was also intended for a Welsh readership. What began with Whitelock's tentative support for Schütt's thesis of a Welsh readership ('I think that he had in part Welsh readers in mind')[225] later developed on no further evidence into a definite statement by the Penguin translators of King Alfred's *Life* that its author's provision of the Welsh forms of eleven English names was 'a sure sign that he was writing with a Welsh audience in mind'.[226] Elsewhere, these same commentators proclaimed: 'It is evident that the *Life of King Alfred* was written principally for the benefit of readers (and listeners) in Wales.'[227] We may well ask what benefit Welsh 'listeners' would have derived from a garbled account of the Anglo-Saxon Chronicle, written, on its editors' own admission in a bombastic and atrociously convoluted Latin which defies the scrutiny of modern scholarship. We might ask, too, what Welsh listeners—or indeed the few Welsh 'readers' who were capable of reading Latin—would have made of the neologisms, Grecisms, and archaic Latin words deliberately inserted in the chaotic text to confuse and to impress the most erudite scholars. As for Welsh princes, they had other and infinitely superior forms of literary entertainment to while away evenings in their halls, rather than being assailed with a garbled story in unintelligible Latin of a Welsh monk who had gone over to the hated West Saxons to be rewarded with pots and pans in Congresbury and Banwell. Welsh princes were very unlikely to warm to a West Saxon tale of how in 853 King Alfred's father, Æthelwulf, 'assembled an army and went with King Burgred [of Mercia] to Wales, where immediately on entry he devastated that race and reduced it to Burgred's authority'.[228] One can only hope for the sake of the personal safety of the reader of the *Life* of Alfred, that his sentence *gentem illam devantans, dominio Burgredi subdit* was either lost on an uncomprehending audience, or else drowned out in derision along the benches of the halls in Glywysing and Gwent. There is, of course, nothing whatever in the *Life* of King Alfred which was either written for, or of interest to a Welsh audience—apart from the material in chapter 80 which was borrowed from a Welsh source.[229] There may indeed have been little in the *Life* of Alfred which was of interest even to the English warrior aristocracy of the later Anglo-Saxon era, since that work of hagiographical fiction portraying a pious and neurotic king was essentially the product of early eleventh-century English monastic reformers who were experimenting with a genre which had been brought to them from Fleury and from elsewhere in Francia. Yet the assumption that the *Life* of Alfred was essentially Welsh in origin has given rise to a penumbra of unscholarly comments on this text, which have served only to enmesh the subject yet further in a tangle of prejudiced half-truths. Take for instance, the Pseudo-Asser's description of Alfred fighting 'like a wild boar (*aprino more*)' against the Danes at Ashdown.[230] Williams[231] followed by Keynes and Lapidge[232] believed that this simile was inspired by the vocabulary of early Welsh poetry where the word 'boar' is synonymous with brave warrior. But the early medieval Welsh—and indeed Celtic peoples generally—did not possess a monopoly on boar similes. The valour of the wild boar provided clichés for a wide variety of warrior societies throughout the Middle Ages. Boar-crested helmets are described in *Beowulf*, and an actual specimen of just such a seventh-century Anglo-Saxon helmet from Benty Grange in Derbyshire may be seen in the Sheffield City Museum.[233] When Geoffrey le Baker referred to Edward, the Black Prince, as 'the boar of Cornwall (*aper Cornubiensis*)' in his account of the campaign at Poitiers in 1356,[234] was he also alluding to the valour of a Celtic boar? And when Geoffrey changed his metaphor a few lines further on, to describe how 'the prince of Wales charged into the enemy with the wild courage of a lion'[235] was he then abandoning his encoded Celtic imagery and moving on to some equally obscure alien motif? It is only when scholars have fallen prey to the Welshness of the *Life* of Alfred, that Celtic boars are seen to emerge from the undergrowth of its sub-text.

The tale of King Alfred, burning the cakes of the swineherd's wife on Athelney, has led us through an analysis of the *Life* of St Neot, back to Ramsey and to the prolific output of Byrhtferth. For the *Life* of Neot not only shares King Alfred in its central subject-matter with the Pseudo-Asser's *Life* of Alfred, but both texts in their vocabulary and style of their Latinity, as well as in the historiographical and hagiographical contexts which they embody, can be shown, independently, to belong to the early eleventh century and to the circle of Byrhtferth of Ramsey in particular. In addition to the general closeness of these two texts to other works currently attributed to Byrhtferth, they also display peculiarly antiquarian Brittonic (i.e. Welsh or Cornish) features which in the case of the *Life* of Alfred were designed to convey the definite impression of a Welsh authorship. In the case of Neot's *Life*, the purpose of the Brittonic element may have been to convey the impression that the author was a Cornish monk, familiar with the original homeland of a saint, about whom nothing of any historical reliability was known. In both cases, the semblance of a British dimension can either be explained by the author's obsession with antiquarianism, and a passion for glossing his narrative with antiquarian detail or alternatively, it may indeed be that both works were written by a British monk who had joined Byrhtferth's circle at Ramsey. The Welsh antiquarian dimension is also intimately related to a love of archaic Latin vocabulary and of Grecisms culled from lexicons. The author's knowledge of Welsh language and history may have been slight, and dependent on his restricted access to a Latin–Welsh glossary and to a Latin text containing king-lists for Welsh rulers in the ninth century. At the time when Byrhtferth and his associates were writing at Ramsey, just after the turn of the millennium, Latin works from Wales were circulating among English monastic libraries, and at Glastonbury in particular. We need only to point to the Anglo-Latin 'Vatican' recension of Nennius's *Historia Brittonum* to appreciate how interested tenth-century English scholars had become in Welsh historical works.[236] That English recension of the Cambro-Latin text of Nennius was compiled as early as *c*.944 in the reign of Edmund and is suggestive of a new antiquarian interest in things Welsh, on the part of Anglo-Saxon scholars, which can only have increased as the tenth century advanced and as Wales was brought ever closer into the English political sphere. Alternatively, the author (or authors) of the *Life* of St Neot and the *Life* of King Alfred may have been a Cornish or Welsh-speaking monk—or at least someone who had access to such a Briton—who had joined the Ramsey community through Ealdorman Æthelwine's contacts with Glastonbury and his West Country estates.

The *Life* of St Neot and the *Life* of King Alfred constitute two facets of the same ambitious hagiographical enterprise. The *Life* of Alfred attempted to show how the hero who saved England from conquest at the hands of heathen Dane was an obsessively pious invalid whose Heaven-sent diseases were self-invited in order to control his sexual passion. Alfred in this portrayal was a king, whose secular scholarly interests and vernacular translations had been forgotten or submerged under a conscious attempt to transform him into a promoter of tenth-century monastic reform. In this respect, Alfred, in the Pseudo-Asser's *Life*, was a king who ruled a whole century before his time. And so John, a dimly remembered scholar at King Alfred's court, was transformed into a pioneering abbot in the role of Odo of Cluny, who was set-upon by his unreformed monks. The king whom we see in the *Life* of St Neot is not so different. He is still the pious and faithful son of the Church, who heroically mans the last ditch in his struggle against the Danish Guthrum. But in this rendering of an equally legendary Alfred, the idea of the king's wicked inclinations was developed further than in the *Life* of Alfred, but this was done in order to allow St Neot to take centre stage. For Neot's crowning glory was to reform Alfred and turn him into a Christian champion who then went on to save England in that final stand against Guthrum at Edington in 878. It is the reformed king, on the other hand, which is presented to us in the *Life* of Alfred—a ruler, who as young man, travelled to St Neot's church in Cornwall and prayed for a Heaven-sent disease.

The *Life* of St Neot has been described by Dumville and Lapidge as 'the work of . . . one ambitious, mannered and occasionally incompetent author'.[237] Precisely the same language has been used by Keynes and Lapidge to describe the qualities of the Pseudo-Asser's *Life* of Alfred, and Lapidge has repeated these same phrases in describing the works of Byrhtferth of Ramsey. Keynes and Lapidge described the author of the *Life* of King Alfred 'as a man with considerable stylistic pretensions but without any mastery of prose style'.[238] Dumville and Lapidge, lapsing into Byrhtferthian unconscious use of stock phrases, wrote in precisely the same terms about the author of the *Life* of St Neot who 'had great stylistic pretensions, but he was not always master of his medium'.[239] They described his syntax as 'bizarre and difficult, so much so that at times it is incomprehensible' and they castigated the author for his 'display of stylistic mannerism'.[240] Precisely the same charges were levelled by Keynes and Lapidge at the Pseudo-Asser:

His sentences are frequently long and sprawling . . . his syntax unclear and his exposition garbled. And as is often the case with authors whose overall command of Latin is insecure, Asser [*sic*] took care to embellish his prose with learned-looking words of various sorts: thus grecisms . . . archaisms . . . and various other rare words . . . adorn his writing.[241]

Lapidge noted the 'eccentric and idiosyncratic' qualities in Byrhtferth's *Life* of St Ecgwine,[242] where Byrhtferth's use of eccentric vocabulary 'betrays the stylistic obsession of one mind that is too self-indulgent to its own ingenuity'.[243] Lapidge pointed to Byrhtferth's weakness in Latin grammar—as evidenced by his inability to master the use of the infinitive[244] and the relative pronoun[245]—defects which have also been observed in the Latin of the Pseudo-Asser.[246] Stevenson described the style of the Pseudo-Asser as 'highly rhetorical, and gives one the impression that the author thought more of the display of his powers of composition and command of recondite words than of the matter conveyed by them'.[247] He spoke of the Pseudo-Asser's 'cloud of verbiage' and the 'bewildering arrangement of his materials',[248] 'the perverted sense in which the words [of his text] are employed',[249] and 'his tendency to wander off into side issues that considerably perplex his narrative'.[250] Byrhtferth of Ramsey, in spite of his ambitious output, exhibits all these perverse tendencies, to obfuscate and to wander, more especially in his *Enchiridion* and in his *Lives* of Ecgwine and of Oswald. The *Enchiridion* is little more than a jumbled mass of pedantic display, and since it was clearly intended as a class book, we can only agree with Hart 'that one would have felt sorry for his pupils'.[251] Armitage Robinson wrote of the 'exaggerated style' in Byrhtferth's writings and of 'the efflorescent rhetoric which he delighted to employ'.[252] Crawford, who knew Byrhtferth's Latin best of all scholars, wrote of Byrhtferth's 'predilection for turgidity and bombastic rhetoric',[253] while Hart who understood his subject best at a psychological level has the last word:

In spite of his [Byrhtferth's] obsession with pattern . . . he was sometimes unable to order his thoughts sufficiently to bring all his many sources into a coherent whole, nor could he always develop argument in a logical way. All this is surprising in a pedagogue, and one would have felt sorry for his pupils. His enthusiasm was constantly outstripping his ability and one respects the way in which he so obviously fought to overcome his difficulties. That he succeeded at all must have been due to a strong inner drive, a sense of duty and above-average application. . . . And he had a sense of humour. All this adds up to a strongly individualistic personality, and his known Latin works are permeated with these traits, making his style easier to identify than that of most of his contemporaries.[254]

All these failings—and the strengths too—are evident in the *Life* of King Alfred and the *Life* of St Neot. We see there the author's attraction to a good story, however irrelevant it may have been, such as that of the profligate Mercian queen, Eadburh, being asked to choose between the ageing Charlemagne and his young son. We see the backtracking and wandering so evident in the *Enchiridion*, and we read the author's repeated apologies for failing to stick to his account of Alfred's *Life*. Above all we see the author's failure to follow any semblance of an overall plan for his work. The *Life* of St Neot was also the invention of a writer who was at his best at an anecdotal level, and at his weakest when expected to deliver a sustained narrative covering the whole life of his subject. So we are told little or nothing of interest about St Neot, but we are treated to the memorable tale of Alfred and the burning cakes. This story—as irrelevant to the *Life* of Neot as the tale of the Mercian Eadburh was to the *Life* of Alfred—also has its pathos and its humour, and it shows its author to be the master of the literary vignette. It is a tale that ought no longer to be treated as somehow inferior to the yarns that we read in Alfred's own *Life*. The legend of the burning cakes, as a piece of pseudo-historical writing, is no worse than other stories invented by King Alfred's biographer. As a folk-tale it is better than most, and provides us with an enduring image from the early eleventh century, of one of England's greatest medieval kings.

Whichever member of the Ramsey circle compiled the *Life* of King Alfred in the early eleventh century, we now know enough about his training and background—and of the strong Frankish influences under which he worked—to have to revise radically our assessment of him and of the *Life* of the king which he wrote. In the past, it has been possible to blame all the shortcomings of the *Life* of Alfred on the rusticity and 'Welshness'—meaning backwardness—of the author. The author may have been a Welshman or a Briton, but if he were, he was neither backward nor stupid and he had access to what was then probably the best library in Britain, at Ramsey, as well as to that most extensive archive at Worcester. He shared with others in the Ramsey circle—and especially with Byrhtferth—very wide reading, impressive scholarship, and a marked antiquarianism. Those anti-quarian interests were related to his besetting weakness—his inability to rise beyond the creation of a literary or historical vignette, and to construct a sustained episodic narrative. Consequently the *Life* of King Alfred shares that same irritating and paradoxical quality so evident in the works of Byrhtferth—the interest of a scholarly and antiquarian mind handicapped by chaotic narration. It was once thought that the chaos so evident in the *Life* of King Alfred reflected a work left unfinished after a first or second draft. There is no longer any reason to entertain such an idea. The *Life* of Alfred was compiled in the same hasty and careless way as the *Life* of St Ecgwine or Byrhtferth's *Manual*. Nor is there any room left for a related idea, that embedded in the chaos of the *Life* of Alfred, a core text may lurk which was indeed a draft left behind by the elusive Bishop Asser—that historical scholar who did indeed assist King Alfred with his translations. No such illusions can be treasured any longer. When we divest the Pseudo-Asser's text of the Anglo-Saxon Chronicle of its Frankish-derived hagiographical accretions, its folk-tales, rhetorical inventions, and bland generalities, there is no identifiable core text remaining which we might plausibly associate with an unfinished draft compiled in the late ninth century.

PART THREE

Charters and Wills

XIV

The Charters of King Alfred
A Higher Order of Scholarship or Speculation?

ALFRED'S TWENTY-EIGHT-YEAR REIGN WAS COMPARATIVELY LONG, BUT in spite of that, surprisingly few charters of this king survive. The same is true of his son and successor, Edward the Elder, of whom no contemporary charter manuscript remains, and several of whose charters are forgeries. The modest scale of the surviving collection of Alfredian charters can only properly be appreciated when set against the size of the surviving corpus of Anglo-Saxon charter material as a whole. Out of a total of some 1,600 charters which survive from the Anglo-Saxon period (forgeries included), only seventeen claim to have been issued in the name of King Alfred. Of these, fourteen were issued in the king's name alone, with the remaining three issued jointly by the king along with other magnates— Archbishop Æthelred of Canterbury (Sawyer 344, Birch 536), Æthelred, Lord of the Mercians (Sawyer 346, Birch 561), and Archbishop Plegmund of Canterbury together with Æthelred of the Mercians and his wife, Æthelflæd (Sawyer 1628, Birch 577/8). It is not possible to attach any significance to the ratio between the reign-length of an Anglo-Saxon king and the number of charters issued under his rule, for the survival rate of documents may bear little relationship to the original charter output in any given period. Charters issued by kings to individual lay magnates had little or no chance of surviving, unless the estates involved eventually reverted to, or fell into the hands of ecclesiastical lords. Churches maintained archives and ecclesiastical documents had a far higher chance of surviving within the eternal family of a monastic community than among a semi-literate or illiterate lay aristocracy. Very occasionally we glimpse evidence for the loss of a 'book' in spite of its high evidentiary value in relation to the all-important business of proving one's title to landed wealth. In 833, Alfred's grandfather, King Ecgberht, granted a new charter (Sawyer 277, Birch 410) on the day after Christmas to three sisters, the old charters having been lost.[1] In a rare example of a tenth-century parchment for a charter of Edward the Elder (Sawyer 367, Birch 603), that king renewed a charter at the request of his *dux*, Æthelfrith, in 903. The original grant by a certain Athulf to Æthelgyth, his daughter, had been destroyed by fire.[2] No doubt the barbarity of the Viking wars in the years after 865 intensified the rate of destruction of all written records. King Alfred himself speaks in his prose preface to Gregory's *Pastoral Care* of 'how—before everything was ransacked and burned—

Charters and Wills

the churches throughout England stood filled with treasures and books'.[3] We can be certain that in addition to works of piety, scholarship, and leisure, monastic libraries held collections of their own charters, and perhaps they also acted as repositories for the treasures and title deeds of neighbouring lay magnates. Survival of documents within church archives depended not only on the chance accident and ravages of time throughout the Middle Ages, but also on the varying fate of monastic libraries in the cultural and religious mayhem which befell English monasteries in the sixteenth century. The fact that the great majority of King Alfred's seventeen charters or supposed charters, have a connection with the churches of Malmesbury, Shaftesbury, Athelney, Glastonbury, and Wilton, and with the bishoprics of Canterbury, Winchester, and Rochester ought to alert us to the very special nature of this survival pattern. We know from the chance survival of a precious Kentish original (not even issued in the king's name), that Alfred granted charters in favour of laymen such as Eardwulf (Sawyer 1203, Birch 539),[4] from very early in his reign, but the few charters issued by Alfred to laymen which survive, all date from later in the reign and most were eventually preserved in cartularies of great monasteries.

When we exclude forgeries and later copies in cartularies and other collections, we are left—for the entire charter collection from the Anglo-Saxon period—with a total of some two hundred contemporary or near-contemporary charters written on their original parchments.[5] But of that number only two of King Alfred's charters can claim to be contemporary or near-contemporary documents. This statistic may be due entirely to chance survival within the Canterbury archive, while fire, floods, and rats may account for the loss of numerous original documents from within Wessex proper. On the other hand, it may be that Alfred was more of a taker than a giver, when it came to ecclesiastical estates. It should not surprise us to find that a king, who needed all the landed wealth at his disposal to fight off Danish attacks, has not filled the monastic archives of southern England with records of his generosity to churchmen. One of the two possible Alfredian originals is a charter issued jointly by King Alfred and Archbishop Æthelred of Canterbury in 873, granting land at Ileden in Kent to a certain Liaba son of Birgwine (Sawyer 344, Birch 536). Although the parchment is original and the hand is ninth century, two witness lists from earlier charters in the reign of King Æthelwulf (*c*.840) have been copied onto this document. A second early parchment contains a record of a grant made by King Alfred in 898 to his *dux* Sigehelm of land at Farleigh in Kent (Sawyer 350, Birch 576). This document, issued in favour of one of the two ealdormen of Kent and preserved in Canterbury Cathedral archive, cannot be original, since the language is later than Alfred's time and it would seem to date to the tenth century.[6] Ironically, a charter which was issued in 839—long before King Alfred was born—has one of the better claims to having a contemporary connection with that king. This is a charter issued by King Æthelwulf of Wessex granting land to a certain Ithda at Canterbury (Sawyer 287, Birch 426). It was witnessed originally by King Æthelwulf, Archbishop Ceolnoth of Canterbury, by Æthelwulf's son, King Æthelstan, and by a large number of other magnates in 839.[7] What few students of King Alfred have observed is that this grant was later confirmed by Alfred and his then archbishop, Æthelred, sometime between 871 and Æthelred's death on 30 June 888. If as Birch observed,[8] the confirmation by Alfred and Archbishop Æthelred is indeed in the same hand as the main body of the charter, then this manuscript may well have been drawn up in King Alfred's reign as a late ninth-century copy of Æthelwulf's original grant, and confirmed by Alfred during a visit to Canterbury early in his reign.

Of the remaining charters issued under Alfred's name, the next oldest manuscript dates from the eleventh century—a copy of a charter issued jointly by King Alfred with his son-in-law, Æthelred, Lord of the Mercians in 889. It records a grant to Wærferth, bishop of Worcester—one of Alfred's scholarly team—of land in London (Sawyer 346, Birch 561). But even this, the third oldest manuscript of the Alfredian charter collection, cannot be accepted as authentic in its present form and has been considered by some scholars as a possible forgery.[9] Nine of the remaining charters of King Alfred survive in twelfth-century copies, while five others survive in even later form. The acknowledged forgeries are found on the whole in later manuscripts—a grant to the church of Shaftesbury (Sawyer 357; fifteenth century), to Chertsey Abbey (Sawyer 353; thirteenth century), to Athelney Abbey (Sawyer 343; seventeenth and eighteenth centuries),[10]—but this is not universally the case. Forgery was the stock in trade of all those who were concerned with evidence for ownership and the precise extent of landed estates, and charters were a prey to forgers ever since such early English records began. Stenton's warning in relation to the semblance of antiquity presented by the palaeography of several charters of King Edward the Elder needs to be constantly borne in mind in relation to religious houses, which in later times would claim to have benefited from his more famous father, King Alfred: 'The fact that some of them [i.e. charters] exist in pre-Conquest handwritings merely proves that the art of fabrication was practised at Winchester before 1066.'[11] The relatively early date of a charter text—even of some of those copied onto separate parchments is not always necessarily a reliable indication of authenticity. While three twelfth-century copies of Alfred's supposed charters are included among possible forgeries (Sawyer 349, 351, and 354), some other Alfredian charters on the other hand, surviving in much later copies, have been pronounced genuine. Whitelock argued—although not convincingly—for the authentic character of three charters (Sawyer 347, 348, and 356), the first two of which are found in fourteenth-century copies only, preserved in the Glastonbury and Wilton cartularies, respectively.[12] The date of a manuscript is clearly only one of several criteria for judging its historical worth, and comparison of charter texts copied into later medieval cartularies, with earlier versions of the same texts where they exist, shows that it was possible for some documents to have been faithfully preserved over centuries of copying. Equally, it was in the interests of forgers to imitate the most authentic and earliest formulae which came to hand. The age of a manuscript, therefore, is clearly a leading indicator as to its authenticity, particularly in a class of documents where forgery could and did offer rich rewards. Forgery was not a scribal game. It was a process designed to provide conclusive 'evidence' for the entitlement to possess vast wealth, and that being so, it must have been practised almost as soon as charters had come into use. We shall see that in the dispute over an estate at Fonthill in Wiltshire, during the reign of Alfred,[13] the production of the charter for scrutiny by one of the disputants swayed the argument in his favour: 'And when we were reconciling them (i.e. the opposing parties in the law suit) at Wardour, the charter (*boc*) was produced and read, and the signatures were all written on it. Then it seemed to all of us who were at that arbitration that Helmstan was the nearer to the oath on that account.'[14]

Too often in Alfredian studies, scholars appeal to charter evidence as if it offered some superior form of historical testimony, without showing an awareness of the limitations this documentation involves. In the case of King Alfred's seventeen charters, we can dismiss five or six[15] as forgeries and accept only one or two as originals. But an evaluation of the material in between the five or six obvious forgeries and the two early (if not contemporary) manuscript charters is a subjective and risky scholarly business. In spite of the scrutiny to which Alfred's charters have been subjected by generations of leading scholars in the field of Anglo-Saxon diplomatic, it is a sobering fact that at least fifteen of the seventeen Alfredian charters have failed to escape the charge of containing suspicious elements, and there is no unanimity as to which Alfredian charters are unassailably genuine. The uncertainty pertaining to this body of Alfredian material has inevitably resulted in its falling prey to scholars who have sought to harness it in their pursuit of partisan debates in other areas of Alfredian studies. Two charters that have fared well at the hands of the critics are curiously not the two earliest surviving charter manuscripts, but the grant to Deormod—one of Alfred's leading thegns—in 892–9 (Sawyer 355, Birch 581)[16] and a grant to Bishop Swithwulf and the church of St Andrews, Rochester, in 880 (Sawyer 321, Birch 548). These last two charters survive in copies no earlier than the twelfth century, and in the case of the Rochester example the charter as it survives was issued in the name of Alfred's father, King Æthelwulf,[17] although otherwise this document, including its witness list, is in keeping with an Alfredian date.[18] Analysis of Sawyer's invaluable survey of scholarly opinion relating to the merits of Alfredian charters reveals a bewildering mass of contradictory pronouncements from Plummer, Stevenson, Stenton, Finberg, Whitelock, and other researchers, who have disagreed with regularity on the merits of individual documents. Patterns can be discerned which underline the subjective nature of the exercise involved. While Stevenson identified seven forgeries and four other doubtful charters issued in Alfred's name, Finberg, who represented a more credulous extreme, accepted seven charters which had been rejected by Stevenson, and even accepted the Athelney charter listed by Whitelock among those which 'can be rejected outright as forgeries'.[19] But Whitelock, having established the 'rigour' of her own scholarship and having secured a position of dominance within the subject, later felt free to indulge in her own brand of scholarly speculation regarding Alfredian charters. Towards the end of her career, her attitude shifted towards a more liberal treatment of those charters preserved in later copies, as shown, for instance, in the radical revision of her opinion of what she termed Wilton I, a charter claiming to have been issued by King Alfred to his faithful *comes* Æthelhelm in 892 (Sawyer 348, Birch 567). In 1979 Whitelock sought to demonstrate the authenticity of this charter, preserved in the fourteenth-century Wilton cartulary,[20] although earlier, in 1955, she had gone on record to claim it as a forgery.[21] Whitelock also attempted to reverse a judgement of Finberg in relation to yet another charter in the Wilton cartulary. Finberg had pronounced in favour of the authenticity of a charter of Alfred's grandson, King Athelstan, supposedly issued for the benefit of St Mary's minster at Wilton in 933 (Sawyer 424, Birch 699).[22] Whitelock, in her anxiety to show that this text was a forgery, based on her Wilton I charter of King Alfred (Sawyer 348, Birch 567), used the weight of two formidable scholarly reputations to sway an otherwise unresolved issue in her favour. She claimed to have inspected Stevenson's personal copy of Birch's *Cartularium Saxonicum* shown to her by A. L. Poole, in which Stevenson (in a marginal note) was reported to have queried the authenticity of that charter (Sawyer 424).[23] Such cautionary tales of scholarly changes of mind—not to say over-zealous treatment of the evidence—are a necessary introduction to the quagmire of diplomatic studies in relation to King Alfred's reign.

The most authentic charter which can be firmly associated with Alfred during his reign as king was not actually issued under the king's name as such. It records a transaction in Kent between two laymen in 875 in which King Alfred heads the witness list (Sawyer 1203, Birch 539). This is a record of a grant of land at *Hamme*—probably Ham in the Romney Marsh in Kent—by Eardwulf to Wighelm. Eardwulf's grant was drawn up in Latin in the format of a royal diploma and the witness list including King Alfred, Archbishop Æthelred of Canterbury, a certain *Oswealdus*, who was a king's son, two ealdormen or *duces*, thirteen thegns or *ministri*, and one Wulfhere, a priest-abbot, clearly represented the court which attended on the king at the time, most likely in Canterbury.[24] This charter provides evidence for the earlier grant of this land by King Alfred to Eardwulf, who in 875 was passing the estate on to his friend Wighelm. It is one of nine documents—seven charters and two wills—which were either witnessed formally by King Alfred or which appealed to his authority. Taken as a group, documents such as this have more to offer the historian than many of the charters which claim to have been formally issued by the king. A ruler of Alfred's posthumous fame inevitably attracted the attention of forgers anxious to lend the weight of Alfred's name to their claim on landed property. Charters which were not issued by Alfred, but where that king is appealed to in the role of a third party within the body of the document, or where his name appears in the witness list only, are less likely to have been forged *ex nihilo* or to have attracted the attention of later revisers. Of the seven charters from Alfred's time as king, in which his witness or cognizance is appealed to, it is significant that five[25] deal with lands in Mercia. This was a region which, although under Alfred's overlordship, enjoyed considerable autonomy under the rule of Æthelred and his wife Æthelflæd, the daughter of King Alfred. Mercia had been an independent kingdom until the deposition of its king, Burgred, in 874, and Alfred's subsequent political relationship with Mercia must have been a delicate one. Alfred's role as overlord in Mercia must have been constantly developing throughout his reign, and the ambiguous status of the king of Wessex *vis-à-vis* the Mercians is reflected in these five charters which were not actually issued by Alfred, and in two others (Sawyer 346 and 1628) issued either jointly by King Alfred with Æthelred, lord of the Mercians, or involving Æthelred in the transaction.

Alfred's posthumous notoriety, promoted by the Anglo-Saxon Chronicle, by the biography of the Pseudo-Asser, and by later historians such as William of Malmesbury ensured that his name would attract the unwelcome attention of forgers anxious to promote their claims to landed estates in a later age. Indeed, Alfred's posthumous reputation was so potent that one forger in his zeal to associate Alfred with a grant of his father, King Æthelwulf, included Alfred's name in the witness list of a charter which was issued some eight years before Alfred was born! Æthelwulf's grant to the deacon, Eadberht, of land at Halstock in Dorset (Sawyer 290, Finberg 567), which was issued on 26 December 841, cannot be accepted as it stands, since it includes the names of Alfred and his brother Æthelred—neither of whom were then born.[26] Finberg, followed by Keynes, argued that the list in which Alfred's name appears was out of place in this charter and originally constitued a confirmatory list of witnesses who attested that same charter 'not later than 854'.[27] As the documents stands, however, Alfred is made to attest a transaction which is dated to 841, and the list can be shown, on other grounds, to be spurious. This bogus witness list, which duplicates virtually in its entirety, a list from an equally fraudulent charter of Æthelwulf, supposedly issued in 854 (Sawyer 308, Birch 469), helps us to unravel a whole series of fake charters relating to Alfred's childhood. The lists in Sawyer 290 and Sawyer 308 have 28 names—or garbled versions of them—in common. The only significant difference between the lists is that the name *Wulfhere dux*, present in Sawyer 290,[28] has been dropped from Sawyer 308.[29] Sawyer 308 relates to the so-called Second Decimation of King Æthelwulf in AD 854[30] and purports to be a grant by that king to his thegn, Wiferth, of land at Hardenhuish, Wiltshire. It was condemned as a forgery by Stevenson, Stenton, and Robertson, with the credulous Finberg alone supporting it.[31] Keynes, while admitting to the 'disreputable appearance and uncertain date' of the single-sheet manuscript of Sawyer 308, nevertheless left the door open to allow for an authentic basis for this and other related forgeries.[32] Alfred and his brother Æthelred were unique in their time, in supposedly having their names included in witness lists of their father's charters while still in their infancy. West Saxon princes did witness their fathers' charters when they had become old enough to participate in the business of the *witan*. It was the *witan* whose consent, along with that of the king, gave validity to the oral transaction embodied in written form in the charter. Such deliberations conducted by a hard-headed warrior aristocracy can have left little room for the participation of senseless infants. Æthelwulf had himself witnessed King Ecgberht's charters jointly with his father when he became a sub-king in Kent—but at a time when he was old enough to participate in the government of Wessex.[33] Æthelwulf also issued and witnessed charters in his own right as king of Kent while his father still ruled as overlord of Wessex.[34] But such practices must not be confused with the fraudulent notion that Alfred participated in King Æthelwulf's government before he had come of age as a warrior—an event which cannot have occurred before Alfred was about 14 in c.863, by which time his father was already long dead.

The first appearance of Alfred's name as a witness in a charter occurs, as we have seen, in the spurious document relating to Halstock in Dorest (Sawyer 290) dated to 841. After a pause, allowing time for the future king to be born, there follows a spate of no less than fourteen charters covering the years 854–6 in which the 4- to 6-year-old infant Alfred's name appears. The possibility of Alfred's genuine association with any of these charters can no longer be seriously entertained. The reason why forgers were prompted to include his name in the witness lists to these documents is clear enough. Eleven of the fourteen charters in question were supposed grants from King Æthelwulf to the church—the Second Decimation[35]—and their dating to 854 was designed by ecclesiastical forgers to exploit the record in the Chronicle of King Æthelwulf's granting 'by charter the tenth part of his land throughout all his kingdom to the praise of God and his own eternal salvation'.[36] Few ecclesiastical forgers could resist such an opportunity to include his church or monastic home among King Æthelwulf's beneficiaries. And so a spate of charters were manufactured—the majority associated with Wilton at Easter, on 22 April 854—in which King Æthelwulf allegedly parcelled out one-tenth of his landed inheritance to various churches.[37] Some eight other forgeries or interpolated charters for the period 854–6 also claim an association either with King Æthelwulf's tithing or with his subsequent pilgrimage to Rome. Since the Chronicle followed on immediately from the record of Æthelwulf's gift to the church with the account of his pilgrimage to Rome, and since the Pseudo-Asser's version of this Rome episode quite wrongly included the infant Alfred in his father's entourage, forgers would have been prompted to associate Æthelwulf's famous son in their fabrications dating to this period.

It is significant that in twelve of the fourteen charters in question Alfred's name appears along with that of his brother Æthelred in the witness lists. Since Æthelred's name never appears on its own without that of Alfred, in the entire period from 841 down to c.862, it is obvious that Æthelred's name was used by forgers as a mere adjunct to that of his younger brother—prompted by the Chronicle's harping on the formula 'King Æthelred and his brother Alfred', which occurs, as we shall see, no less than five times in the Anglo-Saxon Chronicle in the period 868–71.[38] Æthelred, like Alfred, was also too young to participate with the *witan* of King Æthelwulf in the years 854–6, and although he was a few years older than Alfred, his name never appears without that of Alfred or as often as Alfred's in the witness lists for that particular time. The first genuine historical reference to Æthelred appears in a charter of his older brother, King Æthelberht, where Æthelred witnesses a grant of land at Dinton in Wiltshire to a certain thegn, Osmund, in 860 (Sawyer 329, Birch 499). Another charter of Æthelberht's from about this time

(Sawyer 327, Birch 502) does contain the names of Alfred and Æthelred in its witness list, but whatever the merits of the original format of this charter, its dating to AD 790 shows it to have been tampered with, while the appearance of the abbots Wullaf and Wærferth among the witnesses does not inspire confidence.[39] The names of that same pair are found among the witnesses of most, if not all, the forged charters relating to King Æthelwulf's Second Decimation at Wilton, supposedly dating to 854, and this charter of Æthelberht contains their last mention. Yet another charter of King Æthelberht containing the names of Alfred and Æthelred as witnesses (Sawyer 331, Birch 506) has been challenged by Deanesly and Ker as a tenth- or eleventh-century imitation of a ninth-century charter. Whitelock's argument[40] that a tenth-century forger could not reproduce earlier Kentish forms in the boundary clause carries little weight. A Kentish forger in the tenth century who knew his business well could easily have availed himself of the splendid archives in Canterbury and Rochester, providing him with ample material to reproduce archaic Kentish forms for any document he wished to invent. What may be significant about the occurrence of Æthelred's name in his brother Æthelberht's charter to Osmund, granting the lands at Dinton (Sawyer 329, Birch 499), is that Æthelred appears for the first time in his own right and not as Alfred's keeper, although it must be pointed out that the surviving witness list for Sawyer 329 is truncated.[41] Æthelred's name certainly appears without that of his younger brother, Alfred, in an authentic and contemporary charter of King Æthelberht, granting land at Mersham in Kent to his 'faithful minister and prince Æthelred (*meo fideli ministro et principi meo Eðelredo*)' in 863 (Sawyer 332, Birch 507). The charter is witnessed by both Æthelred (*Eðered*), a 'king's son', and by another *Eðered dux*, so the identity of the grantee is ambiguous. But since Æthelred the brother of King Æthelberht was indeed both a prince and a king's son, the grant may have been made by King Æthelberht to his brother, who in any event, witnessed the charter. Whether or not it was the future king, Æthelred I, who was the grantee, what is significant is that Alfred did not witness along with his brother, Æthelred. The recognition that King Æthelberht's charters for Dinton and Mersham contain the earliest instances of Æthelred's name in the witness lists tallies with the chronology of Æthelred's career. Accepting that Æthelred was only a few years older than Alfred, he was about 14 when he witnessed the Dinton charter in 860 and he was perhaps as old as 17 when he put his name to witness the grant for Mersham in 860—precisely the age at which we should expect an ætheling to begin his active role with the *witan*.

The first genuine reference to Alfred in a document, but one in whose doings he did not actively participate, occurs in yet another charter of King Æthelberht in 861, in which he granted lands at Martin in Kent to Abbot Diernoth of St Augustine's in Canterbury (Sawyer 330, Birch 855 (501b)). King Æthelberht made this grant to Diernoth and his monastic *familia* conditional on their fidelity not only to him, but also to his brothers Æthelred and Alfred.[42] The formula associating his younger brothers with the condition of fidelity is doubtless genuine and is echoed three years later in another charter of King Æthelberht (Sawyer 333,

Birch 510) in which he associated his brothers Æthelred and Alfred in a grant to the church of Sherborne, for the benefit of the souls of their father Æthelwulf, and his brother, Æthelbald. This charter for Sherborne, dealing with a matter of family and filial piety, has the names of Æthelred and Alfred associated both in the body of the charter and in the witness list,[43] and it was at precisely this time, when Alfred was about 15, that we should expect to find his name, in his capacity as a *filius regis*, in genuine charter texts for the first time.

A powerful indictment of all those charters which pretend to contain the infantile witness of Alfred and his brother Æthelred emerges from a study of the chronological distribution of the names of King Æthelwulf's other sons as they appear in the witness lists to their father's charters. The eldest son Æthelstan was already witnessing as *rex* in the first year of King Æthelwulf's reign, back in 839, as we find from that near-contemporary charter (Sawyer 287; Birch 426) which was later confirmed in Alfred's reign.[44] Æthelstan witnesses as king (sub-king of Kent) seven times in all between 839 and 850—two of those charters being on contemporary parchments and one being a near-contemporary document.[45] The first occurrence of the name of Æthelbald, second oldest of Æthelwulf's sons, appears at 844 (Sawyer 319, Birch 538), and with greater certainty in a contemporary charter of 847 (Sawyer 298, Birch 451). His name appears seventeen times in all in the witness lists of his father's charters, from 844 to 856-9, usually designated *filius regis,* or simply as *dux* (Sawyer 301, Birch 457), and on one occasion (Sawyer 300, Birch 459) as *dux filius regis.* Æthelbald's presence in the witness lists overlaps with his older brother, King Æthelstan, in two suspect charters dating to 850 (Sawyer 299, 300), after which time Æthelstan disappears from the record, and four years later, in 854, Æthelbald is joined for the first time in the witness lists by Æthelberht, the next brother in line, in that spate of dubious charters connected with King Æthelwulf's tithing. The appearance of all three of Alfred's older brothers in Æthelwulf's witness lists is, however, compatible with their ability to assist their father, either as ealdormen or sub-kings, in the business of government. Æthelstan's name occurs at a time when he ruled as sub-king of Kent. Æthelbald first appears some eight or eleven years before he assumed the kingship in 855. If he were 14 in 844, he would have been 25 when he became king, and his appearance eight or eleven years prior to his own kingship is in line with the earliest authentic references to Alfred in charters of *c.*862, some seven or nine years before he became king in 871. Æthelberht's first appearance as an ealdorman in 854 was only one year before he took over the rule of Kent and some six years before he became king of all Wessex. We do not know at precisely what age Æthelbald first began to witness his father's charters in 847, but we do know he was old enough to rule Wessex in his father's absence eight years later, in 855. What is clear from a study of Æthelwulf's charters is that his three older sons followed each other in a logical sequence, and certainly in the case of Æthelstan and Æthelberht, we can see that the sequence was based on their real ability to share the burdens of office with their father. There is no room in this pattern— whatever the value of the individual charters—for the presence of 4- or 6-year-old

infants, and the only reason why historians have allowed the name of Alfred and
Æthelred to stand in all of those patently suspect documents for 854–6 is that they
have fallen under the influence of the Anglo-Saxon Chronicle and later of the
Pseudo-Asser in believing that Alfred, even from infancy, was different from his
brothers—destined from the cradle for the kingship of Wessex.

The chronological distribution of Alfred's name throughout the witness lists of
his father's charters is not a consistent one. Not only does Alfred's name appear
too early, but after the fourteen 'premature' or infantile occurrences in the period
854–6, there is a significant pause until 861, when Alfred's name reappears in the
body of that charter by King Æthelberht to Abbot Diernoth (Sawyer 330, Birch
855).[46] Why does the infant Alfred enjoy such a high profile in the earlier cluster
of charters dating to 854–6, and why is his name absent from later documents
where we might expect an older and wiser young man to participate? In a contemporary charter of *c*.859, where a grant of land near Canterbury was made by
Æthelmod *dux* to one Plegred (Sawyer 1196, Birch 497), the witness list included
King Æthelwulf and his son, Æthelbald, who signed as *filius regis*.[47] In this authentic and contemporary document there is no mention of Æthelberht or of Æthelred,
much less of the precocious Alfred. Similarly, as we have seen, Æthelred signed as
a 'king's son' without Alfred in the grants by King Æthelberht to Osmund in 860
and in the contemporary document for Mersham in 863. In King Æthelred's reign
as king of Wessex, of nine charters issued in his name, his brother Alfred witnessed only two. Yet, if we were to believe the record of the Anglo-Saxon Chronicle, Alfred was by then inseparable from his older brother, supporting him in all
his campaigns.[48] Significantly, Alfred was a witness along with King Æthelred to
a charter of Queen Æthelswith of Mercia in 868 (Sawyer 1201, Birch 522), at a
time when we know from the Chronicle he accompanied Æthelred into Mercia.[49]
But Alfred's name is conspicuously absent from two contemporary charters of
King Æthelred I. The first is a contemporary parchment containing a grant from
Æthelred as king of Wessex and Kent, issued in Canterbury to the priest Wighelm
(Sawyer 338, Birch 516), and containing forty-one names in its witness list. The
second is another Canterbury grant of 868 by a certain Cialwulf to Eanmund
(Sawyer 1204, Birch 519) which was witnessed by twenty-one magnates, including
King Æthelred and Archbishop Ceolnoth, without any reference to Alfred. The
absence of Alfred's name from the witness lists of his brother's charters and the
erratic occurrences of Alfred's name in the years before he became king, only
serves to highlight the fraudulent nature of the dense distribution of his infantile
witness back in 854–6.

The fact that we cannot accept the presence of Alfred's name on documents
dating to before *c*.862 does not necessarily mean that all of those charters from
854–6 must be fraudulent in their entirety, even if the great majority of them have
been pronounced forgeries at some point in time by leading scholars of early
English diplomatic. Nevertheless, Finberg, followed by Keynes, can scarcely have
been correct in believing that the clutch of forgeries pretending to have been
issued by King Æthelwulf at Wilton, during Easter 854, may have rested on a

genuine basis.[50] The great majority of the Wilton charters of 854 survive in twelfth-century or later copies. In support of Finberg's and Keynes's argument, we might cite a fragmentary copy of a charter which does indeed claim to have been issued at Wilton on 23 April 854, and which survives in a tenth-century strip of parchment (Sawyer 1862, Birch 480). This fragment, dating from sixty to perhaps a hundred years after the events it describes, may suggest that Æthelwulf did in fact issue charters at his Easter court, held at Wilton in 854. But the same document has nothing to say of the supposed Second Decimation, nor does it contain the phrase *in palatio nostro* ('in our palace'), of later forgeries relating to the Second Decimation at Wilton.[51] Alternatively, the tenth-century fragment (Sawyer 1862) may show us that even by that early stage, the tradition of Æthelwulf's benefaction back in 854–5 was already providing a basis for the production of bogus charters. It does not show whether those charters were based on original texts from Æthelwulf's time, or whether they arose from a genuine or false interpretation of the text of Chronicle's annal for AD 855 or from King Æthelwulf's will.[52] Historians may never be able to identify or reconstruct the authentic prototypes which lay behind such later copies of charters, and whatever status the parent documents may have had, we must regard the surviving evidence as either fraudulent, or—in the absence of corroboration from demonstrably contemporary material—unsound.

Of the fourteen charters in which the infant Alfred's name appears in the period 854–6, only three deserve close attention. The first (Sawyer 317, Birch 491) is a grant by King Æthelwulf of land at *Æscesbyrig*, in Woolstone, Berkshire, to his thegn, Ealdred. This grant, dated to 856, is of interest in that like the two following, it was made by the king to a secular lord rather than to the church. The witness list includes the name of the boys, Alfred and Æthelred, but the surviving twelfth-century manuscript shows this list has been corrupted in transmission, and therefore cannot be accepted as reliable testimony of Alfred's witness. The names of Æthelwulf's older sons, Æthelbald and Æthelberht are also present in the list, but whereas Æthelberht is described as *dux*, Æthelbald is designated *episcopus* in error, while Wullaf who is designated *dux* may have appeared in the original version of this forgery under his usual title of *abbas* to match that of his companion, Wærferth.[53] Originally, then, this list contained the names of Wærferth and Wullaf, each described perhaps, as *abbas*, and Æthelbald and Æthelberht, each described as *dux*, together with the names of Æthelred and Alfred, each described as *filius regis*. It is in this form that all six—Wærferth, Wullaf, Æthelbald, Æthelberht, Æthelred, and Alfred—witness the spate of Wilton forgeries dating to 854, and it is clear that this witness list to the grant to Ealdred was based on a version of those lists attached to forgeries, supposedly issued at Wilton on 22 April 854. If this charter to Ealdred really did date to 856, then, since it was King Æthelwulf's grant, it must have been issued after his return from Rome, which must have been late in 856, and both Æthelbald and Æthelberht ought by then to have witnessed as kings. Keynes rejected this charter on the grounds that its 'operative formulas seem to have derived from a tenth-century text'.[54] If that is so, then it affords us added proof that forged Alfredian-type charters were being produced as early as the tenth century. That in itself need not cause surprise. The tenth century was a time of major expansion and upheaval for the West Saxon church and aristocracy alike. It was a time when alternative versions of the West Saxon past had to be invented, and it was also a time when forgers of Alfredian biography and charters alike could make use of genuine information culled from the Anglo-Saxon Chronicle and from other genuine ninth-century charter texts.

The second charter deserving of closer study (Sawyer 316, Birch 467) is regarded as a contemporary or near-contemporary document of a grant by King Æthelwulf to Ealdhere of land at *Ulaham* in Kent. The witness list includes Æthelberht *rex*, and Alfred as 'king's son (*Elfred fili regis*)'. The charter is dated to 855, but the indiction ought then to be the third, whereas it is given as the first, which suggests the correct date ought to be 853.[55] Alfred was a younger and even more helpless infant in 853 than he would have been in 855. Since Æthelberht witnessed as king, we should expect the grant to date to 855 or after, when Æthelberht had assumed the sub-kingship of Kent. Whatever the true date of this charter, the document as it stands would appear to be a later copy, even if from the late ninth century, which would also fit with Birch's comment that the endorsement is in a contemporary hand.[56] Stevenson believed this charter was part of the collection relating to Æthelwulf's tithing or Second Decimation, on account of the reference to Æthelwulf's seeking of forgiveness for his sins and the exemption from worldly services. He believed that this grant—like that of the grant to Dunn (discussed below)—was made with an understood reversion to a religious house.[57] But in this charter to Ealdhere, the grantee was given power to bestow the estate on whomsoever he wished, and it is curious if a reversion to a church were intended by King Æthelwulf, that the church in question would have been content to allow its rights to appear solely in such encoded and unspecified form. The truth is that we can never be certain what the Chronicle meant when it reported how King Æthelwulf 'booked a tenth part of his land' in 855, and we are not permitted to follow the Pseudo-Asser's later monastic and early eleventh-century interpretation to the effect that Æthelwulf 'freed a tenth part of his whole kingdom (*totius regni*) from every royal service and tribute', and handed it over to the church.[58] Keynes was correct in noting that the charter evidence—for what it is worth—shows lay magnates also stood to benefit from Æthelwulf's generosity as well as churchmen.[59] But the details may forever elude us, and there is no good evidence to show convincingly that Æthelwulf's grant to Ealdhere in Kent had anything to do with a so-called Second Decimation. There is even less evidence to show that Æthelwulf gave away vast quantities of land prior to his departure for Rome in 855 'to secure the loyalty of his people in his absence'.[60] The possession of great estates by medieval magnates invariably strengthened their claim to independent action, and the handing over of such a vast number of estates by an absentee king might even have been construed by all parties, as an irresponsible gesture.

The last of the three charters with Alfred's name in the witness list and which has a claim to a measure of authenticity is the grant by King Æthelwulf to his *minister*, Dunn, of land at Rochester in 855 (Sawyer 315, Birch 486). This was the one charter relating to Æthelwulf's tithing of lands, on which Whitelock pinned her hopes for its authentic nature, and by printing its translation in the first volume of *English Historical Documents*, she conferred upon it an imprimatur which it does not necessarily deserve.[61] In this charter, Æthelwulf declares that his gift to Dunn was inspired 'on account of the tithing of lands which, by the gift of God, I have decided to do for some of my thegns', The grant was witnessed by his sons, Æthelberht *rex*, and by Alfred, *filius regis*,[62] and the document was dated by Æthelwulf to 855 'when by the grant of divine grace, I proceeded across the sea to Rome', There could not seem to be clearer support for the Chronicle's record of King Æthelwulf's tithing and for his pilgrimage to Rome along with his infant son, Alfred. The presence of Æthelberht witnessing as king would also suggest that he had been placed in charge of Kent, Sussex, Surrey, and Essex in preparation for his father's absence. Indeed, it would appear that this charter affords perfect evidence for the progress of King Æthelwulf, and of his son Alfred, through East Kent on their way to catch the Frankish ferry. But like all spurious information, the evidence seems too perfect. The Chronicle does not tell us that Alfred accompanied his father to Rome in 855—on the contrary, it dates his supposed pilgrimage to 853, and it was the Pseudo-Asser, as part of his confused translation and copying from the Chronicle, who sent Alfred to Rome a second time in 855. The very presence of Alfred's name in this document arouses suspicion that it was inserted on an erroneous assumption, supplied by the Pseudo-Asser, to the effect that if Æthelwulf were on his way to Rome when this charter was issued, then the infant Alfred simply had to be in his entourage. We know from other evidence that the text of the *Life* of Alfred inspired details for later forged charters pretending to derive from the Alfredian age.[63] As for the dating clause *quando ultra mare Romam perrexi* ('when I proceeded across the sea to Rome'), its use of the past tense may betray a retrospective tone. It is rare to find a ninth-century charter dated by such an event as Æthelwulf's pilgrimage, and it was this very mention of the Rome pilgrimage which prompted Stevenson to brand this charter as 'suspicious' on two occasions in his discussion of it, in spite of that scholar's acceptance of other elements in the document as being genuine.[64] Æthelwulf's Rome pilgrimage was an exotic affair which attracted the attention of forgers not just within his own West Saxon realm. A later generation of monks at St Denis invented a whole embassy from that Frankish monastery and from the court of an 'Emperor Louis' which was supposedly received by King Æthelwulf in London (then a Mercian town!) in 857, 'amid great rejoicings'.[65] Even monks of a distant Frankish house found a use for Æthelwulf's genuine Roman and Frankish connections in their fake charters.

The charter from Æthelwulf to Dunn does nothing to help our understanding of Æthelwulf's tithing. We are not told that King Æthelwulf granted the tithe in this instance to the church. On the contrary, it was something which in Æthelwulf's own words he had 'decided to do for some of my thegns'. The fact that Dunn later bestowed this same grant on the community of the church of Rochester may well have been fortuitous. He had received this estate with full power of disposal from King Æthelwulf in the first instance. It is possible that the main body of this charter and even most of the names in its witness list were copied from an earlier and genuine document. The witness list as it stands, however, is that of a twelfth-century manuscript copy and betrays the hand of an editor. Eleven signatories, each described as a *miles* conclude the list of witnesses. The usual Latin translation of *thegn* was *minister* in charters of the ninth century. *Miles* entered witness lists of the mid-tenth century, and there is no contemporary textual evidence for the occurrence of this word in such contexts until the eleventh.[66] Its presence in Æthelwulf's charter to Dunn does not brand this twelfth-century copy as forgery, but it does proclaim significant editing in its witness list, and that being so, this charter cannot be used to support any argument for Alfred's presence in East Kent in 855, much less for his participation in his father's government at so early a time in his young life.

A study of the titles adopted by King Alfred in his charters sheds some light on how the king, his councillors, and clergy, perceived the terms of Alfred's kingship. That study is hampered, however, by the relatively small number of Alfredian charters which survive, and by the even smaller number of original or genuine documents within that collection. The earliest surviving charter manuscripts of Alfred's reign do not contain the formula *Anglorum Saxonum rex* ((?) 'king of the Anglo-Saxons') or its variants. The late-ninth century parchment of the charter issued jointly by Alfred and his archbishop, Æthelred, in 873, granting land at Ileden in Kent to Liaba son of Birgwine (Sawyer 344, Birch 536), refers to Alfred in the body of the charter simply as *rex,* and (in the witness list) as *Æðelulf* (recte *Ælfred*) *rex occidentalium Saxonum* ('king of the West Saxons').[67] It was on a visit to Canterbury either on that very occasion or sometime close to it, that Alfred and Archbishop Æthelred confirmed the earlier grant of King Æthelwulf to Ithda (Sawyer 287, Birch 426). The contemporary parchment of Alfred's confirmation of that older charter of AD 839 styles Alfred 'king of the West Saxons (*rex Occidentalium Saxonum*)' a formula which not only conforms to Alfred's other authentic titles but which is also in line with the titles taken by his father and older brothers in the kingship of Wessex.[68] The early Canterbury parchment with its grant to Sigehelm (Sawyer 350, Birch 576) describes Alfred as 'king of the Saxons (*rex Saxonum*)' both in its text and in the witness list.[69] In what appears to be a near-contemporary Kentish parchment (Sawyer 1203, Birch 539), Alfred is referred to in the capacity of a third party as *rex occidentalium Saxonum necnon æt Cantwariorum* ('king of the West Saxons and [also] of the men of Kent') and in the witness list of that same charter, he appears simply as *rex.*[70] This charter dates to 875, so it might appear from this and from the charter issued with Archbishop Æthelred in 873, that the simple title of 'king of the West Saxons' or ' king of the Saxons' dates from early in the reign. But the grant to Sigehelm dates to the closing years of the reign (898) and other late copies of genuine charters such as that to Bishop Swithwulf and the Church of Rochester in 880 (Sawyer 321, Birch 548) also carry the title of 'king of the Saxons'.[71]

It is not that simpler or more primitive titles are, on their own, necessarily a proof of authenticity. The Rochester forgery issued to Bishop Burhric (Sawyer 349, Birch 571) alleges modestly to be in the name of 'Alfred, king of the Saxons (*Æluredus rex Saxonum*)'.[72] But of the six obviously forged charters from Alfred's reign, no less than four (Sawyer 351, 353, 354, and 356) refer to Alfred as 'king of the English' (*rex Anglorum*), or 'of the Anglo-Saxons (*Angulsaxonum rex*)', or even as 'king of all Britain (*Rex tocius Bryttanniæ*)'.[73] That the simpler designation of 'king of the Saxons (*rex Saxonum*)' or 'king of the Western Saxons (*rex Occidentalium Saxonum*)' was the more usual if not indeed the more genuine title is supported by contemporary evidence from Alfred's own writings and from the Anglo-Saxon Chronicle. In his *Will*, Alfred refers to himself as 'king of the West Saxons by the grace of God (*Westseaxena cingc mid Godes gyfe*)' or even more simply as 'king by the grace of God'.[74] This does not in itself prove that Alfred did not aspire to loftier titles. His grandson, Eadred, who also left a will, introduced it with the modest formula: 'This is King Eadred's will (*Dis is Eadredes cinges cwide*)'.[75] Yet that same Eadred aspired to honours which Alfred would never have dared to claim, and which were expressed in the rhetorical verbiage of the mid-tenth century. Eadred in his charters is described as a king guiding 'the government of the diadems of the Anglo-Saxons with the Northumbrians, and of the pagans with the Britons'—'orthodoxly consecrated king and ruler to the sovereignty of the quadripartite rule'.[76] But, as in the case also of Athelstan, these bombastic tenth-century formulae were a more appropriate reflection of Eadred's real political power than any anachronistic compliments paid to Alfred by later forgers. In the prefaces to the translations of Gregory's *Pastoral Care* and of Boethius's *Consolation of Philosophy*, Alfred styled himself simply as 'king'.[77] In introducing Gregory's *Dialogues* he used the more elaborate formula of 'Alfred, honoured with the dignity of kingship through Christ's gift'. Whitelock suggested that the choice of wording here revealed Mercian influence on the preface to the *Dialogues* as evidenced by the styles accorded to Æthelred, lord of the Mercians, in a charter of 883 (Sawyer 218, Birch 551), where Æthelred is described as 'by the inspiration of God's grace endowed and enriched with a portion of the realm of the Mercians'.[78] Alfred did indeed benefit from the help of Mercian scribes and scholars, but we need to distinguish clearly between a rhetorical flourish as in the case of 'honoured with the dignity of kingship through Christ's gift' and more strident political assertions embodied in such *titles* as 'king of all Britain' or 'king of the Anglo-Saxons'. Alfred's embellishment of his title in the preface to the *Dialogues* reminds us more of the formula *gratia Dei rex* which occurs frequently in his charters and which is also echoed in the vernacular of his *Will*, and this needs to be distinguished from those titles which lay claim to political authority or jurisdiction over specific peoples or their territories.

The Anglo-Saxon Chronicle, reporting the beginning of Alfred's reign, records that he 'succeeded to the kingdom of the West Saxons (*feng . . . to Wesseaxna rice*)' ignoring the appendages of Surrey, Sussex, Essex, and Kent in the east.[79] This was also the formula used in the Anglo-Saxon Chronicle for the succession of Æthelred in 866.[80] The kingship of Æthelbald and of Æthelberht were described differently to take account of the division of the greater kingdom of Wessex between those two older brothers. Thus, Æthelbald succeeded to the kingdom of the West Saxons in 855 'and Æthelberht to the kingdom of the people of Kent and the kingdom of the East Saxons, and of the people of Surrey, and to the kingdom of the South Saxons'.[81]

In 860, by contrast, 'Æthelberht succeeded to the whole kingdom (*feng ... to allum þam rice*)',[82] and it was to the kingship of that same expanded kingdom of Wessex that Alfred succeeded in 871. Æthelwulf described himself in his charters either as *rex*, *rex Saxonum*, or as *rex occidentalium Saxonum*, or—specifically to include the Men of Kent—as *rex occidentalium Saxonum necnon et Cantuariorum*. In a few instances, Æthelwulf is described as 'king of Kent (*rex Cancie* or *rex Kanciae*)',[83] but by far the most common of his titles was that of 'king of Wessex' or 'king of the West Saxons (*Occidentalium Saxonum rex*)'. In the case of Æthelwulf's sons and successors—Æthelbald, Æthelberht, and Æthelred—the same titles of 'king', 'king of Wessex', or 'king of Wessex and Kent' are found throughout their charters continuing in the tradition of their father's reign. In three contemporary or near-contemporary charters from King Æthelberht's reign, he appears as simply 'king' in 858 (Sawyer 328, Birch 496), as 'king of Wessex and Kent (*rex occidentalium Saxonum nec non et Cantuariorum*)' in 863 (Sawyer 332, Birch 507), and as 'king' in the witness list of the grant of Ealhere to Oswig in 858–66 (Sawyer 1199, Birch 515). Alfred's immediate predecessor, King Æthelred, is styled 'king of Wessex' in five of his surviving charters and he also witnesses a Mercian charter of Queen Æthelswith (Sawyer 1201, Birch 522) in 868 as *Æthelred rex occidentalium Saxonum*—the standard title employed by his father, King Æthelwulf. Æthelred also appears as 'king of Wessex and Kent' in two charters; 'king of the Saxons' in one, and simply as 'king' in yet another. He witnessed an original grant by Cialwulf to Eanmund of land in Canterbury (Sawyer 1204, Birch 519) as *Æðered rex*, and in the one contemporary charter of this king (Sawyer 338, Birch 516) dealing with a grant of a sedes or 'seat' in St Martin's church in Canterbury to a certain Wighelm, Æthelred used his father's Kentish formula of 'king of Wessex and of Kent (*rex occidentalium Saxonum non et Cantwariorum*)'.

We have seen, that Alfred, too, in his contemporary or near-contemporary charters also used these exact same titles. Alfred's position *vis-à-vis* his neighbouring English kingdoms eventually became radically different, however, from that of his father and older brothers. Just as the political map of England was violently redrawn by the Danish conquerers in the 860s and 870s, so too, Alfred emerged from his final confrontation with Guthrum in 878 as the sole surviving native English king. It was inevitable that an awareness of the unique nature and Englishness of his kingship should gradually develop in Alfred's own consciousness and in that of his political advisers over the next decade. Already, a sense of polarity between those who lived under English kingship and those who lived under Danish rule is apparent in the treaty between Alfred and Guthrum which may have been drawn up soon after Alfred's taking of London in 886: 'This is the peace which King Alfred and King Guthrum and the councillors of all the English race and all the people which is in East Anglia have agreed on.'[84] Here then, it is not only Alfred's traditional body of West Saxon councillors, but 'the *witan* of all the English race (*ealles Angelcynnes witan*)' who are now headed by the king of Wessex, whereas the people or nation (*þeod*) in East Anglia are represented by the Danish Guthrum. In other words, Alfred's kingship now applied to all those English not under Danish rule, which is precisely what the Chronicle—that accurate barometer of political thinking at Alfred's court—recorded for the year 886: 'That same year King Alfred occupied London; and all the English people (*Angelcyn*) that were not under subjection to the Danes submitted to him.'[85] It is not clear whether this sweeping statement applied equally to the inhabitants of English Mercia, as it did say, to the people of Essex. It was in the interest of the chronicler to make vague and ambiguous political assertions which showed Alfred up in the best possible light. After the death or abdication of Ceolwulf, who ruled in Mercia as a sub-king of the Danes until *c.*879, if not later, Alfred may have come to be regarded as overlord of England south of Watling Street. But Alfred's position in Mercia must have been a delicate one, and there are clear indications that English Mercia preserved its own *witan* as well as a sense of its own regnal independence—reflected in its charters—down to the end of Edward the Elder's reign. Nevertheless, Alfred's overlordship in English Mercia can scarcely be doubted. Indeed the most impressive list of charters from the Alfredian period (when taken as a group) are those Mercian charters issued jointly by King Alfred along with his son-in-law Æthelred of Mercia, or those Mercian charters issued by Æthelred (or jointly with his wife, Æthelflæd) in which King Alfred's authority or cognizance is appealed to. An agreement drawn up in 896 between Bishop Wærferth of Worcester and a certain Æthelwold concerning lands in Gloucestershire (Sawyer 1441, Birch 574) provides more powerful evidence for Alfred's standing in Mercia than any statement of the Anglo-Saxon Chronicle.

In that year [896] Ealdorman Æthelred summoned all the counsellors *weotan* of the Mercians together at Gloucester—bishops and ealdormen and all his chief men—and did that with the knowledge and leave of King Alfred (*be Ælfredes cyninges gewitnesse 7 leafe*). And they there deliberated how they might most righteously govern their people, both before God and before the world.[86]

The year in which this important assembly convened at Gloucester to review Mercian government under Alfred's overlordship coincided with the end of Alfred's so-called Last War. It was a war which had ended inconclusively, but which saw the final withdrawal of Hæsten and his armies from Wessex. It had also been a war, which from 893 at least, had involved the active co-operation of West Saxon and Mercian levies. We are specifically told in the Chronicle that Ealdorman Æthelred of Mercia had the assistance of the West Saxon ealdormen, Æthelhelm and Æthelnoth 'and the king's thegns who . . . assembled from every borough east of the Parret, and both west and east of Selwood, and also north of the Thames and west of the Severn.'[87] That was the muster which had successfully taken on the Danish warband at Buttington on the banks of the Severn.[88] So, in this last struggle with an elusive Danish enemy, the kingdom of the West Saxons and that of the Mercians acted as one extended kingdom, almost certainly under Alfred's overlordship. It is in this context that we need to interpret not only the assembly at Gloucester in 896, but also the remarkable comment in the Chronicle on the conclusion of the Last War: 'By the grace of God, the [Danish] army had not on the whole afflicted the English people (*Angelcyn*) very greatly.'[89] By 896 the emphasis had moved from a preoccupation with West Saxon affairs to those of the 'English people (*Angelcyn*)', and clearly as Alfred's reign neared its end, his survival as an indigenous English king, rather than just his West Saxon ancestry, must have been apparent to all who enjoyed his protection. This awareness of the novel and wider role for Alfred's kingship is clearly stated in his obituary in the Chronicle: 'He was king over the whole English people (*Ongelcyn*) except for that part which was under Danish rule.'[90] The qualification was of course a major understatement, typical of the Chronicle's reporting, and it was something of which Alfred himself had he been alive would have approved. 'That part which was under Danish rule' consisted of the major portion of what had once been English Northumbria, Lindsey, other parts of Mercia, and most of East Anglia. Nevertheless, in this statement we can already perceive a clear political awareness that Alfred's survival during the viking chaos left him not only master of Wessex, but potentially master of all other English regions which had been liberated from Danish control. It was left to his son Edward and his grandson Athelstan to capitalize on that status, by rolling back Danish frontiers and eventually claiming all of England for the kings of Wessex. But those triumphs were still very much in the future, and indeed Alfred's own future was, until 896, still in the balance. Nevertheless, towards the end of his reign, because of the acknowledgement of his overlordship—however delicate—in Mercia, and because of his eventual triumph over Hæsten's army, the terms of Alfred's kingship had irrevocably changed. He had progressed from what had been virtually a tribal kingship, to that of an overlordship of different peoples from different English traditions, who looked to him for support and defence against a common Scandinavian foe. Alfred was no longer merely a West Saxon king, even if he could never be described with any degree of credibility as king of the Anglo-Saxons, much less as king of all Britain.[91] But just as his father, and later Alfred himself, described themselves as 'king not only of the West Saxons but also of the Men of Kent', so too, a formula was found to describe Alfred's new influence north of the Thames. There is some evidence to suggest that as King Æthelwulf consolidated his own father's hold over all of southern England, his clerks toyed with a new formula to match the emerging pretensions of the West Saxon dynasty. As early as 842, Æthelwulf in granting land near Rochester (Sawyer 291, Birch 439) described himself as 'king of the Southern Peoples (*rex australium populorum*)',[92] and the formula recurs in more elaborate form in a doubtful charter to Malmesbury Abbey which may properly date to 844 (Sawyer 320, Birch 444).[93] In this grant Æthelwulf is styled 'king of the West Saxons and of the Men of Kent and of all the southern English people'.

These genuine experimental titles for Æthelwulf ought not to be confused with the one extravagant instance where this king is styled *rex Anglorum*, which occurs, significantly in the notorious French forgery of a spurious grant by Æthelwulf to the Abbey of St Denis (Sawyer 318, Birch 494).

It is significant that in not a single charter or the Anglo-Saxon Chronicle—or indeed any other document—is Alfred ever designated 'king of the Mercians'.[94] The pride of the Mercian *witan* whose ancestors had been ruled by Offa, and some of whom may even have claimed kinship with Offa and other Mercian kings, would surely not allow Alfred to be so bold. The last ruler to have been unequivocally accorded a royal title (*rex Merciorum*) in Mercian charters was Ceolwulf, the Danish sub-king,[95] but Æthelred and his wife Æthelflæd adopted quasi-regnal formulae in their charters whose style may have been deliberately ambiguous. The fact that this couple issued charters in their own right is itself an indication of their regal status and clearly shows that Æthelred was no ordinary 'ealdorman'. Æthelred, like Alfred, ruled 'by the grace of God'.[96] and any Anglo-Saxon king would have been pleased to be recognized as the holder of the *principatus* and *dominium* ('lordship') of the Mercian people.[97] Æthelred's place, following Ceolwulf II, in the Mercian king-list preserved in Worcester affords us positive proof that in English Mercian circles at least Æthelred was acknowledged as a king.[98] The chronicler, Æthelweard, once referred to Æthelred of Mercia as an ealdorman (*dux*), who had been established by Alfred in London, after the recapture of that town in 886. But in two other instances, Æthelweard unambiguously styles Æthelred as *rex*.[99] Æthelred, lord of the Mercians (*Myrciorum superstes*)[100] was clearly a Mercian aristocrat, who like Ceolwulf, and in spite of West Saxon prejudice, was almost certainly of royal Mercian stock.[101] In spite of Æthelred's undoubted royal status within his Mercian kingdom (referred to in his charters as the *regnum Merciorum* or *Mercna rices*), it is significant that no coinage survives for this ruler. Furthermore, we do have coins from the Mercian mints at Gloucester and Oxford and perhaps from elsewhere in Mercia, which were struck in the name of Alfred at a time when Æthelred was in power.[102] London, Worcester, Gloucester, and Oxford—all key centres in English Mercia—can be shown to have had Alfredian connections through numismatic, charter, or other manuscript evidence, by the late 880s. Æthelred clearly accepted the role of *sub regulus* or 'under-king' in relation to Alfred, while enjoying loftier titles as opportunities presented themselves among his own Mercians. His ambiguous position is reflected in the variety of titles which he was accorded, or which he himself adopted in his charters—titles ranging from the more modest *dux* (ealdorman), through *patricius* and *procurator* to that of *sub regulus* and a man who exercised the power of *hlaford dome* or the 'sovereignty' associated with kings.[103]

If Æthelred's position *vis-à-vis* Alfred was a delicate one, then the reverse was equally true, and Alfred's claims to overlordship, over what in ancient times had been enemy territory, had to be handled with care. The Pseudo-Asser oversimplified what must have been a complex relationship, and he was blissfully unaware that Mercia and Wessex in the age of Alfred had been thrown together by

necessity in the face of a powerful Danish threat. His statement that the Welshman, Anarawd ap Rhodri 'submitted with all his followers to the king's [i.e.
Alfred's] overlordship on such terms that he would be obedient to the king in all
things, just like Æthelred with the Mercians'[104] can be dismissed as fiction. It was
a fiction, however, which has caused much mischief and which has led historians
into accepting Alfred as unqualified master of Mercia and all Wales, and it has
prompted historians, too, to seek a definite date, for this so-called submission of
Æthelred to Alfred. Circumstances in the 880s were such that it was in Æthelred's
interest to stand together with the West Saxons, unless he were to accept the
overlordship of Danish East Anglia. The rump Mercian kingdom which had
survived the ravages of the Great Army was in no position to stand alone. Indeed,
it had begun life as a satellite of the Danelaw. Mercian churchmen, led by the
bishop of Worcester, may have been quick to urge their leaders to co-operate with
Wessex or face going out of business altogether. Such co-operation may or may
not have entailed formal submission. It was an alliance which was cemented in or
before AD 887, by the marriage of Alfred's daughter, Æthelflæd, to Æthelred of the
Mercians. On the other hand, western and southern Mercia had preserved its
witan and presumably its land-holding aristocracy intact, and a strong sense of old
tribal identities remained as can be seen from the wording of Mercian charters
from this time. But Alfred's overlordship of English Mercia must have been
inevitable, and his overkingship of the Mercian Angles was delicately covered by
a new formula—that of *Anglorum Saxonum rex*. This ought more properly to be
translated 'king of the Angles and the Saxons' rather than 'king of the Anglo-
Saxons'. For just as the annexation of Kent made the West Saxon ruler 'king not
only of the West Saxons but also of the Men of Kent', so now Alfred could claim
to be king of the Saxons and of the [Mercian] Angles. In Alfred's charter to Bishop
Wærferth of Worcester (Sawyer 346; Birch 561), which he issued jointly with
Ealdorman Æthelred of Mercia, Alfred's kingship is spelt out twice in the form *rex
Anglorum et Saxonum* ('king of the Angles and of the Saxons').[105] Æthelred's
specifically Mercian credentials, on the other hand, are underlined in that same
charter by the titles *sub-regulus et patricius Merciorum* ('sub-king and *patricius* of the
Mercians').

We are witnessing here the birth of a formula to describe a kingship which
accommodated a number of older tribal loyalties within England. It would seem
that this same process was at work in the minds of those who composed the
inscriptions for Alfred's coinage. While the title *rex Sax[onum]* ('King of the
Saxons') appeared on Alfredian coins throughout the reign, the style *rex Anglo[.]*
appears on Alfred's 'Two Emperors' coin type. This has been expanded by historians to read *rex Anglorum* ('King of the English') and has been taken to reflect
Alfred's claims to rule Mercia in succession to Ceolwulf (874–9).[106] But the title
rex Anglorum is ambiguous, since it might mean nothing more at this period than
an 'English king', and might not necessarily lay claim to overlordship of Anglian
peoples or their territories. Whitelock may have been correct in observing that
'unnecessarily heavy weather is made of the title *rex Angulsaxonum* given to Alfred'

by the author of that king's *Life*.[107] Yet much of the scholarly debate on Alfredian charters conceals a hidden agenda in which the spectre of the Pseudo-Asser has loomed large. Put simply, the question is: do the titles accorded King Alfred in the charters tally with those accorded him in the *Life* of the king ascribed to Asser? The Pseudo-Asser described King Alfred as *Anglorum Saxonum regi* not only in his dedication but at some nine other points throughout the *Life* of Alfred.[108] How does this usage tally with how Alfred is described in his charters, and with descriptions of the king in the Chronicle and in Alfred's own writings? There is nothing inherently fraudulent in the title *Angul-Saxonum rex* which the Pseudo-Asser accords King Alfred, but it is the consistency with which this title is applied throughout the *Life* of Alfred that stands out in contradiction to the ubiquitous *rex Saxonum* or *rex occidentalium Saxonum* of contemporary late ninth-century usage. For even if we allow as genuine the formula *rex Anglorum et Saxonum* in Alfred's charter to Bishop Wærferth (Sawyer 346), such a formula cannot be regarded as the norm. Keynes followed Whitelock in using the Pseudo-Asser's dubious evidence for Alfred's titles to prop up a series of five charters in which Alfred is styled 'king of the Anglo-Saxons'.[109] None of these charters (Sawyer 347, 348, 354, 355, and 356) survive in a manuscript which is older than the twelfth century, while two (Sawyer 347 and 348) survive only in fourteenth-century copies. Of this entire collection, only Sawyer 355 (Birch 581) can be regarded as plausible, the remaining four being branded as forgeries by a procession of leading scholars. Two other charters (Sawyer 351 and 353) which describe Alfred as 'king of the English' have so far failed to find a modern sponsor willing to risk an academic reputation in support of their claims to authenticity.

The Pseudo-Asser used the word *rector* ('ruler') in relation to King Alfred in the opening dedication of the king's *Life* and he addressed the West Saxon king, supposedly in 893, with the outrageous title of 'ruler of all the Christians of the island of Britain (*omnium Brittanniae insulae Christianorum rectori*)'.[110] Here we are reminded of the contemporary record of the presentation of Mac Dornain's Gospels by King Athelstan (924–939) to the metropolitan church of Canterbury.[111] The inscription in the gospels describes King Alfred's grandson as *Æthelstanus, Anglosaexana rex et rector*. The title *rector* may be echoed in the vernacular form in a very doubtful charter of Athelstan,[112] and the word is regularly found in charters of King Eadred from 946 onwards.[113] But the use of this word and its related phrase 'ruler of all Britain' relates to the later tenth century, when Alfred's grandsons and great-grandsons were extending their overlordship over Danish and Celtic inhabitants of Britain. We are reminded of Byrhtferth of Ramsey's early eleventh-century description of a king who lived back in the time of St Ecgwine (*c.* AD 700), as *rector regni* ('ruler of the kingdom').[114] With the exception of one forgery, none of the the charters of King Alfred describe that king as ruler of all Britain, or the like. The forgery in question, alleged to have been issued by Alfred in favour of the thegn, Heahferth (Sawyer 351, Birch 740), describes Alfred as *basileus* or 'emperor of the English and of all peoples round about', and lest the matter should appear in any doubt, the king is made to sign as *Ælfred Rex tocius*

Bryttanniæ. The use of the Greek *basileus* and the flamboyant reference to the whole of Britain, marks this charter off, in company with the Pseudo-Asser's dedication in the *Life* of Alfred, as a forgery which cannot be earlier than *c.*950 at the earliest.[115] The Greek *basileus* reminds us that we have moved forward into the tenth century and to the world of hermeneutic writers, of whom Byrhtferth of Ramsey was a leading exponent at the turn of the milennium. So, we have in the dedication of the Pseudo-Asser's work, not one but several usages which were inappropriate and anachronistic for the reign of Alfred and which were derived from the second or third quarter of the tenth century, if not later.

In addition to those charters in which Alfred's name appears during his life, there are some five documents from the reign of Edward the Elder containing posthumous references to King Alfred. One of these is a very doubtful grant from Edward to the *familia* of Winchester Cathedral supposedly in AD 900 (Sawyer 359, Birch 594), but which was compiled more likely in the eleventh century. Keynes pointed to the 'suspiciously circumstantial clause' referring to Edward's succession to Alfred, which this charter shares in general terms with Sawyer 358 (Birch 592) and Sawyer 1284 (Birch 590). But Keynes accepted Sawyer 359 as a genuine 'routine text formulated within the general context of the "West Saxon" diplomatic tradition'.[116] Two other agreements supposedly drawn up between Edward the Elder and churches in Winchester (Sawyer 1443, Birch 605; and Sawyer 366, Birch 598) refer to the same project—the building by King Edward of a monastery in Winchester for the benefit of his soul and that of his 'venerable father', King Alfred. The first of these two charters (Sawyer 1443) records the acquisition of land by King Edward from Bishop Denewulf of Winchester for the building of the monastery (New Minster), while the second charter (Sawyer 366) records a grant by Edward of land at Chiseldon in Wiltshire for the same New Minister at Winchester—'for the church which I [Edward] have ordered to be newly built, raising it from the foundations for the redemption of my soul and that of my venerable father [Alfred]'.[117] This latter is a poor copy preserved in the fourteenth-century *Liber Monasterii de Hyda* with a garbled witness list. Whitelock believed that when one 'corrected' the witness list of this Chiseldon charter (Sawyer 366) one arrived at a list 'very like that' of the list in Edward's acquisition of land from Bishop Denewulf (Sawyer 1443; Birch 605 and 1338). She suggested that the Chiseldon Latin grant (Sawyer 366) contained a curtailed version of the witness list attached to the Old English charter of Denewulf (Sawyer 1443).[118] Even accepting the drastic corrections that have to be made—(*Elfredus* (Alfred) *filius regis* to *Ælfweardus filius regis* together with five other textual emendations)—we still have to explain why the important names of that same Ælfweard and of Athelstan (the sons of King Edward) are included in Sawyer 366 but are absent in Sawyer 1443 and we also have to account for other bewildering discrepancies between the names in each list. The best that Whitelock could conclude about these charters was that if they were forgeries 'it nevertheless shows that a forger at New Minster had access to a charter similar to those which survive from Wilton, Malmesbury, and Glastonbury'.[119] But those three charters to which she referred (Sawyer 347,

348, and 356) cannot themselves be proven to be genuine, and we are faced here with an essentially unscholarly method of bolstering one set of spurious documents by reference to other equally suspect material. Keynes, building on the sand of Whitelock's speculative discussion, assumed that a group of no less than six Edwardian charters supposedly issued in 901 had at least a genuine basis.[120] He claimed that because Sawyer 365 and Sawyer 366 had identical witness lists, they were 'probably produced by a single agency', but only 'if both are assumed to be genuine'.[121] He claimed furthermore, that the two Malmesbury charters (Sawyer 363 and Sawyer 1205) were also produced by a single 'agency' and suggested that was the same agency as was responsible for the New Minster productions (Sawyer 365 and Sawyer 366).[122] By identifying a supposed 'central agency', which seems to have enjoyed a monopoly of the production of royal charters in ninth-century Wessex, as the body of priests who served in the royal household,[123] Keynes had accepted Whitelock's tolerance of a whole collection of charters—some genuine, some forged—and developed her arguments to their logical but unsound conclusion. The reality behind the 'central agency' may be nothing more than a series of basic formulae proliferated by forgers anxious to lend an air of authenticity to their texts, and based on a few key genuine documents copied and disseminated at an early stage among centres such as Winchester, Malmesbury, Sherborne, and Glastonbury. We know that prominent churchmen such as Dunstan, Æthelwold, and Ælfheah moved with regularity between such communities as Glastonbury, Winchester, Abingdon, and Canterbury in the later tenth century. There is no reason to believe that lesser men did not move in their train, and that copies of genuine charters as well as other documents from the ninth century did not move with them. Uniformity may be the norm we should expect in the texts of solemn diplomas, but as well as providing evidence for a central agency, it may equally reflect a common cause among later tenth-century forgers.

Two remaining charters containing posthumous references to King Alfred provide much more promising material for the historian. One is a grant made in 901 by King Edward in favour of Æthelwulf in which the king gives an estate at Wylye in Wiltshire (Sawyer 362, Birch 595) which had been formerly confiscated from Ealdorman Wulfhere (and his wife) who had 'deserted without permission both his lord, King Alfred and his country in spite of the oath which he had sworn to the king and all his leading men'.[124] Stenton considered this to be one of the more reliable charters of Edward's reign on the grounds that it contained an authentic circumstantial detail relating to the crisis of the Danish wars in Alfredian Wessex.[125] This may indeed be the case, and the fact that the document survives only in a twelfth-century copy in the Winchester cartulary is a reminder of the importance of historical judgement in relation to the study of Anglo-Saxon and Anglo-Latin texts. This is particularly the case in the study of Alfredian charter evidence, where the manuscript material is of such varied date, where preservation was so random, and where forgery and revision were rife.

The last of the five documents from Edward's reign containing posthumous references to King Alfred is what is known as the Fonthill Letter (Sawyer 1445,

Birch 591). Although this piece has been consistently associated with charter material, it is not in any sense a charter or diploma conferring either property or privileges on its recipient. The document does however deal with the history of judgements, royal and otherwise, handed down in relation to a particular dispute over an estate at Fonthill in the extreme south of Wiltshire. The fact that the manuscript carried an endorsement recording a final settlement brought about by the retirement of one of the parties from the suit may have ensured that the parchment was kept as evidence for a proper title for the lands in question. But this is in essence a letter written to King Edward the Elder summarizing the course of a dispute over the possession of the Fonthill estate, and above all else, it is a letter petitioning the king to act in favour of the writer, on the basis of his account of the dispute. The writer's identity is nowhere revealed, but Whitelock was probably correct in assuming him to have been Ordlaf, since it was Ordlaf who succeeded to the Fonthill lands after their confiscation, they having earlier been leased from him.[126] Ordlaf was the grandson of Eanwulf, who had served under King Æthelwulf as ealdorman of Somerset.[127] Ordlaf was himself an ealdorman, probably of Wiltshire, who held office in the last years of Alfred's reign and later under Edward the Elder. Because the dispute over the Fonthill estate arose in King Alfred's reign, the incidental detail which the account of it offers, affords us an invaluable glimpse of the workings of Alfred's rudimentary day-to-day administration. The Fonthill Letter is so important and its narrative so involved that it is useful to summarize its contents thus:[128]

SUMMARY OF FONTHILL LETTER

Addressed to King Edward:

'Sire, I will inform you what happened about the land at Fonthill . . .'

Æthelhelm Higa claims five hides at Fonthill.

Higa brought the case for the land against Helmstan when Helmstan stole Æthelred's belt.

Æthelhelm Higa claimed the land from Helmstan.

Helmstan approached the writer who had previously become his sponsor at Confirmation and asked him to intercede in the dispute.

The writer interceded for Helmstan with King Alfred.

Alfred allowed Helmstan to 'prove his right' *vis-à-vis* Æthelhelm Higa in connection with the land at Fonthill.

The writer and others were appointed to bring the parties to agreement.

These mediators were:

> Wihtbord, Ælfric (then keeper of the wardrobe),
> Brihthelm and Wulfhun the Black of Somerton,
> Strica, Ubba, and others.

Helmstan proved his right to the land with title deeds (*bocon*).

The previous history of the estate went thus:

> Æthelthryth had received it from Æthelwulf as her morning gift.
> Æthelthryth sold it to Oswulf.

King Alfred witnessed Oswulf's purchase of the land from Æthelthryth 'with his signature (*hondsetene*)'.

Other witnesses were Edward, Æthelnoth, and Deormod.

This reconciling of Helmstan with Æthelhelm Higa took place at Wardour.

Helmstan was 'nearer to the oath'.

Æthelhelm insisted on going in to the presence of the king and explaining what had been done.

The king stood in the chamber at Wardour, washing his hands.

King Alfred insisted that Helmstan be allowed to give the oath.

The writer agreed to help Helmstan obtain justice on condition that Helmstan granted the estate to the writer.

The writer, Wihtbord, and Brihthelm accompanied Æthelhelm when he gave the oath.

The oath was given. The suit was closed.

'And Sire, when will any suit be ended if one can end it neither with money nor with an oath? And if one wishes to change every judgement which King Alfred gave, when shall we have finished disputing?'

The oath given, the deeds of the land were given by Helmstan to the writer.

The writer leased the lands back to Helmstan for his lifetime, provided he kept out of disgrace.

One-and-a-half or two years later:

Helmstan stole untended oxen at Fonthill and drove them to Chicklade.

Helmstan was tracked down and fled.

The reeve, Eanwulf son of Peneard, confiscated Helmstan's property at Tisbury for the king because he [Helmstan] was the king's man.

Ordlaf [the writer ?] succeeded to the land at Fonthill, for since it was held by Helmstan only on lease, then Helmstan could not forfeit that particular estate.

You [King Edward] pronounced Helmstan an outlaw.

Helmstan appealed over the tomb of King Alfred ('your father's body').

Helmstan came to the writer, taking a 'seal (*insigle*)' to him, when the writer was with King Edward at Chippenham.

King Edward removed Helmstan's outlawry, and gave him the estate 'to which he still has withdrawn'.

The writer succeeded to 'my land' [at Fonthill].

The writer gave the land at Fonthill to the bishop [Denewulf of Winchester]—five hides in exchange for five hides at Lydiard in the witness (*gewitnesse*) of the king 'and all your councillors'.

The writer appeals to King Edward to maintain the *status quo* regarding the writer's title to the lands in question.

Endorsement:

Æthelhelm Higa retired from the suit when the king was at Warminster. The witnesses [to Æthelhelm Higa's withdrawal] were:

Ordlaf, Osferth, Odda, Wihtbord, Ælfstan the Bald
and Æthelnoth.

The Fonthill letter contains such a wealth of circumstantial detail on the history of a particular legal wrangle over an estate in south Wiltshire, that it would be difficult to dismiss it as a forgery. Not only is much of this detail apparently irrelevant to the needs of a forger, but the format of an historical review of a lawsuit is scarcely that which we would expect a forger of charters to adopt. Even if we were to concede that the document had a spurious origin, since the manuscript in the Canterbury cathedral archive dates to the early tenth century, then as a forgery it would still be sufficiently near the Alfredian era as to be of major significance to the historian.[129] Most of the players in this localized legal drama can be identified from other contemporary sources, and the topographical details are consistent with an authentic account. Fonthill, the estate at the heart of the wrangle, is indeed close to Chicklade where the rustled cattle were driven off to. It is close too, to Old Wardour, where Alfred gave a judgement on the dispute, and to Tisbury, where Helmstan owned another property.

There are, however, many questions which remain unanswered by this letter, in spite of its tantalizing detail. They range from more fundamental issues such as the identity of the writer and the social standing of Helmstan—the defendant in the dispute—to other issues such as the significance of Æthelred's belt and why it was that Æthelhelm brought the case against the supposed thief, Helmstan. The writer of this letter was clearly a man of high social standing. He was sufficiently well placed in aristocratic West Saxon society as to intercede on the defendant's behalf with King Alfred. He clearly had access to the king's chamber at Wardour, and in the next reign he reminds King Edward that he was in that king's company at Chippenham when Helmstan came to them both, with evidence that he had taken an oath at King Alfred's tomb. This writer clearly had great influence at the court of both Alfred and his son, and it is evident from the letter that his influence continually swayed the judgements of both Alfred and Edward in regard to his protége, Helmstan, in the Fonthill affair. The writer also seems to imply that he was influential enough to have a royal diploma drawn up in his own favour and issued with the consent of the King Edward and his *witan*.[130] He was clearly a leading West Saxon magnate, and Ordlaf's position as an ealdorman who had served under Alfred and later under his son, Edward, is consonant with the standing of the writer of this legal memorandum. What is true of the standing of the writer of this document applies to all the persons mentioned in this dispute who can be identified from other sources. Of the men appointed to bring the parties to agreement at Wardour, Wihtbord was an Alfredian thegn who witnessed a charter of that king in 882 and who rose to prominence under Edward the Elder.[131] Ælfric, as keeper of the wardrobe under Alfred, was clearly a household thegn of that king, and we find his name in the witness lists of the charters of Edward down to *c*.910. Brihthelm was also a thegn who served under Alfred and his son, and the same would seem to have been true of Wulfhun, Strica, and Ubba.[132] When Æthelhelm Higa withdrew from the suit at a time when King Edward was at Warminster, he did so in the 'witness' of a group of men of the same powerful standing as those who had been involved from the beginning. Indeed, Ealdorman Ordlaf and the thegn, Wihtbord, were among them still, lending their support to the unfortunate Helmstan. But other men of equally high standing had now been drawn in, such as Odda, a thegn who began his career under Edward the Elder and who survived to serve under King Edmund in the early 940s. Æthelnoth and Ælfstan the Bald almost certainly served under Edward as thegns, while Osferth was a kinsman of King Alfred who served as an ealdorman (*dux*) under Edward and later under Athelstan.[133] Given the personal involvement of leading men of Wessex in this dispute, we must conclude that Helmstan, the alleged thief and cattle rustler, was no ordinary criminal. The writer, Ealdorman Ordlaf, had acted as his sponsor at Confirmation and was bound to the defendant by ties so close, that he felt obliged to intercede with two kings on his behalf. Helmstan must himself have enjoyed a high social and political standing which was worthy of Ealdorman Ordlaf's advocacy. Otherwise it would be impossible to explain this affair as a dispute involving great men who, like Ælfric, the keeper of Alfred's wardrobe, were so close to the king. We are specifically told that Helmstan 'was the king's man (*he wæs cinges mon*)'[134]—and therefore bound to Alfred by bonds of loyalty, confirmed by solemn oaths. Helmstan not only occupied an estate at Fonthill—he held yet another at nearby Tisbury. Keynes tentatively suggested that Helmstan's Tisbury estate might have been as large in the ninth century, as we know it to have been from the mid tenth-century onwards, when it covered several parishes in south Wiltshire.[135] He suggested if that were so, that 'our conception of his [Helmstan's] standing in Alfred's kingdom would be transformed, and certain aspects of the story would appear in a different light'.[136] To begin with, we might conclude that when Alfred gave a judgement which was favourable to Helmstan, during the king's stay at Old Wardour, Alfred was then visiting an estate which that king may have leased in part, to none other than his 'man', Helmstan. But we are not dependent on such speculation—however reasonable—to appreciate the obvious importance of Helmstan, as proved by the status of his supporters and by the personal involvement of two kings in his lawsuit. This in turn leads us back to the issue which triggered off that suit in the first instance, namely the stealing of Æthelred's belt. Since the alleged theft of the belt by Helmstan provoked Æthelhelm Higa into bringing a case against him, it seems clear that the original owner of the belt was no longer in possession of it. In other words, Æthelred was by now, very probably, dead, but he had been a sufficiently notable person for his name to have been associated with the belt, even after it had left his possession. The belt was obviously a precious heirloom—so precious that it was considered to have been worth as much as the five hides of land at Fonthill. If Helmstan, in terms of his social standing, were no ordinary criminal, then clearly Æthelred's belt was no ordinary belt. We are reminded of the silver-hilted sword, 'the gold belt (*gyldenan fetels*) and the armlet which Wulfric made' and 'the sword that Offa owned'—all of which were bequeathed as heirlooms in the *Will* of the atheling, Athelstan, eldest son of Æthelred the Unready in *c*.1015.[137] We are reminded also of two gold-hilted swords named among bequests in King Eadred's *Will* in the middle of the tenth century,[138] and of William of Malmesbury's mention of 'a jewelled belt and a Saxon sword with a golden scabbard' which King Alfred was supposed to have given as a gift to his infant grandson—the future king, Athelstan.[139] Malmesbury's tale of that jewelled belt was part of an apocryphal tradition, designed to lend Alfred's posthumous seal of approval to the conquests of Athelstan. But the notion of the jewelled belt and golden scabbard as being part of aristocratic and royal insignia in the ninth and tenth centuries was clearly accurate. We need only point to the great golden belt-buckle from the battle-harness found at Sutton Hoo, or to the gold and garnet-inlaid belt buckle from Taplow in Berkshire, to appreciate the immense wealth that Anglo-Saxon warlords were prepared to lavish on personal items of battle-dress which were designed to reflect their own high, if not royal status.[140] The Frankish aristocracy was no different from its early English counterpart in its fondness for gaudy display. One of the hallmarks of Count Gerald's sanctity as observed by his early tenth-century biographer, Odo, was that nobleman's aversion to parading the very status symbol which was at the heart of the Fonthill dispute:

He [Gerald] would not change or renew his sword-belt for twenty years if it would last so long. What shall I say of the belts (*de balteo*), the twisted cinctures (*ambitiosis cinctoriis*), the buckles (*fibula*), the decorated medallions for horses (*de equorum phaleris*), when he not only forbade himself to wear gold, but even to possess it?[141]

Elsewhere in Gerald's *Life* we are told that he 'despised the trappings of his position', and that 'from early on, he had a gold cross made for his belt or his girdle (*de balteo vel cinguli*)',[142] which was no doubt understood to be in lieu of the barbaric display of worldly treasures normally associated with the baubles of Sutton Hoo style ornament. Alfred and his warriors clearly shared no such scruples over the enjoyment of high-status objects. King Alfred in his *Will* left a special sword to his son-in-law, Æthelred, Lord of the Mercians. It was a sword worth one hundred mancuses, valued at the same amount as each of the legacies which the king bequeathed on the æthelings of Wessex and on each of his ealdormen.[143] In cash terms, the sword which Alfred left to the Mercian Æthelred was worth some 3,000 silver pence or over a hundred oxen—sufficient to purchase an estate of 300 acres if not much more, depending on the quality of the land.[144] Deormod, one of Alfred's leading thegns, purchased an estate of five hides at Appleford in Berkshire for fifty mancuses of gold (Sawyer 355; Birch 581).[145] So, Deormod's estate, which like that at Fonthill consisted of five hides, was worth only half the value of the treasured sword which King Alfred left to his son-in-law. Æthelred's belt was equated in value with the estate at Fonthill, and therefore, it too must have been of extraordinary value—a garnet-inlaid gold or silver belt, worn by a nobleman or a king—the original owner in this case being most likely Æthelred I, the deceased brother of King Alfred. Once we accept the high social status of Helmstan, together with the crucial significance of the belt, then we can also explain the keen personal interest taken in this case by both King Alfred and his son. It is quite impossible to accept that two successive kings of Wessex, together with a whole company of their leading men—including Osferth, a kinsman of Alfred and Edward—would have involved themselves in a squabble concerning a petty thief.

'Fonthill' is clearly no ordinary letter. It is not written in the style or stunted format of royal diplomas, and its writer was a great man of the kingdom. We can say of that writer, with far greater certainty than of the Pseudo-Asser, that he shared the king's chamber, and we need to pay the closest attention to evidence offered by this confidant of King Alfred. It may seem difficult to understand why, since the writer enjoyed the confidence of King Edward also, that he had to resort to writing a long account of this dreary and envenomed dispute between Helmstan and Æthelhelm Higa. It would have been easier if not more usual—in an era of personal government—for the writer to argue his case face to face with the king. The fact that he chose to put his thoughts on paper, and that he constructed a coherent argument, set out episodically and at such length, shows he was a well-educated man of some literary ability. He was also a man who appreciated the efficacy of a written statement in a legal dispute. This letter is one of the few tangible examples which survive, outside the body of learned Alfredian translations, of a work written by a layman, who had clearly benefited from the increased interest in writing in the vernacular during Alfred's reign.[146] He is therefore a writer who needs to be read with care, and whose account ought not to be interpreted too simplistically in view of the contemporary witness he offers us. His portrait of King Alfred washing his hands in the chamber at Wardour while giving a judgement[147] needs to be set in the context of this author's training and experience in the writing of Old English prose. First, the writer appears to view that event as being in the distant past. It was one or two years afterwards—the writer could not quite remember how long—that Helmstan disgraced himself again, and by then King Alfred had died. The account may have been written many years later, perhaps towards the end of Edward's reign *c.*920.[148] Distance may have lent a folkloric dimension to this account of Alfred. A member of Alfred's court circle who enjoyed the confidence of that king and who clearly could write lucidly in the vernacular was most likely a well-read man who may have shared Alfred's own literary tastes. Such a writer might well have been aware of Suetonius's portraits of those busy emperors of Rome whose work as judges and administrators was never done. Suetonius's account of Augustus sitting in court until nightfall or delivering judgements from his sick-bed in his own house, or reading and making notes while having a haircut and shave in the barbers, was not lost on the imagination of writers in the early Middle Ages.[149] Suetonius also left behind his image of the conscientious Claudius sitting in court on his birthday, or of the worthy Vespasian who got through his daily correspondence before dawn, and who received visitors while he put on his shoes and dressed.[150] None of this was lost on Einhard who cast his hero Charlemagne firmly in the Suetonian mould:

When he was dressing and putting on his shoes he would invite his friends to come in. Moreover, if the Count of the Palace told him that there was some dispute which could not be settled without the emperor's personal decision, he would order the disputants to be brought in there and then, hear the case as if he were sitting in tribunal and pronounce a judgement.[151]

Dynamic warlords such as Charlemagne and Alfred may well have set the world to rights while they washed and dressed, and both men being well versed in Classical lore may also have consciously imitated what was said of their Roman betters. But before we rush to the conclusion that the Fonthill letter lends support to the Pseudo-Asser's vague account of Alfred the conscientious judge, we need to be aware of the literary *topoi* that may underline these accounts. Whitelock, who viewed the Fonthill letter in isolation from the literate *milieu* of Alfred's circle, seized on it as a prop for her arguments relating to the veracity of Asser: 'It supports Asser's statement about the interest taken by Alfred in the administration of justice, and about the readiness of litigants to appeal to him.'[152] It comes as little surprise that one of King Alfred's magnates remembered him in the reign of his son as a king concerned with the administration of justice. Alfred did, after all, compile his own law code, which suggests a major concern with the administration of justice. A king of his deeply spiritual bearing must have been concerned with the notion of *justitia* as the prerogative of the Christian king—a theme hammered home by Alcuin in his letters haranguing the rulers of Northumbria a century before Alfred's own time. As for the readiness of the litigants in the Fonthill dispute to appeal to the king, that may well relate to the high social status of the parties in dispute and to the peculiar family interest which Alfred and Edward may well have had in the case. Every medieval king's court, as a final court of appeal, attracted litigants, who as in this case may have failed to obtain a favourable verdict in the lower reaches of the legal system. A major reason why Ordlaf referred to Alfred's earlier judgement was simply because that king had come down on the side of Ordlaf's protégé, Helmstan. The writer's comment on King Alfred's judgements deserves closer scrutiny: 'And if every decision which King Alfred gave is to be set aside, when shall we be done with negotiating?'[153] This statement comes in the letter (see Summary above) as a protest to King Edward by the writer, who says that the case was closed in King Alfred's time with the judgement going in his favour. Clearly there was now a danger that King Edward, under pressure from the old protagonist, Æthelhelm Higa, might overturn his father's judgement in favour of Helmstan. If this statement means anything to the historian, it suggests that King Edward was liable to overturn a judgement handed down by his father, Alfred, in a desire no doubt to consolidate and extend his own patronage as king. It is surely silly to suggest that this passage implies that Alfred was conscientious in his judgement—which it does not necessarily do—or that it shows Alfred delivered great numbers of judgements of whatever quality. Of course a king who had reigned for twenty-eight years in ninth-century Wessex had chalked up a formidable list of judgements, but a writer of the Fonthill letter's experience and intelligence was not making so obvious or banal a point. As for the justice of Alfred's verdict delivered at Old Wardour, there is a strong argument to show that that particular outcome was influenced by the powerful intervention of the defendant's patron, Ordlaf. Far from supporting the Pseudo-Asser's hagiographical portrait of a saintly king committed to exposing corruption in the law courts,[154] the Fonthill letter may show us the 'genuine' Alfred, being swayed by the influence— not to say by the wealth—of those great men in whom he put his trust.

King Alfred's Will

A Disputed Inheritance

I, KING ALFRED, BY THE GRACE OF GOD, AND WITH THE ADVICE OF ARCHBISHOP
Æthelred and with the witness of all the councillors of the West Saxons, have been
enquiring about the needs of my soul and about my inheritance which God and my
ancestors gave to me, and about the inheritance which my father King Æthelwulf bequeathed
to us three brothers . . .[1]

Thus, Alfred speaks to us across more than a thousand years of time in the opening
words of what he claims to be his last *Will* and testament. As ever in the case of
documents which are closely associated with this king, we are confronted with a
text whose qualities are unique and dramatic but which also present the historian
with formidable difficulties of interpretation. Although King Alfred was not the
first English king to make a *Will*, Alfred's is the earliest royal *Will* to survive in its
entirety from the Anglo-Saxon world. Its importance for the historian can scarcely
be exaggerated, since it not only tells us how Alfred distributed his personal
wealth, but it also sheds a flood of light on how he perceived his relationship with
his father, King Æthelwulf, his older brothers, and his surviving nephews, and on
how he sought to manipulate arrangements relating to their inheritance to the
advantage of his own sons and daughters. This is the document, which in relation
to family matters, takes us closer to the mind of the king than any other, and yet it
has been one of the least studied of all sources which survive from the Alfredian age.[2]

The immense complexities relating to our understanding of Alfred's *Will* confront us in the opening words of its text. For this is no simple catalogue of *post
obitum* gifts made by a king to his family and retainers, nor is it the record of hasty
deathbed arrangements incorporating the *verba novissima* of a dying man. As in the
case of all *Wills*, Alfred's intention was not only to settle his inheritance on his
family and friends, but also to exclude rival kinsmen from getting their hands on
his property, or at least to curtail their participation in its division. But there is also
far more to Alfred's *Will* than this. A major objective in the document was to
answer charges, previously levelled against Alfred, that he had treated his young
nephews unfairly in the division of the inheritance of his older brothers and of his
father, King Æthelwulf. Alfred's interest in this family wrangle was neither historical nor academic. He knew full well that the sons of his brother, King Æthelred
I, who dared to challenge Alfred's handling of their father's inheritance while

Alfred lived and ruled as king, would not hesitate to challenge Alfred's own *Will*
when he was dead. For the logic of their protest would be to claim that property
which ought rightfully to have come to them from their father, Æthelred, and which
had been wrongfully retained by Alfred, was therefore subsequently distributed
unjustly by him to his own beneficiaries. A lengthy introduction to Alfred's *Will* is
designed to justify why Alfred either inherited or seized property from the estate
of his deceased brother, Æthelred, to the exclusion of Æthelred's sons. Connected
with this justification of Alfred's actions is an appeal in Alfred's own *Will* to an
earlier *Will* of his father, King Æthelwulf, who died in 858.

The first half of Alfred's *Will* is in effect a preamble latent with special pleading
to prepare us for his *Will* proper, in the second half—a *Will* which even Alfred—
or most of all Alfred—realized would be vigorously contested by some of his
kinsmen. The complexities of the preamble are such that this part of Alfred's *Will*
is best summarized as follows:

Alfred, consulting Archbishop Æthelred [of Canterbury] and his West Saxon councillors
prepared to settle his inheritance, and conducted an enquiry into 'the inheritance which my
father King Æthelwulf bequeathed to us three brothers, Æthelbald, Æthelred and myself,
stipulating that whichever of us should live longest was to succeed to the whole'.

When Æthelbald died, Æthelred and Alfred entrusted their share to their brother
Æthelberht [who had succeeded Æthelbald as king of the West Saxons in 860]. Then
Æthelred succeeded to the kingship [on the death of Æthelberht in 865]. Alfred, on asking
for his share in their father Æthelwulf's inheritance, was told by King Æthelred that it was
not practicable to divide the property while Æthelred lived, but that on his death he would
leave it to Alfred both 'our joint property and whatever he acquired.' Alfred agreed.

Æthelred and Alfred made a further agreement before the West Saxon councillors at
Swinbeorg in which they made provision for their children in the event that they themselves
were slain 'in those disasters [of the viking wars].' [Cf. Fig. 9, p. 412 below].

'We then agreed . . . that whichever of us should live longer should grant to the other's
children the lands which we had ourselves obtained, and the lands which King Æthelwulf
gave to us in Æthelbald's lifetime except those which he bequeathed to us three brothers.

And each of us gave to the other his pledge, that whichever of us lived longer should
succeed both to lands and treasures and to all the other's possessions except that part which
each of us had bequeathed to his children.'

King Æthelred died [in 871] and subsequently 'many suits about the inheritance'
(*yrfegeflitu*) were heard. Alfred had King Æthelwulf's [his father's] *will* read out before the
West Saxon assembly at *Langandene*. Alfred challenged anyone present to declare if he
(Alfred) had 'treated my young kinsmen wrongfully, the older or the younger' [a reference
to Æthelhelm and to Æthelwold, the sons of King Æthelred, and the nephews of Alfred,
who disputed King Alfred's handling of what they saw as their portion of King Æthelwulf's
inheritance through their father, Æthelred].

The assembly at *Langandene* found in favour of King Alfred. [The second half of the
document consists of Alfred's own *Will* and proceeds with a record of Alfred's distribution
of his property to his kinsmen and friends.][3]

Unless we understand the preamble to King Alfred's *Will* then we can scarcely
hope to understand the origin of the dispute between Alfred and his sons as the

one party, and the sons of King Æthelred as the other—a dispute which may have endured for thirty years or more and which ended in the rebellion of Æthelwold, son of King Æthelred I, and in his slaying by his first cousin, Edward the Elder, son of Alfred, in 903. The preamble holds the key not only to understanding the terms of the provisions which Alfred made for his family and friends after his death, but it also affords us a precious insight into Alfred's own perception of how he eventually came to kingship and power—or at least that particular perception which he wished us to share with him. Since Alfred's major prop in defence of his own position was an appeal to the *Will* of his father, King Æthelwulf, all studies of Alfred's own *Will* must begin with examining the fragmentary remains of the *Will* of his father.

The Pseudo-Asser tells us that during the last two years of Æthelwulf's life, after returning from Rome, he had 'a testamentary, or rather an advisory, letter (*hereditariam, immo commendatoriam, epistolam*)' drawn up 'so that his sons should not dispute unduly among themselves after their father's death'.[4] This document contained, on the Pseudo-Asser's evidence, three main provisions—a division of the kingdom between his two eldest sons, a division of his personal inheritance (*propriae hereditatis*) between his sons, his daughter, and his relatives, and finally, provision for the welfare of his soul. The compiler of the *Life* of Alfred (quoting from Einhard) declared he did not wish to bore us with details of the first two provisions and settled for summarizing the arrangements Æthelwulf made for 'the necessities of the soul'. One poor man, native or foreign, was to be clothed and fed at the expense of every ten hides throughout all Æthelwulf's hereditary land (*hereditariam terram*).[5] This provision would seem to mirror what the Anglo-Saxon Chronicle says of Æthelwulf's conveying 'by charter (*gebocude*) the tenth part of his land throughout all his kingdom for the praise of God and for his own eternal salvation' back in 855 *before* the king left on his Rome pilgrimage.[6] If the two transactions were one and the same, then we have here additional support for Dumville's view that Æthelwulf's *Will* must date to the period before his departure for Rome rather than after his return.[7] The Pseudo-Asser can never be trusted on detail when he departs from slavishly following the text of the Chronicle, and least of all at a point where he echoes the text of Einhard's *Life* of Charlemagne. For how could Æthelwulf hope to impose a settlement on his sons in 858, at a time when on the Pseudo-Asser's own testimony, Æthelwulf had been supposedly excluded from his Wessex kingdom by Æthelbald and was living in virtual exile in Kent or elsewhere in the east of the extended kingdom?

The compiler of the *Life* of Alfred does indeed elsewhere translate—or mistranslate—the Chronicle's account of Æthelwulf's earlier 'booking' of a tenth part of his lands 'to the praise of God and his own eternal salvation' in 855. But whereas the Chronicle must be referring to King Æthelwulf's personal estates— the only sort of lands he was entitled to alienate by 'book'—the Pseudo-Asser took the passage to mean that the king 'freed the tenth part of his whole kingdom from every royal service and tribute'.[8] So the Pseudo-Asser's careless handling of the Chronicle gives the false impression that Æthelwulf freed a tenth part of his entire kingdom (*totius regni*) (rather than his own hereditary estates) from customary obligations, thereby reducing the land assessed for taxation purposes by a tenth. The Pseudo-Asser's text returns to the notion of a tithing in chapter 16, where summarizing the provisions of King Æthelwulf's *Will*, it informs us that Æthelwulf 'enjoined on his successors after him that for every ten hides throughout all his hereditary land, one poor man . . . should be sustained with food, drink and clothing.'[9] Stevenson,[10] as a champion for the veracity of the *Life* of Alfred, could never admit that the Chronicle's account of Æthelwulf's gift to the Church in 855 was one and the same transaction as that described in the *Life* in 858. The Pseudo-Asser's notice of King Æthelwulf's booking of a tenth part of his lands—the so-called Decimation of 854–5—in chapter 11 of the *Life* of Alfred is a slavish but sloppy translation of the Chronicle, while his record of the same event in chapter 16 was typical of the backtracking and recapitulation employed by the Pseudo-Asser. This careless conflation of material is only one of numerous instances in the *Life* of Alfred of hasty editorial work in which no attempt was made to reconcile supposedly additional information with the basic narrative of the Anglo-Saxon Chronicle. There is nothing unique about the doubling of the account of Æthelwulf's bequests in the *Life* of Alfred. Such duplication is already present in chapter 11, where the Pseudo-Asser sends the infant Alfred off to Rome for a second improbable trip in 855.[11]

Finberg needlessly complicated our understanding of King Æthelwulf's so-called decimation, donation, or tithing of his lands, by positing the existence of not one, but two decimations—one issued at Winchester on 5 November 844, and a second issued at Wilton during Easter (22 April 854).[12] In addition to these two general proclamations of largesse, Finberg regarded the charitable provisions in Æthelwulf's *Will* as a third and separate arrangement dating to *c.*858.[13] He regarded all three donations as being quite independent of each other. In Finberg's view, the 844 Decimation allowed exemption for a tenth of all hereditary land belonging to churchmen and laymen from public dues in perpetuity.[14] Ten years later, at Wilton, Æthelwulf (again, in Finberg's view) proclaimed that he was granting one-tenth of 'the private domain of the royal house' of Wessex to the church.[15] But by some obscure process, those estates that had already been leased by the king to his thegns would pass 'with power of free disposal' to those same thegns 'who would' however also 'pass with his [Æthelwulf's] gift under ecclesiastical lordship'.[16] The appalling confusion—so rife in the literature on Æthelwulf's church donations—stems from the Stevenson's thesis that although lay magnates may have benefited from King Æthewulf's donations, those grants to laymen were somehow made on the understanding that the estates so granted by the king would revert to the church.[17] We do not possess a single genuine charter issued by Æthelwulf to a lay magnate where this donation or charitable tithing is unequivocally spelt out together with the right of reversion to a particular church. It seems highly unlikely that churchmen would have been content to allow their ultimate rights to vast amounts of landed wealth to hinge on an unwritten understanding. Nor would those same shrewd churchmen ever have agreed to allow important reversion rights to lie encoded in charter texts, hiding under vague sentiments in which King Æthelwulf merely expressed a pious hope that his grant would assist in the remission of his punishment for his own sins. Heaven might, after all, just as easily have forgiven the king his sins in return for a generous grant towards a layman as it would for a grant towards a particular church.

Finberg believed that the differences in substance and form were so great in the two versions of Æthelwulf's Decimations as outlined in the *Life* of Alfred, they could not refer to the same transaction. But the differences between the versions are more apparent than real. All the provisions focus on the central notion of laying aside a tenth of Æthelwulf's hereditary lands for charitable purposes. In the 844 charters, that tenth part was supposedly freed from taxation; in 855 it was allegedly given to the church, and in Æthelwulf's *Will* it was set aside for provision for the poor.[18] On Finberg's own admission, the best textual evidence for the 844 Winchester donation (Sawyer 322 and cf. Sawyer 314; Birch 447) dates to sometime after *c*. AD 1393 and was described by Robertson as 'highly suspicious'.[19] The earliest extant record of this supposed Decimation dates to William of Malmesbury's *De Gestis Regum Anglorum* of *c*.1130. William has the 844 Decimation issued at Winchester and witnessed by Swithun, who did not succeed to the bishopric of Winchester until 852.[20] The earliest manuscript charter (Sawyer 308, Birch 469) for the Second, or Wilton Decimation, dates to the late eleventh century, and in the opinion of Stevenson, Stenton, and Robertson was based on a false or doubtful original.[21] Stevenson believed it to be a copy of a spurious original drawn up by a foreigner *c*.1100, who had little knowledge of Old English script.[22] The great majority of all those charters dealing with Finberg's so-called First and Second Decimations have been pronounced forgeries. Most appear in the cartularies of Malmesbury, Winchester, and Glastonbury, described by Stevenson as cartularies 'of the lowest possible character'.[23] Even more damaging was Stevenson's assertion that the formulae of these donation charters relate to the tenth rather than to the ninth century. Finberg's quotation of Stenton's remark that 'set phrases might be preserved in the king's writing office for many years without use in any charter which has survived' was citing a scholarly comment taken grotesquely out of context.[24] Stenton was discussing later tenth-century charters *vis-à-vis* each other.[25] He never implied that it was possible for the flamboyant formulae of later tenth-century charters to have existed undetected in scriptoria of the century before. In short, these Decimation charters are all so faulty in their textual transmission, and their internal dating criteria are so flawed with indictional and other dating errors, that it is not possible to identify an earlier Winchester Decimation of 844 as distinct from the Wilton Decimation of 854. To confuse matters yet further, the Anglo-Saxon Chronicle would appear to date Æthelwulf's decimation to 855, while the Pseudo-Asser states that some at least of Æthelwulf's bequests were made out after his return from Rome (in 856) and before his death in 858. Finberg was closest to the truth when he claimed that the plethora of charters relating to these so-called charitable grants by Æthelwulf all probably went back to one original enabling document—an idea that was also expressed in vaguer terms by Robertson.[26]

But that supposedly original enabling document may not have been a charter as we understand it. It may have been a series of provisions in King Æthelwulf's *Will*, and it was a summary of such provisions which was recorded by the compiler of the Anglo-Saxon Chronicle under AD 855. That was the year in which Æthelwulf departed for Rome—the most appropriate time for drawing up such charitable provisions, and not—it should be stressed—in 844, the date offered by so many dubious charters. The brief record of Æthelwulf's conveying 'by charter the tenth part of his land throughout all his kingdom for . . . his own eternal salvation' and the later elaboration of that text by the Pseudo-Asser may well have prompted the entire spate of charter forgeries. The vague record of Æthelwulf's open-ended generosity, prompted by Christian piety, was too good an opportunity for later monastic and other ecclesiastical forgers to miss.

The text of Æthelwulf's *Will* has not survived and we are dependent for accounts of it from the *Will* of Æthelwulf's son, King Alfred, from a garbled discussion by the Pseudo-Asser, and from that brief mention of it in the Chronicle under the year 855. Common sense suggests a great lack of economy in the triple display of Æthelwulf's bounty as Finberg envisaged it. Finberg was himself conscious that the king might not have commanded sufficient resources to sustain such lavish benefactions over two decades of his reign and suggested that the Second Decimation of 854 may have arisen as a result of the collapse of an earlier initiative in 844.[27] He was also embarrassed by the excessive liturgical conditions laid down in these provisions. In what Finberg regarded as the First Decimation at Winchester, fifty Psalms were to be chanted in all the minsters of Wessex every Wednesday, and every priest was to offer two Masses, one for the king and the other for his ealdormen. In the Wilton Donation of 854, these same services were specified for every Saturday. As a way out of his dilemma, Finberg suggested that by 854, the provisions of 844 had either never been implemented or had lapsed.[28] Finberg in developing his elaborate theories of multiple Donations was compelled to take the reader into his confidence because he was acutely aware that he was building an edifice on the poorest of evidence. His reconstruction of what the original elusive Winchester grant might have looked like is based on speculation piled upon speculation, and he admitted that 'in the end we are thrown back on probabilities'.[29]

The Pseudo-Asser's doubling of the record of King Æthelwulf's bequests for the benefit of his soul and the glory of God should be treated as two versions of the same incident, and the most compelling date for this provision together with other bequests for Æthelwulf's family and kin must be the Chronicle's date of 855 rather than 844, 854, or 856–8. The Rome pilgrimage was one from which many travellers were unlikely to return. Wigheard, archbishop-elect of Canterbury, had died there of the plague before his consecration in 668, losing 'almost all the companions who had travelled with him'.[30] Three of Wigheard's successors did make the journey successfully between his time and that of King Æthelwulf, but that number, as Brooks reminded us, was relatively small, and the hazardous journey which might take up to two years to accomplish was usually only embarked upon with a view to resolving some crisis in the Canterbury archbishopric.[31] While bishops went to Rome on business, the motive for kings was paradoxically, pilgrimage—a penitential journey after a *de facto* if not *de jure* abdication, to make up for a life of violence as warrior-kings. Æthelwulf must have known, however vaguely, that royal visitors to Rome had a hopeless track-record for returning home, and most of his predecessors must have left their kingdoms with a view to dying there in penitence. So Cædwalla of Wessex—a young man compared with Æthelwulf—died in Rome in 689, while Ine of Wessex went the same way after abdicating in 726.[32] King Cenred of Mercia retired to a religious life in Rome after his abdication in 709,[33] while one of Cenred's successors, Burgred, the son-in-law of King Æthelwulf, abandoned his Mercian kingdom to the Danes and to Ceolwulf II, in favour of retirement in Rome in 874. There was every reason why Æthelwulf should have made his *Will* in 855, just as there was an even more pressing need for the *witan* and the royal kindred to sort out the succession during his absence.

Wills must have been commonly drawn up immediately before some impending crisis or ordeal. Alfred reminds us in his *Will*, that confronted with the crisis of viking invasion (in 870–1), he and King Æthelred 'spoke about our children, that they would need some property, happen what might to the two of us in those disasters (*brocum*)',[34] and so a *Will* was agreed upon before the West Saxon council at *Swinbeorg*. Several examples survive of Anglo-Saxon testators who put their affairs in order before setting out on pilgrimage, and we do know that some at least, such as Æthelric a landowner from Mercia in the early ninth century, returned to enjoy his estates after the Rome journey.[35] But safe return can never have been regarded as a foregone conclusion. The *Will* of a certain Ketel from East Anglia (*c*.1052–1066) and of Siflæd from Norfolk (*c*. AD 1000) both contain references to the uncertainties of their respective journeys. Ketel declared: 'and if death befall us both [i.e. Ketel and his stepdaughter] on the way to Rome, the estate is to go to Bury St. Edmunds'.[36] Siflæd in a more optimistic mood stipulated that 'if I come home, then I wish to occupy that estate (at Marlingford) for my life; and after my death the *will* is to take effect'.[37] Such then is the context of uncertainty in which we must view the lost *Will* of King Æthelwulf—a *Will* that was to be a bone of contention among his sons and grandsons for almost 50 years. On the one hand, it was a *Will* drawn up by a king during life, but *de facto* it also had the qualities of a deathbed gift, since the king was uncertain of his return. To complicate matters further, Æthelwulf turned out to be the earliest known Anglo-Saxon king who did indeed return from the Rome pilgrimage—and with a new and exotic wife into the bargain. Consequently, he had to be readmitted by his heirs and beneficiaries into the scheme of things in Wessex.

King Æthelwulf had drawn up a *cwide* before leaving his kingdom—a composite rehearsal of various *post obitum* gifts to his kindred, to the church, and to his faithful retainers, all of which would have been read out before the councillors of Wessex to be witnessed by them and backed up by a document, copies of which would have been kept by leading witnesses. That, at least, was the procedure followed by Alfred in drawing up his *Will* in *c*.885 and it is implied by Alfred that his predecessor, King Æthelred, also followed similar procedures involving the West Saxon *witan* at *Swinbeorg* in *c.* 870–1. Alfred also informs us of an earlier *Will* which he himself had once made and subsequently superseded: 'I had entrusted the documents to many men, and in these same mens' witness they were written.'[38] The witnesses then as later were presumably the members of his council. It was a copy of his father King Æthelwulf's *Will* that Alfred some thirty years later caused to be read before the West Saxon council at *Langandene* when the councillors declared they 'could not hear a juster title' to King Alfred's claim than that which they had heard in his father's *Will*. On the basis of Æthelwulf's *Will*, which was read aloud at an assembly at *Langandene*, the councillors of the West Saxons supported Alfred in his dispute with his nephews over the inheritance of King Æthelwulf.

In spite of its shortcomings, King Alfred's own *Will* provides us with enough information to conclude that Æthelwulf's *Will* was a composite affair involving among other things a special entailment of a particular bequest on three of his sons—Æthelbald, Æthelred, and Alfred—with a reversion clause benefiting the survivor. It was in King Alfred's interest to emphasize and isolate that particularly complicated detail of his father's *Will*, since Alfred as the longest surviving of the three sons named in that gift, claimed to inherit everything stipulated in the terms of that particular bequest. Indeed, Alfred informs us in the opening words of his own *Will* that he had made a special enquiry into the terms of that bequest in his father's *Will* relating to Æthelbald, Æthelred, and himself. But even Alfred reveals in his *Will* that there was more to King Æthelwulf's *Will* than the entailed bequest involving Æthelbald, Æthelred, and Alfred. There was mention, for instance, of 'lands which King Æthelwulf gave to us [Alfred and Æthelred] during Æthelbald's lifetime *except* those which he bequeathed to us three brothers'.[39] In other words, those lands were quite distinct, and remained distinct, from an additional inheritance which King Æthelwulf settled on Æthelbald, Æthelred, and Alfred, with a view to the survivor of that trio inheriting all of that particular bequest. The distinction between those two bequests (both of which involved Alfred) in Æthelwulf's *Will* was so clearly marked that Alfred chose to treat them separately when he came to finalize his own *Will* some thirty years later. There are other references in Alfred's *Will* to separate bequests in the earlier *Will* of his father. Alfred's *Will* mentions 'lands at the lower Hurstbourne [Hampshire] and at Chiseldon [Wiltshire]' which were to be given to Winchester 'on the terms on which my father bequeathed it'.[40] Those lands, granted by Æthelwulf to the church in Winchester, may have been quite distinct from Æthelwulf's more general arrangements for the maintenance of churches and for the poor—his so-called Decimation. It is likely that Æthelwulf's grant to Winchester, mentioned in Alfred's *Will*, formed part of a specific *post obitum* gift in Æthelwulf's *Will* which eventually came into Alfred's possession, with a reversion clause in favour of Winchester. Yet another echo of separate provisions in Æthelwulf's *Will* is found in Alfred's gift of 200 pounds 'to be distributed for my sake, for my father and the friends for whom he used to intercede and I intercede'.[41] Money was being set aside here either as alms or as offerings to clergy, to pray for the souls of deceased friends of Æthelwulf and his son, Alfred. Alfred may have been reviving or reinforcing a provision from his father's *Will* which allocated money for this purpose and which formed part of a larger section of Æthelwulf's *Will* dealing—as the Pseudo-Asser speculated—with 'provision for the welfare of his soul'. Yet another—and it has to be said doubtful—bequest which was recorded by the Pseudo-Asser, under the wider heading of spiritual provisions, was Æthelwulf's supposed gift of 300 mancuses to be divided evenly, three ways, between the pope and the churches of St Peter and St Paul in Rome.[42] Stevenson was rightly concerned[43] that Æthelwulf could not have committed his heirs to paying such huge annual sums to Rome, not least because his interest in his family estates was only a life one. There were yet other provisions from Æthelwulf's *Will* which were itemized by the Pseudo-Asser but which were ignored by King Alfred. These include mention of bequests to Æthelwulf's sons, daughter [Æthelswith, queen of Burgred of Mercia], and to other kinsmen (*propinquos*). Furthermore, the Pseudo-Asser distinguished between Æthelwulf's division of his personal inheritance (*propriae hereditatis*)—mostly no doubt in land—between his sons, daughter and kinsmen, and other separate bequests of money which remained after his death for the benefit of his soul, sons, and nobles (*nobiles*).[44] It is possible, then, to identify some ten or more separate bequests and legacies reportedly embodied in Æthelwulf's *Will*, of which the obscure arrangement entailed on Æthelbald, Æthelred, and Alfred constituted but *one* out of a whole package of those gifts. This tentative reconstruction of the contents of Æthelwulf's *Will* and our understanding of the wider context in which the reversion clause relating to Alfred ought to be seen is of paramount importance. For Alfred, in his devious and masterly way, befuddled his own contemporaries and has confused modern historians by exaggerating his own role as beneficiary of his father's estates.

Not only was the particular bequest of which Alfred eventually became the beneficiary, one of several mentioned in Æthelwulf's *Will*, but it related neither directly to the kingship of Wessex nor to the lands which were set aside for the support of that office. Even the Pseudo-Asser assumed that Æthelwulf divided up his property between his sons and daughter from 'his own inheritance (*propriae hereditatis*)', a phrase echoed yet again when we are told that Æthelwulf's alms for the maintenance of the poor came from his 'hereditary land (*hereditariam terram*)'. The compiler of the *Life* of Alfred may have had no good documentary evidence to back up such a statement, but he was at least basing his speculation on what he would have considered plausible practice for an English king at the turn of the millennium. Alfred himself refers to his father's *Will* as *Apulfes cinges yrfe gewrit* or 'King Æthelwulf's writing concerning his private inheritance'.[45] It is Alfred's own personal inheritance—his *yrfe*—which he also disposes of in his own *Will*. Yet in spite of this, historians continue to confuse the kingship of Wessex and its concomitant royal demesne with the personal property of individual members of the royal family. The confusion is fatal to our understanding of West Saxon history, because if we accept that the kingship was included in the bequest which Æthelwulf entailed on three of his sons, then we must also accept that Æthelwulf deliberately engineered a succession which would come to his youngest son, Alfred, should he survive his brothers. Such an 'arrangement' by Æthelwulf would have excluded all children who might be born to Alfred's older brothers then, or at any time in the future. Under such circumstances, Alfred would indeed have been a 'chosen child'—an heir apparent from as early as AD 855—as later on, the compiler of the Anglo-Saxon Chronicle and more specifically the author of Alfred's *Life* would have wished us to believe. Alfred did his job so well, and his later biographer lied so successfully, that their combined smokescreen has continued to confound historical analysis for over a thousand years. What students of Alfredian history have overlooked is that there is no mention of the kingship of Wessex among the bequests in King Alfred's *Will*, nor indeed is there any mention of that kingship in that other surviving *Will* from Anglo-Saxon England—that of Alfred's grandson, King Eadred. As testators, neither Alfred nor his grandson were in a position to dispose unilaterally, or contractually, of the West Saxon kingship in the way they might dispose of a privately owned farm or an antique sword. Had it been otherwise, Alfred—above all kings—would not have failed to exercise such an extraordinary right, and he would have put the kingship 'up front' in those extravagant opening gifts which he settled on his elder son, Edward. We shall see that Alfred's ruthless generosity shown to Edward was calculated to help him secure the kingship against his rivals, but the kingship as such was never in Alfred's gift, nor indeed could it ever have been in the gift of his father, King Æthelwulf.

Alfred speaks in his *Will* of 'the inheritance which my father King Æthelwulf bequeathed to us three brothers, Æthelbald, Æthelred and myself, stipulating that whichever of us should live longest was to succeed to the whole'.[46] The 'inheritance (*yrfe*)' to which the last surviving brother was to succeed *in toto* was argued by Eric John to include both property and the kingship of Wessex: 'It is inconceivable that the kingship was not included in the "everything", otherwise we should have to believe that Æthelwulf thought one of his grandsons might be king whilst one of his younger sons held the property.'[47] Dumville went along with this argument, for by doing so, both he and John accepted the notion that Æthelwulf wished to entail the royal landed inheritance intact on the surviving son. Dumville concluded that from as early as 855 Æthelwulf had already planned to settle the kingship (as well as the family inheritance) on either or both Æthelred or Alfred, whichever lived the longer and, therefore, by implication 'Asser' was quite justified in referring to Alfred as the heir apparent or *secundarius*.[48] John went even further and saw the papal coronation of the infant Alfred in Rome as not only historical fact, but as a means of providing validation for Æthelwulf's complicated scheme, for which the pope was bribed with 300 mancuses—those gifts, specified in the *Life* of Alfred among the bequests in King Æthelwulf's *Will* in favour of the papacy and two Roman churches.[49] But John's argument that 'the property' (in his quotation above) must also have included the kingship, only holds good if we accept that the inheritance which Alfred claims his father, Æthelwulf, left to

Æthelbald, Æthelred, and Alfred consisted of *all* the lands Æthelwulf possessed, or at least the great majority of those lands, both in his private capacity and as king of Wessex. Despite the fragmentary nature of the evidence relating to the original contents of Æthelwulf's *Will*, that is not an assumption we are entitled to make.

Not all scholars are agreed that the inheritance (*yrfe*) which Æthelwulf is alleged by Alfred to have left to his longest surviving son included the West Saxon kingship. Keynes and Lapidge believed that Æthelwulf's inheritance bequeathed to Æthelbald, Æthelred, and Alfred consisted of the king's personal holdings of 'bookland' which he could have disposed of as he wished.[50] Those lands were distinct from the royal estates proper which originally at least, had been set aside for the maintenance of the king in his public office, for the support of his retinue, and to help finance those obligations incumbent on him in his role as war-leader and overlord and representative of his nobles. Those royal lands could not have been alienated by Æthelwulf any more than he could have personally and unilaterally designated his successor. Similarly, there were lands owned by the royal kindred ('folkland') which were controlled by tribal law and were not in Æthelwulf's personal gift.[51] So while the personal or folklands held by a reigning king would pass on his death to his male heirs, the mensal or demesne lands were set aside for his successor in the kingship. To hold that the Anglo-Saxon situation was otherwise would be to concede that any Early English king might strip the kingship of its resources and leave his successors bereft of the wherewithal to exercise patronage, sustain their household, and defend the kingdom from external enemies.

This is not the place to enter into lengthy discussion on the distinction between *bocland* and *folcland*—a constitutional quagmire which will probably remain forever such, due to the paucity and ambiguity of evidence. There must, however, be universal agreement, that whatever special status land acquired by the granting of a *book*, over land-grants which were not so documented, and whatever courts held jurisdiction over cases involving such lands, there must have been a clear distinction (after the coming of Christianity at least) between lands which belonged collectively to the kin and land which a person might own privately and dispose of to whomsoever he wished. Similarly, for those who held the office of kingship, there must have been a distinction between lands pertaining to the royal demesne and lands which the king had at his personal disposal. There may have been a third category of lands pertaining to the royal kin as distinct from either the kingship or the king's personal property. The compiler of Alfred's *Life*, in his account of King Æthelwulf's *Will*, distinguished between the settlement of the kingdom on the king's two eldest sons (Æthelbald and Æthelberht) and the distribution of Æthelwulf's 'own inheritance between his sons, daughter and kinsmen'.[52] We shall see that the Pseudo-Asser was wrong in giving the impression that King Æthelwulf could personally and unilaterally have bestowed the kingship on any one of his children, but nevertheless, the broad distinction which is made in the Pseudo-Asser's text between private and public matters in relation to the *Will* of this king is important.

The analogy with the case of Anglo-Saxon episcopal property is instructive because we have clearer evidence from some episcopal *Wills* relating to property

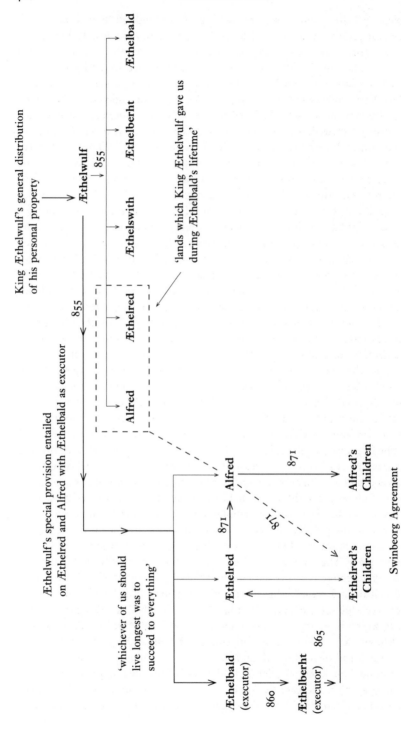

Fig. 9. King Alfred's interpretation of his father's *Will*

pertaining to the episcopal office as distinct from the personal possessions of a bishop. Theodred, bishop of London (942–51) in the reign of King Alfred's grandsons, left a *Will* in which he was careful to distinguish between his episcopal demesne (*biscopriche*) in London and at Hoxne in Suffolk, and what the bishop describes as 'my property (*erfes*), what I have acquired and may yet acquire'.[53] Among the latter, Theodred included extensive estates in Suffolk as well as, for instance, 'my house in Ipswich which I bought (*and min hage þat ic binnin Gypeswich bouhte*)'. On the other hand, he stipulates that all stock which he found on the episcopal demesne lands at London, Hoxne, and elsewhere, when he came to office, were to remain intact on those estates, while other stock on those same episcopal estates which he had (personally) 'added to them' were to be disposed of according to the terms laid down in his *Will*.[54] This *Will* of Bishop Theodred, so much more clearly stated than either the Pseudo-Asser's or Alfred's account of King Æthelwulf's inheritance, places the distinction between property pertaining to public office in Anglo-Saxon England and property acquired in a personal capacity by the holder of that office, in no doubt. It is also clear from the Pseudo-Asser's emphasis on the hereditary nature of Æthelwulf's inheritance, and the distinction which he makes between that and the 'kingdom (*regnum*)', that the gifts which are referred to in the king's *Will* were made, in the Pseudo-Asser's opinion, from King Æthelwulf's personal property. Alfred makes a comment in his *Will* which puts the matter beyond any shadow of doubt. He tells us that after King Æthelwulf's *Will* had been read out before the assembled *witan* at *Langandene*, and after the councillors found in Alfred's favour against his nephews, they proclaimed: 'Now that everything in it has come into your possession, bequeath it and give it into the hand of kinsman or stranger, whichever you prefer.'[55] The entire dispute—we need to remind ourselves—turned on 'the inheritance which my father King Æthelwulf bequeathed to us three brothers . . . (stipulating) that whichever of us should live longest was to succeed to the whole.'[56] Now that Alfred had 'succeeded to the whole' (or 'to everything', *to eallum*) and since he was entitled to bequeath it even to a stranger (*fremdre*), we have at last conclusive proof that neither his *Will* nor the relevant section of King Æthelwulf's *Will*, to which Alfred was appealing, had anything whatever to do, either with lands from the royal demesne or with the kingship of Wessex. And this being so, all the conflicting and elaborate hypotheses put forward by historians relating to Alfred's special position as heir apparent from childhood within the House of Wessex collapse in their turn like a house of cards.

But if Alfred were referring to his father's personal property as Keynes and Lapidge believed, it does not even follow that Æthelwulf intended *all* his personal estates to pass intact to his longest surviving son. In this instance, Æthelwulf intended that a portion of his personal wealth should pass to the longest surviving of only *three* of his sons. We do not possess the full text of Æthelwulf's *Will*—all we have here is a reference by Alfred to a clause within it—and therefore we shall never know precisely how Æthelwulf wished to divide all his inheritance. We are certainly not justified in following the assumption of Keynes and Lapidge that

'Æthelwulf clearly intended that his "personal" property should be kept intact', much less accept their conclusion that he wished that property to pass along with the kingship from Æthelbald 'to each of his brothers in turn'.[57] Not even the Pseudo-Asser, in one of his more creative moods, ever dreamt of such an arrangement. On the contrary, he speaks of Æthelwulf's 'division of his own inheritance between his sons, daughter and kinsmen and of such money as should remain after his death between his soul, sons and nobles'.[58] There is no word here of that complicated arrangement involving only three of Æthelwulf's four surviving sons to the exclusion of all other kin, which would ultimately benefit Alfred, and of which Alfred is, significantly, our only witness.

Let us look now at another aspect of the bequest which King Æthelwulf settled on Æthelbald, Æthelred, and Alfred and which Alfred was claiming as a reversionary right. Scholars have been quick to point out that the noticeable absentee in this provision of King Æthelwulf, was his son, Æthelberht. This son was already old enough to rule the kingdom of Kent by 855 when Æthelwulf made the provision for his other sons. His absence from the reversionary clause involving his three brothers would therefore seem to be all the more remarkable. It certainly cannot be explained away as a scribal omission from the text of Alfred's *Will*, since Alfred, in addition to naming his brothers in the opening lines of his *Will*, later refers to this same bequest as the lands which King Æthelwulf 'bequeathed to us *three* brothers'.[59] So, the omission of Æthelberht's name was clearly intentional. Eric John concluded that Æthelberht 'was excluded from Æthelwulf's *will*'[60]—an assumption which seems unlikely in the extreme, not least because he was entrusted in his father's lifetime with the sub-kingdom of Kent. Æthelberht's favoured status during Æthelwulf's reign is confirmed by his title, first of ealdorman (*dux*) and later by that of *rex*, in the witness lists of his father's later charters. All that we are entitled to conclude is that Æthelwulf found no need to include Æthelberht in the particular *post obitum* gift which he settled on Æthelbald, Æthelred, and Alfred. Dumville, also relying on Alfred's restrictive reporting of his father's *Will*, decided that in the absence of any mention of either Æthelberht or his eastern kingdom, 'we are left to presume that it was expected to go its own way, with Æthelberht as king.'[61] Keynes and Lapidge followed this speculative vein further by suggesting that Æthelberht was intended by his father to 'establish a permanently separate and distinct dynasty' in Kent.[62] What early medieval kingdom— indeed what early medieval estate, however small—was ever 'expected to go its own way'? As for Æthelberht's supposed establishment of a separate dynasty in Kent—surely that ran contrary to West Saxon practice, albeit recently established, since Æthelwulf himself had once ruled as king of Kent under his father Ecgberht.[63] Would not Æthelwulf have intended his son in turn to graduate, with the assent of the *witan*, from the eastern kingship to that of the whole of Wessex—should the opportunity arise? Since Æthelberht did indeed eventually succeed to the whole kingdom, we are justified in that assumption. Æthelwulf could scarcely have parted the territory of the eastern kingdom from that of greater Wessex in 855 without the consent of his *witan*. If that had been so, it is difficult to reconcile such a major political decision with the fact that when Æthelberht himself succeeded to the kingship of Wessex he decided *against* sharing power with any kinsman in Kent much less alienating that kingdom from Wessex. His brothers Æthelred and Alfred followed the same policy of ruling a united kingdom, which makes further nonsense out of any suggestion that Kent or the eastern region 'was expected to go its own way'. There is in fact positive evidence to refute such speculation. King Æthelwulf's controversial charter to Dunn of lands near Rochester (Sawyer 315, Birch 486) suggests that while Æthelberht may have ruled as king of Kent even before 855, there was nevertheless a clear sense in his father's mind that Kent and Wessex proper, still formed one kingdom, united under the rule of Æthelwulf, who described himself in that Kentish charter as 'king of the West Saxons and also of the people of Kent'.[64] Æthelberht is also described as 'king' in the witness list of that same charter, but no territorial label—Kentish or otherwise—is attached to his kingship.[65] Æthelwulf granted land at Lenham and at Blean (near Canterbury) in a charter of AD 850 (Sawyer 300, Birch 459) which was witnessed by his son, King Æthelstan, who is then assumed to have been king of Kent.[66] But that Kentish charter was drafted in West Saxon formulae and was issued at the West Saxon estate at Wilton in Wiltshire, and Æthelstan, who was clearly attending on his father at Wilton, is given the undifferentiated title of *rex* (without reference to Kent) in the witness list.[67]

One of the few trends which historians of Dark Age kingship in the British Isles are confident of recognizing in the ninth century is the decline of tribal or provincial kingship and the concomitant growth of more ambitious centralized monarchy. This is true of Ireland and Scotland and it is especially true of the house of Æthelwulf of Wessex. It would seem perverse, then, to argue that Æthelwulf was deliberately devising a scheme which would help to atomize the political and territorial gains made by his father, when the relentless process points the other way to strong centralized kingship—supported by the church of Canterbury—culminating in the reigns of Athelstan and Edgar in the next century. It is even more illogical to argue, on the one hand, that King Æthelwulf hoped to establish a separate dynasty under Æthelberht in Kent, while he otherwise hoped to settle the kingship eventually on his infant son, Alfred—and all in the apparent knowledge or foreknowledge that none of his elder sons (especially Æthelbald and Æthelberht) would leave any heirs at any time in the future. Nor are we justified in assuming with Dumville that King Æthelberht 'died childless'.[68] Such gratuitous and additional speculation was necessary in order to explain how the supposedly 'breakaway' kingdom of Kent under Æthelberht was eventually reunited to Wessex proper.

If we reject speculation that Æthelberht was cut off from his West Saxon inheritance by his father, or that he was shunted into a siding in Kent to found an incongruously new and potentially rival dynasty, we are still left to explain the conspicuous absence of Æthelberht's name from the gift which Æthelwulf so complexly entailed on three of his sons, and which Alfred ultimately claimed as his own. There is a simple explanation for the absence of Æthelberht's name from this particular gift involving Alfred, and the key to our understanding of it lies in appreciating the ages of Æthelwulf's sons at the time when their father set off for Rome in 855. We have seen how Æthelstan was already dead by 855 and Æthelbald and Æthelberht were two grown men who had to be accommodated into a share in the kingship of greater Wessex. That reason and that alone is sufficient to explain why the ageing Æthelwulf, with the consent of his magnates, set Æthelbald over Wessex and placed Æthelberht over Kent in succession to Æthelstan before he set out on pilgrimage. But Alfred was then perhaps only 5, and his brother Æthelred was perhaps about 7. A veritable tide of scholarly opinion has pleaded on the basis of the Pseudo-Asser's testimony alone, and on one highly suspicious entry in the Chronicle regarding Alfred's pilgrimage to Rome in 853, that Æthelwulf showed special favour to the infant Alfred. The only solid evidence which we possess—namely that of the charters and the known sequence of West Saxon royal succession—strongly suggests that Æthelwulf was preoccupied with settling the kingship on his two older sons, Æthelbald and Æthelberht. These were the sons, after all, who did first succeed their father and who eventually succeeded each other in the kingship of Wessex. Since they (and not Alfred) came to kingship— as the charters attest—while their father was still alive, we may assume that Æthelwulf—with the consent of his magnates—was largely instrumental in bringing these men to power. As for Æthelred and his brother Alfred, Æthelwulf's only reasonable concern for those two infants would have been to provide for them first during their minority, while he was absent in Rome (855–6), and secondly to ensure that if they should ever achieve majority age, they would come into an inheritance commensurate with their status as æthelings, or sons of a king. What- ever role they might play in the future kingship of Wessex can scarcely have exercised Æthelwulf's mind. In the first place, their very survival to manhood was in doubt, and secondly that prospect was so far into the future of an uncertain viking age that Æthelwulf could never have hoped to envisage the needs or the mood of the West Saxon *witan* at that time of 'disasters'[69] when Alfred would have reached manhood. Nor could Æthelwulf envisage what claims would be made on the kingship of Wessex by any sons born to Æthelbald, Æthelberht, or Æthelred either in his lifetime or at some time in the future.

The special inheritance, bequeathed by King Æthelwulf, which Alfred made so much play of in his own *Will*, related neither to kingship nor to Æthelwulf's private property as a whole, but to a wise and simple arrangement to provide for Æthelred and Alfred after they attained to manhood. Æthelbald alone of the two older brothers is mentioned in this bequest which was specifically designed for the infant brothers. Æthelwulf needed to appoint a *mundbora* or guardian over his two youngest boys who were still minors—and what better guardian than their eldest surviving brother who was already acting as king of Wessex during his father's absence? Æthelbald had a dual involvement in this particular bequest. As guardian he was to play the role of a quasi-trustee or executor of the estates entailed in the gift, but Æthelwulf wisely included him as a possible beneficiary in the not unlikely event that both Æthelbald's infant brothers died in infancy. The inheritance would then revert to Æthelbald—a sensible arrangement in view of his role as king of

Wessex and his consequent need to command all the resources available to him. On the other hand, if his brothers should grow to maturity and outlive Æthelbald, they would then be provided with a reversionary inheritance at a future time, when far from enjoying kingship, they might find themselves on the fringes of the succession, and in need of estates to keep them in comfort as junior male heirs of a former king. Æthelberht had never been 'excluded' from this arrangement—it simply did not concern him, at the time, in 855, when it was first drawn up. It is clear from Alfred's *Will* that when Æthelbald died in 860—Alfred was then about 10 and Æthelred about 12—since the two younger boys were still minors, Æthelberht as the new king of Wessex was co-opted to replace Æthelbald as guardian of the estates held in trust for the younger brothers. This according to Alfred was arranged 'with the witness of all the councillors of the West Saxons'[70]— those same councillors who would afterwards be called upon to witness King Alfred's own *Will*.

King Alfred's discussion of his complicated inheritance is ambiguous and vague —and deliberately so. Although the longest lived of the three brothers named in the bequest 'was to succeed to everything', Alfred implies that during life each of the younger brothers at least, could benefit from the gift. He tells us that King Æthelberht was entrusted with 'our share on condition that he should return it to us as fully at our disposal as it was when we entrusted it to him, and he then did so, both that inheritance (*yrfe*) and what he had obtained from the use of the property we two held jointly, and what he had himself acquired'.[71] There is a sense here when Alfred says 'then he did so' that Æthelberht allowed Æthelred and Alfred to benefit from the joint properties while Æthelberht was still alive. This may be connected with the fact that Alfred, the younger of the two junior brothers must have come of age (about 14) sometime late in Æthelberht's reign, perhaps in 864.[72] This is also in keeping with Alfred's claim that when 'Æthelred succeeded to the kingdom, I asked him in the presence of all the councillors that we might divide that inheritance and he should give me my share'.[73] Æthelred refused. It would appear to have been King Æthelwulf's wish that this property held in trust could not be finally disposed of until it reverted *in toto* to a sole surviving son, but on the other hand it could provide an income for the two younger sons, while it was held in trust by an older brother. Alfred went before the *witan* as he claims and demanded his share of the inheritance from his fellow younger brother, Æthelred, who was then king. Alfred was in effect trying to renegotiate an earlier contract established in his father's *Will* back in 855. For a doubly unexpected set of circumstances had developed. The two younger sons had both survived to manhood, and the older of them, had, equally unexpectedly, become king. Since Æthelred had acquired all the wealth pertaining to the kingship of Wessex, Alfred, understandably tried to anticipate the reversionary clause in his father's bequest and asked for his share, there and then, regardless of which brother should live the longest. King Æthelred shrewdly held out for the original terms, which were that the longest surviving brother would inherit the entire gift. And meanwhile, Æthelred enjoyed the benefits and interest which accrued from his role as manager of the trust—a role which he argued meant that 'he could not easily divide it'. This, then, was the arrangement which Æthelwulf had prudently made for his two younger sons for that time when they would have reached their majority—an arrangement which in no way anticipated their eventual succession to the kingship of Wessex. On the contrary, this inheritance was devised for those sons who were least likely to succeed to kingship—hence Alfred's desire, as the least fortunate of Æthelwulf's five sons, to get his share—capital and all(?)—of that entailed inheritance, when the kingship unexpectedly came down as far as Æthelred.

Æthelwulf also left a number of estates to Æthelred and Alfred to tide them over their minority and to sustain their modest needs while they were still under the guardianship of King Æthelbald's household. These were 'the lands which King Æthelwulf gave us *during Æthelbald's lifetime* [855–60] except those which he bequeathed to us three brothers'. It was these estates—earmarked by King Æthelwulf for use during his sons' minorities—that appropriately Alfred and Æthelred agreed at the council of *Swinbeorg* (*c*.871) to pass on to each other's children depending on whether Æthelred or Alfred died first.[74] Because Æthelred died before Alfred, King Alfred's nephews—Æthelhelm and Æthelwold the sons of King Æthelred—stood to gain those estates which their father and King Alfred had obtained, together with those estates which their grandfather, King Æthelwulf, had set aside some sixteen years earlier for the maintenance of their father and their uncle during their minorities. Alfred, on the other hand, as the longest lived of all King Æthelwulf's sons, claimed that other gift in its entirety, which his father had entailed on Æthelbald, Æthelred, and himself. When the nephews of King Alfred came of age, they clearly felt cheated of their father's inheritance and so 'many disputes' arose within the kingdom which resulted in their confrontation with Alfred before the *witan* at the assembly at *Langandene*. Alfred, not surprisingly, because he was by then king, won that legal round, and not necessarily because as he protested, justice was on his side.

King Alfred drew up that version of his own *Will* that survives, sometime between 871 (when he became king) and the death of Archbishop Æthelred of Canterbury in 888, but his *Will* most likely dates from *c*.885, since he included provisions for his five children (all born after *c*.868) and for his eventual son-in-law, Æthelred, Lord of the Mercians. The council at *Langandene* in which Alfred was challenged by his nephews to undertake a fairer distribution of their deceased father's estates would seem to have taken place closer to the time of the final version of Alfred's *Will* than to the time of King Æthelred's death. When Æthelred died, Alfred claims that no one then disputed the terms that had been agreed at *Swinbeorg*, while the assembly at *Langandene* was convened 'when we *now* heard many disputes'.[75] There is a sense that Alfred drew up his final *Will* in the aftermath of his triumph at *Langandene*—a conclusion which is supported by his own admission that 'I had previously written differently concerning my inheritance'. By *c*.885 King Æthelwulf was already nearly thirty years dead, and all four of his older sons—each of them kings in their turn—had also all died. Alfred, by then in full control of Wessex and at the height of his power, was clearly bent on trying to settle the kingship on his son, Edward, to the exclusion of his brother Æthelred's heirs. That kingship was never in Alfred's gift, but clearly the greater amount of landed wealth he could entail on Edward, the stronger he made that son's position in any future contest for the kingship. We must, therefore, treat anything Alfred tells us of the terms of the disputed inheritance of his rival nephews with the utmost caution, if not with scepticism. The support which Alfred tells us he received from the *witan* counts for little. As king, Alfred controlled immense patronage in relation to his thegns, who stood to benefit from backing their lord against claims which his nephews made on his property. It is significant that the case ever came before the *witan* at all. That it did, suggests that Æthelhelm and Æthelwold were by then young men who commanded some independent support and sympathy within Wessex.

Judgements could always be swayed by bribery, or the threat of violence—whatever the legal language in which that might be couched. Alfred's protest that 'I prayed them all [i.e. the West Saxon councillors] for love of me—offering them surety that I would never bear a grudge against any of them on account of any conscientious expression of opinion—that none of them for love or fear of me should hesitate to declare what was the customary law in such a case' reads like so much special pleading and merely highlights the awesome challenge involved in confronting the 'terror' of an early medieval king in his own assembly. The abbot of Ramsey Abbey appealed to Alfred's son, King Edward the Elder, and to his queen, to uphold the terms of a *Will* made by one Ailwin the Black in favour of Ramsey. A decision in favour of the abbot was helped along by a bribe.[76] Bribery and the misuse of patronage was probably rife in the handling of such disputes involving the higher aristocracy in the early Middle Ages. King Alfred was in a much stronger position at *Langandene* than the abbot of Ramsey. He was that king who was hailed by one of his bishops as 'his ring-giver'—'the greatest treasure-giver of all the kings he has ever heard tell of, in recent times or long ago, or of any earthly king he had previously learned of '.[77] That same bishop would have taken a leading role in the very *witan* which decided the fate of the inheritance of Alfred's nephews. Such a well-rewarded man was unlikely to go against his lord, and the young disenchanted if not disinherited, Æthelwold, would have to bide his time until he might seek to redress the injustice he believed had been done to his brother and to himself.

As matters stood in King Alfred's *Will*, Æthelwold and his brother were given a very poor deal indeed, compared with the generosity shown by Alfred to his immediate family. Alfred left eight estates to Æthelhelm son of King Æthelred, and to Æthelhelm's brother, Æthelwold, he left only three. This contrasts with the gifts which Alfred settled on his own sons. He left seventeen estates to his younger son, Æthelweard, including 'all that I have in Cornwall except in Triggshire',[78] and he left some fifteen estates to his eldest son, Edward, together with 'all the booklands which Leofheah holds' and the vast estates which must have been encompassed in the gift of 'all the booklands which I have in Kent'.[79] While Edward's inheritance ranged across nothern Wessex from Triggshire in north-east Cornwall to Kent, his brother's holdings stretched from the Cornish border to Dean in Sussex. These two princes, between them, controlled key locations scattered across the greater kingdom of Wessex. The estates left to the sons of Æthelred I were conspicuously cut off from Wessex proper and were confined almost exclusively to Surrey and Sussex.[80] Æthelwold was the most poorly treated of the two sons of Æthelred, gaining only Godalming and Guildford in Surrey, together with Steyning in Sussex.[81] While these estates may have been substantial holdings, they compared poorly with the great inheritance which had been settled on the sons of Alfred. And while the sons of Æthelred I had no doubt been treated generously in their father's *Will*, it is clear from King Alfred's own testimony that these princes felt disadvantaged by Alfred in his handling of part at least, of their father's inheritance. Alfred left 100 mancuses or 12.50 pounds to each of the sons of Æthelred, compared with 1,000 pounds to Edward and 500 pounds to Æthelweard.[82] Æthelwold's subsequent rebellion against Edward should be seen in relation to the smallness of the gifts which Alfred left to Æthelwold in his *Will*, and in relation to the isolated location of Æthelwold's three estates in Surrey and Sussex. Alfred's special pleading in defence of his inheritance in his own *Will*, together with the apparent meanness with which he treated his nephews, shows the Truth-Teller in an altogether different light from that in which the Anglo-Saxon Chronicle or the Pseudo-Asser would have us see him.

King Alfred's Witan

Kingmakers and Wise Men in the Council of a King

IN 757, ABOUT A HUNDRED YEARS BEFORE KING ALFRED'S TIME, THE Anglo-Saxon Chronicle records that 'Cynewulf and the councillors of the West Saxons deprived Sigeberht of his kingdom because of his unjust acts'.[1] Who were these West Saxon 'Wise Men (*Westseaxna wiotan*)' who had the collective power to depose a king, for what they judged to have been his unlawful deeds *unryhtum dedum*? In 868, when Alfred was already a young warrior, he marched with his brother King Æthelred to help King Burgred of Mercia dislodge the Great Army of Danes from Nottingham. The West Saxon leaders were responding, according to the Anglo-Saxon Chronicle, to a request not just from Burgred, but also from his Mercian councillors (*7 his wiotan*).[2] We can be certain that Æthelred and Alfred did not set off on the hazardous march to Nottingham without having also consulted their own 'wise men'. When Alfred came to make his *Will*, he announced that he did so with the witness 'of all the councillors of the West Saxons'. Already, a picture begins to emerge of the *witan* as royal councillors who had the power to depose kings; who helped to decide on the crucial business of making war, and who helped kings to settle their personal inheritance. This was a body of influential magnates whose presence, as historians, we ignore at our peril. Yet too often students of Alfred's reign have treated those great men of the shires—ealdormen and thegns—whose names appear as witnesses to Alfred's charters, as mere names which can be manipulated statistically in order to provide a date or to otherwise authenticate a particular document. We shall see that some at least, of those magnates who witnessed Alfred's charters were among those *witan* or 'wise men' who assisted the king in the rudimentary government of his kingdom. Some would have attended on the king in his household, holding a position of honour and trust there. Such a man was Ælfric, Alfred's *hrælðen* or 'keeper of the wardrobe' who appears in the Fonthill Letter.[3] Ælfric is also described as Alfred's treasurer or *thesaurarius* in a doubtful charter (Sawyer 348, Birch 567) issued by King Alfred in favour of his ealdorman, Æthelhelm of Wiltshire, in 892.[4] That charter was also supposedly witnessed by Sigewulf, the king's cup-bearer or butler (*pincerna*) and by Deormod his supplies officer (*cellerarius*).[5] Whatever the merits of that particular charter, Sigewulf and Deormod were real enough. Sigewulf witnessed other documents and was probably the relative of Ealdorman Alfred who rescued the

Golden Gospels from viking invaders.[6] Sigewulf probably ended his career as an ealdorman of Kent and was slain while fighting for the cause of Edward the Elder against Alfred's nephew in the battle of the Holme in 902. Deormod was one of the parties who negotiated in the Fonthill dispute and who turns up elsewhere as a *fidelis* of King Alfred who survived to serve under Edward the Elder.[7] That charter issued by Alfred in 892 was made out in favour of Ealdorman Æthelhelm of Wiltshire who died two years before King Alfred in 897. Æthelhelm must have been one of Alfred's trusted men, and presumably a veteran of the wars against Guthrum. Alfred had entrusted Æthelhelm with the embassy to Rome in 887, when he 'took the alms of King Alfred and the West Saxons'.[8] The importance of Alfred's great men whose loyalty he could count on is nowhere better illustrated than in the Anglo-Saxon Chronicle's note of personal regret in the record of the deaths of several thegns in 896. There we are told that the catastrophe of Alfred's Last War with Hæsten 'had not on the whole afflicted the English people very greatly, but they were much more seriously afflicted . . . by the mortality of men, and most of all in that many of the best king's thegns who were in the land died in those three years'. The list of Alfred's friends include the bishops of Rochester and Dorchester; ealdormen of Hampshire, Kent, and Essex; a Sussex thegn; the town-reeve (*wicgerefa*) of Winchester; and Ecgwulf, the king's horse-thegn (*horspegn*).[9] In 896, the Chronicle also records the death of another of Alfred's horse-thegns 'who was also the Welsh reeve (*Wealhgerefa*)'—in charge, no doubt, of the West Saxon borders with the Cornishmen. These were men whom Alfred relied upon to run his kingdom. There were other great men, whose loyalty may not have been so assured, and with all of them, Alfred must have established bonds of mutual obligation in which they enjoyed his patronage and he in his turn relied on their support.

Because sources such as the Anglo-Saxon Chronicle and the Pseudo-Asser focus to such a great extent on Alfred and his family, there has been an understandable tendency to study West Saxon history in terms of individual members of the Alfredian royal house. We must resist this pressure, generated by Alfredian sources themselves, to view the history of Wessex in the ninth and tenth centuries, exclusively in terms of one family, and in isolation from the West Saxon aristocracy. Not only does a detailed study of Anglo-Saxon documents show the falsity of this approach, but we know that elsewhere in ninth-century Europe—from Norway to the Pyrenees—warlords, great and small, ruled with the support of their warrior élites. Alfred's dynasty was no exception, and we shall never understand the peculiar circumstances which brought Alfred to power, and the way in which he held on to power, if we persist in viewing the king in splendid isolation from the great men of his kingdom. Leading questions relating to how Æthelwulf supposedly settled the kingdom on his sons; how Alfred came to kingship and how he secured the succession on his son Edward to the exclusion of his cousins—all these questions cannot be properly answered unless we study them in relation to the role of the landed aristocracy in Wessex and the significance of the royal council made up of the *witan* or 'wise men' who were drawn from among the leading magnates

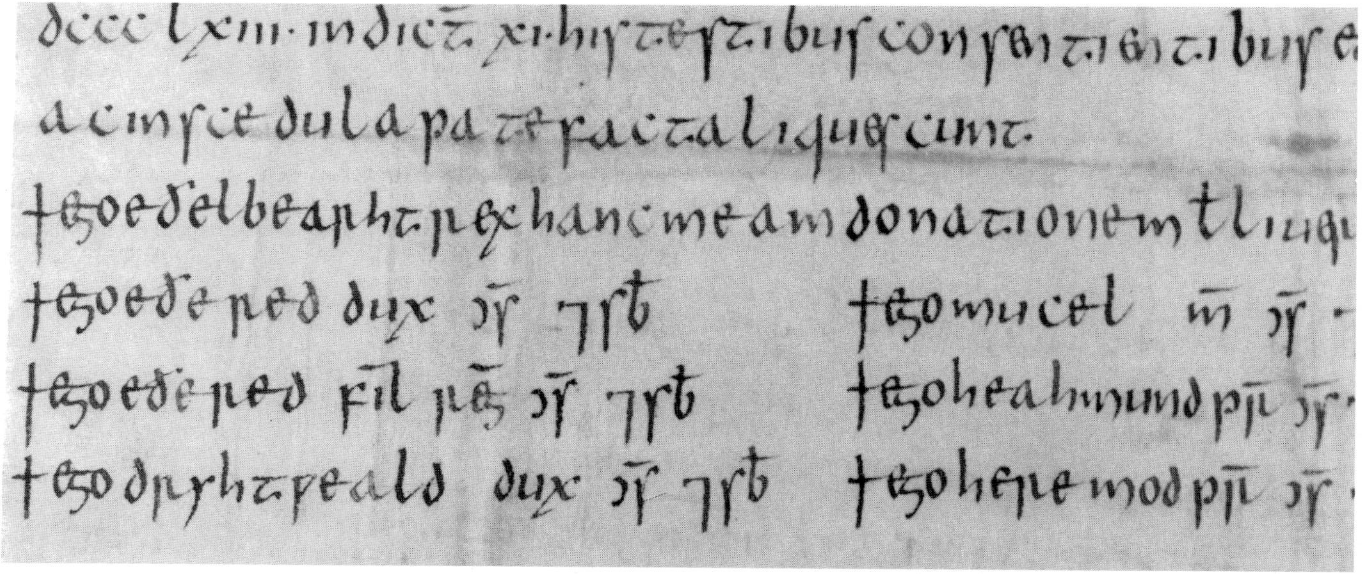

PLATE 19. A record of Alfredian family business preserved in Canterbury Cathedral for over 1100 years. Detail showing the head of the witness list of a charter issued in 863 by Alfred's older brother, Ethelberht, king of the West Saxons and of the Men of Kent. The name of King Ethelberht heads the list, followed by that of Ealdorman Ethelred (*Eðered dux*), followed by Ethelred, 'the king's son' (*Eðered filius regis*). This king's son was Alfred's next older brother and his immediate predecessor in the kingship of Wessex. Alfred—whose name does not appear in this list—was about 15 when it was drawn up. This charter deals with a grant of land at Mersham in Kent.

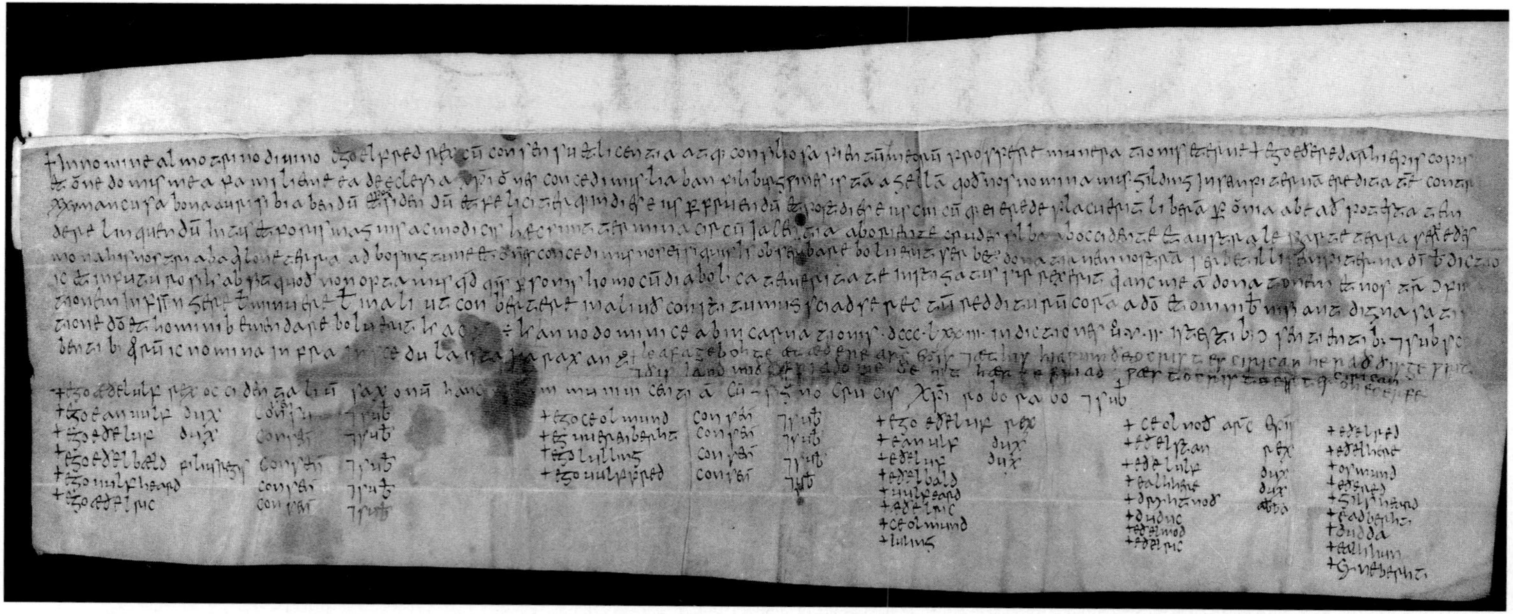

PLATE 20. Charter issued in 873 by Archbishop Æthelred of Canterbury in association with King Alfred. Although this is one of the very rare ninth-century charter manuscripts which survives from King Alfred's reign, it epitomizes the problems relating to charter studies in this period. The Latin and the handwriting are poor, and the witness list is copied twice over from an earlier charter of Alfred's father, King Æthelwulf. So this document, although perhaps dating from the late ninth century, can scarcely be the original parchment on which the grant of land to Liaba, son of Brigwine, at Ileden in Kent, was first recorded.

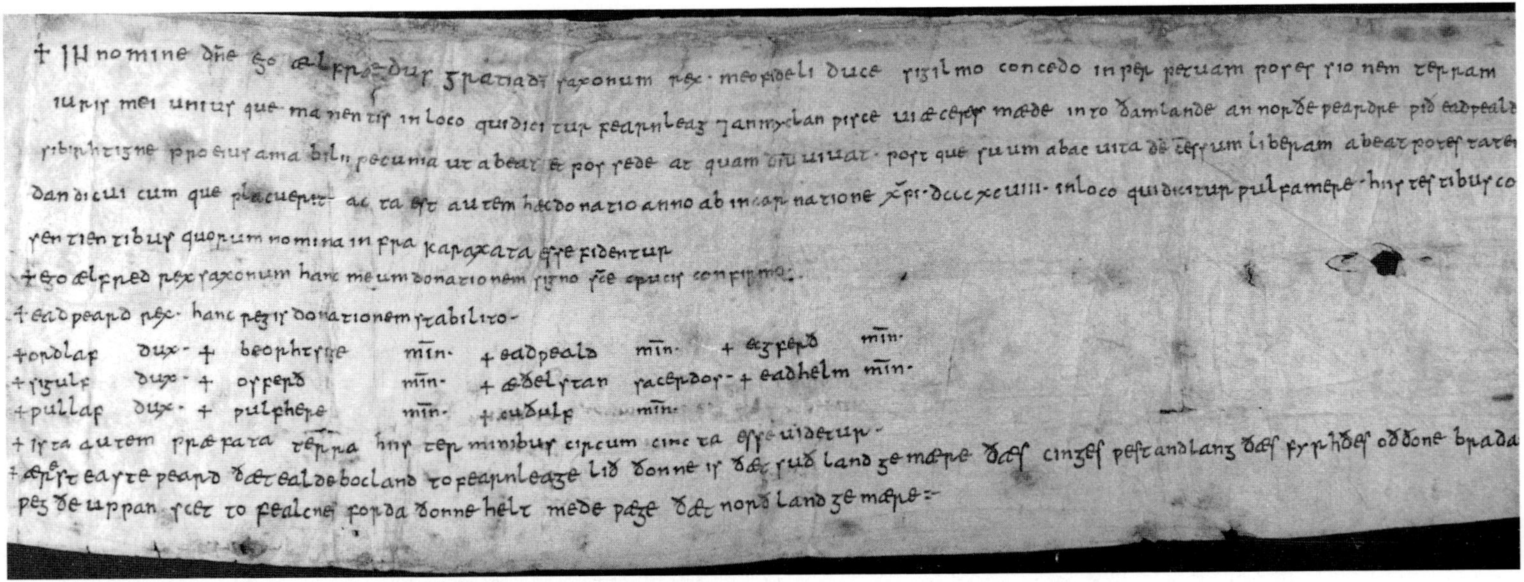

PLATE 21. Charter of Alfred, King of the Saxons, in favour of his 'faithful ealdorman', the Kentish Sigehelm, of land at Farleigh on the Medway, near Maidstone in 898. This single-leaf manuscript may represent a very early copy of the original and was probably drawn up at Rochester. The recipient, Sigehelm, gave his life four years later in the service of King Alfred's son, Edward, when he fell fighting in the battle of the Holme against King Alfred's nephew, Æthelwold, in 902. Sigehelm's daughter, Eadgifu, became the third wife of King Edward. Later versions of the Chronicle claim a certain Sigehelm took the alms of King Alfred to Rome in 883 (See Plate 12b above).

PLATE 22. Archaeological reconstruction of the *Crannog* or lake-dwelling on Langorse Lake, near Brecon. This site has long been associated with *Brecenanmere* a royal Welsh fortress attacked by King Alfred's daughter, Æthelflæd, Lady of the Mercians, in 917. Timbers used in the construction of this crannog have been dated to 892–3. Æthelflæd's attack casts doubt on the Pseudo-Asser's statement that in effect all of the Welsh kings had submitted to Alfred before 893 and that South Wales had already 'belonged' to the West Saxon king 'for a considerable time' before the late 880s.

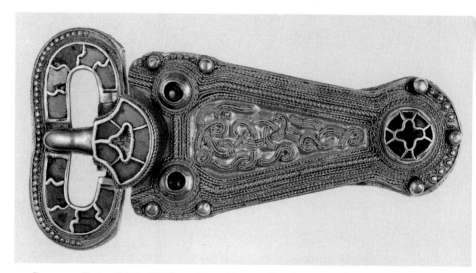

PLATE 23. Taplow Belt Buckle. One of several luxury pieces from an early seventh-century barrow overlooking the Thames at Taplow in Berkshire. Gold with filigree work and garnet inlay, this priceless piece of belt furniture reminds us that King Alfred and his son Edward the Elder were both called upon to adjudicate in a dispute involving Æthelred's belt in the Fonthill law-suit. That valuable object may have belonged to Alfred's older brother, King Æthelred I. Æthelhelm Higa who brought the charge against the man who stole the belt had the same name, *Ælthelhelm*, as King Æthelred's son. The same, or a different Æthelhelm was ealdorman of Wiltshire when he died in 897.

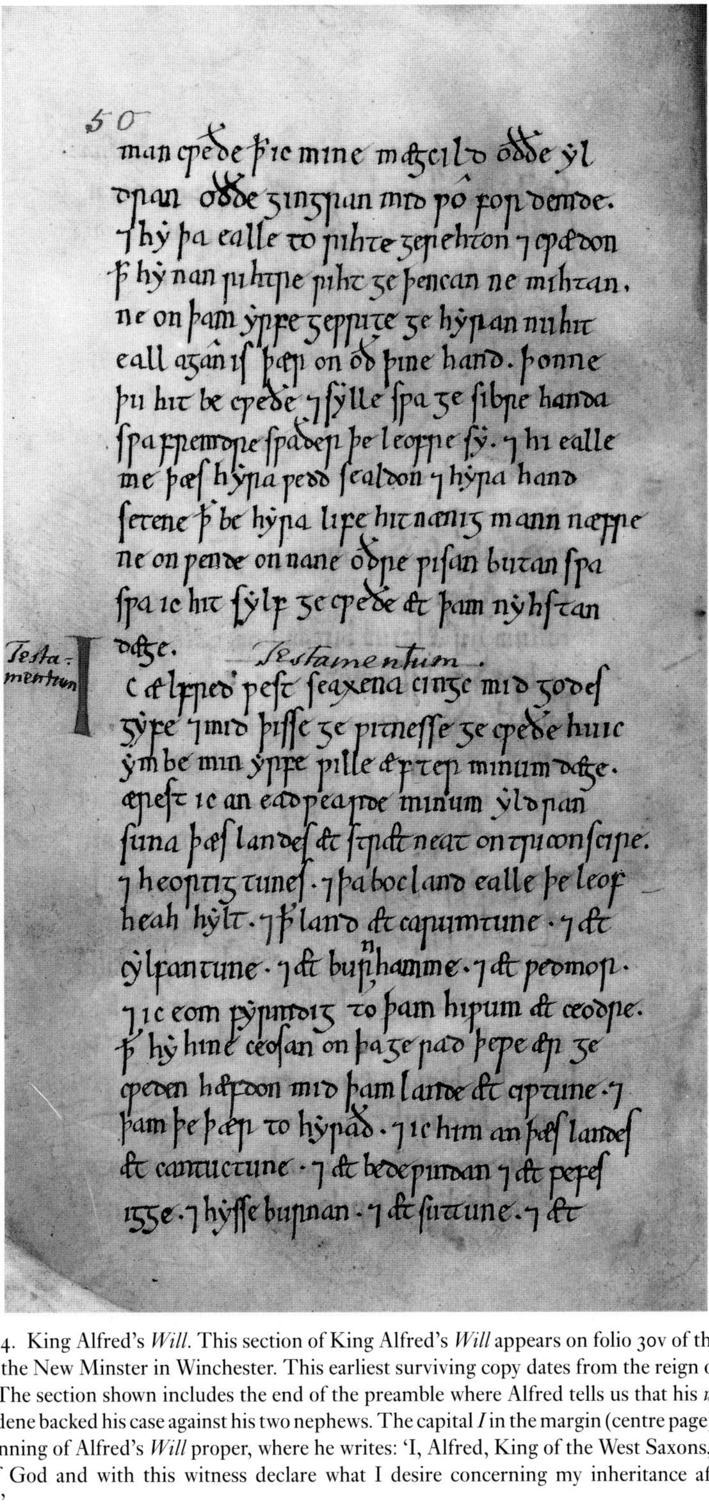

man cweðe þ ic mine mægcild oððe yl
cnan oððe zinzean mid þon for demde.
þhy þa ealle to rihte zerehton ⁊ cwædon
þ hy nan rihtre riht ze þencan ne mihtan,
ne on þam yrfe zeryhte ze hyran nuhit
eall azan if þær on oð þine hand. þonne
þu hit be cweðe ⁊ sylle spa ze sibre handa
spa frēmde spader þe leorre sy. ⁊ hi ealle
me þæf hyra peðð sealdon ⁊ hyra hand
serene þ be hyra lire hit næniz mann næfre
ne on pende on nane oðre pisan butan spa
spa ic hit sylf ze cweðe æt þam nyhstan
dæze.   Testamentum.

Ælfred wesc seaxena cinze mid zodes
zyre ⁊ mid þisse ze pitnesse ze cweðe huic
ymbe min yrre pille ærter minum dæze.
ærest ic an eadpearde minum yldran
suna þæs landes æt strætneat on tricon scire.
⁊ heortiz tunes. ⁊ þa boc land ealle þe leor
heah hylt. ⁊ þ land æt carumtune. ⁊ æt
cylrantune. ⁊ æt burhhamme. ⁊ æt peomor.
⁊ ic eom pyrndiz to þam hipum æt ceoðre.
þ hy hine ceosan on þa ze pad þepe ær ze
cpeden hærdon mid þam lande æt cirptune. ⁊
þam þe þær to hypað. ⁊ ic him an þæs landes
æt cantuctune. ⁊ æt bedepinzan ⁊ æt peres
155e. ⁊ hysse burnan. ⁊ æt surtune. ⁊ æt

PLATE 24. King Alfred's *Will*. This section of King Alfred's *Will* appears on folio 30v of the *Liber Vitae* of the New Minster in Winchester. This earliest surviving copy dates from the reign of Cnut *c*.1031. The section shown includes the end of the preamble where Alfred tells us that his *witan* at Langandene backed his case against his two nephews. The capital *I* in the margin (centre page) marks the beginning of Alfred's *Will* proper, where he writes: 'I, Alfred, King of the West Saxons, by the grace of God and with this witness declare what I desire concerning my inheritance after my lifetime.'

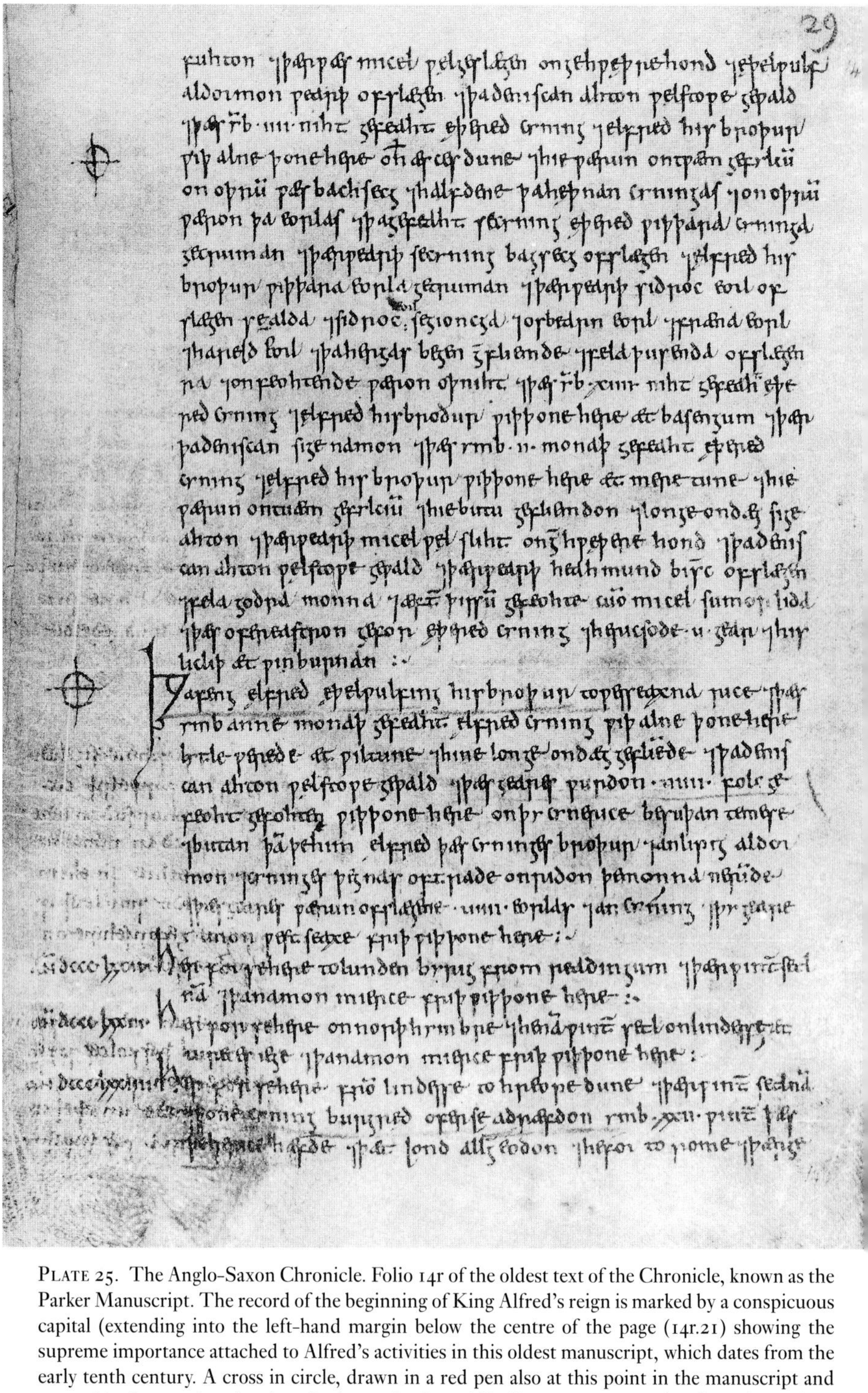

PLATE 25. The Anglo-Saxon Chronicle. Folio 14r of the oldest text of the Chronicle, known as the Parker Manuscript. The record of the beginning of King Alfred's reign is marked by a conspicuous capital (extending into the left-hand margin below the centre of the page (14r.21)) showing the supreme importance attached to Alfred's activities in this oldest manuscript, which dates from the early tenth century. A cross in circle, drawn in a red pen also at this point in the manuscript and entered in the margins elsewhere in the work where Alfred's name appears, also shows how a later annotator (in the early tenth century?) sought to highlight the career of Alfred the Great.

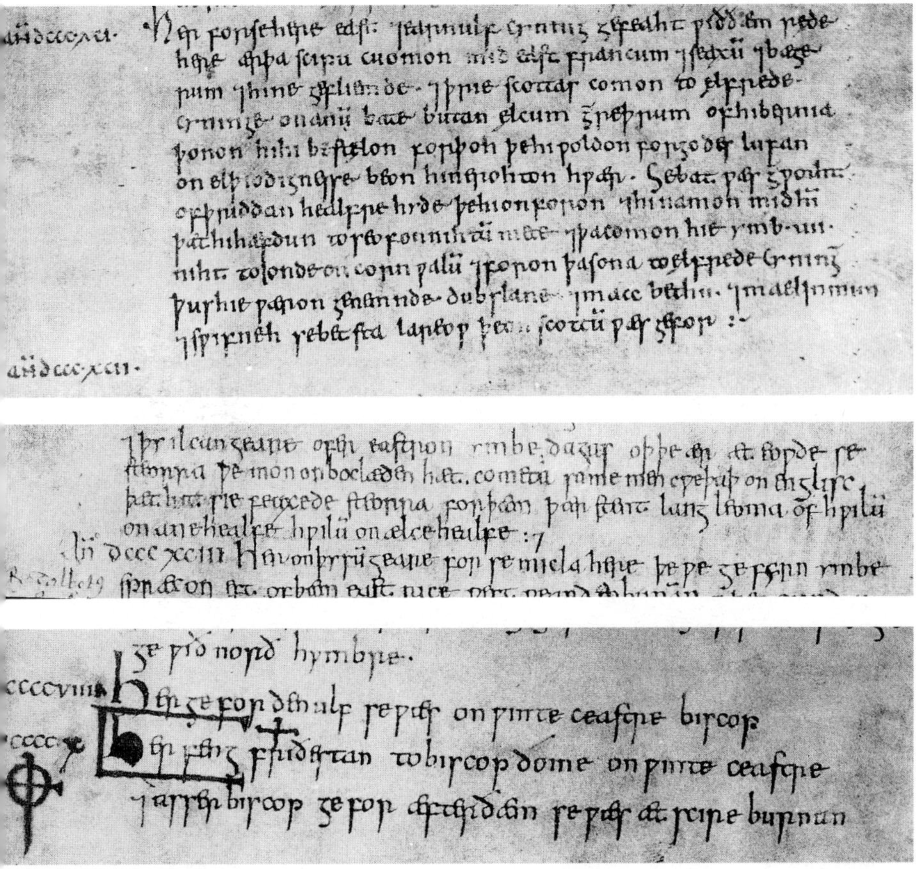

PLATE 26. Details from the Anglo-Saxon Chronicle (MS. A). (*top*) The last lines on folio 16r of the Parker Manuscript recording the arrival of three Irish travellers at the court of King Alfred. This represents the last entry by Hand One who copied the entire record from the beginning of the Chronicle down to here. Hand One also wrote the year number 892 in the margin. Hand Two took over on the top of folio 16v (*middle*) and ignoring Hand One's notice of 892, he continued with additional material for 891, recording the appearance of a comet. It does not necessarily follow that because two copiers of the original Chronicle ended and began their respective copying at this point that the original Chronicle itself ended in 891. (*bottom*) The notice of the succession of Frithestan to the bishopric of Winchester (in A.D. 909) on Folio 20v of the Parker Chronicle. The boxing of the entry, combined with the cross placed over Frithestan's name and the cross in circle in the margin are all designed to highlight this record. Frithestan may have been one of the scribes who was responsible for compiling the original Chronicle. The cross in circle is especially associated with the exploits of King Alfred in this manuscript of the Chronicle. (For Frithestan's vestments, see Plate 29.)

PLATE 27. Clonmacnoise, Co. Offaly, Ireland. Home of Suibne mac Maelumhai, the scholar whose death is reported in the Anglo-Saxon Chronicle at 891. News of Suibne's death reached the West Saxon chronicler through Irish pilgrims who visited King Alfred's court in that year. The Round Tower at Clonmacnoise was built as a look-out and a refuge against viking attack. The Cross of the Scriptures dates from the early tenth century.

(*inset*) This shows Suibne's grave-slab which was once at Clonmacnoise.

PLATE 28. Fragment of sculpture from St. Peter's Britford, Wiltshire. Little has survived in the way of stone buildings or stone carving from Alfredian Wessex. This panel showing the vine motif is one of the few examples of the West Saxon sculpture's art which has been preserved from the ninth century.

PLATE 29. The Vestments of Bishop Frithestan. The end panels of the stole (*top*) and maniple (*bottom*) bear an inscription which reads: *ÆLFFLÆD FIERI PRECEPIT / PIO EPISCOPO FRIÐESTANO* ('Ælfflæd ordered [me] to be made for the worthy bishop Frithestan'). Ælfflæd, second queen of Edward the Elder, had these vestments made for Frithestan sometime between his becoming bishop of Winchester in 909 and her death in 916. The vestments were later presented to the shrine of St. Cuthbert at Chester-le-Street, in Co. Durham, almost certainly by Alfred's grandson, King Athelstan in 934. Hence they are also known as St. Cuthbert's Vestments.

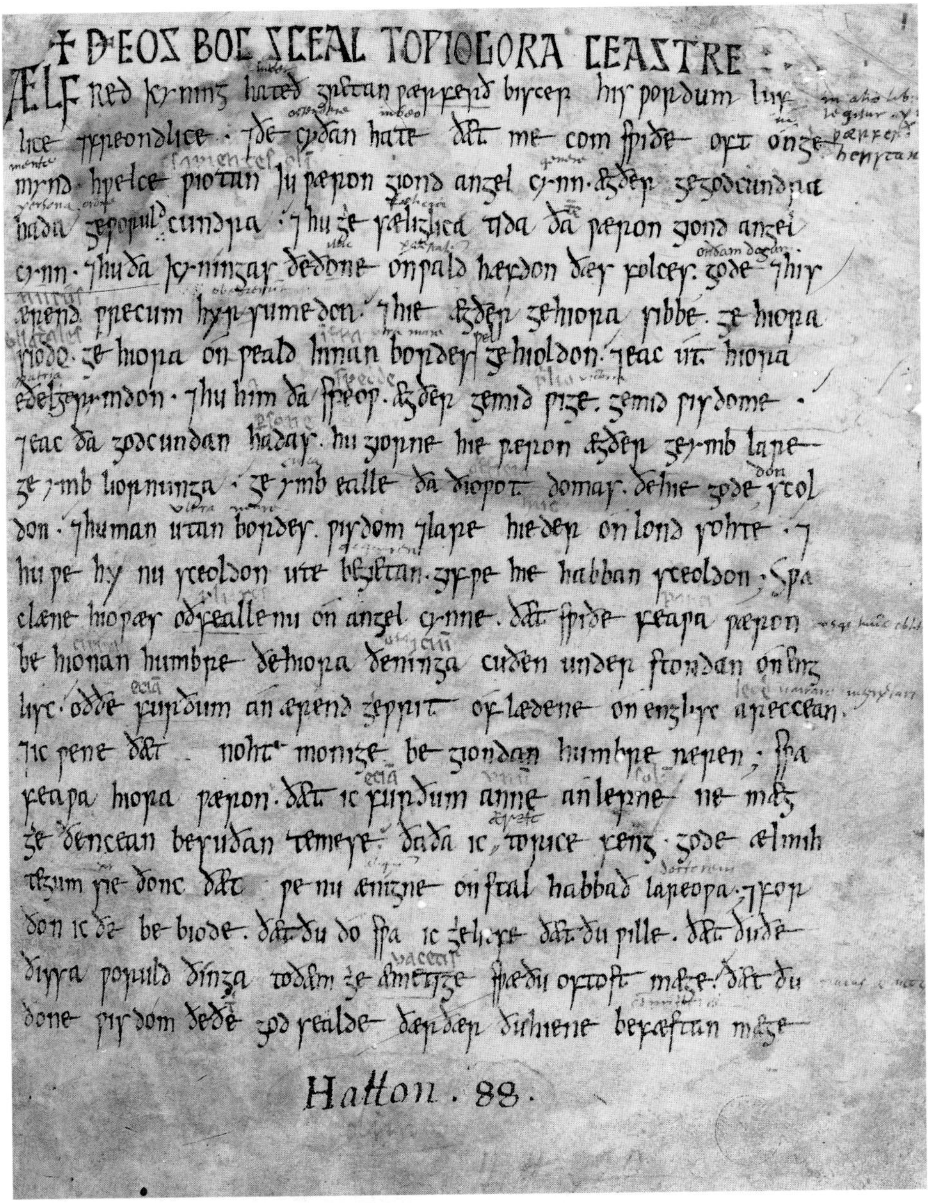

ÆLF red kyning hateð gretan Pærferð biscep his pordum luf
lice 7 freondlice · 7 ðe cyðan hate ðæt me com spiðe oft on ge
mynd · hpelce piotan iu pæron geond angel cynn · ægðer ge godcundra hada
ge poruld cundra · 7 hu gesæliglica tida ða pæron geond angel
cynn · 7 hu ða kyningas þe ðone onpald hæfdon ðæs folces gode 7 his
ærend precum hyrsumedon · 7 hie ægðer ge hiora sibbe · ge hiora
siodo · ge hiora on peald innan borde · ge hiora hiold on · 7 eac ut hiora
eðel gerymdon · 7 hu him ða speop ægðer ge mid pige · ge mid pisdome ·
7 eac ða godcundan hadas hu giorne hie pæron ægðer ge ymb lare
ge ymb liornunga · ge ymb ealle ða ðiopotu domas · ðe hie gode scol
don · 7 hu man utan borde pisdom 7 lare hieder on lond sohte · 7
hu pe hy nu sceoldon ute begietan gyf pe hie habban sceoldon · Spa
clæne hio pæs oð feallenu on angel cynne · ðæt spiðe feapa pæron
be hionan humbre ðe hiora ðeningca cuðen understondan on englisc
oððe furðum an ærend geprit of ledene on englisc areccean ·
7 ic pene ðæt noht monige be gondan humbre næren · spa
feapa hiora pæron · ðæt ic furðum anne anlepne ne mæg
geðencean besuðan temese ða ða ic to rice feng · gode ælmih
tegum sie ðonc ðæt pe nu ænigne onstal habbað lareopa 7 for
ðon ic ðe bebiode ðæt ðu do spa ic gelyfe ðæt ðu pille ðæt ðu ðe
ðissa poruld ðinga to ðæm geæmetige spa ðu oftost mæge ðæt ðu
ðone pisdom ðe ðe god sealde ðær ðer ðu hiene befæstan mæge

Hatton. 88.

PLATE 30. The opening of Alfred's Introductory Letter to his translation of Gregory's *Pastoral Care*. The text of the letter begins: 'King Alfred sends greetings to Bishop Wærferth in loving and friendly words' and across the top of the page is written in capitals: 'This book is for Worcester'. This is the original copy of the translation which the king intended for Bishop Wærferth of Worcester.

PLATE 31. King Alfred was not known as 'the Great' before the sixteenth century, but his cult as a wise and powerful king was already being promoted by Anglo-Norman writers such as Florence of Worcester, William of Malmesbury, and Henry of Huntingdon. Alfred is shown in this illustration seated (on the left) alongside the kings Edgar and Æthelred the Unready. The drawing is from a Westminster manuscript *Life* of Edward the Confessor, dating to c.1255–60 and once attributed to the chronicler Matthew Paris. King Alfred's reign was seen by later medieval illuminators and writers alike as a milestone in the development of the English monarchy.

PLATE 32. The constellation Eridanus in a Fleury manuscript of Cicero's *Aratea*.

PLATE 33. Portrait of St. Luke in a St. Vaast Gospels manuscript. The *Life* of Alfred was compiled
by a monk of the Ramsey circle (in Huntingdonshire) under the reforming and scholarly influence
of the Frankish monastery at Fleury. At that very time, other gifted English monks were in their turn
visiting Fleury. The drawing of the constellation Eridanus, found in a copy of Cicero's *Aratea* (Plate
32) was executed at Fleury by a visiting English monk who came perhaps from Winchester. That
same monk added the picture above to a Frankish Gospel book while on his way through St. Vaast at
Arras, and he performed even greater artistic marvels at St. Bertin near the Channel coast. Men and
women such as this—well travelled and steeped in the principles of Monastic Reform—were ideally
placed to carry works of Frankish hagiography and collections of Frankish annals back to centres
such as Ramsey. Such are the Frankish influences that can be seen at work in the composition of the
Life of King Alfred.

PLATE 34. Matthew Parker, archbishop of Canterbury (1559–75) was a scholar and antiquary who used his great learning to promote the cause of the Anglican Church. Archbishop Parker gave his name to the oldest manuscript (MS. A) of the Anglo-Saxon Chronicle (see Plates 25 and 26) and he published an edition of the *Life* of King Alfred in 1574. It was Parker who rescued the *Life* of Alfred from medieval obscurity and who gave it, and its royal subject, to the world.

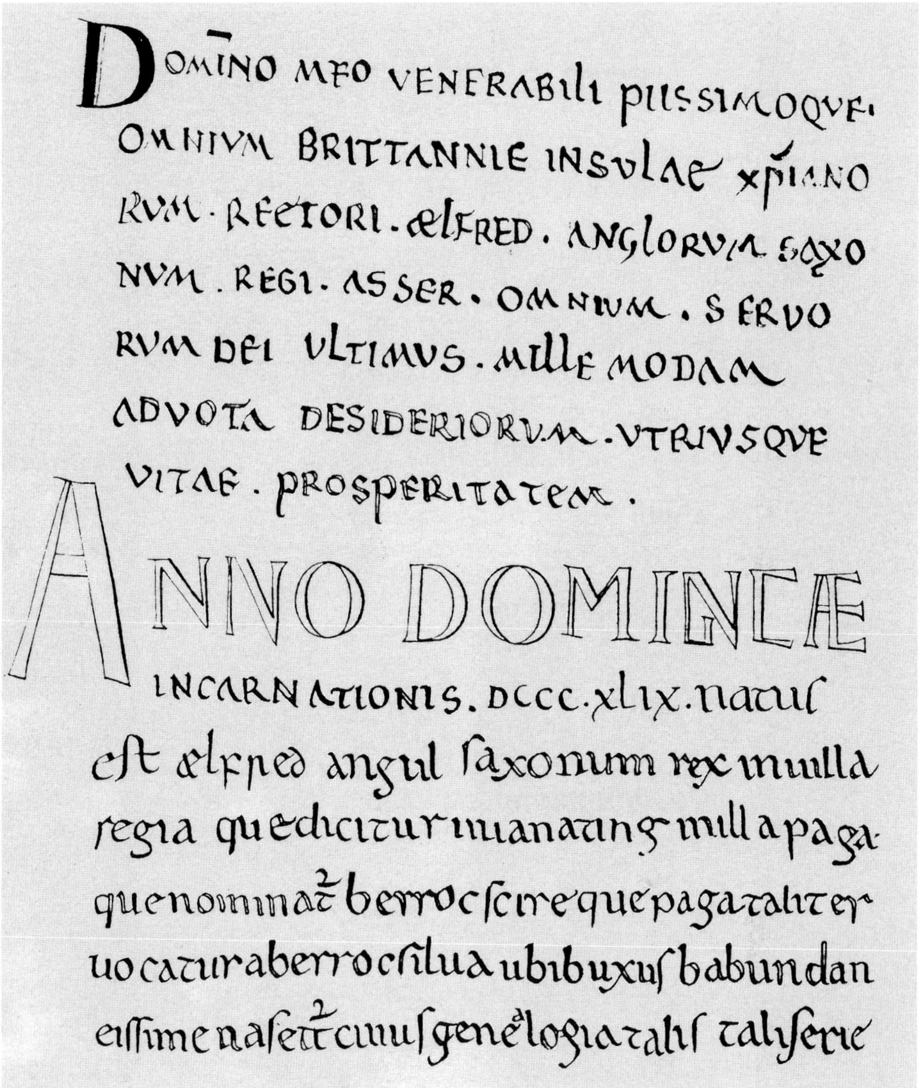

DOMINO MEO VENERABILI PIISSIMOQVE·
OMNIVM BRITTANNIE INSVLAE XPIANO
RVM · RECTORI · ÆLFRED · ANGLORVM SAXO
NVM · REGI · ASSER · OMNIVM · SERVO
RVM DEI VLTIMVS · MILLE MODAM
ADVOTA DESIDERIORVM · VTRIVSQVE
VITAE · PROSPERITATEM ·

ANNO DOMINCÆ
INCARNATIONIS · DCCC · XLIX · natuſ
eſt ælfred angul ſaxonum rex in villa
regia que dicitur in anating mill a paga
que nominat berroc ſcire que paga taliter
uocatur a berro cſilua ubi buxuſ babundan
eiſſime naſett cuiuſ genelogia taliſ talyſeric

PLATE 35. Facsimile of opening lines of *The Life of King Alfred* attributed to Asser. This record does not represent a facsimile in the modern sense. It was published by Francis Wise in his 1722 edition of the *Life* of King Alfred and provides us with a drawing supplied for Wise's edition by the antiquary, James Hill. The drawing includes the Dedication and the first seven lines of the *Life* proper, recording the birth of Alfred supposedly at Wantage in Berkshire. The evidence from this drawing would suggest a date for the Cotton Otho A.xii manuscript of c.1000–25 and its importance rests on the fact that the original manuscript was destroyed by fire in 1731—only nine years after the publication of this precious drawing.

PLATE 36. Statue of King Alfred in Winchester. Erected in 1901 to mark the millennial celebrations of Alfred's death. Queen Victoria and Prince Albert had named their younger son after Alfred the Great, and in 1901 a grateful and self-confident nation saw in Alfred of Wessex the genius of Anglo-Saxon civilization and the beginnings of imperial greatness.

of the kingdom. Use of naïve language has not always been helpful, where words such as 'dish-thegn' and 'cup-bearer' have helped to conjure up images of an unreal world peopled by a king who supposedly received unswerving loyalty from gnome-like followers whose only function in life would appear to have been attendance on their lord. Nothing could be further from the reality of a warrior class, bred to independence of action and life-style, and many of whom ruled vast stretches of inaccessible countryside with the powers of kings all but in name.

Historians ascribe to King Æthelwulf a key role in setting the West Saxon dynasty on a new course in the middle of the ninth century. He is seen to have treated the kingship of Wessex in an absolute manner, first by bequeathing the kingdom in his *Will* to his two older sons, and secondly by a bizarrely complicated and novel arrangement whereby his older boys were granted the kingship for their lifetimes only, and in which Æthelwulf planned that 'what amounts to the reversion of Wessex' should eventually come—kingship and all—into the hands of his younger sons, Æthelred and Alfred.[10] Æthelwulf, then, is seen to disinherit the descendants of his older sons in favour of his infant children, and he is seen, too, as striving to hold together the estates of the royal kindred of Wessex, consciously forming an undivided inheritance to finance the treasury of that strong monarchy which he presumably foresaw would come into being in the mid-tenth century. All this is supposed to have been achieved unilaterally by a West Saxon king, with the acquiescence of his royal kindred, and in detachment from his *witan*, who as the representatives of the interests of the warrior aristocracy had their rights presumably abrogated by an unstoppable ageing king. This myth relating to the providential progression of the House of Alfred from strength to strength, and from king to king, was not invented by modern historians. It was already built into the medieval historiography of the subject. It began with Alfred's own conscious reconstruction in his *Will*—and perhaps also indirectly at least in the Chronicle—of what he wished us to see of his special relationship with a father, whom he probably only dimly remembered. Alfred's purpose in inventing recent family history was designed to consolidate his own position within the kingdom. The compiler of Alfred's *Life* took up that theme and expanded on it in a grotesque way by resorting to folklore and to further invention. While the Pseudo-Asser and perhaps even Alfred himself wished us to believe that Æthelwulf had planned by means of a *Will* for the ultimate succession of his infant son, later Anglo-Norman chroniclers added their own contemporary views of royal succession to complicate the Alfredian saga yet further. Florence (*alias* 'John') of Worcester claimed that Edward the Elder bequeathed (*reliquit*) his kingdom to Athelstan.[11] William of Malmesbury, writing in the second quarter of the twelfth century, took the mythology of the House of Alfred a considerable stage further. According to Malmesbury, Alfred's son and heir, Edward the Elder, arranged by his 'command and testament (*jussu et testamento*)' for the succession of his son, Athelstan to the kingship of Wessex, and we are told that Athelstan's grandfather, King Alfred, 'had formerly prayed for a prosperous reign for him' marking the infant off for special favours by making him a 'knight (*militem fecerat*)' and presenting him with special regalia.[12]

Already by the twelfth century, a historical pattern had been invented, involving Æthelwulf's special favour shown to Alfred, which continued in turn from Alfred to Athelstan, thereby endowing the pre-Norman kingship of England with a specious harmony and unchallenged succession which in reality it never possessed. From the time of Stevenson onwards, the parallel was not lost on modern historians between the regalia supposedly given by Alfred to Athelstan, and the insignia of the consulship which Pope Leo IV allegedly gave to the infant Alfred in Rome in 853.[13] The otherwise cautious Stevenson even toyed with the outlandish idea that the regalia given by Alfred to Athelstan 'were the very ornaments that Alfred received from the pope', noting also the 'striking coincidence' that Athelstan was then about the same age as Alfred when he was supposedly clothed in the consular vestments in Rome.[14] More recent historians have fallen for the constitutional implications in this elaborate myth, by concluding that the continuity of the royal succession 'was made effective by *wills* of successive rulers—Æthelwulf, Alfred and Edward the Elder'.[15] Yet this speculative conclusion was reached in the face of evidence which shows that both Edward and Athelstan had their right to the kingship seriously challenged; that both resorted to bloodshed to defend it; and that Athelstan's succession to the kingship may have been as great an accident of history as the succession of his grandfather, King Alfred.

So much modern interpretation of the Anglo-Saxon past hinges on the optimistic assumption that West Saxon society progressed relentlessly and steadily from more primitive to more developed forms of kingship and government. The *post hoc propter hoc* argument is disguised in a welter of assumptions generated by an overall thesis that not only were there evolutionary forces relentlessly working towards more advanced forms of kingship, but that rulers of that age were also consciously manipulating those forces in their favour. We can, of course, identify major changes in kingship right across north-western Europe in the ninth and tenth centuries—changes imposed on Scandinavian, English, and Celtic societies by the two major forces for change at that time, namely, the overwhelming cultural influence of the Carolingian Empire and the upheavals of the viking wars. Carolingian ideology on the role of emperors as super-kings with a mandate to defend Western Christendom, together with the widespread elimination of tribal and provincial kings in the face of viking attack in the later ninth century, left the way open for survivors in the next century to established dynasties on a much more ambitious territorial basis. But there is no evidence to show that Æthelwulf of Wessex was consciously exploiting those forces for change to the advantage of his own posterity. Carolingian influence of Æthelwulf's court may have been comparatively slight, and the outcome of the viking onslaught was still far in the future during Æthelwulf's reign. His aims, in so far as we can understand them at all, were much more immediate, more modest, and personal. His concern, and that of his magnates for the safety of Wessex during his absence abroad, prompted him prudently to secure the kingship on his two older sons who were best suited to defending Wessex from viking attack. We have seen that Æthelwulf's provision in his *Will* for his infant sons during their minority, and eventually when they would come of age, only formed one of many bequests within his *Will*. We have seen, too, how this provision was prompted by a desire on the part of King Æthelwulf to provide land for all his male children, even for those who had not yet reached manhood, and that it had nothing whatever to do with the kingship of Wessex. Those historians who follow King Alfred's restricted reporting and interpretation of his father's *Will* have come to regard the role of Æthelbald and Æthelberht as mere caretakers set up by their father to hold the West Saxon kingship in trust until such time as the boy Alfred—already 'heir apparent'—would come into the fullness of his royal inheritance. By this far-fetched interpretation, any children whom Æthelbald might have had, or planned to have, by the Carolingian Judith, would be disinherited under the terms of King Æthelwulf's *Will*. Æthelbald's apocryphal rebellion against his father was consequently seen by Ann Williams, for instance, as an attempt to assert his right to found a dynasty of his own in Wessex.[16] We are reminded of the competing theory of Dumville, whereby Æthelbald's brother, Æthelberht, was positively encouraged by his father King Æthelwulf to found just such a separate dynasty in Kent.[17] On the basis of such competing speculations, the wonder is how the ninth-century kingdom of Wessex did not fragment and revert into the constituent parts from which it had emerged in the century before.

Few if any modern commentators on West Saxon royal succession have shown an awareness of the important role played by the West Saxon royal council. Historians invariably treat the subject of royal succession as if it were a private family matter of no concern to anyone apart from King Æthelwulf and his sons. We seem to have reached the ludicrous situation where we accept that concern for the eventual succession of the infant Alfred had assumed a greater urgency in the 850s than the day-to-day survival of the West Saxon aristocracy in the face of the viking menace. The thorny problem of just who was eligible to succeed to the kingship of the West Saxons and precisely how the succession was decided is so central to any study of King Alfred's place in English history that it must be looked at in some detail. Unfortunately, little early English documentation survives which has an immediate bearing on established custom in relation to royal succession in Alfredian times, and we are thrown back largely on evidence from contemporary medieval societies elsewhere within Europe and on reviewing English evidence both before and after Alfred's reign. In trying to answer the question as to how West Saxon kings were chosen for their office, the comparative approach while useful is also fraught with difficulty. Practice varied widely across Early Germanic Europe[18] and when studying English evidence from the eighth to the eleventh centuries, we need to allow for due process of change and for variation in regional custom. While the Visigoths had an elective kingship in the eighth century, King concluded that: 'it is more accurate to speak of an occupative throne, for prior association, designation and simple usurpation all played significant roles'.[19] The Frankish kingship was hereditary but it experienced the fate of other partitive inheritance followed by that people, and a study of the Frankish succession cannot be said to show that it conformed to a given set of rules. As Wood reminded us, while 'any prince had a claim to the throne', succession to Merovingian Kingship depended in part on the ability of a successful candidate making good his 'claim with the support of some portion of the aristocracy or by gaining the approval of one of the kings already in power'.[20] It is also difficult to decide—especially among the Goths—which aspects of their succession procedures were influenced by Roman and Byzantine practice, and which were truly Germanic.[21]

The starting-point which receives general agreement among scholars is that where a hereditary royal succession was practised, then all those male members who were recognized to belong to the *stirps regia* were regarded as being 'throne worthy' or eligible for office. In Anglo-Saxon England a male member of the royal kindred was called an *ætheling*, a word which may be translated as 'prince of the royal house'.[22] While Dumville successfully demonstrated the term has nothing whatever to do with the notion of an 'heir apparent', it is equally clear that æthelings were no ordinary princes, for all the indications are that they were princes who were eligible for kingship and it is to that fact that they owed their special status and title. Dumville's observation that an ætheling 'shared with the reigning king descent from a common grandfather at least'[23] is paralleled by the practice if not indeed the theory of contemporary procedures in relation to Irish royal succession. In Ireland, members of the royal kindred or *derbfhine* ('certain family') were described as *rigdamnai* or 'king-material', and formed a kin-group claiming descent from a common great-grandfather and extending to second cousins.[24] Recognition of 'throne worthiness' both in Ireland and Anglo-Saxon England depended on possession of a genealogy which traced a candidate's immediate royal descent back to a remote common royal ancestor and ultimately to the tribal gods. In the case of Wessex, the house of Alfred claimed descent from Cerdic and indeed from the Germanic wargod, Woden. In practice, those male heirs whose fathers or grandfathers had held the kingship were considered throne-worthy, but more distant relatives or rank outsiders might also seize the kingship and by a genealogical fiction claim descent from a common royal ancestor. The descent of several Northumbrian and Mercian kings in the eighth and early ninth centuries is not at all clear, and Alfred's own genealogy at seventh and eighth-century levels is not beyond suspicion. In Alfred's lifetime, and only four years before he became king, his own West Saxon chronicle informs us that the Northumbrians in 867 'had deposed their king, Osberht, and taken a king with no hereditary right (*ungecyndne cyning*), Ælla'. This record can be read in different ways. On the one hand, it shows it was considered proper for a king to descend from a line of known royal ancestors: on the other hand, kingship might go to the strongest contender among a group of outsiders. Within the royal kindred, both in Anglo-Saxon England and in Celtic Ireland there may have been a preference for the eldest son to succeed, but primogeniture as such was never formally practised. Since the king had to fulfil the all-important function of war-leader, youthful eldest sons might be passed over in favour of more experienced older uncles or cousins, or an elder son might be passed over in favour of a more capable younger brother. The Old Irish adage from the law tract, *Seanchas Már*, would have found ready assent in contemporary England: 'Elder for kin, worth for rulership, wisdom for the church'[25] and in citing that adage, early Irish jurists justified the giving of kingship to more able junior members of royal kindreds. It is true that from the time of Ecgberht of Wessex (802–39) down into the second half of the tenth century, the West Saxon dynasty was practising a *de facto* form of primogeniture, but the special circumstances in which this developed needs identifying. First, there was a ready supply of mature elder sons, and secondly, in Wessex as in Ireland, one of the effects of the constant emergency caused by the viking wars was to promote a narrowing of the succession to within one cellular family, and (in the case of Wessex) from father to elder son within that family. It is rarely pointed out, however, that Alfred's own succession to the kingship broke that very pattern in Wessex, for if primogeniture had been rigorously followed at that time, either the ætheling, Æthelwold or Athelhelm would have followed their father King Æthelred in the kingship, and their uncle, Alfred, and all Alfred's descendants—including Athelstan—might never have come to power.

This brings us to the problem that however much the term 'ætheling' came, for all practical purposes, to mean 'royal candidate', we still do not know how the successful royal candidate was chosen from among other æthelings. The solution to this problem must lie in our understanding of the relationship between the king and his council, which in Wessex included leading churchmen—the bishops of Winchester and Sherborne as well as the archbishop of Canterbury—and leading aristocrats from the shires—the earldormen and greater thegns. Did these men have a say in the choosing of their king? If they did, then we have yet another reason to dispose of the notion that kingship was passed on by means of a royal *Will* from father to son or grandson rather like the apocryphal regalia which Alfred is said to have presented to Athelstan.

The reign of Alfred is pivotal to our understanding of Anglo-Saxon history, and an understanding of the role of his *witan*, therefore, is essential for any study of this king. The evidence relating to the function of any Anglo-Saxon king's councillors is at best scrappy and is usually recorded by way of references which are tangential to the interests of the medieval recorder. That being so, our investigation of this crucial issue must often lead us away from the person of Alfred into the reigns of his descendants and successors before we can eventually draw conclusions about that king's relationship with his own 'wise men'. The digression is both necessary and rewarding, however, if we are ever to understand Alfred's political relationship with the great men of his kingdom. There can be few institutions more poorly understood by modern historians than the royal council or *witenagemot* of Old English kings. Indeed the very existence of this body of councillors is called into question by Oleson who held that 'strictly there is no witenagemot, there are only witan'[26]—in other words, there was no corporate body of councillors as such, only the individual 'wise men (*witan*)' who deliberated with the king. As for the function of the *witan*, that, too, in Oleson's view was equally vague—'they might participate in all the acts of government or in none'.[27] Oleson would, of course, agree that even to speak of 'acts of government' in relation to ninth-century Wessex, where a state as we know it did not exist, is in danger of pointing any enquiry in the wrong direction. Stenton's opinion on the function of the council was equally vague if not deliberately ambiguous: 'It was the duty of the council to advise the king on any problems which he might choose to bring to its notice.'[28] But in Stenton's view, the initiative lay with the king who had the council—however powerful its individual members might be—securely in his pocket. Prior to Oleson's study of the *witenagemot* in the Confessor's reign, there were two schools of thought relating to the function and power of the royal council. What may be described as the 'positive' school represented by Kemble, Liebermann, Freeman, and Stubbs held that the council enjoyed 'a consultative voice, and the right to consider every public act, which could be authorised by the king'.[29] The *witan* were involved in the promulgation of new laws, entering into treaties, the election and deposition of kings, the appointment of bishops, the levying of taxes, and the conversion of folkland into bookland.[30] The 'negative school', on the other hand, led by Purlitz and Chadwick denied the power of the *witan* in varying degrees especially in relation to the election and deposition of kings, the election of bishops, the promulgation of laws, and the levying of taxes.[31]

Oleson favoured the more negative position of Chadwick in denying both the corporate nature of the *witenagemot* and the power which individual *witan* were believed by Kemble to have exercised over the king. Oleson regarded discussions relating to the number of *witan* who attended councils as of central importance, for he denied any distinction between larger and smaller councils. Setting out from the assumption that it was a burden for most thegns to attend at court, he con- cluded that normally, a council was attended only by officials of the royal household and by those greater and lesser thegns of that region which the king and his household might happen to be visiting at any particular time.[32] Oleson denied the idea of great councils which were 'summoned', as opposed to more *ad hoc* gatherings which gravitated about the court of the king as it moved through the shires, although he did concede some councils might have constituted larger *witenagemots* by virtue of their being held 'on one of the high feasts of the church'—Christmas, Easter, or Michaelmas.[33] Discussions on constitutional issues which are held in the abstract are liable to lose touch with reality. It is difficult to envisage any meeting of Alfred's council which was not summoned in some sense—if only to let those present know that it was to take place in the first instance. As it happens, we learn from Bishop Wærferth of Worcester, that when King Alfred's son-in-law, Æthelred, became Lord of the Mercians in *c*.883, 'he summoned (*gesamnode*) the Mercian council (*Mercna weotan*) to Droitwich'.[34] The context of that Mercian gathering suggests it was a solemn affair 'dealing with many necessary matters both spiritual and temporal'. While Stubbs put the numbers present in pre-ninth-century meet- ings of the council at about 20, he reckoned on tenth-century gatherings approaching 100 members. Morris reckoned the number of councillors in any one assembly at anything from fifty to a hundred.[35] Oleson approached the subject from a different perspective. Starting from the premise that every act of the king must be in conformity with the law, it was clearly in the king's interest to consult those who spoke for the community, but consultation with the *witan* did not, in Oleson's opinion, lend legality to the actions of the king.[36] The king might seek to consult his council or he might act alone, and he might choose to consult few or many of his councillors: 'An Anglo-Saxon king may consult all his witan or only a few of them, but the meeting whether large or small, will, according to the ideas of the Anglo-Saxons, rank as a witenagemot.'[37] Oleson would have to qualify his own statement by claiming that the councillors would not have been conscious of their collegiality when consulted by their king.

So far so good. Most historians would, I think, agree with Oleson that the *witan* either in the Confessor's reign or in the reign of Alfred or his father, did not constitute a national assembly 'with definite rights and fixed functions'.[38] We would also emphatically agree that 'they were not representatives of the nation in the nineteenth-century meaning of that word'. But safe assertions about what the royal council was not, may not help us to understand what in reality it was. Alfred's own writings reflect a view of the royal council which does not bear out Oleson's discussion in the abstract. Oleson saw the *witan* as nothing more than a number of local magnates dropping in on the king's household, whenever he happened to be in the locality, and he saw it as their function to 'counsel' the king, which in effect was to rubber-stamp whatever public actions the king wished to propose. Alfred himself sketched a very different picture for us in his own writings. His version of Augustine's *Soliloquies* portrays a royal assembly as an awesome occasion, where the magnates make great efforts and overcome great obstacles to assemble in the king's presence:

Consider now whether many men ever come to the king's estate (*ham*) when he is in residence there, or to his assembly (*gemot*), or to his army (*fird*), and whether it seems to you that they all come thither by the same road. I think, however, that they come by very many different roads: some come from a great distance and have a very long, very bad and very difficult road; some have a very long and very straight and very good road; some have a very short, yet crooked, narrow, and miry road; some have a short and smooth and straight one. . . . Some are in greater honour and greater comfort than others. . . . Some men are in his [the king's] chamber (*on bure*), some in the hall (*on healle*), some on the threshing floor (*on odene*), some in prison (*on carcerne*).[39]

This account of a journey to a royal assembly is presented with a very real sense of purpose, which contemporary readers of Alfred's difficult philosophical text were expected to instantly recognize and identify with. There is surely implicit in this passage the sense, that all those engaged on the weary and difficult journey to the court of their king had been summoned or were otherwise obligated to travel. Not only were the thegns and ealdormen of this literary image converging on the king's estate from all quarters, but their numbers were so great that many had to make do by cramming into the out-buildings on the king's farm. We shall see, that while Alfred had a highly developed sense of the exalted status of his own kingship, he also indicates in his writings that such gatherings at the court might be fraught with tension and involve decisions being imposed on the king against his own will and judgement.[40] Common sense dictates that the politics of power and patronage must have involved the king and his great men in a two-way relationship,

where on occasion at least, the ruler had to bow to the wishes of his leading
supporters in matters where their loyalty had to be ensured.

Not all meetings between Alfred and his magnates saw the king on his dignity.
We have already encountered Alfred adjudicating between his great men when 'the
king stood in the chamber (*innan ðon bure*) at Wardour, washing his hands'.[41] But
if we accept, with Oleson, that councils convened on great festival days of the
church were conspicuously better attended than those held at other times, then by
analogy with the significance of the liturgical calendar, the greater councils must
have assumed greater solemnity and sense of purpose than those associated with
the day-to-day running of the shires. In other words, such councils would have
suggested themselves both to the king and to his *witan* as opportunities to convey
specially important information or to transact specially important business. So, for
instance, it seemed plausible to the Pseudo-Asser, writing at the turn of the
millenium, to make Alfred reward his tutor with grants of monasteries and monastic estates on Christmas Eve, when the king would be understood to be holding his
Christmas court.[42] Alfred's father, King Æthelwulf, was understood by forgers to
have issued a whole series of grants involving his so-called First Decimation at his
Easter court, held at Wilton in April 854. Two charters survive from the early
ninth and mid-tenth centuries respectively, which were issued on the day of an
Anglo-Saxon king's consecration. The earlier is a grant (Sawyer 186, Birch 370)
issued by Ceolwulf I of Mercia to Archbishop Wulfred of Canterbury, on the day
(17 September 822) that Ceolwulf was consecrated by the archbishop.[43] The second
example is a grant (Sawyer 520, Birch 815) by King Eadred to Wulfric in 946, in
which document, incidentally, we are informed that Eadred had been 'chosen by
the election of the nobles (*electione optimatum subrogatus*)'.[44] It was probably expected that a new king should inaugurate his reign by a display of largesse to his
electing nobles.

If we concede that it was incumbent on the king to be seen to act within the law,
then it follows that it was in the king's best interest to gain the assent of as many
of his great men as possible if he were about to embark upon an enterprise, the
legality of which might be in some doubt. On King Alfred's own evidence, his
handling of the inheritance of his deceased brother, King Æthelred, was just such
a case in point. While the fate of Æthelred's private property did not relate to the
kingship of Wessex *per se*, clearly whoever controlled that property had access to
political power and patronage, and the matter was therefore one which impinged
not only on the interests of the king, but on that of the magnates of Wessex as well.
Alfred tells us that when disputes arose relating to his handling of his brother
Æthelred's inheritance, he had his father Æthelwulf's *Will* 'read before all the
councillors of the West Saxons (*eallum Westseaxena witum*)'—councillors who had
assembled at the *gemot* at *Langandene*.[45] While accepting Oleson's warning in
another context of the vague usage of the word *all* in medieval documents, there
is no doubt that King Alfred wished to convey the sense in his *Will* that he had the
support of the great majority of his *witan* in relation to this family dispute. Indeed
he uses the phrase 'all the councillors of the West Saxons' in his *Will* no less than

four times, referring more generally to 'the councillors of the West Saxons' in two further instances. Alfred's *Will* provides powerful evidence for the high profile of the *witan* in the political life of this Early English king. There is also the strong suggestion in Alfred's *Will* that two of the witenagemots attended by all the *witan* were those convened at the election of Æthelberht and later at the election of Æthelred to the West Saxon kingship—councils convened to elect successors to the kings Æthelbald and Æthelberht respectively. If we accept this evidence from Alfred himself—and there is no reason why we should not—then it is difficult to avoid the conclusion that such gatherings, affecting the affairs of all the magnates of the kingdom, were not in some way 'summoned'. Equally, if we accept that greater gatherings of *witan* were expected on the great church festivals, then those meetings, too, were *de facto* 'summoned' if only by virtue of their place being fixed at set points in the church's calendar. But Alfred tells us much more. When his father's *Will* was read aloud to all the *witan* at *Langandene*, Alfred urged his councillors 'to declare what was right' and 'to expound the common law (*folcriht*)' in relation to his treatment of his nephews' share in his dead brother's property.[46] What is crucially important here is Alfred's own assertion that his *witan* sat in judgement and heard the case brought before it either by Alfred or by his nephews. This would seem to undermine Stenton's cautious idea that the initiative always lay with the king in matters relating to consultation with his council. On Alfred's own authority the council is seen to have had a judicial role in matters even pertaining to the king's private inheritance, for they heard the case, considered the evidence of his father's *Will* and then gave a judgement based on the *folcriht* or customary laws of the West Saxons. Indeed, Alfred's Law Code—according to the king's own Introduction to that Code—was drawn up with the advice of his *witan*, and when completed was presented to them for their acceptance. It is not possible in the face of this evidence to accept the view of Chadwick and Oleson that the *witan* in Alfredian times at least, acted merely as individuals and cannot have been conscious of their collective role *vis-à-vis* their king. As soon as we move away from confining the role of Alfred's *witan* to merely assenting to royal acts, and acknowledge their judicial and deliberative function, then we must concede an element of corporate identity to the members of the king's council. That in turn leads on to recognizing the *witan* as a faction within the kingdom, with whom the king had to establish a working relationship. This is in no way to see the *witan* as a 'college' which towered above the king,[47] but it does involve a retreat to a common-sense position much closer to that of Stubbs than to that of Chadwick.

Even if we were only to accept a state of partnership between the king and his councillors, in which the latter were a pliable party, we are compelled to recognize the special status of the *witan* at that one crucial point in the political life of a kingdom—namely on the death of a king.[48] For if the *witan* were conscious—as they must have been—of their corporate power as an influential group within the kingdom during the life of the king, how much more conscious must they have been of their key role *vis-à-vis* the royal kindred at the moment of a king's death.

Chadwick strenuously denied, in the face of all the evidence, that the *witan* had
any meaningful role in the election of a king. He argued that while members of the
council had individual obligations and privileges in relation to the king, who was
their immediate lord, as a body the council as such had little or no consultative or
constitutional role. At most Chadwick grudgingly conceded: 'There is no necessity
to believe that a formal vote took place at all. Most of the king's thegns individually
selected for themselves a new lord and carried with them the provinces which they
governed.'[49] Oleson fully endorsed Chadwick's view that 'election very likely meant
simply recognition by the witan . . . through some such act as the swearing of an
oath of allegiance'.[50] He pointed to the Anglo-Saxon Chronicle's record of how in
920, the Scots, Strathclyde Britons, and English and Northmen of Northumbria
all 'chose (Edward the Elder) as father and lord (*hine geces þa to fæder 7 to
hlaforde*)'[51] to show that whatever else was meant by that record it could not be
referring to an election 'in our sense of the word'.[52] But that particular entry in the
Chronicle does not pretend to record a royal election to a tribal or provincial
kingship such as that of the West Saxons. It is rather a complex record of the
acceptance of Edward's overlordship by different peoples in the north of Britain,
perhaps even at different times.[53] It may well have involved not only kings, incidentally, but their *witan* also.[54] As for the choosing of a king on the death of his
predecessor, an election 'in our sense' did not necessarily have to involve the
formal casting of votes in an assembly. It could have meant simply the lobbying of
members of the *witan* to the extent of securing a majority backing from the great
landowners of the kingdom. How precisely such a majority was secured or recognized matters little. What is crucial is our recognition that the *witan* had a meaningful
say in the choosing of the new king.

Bede[55] relates how the Mercians threw off the overlordship of Oswiu of Northumbria in 657 when three of their ealdormen rose in rebellion and 'set up as their
king (*levato in regem*) Wulfhere, Penda's young son, whom they had kept concealed'.
Here we see, both the importance of royal blood and the crucial role of the leading
magnates in staging a *coup* and organizing the succession. The evidence from Bede
was treated in a cavalier way by Chadwick, who dismissed Bede's implied election
of Wulfhere to the Mercian kingship on the grounds that 'this was a case of
revolution'—all this in spite of Chadwick's own warnings elsewhere, against labelling
some cases of succession as 'constitutional' and others as 'revolutionary'![56] It is true
that the successful 'election' of a rival candidate for kingship might have been
nothing more than successful rebellion. Nevertheless, the fact that such rebellions
were spearheaded by the *witan*—or by that class from which the *witan* were
drawn—shows that the leading aristocrats were possessed of a forum through
which they could effectively organize, when and if a political crisis demanded it.
Whitelock was clearly not convinced of Chadwick's arguments. She accepted that
in 757 the West Saxon council played a major role in deposing Sigeberht from the
kingship and replacing him by Cynewulf, and that in 774, King Alhred of
Northumbria as reported in Byrhtferth's Northumbrian Chronicle in the *Historia
Regum* 'was deprived of the society of the royal household and nobles, by the

counsel and consent of all his people'.[57] The mention of *concilium* ('council' or 'assembly') and *consensus* ('agreement') in the account of Alhred's deposition points to the involvement of the Northumbrian *witan* in this affair. Earlier in 759, that same *witan* had again taken the initiative and elected Æthelwold Moll to the kingship of Northumbria after the assassination of King Oswulf by his own thegns (*a suis ministris*).[58] Æthelwold we are told 'was elected by his people (*a sua plebe electus*)'. Nor does the evidence rest here, however much Chadwick tried to explain it away. In the Northumbrian Danelaw in the tenth century it is clear that the *witan* as an institution had survived the conquest by the Great Danish Army back in 866–7, and that it continued to play a leading role in the making and breaking of kings, even if now those leaders were Danes rather than Angles. 'Archbishop Wulfstan and all the councillors of the Northumbrians (*Wulstan se arcebiscop 7 ealle Norðhymbra witan*)' are specifically named in the Anglo-Saxon Chronicle in 947 and 948 as changing their allegiance from King Eadred of Wessex to the Norwegian, Eric Bloodaxe, and from Eric back to Eadred yet again.[59] Several of those councillors, if not indeed their archbishop, may have been Englishmen, and they were still known collectively, almost a hundred years after the conquest of the Danelaw, by their English title of *witan*.

There is no reason to assume that the situation regarding royal succession and the power of the *witan*, together with its peripheral thegns in Wessex, was any different from that in Northumbria, with the important proviso that in Wessex the house of Ecgberht had managed to get a hold on the kingship which no single kindred in Northumbria had managed to achieve. References to the West Saxon *witan* either choosing their king, or offering or withholding their support for kings are too frequent and too significant to be ignored. The Anglo-Saxon Chronicle's reporting of the deposition of Sigeberht by the councillors of Wessex back in 757 yields further information on closer inspection. Sigeberht's brother, Cyneheard, eventually avenged Sigeberht's deposition and slaying by killing, in his turn, King Cynewulf who had succeeded Sigeberht. Cyneheard was seeking more than just revenge. He also wanted the kingship of the West Saxons which had once been enjoyed by his brother. But he could not achieve this on his own. When the stronghold at *Meretun* where Cyneheard was holding out was surrounded by the thegns who had remained loyal to their slain lord, King Cynewulf, Cyneheard 'offered them money and land on their own terms if they would allow him the kingdom'.[60] Here we see a royal candidate striving to buy the support of the thegns, and the evidence of the Anglo-Saxon Chronicle reiterates yet again, that no contender for kingship could come to power or rule without that support. Oleson, paradoxically, admitted this very point that 'no man could be king until he had secured the support of the *witan*',[61] but failed to realize that the securing of that support from representatives of the thegnly class was tantamount to an election of some sort.

It follows, therefore, that the notion of King Æthelwulf unilaterally bequeathing his kingdom in a *Will* to Æthelbald or Æthelberht—not to speak of to his infant son, Alfred—is a complete nonsense. Whatever arrangements Æthelwulf made for the succession of Æthelbald, before he left for Rome in 855, can have had little or nothing to do with his *Will* and everything to do with seeking the assent of his West Saxon *witan*. We have seen how in Alfred's own *Will* he never once dared to refer to the kingship by way of bequest, since he and all his councillors knew full well that his successor would have to be chosen—and indeed formally chosen—by the *witan*. That is precisely what eventually did happen, for according to the chronicler Æthelweard, on King Alfred's death, 'Edward . . . was crowned with the royal crown on Whitsunday, having been elected by the chief men (*a primatis electus*).'[62] It was however, the Pseudo-Asser's flawed account of Æthelwulf's supposed settling of the succession on his sons by means of a *Will* that bedevilled Chadwick's and subsequent scholars' understanding of the role of the *witan* in relation to early English royal succession. If, after all, Alfred's personal tutor had indeed told us that the West Saxon kingship had been disposed of by *Will*, then such evidence would take precedence over any other. Not only can the Pseudo-Asser's text be shown to be hagiographical and late, but it can also be seen to contain worthless and irresponsible fictions, of which the tale of Æthelwulf's *Will* is one.

Chadwick viewed the evidence from Bede as suggesting that royal succession was sorted out beforehand by the reigning king, and concluded that in the case of Alfred's father: 'Æthelwulf's action in bequeathing his kingdom by will can therefore hardly be regarded as a startling innovation.'[63] In this Chadwick was supported by Oleson who pointed to the succession of Edward the Confessor being settled in the lifetime of Hardacnut and who also noticed that 'Æthelwulf is said to have disposed of the kingdom in a will'.[64] Oleson summarized his views on royal election thus: 'It would probably have been settled before the death of the king by him and his closest advisers, or after his death by the members of the royal family and a few of the leading men in the kingdom.'[65] The involvement of 'all the councillors' of the West Saxons, or of England as a whole—a phrase which recurs throughout contemporary sources from the ninth through to the eleventh century—belies any idea that royal elections or other major decisions which affected the well-being of the whole kingdom were ever settled in a royal *Will* or fixed by a small number of magnates acting behind the scenes. Those thegns such as Wulfric Spot, who controlled vast estates in northern Mercia and southern Northumbria in the late tenth century, or ealdormen such as Ælfstan who served under King Alfred as well as under Alfred's older brothers, Æthelberht and Æthelred, had too great an economic stake in the kingdom for their opinions, as a class, on the royal succession to be ignored.[66]

When confronted by the unambiguous evidence for the election by the *witan* both of Edmund Ironside and of Cnut within a few days of each other in April 1016, and the similar election of Cnut's successors by the *witan* in 1035, Chadwick argued that the powers enjoyed by such assemblies in the late tenth and early eleventh centuries may not have existed in earlier times.[67] He dismissed Ælfric's famous remark, 'No man can make himself king, but the people has the choice to elect whom they like', with the highly unlikely suggestion that the idea was prompted by the election of Hugh Capet to the Frankish kingship in 987.[68] The reporting of the succession crisis which followed Cnut's death in 1035 may tell us something of the internal workings of the council in spite of its eleventh-century context. Admittedly, by then the country and its leading magnates had been heavily affected by Scandinavian rule, but in Wessex at least, traditional procedures and more especially the constituency of the *witan* cannot have changed greatly since Alfredian times. On Cnut's death, 'an assembly of all the councillors (*ealra witena gemot*)' met at Oxford and the *witan* were divided as to how to proceed:

Earl Leofric and almost all the thegns north of the Thames and the shipmen in London chose Harold [son of Cnut] to the regency of all England, for himself and for his brother Hardacnut, who was then in Denmark. And Earl Godwine and all the chief men in Wessex opposed it as long as they could, but they could not contrive anything against it. And it was then determined that Ælfgifu, Hardacnut's mother, should stay in Winchester with the housecarls of her son the king, and they should keep all Wessex in his possession; and Earl Godwine was their most loyal man.[69]

Here, then, we are allowed a glimpse of the internal political manœuvres at a *witenagemot*. The men of the Danelaw and the Scandinavian crews from the fleet at London favoured Harold for the kingship, while 'all the chief men in Wessex (*ealle þa yldestan menn on West Seaxon*)'—those descendants of the Alfredian *witan*—backed the absent Hardacnut and his mother (Ælfgifu or Emma) who was guarding the royal treasure at Winchester. Those opposing lobbies were led by two leading magnates, the earls Leofric and Godwine. The circumstances in which the *witan* met to elect a successor to Cnut in 1035 were highly unusual. Hardacnut, the leading candidate for kingship, was absent in Denmark and the rival claims of Hardacnut and his brother Harold can only have helped to strengthen the mediatory and electoral role of a *witan* which had clearly become a more diverse body than in the time of Alfred. But what is surely significant is that the issue was neither seen nor handled as a private family quarrel between the two young kings and the dowager queen, Emma. It was a matter in which the magnates had a major say. Oleson's citing of the case of the Confessor's succession to the kingship merely complicated the issue but if anything, points to the importance of some form of election.[70] Whether or not Edward's succession was settled in the lifetime of Hardacnut (in 1041), various versions of the Chronicle are unanimous that after Hardacnut's death in 1042 and 'before he was buried, all the people chose (*ge ceas*) Edward as king in London'.[71] Florence of Worcester would have us believe that far from Edward's succession being a private family matter, it was brought about 'chiefly by the exertions of Earl Godwine and Lifing, bishop of Worcester'.[72] It is little wonder than Oleson had second thoughts over these events and admitted that he could not rule out participation by the *witan*.[73] Godwine and Lifing were leading members of the *witan* within Wessex and Mercia respectively.

Edward the Elder was crowned on Whitsunday, AD 900, but his father, King Alfred, had died on 26 October 899. The long interval between the death of Alfred and the crowning of Edward may have had little to do with decorum. It suggests rather that the kingdom had been plunged into political turmoil as soon as Alfred had died. Since the Chronicle records the rebellion of Æthelwold, the nephew of King Alfred, immediately after reporting that 'Edward succeeded to the kingdom', we may assume that the six-month interval between the death of Alfred and the crowning of Edward was filled with attempts by Edward and by his rival first cousin to win over a majority of the *witan* to their cause. The ætheling, Æthelwold, would never have come out in open rebellion against Edward had he not significant support from a portion of the magnates of Wessex. When he eventually fled from Wessex, his royal status alone would not have been sufficient to account for his subsequent success. The fact that the Danish army of Northumbria 'accepted him as king and gave allegiance to him'[74] shows that they received him, not as a fugitive without a following, but as a formidable leader who, if he could not convince them of the justice of his cause in Wessex, could at least convince them of his support there. Otherwise we cannot explain how Æthelwold sailed south from the Humber 'with all the fleet he could procure' and won the submission of the men of Essex, and by implication those of East Anglia also. It has usually been understood by historians that the York Danes accepted Æthelwold as king of Danish York on the assumption there was a vacancy in their own Scandinavian kingship at that time. The Chronicle's account of Æthelwold's reception at York is ambiguous and could equally be taken to mean that the Northumbrians—including their king or kings— accepted Æthelwold's claim as king of the West Saxons, and in order to exploit the civil war in Wessex, lent him military support. The men of the Danelaw would then have been continuing their earlier policy of supporting trouble-makers in Wessex and English Mercia, as when they aided and abetted Hæsten's army in its ravaging of Kent, Essex, Wessex, and Mercia, back in 893–6.[75]

Æthelwold lacked sufficient immediate support from the great men of Wessex in 900 to make good his claim to the kingship, but he may have hoped that in time he would rally far-flung supporters to his defence. He was clearly not bereft of friends within Wessex as the presence of those loyal followers 'who had given alliegance to him' at Wimborne and at Christchurch attests. Similarly, the presence of a certain Brihtsige, 'son of the ætheling Beornoth' who fell fighting in Æthelwold's cause at the battle of the Holme in 903, shows that right up to the end of this bloody struggle, a leading member of an English royal kindred supported Æthelwold against Edward son of Alfred.[76] Stenton,[77] who shared the Anglo-Saxon chronicler's reluctance to admit to any hint of dissent within the House of Alfred, speculated that Brihtsige may have been a landless descendant of a Mercian royal house. Since the struggle primarily involved Wessex, it is much more probable that this son of an ætheling was a descendant of King Æthelwulf of Wessex or of his father King Ecgberht. In that battle at the Holme in which Æthelwold lost his cause and his life, the brunt of the conflict there was borne by the men of Kent who had remained loyal to Edward. That loyalty may have been bought at a price. We are reminded of how Alfred's powers of patronage may have been greatly increased by the demise of the Kentish coastal monasteries during the Viking wars, and the consequent ability of the king to redistribute abandoned monastic estates in Kent to his more loyal followers.[78] It would have been in Alfred's interest to secure the loyalty of that distant but strategic region by means of generous land grants to the Kentish aristocracy.

The leading role of the *witan* and the warrior aristocracy in the civil war between Edward and Æthelwold in Wessex is not far from the surface of the Chronicle's narrative, however much that source was biased in favour of Edward. We are told Æthelwold 'seized the residence at Wimborne and at Christchurch (*Twinham*) against the will of the king [Edward] and his councillors (*witena*)'.[79] For the *witan* to have been involved, Æthelwold must have disputed Edward's right to those two places, and he must have brought the dispute before the *witan* for a judgement which eventually went against him. Christchurch in Hampshire is listed as a fortress in the *Burghal Hidage*[80] and it was a royal estate in the Confessor's time,[81] while Wimborne only ten miles to the west in Dorset was significantly the place of burial chosen for Æthelwold's father, King Æthelred, in 871, and it also reappears as a royal estate in the reign of the Confessor.[82] Considering the popularity of Sherborne and Winchester as royal burial places in the ninth century, Æthelred's burial at Wimborne suggests the king had been prominently associated with that place during life. Æthelwold's claim on Wimborne would then have been understandable, if not just. The fact that King Æthelred was eventually buried there suggests that he may have earlier lavished his patronage on its monastic church. Wimborne's estate was very likely a major power centre in the reign of Æthelred I—surrounded no doubt by landowning magnates who were especially loyal to that king. It is not surprising, therefore, that Æthelwold chose to make his stand in south Dorset 'with the men who had given allegiance to him (*mid þæm monnum þe him to gebugon*)'[83]—in other words with those men who had acknowledged him as king. Assuming that Wimborne, and perhaps also Christchurch, were royal estates (or at least farms owned by members of the royal kindred) in Alfredian times—and Æthelred's burial at Wimborne would confirm that assumption—then the involvement of the *witan* in the civil war may have an added significance. Æthelwold's dispute over these estates may have sprung from his claim to the kingship of his father, Æthelred I, and his seizure of those places 'against the will of the *witan*' could be taken to mean that the *witan* had upheld the claim of Edward against that of Æthelwold for the kingship of Wessex. However we interpret these events, the Chronicle appeals to the authority of the *witan* and not just to that of King Edward alone, which is indicative of the importance of the councillors in settling disputes between royal claimants in Alfredian Wessex.

We have seen how William of Malmesbury would have us believe that the succession of Athelstan to the kingship (in 924) was arranged not only by his father Edward but also by his grandfather Alfred. There is, however, the possibility that it was Athelstan's brother, Ælfweard, and not Athelstan himself who was regarded as king of the West Saxons when Edward died. If we can trust the Hyde Register, Ælfweard either enjoyed the title of king during his father's lifetime or he was acknowledged as king during the days immediately following Edward's death.[84] Either possibility challenges the mythical view of Athelstan being groomed for kingship by no less a figure than King Alfred. Ælfweard had a half-brother, Edwin, and the little we know of Edwin suggests that he challenged Athelstan's right to the kingship, and that challenge was only resolved by the drowning of Edwin in the English Channel as late as 933. According to the Northumbrian Chronicle in the *Historia Regum*, Athelstan was responsible for his brother's death[85]— a brother who is styled 'king' by the near-contemporary Folcwin, a monk of St Bertin.[86] Among those older sons of Edward, we may also have to include Æthelweard, who witnessed charters along with Athelstan and Ælfweard in King Edward's lifetime but who probably predeceased Edward.[87] Alfred's role in the so-called designation of Athelstan as a future king can be dismissed out of hand. If Athelstan were 30 when he came to the throne (as William of Malmesbury asserts[88]), then he was only 5 when King Alfred died in 899. Alfred and Edward the Elder were more preoccupied with the challenge of King Æthelred's sons at that time of crisis than with settling the succession a quarter of a century hence, on a boy who was still only an infant and who was, on Malmesbury's own reporting, regarded by some as Edward's illegitimate child.[89] Malmesbury's idea that Edward nominated Athelstan as his successor in a testament (*testamento*) may well have been suggested by the Pseudo-Asser's use of the same word for Æthelwulf's settlement of the kingdom on his sons.[90] Edward the Elder would have been no more entitled to dispose of the kingship in a *Will*, than his father or grandfather. That did not deter Williams from concluding that 'The custom governing the succession arose out of a series of family agreements within the West Saxon royal kin, and was made effective by the wills of successive rulers—Æthelwulf, Alfred and Edward the elder.'[91] The Pseudo-Asser is our only witness to Æthelwulf ever having mentioned the West Saxon kingship in his *Will*. King Alfred, who quoted from his father's *Will* makes no mention of Æthelwulf having included his kingship in that document. Alfred, himself never once mentions the West Saxon kingship in his own *Will* either in relation to his sons or to anyone else. And as for any *Will* of Edward the Elder—no such document survives either in whole or in part. William of Malmesbury's motive for linking Athelstan's career to that of his famous grandfather, and for generally glorifying Athelstan's ability as a king, was prompted by his own belief that Athelstan had been a great benefactor to the monastery at Malmesbury and that the king had declared that he wished one day to be buried there.[92] William had grown up in the monastery at Malmesbury from childhood, and was devoted to its cause.

The record of Athelstan's succession as found in the Mercian Register suggests a different order of events and a different procedure from that envisaged by William of Malmesbury: 'In this year (924) King Edward died at Farndon in Mercia, and his son Ælfweard died very soon after at Oxford, and their bodies are buried in Winchester. And Athelstan was chosen by the Mercians as king (*wæs of Myrcum gecoren to cinge*) and consecrated at Kingston.'[93] The long-dead Alfred can scarcely have had a hand in these events. Given the economy of recording that pervades the Mercian Register, the record of the death of Edward's son, Ælfweard, and the naming of that son, clearly carried special significance. The implication would seem to be that Ælfweard (who only survived his father for sixteen days) was expected to succeed him in the kingship, and that Athelstan's election was something of an after-thought. William of Malmesbury's narrative does reveal that Athelstan's succession may have been as unexpected as it was clearly a cause of discontent. William informs us that 'a certain Alfred (*Eluredus*) with his factious party' tried to prevent the coronation at Kingston on the grounds that Athelstan was Edward's illegitimate son.[94] Malmesbury almost certainly found the record of the magnate Alfred's rebellion in an earlier source, for it was not in his interest to invent or even to include such material in a eulogy on his hero-king. All this flatly contradicts the idea of King Alfred and Edward 'fixing' the infant Athelstan's succession back in the 890s, as indeed it contradicts Malmesbury's other conflicting statements that Athelstan was 'elected king with great unanimity by the nobles', 'after the death of his father and the decease of his brother [Ælfweard]'.[95] It is Malmesbury who gives us the clearest statement regarding Athelstan's election, and it will be noted that his statement that the election took place only after the deaths of his father and his brother is again suggestive that Ælfweard had been the first choice of the *witan*.

Elections of course could also be fixed, but the fact of their taking place at all did serve to acknowledge the formal role of the *witan* in the choosing of a king. Williams drew attention to a possible reference to the dispute over the acceptance of Athelstan as king by the Mercians in a charter (Sawyer 395; Birch 642) issued by Athelstan in 925, in which he granted an estate near Lichfield in Staffordshire, to the thegn, Eadric, and in which there is an enigmatic reference to the king 'investigating the matter of discussed obedience brought to notice by the careful sagacity of my *fideles*'.[96] Edward had died on 17 July 924, and no doubt because of the succession struggle which followed, Athelstan was not crowned until 4 September 925. We are dealing, therefore, with a hiatus in the West Saxon kingship of well over a year. The Mercian grant in favour of Eadric was issued in the immediate aftermath of what may have been a prolonged struggle between the followers of Athelstan, on the one hand, and those of his brother Edwin and the magnate Alfred, on the other. It is in the context of the West Saxon and Mercian councillors' involvement in that struggle that the charter to Eadric may be relevant.[97] As Williams rightly concluded: 'The reference in Athelstan's charter, if indeed it does relate to Athelstan's election, implies a formal assembly and a debate, rather than simple recognition.'[98]

Events of Athelstan's reign—especially relating to that king's disputed hold on the kingship—have no small bearing on our understanding of the reign of King Alfred. It was from Athelstan's reign onwards that the Alfred myth began to take shape, eventually crystallizing by the end of the tenth century in the Pseudo-Asser's crude pastiche which tried to show the predestined nature of Alfred's rule, his unique relationship with his father, his superiority over his brothers, and above all his unchallenged grip as a saintly and beloved king over a united Wessex. This propaganda probably began life at a time when Athelstan was himself struggling to overcome opposition to his own kingship from within his family and from a section of the magnates. Athelstan, like Alfred before him, had to cope with internal dissent within his own dynasty, and at the same time fight off the supreme challenge posed by the York Danes in the person of Olaf Guthfrithsson.[99] With the benefit of hindsight historians view Athelstan and Alfred as 'winners' whose success was seen to be assured by men of their own generation. The evidence, meagre though it is, suggests that Athelstan needed Alfredian propaganda to prop up his own insecure hold on the kingship. We shall never know for certain the precise identity of that Alfred who initially opposed Athelstan's succession. The name, although an aristocratic one, was common among magnates of tenth-century Wessex. No less than four Alfreds, each described as a *minister* or thegn, witnessed the same charter (Sawyer 378; Birch 624) supposedly issued by Edward the Elder in 909.[100] Athelstan's enemy was such a magnate who had enjoyed prominence during the reign of King Edward, and he is likely to have been of royal blood if he were the leader of the opposition who sought the kingship for himself. The *Book of Hyde* mentions a certain Alfred or *Elfredus* as a son of Edward the Elder who was king during Edward's lifetime and, whose name has otherwise been taken to be an erroneous form of Ælfweard, that son of Edward who died within a few weeks of his father.[101] The Anglo-Saxon Chronicle provides the most meagre account of Athelstan's reign and such 'official' accounts as survive have seen to it that little or no information remains on those older sons of Edward who were rivals of Athelstan in the struggles for succession. The rebellious Alfred was probably Athelstan's half-brother or cousin. Ælfweard and the unfortunate Edwin were more certainly half-brothers.

In 924 Athelstan 'was chosen by the Mercians as king' perhaps because it was the Mercian *witan* who were nearest to hand when Edward died in their territory, or more likely because it was still necessary for a West Saxon overlord to secure the assent of the Mercian council. Although there is no mention of the Mercian *witan* as such in the Mercian Register's record of Athelstan's succession, their involvement is implicit. Chadwick dismissed this idea on the grounds that 'As a matter of fact we have no evidence that the Mercian council continued to meet as a separate body'.[102] Chadwick in truth disliked the notion of any council meeting anywhere as a separate body. He was presumably unaware that the Mercian council preserved its separate identity in Alfred's reign under the rule of his daughter Æthelflæd and of her husband Æthelred, Lord of the Mercians. King Alfred, in his dealings with the Mercians, was not only involved with his daughter and son-in-law: he also had to take account of their wise men. A charter (Sawyer 223, Birch 579) setting out arrangements for the building of fortifications in Worcester sometime during the last ten last years of King Alfred's life, twice calls to witness 'all the councillors who are in the land of the Mercians (*ealra ðæra witena ðe on Myrcna land syndon*)'.[103] This charter also informs us, that those members of the Mercian *witan* who witnessed the transaction along with King Alfred had their names attached to the charter.[104] This last piece of information confirms what we might already have guessed, namely that some of the names at least which appear in the witness lists of Alfred's own charters were those of members of his *witan*. Yet another charter dating to 903 or 904 records that Æthelred when he became 'lord of the Mercians (*Myrcna hlaford*) . . . summoned the Mercian council (*Mercna weotan*) to Droitwich to deal with many necessary matters both spiritual and temporal'.[105] It would be perverse to suggest that the Mercian council did not survive at least until the death of Æthelflæd. Lady of the Mercians, in 918 and the abduction of her daughter, Ælfwyn, by King Edward of Wessex in the following year. But Athelstan's 'choosing' by the Mercians in 924 and the election of Edgar in 957 (see below) strongly suggests that as in Northumbria, so too in Mercia, the *witan* not only survived, but retained something of its power to choose kings of the Mercians or at least to formally assent to the overlordship of each individual West Saxon ruler. The Chronicle records the succession of Edgar in 957 with the non-commital phrase: 'In this year the ætheling Edgar succeeded to the kingdom of the Mercians (*feng to Myrcena rice*)'.[106] The re-emergence of the Mercian kingdom as a separate entity at this time shows that the Mercian aristocracy had not only retained its regional identity but was also politically organized. That political organization unquestionably centred on the survival of the Mercian *witan*. What the Chronicle does not tell us is that by accepting Edgar as king in 957, the Mercians were withdrawing their allegiance from his older brother Eadwig, who had succeeded to the united English kingship in 955. The oldest or B *Life* of St Dunstan provides crucial details of the circumstances in which the Mercians withdrew their alliegance from Eadwig:

It came about that the aforesaid king [Eadwig] in the passage of years was wholly deserted by the northern people, being despised because he acted foolishly in the government (*regimine*) committed to him, ruining with vain hatred the shrewd and the wise. . . . When he [Eadwig] had been thus deserted by the agreement of them all, they chose as king for themselves . . . the brother of the same Eadwig, Edgar.[107]

The phrase 'by the agreement of them all' suggests that the desertion of Eadwig and the choosing of Edgar lay with the *witan*—those Mercian *sagaces vel sapientes* ('the shrewd and the wise') whom Eadwig had attempted to ruin. The matter is put beyond all doubt in that same *Life* of Dunstan which continues: 'And thus, in the witness of the whole people (*universo populo testante*) the state was divided between the kings as determined by wise men (*ex diffinitione sagacium*), so that the famous River Thames separated the realms of both.'[108] The use of the terms *sagaces* and *sapientes* is a direct translation into Latin of the Old English *witan*, and this passage shows that in its author's opinion, a tenth-century *witan* could not only act as a brake on the king's handling of *regimen* or 'government', but could also reject or depose a king in favour of another candidate. A charter (Sawyer 1447; Birch 1063) dealing with a legal dispute relating to an estate at Sunbury in Middlesex, drawn up between 968 and 988, refers to that time (in 957) 'when the Mercians chose Edgar as king, and gave him control of all the royal prerogatives'.[109] We have here, yet again, a clear statement that as late as 957 the Mercians considered that the power or *anweald* relating to their 'king-rights (*cynerihta*)' was in some sense vested in their *witan*.

Chadwick would have had us believe that the phrase *feng to rice* so frequently used for the succession of kings by the Chronicle—or its Latin equivalent *succedere in regnum* used by Bede—were at best ambiguous.[110] The Chronicle's standard phrase *feng to rice* can, in Edgar's case, be shown to have involved the Mercian *witan* withdrawing their allegiance from Eadwig and choosing Edgar as their king. That same council of 'wise men'—this time presumably from Wessex, as well as from Mercia—then set the Thames as the boundary between the two kingdoms. References to *sapientes* or *sagaces* meaning 'royal councillors' in the *Life* of St Dunstan suggest that a detailed search for similar usage elsewhere in Anglo-Latin sources ought to shed more light on the question of the composition, function, and powers of the elusive body of 'wise men'. The Pseudo-Asser, for instance, presents us with a set-piece in which King Alfred is alleged to have scolded his judges (*iudices*) for their lack of literacy: 'I am amazed at your presumption, that you have by God's favour and mine assumed the office and status of wise men, but have neglected the study and practice of wisdom.'[111] The speech was unquestionably apocryphal and originated with the early eleventh-century author of Alfred's *Life*, but the context is plausible for the time of writing. We note that although the men in question were judges (*iudices*) they were being castigated for enjoying 'the office and status of wise men (*sapientium ministerium et gradus*)'. That *ministerium* or office may not have automatically accompanied the aristocratic status of these magnates, for Alfred ordered his recalcitrant *sapientes* 'to resign on the spot the exercise of the worldly authority you hold (*terrenarum potestatum ministeria*)'.[112] Who were these 'wise men'—the *iudices* who, in the mind of an early eleventh-century writer, presided over the courts in King Alfred's realm? That same compiler lists them for us as earldormen (*comites*), reeves (*praepositi*), and thegns (*ministri*)[113]—these were categories of magnates, then, who as we might expect, made up the *witan*, and we must also include among their ranks the bishops, and perhaps some other leading churchmen. The judicial function of the *witan* as assumed by the Pseudo-Asser is supported by the evidence from King Alfred's *Will*, where that king expected his *witan* to expound the common law (*folcriht*), and by the Sunbury charter (quoted above), where the *witan* were seen to arbitrate in relation to *cyneriht*, or the law pertaining to kingship and to royal succession. Indeed, all the powers of the *witan*—including whatever political clout they possessed—may well have derived from their primary function as the custodians of *riht* in relation not only to the king, but to tribal custom generally. The ninth-century Mercian evidence[114] that it was the *witan* who appended their names to charters, is in keeping with the added legal force which the names of those men in their capacity as *judices* lent to the witnessing of such transactions. In other words, charters were not just witnessed by the warriors who happened to be attending on the king at any given time, but some of the witnesses at least, would have constituted the membership of a legal assembly.

The description in the Chronicle ascribed to Florence of Worcester of the election of Edward the Martyr, great-great-grandson of King Alfred, in 975, confirms all the evidence we have reviewed thus far:

In the meantime the nobles of the kingdom were very much at variance in the matter of electing a king: for some chose the king's son, Edward, and some chose his brother, Æthelred. On this account the archbishops Dunstan and Oswald, with a great number of bishops, abbots, and ealdormen, met in a body and chose Edward, according as his father had desired; and after his election crowned and anointed him king.[115]

So that same class of leading clergy and ealdormen are to be found here, yet again, electing a successor to King Edgar. Edgar had died suddenly in July 975 when only 'a few men and thegns' were about him. He left two sons who were still too young to rule, a fact which must have strengthened the hand of the *witan* as arbitrators and king-makers in the ensuing struggles for power. Edward, 'a child ungrown' was the son of Edgar's first wife, Æthelflæd Eneda, while his half-brother Æthelred the Unready, who was then only about 10, was the son of Ælfthryth, daughter of a magnate of Devon. According to Eadmer, who wrote in the early twelfth century, Edward who was eventually elected was opposed by the party of Queen Ælfthryth and of Ælfhere, ealdorman of Mercia.[116] This same Ælfhere appears in Byrhtferth's *Life* of St Oswald as leading the anti-monastic reaction in Mercia on the death of Edgar, and is seen to be opposed there by Æthelwine, ealdorman of East Anglia, by Æthelwine's brother Ælfwold and by Byrhtnoth, ealdorman of Essex and hero of the battle of Maldon. As these leading ealdormen and the great men of the shires found themselves in opposing camps, it is little wonder that as the writer of the *Life* of Oswald tells us, on Edgar's death 'the state of the whole kingdom was thrown into confusion, the bishops were agitated, the noblemen (*principes*) stirred up, the monks shaken with fear, the people terrified'.[117] Whether or not Ælfthryth, the mother of the boy-prince Æthelred, was involved in these factions, it is clear from the *Life* of Oswald (which provides the earliest account of these proceeding) that the initiative lay not with the royal family but with those magnates of the kingdom who constituted the *witan*. We are told that when Edgar, 'the emperor of the whole of Albion' died

there began to approach on all sides dissension and tribulation, which neither bishops nor leaders in ecclesiastical and secular affairs (*praesules nec duces ecclesiarum et saecularium rerum*) could allay. . . . Certain of the chief men (*ex primatibus*) of this land wished to elect as king (*eligere ad regem*) the king's elder son, Edward by name; some of the nobles wanted the younger, because he appeared to all gentler in speech and deeds.[118]

Earlier during the lobbying which preceded this crucial gathering of the *witan*, in which ealdormen were ranged against ealdormen (*duces adversum duces*), Æthelwine of East Anglia had been approached by 'all the more noble thegns (*milites nobiliores*) and the illustrious sons of leading men (*principum*)'. Æthelwine, having 'assembled a noble army (*digno exercitu*)', convened a 'synod (*synodo*)' at which the opposition was also represented, and at which the problems regarding monastic lands were discussed. Given the ambiguity of the term, it matters little whether we regard that meeting as a *witenagemot*, a church synod, or a council of war. What does matter is that it demonstrates the power of the 'noble thegns' and 'leading men' to avert civil war within a kingdom. Byrhtferth of Ramsey, the author of the

Life of Oswald, clearly viewed that assembly at which Æthelwine and his brother Ælfwold, opposed the party of Ealdorman Ælfhere of Mercia, as a meeting of the *witan*. Byrhtferth tells us that the leading magnates approached Æthelwine because in him was 'wisdom to do judgement (*in eo sapientia ad faciendum judicium*)'. The quotation from I Kings 3: 28 was punning on the role of Anglo-Saxon 'wise men' as arbitrators between magnates who were in serious dispute over the 'appropriation of enormous revenues (*sumens munera enormia*)', and between rival candidates for kingship.[119] The judicial function of the *witan* was clearly taken by the author of the *Life* of St Oswald, as being central to its make-up. If we can trust Florence of Worcester, Edward was his father's choice for the kingship, but his election was clearly unpopular, and he fell by the hands of assassins from his brother's household about two years later. While Edward may have been his father's choice, it is important to recognize that he was elected by the *witan*. Williams believed that Edward's '"election" . . . was a little more than the formal agreement of the nobles to a previous decision by the royal kin'.[120] We have to accept on the evidence of early and reliable sources, that whatever circumstances brought Edward the Martyr to the kingship, it proved disastrous to ignore the wishes of the majority, or at least the more influential of the *witan*. For in spite of what contemporary and later historians thought of Æthelred the Unready's problematic reign, there is little doubt that he came to kingship as the popular choice of the magnates. The *Life* of Oswald vouches for rejoicing at Æthelred's consecration at Kingston, and Version D of the Chronicle, in spite of deploring the martyrdom of Edward, goes on to record that Æthelred's consecration followed 'very quickly (*swiðe hrædlice*)' on his succession, and was accompanied 'with much rejoicing by the councillors (*witon*) of the English people'.[121]

It is difficult to accept, without major qualification, the statement by Williams that 'in the tenth century, the kingship of England was the inheritance of the West Saxon royal house'.[122] It is of course true, that prior to the return of Scandinavian invaders in the early eleventh century, there was only one (West Saxon) dynasty which controlled the kingship of England throughout the latter half of the previous century. But evidence for the continued and central role of the *witan* shows that while the dynastic principle was paramount in relation to candidature for kingship, the *witan* played a crucial role in deciding between candidates. For even when, as in late ninth-century Wessex or in late tenth-century England as a whole, one dynasty enjoyed a monopoly of power, there was always the problem of distributing that power equitably between potentially rival segments of a royal kindred. We might expect that as the tenth century wore on, and as the House of Alfred obtained a monopoly not only on the kingship of Wessex but of all England, the dynastic principle would have triumphed at the expense of the elective element. But that was clearly not the case, and however powerful the West Saxon dynasty became, princes of that house ignored the wishes of their *witan* at their peril. Even Chadwick, who considered only a fraction of the complex evidence, was forced to make the grudging if vague concession: 'There seems to be traces . . . of a feeling that election of some sort was required.'[123]

If we accept that the West Saxon royal council played a role in the choosing of kings, and if consequently we view the ninth-century *witan* as a consultative assembly capable of advising and exercising an element of control on kingship, then several important conclusions follow. First, we can confirm yet again that the statement in the Anglo-Saxon Chronicle that Alfred was consecrated king by Pope Leo in Rome in 853 was a nonsensical claim. To accept otherwise would be to conclude that the *witan* had been persuaded by Æthelwulf to accept his youngest infant son as king, while Æthelwulf was still reigning and while he was simultaneously persuading the *witan* to accept his two older sons to reign in Wessex during his absence! Alternatively, we would have to conclude that Æthelwulf made one deal with his *witan* regarding the succession of Æthelbald and Æthelberht, and then made another one with the pope regarding the infant Alfred. It is time, once and for all, to recognize that only after Alfred had become king could this claim regarding his infant kingship have been successfully foisted on the historical record. The compiler of Alfred's *Life* took this myth a stage further by building on Alfred's bogus role as 'heir apparent' or *secundarius* from infancy. We must also conclude that the compiler of the *Life* of Alfred was quite mistaken in assuming Æthelwulf included the kingship of Wessex among the other bequests to his children and kinsmen in his *Will*. Since Æthelwulf was going on a long journey from which he was likely not to return, then it must have been necessary to consult the council before his departure, to arrange for a temporary or permanent succession. It is possible that while the public deliberations and findings of the *witan* were binding on the participants, that a written document was indeed drawn up, recording the division of the kingdom between Æthelbald and his brother Æthelberht. Such a document would have been evidentiary to the findings of the *witan*, but it ought not to be confused with Æthelwulf's *Will*. What Æthelwulf did with his personal property was one thing, how the kingship was disposed of, was quite another.

Chadwick, although he denied the collective responsibility of the council as a deliberative body, and although he viewed the relationship between the thegns and their king as strictly personal and individual, nevertheless glimpsed the crucial economic element relating to patronage that lay at the heart of the system. Recognizing that all the thegns of the shires were individually under the lordship of the king, he concluded that on the death of the king, each thegn became *hlafordleas* and had to select a new lord. 'The need for doing so was no mere convention, since the possession of office and all the profits arising therefrom were at stake.'[124] The great men of the kingdom stood not only to gain from high office, but as members of a warrior aristocracy they expected their king to share with them the spoils of war both in the form of movable loot and of land. Such was the *quid pro quo* for their loyalty—so often vaunted as voluntarily given in *Beowulf* and elsewhere. The loyalty which the *witan* might show to a king was rooted in hard economic realities. In spite of the over-rich narration in the Anglo-Saxon Chronicle, covering the struggle for the West Saxon kingship in 757, the economic dimension was clearly admitted: 'Then the ætheling (Cyneheard) offered them money and land on their

own terms, if they would allow him the kingdom.'[125] Even the Irish, who maintained the greatest pretence of heroic values, showed in their legal tracts that more
mundane matters could take precedence over valour. A later gloss on the adage
that kingship ought to be decided on worth, reads: 'That is, to put the person who
possesses most clients and power, if he is as noble as his elder, into the sovereignty.'[126] MacNiocaill reminded us that in early Ireland 'clientship was the basic
economic underpinning of the upper classes, aristocracy or kings, and a basic social
necessity for the lower classes'.[127] The greater client or *céle* was bound to his lord
through generous landed endowments and there is little doubt that such practices
prevailed in Anglo-Saxon England also. King Alfred may have won the loyalty of
the Kentish magnates, by means of grants from derelict monastic estates, and it
was those men who eventually supported his son, Edward, against his cousin,
Æthelwold.[128] For a king might not only buy loyalty with land grants: he might
also find an excuse to confiscate estates and thereby free revenue for other purposes. A charter of Edward the Elder (Sawyer 362, Birch 595) shows how King
Alfred had confiscated an estate of ten hides from an Ealdorman Wulfhere, at
Wylye in Wiltshire, when Wulfhere and his wife 'deserted without permission
both his lord King Alfred and his country in spite of the oath (*jusjurandum*) which
he had sworn to the king and all his leading men (*suis omnibus optimatibus*)'. So a
great man in Alfredian Wessex was bound by oath, not just to his king, but to
fellow members of the *witan* as well. And it was 'by the judgement of all the
councillors (*cum omnium juditio sapientium*) of the West Saxons and of the Mercians'
that Wulfhere 'lost the control and inheritance of his lands'.[129] The 'wise men'
were acting, yet again, in their capacity as judges, and their assembly, in this
instance, functioned as a law court. Meanwhile, Edward the Elder continued to
benefit from Ealdorman Wulfhere's disloyalty to King Alfred, for the confiscated
estate at Wylye came into Edward's 'rightful ownership', which left that king free
to grant its 'meadows, pastures, woods and water-courses' to a certain Æthelwulf
'on account of his pleasing obedience'. The West Saxon *witan* must have been torn
between greed for the redistribution of confiscated lands, and their sense that
Wulfhere had once been one their own number. Wulfhere's name appears in
charter witness lists from 854 in the reign of King Æthelwulf down to 869, when
as the 'dear and venerable *princeps*, Wulfhere (*dilecto et venerabili meo principi
Wulfhero*)'[130] he received an estate (Sawyer 341, Birch 886) at Winterbourne in
Wiltshire, from Alfred's brother, King Æthelred I. Wulfhere received an earlier
grant (Sawyer 336, Birch 508) of lands at Buttermere in Wiltshire from King
Æthelred, or more likely from Æthelberht in 863. Wulfhere was a typical example
of those leading West Saxon magnates, such as the ealdormen Ordlaf, Sigewulf,
and Deormod, who presided over the confiscation of his lands, in that they all had
established roots within the West Saxon system of royal patronage. These men
stood for continuity within that system which they helped to establish and maintain—some like Wulfhere going back into Æthelwulf's reign, and others like
Deormod and Ordlaf surviving into the reign of Edward the Elder. It was in the
interests of such men to sustain continuity of patronage by bringing about an

amicable succession from one royal member of Æthelwulf's family to the next. Wulfhere in a moment of panic or necessity had clearly backed the wrong horse.

Alfred's eventual triumph over the Danish Guthrum in western Wessex in 878 may have left the English king in an enviable position. If many of the magnates of north Wiltshire had indeed submitted to the Danish invaders who overran their lands early in 878, Alfred, later on, would have been able to take retaliatory action against those thegns and to redistribute their land to others whose loyalty he considered either to be more secure or more desirable. The confiscation of Ealdorman Wulfhere's property (and that of his wife) may have been only the tip of an iceberg. Alfred's son and successor, Edward the Elder, also appears to have carried on his father's independent attitude towards the church, as the complaint over Edward's 'unwelcome demand', addressed to that king by Bishop Denewulf of Winchester, shows.[131] It was Athelstan and Edgar who were seen by contemporaries as darlings of the Church party and of monasticism in particular, while Alfred and Edward the Elder—who were in much greater need of revenue— treated the Church in a more pragmatic way. Alfred's treatment of Archbishop Æthelred of Canterbury, for instance, can be compared with Athelstan's attempts to woo the troublesome Wulfstan, archbishop of York in 934 with a generous grant of lands in Amounderness.[132] The circumstances and the archbishops involved in these incidents were very different. Æthelred, as archbishop of Canterbury, was beholding to his West Saxon overlord for support against the Great Army of Danes, while Wulfstan was head of a distant and hostile Northumbrian *witan* which supported the Danish cause. While West Saxon kings could deal more ruthlessly with those bishops and magnates who were within their own kingdom, they had to proceed with caution and diplomacy when dealing with leaders in the Danelaw. So, we may compare Edgar's generosity in confirming the Anglo-Danish magnates of the Danelaw in their rights and privileges, with Alfred's harsh treatment of Ealdorman Wulfhere who presumably defected from his allegiance under the great stress that the Danish invasion and occupation of Wessex in 878 must have imposed. That is not to say that Alfred was not good to his thegns or to his archbishop of Canterbury. On the contrary, given his resources which were much more limited than those of his tenth-century successors, he must have treated them with some skill to secure their loyalty in the fight to save his kingdom. But in the partnership between the king and his magnates and bishops, a balance had to be found which satisfied both parties and which, to them, made equitable use of the resources available.

Half a century later, Edgar may have got the balance wrong, for although he died lamented by his bishops and his 'faithful monks', he left his Church over-endowed at the expense of his warrior aristocracy. And so, the *Life* of St Oswald tells us that on Edgar's death, Ealdorman Ælfhere of Mercia 'appropriating enormous revenues (*sumens munera enormia*)' and 'with the advice of the people' ejected the monks from their monasteries. Ælfhere was not acting alone, for we are told of 'people who were gathered to him' and who stood to gain from his redistribution of monastic land. King Alfred, too, must have had his problems in squeezing resources from a reluctant church and aristocracy. The unrelenting sycophancy of the Pseudo-Asser's text blinds us to the very few genuine traditions that this later work may contain. In spite of the portrayal of King Alfred by the compiler of his *Life*, as a blameless super-king, there are nevertheless several forthright statements made about the difficulties which Alfred encountered in persuading his magnates to co-operate in certain crucial programmes undertaken by him. Alfred's fortress-building initiative was seen as being only partly successful because of the lack of co-operation by those magnates who put their own personal interests before that of 'the common good',[133] and we have already encountered those ealdormen, reeves, and thegns, who were supposedly upbraided by Alfred for their lack of enthusiasm for literacy. Even if such difficulties were merely guessed at by the Pseudo-Asser, his narrative may have value in so far as it offers us an early eleventh-century perspective on Alfred's reign. Although Edward and Athelstan developed and perfected the fortress-building programme, it was undoubtedly Alfred who began this crucial but very costly tactic of defending Wessex from Danish attack. It was the great landowners of Wessex rather than the king himself who must have borne the brunt of the financial and organizational burden of building the *burhs*. The fact that Alfred's policies triumphed and continued under his son and grandson was due to their demonstrable success in the face of the Danish menace, and due no doubt also to the handsome rewards which the magnates reaped in the form of loot and land won back from the Danes.

It is no surprise that Alfred opens his *Will* with the solemn declaration that he was acting 'with the advice of Archbishop Æthelred and with the witness of all the councillors of the West Saxons'.[134] The mention of the archbishop of Canterbury in this context is strongly suggestive of his role as leader of the West Saxon council and reminds us of the Chronicle's unequivocal portrayal of 'Archbishop Wulfstan [of York] and all the councillors of the Northumbrians' as the leaders of Northumbria whose allegiance was a *sine qua non* for anyone who claimed the kingship of that people by the middle of the tenth century.[135] A bishop or archbishop, by virtue of his training and his office, had administrative skills which were invaluable to king and magnates alike. There is no doubting the conspicuous political role of the archbishop of Canterbury within Alfred's kingdom, and indeed next after the king. The prominent mention accorded Archbishop Æthelred in King Alfred's *Will* can be compared with the even more prominent place which the archbishop occupies in King Alfred's Laws. The fine for drawing a weapon in the presence of the archbishop was set at 150 shillings, while if the same crime were committed in the presence of a bishop or ealdorman, the fine was set at only 100 shillings.[136] Similarly, forcible entry into the king's residence was set at 120 shillings; into the archbishop's residence, at 90 shillings; and the residence of another bishop or an ealdorman, at 60 shillings.[137] Earlier codes—even that of King Wihtred of Kent which was witnessed by Beorhtwald (or Brihtwold), archbishop of Canterbury (692–731)—make no specific provision for offences against the metropolitan as opposed to lesser bishops. The annexation of Kent by Wessex in the early ninth century, and the consequent enlistment of the archbishop of Canterbury onto the

West Saxon council had a much more profound effect on the West Saxon dynasty than anything supposedly brought about by royal *Wills*. The kings of Wessex now acquired the services of a succession of churchmen, who by virtue of their metropolitan status were heirs to an ideology of universality and expansionism. A church which aspired to dominate the dioceses scattered throughout the kingdoms of England, and which might on occasion even presume to speak for Welshmen and Scots as well, was surely likely to suggest a broadening of the remit of its new masters in the kingship of Wessex. When seeking to explain Alfred's uncertain transition from king of the West Saxons to king of 'the whole English people except for that part which was under Danish rule', we need to bear in mind the influence of his metropolitans, Æthelred and later Plegmund, who were leaders among his *witan*.

The evidence from northern and southern England regarding the high political profile of their two archbishops is brought nicely together in the Northumbrian Chronicle in the *Historia Regum c.*940. Describing the invasion of the southern Danelaw by Olaf Guthfrithsson, and the eventual confrontation between him and King Edmund (the grandson of King Alfred) before Leicester, the annalist continues: 'There was no severe fighting, for the two archbishops, Oda [of Canterbury] and Wulfstan [of York] reconciled the kings to one another and put an end to the battle.'[138] This was not a treaty arranged by two holy men who were strangers to war. Wulfstan accompanied the pagan Olaf on his invasion, while Oda may have earlier fought at Brunanburh, when he was then bishop of Ramsbury. This was a treaty concluded between two kings—and perhaps forced on two kings—by their respective *witans*, of which the two archbishops were the spokesmen and leading negotiators. For if we concede a deliberative and advisory role to the royal council as a corporate body, it is necessary to accept that such a council had a spokesman. What better candidate for this job than a warrior archbishop, who shared the vested interests of the thegnly class in protecting and acquiring his vast landed estates.

Anglo-Saxon heroic literature, supported by the rhetoric of the Chronicle, reiterates the king's role as the giver of movable treasure to his men. King Alfred was described by one of his grateful bishops as 'his ring-giver (*his beahgifan*)—the best treasure-giver he ever heard of among earthly kings'.[139] Alfred's grandson Athelstan was eulogized as 'lord of nobles, dispenser of rings to men (*beorna beahgifa*)',[140] and his great-grandson Edgar was also remembered as a *beorna beahgyfa*.[141] Alfred and his progeny were cast in the same heroic mould of generous lords who rewarded their faithful war-dogs—bishops and thegns alike—from the royal hoard. But that image may only have been a small part of the reality. Alfred, his son and grandson, were above all else, kings who bought the loyalty of their thegns with grants of land, as the surviving charters bear witness. Treasure might indeed be handed over from king to man, in a moment of gratitude and macho emotion in a royal hall— rather as Athelstan is portrayed in *Egil's Saga*, presenting the warrior Egil with a gold arm-ring on the point of his drawn sword. Egil is said to have received in addition from the English king, two chest-fulls of silver coin, two more gold arm-rings, each weighing a mark, and a 'costly mantle which the king himself had formerly worn'.[142] All that was supposedly for services rendered to Athelstan by Egil in the battle of Vin-Heath in 937.[143] We are reminded of the 'very costly silk robe (*sericum pallium*)' which the Pseudo-Asser claimed Alfred had given him as a gift.[144] While the exotic gift of some costly bauble no doubt cheered up King Alfred's followers when the need arose, nevertheless, gifts of land constituted the most prized and enduring form of payment under Alfred and his successors. According to the Northumbrian Chronicle in the *Historia Regum*, estates— undoubtedly conferred by charter—were among the 'many gifts befitting a king' given by Athelstan to the church of Chester-le-Street in 934.[145] That was all part of Athelstan's bid for the loyalty of the diocese of Lindisfarne, and his frantic efforts to exclude a Danish dynasty from York, and Scottish overlordship from Bernicia.[146] Significantly, the compiler of Alfred's *Life* itemizes the monasteries of Congresbury and Banwell as well as the notorious gift of 'Exeter with all the diocese belonging to it' as the three major rewards he supposedly received from his king. Leaving aside the controversial details surrounding the authenticity of those gifts, what is clear is that an early eleventh-century writer considered it appropri- ate for Alfred to have rewarded his tutor with the assets and revenues arising out of such places. We are told that the monasteries of Congresbury and Banwell were conveyed to Bishop Asser by King Alfred on Christmas Eve morning, by way of 'two letters, in which there was a detailed list of all the things belonging to the two monasteries'.[147]

While the giving of trinkets to warriors may have been a personal matter be- tween lord and man, the conveying of land by charter, on the other hand, involved witnesses to a document—witnesses, who as we have seen, were members of the council. And the conveying of great tracts of land by charter must have involved not only the witness of the council, but also by implication its consent. Herein Chadwick's notion of the lack of collectivity within the *witan* comes to grief. A body of councillors which had huge vested interests in landed estates—the record of whose ownership was registered in documents witnessed by members of that same council—could not but have had a collective sense of its own powers. It was essential to the interests of the *witan* to monitor all major land-owning transac- tions, since all such transactions involved the redistribution of a finite and crucially important resource. Alfred informs us that he and his brothers either severally or individually brought the matter of King Æthelwulf's disputed family inheritance before the whole West Saxon council no less than five times. Alfred's own *Will* in which he disposed of his personal estates was also witnessed by the council cer- tainly once, and almost certainly twice. For those 'many men, with whose witness they—[i.e. the multiple copies of Alfred's first *Will*]—had been drawn up' were surely members of that same West Saxon council which witnessed the final version some years later. It goes without saying that Æthelwulf's *Will*, which was later to cause so much bother, was itself initially witnessed by the council back in 855— a conclusion which we have already reached regarding Æthelwulf's quite separate division of the kingdom. A document which had been dragged before the council five times for elucidation and judgement, almost certainly began life in that same assembly. If there is one single significant conclusion to draw from a study of King Alfred's *Will*, it is the remarkably prominent role accorded there to the *witan*, and the repeated evidence in that document of the *witan*'s crucial involvement in ratifying the inheritance of the kings Æthelwulf, Æthelbald, Æthelberht, Æthelred, and Alfred. And if the royal kindred relied on the backing of the council to resolve their family ownership squabbles, how much more powerfully and decisively must the council have loomed in matters relating to the royal succession. The *witan* cannot have been mere 'yes-men' of the king. They helped to bring him to power initially, in deciding between him and other æthelings, and they brought him to power with the expectation of being eventually rewarded for their pains. The reign of every king must have settled down to become a working partnership between king and *witan*, since a balance needed to be maintained between church, greater lords, and king, in monopolizing and sharing the landed wealth of the kingdom. When the system worked well—as in ninth-century Wessex—it would indeed, have been rare for the *witan* to oppose their king, and in that sense the loyalty of those 'wise men' had been bought. When the system went out of balance—as in the case of ninth-century Northumbria or later tenth-century England—then deposition, assassination, and anarchy might ensue. So, while Alfred no doubt successfully manipulated his council, he could never, on the other hand, ignore the obvious collective power of his wise men.

PART FOUR

The Writings of a Court

XVII

The Anglo-Saxon Chronicle
Search for a West Saxon Dynastic and Christian Past

A Tour around the Chronicle

THE ANGLO-SAXON CHRONICLE COVERS THE HISTORY OF ENGLAND FROM
the time of the earliest English invaders down to AD 1155. The work begins
even earlier, with the record of Caesar's invasion of Britain in 60 BC, followed (as
in Versions A and B for instance) by a continuous numbering of years by AD
reckoning from the birth of Christ (AD 1) onwards. Stenton summed up the
supreme importance of this source thus: 'From the age of the Saxon migration to
the Anarchy of Stephen's reign, they [the various recensions of the Chronicle]
continue to offer information which may be rejected but cannot be ignored. The
criticism of the Chronicle is the basis of Early English Historiography.'[1] There are
seven recensions of the Anglo-Saxon Chronicle, labelled A to G by Plummer and
Earle.[2] The oldest version, A,[3] is also known as the Parker Chronicle, after Archbishop Matthew Parker, who once included that manuscript in his library. The
manuscript of version A is written in one hand down to near the end of AD 891,
and that hand is dated to the late ninth or early tenth century.[4] The place of origin
within Wessex of Manuscript A is disputed, with Parkes's case for a Winchester
origin not having received general approval.[5] Manuscript A may have been at
Winchester from at least as early as the mid-tenth century when the annals for
925–55 were added there. A set of four local Winchester annals for 932–5 (931–
4)—all concerned with bishops of Winchester—points to one of the monastic
houses in that town as a possible home for the manuscript at this period. The
evidence may not be strong, but this island of local interest stands out in contrast
to the lack of detail relating to any other centre in the last three-quarters of the
tenth century. While the scribe of the annals in A for 924 to 946 was also the scribe
of Bald's Leechbook and of the Old English Bede (BL Cotton Otho B.xi), and
while a copy of the West Saxon Laws may belong to the same scriptorium, there
is no certainty that any of these works emanated from Winchester.[6] The date of
Abbot Æthelwold's consecration in the bishopric of Winchester is precisely dated
in the Chronicle to Sunday, the eve of St Andrew's Day in 963 and that record is
allocated a new paragraph on folio 28v of Manuscript A with an initial O—two
lines deep—set in the margin. In the following annal for 964, the fact that monastic disturbances in 'the city (on ceastre)' are assumed to relate to Winchester, which

is not actually named in the text, points to Winchester as the place of writing—as does the familiar but indeterminate reference to the Old and New Minsters.[7] Winchester was the home of Manuscript A at whatever time the annals for 963 and 964 were entered in its text. Manuscript A continues its record down to AD 973, with entries added erratically thereafter. The last entries (in the Second Booklet of A) written in a Winchester hand, belong to the period 973 to 1001. It was removed to Christ Church, Canterbury during the eleventh century and arrived there not later than c.1070. Parkes suggested that Manuscript A may have been taken from Winchester to Canterbury by Bishop Ælfheah of Winchester when he was translated to the archbishopric in 1005.[8] The annals in A from 1005 to 1066 were inserted by a Canterbury scribe (Hand 9) of the early twelfth century.[9]

Manuscripts B and C of the Chronicle are grouped together because of the fact that they have long been considered to derive from a common archetype and because of their supposed Abingdon connection. B[10] continues down to 977 in one hand, while C[11] is an eleventh-century version related to B which was continued down to 1066.[12] B and C are so close to each other that Ker believed the early part of C down to annal 652 to be a direct copy of B. From 653 onwards, C either copied from another version of the Chronicle, as well as from B, or copied, as Bately suggested, from an ancestor of B.[13] B and C contain substantially the same material as A down to 914, and again from 934 to 975, but B and C also contain a few entries from 957 to 977 exclusive to them alone, which led Plummer to believe that B and C derived from a common exemplar at Abingdon. Whitelock had some doubts regarding an Abingdon home for B and C and did not see a copy of the Chronicle reaching Abingdon before c.975.[14] Hart argued for Ramsey rather than Abingdon as being the home of the B text and he made the more radical suggestion that the major distribution of copies of the Chronicle took place not around AD 890 as was once supposed, but in the closing years of the tenth century.[15] Hart also concluded that even Æthelweard's late tenth-century Chronicle showed signs of a Ramsey association[16] and that the precursor of Version D—once considered to have begun life in Northumbria—also derived from a Ramsey milieu.[17] The Mercian Register—a set of Mercian annals running from 902 to 921—was copied into the B text or its precursor B* (and later into C) at some point before the copy of B was produced from its archetype. Hart suggested the Mercian Register was produced at Worcester which was probably also Æthelflæd's centre of power within the kingdom of English Mercia.[18] Gloucester, however, was another possible location, for it was there that Æthelred and his lady, Æthelflæd, were buried. Hart developed a case to show that the B text of the Chronicle originated in Ramsey under the very hand of Byrhtferth and that the B text copied either the 'A text Precursor' or A itself, from the beginning of the Chronicle until 845 and from 934 to 958, rather than an exemplar which was independent of A. Hart also held that the C text (down to 977) derived from A and B and the Mercian Register. That 'A text Precursor' had been taken to Ramsey from its home in Winchester, where Hart surmised that its text of annals stopped at 914.[19] Bately rejected the possibility of B being based on version A or on the Northern Recension which lies behind D and E.[20] She saw the B text as not deriving directly from A, and considered the B text to be as many as perhaps four stages removed from the archetype of the original compilation of the Chronicle.[21]

Hart's ideas were driven by a desire to reach too firm conclusions on a topic, which because of a multitude of unknown factors is of its nature incapable of detailed resolution. So many of the exemplars which once lay behind surviving recensions of the Chronicle have been lost and there has been so much mutual textual interaction between those lost recensions, that it will always remain easier to establish from textual analysis what could not have happened rather than what did happen. But some of Hart's basic ideas in relation to the development of the Chronicle in the late tenth century may well stand the test of scholarly enquiry. His basic tenet, which historians have overlooked for too long, is the undoubted fact that Ramsey lay at the heart of an intellectual and spiritual revival which enjoyed the unrivalled patronage of both the reformers Æthelwold of Winchester and Oswald of Worcester and York, at the end of the tenth century. That patronage and spiritual idealism underpinned the hagiographical and computistical outpourings of Byrhtferth and his Ramsey school. It may well be that the proliferation of the various surviving recensions of the Chronicle stem from that phenomenal cultural movement in the fens in the late tenth and early eleventh centuries. We have already seen how Æthelweard's Chronicle forms part of a wider effort, exemplified also by the Pseudo-Asser, to make the Anglo-Saxon past more accessible through Latin translations of part of the Chronicle's text. This was only one of many facets of a monastic cultural movement in Anglo-Latin which went counter to all that Alfred had being trying to achieve in the vernacular in the century before. We have seen, too, how the Pseudo-Asser, who was one of the Ramsey circle, had access to a text of the Chronicle which ended *c*.892–3 and which prompted the idea of a further work pretending to portray the *Life* of King Alfred, supposedly written in that very year, and based on a Chronicle text. As it happens, Hart argued for two texts of the Chronicle to have been taken from Winchester to Ramsey between 965 and 1002 and at the time when Abbo of Fleury was visiting Ramsey in 985–7.[22] Hart may not have been correct in believing those Chronicle texts to have been the existing A text and an 'A text Precursor' or archetype of A, which Hart argued had then ended at 914.[23] But a foreshortened version of A's exemplar is what we have seen from other evidence, lay behind the text of the Pseudo-Asser's *Life* of Alfred, which was written up at Ramsey in *c*.1000 or soon after. Hart argued for the continuation of the A text precursor down to 914. But if that precursor consisted of two proto-booklets—one of which ended in 892–3, we would then have the necessary conditions for the production of the *Life* of Alfred.[24] Hart explained Stevenson's finding that 'Asser's [*sic*] source was much closer to B than to A'[25] as due to the fact that 'Asser and the B chronicler had available the same chronicle source for this period'.[26] Bately, while acknowledging similarities between the *Life* of Alfred and Versions B and C of the Chronicle has also shown, however, that the vernacular text of the Chronicle used by the author of the *Life* of Alfred was not immediately related to versions B, C, D, or E.[27] On

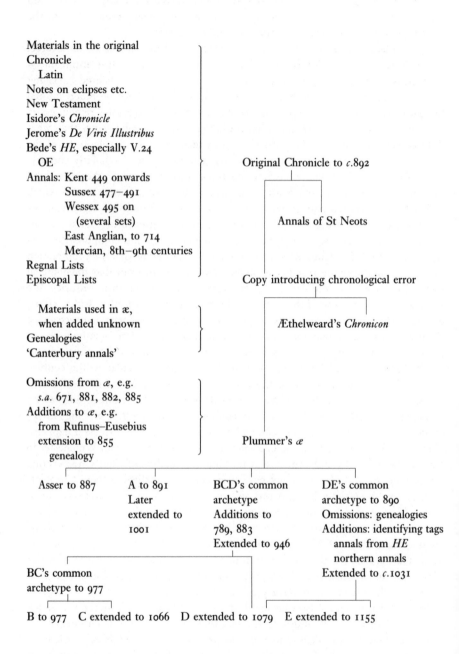

Materials in the original
Chronicle
  Latin
Notes on eclipses etc.
New Testament
Isidore's *Chronicle*
Jerome's *De Viris Illustribus*
Bede's *HE*, especially V.24
  OE   Original Chronicle to *c.*892
Annals: Kent 449 onwards
      Sussex 477–491
      Wessex 495 on
        (several sets)   Annals of St Neots
      East Anglian, to 714
      Mercian, 8th–9th centuries
Regnal Lists
Episcopal Lists   Copy introducing chronological error

  Materials used in æ,
    when added unknown   Æthelweard's *Chronicon*
Genealogies
'Canterbury annals'

Omissions from *æ*, e.g.
  s.a. 671, 881, 882, 885
Additions to *æ*, e.g.
  from Rufinus–Eusebius
  extension to 855
    genealogy   Plummer's *æ*

| Asser to 887 | A to 891 Later extended to 1001 | BCD's common archetype Additions to 789, 883 Extended to 946 | DE's common archetype to 890 Omissions: genealogies Additions: identifying tags annals from *HE* northern annals Extended to *c.*1031 |

BC's common
archetype to 977

B to 977   C extended to 1066   D extended to 1079   E extended to 1155

FIG. 10. Meaney's interpretation for the development of the Anglo-Saxon Chronicle

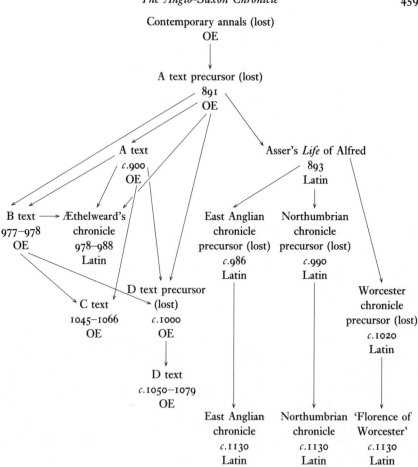

FIG. 11. Hart's interpretation for the development of the Anglo-Saxon Chronicle

the other hand, the acknowledged similarities between Version B and the Latin text of the Chronicle in the *Life* of Alfred would make good sense within the context we have uncovered of the Pseudo-Asser belonging to that very Ramsey school where the B text may have been produced. The arrival also in Ramsey of a fuller version of the Chronicle—(not necessarily the A text as Hart believed)—allows for the development and continuation of further copies of the Anglo-Chronicle in the Ramsey scriptorium.

Versions D and E of the Chronicle are also linked to each other—both deriving from the same northern recension which Whitelock believed originated in York. There is little doubt that the Northumbrian annals which were incorporated into northern versions of the Chronicle did indeed originate in York. But Hart's argument that those northern annals were taken south to Ramsey in the time of Byrhtferth who incorporated them into his *Historical Miscellany* and that at Ramsey

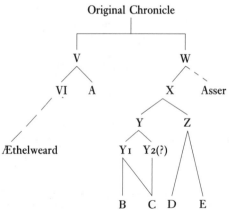

A – E = extant versions of the Chronicle

FIG. 12. Bately's interpretation for the development of the Anglo-Saxon Chronicle

Note: Professor Bately did not in her published stemma of the Chronicle's manuscript development show a direct link between the Æthelweard-A tradition (deriving from V) and the Asser-B/E tradition (deriving from W).

also they provided the basis for the precursor of version D of the Chronicle makes excellent sense.[28] The palaeography of D[29] dates to the second half of the eleventh century and its annals sustain their northern interest until the end of that particular manuscript's record in 1079. Version E[30] or its precursor E*, embodying its version of the northern recension, arrived in St Augustine's, Canterbury *c.*1043 and later came to Peterborough sometime between 1116 and 1121, when the surviving copy of E was produced there and where it was continued down to 1155.[31] Version F[32] is a bilingual version of the Chronicle in Latin and Old English, extending down to 1058 and produced at Canterbury *c.*1100. It represents a Canterbury collation of its archetype—version E*—with version A, together with Canterbury and other material extending down to AD 1058. Version G[33] was copy of A, which was largely destroyed in the Cottonian fire of 1731. Our knowledge of that text depends on an edition of Whelock in 1644 and on a transcript made by Nowell[34] in the sixteenth century. G provides important evidence for the condition of the A text before it left Winchester and before it was altered in some of its annals at Canterbury by the scribe of F. Version H[35] is fragmentary, covering the late period, 1113–14, and is independent of E.[36] Several other versions of the Chronicle survive over varying chronological ranges in Latin translations of the works of other medieval English historians. The Chronicle of Æthelweard, which was written at the end of the tenth century by a descendant of one of King Alfred's troublesome nephews—the sons of Æthelred I—extended down at least as far as AD 975, and was considered by Whitelock to be 'in some respects closer to the original than any surviving manuscript'.[37] The *Life* of Alfred, compiled by the Pseudo-Asser at the same time or soon after Æthelweard was writing, also contains a translation of the Chronicle covering Alfred's life from 851 down to 887.[38] The

Annals of St. Neots represent yet a fuller Latin version of the Chronicle which was free from the chronological error which is found in other extant versions from 756 to 845. Stevenson believed that the version of the Chronicle used by the compiler of the Annals of St Neots was closest to the original Chronicle text and also closest to versions B and C.[39] Other medieval chroniclers such as Henry of Huntingdon, Florence (*alias* John) of Worcester, William of Malmesbury, and works ascribed to Symeon of Durham all used versions of the Chronicle text.[40]

When we refer then, to the Anglo-Saxon Chronicle, we refer to a whole series of manuscript versions of a work which was first compiled at some point in the later ninth century and which was continued and sometimes re-edited at different centres and for different lengths of time, down to the middle of the twelfth century. There is no one definitive manuscript version of the Anglo-Saxon Chronicle because not even the oldest Parker Manuscript (A) provides us with the earliest text, and from the tenth century onwards, most of the surviving versions begin to develop their own independent record of events. On the other hand, all versions of the Chronicle derive from a core text down to 891 and all the main versions of the Chronicle contain essentially editions—with significant additions and omissions— of the same work down as far as *c*. AD 1042, after which those versions which were still being added to, tend to go their own way. Because of the organic nature of the Chronicle—the fact that it began life in the ninth century with its record projected backwards by its first compilers to the time of Julius Caesar and the birth of Christ, and because of its survival as a national chronicle well beyond the Norman invasion—we need to be clear in our minds about the different order of entries in this complex historical source. There are several basic levels at which information is preserved within the Chronicle. It is a source which preserves stratigraphical components of text, and confusion on the part of Chronicle students in regard to the chronology of these many layers of recording has too often led to serious distortion in our understanding of the Chronicle as a whole. The first layer relates to source material which pre-dates the compilatory stage of the Chronicle in the ninth century. This material which was gathered by the ninth-century compilers may contain an accurate or contemporary recording of an event. Such information may have been gleaned by the compilers of the Chronicle from Bede, from king-lists, from a lost set of genuine annals, or from less reliable earlier sagas or oral tradition. But this information whatever its worth to the historian—unless it had been invented or radically edited—pre-dates the period of compilation of the Chronicle. An example of this kind of entry, which reveals the contrast between the most important versions of the Chronicle, is the record of the victory of Æthelfrith, king of the Northumbrians, over Áedán mac Gabhráin, king of Dál Riata in 603. The laconic record preserved in versions B, C, and originally in A reads: 'in this year was the battle of *Dagsastan (Her wæs gefeoht æt Egesanstane)*.'[41] The original Chronicle followed Bede's Epitome in its brief record under 603 of *pugnatum ad Degsastanae*. Version E, on the other hand—being a copy of a northern recension which added in early Northumbrian annals and material from the main body of Bede's *Ecclesiastical History* to the original core text of the Chronicle—

expanded its account of *Degsastan*. The E version names the two main protagonists
in this fight; identifies the place of the victory as *Degsastan*; and tells us that
'Theodbald, Æthelfrith's brother, was killed with all his troop'. Version E even
copied Bede's triumphant statement that 'no king of Scots dared afterwards lead
an army against this nation'.[42] The E chronicler does add one crumb of information on *Degsastan* which had not been found in Bede, namely the record that
'Hering son of Hussa, led the army thither'. Here then, in the pre-contemporary
section of the Chronicle, we have additional early material from the latest and
longest continued of the manuscript versions. This material was lifted with almost
word-for-word translation (albeit a corrupt translation) from Bede's Latin narrative
of his *Historia*, but we are also presented with a Northumbrian tradition which is
likely to derive from some early oral or written source available to the compiler of
the archetype of the northern recension. Another example of early material pressed
into service by the ninth-century compilers is the account of the rebellion of
Cyneheard against the West Saxon king, Cynewulf, narrated under AD 755 in MS
A.[43] Some of that narrative at least was inspired by a saga or lay, which initially
may have been an oral source.[44]

A second major layer in the textual stratigraphy of the Chronicle relates to that
time when the ninth-century compilers, having assembled their historical material,
then added their own personal contribution by way of a contemporary or near-
contemporary record of events. This material divides in turn into two main categories—a very short period of strictly contemporary reporting of events which
had just occurred at or immediately before the time of compilation, and a much
longer period extending back over the living memories of the compilers' generation. The first strictly contemporary material, covered by a small number of annals,
represents the earliest continuous contemporary record within the Chronicle,
and its identification is of crucial importance for the historian. The second category of entries within the compilatory horizon relates to events of the compilers'
own immediate past. Although this material was technically historical in relation
to the compilers' own day, it related to a recent era for which they needed few
historical sources to guide them. The great bulk of the record relating to the
second half of the ninth century—from the reign of Æthelwulf down to Alfred—
falls into this category. Since this phase in the Chronicle's make-up has such an
important bearing on Alfredian studies, we shall return to it in detail, later on. We
may pursue the archaeological metaphor further, in our attempt to understand the
evolution of the Chronicle's text. For just as archaeological stratigraphy can be
disturbed by later intrusions and diggings through earlier deposits of soil and
accumulated debris, so, too, the textual layers of the Chronicle are not always
neatly separated from each other. The mid-ninth-century compilers, in their role
as gatherers of the earliest material in the first layer of world history and other
prefatory matter, will have inevitably interfered with any original narrative through
the process of editing and translating. Later editors in their turn reviewed the text
of the ninth-century compilers and filled in lacunae which they found there with
alternative information from other sources.

The third major layer of material in the Chronicle is that which makes up the ongoing process of compilation, and may therefore be peculiar to a particular manuscript preserved in one particular location, or it may contain information shared by several subsequent recensions of the continuation. In the case of recensions A, B, and C, for instance, they share a core text up to *c*.891–2 with varying continuations from then until 914. Assuming—at this stage in our discussion— that the first compilation was accomplished by 914 at the very latest, the material post-914 in A, B, and C clearly constitutes subsequent continuations to the original compilation. So, for instance, while B and C have no entries for the year 925 to 933 inclusive, version A, on the other hand—although also blank from 925 to 930 inclusive—does have annals for 931 and 932. A's annal for 933 (recording Athelstan's invasion of Scotland) corresponds to the annal for 934 in B. But while B and C share A's information on the Scottish invasion, A alone has two additional brief notices of the death of Bishop Byrnstan of Winchester on All Saints' Day (933) and the succession of Ælfheah to 'the bishopric'—i.e. that same bishopric of Winchester in 934. Such additions as this to version A are suggestive of its Winchester location at the time when these entries were added by the scribe of Hand Three in or soon after 955.[45] Not all continuations represent contemporary recording of events—many constitute the retrospective writing up of extensive periods of time in an effort to take a particular version of the Chronicle up to date. The summary account of the reign of Alfred's grandson, Athelstan, for instance, can scarcely have derived from contemporary annals and was written up retrospectively. The entries for Athelstan's reign are written in the same hand of mid-tenth-century date (*Hand Three*) in Manuscript A, as wrote up all the annals from 924 to 955 inclusive.[46] Since this period of continuations in all versions, stretching from *c*.900 down to 1155, lies outside the span of Alfred's life, we are not, on the whole, concerned with it, except in so far as the Alfredian record in earlier versions of the Chronicle may have been altered or edited at a later time, or when a later manuscript version of the Chronicle contains a record from the Alfredian era which may be closer to the prototype of the original core section of the Chronicle, than that preserved in the Parker Manuscript (A).

A fourth class of entries in the Chronicle, which may relate to any section within the compilation, represents the work of later editors of the post ninth-century compilatory era, carrying out revisions or additions to the earlier record. The scribe of the Parker Chronicle left four years (710 to 713 inclusive) devoid of any annalistic entries, but listed—as was usual for the scribe of version A—each barren year with its AD dating. The same scribe left space after AD 710 however, for material from his exemplar, which he had perhaps intended to insert there. Later in the mid-tenth century, the scribe of Hand Three inserted the annal relating to 710 in the blank space left for it in version A on folio 9r. This is the record of Ealdorman Brihtferth's battle with the Picts and of Ine and Nunna's battle with Geraint.[47] These retrospective additions of material in the Anglo-Saxon Chronicle usually arose from the later collation of one recension with that of another. For instance, the record of the death of Alfred's son, King Edward, in 924, is thought to have been added to a prototype of version E (E*) and to version F of the Chronicle when they were at Canterbury and when they were collated there with the Parker Manuscript (version A).[48] It is against the background of this complex classification of textual layers of entries that we must now attempt to identify the period of first compilation, when the Anglo-Saxon Chronicle came into being as the result of an elaborate programme of research on the part of its original compilers.

The Years before Alfred

The world chronicle which follows the preface to the Anglo-Saxon Chronicle consists of a summary of events from Hebrew, New Testament, Roman, and Early Christian history. Although this introductory material was supplied by the compilers with its succession of *Anno Domini* dates, the great majority of these years were left void of annalistic material for that historical hiatus between Classical Antiquity and the early fifth century.[49] Whether or not the compilers' original plan envisaged the possibility of the later filling in of these blank years, remains debatable. It was once thought that that section of the world chronicle from the birth of Christ to the arrival of Hengist and Horsa was based in part at least, on the Old English translation of *Orosius*, a work which was then ascribed erroneously to King Alfred.[50] Bately ruled out any direct influence from the Old English *Orosius* on this early section of the Anglo-Saxon Chronicle and identified the main sources which lay behind its introductory world chronicle as derived from Isidore's *Chronicon*, Rufinus's translation of Eusebius's *Ecclesiastical History*, the *Liber Pontificalis*, and Jerome's *De Viris Illustribus*.[51] Other material relating to early English history in this introductory section was derived from Easter tables, early annals, regnal and episcopal lists, and the Epitome or Recapitulation at the end of Bede's *Ecclesiastical History*.[52] It was this summary at the end of Bede's work, rather than the main narrative of Bede's *History* which was pressed into service by the compiler of the Chronicle with little attempt at adaptation.[53] The earliest extant version of the Chronicle—that of the First Booklet of Manuscript A ending on fol. 25v at AD 920—is written in a West Saxon dialect of Old English and is dated (from its latest hand) on palaeographical grounds to somewhere before c.930. The final entry in Hand One could not have been made before AD 891 (when that hand finishes on fol. 16r) and this hand is likely to date from the early tenth century rather than from the late ninth.[54] In spite of the uncertainties in dating Hand One and Hand Two in Manuscript A, we may conclude on palaeographical grounds alone that the earliest compilation of the Chronicle must have taken place either before the end of King Alfred's reign or not later than the reign of his son, Edward. As long as the Pseudo-Asser's text (which followed the Chronicle closely down to 887) was accepted as a contemporary biography compiled in AD 893, that year provided a *terminus ante quem* date for the compilation of the Chronicle. There is universal agreement that the Chronicle began life within the kingdom of Wessex, and while the majority of scholarly opinion now favours a compilation date from the reign of

Alfred, there has been a serious minority view in favour of a first compilation in the reign of his father, King Æthelwulf (835–66). While there is disagreement over when the Chronicle was compiled, there has been nothing less than acrimonious conflict over who compiled the work and where. This debate with its conflicting lobbies has led in turn to unsatisfactory scholarly compromises. A lobby which had its most able champion in Plummer and which won later adherents such as R. H. C. Davis held that King Alfred or someone in his immediate court circle produced the work, while another led by Stenton preferred a south-western English provenance and saw the author as a politically disinterested West Saxon ealdorman of one of the western shires. Whitelock modified Stenton's theory of a West Country authorship but held to the fundamental orthodoxy of Stenton in rejecting any Alfredian involvement in the Chronicle.[55]

It may be useful to enter the maze of Chronicle scholarship at the point where Chadwick, Liebermann, Brandl, and—more recently Barker—have identified the reign of Alfred's father, King Æthelwulf, as the period of compilation.[56] Scholars holding this minority view see the first period of compilation taking place during or at the end of Æthelwulf's reign, and see the period from 855 to 899 as a continuation of that earlier compilation. While it is not impossible to reconcile this thesis with an Alfredian inspiration for the further development and circulation of the Chronicle, nevertheless a mid–ninth-century origin would allow King Alfred, or any one of his circle, or even someone working independently of Alfred during his reign at best only a marginal role in the creation of this great historical record. The reasons which prompted some scholars to see a major landmark in the development of the Chronicle in Æthelwulf's reign are valid and instructive. First, there is the remarkable prominence afforded the notice of the death of King Æthelwulf in the composite annal covering the years 855–8. After stating that the king was buried in Winchester and had reigned for eighteen and a half years, we are presented with a genealogy which traces the descent of the dead king not only back through the legendary Cerdic to Woden, but from that Germanic wargod back through Noah's son to Adam. The rounding off of this lengthy genealogy with the phrase 'Adam the first man and our father, i.e. Christ. Amen'[57] might indeed suggest that a landmark had been reached in the compilation here, and the word 'amen', which is peculiar to the Parker Chronicle, is again indicative of a 'rounding off' of a narrative which might pre-date that earliest surviving manuscript copy of the original compilation. The second notable feature relating to the Chronicle narrative immediately after the death of Æthelwulf is the surprising lack of information on the reigns of his immediate successors—the kings Æthelbald and Æthelberht. This dearth of information following the apparent detail on the last years of Æthelwulf, together with his elaborate genealogy, might be taken to suggest a break in the recording process at this point. This in turn could be explained by dating the earliest period of compilation to the end of Æthelwulf's reign, and seeing the next period of continuation or updating, as commencing in Alfred's reign from 871, with a period of annalistic neglect in the interim from 858 to 870. Barker believed that the first compilation of the Anglo-Saxon Chronicle

was a pre-Alfredian work written in one hand down to the annal for 855 and that
this pre-Alfredian version was used by Æthelweard. Barker suggested further, that
the original compilation and its earliest continuation as used by Æthelweard did
not contain a set of Canterbury annals which were later added into the surviving
core text of other extant versions of the Chronicle.[58] Barker's views on a 855
horizon for the first compilation and for a Mercian origin for Æthelweard's copy
of the Chronicle were challenged by Meaney[59] who pointed to the retrospective
nature of much of the Chronicle's record in the period *c*.840–60—not least in the
notice of Alfred's consecration in Rome.[60] If the compilation had indeed come into
being in 855–8, we should expect clear evidence for contemporaneity of recording
for the years immediately preceding, and such evidence is singularly lacking.

There is an alternative explanation for the undoubted importance of Æthelwulf's
genealogy and for the poor documentation on Æthelbald and Æthelberht, and an
analysis of the erratic record supplied by the Chronicle for the period 802 to 858
shows that no serious case can be made for the first compilation of a chronicle at
that time. First, there is not sufficient information given on either Æthelwulf's or
on his father Ecgberht's reign to warrant an argument for ascribing the period of
compilation to 802–58. There may well have been an annalistic source available to
a later compiler which supplied him with information on the reign of Ecgberht
(802–39),[61] but the coverage of events from this period is too erratic and too laconic
to suggest a compilatory phase at such an early time. Any annals surviving from
Ecgberht's reign could have been put to use by a later compiler in the same way
as he had used Bede's Epitome. There is no doubt that the compilers of the
Chronicle were in possession of more uniform coverage on the reign of Alfred's
grandfather, Ecgberht, than they were on his father, Æthelwulf, and they certainly
provided an abundance of information on Ecgberht, compared with the dismissive
treatment of his grandsons, Æthelbald and Æthelberht. But that record on Ecgberht
differs significantly both in quantity and in format, from what we shall recognize
as the Chronicle's contemporary narrative from the time of the first compilation.
Thorogood, who recognized the existence of a set of annals covering Ecgberht's
reign, also recognized a hiatus in the record from what she saw as 'a definite break'
at 839 (*recte* 842): 'The annals after this date have all the marks of retrospective
writing, and seem like stop-gaps to fill in the years between the end of an existing
Chronicle and the point, early in Alfred's reign, when contemporary annalistic
writing began again.'[62] Leaving aside the confusion here between chronicles and
annals, and also the precise point in Alfred's reign when strictly contemporary
recording began, this statement still holds good in general terms. Thorogood also
showed that from 796 through 825 the annals of Ecgberht's reign reckoned the
beginning of each year on 25 December, in line with practice in the Northumbrian
annals for this same period, as preserved in Byrhtferth's *Historical Miscellany*.[63]
The change from reckoning the beginning of a new year in the Chronicle from 25
December to the Caesarean Indiction on 25 September or to any other date in
September–October occurred somewhere between 839 and 851. Thorogood argued for that change in dating to have coincided with the break which she had

otherwise recognized at c.842, and to have been associated with the compilation of the earliest version of the Chronicle, not in Æthelwulf's but in Alfred's reign.

Thorogood's observations on the stop-gap nature of the record covering Æthelwulf's later years and the reigns of his three immediate successors were essentially correct—and in particular her key observation that (in Manuscript A) there are only six entries in the Chronicle covering the quarter century from 840 to 865.[64] The elaborate entry (under 855) relating to Æthelwulf's death is especially indicative of the retrospective tone of the reporting on that king. It summarizes a whole sequence of events which stretched over several years, but which were all entered under 855—the vikings' wintering on Sheppey, Æthelwulf's so-called Decimation, his pilgrimage to Rome, his marriage to the Carolingian Judith, his death and genealogy, the succession of Æthelbald to Wessex and of Æthelberht to the eastern region. The very tone of the narrative is also strongly retrospective: 'and two years after he had come from France, he died, and his body is buried in Winchester.' The statement in this summary that 'Æthelbald reigned five years' not only writes off the reign of that king as an historical black hole in early English history, but it shows that the entry as it stands in the Parker Manuscript cannot have been compiled before AD 860, and since the Danish wintering on Sheppey must have happened in the autumn of 864,[65] this retrospective summary of West Saxon history covers no less than six years.

The insertion of the elaborate West Saxon genealogy in connection with the notice of King Æthelwulf's death can be interpreted to reflect as much credit on King Alfred as it does on his father. While it might be reasonable to view this formal demonstration of royal descent as the epilogue to a completed compilation, there are more compelling reasons to view it as a beginning. Whitelock believed that this could have been a suitable place for a compiler working in Alfred's reign 'to insert the family tree of the reigning house',[66] although she conceded that it would have been more logical to place it after the death of Ecgberht, the first king of his dynasty. Bately identified elements of vocabulary in the 855 entry which marked it off from surrounding material and suggested it might have been written by the same person—'the first Alfredian annalist'—who compiled the annals of the 870s.[67] Sisam regarded Æthelwulf's pedigree at 855 as 'additional material, artlessly tacked on' and in no way providing evidence for the ending of a compilation at 855.[68] When we recall Alfred's virtual obsession in his *Will* with striving to establish a special relationship between himself and his father Æthelwulf, and the special appeal in that document made by Alfred over the heads of his older brothers to the *Will* of his father, and to the implied special relationship he believed he enjoyed with Æthelwulf, we begin to see the significance of the elaborate genealogy accorded that king in the Anglo-Saxon Chronicle. Sisam's suggestion that the pedigree of Æthelwulf was inserted in the Chronicle under annal 855 in order to flatter one of Æthelwulf's sons—'particularly Alfred'—has much to recommend it.[69] The prominence accorded to Æthelwulf in the Chronicle's notice of his death forms part of the same strategy of recording demonstrated in the extraordinary account of Alfred's crowning in Rome under the year 853. If we were to believe that record, it was after all 'King Æthelwulf' who 'sent his son Alfred to Rome' to be consecrated king by the pope in that year. Whitelock's naïve argument that Alfred could possible have mistaken the significance of this ceremony was sensibly countered by Davis who believed: 'It is surely obvious that Alfred stood to gain by the mis-statement. . . . The notion that Alfred was predestined to rule Wessex because he had been consecrated by the pope must surely have been convenient to Alfred.'[70] The record of Alfred's consecration as king by the pope could scarcely have entered the Anglo-Saxon Chronicle without Alfred's connivance, and the underpinning of this claim by association with Alfred's father, Æthelwulf, was an attempt to lend an air of legitimacy to the premature conferring of kingship on an infant ætheling. This record of Alfred's infantile consecration in the kingship is yet another instance of retrospective reporting on the reign of Æthelwulf.

According to versions A and B of the Chronicle, King Æthelwulf was buried in Winchester. The *Annals of St. Neots* however—which contain yet another version of the core text of the earliest Chronicle—claim Æthelwulf was buried at Steyning in Sussex.[71] Steyning reappears in the text of King Alfred's *Will* as part of that king's complicated inheritance which he left to his nephew, Æthelwold.[72] The place may also have formed part of the royal inheritance of Æthelwulf, and so its church would have enjoyed his royal patronage. The record of the burial of Æthelwulf was in nobody's interest to invent, so it would seem that Æthelwulf was first buried at Steyning when he died in 858, and his body was later moved to Winchester where it was to form the centre of a royal mausoleum for the newly established House of Alfred. The removal to Winchester must date to Alfred's reign. It was Alfred and his son, Edward, who singled out the church of Winchester for their royal patronage, and it was Alfred who, in his *Will*, chose to be buried in Winchester, while his brothers who preceded him in the kingship were interred in Wimborne and Sherborne minsters. The creation of this royal mausoleum which clearly dates from Alfred's time and which was eventually to contain the remains of Alfred himself, of his queen, his son Edward, and several of his grandsons, may have been consciously modelled on the West Frankish mausoleum at St Denis or the earlier Carolingian mausoleum at Aachen.[73] If the record of Æthelwulf's earlier burial at Steyning can be trusted, then the subsequent burial of that king in Winchester formed part of a wider picture in which Alfred developed his public position in relation to the close association he was supposed to have enjoyed with his father. However we interpret the reinterment of Æthelwulf in Winchester, the notice of a Winchester burial was almost certainly entered in the Chronicle during Alfred's reign.

A version of the genealogy associated with King Æthelwulf in the 855 annal is reproduced in the king-list at the very beginning of Manuscript A's text of the Chronicle. The earliest section of the Anglo-Saxon Chronicle—an introductory world chronicle—is preceded by a king-list and parts of a genealogy which, in the oldest Manuscript A, follows the West Saxon royal succession from its alleged origins with Cerdic in the Migration age, down to King Alfred.[74] The figures of

Alfred and his father, Æthelwulf, loom large in the Chronicle's prefatory genealogy in the oldest extant manuscript, for not only does that genealogy end with Alfred, but when Alfred's name is reached in the king-list, the compiler of the genealogy presents him as a ruler representing the culmination of English history thus far. And when the name of Æthelwulf is reached in the king-list, Æthelwulf's genealogy is inserted there, tracing his line back to Cerdic, before the list moves on to name Æthelbald as his immediate successor. The preface begins with the supposed origins of the English or at least of the West Saxon people: 'In the year when 494 years had passed from Christ's birth, Cerdic and his son Cynric landed at *Cerdicesora* with five ships.'[75] Cerdic's genealogy is next traced back to Woden and we are told that Cerdic (and his son, Cynric) 'were the first kings who conquered the land of the West Saxons from the Britons'. The West Saxon king-list then follows down to Alfred's father, Æthelwulf, whose genealogy is then inserted and traced back to Cerdic. So, whoever inserted this West Saxon king-list at the beginning of the Chronicle's oldest text, designedly broke the West Saxon pedigree into two parts, basing the earlier part on Cerdic and the more recent half on King Æthelwulf. By so doing, Æthelwulf—of all West Saxon kings—was placed on a par with the supposed founder of the West Saxon kingship and the first king of his line who supposedly conquered Wessex. The succession of Æthelwulf's sons—Æthelbald, Æthelberht, and Æthelred—is next noted without comment, and the preface closes with a fanfare on Alfred: 'Then their brother Alfred succeeded to the kingdom, and then 23 years of his life were past, and 396 years from when his race first conquered the land of the West Saxons from the Britons.'[76] Alfred is unique among all kings in this prefatory material in having his age noted at the time when he came to the kingship. Unlike other kings in the list, his reign-length was not given, because Alfred was still ruling when this introductory section of the Chronicle was compiled. This rounding off of the prefatory material with Alfred seen as succeeding 396 years after Cerdic's conquest, and with Æthelwulf presented in the image of a second Cerdic, may suggest that the compiler of this preface also shared the notion of the special relationship that was supposed to have existed between Æthelwulf and his youngest infant son, Alfred. It could of course be argued that the prominence accorded to Æthelwulf in the body of the text of this prefatory material might suggest it was composed during Æthelwulf's reign and that the note on Alfred was tagged on later during Alfred's rule. In the version of this same preface which survives on a separate leaf once appended to version B of the Chronicle, the special 'rounding off' at Alfred's place in the king-list is edited out and the list is continued down to include Edward the Martyr.[77] But however we date the original composition of the prefatory matter in the Chronicle there is no denying the special emphasis accorded to Æthelwulf and to his son Alfred, in that oldest surviving version of it in Manuscript A, which clearly comes from Alfred's reign.

The special treatment accorded to Æthelwulf in the Anglo-Saxon Chronicle and the diminution of the roles allotted to Alfred's older brothers and predecessors in the kingship reminds us of the special relationship that the Pseudo-Asser pretended

to have existed between the infant Alfred and his father.[78] It is true as Stenton
noticed, that the Chronicle is significantly silent on Æthelbald's supposed rebellion
against his father, whereas this episode was played up and almost certainly invented by the compiler of the *Life* of Alfred. But Stenton failed to recognize the
deliberate diminution of the role of Alfred's brothers in Alfredian and later tenth-
and eleventh-century sources alike, and while this process had reached grotesque
dimensions in the hands of the Pseudo-Asser, it was none the less already present
in the Chronicle also. The reason, therefore, that the record for the years immediately following Æthelwulf's death looks scrappy ought not to be attributed either
to the end of an earlier period of compilation, nor solely to the notion of this being
a stop-gap period between Alfredian contemporaneity and the ending of earlier
annals *c*.840. It is due to a large extent to the later chronicler's deliberate silence on
the achievements of the kings Æthelbald and Æthelberht. The Chronicle tells us
nothing of Æthelbald other than that he ruled in Wessex for five years and that he
was buried in Sherborne. It leaves a void for the history of Æthelbald's reign from
855–60, and the meagre information it supplies on this king might easily have been
gleaned from a king-list which had been glossed with a notice of the place of burial.
The reign of Æthelbald's brother and successor, Æthelberht, is treated in no
greater detail. He is said to have held the whole kingdom (of Wessex and the east)
'in good harmony and great peace'—and was buried in Sherborne after a reign of
five years. During Æthelberht's reign a Danish army stormed Winchester and in
865 the Danes are recorded ravaging in East Kent, but Æthelberht was not associated by the chronicler with either campaign.[79] It is a remarkable fact that from
the death of King Æthelwulf (recorded under 855 for 858) up to the Nottingham
expedition in 868, no West Saxon king is recorded as doing anything in the
Chronicle apart from reigning or dying. And it is surely significant that after a
lapse of ten years from the death of Æthelwulf, it is none other than Alfred who
is pointedly introduced to the Chronicle record while not yet king, but associated
with his brother, King Æthelred. Alfred and Æthelred are seen there—quite
unlike Æthelbald or Æthelberht—to be acting in a positive way. It was Davis who
first observed the phenomenon that although Æthelred's succession is noted in the
Chronicle in 866 'we are not told anything about King Æthelred alone'.[80] So
'Æthelred and his brother Alfred' were jointly approached by the Mercians and
then went to the help of the Mercians at Nottingham in 868, while the same
formula (*Æþered cyning 7 Ælfred his broþur*) is used four more times of the royal
brothers in relation to their campaigns at Reading, Ashdown, Basing, and Meretun,
in the hectic year of 871.[81] This brings the chronicler conveniently to record the
death of Æthelred I after Easter in 871 and to the succession of 'his brother Alfred,
the son of Æthelwulf' (*Ælfred Æþelwulfing his broþur*) to which virtually everything recorded in this chronicle so far has been leading. We notice too, that at the
record of his succession, Alfred changes from being not only the brother (*his
broþur*) of King Æthelred, but also to being the son of that renowned Æthelwulf
whose death and genealogy was entered in the record back in 855.

A study of the events of Æthelred's reign shows that while the compiler treated all records which may have survived from the reigns of Æthelbald and Æthelberht by silence and omission, the message given for the reign of Æthelred is that although he was a worthy ruler, he never once functioned as king without the close association of 'his brother Alfred'. While Alfred's name is paired five times in association with all of King Æthelred's campaigning, he is referred to on three further occasions in the A text as 'his [i.e. Æthelred's] brother Alfred'.[82] This prominent treatment of a younger brother of a reigning king is unprecedented in the Anglo-Saxon Chronicle.[83] The inevitable conclusion to be drawn from this record is that the compiler of the Chronicle was anxious—within the limits imposed by his formulaic annalistic genre—to accord Alfred the highest possible profile in his narrative, even before he became king. We can see how, when a writer of the Pseudo-Asser's inventiveness perused the Chronicle in his desperate quest for information on the early Alfred, he was led to ever more extravagant distortions of the truth: 'He [Alfred] could easily have taken it [the kingship of Wessex] over with the consent of all while his brother, Æthelred, was alive, had he considered himself worthy to do so, for he surpassed all his brothers both in wisdom and in all good habits; and in particular because he was a great warrior and victorious in virtually all battles.'[84] This was precisely the effect which the chronicler of the reign of Æthelred I intended his narrative to have on his readers.

The Stenton Thesis

As early as 1925, Stenton, in a brief and—what was even by the standards of the time—a poorly argued paper laid a false trail in Alfredian studies which has rarely been openly and comprehensively challenged even by that growing number of scholars who otherwise rejected Stenton's findings on this subject on points of detail. Stenton was not comfortable with annalistic research. He lacked Plummer's intuitive understanding of the recording of early medieval dynastic struggles, and he was insensitive to the true significance of topographical detail in annalistic recording. In his paper on 'The South-Western Element in the Old English Chronicle',[85] Stenton proclaimed that not only was the Chronicle compiled in the south-west of Wessex, but it was created in isolation from King Alfred and his court by some unknown ninth-century nobleman for 'personal reasons not now to be discovered'.[86] The approach was methodologically flawed from the outset. Not only was he investing material which had been conflated from a wide variety of sources with a coherence which it had never possessed, but he also chose largely to ignore the complex interrelationships between the surviving versions of the Chronicle. Stenton based his analysis of annalistic entries on the period 754–891, although he and all leading scholars on the Chronicle were already well aware by that time of the possible changes which may have taken place within the record at c.855 and later in the 870s and 880s. Stenton was analysing a composite sample of entries brought together by compilers from diverse sources which may indeed have included south-western material from annals pre-dating the Chronicle's first compilatory phase, as well as other diverse material from different regions within southern England.

Stenton singled out only five annals from the period 754 to 891 to prove his theory of a West Country authorship. Those annals covered events from 789, 845, 851, 867, and 878. The first of these described the arrival of three ships on the Wessex coast in 789 whose crews slew a local reeve who tried to bring them before the West Saxon king, Brihtric.[87] The *Annals of St. Neots* identified the newcomers as Northmen and their port of call in Wessex as Portland.[88] Æthelweard identified the reeve as Beaduheard and claimed he was in Dorchester when news of the ships' arrival reached him.[89] An eighth-century entry such as this, if it were a contemporary record—as Stenton believed it to have been—might tell us little about the location of a compiler or continuator of the Chronicle proper who worked in the second half of the ninth century. Nor could we necessarily argue that a ninth-century compiler who used late eighth-century material relating to the West Country had himself an abiding interest in that part of England. The compilers of the Anglo-Saxon Chronicle had so little information on any part of England, that prior to their own period of compilation, they used whatever annals or documentation that came to hand. A compiler who included records of far-off Pictish battles such as *Degsastan* or the doings of Bishop Ceolwulf of distant Lindsey (*sub anno* 794 for 796) would have seized on this exotic account of the first Danish raid on Wessex, regardless of where he was himself located within the kingdom. The comment in this 789 annal—'Those were the first ships of Danish men who came to the land of the English' which is common to A, B, and to Æthelweard, clearly shows it to have been a retrospective entry, and the fact that the later chronicler, Æthelweard, brings additional local information to bear on the record does not as we shall see, prove that the Anglo-Saxon Chronicle was either compiled in Western Wessex or that it was compiled in isolation from the king and his court. Stenton's approach to the annals for 845 and 851 was essentially speculative:

> The suspicion that the chronicler's interest lay in the south-western shires is materially strengthened by the annal of 845, which tells how the ealdormen of Somerset and Dorset defeated the Danes at the mouth of the Parret, and by the annal of 851, which opens with the record of a victory won at Wigborough in the west of Somerset by Ceorl the ealdorman of Devon.[90]

Stenton was selective and uncritical in his handling of this material, and his argument carries no weight here. The two incidents in question referred to West Saxon victories over marauding Danish invaders. Unlike Ireland and Francia which suffered relentless piratical raiding from Norsemen at this time, the West Saxons got off relatively lightly prior to 871. All Danish raids on Wessex were memorable events, therefore, and West Saxons' victories would have provided even more memorable material for an annalist. The annalist's interest in the incident at *Wicganbeorg* in the west in 851 is more than countered by his observation under the same year of the first Danish wintering on remote Thanet in the Kentish east, and of the storming of Canterbury and London together with a precise record for the number of Danish ships on the Thames.[91] The entry for 851 has, if anything, a south-eastern or Kentish bias, recording not only King Æthelwulf's major victory over the vikings at *Aclea*, but also including a detailed account of King Athelstan's sea-battle at Sandwich in East Kent, where Ealdorman Ealhhere is named among the leaders, and where eight or nine enemy ships were said to have been captured.[92]

Stenton was well aware that the majority of notices in the Chronicle about battles or kings and ecclesiastics—whether they related to the western shires or not—were too important and too well known to be indicative of the geographical location of an individual compiler. This did not deter him from attaching the greatest importance to the notice of the death of Bishop Ealhstan of Sherborne in 867 because of the specific mention of *on tune* as the burial place of the bishop.[93] Whitelock translated the term simply as 'in the cemetery [of Sherborne]',[94] but for Stenton, the phrase betrayed local knowledge on the part of 'an annalist who . . . did not live many miles from Sherborne'.[95] For all we shall ever know, the annalist may even have been a clerk of Sherborne, for that bishopric was one of the few key West Saxon centres capable of producing such a scholar. There were few political or ecclesiastical *foci* within ninth-century quasi-tribal kingdoms such as Wessex, and apart from royal estates, the bishoprics at Winchester and Sherborne would have been the best known centres in the kingdom, and they were known—it may be said—to all leading members of the *witan* and those clerks who must have accompanied King Alfred's household across the land. The bishop of Sherborne was a powerful magnate whose death and funeral was too major an event to provide us with any firm evidence as to the precise location of the Anglo-Saxon chronicler. This notice of Ealhstan's death in 867, like the annal of 789, may not be a contemporary record as it stands, since the fifty years ascribed by the chronicler to Ealhstan's episcopacy is in conflict with the testimony of other sources.[96] Finally, Stenton argued from the Chronicle's silence on Bishop Ealhstan's part in King Æthelbald's rebellion against his father, that this proved to be a peculiarly embarrassing issue to a south-western chronicler. The silence may now be more plausibly ascribed to the fact that such a rebellion never took place. Even Stenton admitted that the evidence from the Anglo-Saxon Chronicle went against that of the *Life* of Alfred. We are told in the *Life* of Alfred that King Æthelwulf, on his return from Rome and Francia (in 856) acceded to accepting the rule of his supposedly rebellious son, Æthelbald, over Wessex, while Æthelwulf took charge of 'the eastern districts'.[97] The Chronicle, on the other hand, not only ignores Æthelbald's rebellion, but flatly denies the Pseudo-Asser's account of how King Æthelwulf was shunted into Kent 'with the agreement of all the nobles', by telling us that 'afterwards he came home to his people and they were glad of it'.[98]

The major plank in Stenton's argument for a south-western origin for the Chronicle centred on his interpretation of the annal for 878. Stenton held that the remarkable topographical detail in the account of Alfred's retreat to Athelney; the rallying of his followers at Ecgberht's Stone east of Selwood; their encampment at Iley; their victory at Edington; Guthrum's baptism at Aller; and the finale at Wedmore—all revealed a personal knowledge of this part of the West Country on the part of the annalist.[99] Yet even Stenton conceded that 'nothing in Early English history is more familiar than the story of Alfred's retreat to Athelney, Guthrum's baptism at Aller, and his chrism-loosing at Wedmore'.[100] We might add, that either Alfred himself, or others in his circle, had intended this to be so, for we have seen how the account of the 878 campaign was designed by the chronicler to mark the highest achievement in Alfred's kingship, that it was purposely invested with dramatic qualities, and that any negative aspects of the outcome at Edington had been carefully suppressed.[101] However we interpret events at Edington and Aller, there is no denying that they marked a turning-point in Alfred's kingship. Alfred himself and all the veterans of that campaign must, in later years, have invested those places—where the destiny of the West Saxons had hung in the balance—with something of the same heroic and emotional resonance as twentieth-century veterans looking back at Dunkirk, Omaha Beach, or El Alamein. Those signposts in Alfred's march back to power in Wessex—Athelney, Ecgberth's Stone, Iley, and Edington—were engraved on the memories of everyone involved in the struggle for West Saxon survival, and those obscure names now stand out as islands of detail in an otherwise terse Chronicle narrative, because whoever wrote up the annal for 878 was either an eye-witness with personal memories of that campaign or else acquired his information from someone who was an eye-witness. We shall also see, that the great detail offered in the 878 annal—both in relation to chronology and topography—is paralleled by the similar detail offered on the opening of the First War at Reading in 871 and in the detailed account of the Last War in Kent and in Mercia (892–6). However we interpret the significance of that fact, we must accept that all such detail relates to military matters involving Alfred and his Danish adversaries. That being the case, all of this material—and especially the 878 annal—was of 'national' significance, and therefore on Stenton's own criteria is not in any way suitable material to provide an indication of the chronicler's own geographical base. To sum up thus far: Stenton's five so-called diagnostic annals are neither numerous enough nor conclusive enough to tell us anything of the regional origins of the Anglo-Saxon Chronicle or of the person or persons who compiled it.

Stenton's interpretation of the south-western element in the chronicle of the late tenth-century West Saxon magnate, Æthelweard, was as flawed as his investigation of the mainstream texts of the Anglo-Saxon Chronicle. Since Æthelweard had attempted a Latin translation of the Anglo-Saxon Chronicle *c.* AD 1000, Stenton turned to that text in the hope of turning out further evidence for a West Country origin for its Old English prototype. He assumed that Æthelweard's eccentric Latin compilation represented an earlier text of the original Chronicle than the Parker version preserved in Manuscript A. He viewed the additional material in Æthelweard's work not only as predominantly south-western in orientation, but he also saw it as originating in the archetype of the text of Æthelweard's Chronicle 'which was fuller than any [version of the Anglo-Saxon Chronicle] that is now extant'.[102] This approach involved a whole series of assumptions, all of which can be challenged, and most of which can be discounted. Bately, in a detailed study, rejected the notion that Æthelweard was translating a version of the Chronicle which was significantly older than the surviving vernacular versions.[103] Even if we were to accept that the additions to Æthelweard are predominantly south-western in orientation, Stenton overlooked one possibility as to the origin of that south-western material. He discounted the notion that Æthelweard was himself a diligent researcher, but he was rash in concluding that much of his additional information went back to the original stratum of his source. It is highly probable, since Æthelweard was himself based in the western shires, that he consulted a version of the Chronicle which had already accumulated a number of accretions reflecting the western home of that particular manuscript over the tenth century. Additional details of a south-western nature in Æthelweard do not necessarily, therefore, go back to a precursor text of the Chronicle. But Æthelweard's additional information was not exclusively western—far from it. It is Æthelweard who informs us that Alfred's son, Edward, was in charge of the English levies at Farnham in Surrey in 893[104]—a piece of information relating to what the Pseudo-Asser described in another context as the 'eastern regions (*orientales plagae*)' of the kingdom.[105] Æthelweard's account of the siege of Rochester in 885 provides a fuller account than that offered by extant vernacular versions of the Chronicle, and its additional information that the East Anglian Danes collaborated with the newly arrived Danish garrison at Benfleet, provides a motive for Alfred's attack on East Anglia.[106] This passage in Æthelweard provided Stenton with 'the most convincing evidence that Æthelweard's version of the Chronicle was fuller than any that is now known'[107] and in this he was followed by Whitelock.[108] Bately questioned Stenton's theory that Æthelweard's additional information in the Rochester annal of 885 was original to the archetype of the Anglo-Saxon Chronicle and that it was subsequently lost by a copier through *homoeoteleuton*, pointing out that the now lost source which supplied Æthelweard with information on the battle of Farnham in 893 could also have included material relating to 885 and earlier annals.[109] However we interpret the additional information in Æthelweard's account of events in 885, we should not lose sight of the fact that Æthelweard's expanded and detailed text relates in this instance to a campaign in East Kent and the Thames estuary—far to the east of Wessex proper—and no scholar has as yet used this fact to urge the case for a Canterbury origin for the earliest version of the Anglo-Saxon Chronicle.[110] Stenton did not make sufficient allowance for the possibility of Æthelweard himself adding material to his chronicle from other sources. We know that Æthelweard was capable of incorporating relatively recent material into his text. Æthelweard's assertion that Ealdorman Eanwulf of Somerset was buried at Glastonbury in 867 may be matched by his record of the burial of King Edmund of East Anglia at Bury St Edmunds on the other side of England.[111] Since Edmund's body was not taken to Bury until *c*.925, if not later—and more than half a century after that king's death—this record at least, shows that not all of Æthelweard's additional information can derive from the earliest stratum of the original version of the Chronicle which he consulted.[112]

Stenton read too much significance into Æthelweard's record of the burial of Bishop Heahmund at Keynsham (in Somerset) in 871. Heahmund had been a warrior-bishop who, unusually, had lost his life fighting the Danes alongside King Æthelred and his brother Alfred, and Sherborne was—as we have seen—a most important centre for the West Saxons in the ninth-century. Two of Alfred's older royal brothers—the kings Æthelbald and Æthelberht—had been buried there, and Alfred himself possessed numerous estates elsewhere in the West Country in Somerset and Devon.[113] In West Saxon eyes, Sherborne's bishop may have been almost as important as the archbishop of Canterbury, who was based far outside Wessex proper. Æthelweard's notice therefore of the burial of Heahmund, bishop of Sherborne in 871, like that of the Chronicle's record of the burial of Ealhstan in 867, ought not to prompt speculation about the origins of the Chronicle. Æthelweard's notice of the place of burial of Heahmund need tell us no more about the place of origin of the Chronicle than Æthelweard's similar record of the burial of Archbishop Ceolnoth in Canterbury in the previous year.[114] Indeed Æthelweard's phrase—that Ceolnoth was 'buried in the city of Canterbury (*sepultus est in urbe Cantuariorum*)' more than offsets the detail in the Chronicle that Bishop Ealhstan was buried in the minster enclosure (*on tune*) in Sherborne. Of course Æthelweard, who was himself of West Saxon royal stock, and who ended his career as ealdorman of the western shires must have had a keen interest in West Country affairs and especially in his predecessors—the ealdormen of Somerset and Devon.[115] Æthelweard's additional information therefore, on Hun, ealdorman of Somerset (823)—whom we are told incidentally was buried in Winchester; his successor, Eanwulf (867); on Odda, ealdorman of Devon and on Æthelnoth, ealdorman of Somerset (in 878) are what we should expect from an ealdorman turned chronicler, who introduces himself to us in his own chronicle as *patricius, consul,* and *quæstor.*[116]

What Stenton overlooked in his study of Æthelweard's Chronicle is that not only is its West Saxon reporting concerned with detail in relation to events in the eastern part of the kingdom, but the Chronicle adds significantly to our understanding of events in Mercia and the Danelaw as well. It is Æthelweard who tells us of the burial of Ealdorman Æthelwulf—who fell before the Danish onslaught at Reading in 871—at distant Derby in the north midlands. It is Æthelweard who tells us of the Danish encampment at Gloucester in 877 and of the burial of Æthelred, Lord of the Mercians in that same town in 910 (*recte* 911). He confirms the Mercian Register's report of the burial of Æthelred's wife, Æthelflæd, in Gloucester in 917. Æthelweard also refers to Æthelred of the Mercians as king (*rex*) in marked contrast to the Anglo-Saxon Chronicle which consistently downgrades this *hlaford* or 'lord' of the Mercians to the rank of ealdorman—with implied inferiority and subservience to Alfred.[117] The added detail on Mercian events and the upgrading of Æthelred's status suggests that the copy of the Chronicle which Æthelweard used for his translation may well have been housed at some Mercian centre at some time in the tenth century before it came into Æthelweard's possession. This transient Mercian location would also explain the few key entries relating to the Scandinavian invaders and colonists which we do not find elsewhere in the Anglo-Saxon Chronicle—the naming of Ivar (*Iguuares*) as one of the leaders of the Great Army (866), and the notice of Ivar's death (870); the burial of St Edmund (870); the invasion of [Wessex by] Sigeferth, a pirate from Northumbria (893), and the appointment of Æthelbald to rule the church of Danish York in 900.[118] This Mercian and Danelaw dimension to Æthelweard's text was ignored by Stenton, and while it by no means can be used to argue for a Mercian origin for Æthelweard's Chronicle, it does show how Æthelweard's vernacular exemplar gathered accretions to its original text of the Anglo-Saxon Chronicle at some time when it was taken from Wessex to Mercia in the tenth century. This Mercian and Danelaw association with Æthelweard's text may lend support to Hart's thesis that the production of Æthelweard's Chronicle owed something to the influence of Ramsey.[119] The south-western additions—which are no more numerous than those from Mercia—can be accounted for in the same way, and their emphasis on the careers of ealdormen from the western shires may even suggest that they were collected by Æthelweard himself. Under no circumstances can any of Æthelweard's additional south-western material be conflated with mainstream versions of the Chronicle to prove a south-western preponderance of information in the Chronicle's core text. The time is long overdue to consign Stenton's hypothesis of a south-western origin for the Anglo-Saxon Chronicle to the historiographical archive. There is no room for a compromise which pays homage to Stenton while at the same time pointing to alternative solutions to the question of origins. So, while Dumville 'remained attracted by Stenton's hypothesis' and held that 'it seems to me that Stenton's case is clear and far from incredible', he nevertheless acknowledged a strong Canterbury dimension in the early Chronicle, and conceded that 'the compiler was interested in the court and its concerns'.[120] Stenton's speculation that the work was 'composed for an ealdorman of Somerset, or at least for some prominent thegn of this region'[121] was a regrettable misunderstanding of, and misrepresentation of Æthelweard's personal imprint on a version of the Chronicle, and would never have gained credence were it not for Stenton's extraordinary scholarly reputation.

The Hand of an Editor: The Shadow of a Censor

A study of political and topographical detail in the Anglo-Saxon Chronicle's entries prior to the mid-ninth century can tell us little about the whereabouts of the later compilers of the Chronicle itself. To establish where the Chronicle was written, and by whom, we need to examine its record for the second half of the ninth century, when there is general agreement that the first compilation was accomplished. To look at earlier sections (of the pre-850 period) *en masse* is to examine a mixed bag of material drawn from a whole range of sources, involving different authors who were presumably located in different centres. Even attempts to isolate entries which are considered to derive from a particular annalistic source—

such as the Canterbury matter in the Chronicle *c.*670–833—are fraught with difficulty.[122] Such studies may shed light on places where annals were being kept prior to the compilatory phase. They do not necessarily tell us anything about where the later compilation was accomplished, or by whom. The reason why the authorship and place of compilation of the Anglo-Saxon Chronicle is virtually impossible to determine is that its record—when the compilatory phase has been reached—does not concern itself with local events. Dumville's observation that the Chronicle narrative from *c.*891 to 896 'lacks the signs of localisation, whether geographical or institutional, for which one normally searches in any set of annals'[123] has implications for the earlier historical sections of the compilation.[124] For even where those earlier annals may have reflected regional bias, it was inevitable that regional emphasis should become diluted and mixed in the textual melting-pot of the late ninth-century compilers. It was in the very essence of the Chronicle to deal with the wider picture of Alfred's conflict with the Danes. And its earlier sections were used by the compilers to show how the story of the West Saxons and their kings was related to world history and an unfolding Christian destiny which would eventually overcome the pagan Danes. Not only did such a grand design make no accommodation for local or tribal loyalties, but it was also beyond the vision of Stenton's 'prominent Somerset thegn'. The Chronicle, in this respect, is much closer to the Frankish Annals than it is to other sets of annals in the Christian West.[125] It is for this reason that the annals which lie behind the Northumbrian Chronicle of Byrhtferth of Ramsey, for instance, have much more in common with contemporary Irish annals or with later Welsh annals, than they have with the Anglo-Saxon Chronicle's narrative of events for the later ninth century. For just as the Frankish Royal Annals concentrate on the movements of the Carolingian court and on the prolonged campaign against the Saxons, and while succeeding Frankish chronicles in the late ninth century also focus on the movements of the court and the viking wars, so too, the Anglo-Saxon Chronicle in the Alfredian era reads like a military journal of that king's involvement in the Danish wars.

This obsession with military matters—in which King Alfred was at the centre—excluded not only mention of local events, but also cut down dramatically on the notice of natural phenomena and disasters so characteristic of monastic chronicles elsewhere throughout Christendom. The compiler of the Anglo-Saxon Chronicle did incorporate such miscellaneous information when he was compelled to rely on earlier sources to fill out his barren record for the seventh and eighth centuries, but as soón as he reached the Viking Age and the threat it posed to the West Saxon kingdom, he had little further need for natural disasters. So, for the seventh century the chronicle records, for instance a solar eclipse in 664, a mortality of birds in 671, and the appearance of a comet in 678. A comet reappears in 729, followed by a solar eclipse in 733 and by a blood-red moon in 734. Later in the eighth century we are told of 'the great winter' of 763 and of a red cross in an evening sky of 776 as well as 'marvellous adders' in Sussex in that same year.[126] Such records are extremely rare in the ninth-century section of the Anglo-Saxon Chronicle and confirm the retrospective nature of much of this account as well as the more confined terms of reference of its narrative. The great storms and hard winters during 855–7, which were recorded by Frankish and Irish annalists went unnoticed in the West Saxon record, as did the Irish storms of 868, 878, and 892. Western Francia experienced a 'long winter with continuous snowfalls and hard frost from November to April' in 860, which must surely have left its mark on southern England, but the West Saxon chronicler made no mention of it. A dramatic solar eclipse which rendered the stars visible in the daytime sky in Ireland in 885 (on 16 June) was not recorded by the Anglo-Saxon chronicler, who did, however, in his retrospective account of Frankish affairs under 885, refer to an earlier Frankish eclipse of 878–9. The Chronicle does elsewhere record that solar eclipse of 29 October 878 (under 879), where it may have been taken to mark the end of Alfred's struggles with Guthrum. But 878 witnessed two eclipses in that October—a lunar eclipse on the 15th and the solar eclipse on the 29th—both of which are accurately recorded and exactly dated in the *Annals of Ulster* and the *Annals of Fulda*.[127] Dynastic and inter-tribal rivalries within Wessex dominate the record for the eighth century and no doubt they continued in reality into the ninth, even though they are no longer mentioned in the Chronicle. Succession to kingship and the distribution of power in all early medieval European societies involved endless struggles between competing segments of leading kin groups, with assassination and internecine strife being the order of the day. The absence of any reference in the Chronicle to such dynastic conflict within ninth-century Wessex reflects the attitude of that team which first put the Chronicle together. By the later ninth century Alfred was personally engaged in stifling opposition from his nephews and with founding his own dynasty within the House of Ecgberht, and we know from his *Will* and from the violent struggle at the opening of his son, Edward's, reign, that Alfred's ambitions had not gone unopposed. Yet the Chronicle tells us only what its editors wanted us to know—and what so many Victorian and twentieth-century historians liked to read—that ninth-century Wessex saw the inevitable evolution of a strong, peaceful, unopposed kingship which was destined to govern all England under Alfred's successors.

The editorial hand of the compiler of the Anglo-Saxon Chronicle can be seen at work from the beginning of the reign of King Ecgberht. Ecgberht's campaigns against Cornishmen, Kentish men, Mercians, and Danes are recorded in a manner calculated to demonstrate this king's role as *Bretwalda*—that elusive title of 'Wide Ruler' or 'Ruler of Britain'—an over-kingship which Bede had accorded to seven kings when writing in the early eighth century. Bede's list of early rulers who exercised this coveted but nebulous *imperium* was as follows:

Ælle, king of the South Saxon
Ceawlin, king of the West Saxons
Æthelberht, king of Kent
Rædwald, king of the East Angles
Edwin, king of the Northumbrians
Oswald, king of the Northumbrians
Oswiu, king of the Northumbrians.[128]

The notion of a *Bretwalda* can never have meant much more than that of 'over-king'—a ruler who might on occasion extract tribute and ritual acts of submission from lesser kings, and who might also on occasion interfere in the internal affairs of an under-kingdom, particularly in matters of granting land to the church. The names of Ælla and Ceawlin belong essentially to an era of prehistory, but the criterion for who was 'in' and who was 'out' of this list clearly varied according to the political perspective of the writer. The compiler of the Chronicle boldly proclaimed under 829 that Ecgberht of Wessex 'was the eighth king who was *Bretwalda*' having 'conquered the kingdom of the Mercians, and everything south of the Humber' and having received the submission of the Northumbrians at Dore in North Derbyshire.[129] Clearly Ecgberht could justifiably be claimed to have joined the gallery of overlords, but it was a gallery which by the ninth century had taken on an antiquarian ring. To underline this achievement of King Alfred's grandfather, the chronicler lists off all previous *Bretwaldas* before Ecgberht's time. The list repeats the seven rulers offered by Bede—hence Ecgberht is presented as eight in the line—but it wilfully ignores the period of Mercian supremacy, and of Mercian domination of Wessex from the late seventh century and throughout the eighth. So, Bede and the Anglo-Saxon Chronicle chose to exclude Wulfhere of Mercia (658–75) from the list of overlords, while the chronicler continued to turn a blind eye to Mercian achievements under Æthelbald (716–57) and later under Offa (757–96). Even Bede grudgingly conceded that Æthelbald was overlord of the southern English—although he did not include him among the *Bretwaldas*—when Bede was writing his *History* in 731.[130] Æthelbald's title of *rex Britanniae* and 'king not only of the Mercians, but also of all provinces which are called by the general name "South English" (*Sutangli*)' in a contemporary charter of 736 (Sawyer 89; Birch 154) shows that however inflated that title may have been, the Mercian king viewed himself in a role similar to that of *Bretwalda*.[131] It is clear that at no point in King Alfred's reign could he have been said to have matched the political power of his Mercian predecessors and of the mighty Offa in particular. Nor could Alfred ever have described himself as *Rex totius Anglorum patriae* with the same justification as Offa had done in his charter of 774 to Archbishop Jænberht of Canterbury.[132] But it was not in the interests of the compilers of the Chronicle to admit to the decline of the West Saxon kingdom after the abdication of Ine in 726, and it would have been especially embarrassing for them to admit to former Mercian glories at a time when Alfred was inching his way forward to annexe what was left of English Mercia into the West Saxon realm. The annexation by Wessex of Mercia was a slow process, achieved through a combination of diplomacy, successful inter-dynastic marriages and above all by the intervention of Danish invaders. The absorption of the old Mercian enemy was not fully achieved in Alfred's lifetime and it was not until 919 that Alfred's son, Edward, heavy-handedly snuffed out the last glimmer of Mercian dynastic independence.

The only concession which the Chronicle makes to Offa's interference in West Saxon affairs is the admission (under 839) that Offa, in alliance with Brihtric king of Wessex, drove Ecgberht into a three-year exile in Francia, at a time before

Ecgberht had himself become king. Brihtric's conduct is explained or excused by the note that he had married Offa's daughter. That marriage of Brihtric to Eadburh of Mercia is recorded elsewhere in the Chronicle at 789 and the relative prominence given it in the Chronicle prompted the folk-tale of Eadburh as the wicked poisoner, recorded in the early eleventh century by the Pseudo-Asser.[133] Significantly the admission that Ecgberht was himself engaged in a struggle with his predecessor for control of the West Saxon kingship is mentioned in the Chronicle retrospectively, at the very end of Ecgberht's reign. It is difficult to envisage from a reading of the Chronicle alone that Alfred's grandfather was the founder of a new dynasty in Wessex, if not indeed something of a usurper. Whatever else we may say of those West Saxon annals which cover the reign of Ecgberht and the first two decades of the reign of his son, Æthelwulf, is that they provide a heavily edited account of the West Saxon past. Those annals display not only a predictable and understandable West Saxon bias. They also represent what might be termed an official version of West Saxon history, imposed on them by a compiler who had the interests of Ecgberht's descendants and successors very much at heart.

The late ninth-century compilers of the Chronicle decided to identify the fortunes of the West Saxon kings with the struggle against the pagan invaders from about the time they recorded the Danish raid on Sheppey in 835. It is no coincidence that the Chronicle may be said to have assumed its editorial format from that time onwards. From the notice of the viking raid on Sheppey in 835 until a battle at Sandwich in 851, a relatively full record is devoted almost exclusively to recording the progress of the viking wars in the greater kingdom of Wessex.[134] The only exceptions to this pattern is the notice of the deaths of two Winchester bishops and two ealdormen (all in 836); the death of a certain Wulfheard in 840 and of King Ecgberht in 839, together with the record of the succession of Alfred's father, King Æthelwulf, in that same entry. This is why we should not draw any conclusions whatever in regard to the place of compilation of the Chronicle from the fact that no Winchester bishops are mentioned after 836 because after that time the compilers of the Chronicle had narrowed the remit of their project to recording the involvement of West Saxon kings in the viking wars.[135] In the sixteen-year interval from 835 to 851, no less than seventeen separate West Saxon (including Kentish) engagements with the vikings are recorded. This method of recording, so conspicuous in this section of the Chronicle, sets the format for all later reporting, up until the end of the reign of Edward the Elder in 924. That this format was deliberately chosen by the first compilers of the Chronicle in King Alfred's reign, there can be little doubt. The account of the progress of the viking wars from 835 until Alfred's own time is interrupted only by a handful of events—all of which deal with Æthelwulf's dynasty and include some details which are relevant to the story of how Alfred himself eventually came to the kingship. The first of these is the notice in 853 of how Æthelwulf of Wessex helped King Burgred of Mercia subdue the Welsh. Alfred's so-called consecration by Pope Leo is next recorded, as is the marriage of Burgred of Mercia to the daughter of Æthelwulf of Wessex. The next composite annal for 855–8 records Æthelwulf's journey to Rome, his marriage, return to England, and his death, together with his elaborate genealogy. The progress of the viking wars was followed alongside a brief mention of the reigns of Alfred's older brothers, Æthelbald and Æthelberht, and in particular the arrival of the 'Great Heathen Army' is noted in 866, and its progress is followed laconically but with conspicuous regularity, from East Anglia to Northumbria, up to the succession of King Alfred to the kingship of Wessex in 871.[136]

Alfred's succession was, as we have seen, anticipated through the device of the chronicler associating him with all the actions of his older brother and immediate predecessor, Æthelred I. The only event recorded between 851 and 871 which might seem to fall outside the dynastic story of Wessex and the progress of the war against the Danes is the death of Bishop Ealhstan of Sherborne in 867—that record into which Stenton, as we have seen, misread so much significance. When we take Ealhstan's long service as a bishop and a warrior into account—he served under Alfred's four older brothers, his father, and his grandfather—we realize that few other men could have been as influential within the House of Ecgberht. Back in Ecgberht's reign in 825, Bishop Ealhstan helped Alfred's father, Æthelwulf, drive the last king of Kent out of that kingdom. The notice of Ealhstan's death, may be said to conform then, to the central dynastic and military narrative adopted by the compiler of the Chronicle in Alfred's reign. During the thirty-seven years from 851 to 888, the deaths of only four West Saxon magnates (apart from Alfred's royal kindred) are recorded—that of Bishop Ealhstan in 867, of Archbishop Ceolnoth in 870 and of Archbishop Æthelred and Ealdorman Æthelwold in 888. A chronicle now exclusively devoted to the West Saxon dynasty and its struggle with the Danes had abandoned the staple of all other western annals—the obituaries of leading ecclesiastics and of the warrior aristocracy. It is the scarcity of these obituaries and of localized records relating to marvellous happenings in the period 851 to 891, combined with preoccupation with dynastic matters and with West Saxon royal involvement in the viking wars, that not only render the Chronicle impervious to any analysis which might yield up its place of composition, but which also marks it off as essentially a court document.

Alfred in the Chronicle

That the Anglo-Saxon Chronicle was compiled in Alfred's reign becomes apparent as soon as we follow the narrative down beyond Alfred's succession in 871. We have seen how the compiler appeared to have lost interest in the deeds of Alfred's older brothers when they succeeded their father, Æthelwulf, in the decade after 858, and how the emphasis switched more and more to the threat posed by the Danish invaders. Yet prior to 871, even the progress of the Great Army of Danes is narrated in a summary fashion. The record for 870 when compared with 871 is especially illuminating. Under 870 the chronicler records the return of the Great Army to East Anglia. The fall of that neighbouring English kingdom, together with the death of its king—soon to be revered as a saint—is summarized, if not dismissed, in a few words: 'And that winter King Edmund fought against them, and the Danes had the victory, and killed the king and conquered all the land.'[137] East Anglia was the second of the Old English kingdoms to have fallen to the Danes—Northumbria having collapsed in 867—and the death of its king, Edmund, was regarded as a famous martyrdom at the hands of the heathen, almost certainly within Alfred's own lifetime.[138] But the compiler of the Chronicle was still not too concerned because Wessex was not yet involved. All that was to change in the very next year (871):

In this year the [Danish] army came into Wessex to Reading, and three days later two Danish earls rode farther inland . . . the four days later King Æthelred and his brother Alfred led a great army to Reading . . . and four days later King Æthelred and his brother Alfred fought against the whole army at Ashdown . . . and a fortnight later King Æthelred and his brother Alfred fought against the army at Basing . . . and two months later King Æthelred and his brother Alfred fought against the army at *Meretun* . . . and Bishop Heahmund was killed there and many important men. And after this a great summer army came to Reading. And afterwards after Easter King Æthelred died, and he reigned five years, and his body is buried in Wimborne Minster.

Then his brother Alfred, the son of King Æthelwulf, succeeded to the kingdom of the West Saxons. And a month later King Alfred fought with a small force against the whole army at Wilton.[139]

Nothing better illustrates the stark change that took place within the Chronicle at this point, than to compare this entry of 871 with the brief account of the major catastrophe which befell the East Angles and their king in the year before. We have noted how the twinning of Alfred with all the exploits of his brother, King Æthelred, may well have been devised by the compiler to enhance Alfred's profile within the Chronicle and even to convey the illusion that he had already assumed kingly powers before actually being elected king. But it is the detailed reporting of the Danish invasion of Wessex in 871, and in particular the recording of campaign details by numbers of days, that shows above all else that the year 871—the year in which Alfred became king—was deliberately chosen by the compiler of the Anglo-Saxon Chronicle as the year in which he would begin his detailed record. The compiler did not actually begin his work of contemporaneous recording in 871. He chose, rather, to provide much fuller retrospective detail for that particular year. That much seems clear from the retrospective tone of the summing up at the end of this long and detailed entry: 'And during that year, nine general engagements were fought against the Danish army in the kingdom south of the Thames, besides the expeditions which the king's brother Alfred, and [single] ealdormen and king's thegns often rode on, which were not counted.'[140] This is the record of a compiler looking back from some distance to the beginning of Alfred's reign. For although he is deliberately filling out his narrative with details, he is not only writing retrospectively, but he is also vague. Although he claims nine major battles were fought against the vikings, apart from more minor skirmishes in this year, he itemizes only six. What gives this entry its true significance is that it is the first of a series of detailed reports on Alfred's campaigns against the Great Army which culminated in his victory over Guthrum in 878. The reporting for

871 contains islands of remarkable detail on a par with those supplied for the
Edington victory in 878. Even Stenton conceded that 'wherever he lived, the
annalist certainly drew his information about the earlier struggle which followed
the Danish occupation of Reading in 871, the war of Ashdown and Basing, from
some one who had been intimately concerned in it.'[141] The same holds true for
the details of the 878 campaign and for the most detailed reporting of all—namely
that of Alfred's Last War from 892 to 896. In other words, the compilers of
the Chronicle who covered the quarter of a century from 871 to 896 must have
either themselves experienced the major military events they reported on, or at
least have consulted those who were at the centre of those events. Whichever way
we look at it, the argument points in the direction of the Chronicle at this section
being interpreted in some measure as a 'court' document, and we are entering here
into that layer of recording which represents memories from the lifetime of the
recorders.

There are several characteristics in the Chronicle narrative which might suggest
that either the king himself or a clerk working under his editorial eye was responsible for the retrospective recording of near-contemporary events at the time of
compilation. We have already noted the editorial minimizing of the role of eighth-
and early ninth-century Mercian rulers; the ignoring of any achievements of Alfred's
older brothers; and the deliberate and consistent association of Alfred with all the
exploits of Æthelred I. The first eight years of Alfred's own reign were fraught
with personal danger for the king while his West Saxon kingdom was under
constant threat from Danish invaders who were liable to conquer and overrun it at
any moment. A reading of all the available sources shows that the initiative for
much of this time lay with the Danes, flushed with their recent victories against all
neighbouring Anglo-Saxon kingdoms.[142] Yet the narrator in the Chronicle skilfully
tried to conceal Alfred's difficulties and perhaps also his shortcomings as a commander, and by a sleight of hand he presented his military book-keeping in a way
which suppressed the true gravity of Alfred's position. Notice, for instance, how
Alfred's first battle fought as king—surely a crucial encounter in the eyes of his
own warband—although it was a military defeat, is presented in the most favourable light possible: 'Then his [Æthelred's] brother Alfred, son of Æthelwulf,
succeeded to the kingdom of the West Saxons. And a month later King Alfred
fought with a small force against the whole army at Wilton and put it to flight far
into the day; and the Danes had possession of the battlefield.'[143] We notice how the
beginning of Alfred's reign as king is linked to the credentials of his father Æthelwulf;
how Alfred's 'small force (*lytle werede*)' is set in apposition to 'the whole army (*alne
þone here*)'—meaning the Great Army which combined with the recently arrived
'great summer army (*micel sumorlida*)' of Danes at Reading; and finally, how the
emphasis on Alfred's initial victory 'far into the day' attempts to soften—if not
indeed to obscure—the stark fact of his ultimate defeat. There is a skilful editorial
hand at work here, which is of a different order from what we might expect of a
country gentleman writing disinterestedly in the western shires. It is doubtful
whether the Chronicle tells us even half the story in relation to Alfred's negotiations

and struggles with the Danes in the 870s. For instance, if we were to rely solely on the Chronicle we would never have been able to explain, how when the Danes had just defeated the new king, Alfred, they inexplicably withdrew from Wessex—first to London in 871–2 and then on to Northumbria in the following year. The reason for this Danish withdrawal, which can be supplied from northern chroniclers and later sources, was because of a revolt against Danish rule in Northumbria which took the Danes the next four years to sort out, and which accounts for their absence from Wessex until 875–6.[144] When the chronicler informs us that 'the West Saxons made peace with the enemy' before their departure from Wessex in 872 he is almost certainly concealing the humiliating fact that Alfred was forced to accept some form of client status.[145] The Chronicle reveals nothing of Alfred's submission to the Danes in 871 or of the accompanying exactions which must have stripped the embattled West Saxon king of much of the bullion and coin from his royal hoard. Instead, it has an unrealistically upbeat account of how the Danes, on their ominous return, gave Alfred hostages 'who were their most important men next to their king in the army' and of how they swore oaths on their holy ring— 'a thing which they would not do before for any nation'. The latter comment, as I have shown above, is ridiculous. It would have been normal for pagan Danes to swear oaths on their own cult objects. Oath-swearing would only have been a *coup* for Alfred if he had forced the Danes to keep their oath or to swear with him in good faith on his Christian gospels and reliquaries. Even that most careless of writers, the Pseudo-Asser, understood that point and silently lost the embarrassingly pagan detail of the holy ring (*halgan beage*) by substituting Alfred's Christian relics.[146] As things turned out, the oaths cannot have been taken very seriously, since the Danes—having sworn to leave Alfred's kingdom at Wareham in 875–6— 'stole away by night from the English army to Exeter'.[147] As for the hostage-giving, since the Danes were clearly on top in these negotiations, the high quality of their hostages may have been difficult if not impossible to establish. All Alfred could have hoped for was an exchange of hostages, but the Chronicle, written up after Alfred's final victory over Guthrum in 878, was never intended to let us in on the secrets of such realpolitik. Finally, we have seen how the record of Alfred's ultimate triumph over Guthrum and his Danes at Edington in 878 was deliberately presented to the reader as a resounding victory against all odds, and for which no explanation was offered. We are merely told that the Danes withdrew into Mercia in the harvest season in 877; that they returned to surprise Alfred at Chippenham in the winter of 878; that he was forced to fly 'with a small force' to Athelney and the Somerset marshes; but that quite mysteriously after Easter he managed to rally men of the western shires to secure a lasting victory at Edington. One can only agree with Davis's comment: 'Everyone knows that the easiest way of enhancing the significance of a victory is to exaggerate the perils and dangers endured before it was won.'[148] Clark's comment that the initial compilation of the Chronicle (in her reckoning prior to 892) provides an 'unadorned, unqualified record [which] is as near absolute fact as history can get'[149] was shockingly naïve, even if it may be otherwise excused as a comment on a certain literary style of reporting in the early record. Operating within the constrictions of that annalistic style, the disarmingly terse narrative of events from 871 to 878 presents a sophisticated cover-up of a whole series of difficulties—not to say blunders—made by a young king who had never expected to rule the West Saxon kingdom, much less defend it against a dynasty of ruthless and battle-hardened Danish overlords.

A second dramatic change occurs in the Chronicle narrative after the account of Alfred's final victory over Guthrum in 878. We are told that Guthrum's army withdrew from Chippenham to Cirencester in 879, and from Cirencester to East Anglia in the following year. Guthrum and his followers then disappear from the record—apart from obscure references to the occasional breaking of the peace— until the death of Guthrum is recorded in 890. It might well be argued that the reason for the change in the record was dictated by the events themselves. Since Guthrum had withdrawn his challenge to Wessex, perhaps there was little left of a Danish menace to report within the kingdom, but that can scarcely account for the fact that the compiler of the Chronicle decided to fill out his narrative of events for the period 880–91 by focusing on Frankish affairs.[150] So, while the annals from 871 to 878 begin and end with narratives replete with remarkable topographical and chronological detail on the progress of Alfred's wars, and while the whole period from 871 to 878 is devoted to following the progress of the First and Second War, the focus of attention after 878 shifts abruptly to Francia. The features in regard to content, which distinguish the record for the 870s from that of the 880s are paralleled by differences in the use of Old English vocabulary and constructions which are found between the same two consecutive sets of annals. Bately identified what she described as the first and second Alfredian annalists covering precisely the same periods in the Anglo-Saxon Chronicle, on the basis of a linguistic study.[151] The first annalist who reported on Alfred's First and Second War (871–8) may also have been responsible for the expanded entry on the feud between Cyneheard and Cynewulf in 775 and for the entry on Æthelwulf's last years and death under 855.[152] The annals for the 880s—including 882, 883, and 884[153]—extending down to 890 (the viking fight with the Bretons at St Lô) display their own discrete linguistic characteristics which suggest that a second Alfredian annalist was at work here—presumably translating and editing a Frankish source.[154] We are told that as Guthrum's followers withdrew to Cirencester in 879, yet another Viking warband encamped at Fulham, and that in 880 this Fulham army 'went overseas into the Frankish empire to Ghent and stayed there for a year'. The progress of this army is followed in detail 'farther inland into the Frankish empire' in 881, along the Meuse in 882, up the Scheldt to Condé in 883, and up the Somme to Amiens in 884. In the following year, this army is reported to have divided into two—one part going east (to Louvain, according to Æthelweard) while the other part returned across the Channel to make an abortive assault on Rochester. Eventually these invaders of Kent and Essex withdrew back over the Channel, and meanwhile under 886, the chronicler takes up the story of the eastern portion of the Continental army which went to Louvain. It turned west again, going up the Seine and wintered at Paris. In the annal of 887 we are told this force moved from Paris to the Marne as far as Chézy and the Yonne area, 'spending two winters in those two places'. In 890 we are told the army moved from the Seine to St Lô between Brittany and France where it was defeated by the Bretons. In 891 the movement of this viking warband is relentlessly followed back east where it was defeated by King Arnulf and the East Franks. Finally, under 892, 'the Great Danish Army which we have spoken about before' is followed from the kingdom of the East Franks westward to Boulogne and across the Channel to east Kent, where it introduces the Chronicle's account of King Alfred's Last War. This Frankish record forms a great block of material from 880 to 892 which has no counterpart elsewhere in the entire record either in terms of detail or of sustained reporting over a twelve-year period. The detail is indeed remarkable.[155] At St Lô we are informed that the Bretons drove the vikings 'into a river and drowned many of them'. Under 885 a Frisian contingent is identified as helping to bring about a Saxon victory over a viking naval force, while in 891, the chronicler was aware that Arnulf's army consisted of East Franks, Saxons, and Bavarians and that it 'fought against the mounted force before the ships arrived'. Earlier, under the annal for 881, we were informed that the Danish army had provided itself with horses after a battle fought in that year.[156] This collection of Frankish annals is in all respects more detailed than most of the Alfredian Chronicle's reporting on English events from outside of Wessex, and it is patently more regular and more detailed in its reporting than the Chronicle's treatment of the reigns of the ninth-century West Saxon kings Æthelbald and Æthelberht. Indeed, the Frankish detail compares favourably with the Alfredian chronicler's reporting of West Saxon events for the 870s and it raises the crucial question as to the origin of this Frankish material in the Anglo-Saxon Chronicle.

Those scholars who accepted Pseudo-Asser as a contemporary witness on Alfredian affairs also accepted the possibility that he had independent access to contemporary Continental information. Keynes and Lapidge speculated on the nature of the Pseudo-Asser's Frankish contacts, holding that 'it is conceivable that his [Asser's] knowledge was direct and personal, but it is perhaps more likely that he derived it from a Frankish informant such as Grimbald'.[157] There is little in the Pseudo-Asser's version of the Chronicle's Frankish section to warrant the notion of 'Asser's superior knowledge of Frankish affairs', although it is possible that the Pseudo-Asser may have consulted a set of late ninth-century Frankish annals.[158] But in this as in so much else, the compiler of the *Life* of Alfred slavishly followed his version of the Anglo-Saxon Chronicle. Indeed, he was, as ever, careless, for the Pseudo-Asser omitted altogether the Chronicle's annal for 884 which recorded the movement of the army from the Somme to Amiens.[159] The additional information offered by the Pseudo-Asser may be explicable solely in terms of the version of the Anglo-Saxon Chronicle which he used, together with his characteristic guesswork which was prompted by his Chronicle text. The Pseudo-Asser's contemporary, Æthelweard, also used a version of the Alfredian chronicle which had its own more detailed readings or interpolations for this Frankish section than those of the Parker Chronicle, yet no scholar has as yet claimed that Æthelweard either had 'direct and personal' knowledge of those events or that he had a Frankish friend and confidant. The Pseudo-Asser's information on the nunnery at Condé or the royal estate at Chézy reminds us of his speculative glosses on the royal estates at Chippenham and Reading, and that information is more than matched by Æthelweard's additional and more specific knowledge of the movement of one section of the Danish army to Louvain in 885 or the earlier encampment at Elsloo in 882.[160] Nor should the Pseudo-Asser's detail on the location of Paris and the blockading of its bridge lead us to any rash conclusion about the originality of his source. The Pseudo-Asser's detail on Paris in 886, when distilled and isolated from his customary verbiage, relates solely to the bridge and the island on the Seine. That detail was most probably inspired by the Anglo-Saxon Chronicle's mention of the bridge at Paris under the following year, 887.[161] For those who set great store by the Pseudo-Asser's supposed detail, it can be pointed out that the Pseudo-Asser's information in relation to the bridge at Paris in 886 is far less significant than Æthelweard's account of the campaign of that same Continental army in Kent in 885. And however we explain the fuller nature of Æthelweard's text here, he clearly had access to more detailed and more reliable information than anything we find among the additions in the Pseudo-Asser's text.

The account of the division of the Frankish territories into five parts on the succession of Arnulf in 887 is found in the Chronicle, in Æthelweard and in Pseudo-Asser. All three versions unquestionably derive from the record of the earliest version of the Chronicle. It is misleading to describe the Pseudo-Asser's remarks about the priority of the Carolingian, Arnulf, over those of his co-rulers in 887 as 'derived but also developed' from the Anglo-Saxon Chronicle.[162] This implies that the Pseudo-Asser had yet again, some 'superior knowledge' of Frankish affairs, when in fact his information on Arnulf, precisely like Æthelweard's information on the same king, was solely reliant on an early version of the Chronicle.[163] The Pseudo-Asser's only contribution was to pad out his text of the Chronicle with a gloss moralizing on Arnulf's wickedness in expelling his uncle, Charles the Fat. The Pseudo-Asser's condemnatory gloss on this Carolingian family succession struggle was typical of that compiler's monastic preaching against dynastic squabbles. He showed similar disapproval of the dynastic troubles in ninth-century Northumbria.[164] In addition to the Frankish annalistic material from 880 to 892, there are also two Frankish dynastic and genealogical passages in this Frankish section of the Anglo-Saxon Chronicle under 885.[165] Both passages are closely related in content and they both trace the family relationships of Carloman and Charles the Fat back through the emperor Charles the Bald to that ruler's daughter, Judith, whom 'Æthelwulf, king of the West Saxons had married'.[166] The repeated emphasis on the marriage of King Alfred's father, Æthelwulf, to the princess of the House of Charlemagne ('Old Charles'), and the obvious pride with which the chronicler draws our attention to it, helps to explain the existence of this detailed Frankish section in the Anglo-Saxon Chronicle in the first instance. This information on King Æthelwulf's last marriage was recorded after a safe period of time had elapsed since the event had taken place. What the chronicler does not repeat under the 885 annal is that the same Carolingian Judith, later married Alfred's older brother, King Æthelbald. That piece of information—like all other details on Æthelbald's reign—was quietly forgotten. By the 890s, Æthelwulf and his son, Æthelbald, were long dead, and the Carolingian Judith had left no heirs that we know of to complicate the royal succession within Wessex. By this time, too, what once was a marriage which might have embarrassed or overshadowed Alfred could now be turned to advantage by ignoring Æthelbald and by stressing Judith's Carolingian credentials and her union with Alfred's father. This highlighting of the marriage of Alfred's father to the Carolingian house had by now become most flattering to Alfred. The emphasis accorded it in the Anglo-Saxon Chronicle—like the account of the infant Alfred's consecration in Rome—is suggestive once more of a compiler who was in the business of presenting Alfred in the most favourable light.

Sawyer correctly pointed out that the purpose of the Anglo-Saxon chronicler's relentless following of the Danish army in Francia was the certain knowledge that it would eventually return to Kent in 892.[167] The notion that this Frankish record was kept up to date because of the chronicler's anxiety that a Danish warband on the Continental side of the English Channel just might return is not convincing.[168] The *raison d'être* of the Chronicle, as we have seen, was to follow King Alfred's personal struggle with the Danes. The inclusion of relentlessly detailed information on a Great Army of Danes, which was eventually to return from Francia and challenge Alfred in the east of his kingdom, was entirely in keeping with the brief of the chronicler. But the presence of this Frankish material in the record is only meaningful if we view it as a retrospective record. In other words, it makes good sense to conclude that this section of the Chronicle could only have been compiled at some time after the invasion of East Kent by the returning Continental army in 892. This retrospective aspect of the Frankish material is evident from the frequent summarizing of events from several years under one annal in the Chronicle. For instance, the death of Charles (*recte* Carloman) in 884, of his brother, Louis in 882, and of their father, Louis the Stammerer in 879 are all recorded under the annal for 885.[169] The inclusion of this Frankish material served other purposes as well. It filled out a bare narrative of English events for the period 880 up to 892 and as a bonus it gave the Anglo-Saxon chronicler an opportunity both to stress the genealogical ties between King Alfred and the House of Charles the Bald, as well as seeming to allow the men of Wessex to participate in events in the wider and more prestigious Carolingian world. The Danish menace which posed a common threat to Alfredian Wessex and to the Carolingian Empire was used by the English chronicler in the same way as he, or one of his collaborators, used the world history and the Bede Epitome to tie in West Saxon culture with its Continental Christian and Roman origins in the Late Antique past. Viewed in this light, it is impossible not to see this Frankish material—coherent and detailed as it is—as having reached the West Saxon chronicler as one continuous text of a Latin manuscript version of Frankish annals from 880 to 892. This text was conveyed to the West Saxon chronicler by a Frankish scholar who was most likely at the court of King Alfred or otherwise it was obtained by a West Saxon visitor who encountered it while in Francia. The West Saxon chronicler then added in his own additions relating to the papacy and other matters.[170] The material is far too consistent and concise to have been fed piecemeal and year by year to an English chronicler by some 'lookout' on the Frankish side of the Channel. Besides, the Frankish material is not presented in a logical chronological sequence. It is inconceivable that such detail relating to places as far apart as St Lô in the west and Elsloo in the east, and from Ghent and Louvain in the north to the river Yonne in Burgundy, could possibly have been transmitted over a twelve-year period to a chronicler in Wessex. All we can say about the identity of the Frankish annalist whose work ultimately lay behind this section of the Chronicle is that he was probably based at some centre between the Seine and the Rhine and that his comments on Arnulf in 887 may show him to have been partisan to that ruler's claim on the Carolingian succession.[171] The presence of this sustained and detailed Frankish section in the Anglo-Saxon Chronicle provides yet further argument against the notion of the compiler of the Chronicle being a disinterested gentleman of the western shires and suggests the possibility of this project having been undertaken at the West Saxon court. The presence of this Frankish material also suggests that the notion of compiling the Anglo-Saxon Chronicle in the first instance may have been inspired by first-hand knowledge of a Frankish chronicle of the sort which lies behind the record for 880 to 892. We have already observed that the uncompromisingly military nature of the entire Alfredian record, while not identical with Frankish models, is much closer to a Frankish format than to anything in contemporary Northumbrian or Irish annals.

Three Men in a Boat: The Beginnings of Contemporaneity

The section of the Chronicle which provides the most detail on the progress of the Danish wars and which tells us most about its author is that which covers the account of King Alfred's Last War from 892 until 896. The detail in this narrative is all-embracing and its distinctive characteristics in regard to its use of language and its content have been acknowledged by several scholars. This is detail that extends to the military narrative in general, to topographical description, to strategy and political commentary, to the listing of English casualties, and to the close observation of Danish movements and tactics. Although the annalist's sights continue to remain firmly fixed on the progress of the Danish wars, there is nevertheless a modest but significant return to an awareness of natural phenomena which points to contemporary reporting here. This is shown by the record of the comet noted in the last portion of the entry for 891, and especially in the reference to the 'mortality of cattle and men' at 896. There is unquestionably a profound change in the manner of recording events in the Chronicle from 891 onwards. Take, for instance, the remarkable topographical description of the Lympne estuary and of the nearby Kentish Weald which opens the account of the last great Danish invasion of Alfred's reign in 892:

That estuary [of the Lympne] is in East Kent, at the end of that great wood which we call *Andred*. The wood is from east to west 120 miles long, or longer, and 30 miles broad. The river of which we spoke before, comes out of the Weald. They rowed their ships up the river as far as the Weald, four miles from the mouth of the estuary, and there they stormed a fortress. Inside that fortification there were a few peasants (*cirlisce men*) and it was only half made.[172]

This account although relating to the furthest eastern corner of the kingdom—far outside Wessex proper—sets the detailed tone for much of what follows. The information on the half-prepared state of the defences may be incidental or it may be a veiled reprimand. It can be compared with the account of Alfred's men who raised the siege of a Danish fort on the Colne in 893 because 'they had completed their term of service and used up their provisions'.[173] Detail in the reporting of that particular incident may perhaps be seen more clearly to convey disapproval on the part of the writer. We are told that the English levy which had cornered the Danes on the Colne had given up the struggle even though the beleaguered Danish leader had been so severely wounded he could not be moved, and even though Alfred himself 'was then on the way there with the division which was serving with him'. This form of reporting was not necessarily a reversal of the style employed in the 870s when the compiler then played down successive West Saxon defeats and diminished the achievement of Alfred's older brothers by a devious economy with the truth. In the case of reporting in the 890s, mistakes and failures were likewise seldom admitted, but when they were, organizational failure at local level or lack of loyalty to the king himself was hinted at as the cause for blame. If the earlier narrative of the 870s centred on Alfred's personal military achievements—even as we saw, before he had become king—then the account of his Last War focused yet more sharply on the person of the king and can be said to have been written from Alfred's own perspective. While this section of the Chronicle, more than any other, allows us the most detailed insights into the strategies and objectives of both sides in the Danish wars, it is Alfred's own personal policies and decisions that the reader is invited to study and admire, and it is Alfred now more than ever, who is at the heart of the narrative. It was Alfred who in 893 'advanced to take up a position between the two enemy forces [in East Kent] . . . so that he could reach either army, if they chose to come into the open country'.[174] Not even Alfred's son and heir, the prince Edward the Elder, was allowed by the chronicler to diminish in any way the king's personal achievement in 893, although Æthelweard had access to a report which named Prince Edward as the leader of an English army which was victorious over the Danes at Farnham in Surrey at that very time.[175] Even if we were to accept that Æthelweard's note on Edward derived from the archetype of the Chronicle, it remains a remarkable fact, that Alfred's eldest son, who was by now a warrior in his own right, is virtually excluded from the Chronicle's narrative of Alfred's Last War. It was Alfred again in 893 who 'had divided his army into two, so that always half its men were at home, half on service, apart from the men who guarded the boroughs'.[176] And in that extraordinarily lengthy entry of the same year, the narrative is essentially an account of how Alfred personally handled this last invasion crisis. Alfred, we are told, first collected an army and marched east to prevent the two Danish invading forces from joining up in the Kentish peninsula. Later in the same campaign, when a fleet of Northumbrian and East Anglian Danes created a diversion by trying to cut off western Wessex, we are informed 'when the king heard that, he turned west towards Exeter with the whole army, except for a very inconsiderable portion of the people (who continued) eastwards'.[177] The capture of the fortress of the Danish king, Hæsten, at Benfleet together with his wife and children is next recorded—where Alfred plays a central role yet again—but the annalist, fearing his readers may have lost sight of Alfred, reminds them 'when the king had turned west with the army towards Exeter, as I have said before'.[178]

We have seen when examining Alfred's role as a warrior, that the king is not recorded as having taken part in any pitched battles in his Last War, and the wordy accounts of his doings in this campaign may have been partly designed to obscure that fact. Edward's victory at Farnham would be unknown were it not for Æthelweard, and in the Chronicle itself an English victory over the Danes at Buttington in 893—in which Alfred played no part—is treated in a revealing way. While Alfred was tied up with a Danish force at Exeter, the Danish army at Shoebury in Essex moved up the Thames and from there it moved up along the Severn. This Danish warband was eventually crushed by a combined force of Mercians, West Saxons, and Welshmen at Buttington, when the Chronicle records that 'the Christians had the victory . . . and a very great slaughter of Danes was made'. Yet Alfred had no part in this crucial victory which clearly made a significant contribution to the overthrow of Hæsten and his hordes. Æthelweard, who understood the importance of this battle tells us: 'these events, which occurred at Buttington, are vaunted by aged men',[179] and ascribes the victory, as does the Chronicle, to Æthelred of Mercia and to the two ealdormen, Æthelhelm and Æthelnoth. And while Æthelred is styled *ealdorman* in the Chronicle, this ruler is significantly called 'king (*rex*) of the Mercians' by Æthelweard; his ally Æthelhelm is described as 'the famous ealdorman (*dux præclarus*)', and Æthelnoth was said to have been in charge of the West Saxon army. The Anglo-Saxon chronicler is at pains however to exonerate Alfred from any taint of cowardice or inactivity in the matter of this victory at Buttington. The episode is introduced with the reminder: 'when he [Alfred] was occupied against the army there in the west' it was 'the king's thegns who then were at home at the fortresses [who] assembled from every borough' to confront the invaders of the Severn basin.[180] So, it was thanks to King Alfred's planning for the manning of fortresses that a contingent was available to take on and defeat this enemy. Lest we should lose sight of the king's role in this war, where the king led from behind and involved himself in damage limitation, his being tied up at Exeter is referred to yet again, and with obvious effect, immediately before the victory at Buttington is recorded: 'When they [the English] had encamped for many weeks on the two sides of the river [Severn at Buttington], and the king was occupied in the west in Devon against the naval force, the besieged [at Buttington] were oppressed by famine. . . . Then they came out . . . and the Christians had the victory."[181] Alfred may not have been present at Buttington, but the Chronicler somehow managed to present the English victory as part of the king's personal overall success against the Danes.

The account of Alfred's attempts at shipbuilding in 896 is firmly logged as one of the king's personal achievements. It is true that an element of failure is admitted, redounding on the poor design of the ships which left them out-manœuvred and prone to run aground, but such shortcomings are only inadvertently referred to, and offered as an excuse for any mishaps in this incident, which on the whole is reported as an unqualified success. We are told

King Alfred had 'long ships' built to oppose the Danish warships. They were almost twice as long as the others. Some had 60 oars, some more. They were both swifter and steadier and also higher than the others. They were built neither on the Frisian nor the Danish pattern, but as it seemed to him himself that they could be most useful.[182]

Here we are presented with Alfred, the innovator and the strategist. In spite of serious English casualties, the first engagement involving these ships (off the Isle of Wight) in 896 is reported as an overall triumph resulting in 120 Danish crewmen being slain. Out of a modest Danish fleet of six ships, four were captured or destroyed. One ship escaped with only five survivors, while the 'greatly wounded' crew of a remaining vessel escaped past Sussex and back to East Anglia. The role ascribed to Alfred in this section of the Chronicle is that of the clever strategist who triumphs over his enemies through wisdom and laudable military cunning, and who successfully organizes his warriors to ensure their victory. As in the Buttington campaign, Alfred was not present during what was a modest naval engagement in the Solent. But by telling us Alfred was at Winchester, when the captive Danes from this incident were later brought before him, the chronicler again manages to involve Alfred personally in this seeming triumph.[183]

Alfred's role as the clever tactician is illustrated most clearly in the account of the campaign at the river Lea in Essex in 895. That Danish warband, which had been defeated at Buttington in 893 and again near Chester later in that year, had used Essex as the springboard for their raids directed against English Mercia and Wessex. In 895 this warband built a fortress on the Lea, some 20 miles north of London, and the Chronicle informs us that Alfred moved his army in the vicinity of the fortress so that local English inhabitants could save their corn harvest. It is in this account that the narrator reveals how much he shared the king's own angle of vision:

Then one day the king rode up along the river, and examined where the river could be obstructed, so that they [the Danes] could not bring the ships out. And then this was carried out: two fortresses were made on the two sides of the river. When they had just begun that work, and had encamped for that purpose, the enemy perceived that they could not bring the ships out. Then they abandoned the ships and went overland.[184]

This record can only have been based on the eyewitness account of someone who had taken part in this campaign. Its author was someone very close to Alfred, since it is the king's personal motivation and superior strategy that lie at the centre of this narrative. The approach and perspective of the writer of this passage is entirely consistent with what is recorded elsewhere in the account of the Last War, and there is no reason to suppose that more than one annalist was involved. Clark's analysis of the narrative style of the Chronicle identified these annals from 892 to 896 as a discreet section within the compilation, showing a marked departure from the 'terse formulas' and 'formulaic language' of earlier recording.[185] Stylistically, the syntax becomes more complex, there is a wider range of connectives between clauses, with a proliferation of subordinate clauses to facilitate greater detail of expression. But Clark went further and saw the burgeoning of subordination and elements of rhetoric as tools to provide an 'insight . . . into purpose and motivation, usually those of King Alfred himself' and where 'syntax is here being used to give an illusion of insight into the motives underlying King Alfred's various acts'. She saw this section of annals as being 'united by some common themes . . . and with the king's own ideas and methods'.[186] Clark's researches into the use of style led her to the remarkable recognition of Alfred's involvement, directly or indirectly in the annals for 891–6, but she shrank from the consequences of her own findings with a disclaimer which ensured she did not overstep the bounds of orthodoxy: 'The insights of his [i.e. Alfred's] motives cannot be more than conjectural. Further, although his mind is suggested behind many individual developments, there is little sense of any control of events as a whole, nor is the formal continuity controlled by any real plan.'[187] These observations, valid and perceptive in themselves, are explicable not in terms of the narrative style of the Chronicle, so much as in the problems facing Alfred on the ground. We have seen that extraordinary Danish mobility which outmanœuvred Carolingian armies also dictated the progress of all Alfred's wars. Alfred, even in his more successful and later stages of the Second War as well as in his Last War, was constantly reacting to Danish initiatives. He was never properly in control, nor were the English in a position to implement a master plan, other than that of very successful damage limitation. The very full narrative of events from 892 to 896 reflects those realities perfectly, and we are not compelled to insist on Alfred's personal authorship of this material to retain the essence of Clark's discovery—namely that this section was written by someone who knew the mind of the king and who wished to portray Alfred in a favourable light. Dumville, too, recognized that the Chronicle's account for 891–6 was 'written by people close to the events which the annals describe— royal military operations, responses (whether royal or local) to Scandinavian assaults, and the fortunes of members of the royal dynasty'. And these annalists Dumville would identify as 'royal priests' or 'court chaplains'. But the shades of the mentors dictated equivocation was necessary to prevent the logical admission that this record sprang directly or indirectly from Alfred himself: 'This need not mean that the annals were written at court (although that is no doubt the most economical hypothesis), but merely by people who had access to the court and the collective knowledge of high politics which would be available there.'[188] If by this, Dumville meant that the Chronicle was written by someone who had access to King Alfred's household, then we are in complete agreement.

The personal involvement of the king or of one of his close associates in this section of the Chronicle is supported by the evidence of a number of passages which suggest that the annalist was working at the king's court, and at the king's behest, rather than in isolation from the royal circle. After the sea-fight off the Isle of Wight in 896, we are told that two Danish ships' crews were cast ashore on the Sussex coast 'and the men were brought to Winchester to the king and he ordered them to be hanged'.[189] The fact that the annalist knew where the king was at this juncture may be significant because Alfred had not been personally involved in the engagement in the Solent which had just been described by the writer in such detail. Winchester, although an important town, was still only one of many centres which housed the royal court in the late ninth century. The list of casualties in the Solent contains details which point back once more to the king's personal interest in the record. We are told of the slaying of Lucuman, the king's reeve (*cynges gerefa*), and of Æthelfrith, the king's *geneat*, together with two Frisians who are mentioned by name—Wulfheard and Æthelhere.[190] This listing of two of the king's royal servants, together with two Frisians who must have helped Alfred with the design, building, and crewing of his ships, shows just how close the record keeps here to the personal interests of the king. When the chronicler digresses to describe the capture of the Danish fortress at Benfleet in 893, he has to momentarily leave his account of Alfred's tactical retreat to Exeter in order to narrate this English success in the east. The chronicler tells us that of the Danish king's family which was captured at Benfleet in Essex: 'Hæstan's wife and two sons were brought to the king; and he gave them back to him [Hæstan], because one of them was his godson, and the other the godson of ealdorman Æthelred [of Mercia]. They had stood sponsor to them before Hæstan came to Benfleet.'[191] Hæstan's wife and sons must have been baptized in Alfred's presence sometime after Alfred had sorted out the crisis in East Kent, earlier in 893 and at a time when he had established a diplomatic if not friendly relationship with Hæstan.[192] Whoever wrote this account knew of Alfred's involved negotiations with the Danish leader and he was aware of Alfred's personal contact with Hæstan or his family on at least three occasions—at the baptism, after the capture of the wife and sons at Benfleet, and at the restoration of the captives to Hæsten.

There is one entry in the Anglo-Saxon Chronicle more than any other which points to King Alfred or his immediate circle as the point of origin for the Chronicle. This entry is the first major English-based event to be recorded at the end of the Frankish section and relates to the arrival of three Irishmen in Cornwall in 891:

And three Irishmen came to King Alfred in a boat without any oars from Ireland, which they had left secretly, because they wished for the love of God to be in foreign lands, they cared not where. The boat in which they travelled was made of two and a half hides, and they took with them enough food for seven days. And after seven days they came to land in Cornwall, and went immediately to King Alfred. Their names were as follows: Dubslane, Mach-bethu, and Maelinmum. And Swifneh, the best scholar among the Irish, died.[193]

However improbable this account may seem, it can be shown to be circumstantially accurate in every respect. We know from independent Irish sources that it was common for zealous monks to set out as *peregrini* or pilgrims seeking a 'white martyrdom' by way of exile from their native home. They undertook penitential journeys to Rome and Jerusalem or else they sought the solitude of a hermit's life in the 'desert' of the ocean or in the forested wilderness of Francia or Germany. Æthelweard informs us that the ultimate destination for these Irish pilgrims was Rome and eventually, Jerusalem.[194] The description of their boat and the bizarre details of their voyage can also be corroborated from contemporary Irish evidence. The currach in which they drifted may have been small, but its construction—as we know from Adomnán's late seventh-century accounts[195]—was typical. The decision to travel with a limited food supply and without oars is also vouched for in early Irish sources, where we learn that it was left to Divine Providence to guide and power the voyage.[196] All these details not only vouch for the accuracy of the West Saxon annalist, but show that he had access to a first-hand account of this expedition. At first glance, the landing in Cornwall might seem to lend support to Stenton's West Country theory for the place of origin of the chronicler. But the Irish party reached Cornwall, not because it was near the home of a chronicler, but because that was their nearest landfall. We note how the annalist introduces his account of the episode with the remark: 'And three Irishmen came to King Alfred' and that he then goes on: 'and . . . they came to land in Cornwall, and went immediately to King Alfred.' Unlike Æthelweard, the compiler of the Chronicle sought to give the impression that these pilgrims were more bent on seeking out the court of the West Saxon king than on going on to Rome—a destination which in this account is not even mentioned. So, Alfred, is drawn in, yet again, to the centre of a narrative, which on first reading did not seem to involve the king directly. The notice of the death of the Irish scholar *Swifneh* was clearly passed on by these Irish visitors to the chronicler or directly to King Alfred who had one of his clerks make a brief record of the visit. We are reminded of the account inserted into the Old English *Orosius* of Ohthere's voyage. This deceased Irish scholar was Suibhne mac Máelhumai, the anchorite and 'excellent scribe' of the monastery of Clonmacnoise in the Irish midlands, whose death is registered independently in the *Annals of Ulster* in 891 and whose grave-slab was once extant at Clonmacnoise.[197] The notice of the death of this foreign ecclesiastical scholar in this Alfredian section of the Chronicle stands in glaring contrast to the absence of West Saxon ecclesiastical obituaries in the same source. How did it come about that the death of this Clonmacnoise scribe was noted by an Anglo-Saxon chronicler who otherwise ignored the demise of some West Saxon bishops of Sherborne and even Winchester, and who scarcely ever recorded the death of a leading ecclesiastic from West Saxon monasteries such as Winchester, Glastonbury, Malmesbury, or Wimborne? Few scholars have shown amazement that while the Chronicle maintains total silence on the abbots of St Augustine's in Canterbury, it introduces us by name to three wandering Irishmen and informs us of the death of a fourth, Suibhne, in his far country. This record of Suibhne's death not only reinforces the veracity of the Chronicle's account, but shows yet again how the West Saxon annalist either had himself a great personal interest in these Irish travellers or that he was writing under instructions from someone who had. Proof that the writer personally met the three Irish mariners or that he had access to notes on their visit drawn up by Alfred himself or by one of his clerks is made virtually certain by the record he has left us of their names. The accuracy of the Old Irish orthography holds the key to this episode. *Dubsláine*, an authentic early Irish name would, if it were written from oral information, have been transcribed into Old English as *Dufslaneh*, while the somewhat less accurate *Maelinmun* (recte *Máelinmain*) would have been written via oral information as *Mailinvun* or *Mailinwun*. The Old Irish name *Macbethad* is given with orthographic precision in Manuscript B of the Chronicle as *Macbethath* and in Æthelweard's version as *Macbeathath*—both of which readings are superior to *Macbethu* of version A.[198] The orthography of these names in surviving versions of the Chronicle places the written accuracy and immediacy of all this linguistic information in no doubt. These names must have been written down by the Irish travellers and passed on to the English annalist. In contrast to the written origin of the names of the three visitors, the reporting of the death of Suibhne (which took place in Ireland in the previous year) was conveyed orally at King Alfred's court. The Anglo-Saxon rendering *Swifneh* of version A and *Suifne* of version B represents an accurate phonetic rendering of Old Irish *Suib(h)ne*. The news of Suibhne's death was clearly conveyed orally to the chronicler by his three Irish informants. But why should this have been done, and where was it most likely to have taken place? Why should a chronicler who was relentlessly following the story of King Alfred and the Danish wars to the exclusion of so much West Saxon news, just once, and only once, leave his narrative to accommodate a seemingly bizarre digression? The reasonable answer can only be that the chronicler encountered the travellers at King Alfred's court. He twice tells us that they either arrived there or that they wished to be there, and a reasonable conclusion must be that these men met the Anglo-Saxon annalist himself while lodging in Alfred's household. The internal evidence of the Chronicle's own narrative goes against the possibility of a meeting with an annalist in the West Country. The emphasis, as we have noted, is twice laid on the court of the king, and Æthelweard reinforces the court dimension with his unexpected comment that 'the *witan* rejoiced equally with the king at their arrival'.[199] Even if we were to argue that the chronicler derived his record of this visit from a set of notes written up by Alfred or one of his household, we would still have to accept that the chronicler encountered that record either during or not long after the visit and we would still have to account for why he incorporated such exotic material into his very confined narrative. And why the great interest in their quest? Of all men in ninth-century Wessex, it was Alfred himself who was most likely to have had a deep personal interest in these wanderers. Alfred was at this time engaged on his programme of scholarly writings, some of which involved grappling with philosophical problems beyond the intellectual reach of himself and his helpers. Æthelweard informs us that of the three visitors to Alfred's court, *Magilmumen* or Máelinmain was 'a man blossoming in the arts, learned in literature, an eminent teacher of the Irish'. In 891, at the time of their visit, the reputation of Irish monks for Latin learning was not only high within Ireland, but thanks to the scholarship of men like Eriugena and Sedulius, Irishmen had been taking a leading part in philosophical and other scholarly endeavours at the Carolingian court of Charles the Bald. Alfred must have been aware of such matters, and it was in his interest to befriend visiting scholars who might prove of use in his own programme. The arrival of these castaways from the western sea reminds us of the account in the *Life* of Charlemagne attributed to Notker the Stammerer, a monk of St Gall. Notker began his *Life* of Charlemagne at about the very time when Alfred befriended his Irish guests, with a tale of two other Irishmen 'who happened to visit the coast of Gaul in the company of some British traders' sometime after 771: 'These men were unrivalled in their knowledge of sacred and profane letters, at a time when the pursuit of learning was almost forgotten throughout the length and breadth of Charlemagne's kingdom and the worship of the true God was at a very low ebb.'[200] The parallel with Alfred's own rhetorical lament on the decline of learning in the England of his day is notable. According to Notker, these two Irishmen would shout to the crowds in the market-place: 'If anyone wants some wisdom, let him come to us and receive it: for it is wisdom which we have for sale.'[201] The challenge was too much for Charlemagne 'who was always an admirer and a great collector of wisdom' and he summoned the scholars to his court, rewarding them handsomely according to their own modest wishes.[202] It was just such gurus who would have excited King Alfred's curiosity and scholarly interest. The fact that they were afforded such an extraordinarily high profile, with their names transcribed accurately from Old Irish into Old English, suggests in a most immediate way that Alfred himself was ultimately responsible for having the account of their visit to his court preserved in a chronicle which at this point dealt almost exclusively with the king's own royal and military affairs.

The Birth of a Chronicle

So far we have identified the special nature of this detailed late Alfredian record from 891 to 896, and we have ascribed its authorship, if not to Alfred himself, then to someone highly partisan to the king's position and being either a member of the king's circle or having access to the 'court' archives. It is necessary to attempt to set this collection of annals (from 891 to 896) within the wider context of the Anglo-Saxon Chronicle as a whole. The end of the Frankish section at 891 marks a watershed in every respect in the development of the Chronicle. It is as if the chronicle had been marking time from when Alfred overcame Guthrum back in 878, until a new menace—in the form of a returning Continental Danish warband—confronted the West Saxon king yet again in 892. From 891 to 896 inclusive, the narrative of events returns firmly to English soil. The account of King Alfred's Last War, beginning in 892, forms the most detailed and coherent section in the whole of the Chronicle prior to Alfred's death, and of all sections of the Chronicle it is especially this which bears the hallmark of contemporary reporting and perhaps also of Alfred's own personal involvement. The record for these six years is, as we have seen, fuller than for any gone before—even for 871, when Alfred became king, or for 878 when he established his supremacy in Wessex. Yet paradoxically, it is this very section of the Chronicle—with its first demonstrably contemporary annals and first strong Alfredian associations—which has come to be regarded by scholars as not forming an integral part of the original or so-called core text of the earliest compilation. There are three major reasons why the 891–6 annals have been excluded from the notional core text and viewed instead as later continuations to a compilation which was produced in *c*.891. First, the work of the first scribe (Hand One) comes to an end in Manuscript A towards the end of its 891 annal, and secondly, this break coincides very roughly with a point in the Chronicle text where material entered in Hand Two after 891 is not reproduced in some other versions—namely Æthelweard and Version E.[203] The implication of this would seem to be the compilation of the core text was effected by *c*.891 and that everything after that date represents continuations in the various recensions. But the third and most substantial reason for treating the post-891 material even in Manuscript A as a later continuation is because those who held to the 'Genuine Asser' thesis were compelled to accept that the Chronicle had to be completed prior to 893. That after all was the year in which the Pseudo-Asser claimed to be writing his *Life* of King Alfred, and that same life depended on a close translation of the Chronicle down to 887 for the great bulk of its narrative.

Once the Asser bogey has been removed, the first two arguments for a 890–2 compilatory horizon are not as compelling as they at first sight seem. So far in our study, we have concentrated on the historical content of the Chronicle and on the internal evidence of the text, without getting too involved in linguistic and palaeographical considerations, although we have noted a distinct change in the style of reporting and in the Old English syntax and vocabulary employed by the annalist for the 891 to 896 section. Remarkably, too, the manuscript layout and the palaeography of the oldest Manuscript A, also point to a change in the evolution of the Chronicle at this point. The oldest surviving manuscript of the Chronicle (MS A) is only a copy or a copy of a copy of the archetype. It is at least two stages removed from those earliest notebooks or proto-booklets which went to make up the exemplar.[204] Changes in handwriting within Manuscript A may provide nothing more than evidence for scribal arrangements for the production of this particular copy of our text at sometime between *c*.900 and *c*.930—the date of Hand One and Hand Two in Manuscript A. Changes in hands within the A manuscript cannot, therefore, be assumed to replicate changes in the archetype in all respects. Too much effort has been spent on deciding the time which may have elapsed between the completion of the work done by Hand One and the commencement of Hand Two.[205] Because we are dealing with a copy only, the relevant question surely hinges not on the timetable between Hand One and Hand Two, but on how far the change in hands replicates any original features within the exemplar. There is evidence to suggest that the layout and palaeography of Manuscript A have preserved some essential features of its exemplar, but that they do not reflect those features in exact detail. The very process of copying—however carefully it may be done—inevitably leads to a gradual drift away from the organization of an exemplar. We shall see, furthermore, that the change at *c.*891 may not relate to a division between a core chronicle completed in 891 and its continuation, but rather to a physical division between a proto-booklet containing an historical introduction from BC 60 down to 891, and a set of contemporary annals from 891 to 896—all of which were produced simultaneously soon after 896.

Manuscript A is written in one hand (Hand One) from the opening genealogical regnal list of the Chronicle down to the end of the second item (the arrival of the three Irishmen) recorded under the year 891. This takes the narrative down to within three lines from the bottom of fo. 16^r, and on the next page (16^v) a second scribe (Hand Two) continued the record, beginning with the last episode for 891 (the sighting of a comet after Easter) and continuing perhaps to the end of 911. Parkes believed Hand Two ended his work six lines from the foot of fo. 21^r at the end of the annal for 911.[206] Bately saw her Hand 2b also ending at the same point in the manuscript.[207] Yet another scribe (Parkes's Hand Three or Bately's Hand 2c) continued from 912 until 923, towards the end of the reign of Edward the Elder (*sub anno* 923, *recte* 920). Parkes believed Hand Three took over at the annal for 912 and continued to the end of the First Booklet of Manuscript A on fo. 25^v.[208]

Although Hand One of the oldest Manuscript A broke off before the end of 891, that scribe did write the annal number for 892 in his own hand, and left three blank lines for that annal at the bottom of fo. 16^r. His successor, Hand Two, finished the entry for 891 on the top of the verso page, ignoring the notice for 892 at the end of the text on the page before.[209] It is as if Hand One in Manuscript A had information on 892 in his possession and had planned to enter it under its appropriate year number. But even if that were the case, it does not necessarily tell us anything about how far the work of Hand One was separated from that of Hand Two in time.

Evidence for overlap or continuity between the first two scribes of Manuscript A is reflected in the palaeography, layout, language, and style of the Chronicle itself. Parkes drew attention to the palaeographical association between other manuscripts associated with Hand One and those associated with Hand Two, and he observed that an annotation of a cross-in-circle device marking work copied by Hand One and Hand Two in MS A is only found elsewhere on folio 20^r of the Trinity Isidore—a work otherwise related palaeographically with Hand One of MS A.[210] While the last mention of the Danish army in Francia is found (in Hand Two) introducing the annal for 892, the first item in the extensive reporting of Alfred's later years occurs in the work of Hand One, under 891. The remarkable account of the arrival of the three Irishmen at Alfred's court, providing their names, the purpose of their visit, the account of their boat and their voyage, all belongs stylistically to the annals for 891 to 896, and has no place in terms of either style or content with the Frankish section. The fact that this Irish information is not actually part of the narrative on the Last War cannot divorce it on general stylistic grounds from the 892–6 material. The detailed narrative dealing with the arrival of the Irishmen heralds the end of the Frankish interlude and the beginning of a new and involved style of reporting. Clark significantly allowed that the 'syntax is complex and the description ample in 891 A, both in the section by the first scribe and in that by the second'.[211] Her comment that 'stylistically the break [between the terse annalistic mode of the Frankish section and the fuller style of the Last War] is not sharp' needs correcting. It is not that the two styles of the chroniclers' reporting are blurred but that organizationally, and palaeographically, these two different styles were dovetailed into each other by a team of scholars who sought to hammer out a continuous narrative. The break between the Frankish account and the reporting on the arrival of the Irishmen is as sharp as can be. The content of the account of the Irishmen's voyage does not fit with the material on the Last War, but stylistically, it forms a unity with it as Clark observed. Since the account of the Irishmen was written in the First Hand and subsequent material for 891 was written in the Second Hand, this in turn leads us back to the essential continuity within the A manuscript and the possibility that too much weight may have been given to the variation in hands discerned within the manuscript. In other words, we should allow for the possibility of simultaneous production of different sections of the Chronicle by a team of compilers who worked in 896–7. That is not to say that the palaeography of the manuscript is not important, but since we are dealing (in the case of Manuscript A) with a copy—or a copy of a copy—changes in hand are unlikely to correspond exactly and in all cases with changes in the exemplar.[212]

The layout of the account of Alfred's Last War in Manuscript A could suggest that this section was copied from an earlier proto-booklet covering the period 891 to 896. From the entry for 894 onwards, on fo. 18[r], Hand Two centred the year number on a line all to itself and the narrative of this scribe filled up the entire width of the page, leaving no margin for year numbers to the side, as in the earlier layout followed by Hand One. The new arrangement continues down to the end of the account of the Last War in 896 on fo. 19[v], when Hand Two then reverted to a layout resembling, but not exactly the same as Hand One's format. The entry of the death of Ealdorman Æthelhelm of Wiltshire in 897 is laid out with the year number extending into the left-hand margin. This confirms yet again, that this 897 entry was written up after the death of Alfred and sometime in the reign of Edward, and that the summing up at the beginning of 896 followed by the account of the sea-fight near the Isle of Wight in that year, does indeed represent the end of the Alfredian Chronicle. But the layout of the entire section for 891 to 896 in Manuscript A makes us aware how the copying process—and in particular the dovetailing of material between what were originally separate notebooks made up by compilers of different sections of the Chronicle—may have distorted original arrangements within the exemplar. The arrangement of full lines begins on fo. 17[r] in the middle of the extensive narrative for 893, and the first year number which is centred on the page is that of 894 on fo. 18[r]. There is reason to assume that Hand Two would have begun centring his year numbers from 891 onwards were it not for the fact that he was following on immediately from Hand One and that the two scribes may have been dovetailing their accounts from two separate proto-booklets or exemplars. Hand Two found that Hand One had already begun copying the entry for 891 onto the single leaf (fo. 16ʳ) at the end of the second quire, and Hand Two felt constrained to follow the ruling according to Hand One's layout on the verso of that singleton (fo. 16ᵛ), and so for 892 and for the beginning of 893, Hand Two conformed to Hand One's layout, placing the year number extending somewhat into the left-hand margin. At the first opportunity—as soon as he began writing in his new quire on fo. 17ʳ—Hand Two expanded his lines to accord with a new format, and one which he may have had before him in his exemplar or proto-booklet containing material for 891–6.[213] And just as Clark vouched for the stylistic change from terse annalistic formulae to a more elaborate chronicle-type narration in 891, so Parkes saw in the changed format of the page for this section, a 'history' layout comparable with that for the Old English Orosius or the Old English Bede.[214]

The break in the oldest version of the Anglo-Saxon Chronicle at *c*. AD 891 is also apparent in the physical preparation of the A manuscript. The scribe responsible for Hand One ruled his sheets after folding, in insular fashion, while his successor ruled before folding, in Continental fashion. So too, the insular practice of having hair sides of the parchment facing flesh (HFHF) throughout the bound book was followed by Hand One, while Hand Two in the third quire followed the Continental arrangement of having flesh face flesh, and hair face hair (HFFH).[215] Bately has also pointed to the change in pricking arrangements designed to guide the ruling on the sheets, which remains constant on the first sixteen folios, and changes on fo. 17 at the beginning of the third quire.[216] This must not lead us into a false assumption, however, that everything now found in the first three quires of Manuscript A mirrors precisely all the arrangements in its exemplar. Nor should we assume that the third or last quire (fos. 16ᵛ–25ᵛ) of that First Booklet of Manuscript A—namely all the annals from 892 down to 920 (923 A)—were compiled at the end of the reign of Edward the Elder, or that all of them must inevitably be regarded as continuations of an 892 Chronicle. On the contrary, regardless of the number of hands at work in this third quire, it is still only a copy of a composite second proto-booklet, containing annals from 892 to 896 which were almost certainly written up contemporaneously with the completion of the first proto-booklet, followed by continuations of the original Alfredian Chronicle from 897 to 920. The material for 891/3–896/7 was clearly all written up, in or soon after 896 and intended to form an integral part of the first compilation of the Chronicle. I would argue that there was one (master) copy, preserved at one centre where the 891–6 material and all subsequent additions were inserted in a second proto-booklet as part of a continuous process of recording. The separate first proto-booklet which contained the strictly historical part of the compilation remained detached from the contemporary chronicle which began in 891. It was just such an isolated copy of the first proto-booklet that Æthelweard and Pseudo-Asser encountered in the late tenth and early eleventh centuries. A centre such as Winchester, on the other hand, kept its master copy of the Chronicle intermittently up to date, filling up the blank pages in the second proto-booklet, which followed the account of Alfred's Last War. The various hands in the third quire of the First Booklet of Manuscript A do not necessarily coincide with each individual addition to the Chronicle in that manuscript, since these hands, however they are deciphered, represent merely copiers, transcribing a copy of the exemplars of the first two proto-booklets of the Chronicle text, together with its continuations and additions.

The evidence for a break, therefore, at 891–2 is impressive but ambiguous. We see how this coincides with a major palaeographical division within the layout of the earliest Manuscript A; that 891 marks a fundamental division between the Frankish interlude and the return to reporting on English affairs; and that the account of the Irishmen's arrival and of King Alfred's Last War marks a stylistic change in Old English usage in the Chronicle. Keynes and Lapidge argued for the precise point of this break at 892 rather than 891, on the grounds that although Manuscript E of the Chronicle omits the 891 annal, it does include 892, and then omits all that follows of Alfred's reign. Æthelweard also omitted the annals for 893 to 896 inclusive, providing instead his own distinctive version but showing some knowledge of A's account of 893 in abbreviated form.[217] We may envisage, therefore, that the earliest compilation of the Anglo-Saxon Chronicle involved the production of two proto-booklets—one full proto-booklet covering the work from its prefatory matter down to 891–2, with a second proto-booklet containing the latest contemporary narrative for 891–6, covering the years immediately prior to the moment of compilation. The origin of the overlap for the year 891 went back to the original process of collecting information on the part of the team of compilers. The scribe in charge of the compilation of the Frankish section took his Frankish annals down through the note of Arnulf's victory in 891 to the departure of the Danes from Boulogne in 892. This now effected a tie-up with the remarkably detailed narrative by the contemporary narrator of Alfred's Last War who began with the Danish landing at the Lympne estuary in Kent in 892. But that scribe in charge of the detailed account of Alfred's Last War had actually begun his narrative with two prophetic events in 891 in which he recorded the arrival of the Irishmen and the appearance of the comet—both of which marvellous happenings may have been taken by the medieval writer as presaging terrible disasters in the following years. Byrhtferth of Ramsey, as Hart reminded us, went on record in his *Manual* to associate comets with the onset of famine.[218] Early medieval Frankish and Irish annalists regarded prodigious landings on the seashore as omens to be reported and as events which by implication pointed to forthcoming disasters. Witness, for instance, the Frankish reporting of an exotic palm-tree which was washed ashore on the Gaulish coast in 858, or the marginal note in the Annals of Ulster giving an account of a stranded whale on the Ulster coast, whose 'golden' teeth were placed on the altar of Bangor in 753.[219] The arrival of the scholarly Irishmen, rescued by Heaven from the perils of the ocean and taken—as it would seem—by divine destiny to Alfred's court, was viewed by the Anglo-Saxon chronicler, as prelude to great events—not necessarily disastrous—in the career of King

Alfred. The notice of the comet, unlike other events under their year numbers, points forward to the Danish invasion in the following year and to the plague of cattle and men (893–6) in which Alfred is reported to have lost some of his best thegns.

When it came to tying up these two sections of the Chronicle—one historical and the other contemporary reporting—the different compilers each overlapped for the years 891 and 892, and an echo of that original process of compilation may be imperfectly preserved in the palaeography of Manuscript A. Whatever the difference in time between when Hand One left off on fo. 16^r, and when Hand Two commenced his writing over the page, a conscious effort had nevertheless been made to achieve an overlap. So, Hand One dealt with Arnulf's victory over the vikings and then entered the lengthy piece on the three Irishmen and their boat, which belonged originally to the contemporary 891–6 proto-booklet. Hand One also entered the annal number for 892, which was ignored by his continuator (Hand Two) who completed the 891 entry by recording the arrival of the comet. Finally, Hand Two completed the Frankish section by noting the departure of the viking army from Boulogne. What we do not know is how many copies of the first proto-booklet were produced in isolation from the annals post-891, and at what time did the distribution of those copies take place. Detailed textual comparisons between the Alfredian record in the Parker Chronicle, and in the copies available to Æthelweard and to the Pseudo-Asser, now show that each of those three versions were not necessarily as far removed from the archetype as was once thought.[220] If the palaeography of the Parker Manuscript (A), in showing a major break in the text at 891–2, suggests that manuscript has preserved—albeit imperfectly—the layout of its exemplar, then we must surely accept the Parker Manuscript to be a reasonably close copy of its exemplar—close at least in the general morphology of its layout if not in time. If the exemplar of A, and the exemplars which were used by Æthelweard and by the Pseudo-Asser were very close—if not indeed one and the same exemplar—we do not need to assume that a multiplicity of booklets were produced, which ended at AD 891–2. Nor indeed do we necessarily need to hold that this first booklet was produced earlier than or in isolation from the second booklet covering Alfred's Last War in the period 892–6. As long as the Pseudo-Asser's *Life* of Alfred was retained as a contemporaneous text for the Alfredian period, it was necessary for scholars to hold that the first booklet of the Chronicle was in circulation by 893.[221] It is true as we have seen[222] that a very real connection existed between the time when the Pseudo-Asser claimed to write his *Life* of Alfred, and his particular text of the Anglo-Saxon Chronicle. Because the Pseudo-Asser had access to a text of the first proto-booklet of the Chronicle—whose last annal came down to *c*.892, he was prompted to pretend that as 'Asser' he was taking up his pen on Alfred's biography in or soon after the final year of his particular truncated version of the Chronicle text.[223] The removal of the Pseudo-Asser's text from the Alfredian canon, no longer pins the production of the Anglo-Saxon Chronicle to a date prior to 893, nor can so early a date be sustained in view of the inclusion of the Frankish material down to 892. Some time was needed for a compiler to acquire the Frankish text, to translate it, and, more importantly, to knead it into the complex Old English compilation. The Frankish material, after all, involved no mere synthesis or conflation on the part of the compiler. It involved a major policy decision relating to the format of the entire Chronicle. The insertion of this Frankish matter not only formed a bridge between the 870s and 890s, but it also confirmed the status of the Chronicle as a record of Alfred's struggles with a series of Danish Great Armies. The timetable imposed by the acceptance of a 'Genuine Asser' was too tight in the extreme to allow for such a development. Besides, the Frankish text, even if it had arrived as early as 892, would have come hard on the heels of a Danish army which was to cause major dislocation within the West Saxon kingdom until its departure in 896. Who, in the alarm and chaos in Wessex in 892 and immediately thereafter, would have sat down and transcribed a set of Frankish annals in order to tie them into an account of an on-going war which no one was sure that Alfred could win? The only sensible time when the consecutive Frankish material of 880 to 892 could have been written up was when West Saxon observers had put the Last War confidently behind them in 896. If we accept a production date of 890–1 for the first proto-booklet of the Chronicle, we are forced into an even more extreme position. We have then to conclude that an Anglo-Saxon compiler went to all the trouble in following a bizarre interest in a Frankish episode, without knowing that the Danish army which he followed in such great detail in Francia for twelve years would eventually constitute Alfred's opponent in his Last War. That is impossible to accept. Common sense points to 896–7 as the time when the first proto-booklet of the Anglo-Saxon Chronicle was produced, and we should see it as being produced simultaneously with the set of annals covering Alfred's Last War.

If this is indeed the case, then when the Chronicle was first put together in 896–7, it consisted of a self-contained first proto-booklet covering the period from 60 BC down to 891–2. This was in every sense a closed book, put together by perhaps two or more compilers, and dealing with historical events of the remote and recent past. A second proto-booklet was begun simultaneously to serve as a chronicle of contemporary events which would be brought up to date from time to time and which of course formed a unity with the historical chronicle covering all that had gone before. This second proto-booklet began with the record of the Irishmen and the comet, by way of introduction to the account of Alfred's Last War, and the last entries which were made while the king was still alive dealt with the summing up after the war in 896, the deaths of the king's best thegns, and an account of the sea-battle in the Solent—all in that same year. Because the material covering Alfred's Last War was entered at the beginning of a separate and second proto-booklet, that relatively compact material stood at the beginning of a potentially on-going record in a booklet which was as yet, virtually empty of annalistic material. This second booklet with 'work in progress' was therefore tied more closely to its home scriptorium than the completed first booklet. For this reason the second proto-booklet would not have been available for circulation and copying in the same way as the first proto-booklet, but was retained as a master copy for continuation at its centre of origin, such as Winchester. The exemplar of the second proto-booklet was eventually continued to become the archetype of the Parker Manuscript's (A) text from 892 to 923 (A) (down to fo. 25^v). The Pseudo-Asser and Æthelweard in the late tenth and early eleventh century (together with that northern recension which lies behind E) derived their accounts, on the other hand, from the more freely available copies of the first proto-booklet only, which in the Pseudo-Asser's case had not been continued beyond *c*.892.

It was inevitable, in spite of the coherence of the Chronicle, that the existence of a separate proto-booklet covering all the pre-contemporary material down to 891–2 would lead eventually to the copying and independent continuation elsewhere of that core text. Precisely when the earliest copies of the first proto-booklet were made is not possible to deduce with certainty. The production of several copies of the first proto-booklet soon after 896 would conform well to what Alfred tells us of his own arrangements for the distribution of copies of his translation of Gregory's *Pastoral Care*. The king informs us that he was sending a copy 'to every bishopric in my kingdom' and although he specifically ordered that no one should ever remove the copy sent to those centres, he does nevertheless make allowance for the book being on loan or being copied or travelling in the bishop's company.[224] Parkes believed that the Parker Manuscript may well have been the bishop's copy, once kept at Winchester and produced in the scriptorium there.[225] On the other hand, if every West Saxon and Mercian bishop's seat had been sent a copy of the original compilation of the Chronicle in the late ninth-century, it seems odd that Canterbury had to wait until the eleventh century to receive its version A from Winchester. And it seems odd, too, that Mercia has only the meagre and truncated record of the Mercian Register to show by way of tenth-century annals, if indeed Worcester had been sent a copy of the Alfredian Chronicle with the implied instruction to keep its record up to date. Hart highlighted an uncomfortable truth that all versions of the Chronicle, apart from A, exhibit a text history which cannot be proven to go back earlier than the late tenth century and which seem to derive not from the Alfredian era, but from the milieu of the monastic reformers at the end of the tenth century. Hart's most persuasive point was to argue against the circulation of supposedly official continuations of the Chronicle within the southern and northern Danelaw during the turbulent years of the first three quarters of the tenth century.[226] His case therefore, rested on seeing the origins of versions B, C, D, and E as stemming from a compilatory horizon based on Ramsey in the late tenth and early eleventh centuries. The recognition of the Pseudo-Asser's text of the *Life* of Alfred as also belonging to an early eleventh-century Ramsey scenario may not validate the details of Hart's complex arguments, but it does strengthen his case overall. This does not mean there were no copies available of the exemplar of the Chronicle in pre-tenth-century Wessex, but it may suggest that the Chronicle was never published in the same way as the *Pastoral Care* and perhaps some other works of translation completed by Alfred and his circle.

In spite of the separate text history of the first proto-booklet, it is important not to lose sight of the essential continuity between the annals from that first proto-booklet and the narrative for the 890s. We have seen how the Frankish record of the 880s anticipated the return of the Danes from Francia to England and all the drama of King Alfred's Last War, which makes up the record for the 890s. The annal of 892, on the other hand, glances backwards, speaking of the Danish invaders of Kent as 'the great Danish army, which we have spoken about before'—namely the account of the lengthy campaign in the Frankish empire in 880s.[227] The subsequent years—893, 894, and 895—are identified in terms of the number of years since the Danes 'had come hither across the sea'. And if the account of Alfred's Last War was bonded editorially into that of the 880s, then so, too, does Frankish material from the 880s refer back to the earliest Alfredian record of the 870s. We might cite, for instance, the notice of the death of Louis the Stammerer under 885, which is dated to 'the year of the eclipse of the sun'—an event recorded back in 879.[228] So, it can be misleading to make too much of the different styles of reporting in the Chronicle during the Alfredian period, since we are most likely dealing with a work which was put together simultaneously by a team of compilers who worked on different sections of the Chronicle. Much of the very valuable evidence for the use of vocabulary and syntax in the distinctive sections of the Alfredian chronicle seems to point to different writers perhaps coming from different regional and scholarly backgrounds who were collaborating on the same project at the same time.

There is clearly stylistic continuity between the annals from 891 to 896. Yet the beginning of the 891 annal occurs, as we have observed, in Hand One in Manuscript A, while Hand Two begins with a remaining part of the 891 entry. However distinct the Frankish section may be from the detailed reporting on English events which follows it in 891, due to dovetailing of quite separate material, there is no clear-cut organizational division in Manuscript A between where the compilation of the first proto-booklet of Manuscript A's exemplar ended, and where the first period of contemporary reporting in the second proto-booklet began. Some members of the Chronicle team, then, were working on a World Chronicle, others on annals of the 870s, yet others on the 880s, and yet another individual worked on the contemporary record for the period 891 to 896. The completion of the first proto-booklet with the annals for *c*.891–3 may have been part of a deliberate decision to keep the historical section of the compilation separate from the contemporary chronicle. Equally, it may have been only coincidental that the end of the historical section which came down as far as *c*.891 happened to fill up, or almost fill, a proto-booklet all to itself. The fact that the first booklet allowed for sufficient material down to *c*.891 ought not obscure the fact for us that the first compilation of the Chronicle as a whole, extended into a second proto-booklet as far as 896. It was only because the earlier historical section of the Chronicle apparently became available for separate copying that it took on a life of its own as a so-called '890 Chronicle', and belief that the Pseudo-Asser had access to that work prior to 893 ensured its acceptance as a compilation in its own right. This inevitably led to the relegation of the most crucial section in the earliest compilation—covering that detailed Alfredian record from 891 to 896—to the incongruous status of an addition.

The Case for Winchester

Stenton rejected the possibility of the Chronicle having been compiled in Winchester and in this he was followed by Davis[229] who otherwise rejected Stenton's views on the origins of the Chronicle. Dumville rejected the notion of the compilation of 'the Chronicle to *892' at Winchester and he also regarded evidence for a Winchester origin for Manuscript A and related texts written in early square minuscule, as 'far from certain'.[230] Stenton's reasons for excluding Winchester as the home of the compilation were even weaker than his arguments for its southwestern origin, and they were inspired by a need to support that shaky southwestern thesis and to keep the Chronicle as far removed from Alfred's personal influence as possible. Stenton argued that there is little detail offered on Winchester for the period 754–891; that no attempt is made in the Chronicle to supply a complete list of bishops of Winchester or of ealdormen of Hampshire, and that a Chronicle which got its reporting wrong on the burial of King Æthelwulf in Winchester in 858 could not have been put together in that town. All of these points would carry weight, if we worked from the assumption that the Chronicle evolved over several centuries in one scriptorium and from one cumulative, continuous, and contemporaneous record of events. But the Chronicle is—it must be repeated—a compilation put together at the end of the ninth century from a plethora of earlier sources—including earlier West Saxon annals. What particular sets of annals were used by the late ninth-century compilers depended on availability, which might not necessarily coincide with their own geographical location. By the time the compilers set to work at the end of Alfred's reign, Wessex had been ravaged by three viking wars—the second of which (875–8) resulted in the overrunning of a whole section of the kingdom. When Winchester was sacked by an army of Danes from the Somme in 860, we do not know what early records were lost at that time, and later compilers—wherever they were based—must have been constrained to work with whatever early annals and succession-lists that then came to hand. Stenton's observations on entries relating to the eighth and early ninth centuries may tell us something of the location of early annalists whose records survived the Danish wars, and nothing whatever about the compilers who assembled that material in c.897. Winchester's bishops are not inconspicuous in the early record, and we are given information other than obituaries such as that concerning Cyneberht, 'bishop of the West Saxons', who went to Rome with Æthelheard, archbishop of Canterbury, in 801.[231] Two of Winchester's bishops, Herefrith and Wigthegn are mentioned in 836, and the Chronicle is then silent on six of their successors, including Swithun who died in 862 and Tunbeorht, the first Winchester prelate of Alfred's reign who ruled the see from c.871 to 879.[232] But the nature of the Chronicle's record changed radically from 835 onwards, ceasing to provide annals in the conventional sense and concentrating on the West

Saxon dynasty's involvement in the Danish wars. It was only when in the tenth century that the Chronicle's continuators departed from that central Alfredian theme and reverted to the recording of miscellaneous information, that Winchester's bishops re-entered the record. On the other hand, warrior bishops of Sherborne and ealdormen who led shire armies were mentioned in the Alfredian Chronicle because they were involved in the business of fighting Danes. Stenton, as we have seen, inflated the statistics in relation to ealdormen from the West Country by including annals found only in Æthelweard's Chronicle, and he otherwise exaggerated the predominance of West Country ealdormen in the records. An analysis of entries from 835—when a coherent sequence of entries on the Danish invaders begins—shows no preponderance of rulers from Somerset, Dorset, and Devon in the mainstream versions of the Chronicle. During this time the list of ealdormen reads as follows:

836 Duda and Osmod [shire unspecified]
840 Wulfheard (Hampshire)
840 Æthelhelm (Dorset)
841 Hereberht (Kent)
845 Eanwulf (Somerset)
    Osric (Dorset)
851 Ealhhere (Kent)
    Ceorl (Devon)
853 Ealhhere (Kent)
    Huda (Surrey)
860 Osric (Hampshire)
    Æthelwulf (Berkshire)
871 Æthelwulf (Berkshire)
883 Sigelm and Æthelstan [shire unspecified]
886 Æthelred of Mercia
887 Æthelhelm (Wiltshire)
888 Beocca [shire unspecified]
    Æthelwold [shire unspecified]
893 Æthelred of Mercia
    Æthelhelm and Æthelnoth [(?) West Country]
896 Ceolmund (Kent)
    Brihtwulf (Essex)
    Wulfred (Hampshire)
    Eadwulf (Sussex thegn)
    Beornwulf (Reeve of Winchester)
    Wulfric (Welsh reeve)

There is nothing here—even if we were to identify firmly some of those unlocated rulers with western shires—to suggest any preponderance whatever on the West Country. The list of ealdormen is evenly distributed with strong representation for Kentish leaders in the far east of the kingdom. There is nothing in this list—which

includes three Hampshire ealdormen and one town-reeve of Winchester—to provide an argument against a Winchester location for the compilers who assembled
this record. There is also the clear sense from the record, that men who are
mentioned in a context other than a death notice were involved either in the
Danish wars and or in taking alms to Rome for King Alfred. Stenton was also
selective, as we have seen, in his handling of Æthelweard's information. He did not
comment, for instance, on Æthelweard's note on the slaying of Ealdorman Hun of
Somerset in the battle of Ellendun in 825, in which we are told that Hun was
buried in Winchester.[233]

It was not the Chroniclers' task to supply a list of Winchester's bishops or of
Hampshire's ealdormen. The brief was to anchor the history of Wessex single-
mindedly into that of the ancient world and to tie the fragmentary records of early
Wessex into a narrative of military affairs centred on Alfred and his immediate
royal ancestors. Reference has already been made to the original burial of King
Æthelwulf at Steyning in Sussex, and his later reinterment in Winchester. Stenton
used the fact that the Chronicle names Æthelwulf's burial place as being in
Winchester to indicate that Winchester could not have been the place where such
a record was recorded. That argument was surely perverse. If, as seems likely, the
Annals of St Neots were correct in naming the original burial at Steyning, then the
final editing of that account, which states that the king lay at Winchester, reveals
that the compiler was at least up to date with affairs in Winchester at the time of
compilation *c.*897. Much of the confused thinking regarding the origins of the
Chronicle centres on a lack of distinction between the time of compilation and
earlier information used by the compilers. Scholars who have reviewed the evidence since Stenton's time and who have accepted his reasoning have failed to
observe that Stenton worked within an overall assumption of a Chronicle which
was compiled 'soon after King Alfred's accession in 871' when 'the archetype of
the Chronicle which we possess was brought down to the death of King Æthelwulf
in 858' and of a later continuator who brought the narrative down to 891.[234]
Stenton saw, then, the earliest compilers working soon after 871, and he left the
door open for the existence of a proto-chronicle, first compiled at the end of
Æthelwulf's reign. This in turn meant that he viewed Chronicle entries of the
840s and 850s as being much closer to the time of compilation than in fact they
were.

What Stenton saw as 'far [the] more suggestive' of the four major reasons he
gave for a non-Winchester origin for the compilation, was the absence in the
Anglo-Saxon Chronicle of any mention of 'the Danish descent upon Southampton
in 842, recorded by a contemporary Frankish writer'.[235] His remark has been cited
regularly since, and used to tilt the argument against a Winchester, and therefore
against any Alfredian connection with the Chronicle. The record of the Danish
raid on *Hamvic* is found in the Fourth Book of Nithard's 'Books of Histories (*Libri
Historiarum*)', where that contemporary Frankish chronicler tells us that in May
842, 'the Northmen devastated *Contwig* and crossed the sea from there and ravaged *Hamwig* and *Nordhunnwig* in the same manner'.[236] *Contwig* may well be

Quentovic, and from there Nithard suggests the Northmen crossed over to attack Southamptom (*Hamwig*) and the enigmatic *Nordhunnwig*, which has been variously identified with Norwich or Harwich. The record presents problems in relation to identification and topographical coherence. Southampton seems too far west for a raiding party coming directly from Quentovic, and the unidentified location of *Nordhunnwig* does nothing to confirm a Southampton identification. Precisely the same problems are encountered and indeed compounded, when we read the corresponding annal in the Anglo-Saxon Chronicle. Under 842 we read of a great slaughter 'in London and Quentovic and in Rochester'.[237] Here the evidence points more coherently to the Thames estuary as the landfall for the invaders from Quentovic. The irregular order in which the towns are listed, however—with the continental Quentovic sandwiched between London and Rochester—suggests that we have here a conflation of two annals—one of which definitely recorded a raid on the Thames and East Kent, and another which may have referred to a raid on Quentovic in the same year. Versions A,[238] and B[239] of the Chronicle have the form *Cwantawic* for Quentovic supporting *Quantauuic* in the Annals of St Neots[240] and in Æthelweard.[241] But version C, which not unreasonably understood the middle town in the list to refer to Canterbury rather than Quentovic, has the reading *Canwarabirig*, while B has an emended reading of *Cuntawic*.[242]

Given the confused nature of the Frankish and English evidence, there is little certainty regarding the identification of Southampton as the target of the raiders. Even if Nithard's record were less obscure, it would still be questionable to prefer the statement of a Frankish observer so far removed from England, to a late ninth-century Anglo-Saxon record referring to the same incident and which was almost certainly based on an earlier annal. It is unfortunate that a major argument regarding the origins of the Anglo-Saxon Chronicle should have been allowed to hinge on evidence so indeterminate as this. The question as to what a record relating to 842 does or does not reveal of a Winchester provenance may be irrelevant. The supposed raid on Southampton may never have taken place, and even if it did, it happened perhaps over fifty years before the time when the Chronicle was compiled, and some eight years before Alfred was even born. The question we need to ask is what does the material for 891–6—rather than earlier edited annals—reveal of the chronicler's whereabouts, since that is the first section of the entire work to reflect contemporaneous recording. Even for this period with its contemporary observations, certainty in locating the centre of recording is difficult, because of the Chronicle's preoccupation with national themes and with Alfred's military career. We are told towards the very end of 896 that Alfred was based in Winchester when Danish castaways were brought before him to be hanged. That was the last act which the king is credited with during his life. Earlier in that same year we are told of the death of Beornwulf, the town-reeve of Winchester, and (in version A) we read of the death of Wulfred, ealdorman of Hampshire. Twice the chronicler digresses from his extraordinarily full record of a Danish war which took his narrative far outside Wessex proper, into Kent, Essex, and the heartlands of English Mercia. We are told that in 894, those Danes who had been besieging

Exeter raided 'up in Sussex near Chichester' and in 896, those wounded survivors of a sea-battle in or near the Solent were also shipwrecked on the Sussex coast and taken, as we saw, to Winchester.[243] A Winchester chronicler who knew of the hanging of Alfred's captives in 896 would also have been well placed to know of their landing-point and of the earlier raid near Chichester in 894.

Stenton summarized the case for an Alfredian connection with Winchester by stating that along with Exeter, Alfred had a mint there, that he was buried there and that he may have proposed to found a monastery there.[244] To say that Alfred was buried in Winchester was one thing, but to know that he actually chose to be buried there is quite another. Alfred was buried first in the Old Minster in Winchester and his body was later removed for reinterment in the New Minster or Hyde Abbey. In his *Will* he left 50 pounds 'to the church in which I shall rest'[245]— a provision which should be set against Campbell's shrewd observation that 'the most sensitive nerve which great monasteries touched in their dealings with the aristocracy was in the grand provision they made for burial'.[246] Alfred's generous burial gift to Winchester amounted to no less than half the legacy in coin which he bequeathed to his wife and to each of his daughters. Edward's completion of a New Minster at Winchester, as one of the earliest acts of his reign, was surely sustaining a commitment to a church which had earned the special favour of his father. Alfred's queen, Ealhswith, who died only three or four years after Alfred, was also buried in Winchester. She was credited by Florence of Worcester with founding the convent at Nunnaminster in Winchester, and her obituary (5 December) along with that of Alfred (26 October) appears in the Junius 27 calendar.[247] Their son King Edward, and their grandson Ælfweard, were both buried in Winchester in 924. Winchester, which acquired three major monastic centres, was clearly the holiest place for the earliest generations of the Alfredian house. Since Edward's name does not appear in the Junius 27 calendar, that work was very probably produced before 924, and because of its information on Alfred and Ealhswith, there is also a strong possibility that it was produced in a Winchester scriptorium. The manuscript containing this calendar (Oxford Bodley MS Junius 27) also contains the much more extensive Junius Psalter, whose main scribe has been identified with Hand Two of Manuscript A of the Chronicle and of the Old English Orosius (BL MS Add. 47967).[248] A Winchester origin for the Junius 27 calendar is unlikely to be capable of absolute proof, but it remains more likely than Dumville's suggestion of Shaftesbury—a supposedly Alfredian foundation ruled by Alfred's daughter and for which we are reliant on the speculations of the Pseudo-Asser.[249]

There is no obituary in the Chronicle for a bishop of Winchester during the 891–6 period because Bishop Denewulf, who ruled the see from *c.*879, outlived Alfred and did not die until AD 908. But unusually, the Chronicle in 909 notes that 'Frithestan succeeded to the bishopric in Winchester' and a tenth-century annotator boxed in the notice of Frithestan's succession with red ink and placed an elaborate cross in the margin and a small cross above Frithestan's name in the text.[250] The same annotator who marked the name of Frithestan with his red pen, similarly highlighted the notice of Alfred's consecration as king in Rome in 853, and placed other crosses near Alfred's name at various places throughout the record of his reign in the A text.[251] Dumville commented on the significance of the red crosses thus: 'The interests of the mind behind this notation . . . appear to be essentially royalist, particularly concerned with the West Saxon dynasty, and eager to draw attention to its connections with Rome.'[252] If we modify this statement to read that the interests behind the crosses were essentially Alfredian, we may then proceed with Dumville to conclude that 'Bishop Frithestan seems to be the odd man out. Should we therefore associate the mind and the manuscript with him?'[253] A tenth-century inscription, *Friðestan diaconus*, is placed across the top of the booklet containing an eighth-century text of the *Carmen Paschale* by Sedulius, and that booklet was later attached to the manuscript containing the A text of the Parker Chronicle. The deacon, Frithestan, witnessed Winchester charters in 904:[254] he is almost certainly the man who became bishop of that see in 909 and whose name is inscribed on the maniple and stole of St Cuthbert's vestments. In 934, two years after Frithestan's death, those vestments were presented to the church of Lindisfarne at Chester-le-Street by King Athelstan, and they eventually found their way into St Cuthbert's reliquary. The vestments, as their inscription proclaims, were a gift to Frithestan from Queen Ælfflæd of Wessex.[255] They were made between Frithestan's succession in 909 and the death of Ælfflæd in 916, and their inscription is embroidered in a display script related to that employed by Hand One in Manuscript A of the Chronicle, the Trinity Isidore, and the Alfredian translation of the *Pastoral Care* in Oxford Bodley manuscript Hatton 20. Parkes saw all this evidence as grist for his mill to provide a cumulative argument for a Winchester origin for the Parker Manuscript if not indeed for the Chronicle.[256] Dumville saw it almost as a duty to argue that evidence away.[257]

Parkes identified Hand One of MS A of the Chronicle as being the same as that of the scribe who made additions to the Latin booklet of Caelius Sedulius's *Carmen paschale* which is now bound up with the Parker Manuscript, and Dumville conceded that the two scribes could, at least, have come from the same scriptorium.[258] The hand of that annotator of Sedulius is in turn related to the hand of the second scribe of Isidore of Seville's *Etymologiae* in Trinity College Cambridge (MS 368). The bounds of an estate in Winchester, on which St Mary's, Nunnaminster, was established, are entered in a hand which Parkes described as 'closely resembling scribe 1 of the Parker manuscript'.[259] Those bounds were entered in the tenth century into an eighth-century prayer book (BL MS Harley 2965), which from the format of its prayers shows it had been used in a nunnery. The bounds refer to an estate which Alfred's queen, Ealhswith, 'has' in Winchester, and therefore the note can be taken to refer to a situation before the time of Ealhswith's death in 902. Dumville sought to diminish the significance of this evidence by suggesting the note was more likely to have been entered in the book after the lands in question had come into the possession of Nunnaminster 'in the first half of the tenth century'.[260] Whatever the precise date of the boundary note in this manuscript, its Winchester and Alfredian association (through Ealhswith) are secure, even if those associates are less direct than we might wish, and Dumville accepted the close resemblance between the hand of the scribe who entered this boundary note and Hand One of Manuscript A of the Chronicle.[261] Hand Two of MS A was the same as that of the scribe of the Lauderdale Manuscript of the Old English (Tollemache) Orosius (BL MS Add. 47967), whose elaborate initials are in turn related to those of the Old English Bede (Oxford Bodley MS Tanner 10) and the Junius Psalter (Oxford Bodley MS Junius 27).[262] While Parkes did not argue for a common Winchester origin for all these manuscripts, he did argue for their being together at one time in the Winchester scriptorium in the tenth century,[263] and he hinted at a connection between Hand One of MS A—that same hand which filled in lacunae in the Sedulius manuscript—and the deacon, Frithestan of Winchester.[264] Dumville's agnosticism regarding the possibility of a Winchester home for Manuscript A was overstated, even if Parkes's enthusiasm may have been premature. Bately's conclusions are as far as the evidence at this stage in our knowledge will allow us to go: 'I would suggest that what little evidence there is appears to support but not confirm the theory of a Winchester provenance for hands 1 and 2 [of Manuscript A of the Chronicle].'[265] We also have to note that even if we were certain of a Winchester provence for Hands One and Two of Manuscript A, we would still not be certain of a Winchester origin for their exemplars—although that prospect would then have drawn closer. We may never be able to prove that Winchester was the ultimate place of origin for the Anglo-Saxon Chronicle, but it is more likely to have been Winchester than any other centre in Wessex. We can be certain that the organization and resources needed to compile the Chronicle—in terms of a team of researchers, library and writing materials—was beyond the capacity of any one individual. However much we may rightly attribute the Chronicle to Alfred's circle and to those associated with his household, we must come back eventually to the practicalities of book production and writing which required a well equipped library and scriptorium—a place where the necessary research materials could be accumulated and consulted; where parchments could be prepared, and where experienced scribes were available for the writing up. It is difficult to believe that the Anglo-Saxon Chronicle could ever have come into being on a farm in the West Country or even among court scholars camping out with an itinerant king.

The Case for Alfred

When we appreciate Alfred's own great sense of history, and the personal concern for the English past which he displays especially in the preface to the *Pastoral Care*, it is difficult to dissociate the king from the production of the earliest proto-booklets of the Chronicle. A king who in his own admission was preoccupied with 'those wise men who were in former times throughout England' and who lectured his bishops and thegns on those 'happy times when throughout England . . . kings who had rule over people in those days were obedient to God'—such a king, as we shall see, is surely a likely person to have had the historical vision and capability of organizing the compilation of an ambitious record of his country's past.[266] Whether

Alfred's perception of his peoples' past was accurate is open to doubt, but what cannot be disputed is the king's abiding interest in English history as such. His own personal pronouncements testify to this as does the remarkable achievement of directing the translation of so many works of Late Antiquity into Old English.[267] That Alfred had a personal interest in historical research is manifest from his own statements regarding his detailed investigations into the law codes of Æthelberht of Kent (+616), of Ine of Wessex (resigned 726), and of Offa (+796) of Mercia. He tells us several times in the Introduction to his own Code that he collected, reviewed, and edited the laws of those predecessors.[268] This detailed research into legal history brought Alfred personally into contact with the history of three major English kingdoms over the three centuries which English historical documentation had stretched before his time. A scholarly ruler, endowed with Alfred's organizational ability was very likely to channel his historical interests into a formal record of past events, and by the standards of his time, a chronicle or book of annals on the Anglo-Saxon past—influenced by Frankish models—fulfilled the requirements for such an ambition. When we bear in mind that the Anglo-Saxon Chronicle focuses first on Alfred's own dynastic ancestors and later concentrates almost exclusively on his own personal exploits against the Danes, there can scarcely be much doubt about the king's personal association—directly or indirectly—with the work.

The fact that the Chronicle was written from the start in Old English rather than in Latin is surely significant. Contemporary chronicles and annals in the Christian West were almost universally preserved in the Latin of the monastic schools. This is true of the varied contemporary collection of Carolingian annals which otherwise may have provided Alfred with his model for a West Saxon chronicle. Contemporary Irish annalists who were contributing to the precursor of the *Annals of Ulster* at this time, although by now turning to the vernacular, still clung to Latin terminology for their key formulaic annalistic phrases, and still continued to write in a laconic monastic tradition, in stark contrast to the more expansive vernacular style and the essentially secular narrative of the Chronicle in Alfred's reign. A comparison of the Alfredian chronicle with contemporary Irish annals is especially instructive in relation to content. At the time when the Anglo-Saxon Chronicle was being compiled, Irish annalists, recording in an older and more conservative monastic tradition, were busy observing a plethora of happenings under each successive year. The deaths of rival kings, great and small, of ecclesiastics and notorious vikings, are all recorded. But so also are minor events and characters whose identity and historical significance will forever elude us. And cluttering up that fascinating hotch-potch which contemporary Irish annals present us with is a web of observations on weather, plagues, and other more bizarre phenomena, which the West Saxon chronicler has very noticeably either edited out, or otherwise excluded from his narrative.[269] Ninth-century Irish records lack the relentlessly observant editorial hand so evident in the Anglo-Saxon Chronicle, where the single-minded policy in the Alfredian period was to concentrate on King Alfred and his Danish wars, to offer us a study of Alfred's strategies and motives as well as his military achievements, and to preserve that record in the vernacular. Even late ninth-century Frankish chronicles, although concerned with the court and with the fate of factions within the Carolingian empire are conspicuously lacking in editorial focus and retain the monastic Latin tradition. Whatever King Alfred's personal contribution to the actual writing of the Chronicle may have been, that he had a role in the overall conception of the scheme and its vernacular presentation, and that he retained an editorial interest in it can scarcely be disputed.

Alfred appears to have had the greatest influence in the final record dating from his reign—i.e. the annals for 891 to 896. The entire account for 891–6 (and not just the Last War) centres on the person of the king and shows him in the best possible light. The fact that it breaks off in 896 suggests that it was compiled either in or soon after that year. That we are missing similarly detailed annals for the last three years of Alfred's life may suggest that by 897 the king was either already too ill to proceed with the project, or that he did not survive long enough to supervise the writing up of a further detailed continuation at the end of say, another five-year interval. As things turned out, continuations of the record remained scrappy and erratic until the end of 911. A new phase of recording is introduced with the annal for 912, beginning with the account of Edward's building of the *burh* at Hertford, whereupon the Chronicle reverts to a mode of detailed reporting, not unlike that employed in the account of Alfred's Last War. This obvious break in the style and density of recording coincides palaeographically with where several scholars have recognized the beginnings of a new scribe in Manuscript A, in the annal for 912 on folio 21.r.22. Dumville saw only one hand at work from folio 16ᵛ and throughout the third quire of Manuscript A down to folio 25ᵛ, holding that apparent differences in hand were due the same scribe working at different times. He did however see a break in palaeographical terms between 911 and 912, which he identified as the period between the first and second stint of his Scribe 2, who in his opinion copied all the material in the third quire in Manuscript A.²⁷⁰ Parkes saw the break at 911 as being more fundamental, and identified a new hand (his Scribe 3) as beginning on folio 21.r.22, as did Bately (her Hand 2c).²⁷¹ The evidence for a break, therefore, on folio 21ʳ is formidable. As in the case back on folio 16ʳ, when the new scribe of the Edwardian annals took over at the 912 entry—five lines from the foot of folio 21ʳ—he ignored the year numbers already inserted by his predecessor, and his long account of events for 912 overran three existing year numbers in his manuscript. We may be dealing here with a break which again reflects the organization of the exemplar.

Dumville observed that 'the annals *897–*911 seem to belong together'.²⁷² Those annals clearly reveal a falling off in detailed reporting after 896. A piece of editorial summing up in the 896 annal points to the king as being the prime mover in the organization and completion of the record at that time. There is a very conscious rounding off of the record in 896, where the narrator more than at any other point in the Chronicle allows himself a liberty to address his reader with what is almost a thanksgiving prayer as well as an epilogue: 'By the grace of God, the [Danish] army had not on the whole afflicted the English people very greatly;

but they were much more seriously afflicted in those three years by the mortality of cattle and men, and most of all in that many of the best king's thegns who were in the land died in those three years.'[273] The notion of summarizing and writing up several years retrospectively—albeit contemporaneously for 896—is confirmed by the repeated reference to three years of campaigning. The chronicler's concern for the entire indigenous population and his reference to it as 'English people (*Angelcyn*)'[274] as opposed to West Saxons or say, 'West Saxons and Mercians', may well reveal something of King Alfred's own growing political awareness of his role, not only as king of the West Saxons, but of all English folk who were free of Danish rule or who wished to be free of it. The annalist's concern for the demise of 'the best king's thegns' and the detailed list of no less than nine of them, including the town-reeve of Winchester and two of the king's marshals or 'horse-thegns' reflects Alfred's personal concerns in this particular record.[275] This extensive list of obituaries of Alfred's friends should be compared with the conspicuous absence of such entries at earlier points in this record from 858 onwards.[276] The people who have survived the Danish onslaught are English people under the protection of King Alfred: the officials whose deaths are lamented are the king's own royal servants; and God is thanked for the saving of King Alfred's realm. There could be no clearer statement than that this is an official record of events in the reign, or that it was composed at least, by someone close to the very heart of government.

Previous concentration by scholars on an '890 Chronicle' was, as we have seen, determined by the necessity to accept a publication or distribution date prior to Asser's supposed use of the Chronicle in 893. When we remove the Pseudo-Asser's false claim and its accompanying *terminus ante quem* for the production date of the first compilation, we are free to move that date forward to 896–7. Even Keynes and Lapidge, following Dorothy Whitelock, who set their clocks for the compilation of the Chronicle according to the timetable determined by the *Life* of Alfred, accepted that 'the 893–6 chronicler was written at one time, presumably in or soon after 896', and that 'the annals for 897 and 900 belong to what might be called the second continuation'.[277] Here we have a rare case of agreement that the 893–6 annals were indeed compiled in Alfred's reign and that the isolated annal for 897 and the notice of Alfred's death in 900 form part of an Edwardian—and what I would see as a first—continuation. It is unfortunate that so much valuable scholarly analysis which has been done in recent years has concentrated on the so-called 890 Chronicle to the exclusion of the 891–6 section. Professor Bately's reasonable requirement, for instance, that if Alfred were in any way involved with the production of the Chronicle we should expect to find 'Alfred the strategist and Alfred the general' revealed somewhere in its account,[278] while in no way fulfilled in the pre-890 Chronicle, is met in full in the 890–6 section. The pre-890 section does indeed record the events of Alfred's reign to the advantage of the king, but it does not provide evidence for the king's personal motives, and in place of strategies we find a cover-up for mistakes made. But in the 891–6 section, the chronicler fulfils Bately's criteria, and in the words of Keynes and Lapidge: 'The chronicler (for 891–6) is not, however, content simply to report events, for he frequently enlarges on the king's *motives* [authors' own italics] for doing something, and is willing to express his own opinions and to offer his own interpretations.'[279] Bately also rightly noted the absence of any reference to 'men of importance in church and state who must have been known personally to King Alfred and played a part in his rebuilding of Wessex—did none of them' she asked—'take up office or die in the period 872–87?'[280] The absence or relative scarcity of such obituaries of Alfredian magnates in the pre-890 section, we have already recognized to be symptomatic of the retrospective nature of that entire record. It is due to some extent also to the relentless focusing by the chronicler on King Alfred's role in relation to the progress of the Danish wars. But that relative scarcity of obituaries of Alfredian magnates is dramatically reversed in the notice of no less than nine obituaries for Alfred's own officers in the 893–6 section. Bately was understandably reluctant to press the requirement for evidence of Alfred's philosophical and scholarly interests within a pre-890 chronicle which might otherwise have been associated personally with the king, in view of the difficulty in dating Alfred's own scholarly works in relation to the compilation-date of the chronicle. We might add that the compilation of a chronicle involved such a different genre of writing, it allowed little accommodation for philosophical interests. Yet in the 891–6 section, we do encounter something of that scholarly curiosity which reminds us of the Alfred who interviewed the Scandinavian explorers, Ohthere and Wulfstan, as described in the Old English *Orosius*. According to Æthelweard, all three of those Irishmen who visited Alfred's court were *magistri*, and one of them (Máelinmain) he described as 'a man blossoming in the arts, learned in literature, an eminent teacher (*artibus frondens, littera doctus, magister insignis*)'.[281] The Chronicle proper also records the death of a fourth Irishman, Suibhne, in that same year, who is described there as 'the best master (*betsta lareow*)'. Here then in this post-890 section, we find a reflection of Alfred's preoccupation with scholarship and his curiosity regarding foreign scholars, which is the type of material we should expect to find, as Bately required, in any section of the Chronicle which might claim an Alfredian association.

Bately[282] itemized three annals in the Alfredian chronicle where lack of information might be taken to exclude a personal Alfredian connection with their composition. The issues centred on

(1) failure to provide a location for Alfred's sea-battle in 882;
(2) failure to explain how the East Anglian Danes broke the peace in 885;
(3) failure to provide detail on how London was reoccupied in 886.

It is true that all three of these annals contain the scrappiest record of English events, embedded in what was essentially a retrospective report on the Danish army in Francia from 880 to 891.[283] The shortcomings in the reporting of such incidents can now be viewed in the knowledge that they may not have been written up until *c*.897. The lack of topographical detail for the sea-battle in 882 may indeed indicate that this was not a contemporary record, but, on the other hand,

Alfred was remembered (in the late 890s) as having been at the centre of this incident. The Danish fleet was put at four ships, two of which were captured and their crews slain, and two of which surrendered. All of that constitutes a relatively detailed account for a report which may have been compiled some fourteen years after the event and which was incidental to a narrative which dealt essentially with Frankish affairs. The Chronicle's account of Alfred's attack on East Anglia in 885 may be deficient in its present form, since Æthelweard supplies information to the effect that the East Angles had earlier broken out of their territory and joined forces with a new wave of invaders at Benfleet.[284] It was clearly because of that breach of their truce that Alfred attacked East Anglia, and that information may have formed part of the original Chronicle text.[285] The account of Alfred's taking of London in 886 has been bedevilled by the Pseudo-Asser who claimed the king took that place 'after the burning of cities and the massacre of people'.[286] Even if London were taken by force by the English, we need to be very careful in our interpretation of the Chronicle's report of this incident. The vagueness on the part of the chronicler may not stem from ignorance, but from a desire to suppress the truth and to accord Alfred a greater role in this episode than he actually deserved. The Chronicle tells us Alfred 'entrusted the borough to Ealdorman Æthelred'.[287] But London had always been a Mercian town, and the fact that the Mercian Æthelred took immediate charge of it could suggest that he had a greater role in its occupation than the West Saxon chronicler would ever care to admit. The precise nature of the relationship between King Alfred and Æthelred, Lord of the Mercians, is open to question and relates to the wider issue of Mercian relations with Wessex down to the end of Edward's reign. Our understanding of that relationship is particularly restricted for this early period after the departure of the Danish sub-king, Ceolwulf II, from the record, in English Mercia. Alfred's son-in-law, as we have seen, was consistently and deliberately graded at the rank of ealdorman in the Alfredian Chronicle, while Æthelweard elsewhere (though not in this instance) refers to him as 'king'. It is possible that Æthelred's occupation of London may have arisen either from his own initiative, or have fallen to him as a right in his capacity as ruler of English Mercia. Alfred's role then, in the so-called 'occupation (*gesettan*)' of London may have been merely supportive, and is not in any case suggestive, in itself, of a battle. The report in the Chronicle that on the death of Æthelred of Mercia in 911, 'King Edward succeeded to London and Oxford and to all the lands which belonged to them'[288] suggests that those two towns and their associated territories had hitherto been firmly under Æthelred's— rather than under West Saxon—control. The phrase *Eadweard cyng feng to Lundenbyrg* couches Edward's 'succession to London' in the same idiom as Alfred's succession to the West Saxon kingdom (*feng Ælfred to Wesseaxna rice*) back in 871. In other words, Æthelred, Lord of the Mercians, may have ruled his Londoners with much, if not all the autonomy of his Mercian predecessors, during some of the time at least, prior to Edward's takeover in 911.

There is finally the point that if Alfred really had inspired the writing up of the Chronicle, then why had he not insisted on the inclusion of a mention of his own marriage and of the marriage of his daughter to Æthelred of Mercia?[289] We may begin by stating that women, however noble, were treated with greater anonymity in medieval records than their menfolk, and most of them—again, however noble—were ignored altogether. King Alfred himself can scarcely be hailed as a promoter of female identity. He never mentioned any of his three daughters by name in his *Will*—settling instead for 'the eldest, the middle and the youngest (*yldstan, medemestan 7 gingestan*)'—a phrase which he resorted to twice.[290] By contrast, the king mentions his son Edward by name, and he also names his two nephews. The lack of mention of Alfred's marriage must be set against the positive information we have on the marriage of his sister to Burgred of Mercia in 853; her death in 887; the death of Alfred's wife, Ealhswith in 903; and of his daughter Æthelflæd in 918. On the other hand, we are told absolutely nothing in the Chronicle of the spouses of Alfred's four older royal brothers. There is no mention, for instance, of Æthelbald's marriage to his stepmother, Judith, in *c*.858, nor of the wife of Æthelred I—the mother of the rebellious Æthelwold. But those women whom we are told about, all relate to Alfred as the central figure—a point nicely brought out in the identification of Queen Æthelswith of Mercia as 'King Alfred's sister (*Ælfredes sweostor cyninges*)'.[291] So although the absence of any mention of Alfred's wife in the Chronicle prior to 896 may appear curious, it does not undermine the case for an Alfredian association with the work. It was an absence which sorely tried the Pseudo-Asser, whose particular working copy of the Chronicle did not stretch down as far as the obituary of Ealhswith in 903, and who was therefore left without a name for Alfred's queen.

One of the most important studies of the text of the Anglo-Saxon Chronicle is that in which Bately demonstrated on grounds of vocabulary and syntax that the author or authors of the Chronicle were different from the author of the Old English *Orosius* and from the known works of King Alfred.[292] Those findings clearly showed that the ideas of Plummer, Hodgkin, and subsequent scholars who saw Alfred's personal involvement in the actual writing of the Chronicle to be mistaken. There is, however, a danger of oversimplifying the issue of authorship by approaching this problem from a modern perspective. Modern preoccupations with copyright and authors' ownership of their own written work did not apply in the Middle Ages, and the question of who wrote the Anglo-Saxon Chronicle is altogether different even from the question of who wrote Shakespeare's plays. The majority of medieval authors and copiers did not feel impelled to put their names to their written works, and some of those whose names do appear have put their names to the labours of an amanuensis. Anonymity among medieval scribes and copiers was not prompted by modesty so much as a lack of consciousness of the need to associate one's name with a particular text. Had things been otherwise, we would not still be so ignorant of the identity of a whole range of chroniclers stretching down into the central Middle Ages. Alfred is exceptional in providing prefaces to his own works and to the work of his friends, in which he reveals his involvement in scholarly output. That might support an argument for excluding the king from any involvement in the Chronicle whatever, on the grounds that had he commissioned the work, he would not have been slow to inform us of his association with it. On the other hand, there are those scholars such as Sisam, who argued—quite wrongly—for Alfred employing an amanuensis even for those works which bear his name.[293] Hart claimed with greater justification that Æthelweard's erudite if tortuous hermeneutic Latin can scarcely have come from the pen of a layman at the close of the tenth century.[294] Bately demonstrated it is likely that not one but several writers were engaged in the compilation of the Chronicle text during Alfred's reign, and some of those writers in turn, were engaged in the editing and translating of earlier material which they pressed into service in the compilation.[295] The fact that Alfred's style and usage cannot be personally detected in the Chronicle narrative is a valuable observation. But it does not mean that Alfred cannot have been involved in some way in the production of the Chronicle. It is difficult to accept that the king did not in some way assist in the production of a work which focused so carefully on the fortunes of his own dynasty and on his own struggle with the Danes. It was a work which, unlike contemporary chronicles, was cast in the vernacular—and therefore fell within the remit of Alfred's own scholarly preoccupation with vernacular texts—and which fitted in perfectly with that whole corpus of works on Late Antiquity which we know to have been produced, if not by Alfred himself, then at least by people who worked closely with the king. And Alfred, finally, was a king possessed of the necessary resources to employ a veritable team of scholars on such an ambitious project. In view of Alfred's obvious candidature as the patron and director of the Chronicle project, the burden of proof must rest on those who would follow Stenton in rejecting Alfred's involvement at any level within the work, and to identify convincingly that 'particular noble of the ninth century who wished for a vernacular rendering of earlier English history'.[296]

It is now time to review briefly how the Anglo-Saxon Chronicle may have come into being. A team of compilers set to work, late in Alfred's reign, with one group providing prefatory matter and writing up a disjointed series of entries from Julius Caesar and the birth of Christ down to c.834. This group worked from a variety of sources, including the Epitome of Bede and at least two sets of early West Saxon annals. A second group was charged with writing up the reign of King Alfred from the critical year of his succession in 871 down to his final triumph over Guthrum in 878. This same group, which may be said to have set the editorial style of the Chronicle by concentrating on Alfred's involvement in the Danish wars, projected the record back to cover the hiatus between 835 and 871. We can give qualified assent to Thorogood's findings in 1933 that a set of annals from the reign of Ecgberht 'lay before the writer of the Alfredian Chronicle, and that to this he added a summary of the rest of Æthelwulf's reign and of the reigns of his two eldest sons in order to connect his new contemporary annals with the earlier texts'.[297]

But this summary concentrated on a clearly defined theme of the Danish wars and was executed with tight editorial control involving the glorification of the infant Alfred and the relegation of his older royal brothers to subsidiary roles. That bridging of the period between earlier annalistic material and the chronicle of Alfred's reign dealt in a cursory way with some of the most formative years in the history of the West Saxon kingdom. Detailed recording of events in the Alfredian Chronicle clearly begins, as we have seen, at 871—the first year of Alfred's reign. Before that time, we can recognize what we might describe as editorial propaganda in the record of Alfred's visit to Rome in infancy, in Æthelwulf's pilgrimage and marriage, and in the meagre press accorded to Alfred's older brothers. Although the record becomes more dense from 871 onwards, it was not quite, as Thorogood suggested, made up of 'new contemporary annals'. It was still clearly retrospective and its purpose was to summarize and present Alfred's struggles with Hálfdan and Guthrum in the best possible light. This was nevertheless a record of events written in the lifetime of whoever recorded it. The chronological detail provided for the battles of 871 and the topographical and chronological detail offered for 878 reflects the interests of veterans from those campaigns. On the other hand, this record of the 870s was written up a long time after the extravagant events which were supposed to have happened in Rome when Alfred was a boy in 853, and it was almost certainly written many years after King Alfred's first war, against Guthrum—which ended in a heavily edited account of Alfred's victory in 878. Since the next section of the Chronicle (879–91) bears even clearer hallmarks of retrospective writing, this largely Frankish record could well have been put together in the later 890s as part of a design to produce a chronicle of Alfred's involvement in the Danish wars down to what was then the present day. These annals of the 880s may have been written up by a different compiler from the person who wrote up the 871 to 878 section. The purpose of inserting the Frankish material was to provide a continuous account of the progress of King Alfred's enemies and to link the narrative of his first two wars with his final struggle against Hæsten. It is difficult if not impossible to envisage the copying of the Frankish material (879–91) from a Carolingian source at any time before the conclusion of Alfred's Last War in 896.

There was almost certainly not one person, but a team of scholars collaborating on such an ambitious project. This is supported by linguistic and lexigraphical evidence pointing to different compilers at work in different sections of the Chronicle, as well as evidence for the distinct nature of the material recorded in these sections. Yet in spite of the evidence for multiple authorship, there is equally strong evidence for a comprehensive plan behind the layout of the Chronicle from its very beginning. One of the features which sets the Anglo-Saxon Chronicle apart from Irish or even contemporary Frankish annals is the strong sense of coherence and overall plan which underlines the entire record down to 920 (on fo. 25ᵛ to the end of 923 (*recte* 920) in MS A). The continued presence of that plan—centring on the king's involvement in the Danish wars—until late into Edward's reign may be put down to the strong influence of the earliest team of compilers who worked in 896, and many of whom may have survived into Edward's reign and beyond. Alfred's scholarly archbishop, Plegmund, who cannot have been indifferent to the compilation of the Chronicle, survived until 923, while Bishop

Frithestan of Winchester, who may well have been involved in the work of compilation as a younger cleric, survived into the reign of Athelstan and died as late as
932. King Alfred clearly needed help with this great endeavour, and the fact that
his own use of language cannot personally be identified within the compilation may
tell us much about the immediate authorship of the Chronicle but little of the
king's personal interest in the project and his very real responsibility for it.

Whoever conceived the original plan for a chronicle of English affairs from the
beginning of things was not merely content to go back to Vortigern, Hengest,
Horsa, or Cerdic. The person who first planned the Anglo-Saxon Chronicle was
determined to go right back to the beginnings of Christian history—to the birth
of Christ—and to follow up through the apostolic age and into the world of Roman
emperors, through Claudius and the conquest of Britain, to the coming of the
English and the establishment of the dynasty of Cerdic in Wessex. In short, the
earliest sections of the Chronicle were intended to serve a specific purpose—they
were designed to anchor the history of Alfred's own royal house into the respectability of an antique Roman and Christian past. The Anglo-Saxon Chronicle is not
by any means alone among medieval annals in trying to link up with World
History, but the peculiar way in which the Chronicle achieves this reveals much
about the aims of its overall editor. As soon as the terra firma of the late seventh
century is reached, the great historical milestones in the record are set out from the
sending of St Augustine by Pope Gregory with the Christian message in 596, the
arrival of Bishop Birinus in Wessex in 634 along with the baptism of the first West
Saxon king in 635, the building of the Old Minster in Winchester in 642, leading
on through the reign of Ceadwalla and his pilgrimage to Rome in 688, followed by
the reign of Ine and his pilgrimage to Rome in 726. And running parallel to the
record of Christianity in Wessex is the equally important and parallel theme of the
succession of West Saxon kings, whose royal credentials to rule are reinforced at
strategic intervals in the Chronicle by genealogical bench-marks which are usually
inserted at the notice of their deaths. Thus, we are offered genealogical vignettes
for Cynric at 552, for Ceolwulf at 597, for Cynegils at 611, for Æscwine at 674, for
Centwine at 676, for Ceadwalla at 685, and for Ine in 688. Conventional genealogical recording for the eighth century is much flimsier than for the seventh, but
genealogical pronouncements nevertheless continue to be made, as when we are
told of Cynewulf in 757 or of Brihtric at 786 that their 'true paternal ancestry goes
back to Cerdic'. Related to this genealogical material, is the questionable list of
Bretwaldas which was borrowed from Bede and built around the name of Alfred's
grandfather, King Ecgberht at 829. It is not that genealogies are confined in the
Chronicle to the alleged West Saxon forebears of King Alfred. Northumbrian and
Mercian genealogies are also included, but in a much more haphazard way. It is the
regularity with which genealogies of quite obscure early West Saxon rulers are
recorded that is remarkable, together with the fact that the entire record is reinforced
and framed by the two great genealogies of the West Saxon house—one in the
king-list in the preface to the whole Chronicle which leads down to Alfred, and
the other at 855-8, which was centred on Alfred's father. In the king-list in the

preface, the name of King Cynegils is glossed: 'he was the first of the kings of the West Saxons to receive baptism'.[298] The genealogy of King Æthelwulf does not include Cynegils, since not even Alfred could claim direct descent for Æthelwulf from the first Christian king of Wessex, but this loss is made good by the comment that Æthelwulf's remote ancestor, Ingild 'was the brother of Ine, king of the West Saxons, who [held the kingdom for 37 years and] afterwards went to St Peter's and ended his life there'.[299] Thus, the genealogy and the mandate it gave Alfred and his ancestors to rule, was combined with historical statements relating to the Christianization of his royal house, to provide a respectable framework and background for the history of the West Saxons. The motive behind the compilation of the strictly historical part of the Chronicle seems clear. It was designed to equip the English—and especially the West Saxons and the House of Alfred in particular—with roots in a Christian and Roman past. Much of what is found in the Chronicle prior to 855 was designed to give its readers respect and understanding for the contribution of Christianity to the English past and to emphasize the continuity in royal succession from Cerdic to Æthelwulf, regardless of what violence had to be done to historical truth. The Chronicle's dubious record of the infant Alfred's meeting with the pope can be viewed as the culmination of a whole series of reported connections between Alfred's ancestors and the centre of Christendom.

Alfred, more than any other Englishman, was interested in recording the successful struggle, in which he as king, led his Christian people against what the Chronicle describes as 'heathen men (*hæþne men*)'. The Danish wars as set in the context of the Chronicle were seen as the culmination of a longer and greater spiritual struggle which began with the very foundations of Christianity and which continued down through the conversion of Alfred's own royal ancestors, and the bringing of civilization to pagan English society. The Chronicle sets Alfred's role in the struggle against the Danes in the wider and more ancient context of the triumph of Christianity over paganism. That is why the baptism of Guthrum is treated in the Chronicle in such circumstantial detail, for Alfred's triumph as the Christian king was seen as part of the fulfilment of a divinely providential plan. The record of the Danish wars provided the *raison d'être* for the Chronicle during Alfred's reign because King Alfred, as the most likely person to have conceived of the idea of a Chronicle, viewed himself as a champion fighting for the cause of Christianity and Christian culture against the powers of heathen barbarism. In this, the Chronicle served not only a useful political purpose for the House of Ecgberht, but it also happily fitted in with Alfred's wider scholarly programme—and more especially with translations not personally undertaken by the king, but apparently executed during his reign—Orosius's *History against the Pagans* and Bede's *Ecclesiastical History of the English Church*. This awareness of cultural sequence and continuity on behalf of the editor of the first compilation of the Chronicle—from early Christians to Romans, from Romans to Romano-Britains, from Romano-Britains to pagan Saxons, from pagan Saxons to Christian kings of Wessex—all bears the hallmark of King Alfred's own intellect.[300] Compare, for instance, how in the preface to the *Pastoral Care* the king spells out his personal awareness and fascination with cultural transmission and continuity:

Then I remembered also how the divine law was first known in the Hebrew language, and afterwards, when the Greeks had learnt it, they translated it all into their own language, and also all other books. And the Romans likewise, when they had learnt them, turned them all through learned interpreters into their own language. And also all other Christian nations translated a part of them into their own language.[301]

Similarly in the introduction to his *Laws*, Alfred first anchored his own Code into quotations from Mosaic law, and later reflected by way of the Acts of the Apostles on how Judaic law was modified by Christian practice.[302] He developed the notion of this historical progression yet further by viewing English laws of his own time as the product of tribal customary law modified by the cumulative weight of Judaic-Christian practice as interpreted by successive synods of the English church. And in all this, he viewed himself and his 'distinguished wise men (*geðungenra witena*)' as the 'secular lords (*weoruld-hlafordas*)', who together with his bishops, dispensed justice to the people—largely in the form of setting monetary compensations.

After it came about that many peoples had received the faith of Christ, many synods were assembled throughout all the earth, and likewise throughout England . . . of holy bishops and also of other distinguished wise men; they then established . . . that secular lords might with their permission receive . . . compensation in money for almost every misdeed.[303]

In all of this, Alfred shows himself to be the great synthesizer and organizer in bringing into being a corpus of Old English laws. He shows himself, too, to be capable of working with a team and explains his role to us as editor and overseer:

They then in many synods fixed the compensations for many human misdeeds, and they wrote them in many synod-books, here one law, there another. Then, I, King Alfred, collected these together and ordered to be written many of them which our forefathers observed, those which I liked, and many of those which I did not like, I rejected with the advice of my councillors (*witena*) and ordered them to be differently observed.[304]

The Chronicle shares the same historical attitudes as those of the compiler of Alfred's *Laws*, and it bears the stamp, too, of the author of the prefatory letter to Gregory's *Pastoral Care*. The Chronicle has to be the work of Alfred because only Alfred had that distinctive perception of cultural transmission which is so conspicuous in the framework of the Chronicle. Only he had the understanding, motivation, and organizational ability to oversee a record which was essentially designed to glorify him and his royal house. Alfred was a man, who characteristically was looking back to an earlier Christian age, inhabited by those intellectual giants whose works he strove to translate into Old English. The essentially historical mind of this king is revealed yet again when he addresses us in the preface to the *Pastoral Care*, seeking to locate England's intellectual golden age in pre-viking times. There, referring to those same Danish invasions which occupy so much of the Chronicle's record, he writes:

Remember what temporal punishments came upon us, when we neither loved wisdom ourselves nor allowed it to other men. . . . When I remembered all this, I also remembered how, before everything was ravaged and burnt, the churches throughout all England stood filled with treasures and books, and likewise there was a great multitude of the servants of God.[305]

The Anglo-Saxon Chronicle, completed near the end of Alfred's reign, was meant to be read along with other great works from Alfred's scholarly circle, and it is a mistaken approach for scholars to study it in isolation from the entire cultural output of Alfred's reign. To treat the Chronicle in isolation invites us to see it merely as an antiquarian work or as a crude piece of propaganda which the king perhaps used to rally support against the invaders. The crude propaganda argument fails to take into account the allegedly low levels of literacy even among the nobility in ninth-century Wessex, not to mention the fact that most if not all the Alfredian record in the Chronicle is retrospective and relates to past military crises and successes. Equally, the notion that the Chronicle was written in isolation from the king and his circle—perhaps as an antiquarian piece—fails to appreciate the grand design which it embodied. The final word on the origins of the Anglo-Saxon Chronicle must go to Plummer whose scholarship in this field, although a century old, has not been entirely superseded and whose powers of scholarly judgement have rarely been surpassed:

I do not mean that the actual task of compiling the Chronicle from earlier materials was necessarily performed by Alfred, though I can well fancy that he may have dictated some of the later annals which describe his own wars. But that the idea of a national Chronicle as opposed to merely local annals was his, that the idea was carried out under his direction and supervision, this I do most firmly believe.[306]

XVIII

King Alfred's Books
Most Necessary for All Men to Know?

THE LIST OF ORIGINAL WORKS FROM THE HAND OF KING ALFRED AS
well as translations of Latin writers from Late Antiquity, supposed to have
been undertaken by the king, has undergone repeated and sometimes drastic
changes since Alfred's time. We may begin with the king's own comments on his
writings. He tells us very definitely in his prefatory letter to the *Pastoral Care* that
he translated that work of Pope Gregory's into English.[1] In his prose preface to
Gregory's *Dialogues*, on the other hand, Alfred claims that he commissioned his
friends to produce the *Dialogues* for him.[2] The prose preface to the *Consolation of
Philosophy* by Boethius opens with the claim that 'King Alfred was the translator
of this book'.[3] Alfred also informs us that he commissioned the Law Code which
bears his name, and we have already encountered the king's *Will* and those genuine
charters which were drawn up for the king if not by his own clerks, then by clerks
appointed for that purpose in Canterbury and elsewhere. These are the only
instances where we have direct evidence for a claim for Alfred's authorship. The
truncated preface to the Old English version of the *Soliloquies* of St Augustine does
not mention Alfred by name, but modern textual scholarship attributes that work,
and the translation of the first fifty Psalms from the Psalter to King Alfred.[4]

We next hear of Alfred's writings a century after the death of the king when the
Pseudo-Asser informs us that the *Dialogues* of Gregory were translated by Bishop
Wærferth of Worcester—an attribution, which as we shall see, may have relied on
a false understanding of the verse preface to the *Dialogues*. At about this time, too,
the chronicler Æthelweard remembered his illustrious ancestor as the translator of
'the tearful passion of the book of Boethius' and that the king 'turned unknown
numbers of books from the ornate Latin tongue into his own language'.[5]
Æthelweard's contemporary, the homilist Ælfric, together with the author of a
later Old English homily on St Neot refer in general terms to the 'many books
(*manega bec*)'[6] attributed to King Alfred, while Ælfric wrongly ascribed the translation of Bede's *Ecclesiastical History* to the king.[7] That work is now recognized to
have been translated under Mercian influence, perhaps during Alfred's reign (if
not before) and perhaps under the king's patronage. These were vague and shaky
memories indeed, and taken as a whole they suggest that while Alfred was recalled
in the folk mind as a great writer, few scholars had actually read those works a

century after Alfred's own time. When we reach the era of William of Malmesbury in the early twelfth century, we find that while that chronicler had a keen interest in Alfred, his opinions on Alfred's precise contribution to scholarship also need to be treated with great caution. William's claim that Alfred translated 'the greater part of Roman writings' inspires little confidence.[8] He repeats the Pseudo-Asser's statement that Wærferth translated the *Dialogues* and adds that the historical Asser assisted Alfred in the translation (or explanation) of Boethius. In addition to Boethius, Gregory's *Pastoral Care*, and an unfinished translation of the Psalms, William also attributes the translation of Bede's *Ecclesiastical History* to Alfred, and he adds the *Histories* of Orosius to the list. Although Orosius's *Histories against the Pagans* contains geographical information supplied to Alfred, Bately has convincingly shown that this West Saxon text was not written by the king himself.[9] William of Malmesbury makes no mention of the Old English version of the *Soliloquies* of St Augustine, a work which can be safely ascribed to King Alfred, but he does refer to a *Handboc* or *Enchiridion* which was probably the same work— in Malmesbury's mind at least—as the *Manualem librum* mentioned in the *Gesta Pontificum*. One possible major addition to the periphery at least of the Alfredian repertoire of original works is the compilation of the Anglo-Saxon Chronicle up to, and including, Alfred's reign. The Chronicle, as we have seen, although dating from Alfred's reign was not personally written by the king. But it is possible, nevertheless, that it was compiled at the king's command and perhaps also under his overall direction.

Writings attributed to King Alfred, may, because of the complexity of the subject, be listed under four categories. The first and most important group consists of prefaces, written in the king's name, to works which he either claimed to have translated himself, alone or with helpers, or to have arranged for their translation. Here we may include the prefatory letter to the *Pastoral Care* and perhaps also the verse preface and epilogue to that work; the prose preface to the *Consolation of Philosophy*, and the fragmentary preface to the *Soliloquies*. This group also contains other original writings or compilations made by the king, such as his *Will*. It is this group which deserves most attention from historians seeking insights into the king's personality and his personal objectives. The second group consists of texts translated into Old English by Alfred himself. Alfred's personal role in the production of these works is vouched for, either on his own evidence in his prefaces to individual translations, or on well-nigh irrefutable evidence on textual grounds. The king's earliest translations are taken to be those, such as Gregory's *Pastoral Care*, which remain closest to the original Latin, while the *Consolation of Philosophy* by Boethius or the *Soliloquies* of St Augustine,[10] which depart progressively further from their Latin originals and contain proportionately more of the king's own ideas, are seen as later works. The translation of the Psalms also belong in this category and were regarded by William of Malmesbury and by some more recent scholars as the king's last work.[11] The third group consists of translations of original works carried out at Alfred's command by a team of scholarly friends. The *Dialogues* of Pope Gregory is the only lengthy translated text which can be placed with certainty in this category, although there may well have been others. Here, too, we might include original works such as the treaty between Alfred and the Danish Guthrum and those charters which can be definitely shown to have been drawn up under Alfred's authority. Alfred's Law Code was also, according to his own *Introduction*, compiled at the king's command. A fourth group consists of those translations from Latin and original works in Old English carried out during Alfred's reign, if not at his command, then at least with his encouragement. These works cannot be included in the third category for want of any positive statement in any preface or epilogue attached to them or for want of any positive internal textual evidence associating them with Alfred. Works in this category range from the Old English translation of Orosius's *Histories against the Pagans*, the earliest draft of the Anglo-Saxon Chronicle, and (with less certainty) the Old English translation of Bede's *Ecclesiastical History of the English Church and People*, and a ninth-century Martyrology. Finally, on the periphery of this list of Old English works is the *Leechbook* of Bald, a medical treatise surviving in a mid-tenth-century manuscript[12] whose text may have been written in Alfred's reign. There are inevitably areas of overlap between these schematized headings under which the works of Alfred may be studied. A king in Alfred's circumstances was unlikely to have undertaken any single one of the works attributed to him, completely unaided. So, we shall see that while Alfred claimed credit for translating the *Pastoral Care* after much acknowledged help, even his prefatory letter accompanying that work may have involved a team effort. And while the Laws were 'gathered together' on the king's own initiative, he tells us that he 'ordered them to be written'.[13] In the case of most of the written works commissioned by Alfred, he could have exercised unlimited powers of censorship and editorial control, using his helpers sometimes as ghost writers, sometimes as research assistants, and sometimes as scribes for the copying of manuscripts. The Laws were clearly an exception, since they pertained to the common weal and since Alfred could not realistically promulgate new laws in the face of established custom or without the consent of his *witan*:

Now I, King Alfred, have collected these laws, and have given orders for copies to be made of many of those which our predecessors observed and which I myself approved of. But many of those I did not approve of I have annulled, by the advice of my councillors, while [in other cases] I have ordered changes to be introduced. For I have not dared to presume to set down in writing many of my own, for I cannot tell what [innovations of mine] will meet with the approval of our successors.[14]

There is one notable characteristic about three major works which were almost certainly not written by Alfred personally. Orosius's *Histories*, Bede's *Ecclesiastical History*, and the Anglo-Saxon Chronicle form such a coherent body of historical writing—all most likely compiled during Alfred's reign—that it would be difficult to argue they were not conceived as part of one broad plan. The translation of Orosius provided a world history with a strong Christian perspective, while the Chronicle anchored West Saxon history and the annals of Alfred's royal house into that same Antique and Christian view of the past. Bede provided for England what Orosius had attempted for Classical history—the story of the triumph of orthodox Christianity among a pagan people. Bede's history of the English church was a narrative with a relentless agenda showing how the English not only converted to Christian ways, but showing also how their Roman orthodoxy triumphed over Welsh and Hiberno-Scottish Christians and enemies. For Bede—as for Alfred later—that adherence to Roman orthodoxy carried with it the seeds of early English political and military greatness as well as spiritual superiority, when as both writers put it, there were 'happy times' for England in that earlier golden age. The very title of Bede's *History* with its notion of 'England people (*gens Anglorum*)'— a term giving a strong sense of ethnic unity to the diverse tribal and provincial kingdoms of England—must also have appealed to Alfred's sense of English unity in the face of Danish invasion and colonization. In these three works, then, we are presented with something of a paradox. For while the Orosius, Chronicle, and Bede were not actually written by King Alfred personally, they do exhibit greater cohesion as a group than the writings which we can definitely attribute to the king. For Alfred's own productions—including works definitely commissioned by him— offer us a mixed bag of hagiography (Gregory's *Dialogues*), devotional works (the Psalms), advice on administration (*Pastoral Care*), and esoteric philosophical studies (Boethius and Augustine). It may be that we ought to view the works definitely associated with the king as an anthology inspired by his personal devotional and intellectual preferences, while other works less firmly associated with Alfred, bear the hallmarks of a more coherent scheme. The rationale behind Orosius's *Histories*, the Old English Bede, and the Anglo-Saxon Chronicle would appear to be the provision of a coherent body of Christian historical writing in which a West Saxon reader could recognize his people's role in English and World history. In that important respect, this group of texts did indeed provide reading 'most necessary for all men to know'.

Alfred was most heavily influenced in his own writings by the works of Gregory the Great, Boethius, and Augustine, and so a study of his translations of their work must entail a survey of the historical significance of these writers. We can certainly learn more of Alfred through the writings of these men than we can ever hope to know about the king from the Pseudo-Asser or from William of Malmesbury. Gregory the Great, who may be said to have founded the medieval papacy and the notion of a Papal State, became pope in 590. His life as a statesman and pope was set against a background of growing anarchy in the Italian peninsula, with the decline in Byzantine power and the growing influence of barbarian Lombard enclaves which threatened the very survival of Roman ways and of orthodox Christianity in the West. Political upheavals and military disasters within Italy were compounded by famine and an increasing sense of isolation from the protecting power of the Eastern Empire. Gregory had come reluctantly to the papacy, and his *Regulae Pastoralis Liber* ('Book of Pastoral Care') was written soon after his accession, partly as an answer to Archbishop John of Ravenna who had reprimanded Gregory for his slowness in accepting the responsibility of the papal office, and partly to serve as a handbook for his bishops, showing them how to cope with problems of leadership in relation to other clergy, lay lords, and the education of all Christian people. The *Pastoral Care* was a work necessary for all men in ecclesiastical authority to know, and it is little wonder that it was paid the great compliment of being translated from Latin into Greek, by Anastasius II, Patriarch of Antioch, as early as 602. The works of Gregory were known and treasured in the Early Irish Church, and the *Pastoral Care* was known to the Whitby author of the *Life* of Gregory the Great. Bede urged Archbishop Ecgberht of York in 734 to read Gregory's *Pastoral Care* 'in which he discoursed very skilfully concerning the life and vices of rulers'.[15] Bede quotes a letter in his *Ecclesiastical History* from Pope Honorius to King Edwin, the first Christian king of the Northumbrians (617–33), in which the pope urged Edwin to occupy himself 'in frequent readings from the works of Gregory'.[16] That letter, like most others, together with extracts from various other documents, was omitted from the Old English translation of Bede.[17] But whatever Alfred's connection with that translation may have been, there is a strong case to be made for Alfred being familiar with the *Ecclesiastical History* in the original Latin. It is inconceivable that a king with Alfred's sense of history and scholarly mission could fail to have read Bede's *History* in the original.[18] Alcuin, writing to Eanbald, archbishop of York, in 796, admonished him: 'Wherever you go, let the handbook of the holy Gregory go with you. Read and re-read it often.' In Francia, soon after Alcuin's time, the work was promoted by Hincmar, Archbishop of Rheims.[19] Early Latin manuscripts of the work survived in England south of the Humber from Worcester and Winchester. King Alfred's translation of the *Pastoral Care*, therefore, should be seen in the context of the popularity of its Latin text long before and up to Alfred's own time, as well as in the immediacy of the book's message for Alfred and his bishops.

Gregory the Great was a pragmatist whose ideas on theology and administration took a very practical form, and he was a master of the use of metaphor which enabled him to deal with conceptual and intellectual matters in the most concrete terms. Such a man, writing a work which dealt essentially with the nature of Christian government and leadership in the widest sense, was an ideal author for Alfred to translate for the benefit of his beleaguered English bishops—and through those bishops for the benefit of his leading thegns. A cursory glance at a few chapter headings conveys at once the compelling practical nature of this work and the obvious use which both Alfred and his bishops could derive from it: '*What kind of man he is to be who is to rule*'; '*What kind of man he is to be who is not to rule*'; '*How often the occupation of power and government distracts the mind of the ruler*'; '*Concerning the burden of government*'; '*How discrete the ruler is to be in his blaming and flattering*'; '*That princes are to be admonished in one way, and subjects in another*'— these and countless other chapters contain valid psychological insights and sound advice on matters of leadership, teaching, and government. There was much benefit to be gained for Alfred himself in this work, and no doubt the profound effect it had on his own mind prompted him to have it translated and distributed among his bishops. Gregory's advice on the moderate and discrete use of power;[20]

on the avoidance of harsh treatment[21] and the ability to relent when one had over-reacted against a subject[22] all reflects the advice of a man endowed with sound judgement and common sense. Gregory's directives on the avoidance of flattery, on the need for a ruler to be popular with his subjects and to rule the wicked not the good; on the benefits of humility along with the caveat not to carry humility to extremes—all sum up the street wisdom of an Early Medieval politician.[23] On a more personal level, Alfred would have warmed to the notion that a ruler ought not to hide his candle under a bushel, and that a scholar has a social obligation to share his learning with his neighbour.[24] All this was in keeping with the spirit of the translator of the Old English Bede who transformed Bede's address to King Ceolwulf of Northumbria into what is seen by some scholars as a statement inspired by Alfred himself: 'Because God chose you as king, it behoves you to teach your people.'[25] Gregory's exhortation to his bishops that they had a moral and social duty to share their learning with their people rather than opting for a life 'of retirement and solitude'[26] strengthened Alfred's hand, as we shall see, in the promotion of cathedral schools for the young. Alfred's seemingly abortive peace negotiations with the heathen Danes found a justification in Gregory's advice to conclude peace with evil men in the hope that 'love and the society of their neighbours may humanise and reform them'.[27] Gregory was no doubt thinking of his problems with the Arian Lombards, but for a king in Alfred's predicament, precisely the same advice applied. The Christian Gregory had the further sound advice to offer, which he justified with reference to St Paul—i.e. to be careful not to consolidate your enemies' position by encouraging peace between them, and he offered a powerful justification for the use of violence against the unjust.[28] A theme of Gregory's, which must have been of major interest to Alfred, was the advice on maintaining a balance between reflection on spiritual and scholarly matters, and the necessity of pursuing an active life as a ruler.[29]

The *Pastoral Care* understandably offered even more advice for Alfred's bishops than it did for the king himself. No doubt, having absorbed Gregory's precepts, the king was anxious to pass a whole body of advice down the line, which would in effect bolster his own royal power in the provinces. Bishops and the few thegns who were able to read this work were lectured on the business of granting away land—that unique source of patronage and power in the Early Middle Ages. Gregory admonished them not to crow over the recipients of their grants—a reminder of the symbolic power of gift-giving—and he urged caution in the amount of the grant and in the choice of person to whom it was given.[30] It was not only kings and secular lords in Anglo-Saxon England who had the power to bestow land grants on their followers. The church was the major landowner in Alfred's realm, and several charters issued in the name of Bishop Wærferth of Worcester, for instance, testify to that prelate's involvement in leasing lands to priests and kinsmen, to reeves and thegns, and to Æthelred and Æthelflæd, the Lord and Lady of the Mercians.[31] Those with power to give or to seize property were reminded by Gregory (and Alfred) that they were merely God's ministrators giving away God's gifts, and that giving to the poor was merely repaying a debt owed to them.[32] Gregory well understood the mentality of those early Germanic warlords who had come to plague sixth-century Italy, and Alfred must have been aware of that distant kinship between Gregory's Lombard enemies and the magnates who ruled over Wessex in his own time. Gregory warned the magnates against the practice of robbing their neighbours in order to give away alms with the ill-gotten spoils, and against following generous grants of lands with a backlash of extortion.[33]

Alfred would have welcomed Gregory's upholding of the *status quo* in relation to the power of kings. What better way to keep his thegns and *witan* in line than by preaching to them the words of that saintly Gregory, who first sent the message of Christianity to their forefathers. There they would hear 'in the language which we can all understand', that it was necessary for a man to fear his lord (*hlaford*) and for the servant (*cniht*) to fear his master;[34] that it was a crime to slay a king, who like Saul, had been consecrated to God (*Gode gehalgodne*);[35] and of the binding power of old allegiance (*ealdum treowum*)—that cement of loyalty which held every Germanic warband together.[36] Gregory reminded his readers that when they sinned against their lord, they sinned against the God who created authority[37]—nor indeed was it considered right for subjects even to criticize their rulers for genuine faults.[38] When we consider the sustained efforts in King Alfred's and in other Anglo-Saxon Law Codes to shore up the power of the king and to protect his person from injury, we realize that Gregory's *Pastoral Care*—as well as being a handbook for bishops, also acted from Alfred's point of view, as a kind of holy writ to bolster his authority as king.

Ninth-century West Saxon bishops were not just spiritual men. They were leading members of the *witan*—the best educated, and men upon whom the king hoped to rely for loyalty and for crucial administrative know-how in the supervision of the courts, the drafting of legal contracts, and the education of youth. These West Saxon spiritual shepherds were also men so heavily committed to the material survival of the king and his warband that they had lost one of their number, Heahmund of Sherborne, in a pitched battle against the Northmen in 871. Gregory's *Pastoral Care* was an ideal work to act as a handbook for key men who were literate and who controlled the spiritual as well as the material destinies of so many of Alfred's subjects in the shires. And Gregory the Great, the author of this work, while being himself a holy man, was also a most gifted administrator who took over the running of post-imperial Rome on the breakdown of Byzantine administration in sixth-century Italy. Gregory's bishops were not so different from those to whom Alfred distributed copies of the *Pastoral Care* in late ninth-century England. They lived in dangerous times, when the old Roman order was crumbling under the anarchy brought on by Arian Lombard attack. Alfred would have read Gregory's own account in the *Dialogues* of the Lombard invasion, where that 'barbarous nation of the Lombards, drawn as a sword out of a sheath', left their own country and invaded Italy. He would have read, too, how this wild people had 'depopulated cities, razed fortifications to the ground, burned the churches, destroyed the monasteries of men and women, and left the farms desolate'.[39] It was a time when the Roman population of the Italian peninsula turned more and more to their local bishops to see them through on-going military and political crises, as well as to save their souls. Alfred's bishops, too, found themselves faced with a flock which was under constant threat of capture or death at the hands of occupying viking armies. They ruled over dioceses in West Mercia and further south, which had been stripped bare from repeated raiding and extraction of Danegeld. In East Anglia and Northumbria several bishoprics and most monasteries had disappeared altogether in the face of impossible burdens imposed by pagan colonists, and where in Alfred's own melodramatic words 'everything had been ravaged and burnt'.

Gregory wrote his *Dialogues* in 594—dialogues between the writer and his friend Peter the Deacon which set out to narrate miracle stories concerning holy men and women in Italy. The purpose of the work was to show how the early medieval church in the Italian peninsula had produced saints which could match those of the Eastern Mediterranean, but it also served to demonstrate the power of Catholic orthdoxy over the Arianism of the Lombards. The *Dialogues* are divided into four books. As in the case of the *Pastoral Care*, the *Dialogues* were translated into Greek—during the pontificate of the Greek pope, Zacharius (741–51), and from the Greek, they were turned into Arabic in 779. They were widely read throughout the Christian West in the early Middle Ages, and their miracle tales provided prototypes for motifs in later saints' lives throughout Christendom, and not least for Bede. The first book of Gregory's *Dialogues* contains a collection of hagiographical anecdotes rather than *Lives* of saints proper, while the second concentrates on the miracles of St Benedict. The third book deals with Paulinus of Nola and anecdotes relating to the popes John and Agapetus, as well as miracle stories relating to the triumph of orthodoxy over Arianism. The fourth and final book deals with tales of ghosts and spirits which were intended to afford proof of the immortality of the human soul. The continued importance of the Gregory's *Dialogues* was assured in Anglo-Saxon England by the lengthy discussion on Gregory's life and the mention of his *Dialogues* by Bede in his *Ecclesiastical History*.[40] Indeed, Alfred's reference to the *Dialogues* as 'the teaching concerning the virtues and miracles of holy men'[41] may well have been inspired by Bede's account of the *Dialogues* as a work where Gregory 'collected the virtues of the most famous saints he knew . . . so by describing the miracles of the saints, he showed how glorious those virtues are'.[42] Alfred's inclusion of the *Dialogues* in his scholarly translation programme tells us much about that king's respect for Gregory's works in general, but it must also tell us of Alfred's personal interest in popular religion and in marvellous tales of miracles performed by holy men and of equally marvellous tales of the Christian afterlife.

Boethius (480–524) was a late Roman philosopher and diplomat in the service of the Ostrogothic king, Theodoric, who dominated northern Italy from his court at Ravenna. Boethius, who was himself of aristocratic Roman family, became Master of the Offices (*magister officiorum*) under Theodoric in 522, but two years later he was imprisoned in Pavia on suspicion of plotting with the Byzantines against his barbarian master, and he was eventually cruelly tortured and executed in 524 or 525. While languishing in prison he wrote his *de Consolatione Philosophiae* (*On the Consolation of Philosophy*) a work in which he came to terms with the apparent misery and hopelessness of his situation by recourse to acknowledging the triumph of Wisdom or Philosophy over all worldly gain and its concomitant loss. The impact of Boethius on later medieval thought was immense, and his *Consolation of Philosophy*, although not overtly Christian, was considered by medieval Christian scholars to be compatible with a genuine Christian spirituality. Boethius had absorbed the philosophical methods of Plato and Aristotle and the Neoplatonists. He had translated several of the works of Aristotle earlier in his career; he had planned to translate Plato's *Dialogues*[43] and he succeeded in passing on a sizeable portion of the philosophical heritage of the Greeks to the early medieval Latin West. He may be said to have accomplished for philosophical studies what Gregory had achieved at the level of ecclesiastical organization and politics for the Western Church.

Alfred found in Boethius not so much good literature which was 'most necessary for all men to know' as a digest of philosophical lore which appealed to the scholarly and contemplative side of the king's nature. There were, of course, meeting-points for Alfred between the practical and moralistic writings of Gregory and the *Consolation of Philosophy*. Boethius, informing us that men become rich from stealing and plundering from their neighbours[44] echoes Gregory's admonitions to magnates on how to control their wealth. King Alfred must have taken a special interest in Boethius's pronouncements on the futility of a magnate having large numbers of followers in order to reflect personal honour, and on the problem of ensuring their loyalty.[45] Boethius returned to this subject of a great household later on in his *Consolation* when he wrote on the unhappiness of a seemingly powerful but insecure king who needs a great bodyguard[46]—a reference in his case, perhaps, to Theodoric, but applicable to any Germanic warrior-king. But Boethius had essentially a philosophical approach to the subject of wealth and power, claiming that not even the richest or most powerful of men could escape poverty[47] or fear of being overthrown,[48] and that it was Wisdom alone which provided man with enduring happiness, because unlike material wealth it could never be lost[49] in the face of adversity. The *Consolation* might be described as a celebration of Wisdom for its own sake and as holding the key to man's happiness. The fact that Alfred spent so much effort in its translation and in the elaboration and significant alteration of so many of its concepts, provides the most eloquent testimony for the mature and scholarly mind of this king. In addition to its central discussion on the nature of Wisdom and of happiness, there are equally important themes in the *Consolation* on the existence of evil, and why God permits evil to exist;[50] on the nature of free will in mankind;[51] of the role of fate;[52] and the meaning of eternity.[53] For Alfred, a Germanic king, whose recreational oral literature paraded heroes who were driven to violent exploits in search of fame, and who were ruled by a cruel fate, Boethius offered a radical and alternative view of the cosmos.[54] For Boethius, the pursuit of excessive worldly fame for its own sake was an empty goal inasmuch as all fame was relative and doomed to oblivion. As for fate—that bogeyman of Germanic literature—it did not rule the cosmos[55] and it did not govern mens' lives at random but was rather part of a greater and wider plan governing mens' actions[56] by way of reward or rebuke.

Just as Alfred could empathize with Gregory, who battled to preserve orthodoxy and Roman organization in the face of Arianism and barbarian attack, so, too, he must have found a special sympathy with the thoughts and personal circumstances of Boethius. Not only had Boethius like Alfred, been born into a ruling family and eventually had come to high office himself, but both men had known dramatic reversals of fortune—Boethius at the hands of the Gothic Theodoric, and Alfred at the hands of the Nordic Guthrum. Although Alfred prepared his translation of Boethius in the late 880s or 890s, his thorough-going treatment of this complex work suggests he is likely to have first encountered it as a younger man. It is likely, too, that his special interest in the *Consolation* stemmed from the inspiration Alfred had derived from this work when all had seemed lost earlier in his career as king, back in the 870s. If Gregory had provided Alfred with a justification for coming to terms with his powerful Danish enemies in the hope of taming them by associating them with a higher Christian culture, then the cries of Boethius showed Alfred and his circle that the victory of men who did not play by Christian rules was nothing new to the world: 'The wicked sit on thrones and trample the saints under their feet; bright virtues abide in hiding, and the unrighteous mock the righteous. False swearing brings no harm to men, nor false guile that is cloaked with deceits.'[57] Alfred and his following were acutely aware that the best the king was able to achieve against his Danish adversaries was to recognize the rule of his enemy, Guthrum, as king of East Anglia—a king who sat on the throne of the saintly Edmund, and who trampled all that supposedly martyred king had stood for, under foot. As for the breaking of oaths (*mane apas*), not even the Chronicle attempted to conceal how Alfred had been duped by Danish oath-swearing at Wareham in 876 and at Exeter—where they swore 'great oaths (*micle apas sworon*)' in the following year.[58] On the other hand, the eventual conversion of Guthrum would, in Gregory's eyes, have been a vindication of Alfred's otherwise misplaced trust in his pagan enemies. Alfred, as the sole survivor of native English kingship, and who himself very nearly went the way of Edmund of East Anglia and Ælla of Northumbria, could relate in a unique way to Boethius's reminder that 'every man now living is aware that many a king has lost his power and riches and become poor again'.[59]

King Alfred's interest in the writings of St Augustine are entirely in keeping with his admiration for Boethius and Gregory the Great. Augustine (354–430), although earlier in time, inhabited essentially the same world of crumbling Roman values as Boethius and Gregory. While the two latter wrote at the end of that era when the Roman order could be seen to be visibly passing, and when Christianity of the Constantinian variety was also threatened by the breakdown of that order, Augustine, on the other hand, was writing at a time when the *Pax Romana* had relatively recently come under serious threat from barbarian neighbours. Augustine was a Christian philosopher, lately converted to Christianity in 387, under the influence of Ambrose, bishop of Milan. He had been schooled in Platonic, Neoplatonic, and Manichaean ideas. He brought a convert's zeal to Christianity, and he strove to reconcile the revealed truths of his adopted religion with his immense philosophical learning. If Boethius and Gregory stood as survivors at the very end of the Classical tradition, struggling to salvage some of its wreckage for a later age, Augustine, on the other hand, was fully in tune with that Classical tradition and wrote with the authority of an ancient philosopher, for whom Christianity, rather than pagan philosophy, was the novelty to be promoted and explained. The writings of Augustine, like those of Gregory the Great, were to form one of the central pillars upon which later medieval Christian ideology was to be based. Apart from the prestige attached to Augustine's authorship, Alfred is likely to have been attracted to the *Soliloquies* because of his obvious personal interest in discussions on the immortality of the soul—an interest which is also evident in his translation of the *Consolation* by Boethius, and which was no doubt stimulated by Gregory's discussion of the same topic in the fourth book of his *Dialogues.*

If Augustine was one of the greatest of Late Antique Christian thinkers and writers, it cannot be said that his *Soliloquies* were among either his most important or better known works. The Latin original of Augustine's *Soliloquies* consists of two books, the first of which sets out to examine the nature of God and the second to discuss the immortality of the human soul. Alfred's translation of the first book is relatively close, though rarely literal, and he resorts to paraphrase and expansion even at this early stage in the work. Alfred followed Augustine's opening prayer of faith and his plea for conversion and salvation,[60] although he added in material here which was inspired by his knowledge of Boethius's *Consolation.*[61] We are presented with Augustine's summary of intent in this work—'to understand God and to know my own soul'[62] or, as reiterated later on—'to see God with the eyes of my mind as clearly as I now see the sun with the eyes of my body'.[63] The means, by which this vision is to be achieved is through the virtues of faith, hope, and charity. Alfred's rendering of the second book of Augustine's work marks a radical departure. The Alfredian version may still be described as a translation—but only in the loosest sense of that term. Book II opens with the two questions raised by Augustine as to whether the soul is immortal and whether the soul will know more after death than it does in life. But from here on, Alfred and Augustine begin to part company in relation to the way the argument is handled. Augustine presents a complex logical discussion on truth and falsity[64] while Alfred falls back on the authority of Scripture. Although Alfred and his scholarly advisers had overreached themselves in choosing to wrestle with Augustinian philosophy, their ambition knew no bounds in the decision to press on with a third book of the *Soliloquies* dealing with the state of intellect and consciousness of the soul after death—a topic promised by Augustine but never completed by him! This radical departure from the original text in Book II and the creation of a third book of the *Soliloquies* may be compared with Alfred's decision to abandon the central argument on foreknowledge and free will in the final book of the *Consolation of Philosophy* by Boethius. The third book of the Old English translation of the *Soliloquies* is at once the most original of all King Alfred's works, while forming a coherent whole with the rest of the translation of the *Soliloquies* proper. The third book of the *Soliloquies*, however original, continues the theme of the first two and has to be considered an integral part of that Alfredian edition. There is no case to be made for identifying this part of the *Soliloquies* or indeed any of that work with the so-called handbook which the Pseudo-Asser describes as being in the possession of King Alfred during his supposed struggles to master the art of reading Latin. It is on the contrary highly probable that the Pseudo-Asser on skimming through King Alfred's *Soliloquies*, and failing to recognize Augustine as their inspiration, concluded that the 'sayings (*cwydas*)' in the 'anthology (*blostman*)' of the first and second books of Alfred's translation[65] constituted a scholarly scrap-book or anthology—hence the Pseudo-Asser's *flosculos*[66]—based on the king's personal reading. William of Malmesbury may also, as Whitelock suggested[67] have seen a manuscript of the *Soliloquies* and mistaken it for the *Enchiridion* or handbook described in such confusing detail by the Pseudo-Asser. The preface to the *Soliloquies* in citing 'the writings of St. Augustine and St. Gregory and St. Jerome and . . . many other holy fathers'[68] as sources (for the Old English version) does appear to promise an anthology of the works of those writers rather than the translation of a work of Augustine alone. It was all too easy for someone skimming through the original preface to the Old English *Soliloquies* to conclude that this work, introduced as it was with an elaborate house-building metaphor, and citing a list of Church Fathers, was in fact an anthology of Christian learning.

The Old English version of Orosius's *Seven Books of Histories against the Pagans* was definitively identified by Bately as not being a work from Alfred's own hand.[69] Bately was equally clear that Orosius had been translated by someone different from the compilers of the late ninth-century core text of the Anglo-Saxon Chronicle.[70] Whitelock, although cautious on the subject of the authorship of Orosius, had earlier allowed for a lingering possibility that this translation was done by the king himself.[71] While it is crucial to know from Bately's detailed scholarly examination of vocabulary and syntax that the West Saxon translator of Orosius could not have been the same person as the translator of Boethius's *Consolation* and Augustine's *Soliloquies*, there are nevertheless other aspects of Orosius which link it firmly with known Alfredian texts. These points of contact do not in any way negate Bately's findings: they merely remind us that a work may be translated by someone other than King Alfred, but still bear the hallmarks of the king's translation programme. Orosius's *Histories* would have held out an obvious interest for Alfred. As a protégé of St Augustine, and as a man who knew Jerome, Paulus Orosius belonged to that circle of Late Antique writers who strove to mould the wisdom of Antiquity into presentable Christian form. As such, his *Histories* must have been of interest to Alfred as the translator of the *Soliloquies* who was also familiar with some works of Jerome and who had himself a strongly developed historical sense. Orosius had been encouraged by Augustine to write a world history in which he tried to refute pagan allegations that the rise of Christianity and neglect of pagan gods had hastened the decline of Rome, which had been captured by Alaric and the Goths in AD 410. The *Seven Books of Histories* covered the annals of the known world from Ninus, king of Assyria, who ruled supposedly 1,300 years before the building of Rome, down to AD 417 in Orosius's own time. Orosius set out to show that wars and natural disasters had plagued the human race from the beginning of its recorded history and long before the advent of Christianity. He presented the Roman empire as the universal successor to the earlier empires of Babylon, Macedonia, and Carthage, and linked the destiny of Rome to the birth of Christ and the spread of Christianity throughout its empire. The fact that Orosius paid scant attention to established Greek and Roman authorities or that his work was overburdened with Christian polemic did nothing to diminish its popularity as a digest of world history in the Early Middle Ages. For early Irish scholars, Orosius provided a bridge between the history of the ancient world and the origins of the Goidelic rulers of Celtic Ireland. Alfred, too, may have seen in Orosius's great survey of antiquity, the prelude to early English history as otherwise outlined in the Old English translation of Bede and as furnished in its West Saxon details in the Anglo-Saxon Chronicle.

The *Seven Books of Histories against the Pagans* not only fitted in generically with other Alfredian works of translation, but there are important aspects of this work which connect it with Alfred and his circle. The opening chapter of Book One contains a geographical survey designed to allow readers to locate events in their physical context. Written into this chapter is an account of two voyages, separately undertaken by Ohthere and Wulfstan—traders whose reports of their experiences found their way into the Old English Orosius. Ohthere's account is introduced with the statement that 'Ohthere told his lord (*his hlaforde*), King Alfred, that he dwelt northmost of all the Northmen'. This key statement reveals the crucial Alfredian connection with these Scandinavian accounts. For while we must accept Bately's verdict that the two accounts, with their different vocabulary and morphology, cannot have been written by one man, we can still be confident of the Alfredian association. Generically, the two narratives—Ohthere's voyage northward along the Norwegian coast to the White Sea and Wulfstan's voyage in the eastern Baltic to Estonia—are clearly linked. They were unlikely to have been narrated by one man or indeed by two men on the same occasion, but the fact that Ohthere is on record for having narrated the account of his voyage to King Alfred, very strongly suggests that both accounts owe their survival to Alfred's personal interest in their subject-matter. That would not preclude the possibility that each account was written down separately at the king's behest by two different scholars or clerks at Alfred's court, or less likely by the narrators themselves. There is no question from the precise numerical and directional details in both of these accounts that they were written down, at the time of narration, most likely by amanuenses at Alfred's court. Wulfstan's use of the first person—'Bornholm was on our port side'[72]—reveals that his report was originally oral, and while that does not tell us when or to whom it was narrated,[73] there must always remain the strong presumption of an Alfredian involvement in the recording of this narrative. We are reminded of how Abbot Adomnán of Iona wrote down his account of the Holy

Places of the Near East at the dictation of the shipwrecked Frankish Bishop Arculf in the late seventh century. This latter work even included a plan of the Church of the Holy Sepulchre and its surroundings which Arculf sketched for Adomnán on a wax tablet.[74] Having acknowledged Alfredian involvement in the Ohthere and Wulfstan narratives, we cannot be certain of knowing how much of the original written version of these voyages was accurately preserved by the translator of Orosius or what precisely that translator's connection was with King Alfred and his court. But the fact that some first-person forms have survived in this Scandinavian insertion, combined with the distinctive linguistic styles of the Ohthere and Wulfstan episodes suggests that the texts as we have them are relatively close to the original.

There is yet another important link between the Old English Orosius and the writings of King Alfred. Orosius ended his *Histories* with a brief account of the presence of the Gothic kings, *Rædgota* (Radagaisus) and *Alrica* (Alaric) in early fifth-century Italy.[75] Whitelock, followed by Bately, observed that there was a connection between the mention of these two rulers at the end of the Old English Orosius and Alfred's account of those same kings *Rædgota* and *Eallerica* who 'won all the realm of Italy from the mountains even to the island of Sicily' at the opening of Alfred's version of Boethius's *Consolation*.[76] Whitelock pointed out, 'the form *Rædgota* is in both works, yet it is not the true Germanic equivalent of *Radagaisus*, which would be *Rædgar*',[77] while Bately observed that both works also linked the two rulers 'as though they ruled together . . . and invaded Italy together, a linking which has no justification in fact'.[78] Since this assumption was prompted by an original passage in Orosius's *Seventh Book*, Bately concluded that Alfred had borrowed the reference to the kings *Rædgota* and *Eallerica* into his *Consolation* from the Old English Orosius.[79] That deduction is also confirmed by the fact that Alfred leaps, at the beginning of his version of the *Consolation*, from his passing mention of *Rædgota* and *Eallerica* in the early fifth century, to announce: 'then after those kings, did Theorodic hold the same empire in sway'.[80] But while Alaric died in 410, Theodoric did not invade Italy until 493 and died more than a century after Alaric's time in 526. Here we have a typical example of Alfred's tidy historical mind and his desire to seek continuity in his historical narration as evidenced elsewhere in his own works and perhaps also in early sections of the Anglo-Saxon Chronicle. In the case of *Rædgota* and Alaric, Alfred was striving to establish continuity between the closing events of Orosius's *Histories* and the era of Theodoric and his minister, Boethius, who was the author of the *Consolation of Philosophy*. None of this is to suggest that Alfred was immediately responsible for the translation of Orosius. But it does suggest that Orosius's *Histories* had been completed before Alfred began his version of the *Consolation* and that Alfred had read that work and was ultimately responsible for contributing the Scandinavian periplus to it.

King Alfred's own introductions to Gregory's *Dialogues* and *Pastoral Care*, to the *Consolation of Philosophy* by Boethius, and to the *Soliloquies* of St Augustine are pieces that we can attribute most securely to the king. Yet the very nature of those prefaces, with the self-conscious solemnity and breadth of purpose of many of them, ensures that even if we were to accept them as the very words of Alfred himself, the mode in which they are cast serves to erect a barrier between us and their author. Nor is the problem of analysing King Alfred's writings as simple a matter as wrestling with the nature of the genre. It is important to establish on textual grounds which works within the Alfredian canon may have been written by Alfred himself and which may not. Nevertheless unreal distinctions can be made between what we have now come to accept as King Alfred's own writings and the outpourings of other late ninth-century scholars who may have translated as part of a team, and who were either directly responsible to the king or were working in some sense—however loosely—under his patronage. In the latter category of works not directly translated by Alfred himself, we have the *Dialogues* of Pope Gregory commissioned by the king, and Orosius's *Histories against the Pagans* which includes information supplied by him. But these categories may be closer than might at first seem to be the case. There may be less of Alfred to be found in works ascribed personally to him, and there may be more of the king's influence in works such as the Anglo-Saxon Chronicle—compiled during his reign—than has been recognized hitherto. We can never exclude the possibility that his scholarly helpers had a hand in shaping those prefaces written in the king's name, or conversely, that they did not implement his wishes in the production of a work such as the Chronicle.

Anglo-Saxon scholars have successfully demonstrated that Alfred did not personally write the Old English Bede or Orosius, and they have shown us, too, the presence of Mercian dialectal elements in the text of the Old English Bede and in Gregory's *Dialogues*.[81] There is also virtual agreement that the translator of Bede was not the same person as the translator of the *Dialogues*, although they have sufficient stylistic characteristics in common to suggest that they may have been trained or worked in the same Mercian scriptorium.[82] On the other hand, Sisam[83] wisely cautioned against hasty conclusions based on poorly understood dialectal usage in ninth-century England, pointing to Alfred's Mercian wife and to perhaps a team of Mercian scholars at his court, as a possible source of Mercian linguistic influence on the king's own use of language. We may sometimes fail, too, to distinguish between dialectal usage in the spoken language of the shires, and the much more complex interaction between dialectal forms of one written text upon another. Students seeking Alfred's personal contribution to a text are prone to forget that, on his own repeated evidence, he worked with scholarly helpers. Alfred tells us in his preface to Gregory's *Dialogues* that he ordered a translation to be made for him by his 'true friends'. In the prefatory letter to the *Pastoral Care* the king claims he translated that work himself, but he says he accomplished the task having mastered the *Pastoral Care* (*ic hie geleornode*)[84] with the help of no less than four named scholars. All members of the king's scholarly team—including Alfred himself—must have shared ideas and probably also technical vocabulary, and they must have learnt from each other. All of them drew on the same Scriptural and limited Classical and Late Antique repertoire, thereby rendering it the more difficult to determine any one individual contribution.

The prefaces to the *Pastoral Care* and the *Soliloquies*, which were supposedly written by the king, exhibit features which may be suggestive of a team effort rather than the work of Alfred alone. Alfred's prefatory letter to the *Pastoral Care* was not written as a spontaneous free-flowing letter from the king to his people. On the contrary, the language is studied and bookish and the piece was clearly intended for consumption by the bishops. Few would dispute that the prefatory letter to the *Pastoral Care* contains many of Alfred's own ideas and that its contents met with the king's approval. There is no reason, either, why we cannot attribute the knowledge of the Psalms, the Vulgate, and other echoes of Jerome, of St Paul's Epistle to the Corinthians, and of Gregory's and Bede's works—which are all evident in this preface—to Alfred himself. But the presence of these authorities together with evidence for other biblical scholarship, and possible oblique references to Old Saxon and Old High German[85] translations and paraphrases of the Scriptures, may also be suggestive of scholarly helpers who supported the king and who may have helped to turn his ideas in the prefatory letter to the *Pastoral Care* into this carefully mannered statement of intent. The assigning of quotations to their precise Scriptural locations, stylistic variations in some quotations, and the correct numbering of the Psalms in the body of the work, also point to the assistance of trained clerks in the production of the king's prefatory letter to the *Pastoral Care*.[86] Alfred himself adds the observation in his rendering of the *Soliloquies* of St Augustine, of a writer's necessity 'to have a few wise and skilful men (*cuðe men and creftige*) with thee who would hinder thee in no wise, but give aid to thy ability (*crefte*)'.[87] Carnicelli pointed out that the king made this observation in defiance of the sense of the Latin in Augustine's original text, and that Alfred was all the more likely, therefore, to be making a personal point. In his preface to the *Dialogues* of Pope Gregory, Alfred refers to his editorial team as his 'true friends (*to minum getreowum freondum*)'.[88] Some of these friends and scholars, at least, are named in the prose preface to the *Pastoral Care* as Plegmund, who became archbishop of Canterbury in 890, Bishop Asser, and the king's Mass-priests, Grimbald and John. There were, almost certainly, others. There is a strong indication in Alfred's contribution to the *Soliloquies* of Augustine that his inner circle of favourites consisted, not of his warriors—his hunting or carousing companions—but of his scholarly advisers. When questioned closely as to whether he loved his friends 'for their own sake or for some other thing', Augustine is made by Alfred to reply: 'I love them for friendship and companionship and above all others I love those who most help me to understand and to know reason and wisdom, most of all about God and about our souls; for I know that I can more easily seek after Him with their help than I can without.'[89] This is what we should expect from a scholarly king, and men such as Plegmund of Canterbury and Wærferth of Worcester must have benefited lavishly from their close friendship with King Alfred. This passage from the *Soliloquies*, relating to deep friendships within a scholarly circle, explains why the bishop who wrote the verse preface to the *Dialogues*—a man associated with the translation programme—celebrated Alfred as 'the greatest treasure-giver of all the kings he has ever heard tell of, in recent times or long ago'.[90] On the other hand, we must avoid the trap laid for us by the Pseudo-Asser, in viewing King Alfred as a well-intentioned semi-literate, constantly in need of an amanuensis. Sisam, because he had accepted the Pseudo-Asser's account of the king's late development could not bring himself to accept 'that Alfred wrote with his own hand'.[91] There is no reason to hold any longer to such a view. On the contrary, a formidable body of textual evidence now exists which enables scholars to identify Alfred's personal contribution to written works on the basis of words and phrases which can be identified with the king. Sisam, himself, pointed to such characteristic Alfredian usage linking the prefatory letter of the *Pastoral Care*, the prose preface to the *Consolation*, and the text of King Alfred's *Will*[92] and was forced to assume that the king 'would dictate his version piecemeal'[93] to his staff. Alfred may indeed have dictated much, but to argue that this practice—by an otherwise semi-literate king—applied across such a huge and varied range of complex textual matter is scarcely worthy of serious consideration. It is impossible to envisage how works such as the *Consolation* or the *Soliloquies* could have been dealt with orally by someone who could not read. Æthelweard implies that Alfred's translations may have been read aloud for those who were not scholars (*ut non tantum expertioribus sed et audientibus*) but his vague claim that 'the tearful passion of the book of Boethius would be in a measure [thereby] brought to light' inspires little confidence.[94]

The difficulties surrounding the interpretation and authorship of the prefaces attributed to King Alfred are compounded by our uncertainty concerning the relationship of surviving manuscript recensions to each other, and by an added complication of the existence of distinct prose and verse prefaces to several of the king's works. While the prefatory letter to the *Pastoral Care* has been considered to be one of Alfred's earliest writings, Sisam, as we saw, showed it to have been written later than the verse preface to that same translation. The verse preface was almost certainly the original and only preface to the *Pastoral Care* whereas the prefatory letter may well have been written some time later than the actual translation of the work as a whole.[95] The prefatory letter is essentially a policy document issued by the king and intended to accompany the distribution of copies of the translation of the *Pastoral Care* among the bishops of Alfred's kingdom. We cannot assume that the proliferation and distribution of copies necessarily took place immediately after the translation was completed. Nor can we assume that there was only one single distribution of all copies from the king's writing office at a fixed point in time. Alfred himself allowed for the possibility of further copies of the *Pastoral Care* being made from those copies distributed to his bishops. We are told in the prose preface to the Alfredian translation of Boethius that King Alfred 'turned it [the *Consolation of Philosophy*] from Latin into English prose (*engliscu spelle*), [and then] he wrought it up once more into verse (*leoðe*), as it is now done'.[96] The two surviving manuscripts of this translation would appear to preserve two separate stages in the production of the work. The Oxford Bodleian Manuscript (Bodley 180) contains a simple Old English prose translation of the Latin prose and metres of Boethius. The British Library manuscript (Cotton Otho

A.vi) contains the same Old English paraphrase of Boethius's prose, but provides an Old English versified rendering of Boethius's metres based on a prose text similar to Bodley 180. See Fig. 13, p. 549. The Cottonian Old English verse translations, therefore, are based not on the original Latin of Boethius, but on an intermediary Old English prose rendering of the original Latin. All this would seem to tie in with the statement in the Alfredian preface to Boethius, that the prose rendering of this work in Old English preceded the versified Old English version. Yet the chance survival of manuscripts has resulted in the Bodley 180 rendering of the earlier prose version dating from the first half of the twelfth century, while the later and final verse form of the translation of Boethius's metres survived in an earlier mid-tenth-century Cotton manuscript. This Cotton manuscript (Otho A.vi) shared in the disastrous fire damage which destroyed so much of the Cotton collection, and much of it is now known only from a transcript made by the seventeenth-century antiquary, Francis Junius. To complicate matters yet further, King Alfred's Prose preface to Boethius survives in the Bodley 180 version of the work. But in that preface, it is stated that the two stages of translation (from Latin verse to Old English prose, and from Old English prose to Old English verse) have already been completed. It is odd, therefore, that this preface should survive attached to what was only the first stage of the translation process—for the Bodley 180 manuscript which preserves the Alfredian prose preface contains only the Old English prose translation of the original Latin metres. Sisam's explanation that this preface was attached to a draft of the whole work at a stage before the Old English verses were interpolated into it is an unsatisfactory gloss on what is essentially a badly preserved and poorly understood manuscript record.[97] Why should a preface which was clearly intended to accompany a finished verse translation survive attached to an earlier prose draft? And if the Old English prose version (MS Bodley 180) represented only a draft of a preliminary stage in the production, how then do we account for the continued survival of such a preliminary stage, to be copied out yet again in the twelfth century? Evidence from surviving records of the text would suggest that we are dealing with two distinct manuscript traditions of the Boethius translation and that the Alfredian preface is clearly not in its original context in MS Bodley 180 at least, whatever that original context may have been. The precise relationship between the extant prose and verse renderings in the translation of the *Consolation of Philosophy* and of Alfred's role in the composition of the verses especially is still a matter that requires detailed study.

The Old English translation of the *Dialogues* of Pope Gregory has always been known, on Alfred's own testimony, to have been the work of the king's helpers rather than his own. But a prose and verse preface associated with the *Dialogues* have been the subject of confusion and disagreement. Alfred informs us in his prose preface that he requested his 'true friends' to produce a translation of the *Dialogues* for his personal edification. This is the most reliable and most important information we possess on this issue. The Pseudo-Asser states that Wærferth, bishop of Worcester, translated the *Dialogues* 'at the king's command'.[98] Hans Hecht, who brought out his Leipzig edition of the Old English *Dialogues* in 1900 presented it, on 'Asser's' authority as *Bischof Wærferths von Worcester Übersetzung der Dialoge Gregors des Grossen*. On the grounds that 'nobody challenges Asser's statement', Sisam, followed by Whitelock, who in turn was followed by Keynes and Lapidge,—all refer to 'Wærferth's translation of Gregory's *Dialogues*'.[99] Speculation has been piled upon speculation along this historiographical trail. Wærferth leased an estate at Ablington in Gloucestershire in 899 to a priest, Wærwulf, who was his old friend.[100] That transaction survives in an eleventh-century manuscript. The Pseudo-Asser mentions a Mercian priest, Wærwulf, as being one of those summoned along with Bishop Wærferth to read aloud 'by day or night' to the, as yet, illiterate Alfred—'for he had not yet begun to read anything'.[101] Whitelock was 'tempted'[102] to identify that Wærwulf who leased land at Ablington with one of those 'friends' whom King Alfred tells us translated the *Dialogues*. She saw Bishop Wærferth and the priest Wærwulf making up that team. That temptation 'inevitably' spread to the commentary of Keynes and Lapidge[103] on 'Werferth's Translation of Gregory's *Dialogues*'. By a weak process of intellectual osmosis, the priest Wærwulf of the Ablington charter had found a secure place in the Alfredian canon. We are no more justified in attributing the Old English *Dialogues* to Wærferth (—not to mention Wærwulf—) than we would be in attributing the Old English translation of the *Consolation of Philosophy* to the historical Asser. William of Malmesbury, after all, boldly claims that Asser explained the *Consolation* to King Alfred in simpler terms,[104] and Whitelock felt it 'unlikely that William would make so factual a claim out of sheer invention'.[105] Malmesbury did not, incidentally, have to invent the idea. He deduced it from his thorough knowledge of the Pseudo-Asser's text, which he took to be genuine and which showed him Alfred as an illiterate king being schooled and read aloud to by the historical Asser. Malmesbury, being wiser than many modern scholars, sensibly concluded that if all that were true, then Alfred never could have mastered the *De Consolatione Philosophiae* on his own. The pronouncement by Keynes and Lapidge that 'Asser mentions that Wærferth was a Mercian'[106] is not correct. The compiler of the *Life* of King Alfred names Plegmund, Æthelstan, and Wærwulf as being 'Mercians by birth (*Mercios genere*)' and he names Wærferth as bishop of Worcester, without stating his kingdom of origin. He then goes on to relate how Alfred 'summoned these four men to him from Mercia (*Quos quatuor . . . de Mercia ad se advocaverat*)'.[107] Since Wærferth was already bishop of Worcester, of course, he would have been summoned from Mercia, but there is no more reason to assume he was a Mercian on this evidence alone, than to hold that the Mercian Plegmund was a man of Kent because he ruled the metropolitan see of Canterbury.

The controversy surrounding the authorship of the Old English *Dialogues* becomes further complicated when we turn to the verse preface to that work, currently labelled in the Alfredian canon as 'Bishop Wulfsige's Preface to Wærferth's translation of Gregory's *Dialogues*'.[108] Students of Anglo-Saxon history who are unfamiliar with 'Bishop Wulfsige's Preface' will be surprised to learn that there is no mention of a Bishop Wulfsige in the only surviving manuscript (Cotton Otho C.i part 2) of the verse preface to the *Dialogues*. Instead they will find that the book [of the *Dialogues* of Gregory] is made to speak to the reader in the verse preface, informing him that Bishop Wulfstan (*Wulstan bisceop*)

'ordered me to be written. The bishop who had this copy made which you hold in your hands and study, begs that you ask help for him of these saints whose memory it records'; and that God may forgive his sins, and grant rest in Heaven to him; 'and also to his lord who gave him the pattern copy (*bysene*)', King Alfred, 'who is the best treasure-giver he ever heard of among earthly kings.'[109]

The message of this preface, thus far, was agreed by Sisam and subsequent scholars to mean that Alfred had sent an exemplar of the *Dialogues* to this bishop, who had a copy made from it and who then wrote the verse preface to introduce that copy which he had made. Sisam argued correctly that only the bishop, writing in his own name, would refer to himself as 'poor servant'; that King Alfred was alive when he wrote, and that the bishop's name (to suit the alliteration) had to begin with 'W'. On discovering that the final three letters of *Wulfstan* had been written into the manuscript over an erasure, Sisam opted for the theory that *Wulfstan* had originally read *Wulfsige*, and so the name referred to Bishop Wulfsige of Sherborne who ruled his see during Alfred's later years (*c*.879–900).[110] The idea was attractive and may even be correct, but the truth is we cannot establish what the original reading in the lost exemplar of this manuscript was. There is yet another and even more reasonable possibility. We can agree that the original text of this preface did not include the name Wulfstan because there was no Alfredian bishop of that name. The only surviving manuscript of the verse preface was in Worcester *c*.1200[111] and that copy of the preface as well as the accompanying text of the *Dialogues* was very probably made at Worcester in the first or second quarter of the eleventh century. We may agree also that a scribe copying a work at Worcester *c*.1025–50 might well have changed the name of an unfamiliar ninth-century West Saxon bishop to that of Wulfstan I, the bishop and sermon-writer who ruled the Worcester diocese from 1002 until 1023.[112] Alternatively, we might hold that the erasure and substitution of the last three letters of the bishop's name was effected during the episcopate of Wulfstan II at Worcester (1062–95), although this, as Sisam pointed out, raises serious problems in view of the eleventh-century date of the manuscript.[113] It might also be that Wulfstan I ordered a copy of the Old English *Dialogues* to be made, and this in turn inspired the change of name when copying out the original verse preface. But whatever the circumstances in which the name of the original bishop was changed to *Wulfstan*, that change took place too late and in too late a manuscript to shed any definite light on the original.

Sisam's insistence that the original name read *Wulfsige* was driven by one major consideration. Wulfsige, bishop of Sherborne, suited the evidence of a case based on the testimony of the *Life* of King Alfred. The Pseudo-Asser had said that Wærferth, bishop of Worcester, had translated the *Dialogues* for Alfred. If that were true—and Sisam reminded us 'nobody challenges Asser's statement'—then the bishop in the verse preface could not have been Wærferth of Worcester because that bishop categorically tells us in his poem that he merely copied the work from King Alfred's exemplar. Wulfsige of Sherborne provided an Alfredian bishop who allowed scholars to cling to the 'genuine Asser' thesis. To support his proposal for a Wulfsige authorship, Sisam argued that because the manuscript shows an emendation for only the last three letters of the name *Wulfstan* that the *Wulfs* element in the name was part of the original text. That did not necessarily follow. The unique manuscript of this text, Cotton Otho C.i, is too late (eleventh century) to provide us with any certainty as to what the original reading might have been. The scribe of this manuscript may simply have written *Wulfstan* and blundered the final letters. Either he or an earlier copyist or some other emendator could have abandoned the name of the original ninth-century bishop, not for any deliberate purpose to falsify but influenced by a more familiar Worcester name of the eleventh or twelfth century than that of a more obscure original.[114]

The prospect of Wulfsige's authorship of the verse preface necessitated very special pleading on Sisam's part. Since the preface survived at Worcester, he had to speculate that in the late tenth century the monastic reformers at Worcester had run out of copies of the *Dialogues* and had to summon up a copy from Sherborne.[115] But why look to Sherborne? Sisam admitted that it was 'likely' that Worcester's own ninth-century copy of the *Dialogues* would have survived there through the tenth century. We might point to the famous Alfredian manuscript (Hatton 20) of the *Pastoral Care* which has the heading *This book is to go to Worcester* still boldly visible across its first page of text. And in that same Hatton text of the *Pastoral Care*, King Alfred greeted Bishop Wærferth of Worcester. If, as was likely, a similar copy of the *Dialogues* existed at Worcester, surely that would have provided a pattern for extra copies that might be needed there in the tenth century? Sisam also had to explain away the fact that yet another (late-eleventh century) manuscript containing a revision of the Old English version of Gregory's *Dialogues* (Hatton 76) had also been a Worcester book.[116] That Hatton text of the *Dialogues* also displays textual affinities with the Cotton text from Worcester which contains the verse preface. On balance, Worcester's library in the late tenth century would seem to have been as well equipped to supply copies of Alfredian texts as Sherborne. A more reasonable and economical argument is to hold with Dobbie that the original text of the verse preface stated that the copy of the *Dialogues* was made from King Alfred's exemplar by Bishop Wærferth of Worcester. The work of translating the *Dialogues* had, as King Alfred himself tells us, been done by his friends. Wærferth of Worcester then made a copy of the *Dialogues* for his cathedral from an exemplar provided by King Alfred and added his own short verse preface. The Pseudo-Asser, because of Ramsey's close connections with Worcester—connections acknowledged by Sisam[117]—had access to that library at the turn of the tenth century and may have lighted upon Wærferth's preface to the Old English *Dialogues*, where he saw the words *Wærferth bisceop* at the head of the preface. He wrongly concluded from this cursory inspection that it was Wærferth who translated the entire *Dialogues*, and told us so in his *Life* of King Alfred. The Pseudo-Asser was a reader of Alfredian prefaces, and Worcester was the obvious library where he encountered them. In that very passage where he tells us Wærferth translated the *Dialogues*, he tells us Wærferth accomplished this *aliquando sensum ex sensu ponens* ('sometimes rendering sense for sense').[118] That phrase may go back ultimately to the sentiments of Jerome or Pope Gregory,[119] but the Pseudo-Asser unquestionably borrowed it from King Alfred's phrase *hwilum andgit of andgiete* repeated in his prefaces to both the *Pastoral Care* and the *Consolation*.[120] We may never know for certain which bishop's name originally appeared in the verse preface to the *Dialogues* of Gregory. It might even have been the name of Wulfsige of Sherborne, although as Dobbie shrewdly observed, 'Sisam's explanation . . . depends on a rather long chain of assumptions'.[121] But the unique manuscript of the verse preface comes from Worcester, and we are no longer constrained by the distorting influence of the Pseudo-Asser. That being so, there is better reason to revert to the idea which Keller proposed in 1900, and tentatively ascribe the earliest Worcester copy of the *Dialogues* together with its verse preface to Bishop Wærferth of that see.[122] And while we may never be so bold as to describe the verse preface categorically as 'Bishop Wærferth's Preface', we must, with much greater justification, refrain from ascribing the translation of the *Dialogues* to Wærferth. The earliest authority for attributing the translation to Wærferth is the Pseudo-Asser who may have misread the original verse preface. If Wærferth's name had appeared in that original preface, he would there have proclaimed himself a copyist rather than a translator. Furthermore, since the verse preface appears in only one of the four extant manuscripts of the Old English *Dialogues* that in itself would suggest that it was not written at the time of translating and did not originally accompany the exemplar.

The manuscript evidence for the Old English translation of the *Soliloquies* of St Augustine is, if not also complex, certainly unsatisfactory. The only surviving manuscript, (BL Cotton Vitellius A.xv) dating from the second quarter of the twelfth century is written in late West Saxon with evidence for early Middle English forms.[123] The scribe in Carnicelli's opinion 'was an Englishman who had adopted many Anglo-Norman orthographic practices'.[124] The preface to Alfred's Old English version of the *Soliloquies* begins abruptly, suggesting that the lost exemplar was acephalus, but the surviving manuscript suggests that its scribe began at the beginning of the text he had before him.[125] The loss of the final words of text at the end of the Cotton Vitellius manuscript has resulted from the loss of a final folio from that manuscript. This lopping of text at the beginning and end in the surviving manuscript of the *Soliloquies* and in its exemplar has left serious doubts about this text unresolved. Is there a missing reference to Alfred as the author of the work in the words that may have been lost at the beginning of the preface? As it stands the preface to the *Soliloquies* is the only preface written by the king in which he fails to reveal his authorship, and Alfred unlike so many writers in the Early Middle Ages chose to take credit for authorship rather than remain anonymous. Tantalizingly at the very end of the work, a concluding sentence breaks off: 'Here end the sayings which King Alfred collected from the book which we call in . . .' This reference to 'the sayings (*þa cwidas*)' of King Alfred does not in itself authenticate the piece as the work of the king—it is likely to be

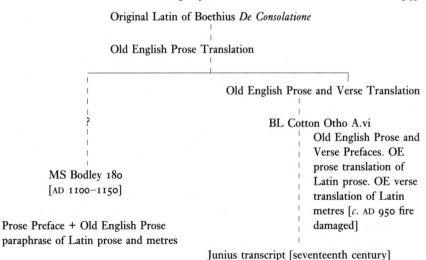

FIG. 13. Text history of the Old English *Boethius*

a later gloss—but it would be interesting to know which book the writer was referring to as the source of Alfred's work. Yet in spite of its unsatisfactory state of survival, the *Soliloquies* have withstood the scrutiny of modern scholarship and retain a secure place in the Alfredian canon.

There are strong personal touches which we may recognize as distinctively Alfredian to be found throughout the prefaces attributed to the king. Some of these relate to minor stylistic mannerisms such as the emphatic 'now . . . now . . . now' recognized by Sisam in the prose preface to the *Consolation* as echoing a similar usage in the prefatory letter to the *Pastoral Care*.[126] Other Alfredian traits are of a more subjective nature, but are none the less real. We find in the prefatory letter to the *Pastoral Care* the rhetorical use of exaggeration to paint as bleak a picture as possible in order to underline Alfred's personal achievement and in order also to persuade the bishops to take action. Alfred would have us believe, when contrasting an earlier golden age with his own time, that when he became king there were so few men capable of understanding 'their Divine Services in English, or translate a letter from Latin into English . . . that I cannot remember a single one south of the Thames'. This exaggeration is employed to provide maximum impact for the statement: 'Thanks be to God Almighty that we have any teachers among us now', and where later he writes of 'learned bishops as now, thanks be to God, they are nearly everywhere'—but all thanks, really, to Alfred's personal exertions and to the continued co-operation which he sought from his bishops. We are reminded of the way in which the compiler of the Chronicle deliberately stressed Alfred's dire straits prior to his unexplained victory over Guthrum back in 878. Scholars who lean on Alfred's every word in relation to the state of Latin learning at the time when he became king would do well to recall the ominously similar lament of the homilist Ælfric (*fl.* AD 1000) in his preface to his Grammar:

Therefore God's ministers and monks should take warning now, lest in our days sacred doctrine should lose its fervour and decay; as happened in England only a few years ago, so that no English priest could compose or thoroughly interpret a letter in Latin, until Archbishop Dunstan and Bishop Æthelwold restored learning in the monasteries.[127]

We are dealing here with the use of exaggerated formulae for getting the point across for the need to have educated clerks. If we were to take Alfred and Ælfric too literally, we would have to write off not only the survival of Latin, but of Early English Christianity itself for much of the ninth century and the first half of the tenth. Alfredian rhetorical exaggeration needs to be properly recognized for what it was—a useful device to bolster the achievement of the king and perhaps also of his scholarly circle. It was a device, too, which was calculated to persuade his bishops to accept the need for education and for his translation programme. Stenton warned in relation to Alfred's comments on the state of English learning that 'impressions like this may be dangerous if they are taken literally',[128] but ironically, Stenton's findings on the decline in standards of Latin scholarship in ninth-century Anglo-Latin charters were frequently used to show that Alfred's lament on scholarly decline was accurately founded.[129] Stenton was correct in pointing to a decline—grammatical and syntactical—in the Latinity of some early ninth-century English diplomas, which he identified as being particularly marked from *c.*825 onwards, especially in Canterbury.[130] But Stenton recognized that the decline was neither universal nor absolute. We might add that it is unsafe to argue that clerks who drew up diplomas were the only people in Anglo-Saxon society who were schooled in Latin.

Sound standards in the Latin of diplomas was maintained throughout the reign of Offa and his successor Coenwulf down to AD 821. Stenton saw a slow decline beginning with a grant by King Coenwulf to Archbishop Wulfred of land near Faversham in Kent in 814 (Sawyer 177), through a similar grant involving Ceolwulf I of land near Kemsing in Kent in 822 (Sawyer 186), and culminating in the 'grotesque' Latin of a grant in 863 by Æthelberht of Wessex of land at Mersham in Kent (Sawyer 332).[131] Arguing from charter evidence is notoriously fraught with the possibility of finding whatever one sets out to seek. This is so, because of the lack of sufficient numbers of such documents to provide a reliable statistical sample, the uneven conditions under which charters were produced, and because of problems caused by later copying and by forgers. We do not possess sufficient evidence to arrive at definite conclusions regarding the state of Latin at the court of the kings Ecgberht and his son, Æthelwulf, based on charters alone. Of some 74 surviving charters (including fragmentary texts) issued in the names of Ecgberht and Æthelwulf, or of West Saxon and Kentish bishops and laity during the reigns of those kings (*c.*802–58), only nine or ten[132] are agreed to survive in contemporary manuscripts. One of these (Sawyer 1195; Birch 403) is in the vernacular, while four others[133] may preserve ninth-century texts in tenth-century copies. The remainder all appear in later medieval copies and can scarcely be used as reliable evidence for the state of ninth-century Latinity. While an element of decline in Latin standards can be detected in Mercian diplomas, the bulk of the evidence for a marked fall in standards comes from Kent at a time when that former kingdom was going through a difficult transition from being a tributary of Mercia to being annexed by Wessex.[134] Stenton noted that Archbishop Wulfred's enforced absence from Canterbury for four years from 817 to 821 may have had a detrimental effect on standards there.[135] The sacking of Canterbury and London in 851 by a viking army backed up with a huge fleet of 350 warships can only have had a damaging effect at a time when Norse paganism was at its most strident, and when invading warriors from a pre-literate society were unlikely to make any concessions towards clerks in a scriptorium.

Evidence from Ireland as well as England would suggest a decline in Latin scholarship in both countries in the early ninth century. This decline appears, at first, to have been part of a natural cycle of crests and troughs within the ongoing evolution of Christian culture in the early medieval West. On the other hand, both Anglo-Saxon and Irish societies experienced a marked development and proliferation of texts in the vernacular in the ninth and tenth centuries—a phenomenon that has not been adequately accounted for, or studied at a comparative level. As to the decline in Latin learning, that was even more true for Francia, where Charlemagne's renaissance was prompted as much by a desire to revitalize scholarly standards and levels of literacy among his clergy, as by any crusade to exhume a Classical past. But there is overwhelming evidence to show that decline in Classical learning was accelerated and exacerbated by the fury of viking attacks as the ninth century wore on. As long as Carolingian defences held, it was Anglo-Saxon and Irish treasure-houses of learning which bore the brunt of viking terror. But those who would rashly take Alfred's words on scholarly decline at their face value would do well to remember that Northumbria was capable of exporting Alcuin to the court of Charlemagne, and that this aged scholar must have left a whole generation of pupils behind him in early ninth-century York; while in Ireland, as we have noted, Sedulius and Eriugena testify to the high standard of teaching in schools that were to serve the second and third Carolingian generation. Nor had the later Carolingians forgotten England's potential for Latin scholarship. Lupus, abbot of Ferrières, was writing to York in 850 in search of Quintilian's *Institutes* and other books. Sisam, who was rightly sceptical of Alfredian views on ninth-century English learning, reminded us that Lindisfarne was capable of producing a sumptuous *Liber Vitae* in the early ninth century, and that the libraries of that house and of others such as Peterborough must have remained intact into the early years of the second half of the century.[136] It can only have been the advent of the Great Army of Danes from 865 onwards, which dealt a death-blow to libraries and scriptoria in East Anglia, Lindsey, and Northumbria, and by then Alfred was edging ever closer to kingship and to developing his translation programme. Alfred's throw-away statement that 'there were very few on this side of the Humber . . . who could translate a letter (*ærendgewrit*) from Latin into English, and I believe there were not many beyond the Humber"[137] can only be taken as a gross overstating of the case. It betrays, too, in its vagueness, the provincial nature of his kingship, since he speaks as a man for whom Northumbria is a remote region about which he is expected to know little.

Alfred was, as ever, being economical with the truth, in order to glorify his own achievement. When he tells us that there were few 'on this side of the Humber' capable of translating Latin letters into English, he overlooks the fact that on his own admission, his personal contribution to the translation enterprise was reliant on help from Mercian scholars such as Archbishop Plegmund. The *Dialogues* of Gregory and the Old English Bede were, as we have seen, also translated by Mercians. Sisam dated the poetry of Cynewulf to the ninth century and located the poet in either Mercia or Northumbria.[138] A *Life* of St Chad and an Old English prose martyrology may also be attributed to Mercia. It is surely wrong to dismiss this achievement as 'meagre' or to describe the ninth century as 'barren' in terms of intellectual achievement.[139] Scholars who hold these views show some confusion in their assessment of literary activity in the ninth century as a whole. Works produced in Northumbria, East Anglia, and eastern Mercia almost certainly date to before the advent of the Great Army, and for those regions the term 'ninth century' means in effect the 65 years prior to 865—a narrow bracket, which if applied to earlier centuries in English literary development would pose equal if not greater problems for identification with firmly datable material. Secondly, the term 'ninth century' for the kingdom of Wessex includes, of course, the entire Alfredian renaissance which drew much of its vitality from Mercian scholarship from the first half of the century. The description, therefore, of this century as 'barren' is an anomaly born of over-zealous attempts to defend every statement made by King Alfred and later by the Pseudo-Asser as enshrining some absolute truth. Whichever bishop—Wærferth or Wulfsige—was the vernacular poet of the preface to the *Dialogues*, it is very likely that he was also well schooled in Latin. It is impossible that the West Saxon scholars who assembled material for the compilation of the Anglo-Saxon Chronicle from earlier Latin annals and other Latin sources were not themselves capable of reading Latin. Such men must have been schooled by others of an earlier (mid ninth-century) generation—unless we resort to the Pseudo-Asser's methods and assume that all of them, including Alfred, were brought up illiterate. King Æthelwulf had a Frankish secretary, Felix, and yet another Frank may have been responsible for Frankish features in a grant of land at Chart in Kent, issued by Æthelwulf in 843.[140] Stenton interpreted the presence of these foreigners in a West Saxon (or (?)Canterbury) writing office as indicative that Æthelwulf 'may have found difficulty in obtaining English clerks skilled enough in *dictamen* to draft his solemn charters'.[141] But charters, constructed as they were according to set formulae, were among the easier of Latin documents to produce. The presence of Frankish clerks in Æthelwulf's kingdom lends itself to an alternative interpretation. The West Saxons were near neighbours to the courts of Louis the Pious and later of Charles the Bald—foremost centres of culture and learning in the Christian West. It was inevitable that Æthelwulf's court should have been influenced to some degree at least by this superior culture. The acquiring by the aged Æthelwulf of a young Carolingian wife provides proof of that. The fact that Frankish clerks appear in Æthelwulf's writing office could suggest that West Saxon scribes and clerks, as well as the young Alfred—far from being educationally deprived—had benefited from this important cultural contact. In the final analysis, Alfred's own interest in learning—however much it may have centred on the vernacular—must have owed a great deal to the Carolingian renaissance. It was Alfred himself who encouraged us by his silence to assess his achievement in isolation both from his contemporary English background and from the influence of his Carolingian neighbours. Alfred in his prefatory letter to the *Pastoral Care* shows himself to be a master at manipulating and projecting a desired image of himself to his own time and to a gullible posterity.

This discussion of Alfred's sweeping statements on the decline of Latin scholarship in early ninth-century England leads to a further interesting conclusion on the status of the Old English vernacular at that time. There was a marked shift from the use of Latin to English in the production of charters from the early ninth century onwards in Mercia and Wessex. This development may not have been driven by any ignorance of Latin. It seems, rather, to have been a natural response to clarifying and coping more efficiently with a growing body of complex on-going legal disputes which required lucidity on the part of those who recorded them.[142] At this time, a new genre of legal text was emerging—the 'statement' or *talu* of a legal case, which was a narrative of the legal twists and turns of the dispute so far, and which provided aids, if not for reaching a judgement—then as guidelines drawn up in the interests of one party to the action. Later ninth and early tenth-century examples of the genre include Alfred's summary of the legal wrangle and involved family history which lay behind his *Will*, and the Fonthill Letter, which is a statement or summing up of a lawsuit spanning more than one reign. The earliest body of English *Wills* also belong at the beginning of the ninth century, and although all this material makes up a specialized corpus of Old English legal texts, 'the finest documents of this class have a vividness of detail which entitles them to rank as literature'.[143] The Mercian court of Ealdorman Æthelred and his wife Æthelflæd, the daughter of King Alfred (*c*.883–918), yields several examples of grants drawn up in the vernacular as well as the continued use of the more formal Latin diploma. An earlier Mercian example of a charter drawn up in the vernacular shortly before Alfred was born is that of King Beorhtwulf's grant of land at Wooton Underwood (Bucks.) dating to *c*.845.[144] When Alfred was as yet only about 15, he witnessed an elaborate grant drawn up in English in favour of the church at Sherborne, by his brother, King Æthelberht in 864.[145] A similar grant in the vernacular was drawn up by King Æthelred for his ealdorman Ælfstan in 870–1.[146] The Alfredian translations of Late Antique writers as well as the compilation of the Anglo-Saxon Chronicle must be seen against the background of this ever growing use of the vernacular across the whole of the ninth century throughout Mercia and Wessex. This is not to diminish Alfred's remarkable personal achievement in the promotion and development of Old English as a language of learning and literature, but instead of leaning on his every rhetorical lament on the decline of Latin, we ought instead to view his achievement with translated texts, as part of, and an extension of, the growing use of vernaculars in the written culture throughout all of England, Scotland, Wales, and Ireland in the ninth century.

Alfred's lament on the poor state of learning is rendered something of a nonsense by the testimony which his own writings offer on his personal learning and on that of his editorial team. Wittig, in his study of the king's translation of the *Consolation of Philosophy* by Boethius[147] concluded that it indicated a knowledge of the fourth *Georgic* (together with a commentary such as that by Servius); Virgil's *Aeneid*, Book VI; the tenth book of Ovid's *Metamorphoses*; and perhaps also the *Etymologiae* of Isidore of Seville.[148] More significantly, Wittig concluded that Alfred or his helpers cannot be shown (as was once thought) to have relied on any known version of the numerous current commentaries on Boethius for the expansion and explanation of that philosophical text. Instead, the Alfredian exposition on Classical mythological lore and on many of the philosophical arguments of Boethius would appear to be the product of painstaking consideration given to these issues prior to and during the translation of the text. Payne demonstrated how thoroughly Alfred must have studied the original Latin of Boethius, in order not only to adapt the original argument, but also in making necessary minor alterations to every section of the work to prepare the ground for more substantial Alfredian alterations towards the end.[149] The sources which lie behind the Old English translation of the *Soliloquies* include, of course, St Augustine's work of that name, as well as Augustine's *De Videndo Deo*, which is acknowledged by name in the Old English translation. Other sources which went into the compilation of the Alfredian *Soliloquies* include Gregory's *Homily on Luke* and Gregory's *Morals*, Jerome's *Vulgate* and a *Commentary on Luke*, once attributed to Jerome.[150] Finally, the influence of Gregory's *Dialogues*, and the Alfredian translations of Gregory's *Pastoral Care* and Boethius' *Consolation of Philosophy* contribute an important element to the argument that the *Soliloquies* were indeed translated by King Alfred.[151] The evidence for this scholarly basis to the translation of Boethius, the *Soliloquies*, and to the *Pastoral Care* is suggestive of a well-educated king working in the company of a highly educated scholarly élite. The chronicler Æthelweard may not have read many of Alfred's works, but he was sufficiently impressed with his ancestor's scholarly output to describe King Alfred as 'learned in speech (*sermone doctus*) and steeped in sacred literature above all things (*sermone doctus, diuinis quippe super omnia documentis imbutus*)'.[152] Æthelweard, unlike the Pseudo-Asser, did not have access among his family records to any tradition which even hinted at the idea of an illiterate ruler struggling with his homework.

The prose preface to King Alfred's *Pastoral Care* is followed by a brief verse preface, which, although recognized as such by Sweet in 1871, was not properly edited until much later. This verse preface has been hesitatingly attributed to King Alfred, while a versified epilogue to the entire work has been treated with even more caution by Alfredian scholars. The verse preface is clearly more closely connected with the translation of the *Pastoral Care* than the prefatory letter, in so far as its content relates to the text and translation of the *Pastoral Care* itself. While the verse epilogue does contain a mention of Gregory, it does not refer specifically to the *Pastoral Care*. Yet the epilogue does contain strong echoes of passages in Alfred's translation of the *Pastoral Care*. The verse preface and epilogue are likely to have been composed at the time of completion of the translation, which is supported by their presence in the late-ninth century Hatton 20 manuscript of that work.[153] It seems logical, too, that we accept the verse preface and epilogue as two of a pair, both in terms of content and in their overall conception. The verse preface is attributed to the book itself, as in the case of the verse preface to the translation of Gregory's *Dialogues*. We are told, 'King Alfred translated every word of me into English and sent me to his scribes south and north; ordered more such to be brought to him after the example, that he might send them to his bishops.'[154] The verse preface opens by telling us that 'This message Augustine over the salt sea brought from the south to the islanders, as the Lord's champion had formerly decreed it, the pope of Rome. The wise Gregory was versed in many true doctrines through the wisdom of his mind.'[155] The author then, suggests that the *Pastoral Care* had first reached England in the baggage of St Augustine in the closing years of the sixth century, and the emphasis on the importance of Pope Gregory and the recourse to the historical perspective on the transmission of the work to the English is all very much part of that Alfredian obsession with cultural transmission from the Mediterranean to the North, from the classical to barbarian, from Christian to pagan. In the Chronicle, too, the sending of Augustine by Pope Gregory in 596, the sending of the *pallium* by Gregory in 601, the death of Gregory in 604 (606A) and detail offered on the names of his parents—all underlines the importance in the mind of the late ninth-century compiler of the man who 'sent us Baptism'.[156] The verse epilogue to the *Pastoral Care* is constructed around the metaphor that 'These [i.e. the words of Gregory's *Pastoral Care*] are now the waters, which the God of hosts promised as a solace to us earth-dwellers. . . . There is little doubt that the source of the waters is in the kingdom of Heaven; that is, the Holy Ghost.'[157] Whence, we are told, the saints have channelled this water to our minds through holy books. The Lord has granted to Gregory to direct this stream to our doors, i.e. to those of us who read the *Pastoral Care*. The reader is admonished to take his water-tight pitcher and fill it with these 'clearest of waters'. Dobbie, drawing attention to the similarities with the style of the preface to the *Soliloquies*, stated that 'if Alfred wrote the Preface to the *Soliloquies*, then he was probably also the author of the epilogue to the *Pastoral Care*'.[158] The Epilogue to the *Pastoral Care* would seem to be Alfred's work, or at least to incorporate his sentiments, and it was certainly written by someone who was steeped in Gregory's metaphorical language as preserved in Alfred's Old English text of the *Pastoral Care*.

Gregory's *Pastoral Care* is assumed to be the earliest of King Alfred's translations. Its scholarly format and bookish vocabulary, and the relative closeness with which it follows the original Latin, may be in keeping with its early status in the translation programme.[159] If the degree of closeness to the original Latin be taken as a yardstick for relative date, then the translation of the *Consolation of Philosophy* may be regarded as the next of Alfred's works. Here, although we are presented in part, with a translation—'sometimes', as Alfred puts it, 'word for word, sometimes sense for sense (*Hwilum . . . word be worde, hwilum andgit of andgite*)'[160]—the translator has taken greater liberties with his original, both in terms of what is left out and what is added in. Alfred or his editorial team decided, for instance, to simplify Boethius's position as a prisoner in the *Consolation*, by introducing him as a good man who was found guilty of plotting against the rule of the wicked Theodoric. In the original text, the position of Boethius is seen as being more complex, with the prisoner protesting his innocence.[161] Alfred also chose to drop a lengthy autobiographical passage in chapter IV of Book I of the original *Consolation*,[162] in which Boethius lashes out at back-stabbers at the court of Theodoric. It was sensibly decided that arguments about a famine in the Campania, the role of a certain Cyprian (an early sixth-century Public Prosecutor) and of more obscure informers—Basilius, Opilio, and Gaudentius[163]—would have done little to endear this translation to a West Saxon reader. So, these lengthy details on the political intrigues which destroyed Boethius were jettisoned, while elsewhere throughout the *Consolation*—and more so as it progressed—the translator indulged himself by adding sometimes lengthy commentaries on the nature of God and of eternity, and of the souls and intelligence of men and angels. On the other hand, Alfred omitted Boethius's crucial central argument in the final or fifth book of the original *Consolation* reconciling God's foreknowledge with free will in men. Alfred's interest in angels and the immortality of the soul reappears in the extraneous material in the translation of the *Soliloquies* of St Augustine, which is regarded as one of the later of Alfred's writings, and one which may have been completed after the *Pastoral Care* and the *Consolation of Philosophy*. The translation of the *Soliloquies* is seen by some scholars as providing a terminus date within the relative chronological scheme for King Alfred's major literary works. There is a marked and progressive falling away in this work from the content of the Latin original—so much so that Alfred provided a third book for this work which Augustine never got around to writing!

As early as 1894, Hubbard demonstrated close similarities between the Old English versions of the *Consolation* and the *Soliloquies*, in terms of content, style, and handling of the original texts. Hubbard was able to show that the *Soliloquies* 'must have been written later than the Boethius'.[164] A key element in what is a detailed textual argument, subsequently reinforced by Carnicelli, is that many additional or 'Alfredian' passages in the *Soliloquies* correspond closely with translated passages in the *Consolation*, while there is only one case in which a translated passage in the *Soliloquies* corresponds to an additional passage of the *Consolation*.[165] This on its own would prove no more than that the author of the *Soliloquies* was already familiar with the translation of Boethius.[166] But there is a powerful cumulative argument for holding that King Alfred was the author of both translations. Despite the differences between the original Latin of Boethius and Augustine, there is often close correspondence in phrasing in the Old English translations of the *Consolation* and *Soliloquies*. Added passages are similar in content in both works, and both texts—as Carnicelli observed—'contain additions that show a thorough knowledge of the life and thinking of a king'.[167] In their original Latin forms, the *Consolation* was constructed around a dialogue between the Lady Philosophy and the captive Boethius, while the *Soliloquies* were presented as a dialogue between Reason (*ratio*) and the mind of Augustine.[168] In the Alfredian or Old English versions, both the *Consolation* and *Soliloquies* retain the dialogue format, simplified as a discourse between Wisdom and the writer. In the *Consolation* the dialogue is largely between *Wisdom* and the mind (*Mod*) of the writer; and in the *Soliloquies* between Reason (*Gesceadwisnes*) and the writer.[169] These dialogues are handled in almost identical ways—in terms of opening remarks, connecting phrases, summarizing of statements, teacher and pupil comments, lexical choices, and general syntax. Since Alfred's authorship of the Old English version of the *Consolation* has never been seriously challenged, then given the remarkable closeness of that work to the *Soliloquies*, Alfred was almost certainly the author of both.

While the evidence points to the *Soliloquies* being relatively later in time than either the *Pastoral Care* or the *Consolation*, there is an argument for holding that the time-span involved in the production of two of these works may have been shorter than some scholars have supposed. While many examples of added or strictly 'Alfredian' material in the *Soliloquies* show a dependence on translated passages (based on the original Latin) in the *Consolation*, there is at least one instance in which an Alfredian addition to the *Consolation* corresponds to a translated passage in the *Soliloquies*.[170] Carnicelli tried to explain away this awkward detail by holding that 'the correspondence here is more of thought than of phrasing'. That is only partly true. There is a detailed correspondence between the two Alfredian texts that goes back ultimately to a vaguer correspondence between the original ideas of Augustine and Boethius. We must at least allow for an alternative explanation. The translated passage in the Old English *Soliloquies* is close to the original Latin of Augustine, while the corresponding piece in the Alfredian *Consolation* does not follow the Alfredian *Soliloquies* in close textual detail.[171] But just as Alfred himself claims that his technique was sometimes to translate 'sense for sense', so too he borrowed material from elsewhere in his translations according to this 'loose' technique. When Alfred's borrowing is seen to be in the opposite direction—from the *Consolation* to the supposedly later *Soliloquies*—then correspondence in ideas, backed by only partial matching in Old English phrasing, has posed no problems for textual scholars eager to pursue a desired conclusion. So, what Carnicelli and Hubbard believed about passages in the *Soliloquies* which were derived from the *Consolation* must equally apply to that passage which was borrowed in the opposite direction:

a man making a free translation of two books, similar in character would, in the second, very naturally make use of expressions he had used in the first, wherever the thought of his second original might suggest them. Expressions that he had worked out *once* as satisfactory forms for rendering the thoughts of the original would inevitably come into his mind, whenever he met the same or similar thoughts in another work, upon whose translation he was working.[172]

This is also the most appropriate explanation for the correspondence between the translated passage from the *Soliloquies* and the Alfredian addition to Boethius. The two passages in question are close enough to show beyond doubt that Alfred or his team must have consulted the *Soliloquies* of Augustine either in the original Latin or, more likely, in their own Old English translation, while they were still working on the translation of Boethius. Augustine in his *Soliloquies* (I. 23) likens the relationship between a student aspiring to Wisdom and a man trying to look at the sun. A man with healthy sight has no difficulty viewing the sun, but 'if he hath unsound eyes (*Gyf he ðonne unhale æagen (h)æfð*), then he needeth that one teach him to look first on the wall, then on gold, and on silver; when he can more easily look on that [then let him look] on fire (*on fyr*), before he looketh at the sun (*ærðam he ongean þa sunnan locie.*)'.[173] Boethius in his *Consolation of Philosophy* (IV. 4) makes Philosophy say of those who cannot see the truth of an argument that 'their eyes are used to the dark and they cannot raise them to the shining light of truth. They are like birds whose sight is sharpened by night and blinded by day.'[174] King Alfred in translating this passage recalled the rather different simile in the *Soliloquies* and added: 'Those men who have not sound eyes cannot gaze with ease full upon the sun (*þa men þe habbað unhale eagen ne magon full eaðe locian ongean þa sunnan*) when he is shining brightest, nor even on fire (*on fyr*) or on aught that is bright do they care to look, if the eyeball be diseased.'[175] This Alfredian passage in the *Consolation* does not show an exact textual dependence on the Old English translation of the *Soliloquies*. Nevertheless, textual similarities in the Old English do exist, and while the order of ideas is reversed, there is very close correspondence between those ideas in both passages. A case can be made for the writer of the *Consolation* having the Old English text of the *Soliloquies* before him, or for having—at the very least—given some thought to the translation of that passage in the *Soliloquies*. Carnicelli was forced to conclude that Alfred 'was familiar with the Latin *Sol*[*iloquies*] at the time he was translating Boethius'.[176] Another possible solution to the difficulty would be to assume that the translations of the *Consolation* and the *Soliloquies* were progressing side by side, with the *Consolation* taking priority and being finished first. This would account for the more dominant influence of the translation of Boethius on the freer and additional prose of the *Soliloquies*, while at the same time allowing for a translated passage in the *Soliloquies* to influence an addition in Boethius. On a more general but important level, Payne observed that the translator's decision to give the name *Mod* ('Mind') to the person to whom Wisdom speaks in the *Consolation* conveys the notion that the dialogue is of an internal nature and that 'the primary literary precedent was doubtless St Augustine's *Soliloquies*, a dialogue where Augustine talks with Ratio, a voice whose origin he cannot identify'.[177] Whitelock believed it to be unlikely that the *Consolation* and the *Soliloquies* 'were far removed from one another in date' and she prudently concluded that 'it is safest to regard the priority of the *Boethius* [over the *Soliloquies*] as probable rather than certain'.[178]

We know from Alfred's prefatory letter that he intended to send a copy of the *Pastoral Care* to every bishopric in his kingdom (*to ælcum biscepstole on minum rice wille ane onsendan*),[179] and we are told in the verse preface, which immediately precedes the translation proper, that Alfred sent copies to his bishops 'for some of them needed it, who knew but little Latin'.[180] The bishops of Wessex, Kent, and parts of Mercia, therefore, were the immediate recipients of the *Pastoral Care* and some of those men (though clearly not Plegmund) may have found the Latin of Gregory's original work difficult if not impossible going. The prefatory letter of the best preserved of the earliest manuscripts of the *Pastoral Care* (Hatton 20 in the Bodleian Library) has the heading *This book is to go to Worcester* (*Đeos boc sceal to Wiogora Ceastre*) and in it the king greets Bishop Wærferth of that Mercian town. The only other contemporary manuscript—the fragmentary Cotton Tiberius B.xi, damaged twice by fire since 1731—has a blank in its prefatory letter for the recipient's name, and so may have been used as a master copy in the king's writing office. Yet another manuscript (Cotton Otho B.ii), dating from *c.* AD 1000, is a copy of the *Pastoral Care* sent to Heahstan of London, while Wulfsige, bishop of Sherborne received an original (now lost) of the later eleventh-century Cambridge University Library Manuscript Ii.2.4. So, in all, some ten copies may have been dispatched to the bishops under Alfred's jurisdiction. While the king did allow for the possibility of the copying of those episcopal manuscripts out in the dioceses, there can be little doubt that he intended the bishops to be the primary reader-ship—and hence his anxiety that each copy which he sent out to his bishops be kept securely in each cathedral church (*mynster*) under their control: 'I command in God's name that no man take the clasp from the book or the book from the minster . . . therefore I wish them always to remain in their place, unless the bishop wish to take them with him, or they be sent out anywhere, or anyone make a copy from them.'[181]

Alfred's prefatory letter embodied two objectives—one by way of an accompanying letter for the *Pastoral Care*, and a second, outlining his hopes for the education of the free-born youth of Wessex. But Alfred did not necessarily envisage young pupils swatting up Pope Gregory's *Pastoral Care*, even if it had been translated into English—that language 'which we can all understand'. Translation of specialized works does not render them any less specialized. It is even more improbable that the *Consolation of Philosophy* or the *Soliloquies* were ever inflicted on West Saxon schoolboys. These were treatises for élitist scholars removed from the world and sharing in largely unresolved philosophical debate that one associates with a closed circle of literati. The *Pastoral Care* was a handbook for bishops —offering prelates 'no better exposition of the pastoral responsibilities of the episcopate and the way they should be exercised'.[182] It is a work which would be lost on elementary pupils of any age. Nor can we argue that the Old English translation of the *Pastoral Care* was reserved for that advanced stream of pupils whom Alfred envisaged as suitable candidates for eventual promotion 'to higher rank (*to hierran hade*)'. The king specifically intended that group should study Latin. His vernacular rendering of the *Pastoral Care* did not provide a consistent word for word translation and was not suitable as a class-book for pupils learning to read the Latin original. Nor was the original *Liber Regulae Pastoralis* ever intended to serve as a Latin primer.

Alfred had in mind that certain boys in his kingdom would be taught from the most rudimentary levels, to read and write in English, and that a few of the more able or ecclesiastically-minded students would proceed eventually to Latin. It is very hard to see how the *Pastoral Care* could have been intended as a book for infant learners or beginners in any language. But neither was it intended, as Potter claimed, 'to be read by contemplatives, [and] by lettered clerks'.[183] While that was true of the *Consolation* and the *Soliloquies*, the *Pastoral Care* was intended for its stated recipients—the bishops of Alfred's kingdom, some of whose own knowledge of Latin (if we are to go by the verse preface) was quite defective. Alfred had, as we have seen, even written into the master copy of his policy document accompanying the *Pastoral Care*, the notion that each copy would be attached to a bishop's minster. The relatively high survival rate of extant manuscripts of the Old English *Pastoral Care* supports the notion of a predominantly episcopal readership. Of the six surviving copies, three are without association and three are associated with the bishops of Worcester, London, and Sherborne. But while the contemporary manuscript, Tiberius Bx.i, had a blank space for the recipient bishop, it did once contain a note to the effect that 'Archbishop Plegmund [of Canterbury] has been given this book, and Bishop Swithwulf [of Rochester] and Bishop Werferth [of Worcester]'.[184] This increases all known associations of the work with five leading bishops and their sees. There is no evidence—in spite of Sisam's speculation to the contrary[185]—to suggest that copies had been distributed to late ninth-century monastic centres, or that the Old English version of the *Pastoral Care* ever established its popularity among monastic foundations of the later tenth century. Had the vernacular work so established itself in reformed monastic circles, we should expect more of those manuscripts which survived into the seventeenth century to have had monastic or lay associations connecting them with supposedly Alfredian monasteries such as Shaftesbury, or with houses of the tenth-century reform such as Abingdon. The reality, however, is otherwise, and copies of the *Pastoral Care* which survive have associations with those bishoprics under Alfred's control, for which the work was intended in the first instance.

The importance of identifying the primary recipients of the prefatory letter to the *Pastoral Care* (and the entire translated work itself) is crucial for a proper understanding of the second objective outlined by Alfred in the preface—namely, his hopes for the education of the young. A careful reading of Alfred's letter to his bishops—for that is what the prose preface actually is—shows that the king's objectives in regard to education were as limited as they were realistic:

Therefore it seems better to me, if ye think so . . . for you to do as we very easily can if we have tranquility enough, that is that all the youth now in England born of free men, who are rich enough to be able to devote themselves to it, be sent to learn as long as they are not fit for any other occupation, until they are well able to read English writing: and let those be afterwards taught more in the Latin language who are to continue learning and be promoted to a higher rank.[186]

This was no comprehensive scheme for schools in ninth-century Wessex. The youth (*gioguð*) in question were inevitably male, free-born (sons of *friora monna*), with enough *sped*—wealth or ability or both[187]—and 'provided they are not fit for any other occupation (*oðerre note*) [or while they may not be fit for any other use]'. And the people Alfred charged with the responsibility to teach these youths were, of course, his bishops, whose cathedrals were expected to house a diocesan school for the instruction of clerks in Christian faith and rituals. Each bishop, who is addressed directly by Alfred in the prefatory letter to the *Pastoral Care*, is told that 'it seems better to me if it seems so to you . . . that we do as we very easily can (*gedon swa we swiðe eaðe magon*) that is, that all the youth . . . be set to learn'. The bishops were to organize this teaching for Alfred in their cathedral schools. Alfred could well have been reading in his copy of Bede's *Ecclesiastical History* how such cathedral schools had existed in Canterbury in the time of Archbishop Theodore (668–90).[188] Later at York, a great cathedral school flourished from the days of Archbishop Ecgberht (732–66).[189] It was incumbent on every bishop to instruct his clergy, and from that obligation arose the development of cathedral schools for the young throughout the medieval West. Not only was King Alfred exhorting his bishops to maintain or revive this tradition—'if we have peace enough' from viking attack—but he also equipped those same prelates with a copy of Gregory's *Pastoral Care* which harped continuously on the bishop's responsibilities and authority as teacher (*lareow*).[190] So much is clear from Alfred's own discussion on this topic. The king must have recognized the necessity of maintaining some schools to provide for a future generation of clerks and ecclesiastical officials. Since, as Alfred himself tells us, the young scholars were all children of free-born men, it was an especially risky business assembling such aristocratic youths in a school situation. Viking slave-raiders were a constant scourge in England, Ireland, and Francia from the second half of the ninth century onwards, and youths of tender age were obviously a prime and manageable prey. Aristocratic youths provided lucrative spoils for raiding parties by way of ransom-money. It is easy to see how formal schooling must have come to a virtual standstill in Wessex in the period 871–8 and 893–6, outside the protection of fortified centres such as Winchester, Canterbury, and Worcester. And it was those very same secure locations which also protected the leading bishops who were briefed by Alfred in his prefatory letter to the *Pastoral Care* to revitalize their cathedral schools.

The Pseudo-Asser wove his mischievous web around the subject of King Alfred's schools, which, because of the high status attributed to the *Life* of Alfred as a historical source, has obscured most of what the king himself has written on this subject. We know that the Pseudo-Asser studied Alfred's accompanying letter to the *Pastoral Care* in some detail. At least two verbal parallels have been established between the Latin text of the *Life* of Alfred and the Old English of the prefatory letter.[191] So, while that so-called prose preface shows that Alfred had exhorted his bishops to educate a limited section of the free-born youth of the kingdom, the Pseudo-Asser extended this brief to include 'all the nobly born children of virtually the entire area (*pene totius regionis*), and a good many of lesser birth as well'[192] in a school under the king's personal tutelage[193] in the royal household, attended by the king's children. While few would dispute that the king's children had access to

tutors at the royal court, there is not a shred of evidence in Alfred's own writings
to support the remainder of the Pseudo-Asser's extravagant claims for Alfred's
role as master in a Palace School which catered for a mass-education programme.
If we were left in any doubt of the veracity of the Pseudo-Asser's embellishments,
we need only turn to his closing observations in the *Life* of Alfred. There we read
that in addition to the noble and non-noble youths of Alfred's kingdom, even the
king's ealdormen and reeves, who failed to pass a reading test, were forced back to
school by the king for fear of losing their jobs. And those who were too old or too
stupid to learn, employed their sons or slaves to read to them 'by day and night'.
If ever there were a recipe for a medieval king to lose his head as well as his throne,
it was surely here. Scholars, such as Bullough, who, in good faith, took the *Life* of
King Alfred at its face value, pointedly chose to ignore the more outlandish
statements in the *Life* of Alfred regarding the mass nature of the school programme and its application to men of all ages.[194] Prudent scholars have silently
ignored this unacceptable face of King Alfred's biography, appreciating full well
the folk element which it entailed. The notion of Alfred as a promoter and master
of his own *schola*, like that of Alfred as monastic founder, was inspired with
hindsight, by the *Regularis Concordia*, that blueprint for reformed monasteries in
England which was drawn up in Winchester *c*.970 and which was studied closely
by the Ramsey school to which the Pseudo-Asser belonged. Alfred's portrayal as
schoolmaster in his court school was part of the hagiographical development of the
king's image in the late tenth century.

Alfred, in his prefatory letter to the *Pastoral Care*, addressed his schooling
programme to the care of his bishops, and the aims of that programme—if such we
chose to call it—were sensibly very limited. When we turn to look at the nature of
the *Consolation of Philosophy* by Boethius and the *Soliloquies* of Augustine, we shall
see that these complex philosophical tracts were never intended as medieval class
primers. In spite of the influence and popularity of Boethius on later medieval
thought, his *Consolation* was not a text for the novice, and Alfred's stylistic and
intellectual tampering with this work, rendered the Old English translation of it
even more unsuited than the Latin original for beginners of any age in whatever
language. The *Soliloquies* of Augustine belonged to the more obscure range of that
theologian's repertoire, suitable only for study and speculative discussion among
an élite group with intellectual pretensions, such as King Alfred's scholarly advisers. In this respect, the king and his scholarly circle, although engaged in the
promotion of the vernacular, resembled their élitist Carolingian contemporaries
who attempted intellectual feats beyond their powers.[195] The Old English versions
of the *Consolation* and the *Soliloquies* pushed the language and thought of the best
educated ninth-century Englishmen to their limits. Alfred's obscure discussions
on predestination and *wyrd* ('fate') in the *Consolation* would have gone far beyond
the grasp of any of those imaginary thegns whom the Pseudo-Asser would have us
believe attended night-school in the king's itinerant court in late ninth-century
Wessex. In keeping with the different ethos of the *Consolation* and the *Soliloquies*,
so, too, the king's introductory preface to these works does not embody the notion

that they were ever considered part of a popular educational scheme. Alfred states in a business-like way in his preface to the *Consolation* that he translated it 'sometimes word for word, sometimes sense for sense' at a time when he was beset with the cares of his royal office. The work was translated 'for each of those whom it pleases to read', and there is no reference whatever to the wider issues which he raised in the accompanying letter addressed to his bishops in the *Pastoral Care*. Likewise, the Alfredian preface to the *Soliloquies* exudes the uncompromising sense that the work was being pursued for Wisdom's sake, and the use of the extended metaphor of building the house of knowledge strongly conveys the notion that Alfred was here addressing his tiny band of scholarly friends who had shared discussions on the meaning of this obscure text with the king.

Scholars studying Alfred's writings in this century have laid too much literal emphasis on what were in fact rhetorical statements by the king. So, when Alfred wrote in his introductory letter to the *Pastoral Care* of translating 'certain books which are the most necessary for all men to know', we ought not necessarily to jump to conclusions that everything translated by the king or produced under his auspices was intended to fit that brief. The *Consolation* and *Soliloquies* certainly did not fit it. Alfred would, himself, have been the first to concede that the New Testament was the most necessary book for all men to know and understand, yet the Scriptures (with the exception of the Psalms) do not seem to have been part of the translated corpus. Furthermore, even if the king had originally intended a translation programme aimed at a popularization of Christian writing, he might well have departed from his original plan.[196] The fact is, that some of the Alfredian Old English translations were suitable for the higher education of aspiring scholars in late ninth-century England, and others most definitely were not. None of the translations were suited as primers. So we need to disentangle Alfred's hopes for the elementary education of some of the youth of Wessex in English—and fewer still in Latin—from his provision of the *Pastoral Care* for the guidance of his bishops in their role as teachers and leaders. And we need also to interpret very cautiously the king's intention to promote the translation of 'certain books which are most necessary for all men to know'. What men did he have in mind?—Certainly not *hoi polloi* in Wessex, nor even those abler youths in a beginners' Latin class. He may have been thinking of a constituency no wider than those young men who would eventually complete their higher learning which would prepare them as clerks in the king's writing office or in the higher echelons of the church. It is even more likely he was thinking of his bishops yet again, some of whose own Latin—not to mention their spiritual lives—may have needed improving. In this respect, we need to concentrate on what we know, rather than on what the Pseudo-Asser would like to have us believe. One of the few fixed points in relation to the readership of Alfred's translations—apart from the *Pastoral Care*—is our knowledge that the *Dialogues* of Pope Gregory were translated for the king's personal use. We also know that the *Dialogues* were read by at least one of Alfred's bishops, who made a copy of the work from an exemplar which the king had sent him.

Alfred's cultural programme was a more modest and yet a more complex phenomenon than many scholars have hitherto supposed. To arrive at a reasonable assessment of it, we need to separate out the advanced scholarly work on translations (*Soliloquies* and *Consolation*) from more popular devotional material (Psalms and *Dialogues*) and we need to separate all the translations in turn from Alfred's hopes for education of the young. Although Whitelock accepted that the *Dialogues* of Gregory were translated for the king's personal use,[197] she implied that the *Pastoral Care* and the other works translated by Alfred himself were intended to provide 'a supply of English textbooks' 'for the education of all young freemen' in the king's schools.[198] Keynes and Lapidge appear to have included not only translations by the king himself, but even peripheral and doubtful ingredients in the Alfredian canon such as Orosius's *Histories* and Bald's *Leechbook* as works which 'served as a basis for a programme of educational reform'.[199] We may exclude all the Alfredian translations, except the Psalms from any imaginary list of class textbooks prescribed in Alfred's cathedral schools. The education of the young was a separate consideration from the production of complex scholarly works in translation which were to be read by mature minds capable of cultivating an interest in philosophy or history. It is still fair to maintain that the king strove to promote the spread of literacy and education throughout his kingdom, albeit to a limited degree. But his specialized translation programme was evidently the outcome of the personal pursuits of a scholar-king eager to share his ideas with a scholarly élite of his own time and with anyone in a later age who might wish to follow him. Indeed, it is remarkable that those works which were clearly not translated by Alfred himself—Orosius and Bede—might be more suitably described as 'books which are most necessary for all men to know' than the more esoteric material pursued by the king himself. The fact that only two medieval manuscripts survive of the *Consolation* and only one of the *Soliloquies* may be an indication of the lack of interest which these works generated and may also suggest that unlike the *Pastoral Care* they were never intended for distribution even among the bishops.[200] It is possible, as we have found in the case of the Anglo-Saxon Chronicle, and as Whitelock suggested in regard to the Old English *Bede*, that scholars have been too ready to assume all Alfredian and related vernacular works of translation were 'published' or distributed in multiple copies during the king's reign. It may only have been the *Pastoral Care*—originally intended by Gregory as a handbook for bishops—which Alfred had copied and circulated to the bishops under his own jurisdiction.[201]

This view of the Alfredian renaissance as an essentially élitist phenomenon finds support in the fact that Alfred's preference for the promotion of the Old English vernacular did not survive as a clearly discernible continuous movement in the century after his death. From the reign of his grandson, Athelstan (924–39), and culminating in the time of Byrhtferth of Ramsey at the turn of the milennium, Latin of a convoluted and bombastic sort had largely replaced Alfredian-type vernacular prose. The origins of this hermeneutic style of Anglo-Latin have still not been satisfactorily resolved. While the immediate forebears of Athelstan's complicated Latin charters are still in some doubt, a convincing case was made by Lapidge for influence from Fleury and Brittany on Anglo-Latin hagiographers from the mid-tenth century onwards.[202] The vernacular tradition was taken up again most notably by the homilist Ælfric and by Byrhtferth in the late tenth-century. The four major manuscript collections of Old English poetry (Beowulf, Vercelli, Junius, and Exeter) all date to the period 970–1000.[203] That revival of writing Old English prose and poetry is unlikely to have owed much to the efforts of Alfred and his circle, a whole century before. We have seen how neither Æthelweard nor Ælfric showed any detailed knowledge of Alfred's translations. If there were a connection between the era of Ælfric and of Alfred, it can only be traced in a tenuous way, not through the monasteries as such, but through the bishops—those original recipients of Alfred's translations. And it can be seen too, not in the survival of some ridiculous notion of a Palace Comprehensive School, but in the survival of isolated cathedral schools as oases of learning for the chosen few. It was Bullough who observed that Oswald, bishop of Worcester and archbishop of York, received his education from his uncle Archbishop Oda of Canterbury.[204] Byrhtferth and his Ramsey school owed everything to Oswald's patronage. Ælfric, the celebrated Old English homilist, tells us that he benefited from the tuition of Bishop Æthelwold of Winchester, who took a personal interest in the monastic school attached to his cathedral church.[205] Bullough rightly suggested that Æthelwold may himself have benefited from earlier Alfredian encouragement given to the establishment of a school in Winchester.[206] But there is no justification for assuming that school was attached to the 'court'—which in Æthelwold's childhood must have had much of the aura of a royal road-show moving from farm to farm across the land. It is much more likely that just as Æthelwold took on himself the role of teacher when he became bishop, he too had once learnt his lessons in the cathedral school at Winchester. Frithestan, who ruled as bishop of Winchester from 909 until his death in 932, was clearly a man who benefited from the patronage of Alfred's son, King Edward, and his queen. The vestments which were presented to him by Queen Ælfflæd testify not only to the high quality of early tenth-century English workmanship but also to Frithestan's high standing at Edward's court.[207] Frithestan was trained for his diaconate in the days of King Alfred and that training—*pace* Dumville—was likely to have been undergone in Winchester. It is highly probable that this bishop, who may have been associated with the compilation of the Chronicle, also continued to promote the Alfredian cathedral school in Winchester during his long episcopate.[208] Frithestan's successor ruled for a mere two years, to be succeeded in 934 by Bishop Ælfheah, the record of whose saintly life would alone suggest that he was a likely prelate to take his role as a teacher seriously. Ælfheah's involvement in the cathedral school in Winchester is vouched for by a statement in the *Life* of Bishop Æthelwold to the effect that he was not only ordained to the priesthood by Ælfheah, but that he 'greatly benefited by the teaching and example of Ælfheah'.[209] Here then, we seem to have continuity, however tenuous, from Alfredian times down to Bishop Æthelwold and to his pupil, Ælfric.

The English monastic reform of the later tenth century, on the other hand, owed its main ideological inspiration to an altogether different source—to Continental reformers at Fleury and elsewhere. That reform was, needless to say, aggressively monastic in its application. It is surely significant, nevertheless, that Dunstan, Æthelwold, and Oswald were all leading members of the episcopacy and that they spearheaded those reforms from the bishoprics (Canterbury, Winchester, and Worcester) that were presumably all recipients of King Alfred's translation of the *Pastoral Care*, and of his plans (in the prefatory letter attached to that work) for the revitalizing of cathedral schools. So, in spite of the decline of monasticism in Alfredian and post-Alfredian England, it may be that Alfred's promotion of cathedral schools ensured the fragile survival of a tradition of teaching in the vernacular. However subdued and modest that survival may have been, it lingered on to glow again under the influence of men such as Ælfric and Byrhtferth, who in turn were supported by the great movement for monastic reform, as England moved towards the millennium. As for the lay lords of Wessex and of England generally—with a few very notable exceptions such as the chronicler, Æthelweard—these warlords seem to have remained illiterate and continued to rely on oral transactions right down to the Conquest—in spite of the Pseudo-Asser's nonsense about Alfred having sent them all back to school in the late ninth century.[210]

XIX

The Genuine Alfred
Pathways through the Mind of a King

Coming to Terms with a Scholarly Alfred

MOST EARLY MEDIEVAL GERMANIC KINGS WERE ILLITERATE. A FEW notable exceptions like Charlemagne and the Northumbrian Aldfrith (685–705) were remembered as patrons of learning who encouraged scholarship and the arts. King Alfred was not only a patron of learning, he was himself a scholarly writer, and through his writings—or those writings which have been attributed to him—we would seem to have a unique opportunity to glimpse the workings of the mind of a ninth-century king. But reading the words of others in the hope of gaining insights into personality and psychological make-up is at any time a parlous undertaking. No sooner has any writer committed his thoughts to paper or parchment than their original inspiration is placed at one or more removes from our grasp. When we go back a thousand years to a society and thought-world about which we understand so little, the task becomes more daunting. Ninth-century Wessex was a land where literacy was exceptional, and where the written word may well have been imbued with a power close to the supernatural. The writings of a ninth-century king were inevitably intended not just to convey his ideas or to instruct. The words of Alfred—no less than those of Gregory or Augustine which he translated—conveyed no ordinary message. They were endowed by association, in Alfred's case, with the awe of kingship, for in his own words, it was 'kings who have the most power (*anweald*) on this earth'.[1] Most ninth-century scholarly writers in the West felt little need to express original ideas of their own—so overshadowed were they by Christian scriptural tradition and by a dimly understood legacy from a Classical past. It was an age, too, when as illuminated manuscripts show, the word—lost in a labyrinth of decoration—might be more important as a vehicle for art than for its literal meaning. It is the illumination of Gospel texts which brings home to us how in Alfred's age, the written word had come to be almost worshipped in its own right. And because of the authority of Antiquity, the words of Scripture and of Classical and Late Antique writers were considered superior to the ideas of any contemporary mind. Alfred wrote in an age when passages from the Bible or from Classical authors provided learned men of his time with building-blocks to construct and adorn a written narrative which, on completion was so galvanized with Classical and biblical allusion as to smother their own thoughts. Because Alfred spent most of his time working on translations of Late Antique writers, it becomes even more difficult to get behind these texts to the mind of the king who translated them. We can, however, hope to learn a great deal from the choice of texts which the king translated and from his handling of that material.

Our understanding and appreciation of Alfred's writings are almost entirely conditioned by whether or not we view this king as an accomplished scholar grounded in the works of Classical writers from childhood, or whether we see him, along with Sisam and Whitelock, as a semi-literate who came late in life to an appreciation of scholarly endeavour. If we see Alfred as a middle-aged student struggling with vocabulary and metaphor, then we incline to interpret his digressions as precocious attempts of a self-taught rustic, striving to think things out for himself and grasping at apparently homely metaphors in his struggle to make sense of his text. Alfred is still seen to come off well from such an approach, since his supposedly homely discourses are taken to reveal the highly original but untrained mind of a man bursting with raw intellectual energy. Such a view has been imposed on modern assessments of Alfred's learning because of the constraints laid down by the 'Genuine Asser' school, which presents us with a king who could not read Latin—if he could read at all—until his thirty-ninth year. If on the other hand, we accept that this exceptional man who translated such difficult philosophical works into the vernacular, and who adapted the texts of his authors so drastically, had been familiar with these authors from his youth, then our assessment of the king's writings changes accordingly. When Alfred is perceived in this light of scholarly maturity, his preference for translating classical terminology into Old English equivalents, for instance, reveals not a man who is struggling to secure his own intellectual grasp, but rather a master, who is in such complete control of his subject, that he wishes to impart the meaning of his exemplar in the fullest possible way. We find, likewise, that however much Alfred's fondness for metaphor may reflect an original mind, it also reveals the mind of a scholar who was himself steeped in that Antique learning which made it feasible for him to attempt such an ambitious programme of translation in the first instance. For Alfred's metaphors, as we shall see, reveal the most thorough knowledge of those Late Antique writers whose works he translated.

Alfred's approach, in his translations, to Roman cultural phenomena and his substitution of Roman offices and titles with what he considered to be West Saxon equivalents is particularly illuminating. He excised references to charioteers, racecourses, and wrestling, from his version of the *Pastoral Care* and he replaced *histriones* or 'actors' in the Roman theatre with Anglo-Saxon *gligmonna*—'jesters' or 'conjurers'.[2] He rendered Gregory's herald (*praeconis officium*) as 'the office of herald (*friccan*) and footmen (*foreryneles*, "forerunners"), who run before kings, loudly proclaiming their journey and will',[3] recalling Bede's account of how King Edwin was preceded by a standard-bearer as he rode about his kingdom in times of peace.[4] So, too, in his translation of Boethius's *Consolation of Philosophy*,[5] Alfred added a local dimension to the argument. When Philosophy holds forth on the vanity of fame and asks

Where now the bones of staunch Fabricius?
Where lies unbending Cato, Brutus where?
A little fame lives on inscribed in stone,
A line or two of empty reputation.[6]

Alfred reinforced the point by substituting an Old English hero for Fabricius: 'Where now are the bones of the famous and wise goldsmith, Weland?'—referring to the Germanic smith-god, whose smithy was believed by the men of Wessex to have been in a neolithic Long Barrow on the Berkshire Downs near Uffington Castle. The Fabricius of Boethius was the Roman consul who conquered the Samnites in the third century BC and although Alfred knew who Fabricius actually was, his name had clearly suggested to the West Saxon king the idea of *fabricator* ('craftsman'), and so put him in mind of the clever artificer, Weland, whose 'smithy' on the Berkshire downs he might well have known. Weland's Smithy is close to that battlefield at Ashdown where Alfred and King Æthelred routed a viking army in 871. Alfred's determination to give his Old English rendering of Boethius a thorough-going vernacular air is seen in his decision to find Old English equivalents for the public offices of the Roman state. So the consul, Boethius, is described as a *heretoga Romana* ('Roman chief'), magistrates and senators are given as *ealdormen 7 geðeahtera* respectively, while elsewhere in the text, Roman senators are referred to as *Romana witan*.[7] We are also introduced to Roman judges (*domeras*), treasurers (*maðmhirdas*), and the 'wisest senators' (*þa wisestan witan*).[8] In the *Soliloquies*, we are introduced to a brief discussion on Roman slaves (*on þeawum*) and St Augustine's servant, Alippius, has become his *cniht*.[9] St Paul, in the *Pastoral Care*, is portrayed as a *ceorl* working as a cultivator (*landbegenga*) in God's orchard.[10] It was commendable that the king excised cultural references which were unintelligible to an English readership and added others of a vernacular nature, and the credit due to him is all the greater when we appreciate the awe in which the words of writers such as Gregory were held in the minds of men throughout the whole of the Middle Ages. Alfred's treatment of Classical terminology contrasts sharply with the policy adopted by the translator of the Old English Orosius. Some vernacular terms are employed in the Orosius translation, and *ealdormon*, for instance, is used to translate *praefectus*,[11] *iudex*,[12] and *comes*.[13] So, too, Scipio Africanus Major is described as 'the best and most excellent of the Roman senators and thegns (*se betsta 7 se selesta Romana witena 7 þegna*)'.[14] But even where the vernacular is employed by the translator of Orosius, there are differences between his usage and that of the Alfredian Boethius. So, while Alfred used *witan* to signify the Roman senators, in the Orosius we find *senatus* denotes senators, who are described as *rædþeahteras* or 'counsellors' of the Romans.[15] The translator of Orosius, unlike Alfred, preferred to retain his Latin nomenclature in regard to *consul*,[16] *senatus/ senatum* ('members of the Senate'),[17] *patricius*,[18] and *philosophus*.[19] And unlike Alfred, too, Roman customs involving the triumph (*triumphan*),[20] or the play (*plega*) and its theatre (*theatrum*)[21] are either explained in some detail or retained by the translator in their Classical form. Alfred's translation methods may reflect, in part at least, that king's personal preference for vernacular terminology and for his desire to accommodate foreign cultural elements into an English context.

Alfred's interest in promoting the vernacular does not in itself vouch for any marked originality in the mind of the king. A man of Alfred's vision and ability very probably had an original mind, but it would be rash to attribute too many of Alfred's similes and metaphors to a mental imagery prompted by his own personal experience. A case in point relates to his liking for nautical metaphors. When translating Boethius's discussion on God's foreknowledge in the *Consolation*, Alfred added the comment:

> He [i.e. God] knows it, not because he wishes it to happen, but because he wishes to prevent it from happening, even as a good steersman, by the raging of the sea, is aware of a great wind ere it come. He bids furl the sail and sometimes lower the mast, and let go the cables, and by making fast before the foul wind he takes measures against the storm.[22]

This metaphor, with its detailed reference to ships' riggings, may indeed have been inspired by personal experience. Alfred, according to the Chronicle not only organized a fleet, but he himself went to sea in 875 and defeated a viking war-party of seven ships. He must have been familiar with the basic crewing of sailing ships and he would have learnt much from his Frisian advisers. But not all recurrent nautical imagery in Alfred's writings can be put down to a consuming personal interest in boats. Alfred's close study of Gregory's works would have made him aware of Gregory's fondness for nautical metaphor. Gregory, in the introduction to his *Dialogues*, compared the journey of his soul to that of a ship battling through a storm and drifting further and further away from the harbour of tranquillity from which it first set sail.[23] That particular metaphor was, as we have seen, taken up by the Pseudo-Asser in his *Life* of King Alfred. Alfred himself had translated a similar ship metaphor of Gregory's in the *Pastoral Care*, which was employed to warn against those who are unsuitable for high office:

> An untaught steersman can very easily steer straight enough on a smooth sea, but the skilled steersman does not trust him on a rough sea and in great storms. And what is sovereignty and rule (*rice 7 ealdordom*) but the mind's storm, which ever tosses the ship of the heart with the waves of the thoughts, and is driven hither and thither . . . as if it were wrecked amongst great and many rocks.[24]

Alfred may well have been prompted by this image of the good and bad steersman to present God as the 'good steersman' who in the *Consolation* prepares his vessel against the coming storm. Alfred was aware that Boethius, like Gregory resorted to nautical metaphors and Alfred's adage: 'Surely you know that if you spread out your boat's sail to the wind, you leave all your journey to the wind's mercy'[25] was firmly based on an original passage of Boethius: 'Commit your boat to the winds and you must sail whichever way they blow, not just where you want.'[26]

It was once thought that there was no known source for Alfred's long digression in the *Soliloquies* in which he likened faith, hope, and charity to three anchors holding the ship of the mind during the terror of the storm.[27] Alfred digressed on the theme that the human soul cannot see God while engrossed in the cares of the body, and it can perceive God only through the pursuit of the virtues of faith, hope, and charity:

These are the three anchors which sustain the ship of the mind in the midst of the dashing of the waves. Yet the mind hath much comfort because it believeth and clearly knoweth that the misfortunes and unhappiness of this world are not eternal. So the ship's master, when the ship rideth most unsteadily at anchor and the sea is roughest, then knoweth of a truth that calm weather is coming.[28]

Alfred's reference here to the 'ship of the mind (*scyp ðes modes*)' is derived from the same phrase in the translation of Gregory's *Dialogues* (*in þam scipe mines modes*)[29] as is the central notion—a homiletic commonplace—of the mind or soul being tossed about by the cares of the world. That same idea resurfaces in Gregory's *Pastoral Care* where Alfred wrote of the 'mind's storm (*modes storm*) which ever tosses the ship of the heart (*ðæt scip ðære heortan*)'.[30] So, too, the notion of the prudent ship's master being able to predict the eventual calm, parallels the prediction of the coming storm by the 'good steersman' in the *Consolation*. The reference to the anchors might appear to be an original Alfredian ingredient in the metaphor, but that may not be the case. Alfred employed the anchor motif earlier in his version of the *Soliloquies*, likening the anchor cables to the way in which we fasten the eyes of the mind on God: 'Just as the ship's anchor-cable is stretched direct from the ship to the anchor, and fasten the eyes of the mind on God, just as the anchor is fastened in the earth. Though the ship be out among the sea-billows, it will remain sound and unbroken if the cable holdeth, since one end of it is fast to the earth and the other to the ship.'[31] Alfred was so fond of this metaphor he employed it a third time in the *Soliloquies* to explain the relationship between 'that which understands and that which is understood . . . as love is between the lover and the one loved. On both it is fastened, as we said before concerning the anchor-cable that the one end was fast to the ship, and the other to the land.'[32] A possible source of this powerful and effective metaphor which clearly exercised Alfred's imagination was Bede's account of Gregory's career in the *Historia Ecclesiastica* where we are told that Gregory, in order to preserve his spiritual life, surrounded himself during his busy time in Constantinople with monks from his old monastery: 'Thus, as he himself writes, through their unremitting example he could bind himself, as it were by an anchor cable, to the calm shores of prayer, while he was being tossed about on the ceaseless tide of secular affairs.'[33]

Bede's *anchorae funis* which acted as a medium to focus his thoughts on spiritual things while his ship of soul 'was tossed on the tide of secular affairs' finds an exact parallel in Alfred's *ancer-strenge* which also provided a life-line for the ship of the soul, while tossed on the ocean of the world, to fasten its eyes of the mind on God. The fact that this passage does not appear in the Old English version of Bede does not mean that Alfred did not have access to it. On the contrary, it suggests that King Alfred, Latin scholar that he surely was, was not dependent on the Mercian translation of Bede, and that he had access to Bede's original and unabridged work. Indeed, when we read Bede's full account of Gregory's career—of his spiritual achievements and his scholarly works—in the Second Book of his *History*, it is difficult to escape the conclusion that it was this source which inspired Alfred to translate the *Pastoral Care* and to have the *Dialogues* translated for him, in the first instance.

Other examples of Alfred's use of imagery, once thought to have been drawn by the king from life, may also have a literary basis rooted yet again in his profound knowledge of Gregory's writings. Alfred tells us, in his prefatory letter to the *Pastoral Care*, that those lamented well-educated English forefathers possessed good libraries and could read books, while a later illiterate generation (of the early ninth century) was made to say: 'In this [the remains of their libraries] we can still see their tracks, but we cannot follow them.'[34] Keynes and Lapidge seized on that Alfredian remark with the comment that 'Alfred's image of following the track refers to hunting; as Asser [*sic*] tells us (chapter 22), Alfred was an enthusiastic huntsman'.[35] Most early medieval kings from Connemara to Kiev were 'enthusiastic huntsmen' and there is no reason to doubt that Alfred was an exception. There is no need either, to attribute Alfred's reference to the *swæþ* ('footprint') of his forefathers, to any obsession on his part with the hunt. Gregory in his *Pastoral Care* speaks of a 'footprint (or track) in the dust (*spor on ðæm duste*)' and yet no one assumes that pope had a passion for the chase. But Alfred, on the other hand, 'translated every word' of Gregory 'into English' and pondered therefore on the expression: 'What can be more foolish than to love footprints made in the dust (*vestigia in pulvere*), and not love Him by whom they were impressed?' Whether Alfred was a hunter or not, it was Gregory who inspired this image.

The author of the verse epilogue to the *Pastoral Care* writes thus of how some readers deal with the saving waters which flow from Gregory's works:

Some damn it within their minds, the stream of wisdom, hold it with their lips, so that it flows not out to no purpose. But the well remains in the man's breast, by the grace of the Lord deep and still. Some let it flow away over the tract of land in rills. That is not a wise thing if so pure water is dispersed in murmuring, shallow streams over the fields, till it becomes a marsh.[36]

The notion of water being a symbol of Divine knowledge which may be imparted to mankind to drink, while being ultimately biblical, is essentially Gregorian. Gregory speaks in his *Pastoral Care* of teachers who 'drink very pure water when they learn the divine wisdom' and of their pupils who 'thirst for instruction but cannot drink it' because the waters of wisdom have been polluted by bad teachers.[37] Towards the end of his work Gregory admonishes that 'the teacher is first to drink of the spring of his own doctrine, and then with his instruction to pour the same water over the minds of his subjects'.[38] Alfred elsewhere in his translation of the *Soliloquies* shows he had absorbed this Gregorian imagery when he refers to God offering us 'the drink of life's well (*lyfes wylle*)' and to God himself as 'the well-spring (*æwilm*) of every good'.[39] The imagery of the stream of knowledge recurs in the prologue to the *Morals* of Gregory and is found also in the prologue to the Old English translation of Gregory's *Dialogues*—that work which Alfred tells us he commissioned to be translated by his 'true friends'.[40] The author of the verse epilogue to the *Pastoral Care* not only borrowed Gregory's motif of waters of divine wisdom, but he followed the Old English version of the *Pastoral Care* in the elaboration of the metaphor by seeing the human mind as a pool that needed to be dammed up to contain its precious contents. For in the Old English version of the *Pastoral Care* we read of dissolute people[41] that they would not 'restrain and dam up their mind as if a man weired a deep pool'. Elsewhere in the Old English text,[42] this metaphor is spelt out with clarity:

The human mind has the properties of water. When water is dammed up, it increases and rises and strives after its original place, when it cannot flow whither it would. But if the dam is thrown open or the weir bursts, it runs off and is wasted, and becomes mud. So does the mind of man . . . burst out into idle loquacity, and so is diverted various ways, as if it were all dispersed in little rivulets.

It was from this passage of the Old English *Pastoral Care* that the author of the verse epilogue unquestionably borrowed his metaphor when he spoke of men damming up the streams of divine wisdom in their minds, while others 'let it flow away over the tract of land in rills . . . in shallow streams over the fields, till it becomes a marsh'.

The author of the epilogue was so steeped in the language of Alfred's translation that even with the constraints of his verse forms, he managed to echo its own turns of phrase. This applied not just to the notion in the epilogue of 'wisdom's stream' which needed to be dammed (*Sume hine weriaⅮ . . . wisdomes stream*),[43] 'as if' according to Alfred's text of the *Pastoral Care* 'a man weired a deep pool (*swelce mon deopne pool gewerige*)'.[44] A comparison of the relevant passage from the Old English translation of the *Pastoral Care* shows how closely the author of the verse epilogue shared in the mental processes of that translator.

EPILOGUE	PASTORAL CARE
Sume hine lætað ofer landscare	*ðonne toflewð hit eall, & ne*
riðum torinnan . . . toflowed æfter	*wierð to nanre nytte, buton to fenne*
feldum, oð hit to fenne werð.	*. . . swelce hit eall lytlum riðum torinne.*

A final Alfredian touch in the epilogue to the *Pastoral Care* is the author's injunction to the would-be disciple of Wisdom: 'Let him now fill his vessel who has brought hither a watertight pitcher. Let him come back soon.' Just as the writer here likens knowledge to a source of water whither the disciple of Wisdom must return to fill his pitcher again and again, so too, in the preface to the *Soliloquies* of St Augustine, Alfred likens knowledge to a forest which yields up its supply of precious timber for those who yearn to construct a house of learning:

I neither came home with a single load, nor did it suit me to bring home all the wood, even if I could have carried it. In each tree I saw something that I required at home. For I advise each of those who is strong and has many wagons, to plan to go to the same wood where I cut these props, and fetch for himself more there, and load his wagons with fair rods, so that he can plait many a fine wall, and put up many a peerless building.[45]

Here then, the supply of water has been replaced by the forest, and the watertight pitcher by the wagon. The biblical and Mediterranean metaphors involving the precious commodity of water and the complexities of damming for irrigation have been replaced in Alfred's mind by the more appropriate English forest and its essential supply of timber for house-building. But although Alfred made his own of the house-building metaphor, he did not invent it out of thin air. That too was ultimately biblical, but could be found in less developed form in Gregory's *Pastoral Care* and in Boethius. Gregory had written: 'A strong wall must be built in a place where the ground has previously been ascertained to be firm, where the foundation is laid'[46] and again 'If a big heavy roof is placed on a new wall before it is dry and firm, not a hall but a ruin is built.'[47] In Alfred's translation of Boethius, Philosophy (personified) is made to declare: 'He that would build a house to last must not place it high on the hilltop . . . he that would build an enduring habitation should not set it on sandhills. . . . No house may stand for long on a high hill if a mighty wind assail it; nor again one that is built on crumbling sand, by reason of the heavy rains.'[48] The theme of house-building is again returned to in Boethius where God is likened to the ideal house: 'Even as the wall of every house is firmly set both on the floor and in the roof, so is every kind of good firmly seated in God, for He is both roof and floor of every form of good.'[49] Gregory's house-building, as in Boethius and later in Alfred's own preface to the *Soliloquies*, had all to do with preparing the mind for the acquisition of knowledge and virtue. The original concept behind Boethius's house-building related to peace of mind,[50] or as Alfred translated it, to securing 'the house of his mind (*hus his modes*)'.[51] It may well be that Alfred's developed hall-building metaphor in the preface to the *Soliloquies* was inspired by childhood memories of days spent watching men carting timber from a Wessex forest and planing down 'staves and props and bars . . . and crossbars and beams for all the structures which I knew how to build'. But ultimately the metaphor derives from his careful reading of Late Antique writers, and it would be rash to use it as evidence for marked originality in the mind of an otherwise naïve and self-taught king. It is the Pseudo-Asser who has prevented us from seeing Alfred as above all else a scholar of long-standing, who got his ideas from books, rather than being a self-made or miraculously-educated genius, whose rudimentary style was overloaded with homely metaphor. On the contrary, we can never overestimate the cumulative influence of ideas of writers such as Gregory and Boethius, working over many years, upon the mind of Alfred. A true picture of the maturity of Alfred's scholarly mind can never be recovered, unless we disabuse ourselves of the preposterous picture offered by the Pseudo-Asser of an eager but illiterate middle-aged man struggling in his Latin class, and replace it with the testimony of Alfred himself speaking to us in the final passages of the *Soliloquies*: 'I myself have seen in the writings of the sacred books more than I can reckon, or even can remember.'[52] Alfred was referring in this particular instance to what he had learnt of the condition of the soul after death. But in this throw-away statement—part of Alfred's own *ex tempore* discussion— we encounter a busy king looking back on life and telling us in effect, that, far from being a neophite to the world of literacy, he had forgotten as much as he had learnt from all that he had ever read 'in the writings of sacred books (*on hǽalgum bocum gewriten*)'. A man who offers us as his life's motto 'I cannot find anything better in man than that he know (*wite*), and nothing worse than that he be ignorant (*nyte*)'[53] is himself highly unlikely to have been ignorant of letters for most of his adult life. Alfred shows us in the *Soliloquies* that he held to a belief that the more one strove after wisdom and learning in this life, the better one's chances were of increasing one's knowledge as well as securing Salvation in the world to come. In contrast to the Pseudo-Asser's confused and contradictory folk traditions regarding Alfred's childhood and youth, the king himself implies that his quest for knowledge had been a deliberately planned and long-term goal: 'Therefore methinks that man very foolish and very wretched who will not increase his intelligence (*andgyt*) while he is in this world, and also wish and desire that he may come to the eternal life, where nothing is hid from us.'[54]

The Pupil of Gregory and Bede

In studying those translated works which are accompanied by an Alfredian preface, we are confronted by material which not only influenced the king's mind, but which he spent months if not years turning from Latin into Old English vernacular. However one views Payne's arguments, for instance, on the element of originality in Alfred's work on Boethius's *Consolation of Philosophy*, she successfully demonstrated the great amount of time and detailed study which Alfred gave to that text.[55] In addition to their spiritual and practical value, Gregory's ideas in the *Pastoral Care* were cast in simple form and driven home with powerful metaphors which reflected not the world of Byzantine court diplomacy which Gregory once inhabited, but that of the farmyards of Latium and Sicily. These were images which the bishops of Wessex could also easily understand. We are introduced to the cunning of curled-up hedgehogs, to the lack of wisdom of young birds learning to fly, to a rooster flapping his wings before crowing to the dawn, to Christian doctrine which is like wheat stored in a barn, to wild horses which are first subdued by soothing hands, and to the desire for riches which is like dust blown into the eyes by a high wind in a dry summer. Through imagery such as this, which was infinitely intelligible to Alfred and the great men of Wessex, a sixth-century pope led his unsophisticated readership step by step, or as Alfred put it, 'rung by rung (*stæpmælum*)', up the ladder (*hlæder*) of the human mind.[56] This ladder image held a particular appeal for Alfred, which he developed and reproduced in almost identical phrasing in his translation of the *Soliloquies*.[57] And Gregory, having beguiled his barbarian readers with a huge register of homely metaphor, led them on masterfully, to ever greater heights into a conceptual world of philosophical and abstract ideas. Alfred and his advisers struggled successfully—with the practical language in the *Pastoral Care* at least—to keep pace with the thought-patterns of this last of the Romans. So, while the mind of man, ever-changing in its make-up[58] might be compared with a deep pool,[59] the thoughts of men were likened to the stretched strings of a harp, or to pictures painted within the mind.[60] Gregory's surface and heart of the human mind are likened by Alfred to bark (*rinde*) and pith (*piðan*)[61] while the Christian church, viewed as both institution and community, was likened to an apple and its pips.[62] The spiritual director was aptly compared with the physician, cajoling and sometimes even resorting to deception in the treatment of his patient, either by concealing his knife or by offering a glass of bitter herbs sweetened with honey. With such metaphors, Gregory advised his bishops on the sensitive issues of reprimanding the powerful in an effort to curb their ambition and greed. And these were images which conditioned Alfred's thinking and powers of expression in his own writing.

We have seen how Bede's account of the letter from Pope Honorius to King Edwin recommended that the Northumbrian king read the works of Gregory. It may be no coincidence that immediately prior to recording the contents of that remarkable letter from a pope to an early English king, Bede and his Old English translator, indulged in a eulogy of the peace and prosperity which the rule of the Christian Edwin brought to his hitherto pagan people. It is here in Bede's *History* that he treats us to the folk-tale of the woman with a new-born child travelling unmolested across Britain from sea and to sea, and of bronze cups left untampered with, at wayside drinking places for travellers free to wander without fear in an idealized Christian kingdom.[63] This overblown image of the benefits of Christianity to God-fearing Englishmen and their earliest Christian warrior-kings was one of those passages in Bede that may have prompted Alfred to exaggerate his own notion of an earlier English golden age, at the opening of his prose preface to the *Pastoral Care*:

It has very often come into my mind, what wise men there formerly were throughout England, both of sacred and secular orders; and how happy times there were then throughout England; and how the kings who had power over the nation in those days obeyed God and his ministers; and they preserved peace, morality, and order at home, and at the same time enlarged their territory abroad; and how they prospered both with war and wisdom.[64]

Alfred's wistful account of those 'happy times (*gesæliglica tida*)' for England is here also echoing that other passage from the *Ecclesiastical History* where Bede—followed by his Old English translator—idealized similar happy times (*gesæligran tide ne fægeran*) at Canterbury when Theodore and Hadrian led the English to new cultural heights with their great learning and great gifts as teachers in the cathedral school: 'Never had there been such happy time since the English first came to Britain; for having such brave Christian kings, they were a terror to all the barbarian nations, and the desires of all men were set on the joys of the heavenly kingdom . . . while all who wished for instruction in sacred studies had teachers ready to hand.'[65] For Alfred, as for Bede, the golden age involved not only advances in learning but also material prosperity and victory for kings in war. Bede tells us in that same chapter of his *History* describing Theodore's Canterbury school, that 'because both of them [Theodore and Hadrian] were extremely learned in sacred and secular literature, they attracted a crowd of students into whose minds they daily poured the streams of wholesale learning'.[66] This may have prompted Alfred's comment in his prefatory letter to the *Pastoral Care* relating to those palmy days—on 'how foreigners came to this land in search of wisdom and instruction'.[67]

The scholarly Alfred shared in, and was heavily influenced by, Bede's antique view of the past, with both men believing in the existence of earlier elusive golden ages. But Alfred also encountered other perspectives on a lost golden age from his own studies of Late Antique writers. In Boethius's *Consolation of Philosophy*, we are presented[68] with an elaborate picture of a primeval age of innocence when, prior to the accumulation of riches, mankind lived in harmony and primitive simplicity. As Alfred translated it, 'each man was content with what the earth yielded'—when men as yet were blissfully ignorant of elaborate architecture, food, and clothing—when 'no merchant had gazed on strand nor island, and no man had heard tell of the pirate host'.[69] His use of the word *sciphere* ('army of ships')[70] shows the king yet again equating in his mind, the advent of the Danish onslaught with the passing of that golden order which had once prevailed in the England of Bede. In his introductory chapter to the *Consolation*, Alfred tells us how Boethius 'perceiving the manifold wrongs wrought by [his royal master, the barbarian] Theoderic upon the Christian faith and upon the chief men of the Romans, began to recall the glad times and immemorial rights they had once enjoyed'.[71] It was natural for a king in Alfred's position, who saw contemporary Christian society in England in constant fear for its survival in the face of viking attack and colonization, to look back to an earlier idyllic age such as that held up to him by Boethius or Bede. The notion of such a golden age also appealed to his political instincts, whereby he could project himself to his people as a saviour-king as well as planting in the minds of his bishops the need for urgent action in the promotion of education. For by evoking an idealized image of England's early Christian past, and by exaggerating the cultural decline in England before his reign, he was able to present himself as the restorer of a golden age which had once supposedly flourished not only in Wessex, but in England as a whole. And the Danes could be clearly seen as a common enemy of God and man against whom all Englishmen might unite under Alfred's leadership in an effort to rid the land of the forces of barbarism and restore the rule of Wisdom and the Christian heritage. The king genuinely saw himself as a champion of Christian culture in the face of barbarian threat. Hence his compelling personal interest in writers such as Gregory, Augustine, and Boethius—all of them wise and holy men living at the end of their time and heroically defending the values of a Christian and Classical past in the teeth of Armageddon. We have seen how Alfred would have sympathized with Gregory's account in his *Dialogues* of how the Lombard invader had devastated Italian monasteries and left towns and farms alike desolate in their path.

A Frustrated Philosopher

If the works of Gregory provided Alfred and his bishops with practical advice on the running of a kingdom and its Christian people, the *Consolation of Philosophy* of Boethius and the *Soliloquies* of St Augustine were more formidable works relating almost exclusively to the interior life of the individual, and which offered little by way of social and practical application. It is mistaken to assume that the Old English translations of Boethius and Augustine represent a popularization of Christian philosophy in digest form, since Alfred's commentary and additions frequently only served to complicate further what were already in themselves difficult treatises. Alfred's original strategy—in the case of the *Pastoral Care* at least—was to translate 'word for word' or 'sense for sense', which was a different matter from condensation or simplification. In the *Consolation* and the *Soliloquies*, he occasionally resorted to over-simplification, confused commentary, and outright omission of difficult passages. That was due to his own difficulties in understanding a philosophical text. This, in turn, served to confirm some modern commentators in their belief that Alfred was indeed a self-made scholar, who was converted late in life to an appreciation of Latin learning. Alfred's difficulties with Boethius and Augustine, however, have little bearing on the timetable for the king's education. They relate instead to the insurmountable difficulties posed by those particular texts. Few writers in the Christian West in Alfred's time could have attempted a translation and commentary of philosophical works, and Alfred's difficulties and failures with this particular aspect of his own work must be seen in relative terms. Alfred's translations do not on the whole set out to simplify, nor do the Alfredian additions always seek to clarify the text. The king's rearranging of material was probably inspired by his own strivings towards a better understanding of the original Latin. But in the *Soliloquies*, for instance, several of Alfred's contributions are by way of the king indulging himself in speculative discussions on topics which personally held great interest for him. The Old English treatment of Boethius's *Consolation* is disjointed and at times wooden, and does not always succeed in preserving the lucidity of the original. Not all of that was Alfred's fault. Old English was not a language which had evolved a philosophical vocabulary, nor did those who spoke and wrote it, share in an indigenous intellectual tradition stretching back over a millennium of time. It was Alfred's achievement to present his native language with the challenge of adapting itself to the requirements of the Classical intellectual tradition. If the results were not always happy, nevertheless the overall positive contribution to the development of Old English prose was incalculable and prepared the ground for the achievement of Ælfric and others a century later. In spite of the complexity of their subject-matter, Alfredian translations still succeed in conveying a powerful sense of the king's personal enthusiasm for the pursuit of knowledge.

Alfred's intellectual capabilities and his standing as a scholar are difficult to assess, not least because students of this subject have laboured for so long with the false legacy left to us by the Pseudo-Asser. Everything Alfred has written has been judged, consciously or unconsciously, on the false understanding that we are dealing with the work of a frustrated genius—of a gifted king, deprived of education in youth, who blossomed in his later life. There is no good evidence from Alfred's own writings or from elsewhere to show that the king was a late starter or a novice with Latin translation. Payne, in her detailed analysis of the Alfredian *Consolation*, on the contrary, remarked on the absence of translation errors or of failings in the use of language.[72] She also pointed to the sound methodology employed by the translator and to evidence for the translator's long and detailed study of the work.[73] We need, however, to distinguish between the technical competence and skills displayed by Alfred and his scholarly advisers, and the intellectual ability inherent in their work. The Old English Bede, in spite of its omissions, provides a stilted translation of the original *Ecclesiastical History*. The omission of documents and of much non-English material—unlike Alfred's omissions in the *Consolation* or the *Soliloquies*—was aimed not at a reworking but at a genuine abridgement of Bede's original work.[74] It has been suggested that the actual translation of Bede was executed, as in the case of the *Dialogues* of Gregory, with an over-literal approach 'retaining Latinate constructions and using a word order unnatural to English, to an extent which suggests that they [the translators] were influenced by the practice of inter-linear glossing of a text'.[75]

Here then, we have scholars—some of whom, at least, may have been working under Alfred's instructions—who were still so new to the translation process that they had not yet shaken off the mechanical approach of the classroom. In Alfred's *Pastoral Care* we still have a bookish but freer translation of a text, where we can occasionally observe the process of a scholar meticulously turning Gregory's Latin into Old English 'word for word'. But there is also greater flexibility in the translation process, and Alfredian additions help to impress the translator's stamp on Gregory's ideas and consolidate the overall vernacular effect.

Alfred's omissions and additions to the *Consolation* and the *Soliloquies* are of an altogether different order from those found in his other translations, and in those found in the translations of his West Saxon and Mercian circle. Scholars such as Schmidt have argued that Alfred was ill served by Old English as a language to express the nuances of Boethian philosophical argument and that he himself lacked the intellectual capability of grasping that argument.[76] Or put more bluntly, Alfredian omissions in the *Consolation* are due to failure and ignorance. Payne, on the other hand, denied both inadequacy of language and Alfred's intellectual limitations as the reasons for his extensive alterations to the *Consolation*. Instead, she argued for Alfred having made a detailed study of his text prior to translation; for his consistent adaptation of the work all through, as being part of an elaborate plan leading to his decision to jettison most of the Boethian material in the final or fifth book of the original work.[77] Alfred, according to Payne, did not need to face the rigours of translating the content of the final book of the original *Consolation* because he had already disposed of the necessity to reconcile divine foreknowledge and human freedom earlier on in his work.[78] Payne constructed a complex argument showing how Alfred had rejected the Boethian concept of eternity, taking God out of that alternative state of existence in an eternal present, and setting Him along with His created cosmos, in time. Alfred, having disposed of a Boethian eternity, envisaged God ruling in time, as a sort of super-king.[79] While this approach may be argued to do justice to Alfred's organizational, linguistic, and stylistic skills, it does not vouch for the king's ability to cope with Platonic philosophy. The fact that Alfred's prose is free of translation errors or that he took elaborate steps all through the text to avoid having to cope with a complex philosophical discussion in the final book, scarcely proves that the king and his scholarly team could understand that discussion. Payne attempted to reconstruct Alfred's own views on fate and freedom, foreknowledge and order, and showed how the king rejected Boethian determinism.[80] But she was forced to rely, not on Alfred's original exposition, but on what she considered was an argument that the king might have wished to present and which she believed he was capable of presenting. On her own admission she was forced to rely on reconstruction and hypothesis: 'An overwhelming mass of wisps of evidence must first be assembled, sifted and pieced together before it is apparent what his views are.'[81]

The key passage in the Alfredian Boethius must surely be the king's views on the definition of the three types of being. The first has a beginning and an end; the second a beginning and no end; and finally, God, who has neither beginning nor end. This was Alfred's cue to proceed to discuss the difference between finite and infinite states of being, and he proved unequal to the task: 'Between these three there is a great difference, but if we are to note every point thereof we shall come late to the end of this book, or never at all.'[82] Alfred's introduction to the *Consolation* (couched in the third person) promised us a translation—not an adaptation or a commentary, but here, in the closing words of his work he dodges a central issue in the Boethian text relating to the nature of the deity and the problem of reconciling foresight with free will. In the end, it comes down to the fact that Alfred and his team could not cope with philosophical discussion, and so avoided following it in detail wherever possible.[83] Their reason was not lack of linguistic skills or for their being novices in Latin, but rather because of their lack of training in dialectic. No amount of Latin grammar or Old English vocabulary could, on their own, allow Alfred or his scholars to penetrate the sense of Boethius's philosophical arguments. Those arguments were wrapped up in syllogisms requiring specialist training to unravel and to transpose from Latin into the vernacular. On Payne's own admission, Alfred tore the Boethian syllogism apart,[84] but by so doing, he precluded all possibility of arriving at a sound understanding of the philosophical core of Boethius's discussion. And so Alfred, and all his team, confronted with the north face of this intellectual Eiger, skirted its problems and arrived at their own conclusions by a much easier route—arguments based on medieval Christian dogma and apologetics. The Christian approach is neatly summed up in Alfred's robust handling of the thorny problem of *wyrd* or 'fate' and forethought in relation to the wider issue of predestination: 'Some sages, however, say that Fate (*wyrd*) rules both the happiness and unhappiness of every man. But I say, as do all Christian men, that it is divine forethought (*godcunde foretiohhung*) that rules them, not Fate.'[85]

The crucial weakness in Alfred's intellectual position is highlighted in his version of the *Soliloquies* of St Augustine by his own statement that while he already believed in the immortality of the soul, he also desired to know rather than just believe.[86] Having raised the reader's hopes for a philosophical proof on this issue, Alfred sinks into a medieval argument relying on hearsay and revelation. If one believes what one is told by one's friends and by one's lord, then how much more does one listen to the Apostles and Prophets—who tell us that the soul is immortal.[87] So, what promised to be a philosophical argument falls back on revelation. Alfred might have been excused for this contradictory approach—he may have been influenced by Augustine's *De Videndo Deo*—if he had not Augustine's text of the *Soliloquies* before him and requiring translation. The fact that he and his advisers did not feel the need to follow that text—perhaps because they failed to understand it—underlines the limitations of Alfredian scholarship. This is not the only point in the *Soliloquies* where a logical argument in the original Latin is abandoned in favour of Christian homily.[88] Even when allowance is made for corrupt textual transmission and possible dislocations in the surviving Old English twelfth-century text, there is evidence in this work at least, for mistranslation[89] as well as confusion and contradiction in the arrangement of material. So, while Alfred in his additions to the original text of the *Soliloquies* goes against Augustine's view that mortal man may attain to full knowledge of God, he makes no effort to reconcile his own opposing statements with the original views which he had translated.[90] Alfred in his efforts to explain why the mind has a natural desire to know what happened in the past—a reflection of his own highly developed historical sense—wanders off into a Platonic discussion where he accepts that the soul 'always existed since the time that God created the first man'.[91] This was a heretical position clearly at variance with Augustinian orthodoxy, which held firmly to the view that the human soul did not exist prior to the creation of the body. This unorthodox element was unintentional, and was arrived at, or rather stumbled upon, not through any intellectual conviction, but from a failure to appreciate the consequences of such a line of speculative enquiry. As in the case of the *Consolation*, while Alfred was capable of jettisoning essential original matter, he also retained inessential material from his Latin original which served only to confuse his own argument.

We are dealing with a scholar who, along with his helpers, were men laudably impelled to grapple with Christian philosophical writing, but who lacked the requisite intellectual training to grasp for themselves the concepts they had set out to translate. This can in no way lend substance to the Pseudo-Asser's contradictory tale of Alfred's status as a late starter in the world of scholarship. The intellectual shortcomings of Alfredian translations reflect not just on Alfred but on his entire team. Nor does that mean that men such as Plegmund or the historical Asser were necessarily feeble scholars. All things are relative, and because Alfred lacked the services of an Alcuin or a Johannes Scotus Eriugena does not brand him or his scholarly team as either charlatans or fools. As for the king's own scholarly ability, he stands head and shoulders above most of his European contemporaries, and he certainly outshone Charlemagne in terms of personal scholarly achievement. Alfred's handling of the *Consolation* and *Soliloquies* shows us a highly intelligent and ambitious man of mature learning, but one who was ill-equipped in striving to grasp the truths of a Late Antique philosophical discussion. The fact that he failed in that was inevitable, given that he and his scholarly helpers were all men of their time—cut off from a training in the dialectic that was crucial for the decoding and formulation of Platonic arguments. Alfred's intellectual achievement compares well with that of Gregory the Great who also attempted to convince his readers of the immortality of the soul and whose methods had a profound influence on Alfred. Towards the close of the third book of the *Dialogues* the deacon, Peter, asks Gregory 'for the spiritual good of many to set down some reason for proof of the immortality of the soul'.[92] Gregory's reply reminds us of how Alfred also raised our expectations in the beginning of the third book of the Old English *Soliloquies*:

Gregory: 'This is a work of great labour, especially for one that is busied with other affairs and hath other things to attend to. Yet if any profit may by my means redound to others, willingly do I prefer that before mine own will and pleasure. And therefore, God's grace assisting me, in this fourth book following I will clearly show that the soul doth live, after the death of the body.'[93]

Gregory's 'proofs' for the immortality of the soul are far less impressive than Alfred's attempts at philosophical discussion, but they are of a genre which had a profound influence on Alfred and on all learned men of his age in the Christian West. Gregory provided a rag-bag of anecdote, folklore, and hearsay relating to near-death experiences and ghostly apparitions. In so doing, Gregory shows us that already by the close of the sixth century, the miracle tale had taken precedence over philosophical and theological argument at the highest levels within the Christian Church. Three centuries later, Alfred, by comparison had risen to the philosophical challenge even if he had, inevitably, proved unequal to the task.

In Alfred's failure to cope with Boethian and Augustinian arguments, we observe a stubborn mind tenaciously striving to convert philosophical niceties into concrete form. Alfred was understandably weak on conceptual issues and strong on the concrete. He seized on Boethius's view of God as the fixed point at the centre of a moving circle or the centre of concentric circles.[94] Alfred transformed this Euclidian metaphor and expanded it to show how all mankind is positioned on a wagon-wheel (*wænes hweol*). Those on the hub are the happiest of men, but significantly, they are still removed from the motionless axle, which is God. 'Midmost' men (*midmestan men*) are in the middle along the spokes, and the wicked endure the full turning of the wheel of Fate out on the rim.[95] The metaphor comes under severe strain, when the axle, as God, is related to the wagon as a whole. Such analogies alone were not sufficient to enable Alfred to gain control of Boethius's argument, and indeed, they sometimes served, as here, to highlight his dilemma. For by claiming for the axle that it 'bears all the waggon and controls (or causes) all its movement' Alfred was ignoring the role of the driver, and his choice of metaphor provides a paradigm for his inability to envisage the role of God outside of time. Yet these Alfredian images, drawn from life in ninth-century Wessex—with the wagon, its wheel, spokes, and fellies—demonstrate the determination of a scholarly mind to present its own interpretation of a metaphysical problem. They also demonstrate that earthy practicality which was so essentially Alfredian. The failure of the Old English *Consolation* as a translation is not the crucial issue. The wonder is that the king who strove to repel the viking invader, and who once stood shoulder to shoulder in the shield-wall at Ashdown, should ever have had the time or inclination to attempt such an intellectual endeavour.

A King's Desire for Learning and Desire for Fame

Few people outside Alfred's immediate scholarly circle may ever have read the translations of the *Consolation* or the *Soliloquies*. Fewer still of Alfred's bishops or thegns having read or heard their king's interpretation of Boethian predestination could have even pretended to have understood it.[96] A larger number, including the Pseudo-Asser in later times, may have read the king's prefaces to these works. But the Alfredian translations, as in the case of the Anglo–Saxon Chronicle, did not have to be widely read in order to promote Alfred's image as a scholar-king. Alfred's translations, read or unread in that largely illiterate age, were sufficient in themselves to demonstrate the king's great learning and to have that learning noised abroad throughout his kingdom. The personal claim to great scholarship, which the translations of Gregory, Boethius, and Augustine undoubtedly proclaimed, must have appealed to Alfred's vanity and served to enhance his position as the Christian scholar-king in contrast to the barbarian Dane whose rule of ignorance dominated Northumbria and East Anglia. Meanwhile, the pursuit of learning for its own sake, as an élitist occupation to be shared by the king with his scholarly friends, allowed for the development of ideas which had practical as well as political ramifications. Alfred, with the help of Boethius, was developing in his own mind a new model of kingship—an essentially Christian model, of a king who relied not on terror or conquest for the enforcement of his authority. Worldly power, and ambition for ever greater glory, had their inbuilt insecurities and inevitable rise and fall, whereas in the new order, men would be ruled by a philosopher-king who had come reluctantly to power in order to prevent the tyranny of the wicked. The scholarly Alfred, as Æthelwulf's youngest son, whom few can have expected to become king, turned his scholarship to political advantage. He developed the idea in his version of the *Consolation* that the acquisition of wisdom led to power[97] and he seems to suggest, perhaps, that his own learning had helped to bring him eventually to the kingship: 'Study Wisdom then, and, when ye have learned it, contemn it not, for I tell you that by its means ye may without fail attain to power [or authority], yea, even though not desiring it. You need not take thought for power [or authority] nor endeavour after it, for if ye are only wise and good it will follow you, even though ye seek it not.'[98] Alfred had read in his original Latin text of Boethius how that scholar justified his ambition for high public office by reference to Plato's *Republic*:

It was you [i.e. Philosophy] who commended Plato's opinion that commonwealths would be blessed if they should be ruled by philosophers or if their rulers should have happened to have studied philosophy. You took your cue from him and said that the reason why it was necessary for philosophers to take part in government was to prevent the reins of government falling into the hands of wicked and unprincipled men to the ruin and destruction of the good. And it was upon this authority that I decided to transfer to public administration what I had learned from you [i.e. Philosophy] in the course of our private leisure.[99]

Alfred must have been well aware that his *witan* and thegns in the shires felt little need for a philosopher-king to combat the ferocity of viking terror. He chose to present a drastic summary of this passage, settling for: 'Is this wise Plato's adage you told me of long ago, that without righteousness no power could be just?'[100]

But however Alfred may have glossed over Boethius's original discussion, he could not have missed the special relevance it held for him. When Boethius returned briefly[101] to affirm his reluctance to assume high office, Alfred chose that statement as a cue to depart from his text and add his own *apologia* for his policies as king of the West Saxons. He followed Boethius in his opening statement that 'you know that I never greatly delighted in covetousness and the possession of earthly power, nor longed for this authority'. Then Alfred added: 'but I desired instruments and materials to carry out the work I was set to do, which was that I should virtuously and fittingly administer the authority committed to me'.[102] There follows Alfred's elaboration on what those instruments for successful government were and on his personal objectives as king. His message was clear. He had not sought the kingship, but having been made king, he demanded the wherewithal, obedience, and co-operation necessary for successful rule. In this he departed significantly from the text of Boethius who relegated the human body and all material things to a secondary position in relation to the mind.[103] Alfred's intervention in the argument at this point to stress the importance of material wealth, of work, and the necessity for action, underlines his personal awareness of the responsibilities of kingship. The motif of the reluctant ruler, who had not sought high office of his own will, ought not to be taken literally. It may have suited Alfred's personal circumstances to adopt it to himself, but it was a literary device he had encountered in the Latin of Boethius. The notion of the reluctant ruler has a long ancestry going back to Suetonius and Tacitus who vouch for the reluctance, feigned or otherwise, on the part of future emperors such as Augustus, Tiberius, and Nero to assume the responsibilities of the principate.[104] Alfred was well aware of Gregory's views on the subject in his *Pastoral Care* where he held Christ up as an example of one who shunned earthly rule,[105] and where he pointed to Moses as an ideal candidate for high office because he refused it out of humility but accepted out of obedience.[106] By the time the Pseudo-Asser had encountered this topos in Alfred's writings in the late tenth century, he crudely transformed it in his *Life* of the king to suggest ludicrously that Alfred 'could easily have taken it [the kingdom of Wessex] over with the consent of all while his brother Æthelred was alive, had he considered himself worthy to do so, for he surpassed all his brothers both in wisdom . . . and as a great warrior', and that when Æthelred died, Alfred 'had begun to reign almost unwillingly (*prope quasi invitus*)'.[107] Here we see a Classical and Late Classical motif of the reluctant ruler transformed into the confused hagiographical caricature of a self-effacing saintly super-king.

The genuine Alfred summarizes his personal attitude towards kingship in his version of the *Consolation* thus:

I have desired material for the exercise of government that my talents and my power might not be forgotten and hidden away, for every good gift and every power soon grows old and is no more heard of, if wisdom be not in them. . . . To be brief I may say that it has ever been my desire to live honourably while I was alive, and after my death to leave to them that should come after me my memory in good works.[108]

Keynes and Lapidge challenged the notion that this celebrated passage in King Alfred's writings can be taken 'as an explicit statement of Alfred's personal *credo*'[109] on the grounds that Wisdom in the *Consolation* goes on to demonstrate the futility of individual fame when set against the extent of the universe and the fact that all men in time are dwarfed by eternity. But this passage forms part of the king's personal contribution to Boethius's text, and can be seen to be a coherent expansion of the original argument. In chapter VII of the second book of the *Consolation*, Boethius begins by very briefly reminding Philosophy that he sought a life in politics, not out of ambition, but 'so that virtue should not grow old unpraised'.[110] Philosophy immediately points out the futility of 'the thought of being famed for the noblest of services to the state'[111] and goes on to remind Boethius of the vast expanse of the earth compared with even the extent of the Roman world whose fame had not penetrated the Caucasus mountains. But Philosophy, in the original text of Boethius, does not condemn the notion of a limited fame. On the contrary, she declares: 'A man should be content when he is famous throughout his own people, and his bright immortal fame will be confined within the bounds of a single nation'.[112] Philosophy is condemning rather the vanity of men who strive for a universal and immortal fame which was the prerogative of the God-head alone. King Alfred accurately rendered that same passage as 'Let every man be content to be well esteemed in his own country, for even if he desire more, he cannot attain to it, since a number of men seldom agree in liking the same thing. This is why the fame of a man remains confined to the country where has his dwelling.'[113] While Boethius does not declare himself desirous of fame—(it is left to Philosophy to accuse him of that)—Alfred, on the contrary, departs from his text of the *Consolation* and informs us of how, having come to the kingship, he strove to 'get full play for his natural gifts' by developing all the human and material resources of his kingdom. Payne rightly observed Alfred's distinction between 'good crafts rather than lying fame', and she defined *cræft* as being 'the virtue that assures that work will last, and "false fame" is the ephemeral accident of men inaccurately judging one another'.[114]

Alfred tells us he was inspired to undertake all his labours as king because 'it has ever been my desire to live honorably while I was alive, and after my death to leave to them that should come after me my memory in good works.' This is not an admission to dishonourable ambition, nor can it be properly construed as part of the original dialogue between the repentant Boethius and the lady, Philosophy. If ever King Alfred were speaking to us of the guiding principles of his life, it is surely here in this very personal and special elaboration of that theme of limited fame permitted by Philosophy in Boethius's original text. This is the statement of a king who admits to his concern for personal reputation and the judgement of posterity. This is the king who may have ultimately directed the tone of manipulative reporting on the Danish wars in the Anglo-Saxon Chronicle. This was the master of the silent argument who presented that shrewd and complicated preamble in his *Will* justifying the exclusion of his brother's children from part at least of their inheritance. This was the king, who above all else, saw History not just as a means of coming to terms with the past, but also of explaining and justifying the present. For Alfred, the judgement of History was paramount. When Boethius wrote that 'many men have been famous in their time but their memory has perished because there were no historians to write about them', he was laying emphasis on the shallowness of that fame which is dependent on the need to be written up by others. Alfred, in his translation, lost sight of the moral argument and was more preoccupied with developing Boethius's comment on the idea of historians who would fail great men by neglecting to write up their deeds! 'It has often cruelly happened, through the bad conduct of the writers [i.e. historians], that because of that sloth and neglect and carelessness, they have left unwritten the virtuous deeds of those men who in those days were most eminent and most desirous of honour.'[115] Alfred himself was leaving little to chance in the matter of writing up his own deeds and the dissemination of those works which would redound to his personal glory.

Boethius, when discussing the evils of avarice in the *Consolation*, points out that as soon as wealth is divided it becomes diminished, unlike the human voice, for instance, which is shared by 'the ears of many hearers to an equal extent'.[116] Alfred was prompted by this statement to momentarily abandon the discussion on hoarding wealth, by adding his own comment which had no place in the original argument of Boethius: 'Surely good report and good esteem are for every man better and more precious than any wealth.'[117] There was nothing novel or peculiar in the notion of a warrior-king of the Early Middle Ages longing for fame and a glorious posthumous reputation. The eulogistic court poetry of German and Celt alike, fed off the warlords' vanity and insatiable greed for immortality in the heroic verses of their bards. The bishop who wrote the verse preface to the *Dialogues* was following convention when he referred to Alfred as 'the best treasure-giver he ever heard of among earthly kings'. So, too, did the author of the poem on *Brunanburh* know how to flatter King Alfred's grandson, Athelstan—'lord of nobles dispenser of treasure to men' who 'won undying glory by the sword's edge' in what was the greatest 'slaughter of a host since the Angles and Saxons came hither from the east'.[118] What made Alfred different from other kings was his genuine love of learning and his Christian piety. His learning—immense by the standards of the day—allowed him to give direction and purpose to his desire for a far loftier type of fame and inspired him to seek after an altogether different kind of reputation from that of his royal peers. For Alfred, steeped as he was in Late Antique Christian learning, wished not to be seen or remembered as a heroic butcher of his enemies. While the Chronicle flatters his ability as a warrior and glosses over his military defeats, it conspicuously avoids the glorification of battle, and the blood-soaked imagery of Germanic epic. Boethius offered Alfred a clear opportunity to expand on the glory that accrues to a warrior who does not shrink from the fight. Boethius writes of a wise man who 'ought no more to take it ill when he clashes with fortune than a brave man ought to be upset by the sound of battle. For both of them their very distress is an opportunity, for the one to gain glory and the other to strengthen his wisdom'[119] Alfred did not rise to this bait. He dutifully recorded Boethius's reference to the warrior (*esne*) and the possibility of his acquiring fame,[120] but in spite of, or because of, Alfred's superior knowledge and bitter personal experience of the bestial and bloody realities of Dark Age warfare, the king refused to be drawn on the subject. There is nothing in Alfredian writings to match the heroic bravado in that Anglo-Saxon poem celebrating Athelstan's victory over the Northmen at *Brunanburh*. We search in vain through Alfred's writings for his thoughts on the personal experience of war and find instead a preoccupation with the life of the soul after death. Other works associated with the king reveal an all-absorbing interest in historical writing and in miracle stories narrating the deeds of long-dead holy men. It is only in the translation of the Psalms that we encounter a text which allowed a Christian warrior-king to pour out his heart on the subject of battle. The king who fought the first unsuccessful engagement of his reign 'with a small force against the whole army [of Danes] at Wilton' in 871, found a special relevance in Psalm 45: 3: 'Our enemies fell upon us so terribly that it seemed to us that all the earth shook with the tumult; and nevertheless they were frightened by God more severely than we; and their kings, lifted up like the mountains were oppressed by God's might.'[121] Alfred in his wretchedness at Athelney knew all about 'those who wish to devour my people like a loaf, who do not beseech God with good works'.[122] And he savoured, too, what he himself called that *stillness*[123] after the killing was done, when his kingdom could be rebuilt and books could be written: 'He drives back from us every attack, far beyond our borders; and he shatters our enemies bows and crushes their weapons and burns their shields. . . . Relax now, and see that I alone am God, and raise me above the foreign peoples.'[124] These allusions to conflict between Christian men and their heathen attackers, filtered as they are through the pious idiom of Scripture, are the closest we are allowed to come to the life and death struggles for hearth and home which Alfred led across the Wessex downland in the 870s.

Alfred sought to be remembered as a Christian king, who translated and disseminated Gregory's handbook on Christian leadership to his bishops, and as the thoughtful strategist in the Chronicle in the 890s, who successfully defended his Christian people against the pagan Dane. In the *Soliloquies* and *Consolation* we encounter the scholar-king who would have us see him struggling with the complex ideas brought forth by the great minds of Late Antiquity. Alfred had an enquiring mind and a natural curiosity about the past, but unlike Bede he never engaged in historical investigation as such, nor was he conscious, as was Bede, of the need to cite historical sources. Alfred justified his interest in and monitoring of historical records with the same standard argument as that used by Bede and other hagiographers—namely that writing up the deeds of a just man would inspire others to imitate them. At the end of the fourth book of the *Consolation*[125] Alfred returned to his ruling obsession—the importance of History for providing us with lessons for the present:

Ah! ye wise men; walk, all of you, in the way pointed out by the famous examples of the noble ones and the ambitious men that lived before you! Why will ye not enquire after the wise men and those that coveted honours, what manner of men they were that came before you? And why will ye not, when you have found out their manner of life, copy them with might and main? For they strove after honour in this world and set themselves to win good report with good works, and wrought a goodly example for those that came after.

Boethius would not have been pleased to find this passage tagged on to his work which was so diametrically opposed to the notion of striving after honour and earthly glory. But here yet again, Alfred reiterates his personal desire for 'striving after honour . . . to win good report'. In passages such as this we draw as near as we can ever hope to come to those ruling principles in Alfred's life—from which the king drew his great strengths and some weakness.

King Alfred's third book of the *Soliloquies* is a speculative discussion on the condition of the soul in the afterlife. In it the king himself attempts to answer questions such as whether the intellect of the soul will be increased in the next life? Will the elect of God be aware of the sufferings of the damned? Will the damned know of the joy of the those who are saved? Will all the elect enjoy the same degree of wisdom? This is not a subject which was ever central to Christian writing and reveals Alfred's speculative mind and a curiosity in relation to the afterlife. It reveals, too, as we have seen, a more sophisticated curiosity than that which is evident in the fourth book of Gregory's *Dialogues* which dealt with the same subject. Although this section of the *Soliloquies* relies on Augustine's *De Videndo Deo* and on the works of Gregory, Alfred offers what is probably his own idea that the more we strive after wisdom in this life, the wiser we shall be in the world to come: 'One is also not to suppose that all men have like wisdom in Heaven; but each has it in that measure which he here yearneth after. As he here toils better and yearns more for wisdom and righteousness, so he has more of it there, and also greater honour and greater glory.'[126] This is a scholar's view of a scholar's Heaven, where one is not only rewarded proportionately for a virtuous life, but where one may enjoy an intellectual superiority as well.

Alfred's View of Kingship

The Old English translation of the *Soliloquies* has been recognized to 'show a thorough knowledge of the life and thinking of a king'.[127] In his preface, Alfred writes (metaphorically) of a man building a home on land leased by his lord.[128] This lease (*læn*) is compared with the permanent tenure attached to *bocland* which is granted 'through the favour of his lord (*þurh his hlafordes miltse)*'.[129] The recipient is seen as a magnate rather than a mere *weorcmann*, who enjoys the hunting, fowling, and fishing rights that go with his lord's property. Several of Alfred's lengthy additions to the *Soliloquies* hinge on the concept of lordly patronage or on an understanding of the relationship between a lord and his magnates. To achieve this, Augustine, in the dialogues of the Alfredian version of the *Soliloquies*, is frequently cast in the unlikely role of a ninth-century king's man. He is asked for his reaction when a letter (*ærendgewrit*) with the seal (*insegel*) from his lord (*hlaford*) should come to him, whether he would understand its message and whether he would be willing to carry out his lord's wishes.[130] It is pointed out that the lord's friendship as the source of all patronage is more important than any riches received, and Augustine is commended by Reason for the loyalty, love, and fear which he exhibits towards his earthly lord:—'very rightly and very becomingly thou dost (*swiðe rihte and swiðe gerisenlice þu dest*)'.[131] While the ultimate argument in the *Soliloquies* is that God deserves so much more love than an earthly lord, nevertheless, the emphasis falls on the power of the earthly ruler as a yardstick for what is worthy of respect, fear, and love in this world.

To survive as king of the West Saxons, Alfred had every need to be wary of his closest and his most powerful thegns, and to penetrate beyond outward appearances to unmask resentment or hidden ambition. There is little by way of direct discussion in Alfred's writings of a king's fear of rebellion and deposition. What discussion there is, tends to concentrate—because of the didactic nature of the original Latin writings which Alfred translated—on the evils of tyranny and the rule of proud kings. But even this material, which at first sight might seem to operate to the disadvantage of those in royal authority, is put to advantage by Alfred. Gregory, while condemning proud kings in the *Pastoral Care*, and showing how Old Testament rulers were punished for their pride, was at pains to show that he was not against legitimate power. Indeed, Alfred could use Gregory's ideas to argue that rival candidates who were morally flawed ought to be excluded from high office in the first instance:

I do not blame great works nor legitimate power, but I blame a man for being conceited on that account; and I would strengthen the weakness of their hearts, and forbid the incompetent such desires, lest any of them presume to seize on power (*rice*) or the office of teaching (*lareowdom*) so rashly, lest those attempt such dangerous paths who cannot stand firmly on level ground.[132]

Alfred could have used this passage with effect against the rival claims of his nephew, Æthelwold, and his followers, who were ultimately to rebel against his son, Edward the Elder. Reason, in the *Soliloquies*, while discussing the degree to which Augustine would like to know God, compares that knowledge with how well Augustine understands his servant, Alippius.[133] Asked whether he understood Alippius with the outer senses or with his mind, Augustine replies: 'I know him now as well as I can know him with the external senses; but I should like to know his mind.' 'Then', adds Alfred in his translation 'I should know what his loyalty was toward me (*Ðonne wiste ic hwilce treowða he hæfde wið me*)'.[134]

A king needed to know his leading thegns individually and collectively, and Alfred reveals the cynicism with which a ruler viewed his court on those occasions when his followers thronged about him. Alfred uses that analogy to explain how the elect after death, and before the final Judgement at the end of time, view the saved and the damned: 'The good, then, who have full freedom, see both their friends and their enemies, just as in this life lords and rulers (*rice men*) often see together both their friends and their enemies. They see them alike and know them alike, albeit they do not love them alike.'[135] Court intrigues are touched upon, with the possibility that the will of an opposing party of magnates may be imposed on a reluctant king. So, we read of how 'some king in this world may have driven one of his favourites (*hys deorlinga*) from him, or he may have been forced from the king against both of their wills'.[136] We are reminded of the exile of Dunstan from the court of Alfred's great-grandson, Eadwig, in *c*.956.[137]

Alfred's concern for the proper government of the shires and for the loyalty of his thegns there is reflected in the *Pastoral Care*. He railed against idle lordship where a slothful ruler remained inactive himself and refused to admit the intervention of his own lord over the neglected territory.[138] Alfred elaborated on Gregory's treatment of the unjust servant in Matthew (24: 48) to warn any of his bishops or ealdormen against abusing their power in the provinces:

He is very rightly accounted a hypocrite who, while seeming to teach, turns the ministry of that authority into lordship (*ða ðenenga ðæs ealdordomes gecierð to hlaforddome*) and causes the reverence of himself and his power to become the regular custom of the country he rules (*to landsida on his scire*). And yet sometimes they sin more by making themselves the companions and equals of the wicked and unrighteous rather than exercising their authority.[139]

Revealing, too, is the evidence that the translator of the *Soliloquies* was neither an ascetic nor a scholarly recluse. On the contrary, he was man of substance obligated to support a following, and those obligations, like the images drawn from the metaphor of the court, reflect the thoughts of one who lived a public life. When Reason cross-examines Augustine as to whether he wishes for wealth, the translator intervenes to make a special case. The original answer was clearly 'no', with the comment 'Though enough should come to me, I would not rejoice very much.' But Alfred adds the qualifier: 'Nor would I gain more to keep than I could fitly make use of, and keep and support the men on, whom I must help.'[140] When Augustine is challenged about his desire for food and meats, Alfred cannot settle for the Augustinian minimum to keep body and soul together: 'Howbeit, I need much more for the wants of those men which I must take care of, and moreover this I needs must have.'[141] This was a firm intervention on the part of a king whose very survival rested largely on his ability to equip, feed, and house his camp followers during peace and war. We are reminded of Alfred's alteration in Boethius's argument to make allowance for legitimate material wealth and his justification there for work and action.

It was natural for men of the early Middle Ages in the Christian West to view the relationship between God and his people in the light of a king's relationship with his subjects and followers. An indication of how close the parallel had been developed in Ireland is found in the term *Céli Dé* as the name given to a group of monastic reformers in the eighth and ninth centuries. *Céli* were the leading companions of a secular lord—equivalent to thegns in West Saxon society—and so *Céli Dé* were the 'Companions of God'. The *Soliloquies* exploit this model of the lord-and-man relationship as applied to the spiritual life, to the full. So, a life of sin is equated with serving 'an unrighteous lord (*unryhtum hlaforde*)' and repentance is seen as joining the household (*hyred*) of God.[142] Alfred refers to God as 'my ruler (*min gemetgyend*) . . . my house (*min hus*) and my landed inheritance (*min eDel*)' and he refers to himself as God's slave or servant (*ðeawa*).[143] We have already encountered Alfred's argument in the *Soliloquies* that a man should believe implicitly what he is told by his lord (*hlaford*)[144] 'whom thou trustest in all things better than thyself'. Such ideas are also apparent in the translation of Boethius's *Consolation*, where Philosophy taunts Mind for reproaching Worldly Fortune when it had let him down, reminding him that once having agreed to serve Fortune, he should take the rough with the smooth: 'If', wrote Boethius, 'after freely choosing her [Fortune] as the mistress to rule your life, you want to draw up a law to control her coming and going, you will be acting without any justification.'[145] Alfred, who viewed the discussion from his viewpoint as a king, translated:

If however you wish to be its [i.e. Fortune's] follower (*þegn*), you must do cheerfully what belongs to its service (*þenungu*), in obedience to its nature and its will; and if you would have it put on other garb than is its will and its wont, are you not then doing yourself a dishonour (*unweorþast*), in that you are rebelling against the lordship (*hlafordscipe*) you yourself have freely chosen?[146]

The obligation on men to accept the authority of their lords is apparent in all the works translated by King Alfred, but we observe a marked shift in the balance of mutual responsibility in this matter as we move from Gregory's *Pastoral Care* to the *Soliloquies*. This is partly due to the nature of the *Pastoral Care* and partly to the fact that Alfred followed it more closely than in his other translations. But since Alfred's treatment of the *Soliloquies* allowed him greater freedom of personal expression, we can assume that the ideas expressed on lordship in the Alfredian passages there conform more closely to the king's own views. In the *Pastoral Care*, Gregory sets out a carefully balanced view of the relationship between lord and man:

The servant (*ðeow*) is to be told to know that he is not independent (*freoh*) of his master (*hlaford*). It is to be made known to the master that he is to understand that he is the fellow-servant (*efnðeow*) of his servant (*ðeowe*). The servant is commanded and thus addressed: 'Be subject to your worldly masters (*worldhlafordum*).' And again, it is said: 'All who are under the yoke of authority (*hlafordsciepes*) must hold their masters worthy of all honour and respect.' And again it is said: 'Ye masters, do the same to your men after their measure, moderating your threats; consider that both their master and yours is in heaven.'[147]

We also need to take into account that in the *Consolation*, Alfred elaborates on Boethius's original sketch of the rule of evil tyrants[148] painting a picture of 'unrighteous kings (*unrihtwisu cyningu*)' who indulge in inordinate displays of pomp and luxury and who become slaves to their own passions. At first sight, Alfred appears to be condemning only the pomp of these rulers: 'seated on high seats; they are bright with many kinds of raiment, and are girt about with a great company of their thegns, who are decked with belts and golden-hilted swords and war dress of many kinds, threatening all mankind with their grandeur.'[149] But Alfred, following Boethius's understanding of Plato, goes on to show that because they are essentially evil men, such rulers cannot achieve any good. His emphasis on the gaudy display of weaponry and on the warrior-king enthroned on his 'high seat (*heahsetl*)' surrounded by 'a great company (*miclon geferscipe*)' of thegns decked out in battle-harness (*heregeat*) echoes Old Icelandic literary images of Norse kings presiding over their warriors from a 'high seat'. It may be that Alfred was equating the rule of evil kings with his enemies in the Danish warband, such as Guthrum who ruled over East Anglia, or more distant Danish warlords who ruled more aggressively from York.

However Alfred may have condemned the unrighteous king, his own preoccupation with the awesome powers attached to kingship cannot be doubted. When we turn to the *Soliloquies*, we find a view of lordship expressed there, which places kings on a plane beyond the reach of other mortals. While comparisons between the omnipotence of God with the impressive powers of an earthly king were commonplace in the Middle Ages, it is the degree to which Alfred develops this theme in the *Soliloquies* which is remarkable. And while the object of the discussion is ever to demonstrate the limitless power of God as creator, lord, and judge of mankind, nevertheless the treatment of the rôle of an earthly king in the *Soliloquies* reveals a preoccupation with the awesome power of kingship. The omnipotence of God is demonstrated by the fact that 'he rules kings, who have the most power (*anweald*) on this earth'.[150] The dreaded effects of a king's justice towards the guilty is used as an analogy for the condition of the damned at Domesday. 'The wicked see God as the guilty man (*scyldiga man*) who is condemned before some king.'[151] The anguish of the condemned is made the greater when he sees the king surrounded by his favourites, while the joy of the king's favourites (*kinges deorlinges*) is proportionately the more, when they view the plight of the damned. So too, the damned in the next life, who suffer the added agony of observing the joy of the blessed, are compared with the powerless plight of 'men in this world brought into the prison of some king'[152] and whose friends are of no avail to them. Kings, by implication, are likened to God in His triumphant rôle as judge at Domesday. This in turn ties in with the Alfredian notion in the *Consolation* that God is 'an exceedingly powerful king (*swiðe rice cyning*)' and that the cosmos is his kingdom, peopled by freemen—angels and mankind.[153]

This powerful image of kingship which Alfred presents us with in the *Soliloquies* is reinforced by the comparison of royal power with that of the sun. This solar metaphor may have been inspired by Gregory who wrote in his *Pastoral Care* of the benevolent ruler 'who is ready to shine over it [his territory] with the sun of good works'.[154] In a justly celebrated passage, in which Alfred discusses how men come to Wisdom in different ways and attain to it in different degrees of excellence, he compares that process with the arrival of men at the court of their king. They come from far or near, by easy or difficult routes, and on arrival they each enjoy a greater or lesser degree of favour from their king: 'Yet all of them', writes Alfred, 'live through the one lord's favour (*be anes hlafordes are*), just as all men live under the one sun and by its light see everything that they see.'[155] Alfred's lofty view of his own kingly position, as revealed in his own writings, contrasts strongly with the Pseudo-Asser's later hagiographical picture of Alfred as a neurotic invalid. The genuine Alfred was indeed a man of great Christian piety. But that piety led him to ever loftier and more robust views of his own God-like rôle as king, along with a corresponding obsession with the unswerving loyalty and service due to him from his thegns. As legitimate king, Alfred saw himself occupying that more dangerous Gregorian high ground (*frecne stige*), while lesser mortals lived out their lives on the level plain (*on emnum felda*).[156] Alfred, as revealed to us through his writings, saw his kingship as a reflection of divine power on earth. And if his kingship were God-like, it was an easy step for Christian men under Carolingian influence to accept that it was God-given. He refers to himself, somewhat ambiguously and twice in his *Will*, as 'king by the grace of God (*cingc mid Godes gife*)'.[157] Such a formula need not surprise us. Alfred's father, King Æthelwulf, referred to himself as *gratia Dei rex*;[158] and as *Deo auxiliante rex*[159] in contemporary charters. Alfred's daughter, the queen (*hlæfdige*) Æthelflæd, and her husband, Æthelred ealdorman of the Mercians, can be seen to aspire to the *Dei gratia* formula in a contemporary charter issued by them in favour of Wenlock Abbey in 901.[160] But in his preface to Gregory's *Dialogues* Alfred presents us with the full weight of his own perception of the Divine origin of what he saw as his immense royal dignity and authority: 'I, Alfred, honoured with the dignity of kingship (*cynehades*) through Christ's gift . . . to whom God has granted such a lofty station of worldly office (*swa micle heanesse worldgeþingða*).'[161] Alfred not only saw his kingship as God's gift, but he saw that the office, once given, entailed immense power. This Alfredian emphasis on the power of the king was a significant advance on Bede's formula addressed to King Ceolwulf of Northumbria whom Bede saw as ruling those 'whom divine authority has appointed you to rule'.[162] For churchmen, kingship was a gift. For Alfred, as king, it was a gift that carried immense power. There is little sense here of the Pseudo-Asser's humble king constantly on his knees and praying for sickness. The king envisaged in Alfred's *Soliloquies* is far removed, too, from the picture of the impractical and all-forgiving Count Gerald of Aurillac as found in the *Life* of that Frankish ruler, which inspired the Pseudo-Asser for his *Life* of King Alfred. While the saintly Gerald ordered his warriors to fight with the blunt edges of their weapons to avoid spilling human blood, Alfred in his preface to the *Pastoral Care* held up early English Christian warrior-kings as an example to follow for having 'extended their territory outside, and how they succeeded both in warfare and in wisdom'. Alfred saw the just king as leader of his warband, who needed an ample supply of *fyrdmen* or 'fighting men' well supplied with weapons (*wæpnu*) to enable him to succeed as a king,[163] and he saw himself as obligated to use legitimate force in the furtherance of Christian kingship. So, while Gerald failed to act against a thief who stole two of his pack-horses, and secretly released other malefactors from his own prison, Alfred's ideal king presided over a prison where its condemned inmates languished without hope of succour or reprieve.[164] That Alfred could make his prisoners pay the ultimate penalty is shown in the Chronicle. When Danish castaways on the Sussex coast were taken to Winchester in 896, Alfred ordered them to be hanged, and he may even have directed that this detail of his firmness be recorded in the Chronicle.

Yet another indication of Alfred's lofty view of his own position in the world is provided by his use on several occasions of the image of society at large as a tool in the hands of God or of a king. He writes of God working through mankind 'as with some powerful tool (*swa swa myd sumum gewealdnum tolum*)'.[165] This is not at all the same thing as the idea of seeing God (as Alfred also protested) as our co-worker (*mydwyrhta*).[166] The passage in Paul's First Letter to the Corinthians (I Cor. 3: 9–10) to which Alfred alludes probably inspired his thoughts in this discussion and may also have helped to develop his ideas on the house-building metaphor which he employed in the preface to the *Soliloquies*: 'For we are partners working together for God, and you are God's field. You are also God's building. Using the gift that God gave me I did the work of an expert builder, and laid the foundation.' But while St Paul saw himself engaged in a partnership with his people, and while Gregory spoke of the master as a fellow-servant (*efnþeow*), Alfred saw his own subjects as tools in his hand—a means to an end to allow him fulfil his awesome task as king. For just as Christian people in the *Soliloquies* were the tools of God, so in the *Consolation*, the people under Alfred's authority were the tools of his kingly trade:

Now no man, as thou knowest, can get full play for his natural gifts, nor conduct and administer government, unless he hath fit tools (*tolu*), and the raw material to work upon. By material I mean that which is necessary to the exercise of natural powers; thus a king's raw material and instruments (*andweorc 7 his tol*) of rule are a well-peopled land, and he must have men of prayer, men of war, and men of work. As thou knowest, without these tools (*tolan*) no king may display his special talent (*cræft*). Further, for his materials he must have means of support for the three classes (*geferscipu*) above spoken of, which are his instruments . . . Without these means he cannot keep his tools in order, and without these tools he cannot perform any of the tasks entrusted to him.[167]

Alfred in this passage refers to his people in terms of a tool (*tol*) or natural resource no less than seven times, as he also refers repeatedly to his craft (*mine cræftas*) as a king.

The House of Knowledge

Alfred returned to the image of himself as the master craftsman in a somewhat different context in his preface to the *Soliloquies* when he writes of gathering the materials 'for each of the tools (*tola*) that I knew how to work with' to build the house of knowledge.[168] The tools in this instance were his team of scholars and the instruments of learning—materials, books, and libraries. That metaphorical house was actually a complex series of structures (*weorca*)—encompassing all knowledge, and therefore including the 'craft' of kingship and the search for wisdom and for Christian Salvation. Alfred tells that in order to construct those buildings 'which I knew how to build' he carted off from the forest of wisdom 'the finest timbers I could carry'.[169] Only a man of the Pseudo-Asser's poor understanding and sensitivity could have interpreted Alfred's metaphor to mean that the king referred to himself literally as a skilled tradesman. In this mishandling of Alfredian metaphor, the Pseudo-Asser reveals himself yet again as a man writing far removed from the time of King Alfred, and as a man wholly reliant on earlier written sources which he so poorly understood. With the opening lines of Alfred's preface to the *Soliloquies* in his mind, the Pseudo-Asser embarked on a fantastic account of Alfred as master-builder: 'Meanwhile the king, in the midst of wars and frequent hindrances of this present life . . . did not cease to govern the kingdom . . . to erect buildings (*aedificia*) to his own new design (*sua machinatione facere*), more stately and magnificent than had been the custom of his ancestors.'[170] The Pseudo-Asser in his frantic attempt to lend an air of originality to his biography repeated his claim for Alfred as the great builder, again and again in the *Life* of the king: 'What of the buildings (*aedificiis*) beyond compare (*incomparabiliter*) made by his instructions with gold and silver? And what of the royal halls and chambers constructed admirably (*mirabiliter*) in stone and timber at his command?'[171] These claims descend to the level of the ludicrous when we read that Alfred even 'freely bestowed many excellent buildings (*multa et optima aedificia*) on him [Guthrum] and all his men',[172] after the defeat of the Danish warband at Edington in 878. Stevenson, although he was well aware that *aedificia* was the word used in the earliest surviving texts for this passage in chapter 56, followed earlier editors of the *Life* of Alfred, and amended the word to *beneficia* ('gifts') although he admitted 'we have failed to find any instance of *aedificia* having the meaning of gifts'.[173] On the other land, Stevenson, quite remarkably, accepted the meaning of 'buildings' for what are clearly legendary gold and silver artefacts described in typical Byrhtferthian Latin in chapter 91 of the *Life* of Alfred.[174] Keynes and Lapidge, on the other hand, while admitting to being baffled by what the author of Alfred's *Life* meant by *aedificia*, doubtfully translated the word in all instances as either 'treasures' or 'craft'.[175] But the same authors cast their reservations regarding Alfred's qualifications as a builder to one side, when they came to comment on the king's use of the house-building metaphor in the preface to his *Soliloquies*. There they invited readers to consult the *Life* of King Alfred where they would learn (chapter 76) that the king constructed *aedificia* 'to his own specifications'.[176] Carnicelli, who was similarly deluded by the ramblings of the Pseudo-Asser, mused that 'Alfred was skilled in woodcraft and in constructing houses'.[177] The wonder is that modern scholarship has not come up with the suggestion—based on that justly famous Alfredian metaphor of the wagon-wheel of Fate in the *Consolation*—that Alfred was a professional wheelwright.

We are told by the Pseudo-Asser that Alfred gave the second portion of half his entire annual revenues from taxation 'to the craftsmen (*operatores*), whom he had with him in almost countless number, collected and procured from many races, who were men skilled in every kind of earthly building craft (*in omni terreno aedificio*)'.[178] We are asked to believe that Alfred assembled this international throng of builders, to whom he gave one-sixth of his entire annual revenues. The notion is of course preposterous, and were we even to begin to take it seriously, we should expect to find Alfred referring to such an army of specialized craftsmen in his detailed exposition on the requirements of a king in the *Consolation*. We seek in vain for any specific mention of builders or other craftsmen among the king's *weorcmen* who clearly worked the land as serfs, and who as such are set in apposition to the king's warriors or *fyrdmen*. We have seen how the Ramsey writer of Alfred's *Life* indulged in an unreal schematization of King Alfred's finances, dividing them first into two, and then dividing the first half into thirds and the second half into quarters. That plan was influenced by the writer's own preoccupation with numerology, which at the time was characteristic of Byrhtferth and his Ramsey school at the end of the tenth century. But those unreal divisions were most likely suggested to the writer of Alfred's *Life* in the first instance from his knowledge of Alfred's own less complicated schematized view of society in the *Consolation*. Alfred's triple division of 'praying men, fighting men and working men' must have appealed to the Pseudo-Asser's obsession with numerology and with the making of unreal divisions. It may well have prompted him to invent the notion in the first instance, that King Alfred divided up his income between the needs of God (*Deo devovit*) and for his fighting men (*bellatores*), craftsmen (*operatores*), and foreign visitors.[179] Significant here is the fact that the Pseudo-Asser's *bellatores* and *operatores*[180] translate Alfred's *fyrdmen 7 weorcmen* respectively, while the Pseudo-Asser's allocation for God with its subdivisions for the poor, for various monasteries, and the royal school, may be said to cover Alfred's own classification of 'those who pray' (*gebedmen*).[181] But Alfred's *weorcmen* were in reality, toilers in general—the equivalent of the Carolingian serfs—those farm labourers upon whom the other two orders—of clergy and warrior aristocracy—depended for their incomes. The Pseudo-Asser, on the other hand, chose to interpret their *weorc* in the narrowest sense of 'building', and so we arrive at the ridiculous notion that King Alfred's *operatores* made up a great army of builders producing *aedificia* all over his kingdom.[182]

Byrhtferth of Ramsey offers us virtual proof that Alfred's house-building metaphor in the preface to the *Soliloquies* was known to him and his circle at Ramsey in the late tenth and early eleventh century. In explaining to his readers how to determine the correct time of Easter, Byrhtferth, in his chaotic way, digresses with a metaphor: 'We first of all survey the site of the house, and also hew the timber into shape, and neatly fit together the sills, and lay down the beams, and fasten the rafters to the roof, and support it with buttresses, and afterwards delightfully adorn the house. These things we say with reference to Eastertide.' Byrhtferth proceeds immediately to develop his bee metaphor, which, as we have seen, recurs in the *Life* of King Alfred.[183] Although the technical terms used in Alfred's house-building (*kigclas, stuþansceaftas, lohsceaftas, bohtimbru,* and *bolttimbru*) differ from those used by Byrhtferth (*syllan, beamas, ræftras,* and *cantlum*), nevertheless, we are dealing with essentially the same figure of speech set out in remarkably similar detail. Since the preface to the *Soliloquies* pre-dates Byrhtferth's *Manual* by more than a century, and since the house-building metaphor was so distinctively Alfredian and so easily accessible at the very opening of Alfred's preface, it is likely to have inspired Byrhtferth's attempt. The difference in the technical terms used for the building beams and planks may be accounted for by dialectal differences between usage in East Anglia and in Wessex, and by the fact that the imagery entailed in this metaphor is so graphic and so close to everyday medieval experience that it encourages freedom of expression and choice of colloquial words on the part of a vernacular writer. Every Old English writer was aware of those dialectal household words used to describe parts of wooden homes in Anglo-Saxon England, but only Alfred and Byrhtferth put those terms to use in precisely the same style of meta-phor. Crawford noted how Byrhtferth's reference in his *Manual* to 'the brook (*burnan*) from which they [young monks who were his pupils] can drink a salutary draft and also leave a fair heritage of learning to others'[184] echoes the sentiments of the epilogue to Alfred's translation of the *Pastoral Care*. Such borrowings in Byrhtferth's prose are what we should expect from a man who belonged to a circle of monastic scholars who had studied Alfred's life and writings in detail. The Pseudo-Asser—a writer from the Ramsey circle—refers to the *Dialogues* of Gregory having been translated at Alfred's command[185] and actually quotes Gregory by name in his *Life* of Alfred,[186] offering a (Latin) rendering of a passage from the *Pastoral Care*, which is not based on Gregory's original Latin and which may represent a resume of Alfred's Old English version.[187] The Pseudo-Asser's know-ledge of the translation of Gregory's *Dialogues*, together with his verbal echoes of King Alfred's own prose preface to the *Pastoral Care* takes on added significance in the light of Byrhtferth's obvious interest in such texts—both the translations from the Alfredian era and their Latin originals. Lapidge observed that Byrhtferth of Ramsey 'had an intimate knowledge of Boethius'[188] and that he had 'absorbed it [the *Consolation*] more enthusiastically than anyone else'.[189] We may add the Alfredian preface to the *Soliloquies*, if not the *Soliloquies* themselves, to the list of books available to Byrhtferth and his circle, and we recall that the Pseudo-Asser was very likely prompted to identify the manuscript which he consulted of the Alfredian *Soliloquies* with a supposed handbook or *enchiridion* of King Alfred.

The Trials of a King

The final and most damaging distortion by the Pseudo-Asser, of Alfred's life and personality, centred on a misunderstanding—wilful or otherwise—of Alfred's rhetorical statements on the trials of a king. Alfred speaks of the need in his preface to Gregory's *Dialogues* to calm the mind 'amidst these earthly anxieties (*betwix þas eorþlican ymbhigdo*)' by reading books that would allow him to reflect on heavenly matters 'amidst these earthly tribulations (*betwih þas eorðlican gedrefednesse*)'.[190] Elsewhere he tells us how he 'began among other various and manifold troubles of this kingdom (*mislicum & monigfaldum bisgum ðisses kynerices*), to translate into English the book which in Latin is called *Pastoralis*, [and] in English "Shepherd's Book".'[191] This emphasis on the cares of government which rested on Alfred's shoulders reappears in the preface to the *Consolation of Philosophy* where it is stated that Alfred's translation has been achieved in spite of 'the various and manifold worldly cares that often troubled him both in mind and body (*for þam mistlicu 7 manigfealdum weoruldbisgum þe hine oft ægðer ge on mode ge on lichoman bisgodan*)'.[192] When Alfred turned his attention to translating the Psalms, he introduced Psalm 3 with the observation that 'everyone who sings this psalm does . . . [like David] lament his tribulations of either mind or body' and he identified Psalm 45 with the comment that 'David sang this forty-fifth psalm, thanking God that he had released him from his many afflictions'.[193] In his preface to the *Soliloquies* Alfred laments that he has not yet achieved the ease of life (*murge and softe*) that he longs for.[194] All of these rhetorical statements occur in prefaces or prologues to works of the king, or to works carried out under his direction. It was a commonplace for authors in antiquity and in the early Middle Ages to plead either rusticity in their literary style or to point to the cares of high office by way of excusing their literary imperfections. Such rhetorical modesty is frequently and for obvious reasons found in prefaces and epilogues. While the Pseudo-Asser interpreted Alfred's complaints about the burden of office as physical weakness and disease in an ascetic ruler, Alfred on the contrary pointed to his 'worldly cares' as sign of strength—underlining the huge responsibilities which he shouldered and which set him above other men as king. Alfred himself had translated that passage in Gregory's *Pastoral Care*[195] where Moses's acceptance of the leadership of Israel is analysed. We are told how Moses was correctly reluctant yet agreeable to accept 'so great a sovereignty (*swæ miclum ealdordome*)'.[196] More ambitious mortals are castigated however for aspiring to undertake the 'dignity and burden (*weorðscipe 7 byrðenne*)' of office while being unable to carry their own burdens much less those of others. Elsewhere, Gregory speaks of those 'who have neither age nor wisdom' who assume 'the burden of so arduous a ministration (*ða byrðenne swa micelre ðenunge*' as that of a bishop.[197] While public duties were envisaged as a burden carried by the conscientious and philanthropic ruler, so too, it was a commonplace of Classical and Late Antique literature to speak of the tranquillity that comes from solitude and peace of mind. Alfred had translated that passage in Boethius which spoke of true happiness as 'the one resting place from all our toils . . . this haven alone is ever calm after all the storms and billows of our hardships'.[198] For Alfred the warrior-king and scholar, there was clearly a very real tension between the conflicting demands of his public life and his personal desire for learning. Few parts of Gregory's *Pastoral Care* can have held his attention as much as the discussion on the balance between a life of action and reflection:

Let not the ruler forsake the inner care of the divine ministration for the occupation of outer works, nor let him diminish his care of inner government for outward occupations; lest he be hampered by the outer or engaged exclusively in the inner occupations, so that he cannot accomplish the exterior duties which he owes to his neighbours.[199]

Gregory was a realist who understood the necessity for offering leadership to others and for participating in public life. He pointed out that those who shirked public responsibility and who 'entirely neglect the care of worldly things, do not at all help their subjects in their need'.[200] Gregory returned to discuss this dichotomy between the contemplative and active life in the introduction to his *Dialogues* where he confessed to being 'oppressed with heavy grief' at the thought of all 'the practical wrongs which were wont to bring upon me grief and sorrow'.[201]

Alfred, who was a keen student of Gregory, latched onto this notion of being afflicted by the cares of office. There is no doubting that Alfred's references to personal sacrifices and sufferings were genuine. Few kings led their people through more difficult times—fighting off an occupying army in three major wars and constantly guarding his realm from an ever-watchful viking enemy. It must also have been true that Alfred's cares were not all of an administrative or mental nature. Years of strenuous military campaigning, and a season of humiliating defeat and flight, must have imposed severe physical hardship on Alfred and his men—hence he refers to cares 'of mind and body (*ge on mode ge on lichoman*)'. Alfred in his introduction to Psalm 2 suggests that he personally identified with David's tribulations: 'The text of the following psalm is called . . . David's Psalm . . . because David in this psalm lamented and complained to the Lord about his enemies, both native and foreign, and about all his troubles. And everyone who sings this psalm does likewise with respect to his own enemies.'[202] Alfred's life was indeed crowded with the cares of state and with worries for his own personal survival and that of his people. But his appeal to those cares was none the less part of a rhetorical tradition. We notice how the formula *mislicum 7 manigfealdum bisgum* is repeated in the prefaces to the *Pastoral Care* and the *Consolation*. These 'various and manifold worldly cares (*weoruldbisgum*)' which Alfred alludes to in his formulaic way, echo the concern of Gregory in his *Pastoral Care* for the 'trouble of rule and government [which] distracts the mind of the ruler'[203] and echo also Gregory's reference to 'the burden of so arduous a ministration' which he ascribes to bishops and teachers.[204] Gregory exaggerates his own cares of high office in the introduction to his *Dialogues* where he describes himself sitting in gloom bemoaning his involvement with the affairs of the world and longing for his monastic solitude. This rhetorical tradition of lamenting the cares of high ecclesiastical office is evident in the epilogue of Adomnán's book on the *Holy Places* of the Near East, where that busy abbot of Iona (*c.* AD 700) excuses his 'lowly style' on the grounds that he was 'daily beset by laborious and almost insupportable ecclesiastical business from every quarter (*inter laboriosas et prope insustentabiles tota die undique conglobatas eclesiasticae sollicitudinis occupationes*)'.[205] Adomnán did not, of course, wish us to understand that he had become so engulfed in administration that he had actually given up his life of prayer or contemplation—far from it. Nor are we to assume that Gregory, in addition to Bede's account of his bowel pain, was also—on his own admission—a manic depressive. So too, Alfred did not wish to convey the impression that his worldly cares were anything other than the onerous duties of a conscientious king who had taken the equally harassed David as his rôle model. The Pseudo-Asser, however, seized on these repeated rhetorical statements relating to the trials and tribulations of Alfred's kingship, and construed them literally to mean that Alfred was a diseased and pain-ridden ruler. Adherents of the 'Genuine Asser' lobby have inevitably been cornered into adopting what was a late tenth- and early eleventh-century invention of King Alfred's sanctified neuroses. This stubborn allegiance to a particular school of thought has resulted in one of the most grotesque distortions in medieval historiography. The resulting injustice done to scholarly assessments of King Alfred's achievement has been incalculable. Common sense alone should lead us back to a view that only a man of extraordinary intellectual and emotional resilience, as well as of great physical stamina, could have achieved so much in terms of literary output and in his military and administrative career.

Taking Leave of a Misunderstood King

Alfred's writings show him to have been a man of profound learning by the standards of his age. His interest not only in didactic works but in philosophical speculation bespeak an education which was broad and deep and which went back to childhood. As the youngest known son of Æthelwulf—a young man whom few would ever have expected to become king—Alfred may have devoted more time than was usual for one in his position, to developing his education. His contemplative nature and enquiring mind must have suggested to his teachers from the beginning that he ought to be given a solid grounding in Latin. But Alfred proved to be much more than a scholar. He possessed that rare temperament which combined the reflective with an ability for organization and action. The sheer quantity of his translations, and the staying power and organization they entailed, would alone tell us that much. We also know from the Chronicle—however biased in Alfred's favour that source may be—that he was a resourceful king who brought his intelligence to bear on the struggle for survival against his enemies. The man who pondered on the mysteries of human consciousness in an afterlife also had the ability to lead in war. For no man, born into Alfred's world, who shrank from treading on the entrails of the dying, could ever hope to gain the respect of his warband in that life and death struggle with the Norse enemy. The conflicting images of the man drenched in the blood of battle and of the philosopher-king, are not as great as they seem, when we recall that Alfred's warrior-bishop, Heahmund of Sherborne, must have endured even greater contradictions in his ecclesiastical life. Alfred was a man of natural piety, but he was also born a king's son, and when he—against all expectations—eventually came to kingship, he brought to that office not only the awesome monopoly of terror attached to early medieval power, but also equally awesome ideological concepts of the God-like nature of a king. So while Alfred strove to follow the path of 'righteous kingship', his was not the rule of a pious wimp, but of a leader already well schooled in the knowledge of the power and responsibility of his office, and conscious from his historical researches of the mandate which he had inherited from his royal ancestors. Alfred's scholarly activity was directed primarily to the encouragement of his bishops whom he rightly understood to have held key positions touching upon every aspect of life within his kingdom. His distribution of copies of his translation of the *Pastoral Care* to his bishops need not suggest that all his translated works, and other works executed under his general direction, were similarly distributed or published throughout his kingdom. While we know that the translation of the *Dialogues* was indeed copied by one of his bishops, there is no compelling evidence to suggest that Alfred's translation programme was anything other than an élitist, scholarly enterprise designed to be shared among the king's own erudite circle. The Anglo-Saxon Chronicle, too, did not have to be read as a modern newspaper to bolster Alfred's claims to military victory over the Danes. The very existence of the Chronicle lent it an iconic value in an illiterate age, which stood like its Frankish counterparts for the deeds of a royal house and of a great king. Alfred's desire to encourage the education of a select number of the sons of the West Saxon élite in the vernacular should neither be confused with a programme for comprehensive education nor with the education of his bishops through his translation of the *Pastoral Care*. Alfred was of course exceptional in his appreciation of the power of the vernacular as a means of acquiring a solid understanding of Late Antique writers and of promoting discussion of their ideas among his friends. But the notion that Alfred translated so many recondite works with a view that 'all men' should know them, involves a naïve interpretation of the king's own rhetoric.

Alfred's true genius—and the one which impressed medieval writers as well as men and women of a modern age—was his ability not so much to excel, as to possess the qualities of a great all-rounder. He lacked the rigorous scholarship of Bede and the uncompromising piety of Cuthbert. He lacked the reforming zeal of Æthelwold and the ability to rival the prose of Ælfric. He lacked, too, the military resources and the ruthless qualities of Offa even if he made up for this by possessing political acumen and the ability to present an argument with cunning. But while he failed to match all those men in any one of their characteristics, he possessed nevertheless the qualities of all of them in great measure. And he possessed more than most of them, perhaps, qualities of moderation which were indicative of his great humanity. It was inevitable that such a gifted ruler, imbued with such obvious principles of Christian piety, should have been held up as a model of Christian kingship by a later generation of writers in Anglo-Saxon England. Alfred's promotion of the vernacular was centuries ahead of its time and doomed to failure in an age when the very few who could read at all were also capable of reading Latin. But when the monastic reformers of the later tenth-century came up against the chaos of the reign of Æthelred the Unready, which threatened the entire programme of monastic recovery, it was natural that they would turn to the example of men in an earlier age who had stood out against the viking menace—the saintly Edmund of East Anglia and the learned and successful warrior, Alfred, who stood alone as the survivor of English Christian kingship in the wars of the 870s. It has remained impossible to gain a realistic assessment of Alfred while he was hedged around for a millennium with the hagiographical accretions of the Pseudo-Asser. But even when we discard the monastic image of the invalid and illiterate king, it is still a daunting task to cross a thousand years in time and hope to recover the picture of the genuine Alfred. Unlike the Pseudo-Asser, we can never make the bold claim of having sat in the royal chamber with this man. There are times however, when Alfred allows us draw near to his presence and when through his own writings, we can observe him as though an opaque screen. And what we perceive then, is no ordinary man, but a gifted ruler who was himself ever concerned with how we in succeeding generations, would view him.

It has ever been my desire to live honourably while I was alive, and after my death to leave to them that should come after me my memory in good works.

King Alfred's translation of Boethius's *Consolation of Philosophy*

NOTES

Chapter I

1. D. Whitelock (ed.), *English Historical Documents*, i. *c.500–1042* (gen. ed. D. C. Douglas; London, 1968), 137 (hereafter referred to as *EHD*, ed. Whitelock).
2. S. Keynes and M. Lapidge (transl.), *Alfred the Great: Asser's Life of King Alfred and Other Contemporary Sources* (Penguin, Harmondsworth, 1983), 228 n. 2.
3. W. H. Stevenson, (ed.), *Asser's Life of King Alfred*, introd. by D. Whitelock (Oxford, repr. 1959), 1·(hereafter referred to as *Life* of Alfred, ed. Stevenson).
4. P. H. Sawyer, *Anglo-Saxon Charters: An Annotated List and Bibliography* (Roy. Hist. Soc., London, 1968), 366, no. 1258 (hereafter referred to as Sawyer, followed by the charter number); W. de G. Birch (ed.), *Cartularium Saxonicum: A Collection of Charters Relating to Anglo-Saxon History* (4 vols; London, 1964; repr. of 1885–99 edn.), i. 405–7, no. 291 (hereafter referred to as Birch, followed by the charter number); *EHD*, ed. Whitelock, i. 23, 468–9.
5. F. M. Stenton, *Anglo-Saxon England*, 2nd edn. (Oxford repr. 1967), 208.
6. Sawyer 1271, Birch 443.
7. Bishop Ceolred's charter, although surviving in a thirteenth-century manuscript, was accepted by Stenton (and later by Whitelock) as authentic (F. M. Stenton, *The Early History of the Abbey of Abingdon* (Reading, 1913), 25–7; *EHD*, ed. Whitelock, i. 480).
8. Stenton, *Early History of Abingdon*, 28–9.
9. Stenton, *Anglo-Saxon England*, 242 n. 4.
10. Keynes and Lapidge (transl.), *Alfred the Great*, 228 n. 2.
11. A grant by Æthelwulf of Wessex, in favour of his thegn, Duda, of land at Ashdown in Berkshire (Sawyer 288, Birch 431) supposedly dating from 840 is of little help to this discussion. Even if that charter were genuine, it relates to a border area between West Saxon northern Wiltshire and the Vale of the White Horse in Berkshire, and is besides, offset by the more authentic evidence provided by Sawyer 1271 which dates to 844.
12. *EHD*, ed. Whitelock, i. 480.
13. Stenton, *Early History of Abingdon*, 26–7.
14. A. J. Robertson (ed. and transl.), *Anglo-Saxon Charters* (Cambridge, 1956), 279. Robertson was presumably referring to Sawyer 331, Birch 506; Sawyer 332, Birch 507; and Sawyer 338, Birch 516.
15. These are Sawyer 327, Birch 502—an eleventh-century forgery dated AD 790 for AD 860; another eleventh-century charter (Sawyer 319, Birch 538), dated AD 874 for AD 844; the 'highly suspicious' Sawyer 322, Birch 447, dated AD 884 for AD 844; and the equally suspicious Sawyer 320, Birch 444, dated AD 880 for AD 844.
16. Sawyer 1271, Birch 443 (AD 843–4); Sawyer 206, Birch 487 (AD 855); Sawyer 1273, Birch 490 (AD 855); Sawyer 212, Birch 513 (AD 866); Sawyer 1201, Birch 522 (AD 868).
17. Birch 395 (Æthelwulf with no title), ibid., nos. 418 (*dux*), 421 (*princeps*), 426 (*dux*), 437 (*dux*), 439 (*dux*), 442 (*dux*), 445 (*dux*); H. P. R. Finberg (ed.), *The Early Charters of Wessex* (Leicester, 1964), nos. 566 (*dux*) and 567 (*princeps*).
18. Sawyer 1438, Birch 421.
19. Sawyer 290; Finberg (ed.), *Charters of Wessex*, no. 567.

20. Sawyer 190, Birch 416; *EHD*, ed. Whitelock, i. 478.

21. Sawyer 206, Birch 487; *EHD*, ed. Whitelock, i. 485–6.

22. A. Campbell (ed.), *Chronicon Æthelweardi: The Chronicle of Æthelweard* (Nelson Medieval Texts; London, 1962), 37 (hereafter referred to as *Æthelweard*, ed. Campbell).

23. J. L. Nelson (transl.), *The Annals of St-Bertin* (Manchester, 1991), 92 (hereafter referred to as *Ann. Bert.*, transl. Nelson); *EHD*, ed. Whitelock, i. 315.

24. *The Anglo-Saxon Chronicle: A Collaborative Edition*, iii. *Manuscript A*, ed. J. M. Bately (gen. eds. D. Dumville and S. Keynes; Cambridge, 1986), (*sub anno* 871), 49 (hereafter referred to as *ASC: MS A*, ed. Bately).

25. *King Alfred's West Saxon Version of Gregory's Pastoral Care*, ed. H. Sweet (Early English Text Society, Original Series, 45; Oxford, 1958; repr. of 1871 edn.), i. 2–3.

26. Stenton, *Early History of Abingdon*, 28.

27. Ibid. 28–9.

28. *EHD*, ed. Whitelock, i. 174.

29. Sawyer 278, Birch 413.

30. Stenton, *Early History of Abingdon*, 30.

31. Robertson (ed. and transl.), *Anglo-Saxon Charters*, 275.

32. See pp. 191, 377, 403–6 below.

33. *Wullaf dux* (recte *abbas* as in Birch 475–8) and *Æthelbald episcopus* (recte *dux* as in Birch 475–8). Cf. Robertson (ed. and transl.), *Anglo-Saxon Charters*, 275–6.

34. *Life* of Alfred, ed. Stevenson, ch. 12, p. 10.

35. Stenton, *Early History of Abingdon*, 28.

36. A. P. Smyth, *Scandinavian Kings in the British Isles 850–880* (Oxford, 1977), 157.

37. *Ann. Bert.*, transl. Nelson, 86 and nn. 5 and 7.

38. *EHD*, ed. Whitelock, i. 194.

39. J. Campbell, E. John, and P. Wormald, *The Anglo-Saxons* (Oxford, 1982), 34, 37; R. H. Hodgkin, *A History of the Anglo-Saxons*, 3rd edn. (2 vols.; Oxford, 1952), i. 107–14, map facing p. 109; Stenton, *Anglo-Saxon England*, 25–6.

40. Ibid. 26.

41. Hodgkin, *History of the Anglo-Saxons*, i. 114.

42. *Æthelweard*, ed. Campbell, 40.

43. *Ann. Bert.*, transl. Nelson (*sub anno* 850), 69.

44. Sawyer 206, Birch 487; text in *Cartularium Saxonicum*, ed. Birch, ii. 88–9; *EHD*, ed. Whitelock, i. 486.

45. Alfred's brother, Æthelberht, issued a charter from Dorchester in 864 (Sawyer 333, Birch 510).

46. *Select English Historical Documents of the Ninth and Tenth Centuries*, ed. F. E. Harmer (Cambridge, 1914), 18, 51 (hereafter referred to as *SEHD*, ed. Harmer).

47. Sawyer 1494, Birch 1288 and 1354; *Anglo-Saxon Wills*, ed. D. Whitelock (Holmes Beach, Fl., 1986; repr. of 1930 Cambridge edn.), 137–41.

48. Sawyer 1515, Birch 912; *SEHD*, ed. Harmer, 35, 65; Keynes and Lapidge (transl.), *Alfred the Great*, 323 nn. 88 and 89.

49. *Life* of Alfred, ed. Stevenson, ch. 2, p. 4.

50. *EHD*, ed. Whitelock, i. 144–5.

51. Sawyer 328, Birch 496; *EHD*, ed. Whitelock, i. 488–90.

52. *ASC* (*sub anno* 839); *EHD*, ed. Whitelock, i. 172.

53. *ASC* (*sub anno* 853); *EHD*, ed. Whitelock, i. 174.

54. *Life* of Alfred, ed. Stevenson, ch. 9, p. 8.

55. *ASC* (*sub anno* 855) ascribes a five-year reign to Æthelbald who died in 860.

56. *Ann. Bert.*, transl. Nelson (*sub anno* 856), 83 and n. 11.

57. Ibid. (*sub anno* 862), 97.

58. *ASC: MS A*, ed. Bately (*sub anno* 853), 45; *EHD*, ed. Whitelock, i. 174.

59. Sawyer 310, Birch 475; Sawyer 311, Birch 476; Sawyer 312, Birch 477; Sawyer 313, Birch 478. Æthelbald and Æthelberht are designated *dux* in other charters—Sawyer 304, 305, 306, 307, and 308.

60. Sawyer 298, Birch 451.

61. Sawyer 301, Birch 457; Sawyer 300, Birch 459.

62. See J. L. Nelson, 'The Problem of King Alfred's Royal Anointing', *JEH* 18 (1967), 146, 157–8, for a good bibliographical summary, providing access to the entrenched positions of Whitelock, Stenton, Stevenson, Plummer, and Hodgkin.

63. Ibid. 156.

64. *EHD*, ed. Whitelock, i. 810; *Life* of Alfred, ed. Stevenson, p. 180 n. 1.

65. *EHD*, ed. Whitelock, i. 572, 810.

66. BL Add. MS 8873.

67. W. Ullmann, 'Nos si aliquid incompetenter: Some Observations on the Register Fragments of Leo IV in the *Collectio Britannica*', *Ephemerides Juris Canonici*, 9 (1953), 280–7.

68. Nelson, 'Alfred's Royal Anointing', 148–9, 150.

69. Ibid. 152.

70. M. Lapidge, 'Byrhtferth of Ramsey and the Early Sections of the *Historia Regum* Attributed to Symeon of Durham', *ASE* 10 (1982), 104–5.

71. Nelson, 'Alfred's Royal Anointing', 151.

72. Nelson suggested that a Latin version of the account of Alfred's visit to Rome reached Rome perhaps from the *Life* of King Alfred, the Chronicle of Æthelweard, or from the *Life* of Grimbald, and that this was accomplished through frequent contacts between English and Roman clergy in the eleventh century. Nelson, 'Alfred's Royal Anointing', 153–4.

73. *Life* of Alfred, ed. Stevenson, ch. 13, p. 12.

74. Keynes and Lapidge (*Alfred the Great*, 232 n. 19) set out Whitelock's position, alongside alternative and sounder conclusions reached by Nelson. They failed however to confront the problem posed by these conflicting historical interpretations.

75. W. Stubbs (ed.), *Willelmi Malmesbiriensis monachi de Gestis regum Anglorum* (Rolls Series; London, 1889), vol. ii, p. xliii.

76. *EHD*, ed. Whitelock, i. 810; cf. ibid. 572.

77. Ibid. 155; cf. Stenton, *Anglo-Saxon England*, 683.

78. C. Plummer, *The Life and Times of Alfred the Great* (Oxford, 1902), 76 ff.

79. G. Sitwell (transl.), *St. Odo of Cluny: Being the Life of St. Odo of Cluny by John of Salerno and the Life of St. Gerald of Aurillac by St. Odo* (London and New York, 1958), [*Life* of Gerald] chs. 29–30, pp. 119–21, [*Life* of Odo], ch. 9, pp. 52–3; chs. 18–20, pp. 61–3.

80. *Life* of Alfred, ed. Stevenson, chs. 8 and 11, pp. 7, 9.

81. Nelson, 'Alfred's Royal Anointing', 162.

82. Ibid. 156, 158–62.

83. It should be pointed out that the pope who anointed the sons of Charlemagne in 781 was not a Leo but Adrian I (772–95) (*Annales Regni Francorum, Quellen z. deut. Gesch. d. Mittelalters*, ed. Rau (*sub anno* 781), v/i, 40).

84. *ASC: MS A*, ed. Bately (*sub anno* 853), 44–5; *The Anglo-Saxon Chronicle: A Collaborative Edition*, iv. *Manuscript B*, ed. S. Taylor (gen eds. D. Dumville and S. Keynes; Cambridge, 1983), 32 (hereafter referred to as *ASC: MS B*, ed. Taylor). All these events in MS B are dated to 854, but the year 853 was clearly meant. Cf. Kirby's important findings on this topic when he concluded that 'if anything, the reference in the *Chronicle* to Alfred's journey to Rome in 853, already part of the text of the annals which Asser used, has priority over Asser's introduction of Alfred into the account of Aethelwulf's visit in 855–6' (D. P. Kirby, *The Earliest English Kings* (London, 1991), 199).

85. *Life* of Alfred, ed. Stevenson, ch. 8, p. 7.

86. Ibid., ch. 11, p. 9.

87. Chronicle entries omitted from the *Life* of Alfred include, for example, the battle of *Meretun* in 871 and the mention of the Raven banner in 878. The Isle of Thanet is confused with Sheppey under the entry of AD 851, and so on. Some of these omissions were due to the biographer's own carelessness and others were inherent in the version of the Chronicle which he translated. See pp. 313, 487 below.

88. *Life* of Pope Benedict III, in L. Duchesne (ed.), *Le Liber Pontificalis* (Paris, 1955–7), ii. 148.

89. *Ann. Bert.*, transl. Nelson (*sub anno* 855), 80; ibid. (*sub anno* 856), 83.

90. Nelson, 'Alfred's Royal Anointing', 161.

91. Sawyer 340, Birch 520.

92. Sawyer 1201, Birch 522.

93. Sawyer 1203, Birch 539. *Cartularium Saxonicum*, ed. Birch, ii. 159. Cf. J. L. Nelson, 'Reconstructing a Royal Family: Reflections on Alfred, from Asser, Chapter 2', in I. Wood and N. Lund (eds.), *People and Places in Northern Europe 500–1600: Essays in Honour of Peter Hayes Sawyer* (Woodbridge, Suffolk, 1991), 59.

94. *Life* of Alfred, ed. Stevenson, ch. 12, pp. 9–10.

95. *The Annals of Ulster (to A.D. 1131)* ed. S. Mac Airt and G. Mac Niocaill (Dublin, 1983), (*sub anno* 841), 298–9 (hereafter referred to as *Ann. Ulst.*, ed. Mac Airt and Mac Niocaill).

96. J. Bronsted, *The Vikings* (Penguin, Harmondsworth, 1965), 38–9, 58–9.

97. J. L. Nelson, *Charles the Bald* (London and New York, 1992), 185–213.

98. *Ann. Bert.*, transl. Nelson (*sub anno* 866), 131.

99. Ibid.

100. N. P. Brooks and J. A. Graham-Campbell, 'Reflections on the Viking-Age Silver Hoard from Croydon, Surrey', in M. A. S. Blackburn (ed.), *Anglo-Saxon Monetary History: Essays in Memory of Michael Dolley* (Leicester, 1986), 98–9.

101. Ibid. 93.

102. P. H. Sawyer, *The Age of the Vikings*, 2nd edn. (London, 1971), esp. 120–47.

103. C. Gillmor, 'War on the Rivers: Viking Numbers and Mobility on the Seine and Loire, 841–886', *Viator: Medieval and Renaissance Studies*, 19 (1988), 79–109.

104. *Ann. Bert.*, transl. Nelson (*sub anno* 845), 61.

105. T. Reuter (transl.), *The Annals of Fulda* (Manchester and New York, 1992), 90 and n. 4 (hereafter referred to as *Ann. Fuld.*, transl. Reuter).

106. *Ann. Bert.*, transl. Nelson (*sub anno* 866), 129.

107. Stenton, *Anglo-Saxon England*, 241 n. 1.

108. *Ann. Bert.*, transl. Nelson (*sub anno* 861), 95.

109. Ibid.

110. *Ann. Ulst.*, ed. Mac Airt and Mac Niocaill (*sub anno* 871), 326–7. Cf. *Annala Uladh: Annals of Ulster*, ed. W. M. Hennessy and B. MacCarthy (Dublin, 1887–1901), (*sub anno* 870), i. 384–5 (hereafter referred to as *Ann. Ulst.*, ed. Hennessy and MacCarthy).
111. *ASC: MS A*, ed. Bately (*sub anno* 885), 52; *EHD*, ed. Whitelock, i. 182.
112. *Ann. Bert., Quellen z. deut. Gesch. d. Mittelalters*, ed. Rau (*sub anno* 862), VII/ii, 108–9; *Ann. Bert.*, transl. Nelson, 98.
113. *Ann. Ulst.*, ed. Hennessy and MacCarthy (*sub anno* 920), i. 440–1.
114. Gillmor, 'War on the Rivers', 106–7.
115. *ASC* (*sub anno* 867); *EHD*, ed. Whitelock, i. 176.
116. A. P. Smyth, *Scandinavian York and Dublin: The History and Archaeology of Two Related Viking Kingdoms* (2 vols.; Dublin, repr. 1987), ii. 130–2, 133–4.
117. *ASC* (*sub anno* 867); *EHD*, ed. Whitelock, i. 176.
118. *Ann. Fuld.*, transl. Reuter (*sub anno* 882), 93; ibid. (*sub anno* 884), 96–7.
119. *Ann. Bert.*, transl. Nelson (*sub anno* 860), 92.
120. Ibid. (*sub anno* 866), 130.
121. Ibid. (*sub anno* 861), 95.
122. Ibid. (*sub anno* 864), 112.
123. Ibid. (*sub anno* 869), 164.
124. *Life* of Alfred, ed. Stevenson, chs. 29, 73–4, pp. 23–4, 54–5.
125. Ibid., p. 228.
126. Stenton, *Early History of Abingdon*, 26 n. 1.
127. Sawyer 190, Birch 416; *EHD*, ed. Whitelock (no. 85), i. 479.
128. Stenton, *Early History of Abingdon*, 26 n. 1. Cf. *EHD*, ed. Whitelock, i. 477.
129. Sawyer 340, Birch 520; Sawyer 1201, Birch 522. See p. 17 above, and Keynes and Lapidge (transl.), *Alfred the Great*, 241 n. 57.
130. Birch 343 to 513.
131. Keynes and Lapidge (transl.), *Alfred the Great*, 240–1 n. 57.
132. Robertson (ed. and transl.), *Anglo-Saxon Charters*, 268.
133. *Life* of Alfred, ed. Stevenson, p. 229 n. 4.
134. Sawyer 197, Birch 454.
135. Sawyer 340, Birch 520.
136. Birch 460, 496, 506, 507, 515, 516, and 873.
137. Sawyer 190, Birch 416.
138. Sawyer 210, Birch 509.
139. Sawyer 212, Birch 513.
140. Sawyer 340, Birch 520; Sawyer 1201, Birch 522; and perhaps Sawyer 337, Birch 1210.
141. Sawyer 340, Birch 520.
142. Sawyer 190, Birch 416.
143. *EHD*, ed. Whitelock, i. 477.
144. Keynes and Lapidge (transl.), *Alfred the Great*.
145. Stenton, *Early History of Abingdon*, 26 n. 1.
146. Sawyer 340, Birch 520.
147. Robertson (ed. and transl.), *Anglo-Saxon Charters*, 275.
148. Ibid. 279.
149. Sawyer 333, Birch 510.
150. Sawyer 338, Birch 516.
151. Sawyer 340, Birch 520.
152. Sawyer 1201, Birch 522.

153. Keynes and Lapidge (transl.), *Alfred the Great.*
154. *Life* of Alfred, ed. Stevenson, ch. 74, p. 54.
155. Ibid., ch. 29, pp. 23–4.
156. *ASC: MS A*, ed. Bately (*sub anno* 902), 62. MS A omits the phrase 'King Edward's mother' which is included in MS B (*ASC: MS B*, ed. Taylor (*sub anno* 903), 46). Cf. *EHD*, ed. Whitelock, i. 190.
157. Sawyer 1442, Birch 575.
158. *Cartularium Saxonicum*, ed. Birch, ii. 218–19.
159. *EHD*, ed. Whitelock, i. 191.
160. C. [R.] Hart, *The Danelaw* (London and Rio Grande, 1992), 27, 48; D. Hill, *An Atlas of Anglo-Saxon England* (Oxford, 1981), 10.
161. Smyth, *Scandinavian Kings*, 205.
162. Ibid. 206–7.
163. C. E. Blunt, 'The St. Edmund Memorial Coinage', *Proceedings Suffolk Institute of Archaeology*, 31/3 (1969), 234–55, and esp. 251–3. The life of the St Edmund Memorial coinage extended from *c.*890 to 910 and some of the issues may have been minted at Canterbury and York as well as within Danish East Anglia (ibid. 253).
164. *Life* of Alfred, ed. Stevenson, ch. 35, p. 27.
165. Smyth, *Scandinavian York and Dublin*, ii. 198–201, 229–34.
166. *Æthelweard*, ed. Campbell, 40–1.
167. Stenton, *Early History of Abingdon*, 26.
168. Ibid. 26 n. 3.
169. Smyth, *Scandinavian York and Dublin*, ii. 249–53 and map p. 247.
170. Ibid. 196–7.
171. Nelson, *Charles the Bald*, 193.
172. *EHD*, ed. Whitelock, i. 177.
173. *Ann. Bert.*, transl. Nelson (*sub anno* 844), 59.
174. Ibid. (*sub anno* 856), 82–3.
175. Ibid. (*sub anno* 882), 226.
176. Ibid. (*sub anno* 871), 174.
177. *Ann. Ulst.*, ed. Hennessy and MacCarthy (*sub anno* 916), i. 434–5.
178. Ibid. 438–9.
179. *Ann. Fuld.*, transl. Reuter (*sub anno* 882), 91.
180. See p. 138 below.
181. *L'Estoire des Engleis by Geffrei Gaimar*, ed. A. Bell (Anglo-Norman Texts, xiv–xvi; Oxford, 1960), ll. 2959–67, pp. 94–5 and p. 242 nn. Cf. *Two of the Saxon Chronicles Parallel*, ed. C. Plummer and J. Earle (2 vols.; Oxford, 1965; repr. of 1892–9 edn.), ii. 87.
182. Smyth, *Scandinavian York and Dublin*, i. 93–4.
183. See pp. 66–7 below.
184. *EHD*, ed. Whitelock, i. 178.
185. Plummer's suggestion (*Two Saxon Chronicles Parallel*, ii. 88) of Marden near Devizes in Wiltshire suits the topographical evidence, but the name derives from *Mercdene* or *Merhdæne* rather than *Meretun*. For the possible identification of this place-name with either Merdon, south of Winchester or with Martin in south-west Hampshire, see M. Hughes, 'Hampshire Castles and the Landscape: 1066–1216', *Landscape History*, 11 (1989), 31–2.
186. *ASC* (*sub annis* 757, 786); *EHD*, ed. Whitelock, i. 162, 166.

187. *ASC: MS A*, ed. Bately (*sub anno* 871), 48.
188. *ASC: MS B*, ed. Taylor (*sub anno* 872), 35.
189. *ASC: MS A*, ed. Bately (*sub anno* 755), 36; *ASC: MS B*, ed. Taylor (*sub anno* 755), 26.
190. Sawyer 513, Birch 817; text in *Cartularium Saxonicum*, ed. Birch, ii. 580.
191. Sawyer 1438, Birch 421; *Cartularium Saxonicum*, ed. Birch, i. 587–92.
192. Sawyer 308, Birch 469; *Cartularium Saxonicum*, ed. Birch, ii. 64–6.
193. *Æthelweard*, ed. Campbell, 37.
194. *ASC* (*sub anno* 718); *EHD*, ed. Whitelock, i. 159. Cf. *Venerabilis Baedae Opera Historica*, ed. C. Plummer (2 vols.; Oxford, 1969; repr. of 1896 edn.), ii. 264.
195. *Two Saxon Chronicles Parallel*, ed. Plummer and Earle, ii. 38.
196. Keynes and Lapidge (transl.), *Alfred the Great*, 292 n. 7.
197. *Æthelweard*, ed. Campbell, 39.
198. Ibid. 39.
199. *ASC: MS A*, ed. Bately (*sub anno* 871), 49; *EHD*, ed. Whitelock, i. 178.
200. *Life* of Alfred, ed. Stevenson, ch. 74, p. 55.
201. Ibid., pp. 54–7.
202. *Æthelweard*, ed. Campbell, 39.
203. *ASC* (*sub anno* 871); *EHD*, ed. Whitelock, i. 178.
204. *Vita Leobae abbatissae Biscofesheimensis auctori Rudolfo Fuldensi*, ed. G. Waitz, *Mon. Ger. Hist. SS.* 15 (1887), 123; *EHD*, ed. Whitelock, i. 719.
205. Ibid. 178.
206. Brooks and Graham-Campbell, 'Viking-Age Hoard from Croydon', in Blackburn (ed.), *Anglo-Saxon Monetary History*, 105.
207. Smyth, *Scandinavian Kings*, 207.
208. King Alfred's *Will* in *SEHD*, ed. Harmer, 17, 50.
209. Sawyer 283, Birch 377; *Cartularium Saxonicum*, ed. Birch, i. 515. The erroneous date ascribed to this problematic charter in the manuscript is AD 924. Finberg (ed.), *Charters of Wessex* (no. 10), 29. It is possible that Æthelwulf's victory took place at Oakley in Hampshire, to the west of Basingstoke. In that case Æthelwulf would have successfully fought off an attack aimed at the heart of his kingdom, and within a few miles of Basing where his sons Æthelred and Alfred were defeated by the Danes some 20 years later.
210. See p. 75.
211. *Æthelweard*, ed. Campbell, 38.
212. Ibid. 40.
213. Brooks and Graham-Campbell, 'Viking-Age Hoard from Croydon', in Blackburn (ed.), *Anglo-Saxon Monetary History*, 107–9.
214. *EHD*, ed. Whitelock, i. 178.
215. *Æthelweard*, ed. Campbell, 40.
216. Ibid. 41.
217. Stenton, *Early History of Abingdon*, 4–6, 30–1.
218. Ibid. 30–1.
219. H. E. Slater, 'A Chronicle Roll of the Abbots of Abingdon', *Eng. Hist. Rev.* 26 (1911), 727–38.
220. *King Alfred's Version of Pastoral Care*, ed. Sweet, i. 4–5.
221. See pp. 549–53.
222. Smyth, *Scandinavian Kings*, 36–100, 189–213.

223. Sawyer 1278, Birch 533, 534.
224. *Cartularium Saxonicum*, ed. Birch, ii. 149; *EHD*, ed. Whitelock, i. 490.
225. Keynes and Lapidge (transl.), *Alfred the Great*, 177.
226. *EHD*, ed. Whitelock, i. 572, 811.
227. Ibid. 812.
228. Ibid.
229. *Ann. Fuld.*, transl. Reuter (*sub anno* 882), 93.
230. Ibid. (*sub anno* 884), 96–7.
231. *SEHD*, ed. Harmer, 18–19, 51–2. Cf. Keynes and Lapidge (transl.), *Alfred the Great*, 324 n. 97.
232. For the Irish evidence, see A. T. Lucas, 'The Plundering and Burning of Churches in Ireland, 7th to the 16th Century', in E. Rynne (ed.), *North Munster Studies: Essays in Commemoration of Mgr. Michael Moloney* (Limerick, 1967), 172–229.
233. *Ann. Bert.*, transl. Nelson (*sub anno* 841), 51–2.
234. Ibid. (*sub anno* 882), 225.
235. Ibid. (*sub anno* 868), 152.
236. Ibid. (*sub anno* 863), 111.
237. Ibid. (*sub anno* 865), 127.
238. *Ann. Fuld.*, transl. Reuter (*sub anno* 881), 90–1.
239. *Ann. Bert.*, transl. Nelson (*sub anno* 853), 77.
240. Ibid. (*sub anno* 882), 226.
241. Stenton, *Early History of Abingdon*, 31–2.
242. N. Brooks, *The Early History of the Church of Canterbury: Christ Church from 597 to 1066* (Leicester, 1984), 197–203.
243. Sawyer 1438, Birch 421–2; Brooks, *Early History of Canterbury*, 199–200.
244. *Cartularium Saxonicum*, ed. Birch, i. 588.
245. Ibid.
246. Brooks, *Early History of Canterbury*, 204.
247. Ibid. 202.
248. Ibid. 204, and see ibid. 367 n. 82 for later medieval traditions regarding the destruction of Lyminge, Folkestone, and Minster-in-Thanet by the Danes.
249. Ibid. 205.
250. Ibid. 206.
251. Sawyer 380; *Cartularium Saxonicum*, ed. Birch, no. 610, ii. 268–9.
252. R. Fleming, 'Monastic Lands and England's Defence in the Viking Age', *Eng. Hist. Rev.* 100 (1985), 247–65; D. N. Dumville, *Wessex and England from Alfred to Edgar* (Woodbridge, 1992), 53–4; and see also 29–54.
253. *EHD*, ed. Whitelock, i. 501; Sawyer 1444, Birch 618, 619.
254. *SEHD*, ed. Harmer (no. vi), 9 and cf. 84–5 nn.
255. Smyth, *Scandinavian York and Dublin*, ii. 191–258.
256. Brooks and Graham-Campbell, 'Viking-Age Hoard from Croydon', in Blackburn (ed.), *Anglo-Saxon Monetary History*, 106.
257. Ibid. 106–7.
258. Ibid. 106.
259. Ibid. 91–3.
260. Ibid. 93.
261. Ibid. 100.
262. Sawyer 1202, Birch 529–30; *SEHD*, ed. Harmer (no. viii), 11–12, 87. Harmer accepted

AD 871—a date ascribed to this transaction in two Middle English versions in Canterbury chartularies—as plausible (ibid. 87).

263. *SEHD*, ed. Harmer (no. x), 13–15, 88–91. Sawyer 1508, Birch 558; *EHD*, ed. Whitelock, i. 495–7.

264. Brooks and Graham-Campbell, 'Viking-Age Hoard from Croydon', in Blackburn (ed.), *Anglo-Saxon Monetary History*, 107.

265. Ibid. 107–10.

266. I am most grateful to Dr Mark Blackburn for allowing me to read his paper on 'The London Mint in the Reign of Alfred', which appears in Blackburn, M. A. S., and Dumville, D. N. (eds.), *Kings, Currency and Alliances: The History of Coinage in Southern England AD 840–900* (forthcoming).

Chapter II

1. *Rogeri de Wendover Chronica sive Flores Historiarum*, ed. H. O. Coxe (5 vols.; English His. Soc.; London, 1841–4), (*sub annis* 872–3), i. 323–5; cf. *Historia Regum*, in *Symeonis monachi opera omnia*, ed. T. Arnold (2 vols.; Rolls Series, 1882–5), ii. 110. *EHD*, ed. Whitelock, i. 251, 256.

2. *ASC* (*sub anno* 873); *EHD*, ed. Whitelock, i. 178.

3. *Rogeri de Wendover Chronica*, ed. Coxe, i. 323–5; *Symeonis monachi opera omnia*, ed. Arnold, ii. 110. My interpretation of events surrounding the Northumbrian revolt differs significantly from that of Stenton (*Anglo-Saxon England*, 248–9) who saw Ricsige as a candidate of the native Northumbrian faction and who believed Northumbria regained its independence from the Danes 'for the next three years [until 875]'. In view of the crushing defeat of Northumbria's armies at York in 866, it is extremely unlikely that the Northumbrians could have supported a rival king in defiance of Hálfdan from 872 to 875. There is little in either the *Historia Regum* or Roger Wendover to support Stenton's interpretation. Given that Archbishop Wulfhere was expelled along with the Danish under-king, Ecgberht, then surely the restoration of the archbishop and Ricsige suggests that Ricsige represented the Danish overlordship in the same way as his predecessor had done. But cf. Kirby, *Earliest English Kings*, 219 n. 32, for yet another interpretation of these events.

4. *ASC* (*sub anno* 874); *EDH*, ed. Whitelock, i. 178.

5. Ibid.

6. Stenton, *Anglo-Saxon England*, 230.

7. A. Williams, A. P. Smyth, and D. P. Kirby, *A Biographical Dictionary of Dark Age Britain* (London, 1991), 78. See also Kirby, *Earliest English Kings*, 134, 191, 214–16.

8. Ibid. 6, 236.

9. *Cartularium Saxonicum*, ed. Birch, ii. 160 and 161; *EHD*, ed. Whitelock, i. 491. Cf. Kirby's assessment of Ceolwulf II in Kirby, *Earliest English Kings*, 215–17.

10. Sawyer 215, Birch 540; *EHD*, ed. Whitelock (no. 95), i. 491–2.

11. Sawyer 216, Birch 541.

12. Stenton, *Anglo-Saxon England*, 249 n. 3.

13. Sawyer (*Anglo-Saxon Charters*, 125), ascribes Daylesford to Gloucestershire.

14. *EHD*, ed. Whitelock, i. 491; Sawyer 215, Birch 540.

15. Whitelock prints *Brihtnoth* (*EHD*, i. 492).

16. *Beornoth* appears in place of *Beorhtnoð*.

17. J. A. Robinson, *St. Oswald and the Church of Worcester* (British Academy Supplemental Papers, 5; London, 1919), 29.
18. Sawyer 1441. See below.
19. Sawyer 212, Birch 513.
20. Sawyer 214, Birch 524.
21. Whitelock has *Beornnoth* (*EHD*, i. 481).
22. Sawyer 1271, Birch 443; *EHD*, ed. Whitelock, i. 481. See p. 4 above.
23. Sawyer 206, Birch 487 (*Beornnoð*); and also Sawyer 207. Birch 488–9 (*Beornoð*).
24. Sawyer 208, Birch 492 (*[Beor]htnoð*).
25. Sawyer 209, Birch 503 (*Biornoð*).
26. Sawyer 211, Birch 514 (*Beornothus*); and Sawyer 212, Birch 513 *(Beornoþ)*.
27. Sawyer 1280, Birch 608.
28. Sawyer 217, Birch 547.
29. Sawyer 218, Birch 551.
30. Sawyer 219, Birch 552.
31. Sawyer 220, Birch 557.
32. Sawyer 1441, Birch 574.
33. *Cartularium Saxonicum*, ed. Birch, ii. 217; *Diplomatarium Anglicum Ævi Saxonici: A Collection of English Charters*, ed. B. Thorpe (London, 1865), 140, 142.
34. Sawyer 361, Birch 607.
35. *Cartularium Saxonicum*, ed. Birch, ii. 265.
36. The Anglo-Saxon year, as reckoned by this section of the Chronicle began in autumn and probably with the Caesarean Indiction on 24 September. *EHD*, ed. Whitelock, i. 116.
37. *Æthelweard*, ed. Campbell, 35–6. Cf. Æthelweard's reference to *Iguuares frater*, p. 57, below.
38. *Corolla Sancti Eadmundi: The Garland of St. Edmund, King and Martyr*, ed. F. Hervey (London, 1907), 7–9; *Memorials of St. Edmund's Abbey*, ed. T. Arnold (3 vols.; Rolls Series, 1890–6), i. 3–4; Smyth, *Scandinavian Kings*, 201–4.
39. *ASC: MS A.*, ed. Bately (*sub anno* 878), 50; *EHD*, ed. Whitelock, i. 180.
40. *L'Estoire des Engleis*, ed. Bell, ll. 3140–52, pp. 100–1.
41. *The Annals of St. Neot's* (*sub anno* 878), in *Anglo-Saxon Chronicle: A Collaborative Edition*, xvii. *The Annals of St. Neots with Vita Prima Sancti Neoti*, ed. D. Dumville and M. Lapidge (Cambridge, 1984), 78 (hereafter referred to as *Annals of St. Neots*, ed. Dumville and Lapidge).
42. *Annales Lindisfarnenses*, ed. G. H. Pertz, in *Mon. Ger. Hist. SS* (Leipzig, 1925; repr. of 1866 edn.), xix. 506.
43. Smyth, *Scandinavian Kings*, 203 and n. 16.
44. Ibid. 204.
45. J. Raine (ed.), *The Historians of the Church of York and its Archbishops* (3 vols.; Rolls Series; London, 1965; repr. of 1879 and 1894 edn.), i. 404.
46. R. W. McTurk, 'Ragnarr Loðbrók in the Irish Annals?', in B. Almquist and D. Greene (eds.), *Proceedings of the Seventh Viking Congress, Dublin 15–21 August 1973* (Dublin, 1976), 104 n. 86 and 120 n. 199.
47. Ibid. 119–20.
48. Ibid. 121.
49. *Æthelweard*, ed. Campbell, 43.
50. Ibid. 35.

51. Smyth, *Scandinavian Kings*, 189–94.
52. McTurk, 'Ragnarr Loðbrók', in Almquist and Greene (eds.), *Seventh Viking Congress*, 117 n. 173.
53. *Æthelweard*, ed. Campbell, p. xxii.
54. Ibid. (Introduction), l. This is not to deny that Æthelweard's version of the Anglo-Saxon Chronicle does not have valuable information to offer the historian on people and events of south-west Wessex. But McTurk, by quoting Whitelock out of context on the issue of additional information provided by Æthelweard (McTurk, 'Ragnarr Loðbrók', 120), has had a misleading influence on the altogether separate argument which turns on Æthelweard's translating technique. In short, the material provided by Æthelweard on Ivar and Hálfdan in his 878 entry is not additional to the main text of the Chronicle. It is, rather, a garbled translation of Æthelweard's exemplar of the Chronicle, and Whitelock's comments on additional material do not therefore apply. For the significance of additional information in Æthelweard's Chronicle, see pp. 474–7 below.
55. *Æthelweard*, ed. Campbell, 43.
56. Ibid., p. xxix.
57. *ASC: MS B*, ed. Taylor (*sub anno* 879), 37.
58. J. de Vries, 'Die historischen Grundlagen der Ragnarssaga loðbrókar', *Arkiv för nordisk Filologi*, 39 (1923), 271.
59. Ibid.
60. The near-contemporary information supplied by the Anglo-Saxon Chronicle (*sub anno* 878) on the relationship between Ivar and Hálfdan should not be confused with speculation on the part of later medieval English chroniclers and annalists on the identification of Ubbe as the unnamed brother of Ivar and Hálfdan who is mentioned in the Chronicle. Nor should later Scandinavian saga traditions which ascribed numerous sons (including Ivar) to the proto-historical Ragnarr Loðbrók, be allowed to detract from the value and clarity of the Chronicle's record.
61. Ibid.
62. *Æthelweard*, ed. Campbell, 42.
63. *Ann. Ulst.*, ed. Hennessy and MacCarthy, (*sub anno* 872), i. 386–7.
64. The *mh* in the Old Irish name *Imhar* was pronounced [v]. Similarly, the Old Irish form *Amhlaibh* was pronounced [avlaiv] and represented an Old Irish form of the Old Norse name *Olaf* (*Óláfr*).
65. Smyth, *Scandinavian Kings*, 169.
66. Ibid. 169–70.
67. *Annales Fuldenses, Quellen z. deut. Gesch. d. Mittelalters*, ed. R. Rau (*sub anno* 873), VII/iii, 88; *Ann. Fuld.*, transl. Reuter, 70–1.
68. *Halbdeni frater Sigifridi regis. Ann. Fuld.* (*sub anno* 873), ibid.
69. *Ann. Fuld.* (*sub anno* 873), ibid.
70. *ASC: MS A*, ed. Bately (*sub anno* 875), 49; *EHD*, ed. Whitelock, i. 178–9.
71. *Ann. Ulst.*, ed. Hennessy and MacCarthy (*sub anno* 874 *recte* 875), i. 388–9; *Ann. Ulst.*, ed. Mac Airt and Mac Niocaill (*sub anno* 875), 330–1. A. P. Smyth, 'The *Black Foreigners* of York and the *White Foreigners* of Dublin', *Saga-Book of the Viking Society*, 19 (1975–6), 101–17.
72. Smyth, *Scandinavian Kings*, 256–8.
73. Ibid. 258–9.
74. *Ann. Ulst.*, ed. Mac Airt and Mac Niocaill (*sub anno* 875), 330–1. Unlike the Anglo-Saxon Chronicle's edited format for the ninth century, the Annals of Ulster do not

normally arrange material according to themes or by following the fortunes of any one political faction. The Annals of Ulster, by way of contrast to the West Saxon record, provide a contemporary set of miscellaneous annals with little attempt made at ordering a wide range of very diverse material. Related happenings, however, are sometimes grouped together.

75. *ASC: MS A*, ed. Bately (*sub anno* 876), 50; *EHD*, ed. Whitelock, i. 179.
76. Smyth, *Scandinavian Kings*, 255.
77. Ibid. 262–3.
78. McTurk, 'Ragnarr Loðbrók', in Almquist and Greene (eds.), *Seventh Viking Congress*, 118. McTurk was unable to arrive at any coherent conclusions on this subject, since he fell a prey to de Vries's convoluted arguments which were in turn based on a poor understanding of the relevant Irish texts. There is, for instance, no chronological difficulty in reconciling the careers of the Irish *Albann* with the Anglo-Saxon *Healfdene* (ibid. 116 n. 166) and there is no justification for confusing *Albann* (i.e. Hálfdan), a *dux* of the Danes (*Dubgenti*), who was slain according to the Annals of Ulster in 877, with *Alba* (genitive *Alban*) meaning 'northern Britain' or Scotland (cf. ibid. 118 n. 175). If such philological absurdities are engaged in, then why not propose that records relating to the career of the Hiberno-Norse king, *Auisle*, who was slain in Scotland according to the Annals of Ulster in 867 (Mac Airt and Mac Niocaill, 322), are no more than garbled references to *Cell Ausili*, the church of Killashee in Kildare, which is also mentioned in the Annals of Ulster in the years 872 and 874! If ninth-century Anglo-Saxon records were subjected to the same absurd iconoclastic scrutiny as applied by foreign scholars to early Irish and Scottish sources, then the history of Alfred's reign might never be written. McTurk was also led astray by arguing that if Hálfdan, the brother of Ivar, were indeed alive in 878—as he misinterpreted Æthelweard to have meant—then Hálfdan of the Anglo-Saxon Chronicle could not, of course, have been the same as the *Albann* (Hálfdan) who is reported as having died off the Irish coast in 877 (McTurk, 'Ragnarr Loðbrók', 120. See p. 57 above). Finally, McTurk followed de Vries in toying with an argument which identified the Anglo-Saxon *Healfdene* with *Albdani* the Danish leader mentioned in the Annals of Fulda in 873—a path which leads to utter confusion (ibid. 103–5, 116, 118, 120).
79. The detailed relationships between the York and Dublin dynasties, and the fortunes of the Grandsons of Ivar, are dealt with in Smyth, *Scandinavian York and Dublin*.
80. While Sawyer conceded that the *micel here* which invaded England in 865 was a large *here*, he argued strongly that a *here* as such was a modest fighting force and that accounts in the Anglo-Saxon Chronicle of 200 viking warships which confronted Alfred in his Last War could not be relied upon for accuracy (Sawyer, *Age of the Vikings*, 120–47, and esp. 123–6).
81. *ASC: MS A*, ed. Bately (*sub anno* 871), 48.
82. Cf. the genealogy of Alfred's father, King Æthelwulf, in the Anglo-Saxon Chronicle *sub anno* 855–8 (*ASC: MS A*, ed. Bately, 45–6; *EHD*, ed. Whitelock, i. 174–5).

Chapter III

1. This estimate assumes that the Danes moved from East Anglia to Reading as at the beginning of the First War. If they had come via London, their march through West Saxon territory may have amounted to about 120 miles.
2. *Ann. Bert.*, transl. Nelson (*sub anno* 861), 96.

3. Cf. P. H. Sawyer, *Kings and Vikings: Scandinavia and Europe* AD *700–1100* (London and New York, 1982), 54–5.
4. Smyth, *Scandinavian Kings*, 240–4.
5. *Æthelweard*, ed. Campbell, 41.
6. *ASC: MS A*, ed. Bately (*sub anno* 875), 49–50; *EHD*, ed. Whitelock, i. 179.
7. *Æthelweard*, ed. Campbell, 42.
8. *ASC: MS A*, ed. Bately (*sub anno* 877), 50; *EHD*, ed. Whitelock, i. 179.
9. *Æthelweard*, ed. Campbell, 41 n. 2.
10. Ibid. 41.
11. *ASC* (*sub annis* 876–7); *EHD*, ed. Whitelock, i. 179.
12. *Æthelweard*, ed. Campbell, 42.
13. *Ann. Bert.*, transl. Nelson (*sub anno* 882), 226.
14. Ibid. (*sub anno* 862), 98.
15. Ibid. (*sub anno* 865), 129.
16. Ibid. (*sub anno* 868), 152.
17. Ibid. (*sub anon* 873), 183.
18. For the influence of Alfred and his circle on the compilation of the Anglo-Saxon Chronicle, see pp. 482–98 below.
19. *Æthelweard*, ed. Campbell, 41.
20. Ibid. 42.
21. Ibid.
22. Ibid.
23. *Ann. Bert.*, transl. Nelson (*sub anno* 860), 92.
24. *Ann. Fuld.*, transl. Reuter (*sub anno* 884), 97.
25. Ibid (*sub anno* 882), 92–3.
26. D. Whitelock, 'The Importance of the Battle of Edington AD 878', in D. Whitelock (ed.), *From Bede to Alfred* (Studies in Early Anglo-Saxon Literature and History, 13; London, 1980), 9.
27. Ibid. 6–7, 10–11.
28. See pp. 325–9 below.
29. *Æthelweard*, ed. Campbell, 43.
30. *ASC: MS A*, ed. Bately (*sub anno* 878), 51; *EHD*, ed. Whitelock, i. 180.
31. *Æthelweard*, ed. Campbell, 42.
32. Whitelock, 'Importance of the Battle of Edington', in Whitelock (ed.), *From Bede to Alfred*, 12.
33. *SEHD*, ed. Harmer, 18; *EHD*, ed. Whitelock, i. 494.
34. Sawyer 646, Birch 999 and 1347.
35. Sawyer 765, Birch 1215.
36. *SEHD*, ed. Harmer, 17–18; *EHD*, ed. Whitelock, i. 494.
37. *SEHD*, ed. Harmer, 32; *EHD*, ed. Whitelock, i. 503. See pp. 395–6 below.
38. Smyth, *Scandinavian Kings*, 189–94.
39. *Annals of Ireland: Three Fragments copied . . . by Dubhaltach Mac Firbisigh*, ed. J. O'Donovan (Irish Archaeological and Celtic Society; Dublin, 1860), (*sub anno* 851), 122–5.
40. *ASC: MS B*, ed. Taylor, 37; *EHD*, ed. Whitelock, i. 180. The mention of the Raven battle-standard is omitted in MS A, and by Æthelweard and the *Life* of Alfred. It occurs in MSS B, C, D, and E.
41. *Æthelweard*, ed. Campbell, 37.

42. *Ann. Fuld.*, transl. Reuter (*sub anno* 885), 98.

43. *ASC: MS A*, ed. Bately (*sub anno* 876), 50.

44. Smyth, *Scandinavian Kings*, 245 and n. 18; id. *Scandinavian York and Dublin*, ii. 267–70. For the election of Guthfrith, cf. *EHD*, ed. Whitelock, i. 261.

45. *Ann. Bert.*, *Quellen z. deut. Gesch. d. Mittelalters*, ed. Rau (*sub anno* 858), VI/ii, 96–7; *Ann. Bert.*, transl. Nelson, 86.

46. *Ann. Bert.*, ed. Rau (*sub anno* 862), VI/ii, 110–1; *Ann. Bert.*, transl. Nelson, 98.

47. *Ann. Bert.*, ed. Rau (*sub anno* 865), VI/ii, 150; *Ann. Bert.*, transl. Nelson, 127.

48. *Ann. Fuld.*, ed. Rau (*sub anno* 891), VII/iii, 152, 154; *Ann. Fuld.*, transl. Reuter, 122, 123.

49. Anglo-Saxon poem on the battle of *Brunanburh*, *EHD*, ed. Whitelock, i. 201.

50. H. R. Ellis Davidson, *Gods and Myths of Northern Europe* (Pelican, Harmondsworth, 1964), 29, 65, 146–7.

51. Smyth, *Scandinavian York and Dublin*, ii. 95–6.

52. Smyth, *Scandinavian Kings*, 270.

53. *Annals of St. Neots*, ed. Dumville and Lapidge (*sub anno* 878), 78; Smyth, *Scandinavian Kings*, 269.

54. Ibid. 269–70.

55. Ibid. 270.

56. F. M. Stenton, *et al.*, *The Bayeux Tapestry: A Comprehensive Survey*, 2nd edn. (London, 1965), plate 55.

57. The papal banner is shown in the Bayeux tapestry being held aloft by Eustace during the Battle of Hastings (ibid., plate 69, and notes (*sub* 54–5), pp. 184–5; (*sub* 68–9), p. 187).

58. Cf. J. M. Wallace-Hadrill, *Early Germanic Kingship in England and on the Continent* (Oxford, 1971), 140–1.

59. *Two Saxon Chronicles Parallel*, ed. Plummer and Earle [MS E] (*sub anno* 793), i. 57; *ASC: MS A*, ed. Bately (*sub anno* 851), 44; *ASC: MS B*, ed. Taylor, 31.

60. *ASC: MS A*, ed. Bately (*sub annis* 853, 855–8), 45.

61. Ibid. (*sub annis* 865, 866), 46–7. MS A has *micel here* (*sub anno* 866) MS B has *mycel hæþen here* ('Great *Heathen* Army'), *ASC: MS B*, ed. Taylor, 34.

62. *ASC: MS A*, ed. Bately (*sub anno* 871), 48.

63. Smyth, *Scandinavian Kings*, 128–9, 222 and n. 36.

64. *Ann. Bert.*, *Quellen z. deut. Gesch. d. Mittelalters*, ed. Rau (*sub anno* 878), VI/ii, 260; *Ann. Bert.*, transl. Nelson, 206–7.

65. *Ann. Bert.*, ed. Rau (*sub anno* 868), VI/ii, 244; *Ann. Bert.*, transl. Nelson, 195.

66. *Ann. Ulst.*, ed. Mac Airt and Mac Niocaill (*sub anno* 847), 306–7.

67. *Ann. Bert*; ed. Rau (*sub anno* 864), VI/ii, 128; *Ann. Bert.*, transl. Nelson, 111. I do not accept Professor Nelson's translation or interpretation of this passage in which she argued that 'apostate' had the technical sense here of a monk who had reverted to lay life (*Ann. Bert.*, transl. Nelson, 111 n. 3). That the phrase *ritum eorum servat* means 'followed their [pagan] rites [or religion]' is amply supported by the same annals under the year 841. We are told there of the Saxon *Stellinga* who, 'always prone to evil, they chose to imitate pagan usage (*ritus paganorum*) rather than keep their oaths to the Christian faith' (*Ann. Bert.*, ed. Rau (*sub anno* 841), VI/ii, 54; *Ann. Bert.*, transl. Nelson, 51). There can be no clearer contrast between the pagan *ritus* on the one hand, and Christian practice (*Christianae fidei sacramenta*) on the other. So, too, in the 864 annal, the contrast is between Pippin's status of *ex monacho* and *laicus et apostata*. His

new role as an apostate was clearly linked to the phrase *et ritum eorum servat*. To conclude otherwise is to go against the sense of the annal not only here, but elsewhere throughout this source. Witness, for instance, the case of yet another apostate monk, who was beheaded by the Franks, not because he had abandoned the cloister, but because 'he had abandoned Christendom, and gone to live with the Northmen (*apostatam monachum, qui relicta christianitate se Nortmannis contulerat et nimis christianis infestissimus erat*)' (*Ann. Bert.*, ed. Rau (*sub anno* 869), VI/ii, 202; *Ann. Bert.*, transl. Nelson, 202).

68. *Ann. Bert.*, ed. Rau (*sub anno* 858), VI/ii, 96; *Ann. Bert.*, transl. Nelson, 87–8.

69. *Ann. Bert.*, ed. Rau (*sub anno* 864), VI/ii, 138; *Ann. Bert.*, transl. Nelson, 119.

70. *Ann. Bert.*, ed. Rau (*sub anno* 869), VI/ii, 202; *Ann. Bert.*, transl. Nelson, 163.

71. *Ann. Bert.*,, transl. Nelson (*sub anno* 864), 117 and n. 13; ibid. (*sub anno* 866), 136.

72. *Ann. Bert.*, ed. Rau (*sub anno* 882), VI/ii, 284; *Ann. Bert.*, transl. Nelson, 224. Cf. Reuter's comment, *Ann. Fuld.*, transl. Reuter, 91 n. 4.

73. *EHD*, ed. Whitelock, i. 191.

74. Ibid. 180.

75. Smyth, *Scandinavian Kings*, 207–9.

76. Ibid. 208.

77. *Ann. Bert.*, ed. Rau (*sub anno* 839), VI/ii, 42; cf. *Ann. Bert.*, transl. Nelson, 43, where the phrase *cum inmensa multitudine navium* is not translated by the editor. The English king who warned the Frankish emperor of this vision may have been Alfred's grandfather, Ecgberht, who died in 839 (Kirby, *Earliest English Kings*, 210).

78. *Ann. Bert.*, transl. Nelson (*sub anno* 841), 51.

79. D. Obolensky, *The Byzantine Commonwealth: Eastern Europe, 500–1453* (Cardinal paperback, London, 1974; repr. of 1971 edn.), 85–95.

80. Ibid. 117–18.

81. Ibid. 89.

82. Ibid. 206.

83. Ibid. 248.

84. Ibid. 252–60.

85. *ASC* (*sub anno* 890); *EHD*, ed. Whitelock, i. 184.

86. O. M. Dalton (transl.), *The History of the Franks by Gregory of Tours* (2 vols.; Oxford, 1927), ii. 69, 498–9. R. Latouche, *Grégoire de Tours: Histoire des Francs* (2 vols.; Paris, 1963), i. 120. I am grateful to the late Michael Wallace-Hadrill for his helpful discussions on the conversion of Clovis.

87. *Ann. Bert.*, ed. Rau (*sub anno* 876), VI/ii, 244; *Ann. Bert.*, transl. Nelson, 195. Nelson (*Charles the Bald*, 244) implies that this audience with the vikings formed part of the concluding session of the synod. The viking visit to the Frankish court is reported after the closing of the synod in the Annals of St Bertin, suggesting that the incident took place after the synod was formally closed.

88. *Ann. Bert.*, transl. Nelson (*sub anno* 862), 99.

89. *Ann. Fuld.*, transl. Reuter (*sub anno* 882), 93.

90. *Ann. Bert.*, transl. Nelson (*sub anno* 864), 118.

91. *Ann. Reg. Franc.*, *Quellen z. deut. Gesch. d. Mittelaters*, ed. Rau (*sub anno* 826), V/i, 144.

92. *Ann. Bert.*, transl. Nelson (*sub anno* 873), 184–5.

93. Ibid. 183.

94. *Ann. Fuld.*, transl. Reuter (*sub anno* 882), 92 and n. 6.

95. Ibid. 92–3, 105.

96. Ibid. 93.

97. Obolensky, *Byzantine Commonwealth*, 117–18.

98. Whitelock, 'Importance of the Battle of Edington', in Whitelock (ed.), *From Alfred to Bede*, 13.

99. *EHD*, ed. Whitelock, i. 180.

100. *Life* of Alfred, ed. Stevenson, ch. 58, p. 47. The text of the *Life* of Alfred is ambiguous and confused here. We are told that although the newly arrived army 'from overseas' made contact 'with the army further upstream', it nevertheless wintered at Fulham.

101. *EHD*, ed. Whitelock, i. 181.

102. *Ann. Bert.*, transl. Nelson (*sub anno* 873), 184–5.

103. *Ann. Fuld.*, transl. Reuter (*sub anno* 882), 105.

104. Ibid. 105. *Ann. Fuld.*, ed. Rau (*sub anno* 882), vii/iii, 132–4.

105. Ibid. (*sub anno* 873), 88; *Ann. Fuld.*, transl. Reuter, 70–1.

106. Ibid. (*sub anno* 882), 93.

107. *Ann. Bert.*, ed. Rau (*sub anno* 873), vi/ii, 230; *Ann. Bert.*, transl. Nelson, 184, puts the number of Norsemen slain, at 500 men (p. 184); *Ann. Fuld.*, transl. Reuter (*sub anno* 873, p. 72), puts the number slain at 800.

108. *Ann. Fuld.*, ed. Rau (*sub anno* 873), vii/iii, 90–2; *Ann. Fuld.*, transl. Reuter (*sub anno* 873), 72.

109. *ASC: MS A*, ed. Bately (*sub annis* 871, 878), 48–9, 51.

110. *Ann. Fuld.*, transl. Reuter (*sub anno* 882), 105.

111. Ibid. 93.

112. Ibid. 105.

113. *Ann. Bert.*, ed. Rau (*sub anno* 839), vi/ii, 48; *Ann. Bert.*, transl. Nelson, 47.

114. *Ann. Fuld.*, transl. Reuter (*sub anno* 873), 71.

115. Smyth, *Scandinavian York and Dublin*, ii. 82.

116. *Ann. Fuld.*, transl. Reuter (*sub anno* 882), 93.

117. *Ann. Bert.*, transl. Nelson (*sub anno* 882), 225. Hincmar (ibid.) identified the church of St Stephen at Metz as one of the targets for paying this treasure.

118. *Ann. Fuld.*, transl. Reuter (*sub anno* 882), 93.

119. See the discussion on the authorship of the Anglo-Saxon Chronicle, pp. 482–98 below.

120. *Ann. Bert.*, transl. Nelson (*sub anno* 845), 61–2.

121. Ibid. (*sub anno* 862), 98.

122. Ibid. (*sub anno* 866), 130; *Ann. Bert.*, ed. Rau, vi/ii, 154.

123. *Ann. Fuld.*, transl. Reuter (*sub anno* 882), 93.

124. *EHD*, ed. Whitelock, i. 380; text, F. L. Attenborough (ed.), *The Laws of the Earliest English Kings* (New York, 1963; repr. of 1922 edn.), 98–101. For a discussion of the date of the text of this treaty, see Dumville, *Wessex and England*, 1–23.

125. *EHD*, ed. Whitelock, i. 381; *Laws*, ed. Attenborough, 100–1.

126. *EHD*, ed. Whitelock, i. 381; *Laws*, ed. Attenborough, 98–9.

127. Keynes and Lapidge (*Alfred the Great*, 312 n. 3) believed that *Alfred and Guthrum* §2 was intended 'to discourage clashes between men of the two races [*sic*] within Guthrum's kingdom itself'.

128. *EHD*, ed. Whitelock (no. 41), i. 401.

129. See pp. 86, 88 above.

130. *EHD*, ed. Whitelock, i. 182.

131. *Ann. Bert.*, transl. Nelson (*sub anno* 873), 185; *Ann. Fuld.*, transl. Reuter (*sub anno* 882), 92–3.

132. *Ann. Fuld.*, transl. Reuter (*sub anno* 873), 70.
133. *Ann. Bert.*, ed. Rau (*sub anno* 836), VI/ii, 30; *Ann. Bert.*, transl. Nelson, 35.
134. *EHD*, ed. Whitelock, i. 200.
135. For a discussion on the authorship of the 878 annal, see pp. 473–74 below.
136. *EHD*, ed. Whitelock, i. 257; *Rogeri de Wendover*, ed. Coxe, i. 385.
137. Smyth, *Scandinavian York and Dublin*, ii. 64–5.
138. *ASC* (*sub annis* 943–4); *EHD*, ed. Whitelock, i. 202–3; Smyth, *Scandinavian York and Dublin*, ii. 110–13.
139. *Ann. Bert.*, transl. Nelson (*sub anno* 862), 99.
140. Ibid. (*sub anno* 863), 111.
141. Ibid. (*sub anno* 876), 195.
142. *Ann. Fuld.*, transl. Reuter (*sub annis* 883, 885), 94, 97.
143. *ASC: MS A*, ed. Bately (*sub anno* 890), 54; *EHD*, ed. Whitelock, i. 184.

Chapter IV

1. See pp. 464–526 below.
2. See pp. 464, 523–4 below.
3. *ASC* (*sub anno* 880); *EHD*, ed. Whitelock, i. 181.
4. Ibid. 181 nn. 6 and 7.
5. *ASC: MS A*, ed. Bately, 52; *Æthelweard*, ed. Campbell, 44; *Life* of Alfred, ed. Stevenson, ch. 65, p. 49.
6. *Ann. Bert.*, transl. Nelson (*sub anno* 860), 92.
7. Ibid. (*sub anno* 861), 95.
8. The Anglo-Saxon Chronicle reports that a viking fleet, attacking in the Severn estuary in 914, departed for Ireland (*EHD*, ed. Whitelock, i. 195). The subsequent history of that fleet can only be traced through contemporary Irish annals (Smyth, *Scandinavian York and Dublin*, i. 65–6).
9. *EHD*, ed. Whitelock, i. 183.
10. *Ann. Fuld.*, transl. Reuter (*sub anno* 888), 115 n. 2.
11. Ibid. (*sub anno* 884), 96. It may be that the original Frankish manuscript source for the Anglo-Saxon Chronicle's material on Francia gave the slain king's name incorrectly as Charles. The form Charles appears in the Anglo-Saxon Chronicle and in the Annals of Fulda. On the other hand, the author of the *Life* of Alfred—normally careless in such matters—gives the correct form of Carloman, which suggests that the early version of the Anglo-Saxon Chronicle on which he relied did preserve that correct form (*Life* of Alfred, ed. Stevenson, ch. 68, p. 51).
12. *EHD*, ed. Whitelock, i. 181, 184.
13. Ibid. 182.
14. *Ann. Fuld.*, ed. Rau (*sub anno* 884), VII/iii, 120; *Ann. Fuld.*, transl. Reuter, 95.
15. *Ann. Fuld.*, ed. Rau (*sub anno* 885), VII/iii, 124; *Ann. Fuld.*, transl. Reuter, 97–8.
16. The question of what Frankish manuscripts may have been available to Alfredian scholars is as yet not fully explored. There is the possibility that geographical additions relating to Continental Europe which are found in the Old English *Orosius* may have been consulted in a Frankish source. Cf. *The Old English Orosius*, ed. J. M. Bately (Early English Texts Soc. Supplementary Series, 6; Oxford, 1980), pp. lxvii–lxx, 12, 167.
17. The exemplar of the Frankish annals for the 880s used by the Anglo-Saxon chronicler

most probably belonged to one of the continuations of the manuscripts in Group 3 of the Annals of Fulda.

18. *ASC* (*sub anno* 887); *EHD*, ed. Whitelock, i. 183.
19. *Ann. Fuld.*, ed. Rau (*sub annis* 887–8), vii/iii, 144–6. *Ann. Fuld.*, transl. Reuter, 114–16.
20. Ibid. 116 n. 7.
21. *EHD*, ed. Whitelock, i. 183.
22. *ASC: MS A*, ed. Bately (*sub anno* 855), 52; *EHD*, ed. Whitelock, i. 182.
23. *Ann. Bert.*, ed. Rau (*sub annis* 858 and 862), vi/ii, 96 and 108; *Ann. Bert.*, transl. Nelson, 86 and 97.
24. See pp. 12–17 above.
25. *ASC: MS A*, ed. Bately (*sub anno* 855), 45–6; *EHD*, ed. Whitelock, i. 174–5.
26. Ibid. 183.
27. Ibid. 176.
28. *King Alfred's Old English Version of Boethius De Consolatione Philosophiae*, ed. W. J. Sedgefield (Oxford, 1899), 7.
29. *EHD*, ed. Whitelock, i. 181–2; *ASC: MS A*, ed. Bately (*sub anno* 887), 52–3; *ASC: MS B*, ed. Taylor (*sub anno* 886), 38–9.
30. *EHD*, ed. Whitelock, i. 155; A. P. Smyth, *Warlords and Holy Men: Scotland AD 80–1000* (London, 1984; repr. Edinburgh, 1989), 26.
31. *ASC: MS A*, ed. Bately (*sub anno* 851), 44; *ASC: MS B*, ed. Taylor (*sub anno* 853), 31–2; *EHD*, ed. Whitelock, i. 173. MS B specifies that the engagement took place 'in ships'.
32. *Einhardi Vita Karoli Magni* [ch. 17], *Quellen z. deut. Gesch. d. Mittelalters*, ed. Rau, v/i, 186–8. *Ann. Bert.*, ed. Rau (*sub anno* 837), vi/ii, 32.
33. *Einhardi Vita Karoli*, ed. Rau, v/i, 186–8; L. Thorpe (transl.), *Einhard and Notker the Stammerer: Two Lives of Charlemagne* (Penguin, Harmondsworth, 1969), 72.
34. *Ann. Bert.*, transl. Nelson (*sub anno* 854), 79.
35. Ibid. (*sub anno* 862), 98.
36. Ibid. (*sub anno* 872), 180.
37. Ibid. (*sub anno* 862), 99.
38. *ASC: MS A*, ed. Bately (*sub anno* 875), 49–50; *EHD*, ed. Whitelock, i. 179.
39. *ASC: MS A*, ed. Bately (*sub anno* 882), 51; *EHD*, ed. Whitelock, i. 181.
40. It is probable, though not certain, that Alfred's punitive expedition had been provoked by an earlier act of East Anglian aggression. See p. 92 above.
41. The notice of the East Anglian Danes breaking the peace is entered after the record of Alfred's naval expedition against them (*ASC: MS A*, ed. Bately (*sub anno* 885), 52; *ASC: MS B*, ed. Taylor (*sub anno* 886), 38; *EHD*, ed. Whitelock, i. 182).
42. Nor should these statistics be used to suggest that elsewhere in the Anglo-Saxon Chronicle and annals from other societies in the Christian West references to viking fleets in excess of a hundred ships must be exaggerated. On the contrary, the existence of modest numbers recorded alongside larger estimates strongly suggests the veracity of both records, especially when chronicles from Anglo-Saxon England, Ireland, and Francia can be shown to have consistently preserved remarkably similar statistics independently of each other.
43. H. [R.] Loyn, *The Vikings in Wales* (Dorothea Coke Memorial Lecture, University College, London, 1976), 5, 8–10.
44. *Ann. Bert.*, ed. Rau (*sub anno* 837), vi/ii, 32; *Ann. Bert.*, transl. Nelson, 37.
45. *Ann. Bert.*, ed. Rau (*sub anno* 846), vi/ii, 68; *Ann. Bert.*, transl. Nelson, 62.
46. *Ann. Bert.*, ed. Rau (*sub anno* 850), vi/ii, 76; *ann. Bert.*, transl. Nelson, 69.

47. *ASC: MS A*, ed. Bately (*sub anno* 896), 60; *EHD*, ed. Whitelock, i. 189.
48. P. Foote and D. M. Wilson, *The Viking Achievement: The Society and Culture of Early Medieval Scandinavia* (London, 1980; repr. of 1970 edn.), 242–56.
49. *ASC: MS A*, ed. Bately (*sub anno* 896), 60–1; *EHD*, ed. Whitelock, i. 189.
50. *ASC: MS A*, ed. Bately (*sub anno* 896), 60.
51. 120 Danes were slain in the skirmish about the stranded Alfredian boats, while the crews of almost three Danish ships had earlier been slaughtered in the same incident. We are told that in that summer of 896, 'no fewer than 20 ships, men and all, perished along the south coast' (*EHD*, ed. Whitelock, i. 189).
52. The Frisians, according to contemporary Frankish observers, fought the Northmen in very small boats, and it would seem that small craft were associated in Frankish eyes with traditional Frisian boat design (*Ann. Fuld.*, ed. Rau (*sub anno* 885), VII/iii, 124).
53. *EHD*, ed. Whitelock, i. 181.
54. *Ann. Fuld.*, transl. Reuter, 121–3.
55. Nelson, *Charles the Bald*, 125, 133, 225–6, and 320–1 map 3.
56. Ibid. 193.
57. *Annales Vedastini, Quellen z. duet, Gesch. d. Mittelalters*, ed. Rau (*sub anno* 882), VI/ii, 302.
58. *Ann. Bert.*, ed. Rau (*sub anno* 882), VI/ii, 284; *Ann. Bert.*, transl. Nelson, 224.
59. *Ann. Bert.*, transl. Nelson (*sub anno* 882), 226.
60. See pp. 116–18 below.

Chapter V

1. Smyth, *Scandinavian Kings*, 54–67.
2. F. Amory, 'The Viking Hasting in Franco-Scandinavian Legend', in M. H. King and W. M. Stevens (eds.), *Saints, Scholars and Heroes: Studies in Medieval Culture in Honour of Charles W. Jones* (2 vols.; Collegeville, Minn., 1979), ii. 266–7; Whitelock accepted the original form as *Hásteinn* (*EHD*, i. 185 n. 3).
3. *Dudonis de moribus et actis primorum Normanniæ ducum*, ed. J. P. Migne (*Patrologiae*, vol. 141; Paris, 1853), 622.
4. Cf. *Ann. Bert., Quellen z. deut. Gesch. d. Mittelalters*, ed. Rau (*sub anno* 857), VI/ii, 94; (*sub anno* 859), 100.
5. Amory, 'Viking Hasting', in King and Stevens (eds.), *Studies in Honour of Jones*, ii. 270.
6. *Reginonis Chronica, Quellen z. deut. Gesch. d. Mittelalters*, ed. Rau (*sub anno* 867), VII/iii, 214–16.
7. *Dudonis de moribus*, ed. Migne, 622–5.
8. Ibid. Cf. Amory, 'Viking Hasting', in King and Stevens (eds.), *Studies in Honour of Jones*, 270.
9. *The Gesta Normannorum Ducum of William of Jumièges, Orderic Vitalis, and Robert of Torigni*, ed. E. M. C. van Houts (2 vols; Oxford, 1992), i. 11, 22–7.
10. *Dudonis de moribus*, ed. Migne, 626.
11. *Gesta Normannorum of William of Jumièges*, ed. van Houts, i. 27, 57.
12. *Reginonis Chronica*, ed. Rau (*sub anno* 874), VII/iii, 244.
13. *Ann. Ved.*, ed. Rau (*sub anno* 882), VI/ii, 302.
14. *Ann. Bert.*, ed. Rau (*sub anno* 882), VI/ii, 284; *Ann. Bert.*, transl. Nelson, 224.
15. Smyth, *Scandinavian Kings*, 64–5.

16. *Ann. Ved.*, ed. Rau (*sub annis* 889–90), VI/ii, 320.

17. *ASC: MS A*, ed. Bately (*sub anno* 890), 54; *EHD*, ed. Whitelock, i. 184.

18. *Ann. Ved.*, ed. Rau (*sub anno* 890), VI/ii, 320.

19. Ibid. (*sub anno* 890), VI/ii, 320–2.

20. Ibid. (*sub anno* 891), VI/ii, 322.

21. *ASC: MS A (sub anno* 891); *EHD*, ed. Whitelock, i. 184; *Ann. Fuld.*, ed. Rau (*sub anno* 891), VII/iii, 151–4; *Reginonis Chronica*, ed. Rau (*sub anno* 891), VII/iii, 294.

22. *Ann. Ved.*, ed. Rau (*sub anno* 891), VI/ii, 322.

23. Ibid. (*sub anno* 892), 324.

24. *ASC (sub anno* 892); *EHD*, ed. Whitelock, i. 184.

25. *Ann. Fuld.*, transl. Reuter (*sub anno* 891), 123.

26. *ASC (sub anno* 892); *EHD*, ed. Whitelock, i. 184–5.

27. B. K. Davison, 'The Burghal Hidage Fort at Eorpeburnan: A Suggested Identification', *Medieval Archaeology*, 16 (1972), 123–7; N. Brooks, 'The Unidentified Forts of the Burghal Hidage', *Medieval Archaeology*, 8 (1964), 81–6; Keynes and Lapidge (transl.), *Alfred the Great*, 284 n. 22; Dumville, *Wessex and England*, 25 n. 121. For the *Burghal Hidage*, see pp. 134–7 below.

28. *ASC: MS A*, ed. Bately (*sub anno* 893), 57; *EHD*, ed. Whitelock, i. 186.

29. *Ann. Bert.*, ed. Rau (*sub anno* 862), VI/ii, 110; *Ann. Bert.*, transl. Nelson, 99.

30. *ASC: MS A*, ed. Bately (*sub anno* 893), 58; *EHD*, ed. Whitelock, i. 187.

31. *ASC: MS A*, ed. Bately (*sub anno* 893), 57; *EHD*, ed. Whitelock, i. 186.

32. *ASC: MS A*, ed. Bately (*sub anno* 896), 59; *EHD*, ed. Whitelock, i. 188.

33. Smyth, *Scandinavian York and Dublin*, ii. 193–5, 212–13, 217 nn. 6 and 7.

34. *ASC (sub anno* 893); *EHD*, ed. Whitelock, i. 185.

35. Ibid.

36. *Æthelweard*, ed. Campbell, 49, where that editor wrongly translated *Hamtunscire* as Northamptonshire. I followed Campbell's error here in my earlier work (Smyth, *Scandinavian York and Dublin*, i. 32).

37. Æthelweard alone names Edward the Elder as the leader of the victorious English army at Farnham (ed. Campbell, 49). The Chronicle proper, tells of the recovery of the booty (*ASC (sub anno* 893); *EHD*, ed. Whitelock, i. 185).

38. Ibid.

39. *Æthelweard*, ed. Campbell, 49–59; *ASC (sub anno* 893); *EHD*, ed. Whitelock, i. 185–6; and ibid. 186 n. 1.

40. *Æthelweard*, ed. Campbell, 49.

41. Ibid. 49–50.

42. *ASC (sub anno* 893); *EHD*, ed. Whitelock, i. 186.

43. Smyth, *Scandinavian York and Dublin*, i. 32–3.

44. *Æthelweard*, ed. Campbell, 50.

45. Ibid. 51.

46. F. M. Stenton, 'Æthelweard's Account of the Last Years of King Alfred's Reign', *Eng. Hist. Rev.* 24 (1909), 81–2. Smyth, *Scandinavian York and Dublin*, i. 33–4.

47. *Ann. Ulst.*. ed. Mac Airt and Mac Niocaill (*sub anno* 837), 294–5; *Ann. Ulst.*, ed. Hennessy and MacCarthy (*sub anno* 836), i. 338–9.

48. *Ann. Bert.*, ed. Rau (*sub anno* 861), VI/ii, 106, Cf. *Ann. Bert.*, transl. Nelson, 95.

49. *Ann. Bert.*, ed. Rau (*sub anno* 859), VI/ii, 98; *Ann. Bert.*, transl. Nelson, 89.

50. *ASC (sub anno* 894); *EHD*, ed. Whitelock, i. 187.

51. Smyth, *Scandinavian York and Dublin*, i. 34–5.

52. *ASC* (*sub anno* 893); *EHD*, ed. Whitelock, i. 187.

53. Ibid.

54. Ibid. 186.

55. Ibid.

56. *ASC: MS A*, ed. Bately (*sub anno* 893), 57.

57. Whitelock's suggestion (*EHD*, i. 186 n. 4) that Alfred and Ealdorman Æthelred had negotiated with Hæsten back in 885 has little to recommend it. She herself admitted there was no evidence that Hæsten was a leader of the expedition launched from Francia against Rochester in that year (*ASC* (*sub anno* 885); *EHD*, ed. Whitelock, i. 181–2). The AD 885 attack was fended off by Alfred's decisive action in coming to the support of the town. Æthelweard alone tells us that not all the viking assailants of Rochester returned immediately to the Continent. A section of them remained and 'renewed their exchange of hostages with the English' (*Æthelweard*, ed. Campbell, 44). Æthelweard's mention of a joint attack by East Anglian Danes allied with viking stragglers from the Rochester expedition, against Benfleet later in 885, does not help in any way (ibid. 45). It is very unlikely that there was any connection between viking action around Benfleet in 885 and events of 893. When the annalist of 893 tells us that Alfred and Ealdorman Æthelred 'had stood sponsor to them [i.e. Hæsten's family] before Hæsten came to Benfleet' (*ASC* (*sub anno* 893); *EHD*, ed. Whitelock, i. 186) he clearly referred—from the context of the discussion—to Hæsten's recent arrival at Benfleet in 893, from his earlier camp at Milton Regis (cf. Keynes and Lapidge (transl.), *Alfred the Great*, 287 n. 11). We may take it, then, that Alfred's peace negotiations with Hæsten had taken place in East Kent—most likely at Milton—earlier in 893.

58. See pp. 96–7 above.

59. *Reginonis Chronica*, ed. Rau (*sub anno* 882), VII/iii, 264; *Ann. Fuld.*, ed. Rau (*sub anno* 883), VII/iii, 120.

60. *Æthelweard*, ed. Campbell, 50.

61. *ASC* (*sub anno* 893); *EHD*, ed. Whitelock, i. 187.

62. Ibid.

63. Ibid. (*sub anno* 887), 183.

64. *Æthelweard*, ed. Campbell, 42, 51.

65. On the other hand, the statement that the Buttington vikings fled back to Essex 'to their fortress and their ships' (*EHD*, ed. Whitelock, i. 186) suggests that the main bulk of their fleet had been left for safety in the east.

66. *EHD*, ed. Whitelock, i. 187.

67. Ibid.

68. Ibid. (*sub anno* 894), 187.

69. Ibid.

70. Ibid. (*sub anno* 895), 188.

71. Ibid. (*sub anno* 896), 188.

72. *Æthelweard*, ed. Campbell, 49.

73. *ASC* (*sub anno* 893); *EHD*, ed. Whitelock, i. 185.

74. Ibid. 186.

75. *Ann. Ved.*, ed. Rau (*sub anno* 884), VI/ii, 304.

76. *Reginonis Chronica*, ed. Rau (*sub anno* 882), VII/iii, 260–2.

77. Smyth, *Scandinavian Kings*, 167; id., *Scandinavian York and Dublin*, ii. 130–1.

78. *Æthelweard*, ed. Campbell, 44.

79. *ASC* (*sub anno* 894); *EHD*, ed. Whitelock, i. 187.
80. *ASC: MS A*, ed. Bately (*sub anno* 893), 57; *EHD*, ed. Whitelock, i. 187.
81. *Æthelweard*, ed. Campbell, 50.
82. Smyth, *Scandinavian York and Dublin*, i. 34.
83. Cf. D. Hill, *An Atlas of Anglo-Saxon England* (Oxford, 1981), 41.
84. *Ann. Bert.*, transl. Nelson (*sub anno* 881), 222.
85. *Ann. Fuld.*, transl. Reuter (*sub anno* 881), 90.
86. *Ann. Ved.*, ed. Rau (*sub anno* 881), VI/ii, 300.
87. Ibid. (*sub anno* 892), 324.
88. *EHD*, ed. Whitelock, i. 194–5.
89. *Ann. Fuld.*, transl. Reuter (*sub anno* 887), 101.
90. *ASC* (*sub anno* 896); *EHD*, ed. Whitelock, i. 188.
91. *Ann. Fuld.*, transl. Reuter (*sub anno* 882), 92, 105.
92. Ibid. 105.
93. See pp. 88–91 above.
94. *ASC* (*sub anno* 893); *EHD*, ed. Whitelock, i. 186.
95. Ibid. (*sub anno* 895), 188.
96. Smyth, *Scandinavian York and Dublin*, ii. 19, 197, 251.
97. *Ann. Bert.*, transl. Nelson (*sub anno* 862), 98.
98. Ibid. (*sub anno* 866), 131.
99. *ASC* (*sub anno* 911); *EHD*, ed. Whitelock, i. 193.
100. Ibid. (Mercian Register, *sub annis* 918–19), 198.
101. Campbell, John, and Wormald, *The Anglo-Saxons*, 152; cf. Keynes and Lapidge (transl.), *Alfred the Great*, 339 and 341 n. 15.
102. See pp. 68, 75 above.
103. *ASC: MS A*, ed. Bately (*sub anno* 893), 56; cf. *EHD*, ed. Whitelock, i. 185.
104. *ASC: MS A*, ed. Bately (*sub anno* 893), 57; *EHD*, ed. Whitelock, i. 187.
105. Ibid. 191.
106. *ASC: MS A*, ed. Bately (*sub anno* 900), 61; *EHD*, ed. Whitelock, i. 190.
107. *SEHD*, ed. Harmer, 18, 51.
108. *ASC: MS A*, ed. Bately (*sub anno* 900), 61–2; *EHD*, ed. Whitelock, i. 190.
109. Ibid. (*sub anno* 895), 188.
110. Campbell, John, and Wormald, *The Anglo-Saxons*, 57–8.
111. *ASC: MS A*, ed. Bately (*sub anno* 755), 36–7.
112. *Ann. Reg. Franc.*, *Quellen z. deut. Gesch. d. Mittelalters*, ed. Rau (*sub anno* 808), V/i, 88.
113. Bronsted, *The Vikings*, 166–85.
114. Smyth, *Scandinavian York and Dublin*, ii. 197.
115. Smyth, *Scandinavian Kings*, 145.
116. Smyth, *Scandinavian York and Dublin*, i. 66, 67–8, 73.
117. *Chronicum Scotorum: A Chronicle of Irish Affairs from the Earliest Times to AD 1135* ed. W. M. Hennessy (Rolls Series; London, 1866), (*sub anno* 845), 144–5.
118. *Ann. Fuld.*, transl. Reuter (*sub anno* 882), 104.
119. *Ann. Fuld.*, ed. Rau (*sub anno* 891), VII/iii, 152; *Ann. Fuld.*, transl. Reuter, 121.
120. *ASC: MS A*, ed. Bately (*sub anno* 885), 52; *EHD*, ed. Whitelock, i. 181.
121. *Ann. Ved.*, ed. Rau (*sub anno* 890), VI/ii, 320.
122. *Einhardi Vita Karoli*, ed. Rau, V/i, 186.
123. *Ann. Bert.*, ed. Rau (*sub anno* 837), VI/ii, 32; *Ann. Bert.*, transl. Nelson, 36–7.
124. *Ann. Bert.*, ed. Rau (*sub anno* 837), VI/ii, 32; Nelson, transl., 37.

125. *Ann. Bert.*, ed. Rau (*sub anno* 839), VI/ii, 38; *Ann. Bert.*, transl. Nelson, 41.

126. *Ann. Bert.*, ed. Rau (*sub anno* 862), VI/ii, 108; *Ann. Bert.*, transl. Nelson, 98.

127. *Ann. Bert.*, ed. Rau (*sub anno* 865), VI/ii, 150; *Ann. Bert.*, transl. Nelson, 127.

128. *Ann. Bert.*, ed. Rau (*sub anno* 862), VI/ii, 110–2; *Ann. Bert.*, transl. Nelson, 100.

129. *Ann. Bert.*, ed. Rau (*sub anno* 866), VI/ii, 156; *Ann. Bert.*, transl. Nelson, 131.

130. *Ann. Bert.*, ed. Rau (*sub anno* 868), VI/ii, 184; *Ann. Bert.*, transl. Nelson, 151.

131. *Ann. Bert.*, ed. Rau (*sub anno* 869), VI/ii, 186–8; *Ann. Bert.*, transl. Nelson, 153–4.

132. *Mon. Ger. Hist.*, *Capitularia regum Francorum*, II, ed. A. Boretius and V. Krause, (Hanover, 1897), (no. 275), 337.

133. *Ann. Bert.*, ed. Rau (*sub anno* 873), VI/ii, 232; *Ann. Bert.*, transl. Nelson, 185.

134. Nelson, *Charles the Bald*, 213.

135. *Ann. Bert.*, ed. Rau (*sub anno* 869), VI/ii, 202; *Ann. Bert.*, transl. Nelson, 163–4.

136. *Ann. Fuld.*, transl. Reuter (*sub anno* 881), 90–1.

137. Ibid. (*sub anno* 883), 95.

138. *Ann. Bert.*, ed. Rau (*sub anno* 882), VI/ii, 286; *Ann. Bert.*, transl. Nelson, 226.

139. *Ann. Ved.*, ed. Rau (*sub anno* 884), VI/ii, 304–6.

140. *Ann. Bert.*, ed. Rau (*sub anno* 860), VI/ii, 102; *Ann. Bert.*, transl. Nelson, 92.

141. *Ann. Bert.*, ed. Rau (*sub anno* 866), VI/ii, 154; *Ann. Bert.*, transl. Nelson, 130.

142. Ibid. 130 n. 4.

143. See p. 41 above.

144. *Ann. Bert.*, ed. Rau (*sub anno* 865), VI/ii, 150; *Ann. Bert.*, transl. Nelson, 127.

145. *Ann. Ved.*, ed. Rau (*sub anno* 884), VI/ii, 304–6.

146. *ASC* (*sub anno* 896); *EHD*, ed. Whitelock, i. 188.

147. See pp. 111–13 above.

148. *EHD*, ed. Whitelock, i. 189.

Chapter VI

1. *Life* of Alfred, ed. Stevenson, ch. 91, p. 76.

2. *EHD*, ed. Whitelock, i. 192.

3. The *Life* of Alfred provides a translation of the Alfredian Chronicle from AD 851—supposedly the third year of Alfred's life—up until AD 887 (*Life* of Alfred, ed. Stevenson, ch. 3, p. 4—ch. 86, p. 73).

4. T. Wright, 'Some Historical Doubts Relating to the Biographer Asser', *Archaeologia*, 29 (1842), 192–201.

5. Ibid. 196, 199–200. Cf. *Life* of Alfred, ed. Stevenson, pp. xlix–l.

6. Ibid., pp. xcix, ciii.

7. Ibid., pp. xiii–xxxii.

8. Ibid., pp. 221–5; 294–6.

9. Ibid., p. xcvi.

10. Ibid., pp. c–ci; cviii.

11. Ibid., p. xcvii and cf. pp. xcvii–xcix.

12. V. H. Galbraith, 'Who Wrote Asser's Life of Alfred?', in V. H. Galbraith, *An Introduction to the Study of History* (London, 1964), 122.

13. F. W. Maitland, 'The Laws of the Anglo-Saxons', *Quarterly Review*, 200 (October 1904), 147–8.

14. Galbraith, 'Who Wrote Asser's Life of Alfred', 90.

15. Ibid. 93–4, 110, 113–14, 120.
16. Ibid. 91–2, 104–10.
17. Ibid. 113.
18. Ibid. 99–103.
19. Ibid. 99–100.
20. Ibid. 111.
21. J. L. Nelson, 'Myths of the Dark Ages', in L. M. Smith (ed.), *The Making of Britain: The Dark Ages* (London, 1984), 155.
22. H. H. Howorth, 'Asser's Life of Alfred', *The Athenæum*, no. 2526 (25 Mar. 1876), 425–6; ibid., no. 2535 (27 May 1876), 727–9; no. 2549 (2 Sept. 1876), 307–9; and ibid., 'Ethelweard and Asser', no. 2597 (4 Aug. 1877), 145–6. Cf. Clifford's reply to Howorth—W. Clifford, 'Asser's Life of Alfred', ibid., no. 2539 (24 June 1876), 859–60. *Life* of Alfred, ed. Stevenson, pp. cx–cxv.
23. Because of the uncorrected dating in the Anglo-Saxon Chronicle, 901 rather than 899 was considered to have been the year of Alfred's death (*Two Saxon Chronicles Parallel*, ed. Plummer and Earle, i. 91).
24. Nelson, 'Myths of the Dark Ages', in Smith (ed.), *Making of Britain*, 149.
25. Stenton, *Anglo-Saxon England*, 261.
26. See Nelson, 'Myths of the Dark Ages', in Smith (ed.), *Making of Britain*, plate 83, p. 156.
27. Stenton, *Anglo-Saxon England*, 269 n. 1.
28. Ibid. 268.
29. D. Whitelock, *The Genuine Asser* (Stenton Lecture 1967; Reading, 1968), 3.
30. D. Whitelock, 'Recent Work on Asser's Life of Alfred', in *Life* of Alfred, ed. Stevenson, p. cxlvii.
31. *Willelmi Malmesbiriensis monachi de Gestis Pontificum Anglorum Libri Quinque*, ed. N. E. S. A. Hamilton (Rolls Series; London, 1870), 177. *Willelmi Malmesbiriensis monachi de Gestis regum Anglorum*, ed. W. Stubbs (Rolls Series; London, 1887), i. 131.
32. See pp. 357–60 below.
33. Whitelock, *Genuine Asser*, 20.
34. Ibid. 8.
35. Ibid. 20.
36. *Life* of Alfred, ed. Stevenson, p. xi.
37. Keynes and Lapidge (transl.), *Alfred the Great*, 50.
38. Ibid.
39. Ibid. 51.
40. *Life* of Alfred, ed. Stevenson, pp. li–liii.
41. Ibid., p. lii.
42. Ibid., pp. liii–liv.
43. Ibid., pp. xxi–xxviii.
44. Ibid., pp. xxviii–xxxi.
45. Ibid., pp. xxxii–xxxiii.
46. Keynes and Lapidge (transl.) *Alfred the Great*, 224–5.
47. *Life* of Alfred, ed. Stevenson, pp. xxxii–xxxiii.
48. Ibid., pp. xv–xvi.
49. Sisam, *Studies in the History of Old English Literature*, 148 n. 3.
50. Whitelock, *Genuine Asser*, 17.
51. *Life* of Alfred, ed. Stevenson, p. xliv.

52. Sisam, *Studies*, 148 n. 3.
53. *Life* of Alfred, ed. Stevenson, pp. xxxviii and n. 1.
54. Stevenson (ibid., index, 383), wrongly described Ussher as archbishop of Dublin.
55. Ibid., p. xli.
56. Ibid., p. xlii and n. 1.
57. Ibid., p. xliii.
58. Ibid., p. xliii; Whitelock, 'Recent Work on Asser's Life of Alfred', p. cxxvii–cxxviii; Sisam, *Studies*, 148 n. 3.
59. *Life* of Alfred, ed. Stevenson, p. xxx, n. 1.
60. Ibid., p. xliii.
61. Ibid., pp. xlvi–xlvii; lv–lvii.
62. C. [R.] Hart, 'The East Anglian Chronicle', *Journal of Medieval History*, 7 (1981), 268; Keynes and Lapidge (transl.), *Alfred the Great*, 52.
63. C. [R.], Hart, 'Byrhtferth's Northumbrian Chronicle', *Eng. Hist. Rev.* 97 (1982), 558–82; M. Lapidge, 'Byrhtferth of Ramsey and the Early Sections of the *Historia Regum* Attributed to Symeon of Durham', *ASE* 10 (1982), 97–122.
64. *Life* of Alfred, ed. Stevenson, p. lix.
65. P. Hunter Blair, 'Some Observations on the "Historia Regum" Attributed to Symeon of Durham', in K. Jackson, *et al.* (eds.), *Celt and Saxon: Studies in the Early British Border* (Cambridge, 1964), 100–2.
66. Lapidge, 'Byrhtferth of Ramsey', 121.
67. Whitelock (*Genuine Asser*, 18 n. 2) discussed the text of chapter 70 of the *Life* of Alfred dealing with events of 885, as copied into the second set of extracts from the *Life* in the later part of the *Historia Regum* (*HR* 2). There she demonstrated that while this second section of the *Life* of Alfred usually follows Florence of Worcester's extracts from that work, in the case of the 885 events, the compiler of the *Historia Regum* (*HR* 2) must have been following that manuscript of the *Life* which had been available to the compiler (Byrhtferth) of the first five parts of the *Historia* (*HR* 1). Furthermore, she held that the particular reading of the manuscript of the *Life* which lies behind the *HR* 2 text of the *Historia* was closer to the reading preserved in the Annals of St Neots version than to that of Cotton Otho A.xii, and that the Cotton text contained an inferior version. She also concluded that the *HR* 2 text in this particular instance had not borrowed from *HR* 1, but from that manuscript of Alfred's *Life* which had also been the source of the *HR* 1 extracts.
68. Keynes and Lapidge (transl.), *Alfred the Great*, 57.
69. *Life* of Alfred, ed. Stevenson, pp. xlviii–xlix; lviii–lix.
70. Ibid., p. lix.
71. Hart, 'Byrhtferth's Northumbrian Chronicle', 563–4.
72. Ibid. 578.
73. Ibid. 575–6.
74. Ibid. 576.
75. The date of compilation of the Annals of St Neots is disputed. See pp. 160–4 below.
76. Hart, 'East, Anglian Chronicle', 249.
77. *Annals of St. Neots*, ed. Dumville and Lapidge, p. xxiii.
78. Hart, 'East Anglian Chronicle', 250–1.
79. Cf. *Annals of St. Neots*, ed. Dumville and Lapidge, p. xiv: 'If we were to rename chronicle-texts to make their conventional (and rarely medieval) titles accurately reflect their origins or concerns, we should in creating chaos, lose more than we might

gain by the exercise.' Those editors failed to follow their own advice when they substituted *John* of Worcester for the familiar, if less accurate 'Florence'.

80. Hart, 'East Anglian Chronicle', 280.

81. Ibid. 250, 280. The surviving text of the Annals of St Neots is found in a composite volume in Cambridge, Trinity College, MS R.7.28 (770) and was written between *c.*1120 and *c.*1140 (*Annals of St. Neots*, ed. Dumville and Lapidge, pp. xv–xvi). For a discussion of the date of compilation of these annals, see pp. 160–4 below.

82. Hart, 'East Anglian Chronicle', 261; cf. *Annals of St. Neots*, ed. Dumville and Lapidge, p. xxxix.

83. Hart, 'East Anglian Chronicle', 261–4.

84. Whitelock, *Genuine Asser*, 18–19; Keynes and Lapidge (transl.), *Alfred the Great* (ch. 70), 88 and 253 n. 135.

85. *Life* of Alfred, ed. Stevenson, pp. xlix, lvii–lviii.

86. Hart, 'East Anglian Chronicle', 264.

87. *Annals of St. Neots*, ed. Dumville and Lapidge, pp. xli–xlii.

88. Ibid., p. xlii.

89. Ibid., p. xxiii.

90. Hart, 'East Anglian Chronicle', 274–7.

91. *Annals of St. Neots*, ed. Dumville and Lapidge, pp. lxiv–lxv.

92. Ibid., p. xlv, n. 49.

93. Ibid., p. xlvii.

94. Ibid., p. xlvii.

95. Ibid., pp. xliii–xlvii.

96. Hart, 'East Anglian Chronicle', 251–3, 260.

97. *Annals of St. Neots*, ed. Dumville and Lapidge, pp. xliii–xlvii.

98. Ibid., p. xlvi.

99. Ibid., p. xlv.

100. *Annals of St. Neots*, ed. Dumville and Lapidge (*sub annis*, 365, 369, 375, 527, 579, 585, 588, and 633), 4–10.

101. Hart, 'East Anglian Chronicle', 252.

102. *Encomium Emmae Reginae*, ed. A. Campbell (Camden Soc. 3rd Series, 72; London, 1949), pp. xix–xxi; xxxv–xxxvii.

103. Ibid. 24–5.

104. *Life* of Alfred, ed. Stevenson, ch. 3, p. 5.

105. *Encomium Emmae*, ed. Campbell, ibid.

106. *Life* of Alfred, ed. Stevenson, ch. 37, p. 28.

107. *Encomium Emmae*, ed. Campbell, pp. xxxvii, 24–5, 96. *Annals of St. Neots*, ed. Dumville and Lapidge, 78.

108. *Encomium Emmae*, ed. Campbell, p. xxxvii.

109. *Life* of Alfred, ed. Stevenson, p. 44.

110. *Annals of St. Neots*, ed. Dumville and Lapidge (*sub anno* 851), 43.

111. Ibid. (*sub anno* 871), 66.

112. Ibid. (*sub anno* 878), 78; Hart, who noted that the Annals of St Neots regularly leave out glosses on place-names from the *Life* of Alfred (Hart, 'East Anglian Chronicle', 262), did not include the omission of the gloss on Sheppey in his list. In view of the tendency on the part of the compiler of the Annals of St Neots to omit such glosses, the inclusion of the gloss on *Æscesdun* is significant, and shows that such omissions were not universal practice on the part of the compiler of the Annals of St Neots.

113. Whitelock, *Genuine Asser*, 8; Keynes and Lapidge (transl.), *Alfred the Great*, 57.
114. *Memorials of St. Edmund's Abbey*, ed. T. Arnold (3 vols.; Rolls Series, 1890–6), i. 341.
115. C. [R.] Hart, *The Danelaw* (London and Rio Grande, 1992), 198 and notes. F. E. Harmer (ed.), *Anglo-Saxon Writs* (Manchester, 1952), 145–7, 435–7. Cf. Sawyer 1069.
116. Sawyer 980.
117. Hart, *Danelaw*, 57–9, 62–6, 471–2.
118. *Encomium Emmae*, ed. Campbell, p. xlviii.
119. Sawyer 997. Harmer (ed.), *Anglo-Saxon Writs*, 246, 257.
120. Whitelock, *Genuine Asser*, 19–20.
121. M. McKisack, *Medieval History in the Tudor Age* (Oxford, 1971), 27–8.
122. Corpus Christi College Cambridge MS 100.
123. *Life* of Alfred, ed. Stevenson, pp. li–liii; Keynes and Lapidge (transl.), *Alfred the Great*, 225. The statement by Keynes and Lapidge that the Corpus 100 transcript 'reproduces the text of Asser as it stood in the Cotton manuscript before Parker's annotations were added and before the passages from other sources had been inserted' (ibid. 225) was a reckless generalization, which departed from the earlier caution of Stevenson (*Life* of Alfred, p. lii) who recognized that it had been tampered with by Parker and copied by an indifferent scholar. If the judgement of Keynes and Lapidge on this transcript were indeed true, then the loss of its exemplar, Cotton Otho A.xii, would be of little consequence.
124. *Life* of Alfred, ed. Stevenson, pp. lvi and lviii; cf. Dumville in *Annals of St. Neots*, ed. Dumville and Lapidge, p. xlii.
125. *Life* of Alfred, ed. Stevenson, p. xii.
126. Ibid., p. xxi.
127. J. Strype, *The Life and Acts of Matthew Parker, the First Archbishop of Canterbury in the Reign of Queen Elizabeth* (3 vols.; Oxford, 1821), ii. 441.
128. Ibid. 245.
129. Ibid. 500.
130. *Life* of Alfred, ed. Stevenson, p. xxi, n. 2.
131. Ibid., p. xxi, n. 2.
132. Ibid., p. xxix.
133. Strype, *Life of Parker*, ii. 441–4.
134. Ibid. 27–8, 53, 372.
135. Ibid. 293–7.
136. Ibid. 245–6, 251–2.
137. McKisack, *Medieval History*, 47.
138. Ibid.
139. Strype, *Life of Parker*, ii. 501.
140. *Life* of Alfred, ed. Stevenson, p. lii.
141. Ibid., p. xix.
142. Ibid., pp. lxvii–lxviii, n. 4.
143. Strype, *Life of Parker*, ii. 456, 518.
144. McKisack, *Medieval History*, 35.
145. *Correspondence of Matthew Parker D.D., Archbishop of Canterbury Comprising Letters Written by and to him, from AD 1535 to his Death, AD 1575*, ed. J. Bruce and T. T. Perowne (Parker Soc.; Cambridge, 1853), 388.
146. McKisack, *Medieval History*, 41.
147. Ibid. 35–6.
148. Ibid. 30–1.

149. V. Sanders, 'The Household of Archbishop Parker and the Influencing of Public Opinion' *JEH* 34 (1983), 535–42.
150. McKisack, *Medieval History*, 28.
151. Sanders, 'The Household of Parker', 538.
152. McKisack, *Medieval History*, 35.
153. Ibid.
154. *Life* of Alfred, ed. Stevenson, p. xxxiv.
155. Ibid., p. xvi and n. 2.
156. Ibid., ch. 88, pp. 73–4.
157. Sanders, 'The Household of Parker', 536.
158. Strype, *Life of Parker*, ii. 501.
159. *Matthaei Parisiensis Historia Anglorum, sive et vulgo dicitur Historia minor*, ed. F. Madden (3 vols.; Rolls Series; London, 1866), vol. i, p. xxxvii. Cf. *Life* of Alfred, ed. Stevenson, p. xix.
160. Ibid., pp. xxxix, xli, n. 1.
161. Cf. Whitelock, *Genuine Asser*, 20.
162. *Life* of Alfred, ed. Stevenson, p. xi.
163. *Encomium Emmae*, ed. Campbell, p. xxi.

Chapter VII

1. See pp. 12–17 above.
2. *Life* of Alfred, ed. Stevenson, ch. 1, p. 19; *EHD*, ed. Whitelock, i. 266.
3. *Einhardi Vita Karoli, Quellen z. deut. Gesch. d. Mittelalters*, ed. Rau, v/i, 170; Thorpe (transl.), *Two Lives of Charlemagne*, 59.
4. *Life* of Alfred, ed. Stevenson, chs. 79, 81, 88–9.
5. This was even the view of Kirby who, in one of the few original studies on the *Life* of Alfred, concluded, nevertheless, that the work was written in different drafts and stages—in 888–9 and 893–4 (D. P. Kirby, 'Asser and his Life of King Alfred', *Studia Celtica*, 6 (1971), 12–35, esp. 23–7).
6. *Life* of Alfred, ed. Stevenson, ch. 73, p. 54.
7. Ibid., chs. 82 to 86 inclusive.
8. Ibid., ch. 29, pp. 23–4.
9. Ibid., ch. 30.
10. The *Life* of Alfred provides a translation of the Alfredian section of the Chronicle from AD 851 (ch. 3) down to AD 887 (ch. 86). Although the continuous biographical section of the *Life* is begun at chapter 73, interrupting the translation of the Chronicle after AD 885, nevertheless chapter 73 deals with Alfred's marriage which was earlier dated by the author of the *Life* to AD 868 (ch. 29).
11. *Life* of Alfred, ed. Stevenson, chs. 12–17, 21–5, 29.
12. Ibid., chs. 37–8.
13. Ibid., chs. 21–5, 29.
14. Ibid., part of ch. 13, and all of chs. 14 and 15.
15. Ibid., ch. 12 and part of ch. 13.
16. Ibid., ch. 17.
17. Ibid., ch. 16.
18. For the author's protests regarding his status as a contemporary observer of the events he describes, cf. chs. 13, 22, 24, 29, etc. (ibid.).
19. Ibid., ch. 8, p. 7.

20. Ibid., ch. 11, p. 9.
21. See pp. 3–9 above.
22. *Life* of Alfred, ed. Stevenson, ch. 1, p. 1.
23. See p. 4 above.
24. *ASC: MS A*, ed. Bately (*sub anno* 855), 45–6; *EHD*, ed. Whitelock, i. 174–5.
25. Keynes and Lapidge (transl.), *Alfred the Great*, 4, 228–9.
26. See p. 3 above.
27. D. N. Dumville (ed.), 'The West Saxon Genealogical Regnal List: Manuscripts and Texts', *Anglia*, 104 (1986), 1–32; *ASC: MS A*, ed. Bately, pp. xxi, 2.
28. The text of the author's exemplar which he omitted read: *Wig Freawining, Freawine Friþogaring, Friþogar Bronding* (*ASC: MS A*, ed. Bately, 45) and that text in the manuscript of the Parker Chronicle (fo. 13a) takes up the space of precisely one line. For while *Wig Freawining* comes at the end of line 23, it occupies about the same space as *Brond Beldæg* which follows on from *Friþogar Bronding* and fills up the end of line 24. R. Flower and H. Smith (eds.), *The Parker Chronicle and Laws* (*Corpus Christi College, Cambridge, MS. 173): A Facsimile* (Early English Text Soc. Original Series, 208; London, 1941), fo. 13a.
29. *ASC* (*sub annis* 530, 534); *EHD*, ed. Whitelock, i. 144–5.
30. *Life* of Alfred, ed. Stevenson, ch. 2, p. 4 and cf. ibid., p. 2.
31. Ibid., p. 4.
32. Sawyer 328, Birch 496; *EHD*, ed. Whitelock, i. 488–9. Nelson ('Reconstructing a Royal Family', in Wood and Lund (eds.), *Essays in Honour of Sawyer*, 56 n. 51) argued that the Oslac who attested Sawyer 328 'seems too low on the list of lay attesters, and the date, 858, too late, for identification as the then king's maternal grandfather to seem likely'. Nelson's arguments were founded on the assumption that the *Life* of Alfred afforded genuine contemporary testimony on Alfred's family.
33. *Life* of Alfred, ed. Stevenson, ch. 12, p. 10.
34. Ibid., ch. 13, p. 11.
35. Ibid., ch. 14.
36. *ASC* (*sub anno* 789); *EHD*, ed. Whitelock, i. 166.
37. *Life* of Alfred, ed. Stevenson, ch. 15.
38. Ibid., pp. 13–14; Keynes and Lapidge (transl.), *Alfred the Great*, 72.
39. *Life* of Alfred, ed. Stevenson, ch. 12, p. 12; Keynes and Lapidge (transl.), *Alfred the Great*, 71.
40. *Life* of Alfred, ed. Stevenson, ch. 15, p. 14.
41. *ASC* (*sub anno* 802); *EHD*, ed. Whitelock, i. 169.
42. Keynes and Lapidge (transl.), *Alfred the Great*, 236 n. 32.
43. *Life* of Alfred, ed. Stevenson, pp. 208–9.
44. Ibid., ch. 13, p. 12; Keynes and Lapidge (transl.), *Alfred the Great*, 71.
45. *Life* of Alfred, ed. Stevenson, p. 206.
46. S[tith] Thompson, *Motif-Index of Folk-Literature*, rev. edn. (Bloomington, Ind., 1966), D.24.1–2, ii. 9.
47. See pp. 325–9 below.
48. A. P. Smyth, *Celtic Leinster: Towards an Historical Geography of Early Irish Civilization AD 500–1500* (Dublin, 1982), 83.
49. *The Annals of Clonmacnoise from the Creation to AD 1408*, ed. D. Murphy (Dublin, 1896), (*sub anno* 905), 145.
50. *Life* of Alfred, ed. Stevenson, ch. 15, p. 14.

51. Ibid., ch. 12.
52. Ibid., opening of ch. 13.
53. Ibid., ch. 17.
54. *ASC: MS A*, ed. Bately (*sub anno* 855), 45.
55. *Ann. Bert.*, *Quellen z. deut. Gesch. d. Mittelalters*, ed. Rau (*sub anno* 858), vi/ii, 96; *Ann. Bert.*, transl. Nelson, 86.
56. *Ann. Bert.*, ed. Rau (*sub anno* 856), vi/ii, 92; *Ann. Bert.*, transl. Nelson, 83.
57. Sawyer 315, Birch 486. *EHD*, ed. Whitelock, i. 483–5.
58. *Cartularium Saxonicum*, ed. Birch, ii. 87; *EHD*, ed. Whitelock, i. 484.
59. Keynes and Lapidge (transl.), *Alfred the Great*, 235 n. 27.
60. The tale of Eadburh takes its place alongside such folk-tales as that of the *Queen expelled for poisoning her step-son* in the Stith Thompson motif-index (Stith Thompson, *Motif-Index*, Q.211.4.1, v. 201).
61. *ASC: MS A*, ed. Bately (*sub anno* 836), 43; *EHD*, ed. Whitelock, i. 172.
62. Stevenson stretched the evidence beyond all acceptable limits by suggesting that Asser might have encountered people who had seen Eadburh in her fallen state in his earlier life either in Wales or Francia (*Life* of Alfred, ed. Stevenson, p. 209).
63. Ibid., chs. 74, 76, 77, 81, 88, 89, 90, and 91.
64. *EHD*, ed. Whitelock, i. 266.
65. Whitelock, *Genuine Asser*, 4.
66. *Notkeri Gesta Karoli* [i. iii], *Quellen z. deut. Gesch. d. Mittelalters*, ed. Rau, vii iii, 324–6. Thorpe (transl.), *Two Lives of Charlemagne*, 95–6.
67. *Life* of Alfred, ed. Stevenson, ch. 23, p. 20.
68. Stith Thompson, *Motif-Index*, H.1242, iii. 484.
69. *Herodotus*, iv. 9–10.
70. G. C. Macauley (transl.), *The History of Herodotus* (London and New York, 1890), [iv. 9–10], i. 295–6.
71. A. P. Smyth, 'Húi Failgi Relations with the Húi Néill', *Études celtiques*, 14/2 (1975), 515–16, 521.
72. Gen. 49.
73. *Adomnan's Life of Columba*, ed. A. O. Anderson and M. O. Anderson (London, 1961), 256–7.
74. *Vitae Sanctorum Hiberniae*, ed. C. Plummer (2 vols.; Oxford, 1968; repr. of 1910 edn.), vol. i, p. clxxi, n. 9.
75. Stith Thompson, *Motif-Index*, D.1819.4, ii. 334.
76. *The Tripartite Life of Patrick with Other Documents Relating to that Saint*, ed. W. Stokes (2 vols.; Rolls Series; 1887), i. 9; ii. 393.
77. C. Grant Loomis, *White Magic: An Introduction to the Folklore of Christian Legend* (Cambridge, Mass., 1948), 24.
78. Whitelock, *Genuine Asser*, 11–12, 20.
79. *Life* of Alfred, ed. Stevenson, ch. 23, p. 20.
80. *Ann. Bert.*, ed. Rau (*sub anno* 856), vi/ii, 92; *Ann. Bert.*, transl. Nelson, 83.
81. See pp. 12–17 above.
82. *ASC* (*sub anno* 839); *EHD*, ed. Whitelock, i. 172.
83. Ibid. (*sub anno* 851), 173.
84. *Life* of Alfred, ed. Stevenson, ch. 16, p. 14. Cf. Keynes and Lapidge (transl.), *Alfred the Great*, 314 n. 3.
85. *Life* of Alfred, ed. Stevenson, ch. 25, p. 21.

86. Ibid., ch. 22, p. 20.
87. Ibid.
88. Ibid. Keynes and Lapidge (*Alfred the Great*, 239 n. 48) accepted the reading *magister adiit et legit* but mistranslated '[he] went to his teacher and learnt it' or 'absorbed its contents'.
89. See pp. 469–71 below.
90. *EHD*, ed. Whitelock, i. 266.
91. Gen. 37: 3.
92. *Bede's Life of St. Cuthbert*, in *Two Lives of Saint Cuthbert: A Life by an Anonymous Monk of Lindisfare and Bede's Prose Life*, ed. and transl. B. Colgrave (New York, 1969), 156–7; cf. the Anonymous *Life* of Cuthbert, ibid. 64–5.
93. *Life* of Gerald, *Patrologiae*, ed. Migne, 645; Sitwell (transl.), *St. Odo of Cluny*, 97.
94. *Life* of Alfred, ed. Stevenson, ch. 22, p. 20.
95. Ibid., ch. 76, p. 59.
96. Ibid., ch. 24, p. 21.
97. *Life* of Gerald, *Patrologiae*, ed. Migne, 645; Sitwell (transl.), *St. Odo of Cluny*, 97.
98. *Life* of Odo, *Patrologiae*, ed. Migne, 48–9; Sitwell (transl.), *St. Odo of Cluny*, 15.
99. *Life* of Alfred, ed. Stevenson, chs. 12, 13, and 17.
100. See p. 34 above.
101. *Life* of Alfred, ed. Stevenson, ch. 37, p. 28.
102. Ibid., ch. 39, p. 30. The reference to a tree in the midst of the battlefield at Ashdown may have been derived from the Book of Samuel's account of David's victory over the Philistines which took place 'near the balsam trees' in the Valley of Rephaim. Before that battle, David heard the Lord's promise: 'When you hear the sound of marching in the tree-tops, then attack, because I will be marching ahead of you to defeat the Philistine army' (2 Sam. 5: 22–24). I am grateful to my student, Miss Kay Gazzard, for suggesting this reference to me.
103. Keynes and Lapidge (transl.), *Alfred the Great*, 37; *Life* of Alfred, ed. Stevenson, ch. 37, pp. 28–9.
104. Translation based on Keynes and Lapidge (transl.), *Alfred the Great*, 79; cf. *Life* of Alfred, ed. Stevenson, ch. 38, pp. 29–30. D. P. Kirby noted the bias in favour of Alfred's rôle at Ashdown as narrated in the Life of Alfred ('Asser and his Life of King Alfred', *Studia Celtica* 7 (1971), 30–1).
105. *ASC* (*sub anno* 871); i. 177.
106. See p. 34 above.
107. *Life* of Alfred, ed. Stevenson, ch. 38.
108. The use of *partes* in this context clearly relates to 'a faction' and therefore would normally apply to West Saxons *versus* vikings (J. F. Niermeyer, *Mediae Latinitatis Lexicon Minus* (Leiden, 1976), 766.). Common sense—if it can ever be applied to the *Vita Alfredi*—requires that *ab utraque parte* refers in this instance to divisions within the West Saxon army. Otherwise we are given to assume that West Saxons and Danes sat down together to work out a battle plan!
109. *Life* of Gerald, *Patrologiae*, ed. Migne, 665–6; Sitwell (transl.), *St. Odo of Cluny*, 127–8.
110. See pp. 199–216 below.
111. *Life* of Alfred, ed. Stevenson, ch. 38, p. 29.
112. Ibid., ch. 29, p. 24.
113. Ibid., ch. 42, p. 32.

114. *Annals of St. Neots*, ed. Dumville and Lapidge, 68.
115. *Life* of Alfred, ed. Stevenson, ch. 11, p. 9.
116. Keynes and Lapidge (transl.), *Alfred the Great*, 80–1; *Life* of Alfred, ed. Stevenson, ch. 42, p. 32.
117. See pp. 37–8 above.
118. *Life* of Alfred, ed. Stevenson, 227.
119. See pp. 470–1 below.
120. See pp. 416–18, 470–1 below.
121. D. A. Binchy, *Celtic and Anglo-Saxon Kingship* (Oxford, 1970), 26–30.
122. *Mediae Latinitatis Lexicon Minus*, ed. J. F. Niermeyer (Leiden, 1976), 951.
123. D. N. Dumville, 'The Ætheling: A Study in Anglo-Saxon Constitutional History', *ASE* 8 (1979), 6.
124. Ibid. 5.
125. Ibid. 4–5.
126. Ibid. 24 and cf. 14.
127. Ibid. 24.
128. Ibid. 24–5.
129. Ibid. 21 n. 8.
130. Ibid. 23.
131. See pp. 410–14 below.
132. Dumville, 'Ætheling', 21–4.
133. See pp. 409–20 below.
134. *Life* of Alfred, ed. Stevenson, chs. 12–17.
135. *ASC: MS A*, ed. Bately (*sub anno* 855), 45; *EHD*, ed. Whitelock, i. 174.
136. *Life* of Alfred, ed. Stevenson, ch. 16, p. 14.
137. See pp. 382–3 below.
138. *Bede's Ecclesiastical History of the English People*, ed. and transl. B. Colgrave and R. A. B. Mynors (Oxford, 1969), [v. viii], 472.
139. See p. 52 above.
140. See p. 11 above.
141. Nelson, *Charles the Bald*, 203–4.
142. *ASC* (*sub annis* 855–8); *EHD*, ed. Whitelock, i. 174.
143. See pp. 470–1.
144. *Annals of St. Neots*, ed. Dumville and Lapidge (*sub anno* 857), 51.
145. *Life* of Alfred, ed. Stevenson, ch. 12, pp. 9–10.
146. *ASC: MS A*, ed. Bately (*sub annis* 855, 860), 45–6; *EHD*, ed. Whitelock, i. 174–5.
147. *Ann. Bert.*, ed. Rau (*sub anno* 856), vi/ii, 92.
148. Ibid. (*sub anno* 858), 96.
149. *Liber Pontificalis*, ed. Duchesne, ii. 148; *Life* of Alfred, ed. Stevenson, p. 194, and n. 2.
150. Keynes and Lapidge (transl.), *Alfred the Great*, 235 n. 27.
151. *Life* of Alfred, ed. Stevenson, ch. 12, p. 10; *EHD*, ed. Whitelock, i. 264.
152. *Life* of Alfred, ed. Stevenson, ch. 17, p. 16; *EHD*, ed. Whitelock, i. 266.
153. See pp. 11–12 above.
154. *Ann. Bert.*, ed. Rau (*sub anno* 858), vi/ii, 96; *Ann. Bert.*, transl. Nelson, 86.
155. *Bede's Ecclesiastical History*, ed. and transl. Colgrave and Mynors, 150–1 and 151 n. 5.
156. See p. 182 above.
157. Gen. 49: 4.

158. See pp. 310–11 below.
159. *Life* of Alfred, ed. Stevenson, ch. 12, p. 10.
160. Ibid., ch. 28, p. 23.
161. *Æthelweard*, ed. Campbell, 36.
162. *Life* of Alfred, ed. Stevenson, ch. 17, p. 16.
163. Ibid., ch. 12, p. 10; *EHD*, ed. Whitelock, i. 264.
164. *Life* of Alfred, ed. Stevenson, ch. 12, p. 10.
165. See pp. 470–1.
166. *Æthelweard*, ed. Campbell, 39.
167. A. Williams, 'Some Notes and Considerations on Problems Connected with the English Royal Succession, 860–1066', in R. A. Brown (ed.), *Proceedings of the Battle Conference on Anglo-Norman Studies I: 1978* (Ipswich, 1979), 227 n. 32.
168. *Life* of Alfred, ed. Stevenson, chs. 21–25, and 29.
169. Ibid., ch. 23.
170. See pp. 24–8 above.
171. For this reason, Nelson's otherwise interesting discussion on Alfred's maternal kin needs to be treated with caution. (Nelson, 'Reconstructing a Royal Family', in Wood and Lund (eds.), *Essays in Honour of Sawyer*, 54–60).
172. See pp. 406–17 below.
173. *Life* of Alfred, ed. Stevenson, ch. 49, pp. 36–7.
174. Ibid., ch. 27, p. 23.
175. Ibid., ch. 9, p. 8.
176. Keynes and Lapidge (transl.), *Alfred the Great*, 246–7 n. 94.
177. *Life* of Alfred, ed. Stevenson, ch. 52, p. 40.
178. Whitelock, *Genuine Asser*, 20.
179. *Life* of Alfred, ed. Stevenson, ch. 21, p. 19.
180. See pp. 304–6 below.

Chapter VIII

1. Galbraith, 'Who Wrote Asser's *Life* of Alfred', 113.
2. *Life* of Alfred, ed. Stevenson, ch. 25, p. 21; *EHD*, ed. Whitelock, i. 267.
3. *Life* of Alfred, ed. Stevenson, ch. 74, pp. 54–7.
4. Ibid., p. 57; Keynes and Lapidge (transl.), *Alfred the Great*, 90.
5. *Life* of Alfred, ed. Stevenson, ch. 76, p. 59; ch. 91, p. 77.
6. *EHD*, ed. Whitelock, i. 272; *Life* of Alfred, ed. Stevenson, ch. 91, p. 76.
7. Ibid., ch. 74, pp. 55–7.
8. Keynes and Lapidge (transl.), *Alfred the Great*, 90; *Life* of Alfred, ed. Stevenson, ch. 74, pp. 56–7.
9. Keynes and Lapidge (transl.), *Alfred the Great*, 89.
10. *Life* of Alfred, ed. Stevenson, ch. 74, p. 55.
11. *Einhardi Vita Karoli* [iii. 26–7], Thorpe (transl.), *Two Lives of Charlemagne*, 79–80; *Einhardi Vita Karoli*, *Quellen z. deut. Gesch. d. Mittelalters*, ed. Rau, v/i, 197–8.
12. *EHD*, ed. Whitelock, i. 267–8; *Life* of Alfred, ed. Stevenson, ch. 76, pp. 59–60.
13. Ibid., p. 60.
14. *Einhardi Vita Karoli* [iii. 24], Thorpe (transl.), *Two Lives of Charlemagne*, 78; *Einhardi Vita Karoli*, ed. Rau, v/i, 196.
15. *Einhardi Vita Karoli* [iii. 21], Thorpe (transl.), *Two Lives of Charlemagne*, 76; *Einhardi Vita Karoli*, ed. Rau, v/i, 192.

16. *Einhardi Vita Karoli* [iii. 26], Thorpe (transl.), *Two Lives of Charlemagne*, 80; *Einhardi Vita Karoli*, ed. Rau v/i, 198.

17. Keynes and Lapidge (transl.), *Alfred the Great*, 89–90; *Life* of Alfred, ed. Stevenson, ch. 74, p. 56.

18. Ibid., p. 55.

19. Ibid., ch. 24., p. 21.

20. *Einhardi Vita Karoli* [iii. 25], Thorpe (transl.), *Two Lives of Charlemagne*, 79; *Einhardi Vita Karoli*, ed. Rau, v/i, 196.

21. Keynes and Lapidge (transl.), *Alfred the Great*, 255–6 n. 143.

22. Galbraith, 'Who Wrote Asser's *Life* of Alfred', 128.

23. *Life* of Alfred, ed. Stevenson, ch. 42, p. 32.

24. Ibid., ch. 74, p. 56.

25. *EHD*, ed. Whitelock, i. 266; *Life* of Alfred, ed. Stevenson, ch. 22, p. 20.

26. See pp. 186–9 above.

27. See pp. 36–7 above.

28. See pp. 586–8 below.

29. See pp. 588–94 below.

30. *Gaius Suetonius Tranquillus: The Twelve Caesars*, transl. R. Graves, introd. by M. Grant (London, 1979), ch. 45, p. 32 (Julius Caesar); ch. 81, p. 87 (Augustus).

31. Ibid., ch. 50, p. 155 (Gaius); ch. 2, pp. 162–3; ch. 30, p. 177; ch. 31, p. 177 (Claudius).

32. *Bede's Life of Cuthbert*, in *Two Lives of Saint Cuthbert*, ed. and transl. Colgrave, 158–61.

33. Ibid. 180–3.

34. Ibid. 272–3.

35. Ibid. 274–5.

36. *Félire Óengusso Céli Dé: The Martyrology of Óengus the Culdee*, ed. W. Stokes (Henry Bradshaw Soc.; London, 1905), 42–5.

37. *Life of St. Magnenn of Kilmainham*, in *Silva Gadelica: A Collection of Irish Tales*, ed. S. H. O'Grady (2 vols.; London and Edinburgh, 1892), i. 39 [Irish text]; ii. 37–8 [transl.].

38. *Life* of Gerald, *Patrologiae*, ed. Migne, 645; Sitwell (transl.), *St. Odo of Cluny*, 97.

39. Ibid.

40. *Life* of Gerald, *Patrologiae*, ed. Migne, 649; Sitwell (transl.), *St. Odo of Cluny*, 104.

41. *Life* of Gerald, *Patrologiae*, ed. Migne, 690; Sitwell (transl.), *St. Odo of Cluny*, 163.

42. *Life* of Odo, *Patrologiae*, ed. Migne, 47; Sitwell (transl.), *St. Odo of Cluny*, 10–1.

43. *Life* of Odo, *Patrologiae*, ed. Migne, 46–7; Sitwell (transl.), *St. Odo of Cluny*, 8–9; 10–1.

44. *Life* of Gerald, *Patrologiae*, ed. Migne, 649; Sitwell (transl.), *St. Odo of Cluny*, 104.

45. The object of Odo's *Life* of Gerald was to show monks of the tenth-century reform, a shining example of a layman who preserved his chastity and who otherwise succeeded in living the life of a monk amidst the distractions of his worldly office (*Life* of Gerald, *Patrologiae*, ed. Migne, 679, etc.).

46. Ibid. 645, 650.

47. Ibid. 650, 693.

48. Ibid. 654.

49. Ibid. 680; Sitwell (transl.), *St. Odo of Cluny*, 146.

50. *Life* of Gerald, *Patrologiae*, ed. Migne, 652, 678; Sitwell (transl.), *St. Odo of Cluny*, 144.

51. *EHD*, ed. Whitelock, i. 269.

52. Stenton, *Anglo-Saxon England*, 417.
53. *The B Life of St. Dunstan*, in *Memorials of Saint Dunstan Archbishop of Canterbury*, ed. W. Stubbs (Rolls Series; London, 1874), 32–3. *The Oldest Life of St. Dunstan*, *EHD*, ed. Whitelock, i. 830.
54. Keynes and Lapidge (transl.), *Alfred the Great*, 90; *Life* of Alfred, ed. Stevenson, ch. 74, p. 57.
55. Ibid., p. 56.
56. Cf. G. Craig, 'Alfred the Great: A Diagnosis', *Journal of the Royal Society of Medicine*, 84 (1991), 303–5.
57. *Life* of Alfred, ed. Stevenson, ch. 91, p. 77.
58. Ibid., pp. 328–9.
59. Ibid., p. 328. See *Bald's Leechbook* in *Leechdoms, Wortcunning and Starcraft of Early England*, ed. T. O. Cockayne (3 vols.; Rolls Series; London, 1864–6) ii. 2–299; esp. 174–5, 288–91. Keynes and Lapidge (transl.), *Alfred the Great*, 33–4, 215 n. 40, 270 n. 220. A. L. Meaney, 'Alfred, the Patriarch and the White Stone', *Journal of the Australasian Universities Language and Literature Association*, 49 (1978), 65–79.
60. *Life* of Gerald, *Patrologiae*, ed. Migne, 645.
61. Ibid. 647; Sitwell (transl.), *St. Odo of Cluny*, 100.
62. *Life* of Gerald, *Patrologiae*, ed. Migne, 649; Sitwell (transl.), *St. Odo of Cluny*, 104.
63. Keynes and Lapidge (transl.), *Alfred the Great*, 89; *Life* of Alfred, ed. Stevenson, ch. 74, p. 55.
64. Ibid., p. 56; Keynes and Lapidge (transl.), *Alfred the Great*, 90.
65. *Life* of Gerald, *Patrologiae*, ed. Migne, 657, 683, 691; Sitwell (transl.), *St. Odo of Cluny*, 116, 151, 163.
66. *Life* of Gerald, *Patrologiae*, ed. Migne, 657; Sitwell (transl.), *St. Odo of Cluny*, 116.
67. *Life* of Alfred, ed. Stevenson, ch. 104, p. 90; Keynes and Lapidge (transl.), *Alfred the Great*, 108.
68. See pp. 272–8 below.
69. Keynes and Lapidge (transl.), *Alfred the Great*, 89; *Life* of Alfred, ed. Stevenson, ch. 74, p. 55.
70. Ibid., pp. 297–9.
71. Keynes and Lapidge (transl.), *Alfred the Great*, 254 n. 142.
72. *Willelmi Malmesbiriensis de Gestis Regum*, ed. Stubbs, i. 148; *EHD*, ed. Whitelock, i. 281.
73. Smyth, *Scandinavian York and Dublin*, ii. 11–12, 64–6.
74. The progress of the West Saxon conquest of Cornwall in the ninth century is poorly understood because of the paucity of documentation. W. G. Hoskins, *The Westward Expansion of Wessex* (Leicester University Occasional Papers, 13; Leicester, 1960), 19–20.
75. *ASC: MS A*, ed. Bately (*sub anno* 813), 41; *EHD*, ed. Whitelock (*sub anno* 815) i. 170.
76. *EHD*, ed. Whitelock, i. 171.
77. Ibid. 172.
78. *Annales Cambriae*, ed. J. W. ab Ithel (Rolls Series; London, 1860), (*sub anno* 875), 15.
79. H. P. R. Finberg, 'Sherborne, Glastonbury and the Expansion of Wessex', *Trans. Roy. Hist. Soc.* 5/3 (1953), 117–18.
80. The Chronicle's silence on the eventual conquest of Cornwall in the tenth century cannot be cited as an analogy for events in Alfred's reign because the fragmentary

nature of annalistic recording in the reign of Athelstan does not compare with the detailed Chronicle record for the reign of Alfred.

81. *SEHD*, ed. Harmer, 17.
82. Finberg, 'Sherborne, Glastonbury', 111–14.
83. Ibid. 114. It is possible that for *Tauistoke*, in Æthelberht's charter, Tavistock on the eastern side of Dartmoor was meant (ibid. 114 n. 5).
84. See p. 330 below.
85. See pp. 330, 334 below.
86. *Vita I S. Neoti et Translatio*, in *The Anglo-Saxon Chronicle: A Collaborative Edition*, xvii. *The Annals of St. Neots with Vita Prima Sancti Neoti*, ed. D. Dumville and M. Lapidge (Cambridge, 1984), 118–20 (hereafter referred to as *Vita I S. Neoti*, ed. Dumville and Lapidge).
87. Bede's *Ecclesiastical History* [*Praefatio*], ed. and transl. Colgrave and Mynors, 2–3.
88. The possible influences of Thegan and the Astronomer on the text of the *Life* of Alfred are discussed by J. Campbell, 'Asser's Life of Alfred' in Holdsworth and Wiseman (eds.), *Inheritance of Historiography*, 117–19.
89. The precise context in which the biographer of Alfred had access to the *Life* of Gerald, and the time and place in which the *Life* of Alfred was written, are discussed on pp. 272–8 below.
90. See pp. 275–6 below.
91. See pp. 597–600 below.
92. *Einhardi Vita Karoli, Quellen z. deut. Gesch. d. Mittelalters*, ed. Rau, v/i, 166; Thorpe (transl.), *Two Lives of Charlemagne*, 52.
93. *The Life of Bishop Wilfrid by Eddius Stephanus*, ed. B. Colgrave (Cambridge, 1927), 3.
94. *SEHD*, ed. Harmer, 49.
95. See pp. 598–9 below.
96. *Life* of Gerald, *Patrologiae*, ed. Migne, 645–6; Sitwell (transl.), *St. Odo of Cluny*, 98–9.
97. *Bischof Wærferths von Worcester Übersetzung der Dialoge Gregors des Grossen*, ed. H. Hecht, (Leipzig, 1900), i. 1.
98. *King Alfred's Version of Pastoral Care*, ed. Sweet, i. 6–7.
99. *Life* of Alfred, ed. Stevenson, ch. 77, p. 62.
100. Ibid.
101. *King Alfred's Old English Version of Boethius De Consolatione Philosophiae* ed. W. J. Sedgefield (Oxford, 1899), 5; *King Alfred's Version of the Consolation of Boethius, done into Modern English*, transl. W. J. Sedgefield (Oxford, 1900), *Proem*, facing p. 1.
102. Keynes and Lapidge (transl.), *Alfred the Great*, 259 n. 164.
103. *Boethius*, ed. Sedgefield, 5; id. (transl.), *Proem*, facing p. 1.
104. *King Alfred's Anglo-Saxon Version of Boethius De Consolatione Philosophiae*, ed. S. Fox (New York, 1970; repr. of 1864 edn.), 260–1.
105. Keynes and Lapidge (transl.), *Alfred the Great*, 89–90; *Life* of Alfred, ed. Stevenson, ch. 74, p. 56.

Chapter IX

1. *Life of Alfred*, ed. Stevenson, ch. 87, p. 73.
2. Ibid., chs. 87–9.
3. Ibid., ch. 89, p. 75.

4. Ibid., chs. 88–9, pp. 74–5.

5. Ibid., ch. 76, p. 59.

6. Ibid., ch. 81; *EHD*, ed. Whitelock, i. 270.

7. Keynes and Lapidge (transl.), *Alfred the Great*, 52.

8. *Life* of Alfred, ed. Stevenson, ch. 76, p. 60.

9. Ibid., ch. 22.

10. Ibid., ch. 22, p. 20; *EHD*, ed. Whitelock, i. 266.

11. *Life* of Alfred, ed. Stevenson, ch. 24, p. 21; *EHD*, ed. Whitelock, i. 266.

12. *Life* of Alfred, ed. Stevenson, ch. 88, p. 73; *EHD*, ed. Whitelock, i. 271.

13. *Life* of Alfred, ed. Stevenson, ch. 75, p. 58.

14. Ibid., ch. 76, p. 60; *EHD*, ed. Whitelock, i. 268.

15. *Life* of Alfred, ed. Stevenson, ch. 77, p. 63; *EHD*, ed. Whitelock, i. 269.

16. *Life* of Alfred, ed. Stevenson, ch. 77, pp. 62–3.

17. Brooks,`*Early History of the Church of Canterbury*, 152–4; 210–14.

18. *Life* of Alfred, ed. Stevenson, ch. 81, p. 67.

19. Ibid., p. 60.

20. Ibid., ch. 75, p. 58; *EHD*, ed. Whitelock, i. 267.

21. *Life* of Alfred, ed. Stevenson, ch. 86, p. 73.

22. See p. 183 above.

23. Keynes and Lapidge (transl.), *Alfred the Great*, 28.

24. Ibid. 239 n. 46.

25. *Life* of Alfred, ed. Stevenson, ch. 88, p. 74.

26. Ibid., p. 74.

27. J. Ryan, *Irish Monasticism: Origins and Development* (Dublin, 1992; repr. of 1972 edn.), 378.

28. *Life* of Odo, *Patrologiae*, ed. Migne, 49; Sitwell (transl.), *St. Odo of Cluny*, 15.

29. The *Life* of Alfred describes the contents of the king's childhood book in chapters 24 and 88, and although it was eventually filled completely 'with various matters' (*Life* of Alfred, ed. Stevenson, ch. 88, pp. 73–4), its contents are twice described as consisting of the Divine Office, Psalms, and prayers. On his miraculous entrance into Latin translation and biblical exegesis, the king was supposedly provided by Asser with yet another book, which was filled with biblical quotations and commentary.

30. See pp. 549–52 below.

31. See pp. 230, 528, 598 below.

32. *Einhardi Vita Karoli* [iii. 25], *Einhardi Vita Karoli, Quellen z. deut. Gesch. d. Mittelalters*, ed. Rau, v/i, 196; Thorpe (transl.), *Two Lives of Charlemagne*, 79.

33. *Suetonius: The Twelve Caesars*, transl. Graves, Julius Caesar, ch. 4, p. 14; Augustus, ch. 8, p. 51 and cf. ch. 89 of Augustus (p. 91) which had a major influence on Einhard's portrait of Charlemagne; Tiberius, chs. 70–1, pp. 131–2; Claudius, chs. 41–2, p. 180; and Nero, ch. 10, p. 187.

34. King Alfred's biographer shows a dependence on Einhard's text in chapters 16, 73, and 81. Cf. M. Schütt, 'The Literary Form of Asser's *Vita Alfredi*', *Eng. Hist. Rev.* 72 (1957), 209–20.

35. *Einhardi Vita Karoli* [iii. 19], *Einhardi Vita Karoli, Quellen z. deut. Gesch. d. Mittelalters*, ed. Rau, v/i, 190; Thorpe (transl.), *Two Lives of Charlemagne*, 74–5.

36. *Life* of Alfred, ed. Stevenson, ch. 75, pp. 58–9; *EHD*, ed. Whitelock, i. 267.

37. *Life* of Alfred, ed. Stevenson, ch. 75, p. 58; *EHD*, ed. Whitelock, i. 267.

38. See pp. 181–2 above.

39. If Einhard's text is taken too literally, then it is possible to conclude that Alcuin taught Charlemagne to write. But Einhard's account of the emperor's adult education programme in chapter 25 of the *Vita Karoli* provides merely a summary of what was in reality a more complex and long-standing endeavour.
40. *King Alfred's Version of Pastoral Care*, ed. Sweet, i. 6–7.
41. *Life* of Alfred, ed. Stevenson, chs. 77–8, pp. 62–3.
42. See pp. 262–4 below.
43. *Life* of Alfred, ed. Stevenson, ch. 73, p. 294; Galbraith, 'Who Wrote Asser's *Life*', 105.
44. *Life* of Alfred, ed. Stevenson, ch. 22, p. 20.
45. Ibid., ch. 24, p. 21.
46. Ibid., ch. 29, p. 24.
47. Ibid., ch. 39, p. 30.
48. *Vita Alchuini auctore anonymo*, in *Monumenta Alcuiniana*, ed. Wattenbach and Dümmler (Bibliotheca Rerum Germanicarum, 6; Berlin, 1873), 17.
49. Ibid. 18.
50. *Life* of Alfred, ed. Stevenson, ch. 79, pp. 63–4. The *Life* of Alfred is conspicuously short on topographical details especially in relation to King Alfred's movements within Wessex. Apart from the tradition that Alfred was born in Wantage, this meeting between king and scholar at Dean and a later encounter between the two men at *Leonaford* (ibid., ch. 81, p. 67) is all that his biographer adds to what we know of King Alfred's movements within his own kingdom. Indeed, this scarcity of topographical information in relation to royal itineraries exposes the poverty of the *Life* of Alfred when compared for instance with the Frankish royal biographies by Thegan, Nithard, Ermoldus, or Astronomus, and points yet again to the relative lateness and derivative nature of the English source.
51. *Vita Alchuini*, ed. Wattenbach and Dümmler, 17.
52. Literally 'of my own [people] (*meorum*)', *Life* of Alfred, ed. Stevenson, ch. 79; p. 64.
53. Ibid., ch. 79, p. 66.
54. Whitelock, *Genuine Asser*, 15 n. 4. Elfodw, 'archbishop' of Gwynedd (died 809) is mentioned in the Welsh annals.
55. *Annales Cambriae*, ed. Ab Ithel (*sub annis*, 840 and 873), 13–14.
56. For an explanation of how Welsh information such as that on 'Archbishop' Nobis found its way into King Alfred's biography, see pp. 354–64 below.
57. *Life* of Alfred, ed. Stevenson, ch. 78, p. 63; *EHD*, ed. Whitelock, i. 269.
58. *Life* of Alfred, ed. Stevenson, ch. 81, p. 68; *EHD*, ed. Whitelock, i. 271.
59. Galbraith, 'Who Wrote Asser's *Life*', 93–103; Whitelock, *Genuine Asser*, 6–8.
60. *Life* of Alfred, ed. Stevenson, ch. 79, p. 64.
61. *Vita Alchuini*, ed. Wattenbach and Dümmler, p. 18.
62. *Anglo-Saxon Chronicle* (*sub annis* 912, 914, 915, 917).
63. The record of the deposition of Charles was copied by Alfred's biographer from his text of the Chronicle a few lines above his record of Alfred's Latin lesson under the same year. Neither the Chronicle nor the *Life* of Alfred give an exact date for Charles the Fat's deposition other than that it took place 'six weeks before he died', but the compiler of Alfred's *Life* might have seen that information in a Frankish chronicle since, as we have seen he was very probably familiar with several Frankish sources, including the Annals of St Bertin and a version of Frankish annals similar to the Annals of Fulda (see pp. 104, 193 above).
64. *Ann. Fuld.*, transl. Reuter, 103 n. 8.
65. The other episode where an exact date is provided in Alfred's *Life* relates to the king's

grant of two monasteries to Asser at daybreak on Christmas Eve (*diluculo vigiliae Natalis Domini*) (*Life* of Alfred, ed. Stevenson, ch. 81, p. 67).

66. *Æthelweard*, ed. Campbell, 51.

67. See pp. 495–8 and 539–40 below.

68. See pp. 560–2 below.

69. *Vita I S. Neoti*, ed. Dumville and Lapidge, 132–3.

70. *The Homilies of the Anglo-Saxon Church: The First Part containing the Sermones Catholici or Homilies of Ælfric*, ed. B. Thorpe (London 1844–6), i. 2–3; *EHD*, ed. Whitelock, i. 850.

71. Ibid. 854.

72. *Homilies of Ælfric*, ed. Thorpe, ii. 116–19.

73. *Æthelweard*, ed. Campbell, 51.

74. See pp. 559–63 below.

75. Sisam, *Studies*, 140.

76. Ibid. 295–7.

77. Sisam, expressed contradictory thoughts on the personal Alfredian element in King Alfred's prose. On the one hand, he believed the amanuenses 'would give his words the written form they thought best' (*Studies*, 140), while elsewhere he sought for personal elements in the king's style (ibid. 295–7).

78. J. M. Bately, 'Old English Prose Before and During the Reign of Alfred', *ASE* 17 (1988), 127.

79. Ibid. 132.

80. Ibid. 130–1.

81. Ibid. 132.

82. Cf. J. Goody, *Literacy in Traditional Societies* (Cambridge, 1968), 48–55, 60, for a discussion of the development of philosophy in a literate culture.

83. The influence of literacy on traditional or oral societies is a huge subject which is fraught with contention. R. Harris, 'How Does Writing Restructure Thought?', *Language and Communication*, 9 (1989), 99–106, although challenging assumptions about the role of the Greeks in the development of literacy, does not apply directly to the particular problem of assessing Alfred's relationship with vernacular and Latin texts. See also W. J. Ong, *Orality and Literacy* (London and New York, 1982).

84. The fragmentary preface to the *Soliloquies* does not name Alfred as the author, but the king's authorship of this work is accepted on stylistic grounds. See pp. 537–8 below. The author of this preface addresses the reader in the first person, as does King Alfred in his introductory letter to the *Pastoral Care*, and in his preface to the *Dialogues*.

85. J. M. Bately, 'Lexical Evidence for the Authorship of the Prose Psalms in the Paris Psalter', *ASE* 10 (1982), 69–95; cf. Bately, 'Old English Prose Before and During the Reign of Alfred', 97, 130–1.

86. D. Whitelock, 'William of Malmesbury on the Works of King Alfred', in *Studies in Memory of Garmonsway*, ed. Pearsall and Waldron, 78–93.

87. *Willelmi Malmesbiriensis de Gestis Regum*, ed. Stubbs, i. 132; Whitelock, 'Malmesbury on the Works of Alfred', 85–6.

88. Smyth, *Scandinavian York and Dublin*, ii. 76. *Willelmi Malmesbiriensis de Gestis Regum*, ed. Stubbs, i. 126.

89. Ibid. 125; see pp. 342–3 below.

90. Whitelock, 'Malmesbury on the Works of Alfred', 82.

91. *Bischof Wærferths Übersetzung der Dialoge*, [preface], ed. Hecht, i. 1.

92. Keynes and Lapidge (transl.), *Alfred the Great*, 123.

93. Whitelock, 'Malmesbury on the Work of Alfred', 89.

94. Ibid. 90.

95. *Willelmi Malmesbiriensis de Gestis Pontificum*, ed. Hamilton, 332–3, 336; Whitelock, 'Malmesbury on the Works of Alfred'. 90.

96. See p. 233 below.

97. Keynes and Lapidge (transl.), *Alfred the Great*, 268 n. 208.

98. The parallel between Alfred's *libellus* and Charlemagne's *tabulas et codicellos* is not, of course, exact. Alfred's notebook was supposed to have been a *florilegium* of spiritual texts. Charlemagne's was a copybook for practising his alphabet.

99. *Life* of Alfred, ed. Stevenson, ch. 89, p. 75.

100. Whitelock, 'Malmesbury on the Works of Alfred', 90–1.

101. *King Alfred's Version of St. Augustine's Soliloquies*, ed. Carnicelli, 47; *King Alfred's Old English Version of Soliloquies*, transl. Hargrove, 1.

102. Whitelock, 'Malmesbury on the Works of Alfred', 90–1.

103. *Florentii Wigorniensis monachi, Chronicon ex Chronicis*, ed. B. Thorpe (2 vols.; English Hist. Soc.; London, 1848), i. 272.

104. Cambridge University Library Manuscript Kk.4.6. Whitelock, 'The Prose of Alfred's Reign', in Stanley (ed.), *Continuations and Beginnings*, 72–3.

105. *Life* of Alfred, ed. Stevenson, ch. 89, p. 75; *EHD*, ed. Whitelock, i. 272.

106. *The Old English Orosius*, ed. J. M. Bately (Early English Text Soc., Supplementary Series, 6; Oxford, 1980), pp. lxxiii–lxxv.

107. Bately, 'Old English Prose Before and During Alfred's Reign', 117 and n. 143.

108. *Old English Orosius*, ed. Bately, pp. lxxii and lxxxi.

109. BL Add. MS 47967.

110. *Old English Orosius*, ed. Bately, p. xxiii; *ASC: MS A*, ed. Bately, pp. xxxii–xxxiv.

111. *Old English Orosius* [I. i], ed. Bately, 13; R. Pauli, *The Life of Alfred the Great: To Which is Appended Alfred's Anglo-Saxon Version of Orosius*, transl. B. Thorpe (Bohn's Antiquarian Library; London, 1889), 249.

112. *Old English Orosius*, ed. Bately, 14–15.

113. Ibid. 15.

114. Ibid. 15.

115. Ibid. [I. i], 16; Pauli, *Alfred the Great*, transl. Thorpe, 253.

116. *Old English Orosius*, ed. Bately, pp. xci–xcii. Bately was confirming Whitelock's suggestion here.

117. Ibid., pp. xciii–c; cf. Whitelock, 'Prose of Alfred's Reign', 89–90, 93.

118. See pp. 471–7 below.

119. See pp. 523–5 below.

120. See p. 541 below.

121. *ASC: MS A*, ed. Bately (*sub anno* 81), 6.

122. Whitelock, 'Prose of Alfred's Reign', 74.

123. *Old English Orosius*, ed. Bately, p. lxxxiv.

124. *Two Saxon Chronicles Parallel*, ed. Plummer and Earle, vol. ii, pp. cvi–cviii, 8.

125. See pp. 521–3 below.

126. *Old English Orosius*, ed. Bately, pp. lxxv–lxxxi.

127. Whitelock, 'Prose of Alfred's Reign', 97.

128. See pp. 502, 512–14 below.

129. Keynes and Lapidge (transl.), *Alfred the Great*, 33.

130. Ibid.
131. Stenton, *Anglo-Saxon England*, 270.
132. See pp. 471–7 below.
133. Keynes and Lapidge (transl.), *Alfred the Great*, 40.
134. Whitelock, 'The Old English Bede', *Proc. Brit. Acad.* 48 (1962), 71.
135. Ibid. 77; id., 'Chapter-Headings in the Old English Bede', 277–8. Cf. 'There is no evidence that a similar circulation [as in the case of Alfred's *Cura Pastoralis*] of the Old English Bede was intended' (ibid. 283 n. 51).
136. See p. 506 below.
137. It is not indeed certain that the Old English Bede was even completed during the reign of Alfred.
138. Stenton, *Anglo-Saxon England*, 269.
139. See pp. 116–45 above.
140. Stenton, *Anglo-Saxon England*, 272–3.
141. Whitelock. 'Prose of Alfred's Reign', 73, 75–6; *EHD*, ed. Whitelock, i. 372.
142. Whitelock, 'Prose of Alfred's Reign', 96–8.
143. See pp. 504–5 below.
144. Sisam, *Studies*, 142.
145. See pp. 559–60 below.
146. Brooks, *Early History of the Church of Canterbury*, 154.
147. *King Alfred's Version of Pastoral Care*, ed. Sweet, i. 6–7.
148. Much of the pre-ninth century annalistic material in the Chronicle may have been originally recorded in Latin. The Cynewulf and Cyneheard annal of 755, once taken to be illustrative of pre-Alfredian prose, is now seen to reveal a vernacular verse background (Bately, 'Old English Prose Before and During the Reign of Alfred', 93 n. 2; 132 n. 219). But the 755 episode—like the poem on Brunanburh in 937—represents an intrusive element in the annalistic format.
149. Whitelock, 'Prose of Alfred's Reign', 74; *Old English Orosius*, ed. Bately, pp. xc, xcii.
150. Ibid., pp. lxxxix–xc.
151. Ibid., pp. lxxxix, xcii.
152. Ibid., p. lxxxix.
153. Ibid., pp. xcii, 83; Pauli, *Alfred the Great*, transl. Thorpe, 379.
154. *Old English Orosius*, ed. Bately, p. xcii n. 4.
155. *King Alfred's Version of Pastoral Care*, ed. Sweet, i. 8–9.
156. Sisam, *Studies*, 145.
157. Ibid. 144–5.
158. Ibid. 143.
159. *King Alfred's Version of Pastoral Care*, ed. Sweet, i. 6–7.
160. See pp. 544–8 above.
161. See pp. 545–8 below.
162. The verse preface of the *Pastoral Care* also speaks of the distribution of copies of that text among Alfred's bishops (ibid., i. 8–9). It may be that the *Pastoral Care* was copied and distributed at two different points in time.
163. See pp. 401–20 below.
164. *SEHD*, ed. Harmer, 52.
165. Sisam, *Studies*, 294, 296.
166. Brooks, *Early History of the Church of Canterbury* 152.
167. The *Swinbeorg* assembly was held while Æthelred was still king, and after the invasion

of Wessex by the Great Army in 871. Hence it was held sometime before mid-April in 871, for Æthelred died after Easter in that year (*SEHD*, ed. Harmer, 49–50; *ASC* (*sub anno* 871); *EHD*, ed. Whitelock, i. 178).

168. See pp. 408–18 below.

169. *SEHD*, ed. Harmer, 18; *EHD*, ed. Whitelock, i. 494.

170. See p. 418 below.

171. *King Alfred's Version of Pastoral Care*, ed. Sweet, i. 6–7.

172. Alfred's acknowledgement of Archbishop Plegmund's help with the translation of the *Pastoral Care* dates that work to after 890 if we take the statement at its face value. If the reference to Plegmund's archiepiscopal status were anachronistic, it is still unlikely that this cleric (who died in 923) joined Alfred's court circle long before 890.

173. Whitelock, 'Prose of Alfred's Reign', 75.

174. Ibid. 95–6; Bately, 'Old English Prose Before and During the Reign of Alfred', 130–1.

175. Keynes and Lapidge (transl.), *Alfred the Great*, 35, 153.

176. Whitelock, 'Prose of Alfred's Reign', 70–1.

177. *Old English Orosius*, ed. Bately, pp. lxxxvi–lxxxvii.

178. Ibid., pp. xc, xcii.

179. Ibid., p. lxxxvii.

180. See pp. 546–8 below.

181. Hargrove (transl.), *Alfred's Soliloquies*, 3.

182. See pp. 557–8 below.

183. *King Alfred's Version of Pastoral Care*, ed. Sweet, i. 6–7.

Chapter X

1. *Life* of Alfred, ed. Stevenson, ch. 77, p. 62.

2. Ibid., ch. 78, p. 63. For John the Old Saxon, see pp. 262–4 below.

3. Ibid., ch. 79, pp. 63–6.

4. *King Alfred's Version of Pastoral Care*, ed. Sweet, i. 6–7. Plegmund did not become archbiship until 890. We have already seen how the Pseudo-Asser had access to Alfred's prose preface to the *Pastoral Care* (see pp. 214–15, 224 above).

5. D. Whitelock, 'Some Charters in the Name of King Alfred', in *Studies in Honour of Charles W. Jones*, ed. King and Stevens, i. 83.

6. *Life* of Alfred, ed. Stevenson, ch. 77, p. 63; *EHD*, ed. Whitelock, i. 269.

7. Sawyer 349, Birch 571. Whitelock, 'Some Charters in the Name of Alfred', i. 93 n. 21.

8. Sawyer 1628, Birch 577–8.

9. Sawyer 1203, Birch 539; *Cartularium Saxonicum*, ed. Birch, ii. 159.

10. Sawyer 350, Birch 576.

11. *Life* of Alfred, ed. Stevenson, ch. 79, p. 63.

12. Ibid., ch. 79, pp. 63–5.

13. Whitelock, 'Prose of Alfred's Reign', 89.

14. D. A. Bullough, 'The Educational Tradition in England from Alfred to Aelfric: Teaching *utriusque linguae*', *Settimane di studio del Centro italiano di Studi sull'alto Medioevo*, 19 (1972), 455–6.

15. *King Alfred's Version of Pastoral Care*, ed. Sweet, i. 8–9.

16. See pp. 544–8 below.

17. Cf. Whitelock ('Some Charters in the Name of Alfred', 81) where she argues in the

case of *Deormod* that the frequent occurrence of his name in Alfredian witness lists 'show that he was often at court'.

18. Sawyer 349, Birch 571.
19. *Life* of Alfred, ed. Stevenson, p. 201 n. 4.
20. Sawyer 348, Birch 567.
21. *EHD*, ed. Whitelock, i. 499.
22. Whitelock, 'Some Charters in the Name of Alfred', 78–83.
23. Ibid. 80.
24. Ibid. 82.
25. Ibid. 93 n. 21. *Life* of Alfred, ed. Stevenson, pp. 304–5.
26. Sawyer 372–3, Birch 613 and 612.
27. *Cartularium Saxonicum*, ed. Birch, ii. 209, 273, 275.
28. Whitelock, 'Some Charters in the Name of Alfred', 79–80.
29. Ibid. 83.
30. Sawyer 356, Birch 568–9.
31. *Life* of Alfred, ed. Stevenson, p. lxvii.
32. Whitelock, 'Some Charters in the Name of Alfred', 84.
33. *Cartularium Saxonicum*, ed. Birch, ii. 210.
34. Sawyer 377, Birch 625.
35. Whitelock, 'Some Charters in the Name of Alfred', 84.
36. Sawyer 1205, Birch, 585.
37. Whitelock, 'Some Charters in the Name of Alfred', 84–5.
38. See p. 269 below.
39. Sawyer 1279, Birch 580.
40. *Cartularium Saxonicum*, ed. Birch, ii. 223.
41. Keynes and Lapidge (transl.), *Alfred the Great*, 259 n. 166.
42. Sawyer 1275 and 352.
43. Sawyer 350.
44. Sawyer 1275, Birch 543.
45. Sawyer 352, Birch 549.
46. *Life* of Alfred, ed. Stevenson, ch. 77, p. 62.
47. Sawyer 352, Birch 549.
48. Sawyer 350, Birch 576.
49. Sawyer 352.
50. Sawyer 1284, Birch 590.
51. Sawyer 1285, Birch 599.
52. Sawyer 350, Birch 576.
53. Sawyer 352, Birch 549.
54. Sawyer 1285, Birch 599.
55. *SEHD*, ed. Harmer, 114.
56. Sawyer 350, Birch 576; Sawyer 352, Birch 549.
57. Sawyer 382, Birch 627; *Cartularium Saxonicum* ed. Birch, ii. 301.
58. *Life* of Alfred, ed. Stevenson, pp. 304–5.
59. Sawyer 368, Birch 600; *Cartularium Saxonicum*, ed. Birch, ii. 253.
60. Sawyer 385, Birch 622.
61. *King Alfred's Version of Pastoral Care*, ed. Sweet, i. 6–7.
62. *ASC: MS A*, ed Bately (*sub anno* 902), 62.
63. *Life* of Alfred, ed. Stevenson, ch. 78, p. 63.

64. *The Monastic Breviary of Hyde Abbey, Winchester*, ed., J. B. L. Tolhurst (6 vols; Henry Bradshaw Soc., 77; London, 1939), iv, fols. 288r–291r.
65. P. Grierson, 'Grimbald of St Bertin's', *Eng. Hist. Rev.* 55 (1940), 538–40.
66. *Breviary of Hyde Abbey*, ed. Tolhurst, iv, fo. 288ᵛ.
67. Ibid.
68. Grierson, 'Grimbald of St Bertin's', 529–30, 532–8.
69. Ibid. 533–8.
70. *Breviary of Hyde Abbey*, ed. Tolhurst, iv, fo. 289ᵛ.
71. Ibid.
72. Ibid., fo. 290ʳ.
73. See p. 189 above.
74. *Breviary of Hyde Abbey*, ed. Tolhurst, iv, fo. 290ʳ.
75. Ibid., fo. 291ʳ.
76. *EHD*, ed. Whitelock, i. 814.
77. Grierson, 'Grimbald of St. Bertin's', 547–8 and 548 n. 2.
78. Keynes and Lapidge (transl.), *Alfred the Great*, 331.
79. J. L. Nelson, '"A King across the Sea": Alfred in Continental Perspective', *Trans. Roy. Hist. Soc.* 5/36 (1986), 48.
80. Ibid. 48–9.
81. *Councils and Synods with Other Documents Relating to the English Church*, I. AD 871–1204, pt. i. 871–1066, ed. D. Whitelock, M. Brett, and C. N. L. Brooke (Oxford, 1981), 10.
82. Ibid.
83. Ibid. 11.
84. *EHD*, ed. Whitelock, i. 816; *Councils and Synods*, ed., Whitelock, Brett, and Brooke, I/i, 11.
85. Keynes and Lapidge (transl.), *Alfred the Great*, 186.
86. Ibid. 332 n. 10.
87. *Councils and Synods*, ed. Whitelock, Brett, and Brooke, I/i, 11.
88. Keynes and Lapidge (transl.), *Alfred the Great*, 332 n. 8.
89. *Councils and Synods*, ed. Whitelock, Brett, and Brooke, I/i, 10.
90. Grierson, 'Grimbald of St Bertin's', 549.
91. Nelson, '"A King across the Sea"', 49.
92. J. M. Bately, 'Grimbald of St Bertin's', *Medium Ævum*, 35 (1966), 4–5.
93. Ibid. 7–10.
94. *Life* of Alfred, ed. Stevenson, ch. 78, p. 63.
95. *EHD*, ed. Whitelock, i. 269.
96. *Life* of Alfred, ed. Stevenson, ch. 94, p. 81.
97. Cf. Bately, 'Grimbald of St Bertin's', 2.
98. *Life* of Alfred, ed. Stevenson, ch. 78, p. 63.
99. Ibid. p. 311.
100. Bately, 'Grimbald of St. Bertin's', 2
101. *Life* of Alfred, ed. Stevenson, chs. 92, 98, pp. 79, 85.
102. Robertson (ed. and transl.), *Anglo-Saxon Charters*, 246 and n. 10, 247, 494–6; Keynes and Lapidge (transl.), *Alfred the Great*, 340 n. 6.
103. L. Alcock, *Arthur's Britain: History and Archaeology* (London, 1971), 73–80.
104. Keynes and Lapidge (transl.), *Alfred the Great*, 340 n. 6.
105. *Life* of Alfred, ed. Stevenson, ch. 93, p. 80; *EHD*, ed. Whitelock, i. 273.

106. Ibid. 274.

107. Bede's *Ecclesiastical History* [v. 24], ed. Colgrave and Mynors, 566–7.

108. *Breviary of Hyde Abbey*, ed. Tolhurst, iv, fo. 288ʳ.

109. *Life* of Odo, *Patrologiae*, ed. Migne, 56–7; Sitwell (transl.), *St. Odo of Cluny*, 32, 34.

110. *Chronicon Abbatiæ Rameseiensis*, ed. W. D. Macray (Rolls Series; London, 1886), 120.

111. *Life* of Alfred, ed. Stevenson, ch. 94, p. 81; *EHD*, ed. Whitelock, i. 274.

112. *Life* of Gerald, *Patrologiae*, ed. Migne, 674; Sitwell (transl.), *St. Odo of Cluny*, 138.

113. *Life* of Gerald, *Patrologiae*, ed. Migne, 674; Sitwell (transl.), *St. Odo of Cluny*, 138.

114. *Life* of Gerald, *Patrologiae*, ed. Migne, 675; Sitwell (transl.), *St. Odo of Cluny*, 139.

115. *Life* of Gerald, *Patrologiae*, ed. Migne, 689–90; Sitwell (transl.), *St. Odo of Cluny*, 162.

116. A. Beaufrère, *Gerbert: Patre a Aurillac, Pontife a Rome* (Aurillac, 1970), 15–16, 41–7.

117. *Life* of Gerald, *Patrologiae*, ed. Migne, 674; Sitwell (transl.), *St. Odo of Cluny*, 138.

118. *Life* of Alfred, ed. Stevenson, ch. 95, p. 82.

119. *Chronicon Abbatiæ Rameseiensis*, ed. Macray, 155–6.

120. Ibid. 124. Two failed attempts to poison St. Benedict are narrated in Gregory's *Dialogues* II.iii and II.viii.

121. *Adomnan*, ed. Anderson and Anderson, 504–7.

122. *Life* of Alfred, ed. Stevenson, ch. 96, p. 82. Whitelock, acting on her innate sense of the historically plausible, refrained from including the account of the attack on Abbot John in the partial translation of the *Life* of Alfred in her *English Historical Documents* (*EHD*, ed. Whitelock, i. 274).

123. *Life* of Odo, *Patrologiae*, ed. Migne, 80–1; Sitwell (transl.), *St. Odo of Cluny*, 80.

124. *Chronicon Monasterii de Abingdon*, ed. J. Stevenson (2 vols.; Rolls Series; London, 1858), ii. 261; *Life* of Æthelwold, *EHD*, ed. Whitelock, i. 835–6.

125. *Life* of Æthelwold, in *Chronicon Monasterii de Abingdon*, ed. Stevenson, ii. 261; *EHD*, ed. Whitelock, i. 836.

126. *Life* of Odo, *Patrologiae*, ed. Migne, 66; Sitwell (transl.), *St. Odo of Cluny*, 53.

127. *Life* of Odo, *Patrologiae*, ed. Migne, 66; Sitwell (transl.), *St. Odo of Cluny*, 52–3.

128. *Life of Alfred*, ed. Stevenson, ch. 97, p. 85; Keynes and Lapidge (transl.), *Alfred the Great*, 105.

129. *Life* of Alfred, ed. Stevenson, ch. 93, p. 81.

130. P. Wormald, 'Æthelwold and his Continental Counterparts: Contact, Comparison, Contrast', in B. Yorke (ed.), *Bishop Æthelwold: His Career and Influence* (Boydell, 1988), 18–19.

131. *SEHD*, ed. Harmer, 17, 51.

132. Ibid. 18, 52.

133. Ibid. 19, 53.

134. Ibid. 17, 50.

135. Ibid. 102.

136. Ibid. 96; Keynes and Lapidge (transl.), *Alfred the Great*, 318 n. 26.

137. E. John, 'The King and the Monks in the Tenth-Century Reformation', in *Orbis Britanniae*, 165–71.

138. *SEHD*, ed. Harmer, 18, 52.

139. *Life* of Gerald, *Patrologiae*, ed. Migne, 672–3, 690; Sitwell (transl.), *St. Odo of Cluny*, 136 and nn. 1 and 2, 162.

140. *SEHD*, ed. Harmer, 17–18, 51.

141. *Life* of Alfred, ed. Stevenson, ch. 75, p. 57.

142. Ibid., ch. 98, p. 85; *EHD*, ed. Whitelock, i. 274.

143. *Life* of Alfred, ed. Stevenson, ch. 75, p. 58; *EHD*, ed. Whitelock, i. 267.

144. *SEHD*, ed. Harmer, 17, 51.
145. While it was understandable for opposition to reform to assert itself very early on in the reform programme of long-established (and therefore lax foundations), Athelney was, by contrast, a new house supposedly founded for fervent monastic recruits.
146. *SEHD*, ed. Harmer, 34, 64.
147. Ibid. 119.
148. Sawyer 343, Birch 545; Finberg (ed.), *Early Charters of Wessex* (no. 415), 123–5.
149. Ibid. 125 n. 1.
150. The argument relating to the doubtful historical association of Alfred with Athelney Abbey is in no way altered by the remarkable paper by Dr Simon Keynes in which he drew attention to two allegedly Alfredian charters which were preserved in a transcript of excerpts from the lost cartulary of Athelney. The transcript, made by George Harbin in 1735, includes two charters supposedly made out by Alfred in favour of Athelney, but Keynes wrote of the first that 'it cannot be authentic in its received form' and of the second that 'one would hesitate before accepting this text as an authentic instrument of King Alfred the Great'. While both charters would appear to be tenth-century forgeries, Keynes still regarded Athelney 'as the abbey founded by King Alfred the Great in gratitude to God for granting him victory over the Vikings' (S. Keynes, 'George Harbin's Transcript of the Lost Cartulary of Athelney Abbey', *Proc. Somerset Archaeological and Natural History Soc.* 136 (1993 for 1992), 155).
151. Sawyer 357, Birch 531–2.
152. Finberg (ed.), *Early Charters of Wessex* (no. 212), 76.
153. *Cartularium Saxonicum*, ed. Birch, ii. 148.
154. *Æthelweard*, ed. Campbell, 54.
155. Ibid.
156. See p. 316 below.
157. See pp. 43–5 above.
158. *Life* of Alfred, ed. Stevenson, ch. 93, p. 81; *EHD*, ed. Whitelock, i. 273–4.
159. See pp. 42–5, 90–2, 124, 142–4 above.
160. See p. 41 above.
161. *Life* of Odo, *Patrologiae*, ed. Migne, 80; Sitwell (transl.), *St. Odo of Cluny*, 79.
162. *King Alfred's Version of Pastoral Care*, ed. Sweet, i. 4–5.
163. Smyth, *Scandinavian Kings*, 250 and n. 39.
164. *Life* of Æthelwold, in *Chronicon Monasterii de Abingdon*, ed. Stevenson, ii. 260; *EHD*, ed. Whitelock, i. 835.
165. Keynes and Lapidge (transl.), *Alfred the Great*, 271 n. 30.
166. There is little possibility that the author of King Alfred's *Life* had ever visited Athelney. Even if he had done, that visit took place *c.*1000 rather than in Alfred's lifetime. The textual evidence from the passage which describes the place exhibits marked features of Byrhtferth of Ramsey and his circle of writers. See p. 299 below.

Chapter XI

1. Galbraith, 'Who Wrote Asser's Life of Alfred?', 98–103; *Life* of Alfred, ed. Stevenson, pp. xxxii–xxxiii, and p. xxxiii n. 1.
2. For a rare but significant passing mention of the *Life* of Gerald and its significance for the development of ideas on English monastic reform, see Wormald, 'Æthelwold and his Continental Counterparts', 19–20.

3. See pp. 280–2 below.
4. *Life* of Gerald, *Patrologiae*, ed. Migne, 644–5; Sitwell (transl.), *St. Odo of Cluny*, 97.
5. *Life* of Gerald, *Patrologiae*, ed. Migne, 645; Sitwell (transl.), *St. Odo of Cluny*, 98.
6. *Life* of Gerald, *Patrologiae*, ed. Migne, 645–6; Sitwell (transl.), *St. Odo of Cluny*, 98–9.
7. *Life* of Alfred, ed. Stevenson, ch. 42, p. 32.
8. Ibid., ch. 76, pp. 59–60.
9. *Life* of Gerald, *Patrologiae*, ed. Migne, 649–50, 653–4; Sitwell (transl.), *St. Odo of Cluny*, 104–5, 111–12.
10. *Life* of Gerald, *Patrologiae*, ed. Migne, 670; Sitwell (transl.), *St. Odo of Cluny*, 134.
11. J. A. Robinson, *The Times of Saint Dunstan* (Oxford, 1969; repr. of 1923 edn.), 134–6; Sitwell (transl.), *St. Odo of Cluny*, p. xii.
12. *Life* of Odo, *Patrologiae*, ed. Migne, 45; Sitwell (transl.), *St. Odo of Cluny*, 6.
13. Smyth, *Scandinavian York and Dublin*, ii. 40–1, 91–4, 102–4, 105–6.
14. Stenton, *Anglo-Saxon England*, 342; Williams, Smyth, and Kirby, *Biographical Dictionary*, 186.
15. *Vita Oswaldi*, in *Historians of the Church of York*, ed. Raine, i. 413.
16. Ibid. 420–1, 435.
17. Byrhtferth of Ramsey prefaced his *Vita* of Oswald with a mini-*Vita* of Oda.
18. *Vita Oswaldi*, ed. Raine, i. 404.
19. Hart, *Danelaw*, 596; Robinson, *St. Oswald and the Church of Worcester*, 15–16.
20. *Vita Oswaldi*, ed. Raine, i. 422–4, 435.
21. Hart, *Early Charters of Northern England*, 337; *Vita Oswaldi*, ed. Raine, i. 468.
22. Hart, *Danelaw*, 30–1, 472; Williams, Smyth, and Kirby, *Biographical Dictionary*, 1.
23. *Byrhtferth's Manual AD 1011*, ed. S. J. Crawford (Early English Text Soc.; Oxford, 1966; repr. of 1929 edn.).
24. S. J. Crawford, 'Byrhtferth of Ramsey and the Anonymous Life of St. Oswald', in Burkitt (ed.), *Speculum Religionis*, 99–111; J. Armitage Robinson, 'Byrhtferth and the Life of St Oswald', *Journal of Theological Studies*, 31 (1930), 35–42; M. Lapidge, 'The Hermeneutic Style in Tenth-Century Anglo-Latin Literature', *ASE* 4 (1975), 91.
25. Lapidge, 'Hermeneutic Style', 91–3; id., 'The Medieval Hagiography of St Ecgwine', *Vale of Evesham Historical Soc. Research Papers*, 6 (1977), 77–93; id., 'Byrhtferth and the *Vita S. Ecgwini*', *Medieval Studies*, 41 (1979), 331–53.
26. See p. 157 above.
27. Lapidge, 'Hermeneutic Style', 94–5.
28. Robinson, *St. Oswald and the Church of Worcester*, 6, 16.
29. *Life* of Odo, *Patrologiae*, ed. Migne, 54; Sitwell (transl.), *St. Odo of Cluny*, 26–7.
30. *Vita Oswaldi*, ed. Raine, i. 446.
31. *Chronicon Abbatiæ Rameseiensis*, ed. W. D. Macray, 159–60.
32. Ibid. 158. A. Gransden, *Historical Writing in England c.550–1307* (London, 1974), 112.
33. *Chronicon Abbatiæ Rameseiensis*, ed. Macray, 158.
34. *Life* of Odo, *Patrologiae*, ed. Migne, 80–2; Sitwell (transl.), *St. Odo of Cluny*, 79–81.
35. Lapidge, 'Hermeneutic Style', 67, 72.
36. Ibid. 73, 78.
37. *Life* of Alfred, ed. Stevenson, p. xcii. Stevenson's list of Frankish borrowings into the text of the *Life* of Alfred (p. xciv) is supplemented elsewhere in his edition on pp. xciii, 255–6, and 312.
38. Ibid., pp. 313, 315–16.

39. Ibid., pp. 255–6.
40. Ibid., pp. 312–13.
41. Ibid., p. 313.
42. Lapidge, 'Hermeneutic Style', 78–81.
43. *Memorials of St. Dunstan*, ed. Stubbs, 3–52. Lapidge, 'Hermeneutic Style', 81–3.
44. Cf. the note on *famen* in M. W. Herren, *The Hisperica Famina: I The A-Text* (Toronto, 1974), 129–30.
45. *Vita Oswaldi*, ed. Raine, i. 410.
46. Lapidge, 'Hermeneutic Style', 99–100.
47. *Life* of Alfred, ed. Stevenson, pp. xcii, 256; and cf. the note on *castellis*, ibid., pp. 312–13. Crawford, 'Byrhtferth and the Anonymous Life of Oswald', 102–3; Lapidge, 'Hermeneutic Style', 71–3.
48. *Life* of Alfred, ed. Stevenson, p. xciii; Keynes and Lapidge (transl.), *Alfred the Great*, 54–5.
49. Ibid. 54.
50. *Life* of Alfred, ed. Stevenson, p. lxxxix.
51. Crawford, 'Byrhtferth and the Anonymous Life of Oswald', 102.
52. Lapidge, 'Hermeneutic Style', 68–9.
53. *Æthelweard*, ed. Campbell, p. xlv.
54. Ibid.
55. Campbell (ibid.) was aware of the danger of over-simplification when it came to classifying Anglo-Latin periods and styles, but his overall view of this subject still stands.
56. *Life* of Alfred, ed. Stevenson, ch. 89, p. 75; *EHD*, ed. Whitelock, i. 272.
57. *Byrhtferth's Manual*, ed. Crawford, 133.
58. Lapidge, 'Byrhtferth and the *Historia Regum*', 99 n. 12.
59. M. L. W. Laistner, 'Notes on Greek from the Lectures of a Ninth Century Monastery Teacher', *Bulletin of the John Ryland's Library, Manchester*, 7 (1923), 421–56, esp. 422–6.
60. Lapidge, 'Hermeneutic Style', 70–3.
61. *Einhardi Vita Karoli, Quellen z. deut. Gesch. d. Mittelalters*, ed. Rau, v/i, 196.
62. *Historia Regum*, in *Symeonis monachi opera*, ed. Arnold, ii. 75 and 84.
63. Ibid. 67.
64. Ibid. 89.
65. Ibid. 75.
66. *Life* of Alfred, ed. Stevenson, ch. 27, p. 22.
67. See p. 294 below.
68. *Vita Oswaldi*, ed. Raine, i. 404.
69. *Life* of Alfred, ed. Stevenson, p. lvii.
70. *A Patristic Greek Lexicon*, ed. G. W. H. Lampe (Oxford, 1964), fasc. iii, 592.
71. Stevenson, ch. 95, p. 82.
72. Keynes and Lapidge (transl.), *Alfred the Great*, 272 n. 234.
73. *Vita Oswaldi*, ed. Raine, i. 418.
74. Lapidge, 'Byrhtferth and the *Historia Regum*', 101. It has to be said that *bellator*, although used by Lapidge as a diagnostic word is not a rarity.
75. [*Life* of St Ecgwine], *Vita Quorundum Anglo-Saxonum*, ed. [J. A.] Giles (London, 1854), 352.
76. *Life* of Alfred, ed. Stevenson, ch. 67, p. 50; ch. 100; p. 86.

77. Ibid., ch. 101.
78. Ibid., ch. 76.
79. Ibid., ch. 1. The word *rector* also appears in the *Life* of St Ecgwine (ed. Giles, 379).
80. *Life* of Alfred, ed. Stevenson, ch. 80.
81. Ibid., ch. 79.
82. Ibid., ch. 91.
83. *Vita Oswaldi*, ed. Raine, i. 462.
84. Lapidge, 'Byrhtferth and the *Vita S. Ecgwini*', 352.
85. *Life* of Alfred, ed. Stevenson, ch. 91, p. 77; *Byrhtferth's Manual*, ed. Crawford, 198.
86. *Life* of Alfred, ed. Stevenson, chs. 15, 96.
87. Ibid., ch. 5.
88. Ibid., ch. 97.
89. Ibid., ch. 88.
90. Ibid., ch. 16.
91. Lapidge, 'Byrhtferth and the *Historia Regum*', 102–3; id., 'Byrhtferth and *Vita S. Ecgwini*', 336.
92. Keynes and Lapidge (transl.), *Alfred the Great*, 54.
93. Lapidge 'Bythferth and the *Vita S. Ecgwini*', 336.
94. Id., 'Byrhtferth and the *Historia Regum*', 106.
95. *Life* of Alfred, ed. Stevenson, chs. 75 and 76.
96. Ibid., ch. 19.
97. *Life* of St Ecgwine, ed. Giles, 383.
98. *Life* of Alfred, ed. Stevenson, ch. 91.
99. Ibid., chs. 71, 76–8, 89.
100. Lapidge, 'Byrthferth and the *Historia Regum*', 102.
101. *Life* of Alfred, ed. Stevenson, ch. 15, p. 13; *Historia Regum*, in *Symeonis monachi opera*, ed. Arnold, ii. 67.
102. Ibid. 86.
103. Ibid. 44.
104. *Einhardi Vita Karoli, Quellen z. deut. Gesch. d. Mittelalters*, ed. Rau v/i, 164.
105. The word *excellentissimae* occurs in ch. 92 of the *Life* of Alfred, ed. Stevenson, p. 79.
106. *Vita Oswaldi*, ed. Raine, i. 427.
107. *Historia Regum*, ed. Arnold, ii. 11.
108. *Life* of Alfred, ed. Stevenson, (dedication), p. 1.
109. See pp. 391–2 below.
110. *Historia Regum*, ed. Arnold, ii. 84.
111. *Life* of St Ecgwine, ed. Giles, 378.
112. *Life* of Alfred, ed. Stevenson, ch. 91, p. 78.
113. Ibid., ch. 92.
114. Ibid., ch. 91.
115. Ibid., chs. 76, 100.
116. Ibid., chs. 92, 104.
117. *Vita Oswaldi*, ed. Raine, i. 412.
118. *Life* of Alfred, ed. Stevenson, ch. 97.
119. *Life* of St Ecgwine, ed. Giles, 394.
120. *Life* of Alfred, ed. Stevenson, ch. 76.
121. *Byrhtferth's Manual*, ed. Crawford, 244.
122. *Immo* appears in the *Life* of Alfred with particular frequency in chapters 12, 13, and

23. It also occurs in the *Life* of Oswald (ed. Raine, i. 412.), and the *Life* of St Ecgwine (ed. Giles, 376).

123. Lapidge, 'Byrhtferth and the *Historia Regum*', 102.

124. *Historia Regum*, ed. Arnold, ii. 90.

125. *Life* of Alfred, ed. Stevenson, ch. 12, p. 10.

126. Ibid., ch. 91.

127. Ibid., ch. 22.

128. *Historia Regum*, ed. Arnold, ii. 42.

129. *Life* of Alfred, ed. Stevenson, chs. 22, 74, 88 for *incessabiliter*; chs. 25, 91 for *incessabilius*.

130. Ibid., ch. 101.

131. *Vita Oswaldi*, ed. Raine, i. 413; *Life* of St Ecgwine, ed. Giles, 352.

132. *Vita Oswaldi*, ed. Raine, i. 473.

133. *Life* of Alfred, ed. Stevenson, chs. 15, 42, 74, 81, 91, 101.

134. *Vita Sancti Wilfridi*, in *Historians of the Church of York*, ed. Raine, i. 105.

135. *Life* of Alfred, ed. Stevenson, ch. 92.

136. There is need for comprehensive computerized word searches to be carried out not only on the works of Byrhtferth of Ramsey but on all tenth- and early eleventh-century Anglo-Latin authors. Present evidence suggests that such an undertaking would reveal an ever closer connection between the Latinity of the Pseudo-Asser and that of other known tenth-century Anglo-Latin authors.

137. *Life* of Alfred, ed. Stevenson, ch. 15.

138. *Vita Oswaldi*, ed. Raine, i. 406.

139. *Historia Regum*, ed. Arnold (*sub anno* 797), ii. 58.

140. *Life* of Alfred, ed. Stevenson, ch. 74.

141. Ibid., ch. 99. For a discussion on the possibility of error through dittography in this passage, cf. Keynes and Lapidge (transl.), *Alfred the Great*, 273 n. 239.

142. *Vita Oswaldi*, ed. Raine, i. 456.

143. Ibid. 464.

144. *Life* of Alfred, ed. Stevenson, ch. 74.

145. *Life* of St Ecgwine, ed. Giles, 390.

146. *Historia Regum*, ed. Arnold, ii. 58.

147. *Life* of Alfred, ed. Stevenson, ch. 74.

148. Lapidge, 'Byrhtferth and the *Historia Regum*', 107.

149. *Life* of St Ecgwine, ed, Giles, 376.

150. *Vita Oswaldi*, ed. Raine, i. 439.

151. *Life* of Alfred, ed. Stevenson, ch. 91, pp. 76–7; *EHD*, ed. Whitelock, i. 272.

152. See Appendix.

153. *Life* of Alfred, ed. Stevenson, ch. 22, p. 20.

154. *Historia Regum*, ed. Arnold (*sub anno* 764), ii. 42.

155. *Life* of Alfred, ed. Stevenson, ch. 22, p. 20; *EHD*, ed. Whitelock, i. 266.

156. Crawford, 'Byrhtferth and the Anonymous Life of Oswald', 108.

157. *Life* of Alfred, ed. Stevenson, p. xci.

158. Ibid., ch. 74, p. 54.

159. *Historia Regum*, ed. Arnold, ii. 53.

160. *Life* of Alfred, ed. Stevenson, chs. 22, 24, 25, 74 ($\times$ 2), 76, 79, 81, 100, 104 ($\times$ 2), 106.

161. Ibid., ch. 104.

162. Ibid., ch. 74.

163. *Byrhtferth's Manual*, ed. Crawford, 244.

164. *Vita Oswaldi*, ed. Raine, i. 430.
165. *Historia Regum*, ed. Arnold, ii. 55. Cf. *diurnus et nocturnus*, ibid.
166. *Life* of Alfred, ed. Stevenson, ch. 74.
167. Lapidge, 'Byrhtferth and the *Historia Regum*', 101.
168. *Historia Regum*, ed. Arnold, ii. 13.
169. *Life* of Alfred, ed. Stevenson, ch. 92.
170. Ibid., ch. 74.
171. Ibid., ch. 103, cf. ch. 99.
172. Ibid., ch. 103.
173. *Historia Regum*, ed. Arnold, ii. 55.
174. *Life* of St Ecgwine, ed. Giles, 390.
175. Lapidge, 'Byrhtferth and the *Historia Regum*', 105–8.
176. *Life* of Alfred, ed. Stevenson, ch. 21.
177. Ibid., ch. 73.
178. *Vita Oswaldi*, ed. Raine, i. 429.
179. Ibid. 442.
180. *Life* of Alfred, ed. Stevenson, ch. 97.
181. *Historia Regum*, ed. Arnold (*sub anno* 793), ii. 55.
182. *Byrhtferth's Manual*, ed. Crawford, 216.
183. Ibid. 40.
184. *Vita Oswaldi*, ed. Raine, i. 403.
185. *Life* of Alfred, ed. Stevenson, ch. 74.
186. Ibid., ch. 92.
187. *Vita Oswaldi*, ed. Raine, i. 454.
188. *Life* of Alfred, ed. Stevenson, ch. 16.
189. *Byrthferth's Manual*, ed. Crawford, 232–3.
190. Ibid. 182–3.
191. Ibid. 180–1.
192. Ibid. 202 (and cf. *Vita Oswaldi*, ed. Raine, i. 462).
193. *Byrhtferth's Manual*, ed. Crawford, 18.
194. *Life* of Alfred, ed. Stevenson, ch. 13.
195. *Byrhtferth's Manual*, ed. Crawford, 232–3.
196. Lapidge, 'Byrhtferth and the *Historia Regum*', 105.
197. [*Life* of Alfred], *EHD*, ed. Whitelock, i. 271; *Life* of Alfred, ed. Stevenson, ch. 81, p. 68.
198. Ibid., ch. 88.
199. *Life* of St Ecgwine, ed. Giles, 378.
200. *Life* of Alfred, ed. Stevenson, p. 326.
201. Crawford, 'Byrhtferth and the Anonymous Life of Oswald', 108–9.
202. The 'place' (*locus*) in the phrase *hoc in loco* both for Byrhtferth and the Pseudo-Asser is not a vague physical or geographical location, but a point in the writer's narrative.
203. *Life* of Alfred, ed. Stevenson, ch. 81, p. 68; *EHD*, ed. Whitelock, i. 271.
204. Lapidge, 'Byrhtferth and the *Historia Regum*', 104; id., 'Byrhtferth and the *Vita S. Ecgwini*', 343.
205. Crawford, 'Byrhtferth and the Anonymous Life of Oswald', 102; Robinson, 'Byrhtferth and the Life of St. Oswald', 36.
206. *Historia Regum*, ed. Arnold, ii. 72.
207. *Life* of Alfred, ed. Stevenson, ch. 16, 15–16.

208. It may also be said that Æthelwulf's annual bequest of 300 mancuses to Rome seems far too high a sum for an annual donation. King Alfred in his *Will* bestowed only 100 mancuses as a once-off legacy to Æthelred, his archbishop of Canterbury (*SEHD*, ed. Harmer, 18, 51).

209. *Life* of Alfred, ed. Stevenson, chs. 21 and 73.

210. Whitelock, 'Prose of Alfred's Reign', 80.

211. Howorth, 'Ethelweard and Asser', *Athenaeum*, no. 2597 (4 Aug. 1877), 146. The ship's metaphor occurs in *Æthelweard*, ed. Campbell, 38.

212. *Life* of Alfred, ed. Stevenson, p. cxvii.

213. Keynes and Lapidge (transl.), *Alfred the Great*, 74; *Life* of Alfred, ed. Stevenson, ch. 21, p. 19.

214. Keynes and Lapidge (transl.), *Alfred the Great*, 88; *Life* of Alfred, ed. Stevenson, ch. 73, p. 54.

215. *Æthelweard*, ed. Campbell, 38–9.

216. *Life* of Alfred, ed. Stevenson, p. cxvii.

217. Howorth, 'Ethelweard and Asser', 146.

218. *Byrhtferth's Manual*, ed. Crawford, 14–17.

219. Ibid. 14–15.

220. Ibid. 142–5.

221. Ibid. 244.

222. *Vita Oswaldi*, ed. Raine, i. 423.

223. *Life* of Alfred, ed. Stevenson, ch. 76; *EHD*, ed. Whitelock, i. 268.

224. *Life* of Alfred, ed. Stevenson, ch. 88, p. 74; *EHD*, i. 272.

225. *Life* of Alfred, Stevenson, pp. 302–3; Keynes and Lapidge (transl.), *Alfred the Great*, 258–9 n. 161.

226. *Memorials of St. Dunstan*, ed. Stubbs, 10.

227. Ibid. 387.

228. *Life* of Alfred, ed. Stevenson, ch. 88, p. 74.

229. Ibid., ch. 53, p. 41.

230. Ibid., pp. 255–6.

231. Sawyer 792, Birch 1297; Hart, *Early Charters of Eastern England*, 165–86. The reference in the charter to *gronnis* is found in Hart (ibid. 166).

232. Ibid. 186.

233. J. Leland, *De Rebus Britannicis Collectanea*, ed. T. Hearne (6 vols.; London, 1774), iv. 23; Crawford, 'Byrhtferth and the Anonymous Life of Oswald', 100.

234. *Life* of Alfred, ed. Stevenson, ch. 88, p. 74.

235. Ibid., ch. 89, p. 75.

236. *Vita Oswaldi*, ed. Raine, i. 423.

237. *Regularis Concordia: The Monastic Agreement*, ed. Dom T. Symons (Nelson Medieval Texts; London, 1953), 3.

Chapter XII

1. Lapidge, 'Byrhtferth and the *Historia Regum*', 114.

2. *Life of Alfred*, ed. Stevenson, p. xcv.

3. Ibid., ch. 1, p. 3; *Vita Oswaldi*, ed. Raine, i. 458; *Byrhtferth's Manual*, ed. Crawford, 178–9.

4. Lapidge, 'Byrhtferth and the *Vita S. Ecgwini*', 348.

5. Ibid. 353.
6. Keynes and Lapidge (transl.), *Alfred the Great*, 54.
7. *Life* of Alfred, ed. Stevenson, pp. 163, 302.
8. Keynes and Lapidge (transl.), *Alfred the Great*, 53.
9. *Life* of Alfred, ed. Stevenson, p. xciv.
10. Ibid., pp. 301–2.
11. Ibid., p. 336.
12. *ASC: MS A*, ed. Bately (*sub anno* 866), 47; *EHD*, ed. Whitelock, i. 176.
13. *Life* of Alfred, ed. Stevenson, ch. 21, p. 19. Keynes and Lapidge (*Alfred the Great*, 74) in this chapter and elsewhere, consistently and misleadingly translated the Pseudo-Asser's *pagani* as 'vikings'. Alfred's biographer, as a monastic opponent of the Scandinavian invaders, used the word *pagani* deliberately to emphasize the heathenism of his enemies.
14. *Life* of Alfred, ed. Stevenson, ch. 21, p. 19.
15. *Bede's Ecclesiastical History* [v. xix], ed. Colgrave and Mynors, 516–17.
16. *Life* of St Ecgwine, ed. Giles, 378.
17. B. Yorke, 'The Kingdom of the East Saxons', *ASE* 14 (1985), 1–36.
18. See pp. 11, 17, 178–9 above.
19. *ASC* (*sub anno* 917); *EHD*, ed. Whitelock, i. 197–8.
20. C. Hart, 'The Ealdordom of Essex', in K. Neale (ed.), *An Essex Tribute for Frederick Emmison* (London, 1987), 65–6.
21. Ibid. 63.
22. Ibid. 76–7.
23. The statement that the Danes came from the Danube to Britain in 865–6 also appears in Byrhtferth's *Historical Miscellany* (*Historia Regum*, ed. Arnold, ii. 73). It is omitted in the Annals of St Neots which name the Danish destination more accurately as *Anglia* or England, rather than *Britannia* or Britain of the Pseudo-Asser (*Annals of St. Neots*, ed. Dumville and Lapidge (*sub anno* 866), 53).
24. Keynes and Lapidge (transl.), *Alfred the Great*, 238 n. 44.
25. *Life* of Alfred, ed. Stevenson, pp. 217–18.
26. *De Moribus et Actis Primorum Normanniæ Ducum auctore Dudone Sancti Quintini Decano*, ed. J. Lair (Caen, 1865), 129–31, 141–4.
27. *De Origine Actibusque Getarum*, in *Iordanis Romana et Getica*, ed. T. Mommsen, *Monumenta Germaniae Historica, Auctorum Antiquissimorum*, v/i [iv–v], 61–6. The reference to Dacia is in *Getica* [v. 33–4], 62.
28. G. Turville-Petre, *The Heroic Age of Scandinavia* (London, 1951), 16–18, 29–31.
29. *Getica* [xxii. 115], ed. Mommsen, 87–8.
30. Ibid. [xxii. 113], 87; Amory, 'Hasting in Franco-Scandinavian Legend', 267–8.
31. Dudo, *De Moribus*, ed. Lair, 130–1.
32. Ibid. 129.
33. *Old English Orosius*, ed. Bately, [I. i], 13.
34. Ibid. [VI. xxvi], 145.
35. Ibid. [I. i], 12–13.
36. Ibid. [I. i], 13–7. See pp. 234–5 above.
37. See pp. 162–4 above. It is interesting to observe in this connection that independent versions of Rollo's vision survive in the *Annals of St. Neots* (ed. Dumville and Lapidge, p. lvii) and in Dudo's *De Moribus* (ed. Lair, 144–7).
38. *Life* of St Ecgwine, ed. Giles, 349–96.

39. Ibid. 376–7.
40. Ibid. 377.
41. Ibid. 378.
42. Ibid. 379.
43. Lapidge, 'Byrhtferth and the *Vita S. Ecgwini*', 344.
44. Ibid. *Life* of St Ecgwine, ed. Giles, 380–2.
45. Lapidge, 'Byrhtferth and the *Vita S. Ecgwini*', 343–4.
46. Ibid. 343.
47. *Life* of St Ecgwine, ed. Giles, 377, 381; *Life* of Alfred, ed. Stevenson, ch. 30, p. 25; ch. 91, p. 76.
48. *Life* of St Ecgwine, ed. Giles, 378–9.
49. Lapidge, 'Byrhtferth and the *Vita S. Ecgwini*', 343.
50. *Bede's Ecclesiastical History* [v. xix], ed. Colgrave and Mynors, 516–17; [V. xxiv], 566–7; Lapidge, 'Byrhtferth and the *Vita S. Ecgwini*', 344.
51. Ibid.
52. Lapidge, 'Hermeneutic Style', 78–81.
53. *Bede's Ecclesiastical History* [v. xix], ed. Colgrave and Mynors, 516–17.
54. *Councils and Ecclesiastical Documents Relating to Great Britain and Ireland*, ed. A. W. Haddan and W. Stubbs (Oxford 1869–78), iii. 350–6; *EHD*, ed. Whitelock, i. 751–6; cf. Lapidge, 'Byrhtferth and the *Vita S. Ecgwini*', 344–5.
55. Ibid. 345.
56. *Councils and Ecclesiastical Documents*, ed. Haddan and Stubbs, iii. 351–3; *EHD*, ed. Whitelock, i. 752–3.
57. *Bede's Ecclesiastical History* [II. iv], ed. Colgrave and Mynors, 148–9.
58. Ibid. [II. v], 149–51.
59. *Life* of Alfred, ed. Stevenson, ch. 26, p. 22.
60. Ibid., ch. 75, p. 58; ch. 80, p. 66.
61. *Life* of St Ecgwine, ed. Giles, 360.
62. Ibid.
63. *Life* of Alfred, ed. Stevenson, ch. 17, p. 16; *EHD*, ed. Whitelock, i. 266.
64. Bede says of Eadbald of Kent that 'he was polluted with such fornication as the apostle declares to have been not so much as named among the gentiles (*sed et fornicatione pollutus est tali, qualem nec inter gentes auditam apostolus testatur*)', *Bede's Ecclesiastical History* [II. v], ed. Colgrave and Mynors, 150–1.
65. *Councils and Ecclesiastical Documents*, ed. Haddan and Stubbs, iii. 353; *EHD*, ed. Whitelock, i. 753.
66. See pp. 192–5 above.
67. *ASC: MS A*, ed. Bately (*sub anno* 867), 47; *EHD*, ed. Whitelock, i. 176.
68. *Life* of Alfred, ed. Stevenson, ch. 28, p. 23.
69. Ibid., ch. 12, p. 10; *EHD*, ed. Whitelock, i. 264.
70. See Appendix.
71. *Vita Oswaldi*, ed. Raine, i. 450.
72. *Life* of Alfred, ed. Stevenson, ch. 46, p. 35.
73. *Historia Regum*, ed. Arnold, ii. 58.
74. Ibid. 65.
75. Keynes and Lapidge (transl.), *Alfred the Great*, 240 n. 55.
76. *Life* of Alfred, ed. Stevenson, ch. 49, pp. 36–7; Keynes and Lapidge (transl.), *Alfred the Great*, 82.

77. *Vita Oswaldi*, ed. Raine, i. 450–2.
78. *ASC* (*sub anno* 979); *EHD*, ed. Whitelock, i. 211.
79. C. E. Fell, *Edward, King and Martyr* (University of Leeds, Texts and Monographs, 1971), pp. xix, xxi, 4–14.
80. See p. 68 above.
81. *EHD*, ed. Whitelock, i. 173; *ASC: MS B*, ed. Taylor (*sub anno* 853), 31; *Æthelweard*, ed. Campbell, 31.
82. *ASC: MS A*, ed. Bately (*sub anno* 851), 44. Cf., ibid., pp. lxxxiii, lxxxviii–lxxxix.
83. *Life* of Alfred, ed. Stevenson, ch. 3, pp. 4–5.
84. *ASC: MS A*, ed. Bately (*sub anno* 855), 45; *ASC: MS B*, ed. Taylor (*sub anno* 856), 32.
85. *EHD*, ed. Whitelock, i. 172; See p. 44 above.
86. *Life* of Alfred, ed. Stevenson, ch. 9, pp. 7–8.
87. *Historia Regum*, ed. Arnold, ii. 3–13.
88. Ibid. 9–10.
89. Lapidge, 'Byrhtferth and the *Historia Regum*', 120.
90. *Life* of Alfred, ed. Stevenson, ch. 27, p. 23.
91. *Vita Oswaldi*, ed. Raine, i. 454.
92. Keynes and Lapidge (*Alfred the Great*, 250 n. 118), acknowledged that the eclipse recorded in the Chronicle under 879 and translated in the *Life* of King Alfred in chapter 59, referred to the total eclipse of 29 October 878.
93. D. J. Schove and A. Fletcher, *Chronology of Eclipses and Comets AD 1–1000* (Woodbridge, 1984), 198–9. I intend to publish a more detailed discussion of the October 878 eclipse shortly.
94. *Ann. Ulst.*, ed. Mac Airt and MacNiocaill (*sub anno* 878), 334–5.
95. *Ann. Fuld.*, ed. Rau (*sub anno* 878), VII/iii, 108; *Ann. Fuld.*, transl. Reuter (*sub anno* 878), 85.
96. *Regino of Prüm*, ed. Rau (*sub anno* 878), VII/iii, 254.
97. *EHD*, ed. Whitelock, i. 180.
98. *Life of Alfred*, ed. Stevenson, ch. 59, p. 48.
99. Schove and Fletcher, *Chronology of Eclipses*, 198.
100. *Life of Alfred*, Stevenson, p. 286.
101. Schove and Fletcher, *Chronology of Eclipses*.
102. *Life of Alfred*, Stevenson, p. 280.
103. *Vita Oswaldi*, ed. Raine, i. 404.
104. Ibid. 404–5.
105. *ASC* (*sub anno* 897); *EHD*, ed. Whitelock, i. 189.
106. *ASC* (*sub anno* 887); *EHD*, ed. Whitelock, i. 183; *Life* of Alfred, ed. Stevenson, ch. 86, p. 72.
107. *Vita Oswaldi*, ed. Raine, i. 406.
108. Ibid. 404.
109. *Life* of Alfred, ed. Stevenson, ch. 94, p. 81; *EHD*, ed. Whitelock, i. 274.
110. *Life* of Alfred, ed. Stevenson, p. 334; Keynes and Lapidge (transl.), *Alfred the Great*, 272 n. 233.
111. Robinson, *St. Oswald and the Church of Worcester*, 41.
112. See p. 176 above.
113. Robinson, *St. Oswald the Church of Worcester*.
114. *Life* of Alfred, ed. Stevenson, ch. 94, p. 81.

115. *Vita Oswaldi*, ed. Raine, i. 413.
116. *Life* of St Odo, *Patrologiae*, ed. Migne, 76–8; Sitwell (transl.), *St. Odo of Cluny*, 72–4; *Regularis Concordia*, ed. Symons, 65.
117. *Life* of Gerald, *Patrologiae*, ed. Migne, 670; Sitwell (transl.), *St. Odo of Cluny*, 134.
118. *Life* of Gerald, *Patrologiae*, ed. Migne, 691; Sitwell (transl.), *St. Odo of Cluny*, 164.
119. *Life* of Gerald, *Patrologiae*, ed. Migne, 652, 658, 692; Sitwell (transl.), *St. Odo of Cluny*, 108, 118, 165.
120. *SEHD*, ed. Harmer, 19, 52–3, cf. note, p. 102.
121. See pp. 260–6 above.
122. *SEHD*, ed. Harmer, 19, 53.
123. Ibid. 18, 52.
124. Ibid.
125. *Life* of Alfred, ed. Stevenson, chs. 100–2, pp. 86–9.
126. Ibid., pp. 86–8.
127. Ibid., pp. 88–9.
128. See pp. 264–6 above.
129. See pp. 41–2 above.
130. *Life* of Alfred, ed. Stevenson, ch. 100, pp. 86–7.
131. Ibid.
132. *ASC: MS A*, ed. Bately (*sub anno* 893), 56; *EHD*, ed. Whitelock, i. 185.
133. Ibid. 186.
134. *Byrhtferth's Manual*, ed. Crawford, 66–7, 86–7, 92–3, 200–5.
135. *Life* of St Ecgwine, ed. Giles, 350.
136. Ibid. 363–4.
137. Lapidge, in his analysis of this apocryphal episode in the *Life* of Ecgwine, followed its fictional account to the point of accepting that swineherds acted as witnesses to Anglo-Saxon charters (Lapidge, 'Byrhtferth and the *Vita S. Ecgwini*', 347–8).
138. *Byrhtferth's Manual*, ed. Crawford, 206–9.
139. Lapidge, 'Byrhtferth and the *Vita S. Ecgwini*', 338; id., 'Byrhtferth and the *Historia Regum*', 109–10.
140. *Life* of St Ecgwine, ed. Giles, 350.
141. Ibid. 363.
142. *Life* of Alfred, ed. Stevenson, ch. 102, p. 88.
143. *Historia Regum*, ed. Arnold, ii. 91.
144. *ASC: MS A*, ed. Bately (*sub anno* 871), 48; *Life* of Alfred, ed. Stevenson, ch. 36, p. 27; ch. 37, p. 28.
145. *Historia Regum*, ed. Arnold, ii. 78.
146. Ibid. 91.
147. *Life* of Alfred, ed. Stevenson, ch. 99, p. 86.
148. *Byrhtferth's Manual*, ed. Crawford, 18–19.
149. *Life* of Alfred, ed. Stevenson, ch. 104, p. 90; Keynes and Lapidge (transl.), *Alfred the Great*, 108.
150. Stevenson shrewdly observed—though with some embarrassment—that 'the author, who is so exceedingly profuse in his explanations in this chapter [on the horn lantern], does not hint at any device for accommodating the candles' (*Life* of Alfred, ed. Stevenson, p. 339).
151. Ibid., p. 338.
152. Ibid., ch. 103, pp. 89–90; Keynes and Lapidge (transl.), *Alfred the Great*, 107–8.

153. *Byrhtferth's Manual*, ed. Crawford, 159.
154. Ibid. 163.
155. Ibid. 156–7, 166–7.
156. Ibid., chart facing p. 116.
157. *Vita Oswaldi*, ed. Raine, i. 405, 442.
158. Ibid. 434.
159. Ibid. 412.
160. *Historia Regum*, ed. Arnold, ii. 40.
161. *Byrhtferth's Manual*, ed. Crawford, 122–5.
162. *Life* of Alfred, ed. Stevenson, ch. 24, p. 21; ch. 76, p. 59.
163. *Byrhtferth's Manual*, ed. Crawford, 112–15.
164. Ibid. 126–7.
165. Ibid. 192–3.
166. *Life* of Alfred, ed. Stevenson, ch. 104, p. 90; Keynes and Lapidge (transl.), *Alfred the Great*, 108.
167. *Life* of Alfred, ed. Stevenson, ch. 104, p. 90.
168. *Life* of Gerald, *Patrologiae*, ed. Migne, 657; Sitwell (transl.), *St. Odo of Cluny*, 116.
169. *Life* of Gerald, *Patrologiae*, ed. Migne, 691; Sitwell (transl.), *St. Odo of Cluny*, 163.
170. *Life* of Gerald, *Patrologiae*, ed. Migne, 657, 683; Sitwell (transl.), *St. Odo of Cluny*, 117, 150–1.

Chapter XIII

1. Keynes and Lapidge (transl.), *Alfred the Great*, 197–8. *Vita I S. Neoti*, ed. Dumville and Lapidge, 125–6.
2. Smyth, *Scandinavian York and Dublin*, ii. 76, 87.
3. *Willelmi Malmesbiriensis de Gestis Regum*, ed. Stubbs, 126.
4. Keynes and Lapidge (transl.), *Alfred the Great*, 198.
5. See pp. 74–98 above.
6. *ASC* (*sub anno* 878); *EHD*, ed. Whitelock, i. 179–80. *ASC: MS A*, ed. Bately, 50.
7. Keynes and Lapidge (transl.), *Alfred the Great*, 198–9; *Vita I S. Neoti*, ed. Dumville and Lapidge, pp. cxvi–cxvii.
8. See pp. 160–4 above, where Dumville and Lapidge's date for the Annals of St Neots in the second quarter of the twelfth century is challenged.
9. *Annals of St. Neots*, ed. Dumville and Lapidge, 76.
10. Ibid.
11. *Life* of Alfred, ed. Stevenson, ch. 53b, pp. 41–2.
12. Ibid., p. 256.
13. *Annals of St. Neots*, ed. Dumville and Lapidge, p. xl.
14. *Life* of Alfred, ed. Stevenson, pp. 98–8, and n. 3; *Annals of St. Neots*, ed. Dumville and Lapidge, p. xxiii and n. 29.
15. *Life* of Alfred, ed. Stevenson, p. xxxvi.
16. *Annals of St. Neots*, ed. Dumville and Lapidge, pp. xxxix, lviii.
17. Ibid., pp. lviii, 76.
18. *Vita I S. Neoti*, ed. Dumville and Lapidge, 120.
19. BL Add. MS 38130. *Annals of St. Neots*, ed. Dumville and Lapidge, pp. lxxxiii–iv, 120.
20. J. Whitaker, *The Life of Saint Neot, the Oldest of All the Brothers to King Alfred* (London, 1809), 68–87.

21. *Vita I S. Neoti*, ed. Dumville and Lapidge, 112.
22. Ibid. 118.
23. Ibid. 120.
24. Ibid. 121–3.
25. Ibid. 128–31.
26. Ibid. 132–4.
27. Ibid. 135.
28. Ibid. 137.
29. Ibid. 138–42.
30. *The Life of Bishop Wilfrid by Eddius Stephanus*, ed. B. Colgrave (Cambridge, 1927), 36–7.
31. See pp. 274–5 above.
32. *Vita I S. Neoti*, ed. Dumville and Lapidge, pp. xcviii–xcix.
33. Ibid. 120.
34. Smyth, *Scandinavian York and Dublin*, ii. 89–125, 173–84.
35. *Vita I S. Neoti*, ed. Dumville and Lapidge, 137.
36. Ibid., p. lxxxvii; cf. C. R. Hart (ed.), *The Early Charters of Eastern England* (Leicester, 1966), 27–9; Hart, *Danelaw*, 606.
37. Ibid.
38. L. Simpson, 'The King Alfred/St Cuthbert Episode in the *Historia de Sancto Cuthberto*: Its Significance for Mid-Tenth-Century English History', in Bonner, Rolleson, and Stancliffe (eds.), *St. Cuthbert, His Cult and Community to AD 1200* (Woodbridge, 1989), 397–411.
39. *Historia de Sancto Cuthberto*, in *Symeonis monachi opera omnia*, ed. Arnold, i. 204–5. The name of the battlefield, where Alfred won his decisive victory over the Danes, is given in the text of the *Historia de Sancto Cuthberto* as *apud montem Assandune* (ibid., i. 205), which is clearly an error for *Ethandune* because the geographical and historical context shows unquestionably that Edington was meant. Arnold argued that the form *Assandune* was prompted by the location of Cnut's victory over Edmund Ironside at Assandune in Essex in 1016 (ibid. 205 n. *a*). I incline to Simpson's view that the account of the Alfred/Cuthbert vision in the *Historia* inspired the Alfred/Neot vision in the *Life* of Neot (Simpson, 'The King Alfred/St Cuthbert Episode', 409–10). While the form *Assandune* may reveal the confusion of an eleventh-century scribe, the propaganda value of the Alfred/Cuthber vision surely had a mid- to late-tenth century origin.
40. *Vita I S. Neoti*, ed. Dumville and Lapidge, 121–2. ASC (*sub annis* 883, 885); *EHD*, ed. Whitelock, i. 181–2.
41. *Vita I S. Neoti*, ed. Dumville and Lapidge, 124–5.
42. Ibid. 115.
43. Ibid. 115 n. 4.
44. Hart, *Early Charters of Eastern England*, 27–8.
45. Keynes and Lapidge (transl.), *Alfred the Great*, 197.
46. *Vita I S. Neoti*, ed. Dumville and Lapidge, p. xcvi.
47. Hart, *Early Charters of Eastern England*, 28.
48. Cf. Hart, *Danelaw*, 610.
49. *Vita I S. Neoti*, ed. Dumville and Lapidge, pp. xciii–xciv.
50. Ibid., p. lxxviii.
51. Ibid., p. lxxxi.
52. Lapidge, 'Byrhtferth and *Vita S. Ecgwini*', 342.

53. Lapidge, 'Byrhtferth and the *Historia Regum*', 119–20.
54. Cf. Hart, *Danelaw*, 610–11.
55. *Vita I S. Neoti*, ed. Dumville and Lapidge, 122, 132.
56. Ibid. 127.
57. Keynes and Lapidge (transl.), *Alfred the Great*, 54.
58. *Vita I S. Neoti*, ed. Dumville and Lapidge, p. xcviii.
59. See Appendix.
60. Ibid., p. xcviii.
61. *Life* of Alfred, ed. Stevenson, ch. 103, p. 90.
62. See Appendix.
63. *Vita I S. Neoti*, ed. Dumville and Lapidge, 124.
64. Ibid. 123.
65. *Life* of Alfred, ed. Stevenson, ch. 15, p. 14.
66. *Vita I S. Neoti*, ed. Dumville and Lapidge, 134.
67. Ibid. 115.
68. Ibid. 140.
69. *Historia Regum*, ed. Arnold (*sub anno* 800), ii. 63.
70. Ibid. (*sub anno* 798), ii. 60.
71. *Vita I S. Neoti*, ed. Dumville and Lapidge, 119.
72. Ibid. 113.
73. Ibid. 140, 141.
74. Ibid. 121.
75. Ibid. 122.
76. *Life* of Alfred, ed. Stevenson, ch. 71, p. 54.
77. Ibid. p. xcix.
78. Lapidge, 'Byrhtferth and the *Historia Regum*', 101 n. 18.
79. *Vita I S. Neoti*, ed. Dumville and Lapidge, 114, 115, 130.
80. *Life* of Alfred, ed. Stevenson, p. xci; *Vita I S. Neoti*, ed. Dumville and Lapidge, 132, 134.
81. Ibid., p. ci.
82. *Byrhtferth's Manual*, ed. Crawford, 172–3.
83. *Vita I S. Neoti*, ed. Dumville and Lapidge, p. cii.
84. *Life* of Alfred, ed. Stevenson, ch. 76, p. 61.
85. Ibid., ch. 90, p. 75.
86. *Vita Oswaldi*, ed. Raine, 458.
87. See p. 301 above.
88. Lapidge, 'Byrhtferth and the *Historia Regum*', 114.
89. Ibid.
90. *Vita I S. Neoti*, ed. Dumville and Lapidge, pp. ciii, cix n. 87, 134.
91. Ibid., p. civ.
92. Lapidge, 'Hermeneutic Style', 85–7.
93. *Vita I S. Neoti*, ed. Dumville and Lapidge, p. cviii n. 86.
94. *ASC* (*sub anno* 885); *EHD*, ed. Whitelock, i. 182; *ASC: MS A*, ed. Bately, 53.
95. *Life* of Alfred, ed. Stevenson, ch. 71, p. 54.
96. *Vita I S. Neoti*, ed. Dumville and Lapidge, 122.
97. Ibid., p. cviii n. 86.
98. The editors of the *Vita Sancti Neoti* point out that 'Asser has no account of Alfred's death, whereas the author of *Vita I* [of Neot] includes in his account of that event

some chronological details which manifestly derive from a version of the Chronicle' (Dumville and Lapidge, p. cviii n. 86). This argument, they claimed, showed that the *Life* of Alfred cannot have been the source of *Vita I* of St Neot. But if the author of the *Life* of Alfred were indeed a forger pretending to be the historical Bishop Asser who was supposedly writing in 893, he would, of course, have excluded any account of Alfred's death in 899. But such a forger, on the other hand, would have been free to incorporate accounts of Alfred's death from the Chronicle into any other works which he may have written, and where he was not pretending to have been writing in the year 893. As for the chronological sequence—given that the *Life* of Alfred is now recognized as deriving from the same early eleventh-century circle of writers as the *Life* of Neot—the relative dating of the two works is no longer such an important issue.

99. *Vita I S. Neoti*, ed. Dumville and Lapidge, 113.
100. Ibid. 116.
101. *Life* of Alfred, ed. Stevenson, ch. 74, p. 54.
102. *Vita I S. Neoti*, ed. Dumville and Lapidge, 125.
103. *Life* of Alfred, ed. Stevenson, ch. 79, p. 63.
104. *Vita I S. Neoti*, ed. Dumville and Lapidge, 113.
105. Ibid. 119.
106. Lapidge, 'Byrhtferth and the *Historia Regum*', 104–5.
107. *Vita I S. Neoti*, ed. Dumville and Lapidge, 119, 133, 140.
108. Lapidge, 'Byrhtferth and the *Historia Regum*', 109.
109. *Willelmi Malmesbiriensis de Gestis Pontificum*, ed. Hamilton, 268–9.
110. *Historia Regum*, ed. Arnold, ii. 83; *The Historical Works of Symeon of Durham*, in *The Church Historians of England*, ed. J. Stevenson (London, 1855), III/ii, 493.
111. Cf. Lapidge, 'Byrhtferth and the *Historia Regum*', 115–16.
112. Simpson, 'The Alfred/St Cuthbert Episode', 410 and n. 45.
113. *Vita I S. Neoti*, ed. Dumville and Lapidge, 112.
114. Ibid., pp. cx, 112, 124.
115. Ibid. 125.
116. *The Chronicle Attributed to John of Wallingford*, ed. R. Vaughan (Camden Miscellany 21, Camden 3rd Series, 90; London, 1958), 33.
117. *Vita I S. Neoti*, ed. Dumville and Lapidge, 129.
118. Cf. Adomnan's denigration of Old Irish as 'a poor and unfamiliar language' *Adomnan's Life of Columba*, ed. Anderson and Anderson, 178–9.
119. In his section of the *Historia Regum* under the year AD 798, Byrhtferth records a battle fought against King Eardwulf of Northumbria 'at a place which is called by the English, Billington [Moor] near Whalley (*in loco qui appellatur ab Anglis Billingahoth, juxta Walalege*)'. *Historia Regum*, ed. Arnold, ii. 59.
120. *Life* of Alfred, ed. Stevenson, ch. 55, p. 45. Cf. Byrhtferth's rendering of this same passage on Selwood from the version of the *Life* of Alfred in the *Historical Miscellany* (*Historia Regum*, ed. Arnold, ii. 83).
121. *Vita I S. Neoti*, ed. Dumville and Lapidge, p. cx.
122. Ibid., pp. cx–cxi.
123. Ibid. 118.
124. Ibid.
125. Ibid. 140.
126. Ibid., pp. cxi, 139.
127. Hill, *Atlas of Anglo-Saxon England*, map 17, p. 12.

128. E. Ekwall, *The Concise Oxford Dictionary of English Place-Names* (Oxford, 1936), 337.
129. Hart, *Danelaw*, 608–10.
130. See Hart's detailed map of *The Fenland in the Time of Hereward*, in Hart, *Danelaw*, map 24.2, p. 632, and see Map 10 on p. 345 above.
131. Hart, *Early Charters of Eastern England*, 182.
132. *Vita I S. Neoti*, ed. Dumville and Lapidge, p. cxi.
133. Ibid., p. cxi.
134. Ibid.
135. Ibid., p. xcix.
136. See p. 277 below.
137. *Life* of Alfred, ed. Stevenson, ch. 42, p. 33.
138. Ibid., ch. 54, p. 43.
139. Ibid., chs. 9, 30, 49, 55, 57.
140. Ibid., chs. 42, 52, 54, 74.
141. Ibid., ch. 35, p. 27.
142. Ibid., ch. 52, p. 40.
143. Ibid., ch. 79, p. 64.
144. Ibid.
145. Ibid., ch. 80, p. 66.
146. Lapidge, 'Byrhtferth and the *Historia Regum*', 105.
147. Thanet, Nottingham, Dorset, Exeter, Selwood, and Cirencester. The Pseudo-Asser supplies four other British place-names, whose meanings are not explained. See p. 348 above.
148. *SEHD*, ed. Harmer, 17–18, 51.
149. Keynes and Lapidge (transl.), *Alfred the Great*, 321 n. 65.
150. Ibid. 241 n. 63.
151. *Life* of Alfred, ed. Stevenson, ch. 84, p. 71.
152. Ibid., ch. 5, pp. 5–6.
153. Ibid., ch. 42, p. 33.
154. Ibid., ch. 57, p. 47.
155. Ibid., ch. 35, p. 27.
156. Ibid., ch. 26, p. 22.
157. *Historia Regum*, ed. Arnold, ii. 74, 77.
158. Lapidge, 'Byrhtferth and the *Historia Regum*', 105.
159. Keynes and Lapidge (transl.), *Alfred the Great*, 51.
160. *Life* of Alfred, ed. Stevenson, p. xci.
161. Keynes and Lapidge (transl.), *Alfred the Great*, 54.
162. *Life* of Alfred, ed. Stevenson, p. 326.
163. Ibid., ch. 89, p. 75.
164. Ibid., p. 326.
165. Sawyer 964 and 967. *Chronicon Monasterii de Abingdon*, ed. Stevenson, i. 438, 441.
166. *Life* of Alfred, ed. Stevenson, p. 255.
167. Ibid. 256. Other possible Celtic Latin words are to be found in the *Vita Alfredi* but they are neither numerous nor conclusively 'Welsh' in origin.
168. Ibid., ch. 18, p. 18; *ASC: MS A*, ed. Bately (*sub anno* 860), 46.
169. *Life* of Alfred, ed. Stevenson, 179.
170. *ASC: MS A*, ed. Bately, 44.
171. *Life* of Alfred, ed. Stevenson, ch. 5, p. 6.

172. *Vita I S. Neoti*, ed. Dumville and Lapidge, 129.
173. *Armes Prydein: The Prophecy of Britain from the Book of Taliesin*, ed. I. Williams and R. Bromwich (Dublin, 1972), 4–5, 12–13.
174. Ibid. 8–9.
175. *Nennius: British History and the Welsh Annals*, ed. and transl. J. Morris (Chichester, 1980), 67. Cf. Keynes and Lapidge (transl.), *Alfred the Great*, 229 n. 6, 232 n. 20.
176. *Life* of Alfred, ed. Stevenson, ch. 30, p. 24, and pp. 230–1 n.
177. Ibid., ch. 79, p. 64. Stevenson (ibid., p. 380) followed by Keynes and Lapidge (*Alfred the Great*, 367) who omit all reference to the Severn in the index to their respective edition and translation of the *Life* of Alfred.
178. *Nennius*, ed. Morris, 60, 74, 81, 82.
179. *Annales Cambriae*, ed. Ab Ithel (*sub anno* 632), 7.
180. *Nennius*, ed. Morris, 81. Cf. *Annales Cambriae*, ed. Ab Ithel (*sub anno* 1257), 92, where the form for the Severn is *Hafren*.
181. *Life* of Alfred, ed. Stevenson, ch. 82, p. 69; ch. 84, p. 71. Cf. *Claudii Ptolemæi Geographia*, ed. C. Müller (Paris, 1883), i. 86.
182. Hart, *Danelaw*, 610.
183. Robinson, 'Byrhtferth and the Life of St Oswald', 40.
184. *Vita Oswaldi*, ed. Raine, i. 431–3.
185. *Life* of Alfred, ed. Stevenson, ch. 79, p. 64.
186. Ibid., ch. 81, p. 68.
187. See pp. 225–7 above.
188. *Life* of Alfred, ed. Stevenson, ch. 79, p. 65.
189. Ibid., ch. 81, p. 67.
190. Ibid., ch. 79, p. 65.
191. Ibid., pp. 313–14.
192. Keynes and Lapidge (transl.), *Alfred the Great*, 94.
193. *Life* of Alfred, ed. Stevenson, p. 339 n. 2.
194. Ibid., ch. 18, p. 17.
195. *ASC: MS A*, ed. Bately (*sub anno* 860), 46; *ASC: MS B*, ed. Taylor (*sub anno* 861), 33; *EHD*, ed. Whitelock, i. 175.
196. *Life* of Alfred, ed. Stevenson, ch. 81, p. 68.
197. Galbraith, 'Who Wrote Asser's *Life* of Alfred', 93–9.
198. *EHD*, ed. Whitelock, i. 822–3.
199. Keynes and Lapidge (transl.), *Alfred the Great*, 264–5 n. 193.
200. Ibid. 264–5 and 50–1.
201. John, *Orbis Britanniae*, 290.
202. Ibid. 290–1.
203. See pp. 122–3 above.
204. The Pseudo-Asser narrated King Alfred's gift of the *parochia* of Exeter in chapter 81 of the *Life* of the king, and then immediately proceeded swiftly to bring his Chronicle translation to a close in chapters 82–5. Having abandoned his Chronicle translation for good, the Pseudo-Asser resumed his fictional account (chapter 87) of his relationship with King Alfred and of the miraculous tale of how the king began to read and to translate in his thirty-ninth year. The intervening chapters in the *Life* of Alfred (chapters 82–5) cover only those annals in the Anglo-Saxon Chronicle for the years 886–7, but although the Pseudo-Asser abandoned his Chronicle at 887, his exemplar most likely contained the record down to 893, as his knowledge of imperfect and

abortive fortress-building—hitherto supposed to be based on contemporary personal knowledge—suggests (*Life* of Alfred, ed. Stevenson, ch. 91, pp. 78–9).

205. Ibid., ch. 80, p. 66.
206. See p. 78 above.
207. *ASC* (*sub anno* 914); *EHD*, ed. Whitelock, i. 194–5.
208. *ASC: MS A*, ed. Bately (*sub anno* 853), 44–5; *EHD*, ed. Whitelock, i. 174.
209. Smyth, *Scandinavian York and Dublin*, i. 109–10; ii. 8–9, 62–72.
210. *ASC: MS A*, ed. Bately (*sub anno* 893), 57.
211. W. Davies, *Wales in the Early Middle Ages* (Leicester, 1982), 114.
212. Smyth, *Scandinavian York and Dublin*, ii. 65–72.
213. *Life* of Alfred, ed. Stevenson, p. 316.
214. D. N. Dumville, 'The "Six" Sons of Rhodri Mawr: A Problem in *Asser's Life of King Alfred*', *Cambridge Medieval Celtic Studies*, 4 (1982), 9 n. 39.
215. Ibid. 9–10.
216. Ibid. 6.
217. Ibid. 14.
218. Ibid. 13–14.
219. Ibid. 15.
220. Ibid. 13.
221. Ibid. 14.
222. Ibid. 13.
223. *Annales Cambriae*, ed. Ab Ithel, 15.
224. Ibid.
225. Schütt, 'The Literary Form of Asser's *Vita Alfredi*', 210; Whitelock, *Genuine Asser*, 5.
226. Keynes and Lapidge (transl.), *Alfred the Great*, 250 n. 115.
227. Ibid. 56.
228. *Life* of Alfred, ed. Stevenson, ch. 7, p. 7.
229. James Campbell ('Asser's Life of Alfred', 122–3) challenged the idea that the *Life* of Alfred was written for a Welsh readership.
230. Ibid., ch. 38, p. 29.
231. *Armes Prydein*, ed. Williams and Bromwich, p. xxix and n. 2.
232. Keynes and Lapidge (transl.), *Alfred the Great*, 242 n. 70.
233. Campbell, John, and Wormald, *The Anglo-Saxons*, 43, 55.
234. *Chronicon Galfridi le Baker de Swynebroke*, ed. E. M. Thompson (Oxford, 1889), 152.
235. Ibid. 153.
236. *The Historia Brittonum*, iii. *The 'Vatican' Recension*, ed. D. N. Dumville (Cambridge, 1985), 18–19.
237. *Vita I S. Neoti*, ed. Dumville and Lapidge, p. cii.
238. Keynes and Lapidge (transl.), *Alfred the Great*, 54.
239. *Vita I S. Neoti*, ed. Dumville and Lapidge, p. c.
240. Ibid.
241. Keynes and Lapidge (transl.), *Alfred the Great*, 54.
242. Lapidge, 'Byrhtferth and *Vita S. Ecgwini*', 348.
243. Ibid. 336.
244. Ibid. Cf. Lapidge, 'Byrhtferth and *Historia Regum*', 103.
245. Lapidge, 'Byrhtferth and the *Vita S. Ecgwini*', 336–7.
246. *Life* of Alfred, ed. Stevenson, pp. 238–9, where *sumere debere sciret* was emended by Stevenson to read *subiret*. Cf. Keynes and Lapidge (transl.), *Alfred the Great*, 242 n.

69. For the Pseudo-Asser's problem with the relative pronoun, see *Life* of Alfred, ed. Stevenson, ch. 89, p. 75; cf. Keynes and Lapidge (transl.), *Alfred the Great*, 269 n. 216. *Life* of Alfred, ed. Stevenson, ch. 91, p. 77; cf. Keynes and Lapidge (transl.), *Alfred the Great*, 270 n. 223. *Life* of Alfred, ed. Stevenson, ch. 99, p. 85; Keynes and Lapidge (transl.), *Alfred the Great*, 272–3 n. 238.

247. *Life* of Alfred, ed. Stevenson, p. lxxxix.

248. Ibid., p. xc.

249. Ibid., p. xc.

250. Ibid.

251. Hart, 'Byrhtferth's Northumbrian Chronicle', 567.

252. Robinson, 'Byrhtferth and the Life of St Oswald', 36.

253. Crawford, 'Byrhtferth and the Anonymous Life of Oswald', in Burkitt (ed.), *Speculum Religionis*, 110.

254. Hart, 'Byrhtferth's Northumbrian Chronicle', 567.

Chapter XIV

1. *Cartularium Saxonicum*, ed. Birch, i. 572.

2. Ibid., ii. 258.

3. See p. 39 above.

4. See p. 375 below.

5. *EHD*, ed. Whitelock, i. 337.

6. *Life* of Alfred, ed. Stevenson, p. 151 n. 2. Sawyer 350 was copied or (if original) was drawn up by a Rochester scribe and the original transaction was enacted at Woolmer in Hampshire (Brooks, *Early History of Church of Canterbury*, 169 and n. 72; S. Keynes, 'The West Saxon Charters of King Æthelwulf and his Sons', 1140–1).

7. *Cartularium Saxonicum*, ed. Birch, i. 598.

8. Ibid., ii. 599.

9. P. Chaplais, 'The Authenticity of the Royal Anglo-Saxon Diplomas of Exeter', *Bulletin of the Institute of Historical Research*, 39/99 (1966), 15.

10. Keynes, ('Charters of King Æthelwulf', 1134) while accepting that Sawyer 343 (Birch 545) was 'a disreputable text . . . not acceptable in its received form', nevertheless believed 'that an authentic charter of the 870s . . . lies not far behind it'.

11. Stenton, *Latin Charters of the Anglo-Saxon Period*, 52.

12. See pp. 252–3 above and p. 375 below.

13. See p. 394 below.

14. *SEHD*, ed. Harmer, 31; *EHD*, ed. Whitelock, i. 502.

15. Sawyer 343, 349, 351, 353, and 357. The status of Sawyer 354 is also very doubtful (*pace* Keynes, 'Charters of King Æthelwulf', 1137–8).

16. See Keynes, 'Charters of King Æthelwulf', 1137 n. 2.

17. *Cartularium Saxonicum*, ed. Birch, ii. 168.

18. Cf. Whitelock, 'Some Charters in the Name of Alfred', in King and Stevens (eds.), *Studies in Honour of Charles W. Jones*, i. 78 and 92 n. 6.

19. Ibid. 78.

20. Ibid. 78–83.

21. *EHD*, ed. Whitelock, i. 499.

22. Finberg (ed.), *Early Charters of Wessex* (no. 239), 83.

23. Whitelock, 'Some Charters in the Name of Alfred', 83, 95 n. 41.

24. *Cartularium Saxonicum*, ed. Birch, ii. 158–9.
25. Sawyer 217, 218, 223, 1441, and 1442.
26. Finberg (ed.), *Early Charters of Wessex*, 162.
27. Ibid. 164. Keynes, 'Charters of King Æthelwulf', 1114 n. 5; 1122.
28. Finberg (ed.), *Early Charters of Wessex*, 162.
29. *Cartularium Saxonicum*, ed. Birch, ii. 65–6.
30. See pp. 377, 403–6 below.
31. Sawyer, *Anglo-Saxon Charters*, 147.
32. Keynes, 'Charters of King Æthelwulf', 1120–1, and 1121 n. 3.
33. Sawyer 279, Birch 852; Sawyer 280, Birch 418. The witness of Æthelwulf as a 'king's son' (*filius regis*) to a charter of Ecgberht in favour of Abingdon Abbey in 835 (Sawyer 278; Birch 413) has been regarded as a post-conquest forgery.
34. Sawyer 282; Birch 396.
35. See pp. 403–6 below.
36. *ASC: MS A*, ed. Bately (*sub anno* 855), 45; *EHD*, ed. Whitelock, i. 174.
37. See pp. 404–6 below.
38. See pp. 470–1 below.
39. *Cartularium Saxonicum*, ed. Birch, ii. 108.
40. Sawyer, *Anglo-Saxon Charters*, 152–3.
41. *Cartularium Saxonicum*, ed. Birch, ii. 105; *Codex Diplomaticus Aevi Saxonici*, ed. Kemble (no. 283), ii. 68.
42. *Cartularium Saxonicum*, ed. Birch, vol. ii, appendix, p. xix.
43. Robertson (ed. and transl.), *Anglo-Saxon Charters*, 16–18.
44. *Cartularium Saxonicum*, ed. Birch, i. 598.
45. Sawyer 287, 289, 291, 293 (contemporary), 296 (contemporary), 299, 300. Æthelstan also supposedly witnessed two other of his father's charters as 'king' but those documents date, in the form in which they survive, to the reign of King Alfred. These are Sawyer 319 (Birch 538), dated AD 874 *recte* 844; and Sawyer 320 (Birch 444), dated AD 880 *recte* 844 or *c*.850. Æthelstan was alive in 851, but he was most likely dead by 853.
46. Alfred's name reappears also in witness lists in 860–2, if we were to allow the erroneously dated grant of Æthelberht to Bishop Wærmund of Rochester (Sawyer 327, Birch 502).
47. *Cartularium Saxonicum*, ed. Birch, ii. 102–3.
48. See p. 470 below.
49. See pp. 23–4 above.
50. Finberg (ed.), *Early Charters of Wessex*, 192–206. Keynes, 'Charters of King Æthelwulf', 1119–23.
51. Keynes's defence of the use of *palatium* in ninth-century West Saxon charters, by reference to later tenth-century usage, was neither helpful nor reassuring for a true assessment of the charters for the Second Decimation (Keynes, 'Charters of Æthelwulf', 1121 n. 2.).
52. See pp. 403–18 below. The error in the indiction of the fragmentary Sawyer 1862 does not inspire confidence. If the fragmentary Sawyer 1862 really did refer to lands in Suffolk as Birch believed (*Cartularium Saxonicum*, ii. 81), then such a charter could never have been issued by Æthelwulf of Wessex who had no jurisdiction in East Anglia. The reference to Æthelwulf's son, Ealdorman Æthelbald, and to his daughter, Queen Æthelswith of Mercia, would suggest that the lands referred to in the charter were located in Wessex.

53. *Cartularium Saxonicum*, ed. Birch, ii. 94.

54. Keynes, 'Charters of king Æthelwulf', 1122 n. 1.

55. *Life* of Alfred, ed. Stevenson, p. 193 n. 3.

56. *Cartularium Saxonicum*, ed. Birch, ii. 62.

57. *Life* of Alfred, ed. Stevenson, pp. 188–9.

58. *Life* of Alfred, ed. Stevenson, ch. 11, p. 9.

59. Keynes, 'Charters of King Æthelwulf', 1119–21.

60. Ibid. 1120 n. 4.

61. *EHD*, ed. Whitelock, i. 484–5.

62. *Cartularium Saxonicum*, ed. Birch, ii. 87.

63. Sawyer, *Anglo-Saxon Charters*, 159 (no. 358), 161 (no. 365). See pp. 253–4 above.

64. *Life* of Alfred, ed. Stevenson, pp. 188 n. 2; 193 n. 4.

65. Sawyer 318, Birch 494. *Cartularium Saxonicum*, ed. Birch, ii. 97–8. 'Sussex Anglo-Saxon Charters: Part II', ed. E. E. Barker, *Sussex Archaeological Collections: Sussex Archaeological Society*, 87 (Oxford, 1948), 132–5.

66. Whitelock, 'Some Charters in the Name of Alfred', 82 and n. 36, 95.

67. *Cartularium Saxonicum*, ed. Birch, ii. 153–4.

68. Ibid., i. 599.

69. Ibid., ii. 219–220.

70. Ibid. 158.

71. Ibid. 168. The king's name is copied wrongly as *Æðelulf*, but the witness list is genuinely Alfredian. Cf. Whitelock, 'Some Charters in the Name of Alfred', 77.

72. *Cartularium Saxonicum*, ed. Birch, ii. 212.

73. Ibid. 203, 205, 457.

74. *SEHD*, ed. Harmer, 15, 17.

75. Ibid. 34.

76. *EHD*, ed. Whitelock, i. 508–9.

77. See pp. 543–4 below.

78. *SEHD*, ed. Harmer, 20, 53.

79. *ASC* (*sub anno*) 871; *EHD*, ed. Whitelock, i. 178; *ASC: MS A*, ed. Bately, 48.

80. Ibid. 47.

81. *ASC* (*sub anno* 855); *EHD*, ed. Whitelock, i. 175.

82. *ASC: MS A*, ed. Bately, 46.

83. Sawyer 286 and 323. Sawyer 286 is dated to AD 838, while Æthelwulf was still ruling as sub-king, under his father Ecgberht.

84. *The Laws of the Earliest English Kings*, ed. and transl. F. L. Attenborough (New York, 1963; repr. of 1922 edn.), 98–9; *EHD*, ed. Whitelock, i. 380.

85. *ASC: MS A*, ed. Bately (*sub anno* 886), 53; *EHD*, ed. Whitelock, i. 183.

86. *SEHD*, ed. Harmer, 24.

87. *ASC* (*sub anno* 893); *EHD*, ed. Whitelock, i. 187.

88. See pp. 125–6 above.

89. *ASC* (*sub anno* 896); *EHD*, ed. Whitelock, i. 188; *ASC: MS A*, ed., Bately, 59.

90. *ASC* (*sub anno* 900); *EHD*, ed. Whitelock, i. 189–90; *ASC: MS A*, ed. Bately, 61.

91. I cannot agree, therefore, with the interpretation of these events by Dr. Keynes, that on Alfred's occupation of London in 886 'this doubtless momentous event was followed by the symbolic submission to King Alfred of all his English subjects in consequence of which he came to be styled "king of the Anglo-Saxons"' (S. Keynes, 'King Alfred and the Mercians', in M. A. S. Blackburn and D. N. Dumville (eds.), *Kings, Currency*

and Alliances: The History and Coinage of Southern England, AD 840–900 (Woodbridge, Suffolk, 1994), forthcoming). There is no evidence to suggest that any, much less 'all' of Alfred's 'English subjects' made a 'symbolic' submission to Alfred or to any other king. Such ideas are driven by Victorian preconceptions, which feed in turn off the Pseudo-Asser's spurious claims for Alfred's 'greatness'.

92. *Cartularium Saxonicum*, ed. Birch, ii. 15.

93. Ibid. 21.

94. Attempts to show that two of Alfred's London coins bear the inscription *rex SM* and that this in turn was meant to declare Alfred's kingship of both the Saxons and Mercians are neither proven nor convincing.

95. See pp. 52–5 above.

96. *gratia domini largiflua concedente* in Sawyer 217, Birch 547; *Cartularium Saxonicum*, ed. Birch, ii. 166. *Gratia Dei disponente* in Sawyer 220, Birch 557; *Cartularium Saxonicum*, ii. 194. *Divina largiente gratia* in Sawyer 219, Birch 552; *Cartularium Saxonicum*, ed. Birch, ii. 174. *in bryrdendre Godes gefe* in Sawyer 218, Birch 551. *SEHD*, ed. Harmer, 20.

97. Sawyer 219, Birch 552; *Cartularium Saxonicum*, ed. Birch, ii. 174.

98. *Hemingi Chartularium Ecclesiæ Wigorniensis*, ed. T. Hearne (Oxford, 1723), i. 242.

99. *Æthelweard*, ed. Campbell, 46, 49, 50.

100. Ibid. 53.

101. See pp. 52–5 above.

102. R. H. M. Dolley and C. E. Blunt, 'The Chronology of the Coins of Ælfred the Great', in R. H. M. Dolley (ed.), *Anglo-Saxon Coins: Studies Presented to Stenton* (London, 1961), 82–3; Blackburn, *MEC*, 314.

103. Sawyer 223, Birch 579; *Cartularium Saxonicum*, ii. 222.

104. *Life* of Alfred, ed. Stevenson, ch. 80, p. 67.

105. *Cartularium Saxonicum*, ed. Birch, ii. 200–1.

106. Keynes and Lapidge (transl.), *Alfred the Great*, 227–8 n. 1; cf. Whitelock, *Genuine Asser*, 15.

107. Ibid. 14.

108. *Life* of Alfred, ed. Stevenson, chs. 1, 13, 21, 64, 67, 71, 73, 83, 87.

109. Keynes, 'Charters of King Æthelwulf', 1147–8.

110. *Life* of Alfred, ed. Stevenson, dedication, p. 1.

111. J. F. Kenney, *The Sources for the Early History of Ireland: Ecclesiastical* (Dublin, 1979; repr. of 1929 edn.), 644–5. Cf. Robinson, *The Times of St. Dunstan*, 55–8.

112. *Life* of Alfred, ed. Stevenson, p. 148 n. 1.

113. *Cartularium Saxonicum*, ed. Birch, ii. 567 (no. 810); 581 (no. 818); 584 (no. 820); 586 (no. 821); 588 (no. 822); 593 (no. 828); 594 (no. 829); 596 (no. 830); 598 (no. 831); 602 (no. 834).

114. *Life* of St Ecgwine, ed. Giles, 379.

115. This forgery, although purporting to have been issued by King Alfred (Sawyer 351) is actally dated to AD 939. *Cartularium Saxonicum*, ed. Birch, ii. 456–7.

116. Keynes, 'Charters of King Æthelwulf', 1142.

117. *Cartularium Saxonicum*, ed. Birch, ii. 250.

118. Whitelock, 'Charters in the Name of King Alfred', 90.

119. Ibid. 91.

120. Sawyer 365, 366, 363, 1205, 362, 364.

121. Keynes, 'Charters of King Æthelwulf', 1142–3.

122. Ibid.

123. Ibid. 1147.

124. *Cartularium Saxonicum*, ed. Birch, ii. 243. *EHD*, ed. Whitelock, i. 499.

125. Stenton, *Latin Charters*, 52.

126. *EHD*, ed. Whitelock, i. 501.

127. Robertson (ed. and transl.), *Anglo-Saxon Charters*, 276.

128. The text is edited in *SEHD*, ed. Harmer, 30–2, and translated in *EHD*, ed. Whitelock, i. 501–3. A text and commentary is provided by S. Keynes, 'The Fonthill Letter', in M. Korhammer, K. Reichl, and H. Sauer (eds.), *Words, Texts, and Manuscripts: Studies in Anglo-Saxon Culture Presented to Helmut Gneuss* (Woodbridge, Suffolk, 1992), 53–97.

129. Cf. Keynes, 'Fonthill Letter', 58–61, 95–6.

130. The writer claims that he gave the five hides of the Fonthill estate to the bishop (of Winchester) in exchange for five hides at Lydiard and that this was done with the witness (*gewitnesse*) of King Edward and his counsellors (*weotena*) (*SEHD*, ed. Harmer, 32; *EHD*, ed. Whitelock, i. 503).

131. Keynes, 'Fonthill Letter', 69.

132. Ibid. 69–70.

133. Ibid. 93–4.

134. *SEHD*, ed. Harmer, 32.

135. Keynes, 'Fonthill Letter', 81–2.

136. Ibid. 82.

137. *Codex Diplomaticus aevi Saxonici*, ed. Kemble, iii. 361–2; *EHD*, ed. Whitelock, i. 549.

138. *SEHD*, ed. Harmer, 34, 64.

139. *Willelmi Malmesbiriensis de Gestis Regum*, ed. Stubbs, i. 145; transl. Giles, 131.

140. Campbell, John, and Wormald, *The Anglo-Saxons*, 32, 39.

141. *Life* of Gerald [I. xvi], *Patrologiae*, ed. Migne, 653; Sitwell (transl.) *St. Odo of Cluny*, 111.

142. *Life* of Gerald [II. iii], *Patrologiae*, ed. Migne, 672; Sitwell (transl.), *St. Odo of Cluny*, 136.

143. *SEHD*, ed. Harmer, 18, 51.

144. Whitelock, *Beginnings of English Society*, 96.

145. *Cartularium Saxonicum*, ed. Birch, ii. 224. *Chronicon Monasterii de Abingdon*, ed. Stevenson, i. 51.

146. The fact that the writer may or may not have been a practised scribe does not affect the argument regarding the ability of the author to compose a coherent narrative of a difficult and entangled lawsuit (Keynes, 'Fonthill Letter', 96).

147. *SEHD*, ed. Harmer, 31, 61.

148. Keynes, 'Fonthill Letter', 56, 93–5.

149. Suetonius, *Twelve Caesars*, transl. Graves, (Augustus) ch. 33, p. 67; ch. 79, p. 87.

150. Ibid., (Claudius) ch. 14, p. 167; (Vespasian) ch. 21, p. 250.

151. *Einhardi Vita Karoli, Quellen z. deut. Gesch. d. Mittelalters*, ed. Rau, v/i, 196; Thorpe (transl.), *Two Lives of Charlemagne*, 78.

152. *EHD*, ed. Whitelock, i. 501. Keynes also saw the Fonthill account of Alfred's involvement in this lawsuit as corroborating 'Asser's' notoriously vague account of Alfred as the conscientious judge (Keynes, 'Fonthill Letter', 74).

153. *SEHD*, ed. Harmer, 31, 62.

154. *Life* of Alfred, ed. Stevenson, ch. 106, pp. 92–5.

Chapter XV

1. The text of Alfred's *Will* is edited and translated in *SEHD*, ed. Harmer, 15–19, 49–53. Cf. the translation in *EHD*, ed. Whitelock, i. 492–5.
2. D. P. Kirby, (*Earliest English Kings*, 201–4) offered new insights in his study of Alfred's *Will*.
3. *SEHD*, ed. Harmer, 15–16; *EHD*, ed. Whitelock, i. 492–3.
4. *Life* of Alfred, ed. Stevenson, ch. 16, p. 14; *EHD*, ed. Whitelock, i. 265.
5. *Life* of Alfred, ed. Stevenson, ch. 16, p. 15.
6. *ASC: MS A*, ed. Bately (*sub anno* 855), 45; *EHD*, ed. Whitelock, i. 174.
7. Dumville, 'Ætheling', 22–3.
8. *Life* of Alfred, ed. Stevenson, ch. 11, pp. 8–9.
9. Ibid., ch. 16, p. 15.
10. Ibid., p. 191.
11. Dumville ('Ætheling', 23) writes of 'Alfred's first visit to Rome' with the implication that he accepted Alfred made the journey twice.
12. Finberg (ed.), *Early Charters of Wessex*, 187–206.
13. Ibid. 193.
14. Ibid. 187.
15. Ibid. 191–2.
16. Ibid. 192.
17. *Life* of Alfred, ed. Stevenson, p. 188; see pp. 377, 382 above.
18. One poor man to be sustained with food and clothing from every ten hides of Æthelwulf's hereditary land. *Life* of Alfred, ed. Stevenson, ch. 16, p. 15.
19. Finberg (ed.), *Early Charters of Wessex*, 194–5; Robertson (ed. and transl.), *Anglo-Saxon Charters*, 275.
20. *Willelmi Malmesbiriensis de Gestis Regum*, ed. Stubbs, i. 119–20.
21. Sawyer, *Anglo-Saxon Charters*, 147.
22. *Life* of Alfred, ed. Stevenson, pp. 187–8 and 188 n. 1.
23. Ibid., p. 187.
24. Finberg (ed.), *Early Charters of Wessex*, 199.
25. Stenton, *Latin Charters of the Anglo-Saxon Period*, 15.
26. Robertson (ed. and transl.), *Anglo-Saxon Charters*, 275.
27. Finberg (ed.), *Early Charters of Wessex*, 190.
28. Ibid. 190, 192.
29. Ibid. 204.
30. *Bede's Ecclesiastical History* [IV. i], ed. Colgrave and Mynors, 328–9.
31. Brooks, *Early History of Church of Canterbury*, 133–4.
32. Cf. *ASC* (*sub annis* 688 and 726); *EHD*, ed. Whitelock, i. 156, 159.
33. See p. 302 above.
34. *SEHD*, ed. Harmer, 16.
35. Sawyer 1187, Birch 313. *Cartularium Saxonicum*, ed. Birch, i. 438; *EHD*, ed. Whitelock, i. 472.
36. D. Whitelock, *Anglo-Saxon Wills* (Holmes Beach, Fl., 1986; repr. of 1930 edn.), 90–1.
37. Ibid. 94–5.
38. *SEHD*, ed. Harmer, 18; *EHD*, ed. Whitelock, i. 494.
39. *SEHD*, ed. Harmer, 16; *EHD*, ed. Whitelock, i. 493.
40. *SEHD*, ed. Harmer, 17; *EHD*, ed. Whitelock, i. 493.

41. *SEHD*, ed. Harmer, 18; *EHD*, ed. Whitelock, i. 494.
42. *Life* of Alfred, ed. Stevenson, ch. 16, pp. 15–16.
43. Ibid., p. 211.
44. Ibid., ch. 16, pp. 14–15.
45. *SEHD*, ed. Harmer, 16.
46. Ibid.; *EHD*, ed. Whitelock, i. 492.
47. John, *Orbis Britanniae*, 40–1.
48. Dumville, 'Ætheling', 24.
49. John, *Orbis Britanniae*, 40.
50. Keynes and Lapidge (transl.), *Alfred the Great*, 314 n. 3.
51. A distinction is made in Early Irish law between lands belonging to the kindred and mensal lands pertaining to the office of kingship (MacNiocaill, *Ireland before the Vikings*, 60). A similar 'extremely clear' distinction between the official and personal property of Visigothic kings is evident from the enactments of Councils of Toledo (Wood, 'Kings, Kingdoms and Consent', in Sawyer and Wood, *Early Medieval Kingship*, 26).
52. *Life* of Alfred, ed. Stevenson, ch. 16, p. 14.
53. Whitelock, *Anglo-Saxon Wills*, 2–4; *EHD*, ed. Whitelock, i. 510–11.
54. Whitelock, *Anglo-Saxon Wills*, 4–5; *EHD*, ed. Whitelock, i. 511.
55. *SEHD*, ed. Harmer, 17; *EHD*, ed. Whitelock, i. 493.
56. *SEHD*, ed. Harmer, 16; *EHD*, Whitelock, i. 492.
57. Keynes and Lapidge (transl.), *Alfred the Great*, 314 n. 3.
58. *Life* of Alfred, ed. Stevenson, ch. 16, pp. 14–15.
59. *SEHD*, ed. Harmer, 16.
60. John, *Orbis Britanniae*, 41 n. 1.
61. Dumville, 'Ætheling', 24.
62. Keynes and Lapidge (transl.), *Alfred the Great*, loc. cit.
63. Ecgberht's grant to Bishop Beornmod of Rochester in AD 838 was issued with the consent of his son, King Æthelwulf (Sawyer 280, Birch 418), and Æthelwulf issued a charter in his own right as king of Kent (*rex Cancie*) in the same year (Sawyer 286, Birch 419), *Cartularium Saxonicum*, ed. Birch, i. 584–7.
64. Ibid., ii. 86.
65. Ibid. 87.
66. Ibid. 46–8.
67. Cf. Brooks, *Early History of Church of Canterbury*, 169.
68. Dumville, 'Ætheling', 24.
69. See pp. 421–51 below.
70. *SEHD*, ed. Harmer, 16.
71. Ibid.; *EHD*, ed. Whitelock, i. 492.
72. Cf. P. D. King, *Law and Society in the Visigothic Kingdom*, (Cambridge, 1972), 244–5.
73. *SEHD*, ed. Harmer, 16; *EHD*, ed. Whitelock, i. 492.
74. *EHD*, ed. Whitelock, i. 493.
75. *SEHD*, ed. Harmer, 16–17; *EHD*, ed. Whitelock, i. 493.
76. Sheehan, *The Will in Medieval England*, 65. Ælfric, an influential relative of this Ailwin contested the *Will* on the grounds that neither royal nor family approval had been obtained to alienate the four estates in question from Ramsey Abbey. The abbot persuaded Edward the Elder to let the *Will* stand. King Alfred's *Laws* [41] required the consent of kinsmen witnessed by the king and a bishop, for the alienation of certain

entailed bookland (Attenborough, *Laws of the Earliest English Kings*, 82–3; *EHD*, ed. Whitelock, i. 379). It is likely that those estates acquired by Ramsey had originally just such a restrictive clause in their documented title or that they were otherwise regarded as inalienable from the kindred or its individual members.

77. Keynes and Lapidge (transl.), *Alfred the Great*, 188; Sisam, *Studies*, 201, 225. See p. 000 above.
78. *SEHD*, ed. Harmer, 17, 51.
79. Ibid. 17, 50–1.
80. Crondall which was allocated to Æthelhelm, although in Hampshire, is but a few miles west of Farnham in Surrey.
81. According to the Annals of St Neots, King Æthelwulf was buried at Steyning (*Annals of St. Neots*, ed. Dumville and Lapidge (*sub anno* 857), 51). Æthelwulf was presumably reinterred by King Alfred in Winchester (Whitelock, *Genuine Asser*, 9).
82. Ibid. 18, 51.

Chapter XVI

1. *ASC: MS A*, ed. Bately (*sub anno* 755), 36. *EHD*, ed. Whitelock, i. 162.
2. *ASC: MS A*, ed. Bately (*sub anno* 868), 47.
3. See pp. 394–5 above, and *SEHD*, ed. Harmer, 30, 61.
4. See pp. 191, 381, etc. above.
5. *Cartularium Saxonicum*, ed. Birch, ii. 209.
6. See p. 47 above.
7. Whitelock, 'Some Charters in the Name of Alfred', 80–2.
8. *ASC: MS A*, ed. Bately (*sub anno* 887), 53.
9. Ibid. 59–60.
10. A. Williams, 'Some Notes and Considerations on Problems Connected with the English Royal Succession, 860–1066', in R. A. Brown (ed.), *Proceedings of the Battle Conference I: 1978* (Ipswich, 1979), 146.
11. *Florentii Wigorniensis monachi, Chronicon ex Chronicis*, ed. B. Thorpe (2 vols.; English Hist. Soc.; London, 1848), (*sub anno* 924), i. 130.
12. *Willelmi Malmesbiriensis de Gestis Regum*, ed. Stubbs, 145; *EHD*, ed. Whitelock, i. 279.
13. Williams, 'English Royal Succession', 150 and n. 35.
14. *Life* of Alfred, ed. Stevenson, pp. 184–5.
15. Williams, 'English Royal Succession', 151–2. Nelson ('Reconstructing a Royal Family', in Wood and Lund (eds.), *Essays in Honour of Sawyer*, 63–4) also accepted the investiture by Alfred of 'his little grandson Athelstan'.
16. Ibid. 148.
17. See pp. 414–15 above.
18. I. N. Wood, 'Kings, Kingdoms and Consent', in P. H. Sawyer and I. N. Wood (eds.), *Early Medieval Kingship* (Leeds, 1977), 7–12.
19. King, *Law and Society*, 24.
20. Wood, 'Kings, Kingdoms and Consent', 14.
21. R. Collins, 'Julian of Toledo and the Royal Succession in Late Seventh-Century Spain', in Sawyer and Wood (eds.), *Early Medieval Kingship*, 44–5. King, *Law and Society*, 26 n. 3, 28 n. 4. There is a suggestion—if nothing more than a suggestion—in J. M. Wallace-Hadrill, *Early Germanic Kingship in England and on the Continent* (Oxford, 1971), 1–20 to the effect that kingship may not have been an indigenous

Germanic institution at all—a notion that is discredited by the known fact that the origin of Iron Age and Early Medieval kingship lay not only deeply rooted and widely spread in the Germanic past, but was widespread throughout the Indo-European world at large.

22. Dumville, 'The Ætheling', 3.
23. Ibid.
24. F. J. Byrne, *Irish Kings and High-Kings* (London, 1973), 35; G. MacNiocaill, *Ireland before the Vikings* (Dublin and London, 1972), 49–50.
25. Byrne, *Irish Kings and High-Kings*, 35.
26. T. J. Oleson, *The Witenagemot in the Reign of Edward the Confessor: A Study in the Constitutional History of Eleventh-Century England* (Oxford, 1955), 77.
27. Ibid. 76.
28. Stenton, *Anglo-Saxon England*, 544.
29. J. M. Kemble, *The Saxons in England: A Short History of the English Commonwealth till the Period of the Norman Conquest*, rev. edn. (2 vols.; London, 1876), ii. 204.
30. Oleson, *Witenagemot*, 8, 82–3. Kemble, *Saxons in England*, ii. 204. W. Stubbs, *The Constitutional History of England in its Origins and Development*, 3rd edn. (3 vols.; Oxford, 1880–4), i. 126–40.
31. H. M. Chadwick, *Studies on Anglo-Saxon Institutions* (Cambridge, 1905), 355–66; F. Purlitz, *König und Witenagemot bei den Angelsachsen* (Bremen, 1892), 12–50.
32. Oleson, *Witenagemot*, 19–21, 42–3.
33. Ibid. 43, 72–3.
34. *SEHD*, ed. Harmer, 26, 58.
35. Stubbs, *Constitutional History*, i. 125–6. Cf. Kemble, *Saxons in England*, ii. 200. Oleson, *Witenagemot*, 11, 12, 20.
36. Ibid. 20.
37. Ibid. 21.
38. Ibid. 112.
39. *EHD*, ed. Whitelock, i. 845; *King Alfred's Version of St. Augustine's Soliloquies*, ed. Carnicelli, 77.
40. See p. 590 below.
41. See pp. 395, 399 above.
42. *Life* of Alfred, ed. Stevenson, ch. 81, p. 67.
43. *Cartularium Saxonicum*, ed. Birch, i. 508–10; *EHD*, ed. Whitelock, i. 474–5.
44. *Cartularium Saxonicum*, ed. Birch, ii. 576; *EHD*, ed. Whitelock, i. 508.
45. *SEHD*, ed., Harmer, 16, 50.
46. Ibid. 17.
47. Cf. Oleson, *Witenagemot*, 82–90.
48. Ibid. 88–9.
49. Chadwick, *Studies on Anglo-Saxon Institutions*, 364.
50. Oleson, *Witenagemot*, 82–3.
51. *ASC: MS A*, ed. Bately (*sub anno* 920), 69.
52. Oleson, *Witenagemot*, 83 n. 1.
53. Smyth, *Scandinavian York and Dublin*, i. 110.
54. The phrase *Rægnald 7 Eadulfes suna 7 ealle þa þe on Norþhymbrum bugeaþ, ægþer ge Englisce ge Denisce ge Norþmen ge oþre* (*Two Saxon Chronicles Parallel*, ed. Plummer and Earle, i. 104) suggests that the Anglo-Danish Northumbrian *witan*—later prominent under Archbishop Wulfstan—were already involved in Northumbrian affairs by 920.

55. *Bede's Ecclesiastical History* [III. xxiv], ed. Colgrave and Mynors, 294–5.
56. Chadwick, *Studies on Anglo-Saxon Institutions*, 361, 364.
57. *Symeonis monachi opera omnia*, ed. Arnold, ii. 45. Cf. Whitelock, *Beginnings of English Society*, 53.
58. *Bede's Ecclesiastical History* (*Continuations sub anno* 759), ed. Colgrave and Mynors, 575.
59. *Two Saxon Chronicles Parallel*, ed. Plummer and Earle (MS D, *sub annis* 947–8), i. 112.
60. *ASC: MS A*, ed., Bately (*sub anno* 755), 37; *EHD*, ed. Whitelock, i. 162.
61. Oleson, *Witenagemot*, 84.
62. *Chronicle of Æthelweard*, ed. Campbell, 51.
63. Chadwick, *Studies on Anglo-Saxon Institutions*, 361.
64. Oleson, *Witenagemot*, 84, 86.
65. Ibid. 82.
66. Stenton, *Anglo-Saxon England*, 545; Robertson (ed. and transl.), *Anglo-Saxon Charters*, 18, 23–4, 279.
67. Stenton, *Anglo-Saxon England*, 385; *Two Saxon Chronicles Parallel*, ed. Plummer and Earle, i. 148–9; ii. 196.
68. Chadwick, *Studies on Anglo-Saxon Institutions*, 354, 357 n. 3.
69. *EHD*, ed. Whitelock, i. 232; *Two Saxon Chronicles Parallel*, ed. Plummer and Earle (MS E, *sub anno* 1036), i. 159.
70. Oleson, *Witenagemot*, 86.
71. *EHD*, ed. Whitelock, i. 235; *Two Saxon Chronicles Parallel*, ed. Plummer and Earle, i. 162–3.
72. *Florentii Wigorniensis monachi, Chronicon ex Chronicis*, ed. Thorpe, i. 196–7; *EHD*, ed. Whitelock, i. 292.
73. Oleson, *Witenagemot*, 86.
74. *ASC: MS B*, ed. Taylor, 46; *Two Saxon Chronicles Parallel*, ed. Plummer and Earle, MS D, i. 93; *EHD*, ed. Whitelock, i. 190.
75. See pp. 122–3 above.
76. *ASC: MS A*, ed. Bately (*sub anno* 904), 63. *EHD*, ed. Whitelock, i. 191.
77. Stenton, *Anglo-Saxon England*, 318.
78. See pp. 44–5 above.
79. *ASC: MS B*, ed. Taylor (*sub anno* 901), 46; *EHD*, ed. Whitelock, i. 190.
80. Robertson (ed. and transl.), *Anglo-Saxon Charters*, 246–7.
81. Keynes and Lapidge (transl.), *Alfred the Great*, 292 n. 8.
82. *EHD*, ed. Whitelock, i. 178; Keynes and Lapidge (transl.), *Alfred the Great*, 292 n. 7.
83. *ASC: MS A*, ed. Bately (*sub anno* 900), 62.
84. *Liber Vitae: Register and Martyrology of New Minster and Hyde Abbey, Winchester*, ed., W. de Grey Birch (Hampshire Records Soc.; London and Winchester, 1892), 6; *Two Saxon Chronicles Parallel*, ed. Plummer and Earle, ii. 121.
85. *Historia Regum* (*sub anno* 933) in *Symeonis monachi opera omnia*, ii. 124.
86. *Folcwini diaconi gesta abbatum S. Bertini Sithensium*, in *Mon. Germ. Hist. Scriptores*, ed. O. Holder-Egger, 13 (1881), 600–35; *EHD*, ed. Whitelock, i. 318.
87. It is, however, likely that the ætheling, Æthelweard, may have been the son of King Alfred and therefore the brother of Edward, who was confused in the Hyde Register with a son of Athelstan. Edmund and Eadred, two infant sons of Edward the Elder, eventually succeeded Athelstan in the kingship.
88. *EHD*, ed. Whitelock, i. 279.

89. Ibid. 277.
90. *Willelmi Malmesbiriensis de Gestis Regum*, ed. Stubbs, i. 145; *EHD*, ed. Whitelock, i. 279. Malmesbury borrowed other information on Alfred from a version or a summary of the Pseudo-Asser's *Life* of King Alfred, from which among other things, he learnt of Alfred's personal handbook and of the tale of Abbot John of Athelney. Whitelock, 'William of Malmesbury on the Works of King Alfred', 81–2, 91–3.
91. Williams, 'English Royal Succession', 151–2.
92. *EHD*, ed. Whitelock, i. 282.
93. *Two Saxon Chronicles Parallel*, ed. Plummer and Earle, i. 105; *EHD*, ed. Whitelock, i. 199.
94. *Willelmi Malmesbiriensis de Gestis Regum*, ed. Stubbs, i. 141–2; *EHD*, ed. Whitelock, i. 277.
95. *Willelmi Malmesbiriensis de Gestis Regum*, ed. Stubbs, i. 141, 145; *EHD*, ed. Whitelock, i. 277, 279.
96. *Cartularium Saxonicum*, ed. Birch, ii. 318; Robinson, *Times of St. Dunstan*, 42–50.
97. Williams ('English Royal Succession', 151) dated this charter (Sawyer 395) to AD 931.
98. Ibid.
99. Smyth, *Scandinavian York and Dublin*, ii. 62–106.
100. *Cartularium Saxonicum*, ii. 295. So, too, an Ealdorman Alfred and two thegns of that name witnessed two other doubtful Edwardian charters—Birch 594, Sawyer 359; and Birch 595, Sawyer 362 (ibid. 241, 244).
101. *Liber Monasterii de Hyda*, ed. Edwards, 113; *Two Saxon Chronicles Parallel*, ed. Plummer and Earle, ii. 121.
102. Chadwick, *Studies on Anglo-Saxon Institutions*, 359.
103. *Cartularium Saxonicum*, ed. Birch, ii. 222.
104. Ibid.
105. *SEHD*, ed. Harmer, 26, 58, 110.
106. *ASC: MS B*, ed. Taylor, 54; *EHD*, ed. Whitelock, i. 205.
107. *Sancti Dunstani Vita auctore B*, in *Memorials of St. Dunstan*, ed. Stubbs, 35–6; *EHD*, ed. Whitelock, i. 830.
108. *Memorials of St. Dunstan*, ed. Stubbs, 36; *EHD*, ed. Whitelock, i. 830.
109. Robertson (ed. and transl.), *Anglo-Saxon Charters*, 90–1.
110. Chadwick, *Studies on Anglo-Saxon Institutions*, 360.
111. *Life* of Alfred, ed. Stevenson, ch. 106, p. 93; *EHD*, ed. Whitelock, i. 276.
112. *Life* of Alfred, ed. Stevenson, ch. 106, p. 93.
113. Ibid. 94.
114. See p. 440 above.
115. *Florenti Wigorniensis monachi, Chronicon ex Chronicis*, ed. Thorpe, i. 144–5; J. Stevenson, *Church Historians of England*, II/i, 249.
116. *Memorials of St. Dunstan*, ed. Stubbs, 214.
117. *Vita Sancti Oswaldi*, ed. Raine, i. 443; *EHD*, ed. Whitelock, i. 839.
118. *Vita Sancti Oswaldi*, ed. Raine, i. 448–9; *EHD*, ed. Whitelock, i. 841.
119. *Vita Sancti Oswaldi*, ed. Raine, i. 445. The 'enormous revenues' arising from monastic lands confiscated from monasteries by Ealdorman Ælfhere of Mercia, are referred to (ibid.) on 443.
120. Williams, 'English Royal Succession', 156.
121. *Vita Sancti Oswaldi*, ed. Raine, i. 455; *EHD*, ed. Whitelock, i. 843. *ASC: MSS D* and

E (*sub anno* 978); *Two Saxon Chronicles Parallel*, ed. Plummer and Earle, i. 123; *EHD*, ed. Whitelock, i. 210.

122. Williams, 'English Royal Succession', 157.
123. Chadwick, *Studies on Anglo-Saxon Institutions*, 359–60.
124. Ibid. 362.
125. *ASC: MS A*, ed. Bately (*sub anno* 755), 37; *EHD*, ed. Whitelock, i. 162.
126. Byrne, *Irish Kings and High-Kings*, 35.
127. MacNiocaill, *Ireland before the Vikings*, 60.
128. See pp. 44–5 above.
129. *Cartularium Saxonicum*, ed. Birch, ii. 243. *EHD*, ed. Whitelock, i. 499.
130. *Cartularium Saxonicum*, ed. Birch, iii. 43.
131. See pp. 45–6 above.
132. Sawyer 407, Birch 703, 1344; *EHD*, ed. Whitelock, i. 505–8.
133. *Life* of Alfred, ed. Stevenson, ch. 91, pp. 78–9.
134. *SEHD*, ed. Harmer, 15, 49.
135. Smyth, *Scandinavian York and Dublin*, ii. 155.
136. *Laws of the Earliest English Kings*, ed. Attenborough, 72–3.
137. Ibid. 82–3.
138. *Symeonis monachi opera omnia*, ed. Arnold (*sub anno* 939, *recte* 940), ii. 94.
139. Sisam, *Studies*, 201, 225.
140. *ASC: MS A*, ed. Bately (*sub anno* 937), 70.
141. Ibid. (*sub anno* 975), 77.
142. *Egils Saga Skalla-Grímssonar*, ed. S. Nordal, in *Íslenzk Fornrit* (Reykjavík, 1933), ii. 144, 147, 161, 173.
143. Smyth, *Scandinavian York and Dublin*, ii. 62–88.
144. *Life* of Alfred, ed. Stevenson, ch. 81, p. 68.
145. *Symeonis monachi opera omnia*, ed. Arnold (*sub anno* 934), ii. 93.
146. Smyth, *Warlords and Holy Men*, 234–5.
147. *Life* of Alfred, ed. Stevenson, ch. 81, pp. 67–8.

Chapter XVII

1. F. M. Stenton, 'The South-Western Element in the Old English Chronicle', in A. G. Little and F. M. Powicke (eds.), *Essays in Medieval History Presented to Thomas Frederick Tout* (Manchester, 1925), 15.
2. Readers are advised to study this chapter in conjunction with the facsimile of Version A in *The Parker Chronicle and Laws (Corpus Christi College, Cambridge, MS. 173): A Facsimile*, ed. R. Flower and H. Smith (Early English Text Soc., os 208; London, 1941). For a description of the various recensions of the Anglo-Saxon Chronicle, a discussion on the origin of the compilation and for extensive bibliography, see J. M. Bately, 'The Compilation of the Anglo-Saxon Chronicle, 60 BC to AD 890: Vocabulary as Evidence', *Proc. Brit. Acad.* 64 (1980 for 1978), 93–129. A. L. Meaney, 'St Neots, Æthelweard and the Compilation of the Anglo-Saxon Chronicle: A Survey', in P. E. Szarmach (ed.), *Studies in Earlier Old English Prose* (Albany, NY, 1986), 193–243.
3. Corpus Christi College Cambridge MS 173, fos. 1ᵛ–32ʳ.
4. M. B. Parkes, 'The Palaeography of the Parker Manuscript of the *Chronicle*, Laws and Sedulius, and Historiography at Winchester in the Late Ninth and Tenth Centuries', *ASE* 5 (1976), 149–71. *EHD*, ed. Whitelock, i. 109–10; Meaney, 'St Neots', in Szarmach (ed.), *Studies*, 194–5.

5. Parkes, 'Palaeography of the Parker Manuscript', 156–71.

6. Dumville, *Wessex and England*, 64–5. Cf. *ASC: MS A*, ed. Bately, pp. xxxiv–xxxv.

7. *ASC: MS A*, ed. Bately (*sub annis* 963–4), 75–6.

8. Parkes, 'Palaeography of the Parker Manuscript', 171.

9. *ASC: MS A*, ed. Bately, p. xli.

10. BL Cotton Tiberius A.vi.

11. BL Cotton Tiberius B.i.

12. *EHD*, ed. Whitelock, i. 110.

13. Bately, 'Compilation of the Anglo-Saxon Chronicle', 97 and n. 1.

14. Meaney, 'St Neots', in Szarmach (ed.), *Studies*, 195–6.

15. C. [R.] Hart, 'The B Text of the *Anglo-Saxon Chronicle*', *Journal of Medieval History*, 8 (1982), 278, 280–2, 290–1.

16. Ibid. 286.

17. Ibid. 279.

18. Ibid. 255.

19. Cf. Meaney, 'St Neots', in Szarmach (ed.), *Studies*, 220–5.

20. Bately, 'Compilation of the Anglo-Saxon Chronicle', 97, and see following note.

21. J. [M.] Bately, *The Anglo-Saxon Chronicle: Texts and Textual Relationships* (Reading, 1991), 3–8, 26–31, 59–62.

22. Hart, 'The B Text', 280–4.

23. Ibid. 278–80.

24. For an explanation of my use of the term *proto-booklet*, see pp. 499 and n. 204 below.

25. *Life* of Alfred, ed. Stevenson, p. lxxxvi.

26. Hart, 'The B Text', 247.

27. Bately, *Anglo-Saxon Chronicle: Texts and Textual Relationships*, 53–5.

28. Hart, 'The B Text', 279.

29. BL Cotton Tiberius B.iv.

30. Bodleian MS Laud Misc. 636.

31. Meaney, 'St Neots', in Szarmach (ed.), *Studies*, 197–8.

32. BL Cotton Domitian A.viii.

33. BL Cotton Otho B.xi; Otho B.x; Add. 34652.

34. BL Add. 43703.

35. BL Cotton Domitian A.ix.

36. *EHD*, ed. Whitelock, i. 112.

37. Ibid. 113. Cf. Meaney, 'St. Neots', in Szarmach (ed.), *Studies*, 201–3. For Bately's reservations on the superior nature of Æthelweard's exemplar in relation to Manuscript A, see p. 475 below.

38. Ibid. 199–201.

39. Ibid. 201.

40. *EHD*, ed. Whitelock, i. 113–14.

41. *ASC: MS B*, ed. Taylor, 19.

42. *ASC* (*sub anno* 603); *Two Saxon Chronicles Parallel*, ed. Plummer and Earle, i. 21, ii. 18–19; *EHD*, ed. Whitelock, i. 147; *Bede's Ecclesiastical History* [I. xxxiv], ed. Colgrave and Mynors, 116–17.

43. See pp. 35, 433 above.

44. Bately, 'Compilation of the Anglo-Saxon Chronicle', 106–7.

45. *ASC: MS A*, ed. Bately, pp. xxxiv–xxxv. See also pp. 513–14 below.

46. *ASC: MS A*, ed. Bately, pp. xxxiv–xxxv.

47. Ibid., pp. xxxiv, xlvii and n. 151; *EHD*, ed. Whitelock, i. 158.

48. Ibid. 199 n. 5.
49. See *ASC: MS A*, ed. Bately, 7–15.
50. R. H. Hodgkin, *A History of the Anglo-Saxons*, 3rd edn. (2 vols.; Oxford, 1952), ii. 625. On *Orosius*, see pp. 234–5, 240 above.
51. J. M. Bately, 'World History in the *Anglo-Saxon Chronicle*: Its Sources and its Separateness from the Old English Orosius', *ASE* 8 (1979), 177–94.
52. J. M. Bately, 'Manuscript Layout and the Anglo-Saxon Chronicle', *Bulletin of the John Rylands University Library of Manchester*, 70 (1988), 39.
53. J. M. Bately, 'Bede and the Anglo-Saxon Chronicle', in King and Stevens (eds.), *Saints, Scholars and Heroes*, i. 233–54 and esp. 240–54.
54. Cf. Dumville, *Wessex and England*, 96. *ASC: MS A*, ed. Bately, pp. xxxiii–xxxiv.
55. Cf. Dumville, *Wessex and England*, 71 n. 71.
56. For bibliography on the 855 horizon for the compilation of the Chronicle, see Bately 'Compilation of the Anglo-Saxon Chronicle', 98 n. 4, 99 n. 2.
57. *EHD*, ed. Whitelock, i. 175; *ASC: MS A*, ed. Bately (*sub anno* 855), 45–6.
58. E. E. Barker, 'The Anglo-Saxon Chronicle Used by Æthelweard', *Bulletin of the Institute of Historical Research*, 40 (1967), 75–8.
59. Meaney, 'St. Neots', in Szarmach (ed.), *Studies*, 205–6.
60. Ibid.
61. A. J. Thorogood, 'The Anglo-Saxon Chronicle in the Reign of Ecgberht', *Eng. Hist. Rev.* 48 (1933), 353–63.
62. Ibid. 359.
63. Ibid. 353, 358–9.
64. Ibid. 359.
65. Ibid. 360–1.
66. *EHD*, ed. Whitelock, i. 114–15.
67. Bately, 'Compilation of the Anglo-Saxon Chronicle', 112–13.
68. K. Sisam, 'Anglo-Saxon Royal Genealogies', *Proc. Brit. Acad.* 39 (1953), 332.
69. Ibid.
70. R. H. C. Davis, 'Alfred and Great: Propaganda and Truth', *History*, 56 (1971), 176.
71. *ASC* (*sub anno* 857); *Annals of St. Neots*, ed. Dumville and Lapidge, 51.
72. See p. 420 above.
73. Cf. Parkes, 'Palaeography of the Parker Manuscript', 167.
74. D. N. Dumville, 'The West Saxon Genealogical Regnal List and the Chronology of Early Wessex', *Peritia: Journal of the Medieval Academy of Ireland*, 4 (1985), 21–66.
75. *EHD*, ed. Whitelock, i. 136.
76. Ibid. 137.
77. The separated leaf (Cotton Tiberius A.iii, fo. 178) once came after two blank folios at the end of version B. See *ASC: MS B*, ed. Taylor, 56–8 (text), pp. xvi–xvii, xix–xx, xxi.
78. See pp. 15–16, 185–6, 190–1 above.
79. *EHD*, ed. Whitelock, i. 175.
80. Davis, 'Propaganda and Truth', 176.
81. *ASC: MS A*, ed. Bately (*sub annis* 868, 871), 47–8.
82. *Ælfred his broþur, Ælfred Æthelwulfing his broþur*, and *Ælfred þæs cynges broþur* (*ASC: MS A*, ed. Bately, 48–9).
83. King Æthelwulf was associated in military campaigns in the Chronicle, first with his father Ecgberht, and later with his sons, Æthelstan and Æthelbald. In the tenth century, King Athelstan was associated with his brother, Edmund, in connection with

the record of the battle of Brunanburh. But the reference to Edmund fighting along-side Athelstan at Brunanburh comes from a praise-poem, and the isolated and varied references to Æthelwulf's association with his father and sons do not compare with the remarkably consistent and frequent linkage of King Æthelred I with his brother Alfred.

84. *Life* of Alfred, ed. Stevenson, ch. 42, p. 32; Keynes and Lapidge (transl.), *Alfred the Great*, 80–1.

85. Stenton, 'South-Western Element in the Old English Chronicle', in Little and Powicke (eds.), *Essays Presented to Tout*, 15–24.

86. Ibid. 23.

87. *ASC: MS A*, ed. Bately (*sub anno* 787), 39.

88. *ASC* (*sub anno* 789); *Annals of St. Neots*, ed. Dumville and Lapidge, 39.

89. *Æthelweard*, ed. Campbell, 27.

90. Stenton, 'South-Western Element', 18.

91. *EHD*, ed. Whitelock, i. 173.

92. Ibid. and nn. 15–17.

93. Stenton, 'South-Western Element', 18.

94. *ASC* (*sub anno* 867); *EHD*, ed. Whitelock, i. 176.

95. Stenton, 'South-Western Element', 18.

96. *Two Saxon Chronicles Parallel*, ed. Plummer and Earle, ii. 71.

97. *Life* of Alfred, ed. Stevenson, ch. 12, p. 10.

98. *EHD*, ed. Whitelock, i. 174.

99. Stenton, 'South-Western Element', 18–19.

100. Ibid. 18.

101. See pp. 73–4, 87–92 above.

102. Stenton, 'South-Western Element', 19–20.

103. Bately, *Anglo-Saxon Chronicle: Texts and Textual Relationships*, 41–53, 59–60.

104. *Æthelweard*, ed. Campbell, 49.

105. *Life* of Alfred, ed. Stevenson, ch. 12, p. 10.

106. *Æthelweard*, ed. Campbell, 44–5.

107. Stenton, 'South-Western Element', 20.

108. *EHD*, ed. Whitelock, i. 182 n. 1.

109. Bately, *Anglo-Saxon Chronicle: Texts and Textual Relationships*, 42–5.

110. For Barker's ideas on the later addition of a set of Canterbury annals to an original Chronicle compiled *c*.855 and its rejection by Bately, see E. E. Barker, 'The Anglo-Saxon Chronicle Used by Æthelweard', 74–80; Bately, 'Bede and the Anglo-Saxon Chronicle', 234–9; Bately, *Anglo-Saxon Chronicle: Texts and Textual Relationships*, 41–2.

111. *Æthelweard*, ed. Campbell, 36.

112. Ibid., pp. xxvii–xxviii. D. Whitelock, 'Fact and Fiction in the Legend of St Edmund', *Proc. Suffolk Inst. Archaeol.* 31 (1969), 222. Cf. Smyth, *Scandinavian Kings in the British Isles*, 205–6.

113. Alfred had few estates in Dorset, but several in Somerset and Devon. Cf. Meaney, ('St. Neots', in Szarmach (ed.), *Studies*, 209) where that writer challenged Stenton's view on a West Country origin for the Chronicle and allowed for royal involvement in its compilation. Meaney was reluctant to dismiss Stenton's views out of hand and settled for an unsatisfactory *impasse*, being unable 'to see how the matter can ever be finally decided one way or another'.

114. *Æthelweard*, ed. Campbell, 36–7.

115. For Æthelweard's background, see *Æthelweard*, ed. Campbell, pp. xii–xvi. Barker, 'The Anglo-Saxon Chronicle Used by Æthelweard', 86–90.

116. Cf. Ibid. 80.

117. I cannot agree with Hart that Æthelweard's references to 'King' Æthelred of the Mercians 'can be put down to his own stylistic quirks' (Hart, 'The B Text', 251).

118. Cf. Barker, 'The Anglo-Saxon Chronicle Used by Æthelweard', 82.

119. Hart, 'The B Text', 286.

120. Dumville, *Wessex and England*, 72.

121. Stenton, 'South-Western Element', 22.

122. Barker, 'The Anglo-Saxon Chronicle Used by Æthelweard', 75–7.

123. Dumville, *Wessex and England*, 69.

124. Dumville saw the 891–6 section of the Chronicle as a continuation of a compilation completed in 890–1, and he would therefore not view the 891–6 section as having any editorial influence on anything which had gone before. Sawyer (*Age of the Vikings*, 19) correctly understood the significance of the 892–6 annals as having had an influence on the writing-up of events from 835. See p. 489 below.

125. Stenton's statement that 'when compared with the great Frankish annals of the ninth century, which seem to descend from an official record, the *Chronicle* has definitely the character of private work' (Stenton, *Anglo-Saxon England*, 683) was fundamentally mistaken. Campbell ('Asser's Life of Alfred', 116) recognized the parallel between the Frankish royal annals and the Anglo-Saxon Chronicle.

126. This entry appears under 773 in MS A.

127. *Ann. Ulst.*, ed. Mac Airt and Mac Niocaill (*sub anno* 877), 334–5; *Ann. Fuld.*, *Quellen z. deut. Gesch. d. Mittelalters*, ed. Rau (*sub anno* 878), VII/iii. 108–9. See p. 507 below.

128. *Bede's Ecclesiastical History* [II. v], ed. Colgrave and Mynors, 148–51.

129. *ASC: MS A*, ed. Bately (*sub anno* 827), 42.

130. *Bede's Ecclesiastical History* [v. xxiii], ed. Colgrave and Mynors, 558–9.

131. *Cartularium Saxonicum*, ed. Birch, i. 222–3; *EHD*, ed. Whitelock, i. 453–4.

132. Sawyer 111, Birch 214; *Cartularium Saxonicum*, ed. Birch, i. 301–3.

133. See p. 179 above.

134. Cf. Sawyer, *Age of the Vikings*, 19.

135. Dumville (*Wessex and England*, 71) followed Stenton in pointing to the relative scarcity of references to Winchester bishops in the Chronicle, without studying that Winchester record against the different textual levels within the Chronicle compilation, and while ignoring key references to Winchester in the 891–6 section.

136. Smyth, *Scandinavian Kings*, 169–213.

137. *EHD*, ed. Whitelock, i. 177.

138. Smyth, *Scandinavian Kings*, 233 and n. 24.

139. *EHD*, ed. Whitelock, i. 177–8; *ASC: MS A*, ed. Bately (*sub anno* 871), 48–9.

140. *EHD*, ed. Whitelock, i. 178.

141. Stenton, 'South-Western Element in the Old English Chronicle', in Little and Powicke (eds.), *Essays Presented to Tout*, 18.

142. See pp. 68–70 above.

143. *ASC: MS A*, ed. Bately (*sub anno* 871), 48–9. *EHD*, ed. Whitelock, i. 178.

144. Smyth, *Scandinavian Kings*, 240–54.

145. See pp. 39–50 above.

146. *Life* of Alfred, ed. Stevenson, ch. 49, p. 37. For the significance of the ring in

pagan Scandinavian ritual, see Smyth, *Scandinavian York and Dublin*, ii. 244, 252–3, 265–71.

147. *EHD*, ed. Whitelock, i. 179.
148. Davis, 'Propaganda and Truth', 172.
149. C. Clark, 'The Narrative Mode of *The Anglo-Saxon Chronicle* before the Conquest', in Clemoes and Hughes (eds.), *Studies Presented to Dorothy Whitelock*, 220.
150. See pp. 99–115 above.
151. Bately, 'Compilation of the Anglo-Saxon Chronicle', 109–15.
152. This first Alfredian annalist may also have written or revised the annals for 835 and 860 (ibid. 112–13).
153. Ibid. 110 and n. 3.
154. Ibid. 110, 114–16.
155. See p. 103 above.
156. See p. 104 above.
157. Keynes and Lapidge (transl.), *Alfred the Great*, 253 n. 134. Cf. ibid. 55.
158. Ibid. 266 n. 201.
159. *Life* of Alfred, ed. Stevenson, p. 287.
160. *Æthelweard*, ed. Campbell, 44.
161. Æthelweard also mentions the bridge at Paris under 887 (*Æthelweard*, ed. Campbell, 46). Even if it were demonstrated that the Pseudo-Asser did possess 'superior knowledge on Frankish affairs', that knowledge would not have come via the ninth-century Grimbald, but from altogether better documented Frankish contacts with late tenth- and early eleventh-century Ramsey.
162. Keynes and Lapidge (transl.), *Alfred the Great*, 267 n. 204.
163. The deposition of Charles by his nephew was reported in the Anglo-Saxon Chronicle, while it was not quite so stated in Æthelweard.
164. *Life* of Alfred, ed. Stevenson, ch. 27, p. 22.
165. See p. 103 above.
166. *EHD*, ed. Whitelock, i. 182.
167. Sawyer, *Age of the Vikings*, 19.
168. Davis, 'Propaganda and Truth', 174.
169. See pp. 103–4 above.
170. See pp. 101, 107 above.
171. Dumville in a publication promised in 1992 believed the compiler of the Anglo-Saxon Chronicle 'drew on a Breton source of information' for his Frankish material of the 880s (cited in Dumville, *Wessex and England*, 89 and n. 165).
172. *ASC: MS A*, ed. Bately (*sub anno* 892), 55; *EHD*, ed. Whitelock, i. 184–5.
173. Ibid. 186.
174. Ibid. 185.
175. *Æthelweard*, ed. Campbell, 49.
176. *EHD*, ed. Whitelock, i. 185.
177. Ibid. 186.
178. Ibid. 186.
179. *Æthelweard*, ed. Campbell, 50.
180. *EHD*, ed. Whitelock, i. 187.
181. Ibid.
182. Ibid. 189.
183. Ibid. 189.

184. Ibid. 188.
185. Clark, 'Narrative Mode of *Anglo-Saxon Chronicle*', 215–24.
186. Ibid. 223.
187. Ibid. 224.
188. Dumville, *Wessex and England*, 69–70.
189. *EHD*, ed. Whitelock, i. 189.
190. *ASC: MS A*, ed. Bately (*sub anno* 896), 60.
191. *EHD*, ed. Whitelock, i. 186.
192. Cf. T. A. Shippey, 'A Missing Army: Some Doubts about the Alfredian Chronicle', *In Geardagum*, 4 (1982), 41–55.
193. *ASC* (*sub anno* 891); *EHD*, ed. Whitelock, i. 184. *ASC: MS A*, ed. Bately, 54.
194. *Æthelweard*, ed. Campbell, 48. Some of Æthelweard's comments on the three Irish travellers look like speculation on the part of that late tenth-century chronicler, who misunderstood elements in this account. Æthelweard does not mention the death of Suibhne as such, but he seems to imply that Suibhne was one of the three pilgrims who died on the journey. This cannot be so, because Suibhne died in 891—most likely in Ireland—before the other three pilgrims set out on their voyage.
195. *Adomnan's Life of Columba*, ed. Anderson and Anderson, 444–5, 454–5.
196. *Two Saxon Chronicles Parallel*, ed. Plummer and Earle, ii. 103–4.
197. *Ann. Ulst.*, ed. Mac Airt and MacNiocaill, (*sub anno* 890), 346–7. A. P. Smyth, *Celtic Leinster: Towards an Historical Geography of Early Irish Civilization AD 500–1500* (Dublin, 1982), 104, fig. 51a.
198. I am grateful to Dr Donnchadh Ó hAodha, Department of Old Irish, University College Galway, for his help with the study of these name forms. See *ASC: MS A*, ed. Bately (*sub anno* 891), 54; *ASC: MS B*, ed. Taylor (*sub anno* 892), 40; *Æthelweard*, ed. Campbell, 48.
199. Ibid.
200. *Two Lives of Charlemagne*, transl. Thorpe, 93.
201. Ibid.
202. Ibid. 93–4.
203. Version E omits 891 but includes 892 and omits 893–6. Æthelweard includes 892 and a summary of 893. See below.
204. I use the term *proto-booklet* to distinguish between the earliest notebooks used by the compilers of different sections of the Chronicle, and the First and Second Booklets of the surviving Manuscript A. Parkes was not always clear in his use of terminology in regard to this distinction.
205. Dumville, *Wessex and England*, 90–1, 113–19.
206. Parkes, 'Palaeography of the Parker Manuscript', 154.
207. *ASC: MS A*, ed. Bately, pp. xxvi–xxxiv.
208. Ibid.
209. Cf. Parkes, 'Palaeography of the Parker Manuscript', 155.
210. Ibid. 156–7. See p. 513 below.
211. Clark, 'Narrative Mode of *Anglo-Saxon Chronicle*', 221 n. 1.
212. The idea that the compiler of the 891–6 section was working contemporaneously with the compilers of the 870 and 880s material is a different concept from Dumville's theory of collaboration between Hand One and Hand Two in the Parker Manuscript (A) (Dumville, *Wessex and England*, 90–1, 116–19). The first relates to the original compilation of the Chronicle in 896, the second relates to the copying of the A text

c.900–*c*.930. For Bately's assessment of Dumville's theory of simultaneous copying and for her reservations regarding it, see *ASC: MS A*, ed. Bately, pp. xxx–xxxii.

213. Cf. Parkes, 'Palaeography of the Parker Manuscript', 155.
214. Ibid.
215. Ibid. 161; *ASC: MS A*, ed. Bately, p. xvii.
216. Ibid., p. xvii.
217. *Æthelweard*, ed. Campbell, pp. xxviii–xxix.
218. Hart, 'The B Text', 264.
219. *Ann. Bert., Quellen z. deut. Gesch. d. Mittelalters*, ed. Rau (*sub anno* 858), VI/ii, 94. *Ann. Ulst.*, ed. Hennessy and MacCarthy (*sub anno* 752), i. 216–17. *Ann. Ulst.*, ed. Mac Airt and MacNiocaill, i. 209.
220. Bately, *Anglo-Saxon Chronicle: Texts and Textual Relationships*, esp. 59–62.
221. Cf. Dumville, *Wessex and England*, 89.
222. See pp. 238–9 above.
223. The Pseudo-Asser's Chronicle text may well have continued down to 892–3 as in the case of the exemplar consulted by Æthelweard, which clearly contained a version of the 893 annal. The Pseudo-Asser almost certainly had access, for instance, to the account of the unfinished fort under AD 892 in Version A of the Chronicle—an account which prompted his speculation on Alfredian fort-building in chapter 91 of the *Life* of Alfred (*Life* of Alfred, ed. Stevenson, ch. 91, p. 78).
224. See p. 543 below.
225. Parkes, 'Palaeography of the Parker Manuscript', 171.
226. Hart, 'The B Text', 279.
227. *EHD*, ed. Whitelock, i. 184.
228. Ibid. 180, 182.
229. Davis, 'Propaganda and Truth', 173.
230. Dumville, *Wessex and England*, 71, 97.
231. Cf. Stenton, 'South-Western Element', 17.
232. F. M. Powicke and E. B. Fryde, *Handbook of British Chronology*, 2nd edn. (London, 1961), 257.
233. *Æthelweard*, ed. Campbell, 29.
234. Stenton, 'South-Western Element', 15.
235. Ibid. 17.
236. *Nithardi Historiarum Libri iiii, Quellen z. deut. Gesch. d. Mittelalters*, ed. Rau, V/i, 450.
237. *EHD*, ed. Whitelock, i. 173.
238. *ASC: MS A*, ed. Bately (*sub anno* 839), 43.
239. *ASC: MS B*, ed. Taylor (*sub anno* 839), 31.
240. *Annals of St. Neots*, ed. Dumville and Lapidge, 42.
241. *Æthelweard*, ed. Campbell, 3.
242. *ASC: MS B*, ed. Taylor, 31, n. under [*839*].
243. See p. 145 above.
244. Stenton, 'South-Western Element', 16.
245. *SEHD*, ed. Harmer, 18, 52.
246. J. Campbell, 'England *c*.991', in Cooper (ed.), *The Battle of Maldon: Fact and Fiction*, 2.
247. Dumville, *Wessex and England*, 104–6 and 106 n. 239.
248. Parkes, 'Palaeography of the Parker Manuscript', 157 and n. 1. Dumville (*Wessex and England*, 72–3, 104–5) attempted to refute Parkes's evidence, but his argument was

premature, for the solution of these issues will depend on further detailed study of the palaeography and art history of the relevant manuscripts.

249. Dumville, *Wessex and England*, 106.
250. *ASC: MS A*, ed. Bately, p. xliii; Parkes, 'Palaeography of the Parker Manuscript', 168.
251. Dumville (*Wessex and England*, 132–3) lists the occurrences of the red crosses in the A manuscript.
252. Ibid. 133.
253. If Frithestan were associated with the insertion of the crosses, Dumville surmised that they were inserted into the A text in the 920s (ibid. 134).
254. Ibid. 162.
255. The inscription reads: *ÆLFFLÆD FIERI PRECEPIT / PIO FRIÐESTANO EPISCOPO* ('Ælfflæd ordered [me] to be made for the pious bishop Frithestan') (ibid. 87).
256. Parkes, 'Palaeography of the Parker Manuscript', 162–9.
257. Dumville (*Wessex and England*, 87, 131–2) stated that we know nothing of Frithestan's movements prior to 909—arguing that he might have had Kentish connections—and that in spite of the obvious Winchester association with the Cuthbert stole and maniple, those artefacts might not have been made in Winchester.
258. Parkes, 'Palaeography of the Parker Manuscript', 156; Dumville, *Wessex and England*, 83.
259. Parkes, 'Palaeography of the Parker Manuscript', 158 n. 3. Cf. Dumville, *Wessex and England*, 86.
260. Ibid. 83–5.
261. Cf. *ASC: MS A*, ed. Bately, p. xxiv.
262. Parkes, 'Palaeography of the Parker Manuscript', 156–7. Cf. *ASC: MS A*, ed. Bately. p. xxxii. See also R. Gameson, 'The Fabric of the Tanner Bede', *Bodleian Library Record*, 14/3 (1992), 176–206.
263. Parkes, 'Palaeography of the Parker Manuscript', 158.
264. Ibid. 162.
265. *ASC: MS A*, Bately, p. xxxiii.
266. Cf. King Alfred's prose preface or introductory letter to his translation of Gregory's *Pastoral Care*, ed. Sweet, i. 1–2.
267. See pp. 527–66 below.
268. Alfred [Introd. 49.9], in *Laws of the Earliest English Kings*, ed. Attenborough, 62–3.
269. A. P. Smyth, 'The Earliest Irish Annals: Their First Contemporary Entries, and the Earliest Centres of Recording', *Proceedings of the Royal Irish Academy*, 72 C (1972), 1–48.
270. Dumville, *Wessex and England*, 67–9, 92.
271. Parkes, 'Palaeography of the Parker Manuscript', 150, 154. *ASC: MS A*, ed. Bately, pp. xxv–xxxiv, and esp. xxviii.
272. Dumville, *Wessex and England*, 69.
273. *EHD*, ed. Whitelock, i. 188.
274. *ASC: MS A*, ed. Bately (*sub anno* 896), 59.
275. The deaths of eight of King Alfred's followers are listed at this point in the annal, and a ninth—the marshal Wulfric—is mentioned at the end.
276. Cf. Bately, 'Compilation of the Anglo-Saxon Chronicle', 127 n. 3 (continued on p. 128).
277. Keynes and Lapidge (transl.), *Alfred the Great*, 280. Cf. Dumville, *Wessex and England*, 69.

278. Bately, 'Compilation of Anglo-Saxon Chronicle', 127–8.

279. Keynes and Lapidge (transl.), *Alfred the Great*, 280.

280. Bately, 'Compilation of the Anglo-Saxon Chronicle', 128 n. 3 from previous page.

281. *Æthelweard*, ed. Campbell, 48.

282. Ibid.

283. See p. 102 above.

284. *Æthelweard*, ed. Campbell, 44–5.

285. See p. 475 above.

286. *Life* of Alfred, ed. Stevenson, ch. 83, p. 69.

287. *ASC: MS A*, ed. Bately (*sub anno* 886), 53; *EHD*, ed. Whitelock, i. 183.

288. *ASC: MS A*, ed. Bately (*sub anno* 911), 64.

289. Bately, 'Compilation of the Anglo-Saxon Chronicle', 127, 128 n. 3.

290. *SEHD*, ed. Harmer, 17–18, 51.

291. *ASC: MS A*, ed. Bately (*sub anno* 888), 54.

292. Bately, 'Compilation of the Anglo-Saxon Chronicle', 116–29.

293. Sisam, *Studies*, 140.

294. Hart, 'The B Text', 285. There would not necessarily have been any element of deceit in a writer such as Æthelweard putting his name to a work in which he had employed a ghost writer. (Cf. Campbell, 'England *c.*991', in Cooper (ed.), *The Battle of Maldon: Fact and Fiction*, 7, where that writer takes the opposite view.)

295. Bately, 'Compilation of the Anglo-Saxon Chronicle', 101, 104–5, 113–15.

296. Stenton, 'South-Western Element', 23.

297. Thorogood, 'The Anglo-Saxon Chronicle in the Reign of Ecgberht', 361–2.

298. *EHD*, ed. Whitelock, i. 136.

299. The material in brackets is not in A. *ASC: MS A*, ed. Bately (*sub anno* 855), 45; *EHD*, ed. Whitelock, i. 174.

300. The awareness shown in the Chronicle for the importance of cultural continuity with the earlier Christian past may help to explain why Manuscript A retains a full succession of blank annals with nothing but their AD numbering to justify their presence in the text.

301. *King Alfred's Version of Pastoral Care*, ed. Sweet, i. 4–7. Cf. *EHD*, ed. Whitelock, i. 819.

302. *Die Gesetze der Angelsachsen*, ed. F. Liebermann (1960 repr. of 1903 Halle edn.), i. 26–47.

303. Alfred [Introd. 49.7]; ibid., i. 44–6; *EHD*, ed. Whitelock, i. 373.

304. Alfred [Introd. 49.8–9]; *Gesetze der Angelsachsen*, ed. Liebermann, i. 46; *EHD*, ed. Whitelock, i. 373.

305. *King Alfred's Version of Pastoral Care*, ed. Sweet, i. 4–5; *EHD*, ed. Whitelock, i. 818.

306. *Two Saxon Chronicles Parallel*, ed. Plummer and Earle, vol. ii, p. civ.

Chapter XVIII

1. *Alfred's Version of the Pastoral Care*, ed. Sweet, i. 6–7.

2. *Bischof Wærferths Übersetzung der Dialoge Gregors*, ed. Hecht, 1. The *Dialogues* are referred to as 'the teaching concerning the virtues and miracles of holy men', but since the preface is attached to the *Dialogues* in the Cambridge Corpus Christi MS 322 and (to the redaction) in the Bodleian Hatton MS 76, and since its description fits Gregory's work, there is no doubt as to what work of translation was being referred to.

3. *King Alfred's Old English Version of Boethius De Consolatione Philosophiae*, ed. W. J. Sedgefield (Oxford, 1899), 1.

4. See pp. 548–9, 557 below.

5. *Æthelweard*, ed. Campbell, 50–1.

6. R. Wuelcher, 'Ein Angelsaechsisches Leben des Neot', *Anglia*, 3 (1880), 113.

7. *Ælfric's Catholic Homilies*, ed. Thorpe, ii. 118–19. Cf. Whitelock, *Prose*, 69.

8. *Willelmi Malmesbiriensis de Gestis Regum*, ed. Stubbs, i. 132.

9. See pp. 538–41 below.

10. Alfred's name does not appear in the preface to the translation of the *Soliloquies*.

11. See p. 246 above.

12. *Leechdoms, Wortcunning and Starcraft of Early England*, ed. Cockayne, ii. 2–299.

13. Keynes and·Lapidge (transl.), *Alfred the Great*, 164.

14. *Laws of the Earliest English Kings*, ed. Attenborough, 62–3.

15. *EHD*, ed. Whitelock, i. 736.

16. *Bede's Ecclesiastical History* [II. 17], ed. Colgrave and Mynors 194–5.

17. *The Old English Version of Bede's Ecclesiastical History of the English People*, ed. T. Miller (Early English Text Soc.; London, 1890), I/i, 146–8.

18. See pp. 561, 576–7 below.

19. S. Potter, 'The Old English "Pastoral Care"', *Transactions of the Philological Soc.* (1947), 115.

20. *Alfred's Version of the Pastoral Care*, ed. Sweet, i. 113, 123, 189.

21. Ibid. 144.

22. Ibid. 165.

23. Ibid. 110, 146–7, 116.

24. Ibid. 44–7.

25. *Old English Version of Bede's History*, ed. Miller, I/i, 2–3; D. Whitelock, 'The Old English Bede', *Proc. Brit. Acad.* 48 (1962), 70–1.

26. *Alfred's Version of the Pastoral Care*, ed. Sweet, i. 44–7.

27. Ibid., ii. 363.

28. Ibid. 353, 360–1, 376–8.

29. Ibid., i. 127.

30. Ibid., ii. 321, 325.

31. Sawyer 1279, 1282, 1281, 1278, 1280, 1283.

32. *Old English Version of Bede's History*, ed. Sweet, ii. 335.

33. Ibid. 340–1.

34. Ibid. 108–9.

35. Ibid. 197.

36. Ibid. 198.

37. Ibid. 200.

38. Ibid. 196.

39. *Dialogues of Gregory* [iii. 38]; *Li Dialoge Gregoire lo Pape* [Twelfth-century French translation with original Latin text], ed. W. Foerster (Halle and Paris, 1876), 187. Cf. G. F. Browne, *King Alfred's Books* (London, 1920), 66.

40. *Bede's Ecclesiastical History* [II. i], ed. Colgrave and Mynors, 122–35.

41. *Bischof Wærferths Übersetzung*, ed. Hecht, 1.

42. *Bede's Ecclesiastical History* [II. i], ed. Colgrave and Mynors, 128–9.

43. V. E. Watts (transl.), *Boethius: The Consolation of Philosophy* (Penguin, Harmondsworth, 1969), 12.

44. *Alfred's Old English Version of Boethius*, ed. Sedgefield, 71; id. (transl.), *King Alfred's Version of the Consolation of Boethius, Done into Modern English, with an Introduction* (Oxford, 1900), 77.
45. Sedgefield (transl.), *Alfred's Boethius*, 30; Watts (transl.), [Original] *Boethius* (II. v), 66–7.
46. Sedgefield (transl.), *Alfred's Boethius*, 71; Watts (transl.), [Original] *Boethius* (III. v), 88.
47. Sedgefield (transl.), *Alfred's Boethius*, 64.
48. Ibid. 70–1.
49. Ibid. 24.
50. Ibid. 119.
51. Ibid. 166.
52. Ibid. 10, 160.
53. Ibid. 147.
54. Ibid. 10.
55. Ibid.
56. Ibid. 160.
57. *King Alfred's Boethius*, ed. Sedgefield [text], 10; Sedgefield (transl.), *Alfred's Boethius*, 5; Watts (transl.), [Original] *Boethius* [I. v], 47–8.
58. *ASC: MS A*, ed. Bately (*sub anno* 877), 50.
59. Sedgefield (transl.), *Alfred's Boethius*, 70.
60. *King Alfred's Old English Version of St. Augustine's Soliloquies turned into Modern English*, transl. H. L. Hargrove (New York, 1904), 4–9.
61. *Alfred's Version of St. Augustine's Soliloquies*, ed. Carnicelli, 53, 100.
62. Hargrove (transl.), *Alfred's Version of Augustine's Soliloquies*, 10.
63. Ibid. 20.
64. *Alfred's Version of Soliloquies*, ed. Carnicelli, 103; *King Alfred's Old English Version of St. Augustine's Soliloquies* [text], ed. H. L. Hargrove (New York, 1902), p. xlv.
65. *Alfred's Soliloquies*, ed. Carnicelli, 83, 92, 97.
66. *Life* of Alfred, ed. Stevenson, ch. 89, p. 75.
67. Whitelock, 'Prose of Alfred's Reign', 71–2.
68. *Alfred's Version of Soliloquies*, ed. Carnicelli, 47.
69. *Old English Orosius*, ed. Bately, pp. lxxiii–lxxxvi and esp. pp. lxxiv–lxxv.
70. Ibid., pp. lxxxiii–lxxxvi.
71. Whitelock, 'Prose of Alfred's Reign', 89–94.
72. *Old English Orosius*, ed. Bately, 16.
73. Ibid. 197.
74. *Adomnan's De Locis Sanctis*, ed. D. Meehan (Scriptores Latini Hiberniae, 3; Dublin, 1958), facing p. 47.
75. *Old English Orosius*, ed. Bately, 155.
76. *Alfred's Version of Boethius* [text], ed. Sedgefield, 7; Sedgefield (transl.), *Alfred's Boethius*, 1.
77. Whitelock, 'Prose of Alfred's Reign', 82 n. 3.
78. *Old English Orosius*, ed. Bately, p. xcii.
79. Ibid., p. xcii.
80. Sedgefield (transl.), *Alfred's Boethius*, 1.
81. *Old English Version of Bede's History*, ed. Miller, II/i, pp. xxxiii, xlix, lvii; Whitelock, 'Old English Bede', 57–8.
82. Ibid. 76, 88 n. 159.

83. Sisam, *Studies*, 294.

84. *Alfred's Version of the Pastoral Care*, ed. Sweet, i. 6–7.

85. Potter, 'Old English "Pastoral Care"', 118.

86. Ibid. 119–20.

87. *Alfred's Version of Soliloquies*, ed. Carnicelli, 49; Hargrove (transl.), *Alfred's Soliloquies*, 3.

88. *Bischof Wærferths Übersetzung*, ed. Hecht, 1.

89. *Alfred's Version of Soliloquies*, ed. Carnicelli, 74; Hargrove (transl.), *Alfred's Soliloquies*, 25.

90. Keynes and Lapidge (transl.), *Alfred the Great*, 188; cf. Sisam, *Studies*, 201, 225.

91. Ibid. 140.

92. Ibid. 295–6.

93. Ibid. 140.

94. *Æthelweard*, ed. Campbell, 50–1.

95. Sisam, *Studies*, 144.

96. *Alfred's Version of Boethius*, ed. Sedgefield, 5; id. (transl.), p. iii.

97. Sisam, *Studies*, 294–5.

98. *Life* of Alfred, ed. Stevenson, ch. 77, p. 62.

99. Sisam, *Studies*, 227; Whitelock, 'Prose of Alfred's Reign', 67; Keynes and Lapidge (transl.), *Alfred the Great*, 123, 187, 292–3.

100. Sawyer 1279, Birch 580.

101. *Life* of Alfred, ed. Stevenson, ch. 77, pp. 62–3.

102. Whitelock, 'Prose of Alfred's Reign', 67–8.

103. Keynes and Lapidge (transl.), *Alfred the Great*, 293 n. 1.

104. *Willelmi Malmesbiriensis de Gestis Regum*, ed. W. Stubbs, i. 131; *Willelmi Malmesbiriensis de Gestis Pontificum*, ed. Hamilton, 177, 332, 336.

105. Whitelock, 'Prose of Alfred's Reign', 83.

106. Keynes and Lapidge (transl.), *Alfred the Great*, 123.

107. *Life* of Alfred, ed. Stevenson, ch. 77, p. 62.

108. Cf. Keynes and Lapidge (transl.), *Alfred the Great*, 187, 333.

109. Sisam, *Studies* (summary translation), 225.

110. Ibid. 226–7.

111. Ibid. 201.

112. *Sermo Lupi ad Anglos*, ed. D. Whitelock (London, 1939), 6–12.

113. Sisam, *Studies*, 202 and n. 1, 226–7.

114. *Wulfstan* may not have been the only name at his finger tips. A scribe *Wulfgeat* who described himself as being 'of Worcester' and who worked on a Worcester manuscript some time after 1076, left his name on a collection of early English church canons (MS Junius 121, fo. 101a, see E. van K. Dobbie, *The Anglo-Saxon Minor Poems* (London and New York, 1942), p. lxxv and n. 3). Such a man would have lived too late in the eleventh century to have influenced the scribe of Otho C.i. part 2, but the fact remains that we cannot assume that *Wulfstan* was the only familiar name in eleventh-century Worcester, beginning with *Wulf-*.

115. Sisam, *Studies*, 228.

116. Ibid. 229.

117. Ibid. 228.

118. *Life* of Alfred, ed. Stevenson, ch. 77, p. 62.

119. Whitelock, 'Prose of Alfred's Reign', 79 and n. 1; Keynes and Lapidge (transl.), *Alfred the Great*, 259 n. 164.

120. *Alfred's Version of the Pastoral Care*, ed. Sweet, i. 6–7; *Alfred's Version of Boethius*, ed. Sedgefield, 1.

121. Dobbie, *Anglo-Saxon Minor Poems*, p. cxvii.

122. W. Keller, *Die littarischen Bestrebungen von Worcester* (Strasburg, 1900), 6–8. I do not, of course, accept Keller's case that Wærferth was the translator of the text of the *Dialogues*.

123. *Alfred's Version of Soliloquies*, ed. Carnicelli, 3–4.

124. Ibid. 19.

125. Ibid. 2–3.

126. Sisam, *Studies*, 296.

127. Ibid. 301.

128. Stenton, *Latin Charters of Anglo-Saxon Period*, 49.

129. Whitelock, 'Old English Bede', 75; Keynes and Lapidge (transl.), *Alfred the Great*, 294 n. 4.

130. Stenton, *Latin Charters of Anglo-Saxon Period*, 39.

131. Ibid. 39–40.

132. Sawyer [?]287, 293, 296, 298, 316, 1195, 1196, 1268, 1436, and 1438.

133. Sawyer 270, 280, 1266, and 1269.

134. Stenton ridiculed two slips in the Latin declensions of a certain Pilheard the 'companion' (*comes*) of Coenwulf of Mercia which appear in a charter of *c*.800 (Stenton, *Latin Charters*, 42). That grant (Sawyer 106) of exemptions to Pilheard is preserved in the form of an endorsement to an earlier grant of Offa's dating to 767 (*Cartularium Saxonicum*, Birch (no. 201), i. 284–6). The immediate circumstances in which such endorsements were executed may have been very different from the more deliberate procedures which lay behind the original diploma.

135. Stenton, *Latin Charters of Anglo-Saxon Period*, 41; cf. id, *Anglo-Saxon England*, 227–8.

136. Sisam, *Studies*, 7.

137. *Alfred's Version of the Pastoral Care*, ed. Sweet, i. 2–3.

138. Sisam, *Studies*, 1–28.

139. Keynes and Lapidge (transl.), *Alfred the Great*, 259–60 n. 167.

140. Sawyer 293; *Life* of Alfred, ed Stevenson, p. 203 n. 1.

141. Stenton, *Latin Charters of Anglo-Saxon Period*, 47; cf. *Life* of Alfred, ed. Stevenson, pp. 203 n. 1, 225–6.

142. Stenton, *Latin Charters of Anglo-Saxon Period*, 43.

143. Ibid. 44.

144. Sawyer 204.

145. Sawyer 333.

146. Sawyer 342. Stenton, *Latin Charters of Anglo-Saxon Period*, 46–7.

147. J. S. Wittig, 'King Alfred's *Boethius* and its Latin Sources: A Reconsideration', *ASE* 11 (1983), 185.

148. Ibid. 172.

149. F. A. Payne, *King Alfred and Boethius: An Analysis of the Old English Version of the Consolation of Philosophy* (Madison, Milwaukee, and London, 1968), 16, 17–18, 145.

150. Whitelock, 'Prose of Alfred's Reign', 88; Keynes and Lapidge (transl.), *Alfred the Great*, 299 n. 4.

151. *Alfred's Soliloquies*, ed. Carnicelli, 28–9.

152. *Æthelweard*, ed. Campbell, 51–5.

153. While the metrical preface is found in Hatton 20; Junius 53; CCCC 12; and Trinity

College Cambridge, R.5.22; the metrical epilogue is only found in Hatton 20 and CCCC 12. But the metrical epilogue does not appear in Junius 53 because its exemplar, the fire-damaged Cotton Tiberius B.xi was incomplete at the end. Dobbie, *Anglo-Saxon Minor Poems*, pp. cxii–cxv.

154. *Alfred's Version of the Pastoral Care*, ed. Sweet, i. 8–9.
155. Ibid.
156. The name of Gregory's father, Gordianus, was known to Bede's *Ecclesiastical History* [II. i], the name of his mother, Sylvia, was probably taken from the Whitby *Life* of Gregory (*Bede's Ecclesiastical History*, ed. Colgrave and Mynors, 122–3, n. 1).
157. *Alfred's Version of the Pastoral Care*, ed. Sweet, ii. 466–7.
158. Dobbie, *Anglo-Saxon Minor Poems*, pp. cxii, 9.
159. While Whitelock agreed that 'very little was omitted' from the original in the Old English *Pastoral Care*, she felt there was little word for word (*hwilum word be worde*) translation. Whitelock, 'Prose of Alfred's Reign', 79.
160. *Alfred's Version of Boethius*, ed. Sedgefield, 5.
161. Cf. Payne, *King Alfred and Boethius*, 59.
162. Watts (transl.), *Boethius: The Consolation of Philosophy*, 41–4.
163. Ibid. 42.
164. F. G. Hubbard, 'The Relation of the "Blooms of King Alfred" to the Anglo-Saxon Translation of Boethius', *Modern Language Notes*, 9 (1894), 339.
165. Ibid. 331–4; *Alfred's Version of Soliloquies*, ed. Carnicelli, 32–4.
166. Ibid. 33.
167. Ibid. 32.
168. Keynes and Lapidge (transl.), *Alfred the Great*, 30–1.
169. Hubbard, 'Blooms of King Alfred', 323.
170. *Alfred's Version of Soliloquies*, ed. Carnicelli, 32–3 n. 49.
171. *Alfred's Version of Boethius*, ed. Sedgefield, 121, lines 9–12; *Alfred's Version of Soliloquies*, ed. Carnicelli, 78, lines 11–14.
172. Ibid. 30.
173. Ibid. 78; Hargrove (transl.), *Alfred's Soliloquies*, 28.
174. Watts (transl.), *Boethius*, 130.
175. *Alfred's Version of Boethius*, ed. Sedgefield, 121; Sedgefield (transl.), 140–1.
176. *Alfred's Version of Soliloquies*, ed. Carnicelli, 33 n. 49.
177. Payne, *King Alfred and Boethius*, 123.
178. Whitelock, 'Prose of Alfred's Reign', 76.
179. *Alfred's Version of the Pastoral Care*, ed. Sweet, i. 6–7.
180. Ibid. 8–9.
181. Ibid.
182. Bullough, 'Educational Tradition in England from Alfred to Aelfric', 457.
183. Potter, 'Old English "Pastoral Care"' 117.
184. Sisam, *Studies*, 142.
185. Ibid. 141.
186. *Alfred's Version of the Pastoral Care*, ed. Sweet, i. 6–7.
187. Bullough, 'Educational Tradition in England from Alfred to Aelfric', 458 and n. 10. Alfred may also have intended some young women to be educated in the vernacular— daughters of the West Saxon aristocracy who had entered a nunnery such as Wimborne.
188. *Bede's Ecclesiastical History* [IV. ii], ed. Colgrave and Mynors, 332–5.
189. Campbell, John, and Wormald, *The Anglo-Saxons*, 112.

190. Cf. *Alfred's Version of the Pastoral Care*, ed. Sweet, i. 3–1, 44–5; ii. 370–3, etc.
191. Keynes and Lapidge (transl.), *Alfred the Great*, 296 nn. 14 and 15.
192. *Life* of Alfred, ed. Stevenson, ch. 75, p. 58.
193. Ibid., ch. 76, p. 60.
194. Bullough, 'Educational Tradition in England from Alfred to Aelfric', 454–6.
195. Cf. ibid. 467.
196. Cf. Whitelock ('Prose of Alfred's Reign', 68), where that scholar presented a related argument on a possible change in Alfred's literary objectives.
197. Ibid.
198. Ibid. 68–9.
199. Keynes and Lapidge (transl.), *Alfred the Great*, 34.
200. For evidence for the existence of a manuscript of at least part of the text of Alfred's version of the *Soliloquies* in eleventh-century Canterbury, see Whitelock, 'Prose of Alfred's Reign', 73.
201. See p. 560 above.
202. Lapidge, 'Hermeneutic Style', 70–6.
203. Sisam, *Studies*, 99.
204. Bullough, 'Educational Tradition in England from Alfred to Aelfric', 282.
205. Ibid. 487.
206. Ibid. 479–80.
207. Dumville, *Wessex and England*, 87; and cf. ibid. n. 153, for Dumville's reservations on the identity of Ælfflæd.
208. See pp. 512–13 above.
209. *EHD*, ed. Whitelock, i. 833.
210. Cf. Keynes and Lapidge (transl.), *Alfred the Great*, 35–6.

Chapter XIX

1. Hargrove (transl.), *Alfred's Soliloquies*, 37; *Alfred's Version of Soliloquies*, ed. Carnicelli, 86.
2. Potter, Old English 'Pastoral Care', 118, 230–1.
3. *King Alfred's Version of Pastoral Care*, ed. Sweet, ii. 90–1.
4. *Bede's Ecclesiastical History* [II. xvi], ed. Colgrave and Mynors, 192. The Old English version of Bede's *History* (ed. Miller, I/i, 145–6) translates the Roman standard or *tufa* of Bede as *tacn*.
5. *Alfred's Version of Boethius*, ed. Sedgefield, 46; Sedgefield (transl.), 48.
6. Watts (transl.), [Original] *Boethius* [II. vii], 75–6.
7. *Alfred's Version of Boethius*, ed. Sedgefield, 7, 22, 34, 43, 50, 61.
8. Ibid. 64.
9. *Alfred's Version of Soliloquies*, ed. Carnicelli, 57–8.
10. *King Alfred's Version of Pastoral Care*, ed. Sweet, ii. 292–3.
11. *Old English Orosius* [I. xii], ed. Bately, 32:18.
12. Ibid. [VI. x], 139:25.
13. Ibid. [VI. xxxvi], 154:9.
14. Ibid. [V. iv], 118:24.
15. Ibid. [II. iv], 42:16.
16. Ibid. [II. ii], 40:12–14.
17. Ibid. [II. iv.], 42:14.

18. Ibid. [VI. ii], 134:23.
19. Ibid. [VI. xii], 140:23.
20. Ibid. [II. iv], 42:1–13.
21. Ibid. [VI. ii], 134:29–31, 135:1–3.
22. Sedgefield, (transl.), *Alfred's Version of Boethius*, 170; [text] *Alfred's Version of Boethius*, ed. Sedgefield, 144.
23. *Bischof Wærferths Übersetzung*, ed. Hecht, 5.
24. *King Alfred's Version of Pastoral Care*, ed. Sweet, i. 58–9.
25. Sedgefield (transl.), *Alfred's Version of Boethius*, 13; [text] *Alfred's Version of Boethius*, ed. Sedgefield, 16.
26. Watts (transl.), [Original] *Boethius* [II. i], 55.
27. Whitelock, 'Prose of Alfred's Reign', 80.
28. *Alfred's Version of Soliloquies*, ed. Carnicelli, 68; Hargrove (transl.), *Alfred's Soliloquies*, 19.
29. *Bischof Wærferths Übersetzung*, ed. Hecht, 5.
30. *King Alfred's Version of Pastoral Care*, ed. Sweet, i. 58–9.
31. *Alfred's Version of Soliloquies*, ed. Carnicelli, 61–2; Hargrove (transl.), *Alfred's Soliloquies*, 14.
32. *Alfred's Version of Soliloquies*, ed. Carnicelli, 67; Hargrove (transl.), *Alfred's Soliloquies*, 18.
33. *Bede's Ecclesiastical History* [II. i], ed. Colgrave and Mynors, 124–5.
34. *King Alfred's Version of Pastoral Care*, ed. Sweet, i. 5.
35. Keynes and Lapidge (transl.), *Alfred the Great*, 295.
36. *King Alfred's Version of Pastoral Care*, ed. Sweet, ii. 468–9.
37. Ibid., i. 30–1.
38. Ibid., ii. 372–3.
39. Hargrove (transl.), *Alfred's Soliloquies*, 6–7; *Alfred's Version of Soliloquies*, ed. Carnicelli, 52, 54.
40. *Bischof Wærferths Übersetzung*, ed. Hecht, 2.; *Byrhtferth's Manual*, ed. Crawford, 132–3. Cf. Whitelock, 'Prose of Alfred's Reign', 77–8.
41. *King Alfred's Version of Pastoral Care*, ed. Sweet, i. 283–4.
42. Ibid. 276–7.
43. Ibid., ii. 469.
44. Ibid., i. 283.
45. *EHD*. ed. Whitelock, i. 237.
46. *King Alfred's Version of Pastoral Care*, ed. Sweet, ii. 308.
47. Ibid. 382–3.
48. *Alfred's Version of the Boethius*, ed. Sedgefield, 26–7; Sedgefield (transl.), 25.
49. *Alfred's Version of the Boethius*, ed. Sedgefield, 110; Sedgefield (transl.), 127.
50. Watts (transl.), [Original] *Boethius* [II. iv], 64–5.
51. *Alfred's Version of the Boethius*, ed. Sedgefield, 27; Sedgefield (transl.), 25; cf. Payne, *King Alfred's and Boethius*, 93.
52. *Alfred's Version of Soliloquies*, ed. Carnicelli, 94; Hargrove (transl.), *Alfred's Soliloquies*, 44.
53. *Alfred's Version of Soliloquies*, ed. Carnicelli, 84; Hargrove (transl.), *Alfred's Soliloquies*, 36.
54. *Alfred's Version of Soliloquies*, ed. Carnicelli, 97; Hargrove (transl.), *Alfred's Soliloquies*, 47. In spite of the evidence offered us by Alfred himself to the contrary, scholars even

of Sisam's stature preferred to follow the testimony of the *Life* of Alfred to the effect that Alfred 'was not a scholar or even well grounded in Latin' (Sisam, *Studies*, 293).

55. Payne, *King Alfred and Boethius*, 16, 145.
56. *King Alfred's Version of Pastoral Care*, ed. Sweet, i. 22–3.
57. *Alfred's Version of Soliloquies*, ed. Carnicelli, 78, 102.
58. *King Alfred's Version of Pastoral Care*, ed. Sweet, i. 272–3.
59. Ibid. 283.
60. Ibid. 156–7.
61. Ibid. 54–5.
62. Ibid. 94.
63. *Bede's Ecclesiastical History* [II. 16], ed. Colgrave and Mynors, 192–3; *Old English Version of Bede's History*, ed. Miller, I/i, 144–7.
64. *King Alfred's Version of Pastoral Care*, ed. Sweet, i. 3–4.
65. *Bede's Ecclesiastical History* [IV. 2], ed. Colgrave and Mynors, 334–5; *Old English Version of Bede's History*, ed. Miller, I/ii, 258–9.
66. *Bede's History* [IV. 2], ed Colgrave and Mynors, 332–3; Cf. *Old English Bede*, ed. Miller, I/ii, 258–9.
67. *King Alfred's Version of Pastoral Care*, ed. Sweet, i. 2–3. The West Saxon, Aldhelm, who was Theodore's pupil at Canterbury, remembered Theodore being surrounded by crowds of Irish scholars there in the seventh century (Stenton, *Anglo-Saxon England*, 181).
68. Watts (transl.), [Original] *Boethius* [II. v], 68–9.
69. Sedgefield (transl.), *Alfred's Version of Boethius*, 33–4.
70. *Alfred's Version of Boethius*, ed. Sedgefield, 34.
71. Sedgefield (transl.), *Alfred's Version of Boethius*, 1.
72. Payne, *King Alfred and Boethius*, 135–6.
73. Ibid. 16, 39, 145.
74. Whitelock, 'Old English Bede', 62–6.
75. Ibid. 76.
76. K.-H. Schmidt, *König Alfreds Boethius-Bearbeitung* (Göttingen, 1934), 62.
77. Payne, *King Alfred and Boethius*, 4, 14, 16, 18, 31, 59, 136, 145.
78. Ibid. 37.
79. Ibid. 18–25, 32, 44.
80. Ibid. 30–48, 78–90.
81. Ibid. 144.
82. *Alfred's Version of Boethius*, ed. Sedgefield, 148; Sedgefield (transl.), 174.
83. Payne, *King Alfred and Boethius*, 18, 143.
84. Ibid. 143.
85. *Alfred's Version of Boethius*, ed. Sedgefield, 131; Sedgefield (transl.), 153.
86. Hargrove (transl.), *Alfred's Soliloquies*, 38.
87. *Alfred's Version of Soliloquies*, ed. Carnicelli, 87–9; Hargrove (transl.), *Alfred's Soliloquies*, 38–40.
88. *Alfred's Version of Soliloquies*, ed. Carnicelli, 61–4.
89. Ibid. 99–100.
90. Ibid. 101–3.
91. Ibid. 90–1, cf. 104; Hargrove (transl.), *Alfred's Soliloquies*, 41.
92. *Dialoge Gregoire lo Pape* [*Dialogues*, Latin text, iii. 38], ed. Foerster, 188.
93. Ibid.

94. Watts (transl.), [original] *Boethius* [IV. vi], 136–7.
95. *Alfred's Version of Boethius*, ed. Sedgefield, 129–30; Sedgefield (transl.), 151–2.
96. Æthelweard implies that some people may have had Alfred's works read aloud to them (*Æthelweard*, ed. Campbell, 51). Even if that were the case, we ought not to envisage 'public readings' of either the *Consolation* or the *Soliloquies*.
97. Payne, *King Alfred and Boethius*, 43.
98. *Alfred's Version of Boethius*, ed. Sedgefield, 35; Sedgefield (transl.), 35.
99. Watts (transl.), [original] *Boethius* [I. iv], 41.
100. *Alfred's Version of Boethius*, ed. Sedgefield, 9; Sedgefield (transl.), 4.
101. Watts (transl.), [original] *Boethius* [II. vii], 72–3.
102. Sedgefield (transl.), *Alfred's Version of Boethius*, 41.
103. Cf. Payne, *King Alfred and Boethius*, 66.
104. J. Béranger, *Recherches sur l'aspect idéologique du Principat* (Basle, 1953), 137–69.
105. *King Alfred's Version of Pastoral Care*, ed. Sweet, i. 32–3.
106. Ibid. 50–1.
107. *Life* of Alfred, ed. Stevenson, ch. 42, p. 32.
108. Sedgefield (transl.), *Alfred's Version of Boethius*, 41–2.
109. Keynes and Lapidge (transl.), *Alfred and Great*, 298 n. 7.
110. Watts (transl.), [original] *Boethius*, 72.
111. Ibid. 73.
112. Ibid. 74.
113. *Alfred's Version of Boethius*, ed. Sedgefield, 43; Sedgefield (transl.), 45.
114. Payne, *King Alfred and Boethius*, 65.
115. *Alfred's Version of Boethius*, ed. Sedgefield, 43–4. Cf. Sedgefield (transl.), 45.
116. Watts (transl.), [original] *Boethius*, [II. v], 65.
117. Sedgefield (transl.), *Alfred's Version of Boethius*, 27.
118. *ASC* (*sub anno* 937); *EHD*, ed. Whitelock, i. 200–1.
119. Watts (transl.), [original] *Boethius* [IV. vii], 144.
120. *Alfred's Version of Boethius*, ed. Sedgefield, 138; Sedgefield (transl.), 162.
121. Keynes and Lapidge (transl.), *Alfred the Great*, 159.
122. Ibid. 158; Psalm 13: 9.
123. *King Alfred's Version of Pastoral Care*, ed. Sweet, i. 6–7.
124. Psalm 45: 8–9; Keynes and Lapidge (transl.), *Alfred the Great*, 160.
125. *Alfred's Version of Boethius*, ed. Sedgefield, 135; Sedgefield (transl.), 162–3.
126. *Alfred's Version of Soliloquies*, ed. Carnicelli, 94, 105. Cf. Hargrove (transl.), *Alfred's Soliloquies*, 43.
127. *Alfred's Version of Soliloquies*, ed. Carnicelli, 32.
128. Ibid. 48.
129. Ibid.
130. Ibid. 62; Hargrove (transl.), *Alfred's Soliloquies*, 15.
131. *Alfred's Version of Soliloquies*, ed. Carnicelli, 63; Hargrove (transl.), *Alfred's Soliloquies*, 16.
132. *King Alfred's Version of Pastoral Care*, ed. Sweet, i. 40–1.
133. *Alfred's Version of Soliloquies*, ed. Carnicelli, 58; Hargrove (transl.), *Alfred's Soliloquies*, 11.
134. *Alfred's Version of Soliloquies*, ed. Carnicelli, 59; Hargrove (transl.), *Alfred's Soliloquies*, 12.
135. *Alfred's Version of Soliloquies*, ed. Carnicelli, 96; Hargrove (transl.), *Alfred's Soliloquies*, 46.

136. *Alfred's Version of Soliloquies*, ed. Carnicelli, 96; Hargrove (transl.), *Alfred's Soliloquies*, 46–7.

137. Stenton, *Anglo-Saxon England*, 360–1.

138. *King Alfred's Version of Pastoral Care*, ed. Sweet, ii. 337.

139. Ibid., i. 120–2.

140. *Alfred's Version of Soliloquies*, ed. Carnicelli, 72; Hargrove (transl.), *Alfred's Soliloquies*, 23.

141. *Alfred's Version of Soliloquies*, ed. Carnicelli, 73; Hargrove (transl.), *Alfred's Soliloquies*, 24.

142. *Alfred's Version of Soliloquies*, ed. Carnicelli, 52; Hargrove (transl.), *Alfred's Soliloquies*, 6.

143. *Alfred's Version of Soliloquies*, ed. Carnicelli, 54; Hargrove (transl.), *Alfred's Soliloquies*, 8.

144. *Alfred's Version of Soliloquies*, ed. Carnicelli, 87; Hargrove (transl.), *Alfred's Soliloquies*, 38–9.

145. Watts (transl.), [original] *Boethius* [II. i], 55.

146. *Alfred's Version of Boethius*, ed. Sedgefield, 16; cf. Sedgefield (transl.), 13.

147. *King Alfred's Version of Pastoral Care*, ed. Sweet, i. 201–2.

148. Watts (transl.), [original] *Boethius* [IV. ii], 123.

149. *Alfred's Version of Boethius*, ed. Sedgefield, 111; Sedgefield (transl.), 128.

150. *Alfred's Version of Soliloquies*, ed. Carnicelli, 86; Hargrove (transl.), *Alfred's Soliloquies*, 37.

151. *Alfred's Version of Soliloquies*, ed. Carnicelli, 94; Hargrove (transl.), *Alfred's Soliloquies*, 43.

152. *Alfred's Version of Soliloquies*, ed. Carnicelli, 96; Hargrove (transl.), *Alfred's Soliloquies*, 46.

153. *Alfred's Version of Boethius*, ed. Sedgefield, 142; Sedgefield (transl.), 166.

154. *King Alfred's Version of Pastoral Care*, ed. Sweet, ii. 336–7.

155. *Alfred's Version of Soliloquies*, ed. Carnicelli, 77–8; Hargrove (transl.), *Alfred's Soliloquies*, 27.

156. *King Alfred's Version of Pastoral Care*, ed. Sweet, i. 40.

157. *SEHD*, ed. Harmer, 15, 17.

158. Sawyer 293, Birch 442; Sawyer 296, Birch 449.

159. Sawyer 298, Birch 451.

160. Sawyer 221, Birch 587.

161. *Bischof Wærferths Übersetzung*, ed. Hecht, 1.

162. *Bede's Ecclesiastical History*, ed. Colgrave and Mynors, *Praefatio*, 2–3.

163. *Alfred's Version of Boethius*, ed. Sedgefield, 40.

164. *Alfred's Version of Soliloquies*, ed. Carnicelli, 96; Hargrove (transl.), *Alfred's Soliloquies*, 46.

165. *Alfred's Version of Soliloquies*, ed. Carnicelli, 68–9; Hargrove (transl.), *Alfred's Soliloquies*, 19.

166. *Alfred's Version of Soliloquies*, ed. Carnicelli, 69; Hargrove (transl.), *Alfred's Soliloquies*, 19.

167. *Alfred's Version of Boethius*, ed. Sedgefield, 40; Sedgefield (transl.), 41.

168. *Alfred's Version of Soliloquies*, ed. Carnicelli, 47.

169. Ibid. 46.

170. *Life* of Alfred, ed. Stevenson, ch. 76, p. 59; *EHD*, ed. Whitelock, i. 267.

171. *Life* of Alfred, ed. Stevenson, ch. 91, p. 77; *EHD*, ed. Whitelock, i. 272.

172. *Life* of Alfred, ed. Stevenson, ch. 56, p. 47, and see footnote ibid., for original textual reading.
173. Ibid., p. 279.
174. Ibid.
175. Keynes and Lapidge (transl.), *Alfred the Great*, 85, 91, 101, 106. Cf. ibid. 249–50 n. 114.
176. Ibid. 299 n. 2.
177. *Alfred's Version of Soliloquies*, ed. Carnicelli, 99.
178. *Life* of Alfred, ed. Stevenson, ch. 101, p. 87.
179. Ibid., ch. 100–2, pp. 86–9.
180. Ibid., pp. 86–7.
181. *Alfred's Version of Boethius*, ed. Sedgefield, 40.
182. We may compare the Pseudo-Asser's poor handling of this Latin usage with the more correct approach of the ninth-century translator of Bede's *Ecclesiastical History*. That Mercian scholar correctly translated Bede's *operatio* (meaning any work, or the 'performance' or 'practice' of a work) with the Old English *wyrcnes* (*Old English Version of Bede's History*, ed. Miller, 1/i, 40); ibid. 1/i, 100.
183. *Byrhtferth's Manual*, ed. Crawford, 142–3.
184. Ibid. 132–3.
185. *Life* of Alfred, ed. Stevenson, ch. 77, p. 62.
186. Ibid., ch. 102, p. 88.
187. *King Alfred's Version of Pastoral Care*, ed. Sweet, ii. 320–1. Alfred is closer in his translation to Gregory's text than the Pseudo-Asser. Cf. Keynes and Lapidge (transl.), *Alfred the Great*, 274 n. 247.
188. Lapidge, 'Byrhtferth and the Early Sections of the "Historia Regum"', *ASE* 10 (1982), 115.
189. Ibid. 114.
190. *Bischof Wærferths Übersetzung*, ed. Hecht, 1.
191. *King Alfred's Version of Pastoral Care*, ed. Sweet, i. 6–7.
192. *Alfred's Version of Boethius*, ed. Sedgefield, 5.
193. Keynes and Lapidge (transl.), *Alfred the Great*, 154, 159.
194. *Alfred's Version of Soliloquies*, ed. Carnicelli, 47.
195. *King Alfred's Version of Pastoral Care*, ed. Sweet, i. 50–2.
196. Ibid. 50–1.
197. Ibid., ii. 382–3.
198. Sedgefield (transl.), *Alfred's Version of Boethius*, 100.
199. *King Alfred's Version of Pastoral Care*, ed. Sweet, i. 126–7.
200. Ibid. 136–7.
201. Brown, *King Alfred's Books*, 41.
202. Keynes and Lapidge (transl.), *Alfred the Great*, 153.
203. *King Alfred's Version of Pastoral Care*, ed. Sweet, i. 36–7.
204. Ibid., ii. 382–3.
205. *Adomnan's De Locis Sanctis*, ed. Meehan, 120–1.

APPENDIX
POLYSYLLABIC ADVERBS IN -*ITER* IN THE *LIFE* OF KING ALFRED

VITA ÆLFREDI ed. W. H. Stevenson. Numbers refer to chapters

VITA S. OSWALDI ed. J. Raine. *Historians of Church of York*, i*

VITA S. ECGWINI ed. J. A. Giles. *Vita Quorundum Anglo Saxonum**

HISTORIA REGUM ed. T. Arnold. Sects. 1–5 in *Symeonis Opera*, i*

VITA S. NEOTI eds. D. Dumville and M. Lapidge*

*(Numbers refer to pages in respective editions)

Manual = *Byrhtferth's Manual*, ed. S. J. Crawford
Epilog. = Epilogue to Byrhtferth's *Manual* (ibid.)

VITA ÆLFREDI	VITA S. OSWALDI	VITA S. ECGWINI	HISTORIA REGUM	VITA S. NEOTI
acriter 67, 97				acriter 121, 131
aequaliter 16, 103	aequaliter 474			
	affabiliter 469			
	agiliter 415	agiliter 391		
amabiliter 19				
	amicabiliter 441			
annualiter 99, 100, 102			annualiter 91	
arbiter 105				
atrociter 27, 33, 36, 56		atrociter 391	atrociter 70	
breviter 21, 74	breviter 420, 428, 442, 453, 454	breviter 350	breviter 11, 28, 33	
	concorditer 414			
corporaliter 74				corporaliter 123
				crudeliter 124
	dapsiliter 464			
	digniter 405	digniter 358, 378, 390	digniter 13 [and *Manual* 202]	
	duriter 450	duriter 391	duriter 62, 71	
	enerviter 405		enerviter 86 [and *Epilog.* 246]	
				equanimiter 116
				familiariter 121

VITA ÆLFREDI	VITA S. OSWALDI	VITA S. ECGWINI	HISTORIA REGUM	VITA S. NEOTI
feliciter 106			feliciter 6, 43, 44, 50	
	fiducialiter 448	fiducialiter 362		
fideliter 99 (x2)	fideliter 404, 405			fideliter 124, 134, 138
firmiter 38, 49	firmiter 416, 419, 454		firmiter 91	
flebiliter 91				
graviter 96			graviter 56	graviter 132, 137
	gaudenter 447	gaudenter 391		
hilariter 101	hilariter 405, 412			
hostiliter 18, 42, 52, 54, 93, 96			hostiliter 75	
honorabiliter 19 (x2), 28, 41, 74, 81	honorabiliter 450		[honorabilia 10] [honorabili 11]	
[honorifice, 46]	honorifice 417		honorifice 51, 58, 65	honorifice 120
	immarcessibiliter 417			
[cf miseri- corditer]	immisericorditer 451	immisericorditer 393	immisericorditer 51, 59	
inaniter 99				
incessabiliter 22, 74, 88				
incommutabiliter 103				incommutabiliter 134
incomparabiliter 91				
	indigniter 408			
	inedicibiliter 413, 422, 454, etc.	inedicibiliter 349 [medicibiliter in Giles's text]	inedicibiliter 60	
	ineffabiliter 453	ineffabiliter 379		
			inenarrabiliter 60 ·	[inenarrabilis 140]
infatigabiliter 42, 55				
inseparabiliter 22, 24				
irrationabiliter 15				
largiter 56, 76	largiter 410	largiter 394		
laudabiliter 101				

VITA ÆLFREDI	VITA S. OSWALDI	VITA S. ECGWINI	HISTORIA REGUM	VITA S. NEOTI
leniter 91, 106		leniter 390		
lugubriter 91		lugubriter 381, 386		
		magnanimiter 394		
memoriter 22, 76	memoriter 419, 423		memoriter 74	
mirabiliter 91, 104, 105	mirabiliter 419, 420, 430, 456	mirabiliter 351, 357	mirabiliter 33, 41, 54	
miserabiliter 15, 91			miserabiliter 53	
misericorditer 82	misericorditer 410, 440	misericorditer 351, 395		
muliebriter 18	muliebriter 417	muliebriter 383		
				muliercule 126
multipliciter 99 (x2)	multipliciter 456			
nequiter 106		nequiter 392	nequiter 41	
		optabiliter 381		
ordinabiliter 16, 38, 93, 100, 103, 105				
pariter 76	pariter 402, 430, 438, 442, 446	pariter 380, 381	pariter 14 [*Manual* 18]	pariter 111, 112, 116 etc.
	paternaliter 447			
		pigriter 383		
	pleniter 418, 459	pleniter 349, 388, 393	pleniter 8, 91	
populariter 42				
	praesentialiter 444			
qualiter 56	qualiter 417, 421, 428, 433, 457	qualiter 352 (x2), 353, 357	qualiter 5, 33, 36 [*Epilog.* 245; *Manual* 222]	qualiter 117
regaliter 9	regaliter 425 (x2), 443	regaliter 351, 393	regaliter 59, 64, 84	
sagaciter 106	sagaciter 416	sagaciter 349		
specialiter, 16				specialiter 114, 140
			spiritaliter [*Manual* 208]	
sollemniter 74	sollemniter 464	sollemniter 390 [Cf. *V. Ecgwini*, 381, for repetition of other forms]	sollempniter 58	

VITA ÆLFREDI	VITA S. OSWALDI	VITA S. ECGWINI	HISTORIA REGUM	VITA S. NEOTI
subtiliter 99				
			sublimiter 47	
suppliciter 30				
				taliter 131
tenuiter 104				
unanimiter 30		unanimiter 377, 392		
utiliter 92, 99				
			terribiliter 33	
			venerabiliter 59	
[venerabilis 76, 77, 78, 89]			[venerabilis 34, 51]	[venerabilis 111]
viriliter 38, 56, 66, 69	viriliter 405, 427, 456 (x2)	viriliter 354 (x2)		viriliter 112, 130
vituperabiliter 15				

NOTE: This Appendix does not endeavour to include a comprehensive list of polysyllabic adverbs in any of the works listed above, apart from the *Vita Ælfredi*.

SELECT BIBLIOGRAPHY

Abbo of Fleury: SEE Hervey, F. (ed.), *Corolla Sancti Eadmundi*; and Winterbottom, M. (ed.), *Three Lives of English Saints*.

Ab Ithel, J. W. (ed.), *Annales Cambriae* (Rolls Series; London, 1860).

Æthelweard: SEE Campbell, A. (ed.), *Chronicon Æthelweardi*.

Alcock, L., *Arthur's Britain: History and Archaeology* (London, 1971).

Alcuin, *Life* of: SEE Wattenbach, W., and Dümmler, [E.], (eds.), *Vita Alchuini auctore anonymo*.

Almquist, B., and Greene, D. (eds.), *Proceedings of the Seventh Viking Congress, Dublin 15–21 August 1973* (Dublin, 1976).

Amory, F., 'The Viking Hasting in Franco-Scandinavian Legend', in King and Stevens (eds.), *Saints, Scholars and Heroes*, ii. 265–86.

Anderson, A. O., and Anderson, M. O. (eds.), *Adomnan's Life of Columba* (London, 1961).

Anglo-Saxon Chronicle: SEE Bately, J. M. (ed.), *The Anglo-Saxon Chronicle*; Dumville, D. N., and Lapidge, M. (eds.), *Annals of St. Neots*; Plummer, C., and Earle, J., *Two of the Saxon Chronicles Parallel*; Smith, A. H. (ed.), *The Parker Chronicle 832–900*; Taylor, S. (ed.), *The Anglo-Saxon Chronicle*; Flower, R., and Smith, H. (eds.), *The Parker Chronicle and Laws*.

Annales Lindisfarnenses: SEE Pertz, G. H. (ed.), *Annales Lindisfarnenses*.

Annales Vedastini: SEE Rau, R. (ed.), *Annales Vedastini*.

Annals of Ulster: SEE Hennessy, W. M., and MacCarthy, B. (eds.), *Annala Uladh*; Mac Airt, S., and Mac Niocaill, G. (eds.), *The Annals of Ulster (to AD 1131)*.

Archibald, M. M., 'Against the Tide: Coin-Movement from Scandinavia to the British Isles in the Viking Age', in *Festskrift til Kolbjørn Skaare i anledning 60-årsdagen* (Norsk Numismatisk Forening; Oslo, 1991), 19–22.

Arnold, T. (ed.), *Memorials of St. Edmund's Abbey* (3 vols.; Rolls Series, 1890–6).

—— *Symeonis monachi opera omnia* (2 vols.; Rolls Series, 1882–5).

Asser: SEE Stevenson, W. H. (ed.), *Asser's Life of King Alfred*.

Attenborough, F. L. (ed.), *The Laws of the Earliest English Kings* (New York, 1963; repr. of 1922 edn.).

Augustine of Hippo: SEE Carnicelli, T. A. (ed.), *King Alfred's Version of St. Augustine's Soliloquies*; and Hargrove, H. L. (ed.), *King Alfred's Old English Version of St. Augustine's Soliloquies*.

Baker, P. S., 'Byrhtferth of Ramsey and the Renaissance Scholars', in Berkhout and Gatch (eds.), *Anglo-Saxon Scholarship*, 69–77.

—— 'Byrhtferth's *Enchiridion* and the Computus in Oxford, St John's College 17', *ASE* 10 (1982), 123–42.

—— 'The Old English Canon of Byrhtferth of Ramsey', *Speculum*, 55 (1980), 22–37.

Bald's *Leechbook*: SEE Cockayne, [T.] O. (ed.), *Leechdoms, Wortcunning and Starcraft of Early England*.

Barker, E. E., 'Sussex Anglo-Saxon Charters', *Sussex Archaeological Collections: Sussex Archaeological Society*, Part 1, 86 (1947), 42–101; Part 2, 87 (1948), 112–63; Part 3, 88 (1949), 51–113.

—— 'The Anglo-Saxon Chronicle Used by Æthelweard', *Bulletin of the Institute of Historical Research*, 40 (1967), 74–91.

Barrett, H. M., *Boethius: Some Aspects of his Times and Work* (Cambridge, 1940).

Bassett, S. (ed.), *The Origins of Anglo-Saxon Kingdoms* (Leicester, 1989).

Bately, J. M., 'Grimbald of St Bertin's', *Medium Ævum*, 35 (1966), 1–10.

—— 'The Classical Additions in the Old English Orosius', in Clemoes and Hughes (eds.), *Studies Presented to Dorothy Whitelock*, 237–51.

—— 'The Compilation of the Anglo-Saxon Chronicle, 60 BC to AD 890: Vocabulary as Evidence', *Proc. Brit. Acad.* 64 (1980 for 1978), 93–129.

—— 'World History in the *Anglo-Saxon Chronicle*: Its Sources and its Separateness from the Old English Orosius', *ASE* 8 (1979), 177–94.

—— (ed.), *The Old English Orosius* (Early English Text Soc., Supplementary Series, 6; Oxford, 1980).

—— *The Literary Prose of King Alfred's Reign: Translation or Transformation?* Inaugural Lecture, King's College, London, 1980. Repr. *Old English Newsletter Subsidia*, 10 (Cemers, Suny-Binghampton, 1984).

—— 'Bede and the Anglo-Saxon Chronicle', in King and Stevens (eds.), *Saints, Scholars and Heroes*, i. 232–54.

—— 'Lexical Evidence for the Authorship of the Prose Psalms in the Paris Psalter', *ASE* 10 (1982), 69–95.

—— (ed.), *The Anglo-Saxon Chronicle: A Collaborative Edition*, iii. *Manuscript A* (gen. eds. D. Dumville and S. Keynes; Cambridge, 1986).

—— 'Manuscript Layout and the Anglo-Saxon Chronicle', *Bulletin of the John Rylands University Library of Manchester*, 70 (1988), 21–43.

—— 'Old English Prose Before and During the Reign of Alfred', *ASE* 7 (1988), 93–138.

—— 'John Joscelyn and the Laws of the Anglo-Saxon Kings', in Korhammer, Reichl and Sauer (eds.), *Studies Presented to Helmut Gneuss*, 435–66.

—— *The Anglo-Saxon Chronicle: Texts and Textual Relationships* (Reading, 1991).

—— 'The *Anglo-Saxon Chronicle*', in Scragg (ed.), *The Battle of Maldon*, 37–50.

Beaufrère, A., *Gerbert: Patre a Aurillac, Pontife a Rome* (Aurillac, 1970).

Beaven, M. R. L., 'The Beginning of the Year in the Alfredian Chronicle (866–87)', *Eng. Hist. Rev.* 33 (1918), 328–42.

Bede: SEE: Colgrave, B., and Mynors, R. A. B. (eds.), *Bede's Ecclesiastical History*; Miller, T. (ed.), *The Old English Version of Bede's History*; Plummer, C. (ed.), *Venerabilis Baedae Opera Historica*.

Bell, A. (ed.), *L'Estoire des Engleis by Geffrei Gaimar* (Anglo-Norman Texts, 14–16; Oxford, 1960).

Béranger, J., *Recherches sur l'aspect idéologique du Principat* (Schweitzerische Beiträge zur Altertumswissenschaft, 6; Basle, 1953).

Berkhout, C. T., and Gatch, M. McC. (eds.), *Anglo-Saxon Scholarship: The First Three Centuries* (Boston, 1978).

Biddle, M., *Excavations near Winchester Cathedral, 1961–68* (Winchester, 1969).

—— (ed.), *Winchester Studies I: Winchester in the Early Middle Ages* (Oxford, 1976).

—— 'The Study of Winchester: Archaeology and History in a British Town, 1961–83', *Proc. Brit. Acad.* 69 (1983), 91–135.

Binchy, D. A., *Celtic and Anglo-Saxon Kingship* (O'Donnell Lectures; Oxford, 1970).

Birch, W. de G. (ed.), *Cartularium Saxonicum: A Collection of Charters Relating to Anglo-Saxon History* (4 vols.; London, 1964; repr. of 1885–99 edn.).

—— (ed.), *Liber Vitae: Register and Martyrology of New Minster and Hyde Abbey, Winchester* (Hampshire Records Soc.; London and Winchester, 1892).

Blackburn, M. A. S. (ed.), *Anglo-Saxon Monetary History: Essays in Memory of Michael Dolley* (Leicester, 1986).

—— 'The Earliest Anglo-Viking Coinage of the Southern Danelaw (late 9th century)', *Proceedings of the 10th International Congress of Numismatists*, London, Sept. 1986 (London, 1990), 341–9.

—— 'The Ashdown (Essex) Hoard and the Currency of the Southern Danelaw in the Late Ninth Century', *British Numismatic Journal*, 59 (1989), 13–38.

—— and Dumville, D. N. (eds.), *Kings, Currency and Alliances: The History and Coinage of Southern England, AD 840–900* (Woodbridge, Suffolk, forthcoming).

Blair, P. Hunter, 'Some Observations on the "Historia Regum" Attributed to Symeon of Durham', in Jackson, *et al.* (eds.), *Celt and Saxon*, 63–118.

Blunt, C. E., 'The St Edmund Memorial Coinage', *Proceedings Suffolk Institute of Archaeology*, 31/3 (1969), 234–55.

Boethius: SEE Fox, S. (ed.), *King Alfred's Anglo-Saxon Version of Boethius de Consolatione Philosophiæ*; Sedgefield, W. J. (ed.), *King Alfred's Old English Version of Boethius de Consolatione Philosophiae*; and Watts, V. E. (transl.), *Boethius*.

Bolton, W. R., 'Boethius and a Topos in *Beowulf*', in King and Stevens (eds.), *Saints, Scholars and Heroes*, i. 15–43.

—— 'How Boethian is Alfred's *Boethius*?', in Szarmach (ed.), *Studies in Earlier Old English Prose*, 153–70.

Bonner, G., Rolleson, D., and Stancliffe, C. (eds.), *St. Cuthbert, His Cult and Community to AD 1200* (Woodbridge, 1989).

Boretius, A., and Krause, V. (eds.), *Mon. Ger. Hist. Capitularia Regum Francorum Occidentalis (Karoli II)* (Hanover, 1897).

Bridgeman, C. G. O., and Wedgwood, J. C. (eds.), *Collections for a History of Staffordshire edited by the William Salt Archaeological Society 1916* (London, 1918).

Brønsted, J., *The Vikings* (Penguin, Harmondsworth, 1965).

Brooks, N., *The Early History of the Church of Canterbury: Christ Church from 597 to 1066* (Leicester, 1984).

—— 'The Unidentified Forts of the Burghal Hidage', *Medieval Archaeology*, 8 (1964), 74–90.

—— 'England in the Ninth Century: The Crucible of Defeat', *Trans. Roy. Hist. Soc.* 5/29 (1979), 1–20.

—— 'The Development of Military Obligations in Eighth- and Ninth-Century England', in Clemoes and Hughes (eds.), *Studies Presented to Dorothy Whitelock*, 69–84.

Brooks, N. P., and Graham-Campbell, J. A., 'Reflections on the Viking-Age Silver Hoard from Croydon, Surrey', in Blackburn (ed.), *Anglo-Saxon Monetary History*, 91–110.

Brown, R. A. (ed.), *Proceedings of the Battle Conference on Anglo-Norman Studies I: 1978* (Ipswich, 1979).

—— (ed.), *Proceedings of the Battle Conference on Anglo-Norman Studies XI: 1988* (Woodbridge, 1990).

Browne, G. F., *King Alfred's Books* (London, 1920).

Brownrigg, L. L., 'Manuscripts Containing English Decoration 871–1066, Catalogued and Illustrated: A Review', *ASE* 7 (1978), 239–63.

Bruce, J., and Perowne, T. T. (eds.), *Correspondence of Matthew Parker D.D., Archbishop of Canterbury Comprising Letters Written by and to him, from AD 1535 to his Death, AD 1575* (Parker Soc.; Cambridge, 1853).

Bullough, D. A., 'The Educational Tradition in England from Alfred to Aelfric: Teaching *utriusque linguae*', in *Settimane di studio del Centro italiano di Studi sull'alto Medioevo*, 19 (1972), 453–94.

Burkitt, F. C. (ed.), *Speculum Religionis: Being Essays and Studies in Religion and Literature from Plato to von Hügel . . . Presented to Claude G. Montefiore* (Oxford, 1929).

Burlin, R. B., and Irving, E. B., *Old English Studies in Honour of John C. Pope* (Toronto, 1974).

Burrow, I., 'The Town Defences of Exeter', *Trans. Devon Association*, 109 (1977), 13–40.

Byrne, F. J., *Irish Kings and High-Kings* (London, 1973).

Cabaniss, A. (transl.), *Son of Charlemagne: A Contemporary Life of Louis the Pious* (Syracuse, n.d.). [The Astronomer's *Life* of Louis the Pious]

Cameron, M. L., 'The Sources of Medical Knowledge in Anglo-Saxon England', *ASE* xi (1983), 135–55.

—— 'Bald's *Leechbook*: Its Sources and their Use in its Compilation', *ASE* 12 (1983), 153–83.

Campbell, A., 'An Old English Will', *Journal of English and Germanic Philology*, 37 (1938), 133–52.

—— *Encomium Emmae Reginae* (Roy. Hist. Soc., Camden Soc. 3rd Series, 72; London, 1949).

—— (ed.), *Chronicon Æthelweardi: The Chronicle of Æthelweard* (Nelson Medieval Texts; London, 1962).

Campbell, E., and Lane, A., 'Llangorse: A Tenth-Century Royal Crannog in Wales', *Antiquity*, 63 (1989), 675–81.

Campbell, J., 'Observations on English Government from the Tenth to the Twelfth Century', *Trans. Roy. Hist. Soc.* 5/25 (1975), 39–54.

—— 'Asser's Life of Alfred', in Holdsworth and Wiseman (eds.), *The Inheritance of Historiography, 350–900*, 116–17.

—— 'England, *c.*991', in Cooper (ed.), *Battle of Maldon*, 1–18.

—— John, E., and Wormald, P., *The Anglo-Saxons* (Oxford, 1982).

Campbell, J. J., 'The Dialect Vocabulary of the OE Bede', *Journal of English and Germanic Philology*, 50 (1951), 349–72.

—— 'The OE Bede: Book III, Chapters 16–20', *Modern Language Notes*, 67 (1952), 381–6.

Carnicelli, T. A. (ed.), *King Alfred's Version of St. Augustine's Soliloquies* (Cambridge, Mass., 1969).

Chadwick, H. M., *Studies on Anglo-Saxon Institutions* (Cambridge, 1905).

Chaplais, P., 'The Anglo-Saxon Chancery: From the Diploma to the Writ', *Journal of the Society of Archivists*, 3 (1965–9), 160–76.

—— 'Some Early Anglo-Saxon Diplomas on Single Sheets: Originals or Copies?', *Journal of the Society of Archivists*, 3 (1965–9), 315–36.

—— 'The Authenticity of the Royal Anglo-Saxon Diplomas of Exeter', *Bulletin of the Institute of Historical Research*, 39/99 (1966), 1–34.

Chronicum Scotorum: SEE Hennessy, W. M. (ed.), *Chronicum Scotorum*.

Clark, C., 'The Narrative Mode of *The Anglo-Saxon Chronicle* before the Conquest', in Clemoes and Hughes (eds.), *Studies Presented to Dorothy Whitelock*, 215–35.

Clement, R. W., 'The Production of the *Pastoral Care*: King Alfred and His Helpers', in Szarmach (ed.), *Studies in Earlier Old English Prose*, 129–52.

Clemoes, P., and Hughes, K. (eds.), *England before the Norman Conquest: Studies in Primary Sources Presented to Dorothy Whitelock* (Cambridge, 1971).

Clifford, W., 'Asser's Life of Alfred', *The Athenæum*, no. 2539 (24 June 1876), 859–60.

Cockayne, [T.] O. (ed.), *Leechdoms, Wortcunning and Starcraft of Early England . . . Illustrating the History of Science in this Country before the Norman Conquest* (3 vols.; Rolls Series; London, 1864–6).

Colgrave, B. (ed.), *The Life of Bishop Wilfrid by Eddius Stephanus* (Cambridge, 1927).

—— (ed. and transl.), *Two Lives of Saint Cuthbert: A Life by an Anonymous Monk of Lindisfarne and Bede's Prose Life* (New York, 1969).

—— and Mynors, R. A. B. (ed. and transl.), *Bede's Ecclesiastical History of the English People* (Oxford, 1969).

Collins, R., 'Julian of Toledo and the Royal Succession in Late Seventh-Century Spain', in Sawyer and Wood (eds.), *Early Medieval Kingship*, 30–49.

Cooper, J. (ed.), *The Battle of Maldon: Fiction and Fact* (London and Rio Grande, 1993).

Coulson, C. L. H., 'Fortresses and Social Responsibility in Late Carolingian France', *Zeitschrift für Archäologie des Mittelalters*, 4 (1976), 29–36.

Courcelle, P., *La Consolation de Philosophie dans la tradition littéraire* (Études Augustiniennes; Paris, 1967).

Coxe, H. O. (ed.), *Rogeri de Wendover Chronica sive Flores Historiarum* (5 vols.; English Hist. Soc.; London, 1841–4).

Craig, G., 'Alfred the Great: A Diagnosis', *Journal of the Royal Society of Medicine*, 84 (1991), 303–5.

Crawford, S. J., 'Byrhtferth of Ramsey and the Anonymous Life of St Oswald', in Burkitt (ed.), *Speculum Religionis: Essays Presented to Claude G. Montefiore*, 99–111.

—— (ed.), *Byrhtferth's Manual AD 1011* (Early English Text Soc.; Oxford, 1960, repr. of 1929 edn.).

Cross, J. E., 'The Influence of Irish Texts and Traditions on the Old English Martyrology', *Proc. Roy. Irish Acad.* 81 C (1981), 173–92.

—— 'The Latinity of the Ninth-Century Old English Martyrologist', in Szarmach (ed.), *Studies in Earlier Old English Prose*, 275–300.

Dales, D., *Dunstan: Saint and Statesman* (Cambridge, 1988).

Dalton, O. M. (transl.), *The History of the Franks by Gregory of Tours* (2 vols.; Oxford, 1927).

Darby, H. C., *The Draining of the Fens*, 2nd edn. (Cambridge, 1956).

Davidson, H. R. Ellis, *Gods and Myths of Northern Europe* (Pelican, Harmondsworth, 1964).

Davies, W., 'Land and Power in Early Medieval Wales', *Past and Present*, 81 (1978), 1–23.

—— *Wales in the Early Middle Ages* (Leicester, 1982).

Davis, R. H. C., 'East Anglia and the Danelaw', *Trans. Roy. Hist. Soc.* 5/5 (1955), 23–39.

—— 'Alfred the Great: Propaganda and Truth', *History*, 56 (1971), 169–82.

—— 'Alfred and Guthrum's Frontier', *Eng. Hist. Rev.* 97 (1982), 803–10.

Davison, B. K., 'The Burghal Hidage Fort of Eorpeburnan: A Suggested Identification', *Medieval Archaeology*, 16 (1972), 123–7.

Deanesly, M., 'The Archdeacons of Canterbury under Archbishop Ceolnoth (833–870)', *Eng. Hist. Rev.* 42 (1927), 1–11.

Dearden, B., 'Charles the Bald's Fortified Bridge at Pîtres (Seine): Recent Archaeological Investigations', in Brown (ed.), *Anglo-Norman Studies XI: Proceedings of Battle Conference*, 107–12.

—— and Clark, A., 'Pont-de-l'Arche or Pîtres? A Location and Archaeomagnetic Dating for Charles the Bald's Fortifications on the Seine', *Antiquity*, 64 (1990), 567–71.

Derolez, R., 'The Orientation System in the Old English Orosius', in Clemoes and Hughes (eds.), *Studies Presented to Dorothy Whitelock*, 253–68.

Diez, G. Martinez, 'Los Concilios de Toledo', *Anales Toledanos*, 3 (1971), 119–38.

Dobbie, E. van K., *The Anglo-Saxon Minor Poems* (London and New York, 1942).

Doble, G. H., *S. Neot: Patron of St. Neot, Cornwall and St. Neot's, Huntingdonshire* (Exeter [1929]).

Dolley, R. H. M. (ed.), *Anglo-Saxon Coins: Studies Presented to F. M. Stenton on the Occasion of his 80th Birthday* (London, 1961).

Dolley, R. H. M. (ed.), 'The Location of Pre-Alfredian Mint(s) of Wessex', *Proceedings Hampshire Field Club and Archaeological Soc.* 27 (1970), 57–61.

—— and Blunt, C. E., 'The Chronology of the Coins of Ælfred the Great 871–899', in Dolley (ed.), *Anglo-Saxon Coins: Studies Presented to Stenton*, 77–95.

—— and Skaare, K., 'The Coinage of Æthelwulf, King of the West Saxons', in Dolley (ed.), *Anglo-Saxon Coins: Studies Presented to Stenton*, 63–76.

Dornier, A. (ed.), *Mercian Studies* (Leicester, 1977).

Duby, G., *The Three Orders: Feudal Society Imagined*, transl. A. Goldhammer, foreword T. N. Bisson (Chicago and London, 1980).

Duchesne, L. (ed.), *Le Liber Pontificalis: Texte introduction et commentaire* (Bibliothèque des Écoles Françaises d'Athènes et de Rome; Paris, 1955–7; 3 vol. repr. of 1886–92 edn.).

Dudo of St Quentin: SEE Lair, J. (ed.), *De Moribus et Actis Primorum Normanniæ Ducum auctore Dudone Sancti Quintini decano*; and Migne, J. P. (ed.), *Dudonis de Moribus et Actis Primorum Normanniæ Ducum*.

Dumville, D. N., 'The Anglian Collection of Royal Genealogies and Regnal Lists', *ASE* 5 (1976), 23–50.

—— 'The Ætheling: A Study in Anglo-Saxon Constitutional History', *ASE* 8 (1979), 1–33.

—— 'The "Six" Sons of Rhodri Mawr: A Problem in Asser's *Life of King Alfred*', *Cambridge Medieval Celtic Studies*, 4 (1982), 5–18.

—— 'The West Saxon Genealogical Regnal List and the Chronology of Early Wessex', *Peritia: Journal of the Medieval Academy of Ireland*, 4 (1985), 21–66.

—— *The Historia Brittonum*, iii. *The 'Vatican' Recension* (Cambridge, 1985).

—— (ed.), 'The West Saxon Genealogical Regnal List: Manuscripts and Texts', *Anglia*, 104 (1986), 1–32.

—— 'English Square Minuscule Script: The Background and Earliest Phases', *ASE* 16 (1987), 147–79.

—— (ed.), *Wessex and England from Alfred to Edgar* (Woodbridge, 1992).

—— and Lapidge, M. (eds.), *The Anglo-Saxon Chronicle: A Collaborative Edition*, xvii. *The Annals of St. Neots with Vita Prima Sancti Neoti* (Cambridge, 1984).

Dunstan, *Life* of: SEE Stubbs, W. (ed.), *Memorials of Saint Dunstan*.

Ecgwine, *Life* of: SEE Giles, J. A. (ed.), *Vita Quorundum* [?] *Anglo-Saxonum*.

Edwards, E. (ed.), *Liber Monasterii de Hyda Comprising a Chronicle of the Affairs of England, from the Settlement of the Saxons to the Reign of King Cnut; and a Chartulary of the Abbey of Hyde in Hampshire, AD 455–1023* (Rolls Series; London, 1866).

Egils Saga: SEE Nordal, S. (ed.), *Egils Saga Skalla-Grímssonar*.

Einhard: SEE Rau, R. (ed.), *Einhardi Vita Caroli*.

Enright, M. J., 'Charles the Bald and Aethelwulf of Wessex: The Alliance of 856 and Strategies of Royal Succession', *Journal of Medieval History*, 5 (1979), 291–302.

Fell, C. E., *Edward, King and Martyr* (Leeds, 1971).

Finberg, H. P. R., 'Sherborne, Glastonbury, and the Expansion of Wessex', *Trans. Roy. Hist. Soc.* 5/3 (1953), 101–24.

—— SEE Hoskins, W. G. (with supplement by H. P. R. Finberg), *The Westward Expansion of Essex*.

—— (ed.), *The Early Charters of Devon and Cornwall* (Leicester, 1963).

—— *Lucerna: Studies of Some Problems in the Early History of England* (London and New York, 1964).

—— (ed.), *The Early Charters of Wessex* (Leicester, 1964).

—— (ed.), *West Country Historical Studies* (Newton Abbot, 1969).

Fisher, D. J. V., 'The Anti-Monastic Reaction in the Reign of Edward the Martyr', *Cambridge Historical Journal*, 10 (1950–2), 254–70.

Fleming, R., 'Monastic Lands and England's Defence in the Viking Wars', *Eng. Hist. Rev.* 100 (1985), 247–65.

Florence *alias* John of Worcester: SEE Thorpe, B. (ed.), *Florentii Wigorniensis monachi.*

Flower, R., and Smith, H. (eds.), *The Parker Chronicle and Laws (Corpus Christi College, Cambridge, MS. 173): A Facsimile* (Early English Text Soc., OS 208; London, 1941).

Foerster, W. (ed.), *Li Dialoge Gregoire lo Pape* (Halle and Paris, 1876), i. [*Dialogues of Gregory.*]

Foote, P., and Wilson, D. M., *The Viking Achievement: The Society and Culture of Early Medieval Scandinavia* (London, 1980; repr. of 1970 edn.).

Forsey, G. F., 'Byrhtferth's *Preface*', *Speculum*, 3 (1928), 505–22.

Fouracre, P. J., 'The Context of the OHG *Ludwigslied*', *Medium Ævum*, 54 (1985), 87–103.

Fox, S. (ed.), *King Alfred's Anglo-Saxon Version of Boethius De Consolatione Philosophiæ* (New York, 1970; repr. of 1864 edn.).

France, J., 'The Military History of the Carolingian Period', *Revue Belge d'histoire militaire*, 26 (1985), 81–99.

Gaimar: SEE Bell, A. (ed.), *L'Estoire des Engleis by Geffrei Gaimar.*

Galbraith, V. H., 'Who Wrote Asser's Life of Alfred', in V. H. Galbraith, *An Introduction to the Study of History* (London, 1964), 88–128.

Gameson, R., 'English Manuscript Art in the Mid-Eleventh Century: The Decorative Tradition', *Antiquaries Journal*, 71 (1991), 64–122.

—— 'The Fabric of the Tanner Bede', *Bodleian Library Record*, 14/3 (1992), 176–206.

Gatch, M. McC., 'King Alfred's Version of Augustine's *Soliloquia*: Some Suggestions on its Rationale and Unity', in Szarmach (ed.), *Studies in Earlier Old English Prose*, 17–46.

Gerald of Aurillac: SEE Migne, J. P. (ed.), *Sancti Odonis Abbatis Cluniacensis II, de Vita Sancti Geraldi Auriliacensis Comitis*; and Sitwell, G. (transl.), *St. Odo of Cluny.*

Gibson, M., Nelson, J. [N.], and Ganz, D. (eds.), *Charles the Bald: Court and Kingdom. Papers based on a Colloquium held in London in April 1979* (BAR International Series, 101; Oxford, 1981).

Giles, J. A. (transl.), *William of Malmesbury's Chronicle of the Kings of England* (London, 1847).

—— (ed.), [*Life* of St Ecgwine] *Vita Quorundum Anglo-Saxonum: Original Lives of Anglo-Saxons and Others Who Lived before the Conquest* (London, 1854).

Gillmor, C., 'War on the Rivers: Viking Numbers and Mobility on the Seine and Loire, 841–886', *Viator: Medieval and Renaissance Studies*, 19 (1988), 79–109.

—— 'The Logistics of Fortified Bridge Building on the Seine under Charles the Bald', in R. A. Brown (ed.), *Anglo-Norman Studies XI: Proceedings of Battle Conference 1988*, 87–105.

Gneuss, H., 'The Origin of Standard Old English and Æthelwold's School at Winchester', *ASE* 1 (1972), 63–83.

—— 'Die Handschrift Cotton Otho A. XII', *Anglia*, 94 (1976), 289–318.

Godden, M., and Lapidge, M. (eds.), *The Cambridge Companion to Old English Literature* (Cambridge, 1991).

Godfrey, J., *The Church in Anglo-Saxon England* (Cambridge, 1962).

Godman, P., *Poetry of the Carolingian Renaissance* (London, 1985).

Goody, J., *Literacy in Traditional Societies* (Cambridge, 1968).

Graham-Campbell, J., *The Viking World* (London, 1989). See also Brooks, N. P., and Graham-Campbell, J., 'Reflections on the Viking-Age Silver Hoard'.

Gransden, A., *Historical Writing in England* c.550 to 1307 (London, 1974).

Graves, R. (transl.), *Gaius Suetonius Tranquillus: The Twelve Caesars*, Book Club Associates hardback edn., introd. by M. Grant (London, 1979).

Gregory, Pope: SEE Foerster, W. (ed.), *Li Dialoge Gregoire*; Hecht, H. (ed.), *Bischof Wærferths Übersetzung der Dialoge Gregors*; Ker, N. R. (ed.), *The Pastoral Care*; Sweet, H. (ed.), *King Alfred's Version of the Pastoral Care*.

Grierson, P., 'Abbot Fulco and the Date of the 'Gesta abbatum Fontanellensium', *Eng. Hist. Rev.* 55 (1940), 275–84.

—— 'Grimbald of St Bertin's', *Eng. Hist. Rev.* 55 (1940), 529–61.

—— 'The Relations between England and Flanders before the Norman Conquest', *Trans. Roy. Hist. Soc.* 4/23 (1941), 71–112.

Grundy, G. B., 'On the Meanings of Certain Terms in the Anglo-Saxon Charters', in G. C. Moore Smith (ed.), *Essays and Studies by the Members of the English Association*, viii (Oxford, 1922), 37–69.

Haddan, A. W., and Stubbs, W. (eds.), *Councils and Ecclesiastical Documents Relating to Great Britian and Ireland* (3 vols.; Oxford, 1869–78).

d'Haenens, A., *Les Invasions normandes en Belgique au IXᵉ siècle: Le Phénomène et sa répercussion dans l'historiographie médiévale* (Louvain, 1967).

Hamilton, B., 'The Monastic Revival in Tenth Century Rome', *Studia Monastica*, 4 (1962), 35–68.

Hamilton, N.E.S.A. (ed.), *Willelmi Malmesbiriensis monachi de Gestis Pontificum Anglorum Libri Quinque* (Rolls Series; London, 1870).

Hammer, C. I., '*Lex Scripta* in Early Medieval Bavaria: Use and Abuse of *Lex Baiuvariorum*', in King and Ridyard (eds.), *Law in Mediaeval life and Thought*, 185–95.

Hargrove, H. L. (ed.), *King Alfred's Old English Version of St. Augustine's Soliloquies* (Yale Studies in English, 13; New York, 1902).

—— (transl.), *King Alfred's Old English Version of St. Augustine's Soliloquies turned into Modern English* (Yale Studies in English, 22; New York, 1904).

Harmer, F. E. (ed.), *Select English Historical Documents of the Ninth and Tenth Centuries* (Cambridge, 1914).

—— 'Anglo-Saxon Charters and the Historian', *Bulletin of the John Rylands Library*, 22 (1938), 339–67.

—— (ed.), *Anglo-Saxon Writs* (Manchester, 1952).

Harris, R., 'How Does Writing Restructure Thought?', *Language and Communication*, 9 (1989), 99–106.

Harrison, K., 'The Beginning of the Year in England, c.500–900', *ASE* 2 (1973), 51–70.

—— *The Framework of Anglo-Saxon History to AD 900* (Cambridge, 1976).

—— 'Easter Cycles and the Equinox in the British Isles', *ASE* 7 (1978), 1–8.

Hart, C. R. (ed.), *The Early Charters of Eastern England* (Leicester, 1966).

—— 'The Ramsey Computus', *Eng. Hist. Rev.* 85 (1970), 29–44.

—— 'Byrhtferth and His Manual', *Medium Ævum*, 41 (1972), 95–109.

—— 'Athelstan "Half King" and His Family', *ASE* 2 (1973), 115–44.

—— (ed.), *The Early Charters of Northern England and the North Midlands* (Leicester, 1975).

—— 'The East Anglian Chronicle', *Journal of Medieval History*, 7 (1981), 249–82.

—— 'The B Text of the Anglo-Saxon Chronicle', *Journal of Medieval History*, 8 (1982), 241–99.

—— 'Byrhtferth's Northumbrian Chronicle', *Eng. Hist. Rev.* 97 (1982), 558–82.

—— 'The Early Section of the Worcester Chronicle' *Journal of Medieval History*, 9 (1983), 251–315.

—— 'The Ealdordom of Essex', in Neale (ed.), *An Essex Tribute for Frederick Emmison*, (London, 1987), 57–84.

—— *The Danelaw* (London and Rio Grande, 1992).

—— 'Essex in the Late Tenth Century', in Cooper (ed.), *Battle of Maldon*, 171–204.

Haslam, J. (ed.), *Anglo-Saxon Towns in Southern England* (Chichester, 1984).

Hearne, T. (ed.), *The Life of Alfred the Great by Sir John Spelman [1643]* (Oxford, 1709).

—— (ed.), *Hemingi Chartularium Ecclesiæ Wigorniensis e codice MS. penes Richardus Graves* (Oxford, 1723).

—— (ed.), SEE ALSO Leland, J., *Joannis Lelandi antiquarii De Rebus Britannicis Collectanea*.

Hecht, H. (ed.), *Bischof Wærferths von Worcester Übersetzung der Dialoge Gregors des Grossen über das Leben und die Wunderthaten italienischer Väter und über die Unsterblichkeit der Seelen*. (Bibliothek der Angelsächsischen Prosa V. 2 vols. i. Text (Leipzig, 1900); ii. Commentary (Hamburg, 1907)).

Henel, H., 'Notes on Byrhtferth's *Manual*', *Journal of English and Germanic Philology*, 41 (1942), 427–43.

—— 'Byrhtferth's *Preface*: The Epilogue of his *Manual*', *Speculum*, 18 (1943), 288–302.

Hennessy, W. M. (ed.), *Chronicum Scotorum: A Chronicle of Irish Affairs from the Earliest Times to AD 1135* (Rolls Series; London, 1866).

—— and MacCarthy, B. (ed.), *Annala Uladh: Annals of Ulster, Otherwise Annala Senait, Annals of Senat, a Chronicle of Irish Affairs from AD 431 to AD 1540* (Dublin, 1887–1901).

Herren, M., *The Hisperica Famina*, i. *The A-Text* (Toronto, 1974).

—— (ed.), *Iohannis Scotti Erivgenae Carmina* (Scriptores Latini Hiberniae xii. Dublin, 1993).

Hervey, F. (ed.), *Corolla Sancti Eadmundi: The Garland of Saint Edmund, King and Martyr* (London, 1907).

Hill, D., *An Atlas of Anglo-Saxon England* (Oxford, 1981).

Hinton, D. A., *Alfred's Kingdom: Wessex and the South 800–1500* (London, 1977).

Hodges, R., 'Trade and Market Origins in the Ninth Century: An Archaeological Perspective of Anglo-Carolingian Relations', in Gibson, Nelson and Ganz (eds.), *Charles the Bald*, 213–33.

—— *Dark Age Economics: The Origins of Towns and Trade AD 600–1000* (London, 1982).

Hodgkin, R. H., *A History of the Anglo-Saxons*, 3rd edn. (2 vols.; Oxford, 1952).

Holdsworth, C., and Wiseman, T. P. (eds.), *The Inheritance of Historiography, 350–900* (Exeter, 1986).

Hollister, C. W., *Anglo-Saxon Military Institutions* (Oxford, 1962).

Horgan, D. M., 'The Old English *Pastoral Care*: The Scribal Contribution', in Szarmach (ed.), *Studies in Earlier Old English Prose*, 109–28.

Hoskins, W. G. (with supplement by H. P. R. Finberg), *The Westward Expansion of Wessex* (Leicester University Occasional Papers, 13; Leicester, 1960).

Howorth, H. H., 'Asser's Life of Alfred', *The Athenæum: Journal of English and Foreign Literature, Science, the Fine Arts, Music and Drama*, no. 2526 (25 Mar. 1876), 425–6; no. 2535 (27 May 1876), 727–9; no. 2549 (2 Sept. 1876), 307–9.

—— 'Ethelweard and Asser', *The Athenæum*, no. 2597 (4 Aug. 1877), 145–6.

Hubbard, F. G., 'The Relation of the "Blooms of King Alfred" to the Anglo-Saxon Translation of Boethius', *Modern Language Notes*, 9 (1894), 321–42 [alternative pagination 161–71].

Hughes, M., 'Hampshire Castles and the Landscape: 1066–1216', *Landscape History: Journal of the Society for Landscape Studies*, 11 (1989), 27–60.

Hunter, J., *Ecclesiastical Documents*: I. *A Brief History of the Bishoprick of Somerset from its Foundation to the Year 1174*, ii. *Charters from the Library of Dr. Cox Macro* (Camden Soc., vol. 8 (Old Ser.); London, 1840).

Jackson, K., *et al.* (eds.), *Celt and Saxon: Studies in the Early British Border* (Cambridge, 1964).

John of Salerno: SEE Migne, J. P. (ed.), *Vita Sancti Odonis*; and Sitwell, G. (transl.), *Life of St. Odo*.

John *alias* Florence of Worcester: SEE Thorpe B. (ed.), *Florentii Wigorniensis monachi, Chronicon ex Chronicis.*

John, E., *Land Tenure in Early England* (Leicester, 1964).

—— *Orbis Britanniae and Other Studies* (Leicester, 1966).

Keller, W., *Die literarischen Bestrebungen von Worcester* (Strasburg, 1900).

Kemble, J. M., *Codex Diplomaticus Aevi Saxonici* (6 vols.; London, 1839–48).

—— *The Saxons in England: A Short History of the English Commonwealth till the Period of the Norman Conquest*, revised edn. (2 vols.; London, 1876).

Kennedy, A. G., 'Disputes about *bocland*: The Forum for their Adjudication', *ASE* 14 (1985), 175–95.

Kenney, J. F., *The Sources for the Early History of Ireland: Ecclesiastical* (Dublin, 1979; repr. of 1929 edn.).

Ker, N. R. (ed.), *The Pastoral Care: King Alfred's Translation of St. Gregory's Regula Pastoralis* (Early English Manuscripts in Facsimile, 6; (Copenhagen, 1956).

—— *Catalogue of Manuscripts Containing Anglo-Saxon* (Oxford, 1957).

Keynes, S., 'King Athelstan's Books', in Lapidge and Gneuss (eds.), *Studies Presented to Peter Clemoes*, 143–201.

—— 'A Tale of Two Kings: Alfred the Great and Æthelred the Unready', *Trans. Roy. Hist. Soc.* 5/36 (1986), 195–217.

—— 'The Fonthill Letter', in Korhammer, Reichl, and Sauer (eds.), *Studies Presented to Helmut Gneuss*, 53–97.

—— 'The Discovery and First Publication of the Alfred Jewel', *Somerset Archaeology and Natural History*, 136 (1993 for 1992), 1–8.

—— 'George Harbin's Transcript of the Lost Cartulary of Athelney Abbey', *Proc. Somerset Archaeology and Natural History Soc.* 136 (1993 for 1992), 149–59.

—— 'The Control of Kent in the Ninth Century', *Early Medieval Europe*, 2 (1993), 111–31.

—— 'King Alfred and the Mercians', in Blackburn and Dumville (eds.), *Kings, Currency and Alliances.*

—— 'The West Saxon Charters of King Æthelwulf and his Sons', *Eng. Hist. Rev.* 109 (1994), 1109–49.

—— and Lapidge, M. (transl.), *Alfred the Great: Asser's Life of King Alfred and Other Contemporary Sources* (Penguin, Harmondsworth, 1983).

King, E. B., and Ridyard, S. J. (ed.), *Law in Mediaeval life and Thought* (Sewanee Mediaeval Studies; Sewanee, Tenn., 1990).

King, M. H., and Stevens, W. M. (eds.), *Saints, Scholars and Heroes: Studies in Medieval Culture in Honour of Charles W. Jones* (2 vols.; Collegeville, Minn., 1979).

King, P. D., *Law and Society in the Visigothic Kingdom* (Cambridge, 1972).

Kirby, D. P., 'The Place of Ceredigion in the Early History of Wales, *c.*400–1170', *Journal of the Cardiganshire Antiquarian Soc.* 6 (1970), 265–84.

—— 'Asser and his Life of King Alfred', *Studia Celtica*, 6 (1971), 12–35.

—— 'Hywel Dda: Anglophil?', *Welsh History Rev.* 8 (1976), 1–13.

—— *The Earliest English Kings* (London, 1991).

—— 'The Political Development of Ceredigion *c.*400–1081', in J. L. Davies and D. P. Kirby (eds.), *The County History of Cardiganshire*, i. *From the Earliest Times to the Coming of the Normans* (Cardiff, 1994), 318–77.

Kitson, P., Review of M. A. O'Donovan's *Charters of Sherborne (London, 1988)*, in *Medium Ævum*, 60 (1991), 104–5.

Klaeber, F., 'Zur altenglischen Bedaübersetzung', *Anglia*, 27 (1904), 399–435.

Knecht, R. J., *Francis I* (Cambridge, 1982).

Korhammer, M., Reichl, K., and Sauer, H. (eds.), *Words, Texts, and Manuscripts: Studies in Anglo-Saxon Culture Presented to Helmut Gneuss on the Occasion of his Sixty-Fifth Birthday* (Woodbridge, Suffolk, 1992).

Lair, J. (ed.), [Dudo of St Quentin] *De Moribus et Actis Primorum Normanniæ Ducum auctore Dudone Sancti Quintini Decano* (Caen, 1865).

Laistner, M. L. W., 'Notes on Greek from the Lectures of a Ninth Century Monastery Teacher', *Bulletin of the John Rylands Library, Manchester*, 7 (1923), 421–56.

Lampe, G. W. H. (ed.), *A Patristic Greek Lexicon*, (Oxford, 1964), 5 fascs.

Lapidge, M., 'Three Latin Poems from Æthelwold's School at Winchester', *ASE* 1 (1972), 85–107.

—— 'The Hermeneutic Style in Tenth-Century Anglo-Latin Literature', *ASE* 4 (1975), 67–111.

—— 'The Medieval Hagiography of St Ecgwine', *Vale of Evesham Historical Soc. Research Papers*, 6 (1977), 77–93.

—— 'Dominic of Evesham: *Vita S. Ecgwini episcopi et confessoris*', *Analecta Bollandiana*, 96 (1978), 65–104.

—— 'Byrhtferth and the *Vita S. Ecgwini*', *Medieval Studies*, 41 (1979), 331–53.

—— 'Some Latin Poems as Evidence for the Reign of Athelstan', *ASE* 9 (1981), 61–98.

—— 'Byrhtferth of Ramsey and the Early Sections of the *Historia Regum* Attributed to Symeon of Durham', *ASE* 10 (1982), 97–122.

—— 'A Frankish Scholar in Tenth-Century England: Frithegod of Canterbury/Fredegaud of Brioude', *ASE* 17 (1988), 45–65.

—— 'The Saintly Life in Anglo-Saxon England', in Godden and Lapidge, *Cambridge Companion to Old English Literature*.

—— and Gneuss, H. (eds.), *Learning and Literature in Anglo-Saxon England: Studies Presented to Peter Clemoes on the Occasion of his Sixty-Fifth Birthday* (Cambridge, 1985).

—— and Sharpe, R., *A Bibliography of Celtic Latin Literature 400–1200* (Dublin, 1985).

—— and Winterbottom, M., *Wulfstan of Winchester: The Life of St Æthelwold* (Oxford, 1991).

Latouche, R. (transl.), *Grégoire de Tours: Histoire des Francs* (2 vols.; Paris, 1963).

[Leland, J.] *Joannis Lelandi antiquarii De Rebus Britannicis Collectanea*, ed. T. Hearne (6 vols.; London, 1774).

Liebermann, F. (ed.), *Die Gesetze der Angelsachsen* (3 vols.; 1960 repr. of 1903 Halle edn.).

[*Life* of Leofgyth] *Vita Leobae abbatissae Biscofesheimensis auctore Rudolfo Fuldensi Mon. Ger. Hist. SS.* 15 (1887), 118–31.

Little, A. G., and Powicke, F. M. (eds.), *Essays in Medieval History Presented to Thomas Frederick Tout* (Manchester, 1925).

Lloyd, D. M., 'William Salesbury, Richard Davies, and Archbishop Parker', *Journal of the National Library of Wales*, 2 (1941), 7–16.

Lloyd, J. E., *A History of Wales from the Earliest Times to the Edwardian Conquest* 3rd. edn. (2 vols.; London and New York, 1948).

Loomis, C. Grant, *White Magic: An Introduction to the Folklore of Christian Legend* (Cambridge, Mass., 1948).

Lotter, F., 'Das Idealbild adliger Laienfrömmigkeit in den Anfängen Clunys: Odos Vita des Grafen Gerald von Aurillac', in *Benedictine Culture, 750–1050* ed. Lourdaux, W., and Verhelst, D., in *Mediaevalia Lovaniensia*, Ser. I (Studia 11) (Leuven, 1983), 76–95.

Louis the Pious, *Life* of: SEE Rau R. (ed.), *Thegani Vita Hludowici*, and *Anonymi Vita Hludowici*; and Cabaniss, A. (transl.), *Son of Tharelamagne*.

Loyn, H. R., 'The Term *Ealdorman* in the Translations Prepared at the Time of King Alfred', *Eng. Hist. Rev.*, 68 (1953), 513–25.

—— 'Gesiths and Thegns in Anglo-Saxon England from the Seventh to the Tenth Century', *Eng. Hist. Rev.*, 70 (1955), 529–49.

—— *The Vikings in Wales* (Dorothea Coke Memorial Lecture, University College London, 1976).

—— *The Vikings in Britain* (London, 1977).

Lucas, A. T., 'The Plundering and Burning of Churches in Ireland, 7th to the 16th Century', in Rynne (ed.), *North Munster Studies*.

Lund, N., 'King Edgar and the Danelaw', *Medieval Scandinavia*, 9 (1976), 181–95.

Lyon, C. S. S., and Stewart, B. H. I. H., 'The Northumbrian Viking Coins in the Cuerdale Hoard', in Dolley (ed.), *Anglo-Saxon Coins: Studies Presented to Stenton*, 96–121.

Mac Airt, S., and Mac Niocaill, G. (eds.), *The Annals of Ulster (to AD 1131)*, i (Dublin, 1983).

Macauley, G. C. (transl.), *The History of Herodotus* (London and New York, 1890).

Mackenzie, M. M., and Roueché, C. (eds.), *Images and Authority: Papers Presented to Joyce Reynolds on the Occasion of her Seventieth Birthday* (Cambridge Philological Soc., Supplementary vol. 16; Cambridge, 1989).

McKisack, M., *Medieval History in the Tudor Age* (Oxford, 1971).

McKitterick, R., 'The Palace School of Charles the Bald', in Gibson, Nelson, and Ganz (eds.), *Charles the Bald*, 385–400.

Mac Niocaill, G., *Ireland before the Vikings* (Dublin and London, 1972).

Macray, W. D. (ed.), *Chronicon Abbatiæ Rameseiensis, a sæc. x. usque ad an. circiter 1200* (Rolls Series; London, 1886).

McTurk, R. W., 'Ragnarr Loðbrók in the Irish Annals?', in Almquist and Greene (eds.), *Seventh Viking Congress*, 93–123.

—— Review of A. P. Smyth, *Scandinavian York and Dublin*, i. in *Saga-Book of Viking Society for Northern Research*, 19: 4 (1977), 471–4.

Madden, F. (ed.), *Matthaei Parisiensis Historia Anglorum, sive et vulgo dicitur Historia minor* (3 vols.; Rolls Series, London, 1866).

Maddicott, J. R., 'Trade, Industry and the Wealth of King Alfred', *Past and Present*, 123 (1989), 3–51.

Maitland, F. W., 'The Laws of the Anglo-Saxons', *Quarterly Review*, 200 (Oct. 1904), 139–57.

Manitius, M., *Geschichte der lateinischen Literatur des Mittelalters* (Munich, 1959–64; repr. of 1911–31 edn.).

Meaney, A. L., 'Alfred, the Patriarch, and the White Stone', *AUMLA. Journal of the Australasian Universities Language and Literature Association*, 49 (1978), 65–79.

—— 'D: An Undervalued Manuscript of the Anglo-Saxon Chronicle', *Papergon* (New Ser.), 1 (1983), 13–38.

—— 'Variant Versions of Old English Medical Remedies and the Compilation of Bald's *Leechbook*', *ASE* 13 (1984), 235–68.

—— 'St Neot's, Æthelweard and the Compilation of the Anglo-Saxon Chronicle: A Survey', in Szarmach (ed.), *Studies in Earlier Old English Prose*, 193–243.

Meehan, D. (ed.), *Adomnan's de Locis Sanctis* (Scriptores Latini Hiberniae, 3; Dublin, 1958).

Metcalf, D. M., 'The Prosperity of North-Western Europe in the Eighth and Ninth Centuries', *Econ. Hist. Rev.* 2/20 (1967), 344–57.

—— 'A Sketch of the Currency in the Time of Charles the Bald', in Gibson, Nelson, and Ganz (eds.), *Charles the Bald*, 53–84.

—— and Northover, J. P., 'Debasement of the Coinage in Southern England in the Age of King Alfred', *Numismatic Chronicle*, 145 (1985), 150–76.

Migne, J. P. (ed.), [*Life* of Count Gerald of Aurillac] *Sancti Odonis Abbatis Cluniacensis II, de Vita Sancti Geraldi Auriliacensis Comitis*, in *Patrologiae Cursus Completus* (series Latina, 133; Paris, 1853), 639–704.

—— (ed.), [*Life* of St Odo of Cluny] *Vita Sancti Odonis Abbatis Cluniacensis secundi, scripta a Joanne monacho, ejus discipulo*, in *Patrologiae Cursus Completus* (series Latina, 133; Paris, 1853), 43–86.

—— (ed.), [Dudo of St Quentin] *Dudonis de Moribus et Actis Primorum Normanniæ Ducum*, in *Patrologiae Cursus Completus* (series secunda, 141; Paris, 1853), 607–758.

Miller, T. (ed.), *The Old English Version of Bede's Ecclesiastical History of the English People* (4 vols.; Early English Text Society, os 95–96 110–111; London, 1890–98).

Millinger, S. P., 'Liturgical Devotion in the Vita Oswaldi', in King and Stevens (eds.), *Saints, Scholars and Heroes*, ii. 239–64.

Mommsen, T. (ed.), *Iordanis Romana et Getica*, in *Mon. Ger. Hist. Auctorum Antiquissimorum* (Berlin, 1961; repr. of 1882 edn.), v/i.

Morris, J. (ed. and transl.), *Nennius: British History and the Welsh Annals* (Chichester, 1980).

Morrish, J., 'King Alfred's Letter as a Source on Learning in England in the Ninth Century', in Szarmach (ed.), *Studies in Earlier Old English Prose*, 87–107.

Müller, C. (ed.), *Claudii Ptolemæi Geographia*, i (Paris, 1883).

Murphy, D. (ed.), *The Annals of Clonmacnoise from the Creation to AD 1408* (Dublin, 1896).

Napier, A. S. (ed.), *Old English Glosses, chiefly unpublished* (*Anecdota Oxoniensia*: Medieval and Modern Ser., 2; Oxford, 1900).

—— and Stevenson, W. H. (eds.), *The Crawford Collection of Early Charters and Documents now in the Bodleian Library* (*Anecdota Oxoniensia* Medieval and Modern Ser., 7; Oxford, 1895).

Neale, K. (ed.), *An Essex Tribute for Frederick Emmison* (London, 1987).

Nelson, J. L., 'The Problem of King Alfred's Royal Anointing', *JEH*, 18 (1967), 145–63.

—— 'The Earliest Surviving Royal *Ordo*: Some Liturgical and Historical Aspects', in Tierney and Linehan (eds.), *Studies Presented to Walter Ullman*, 29–48.

—— 'The Church's Military Service in the Ninth Century: A Contemporary Comparative View', in Shiels (ed.), *Studies in Church History*, 17–24.

—— 'Myths of the Dark Ages', in Smith (ed.), *The Making of Britain: The Dark Ages*, 145–58.

—— ' "A King across the Sea": Alfred in Continental Perspective', *Trans. Roy. Hist. Soc.* 5/36 (1986), 45–68.

—— 'Wealth and Wisdom: The Politics of Alfred the Great', in Rosenthal (ed.), *Kings and Kingship, Acta*, 11, 31–52.

—— 'Translating Images of Authority: The Christian Roman Emperors in the Carolingian World', in Mackenzie and Rouché (eds.), *Papers Presented to Joyce Reynolds*, 194–205.

Nelson, J. L., 'Reconstructing a Royal Family: Reflections on Alfred, from Asser, Chapter 2', in Wood and Lund (eds.), *Essays in Honour of Sawyer*, 47–66.
—— (transl.), *The Annals of St-Bertin* (Manchester and New York, 1991).
—— *Charles the Bald* (London and New York, 1992).
—— and Coupland, S., 'The Vikings on the Continent', *History Today*, 38 (1988), 12–19.
Nennius: SEE Morris, J. (ed. and transl.), *Nennius*.
Niermeyer, J. F., *Mediae Latinitatis Lexicon Minus* (Leiden, 1976).
Nithard: SEE Rau, R. (ed.), *Nithardi Historiarum Libri iiii*.
Nordal, S. (ed.), *Egils Saga Skalla-Grímssonar, Íslensk fornrit*, ii (Reykjavík, 1933).
North, J. J., *English Hammered Coinage* (2 vols.; London, 1963).
Notker: See Rau, R. (ed.), *Notkeri Gesta Karoli*.
Obolensky, D., *The Byzantine Commonwealth: Eastern Europe, 500–1453* (Cardinal Paperback, London, 1974; repr. of 1971 edn.).
Odo of Cluny: SEE Migne, J. P. (ed.), *Vita Sancti Odonis Abbatis Cluniacensis secundi*; and Sitwell, G. (transl.), *St. Odo of Cluny*.
O'Donovan, J. (ed.), *Annals of Ireland: Three Fragments copied . . . by Dubhaltach Mac Firbisigh* (Irish Archaeological and Celtic Society; Dublin 1860).
O'Donovan, M. A., 'An Interim Revision of Episcopal Dates for the Province of Canterbury, 850–950: Part I', *ASE* 1 (1972), 23–44.
Ogilvy, J. D. A., 'Beowulf, Alfred, and Christianity', in King and Stevens (eds.), *Studies in Honour of Charles W. Jones*, i. 59–66.
O'Grady, S. H. (ed.), *Silva Gadelica: A Collection of Irish Tales* (2 vols., London and Edinburgh, 1892).
Oleson, T. J., *The Witenagemot in the Reign of Edward the Confessor: A Study in the Constitutional History of Eleventh-Century England* (Oxford, 1955).
Ong, W. J., *Orality and Literacy* (London and New York, 1982).
Orosius: SEE Bately, J. M. (ed.), *The Old English Orosius* and Pauli, R., *The Life of Alfred the Great*.
Orrick, A. H., *Nordica et Anglica: Studies in Honour of Stefán Einarsson* (The Hague, 1968).
Ortenberg, V., *The English Church and the Continent in the Tenth and Eleventh Centuries: Cultural, Spiritual and Artistic Exchanges* (Oxford, 1992).
Oswald, *Life* of: SEE Raine, J. (ed.) *The Historians of the Church of York and its Archbishops*.
Otten, K., *König Alfreds Boethius* (Tübingen, 1964).
Pagan, H. E., 'Coinage in the Age of Burgred', *Brit. Numismatic Journal*, 34 (1965), 11–27.
—— 'Coinage in Southern England, 796–874', in Blackburn (ed.), *Anglo-Saxon Monetary History*, 45–66.
—— and Stewart, I., 'A New Mercian Moneyer for Alfred's Lunette Type', *Numismatic Circular*, 97 (1989), 8.
Parkes, M. B., 'The Palaeography of the Parker Manuscript of the *Chronicle*, Laws and Sedulius, and Historiography at Winchester in the Late Ninth and Tenth Centuries', *ASE* 5 (1976), 149–71.
—— 'A Fragment of an Early-Tenth-Century Anglo-Saxon Manuscript and its significance', *ASE* 12 (1983), 129–40.
Parson, D. (ed.), *Tenth-Century Studies: Essays in Commemoration of the Milennium of the Council of Winchester and Regularis Concordia* (London and Chichester, 1975).
Pauli, R., *The Life of Alfred the Great: To Which is Appended Alfred's Anglo-Saxon Version of Orosius*, transl. B. Thorpe (Bohn's Antiquarian Library; London, 1889).
Payne, F. A., *King Alfred and Boethius: An Analysis of the Old English Version of the Consolation of Philosophy* (Madison, Milwaukee, and London, 1968).

Pearsall, D. A., and Waldron, R. A. (ed.), *Medieval Literature and Civilization: Studies in Memory of G. N. Garmonsway* (London, 1969).

Pearse, J. W., 'Did Alfred Translate the *Historia Ecclesiastica*?', *Publications of the Modern Language Association Proceedings*, 8 (1893), vi–x.

Pertz, G. H. (ed.), *Annalium Fuldensium pars secunda, auctore Ruodolfo*, in *Mon. Ger. Hist. SS*, fol. (Leipzig, 1925; repr. of 1826 edn.), i. 361–75.

—— (ed.), *Annales Lindisfarnenses*, in *Mon. Ger. Hist. SS*, fol. (Leipzig, 1925; repr. of 1866 edn.), xix. 503–7.

Pirie, E. J. E., Archibald, M. M., and Hall, R. A., *Post-Roman Coins from York Excavations 1971–81* (Council for British Archaeology, London, 1986).

Plummer, C., *The Life and Times of Alfred the Great* (Oxford, 1902).

—— (ed.), *Venerabilis Baedae Historiam Ecclesiasticam Gentis Anglorum. Historiam Abbatum. Epistolam Ecgberctum una cum Historia Abbatum Auctore Anonymo* (2 vols.; Oxford, 1969; repr. of 1896 edn.).

—— (ed.), *Vitae Sanctorum Hiberniae* (2 vols.; Oxford, 1968; repr. of 1910 edn.).

—— and Earle, J., *Two of the Saxon Chronicles Parallel*, introd. by D. Whitelock (2 vols.; Oxford, 1965; repr. of 1892–9 edn.).

Potter, S., *On the Relations of the Old English Bede to Werferth's Gregory and to Alfred's Translations* (Mémoires de la Société Royale des Sciences de Bohème; Classes des Lettres, 1930).

—— 'The Old English "Pastoral Care" ', *Transactions of the Philological Soc.* (1947), 114–25.

Powicke, F. M., and Fryde, E. B., *Handbook of British Chronology*, 2nd edn. (London, 1961).

Prentout, H., *Études critique sur Dudon de Saint-Quentin et son Histoire des premier Ducs Normands* (Paris, 1916).

Prinz, F. E., 'King, Clergy and War at the Time of the Carolingians', in King and Stevens (eds.), *Saints, Scholars and Heroes*, ii. 301–30.

Purlitz, F., *König und Witenagemot bei den Angelsachsen* (Bremen, 1892).

Radford, C. A. Ralegh, 'The Pre-Conquest Boroughs of England, Ninth to Eleventh Centuries', *Proc. Brit. Acad.* 64 (1978), 131–53.

Raine, J. (ed.), *The Historians of the Church of York and its Archbishops* (3 vols.; Rolls Series; London, 1965; repr. of 1879 and 1894 edn.).

Rau, R. (ed.), *Annales Regni Francorum*, in *Fontes ad Historiam Regni Francorum aevi Karolini illustrandam* (*Quellen z. deut. Gesch. d. Mittelalters*, V/i (Darmstadt, 1955), 9–155.

—— (ed.), *Einhardi Vita Karoli*, ibid., V/i, 157–211.

—— (ed.), *Thegani Vita Hludowici Imperatoris*, ibid., V/i, 215–53.

—— (ed.), *Anonymi Vita Hludowici Imperatoris*, ibid., V/i, 257–381.

—— (ed.), *Nithardi Historiarum Libri iiii*, ibid., V/i, 385–461.

—— (ed.), *Annales Bertiniani*, ibid., VI/ii (Darmstadt, 1969), 11–287.

—— (ed.), [*Annals of St-Vaast*], *Annales Vedastini*, ibid., VI/ii, 289–337.

—— (ed.), *Annales Xantenses*, ibid., VI/ii, 339–71.

—— (ed.), *Annales Fuldenses*, ibid., VII/iii, 19–177.

—— (ed.), *Notkeri Gesta Karoli*, ibid., VII/iii, (Berlin, n.d.), 18–427.

—— (ed.), *Reginonis Chronica*, ibid., VII/iii, 180–319.

Regino of Prüm: SEE Rau, R. (ed.), *Reginonis Chronica*.

Reuter, T. (transl.), *The Annals of Fulda* (Manchester and New York, 1992).

Riché, P., 'Les Moines bénédictins, Maîtres d'École VIIIe–XIe Siècles', in *Benedictine Culture 750–1050*, ed. Lourdaux, W., and Verhelst, D., in *Mediaevalia Lovaniensia*, Ser. I, Studia 11, (Leuven, 1983), 96–113.

Robertson, A. J. (ed. and transl.), *Anglo-Saxon Charters* (Cambridge, 1956).

Robinson, J. A., *St. Oswald and the Church of Worcester* (British Academy Supplemental Papers, 5; London, 1919).

—— *The Times of Saint Dunstan* (Oxford, 1969; repr. of 1923 edn.).

—— 'Byrhtferth and the Life of St. Oswald', *Journal of Theological Studies*, 31 (1930), 35–42.

Rollason, D. W., 'Lists of Saints' Resting Places in Anglo-Saxon England', *ASE* 7 (1978), 61–93.

—— 'The Cults of Murdered Royal Saints in Anglo-Saxon England', *ASE* 11 (1983), 1–22.

—— 'Relic Cults as an Instrument of Royal Policy *c*.900–*c*.1050', *ASE* 15 (1986), 91–103.

Rosenthal, R. (ed.), *Kings and Kingship*, Acta, xi (SUNY Colloquium on Medieval Kingship 1984; published 1987).

Rowell, G. (ed.), *The English Religious Tradition and the Genius of Anglicanism: Studies in Commemoration of John Keble: The Second Centenary* (Wantage, 1992).

Ryan, J., *Irish Monasticism: Origins and Development* (Dublin, 1992; repr. of 1972 edn.).

Rynne, E. (ed.), *North Munster Studies: Essays in Commemoration of Mgr. Michael Moloney* (Limerick, 1967).

Salter, H. E., 'A Chronicle Roll of the Abbots of Abingdon', *Eng. Hist. Rev.*, 26 (1911), 727–38.

Sanders, V., 'The Household of Archbishop Parker and the Influencing of Public Opinion', *JEH* 34 (1983), 534–47.

Sawyer, B., Sawyer, P. H., and Wood, I. (eds.), *The Christianization of Scandinavia: Report of a Symposium held at Kungälv, Sweden 1985* (Alingsås, Sweden, 1987).

Sawyer, P. H., *Anglo-Saxon Charters: An Annotated List and Bibliography* (Roy. Hist. Soc., London, 1968).

—— *The Age of the Vikings*, 2nd edn. (London, 1971).

—— *From Roman Britain to Norman England* (London, 1978).

—— *Kings and Vikings: Scandinavia and Europe AD 700–1100* (London and New York, 1982).

—— and Wood, I. N. (eds.), *Early Medieval Kingship* (Leeds, 1977).

Schepss, G., 'Zu König Alfreds Boethius', *Archiv für das Studium der neueren Sprachen*, 94 (1895), 149–60.

Schmidt, K.-H., *König Alfreds Boethius-Bearbeitung* (Göttingen, 1934).

Scholz, B. W., and Rogers, B. (transl.), *Carolingian Chronicles, Royal Frankish Annals and Nithard's Histories* (Ann Arbor, Mich. n.d.).

Schove, D. J., and Fletcher, A., *Chronology of Eclipses and Comets AD 1–1000* (Woodbridge, Suffolk, 1984).

Schütt, M., 'The Literary Form of Asser's *Vita Alfredi*', *Eng. Hist. Rev.* 72 (1957), 209–20.

Scragg, D. G. (ed.), *The Battle of Maldon AD 991* (Oxford, 1991).

Sedgefield, W. J. (ed.), *King Alfred's Old English Version of Boethius De Consolatione Philosophiae* (Oxford, 1899).

—— (transl.), *King Alfred's Version of the Consolation of Boethius, done into Modern English, with an Introduction* (Oxford, 1900).

—— (ed.), *An Anglo-Saxon Book of Verse and Prose* (Manchester and London, 1928).

Seward, D., *Prince of the Renaissance: The Life of François I* (London, 1973).

Sheehan, M. M., *The Will in Medieval England from the Conversion of the Anglo-Saxons to the End of the Thirteenth Century* (Pontifical Institute: Studies and Texts, 6; Toronto, 1963).

Shiels, W. J. (ed.), *Studies in Church History*, xx. *The Church and War* (Oxford, 1983).

Shippey, T. A., 'A Missing Army: Some Doubts about the Alfredian Chronicle', *In Geardagum*, 4 (1982), 41–55.

Simpson, L., 'The King Alfred/St Cuthbert Episode in the *Historia de Sancto Cuthberto*: Its Significance for Mid-Tenth-Century English History', in Bonner, Rolleson, and Stancliffe (eds.), *St. Cuthbert, His Cult and Community to AD 1200*, 397–411.

Sisam, K., *Studies in the History of Old English Literature* (Oxford, repr. 1962).

—— 'Anglo-Saxon Royal Genealogies', *Proc. Brit. Acad.* 39 (1953), 287–348.

Sitwell, G. (transl.), *St. Odo of Cluny: Being the Life of St. Odo of Cluny by John of Salerno and the Life of St. Gerald of Aurillac by St. Odo* (London and New York, 1958).

Slater, H. E., 'A Chronicle Roll of the Abbots of Abingdon', *Eng. Hist. Rev.* 26 (1911), 727–38.

Smith, A. H. (ed.), *The Parker Chronicle 832–900* (London, repr. 1964 of 1951 edn.).

Smith, L. M. (ed.), *The Making of Britain: The Dark Ages* (London, 1984).

Smyth, A. P., 'The Earliest Irish Annals: Their First Contemporary Entries and the Earliest Centres of Recording', *Proc. Roy. Irish Acad.* 72 C (1972), 1–48.

—— 'Húi Failgi Relations with the Húi Néill', *Études celtiques*, 14/2 (1975), 503–23.

—— 'The *Black Foreigners* of York and the *White Foreigners* of Dublin', *Saga-Book of the Viking Society*, 19 (1975–6), 101–17.

—— *Scandinavian Kings in the British Isles 850–880* (Oxford, 1977).

—— *Celtic Leinster: Towards an Historical Geography of Early Irish Civilization AD 500–1500* (Dublin, 1982).

—— 'The Vikings in Britain', in Smith (ed.), *The Making of Britain: The Dark Ages*, 105–16.

—— *Warlords and Holy Men: Scotland AD 80–1000* (London, 1984; repr. Edinburgh, 1989).

—— *Scandinavian York and Dublin: The History and Archaeology of Two Related Viking Kingdoms* (2 vols.; Dublin, repr. 1987).

——: SEE Williams, A., and Kirby, D. P., *Biographical Dictionary of Dark Age Britain*.

Spelman, J., SEE Hearne, T. (ed.), *The Life of Alfred the Great*.

Stafford, P., 'Charles the Bald, Judith and England', in Gibson, Nelson, and Ganz (eds.), *Charles the Bald*, 137–51.

—— *The East Midlands in the Early Middle Ages* (Leicester, 1985).

Stanley, E. G. (ed.), *Continuations and Beginnings: Studies in Old English Literature* (London, 1966).

Stenton, D. M. (ed.), *Preparatory to Anglo-Saxon England, Being the Collected Papers of Frank Merry Stenton* (Oxford, 1970).

Stenton, F. M., 'The South-Western Element in the Old English Chronicle', in Little and Powicke (eds.), *Essays Presented to Tout*, 15–24.

—— *The Latin Charters of the Anglo-Saxon Period* (Oxford, 1955).

—— *Anglo-Saxon England*, 2nd edn. (Oxford, repr. 1967).

—— *The Early History of the Abbey of Abingdon* (University College Reading: Studies in Local History, 1913).

—— 'Æthelweard's Account of the Last Years of Alfred's Reign', *Eng. Hist. Rev.* 24 (1909), 79–84.

—— *The Bayeux Tapestry: A Comprehensive Survey*, 2nd edn. (London, 1965).

Stevenson, J. (ed.), *The Church Historians of England*: [*The Historical Works of Symeon of Durham*] III/ii (London, 1855).

—— (ed.), *Chronicon Monasterii de Abingdon* (2 vols.; Rolls Series; London, 1858).

Stevenson, W. H. (ed.), *Asser's Life of King Alfred*, introd. by D. Whitelock (Oxford, repr. 1959 of 1904 edn.).

Stokes, W. (ed.), *The Tripartite Life of Patrick with Other Documents Relating to that Saint* (2 vols.; Rolls Series; 1887).

—— (ed.), *Félire Óengusso Céli Dé: The Martyrology of Óengus the Culdee* (Henry Bradshaw Soc.; London, 1905).

Strype, J., *The Life and Acts of Matthew Parker, the First Archbishop of Canterbury in the Reign of Queen Elizabeth* (3 vols., Oxford, 1821).

Stubbs, W., *The Constitutional History of England in its Origins and Development*, 3rd edn. (3 vols.; Oxford, 1880–4).

—— (ed.), *Memorials of Saint Dunstan, Archbishop of Canterbury* (Rolls Series; London, 1874).

—— (ed.), *Willelmi Malmesbiriensis monachi de Gestis regum Anglorum*, i (Rolls Series; London, 1887).

Suetonius: SEE Graves, R. (transl.), *Gaius Suetonius Tranquillus*.

Sweet, H. (ed.), *King Alfred's West Saxon Version of Gregory's Pastoral Care* (Early English Text Society, Original Series, 45 (part 1), 50 (part 2); Oxford, 1958; repr. of 1871 edn.).

Symeon of Durham: SEE Arnold, T. (ed.), *Symeonis monachi opera omnia*.

Symons, Dom T. (ed.), *Regularis Concordia Anglicae Nationis Monachorum Sanctimonialiumque: The Monastic Agreement of the Monks and Nuns of the English Nation* (Nelson Medieval Texts; London, 1953).

Szarmach, P. E. (ed.), *Studies in Earlier Old English Prose* (Albany, NY, 1986).

Taylor, S. (ed.), *The Anglo-Saxon Chronicle: A Collaborative Edition*, iv. *Manuscript B* (gen. eds. D. Dumville and S. Keynes; Cambridge, 1983).

Thegan: SEE Rau, R. (ed.), *Thegani Vita Hludowici Imperatoris*.

Thompson, E. M. (ed.), *Chronicon 'Galfridi' le Baker de Swynebroke* (Oxford, 1889).

Thompson, S[tith], *Motif-Index of Folk-Literature*, rev. edn. (Bloomington, Ind. 1966).

Thorogood, A. J., 'The Anglo-Saxon Chronicle in the Reign of Ecgberht', *Eng. Hist. Rev.* 48 (1933), 353–63.

Thorpe, B. (ed.), *Ancient Laws and Institutes of England: Comprising also . . . Monumenta Ecclesiastica Anglicana . . . and the Ancient Latin Version of the Anglo-Saxon Laws* (2 vols.; London, 1840).

—— (ed.), *The Sermones Catholici or Homilies of Ælfric* (2 vols.; London, 1846).

—— (ed.), [Florence *alias* John of Worcester] *Florentii Wigorniensis monachi, Chronicon ex Chronicis* (2 vols.; English Hist. Soc.; London, 1848).

—— (ed.), *Diplomatarium Anglicum Ævi Saxonici: A Collection of English Charters* (London, 1865).

Thorpe, L. (transl.), *Einhard and Notker the Stammerer: Two Lives of Charlemagne* (Penguin, Harmondsworth, 1969).

Tierney, B., and Linehan, P. (eds.), *Authority and Power: Studies on Medieval Law and Government Presented to Walter Ullman on his Seventieth Birthday* (Cambridge, 1980).

Tolhurst, J. B. L. (ed.), *The Monastic Breviary of Hyde Abbey, Winchester* (6 vols.; Henry Bradshaw Soc.; London, 1932–42).

Turville-Petre, G., *The Heroic Age of Scandinavia* (London, 1951).

Ullmann, W., 'Nos si aliquid incompetenter: Some Observations on the Register Fragments of Leo IV in the *Collectio Britannica*', *Ephemerides Juris Canonici*, 9 (1953), 279–87.

van Drat, P. F., 'The Authorship of the Old English Bede: A Study in Rhythm', *Anglia*, 39 (1916), 319–46.

van Houts, E. M. C. (ed.), *The Gesta Normannorum Ducum of William of Jumièges, Orderic Vitalis, and Roger of Torigni* (2 vols.; Oxford, 1992).

Vaughan, R. (ed.), *The Chronicle Attributed to John of Wallingford* (Camden Miscellany 21, Camden 3rd Series, 90; London, 1958).

Vince, A. (ed.), *Pre-Viking Lindsey* (Lincoln Archaeological Studies, 1; Lincoln, 1993).

von Hildegard, L. C. T., 'Ohthere, Wulfstan und der Aethicus Ister', *Zeitschrift für deutsches Altertum und deutsche Literatur*, 111 (1982), 153–68.

Vries, J. de, 'Die historischen Grundlagen der Ragnarssaga Loðbrókar', *Arkiv för nordisk Filologi*, 39 (1923), 244–74.

—— 'Die Entwicklung der Sage von den Lodbrokssöhnen in den historischen Quellen', *Arkiv för nordisk Filologi*, 44 (1928), 117–63.

Vyvers, A. van de, 'Les Œuvres inédites d'Abbon de Fleury', *Revue Bénédictine*, 47 (1935), 125–69.

Waitz, G. (ed.), *Vita Leobae abbatissae Biscofesheimensis auctori Rudolfo Fuldensi, in Mon. Ger. Hist. SS* 15 (1887), 118–31.

Wallace-Hadrill, J. M., 'The Franks and the English in the Ninth Century: Some Common Historical Interests', *History*, 35 (1950), 202–18.

—— *Early Germanic Kingship in England and on the Continent* (Oxford, 1971).

—— *The Vikings in Francia* (Stenton Lecture; Reading, 1975).

—— 'War and Peace in the Earlier Middle Ages', *Trans. Roy. Hist. Soc.* 5/25 (1975), 157–74.

—— 'A Carolingian Renaissance Prince: The Emperor Charles the Bald', *Proc. Brit. Acad.* 44 (1980 for 1978), 155–84.

Wallenberg, J. K. (ed.), 'Studies in Old Kentish Charters', *Studia Neophilologica*, 1 (1928), 34–44.

Waterhouse, R., 'The Hæsten Episode in the *Anglo-Saxon Chronicle*', *Studia Neophilologica*, 46 (1974), 136–41.

—— 'Tone in Alfred's Version of Augustine's *Soliloquies*', in Szarmach (ed.), *Studies in Earlier Old English Prose*, 47–86.

Watts, V. E. (transl.), *Boethius: The Consolation of Philosophy* (Penguin, Harmondsworth, 1969).

Wattenbach, W., and Dümmler, [E.] (eds.), [*Life* of Alcuin] *Vita Alchuini auctore anonymo*, in *Monumenta Alcuiniana, Bibliotheca Rerum Germanicarum*, gen. ed. P. Jaffé, vol. vi (Berlin, 1873).

Webb, J. F. (transl.), *Lives of Saints. The Voyage of Brendan. Bede: Life of Cuthbert. Eddius Stefanus: Life of Wilfrid* (Penguin, Harmondsworth, 1973; repr. of 1965 edn.).

Webster, L., and Backhouse, J., *The Making of England: Anglo-Saxon Art and Culture AD 600–900* (British Museum, 1991).

Wheeler, G. H., 'Textual Emendations to Asser's Life of Alfred', *Eng. Hist. Rev.* 47 (1932), 86–8.

Whitaker, J., *The Life of Saint Neot, the Oldest of All the Brothers to King Alfred* (London, 1809).

Whitelock, D. (ed.), *Anglo-Saxon Wills* (Holmes Beach, Fl., 1986; repr. of 1930 Cambridge edn.).

—— 'The Conversion of the Eastern Danelaw', *Saga-Book of the Viking Society for Northern Research*, 12/3 (1941), 159–76.

—— 'Scandinavian Personal Names in the *Liber Vitae* of Thorney Abbey', *Saga-Book of the Viking Society for Northern Research*, 12 (1937–45), 127–53.

Whitelock, D. (ed.), *Sermo Lupi ad Anglos* (London, 1939).

—— *The Beginnings of English Society* (Penguin, Harmondsworth, 1963; repr. of 1952 edn.).

—— (ed.), *English Historical Documents*, i. c.*500–1042* (gen. ed. D. C. Douglas; London, 1968).

—— 'Recent Work on Asser's Life of Alfred', introduction to Stevenson (ed.), Asser's *Life of Alfred* (1959 edn.), pp. cxxxii–clii.

—— 'On the Commencement of the Year in the Saxon Chronicles', Appendix to Introduction in Plummer and Earle (ed.), *Two Saxon Chronicles Parallel*, pp. cxxxix–cxliid.

—— 'The Old English Bede', *Proc. Brit. Acad.*, 48 (1962), 57–90.

—— 'The Prose of Alfred's Reign', in Stanley (ed.), *Continuations and Beginnings*, 67–103.

—— *The Genuine Asser* (Stenton Lecture 1967; Reading, 1968).

—— 'William of Malmesbury on the Works of King Alfred', in Pearsall and Waldron (eds.), *Studies in Memory of Garmonsway*, 78–93.

—— 'Wulfstan *Cantor* and Anglo-Saxon Law', in Orrick (ed.), *Studies in Honour of Stefán Einarsson*, 83–92.

—— 'Fact and Fiction in the Legend of St Edmund', *Proceedings of the Suffolk Institute of Archaeology*, 31 (1969), 217–33.

—— 'The List of Chapter-Headings in the Old English Bede', in Burlin and Irving (eds.), *Studies in Honour of John C. Pope*, 263–84.

—— 'Some Charters in the Name of King Alfred', in King and Stevens (eds.), *Saints, Scholars and Heroes*, i. 77–98.

—— 'The Importance of the Battle of Edington AD 878', in D. Whitelock (ed.), *From Bede to Alfred* (Studies in Early Anglo-Saxon Literature and History, 13; London, 1980). Also published separately by The Friends of Edington Priory Church, 1977.

—— 'The Pre-Viking Age Church in East Anglia', in Whitelock, *From Bede to Alfred*, 1–22.

—— (ed.) *From Bede to Alfred: Studies in Early Anglo-Saxon Literature and History* (London, 1980).

—— Douglas, D. C., and Tucker, S. I. (eds.), *The Anglo-Saxon Chronicle: A Revised Translation* (London, 1961).

—— Brett, M., and Brooke, C. N. L. (eds.), *Councils and Synods with Other Documents Relating to the English Church*, I. *AD 871–1204*, Pt. i. *871–1066* (Oxford, 1981).

William of Jumièges: SEE van Houts, E. M. C. (ed.), *Gesta Normannorum*.

William of Malmesbury: SEE Hamilton, N. E. S. A. (ed.), *De Gestis Pontificum*, and Stubbs, W. (ed.), *De Gestis Regum*.

Williams, A., 'Some Notes and Considerations on Problems Connected with the English Royal Succession, 860–1066', *Proceedings of the Battle Conference I: 1978*, ed. Brown, 144–67, 225–33.

—— '*Princeps Merciorum gentis*: The Family, Career and Connections of Ælfhere, Ealdorman of Mercia, 956–83', *ASE* 10 (1982), 143–5.

—— Smyth, A. P., and Kirby, D., *A Biographical Dictionary of Dark Age Britain* (London, 1991).

Williams, I., and Bromwich, R., *Armes Prydein: The Prophecy of Britain from the Book of Taliesin* (Dublin, 1972).

Williams, M., *The Draining of the Somerset Levels* (Cambridge, 1970).

Winterbottom, M. (ed.), [*Life* of Edmund] *Three Lives of English Saints* (Toronto, 1972).

Wittig, J. S., 'King Alfred's *Boethius* and its Latin Sources: A Reconsideration', *ASE* 11 (1983), 157–98.

Wormald, P., '*Lex Scripta* and *Verbum Regis*: Legislation and Germanic Kingship from Euric to Cnut', in Sawyer and Wood (eds.), *Early Medieval Kingship*, 105–38.

—— 'The Venerable Bede and the Church of the English', in 'Rowell (ed.), *The English Religious Tradition*, 13–32.

—— 'A Hand-List of Anglo-Saxon Lawsuits', *ASE* 17 (1988), 247–81.

—— 'Æthelwold and his Continental Counterparts: Contact, Comparison, Contrast', in B. Yorke (ed.), *Bishop Æthelwold: His Career and Influence* (Boydell, 1988), 13–42.

Wood, I. N., 'Kings, Kingdoms and Consent', in Sawyer and Wood (eds.), *Early Medieval Kingship*, 6–29.

—— and Lund, N. (eds.), *People and Places in Northern Europe 500–1600: Essays in Honour of Peter Hayes Sawyer* (Woodbridge, Suffolk, 1991).

Wrenn, C. L., *A Study of Old English Literature* (London, 1967).

Wright, T., 'Some Historical Doubts Relating to the Biographer Asser', *Archaeologia*, 29 (1842), 192–201.

Wuelcher, R., 'Ein Angelsaechsisches Leben des Neot', *Anglia*, 3 (1880), 102–14.

Yerkes, D., 'The Text of the Canterbury Fragment of Werferth's Translation of Gregory's *Dialogues* and its Relation to the other Manuscripts', *ASE* 6 (1977), 121–35.

—— 'The Full Text of of the Metrical Preface to Wærferth's Translation of Gregory', *Speculum*, 55 (1980), 505–13.

—— 'The Translation of Gregory's Dialogues and Its Revision: Textual History, Provenance, Authorship', in Szarmach (ed.), *Studies in Earlier Old English Prose*, 335–44.

Yorke, B. A. E., 'The Bishops of Winchester, the Kings of Wessex and the Development of Winchester in the Ninth and Early Tenth Centuries', *Proceedings Hampshire Field Club and Archaeological Soc.* 40 (1984), 61–70.

—— 'The Kingdom of the East Saxons', *ASE* 14 (1985), 1–36.

—— 'Æthelwold and the Politics of the Tenth Century' in Yorke (ed.), *Bishop Æthelwold: His Career and Influence*, 65–88.

—— *Bishop Æthelwold: His Career and Influence*, ed. B. Yorke (Woodbridge, Suffolk, 1988).

—— 'The Jutes of Hampshire and Wight and the Origins of Wessex', in Bassett (ed.), *The Origins of Anglo-Saxon Kingdoms*, 84–96, notes pp. 256–63.

—— ' "Sisters under the Skin"? Anglo-Saxon Nuns and Nunneries in Southern England', *Reading Medieval Studies*, 15 (1989), 95–117.

—— 'Lindsey: The Lost Kingdom Found?', in Vince (ed.), *Pre-Viking Lindsey*, 141–9.

INDEX

NOTE: United Kingdom placenames are identified by their historic shires, many of which prevailed from the early Middle Ages until 1972. The reasons for this are twofold. Redrawing of county boundaries in 1972 did violence to English toponymy by creating novel divisions such as Avon out of parts of historic Somerset and Gloucestershire, and by arbitrarily altering many other shires which survived. So, Wantage, which had lain within Berkshire since the author of the *Life* of King Alfred so described it a thousand years ago, was moved into Oxfordshire in 1972. A second reason for returning to more enduring boundaries is that their replacements in 1972 may well be superseded by equally ephemeral arrangements, created by ever-changing administrative and electoral needs.

DATE DUE